RESEARCH HANDBOOKS IN HUMAN RIGHTS

Elgar Research Handbooks are original reference works designed to provide a broad overview of research in a given field whilst at the same time creating a forum for more challenging, critical examination of complex and often under-explored issues within that field.

Chapters by international teams of contributors are specially commissioned by editors who carefully balance breadth and depth. Often widely cited, individual chapters present expert scholarly analysis and offer a vital reference point for advanced research. Taken as a whole they achieve a wide-ranging picture of the state-of-the-art.

This highly original series offers a unique appraisal of the state-of-the-art of research and thinking in human rights law. Each volume, edited by a prominent expert, either covers a specific aspect of human rights law or looks at how human rights impacts upon, or intersects with, other areas of law. Combining positivist approaches to international and human rights law, with more critical approaches, the volumes also draw, where appropriate, on research from adjacent disciplines. Addressing current and sometimes controversial legal issues, as well as affording a clear substantive analysis of the law, these *Handbooks* are designed to inform as well as to contribute to current debates.

Equally useful as reference tools or introductions to specific topics or issues, the *Handbooks* will be used by academic researchers, post-graduate students, practicing lawyers and lawyers in policy circles.

RESEARCH HANDBOOK ON HUMAN RIGHTS AND HUMANITARIAN LAW

Research Handbook on Human Rights and Humanitarian Law

Edited by

Robert Kolb

University of Geneva, Switzerland

Gloria Gaggioli

University of Geneva, Switzerland

RESEARCH HANDBOOKS IN HUMAN RIGHTS

Edward Elgar

Cheltenham, UK • Northampton, MA, USA

Published by
Edward Elgar Publishing Limited
The Lypiatts
15 Lansdown Road
Cheltenham
Glos GL50 2JA
UK

Edward Elgar Publishing, Inc.
William Pratt House
9 Dewey Court
Northampton
Massachusetts 01060
USA

A catalogue record for this book
is available from the British Library

Library of Congress Control Number: 2012944443

This book is available electronically in the ElgarOnline.com Law Subject Collection,
E-ISBN 978 1 78100 607 8

MIX
Paper from
responsible sources
FSC
www.fsc.org   FSC® C018575

ISBN 978 1 84980 035 8 (cased)

Typeset by Columns Design XML Ltd, Reading
Printed and bound by MPG Books Group, UK

Contents

Contributors

Jean d'Aspremont, University of Manchester, United Kingdom

Giulio Bartolini, University Roma Tre, Italy

Paolo Benvenuti, University Roma Tre, Italy

Michael Bothe, Goethe University Frankfurt/Main, Germany

Antônio Augusto Cançado Trindade, International Court of Justice (The Hague), Netherlands

Enzo Cannizzaro, University of Roma ('La Sapienza'), Italy

Eric David, Free University of Brussels, Belgium

Francesca De Vittor, University of Macerata, Italy

Giovanni Distefano, University of Neuchâtel, Switzerland

Tristan Ferraro, International Committee of the Red Cross, Switzerland

Gloria Gaggioli, University of Geneva, Switzerland

Roberto Giuffrida, University for Foreigners (Perugia), Italy

Robert K. Goldman, American University, Washington College of Law, United States of America

Vera Gowlland-Debbas, Graduate Institute of International Studies (Geneva), Switzerland

Anne-Laurence Graf-Brugère, University of Geneva, Switzerland

Hans-Joachim Heintze, University of Ruhr (Bochum), Germany

Jean-Marie Henckaerts, International Committee of the Red Cross, Switzerland

Maya Hertig Randall, University of Geneva, Switzerland

Ivan Ingravallo, University of Bari 'Aldo Moro', Italy

Walter Kälin, University of Bern, Switzerland

Robert Kolb, University of Geneva, Switzerland

Sandra Krähenmann, University of Geneva, Switzerland

Dan Kuwali, Mzuzu University, Malawi; University of Pretoria, South Africa

Lindsay Moir, University of Hull Law School, United Kingdom

Manfred Nowak, University of Vienna, Austria

Damien Scalia, Geneva Academy of Human Rights and Humanitarian Law, Switzerland

Elke Schwager, District Court, Munich (Langericht München)

Djacoba Liva Tehindrazanarivelo, Boston University Study Abroad Geneva, Switzerland; Institute of Human Rights, Catholic University of Lyon, France

Hélène Tigroudja, Aix-Marseille University, France

Christian Tomuschat, Humboldt University (Berlin), Germany

Godofredo Torreblanca, University of Geneva, Switzerland and OHCHR

Elodie Tranchez, University of Maine, France

Luisa Vierucci, University of Florence, Italy

Cornelius Wiesener, International Committee of the Red Cross, Switzerland

Preface

The present Handbook deals with an eminently topical and important subject-matter, namely the interplay between International Human Rights Law (HRL) and International Humanitarian Law (IHL). This turbulent subject-matter has been of increasing importance since the days of the adoption of the Universal Declaration of 1948 and the Geneva Conventions of 1949. At the beginning, it was the issues of non-international armed conflicts and the protection of civilians under Geneva Convention IV that provided fruitful avenues for interplay and interaction. Later, occupied territories entered the scene, especially when prolonged occupations took place, from 1967. Today, the manifold grey areas opened by (armed) conflicts of different types, the interplay between the conduct of hostilities and the maintenance of order in the interstices of applicable legal regimes, the issues of *jus post bellum* (including occupation law), the mandates of the UN Security Council playing on both legal grounds, and also the evolving missions of modern armies, which are not any more confined to simple combat missions ('conduct of hostilities') – all these considerations imply new reflections on the mutual impact of each of these bodies of public international law. To what extent can they cooperate without accidents and tensions? To what extent does one prevail over the other? By what means does one induce legal developments in the other? How can one provide mechanisms of implementation for the benefit of the other without endangering the integrity of each? How far can one contribute to a better understanding and interpretation of the other? All these questions, among others, posed in concrete circumstances, are today of the greatest importance to the practitioner in the field, as well as to the international lawyer, be he or she an academic or involved in legal advice. It is to these questions that the present Handbook seeks to open the way, by putting some of them under the focus of legal analysis.

The Handbook is structured in four parts.

The first part provides the historical background. It recalls the origins of HRL and IHL and retraces the various stages of the relationship of these two bodies of law. It analyses the different legal theories of the relationship of HRL and IHL and looks at the position of the individual in international law in light of these evolutions.

The second part analyses some issues of particular concern to either one or both of the bodies of international law that constitute HRL and IHL. Key human rights issues such as the applicability of HRL in armed conflicts, the extraterritorial application of HRL, the definition and scope of the human rights principle of proportionality, the question of non-state armed groups as bearers of human rights obligations and the impact of positive obligations in armed conflict situations are discussed. Some specificities common to both HRL and IHL, such as the principle of humanity or specific rules pertaining to State responsibility are also addressed. The question of the interplay between HRL and IHL is not only addressed generally but also more specifically in contributions addressing conflict rules such as the *lex specialis* principle or the most-favorable-to-the-individual rule.

The third part contains contributions showing how and to what extent there is a need for a combined approach in order to provide adequate protection for victims of armed conflicts. A sample of various topics of importance in armed conflict situations, such as the law of occupation, humanitarian assistance or enforced disappearances, are analyzed in that perspective. One contribution even suggests a new concept, that of a 'humanitarian rights' approach, in order to highlight the significance of both HRL and IHL to protect civilians in armed conflicts. Other specific issues pertaining to the role of HRL and IHL in armed conflict situations are also discussed. The question of HRL and IHL as limits to the actions of the Security Council but also as an integral part of UN activities, in the context of UN territorial administrations for example, is analyzed. The impact of HRL and IHL in agreements regulating or terminating internal armed conflicts is also addressed.

Finally, the fourth and last part is dedicated to the monitoring bodies of HRL and IHL. It shows how human rights bodies have been increasingly interested in IHL, sometimes even applying explicitly or implicitly this body of law or at least taking it into account in order to apply human rights instruments in armed conflict situations. The impact of HRL on IHL implementation bodies is also addressed, as well as the place of HRL in the context of international criminal law. Last but not least, the possibility of developing new monitoring bodies for a better implementation of IHL and HRL in armed conflict situations and the question of reparations for victims of armed conflicts are discussed.

From the various contributions, a clear trend towards *rapprochement*, complementarity, and/or mutual influence between these two bodies of law is palpable. It becomes undeniable that, today, the protection of victims of armed conflicts requires a combined approach, looking both at HRL and IHL. However, a tension is still noticeable. While some authors highlight the areas of convergence, others tend, on the contrary, to stress the enduring differences and conflicting approaches of these two bodies of law. The solutions to the conflicts between rules of HRL and IHL are all the more diverse. The richness of the contributions and the variety of approaches adopted demonstrate the continuing complexity of the interplay between HRL and IHL; a topic that continues to interest academics and practitioners alike.

I should like to close the present short Foreword by saying a word of heartfelt thanks to Dr Gloria Gaggioli for having so competently and diligently carried out all the real work in the setting up of this volume. To the publisher, we both offer our gratitude for the proposal to prepare such a Handbook and for the careful editorial work. We hope that the reader will be enriched by the contributions from so many different horizons that are compiled in this volume, and that he or she will find in the multitude of texts a great number of staring points for his or her own reflections.

Robert Kolb
Professor of Public International Law at the University of Geneva

Abbreviations

ACJHR	African Court of Justice and Human Rights
AfCHPR	African Convention on Human and Peoples' Rights
AfCommHPR	African Commission on Human and Peoples' Rights
API	Additional Protocol I to the 4 Geneva Conventions
APII	Additional Protocol II to the 4 Geneva Conventions
AU	African Union
CAT	Convention against Torture and Other Cruel, Inhuman or Degrading Treatment or Punishment
CEDAW	Convention on the Elimination of All Forms of Discrimination against Women
COE	Council of Europe
CPED	International Convention for the Protection of All Persons from Enforced Disappearance
CRC	Convention on the Rights of the Child
CRPD	Convention on the Rights of Persons with Disabilities
ECHR	European Convention on Human Rights
ECtHR	European Court of Human Rights
EU	European Union
FRY	Federal Republic of Yugoslavia
GCI	Geneva Convention I for the Amelioration of the Condition of the Wounded and Sick in Armed Forces in the Field
GCII	Geneva Convention II for the Amelioration of the Condition of Wounded, Sick and Shipwrecked Members of Armed Forces at Sea
GCIII	Geneva Convention III relative to the Treatment of Prisoners of War
GCIV	Geneva Convention IV relative to the Protection of Civilian Persons in Time of War
HR Council	Human Rights Council
HRC	Human Rights Committee
HRL	Human Rights Law
IAC	International Armed Conflict
IACHR	Inter-American Convention on Human Rights
IACommHR	Inter-American Commission of Human Rights
IACtHR	Inter-American Court of Human Rights
ICC	International Criminal Court
ICCPR	International Covenant on Civil and Political Rights

ICERD	International Convention on the Elimination of All Forms of Racial Discrimination
ICESCR	International Covenant on Economic, Social and Cultural Rights
ICJ	International Court of Justice
ICRC	International Committee of the Red Cross
ICRMW	International Convention on the Protection of the Rights of All Migrant Workers and Members of Their Families
ICTR	International Criminal Tribunal for Rwanda
ICTY	International Criminal Tribunal for Former Yugoslavia
IHFFC	International Humanitarian Fact-Finding Commission
IHL	International Humanitarian Law
ILC	International Law Commission
ILO	International Labour Organization
IMT	(Nuremberg) Judgment
KFOR	Kosovo Force
LTTE	Liberation Tigers of Tamil Eelam
NATO	North Atlantic Treaty Organization
NGO	non-governmental organization
NIAC	non-international armed conflict
NSA	non-state actor
OAS	Organization of American States
OAU	Organization of African Unity
OSCE	Organization for Security and Cooperation in Europe
PCIJ	Permanent Court of International Justice
PKK	Kurdistan Workers' Party
POW	Prisoner of War
SOFA	Status of Force Agreements
TA	Territorial Administration
TRNC	Turkish Republic of Northern Cyprus
UDHR	Universal Declaration of Human Rights
UK	United Kingdom
UN	United Nations
UNHCR	United Nations High Commissioner for Refugees
UNMIK	United Nations Mission in Kosovo
UNTAES	United Nations Transitional Administration for Eastern Slavonia, Baranja and Western Sirmium
UNTAET	United Nations Transitional Administration in East Timor
UPR	Universal Periodic Review
US or USA	United States of America

PART I

HISTORICAL BACKGROUND

1.   The history of international human rights law

Maya Hertig Randall*

1. THE CONCEPT OF INTERNATIONAL HUMAN RIGHTS

The Preamble of the Universal Declaration of Human Rights of 1948 (UDHR)[1] reaffirms the 'faith in fundamental human rights, in the dignity and worth of the human person and in the equal rights of men and women', and expresses the conviction that 'human rights should be protected by the rule of law'. Article 1 of the same Declaration proclaims that: 'All human beings are born free and equal in dignity and rights. They are endowed with reason and conscience and should act towards one another in a spirit of brotherhood.' The quoted passages highlight the double nature of international human rights (IHR). They are at the same time legal and moral rights.[2]

As legal rights,[3] human rights are entitlements 'protected by the rule of law', which implies that they form part of positive law. More precisely, so as to be accurately described as *international* human rights, they need to be protected by the *international* legal order. As moral rights, IHR are generally viewed as basic entitlements that belong to every person by virtue of the sole fact of being human. Based on a common, albeit contested[4] classification, they comprise civil and political rights (so-called first generation rights), social, economic and cultural rights (so-called second generation rights) and solidarity rights[5] (so-called third generation rights).[6] According to the traditional view, *first* generation rights are negative rights, protecting life, bodily and physical integrity and individual freedom against state interference, as well as formal equality[7] and the right to political participation. They comprise mainly classical liberty rights, including, for instance, two of President Roosevelt's famous four freedoms,[8] 'freedom of speech and freedom of belief'. *Second* generation rights, by contrast, are primarily positive rights (or welfare rights), reflecting the concern for substantive equality. They impose on the state the duty to provide for people's basic needs, satisfying what President Roosevelt called 'freedom from want'. Contrary to the first and second generation of human rights, *third* generation rights are conceived not as individual but as group rights.[9] They include, for instance, people's rights to self-determination, the right to development and to a clean environment, and contribute, through the right to peace, to the realization of President Roosevelt's fourth freedom, the 'freedom from fear'. The categorization into three generations is not meant to reflect axiological but temporal priority. *Qua* moral rights, the first generation is generally considered a child of 17th- and 18th-century liberalism, the second generation of 19th-century socialism, whilst the third generation reflects the vindications of a fairer political and economic world order, voiced by developing countries in the context of decolonization, and with strong vigour since the 1970s. *Qua* legal rights, the positivation of the first two generations has so far been more successful than the codification of rights belonging to the third generation.

3

An outline of the history of IHR needs to account for their legal as well as their moral nature.[10] Both dimensions are not self-evident. They have emerged from a long struggle, building on, transforming and challenging existing ideas and power structures of their times. The *legal* nature of IHR implied a departure from the Westphalian tradition, which conceived international law as a legal order regulating external relations between sovereign and equal states. The protection of human rights through international norms has questioned the assumption that states are the exclusive subjects and sole concern of international law. Moreover, as these rights protect citizens against their own state, the concept of IHR also departs from two other principles of the Westphalian paradigm, the idea of state sovereignty and reciprocity. States can no longer argue that the way they treat their own population pertains to their reserved domain (*'domaine réservé'*). Neither can they hold that international law's concern is limited to protecting reciprocal national interests through contractual arrangements (treaties) setting out duties and rights which states hold *vis-à-vis* each other.[11]

The concept of human rights as *moral* rights is no more self-evident than their legal nature. It implies, amongst other things, minimal empathy[12] and identification with fellow beings, rooted in the idea that all humans have certain features in common which transcend other loyalties and identities. Persons are not exclusively defined in terms of gender, or as members of a tribe, a caste, a religious community, or a nation, but form part of 'the human family'.[13] They share the capacity to reason and are endowed with a conscience, which grounds their freedom and equality. Viewed as autonomous moral agents, all humans have the capacity to know good from evil and to decide for themselves. Based on this vision, it was possible to make, like Rousseau, the counter-factual claim that '[m]an is born free, and everywhere he is in chains'.[14] Linked to moral autonomy and equality is another essential feature of the human rights idea affirmed in the UDHR, the equal worth, that is the equal dignity,[15] of every member of the human family. The conviction that every human being is of equal worth and as such bearer of the same basic rights runs counter to a rivaling perception: the vision that people's value is dependent on their honor, which is contingent on their social rank and their behavior. Whilst honor, like reputation and merit, strives towards differentiation, is culturally specific, and can be lost, dignity grounds equal basic concern for all human beings, and thus pretends to universality. As it is independent of conduct, dignity can neither be earned nor forfeited.[16]

What exactly the respect of human dignity entails, and what it is grounded on, remains open to debate. Dignity, like the respect for equality and autonomy, is not only an idea but also a cultural practice.[17] It is based both on reason and feeling, intellect and compassion.[18] As often highlighted, our intuitive understanding makes it easier to identify clear violations of human dignity and human rights than to define positively what their precise content is.[19] It comes thus as no surprise that the UDHR was proclaimed against the backdrop of World War II and the 'barbarous acts which have outraged the conscience of mankind'[20] whilst not spelling out the exact significance of human dignity[21] and leaving open its foundation.[22] Like dignity, IHR thus remain indeterminate and open to justifications from different cultural, philosophical and religious perspectives.[23] Different people in different places have different ideas on what human rights are for, where they come from, what their precise content is, and whether and in what sense they are universal or relative to a given community.[24]

Human rights remain an 'incomplete idea',[25] shaped and evolving through the human suffering that has marked the history of mankind. Based on our experience, 'our sense of who has rights and what those rights are constantly changes. The human rights revolution is by definition ongoing'.[26]

Any account of where the concept of IHR came from, how it developed in the past and how it may evolve in future will, like the idea itself, be necessarily incomplete and controversial. Written by a European legal scholar, this chapter aims at sketching the history of 'human rights with modesty'.[27] It will first outline the development of human rights on the national (section 2) and then on the international level (section 3). In both the domestic and international sphere, human rights first crystallized as moral rights which were cast in solemn declarations. At a later stage, they entered the realm of positive law, for example national constitutions and international treaties.

2. THE DEVELOPMENT OF HUMAN RIGHTS ON THE NATIONAL LEVEL

Historical accounts frequently trace the origins of the contemporary human rights idea back to the Enlightenment. Whilst the legacy of the Enlightenment is without doubt crucial for our contemporary understanding of human rights, these did not 'materialize out of thin air' in the 17th and 18th centuries but have 'deep roots'.[28]

2.1 Precursors

Scholars who search for common foundations to underpin the universality of human rights highlight that many values reflected in IHR norms, such as concern for the life and well-being of others, as well as property, can be found in ancient cultures and belief systems.[29] Although these ancient codes of conduct, including, for instance, Hammurabi's Code from the 18th century BC, or the Ten Commandments of the Old Testament,[30] were framed as duties, and not rights, they provided fertile soil on which human rights have been able to grow.[31] The idea of charity or solidarity, for instance, which underpins social rights, finds support in major religions like Islam,[32] Judaism and Christianity,[33] as well as Confucianism[34] and Buddhism.[35] Taking a second example, religious tolerance, an essential component of one of the best known first generation rights, freedom of thought and belief, was advocated in Mesopotamia as early as in the 6th century BC, when Emperor Cyrus pledged to 'honor the religion and custom of all nations under [his] kingdom'.[36] On the Indian subcontinent, the Buddhist Emperor Ashoka (304–232 BC) adopted a similar stance. Almost two millennia later, another Indian ruler, the Muslim Mughal Emperor Akbar (1542–1605),[37] defended tolerance of diverse religions, at a time when Europe was ravaged by religious wars and the Reformators' vindication of religious liberty was far from realized. Akbar's policy of religious toleration was not foreign to Islam. The Koran holds: 'Let there be no compulsion in religion'.[38] In the Western world, Tertullian (ca. 160–ca. 220 AD) vindicated from the Governor of the Roman province of Carthage, for the sake of the Christian community, the 'right belonging to mankind and the natural power of every person to worship as he thinks best'.[39]

Focusing on the Western precursors more generally,[40] the heritage of the Greeks and Romans provided important intellectual strands for the contemporary concept of human rights. They include reason as a distinctive and common feature of all humans, and the related ideas of freedom, equality and universality, as expressed in the Stoic theory of natural law[41] and the Roman notion of '*ius gentium*' (law flowing from human reason and applicable to all people).[42] Under the influence of the Stoa, the Roman philosopher Cicero[43] grounded the worth (*dignitas*) of human nature in reason, a feature men shared with the gods.[44] In his writings, however, this concept of dignity competed with the status and conduct dependent understanding of dignity as honor.[45]

Later, the Christian tradition also oscillated between egalitarian and differentiating conceptions. The first line of thought anchored human dignity and equality in the idea that all humans are made in God's image[46] and partake in God's reason. The second line of thought denied dignity to sinners, heretics and heathens. The perception of the hierarchical structure of the feudal society and the Church as a natural, God-given order further reinforced the differentiating function of dignity. For the emergence of the human rights idea, it was essential that the first conception of human dignity came to prevail over the latter. In addition to acknowledging people's intrinsic equal worth, it was crucial to affirm another characteristic: their freedom. Humanism, the late Spanish scholastic school, and the Reformation made important contributions to this effect,[47] establishing a strong link between freedom, dignity and equality.

The Italian Renaissance scholar Pico della Mirandola's (1463–1494) influential account of human dignity saw man's godlike nature in his creative ability.[48] He held that unlike all other things, human nature is not fixed. Men, like God, are creators, as they are free to shape and determine their own nature, which founds their dignity. Affirming the freedom and equality of all people within an exclusively European and Christian context was one thing; making the same assertion with regard to 'barbarous unbelievers'[49] was a different matter. Unsurprisingly, the conquest of the Americas led to vivid controversies in Spain about the status and the rights of the Indians. In these lively debates, the Dominican priest and Bishop of Chiapas, Bartolomé de las Casas (1484–1566)[50] and Francisco de Vitoria (1483–1546),[51] founder of the Spanish late scholastic doctrine (also known as the School of Salamanca), opposed the enslavement and exploitation of natives justified on the basis that the Indians lacked reason and autonomy.[52] Their defense of the Indians firmly extended the idea of brotherhood and compassion beyond the Christian community, advocating the notion of a common humanity. Later, the most famous representative of the School of Salamanca, Francisco Suárez (1548–1617) also defended the unity of the human race, which was, in his words, 'quasi-political and moral'.[53] It rested on the conviction that all people of this world, independently of their religion or race, were free by nature and endowed with reason.[54] As such, they were entitled to freedom from slavery and from coercion in religious matters, as well as to respect of their property and their family. These entitlements were claimed on the basis of natural law, understood as a set of immutable and universal precepts, which, by virtue of God's will, are inherent in the rational and free nature of men. Occasionally, and far from systematically, these entitlements were referred to as human rights ('*derechos humanos*').[55]

Among these rights vindicated for people outside the jurisdiction of Christian princes, freedom of religion, however, was far from being accepted with regard to the subjects of Christian rulers. Although imposing conditions and limits on the sanctions which could legitimately be imposed on unbelievers, Suárez, for instance, considered that Christian princes could enforce the worship of the true religion within their jurisdiction, as it was in his view an essential condition for the virtues necessary to safeguard peace and justice within the Republic.[56] Another movement – the Reformation – fundamentally challenged this view, affirming the central place of religious liberty. The respect for freedom of creed and conscience was vindicated as a condition for the subjects' duty to obey their rulers.[57]

The above-mentioned lines of thought paved the way for modern secular natural law doctrines (as set out for instance by Grotius [1583–1645] and Pufendorf [1632–1694]),[58] and initiated a gradual shift from a duty-based to a rights-based society, and from a theocentric to an anthropocentric world view. Secularization and an optimistic vision of mankind, emphasizing human capabilities and reason at the expense of sinfulness and fallibility,[59] favored the birth of the human rights idea during the Enlightenment.

2.2   The Birth of the Human Rights Idea

During the religious and political struggles in England in the 17th century, the influence of natural law doctrines resulted in the 'transformation from Christian to political freedom'.[60] Human rights emerged as instruments of social and political change, aimed at combating the privileges of the old feudal order and the absolute power of the monarch. John Locke's 'Two Treaties of Government',[61] published in 1690, offered a new philosophical justification to the political settlements between Parliament and the King following the Glorious Revolution, reflected in the Bill of Rights (1689). Similar to the famous *Magna Carta* (1215), the Petition of Rights (1628) and the *Habeas Corpus* Act (1679), the Bill of Rights did not set out rights derived from natural law and belonging to all human beings. Instead, it vindicated 'ancient rights and liberties' of the members of Parliament, the 'Lords Spiritual and Temporal and Commons'.[62] Locke (1632–1704), by contrast, founded his argument firmly on natural law. Like Hobbes (1588–1679),[63] he distinguished between the state of nature and political society, grounding the legitimacy of the state not on God but on the consent of naturally free and equal individuals. Imagining a state prior to the political community, both authors adopted a more individualistic vision than preceding scholars, who shared the Aristotelian view of man being by nature 'a social animal'. This is however to a larger extent true for Hobbes than for Locke. Unlike Hobbes, Locke did not perceive the state of nature as a perpetual war between antagonistic subjects (*bellum omnium contra omnes*) but as a state governed by natural law which the individuals left not just to insure their survival, but also due to their desire to live in a political community.[64] The two authors also differed on another important point: by contrast with Hobbes's *Leviathan*, Locke's writings did not justify absolute state power but limited government. When individuals decided to abandon the state of nature and to found a political community, they entrusted the state with a specific function: to protect 'life, liberty and property'. These natural rights were bestowed on all men by natural law in the state of nature. It is Locke's theory of *natural rights* which has left a major imprint on the human rights movement. Although Locke grounded these rights, as will be shown, also on duties, the emphasis shifted. Natural law ceased to be mainly concerned with the laying down of duties,[65] but became to be seen as a source of individual rights. These rights preceded political society and were inalienable entitlements protecting the citizens against state power. Conceived as a shield against the coercive power of the state, Locke's theory of natural rights justified the right to abolish tyrannical governments.

Locke's concept of rights built on a broad notion of property (*dominium*), understood as self-ownership.[66] This notion originated in the late Middle Ages and was further developed by natural law thinkers such as Grotius and Suárez.[67] Locke argued that being the property of God, man had a duty and the corresponding right of self-preservation. So as to preserve himself, he is given freedom, in the sense of property over his own body and his actions. The idea of autonomy as self-ownership over one's mind and body is in Locke's writing the foundation of property rights over things, since the ownership of one's body entails the ownership over the fruit of one's labor. The conception of self-ownership was influential in another way. It favored the view of human beings as self-contained, individualized persons whose bodies, previously only held sacred in a spiritual order, became sacred within a secular order.[68] The intangibility of the human body fuelled opposition to torture and similar forms of punishments, previously considered as practices necessary for the redemption and reparation of the religious, political and moral order of the community.[69]

Another sense of autonomy has been more influential for the modern Western human rights idea than that of self-possession: the account of autonomy as moral and political self-legislation, articulated by Rousseau (1712–1778) and Kant (1724–1804). According to the famous German philosopher from Königsberg, humans are autonomous to the extent that they follow the laws dictated by their reason. By contrast with other beings and objects, persons, as rational and therefore autonomous beings, have no instrumental value (a price) but intrinsic worth: dignity. Due to their worthiness, they can never be employed exclusively as objects or means to achieve someone else's ends, but need to be treated likewise as ends in themselves.[70] This notion of autonomy and dignity grounded for Kant the only original, innate right belonging to every individual by virtue of his or her humanity, the right to equal freedom.[71] The latter implies that each person is not entitled to more freedom than is compatible with the same degree of freedom for others, or, conversely, that any limitation of personal freedom needs to be reciprocally applicable to others.

In the 18th century, it was Locke's work which had the biggest political impact. The natural rights to life, liberty and property, and the right to overthrow tyrannical governments, were invoked to justify the revolutionary break of the North American colonies with the English constitutional order. Article 1 of the Virginia Bill of Rights of 12 June 1776, which influenced the American Declaration of Independence drafted by Thomas Jefferson in the same year,[72] clearly echoed Locke. Its first provision stated:

> That all men are by nature equally free and independent, and have certain inherent rights, of which, when they enter into a state of society, they cannot, by any compact, deprive or divest their posterity; namely, the enjoyment of life and liberty, with the means of acquiring and possessing property, and pursuing and obtaining happiness and safety.

A decade later, the solemnly declared natural rights became part of positive law. In 1789, Congress adopted the Bill of Rights, consisting of the first ten Amendments to the Constitution of the United States of 1787.

Meanwhile, the revolutionary impulse had spread in France, and fuelled a series of Rights Declarations, starting with the famous Declaration of the Rights of Man and of the Citizens of 26 August 1789. Like its American counterparts, the Declaration proclaimed in Article 1 that 'Men are born and remain free and equal in rights ...' and affirmed 'the preservation of the natural and imprescriptible rights of man' to be '[t]he aim of all political association'. 'These rights are liberty, property, security, and resistance to oppression.' The subsequent provisions emphasized as 'natural, unalienable, and sacred rights of man',[73] and 'based upon simple and incontestable principles',[74] the rights to political participation, procedural safeguards, including guarantees of fair trial and against arbitrary detention (*habeas corpus*), freedom of opinion, including religious ones, and the 'inviolable and sacred right' of property.

2.3 Contestation, Positivation and Industrialization

Unsurprisingly, the revolutionary dynamic of the human rights movement fuelled controversy and counter-movements.[75] Among the best-known critiques are those of Edmund Burke, Jeremy Bentham and Karl Marx.[76] Whilst Burke challenged natural rights and the French Revolution in his famous controversy with Thomas Paine from a conservative perspective,[77] Bentham's critique was grounded on utilitarianism and positivism.[78] Famously deriding the 'anarchical' idea of natural rights as 'rhetorical nonsense, – nonsense upon stilts', Bentham held that a real right was 'the child of law', a natural right being 'a son that never had a father'.[79] Stripped of their moral dimension, human rights were, pursuant to this view, reduced to instruments of positive law aimed at protecting individual interests with the purpose and within the limits of maximizing overall welfare.

In the 19th century, the rights declared in the previous century were codified in many of the constitutions adopted during that era in Western Europe. To the extent that natural rights became, as fundamental rights, part of positive law, Bentham's criticism lost some of its practical impact. What, however, if natural law and positive law were in conflict? Did positive law always trump considerations of justice, as expressed by natural law theories? The positivist school, which came to prevail during the 19th century, clearly answered in the affirmative. As we will see later, the breakthrough of the international human rights movement in the 20th century was linked to a revival of natural law and a rediscovery of human rights as moral, for example natural, rights.

Despite the impact of positivism, the transformative force of human rights did not die in the 19th century. The idea of the liberty and equality of all human beings was invoked to challenge the dominant conceptions reducing natural rights to the rights of white, middle-class men. Movements vindicating the rights of women or fighting for the abolition of slavery sought to broaden the sphere of moral concern to classes of people who, for allegedly biological reasons, were considered as lacking the central element for being rights holders: rationality and autonomy.[80] The political struggle for universal suffrage – aimed at decoupling political rights from sex, race and wealth – contributed to the contemporary vision of human rights as being not 'rights of men',[81] but rights belonging to all human beings.

At the same time, another movement of the 19th century challenged the universal drive of the human rights movement: historicism and nationalism. Questioning the Enlightenment's rationalism, individualism and cosmopolitanism, nationalist doctrines stressed the importance of the community – the nation – defined by common history, tradition and culture, planting the seeds for the first third generation right, people's right to self-determination. Under the influence of collectivist doctrines, individual rights came to be viewed as relative to a community, and essentially belonging to its members. According to this vision, the emphasis shifted from 'rights of men'[82] to 'rights of citizens'. The controversy between adherents of universalism and relativism has marked the history of human rights ever since.

Another important factor affecting the debates on human rights in different and diverging ways, was Western imperialism. On the one hand, imperialism, which entailed the discovery of foreign regions and cultures, lent empirical support to the relativist account of human rights. On the other hand, the rule over the colonized people fuelled the vision of Western superiority. Reinforced by theories of Social Darwinism, other cultures were expected to advance towards the higher stages of evolution already reached by Western society.

In addition to the opposition between universalists and relativists, another long lasting debate around human rights originated in the 19th century. Its best-known protagonist was Karl Marx,[83] who rejected the human rights declarations of the previous century as proclaiming 'rights of egoistic man separated from his fellow men and from the community',[84] aimed at consolidating the domination of the bourgeoisie over the working class. Whilst Marx rejected the 18th century's main concern with negative liberty rights and formal equality, socialism emphasized solidarity and the need for positive rights: state intervention was necessary in order to fight economic inequity, protect marginalized and vulnerable members of society, and to alleviate the dire poverty generated by the industrial revolution. Under the banner of labor movements and socialist political parties, rights labeled later as 'second generation rights' were born. The vindications of the socialist movement itself showed, however, that first and second generation rights were not clinically isolated but connected: one of the key demands was universal suffrage, which Marx himself heralded as 'a far more socialist measure than anything which has been honored with that name on the Continent'.[85]

3. THE DEVELOPMENT OF HUMAN RIGHTS ON THE INTERNATIONAL LEVEL

Of the ideologies mentioned in the previous section, it was not the international aspirations of the socialist movement, but nationalism and imperialism that marked international relations by the end of the 19th century. Human Rights remained an essentially domestic concern until the second half of the 20th century. Several developments in international law had prepared the ground for the birth of international human rights in the aftermath of World War II. These precursors helped to shape the content of future human rights norms, and, more generally, contributed to making human well-being a direct concern of international law.

3.1 Precursors

As mentioned above, the abolition of slavery was an important objective of the human rights movement on the domestic level during the 19th century. During the same period, the abolitionist cause was also addressed on the international level.[86] The slave trade was first denounced at the Congress of Vienna as early as 1815. European powers recognized for the first time in a multilateral statement that this practice was 'repugnant to the principles of humanity and of universal morality'.[87] In 1885, the General Act of the Berlin Conference affirmed that 'trading in slaves is forbidden in conformity with the principles of international law'.[88] In the 20th century, endeavors to eliminate slavery were undertaken under the auspices of the League of Nations, founded in the aftermath of World War I at the Paris Peace Conference (1919–1920) with the aim of preventing future war. The Slavery Convention of 1926 committed the state parties to suppressing the slave trade and abolishing slavery.[89] In parallel, the League also took measures to fight 'White Slave Traffic' with the purpose of eliminating the traffic in women and children.[90] Although the Slavery Convention was not exclusively motivated by humanitarian concerns but also pursued economic objectives,[91] its adoption was a significant step for the purpose of international human rights: international law had become an instrument to protect victims of human rights abuses.

Other international instruments and institutions were also relevant for the protection of certain categories of persons, and are for this reason considered as precursors of international human rights law. Diplomatic protection, international humanitarian law, the mandate system for the administration of colonies set up by the League of Nations, as well as the regimes for the protection of minorities and workers rights created under the auspices of the same organization need to be mentioned.

Diplomatic protection originated before the 19th century as an instrument enabling a state to take diplomatic measures against another state so as to seek redress for the injury inflicted on one of its nationals. It was based on the premise that 'whoever uses a citizen ill, indirectly offends the state, which is bound to protect this citizen'.[92] In initiating diplomatic protection, the state of origin enforces its own rights vis-à-vis another state and does not assert the right of its nationals. Nonetheless, via the practice of diplomatic protection, designed as a means of enabling states to protect the interests of their nationals living abroad, minimal standards governing the treatment of aliens emerged. They were derived from general principles of international law recognized by civilized nations. Natural law doctrines and diverse systems of private law served as sources of inspiration for these norms[93] which later helped to shape the content of international human rights norms.

The codification of international human rights could also draw on another body of law, international humanitarian law (IHL). Like human rights, IHL, previously known as the law of war (*ius in bello*) has ancient roots. Minimal standards emerged so as to limit the atrocities of armed conflict, laying down certain rules on the admissible means and methods of warfare, and, to a lesser extent, on the protection of the victims of war. As compared with IHR, the codification and emergence of contemporary IHL took place one century earlier. The impetus was provided by the Swiss businessman Henry Dunant (1828–1910), after he witnessed the aftermath of the battle of Solferino in 1859. From his campaigning book, *A Memory of Solferino*, two main ideas emerged:[94] firstly, all the wounded and sick should be protected from hostilities and cared for independently of their allegiance to a party to the conflict; secondly, National Societies should be created to provide assistance to medical personnel on the battlefields. Dunant's campaign led to the creation of the International Committee for Relief to the Wounded in 1863, later renamed International Committee of the Red Cross (ICRC). Thanks to his endeavor, the first Geneva Convention for the Amelioration of the Condition of the Wounded and Sick in Armed Forces in the Field was adopted in the same year, and National Societies were created in many countries, which are today regrouped under the International Federation of Red Cross and Red Crescent Societies (IFRC) established in 1919.

If the 'law of The Hague' was historically considered as regulating the conduct of hostilities, contemporary IHL mainly consists of the four Geneva Conventions and their additional protocols, and customary rules.[95] Although classical IHL was conceived as imposing obligations on states and not as conferring subjective rights on individuals, its emphasis on humanitarian concerns, witnessed in the change of terminology from 'law of war' to 'IHL', and its precise rules applicable to armed conflicts, favored the cause of human rights at the international level. Nevertheless, despite the common human-itarian objective, IHL and IHR are generally considered two separate branches of law. Whilst classical IHL only applied in times of international armed conflict, IHR were mainly conceived to apply in peacetime. These differences have partly been blurred,[96] and the thesis that IHL is a *lex specialis* rule with regard to IHR has come under challenge from scholars stressing the complementarity and the interaction between these two branches of law.[97] From a historical perspective, IHL preceded IHR and helped to shape its content; nowadays, however, there is also a marked influence of IHR on IHL.

Turning to the contribution of the League of Nations to IHR, only moderate progress was made at the Paris Peace Conference following World War I. On the one hand, the victorious powers rejected proposals to include two sets of provisions in the Covenant (the founding document of the League of Nations which formed an integral part of the Treaty of Versailles):[98] firstly, an article on non-discrimination based on race or nationality, and secondly, a provision on state intervention related to religious intoler-ance which posed a threat to peace. Equal treatment independent of race or nationality failed to galvanize sufficient support at a time when the colonial powers widely practiced inequality, and segregation entailed differentiation and exclusion within the United States.[99] On the other hand, the Covenant contained specific provisions protecting the population within the territories subject to the mandate system estab-lished by the Treaty of Versailles.[100] The Allies put in charge of the administration of the former colonies of the defeated powers were held to exercise their mandate in the interest of the population living in the mandated territories. Pursuant to the Covenant of the League, they had to respect freedom of conscience and religion, the prohibition of slave trade,[101] and guarantee humane labor standards.[102] It is important to note that these guarantees only applied to the mandated territories and did not impose any constraints on the Allies as regards their other colonies. Nevertheless, the mandate system was significant for the emergence of IHR, as it marked a departure from unlimited territorial sovereignty.[103] The administrating powers were no longer free to treat all the people subject to their jurisdiction as they pleased.

The Covenant made another important contribution to the development of IHR in providing for the international protection of workers' rights. Based on the premise that universal peace was impossible without social justice,[104] and anxious to avoid revolutionary turmoil within the state parties, the drafters of the Covenant decided to commit the members of the League to 'endeavour to secure and maintain fair and humane conditions of labour for men, women, and children, both in their own countries and in all countries to which their commercial and industrial relations extend', and stated that they 'will establish and maintain the necessary international organizations' for that purpose.[105] To achieve these ends, the Treaty of Versailles enshrined a fairly detailed list of 'methods and principles for regulating labour conditions which all industrial communities should endeavour to apply', including freedom of coalition, equal pay for men and women, the abolition of child labor, and limitations on working time to 48 hours per week.[106] Moreover, the Treaty created a permanent international organization, the International Labour Organization[107] (ILO), which was to become the first specialized agency of the United Nations. The constitutive articles of the ILO entrusted the newly created organization not only with standard-setting powers but also provided for supervisory systems to secure implementation. These can be viewed as a precursor of the monitoring mechanisms established within human rights regimes.

In addition to workers, the victors of World War I decided to protect another category of persons for the sake of preventing both internal and international conflict: national minorities.

Whilst several prior peace – and bilateral – treaties signed as early as the 16th and 17th centuries contained provisions protecting religious minorities,[108] European countries mainly invoked the protection of minorities in the 19th century to justify (often politically motivated) 'humanitarian interventions' in favor of the Christian minorities within the Ottoman Empire.[109] Although the Covenant remained silent on minority rights,[110] the protection of national minorities was an important issue at the Paris Peace Conference. Following the implosion of the Austro-Hungarian monarchy and the Ottoman Empire, a series of new states was created in Central and Eastern Europe in the name of people's rights to self-determination. These rights figured prominently among President Wilson's 'Fourteen Points' Program which formed the basis of the Peace Conference. For geographic, historical and political reasons, most of the newly created states were not, as suggested by the ideal of national self-determination, ethnically homogeneous nation states but contained important minorities within their territories. In this context, the international protection of minority rights was seen as a condition of political stability and peace. For this reason, a system of minority protection was set up under the auspices of the League of Nation. It was based on a series of protean treaties concluded between the Allies and the newly created states.[111] Based on these treaties, individuals belonging to national minorities were granted rights such as religious freedom, linguistic rights in the private and public sphere including education, and the right to non-discrimination based on race, language or religion.[112] Importantly, these provisions were considered as imposing on the state party 'obligations of *international* concern'[113] that were 'placed under the guarantee of the League of Nations'.[114] Along the same line of thought, disputes arising with respect to minority rights were considered as being of international character.[115] Within the decade following the conclusion of the treaties, a petition procedure was set up. It enabled individuals belonging to national minorities to bring infringements of their rights to the attention of the League. Although not of judicial nature, this petition mechanism was a leap forward and influenced the implementation mechanisms established by future human rights treaties. The substantive provisions of the minority treaties had the same effect as regards the content of future human rights norms.

Based on the evolution traced so far, the international legal order had come to protect nationals, workers, victims of slavery and armed conflict, people living in certain colonies, and national minorities. It did not yet, however, protect human beings simply as human beings. Nor had the view come to prevail that individuals were (partial) subjects of international law. The shield of state sovereignty remained strong. It was however weakened by another and more recent evolution within the international legal order, the emergence of international criminal law.

The idea that perpetrators of large-scale atrocities could be held individually liable and be prosecuted for the commission of international crimes first emerged after the massacres of the Armenians, described as 'crimes against humanity'.[116] The breakthrough in terms of international criminal law took place in the aftermath of World War II, when the Allies established two international courts, the Nuremberg and Tokyo Tribunals, to try Nazi and Japanese leaders for international crimes, including war crimes and crimes against humanity. The importance of these trials for the emergence of IHR was manifold. Firstly, as already mentioned, they contributed to weakening the dogma of state sovereignty, as individuals were denied the right to hide behind the sovereignty shield of their state of origin and were considered as direct addressees of international obligations. From this position, it was a less bold step to acknowledge that individuals could also be holders of rights derived directly from international law. Secondly, the concept of 'crimes against *humanity*', prepared the ground for the recognition of rights belonging to all *human* beings (instead of certain categories of persons). Thirdly, the fact that these crimes served to prosecute atrocities committed by the Nazi regime against its own people, further relativized state sovereignty and reinforced the idea that the treatment of nationals by their own state had clearly become a matter of international concern. Lastly, the Nuremberg and Tokyo trials favored a revival of natural law theories and the idea that individuals are owed rights because of their intrinsic worth, independently of positive law. On that ground, the perpetrators' defense based on the legality of their actions under the Nazi regime was rejected. As the legacy of National Socialism had shown, even legitimately elected governments, acting in the name of the majority, could pose a threat to their population and in particular to minorities. Their power needed thus to be constrained not only from within (through domestic constitutions and judicial review) but also from without, by the international legal order. It was in that context – marked by the tragedy of World War II – that IHR were born.

3.2 The Birth of International Human Rights

Before focusing on the breakthrough of IHR, it is worthwhile to briefly sketch the evolution of the human rights movement during the first half of the 20th century.[117] Prior to the outbreak of World War II, voices advocating for the protection of human rights on the international level remained rare. A notable exception was the Declaration of the International Rights of Man, adopted on 12 October 1929 by the International Law Institute in New York. It clearly departed from the traditional conception of international law, making human rights a concern of the international community. In this vein, its Preamble stated 'that the juridical conscience of the civilized world demands the recognition for the individual of rights preserved from all infringement on the part of the state'.[118] Following the outbreak of World War II, human rights became a rationale to fight Nazi Germany and its allies. The war spawned

> a vast movement of public opinion which ... grew incessantly in force and in scope as the war rolled on. Hundreds of political, scholarly and religious organizations have, by their publications, appeals, manifestations and interventions, spread and impressed the idea that the protection of human rights should be part of the war aims of the Allied Powers, and that the future peace would not be complete if it would not consecrate the principle of international protection of human rights in all States and if it would not guarantee this protection in an effective manner.[119]

One of the most influential human rights advocates was the English author Herbert George Wells (1866–1946). His human rights campaign was initiated with a letter published in *The Times* on 23 October 1939, which contained a Declaration of Rights. An amended version was included in his book *The Rights of Man: or What are We Fighting For?*, published in 1940[120] and subsequently disseminated not only in the Western World, but also on the Asian and African continents. Among legal scholars, Hersch Lauterpacht proposed 'An International Bill of the Rights of Man' in 1943.[121] On the political scene, President Roosevelt invoked human rights to seek support for American involvement in the war in his 'State of the Union' address to Congress on 6 January 1941, evoking a future world order founded upon four essential freedoms, the freedom of speech and expression, the freedom of worship, the freedom from want and the freedom from fear.[122] Roosevelt confirmed his vision in a joint declaration issued with Churchill in the same year. By the end of World War II, 26 allied nations and 21 further states had approved the principles of the so-called 'Atlantic Charter'.[123] These states formed together the core members of the United Nations (UN). Whilst 1945 was the 'constitutional moment'[124] of the international society, the founding year of the UN did not yet mark a fundamental breakthrough for the international human rights movement. The UN Charter failed to set out a legally binding catalogue of international human rights. Among the great victorious powers, there was little enthusiasm for the human rights project, as their record was not immune from criticism: 'the Soviet Union had domestic terror and the Gulag; England and France had colonies; and the United States had racism'.[125] Nevertheless, due to the influence of mainly Latin American countries and non-governmental organizations (most of them from the USA), references to human rights were included in six provisions[126] and the Preamble of the Charter. Against the backdrop of the atrocities committed under the Nazi regime, the

Preamble reaffirmed the 'faith in fundamental human rights, in the dignity and worth of the human person ... '. Articles 1 and 55 elevated the promotion of human rights into a purpose and main task of the United Nations, considering the 'universal respect for, and observance of, human rights and fundamental freedoms for all without distinction as to race, sex, language, or religion'[127] as an essential condition for 'peaceful and friendly relations among nations'.[128] So as to further the protection of human rights, the Charter gave the United Nations General Assembly (UNGA) the mandate to 'initiate studies and make recommendations'[129] to that effect, and Article 68 entrusted the Economic and Social Council (ECOSOC) with setting up commissions 'for the promotion of human rights'. Based on this provision, ECOSOC established the UN Commission on Human Rights (UNCHR) in 1946, which was to become for six decades the main Charter-based institution concerned with the promotion and protection of human rights.[130]

The Commission's first task was to draft an international bill of human rights. Within less than two years, this mission was accomplished: on 10 December 1948, one day after the adoption of the Genocide Convention,[131] the UNGA adopted the world's most famous and most cited human rights catalogue, the UDHR.[132] Since 1948, it has been much debated whether the rights proclaimed in the Declaration truly were 'a common standard of achievement for all peoples and all nations'[133] or whether they essentially reflected Western values imposed on the rest of the world. Both strands of this argument – the Western (instead of universal) nature of the Declaration[134] and the imposition thesis – are too simplistic from a historical perspective.[135]

Whilst it is true that the text of the UDHR (with references to 'inherent dignity',[136] 'equal and inalienable rights',[137] freedom and reason[138]) strongly borrows from the language of the Enlightenment and the French Declaration of 1789,[139] the framers deliberately omitted references to natural law or any other philosophy,[140] leaving the moral foundation of human rights undetermined.[141] As regards the 'imposition thesis', it is interesting to point out that the Great Western Powers were, as already mentioned, far from ardent supporters of an international Bill of Rights.[142] In addition, during the drafting process of the UDHR '[t]he "traditional" political and civil rights – the ones now most often labeled "Western" – were the least controversial of all'.[143] The only exception was Saudi Arabia's objection to the right to free marriage and to change one's religion. Moreover, the drafters aimed at avoiding the charge of excessive individualism, often hastily leveled against the tradition of the Enlightenment,[144] without yielding to collectivism.[145] By contrast with the declarations proclaimed in the 18th century, the UDHR contains a general limitation clause (Article 29), enabling rights to be balanced against the public interests (morality, public order, and general welfare) of a democratic society.[146] The same provision also refers to the social nature of human beings in stating that '[e]veryone has duties to the community in which alone the free and full development of his personality is possible'.[147] Not only communist states, but also Christian philosophers and Asian thinkers welcomed the reference to duties. The representatives of Latin America adopted the same position, which was hardly surprising. They had adopted in May 1948 the American Declaration of Rights *and Duties*. The same states and circles also advocated in favor of social, economic and cultural rights, enshrined in UDHR Articles 22 to 27.[148] Based on the experience that economic hardship had prepared the ground for Hitler's accession to power, many

Western European intellectuals also vindicated these rights. In the United States, supporters of second generation rights invoked the experience of the New Deal and President Roosevelt's defense of the 'freedom from want'.[149] Another favorable factor for the inclusion of social and economic rights in the UDHR was the intensive and successful activity of the ILO. In the period between the two wars, it had adopted nearly one hundred conventions on labor standards.[150]

Nevertheless, the UDHR did not place social and economic rights exactly on the same level as civil and political rights.[151] They were not proclaimed as rights inherent to all human beings but as entitlements belonging to '[e]veryone, as a member of society',[152] to be realized 'in accordance with the organization and resources of each State'.[153] Apart from this qualification, a consensus in favor of the inclusion of social and economic rights also emerged due to two other factors: firstly, the UDHR did not provide for enforcement mechanisms, and secondly, the Declaration's aspiration was mainly educational.[154] It was conceived as a political document to be cast into positive law at a second stage. Whilst the emerging tensions between West and East had already overshadowed the drafting process, the iron curtain came down shortly after the proclamation of the UDHR, closing the window of opportunity for a timely codification of the Universal Declaration in a legally binding international instrument.

3.3   The Cold War Era

The ideological confrontation between the Eastern and the Western bloc protracted the drafting process of an international treaty to implement the UDHR for more than a decade. Instead of a single Covenant, as initially requested by the UNGA, two instruments emerged from the work of the Commission on Human Rights, epitomizing the split between East and West.[155] While the first Treaty, the International Covenant on Economic, Social and Cultural Rights (ICESCR),[156] was supposed to express the view of the Communist countries, the second instrument – the International Covenant on Civil and Political Rights (ICCPR)[157] – was considered to represent Western liberal thought. According to the 'Western' view, only the rights and freedoms enshrined in the ICCPR were of primary importance. Once they were realized, the respect of economic and social rights would follow. Pursuant to the 'Eastern' view, first generation rights were declared as being contingent on second generation rights. Moreover, it was argued that the effective realization of economic and social rights may require the limitation of first generation rights (the so-called 'trade-off thesis').[158]

The decision to split the text of the UDHR into two Covenants was not only of ideological, but also of legal significance, although both treaties share commonalities: both Covenants are similarly structured. They both refer to the inherent dignity of the person as the foundation of the proclaimed rights. Reflecting the legacy of the Nazi regime, they both codify Article 2 UDHR and hold, like all subsequent human rights treaties to be adopted, that all individuals are entitled to the protection of the rights recognized in the Covenants, 'without distinction of any kind, such as race, colour, sex, language, religion, political or other opinion, national or social origin, property, birth or other status'.[159] Moreover, both the ICCPR and the ICESCR innovate with respect to the UDHR in enshrining in their first article a third generation right, people's right to self-determination. Their second provision reveals, however, a fundamental difference.

Whilst civil and political rights are to be realized with immediate effect, social, economic and cultural rights are to be achieved progressively, to the maximum of the states' resources, 'by all appropriate means, including particularly the adoption of legislative measures'. Reflecting the Western view, the wording of Article 2 ICESCR implied that second generation rights were not directly applicable and were to be implemented by the legislative, not the judicial branch. In the same spirit, the supervisory mechanism established by the ICESCR consisted exclusively in a reporting procedure.[160] By contrast, the ICCPR provided in addition to the mandatory reporting procedure for an optional, quasi-judicial enforcement mechanism. Subject to the consent of each state, the body of independent experts charged with monitoring compliance with the ICCPR (named the Human Rights Committee) was also given the power to receive and consider communications from state parties.[161] More importantly, the right of individual communications applied to states that had ratified the First Optional Protocol to the ICCPR.[162] The ICCPR, the ICESCR and the Optional Protocol (which form, together with the UDHR and subsequent Protocols to both Covenants, the so-called 'International Bill of Rights), were adopted on 16 December 1966. They only entered into force in 1976, once the necessary number of 35 ratifications had been achieved. To date, both Covenants have been ratified by over 150 states.[163] From a legal point of view, the goal of a legally binding, universally applicable International Bill of Rights has been largely achieved.[164]

Despite the ideological polarization, four other 'core' human rights treaties were adopted during the Cold War in addition to the two Covenants: the International Convention on the Elimination of All Forms of Racial Discrimination (ICERD, 21 December 1965);[165] the Convention on the Elimination of All Forms of Discrimination against Women (CEDAW, 18 December 1979);[166] the Convention against Torture and Other Cruel, Inhuman or Degrading Treatment or Punishment (CAT, 10 December 1984);[167] and the Convention on the Rights of the Child (CRC, 20 November 1989).[168] After the fall of the Berlin War, the UNGA adopted another three 'core' treaties: the International Convention on the Protection of the Rights of All Migrant Workers and Members of Their Families (ICRMW, 18 December 1990);[169] the Convention on the Rights of Persons with Disabilities (CRPD, 13 December 2006);[170] and the International Convention for the Protection of All Persons from Enforced Disappearance (CPED, 20 December 2006).[171] All of these instruments established independent expert bodies to monitor state compliance. These bodies form, together with the supervisory committees of the two Covenants, the so-called treaty-based enforcement mechanisms of the contemporary international human rights regime.

During the Cold War era, supervisory systems based on human rights conventions were also set up at the regional level on the European, American and African continents.[172] In Europe, the main treaty of the regional human rights regime, the European Convention on Human Rights and Fundamental Freedoms (ECHR),[173] was adopted within the framework of the Council of Europe in 1950, only two years after the proclamation of the UDHR, and with the aim of 'securing the universal and effective recognition and observance of the Rights therein declared'.[174] The content of the ECHR presaged the ideological split between first and second generation rights which materialized on the universal level later, during the drafting process of the two

Covenants. The framers only included first generation rights in the European Convention. Second generation rights were codified 11 years later in the European Social Charter (ESC),[175] which provided for a much weaker enforcement mechanism than the ECHR. This affirmation is even more accurate today: the Strasbourg machinery has evolved into the only human rights regime with a compulsory jurisdiction of a judicial authority (the European Court of Human Rights) to decide individual applications.[176]

In the Americas, the regional human rights system was created under the auspices of the Organization of American States (OAS).[177] The Charter of the OAS was adopted on 30 April 1948, the same day the first international Bill of Rights – the American Declaration of the Rights and Duties of Men – was proclaimed. The American Convention on Human Rights (ACHR) was adopted more than two decades later, in 1969, and entered into force in 1978. Drafted after the adoption of the two Covenants, and mainly limited, similarly to its European counterpart, to civil and political rights, the content of the ACHR was partly inspired by the ICCPR. One year after the entry into force of the Convention, the Inter-American Court of Human Rights was created. The Court, which was given both adjudicative and advisory functions, is, together with the Inter-American Commission on Human Rights (established in 1959), the main international institution to uphold human rights on the American hemisphere.

On the African continent, a regional human rights regime emerged in the framework of the Organization of African Unity (OAU), the predecessor of the African Union (AU). As in the Americas, its supervisory machinery consists both of a Commission (the African Commission on Human and Peoples' Rights, created in 1987) and a Court (The African Court on Human and Peoples' Rights, which has been operational since 2009).[178] The main task of both institutions is to secure respect for the rights protected in the African Charter on Human and Peoples' Rights, adopted in 1981 (AChHPR, also known as the Banjul Charter).[179] By contrast with the other two regional human rights treaties, the African Charter protects both first generation and second generation rights. Moreover, as its name implies, it also contains collective rights (e.g. third generation or solidarity rights). Reflecting the legacy of colonialism and the heritage of African culture, the Charter protects, for instance, the right to self-determination, the right to freely dispose of wealth and national resources, the right to development, the right to peace and security and a right to 'a generally satisfactory environment'.[180] Another distinguishing feature of the AChHPR is that it is not limited to spelling out rights but also sets out individual duties.[181]

Returning to the universal level, another evolution has been of vital importance for the international human rights regime: in parallel to the adoption of treaties establishing their own supervisory bodies, a series of institutions, procedures and mechanisms designed to promote and protect IHR developed which have their source in the UN Charter. The major body of the so-called Charter-based system was the Commission on Human Rights. In addition to its standard-setting activity,[182] the Commission's mandate was extended to examining, monitoring and reporting on human rights situations, either by country or by specific issue.[183] According to its members, the mandate and functioning of the Commission reflected the philosophical tradition of human rights beyond the traditional border between Eastern and Western states.[184] However, over the years, the Charter body came under growing criticism due to its politicization and the double standards governing its action. The politicization of the Commission was hard to deny,[185] as well as hard to avoid due to its intergovernmental character. The Cold War, however, exacerbated this problem. In this context, the composition of the Commission led to an 'inevitable and ideological competition between East and West'.[186] During the Cold War era, both the Western bloc and the Soviet bloc mutually tolerated the fact that human rights violators served as members of the Commission.[187] As will be shown shortly, the end of the Cold War brought about the opportunity for criticism and institutional change.

3.4 The Post Cold War Era

A step towards rapprochement between the Western bloc and Eastern Bloc was taken more than a decade before the fall of the Berlin wall within the framework of the Conference on Security and Co-operation in Europe (CSCE, since 1995 OSCE[188]). The so-called Helsinki process resulted in the adoption of the Helsinki Final Act (also known as Helsinki Accords or Helsinki Declaration), which lays down ten 'Principles Guiding Relations between Participating States'. Importantly for IHR, they were not limited to affirming the sovereign equality of the signatory states, the inviolability of frontiers, territorial integrity and non-intervention in internal affairs, but also committed the State Parties to 'promote and encourage the effective exercise of civil, political, economic, social, cultural and other rights and freedoms all of which derive from the inherent dignity of the human person …'.[189] Moreover, the Signatories were called upon to 'respect human rights and fundamental freedoms, including the freedom of thought, conscience, religion or belief …'.[190] The specific reference to this quintessential first generation right was significant, as it helped to bolster dissident movements within the Eastern Blocs. More generally, the Helsinki Accords had the effect of reinforcing civil and political rights in Central and Eastern Europe.

A few months after the breakdown of Communism, the UNGA seized the opportunity to overcome the ideological opposition between East and West and decided to convene a second World Conference on Human Rights to be held in Vienna in 1993.[191] Before the Conference, it became evident that the aim of reaffirming the universality of IHR would be a daunting task. In the meantime, whilst the 'dialogue of the deaf' between East and West had abated, another cleavage, running 'North–South', had become salient since the 1970s.[192] This challenge to the universal nature of IHR was voiced in four Declarations adopted with a view to the World Conference on the regional level, in South-East Asia,[193] Latin America and the Caribbean,[194] Africa,[195] and in the Arab region.[196] The Bangkok Declaration adopted within the framework of The Association of Southeast Asian Nations (ASEAN),[197] for instance, expressed the ongoing debate on specific 'Asian values'[198] to be accommodated within the framework of the international human rights regime. Placing strong emphasis on respect for national sovereignty and non-interference in the internal affairs of States,[199] it urged 'that the promotion of human rights should be encouraged by cooperation and consensus, and not through confrontation and the imposition of incompatible values',[200] and recognized 'that while human rights are universal in nature, they must be considered in the context of a dynamic and evolving process of international norm-setting, bearing in mind the significance of national and regional particularities and various historical, cultural and religious backgrounds'.[201] As regards the various categories of human rights, the Declaration's focus was clearly on second and third generation rights, for example the fight against poverty and the right to development.[202]

Against the backdrop of the 'Southernization'[203] of IHR, the Vienna Declaration and Programme of Action,[204] adopted by consensus at the second World Conference, was generally considered a success in developed countries.[205] The Declaration repeatedly stressed the universality of human rights. Its first point declared that the universal nature of the rights and freedoms guaranteed on the international level was 'beyond question'. Nevertheless, consensus for this bold statement had been achieved through various concessions. For instance, the Declaration only explicitly refers to the ICESCR and emphasizes the issues of poverty and development. No mention is made of the ICCPR or of the quintessential 'Western' liberties of freedom of speech or religious freedom.[206] Furthermore, the duty of all states to promote and protect all human rights was clearly affirmed in the fifth paragraph, with the qualification that 'the significance of national and regional particularities and various historical, cultural and religious backgrounds must be borne in mind'.

In the same section, the framers of the Declaration intended to put to rest the controversy on the status and relationship between the three generations of IHR, affirming that: '[a]ll human rights are universal, indivisible and interdependent and interrelated. The international community must treat human rights globally in a fair and equal manner, on the same footing, and with the same emphasis.'[207] The indivisibility, interdependence and interrelatedness of human rights expressed the vision of equal importance, substantive overlap and mutual supportiveness between the different generations of rights, rejecting implicitly the 'trade-off theory'[208] and the claim that one category of rights takes priority over the others.[209]

This view was in line with a strand of scholarship skeptical of the traditional argument according to which first generation rights imposed on states exclusively negative duties, whilst second and third generation rights required state action. The theory (first articulated by Professor Shue[210]) that all human rights give rise to both negative and positive duties (the duty to respect, protect and fulfill) has gained significant ground. One of the main practical implications of the 'indivisibility, interdependence and interrelatedness' thesis has been sustained advocacy in favor of direct enforceability by domestic courts and treaty bodies of second (and to a lesser extent) third generation rights.[211] A milestone in this development was achieved in 2008, when the UNGA adopted an optional protocol to the ICESCR enabling the CESCR[212] to receive and consider individual communications alleging the violation of a right protected under the Covenant.[213] The truly equal status between the two Covenants will be reached once the necessary number of ratifications (ten) for the entry into force of the Protocol is secured.

The Vienna Conference also made a significant contribution to the global human rights regime from an institutional point of view. Based on The Programme of Action, the position of United Nations High Commissioner for Human Rights (UNHCHR) was created in 1993 with a view to strengthening the United Nations' human rights mandate.[214] A further important institutional change of the Charter-based system was decided 13 years later. On 15 March 2006, after difficult negotiations, the General Assembly established the Human Rights Council.[215] This new body was created to replace the Commission on Human Rights, which had, as already mentioned, come under increasing attack for its over-politicization. The reform did not bring about radical institutional change. Like its predecessor, the Human Rights Council is an intergovernmental body, composed of 47 members (as compared with 53 members of the Commission). With a view to achieving a fairer representation, the reformers opted for a rotation system, which prevents permanent membership of some and constant exclusion of other states. These modest institutional changes were complemented by a true innovation, consisting in a new *peer* monitoring mechanism: the Universal Periodic Review (UPR).[216] This mechanism was aimed at making a contribution to the overall objective pursued by the creation of the Human Rights Council, 'ensuring universality, objectivity and non-selectivity ... and the elimination of double standards and politicization'.[217] To achieve this objective, the UPR subjects all states to regular scrutiny, which is to be 'based on a interactive dialogue, with the full involvement of the country concerned'.[218]

Despite this innovation, the Council has so far not lived up to the high hopes and expectations underlying its creation.[219] In particular the objective of depoliticization has not been reached, for two reasons: firstly, the Council is, like its predecessor, a political institution due to its composition; secondly, the newly created body started to operate in a context marked by the 'War on Terror'. The aftermath of the 9/11 terrorist attack on the United States has been conducive to a new cleavage, with the 'West' placed in opposition to Islamic countries. In this context, the Council became repeatedly a forum for antagonistic debates on the occupied territories in Palestine and the thorny issue of defamation of religion.

The 'War on Terror' also needs to be mentioned for another reason. Apart from raising the well-known challenge of how to reconcile human rights and security, it has squarely confronted the international community with a series of more recent (but not new) problems. Firstly, the aftermath of 9/11 has emphasized the problem of how to secure effective implementation of IHR. Whilst international human rights law has grown into an impressive body of international norms since the adoption of the UDHR, the effectiveness of these rules is far from guaranteed. As the measures taken in the aftermath of 9/11 have shown, even countries with a long tradition of constitutionalism are prone to disregard the most basic human rights in times of crisis. Secondly, the 'War on Terror', including military actions in Iraq and Afghanistan, extraordinary renditions and detentions of terrorist suspects abroad raises the question of the extraterritorial application of IHR[220] and its relationship with IHL.[221] Thirdly, the UN Security Council's sanctions regime targeting members of terrorist groups[222] – widely criticized on human rights grounds[223] – as well as human rights abuses committed by private military and security contractors in Iraq and Afhangistan[224] have highlighted another problem: in a globalized world where the classical distinctions between public and private, and between the domestic and international sphere, have been blurred, the global human rights regime needs to further extend its reach to non-state actors, including international organizations[225] and corporations.[226] Lastly, so as to prevent violent backlashes against symbols of Western hegemony and exclusionary trends within all nations, IHR need to effectively address problems related to globalization, including, for instance, poverty and environmental degradation.[227]

4. CONCLUSION

Whilst human rights have ancient roots and can be viewed as modern expressions of values common to diverse cultural traditions, their contemporary form can be traced back directly to the Enlightenment. The idea that every human being, by the sole fact of being human, holds equal rights which pre-exist the political community emerged as a powerful conviction to challenge the social stratification of the old feudal order and to protect the population against abuses of coercive state power. Based on the experience that governments pose a formidable threat to their citizens and that oppression breeds both internal and external conflict, human rights became a concern of the international community. The legacy of World War II acted as a catalyst for the consecration of human rights on the global and regional level. The content of these rights has crystallized through the experience of human suffering and injustice. Shaped by history, human rights are dynamic and evolve in order to address new threats to freedom and human well-being. Throughout this process of adaptation and change, two countervailing trends have remained constant. On the one hand, like any powerful vision, the idea of human rights, and the promise of freedom and equality they represent, cannot be taken back[228] and fuel demands for social and political change. On the other hand, history has shown that human rights, and the underlying vision of a common humanity, are demanding ideals. The tendency to deny the rights of certain groups of people – be they 'barbarous non-believers', Blacks, women, Jews, or terrorist suspects – calls for eternal vigilance[229] if the idea of human dignity is to prevail in future.

NOTES

*   Maya Hertig Randall is Professor of Constitutional Law at the University of Geneva, Switzerland. I am very grateful to Marc Morel for his valuable research assistance and for his help with finalizing the references.

1.   For more details on the Declaration, *infra* section 3.2.

2.   For the distinction between moral and legal rights, see, e.g., J. Waldron, 'Introduction', in *Theories of Rights*, ed. J. Waldron (Oxford: Oxford University Press, 1984), 4 *et seq*. On the double nature of human rights, see, e.g., K.M. Girardet, 'Menschenrechte, europäische Identität, antike Grundlagen – Einführung in die wissenschaftliche Problematik', in *Menschenrechte und europäische Identität. Die antiken Grundlagen*, ed. K.M. Girardet and U. Nortmann (Stuttgart: Franz Steiner Verlag, 2005), 19–23.

3.   For a detailed study, see M.K. Addo, *The Legal Nature of International Human Rights* (Leiden and Boston: Martinus Nijhoff, 2010); for a critical analysis, see S. Meckled Garcia and B. Cali, ed., *The Legalization of Human Rights: Multidisciplinary Perspectives of Human Rights and Human Rights Law* (Milton Park and New York: Routledge, 2006).

4.   *Infra* section 3.4.

5.   This term was coined by Vasak in 1977, see K. Vasak, 'A 30-Year Struggle – The Sustained Efforts to Give Force of Law to the Universal Declaration of Human Rights', *UNESCO Courier* 30 (November 1977): 29; on solidarity rights, see id., 'Pour une troisième génération des droits de l'homme', in *Studies and Essays on International Humanitarian Law and Red Cross Principles in Honour of Jean Pictet*, ed. J. Pictet, C. Swinarksi and International Committee of the Red Cross (Geneva: International Committee of the Red Cross, 1984), 837–845; N. Roht-Arriaza, 'Solidarity Rights (Development, Peace, Environment, Humanitarian Assistance)', in *Max Planck Encyclopedia of Public International Law* (2008), available at http://www.mpepil.com (accessed 5 February 2012).

6.   On the distinction between three generations of human rights and a critical assessment, see, e.g., C. Tomuschat, *Human Rights: Between Idealism and Realism* (Oxford: Oxford University Press, 2008),

25–68; T. Meron, 'On a Hierarchy of International Human Rights', *American Journal of International Law* 80 (1986): 1–23; and from an African perspective, J.C. Mubangizi, 'Towards a New Approach to the Classification of Human Rights with Specific Reference to the African Context', *African Human Rights Law Journal* 4 (2004): 93–107.

7.   E.g., equal treatment before and under the law, meaning that the law should treat similar situations alike and apply equally to all. Formal equality is to be distinguished from substantive equality, which aims at compensating historical and social disadvantages of marginalized members of society so as to grant equal opportunities to all. Under a more far-reaching understanding, substantive equality goes beyond equality of opportunity and includes equality of outcome. On the distinction between formal and substantive equality, see, e.g., R.L. West, *Re-imagining Justice: Progressive Interpretations of Formal Equality, Rights, and the Rule of Law* (Aldershot: Ashgate, 2003), 157 *et seq.*

8.   President Franklin Delano Roosevelt famously declared in his annual State of the Union address to Congress in 1941 four essential freedoms: freedom of speech; freedom of worship; freedom from want; and freedom from fear, see also *infra* section 3.2 and note 122.

9.   It is controversial whether solidarity rights have the status of human rights and, if so, whether they are reducible to individual rights. For an insightful analysis of the main arguments, see J. Griffin, *On Human Rights* (Oxford: Oxford University Press, 2008), 257–276.

10. For comprehensive accounts of the history of human rights, see, e.g., M.R. Ishay, *The History of Human Rights: From Ancient Times to the Globalization Era* (Berkeley, Los Angeles and London: University of California Press, 2004); A. Haratsch, *Die Geschichte der Menschenrechte*, 4th edition (Potsdam: Universitätsverlag Potsdam, 2010); L.A. Hunt, *Inventing Human Rights: A History* (New York and London: W.W. Norton and Company, 2007); P.G. Lauren, *The Evolution of International Human Rights: Visions Seen* (Philadelphia: University of Pennsylvania Press, 2003); D.J. Whelan, *Indivisible Human Rights: A History* (Philadelphia: University of Pennsylvania Press, 2010); S. Moyn, *The Last Utopia: Human Rights in History* (Cambridge, MA: The Belknap Press of Harvard University Press, 2010); F. Klug, *The Evolution of Human Rights* (London: Routledge, 2010); J.M. Headley, *The Europeanization of the World: On the Origins of Human Rights and Democracy* (Princeton University Press, 2008). For succinct accounts, see A. Clapham, *Human Rights: A Very Short Introduction* (Oxford: Oxford University Press, 2007), 23–56; Tomuschat, *supra* note 6, at 7–24; W. Kälin and J. Künzli, *The Law of International Human Rights Protection* (Oxford: Oxford University Press, 2009), 3–30; T. Buergenthal, 'Human Rights', in *Max Planck Encyclopedia of Public International Law* (2008), available at http://www.mpepil.com (accessed 5 February 2012); M.A. Baderin and M. Ssenyonjo, 'Development of International Human Rights Law Before and After the UDHR', in *International Human Rights Law: Six Decades After the UDHR and Beyond*, ed. M.A. Baderin and M. Ssenyonjo (Burlington, VT: Ashgate, 2010).

11. See the famous admissibility decision of the European Commission of Human Rights, in *Austria v. Italy* (known as the *Pfunders case*), Application No. 788/60, *Yearbook of the European Convention on Human Rights*, 1961, Vol. IV, 138–140, which described the specific nature and purpose of the European Convention on Human Rights as follows: 'The purpose of the High Contracting Parties in concluding the Convention was not to concede to each other reciprocal rights and obligations in pursuance of their individual national interests but to realise the aims and ideals of the Council of Europe, as expressed in its Statute, and to establish a common public order of the free democracies of Europe with the object of safeguarding their common heritage of political traditions, ideals, freedom and the rule of law … it follows that the obligations undertaken … are essentially of an objective character, being designed rather to protect the fundamental rights of individual human beings from infringement by any of the High Contracting Parties than to create subjective and reciprocal rights for the High Contracting Parties themselves; … [I]t follows that a High Contracting Party, when it refers an alleged breach of the Convention to the Commission … is not to be regarded as exercising a right of action for the purpose of enforcing its own rights, but rather as bringing before the Commission an alleged violation of the public order of Europe.'

For a detailed analysis of the specific nature of human rights treaties, with references to other human rights regimes, see Addo, *supra* note 3, at 468 *et seq.*

12. The role of empathy is stressed by Hunt, *supra* note 10, at 28 *et seq.*

13. See the Preamble of the UDHR: 'Whereas recognition of the inherent dignity and of the equal and inalienable rights of all members of the *human family* is the foundation of freedom, justice and peace in the world' (emphasis added).

14. J.-J. Rousseau, *Le contrat social*, first published in 1762; for an English translation, see *The Social Contract*, trans. M. Cranston (New York: Penguin Books, 2006) and http://ebooks.adelaide.edu.au/r/rousseau/jean_jacques/r864s/ (accessed 1 February 2011).

15. Dignity is derived from the Latin term *dignitas*, meaning, among other things, 'worth'.

16. On the distinction between cultures based on dignity and cultures based on honor, see O. Kamir, 'Honor and Dignity Cultures: The Case of *Kavod* and Kvod Ha-Adam in Israeli Society and Law', in *The Concept of Human Dignity in Human Rights Discourse*, ed. D. Kretzmer and E. Klein (The Hague, London and New York: Kluwer Law International, 2002), 231 *et seq*.

17. See Hunt, *supra* note 10, at 29.

18. The importance of sympathy for the distress of fellow beings as a grounding for human rights is stressed by Clapham, *supra* note 10, at 9.

19. For a prominent exponent of this view, see E. Cahn, *The Sense of Injustice: An Anthropocentric View of Law* (Oxford: Oxford University Press, 1949); A. Dershowitz, *Rights from Wrongs* (New York: Basic Books, 2005).

20. See the Preamble of the UDHR.

21. Griffin, *supra* note 9, at 192.

22. More precisely, the foundational value of human dignity is controversial, too. For an overview of the main theories on the foundation of human rights, see J.J. Shestack, 'The Philosophic Foundations of Human Rights', *Human Rights Quarterly* 20 (1998): 201–234; for a comparative analysis of the interpretation of human dignity by constitutional courts, see C. McCrudden, 'Human Dignity and Judicial Interpretation of Human Rights', *European Journal of International Law* 19 (2008): 655–724.

23. For the openness of human rights and dignity to different justifications, which result in an area of consensus, see K. Hilpert, 'Die Menschenrechte – ein christliches Erbe?', in *Menschenrechte und europäische Identität. Die antiken Grundlagen*, ed. K.M. Girardet and U. Nortmann (Stuttgart: Franz Steiner Verlag, 2005), 159; W. Hirsch, 'Menschenwürde,' in *Theologische Realenzyklopädie*, ed. T. Kirchof and C.R. Kraus (Berlin: De Gruyter, 2007), 580. For more general accounts on how to reach agreement within a plural society, see Rawls's theory of 'overlapping consensus' in J. Rawls, *Political Liberalism* (New York: Columbia University Press, 1993), and Sunstein's concept of rights and constitutional texts as 'incompletely theorized agreements' in C.R. Sunstein, 'Incompletely Theorized Agreements', *Harvard Law Review* 108 (1994–1995): 1733–1772. From this perspective, efforts should focus on the justification of human rights from the vantage point of various religions and cultures, which may entail the reinterpretation of existing beliefs, instead of debating whether or not certain belief systems are *per se* compatible with human rights. As the example of the Catholic church shows, a shift from a skeptical to a favorable vision of human rights can be justified 'from within', e.g., based on the religious doctrine itself. For an outline of this evolution, see R. Marx, 'Menschenrechte in christlich-sozialethischer Perspektive', in *Menschenrechte und europäische Identität. Die antiken Grundlagen*, ed. K.M. Girardet and U. Nortmann (Stuttgart: Franz Steiner Verlag, 2005), 214–224; for a Protestant perspective on human rights, see F. Lohmann, *Zwischen Naturrecht und Partikularismus. Grundlegung christlicher Ethik mit Blick auf die Debatte um eine universale Begründbarkeit der Menschenrechte* (Berlin and New York: De Gruyter, 2002).

24. Among the vast literature on universalism and relativism of human rights, see for some recent contributions, e.g., A. Sajó, ed., *Human Rights With Modesty: The Problem of Universalism* (Leiden and Boston: Martinus Nijhoff Publishers, 2004); C. Corradetti, *Relativism and Human Rights: A Theory of Pluralistic Universalism* (New York: Springer, 2009); G. Fellous, *Les droits de l'homme: une universalité menacée* (Paris: La Documentation Française, 2010); J. Donnelly, 'International Human Rights: Universal, Relative or Relatively Universal?', in *International Human Rights Law: Six Decades After the UDHR and Beyond*, ed. M.A. Baderin and M. Ssenyonjo (Burlington, VT: Ashgate, 2010); P.J. Pararas, 'L'impossible universalité des droits de l'homme', *Revue trimestrielle des droits de l'homme* 85 (2011): 3–22. For an interesting focus on universalism and the UN treaty bodies, see M.K. Addo, 'Practice of United Nations Human Rights Treaty Bodies in the Reconciliation of Cultural Diversity with Universal Respect for Human Rights', *Human Rights Quarterly* 32 (2010): 601–664.

25. Griffin, *supra* note 9, at 9 *et seq*. On the indeterminacy of human rights, see also Addo, *supra* note 3, at 19–81.

26. Hunt, *supra* note 10, at 29.

27. This expression is inspired from the title of Sajó's book, *Human Rights With Modesty: The Problem of Universalism*, *supra* note 24.

28. Hunt, *supra* note 10, at 29.

29. On the early ethical contributions to human rights, see Ishay, *supra* note 10, at 16–61.

30. For a comparison of the Dekanon and the content of the rights protected in the UDHR, see Hilpert, *supra* note 23, at 156.
31. For justifications of human rights from diverse cultural and religious perspectives, see, e.g., U.Voigt, ed., *Die Menschenrechte im interkulturellen Dialog* (Frankfurt am Main, Berlin, Berne, etc.: Peter Lang, 1998); A.A. An-Na'im, ed., *Human Rights in Cross-Cultural Perspectives; A Quest for Consensus* (Philadelphia: University of Pennsylvania Press, 1995).
32. Almsgiving (zakāt) is one of the five pillars of Islam, based on which a certain percentage of one's possession (2.5%) shall be given to charity.
33. On Judaism and Christianity, see Hilpert, *supra* note 23, at 157; A. Soetendorp, 'Jewish Tradition and Human Rights', in *The Essential of Human Rights*, ed. R.K.M. Smith and C. van der Anker (New York: Oxford University Press, 2006).
34. The Chinese member of the drafting committee of the UDHR, Peng-Chun Chang, held that 'economic and social justice, far from being an entirely modern notion, was a 2500-year-old Confucian idea', quoted in M.A. Glendon, *A World Made New: Eleanor Roosevelt and the Universal Declaration of Human Rights* (New York: Random House, 2001), 185.
35. Giving for charitable purposes (dana) is one of the so-called paramitas (perfections) to be respected in Buddhist practice.
36. Cited in B.G. Ramcharan, *Contemporary Human Rights Ideas* (London: Routledge, 2008), 2.
37. See A. Sen, *The Argumentative Indian: Writings on Indian History, Culture and Identity* (London: Penguin Books, 2006).
38. See Sura 2:256 of the Koran; see Griffin, *supra* note 9, at 298, note 33.
39. Tertullian, *Ad Scapulam*: 'Tamen humani iuris et naturalis potestatis est unicuique quod putaverit colere', text available at http://www.intratext.com/IXT/LAT0247/_P2.HTM (accessed 4 February 2011); an English translation is available at http://www.tertullian.org/articles/dalrymple_scapula.htm (accessed 4 February 2011).
40. For a detailed study, see Girardet and Nortmann, *supra* note 2.
41. For an evolution of the natural law doctrine from Antiquity to the Enlightenment, see Lohmann, *supra* note 23, at 165–244.
42. H. Cancik, 'Die frühesten antiken Texte zu den Begriffen, "Menschenrecht", "Religionsfreiheit", "Toleranz"', in *Menschenrechte und europäische Identität. Die antiken Grundlagen*, ed. K.M. Girardet and U. Nortmann (Stuttgart: Franz Steiner Verlag, 2005), 97.
43. On dignity, see Cicero's work *De Officiis*; on natural law and the characteristics of men, *De Legibus*; for an analysis of the former work, see H. Cancik, 'Dignity of Man and *"Persona"* in Stoic Anthropology: Some Remarks on Cicero, *De Officiis I* 105–107', in *Concept of Human Dignity in Human Rights Discourse*, ed. D. Kretzmer and E. Klein (The Hague, London and New York: Kluwer Law International, 2002), 19–39, mentioning the influence of Cicero's work on later scholars, such as P. della Mirandola and S. Pufendorf; on *De Legibus*, see, e.g., Lohmann, *supra* note 23, at 175 *et seq.*
44. See Lohmann, *supra* note 23, at 175–177, 424. As this author points out, the resemblance between humans and God can be traced further back, to the Old Testament, Genesis 1:27: 'So God created man in his own image, in the image of God he created him'. This idea is eloquently expressed in the Talmud, which also highlights the uniqueness of every human being: 'A man may coin several coins with the same matrix and all will be similar, but the King of Kings, the Almighty, has coined every man with the same matrix of Adam and no one is similar to the other. Therefore, every man ought to say the whole world has been created for me', quoted in Shestack, *supra* note 22, at 205. For similar ideas expressed in other religions, see *ibid.*, 205 *et seq.*
45. See Cancik, *supra* note 43.
46. See Genesis 1:27, *supra* note 44; see Hirsch, *supra* note 23, at 578.
47. Hirsch, *supra* note 23, at 579 *et seq.*
48. *Oratio de hominis dignitate* (written in 1486); for an English translation, see http://www.panarchy.org/pico/oration.html (accessed 1 February 2011).
49. J.P. Doyle, 'Francisco Suárez: On Preaching the Gospel to People like the American Indians', *Fordham International Law Journal* 15 (1991): 880.
50. For an English translation and collection of de las Casas's writings in defense of the Indians, see B. de las Casas, *In Defense of the Indians: The Defense of the Most Reverend Lord, Don Fray Bartolome De Las Casas, of the Order of Preachers, Late Bishop of Chiapa*, trans. S. Poole (Dekalb: Northern Illinois University Press, 1992).

51. F. de Vitoria, *De Indis et de Iure Belli Relectiones*, trans. J.P. Bate (Washington, DC: Carnegie Institution, 1995), first published in 1532; an English translation is also available at http://www.constitution.org/victoria/victoria_.htm (accessed 21 December 2010).

52. On the contribution of the late Spanish Scholastic School to Human Rights, see I. Murillo, 'Der Beitrag der spanischen Kultur zum Menschenrechtsgedanken', in *Die Menschenrechte im inter-kulturellen Dialog*, ed. U. Voigt (Frankfurt am Main, Berlin, Berne, etc.: Peter Lang, 1998), 141–154.

53. Doyle, *supra* note 49, at 879.

54. See Hilpert, *supra* note 23, at 149–150.

55. Ibid., 148. A catalogue of rights was drafted by Vitoria; see Lohmann, *supra* note 23, at 424; Murillo, *supra* note 52, at 145 *et seq.*

56. Doyle, *supra* note 49, at 941 *et seq.*

57. Hirsch, *supra* note 23, at 580. For an analysis of the contemporary Protestant approach to human rights and a comparison with the natural law tradition, see Lohmann, *supra* note 23.

58. Griffin, *supra* note 9, at 10.

59. See Hirsch, *supra* note 23, at 580; see also Griffin, *supra* note 9, at 11.

60. Hirsch, *supra* note 23, at 582, translated by the author.

61. J. Locke, *Two Treaties of Government*, ed. Peter Laslett (Cambridge: Cambridge University Press, 1988); the text is also available at http://www.lonang.com/exlibris/locke/ (accessed 5 February 2012).

62. English Bill of Rights of 1689, text available at http://avalon.law.yale.edu/17th_century/england.asp (accessed 5 February 2012).

63. T. Hobbes, *Leviathan*, ed. C.B. MacPherson (London: Penguin Classics, 1981), first published in 1651; the text is also available at: http://oregonstate.edu/instruct/phl302/texts/hobbes/leviathan-contents.html (accessed 5 February 2012).

64. See Lohmann, *supra* note 23, at 200, footnote 165.

65. As was for example still the case in Pufendorf's work *De officio hominis et civis iuxta legem naturalem (On the Duty of Man and Citizen According to the Natural Law)* (1673), see Lohmann, *supra* note 23, at 191–196.

66. On Locke's concept of property, see J. Tully, *A Discourse on Property: John Locke and His Adversaries* (Cambridge: Cambridge University Press, 1980).

67. A. Neschke-Hentschke, 'Menschenrechte – Menschenrechtsdoktrin – Natürliche Gerechtigkeit', in *Menschenrechte und europäische Identität. Die antiken Grundlagen*, ed. K.M. Girardet and U. Nortmann (Stuttgart: Franz Steiner, 2005), 130; K. Seelmann, *Rechtsphilosophie*, 4th edition (Munich: C.H. Beck, 2007), 142; R. Tuck, *Natural Rights Theories: Their Origins and Development* (Cambridge: Cambridge University Press, 1979).

68. For more details, see Hunt, *supra* note 10, at 82 *et seq.*

69. Hunt, *supra* note 10, at 82, 94 *et seq.*

70. I. Kant, *Grundlegung zur Metaphysik der Sitten*, first published in 1785; for an English translation, see *Groundwork of the Metaphysics of Morals: a German-English edition*, ed. J. Timmermann (Cambridge and New York: Cambridge University Press, 2011); for an electronic version, see http://evans-experientialism.freewebspace.com/kant_groundwork_metaphysics_morals01.htm (accessed 18 January 2011).

71. I. Kant, *Die Metaphysik der Sitten*, first published in 1797 (see Part I: Metaphysische Anfangsgründe der Rechtslehre); for an English translation, see *The Metaphysics of Morals*, ed. M. Gregor (Cambridge: Cambridge University Press, 1996).

72. The Declaration of 4 July 1776 proclaimed '… these truths to be self-evident, that all men are created equal, that they are endowed by their Creator with certain unalienable Rights, that among these are Life, Liberty, and the pursuit of Happiness. That to secure these rights, Governments are instituted among Men, deriving their just powers from the consent of the governed.' It justified secession from the United Kingdom based on 'the Right of the People to alter or to abolish' destructive governments.

73. See the Preamble of the Declaration of 1789.

74. Ibid.

75. See L. Henkin, *The Age of Rights* (New York: Columbia University Press, 1990), 13 *et seq.*

76. For an edited version of these authors' critique of human rights, followed by a critical analysis, see J. Waldron, *Nonsense Upon Stilts: Bentham, Burke, and Marx on the Rights of Man* (London: Methuen, 1987).

77. E. Burke, *Reflections on the Revolution in France* (Indianapolis: Liberty Fund, 1999), first published in 1790.

78. J. Bentham, 'Anarchical Fallacies; Being An Examination of the Declarations of Rights Issued During the French Revolution', first published in *The Works of Jeremy Bentham*, Vol. II, ed. J. Bowring (Edinburgh: William Tait, 1843), text available at http://oll.libertyfund.org (accessed 31 January 2011); for an analysis, see H.A. Bedau, 'Anarchical Fallacies: Bentham's Attack on Human Rights', *Human Rights Quarterly* 22 (2000): 261–279.

79. J. Bentham, 'Supply Without Burthern', in *Jeremy Bentham's Economic Writings*, Vol. I, ed. W. Stark (London: George Allen and Unwin Ltd., 1952), 334.

80. Hunt, *supra* note 10, at 186 *et seq.*

81. Understood in terms of gender and not in universalist terms.

82. Understood in universalist terms.

83. K. Marx, 'Zur Judenfrage', 1844; an English version of 'the Jewish Question' can be found in *Karl Marx: Early Texts*, ed. D. McLellan (Oxford: Basil Blackwell, 1971), and at http://www.marxists.org/archive/marx/works/1844/jewish-question/ (accessed 2 February 2011).

84. Ibid.

85. Quoted in Ishay, *supra* note 10, at 9.

86. For an overview and critical analysis, see K. Bales and P.T. Robbins, 'No One Shall Be Held in Slavery or Servitude: A Critical Analysis of International Slavery Agreements and Concepts of Slavery,' *Human Rights Review* 2 (2001): 18–45.

87. Declaration of Congress of Vienna, 1815. For an overview of the struggle against slavery in international law, see Addo, *supra* note 3, at 102–115.

88. Article 9.

89. Slavery Convention, Geneva, 25 September 1926.

90. Clapham, *supra* note 10, at 27.

91. E.g., preventing states that practiced slavery from having an unfair economic advantage over abolitionist states; see J.L. Ray, 'The Abolition of Slavery and the End of International War', *International Organization* 43 (1989): 405–439.

92. E. de Vattel, *The Law of Nations, or Principles of the Law of Nature Applied to the Conduct and Affairs of Nations and Sovereigns* (Indianapolis: Liberty Fund, 2008), Book II, chapter 4, para. 71.

93. See T. Bürgenthal and D. Thürer, *Menschenrechte. Ideale, Instrumente, Institutionen* (Baden-Baden and Zurich: Dike and Nomos, 2010), 13.

94. H. Dunant, *A Memory of Solferino* (Geneva: International Committee of the Red Cross, 2001). This book is a new edition of the original French version *Un souvenir de Solferino*, published in 1862.

95. Convention (I) for the Amelioration of the Condition of the Wounded and Sick in Armed Forces in the Field. Geneva, 12 August 1949; Convention (II) for the Amelioration of the Condition of Wounded, Sick and Shipwrecked Members of Armed Forces at Sea, Geneva, 12 August 1949; Convention (III) relative to the Treatment of Prisoners of War, Geneva, 12 August 1949; Convention (IV) relative to the Protection of Civilian Persons in Time of War, Geneva, 12 August 1949; Protocol Additional to the Geneva Conventions of 12 August 1949, and relating to the Protection of Victims of International Armed Conflicts (Protocol I), 8 June 1977; Protocol Additional to the Geneva Conventions of 12 August 1949, and relating to the Protection of Victims of Non-International Armed Conflicts (Protocol II), 8 June 1977; Protocol Additional to the Geneva Conventions of 12 August 1949, and relating to the Adoption of an Additional Distinctive Emblem (Protocol III), 8 December 2005. The texts are available at: http://www.icrc.org/eng/war-and-law/treaties-customary-law/geneva-conventions/index.jsp (accessed 5 February 2012). Also see J.-M. Henckaerts and L. Doswald-Beck, *Customary International Humanitarian Law* (Cambridge: Cambridge University Press, 2005).

96. Whilst contemporary IHL also extends to internal armed conflicts, there has been a trend for IHR applying increasingly frequently to armed hostilities.

97. See in this book, R. Kolb, 'Human rights law and international humanitarian law between 1945 and the aftermath of the Teheran Conference of 1968'. On the relationship and interaction between IHL and IHR, see also G. Gaggioli, *L'influence mutuelle entre les droits de l'homme et le droit international humanitaire à la lumière du droit à la vie* (Paris: Pedone, forthcoming).

98. See Articles 1–30 of the Treaty of Versailles, text available at http://net.lib.byu.edu/~rdh7/wwi/versailles.html (accessed 10 January 2011).

99. See Clapham, *supra* note 10, at 27.

100. On the creation of the mandate system by the League of Nations, see N. Matz, 'Civilization and the Mandate System under the League of Nations as Origin of Trusteeship', *Max Planck Yearbook on United Nations Law* (2005): 47–95.

101. See Article 22 of the Treaty of Versailles.
102. Article 23(a) of the Treaty of Versailles.
103. Bürgenthal and Thürer, *supra* note 93, at 17.
104. See Part XIII, Section I (Arts 387–399) of the Treaty of Versailles, which, under the heading 'Labour', enshrines the Constitution of the International Labour Organization, consisting of a General Conference of Representatives of the Members and an International Labour Office. See Article 388.
105. Article 23(a) of the Treaty of Versailles.
106. Article 427 of the Treaty of Versailles. These principles were not conceived as individual rights but were meant to guide the work of the international organization set up by the Versailles Treaty. See text below and *supra* note 104.
107. *Supra* note 106. Article 23 states that in order to reach the goal of maintaining human working conditions, the State parties 'will establish and maintain the necessary international organisations'.
108. For some examples, see P. Thornberry, *International Law and the Rights of Minorities* (Oxford: Clarendon Press, 1992), 25–33.
109. See D. Rodogno, 'Réflexions liminaires à propos des interventions humanitaires des Puissances européennes au XIXe siècle', *Relations Internationales* 131 (2007): 9–25.
110. For an overview of the drafting of the Covenant from the perspective of minority protection, see A. Spiliopoulou Åkermark, *Justifications of Minority Protection in International Law* (Boston and London: Kluwer Law International, 1996), 102–104.
111. Ibid., 104–108.
112. See the text of the Treaty concluded with Poland (also known as the 'little Treaty of Versailles'), available at http://www.ucis.pitt.edu/eehistory/H200Readings/Topic5-R1.html (accessed 19 January 2011). This Treaty was the first minority treaty concluded at the Paris Peace Conference, and served as a template for the subsequent minority treaties concluded with the newly created Central and Eastern European States.
113. See ibid., Article 12, emphasis added.
114. Ibid.
115. This implied that the Permanent Court of International Justice (PCIJ) was competent to render opinions and decide disputes arising under the minority treaties; see *Rights of Minorities in Upper Silesia (Minority Schools)*, PCIJ, Series A, No. 12 (1928); *Rights of Minorities in Upper Silesia (Minority Schools)*, PCIJ, Series C, No. 14-II (1928); *Minority Schools in Albania, Advisory Opinion*, PCIJ, Series A/B, No. 64 (1935); *Minority Schools in Albania*, PCIJ, Series C, No. 76 (1935).
116. For more details, see Clapham, *supra* note 10, at 34.
117. For a more detailed analysis, see H. Burger, 'The Road to San Francisco: The Revival of the Human Rights Idea in the Twentieth Century', *Human Rights Quarterly* 14 (1992): 447–477.
118. See Ibid., 452.
119. R. Brunet, *La garantie internationale des droits de l'homme* (Geneva: Ch. Grasset, 1947), 93–94, quoted in Burger, *supra* note 117, at 474. The latter text provides an overview of the main initiatives of the human rights movement during World War II, see ibid., 471 *et seq.* Human Rights had previously also been invoked as a rationale for World War I, see Clapham, *supra* note 10, at 24.
120. Published in New York: Penguin Books. For an overview of H.G. Wells's campaign, see Burger, *supra* note 117, at 464 *et seq.*
121. Published in 1945 in New York: Columbia University Press.
122. On Roosevelt's famous four freedoms, see also *supra* section 1 and note 8; Roosevelt's address is published in Ishay, *supra* note 10, at 213.
123. Published in the *American Journal of International Law* 1941 Supplement: 191.
124. The term 'constitutional moment' is borrowed from B. Ackerman, *The Future of Liberal Revolution* (New Haven: Yale University Press, 1992), 48.
125. W. Osiatynski, 'On the Universality of the Universal Declaration of Human Rights', in *Human Rights With Modesty: The Problem With Universalism*, ed. A. Sajó (Leiden and Boston: Martinus Nijhoff, 2004), 36.
126. Articles 1, 13, 55, 62, 68 and 76 UN Charter.
127. Article 55(c) UN Charter.
128. Article 55 UN Charter.
129. Article 13 UN Charter.
130. The UNCHR was replaced in 2006 by the Human Rights Council, *infra* section 3.4.

131. A/RES/260/A (III), 9 December 1948; *Convention on the Prevention and Punishment of the Crime of Genocide*, New York, 1948.
132. A/RES/217/A/III, 10 December 1948. On the drafting process of the Declaration, see Glendon, *supra* note 34; J. Morsink, *The Universal Declaration of Human Rights: Origins, Drafting, and Intent* (Philadelphia: University of Pennsylvania Press, 1999); H. Charlesworth, 'Universal Declaration of Human Rights (1948)', in *Max Planck Encyclopedia of Public International Law* (2008), available at http://www.mpepil.com (accessed 5 February 2012).
133. Preamble UDHR.
134. For an early and prominent view, see the statement of the American Anthropological Association 'Statement on Human Rights', *American Anthropologist* 49 (1947): 539–543.
135. For an analysis of this question from a historical perspective, see J. Morsink, 'The Philosophy of the Universal Declaration', *Human Rights Quarterly* 6 (1984): 309–334; Osiatynski, *supra* note 125, at 33–50.
136. Preamble UDHR.
137. Preamble UDHR.
138. Article 1, *supra* section 1.
139. On the influence of the French Declaration of 1798 on the UDHR, see S.P. Marks, 'From the "Single Confused Page" to the "Decalogue for Six Billion Persons": The Roots of the Universal Declaration of Human Rights in the French Revolution', *Human Rights Quarterly* 20 (1998): 459–514; see also Morsink, *supra* note 135, at 310 *et seq.*
140. Morsink, *supra* note 135, at 312–314.
141. On the indeterminate nature of IHR, *supra* section1. For a different approach to justify human rights than that based on the tradition of the Enlightenment, see for instance the Arab Charter on Human Rights, 2004, reprinted in *International Human Rights Reports* 12 (2005): 893, entered into force March 15, 2008; more pronounced still is the approach of the Universal Islamic Declaration of Human Rights of 19 September 1981, text available at http://www.alhewar.com/ISLAMDECL.html (accessed 18 January 2011), which derives human rights from God.
142. For an interesting analysis of the same phenomenon on the European level, see A. Moravcsik, 'The Origins of Human Rights Regimes: Democratic Delegation in Postwar Europe', *International Organization* 54 (2000): 217–252, at 220. Moravcsik argues that the strongest support for the European human rights regime stemmed from transitional democracies (such as Germany, Italy, Austria) which sought to 'lock in' and consolidate the rule of law, whilst for established democracies (such as the United Kingdom, Denmark, Sweden, Norway, the Netherlands, Luxembourg) 'the benefits of reducing future political uncertainty outweigh[ed] the "sovereignty costs" of membership' in a human rights regime.
143. Glendon, *supra* note 34, at 226. The UDHR enshrines the following civil and political rights: the right to life, liberty and security; protection against slavery; protection against torture and cruel, inhuman or degrading treatment or punishment; the prohibition of discrimination; the right to an effective remedy; protection against arbitrary arrest, detention or exile; the right to a fair and public hearing by an independent and impartial tribunal; the presumption of innocence; the respect of privacy; the right to seek asylum; the right to a nationality and the right to change it; the right to family; the right to property; the right to freedom of thought, conscience and religion; the right to freedom of opinion and expression and the right to freedom of peaceful assembly and association; and the right to take part in the government of one's country. See Articles 3–21, UDHR.
144. As was shown above in section 2.2, important thinkers of the Enlightenment, such as Locke and Kant, insisted not only on rights but also on duties.
145. Morsink, *supra* note 135, at 317.
146. Article 29, para. 2, UDHR; the limitation of rights so as to respect the rights and freedoms of others mentioned in the same provision was already well established in the Enlightenment tradition (see Article 4 of the French Declaration of 1789: 'Liberty consists in the ability to do whatever does not harm another; hence the exercise of the natural rights of each man has no other limits than those which assure to other members of society the enjoyment of the same rights').
147. Article 29, para. 1, UDHR.
148. These provisions protect the right to social security; the right to work; the right to equal pay for equal work; the right to just and favorable remuneration and social protection; the right to form and join trade unions; the right to rest and leisure; the right to an adequate standard of living; and the right to free participation in the cultural life of the community.

149. To what extent 'the West' was opposed to second generation rights is debated; see the controversy between Whelan and Donnelly on the one hand, and Kirkup and Evans on the other hand: D.J. Whelan and Jack Donnelly, 'The West, Economic and Social Rights, and the Global Human Rights Regime: Setting the Record Straight', *Human Rights Quarterly* 29 (2007): 908–949; A. Kirkup and T. Evans, 'The Myth of Western Opposition to Economic, Social, and Cultural Rights? A Reply to Whelan and Donnelly', *Human Rights Quarterly* 31 (2009): 221–237; D.J. Whelan and J. Donnelly, 'Yes, a Myth: A Reply to Kirkup and Evans', *Human Rights Quarterly* 31 (2009): 239–255.

150. Osiatynski, *supra* note 125, at 45.

151. See Morsink, *supra* note 135, at 331–332.

152. Article 22, UDHR.

153. Article 22, UDHR.

154. See Article 26, para. 2, UDHR and the Preamble, which states that 'every individual and every organ of society, keeping this Declaration constantly in mind, shall *strive by teaching and education* to promote respect for these rights and freedoms' (emphasis added); see Osiatynski, *supra* note 125, at 46.

155. On the drafting process of the two Covenants, see Whelan, *supra* note 10, at 59 *et seq.*

156. Adopted and opened for signature, ratification and accession by A/RES/2200/A/XXI, 16 December 1966.

157. Adopted and opened for signature, ratification and accession by A/RES/2200/A/XXI, 16 December 1966.

158. The controversy on the priority of first generation or second generation rights has not yet been entirely overcome. To date, China has not ratified the ICCPR, and the United States is not bound by the ICESCR.

159. Article 2, para. 1, ICCPR; Article 2, para. 2, ICESCR.

160. See Article 16, ICESCR, based on which states shall submit regular reports to the ECOSOC. In 1985, the supervisory function was delegated to the Committee on Social Economic and Cultural Rights (CSECR), see ECOSOC Resolution, 28 May 1985 (UN Doc. E/RES/1985/17).

161. Article 41, ICCPR.

162. See A/RES/2200/A/XXI, 16 December 1966.

163. There are 159 states parties to the Covenant on economic, social and cultural rights and 167 parties to its counterpart on civil and political rights.

164. The two Covenants contain most rights proclaimed in the UDHR. Exceptions are the right to property, the right to asylum and the right to nationality. See Bürgenthal and Thürer, *supra* note 93, at 33.

165. Adopted and opened for signature, ratification and accession by A/RES/2106/A/XX, 21 December 1965.

166. Adopted and opened for signature, ratification and accession by A/RES/34/180, 18 December 1979.

167. Adopted and opened for signature, ratification and accession by A/RES/39/46, 10 December 1984.

168. Adopted and opened for signature, ratification and accession by A/RES/1386 (XIV), 20 November 1959.

169. Adopted and opened for signature, ratification and accession by A/RES/45/158, 18 December 1990.

170. Adopted and opened for signature, ratification and accession by A/RES/61/106, 13 December 2006.

171. Adopted and opened for signature, ratification and accession by A/RES/61/177, 20 December 2006.

172. After the end of the Cold War, and following the Second World Conference on Human Rights (see section 3.4), a rudimentary human rights regime has also emerged in Southeast Asia, see *infra* note 197.

173. ETS No. 5.

174. See the Preamble of the ECHR. On the history and evolution of the ECHR, see E. Bates, *The Evolution of the European Convention on Human Rights: From Its Inception to the Creation of a Permanent Court of Human Rights* (Oxford: Oxford University Press, 2010).

175. ETS No. 163.

176. Individual applications to the European Court of Human Rights became mandatory with Protocol 11 (ETS No. 155), which entered into force on 1 November 1998, established a permanent Court and abolished the European Commission on Human Rights, the counterpart of which still exists in the African and American system, see *infra* the text accompanying notes 177 *et seq.*

177. For an overview of the history and evolution of the Inter-American human rights regime, see R.K. Goldman, 'History and Action: The Inter-American Human Rights System and the Role of the Inter-American Commission on Human Rights', *Human Rights Quarterly* 31 (2009): 856–887.

178. The Court rendered its first Judgment on 15 December 2009, see *Michelot Yogogombaye versus the Republic of Senegal*, Application No. 001/2008, available at http://www.african-court.org/en/index.php/2012-03-04-06-06-00/list-cases/2-home/171-application-no-001-2008-michelot-yogogombaye-versus-the-republic-of-senegal. The Court was established pursuant to the Protocol to the African Charter on Human and Peoples' Rights.

179. OAU Doc. CAB/LEG/67/3 rev. 5, 21 I.L.M. 58 (1982).

180. Articles 18–24, AChHPR.

181. See Articles 27–29, AChHPR.

182. For an interesting critical approach on the mandate of the Commission, see P. Alston, 'The Commission on Human Rights', in *The United Nations and Human Rights – A Critical Appraisal*, ed. P. Alston (Oxford: Clarendon Press, 1992), 127.

183. On the Commission on Human Rights and its birth, see also *supra* section 3.2.

184. Ishay, *supra* note 10, at 17.

185. See G. Oberleitner, *Global Human Rights Institutions: Between Remedy and Ritual* (Cambridge: Polity, 2007), 44–48.

186. K. Boyle, 'The United Nations Human Rights Council: Origins, Antecedents and Prospects', in *New Institutions for Human Rights Protection*, ed. K. Boyle (Oxford: Oxford University Press, 2009), 26–27.

187. P. Alston, 'Promoting the Accountability of Members of the New UN Human Rights Council', *Journal of Transnational Law and Policy* 15 (2005): 57–58.

188. Organization for Security and Co-operation in Europe.

189. Principle VII of the Helsinki Final Act.

190. Ibid.

191. A/RES/46/116, 17 December 1991. The First World Conference on Human Rights took place in Teheran in 1968.

192. A prominent vindication of developing countries is the right to development; on this issue, see the Declaration on the Right to Development, adopted on 4 December 1986, A/RES/41/128, 4 December 1986.

193. *Bangkok Declaration*, 2 April 1993 (UN Doc. A/CONF.157/ASRM/8-A/CONF.157/PC/59).

194. *San José Declaration*, 22 January 1993 (UN Doc. A/CONF.157/LACRM/15-A/CONF.157/PC/58).

195. *Tunis Declaration*, 6 November 1992 (UN Doc. A/CONF.157/AFRM/14-A/CONF.157/PC/57).

196. *Cairo Declaration*, 5 August 1990 (UN Doc. UN GAOR, World Conference on Human Rights, 4th Session, Agenda Item 5, A/CONF.157/PC/62/Add.18 (1993)).

197. Founded in 1967, ASEAN comprises the following ten states: Indonesia, Malaysia, the Philippines, Singapore, Thailand (which are all founding members), as well as Brunei Darussalam, Lao PDR, Myanmar, Vietnam, Cambodia, see http://www.aseansec.org/64.htm (accessed 17 January 2011). Within ASEAN, a rudimentary human rights regime has emerged following the Second World Conference on Human Rights; see Y. Ginbar, 'Human Rights in ASEAN – Setting Sail or Treading Water?', *Human Rights Law Review* 10 (2001): 504–518; P. Malanczuk, 'Regional Protection of Human Rights in the Asia-Pacific Region', *German Yearbook of International Law* 52 (2009): 107–137; I. Bachet, 'La Commission intergouvernementale des droits de l'homme de l'ANASE, premier organe régional dans le domaine des droits de l'homme en Asie du Sud-Est: Avancée historique ou écran de fumé?', *Revue trimestrielle des droits de l'homme* 83 (2010): 617–635.

198. On this debate, see, e.g., A. Pollis, 'Cultural Relativism Revisited: Through a State Prism', *Human Rights Quarterly* 18 (1996): 316–344; B. von Albertini Mason, *Menschenrechte aus westlicher und asiatischer Sicht. Zu den Grundwerten der liberalen Demokratie'* (Zurich: Schulthess, 2004); J.C. Hsiung, ed., *Human Rights in East Asia: A Cultural Perspective* (New York: Paragon House Publishers, 1985); J.R. Bauer and D.A. Bell, ed., *The East Asian Challenge for Human Rights* (Cambridge University Press, 1999); R. Weatherley, *The Discourse of Human Rights in China: Historical and Ideological Perspectives* (London: Macmillan Press, 1999).

199. See the Preamble and point 5 of the Bangkok Declaration.

200. Preamble of the Bangkok Declaration.

201. Point 8 of the Bangkok Declaration.

202. See the Preamble and points 4, 6, 12, 17, 18 and 19 of the Bangkok Declaration; on the right to development, see, e.g., S. Marks, 'Development: Between Rhetoric and Reality', *Harvard Human Rights Journal* 17 (2004): 137–168.

203. This expression is inspired by Osiatynski, *supra* note 125, at 49.

204. Adopted on 25 June 1993 (UN Doc. A/CONF.157/24 (Part I) at 20 (1993)).

205. See Pollis, *supra* note 198, at 329.
206. References to other first generation rights are made in para. 30: 'The World Conference on Human Rights also expresses its dismay and condemnation that gross and systematic violations and situations that constitute serious obstacles to the full enjoyment of all human rights continue to occur in different parts of the world. Such violations and obstacles include, as well as torture and cruel, inhuman and degrading treatment or punishment, summary and arbitrary executions, disappearances, arbitrary detentions, all forms of racism, racial discrimination and apartheid, foreign occupation and alien domination, xenophobia, poverty, hunger and other denials of economic, social and cultural rights, religious intolerance, terrorism, discrimination against women and lack of the rule of law.'
207. Vienna Declaration, para. 5.
208. *Supra*, text accompanying note 159.
209. For an analysis of the concepts of indivisibility, interdependence and interrelatedness, see Whelan, *supra* note 10.
210. H. Shue, *Rights in Light of Duties, Human Rights and U.S. Foreign Policy* (Massachusetts: Lexington Books, 1979), 65–82; for another early contribution, see G.J.H. van Hoof, 'The Legal Nature of Economic, Social and Cultural Rights: a Rebuttal of Some Traditional Views', in *The Right to Food*, ed. P. Alston and K. Tomasevski (Boston: Martinus Nijhoff, 1984), 97–110. The first prominent reference to Shue's trilogy in the human rights system was made by A. Eide's report to the Sub-Commission on the Prevention of Discrimination and the Protection of Minorities 'The Right to Food as a Human Right', 1987 (UN Doc. E/CN.4/Sub.2/1987/23), see M. Dowell-Jones, *Contextualising the International Covenant on Economic, Social and Cultural Rights* (Leiden and Boston: Martinus Nijhoff, 2004), 29.
211. For contributions advocating in favor of direct enforceability of second generation rights, see, e.g., M. Odello and F. Seatzu, *Ensuring and Enforcing Economic, Social and Cultural Rights* (London: Routledge, 2010); M. Ssenyonjo, 'Economic, Social and Cultural Rights', in *International Human Rights Law: Six Decades After the UDHR and Beyond*, ed. M.A. Baderin and M. Ssenyonjo (Burlington, VT: Ashgate, 2010); for an economic perspective, see also S. Kalantry, J.E. Getgen and S. Arrigg Koh, 'Enhancing Enforcement of Economic, Social, and Cultural Rights Using Indicators: A Focus on the Right to Education in the ICESCR', *Human Rights Quarterly* 32 (2010): 253–310; for a study focusing on the Inter-American system, see M. Feria Tinta, 'Justiciability of Economic, Social and Cultural Rights in the Inter-American System of Protection of Human Rights: Beyond Traditional Paradigms and Notions', *Human Rights Quarterly* 29 (2007): 431–459; for the African system, see C. Anselm Odinkalu, 'Analysis of Paralysis or Paralysis by Analysis? Implementing Economic, Social, and Cultural Rights Under the African Charter on Human and Peoples' Rights', *Human Rights Quarterly* 23 (2001): 327–369.
212. On the CESCR, *supra* note 160. On the Optional Protocol, see C. De Albuquerque, 'Chronicle of an Announced Birth. The Coming into Life of the Optional Protocol to the International Covenant on Economic, Social and Cultural Rights – The Missing Piece of the International Bill of Human Rights', *Human Rights Quarterly* 32 (2010): 144–178; A. Vandenbogaerde and W. Vandenhole, 'The Optional Protocol to the International Covenant on Economic, Social and Cultural Rights: An *Ex Ante* Assessment of its Effectiveness in Light of the Drafting Process', *Human Rights Law Review* 10 (2010), 207–237.
213. A/RES/63/117, 10 December 2008.
214. A/RES/48/141, 20 December 1993. On the UNHCR, see, e.g., I. Boerefijn, *Human Rights, United Nations High Commissioner for* (UNHC), in *Max Planck Encyclopedia of Public International Law* (2008), available at http://www.mpepil.com (accessed 5 February 2012); B.G. Ramcharan, *The United Nations High Commissioner for Human Rights: The Challenges of International Protection* (The Hague and London: Martinus Nijhoff, 2002); id., *A UN High Commissioner in Defence of Human Rights: 'No License to Kill or Torture'* (Leiden: Martinus Nijhoff, 2005).
215. A/RES/60/251, 3 April 2006.
216. For an overview of the UPR, see H.J. Steiner, P. Alston and R. Goodman, ed., *International Human Rights in Context* (Oxford: Oxford University Press, 2007), 806–810; Kälin and Künzli, *supra* note 10, at 245–247; Boyle, *supra* note 186, at 34–36. For an in-depth analysis of the UPR, see F.D. Gaer, 'A Voice Not an Echo: Universal Periodic Review and the UN Treaty Body System', *Human Rights Law Review* 7 (2007): 109–139; J. Duggan-Larkin, 'Can an Intergovernmental Mechanism improve the Protection of Human Rights? The Potential of Universal Periodic Review in Relation to the Realisation of Economic, Social and Cultural Rights', *Netherlands Quarterly of Human Rights* 28 (2010): 548–581.

217.   A/RES/60/251, 3 April 2006, Preamble.
218.   A/RES/60/251, 3 April 2006, para 5(c).
219.   For example, see P.R. Baher, 'The Human Rights Council: A Preliminary Evaluation', *Netherlands Quarterly of Human Rights* 28 (2010): 329–331; V. Chetail, 'Le Conseil des droits de l'Homme des Nations Unies: réformer pour ne rien changer', in *Conflicts, Security and Cooperation. Liber Amicorum Victor-Yves Ghebali*, ed., V. Chetail (Brussels: Bruylant, 2007).
220.   On this issue, see M. Gondek, *The Reach of Human Rights in a Globalising World: Extraterritorial Application of Human Rights Treaties* (Antwerp: Intersentia, 2009).
221.   On this subject, see the contribution by R. Goldman in the present volume.
222.   See the famous Resolution 1373 adopted by the Security Council, S/RES/1373, 28 September 2001.
223.   See, e.g., E. Rosand, 'Security Council Resolution 1373, the Counter-Terrorism Committee, and the Fight against Terrorism', *American Journal of International Law* 97 (2003): 333–341; M. Happold, 'Security Council Resolution 1373 and the Constitution of the United Nations', *Leiden Journal of International Law* 16 (2003): 593–610.
224.   See the excellent article of L. Cameron, 'Private Military Companies: Their Status Under International Humanitarian Law and Its Impact on Their Regulation', *International Review of the Red Cross* 863 (2006): 573–598. Also see the Montreux Document On Pertinent International Legal Obligations and Good Practices for States Related to Operations of Private Military and Security Companies During Armed Conflict. Full text available at http://www.icrc.org/eng/resources/documents/misc/montreux-document-170908.htm (accessed 5 February 2012).
225.   See R. Kolb, S. Vité and G. Porretto, *L'application du droit international humanitaire et des droits de l'homme aux organisations internationales: Forces de paix et administrations civiles transitoires* (Brussels: Bruylant, 2005).
226.   See, e.g., D. Kinley and R. Chambers, 'The UN Human Rights Norms for Corporations: The Private Implications of Public International Law', *Human Rights Law Review* 6 (2006): 447–497. For a more comprehensive analysis, see D. Kinley, ed., *Human Rights and Corporations* (Aldershot: Ashgate, 2009).
227.   Among the vast literature on human rights and globalization, see, e.g., Ishay, *supra* note 10, at 246–310.
228.   In that vein, see the famous quote from the play *The Physicists* by the Swiss writer Dürrenmatt, 'Nothing that has been thought can ever be taken back'.
229.   See the famous quote of Justice Holmes' Dissenting Opinion in the no less famous free speech case of the United States Supreme Court, *Abrams v. United States*, 250 U.S. 616 (1919) 'we should be *eternally vigilant* against attempts to check the expression of opinions that we loathe and believe to be fraught with death …' (emphasis added).

2. Human rights law and international humanitarian law between 1945 and the aftermath of the Teheran Conference of 1968

*Robert Kolb**

1. INTRODUCTION

It is taken for granted today that the law of armed conflict, or international humanitarian law (IHL), and international human rights law (HRL) maintain between their respective bodies both subtle and multiple relationships, with one branch of the law complementing, strengthening or filling the other's gaps. This supposes, from a theoretical standpoint, that both branches of the law have some shared or common legal ground on which they can interact. This means, for instance, that HRL has to apply in times of armed conflict (something by no means guaranteed before the 1960s); or that HRL may apply extraterritorially, for example in occupied territory, still to some extent a controversial question,[1] albeit the practice of the sheer majority of States and of international organs admits such extraterritoriality in a wide array of cases. Thus, today, to properly analyze some subject matter, such as the law of belligerent occupation, it is impossible to do otherwise but to consider it in its complex blend between IHL and HRL.[2] However, this closeness (and for some, promiscuity)[3] of HRL and IHL has no time immemorial pedigree. It evolved slowly from the late 1940s to the present times. And indeed, it grew out of a situation where the two branches of the law stood quite unrelated one besides the other, each one championed by an international institution nourishing some mistrust for the other, and each one having its specialized set of lawyers and its particular agenda. The purpose of this short chapter is not to discuss the present situation,[4] on which there is a profusion of literature. Instead, it might be interesting to look to the past and to learn about the reasons why the two branches of the law started with separatism and why they progressively converged. This allows us to develop some deeper insights into these areas of the law and to give more critical mass to the understanding of where we stand today.

2. THE TWO DRUM-ROLLS OF 1948 AND 1949: UNIVERSAL DECLARATION ON HUMAN RIGHTS AND GENEVA CONVENTIONS ON THE PROTECTION OF VICTIMS OF ARMED CONFLICTS

Human rights law emerged in Europe in the wake of the subjectivist revolution[5] of the Enlightenment. Man, with his inalienable and pre-positive rights, was put at the center of the new 'natural law constructions'.[6] However, for a long time, such human rights were limited to 'civil society', that is, to municipal law, where they were guaranteed by Bills of Rights[7] and municipal organs of judicial control. International society was, at least since the Westphalian Peace (1648), progressively restricted to inter-State relations. The individual had no standing in it. He could not enjoy any rights and duties directly under international law. He was at best an object of international regulation, but not a subject of international rights.[8] The turn of the tide[9] arrived with the declaration of war by President Roosevelt of the United States (5 December 1941); with articles 5 and 6 of the Atlantic Charter of 1942; with the United Nations Declaration of 15th January 1942 whereby the aims of the Atlantic Charter were generally endorsed by the Allies; with the Dumbarton Oaks proposals of 1944; and finally with the Charter of the United Nations (Preamble, articles 1, § 3; 13, § 1, lit. b; 55, lit c). It was understood that the Charter contained only some generic referrals to 'human rights'; it could not spell out the body of international human rights in the detail of a bill of rights. Therefore, it was agreed to add to the Charter first of all a solemn proclamation on human rights by the General Assembly, and later to codify in detail in a legally binding fashion the recognized rights. The first step was reached through the Universal Declaration of Human Rights of 1948.[10] The second step was significantly delayed by the outbreak, and later creeping procrastination, of the Cold War. It proved finally possible to adopt in 1966 two Covenants,[11] one on civil and political rights, the other on social, economic and cultural rights. The split into two texts was a glaring hallmark of the then division of the world into two opposite camps. The Declaration of 1948 is a non-binding resolution of the UNGA, numbered 217. It has been elaborated within the Commission of Human Rights, a subsidiary organ of the ECOSOC. It proclaims in a short and aphoristic form the essential freedoms and rights, without venturing into detail which would have been at once incompatible with the aim of solemnity pursued and also with the fact that the Declaration would have to be followed by a more specific positive law text (the 'Covenant'). Today, the Declaration is commonly held to reflect customary international human rights standards. We may thus notice that in 1948 HRL was not a new feature with respect to municipal law, where it could be traced back to the great public law codifications of the Enlightenment period; but that it was a new feature in international law, where the individual had previously been considered at best as an object of international regulation, but not as a subject of international rights (doctrine of domestic affairs or domestic jurisdiction).

International humanitarian law, or more generally the law of armed conflicts, is one of the oldest branches of public international law. Organized collectivities, which are the main object of the *jus inter potestates* called international law, have since time immemorial interacted not only peacefully but also by war; bellicose contacts generally even preceded peaceful ventures; and overall, hostilities between States covered much longer periods than peaceful relations. Hence, it is understandable that international law contained since times immemorial a bulk of rules on the law of war. In the famous and seminal treatise of Hugo Grotius, not infrequently called the 'founding father' of international law, *De jure belli ac pacis* (1625), the law of war still precedes the law of peace and is also largely predominant in the substantive developments in the book. What was new in the law of armed conflict after 1945? The main point is that this branch of the law witnessed – as it had after World War I – a profound crisis; it had proved inadequate in some respects; and it showed terrible gaps of protection, which had to be filled. This effort has been accomplished through the Geneva Conventions of 1949.[12] Essentially, the Geneva Conventions (hereinafter: GC) transform at least partially the law of armed conflict into a 'humanitarian law'. The protection of the individual war victims becomes the pivotal centre of the system; IHL ceases to be merely (or even essentially) the old 'military law'. This new IHL, with its humanitarian outlook, would in due course necessarily come closer to the nascent and growing arm of international HRL. To be able to perform the function of protection of all the victims of modern war, the old conception of international model norms for legislation on the municipal level (19th century) or of minimum codification as in the Hague (at the turn of the centuries) had to be abandoned.[13] The law is now clearly predicated on the idea of a thorough international codification with mandatory norms of behavior, locked up against derogation and reprisals. The GC represent in this respect the ideal of 'maximal' codification with a protective aim; they are opposed to the 'minimal' codification of the Hague period, geared towards leaving the belligerent some appreciable freedom of action in situations where, as in armed conflict, vital interests are at stake. There is here a neat paradigm shift within the underlying reasons of the law.

World War II had glaringly shown that the traditional law of armed conflicts had been insufficient, especially in the protection of persons *hors de combat*. The treatment of prisoners of war (e.g. Russian prisoners in Germany or Allied prisoners in Japan) and the deportation of civilians were tragic testimony to this. For the wounded and sick military personnel and for prisoners of war, there was already a set of GC which needed only to be developed: the Geneva Conventions of 1929. However, there had been a complete absence of conventional protections for civilians, if some scattered provisions applying to occupied territories are bracketed out (Hague Convention IV, Regulations, articles 42ff.). Overall, it was therefore thought, in 1949, that a new codification effort was necessary on four accounts:

(1)   The law of armed conflict had suffered since 1919 from regular attacks as to its viability: can there truly be a law in armed conflict? Is the law of armed conflict not always delayed by a war? Is it not chimerical to think that a law of armed conflict can work? That law had also suffered heavy breaches during World War II. It was thus felt necessary to solemnly reaffirm that branch of international law and to give it a new impetus starting from a clean slate.

(2)   World War II had shown that there existed a considerable urgency in protecting persons *hors de combat*. Thus, the new law was centered on that humanitarian issue, largely leaving aside the properly military branch of the law of armed conflicts (conduct of hostilities). For the conduct of hostilities, the old Hague Regulations of 1907 were still applicable.

(3)   World War II had shown the tendency of some belligerents to manipulate and to try to escape the law, as well as to use all the gaps and uncertainties for self-serving interpretations (e.g., on hostages). It was consequently considered in 1949 that the new law should be much more detailed than the old, summary and optimistic law of 1907. This produced a codification with a much greater number and length of provisions. Second, the drafters prohibited any opting out of the conventional protections by agreement between or among the belligerents, or

unilateral renunciation of the accorded protections by the beneficiaries (see articles 6–7 GC I-III, and 7–8, 47 of GC IV).

(4)   Experience had shown, especially through the Spanish Civil War (1936–1939), that some regulation was needed also for non-international armed conflicts (roughly speaking civil wars). Thus, common article 3 of the four GC was adopted. It provided a sort of 'minimum convention' within the Convention, granting some elementary protections in the context of non-international armed conflicts.

To these distinctive features, one further has to be added. The system of the law of war in the 19th century, and up to 1949, was based on a subjective rather than an objective trigger for determining the applicability of that body of the law. Traditionally, the application of the law of war depended on the existence of a state of 'war'. Since the concept of war was far from a clear-cut one, modulating between formal (declared) and material (intensity) war, international and civil war, the necessary legal certainty on what was going to be applied to whom was, in practice, achieved through some distinctive acts of will by the concerned States. An international war was held to exist essentially when it was declared (this being a unilateral legal act, expressing a will) or at least when there was an ascertainable subjective *animus belligerendi* of at least one State to the violent contest. This explains the extraordinary importance of the declaration of war in the 19th century.[14] It was of the essence, especially for all the neutral States and their commerce at sea, since their rights and duties towards the warring States would be altered from the declaration of war onwards. A civil war could also bear heavily on the rights of neutral States. Therefore, it was accepted that through a 'recognition of belligerency' (again a unilateral legal act embodying an expression of will) the two parties in a civil war could be treated as belligerents placed on the same footing. Hence, the laws of war, especially neutrality, would apply to both.[15] This recognition could emanate from the local government or from third States. A civil war could thus be transformed, from the legal point of view, into a fully-fledged 'war' between the recognizing State and the recognized entities. Concretely, this means that the rules of the laws of war and of neutrality would apply to such civil wars between the recognizing entities.[16] In short: the application of the law of war depended on a potestative or subjective act.

This subjective system was abandoned in 1949. With the Geneva Conventions, through their common article 2, the trigger for the applicability of the law of armed conflicts now becomes neatly objective. The law of armed conflicts applies, apart from 'declared wars', in cases of 'international armed conflicts' or 'occupation of territories without resistance' (hostile occupation even without hostilities); it also applies to 'non international armed conflicts' (common article 3). All these concepts, but the first one, 'declared war', are objectively defined and do not depend on a declaration or on an act of recognition. Thus, for example, the concept of 'armed conflict' makes reference to effective hostile contacts between armed forces, or even simply to the existence of wounded and sick, prisoners of war, enemy civilians in need of protection (international armed conflicts); or to a military organization of the armed forces and a certain intensity of the armed contest (non-international armed conflicts). If there is such a situation on the field, which is to be objectively determined through the key concept of the modern law, i.e. effectiveness, then the law of armed conflict applies. It is not by accident that the term 'law of war' was now progressively abandoned in favor of the larger term 'law of armed conflict', in order precisely to underscore this shift from a subjective to an objective system. The concept of 'war' essentially depended on a subjective will to be at war; 'armed conflict' refers to a fact on the ground. The main aim of this shift is to ensure the applicability of the IHL to all situations of effective hostile contacts in favor of the protected persons. This reflects the already discussed major shift of the law from military matters (pre-1949) to the humanitarian protection of the victims of the war (post-1949). Lacunae in applicability could easily be accepted before 1949, when the questions turned around military matters to be sorted out between professional armies; since 1949, lacunae in protection could no longer be accepted, in view of the new paramount humanitarian aim of the law.[17] No victim may be left without protection because of legal subtleties turning around the proper concept of war![18]

Thus, overall, the Geneva law is geared towards gapless 'protection' of potential war victims from abuses by belligerents (i.e. especially for persons under the control of the adverse belligerent). It appears understandable that this new outlook of IHL predestined it to enter into fruitful relations with the growing arm of international HRL, at least from the moment that HRL became consolidated into a positive body of international law.

3. TRACES OF CROSS-REFERENCE IN THE TRAVAUX PRÉPARATOIRES: THE MAKING OF THE DECLARATION AND OF THE CONVENTIONS[19]

3.1 Universal Declaration

During the preparation of the Universal Declaration of 1948,[20] the issue of IHL was only very cursorily raised. In contrast with the Geneva Conventions and HRL, it is first of all in the general outlook offered by the Preamble that armed conflicts are mentioned. In § 2 of the Preamble, it is recalled that respect for international HR is a precondition for a lasting peace, that is, for the avoidance of war.[21] However, as can immediately be seen, it is not IHL that features in this paragraph, but rather the question of the maintenance of peace. This latter question is part and parcel of the law of peace (*jus contra bellum* of the UN Charter and related customary international law). However, IHL was implicitly raised when several delegates affirmed that the protection of international HR supposes a condition of peace. This implies the view that HR are doomed to suffer if an armed conflict erupts.[22] There was further direct reference to IHL when the delegate from Lebanon stated that the fundamental rights proclaimed in the Declaration shall also be respected in time of war.[23] This point was, however, not belabored, since the general philosophy in the UN at that time was that the organization would be able to maintain the peace, and that it was self-defeating to venture into speculations that it would not be able to do so. Moreover, the Lebanese delegate did not truly refer to IHL, but rather affirmed that HRL itself should remain applicable in times of armed conflict. There were no further mentions of 'armed conflicts' and their legal regulation during the debates. The question of derogation of HR in periods of public emergency (including war) was left to the elaboration of the Covenant of HR; it was not thought fit to enter into such details in the context of the Declaration.

3.2   Geneva Conventions

During the making of the GC, mentions of international HRL were almost as rare as mentions of armed conflicts and IHL in the context of the Declaration. The main item on which HRL appeared was the Preamble,[24] that is, a non-operational provision stating the general aims and underlying philosophy of the four conventions. The representative of the Holy See wanted to insert into the Preamble phrases such as 'le respect de la personne et de la dignité humaines';[25] there was finally an amendment for inserting the words 'droit humain universel'[26] ('universal human law'). Moreover, a series of delegates stressed that particularly GC IV, on civilians, should be viewed in the light of the Universal Declaration, and that a mention of this fact in its Preamble would be useful.[27] Another place where the question of international HRL was raised was common article 3 to the GC. This enshrined the minimum principles of humanity applicable in all armed conflicts (and even beyond), including particularly non-international armed conflicts. The Special Committee of the Second Commission of the Conference had proposed to add a third paragraph to article 3 in the prisoners of war convention to the effect that if the benefits of the convention could not be extended to a prisoner, this person should in any event remain under the safeguard of the principles on human rights as flowing from the rules established between civilized nations.[28] The link of this proposal with the Martens Clause is apparent. The Danish delegate further underscored that common article 3 should be understood as not affecting in any way the protections an individual could hold under other sources of international law, in particular international HRL.[29] Finally, international HRL was mentioned in the context of the protection of the civilian population in occupied territories. For the Mexican delegate, a clause would have to be inserted into GC IV, providing that the occupying power could modify the local legislation only if it was contrary to the principles of the Universal Declaration.[30] The most solemn invocation of HR occurred, however, during the ceremony for signature of the GC. Mr Petitpierre, from Switzerland, stressed the parallelism and common ideals of the Universal Declaration and the Geneva Conventions. He further uttered the conviction that certain rights recognized by the Declaration had been inserted into the GC.[31]

Overall, it can thus be said that the two sets of texts were not cast into the mould of complete mutual ignorance, but it must also be recognized that the cross-fertilizations between them remained extremely marginal. In the late 1940s, IHL and international HRL were set largely on separate tracks. Their meetings were at once short, exceptional and marginal.

3.3   Legal Writings

Legal doctrine of the 1940s, and 1950s' writing on HRL, hardly mentions IHL at all, being utterly averse to war (at most it is recalled that HRL applies or does not apply in time of armed conflict). Legal writers specializing in IHL rarely mentioned international HRL, which they considered at once too young (and still largely non-positive), too uncertain, too impractical and too political. It was given little place in the centuries-old edifice of the law of war. At the same time, the shift of the law of war to an IHL perspective, in the narrow sense of the term – especially in GC IV dealing with civilians – slowly opened the door to building bridges. What could be closer, within IHL, to HRL, than the suffering 'civilian', the defenseless human being facing the arbitrary measures of war? To be sure, GC IV does not protect all civilians whatever their nationality; it is not about 'all human beings' as typically HRL is; it is rather mainly geared to the protection of adverse or enemy civilians. However, there is assuredly some family link between the two, the 'civilian' and the 'human being'. It is indeed in the context of GC IV that mentions of international HRL are most frequently made in the late 1940s and 1950s.[32] Another aspect over which the two bodies of the law were often linked is common article 3 to the GC.[33] Moreover, Pictet's Commentaries contain a number of mentions of HRL, for example in the context of the general treatment of protected persons, of torture or fair trial.[34] A US military lawyer in an American Society of International Law meeting also favorably mentioned HRL. He compared the GC to 'human rights operating on the wartime scene'.[35] Finally, G.I.A.D. Draper emphatically mentions HRL in the two most obvious contexts, namely the civilian Convention IV ('a legal charter of fundamental and detailed human rights in time of armed conflict'), and common article 3 (implicitly treated as a sort of declaration of human rights in miniature).[36]

4. REASONS FOR INITIAL SEPARATISM

What were the main reasons for the quite neat separatism prevailing in the 1940s and 1950s? There are a series of reasons, warranting some short analysis.[37]

(1) *Time Lag in the Modified Conception of IHL.* In the late 1940s, the law of warfare was still seen essentially through the lens of the old military law that it had previously been. The GC of 1949 were still to display their discreetly subversive action in order to transform this age-old conception and to instill into people's minds a fresh orientation towards a humanitarian law properly so called (centered on protected persons). It is manifest that a military conception of the law of armed conflict favors maintaining a gulf between it and international HRL, whereas a humanitarian conception of IHL facilitates a co-operative conjunction of both branches of the law. There is in this regard a confirmation of the well-known principle that ideological conceptions do not change overnight, but do need some time to adapt to new realities. Thus, a new conception, such as a shift from a militarily-oriented law to a protected persons-oriented law, will need some years to really take root in the minds of the policy-makers and specialized lawyers. This time lag is inevitable. It operated during the 1950s.

(2) *Infancy of International HRL.* In the 1940s and 1950s, international HRL was still in its infancy. There was hardly any positive law in this new area of regulation. The Universal Declaration is a non-binding resolution, that is, a recommendation of the UN General Assembly. The Covenants had not yet been adopted. On the universal level,

there existed only some scattered conventions dealing directly (e.g. issues of stateless-ness) or indirectly (e.g. genocide as a criminal offence) with human rights. The power of the UN itself to deal with HR was largely limited to 'promoting' HR,[38] a term which has led to much quibbling in the context of the domestic jurisdiction clause inserted in article 2, § 7, of the Charter. The power of the UN bodies to take a direct stand on concrete human rights violations has been contested during all the years under scrutiny here. A customary HRL hardly existed, apart from perhaps the rule of non-discrimination contained in article 1, § 3, of the UN Charter. Therefore, an international HRL was at best viewed by international lawyers as a law in *statu nascendi* which was not yet a positive part of international law. It can be understood that therefore no fruitful interactions could be constructed with a branch of the law such as the law of armed conflicts, which had a distinguished pedigree in international law, and was codified in a series of undoubtedly hard law texts. HRL would first have to leave its infancy stage and be consolidated as a true legal body, before being able to meaningfully enter into relations with IHL.

(3) *Distinct 'Guilds' of Lawyers.* IHL and HRL have initially been championed by neatly distinct classes of lawyers, who somewhat mistrust each other. The law of armed conflict (only recently shifted to IHL) was essentially the business of military lawyers working for the State. Moreover, the law of armed conflict was essentially a technical body of rules for hostile relations of a State with other polities. The lawyers practicing it were essentially pragmatic and not too politicized. These persons, in the 1940s and 1950s, were as remote as could be imagined from the world of human rights law, when they were not hostile to it. In their circles, sympathy for HR was rare; neutrality frequent; benevolent neutrality existed; and outright skepticism was not at all uncom-mon. Conversely, HRL had been for centuries a product of Enlightenment thinking and ultimately of political movements fighting for the causes of man in civil society. The orientation of the persons championing such causes was profoundly political. Their action was inscribed at the heart of legal-political reform of civil society. Civil society is about peace; it is not a natural society, with its endemic war. War is thus utterly disliked by HR lawyers and ideologists. Quite naturally, at the international level, the movement of HR was since its beginnings heavily politicized (notably in the UNGA debates). This could only arouse the skepticism of the military lawyers, who feared such 'pollution' of their branch of age-old law. Conversely, the HR lawyers, utterly disliking war, could not but be highly unenthusiastic about a 'law of war', considering it to be a sort of cynical misnomer. The fact cannot be escaped that the concrete law is made by human beings; their state of mind profoundly influences its shape. And the state of mind in the relevant circles in the 1940s and 1950s was favorable to the separation, not the convergence, of HRL and IHL.

(4) *Distinct Institutional Backgrounds.* International HRL was at the time under scrutiny essentially developed within the UN political organs; the ICRC guarded IHL over the same period. Both organizations at that time distrusted each other and did not seek close co-operation. The ICRC feared that an opening of IHL to the new HRL utterances at the UN would politicize this branch of the law and hence would discredit it in military circles and deprive it of its operational character. The law of armed conflict is made for a time of utmost emergency, where hostility between States and peoples is pitched at its maximum level. In such a highly delicate context, any effort to

make the law operational must strive for keeping it as aloof as possible from staunch political debates. The law of armed conflict thus has the best chance to be applied if it is considered a technical law made by specialists of war and well-tailored to the real needs of fighting armies, occupying States, etc. Conversely, the UN did not welcome the efforts of the ICRC to prepare for and draft rules for war. Such a stance somewhere suggested doubts in the capacity of the world organization to carry out its principal aim which was (and is) to maintain the peace. This quite problematic argument, known already in the League of Nations phase,[39] was indeed used in 1949 by the International Law Commission in order to refuse consideration of the law of armed conflict.[40] These institutional obstacles had first to be overcome. This would inevitably take some time.

(5) *Problems Related to the Material Scope of Application.* According to the predominant conception of the period under scrutiny, international HRL applied in peacetime, and IHL applied in times of armed conflicts. The two were thus thought to be mutually exclusive. The *jus belli* took over when the peace was breached; HRL ruled when peace was still present. It is the considerable upsurge of non-international armed conflicts (civil wars) that progressively persuaded States and international organs of the necessity to apply HRL to internal armed conflicts. That was the only way to provide some legal protection to the suffering civilians, since common article 3 of the GC IV was too sketchy to be of sufficient help (and moreover concerned mainly persons *hors de combat* in the immediate control of a belligerent, not the civilians at large). In order to affirm the applicability of international HRL to periods of armed conflict, the derogation clauses for 'times of emergency' contained in HR Conventions[41] were now read as confirming that HRL would have to apply in times of internal warfare. Why adopt a clause suggesting that HRL normally applies, since States may only derogate from certain guarantees in times of 'emergency', if HRL did from the very beginning, *ipso facto* and *ipso jure*, not apply in times of emergency? That would have been contradictory. Was 'war' not the most obvious example of an emergency situation? To the foregoing, it must be added that in the period under consideration (the 1940s and 1950s) HRL was held to apply territorially and not extraterritorially. States assumed their HRL obligations for the territories under their jurisdiction in peacetime, thus excluding occupied territories. This was interpreted narrowly as meaning the ordinary and plenary jurisdiction of territorial sovereignty. It is only later that the concept of a split and partial jurisdiction abroad was advocated, so that HRL obligations could be exported to foreign territories according to the different types of State functions performed there, such as abductions, military occupation, holding persons in captivity, raiding operations, etc. Even today, the precise extent of such an outwardly projected jurisdiction is controversial, as the unhappy ECtHR *Bankovic*-case has illustrated.[42]

All these factors, among others, explain why IHL and international HRL largely ignored each other in the formative stage of the 1940s and 1950s. The situation was, however, soon to change.

5.   REASONS FOR PROGRESSIVE CONVERGENCE

A variety of motives progressively led to an increasingly stronger convergence of IHL and international HRL. The uncertainties and gaps of IHL have been filled by an increasingly strong international HRL during the 1960s and 1970s. After the two Covenants of 1966 had been adopted, international HRL had become a fully-fledged positive international law. The sweeping character of the Covenants decisively rolled back the notion of domestic jurisdiction in this area. Gone were the debates of the 1950s to determine to what extent the UN could act in the context of the 'promotion' and 'study' of human rights. The heyday of HRL was beginning. The fact that warfare occurred during this later time-span mainly in the form of non-international armed conflicts, for which there existed hardly any norms of applicable IHL, explains why HRL quickly took the lead in the progressive legal development of the protection of persons during armed conflict. As one author[43] wrote in 1972, the law of armed conflict or IHL evolved since 1949 (and up to the 1970s) essentially under the banner of human rights law and of resolutions of the UN General Assembly. Let us consider what political, ideological and legal tectonic shifts built up an initially narrow bridge between the two bodies of the law, before that bridge expanded into a comfortable six-lane highway.

(1) *The Gently 'Subversive' Action of the Geneva Conventions of 1949.* The adoption of the GC, and especially of GC IV on civilians, progressively ventilated a new conception of the old law of warfare, namely a 'humanitarian' law for protected persons. A common ground was thus created for HRL and IHL, both predicated, totally or at least partially, on the protection of the human. As already discussed, GC IV most visibly bears the hallmark of the shift: it codifies a 'non-military' subject-area; the civilian is typically the innocent (*non nocentes*), the person not bearing arms, the defenseless individual facing military violence. This situation of persons to be protected against State-originating violence corresponds quite ideally to the genetic code of many HR. Seminal relationships could thus be constructed between IHL and HRL in this area. It therefore comes as no surprise that the General Assembly of the UN could build on both sources, GC IV and international HRL, in its resolutions about the occupied territories resulting from the 1967 Israeli–Arab war. The new conceptions of the GC thus went a long way to prepare and then to foster a closer knit of relationships between the two branches of the law considered here.

(2) *The Upsurge of Non-International Armed Conflicts.* Due to the intricate Cold War equilibrium of powers, international warfare was quite rare in the period under review. Some international armed conflicts erupted, such as those in Korea (1950), India–China (1962), Morocco–Algeria (1962), India–Pakistan (1965), or in the Vietnam of the 1960s. However, non-international armed conflicts (sometimes partially international-ized) were incomparably more frequent, especially in Asia and Africa. These were, to some extent, 'wars by proxy' of the two Superpowers, who confronted each other through governments and rebel movements in the so-called third world.[44] At the time, IHL contained only common article 3 for dealing with these highly complex civil wars which caused intense suffering (e.g. the well-known Nigeria/Biafra war in 1967). It was here strongly felt that the growing arm of international HRL could fill some gaps left glaringly open by IHL.

(3) *Other 'Untrue' Gaps in IHL.* Under the lead of the international HRL movement, other gaps within the law of armed conflict were identified and subjected to an attempt at closing them. These gaps were not true gaps, that is, an absence of legal answers on questions where such a legal answer should exist. They were rather untrue or ideological gaps, since the answer provided by the traditional law of armed conflicts was no longer thought to be appropriate, rather than simply lacking. The law was held to be defective with respect to the enhanced level of protection desired for war victims. Such defaults were identified in the prohibition of certain weapons of indiscriminate reach; or through the attempt at narrowing the scope of 'military necessity' clauses, of allowed reprisals, etc.[45] Overall, the HRL movement was used to push back the State-centeredness of the old law of warfare, ushering in a more welcome, new, individual-oriented approach.[46] HRL here exerted pressure on IHL.

(4) *The Fading Away of the old Mistrust Between the ICRC and the UN.* Faced with the enormous suffering of the civilian population in the protracted conflicts in Africa and Asia, the UN showed increasing interest in providing them with some material, but also some legal, assistance. Its old, somewhat naïve, conception, whereby the UN should not deal with wartime protections but only fight, *en amont*, for maintaining the peace, had had its time. Thus, the UN now convened the Teheran Conference – on 'human rights in armed conflicts' (1968)[47] – at the very time of the Nigerian disaster. Following that Conference, a series of reports by the Secretary General and resolutions of the General Assembly of the UN were devoted to the topic of furthering human rights in times of armed conflicts.[48] It had become accepted that HRL does not apply only in times of peace. By this process within the UN, the question of relationships between the two branches of the law had been plainly posed and could no longer be escaped. It is also from this time that the normalization of the relations between the UN and the ICRC dates. The ICRC could not remain aloof from the discussions in the UN on a subject matter, which interested it at the highest degree. Thus, an agreement for close collaboration was eventually concluded at the end of the 1960s.[49]

(5) *The Adoption of the Two Human Rights Covenants of 1966.* With the adoption of the Covenants on Civil and Political Rights (Covenant II), and on Social, Economic and Cultural Rights (Covenant I), the universal HRL movement has taken the last step to become a fully-fledged positive law. The question of the application of this HRL in times of armed conflict now appeared on the very level of positive law. Thus Covenant II on Civil and Political Rights contains a clause, in article 4, for suspension of some of its HR guarantees in times of public emergency.[50] It thereby supposed that the rights enshrined in the Convention would apply also in states of emergency, unless and to the extent that a State party had made a declaration of derogation within the limits imposed by article 4. This was quickly turned into an admission that HR applied in times of armed conflict.[51] The new interpretation just presented was emphatically confirmed in the Tehran Conference. This evolution brought HRL plainly in the halls hitherto reserved for the law of armed conflict. At least, the question of interactions between the two bodies of the law could no longer be ignored.

All these factors, among others, pulled consistently towards a convergence and some form of co-operation between both branches of the law. It will be left to the future to figure out the exact lines of that co-operation. It must be said that this has not been entirely successful up to now. We are still in the phase where the two tectonic plates are shifting and adjusting to one another. Probably, the question is too complex and shifting to ever receive a definitive answer.

6. CONCLUSION: OUTLOOK ON THE RELATIONSHIPS BETWEEN HRL AND IHL

The IHL of the Geneva period is rooted in the ideal of 'humanitarianism'. Hence, progressive interrelationships with HRL quickly became unavoidable. The interaction of the two areas of the law, IHL and HRL, has today become at once pervasive, intimate and highly sophisticated.[52] In some areas, HRL complements IHL; in other areas, IHL strengthens or inspires HRL. One branch of the law frequently serves to interpret the other. This is the case with respect to the detention of protected persons, fair trial, occupied territories, etc. The question as to the limits of the relationship is also asked: where does welcome co-operation end and where does self-defeating promiscuity start? Where do fruitful complements stop and where do cancerous metastases begin? Should it not be said: co-operation yes, fusion and erasing of the differences no? But if that is accepted, where is the line to be drawn? Moreover, the issue of *lex specialis* (in a '*compleat*' version rather than in a '*derogat*' version, that is, as mutual complements not as mutual derogations) has been raised by the ICJ and then by legal doctrine.[53] It opens up an array of further intricate questions.

Today, the existence of the many HRL monitoring bodies and tribunals also accounts for the contribution of HRL to the protection of persons in the context of armed conflicts. Since there are no true monitoring bodies (and even fewer tribunals) for the respect of IHL, it is quite natural to bring abuses of force during armed conflicts within the ambit of HRL, and to seek the jurisdiction of a HRL court in order to ensure a sanction.[54]

Legal doctrine has ventured subtle and multiple comments upon the relationships of the two areas, and although it is beyond the scope of this introductory and historical chapter to go into them, many of these aspects will be discussed in subsequent topical contributions to this Handbook. The only point which needs to be stressed at this juncture, is how the two areas of the law under consideration have undergone a profound technical, ideological and structural transformation since 1945, which in turn has cast their mutual relations in an entirely new light. Hardly any branches of international law have undergone such changes; hardly any have proved to be so chameleon-like. Thus, dealing with the relations of IHL and HRL is first of all dealing with the profound nature and vision of each of these branches at a given moment in history. It allows, by contrast, a greatly enhanced understanding of where we stand today and why. Essentially, IHL shifted at least partially from 'military' law to 'humanitarian' law (protection of war victims); this humanitarian law progressively opened itself to human rights law. The Martens Clause now found a fertile soil for growth and grew in importance, whereas the rule for residual freedom of the State was resolutely pushed back (i.e. the old rule that 'any act not prohibited is permitted'). Conversely, international HRL shifted from an 'aspiration-law', enmeshed in politics, into a fully-fledged branch of positive international law, albeit with some specificities (e.g. the existence of monitoring organs, their mostly recommendatory actions, etc.).

The 'humanization' of the law of armed conflict and the 'positivation' of HRL opened the way for a partial merger of the two areas of the law, each one making its distinct but joint contribution to the attempt to create an optimum protection for persons and property during the distressing reality of armed turmoil. Overall, this represents the most powerful attempt of humanity to impose some barriers to the barbarity of war by providing some humane regulation to wartime situations. This in turn responds to the quest of modern man towards securing, as far as possible, the goal of human dignity. We are here confronted with a distinct cultural effort, fitting so graphically the civilization ideals of the end of the 19th and the second half of the 20th centuries. It remains to be seen to what extent the man of the 21st century will remain indebted to this outstanding (if not always efficient or effective) edifice of legal-political craftsmanship.

NOTES

* Robert Kolb is Professor of Public International Law at the University of Geneva, Switzerland.
1. For quite obvious political reasons the US government has shown restraint and fear in the face of such an extension of HRL, e.g., in occupied territories or in Guantanamo situations. See H.J. Dennis, 'Application of Human Rights Treaties Extraterritorially in Times of Armed Conflict and Military Occupation', *American Journal of International Law* 99 (2005): 119ff.
2. See, e.g., R. Kolb and S. Vité, *Le droit de l'occupation militaire. Perspectives historiques et enjeux juridiques actuels* (Brussels: Bruylant, 2009).
3. H. Meyrowitz, 'Le droit de la guerre et les droits de l'homme', *Revue du droit public et de la science politique en France et à l'étranger* 88 (1972): 1095ff.
4. To this effect, see the present writer's presentation in the EPIL, online: 'Human Rights and Humanitarian Law', in *Max Planck Encyclopaedia of Public International Law* (2008), available at http://www.mpepil.com (accessed 5 February 2012). See also this contribution for an extended bibliography.
5. See, e.g., E. Opocher, *Lezioni di filosofia del diritto* (Padua: CEDAM, 1983), 101ff., 135ff.
6. See, e.g., J. Locke, *Two Treatises on Government* (1690), II, 123ff. On the subject-matter, see P. Pavan, 'Diritto dell'uomo e diritto natural', *in Apollinaris* XXXIX (1996), 355ff.; F. Castberg, 'Natural Law and Human Rights', *Revue des droits de l'homme* 1 (1968): 14ff.; R. Marcic, *Geschichte der Rechtsphilosophie* (Freiburg im Breisgau: Rombach, 1971), 67ff.; E.B.F Midgley, 'Natural Law and Fundamental Rights', *American Journal on Jurisprudence* 21 (1976): 144ff.; G. Oestreich, *Geschichte der Menschenrechte und Grundfreiheiten im Umriss*, 2nd edition (Berlin: Duncker & Humblot, 1978); M.C. Peces Barba, *Teoria dei diritti fondamentali* (Milan: Giuffrè, 1993); D. Merten and H.-J. Papier, eds., *Handbuch der Grundrechte*, Vol. I, *Entwicklung und Grundlagen* (Heidelberg: Müller, 2004), 3ff.; A. Facchi, *Breve storia dei diritti umani* (Bologna: Il Mulino, 2007); F. Rigaux, 'Les fondements philosophiques des droits de l'homme', *Revue trimestrielle des droits de l'homme* 18 (2007): 307ff.
7. E.g., the Petition of Rights (England, 1628) or the Habeas Corpus Act (England, 1679); the Virginia Bill of Rights (1776); or the *Déclaration des droits de l'homme et du citoyen* (France, 1789). Such a Bill of Rights was proposed also for international law (and it became reality with the Declaration of 1948): H. Lauterpacht, *An International Bill of the Rights of Man* (London: Columbia University Press, 1945). On the English Bills of Rights, see W. Hubatsch, *Die englischen Freiheitsrechte* (Hanover: Pfeiffer, 1962). On the US Bills of Rights, see R.A. Rutland, *The Birth of the Bill of Rights*, 1776–1791 (Chapel Hill: University of North Carolina Press, 1955); G. Ostrander, *The Rights of Man in America, 1606–1861* (Columbia: University of Missouri Press, 1960). On the French Declaration, see G. Del Vecchio, *La déclaration des droits de l'homme et du citoyen dans la révolution française* (Paris: Librairie générale de droit et de jurisprudence, 1968); S.J. Samwer, *Die französische Erklärung der Menschen-und Bürgerrechte von 1789–91* (Hamburg: Heitmann, 1970); S. Rials, La déclaration des droits de l'homme et du citoyen (Paris: Hachette, 1988); J. Morange, *La déclaration des droits de l'homme et du citoyen* (Paris: PUF, 1988); C.-A. Colliard, ed., *La Déclaration des droits de l'homme et du citoyen de 1789* (Paris: Documentation française, 1990).

8.   L. Oppenheim, *International Law*, Vol. I, *Peace*, 3rd edition, ed. R.F. Roxburgh (London: Longmans, Green & Co., 1921), 460.
9.   See R. Cassin, 'La déclaration universelle et la mise en œuvre des droits de l'homme', *Receuil des cours de l'Académie de droit international de La Haye (Hague Recueil)* 79 (1951-II): 237ff.
10. On this important Declaration, see A. Eide et al., eds, *The Universal Declaration of Human Rights: A Commentary* (Oslo: Scandinavian University Press, 1992). See also Cassin, *supra* note 9, at 237ff.; A. Verdoort, *Naissance et signification de la Déclaration universelle des droits de l'homme* (Leuwen and Paris: Société d'Études Morales, Sociales et Juridiques, 1964); N. Robinson, *The Universal Declaration of Human Rights* (New York: Institute of Jewish Affairs, World Jewish Congress, 1958). On the draft Declaration, see R. Brunet, *La garantie internationale des droits de l'homme* (Geneva: Ch. Grasset, 1947), 197ff. For a recent account, see U. Villani, ed., *A tutti in membri della famiglia umana, Per il 60 anniversario della Dichiarazione universale* (Milan: Giuffrè, 2009).
11. See, at the time of the conclusion, J. Mourgeon, 'Les Pactes internationaux relatifs aux droits de l'homme', *AFDI* 13 (1967): 326ff.
12. On the Geneva Conventions of 1949, see J.A.C. Gutteridge, 'The Geneva Conventions of 1949', *British Yearbook of International Law* 26 (1949): 294ff.; L. Orcasitas Llorente, 'La Conferencia de Ginebra de 1949 para mejorar la suerte de la victimas de la guerra', *Revista española de derecho internacional* 2 (1949): 605ff.; F. Siordet, 'La Conférence diplomatique de Genève', *Revue internationale de la Croix-Rouge* 31 (1949): 475ff., 554ff.; J. Pictet, 'La Croix-Rouge et les Conventions de Genève', *RCADI* 76 (1950-I): 1ff.; M. Bourquin, 'Les Conventions de Genève du 12 août 1949', *Revue internationale de la Croix-Rouge* 32 (1950): 90ff.; E. Djafari, *Les Conventions de Genève du 12 août 1949 sur la protection des victimes de la guerre* (thesis, Paris, 1950); S. Tschirkovitch, 'Les nouvelles Conventions internationales de Genève relatives à la protection des victimes de la guerre du 12 août 1949', *RGDIP* 54 (1950): 97ff., 525ff.; P. De La Pradelle, *La Conférence diplomatique et les nouvelles Conventions de Genève du 12 août 1949* (Paris: Les éditions internationales, 1951); R.D. Paine, *The 1949 Geneva Conventions Concerning War Victims* (thesis, Northwestern University, Evanston, Illinois, 1951); A. Schickelé, 'L'avenir des Conventions de Genève', *Revue internationale de la Croix-Rouge* 33 (1951): 496ff.; R.T. Yingling and R.W. Ginnane, 'The Geneva Conventions of 1949', *American Journal of International Law* 46 (1952): 393ff.; J. Kunz, 'The Geneva Conventions of August 12, 1949', in *Law and Politics in the World Community*, ed. G.A. Lipsky, Part III (Berkeley and Los Angeles: University of California Press, 1953): 279ff.; E. Lodemann, 'Die Genfer Rotkreuzabkommen vom 12. August 1949', *Archiv des Völkerrechts* 4 (1953): 72ff.; G.I.A.D. Draper, *The Red Cross Conventions* (London: Stevens & Sons Limited, 1958); H. Coursier, *Cours de cinq leçons sur les Conventions de Genève* (Geneva: ICRC, 1963); G.I.A.D. Draper, 'The Geneva Conventions of 1949', *RCADI* 114 (1965-I): 59ff.; A. Maresca, *La protezione internazionale dei combattenti e dei civili: Le Convenzioni di Ginevra del 12 agosto 1949* (Milan: Giuffrè, 1965); D. Schindler, 'Die Anwendung der Genfer Rotkreuzabkommen seit 1949', *ASDI* 22 (1965): 75ff.; C. Pilloud, 'Les Conventions de Genève 1949–1969. Bilan et perspectives', *Revue internationale de la Croix-Rouge* 51 (1969): 465ff.; C. Pilloud, 'Les Conventions de Genève, 1949–1969', *Revue internationale de la Croix-Rouge* 51 (1984): 465ff.; T. Meron, 'The Geneva Conventions as Customary Law', *American Journal of International Law* 81 (1987): 348ff.; F. Bugnion, *Le Comité international de la Croix-Rouge et la protection des victimes de la guerre* (Geneva: ICRC, 1994), 354ff.; G. Best, *War and Law since 1945* (Oxford: Clarendon Press, 1994), 80ff.; Y. Sandoz, 'Le demi-siècle des Conventions de Genève', *Revue internationale de la Croix-Rouge* 81 (1999): 241ff.; C. Rey-Schyrr, 'Les Conventions de Genève de 1949: une percée décisive', *Revue internationale de la Croix-Rouge* 81, no. 834 (1999): 209ff.; F. Bugnion, 'Les Conventions de Genève du 12 août 1949', *RSDIE* 9 (1999): 371ff.; D. Schindler, 'Significance of the Geneva Conventions for the Contemporary World', in *A Manual of International Humanitarian Laws*, ed. N. Sanajaoba (New Delhi: Regency Publications, 2004), 42ff.; D. Forsythe, '1949 and 1999: Making the Geneva Conventions Relevant after the Cold War', in ibid., 56ff.; C. Rey-Schyrr, *De Yalta à Dien Bien Phu, Histoire du Comité international de la Croix-Rouge, 1945–1955* (Geneva: Georg, 2007), 239ff. One may further consult the commentaries to the four Geneva Conventions edited by the CICR under the direction of Jean Pictet in the 1950s: J. Pictet, ed., *Commentary I, Geneva Convention for the Amelioration of the Condition of the Wounded and Sick in Armed Forces in the Field* (Geneva: International Committee of the Red Cross, 1952); J. Pictet, ed., *Commentary II, Geneva Convention for the Amelioration of the Condition of Wounded, Sick and Shipwrecked Members of Armed Forces at Sea* (Geneva: International Committee of the Red Cross, 1960); J. Pictet, ed., *Commentary III, Geneva Convention relative to the Treatment of Prisoners of War* (Geneva: International Committee of the Red Cross, 1960); J. Pictet, ed.,

Commentary IV, Geneva Convention relative to the Protection of Civilian Persons in Time of War (Geneva: International Committee of the Red Cross, 1958). For the Additional Protocols of 1977, see essentially Y. Sandoz, C. Swinarski and B. Zimmermann, eds, *Commentary on the Additional Protocols of 8 June 1977 to the Geneva Conventions of 12 August 1949* (Geneva: ICRC, 1987); M. Bothe, K.J. Partsch and W. Solf, ed., *New Rules for Victims of Armed Conflicts* (The Hague, Boston and London: Martinus Nijhoff Publishers, 1982).

13. See R. Kolb, 'The Main Epochs of Modern International Humanitarian Law since 1864 and their Related Dominant Legal Constructions', in *Sixty Years of Humanity: Anniversary of the Geneva Conventions of 1949*, ed. Norwegian Centre for Human Rights (forthcoming).

14. The Congress of Paris of 1856 (after the Crimean War) recognized that the declaration of war is necessary and thus required, except in the case of invasion and spontaneous self-defense: see C. Calvo, *Le droit international théorique et pratique*, 5 éd. (Paris, 1896), t. IV, 47. Declarations of war have completely fallen into disuse since 1945: see A. McDonald, 'Declarations of War and Belligerent Parties: International Law Governing Hostilities Between States and Transnational Terrorist Networks', *NILR* 54 (2007): 279ff., 287ff.

15. E.C. Stowell, *International Law* (New York: Holt, 1931), 401: '[S]ome intercourse with the insurrectionists is often necessary. In the troubled conditions of civil warfare it becomes especially urgent for other States to look out for the protection of their nationals within the zone of operations, and the economic demands of war greatly increase the trade in contraband and a variety of articles. In these circumstances, forced by the necessity of providing for effective protection of their nationals, and urged by the desire to continue and extend an authorized trade with all portions and parties of the state engaged in the conflict, other states accord what is called Recognition of Belligerency.' See also H. Wheaton, *Elements of International Law*, 8th edition (Oxford: Oceana, 1866), 35.

16. These two devices (declaration of war, recognition of belligerency) fitted perfectly into the sovereignist and positivist frame of the 19th century:(1) Humanitarian protection was not paramount – thus, gaps in protection were not felt as being inadmissible; if a particular violent contest was not formally classified as 'war' (e.g., armed reprisals), the law of war would simply not apply. The formal aspect dominated the material one.(2) The sovereign will of the different States was decisive, each State remaining free in the application of the legal rules according to its vision of a particular violent struggle (if it declared or recognized the war, there was applicability of the law of war; if not, there was no applicability of the law of war).(3) This will is expressed through a unilateral act (declaration of war, recognition of belligerency), not through an agreement between the belligerents. We here confront again a projection of the 'I' which reflects very well the already discussed paradigm of the primacy of municipal law.(4) The legal picture ensuing from such a system is fraught with relativity: the war formally exists or does not exist according to the will of each State. Thus, the war does not exist objectively but only subjectively. It must be added that the sharp edges of such a doctrine were sometimes smoothed in legal writings, e.g., by the development of a category of 'material war' to be treated as war analogously to a 'formal' or declared war. However, the essence of the system was subjective in the described sense and therefore material criteria could take hold only with many difficulties.

17. H.J. Taubenfeld, 'The Applicability of the Laws of War in Civil War', *in Law and Civil War in the Modern World*, ed. J.N. Moore (Baltimore and London: Lawbook Exchange, 1974), 502ff.

18. It may be added that the subjective aspects have, however, not completely disappeared, especially in the context of non-international armed conflicts. The governments fighting internal rebellion are often reluctant to accept that an 'armed conflict' is ongoing; they prefer to claim that they face at most internal disturbances. By this device, they seek to evade the application of international obligations under the Geneva Convention; the droit de regard of the international community and of the ICRC which this inevitably triggers (resented as interventions in internal affairs in an extremely sensitive moment); and the granting of an unwelcome political and legal status to the insurgents, henceforth treated as 'belligerents'.

19. For the details, see R. Kolb, 'Relations entre le droit international humanitaire et les droits de l'homme. Aperçu de la Déclaration universelle des droits de l'homme et des Conventions de Genève', *Revue internationale de la Croix-Rouge* 80 (1998): 437–447 (English version in R. Kolb, 'The Relationship between International Humanitarian Law and Human Rights Law: A Brief History of the 1948 Universal Declaration on Human Rights and the 1949 Geneva Conventions', *International Review of the Red Cross* 38 (1998): 409–419). See also C. Pilloud, 'La Déclaration universelle des droits de l'homme et les Conventions internationales protégeant les victimes de la guerre', *Revue internationale de la Croix-Rouge* 31 (1949): 252ff.; J.-G. Lossier, 'La Croix-Rouge et la Déclaration

universelle des droits de l'homme', *Revue internationale de la Croix-Rouge* 31 (1949): 259ff.; D. Schindler, 'Le Comité international de la Croix-Rouge et les droits de l'homme', *Revue internationale de la Croix-Rouge* 61 (1979): 7.

20.   For a synopsis of these works, see Eide et al., *supra* note 10, at 3. The work of the Third Committee of the UN General Assembly can be added: A/C.3/SR. 88–116,119–170,174–178. See also Cassin, *supra* note 9, at 271ff. Verdoort, *supra* note 10, at 45ff.; Robinson, *supra* note 10, at 25ff.; J.P. Humphrey, 'The Universal Declaration of Human Rights: Its History, Impact and Juridical Character', in *Human Rights: Thirty Years after the Universal Declaration*, ed. B.G. Ramcharan (The Hague, Boston and London: Martinus Nijhoff, 1979), 21ff. One may also mention the *Yearbook on Human Rights for 1947* (New York: United Nations, 1949), 430ff.

21.   This was proposed by France (R. Cassin): UN Doc. E/CN.4/21, 29; UN Doc. E/CN.4/21, 36; and the reaction of Mexico, UN Doc. E/CN.4/85, 8.

22.   E.g., UN Doc. A/CN 3./SR. 116, 268.

23.   UN Doc. A/CN.3/SR. 152, 639.

24.   See also Best, *supra* note 12, at 70–71.

25.   *Actes de la Conférence diplomatique de Genève de 1949*, Vol. II, sect. A, 313.

26.   Ibid., 797, and see also, 676ff.

27.   De Alba (Mexico), ibid., 676; De Geouffre de la Pradelle (Monaco), ibid., 677; Cohen-Salvador (France), ibid., 681, Nassif (Lebanon), ibid., 679–680. See also the remarks by the Rapporteur, ibid., 762–763.

28.   Ibid., p. 455.

29.   Ibid., 468: 'Rien dans le présent article ne peut être interprété de manière à priver les personnes qui tombent en dehors des clauses de cet article, de leurs droits de l'homme et notamment de leur droit de légitime défense, vis-à-vis des actes illégaux, sanctionnés par leur législation nationale en vigueur avant le commencement des hostilités ou de l'occupation' (Danish Amendment). See the critical remarks of Mr Gardner (United Kingdom), ibid., 398 and the response of Cohn, Actes ... [*supra* note 25], Vol. II, sect. B, 260–261. The UK delegate indeed admitted the point: 'Le délégué au Danemark a ensuite commenté cette déclaration. Je me permets toutefois d'observer que son argumentation n'est pas tout à fait pertinente. En effet, le but de l'article 3 n'est pas de priver qui que ce soit de quoi que ce soit, mais de déterminer les personnes qui, en vertu de l'article 3, peuvent bénéficier de la protection de la Convention' (Sir R. Craigie, *Actes* ..., Vol. II, sect. B, 261).

30.   *Actes* ... [*supra* note 25], Vol. II, sect. A, 655.

31.   *Actes* ... [*supra* note 25], Vol. II, sect. B, 541: 'Après-demain, nous célèbrerons l'anniversaire de la Déclaration universelle des droits de l'homme, qui fut adoptée par l'Assemblée générale des Nations Unies le 10 décembre 1948. Il nous paraît intéressant de rapprocher cette déclaration des Conventions de Genève. Certains des droits fondamentaux proclamés par elle sont à la base de nos textes: ainsi le respect de la personne humaine, garantie contre la torture, les peines ou traitements cruels, inhumains ou dégradants. Ces droits trouvent donc une sanction juridique, au moins partielle, dans les engagements contractuels que vos Gouvernements ont accepté de prendre aujourd'hui. La Déclaration universelle des droits de l'homme et les Conventions de Genève procèdent du même idéal ... '.

32.   See, e.g., Gutteridge, *supra* note 12, at 325.

33.   Ibid., 300: these provisions are the 'expression of concern that even in internal conflicts the observance of certain fundamental human rights be guaranteed'.

34.   See R. Kolb, 'Aspects historiques de la relation entre le droit international humanitaire et les droits de l'homme', *Canadian Yearbook of International Law* 37 (1999): 74–75.

35.   *Proceedings of the American Society of International Law* 43 (1949): 121.

36.   Draper, *supra* note 12, at 48, see also 45. Quoted in Best, *supra* note 12, at 72.

37.   See also R. Kolb, *Ius contra bellum – Précis de droit international relatif au maintien de la paix*, 2nd edition (Bâle and Brussels: Helbing & Lichtenhahn, 2009), 127–129.

38.   See, e.g., U. Villani, 'La Dichiarazione 60 anni dopo', in *A tutti i membri della famiglia umana*, ed. U. Villani (Milan: Giuffrè, 2008), 20–21.

39.   See Anonymous, 'The League of Nations and the Laws of War', *British Yearbook of International Law* 1 (1920–1921): 114–115; E. Dickinson, 'The New Law of Nations', *West Virginia Law Quarterly* 32 (1925–1926): 25, 29; M. Huber, 'Der Wert des Völkerrechts', *Neue Zürcher Zeitung* (20 November 1916). For the argument that devoting attention to the *jus in bello* may weaken the belief in *jus contra bellum*, see Politis (Greece) and Sokal (Poland) in the disarmament commission of the League of Nations, *Documents de la Commission préparatoire de désarmement*, series VIII (Société des Nations, 1929): 87 [Sokal], 91 [Politis]. *Contra*, Rutgers (Holland), ibid., 90. For a criticism, see A. De La

Pradelle, 'Négligera-t-on longtemps encore l'étude des lois de la guerre?', *Revue de droit international* (Paris) 12 (1933): 511ff.; J. Kunz, 'Plus de lois de la guerre?', *RGDIP* 41 (1934): 22ff., the perplexity of both authors emerging clearly through the use in both cases of question marks.

40. *YbILC* (1949): 281, sect. 18: 'It was considered that if the Commission, at the very beginning of its work, were to undertake this study [on the laws of war], public opinion might interpret its action as showing lack of confidence in the efficiency of the means at the disposal of the United Nations for maintaining peace'. See the criticisms in *Ann. IDI* 47-I (1957): 323ff., and the opinion of the Rapporteur, J.-P.A. François ibid., 367ff. See also J. Kunz, 'The Chaotic Status of the Laws of War and the Urgent Necessity for their Revision', *American Journal of International Law* 45 (1951): 37ff.; J. Kunz, 'The Laws of War', *American Journal of International Law* 50 (1956): 313ff.; H. Lauterpacht, 'The Revision of the Laws of War', *British Yearbook of International Law* 29 (1952): 360ff.; A.P. Sereni, *Diritto internazionale* IV (Milan: Giuffrè, 1965), 1823–1826.

41. E.g., Article 4 of the Covenant on Civil and Political Rights (1966). See M. Nowak, *UN Convention on Civil and Political Rights*, 2nd edition (Kehl and Strassburg: N.P. Engel, 2005), 83ff.

42. *Bankovic and others v. Belgium and others*, ECtHR, Application No. 52207/99, Decision on Admissibility, 12 December 2001. On extraterritorial application of HRL, see in this volume: Robert K. Goldman, 'Extraterritorial application of the human rights to life and personal liberty, including habeas corpus, during situations of armed conflict'; V. Gowlland-Debbas and G. Gaggioli, 'The relationship between international human rights and humanitarian law: an overview'. See also R. Kolb, G. Poretto and S. Vité, *L'application du droit international humanitaire et des droits de l'homme aux organisations internationales, forces de paix et administrations civiles transitoires* (Bruxelles: Bruylant, 2005), at 419–428.

43. A. Migliazza, 'L'évolution de la réglementation de la guerre à la lumière de la sauvegarde des droits de l'homme', *RCADI* 137 (1972-III): 141ss, 189.

44. B. Duner, 'Proxy Intervention in Civil Wars', *Journal of Peace Research* (Oslo) 18 (1981): 353ff.

45. Migliazza, *supra* note 43, at 192ff.

46. Ibid., 207–208.

47. See D. Schindler and J. Toman, *The Law of Armed Conflicts* (Leiden and Boston: Martinus Nijhoff Publishers, 2004), 347–348. See also F. Capotorti, 'La Conferenza di Teheran sui diritti dell'uomo', *Comunità internazionale* 23 (1968): 609ff.; A. Cassese, 'La Conferenza internazionale di Teheran sui diritti dell'uomo', *Rivista di diritto internazionale* 51 (1968): 669ff.; R. Cassin, 'The Teheran Proclamation', *Revue des droits de l'homme* 1 (1968): 325ff.; V. Chkhikvadze and Y. Ostrovsky, 'International Human Rights Conference', *International Affairs* (Moscow) 14 (1968): 16–21; G. Rulli, 'La Conferenza di Teheran – La Dichiarazione universale dei diritti dell'uomo', *Civiltà cattolica* 119 (1968): 598–604; E. Lawson (ed.), *Encyclopedia of Human Rights*, 2nd edition (Washington: Taylor & Francis, 1996), 1433–1434.

48. A/RES/2444 (XXIII), 19 December 1968; A/RES/2597 (XXIV), 16 December 1969; A/RES/2674 (XXV), 9 December 1970; A/RES/2675 (XXV), 9 December 1970, A/RES/2676 (XXV), 9 December 1970; A/RES/2677 (XXV), 9 December 1970; A/RES/2852 (XXVI), 20 December 1971; A/RES/3032 (XXVII), 18 December 1972; A/RES/3102 (XXVIII), 12 December 1973; A/RES/3103 (XXVIII), 12 December 1973; A/RES/3318 (XXIX), 14 December 1974. As to the reports of the Secretary General: Report of 20th November 1969, A/7720 and 18th September 1970, A/8052. See also the reports under: Doc. A/8589 (3rd Committee, 1971); Doc. A/8966 (6th Committee, 1972); Doc. A/9412 (6th Committee, 1973); Doc. A/9948 (6th Committee, 1974); Doc. A/10463 (6th Committee, 1975). See also Docs A/31/295 (1976) and A/32/396 (1977). See also the Reports of S. McBride at the San Remo Institute: *Actes du Congrès international de droit humanitaire*, Conférence internationale sur le droit humanitaire de San Remo, 1970, San Remo, 1971. For more details, see the brief account in Kolb, *supra* note 37, at 130–132.

49. See Migliazza, *supra* note 43, at 171, 231.

50. Nowak, *supra* note 41, at 83ff.

51. Ibid.

52. See, among so many other authors, L. Doswald-Beck and S. Vité, 'International Humanitarian Law and Human Rights Law', *International Review of the Red Cross* 293 (1993): 94ff.; R. Provost, *International Human Rights and Humanitarian Law* (Cambridge: Cambridge University Press, 2002); H.P. Gasser, 'International Humanitarian Law and Human Rights Law in Non-international Armed Conflict: Joint Venture or Mutual Exclusion?', *German Yearbook of International Law* 45 (2002): 149ff.; T. Meron, 'International Law in the Age of Human Rights', *RCADI* 310 (2003): 68ff.; H.-J. Heintze, 'On the Relationship between Human Rights Law Protection and International Humanitarian

Law', *International Review of the Red Cross* 856 (2004): 789ff.; F.F. Martin, S.J. Schnably, R. Wilson, J. Simon and M. Tushnet, *International Human Rights and Humanitarian Law: Treaties, Cases and Analysis* (Cambridge: Cambridge University Press, 2006); R. Arnold and N. Quénivet, ed., *International Humanitarian Law and Human Rights Law: Towards a New Merger in International Law* (Boston: Brill, 2008). The ICJ itself analyses situations under both headings, HRL and IHL, adding one perspective to the other. See, e.g., *Legal Consequences of the Construction of a Wall in the Occupied Palestinian Territory*, Advisory Opinion, I.C.J. Reports 2004, sect. 89ff., 102ff.; and *Armed Activities on the Territory of the Congo case* (D.R. Congo v. Uganda), Judgment, I.C.J. Reports 2005, sect. 181ff., 216ff.

53.   On the Court's treatment of lex specialis, see *Threat or Use of Nuclear Weapons*, Advisory Opinion to the UNGA, I.C.J. Reports 1996, sect. 25; *Legal Consequences of the Construction of a Wall in the Occupied Palestinian Territory*, Advisory Opinion, I.C.J. Reports 2004, sect. 106; *Armed Activities on the Territory of the Congo case* (D.R. Congo v. Uganda), Judgment, I.C.J. Reports 2005, sect. 216. See also G. Gaggioli and R. Kolb, 'A Right to Life in Armed Conflicts? The Contribution of the European Court of Human Rights', *Israel Yearbook on Human Rights* 37 (2007): 118 et seq.

54.   As to the contribution of the ECtHR, see, e.g., G. Gaggioli and R. Kolb, 'A Right to Life in Armed Conflicts? The Contribution of the European Court of Human Rights', *Israel Yearbook on Human Rights* 37 (2007): 115ff. See generally the case-law of these tribunals, in particular: (1) UN Human Rights Committee: *Pedro Pablo Camargo v. Colombia* [known as the *Guerrero case*], HRC, 31 March 1982 (UN Doc. CCPR/C/15/D/45/1979); *Baboeram et al. v. Suriname*, HRC, 4 April 1985 (UN Doc. CCPR/C/24/D/146/1983); Concluding Observations on Israel, HRC, 21 August 2003 (UN Doc. CCPR/CO/78/ISR); Concluding Observations on United States, HRC, 15 September 2006 (UN Doc. CCPR/C/USA/CO/3); (2) European Commission of Human Rights: *Cyprus v. Turkey*, Application Nos 6780/74 and 6950/75, Judgment of 10 July 1976; (3) European Court of Human Rights: *Kaya v. Turkey*, ECtHR, Application No. 22535/93, Judgment of 19 February 1998; *Ergi v. Turkey*, ECtHR, Application No. 23818/94, Judgment of 28 July 1998; *Ahmet Özkan and others v. Turkey*, ECtHR, Application No. 21689/93, Judgment of 6 April 2004; *Isayeva, Yussoupova and Bazayeva v. Russia*, ECtHR, Application No. 57947/00, Judgment of 24 February 2005; *Isayeva v. Russia*, ECtHR, Application No. 57950/00, Judgment of 24 February 2005; *Khatsiyeva v. Russia*, ECtHR, Application No. 5108/02, Judgment of 17 January 2008; *Akkum and others v. Turkey*, ECtHR, Application No. 21894/93, Judgment of 24 March 2005; (4) Inter-American Commission of Human Rights: *Arturo Ribon Avila v. Colombia*, IACommHR, Case 11.142, Report No. 26/97, 30 September 1997; *Juan Carlos Abella v. Argentina* [known as the *La Tablada case*], IACommHR, Case 11.137, Report No. 55/97, 18 November 1997; *Guerrero et al. v. Colombia*, IACommHR, Case 11.519, Report No.61/99, 13 April 1999; *Coard et al. v. United States*, IACommHR, Case 10.951, Report No. 109/99, 29 September 1999; *Report on Terrorism and Human Rights*, IACommHR, 22 October 2002; (5) Inter-American Court of Human Rights: *Bámaca-Velásquez v. Guatemala*, IACtHR, Merits, Judgment of 25 November 2000; *Mapiripán Massacre v. Colombia*, IACtHR, Merits, reparations and costs, Judgment of 15 September 2005; *Pueblo Bello Massacre v. Colombia*, IACtHR, Merits, reparations and costs, Judgment of 31 January 2006; *Ituango Massacre v. Colombia*, IACtHR, Preliminary objections, merits, reparations and costs, Judgment of 1 July 2006; *La Rochela v. Colombia*, IACtHR, Merits, reparations and costs, Judgment of 11 May 2007; *Myrna Mack Chang v. Guatemala*, IACtHR, Merits, reparations and costs, Judgment of 25 November 2003; *Plan de Sánchez Massacre v. Guatemala*, IACtHR, Merits, Judgment of 29 April 2004; *Moiwana Community v. Suriname*, IACtHR, Preliminary objections, merits, reparations and costs, Judgment of 15 June 2005; (6) African Commission of Human and People's Rights: *Commission Nationale des Droits de l'Homme et des Libertes v. Chad*, Communication No. 74/92 (1995); *Free Legal Assistance Group and others v. Zaïre*, Communication No. 25/89, 47/90, 56/91, 100/93 (1995); *Organisation Mondiale Contre La Torture v. Rwanda*, Communication Nos 27/89, 46/91, 49/91, 99/93 (1996); *Civil Liberties Organisation, Legal Defence Centre, Legal Defence and Assistance Project v. Nigeria*, Communication No. 218/98 (1998); *Amnesty International and others v. Sudan*, Communication No. 48/90, 50/91, 52/91, 89/93 (1999); *Social and Economic Rights Action Center and Center for Economic and Social Rights v. Nigeria*, Communication No. 155/96 (2001).

3. Theories on the relationship between international humanitarian law and human rights law

*Hans-Joachim Heintze**

The relationship between human rights law and international humanitarian law has been the subject of extensive discussions over the last 40 years. In particular, the experts on international humanitarian law were quite reluctant to accept the application of human rights law during armed conflicts. They argued that the two systems of rules were assigned to two distinct legal regimes, and close ties did not exist from the outset. Many scholars argue that connections 'between the two branches of the law are not in any sense natural or necessary'.[1] This may be true for a historical analysis but after the ICJ 'Advisory Opinion on Nuclear Weapons'[2] the viewpoints centre upon the applicability of human rights law in cases of armed conflicts.[3] The viewpoints of the ICJ reflect the overcoming of the rift between the two branches of the law, which was, in the first place, a consequence of the appearance of non-international armed conflicts after the end of the Second World War. A precondition for the legal regulation of these conflicts was the applicability of human rights law together with international humanitarian law.

Regardless, the whole debate is surprising against the background of the 'openness'[4] of international humanitarian law articulated by the Martens Clause. According to the clause, in the absence of specific regulations, populations and belligerents remain under the protection and empire of the principles of international law, as they result from the usages established between civilized nations, from the laws of humanity, and the requirements of public conscience.[5] The same approach characterizes Article 72 of Additional Protocol I: 'The provisions of the Section are additional ... to other applicable rules of international law relating to the protection of fundamental human rights during international armed conflicts.'

Taking into account the reluctance of the community of States to codify the principle of humanity in detail, the question is posed as to which developments have been made in the abutting bodies of law, and how they influence international humanitarian law.[6] Particular attention must be paid to international human rights law, as today human rights are an integral part of international law for the common welfare of humanity and represent common values that no State may revoke, even in times of war.[7] While international humanitarian law and human rights law vary in terms of origin and the situations in which they apply, the two bodies of law share the objective of protecting and safeguarding individuals in all circumstances.

It seems that the co-existence or even merger of international humanitarian law and human rights law is much more advanced in practical terms than in legal theory. Some scholars still regret that the detailed debate did not succeed in a common conclusion as to how the normative wealth of both branches of the law can combine to serve the protection of human beings.[8] Therefore it makes sense to deal with the different dominating theories on the relationship.

1.   THE TRADITIONAL APPROACH: THE SEPARATION THEORY

Traditional international public law used to be divided into two different branches of law. There was a clear separation between the law of peace and the law of war. Depending on the state of international relations, either the *corpus juris* of the law of peace or that of the law of war was applied. Therefore it was possible to speak of a separation theory.

1.1   Human Rights as Challenge

The appearance of human rights law after the Second World War challenged the traditional approach of international law because the protection of the human being became step-by-step part of two branches of law. Things started to change. Some experts in the field of the law of war feared a politicization of international humanitarian law since they considered human rights law an issue of politics.[9] However, through the UN Charter, human rights left the status of political/moral obligations and became part of international law. Thus the question arose of the relationship between human rights and international humanitarian law.

   The adoption of the UN Charter in 1945 and of subsequent major human rights documents changed the surgically clear division, at least in theory. Since then there have been norms which are valid both in peacetime and in times of war. However, in practice the two branches were nearly completely separated. This can be illustrated by the lack of interest in each other of the experts involved in the elaboration of the Geneva Conventions of 1949 on the one hand, and those drafting the Universal Declaration of Human Rights on the other hand. In practice, the conferences took place simultaneously but ignored each other. They did so quite deliberately, as the UN expressed at this time, again and again, that their task was to build a peaceful international society and to save succeeding generations from the scourge of war. Furthermore, the UN described human rights as a condition for the maintenance of peace, and consequently as part of the *ius contra bellum*. From this viewpoint the UN was not ready to deal with the *ius in bello*. Yet, during the debates in the Third Committee of the UN General Assembly only one delegate (Lebanon) mentioned that human rights should also be guaranteed in times of war,[10] but there was no discussion. This can only be explained by the self-image of the UN as guarantor of international peace.[11] By contrast to Article 25 of the Covenant of the League of Nations, which dealt with humanitarian law and the Red Cross, nothing was said in the UN Charter. The authors thought that this was unnecessary since war had been outlawed.[12]

   As with every innovation, this development was not immediately accepted by all. In particular, those who subscribed to the so-called separation theory rejected the application of human rights norms during armed conflicts, with the argument that these and the norms of the *jus in bello* were two separate fields, which could not be applied at the same time.[13] G.I.A.D. Draper, a leading international law scholar, opposed the fusion of the two bodies of law, arguing that they had fundamental distinctions based upon their origin, theory, nature and purpose:

The attempt to confuse the two regimes of laws is unsupportable in theory and inadequate in practice. The two regimes are not only distinct but are diametrically opposed ... At the end of the day, the law of human rights seeks to reflect the cohesion and harmony in human society and must, from the nature of things, be a different and opposed law to that which seeks to regulate the conduct of hostile relationships between states and other organized armed groups, and in internal rebellions.[14]

He presents a legal construct whereby human rights are the normal regime and international humanitarian law the derogation. There is no common ground because the two bodies of law can only apply in a mutually exclusive fashion.[15] Draper's logic is not supported given the recent historical development of the law of armed conflict as practical and persona-oriented. Of course, the law of armed conflict was always characterized by the dominance of the methods and means of warfare rather than by regulations concerning humanity. However, humanity always played a role too. Even in the classic law of armed conflict, humanitarian and human rights considerations – on the basis of natural law – were taken into account. In this vein, J.C. Bluntschli argued in 1872 that the declaration of war did not rescind the legal order but 'on the contrary, we recognize that there are natural human rights that are to recognized in times of war as in peacetime'.[16] Furthermore, several conventions drafted during the Second Hague Peace Conference of 1907 reflect this practically. The 1907 Hague Convention on Land Warfare refers to the parties to the treaty as 'animated by the desire to serve, even in this extreme case, the interests of humanity'.[17] The 1907 Convention on Naval Mine Warfare is another example, even if one has to accept against the background of the *travaux préparatoires* that considerations of humanity did not especially drive the initial codification of international humanitarian law. Britain's motivation to outlaw naval mines was rooted in retaining its naval dominance rather than in any sense of altruism.[18]

However, even the lip service of the leading military powers reflects that humanitarian concerns began to influence the development of the law of armed conflict. Thus, it can be taken for granted that the principle of humanity is a fundamental principle of the law of armed conflict and part of numerous treaty provisions. The principle protects combatants from unnecessary suffering, as well as individuals who are no longer, or never were, active participants in hostilities, by mandating that they be treated humanely at all times.[19] In the light of the customary international law status of the principle of humanity and the statements in this regard by some scholars, one can have doubts about the justification of the separation theory. Thus, one can argue that separation is an old position, 'which has recently not been maintained'.[20] This is only partly true. It seems that there are still some supporters of the separation theory, even today. For instance, W. Heintschel von Heinegg argues, 'it would not make much sense to complicate the situation by demanding ... the obligations provided for by human rights instruments'.[21] One may wonder which kind of complications is meant. To respect legal obligations is always a challenge for parties to an armed conflict. However, the obligations according to the principle of humanity are binding independently of how complicated the implementation may be for the parties.

1.2   State Practice Enables Clarification

This application of the principle of humanity in time of peace and war is in line with the opinions of the International Court of Justice. The ICJ dealt in the 'Nuclear Weapons Advisory Opinion' and in 'Legal Consequences of the Wall Advisory Opinion'[22] with the relationship between the two bodies of law. In these Advisory Opinions the Court clearly rejected the position that human rights, first and foremost Article 6 of the ICCPR of 19 December 1966, could only be applied in peacetime. The wording of relevant human rights treaties supports the ICJ jurisprudence on the subject. Indeed, these treaties contain clear stipulations concerning the observance of human rights obligations by States Parties in times of armed conflict. For example, Article 15 of the ECHR of 4 November 1950 deals with the fate of human rights norms in situations in which the life of a nation is threatened by war or other public emergencies.

Under such circumstances the respective State Party is allowed to 'take measures derogating from its obligations under this Convention'. However, the human rights enshrined in the ECHR may be limited only to the extent strictly required by the exigencies of the situation. Some of the rights explicitly mentioned in the foregoing articles may never be derogated from (*inter alia* the right to life, the freedom of belief and the prohibition of torture). These human rights are called non-derogable, which means that they are to be applied in all circumstances, without exception. The traditional impermeable border between international humanitarian law, which applies during armed conflicts, and the law of peace, is thereby crossed. This 'crossing of the border' is further supported by Article 3 common to the Geneva Conventions of 12 August 1949, containing a list of rights which are to be protected in all circumstances. Interestingly, these rights broadly cover the non-derogable human rights. This very configuration is what led academics to draft the 'Turku Declaration',[23] which called for the legal grey zones – in the border areas between the law of peace and the law of war – to be filled by the cumulative application of human rights law and international humanitarian law, thereby guaranteeing at least minimum humanitarian standards.[24]

The ECHR is not the only instrument referring to the applicability of human rights in wartime. A further regional human rights instrument, the American Convention on Human Rights of 22 November 1969, lists in its Article 27 non-derogable rights which cannot be abrogated in times of war.

Universal human rights treaties also refer to non-derogable rights. For example, Article 4 of the ICCPR includes an emergency clause similar to that formulated in regional instruments. All these human rights instruments show that human rights are an intrinsic part of the legal rules governing wars and other emergency situations.

Taking into account the obligation of States to respect non-derogable rights in all circumstances, according to human rights instruments and the final document of the First World Conference on Human Rights in Teheran in 1968, C.M. Cerna concluded in 1989 that international humanitarian law had already been 'transformed into a branch of human rights law and termed "human rights in armed conflicts"'.[25] Against this background of the legal regulations concerning states of emergencies it becomes quite obvious, that the separation theory is out of fashion.

2. COMPLEMENTARITY THEORY

When examining which duties are incumbent on a State in times of armed conflict, it is not possible to avoid taking international human rights law into consideration. Even if one accepts that both branches have different roots and approaches as well as functions they can complete each other on specific points.[26] This implies the complementarity of both bodies of law. The theory of complementarity[27] is especially acceptable for those scholars who are against a merger of the two bodies of international law. According to this theory, human rights law and international humanitarian law are not identical bodies of law but complement each other and ultimately remain distinct. This is undoubtedly true, but the point is that they do overlap.

2.1 ICRC Supports the Complementarity Theory

Although the ICRC has in the past approached the subject cautiously, it is nowadays involved in the establishment of common values that transcend legalistic arguments and distinctions. At the end, the ICRC supports the concept of complementarity of international humanitarian and human rights law.[28] Based on the concept of complementarity the ICRC has produced a number of institutional doctrines and directives to its involvement in non-international armed conflicts and situations below the threshold of applicability of international humanitarian law. The most recent doctrine (DOCT/63-2006/1) 'The Invocation of International Human Rights Law by the ICRC' has formulated an overarching approach and mentions the range of human rights which may be invoked by the ICRC. The idea is, on the one hand, to enable the ICRC to use human rights, where appropriate, in its humanitarian work. On the other hand, the ICRC wants to ensure that it remains distinct from doing human rights advocacy and to maintain its unique identity.

In accordance with the concept of complementarity, the ICRC has no obligation to act as a human rights defender. If the application of human rights law would be detrimental to its operational activities the ICRC may decide not to refer expressly to these regulations. Thus, the ICRC in the first line of its operational argumentation takes international humanitarian law into consideration and complements this, when appropriate, by reference to selected sources of human rights law.

Against this background it is convincing that the ICRC took part in the UN discussions on fundamental standards of humanity. The ICRC suggested that there is need for clarification of their desired content and argued:

> The first issue regarding the content related to the question of whether an attempt to merge norms of international humanitarian law and human rights law was the way forward. ICRC expressed concern that such a merger would risk confusing two distinct, albeit complementary, areas of law to the detriment of legal obligations contained in each.[29]

This approach has been reaffirmed by the ICRC Study on customary international humanitarian law. The Study notes that human rights law may serve 'to support, strengthen and clarify analogous principles of humanitarian law'.[30] An example is the term 'fair trial' which is obviously a human rights issue. If one wants to apply that concept in international humanitarian law it is useful to take stock of the human rights case law.

This situation justifies speaking of a convergence of both branches of law, which is more far-reaching than only 'a natural convergence of humanitarian principles under-lying these two bodies of law'.[31] Convergence here means an overlap in terms of the scope of protection. However, the distinction between the two areas of law, which is primarily procedural, must be borne in mind. According to Sperber, human rights law is invoked by an individual against a State. However, humanitarian law is not at present enforced against a State by individuals.[32] The convergence approach opens the possibility for the cumulative application of both bodies of law. Some obligations in human rights treaties remain in force during armed conflicts. The result is undoubtedly a substantial overlap of both bodies of law. However, the response of legal opinion to this situation differs.

2.2   Application by UN Rapporteurs

The somewhat more assertive convergence theory is gaining in influence. It goes further than mere complementarity and aims at providing the greatest effective protection of the human being through the cumulative application of both bodies of law. Reference can consequently be made to one unified complex of human rights beneath different institutional umbrellas.[33]

A glance at the most recent State practice shows that this is not merely theory. Examples are Kuwait in 1991 and Iraq in 2003–2004. The cumulative application of both bodies of law during the armed conflict in Kuwait was both 'feasible and meaningful' and clarified the practical meaning of the convergence theory applied to the occupying regime in Kuwait in 1990/91.[34]

Parallels can be drawn between this and the situation in Iraq in 2003–2004. Security Council Resolution 1483 (2003), which lays down the basic principles for the occupation and reconstruction of Iraq, requires all 'involved' to fulfil their obligations under international law, especially those according to the Geneva Conventions (para. 5), and requests the Secretary-General's Special Representative for Iraq to work for the promotion of human rights protection (para. 8(g)). It goes without saying that such duties require the cumulative application of international humanitarian law and human rights law. With regard to cumulative application, three points need to be underscored:

(1)   The interpretation of rights and duties must refer to both areas of law. It is, for example, difficult to interpret the term 'inhuman treatment' found in human rights law in any other way than according to the requirements of the Third Geneva Convention, as it has a specific meaning in the context of a prisoner-of-war camp. On the other hand, the requirements of paragraph 1(c) of Article 3 common to the four Geneva Conventions could not be fulfilled, after considering 'the legal guarantees deemed imperative by civilized nations' in criminal proceedings, without applying the human rights instruments.

(2)   Human rights law strengthens the rules of international humanitarian law by providing a more exact formulation of State obligations. Thus the duties arising

from Article 55 of the Fourth Geneva Convention pertaining to health care have to be applied in the light of the right to health contained in the International Covenant on Economic, Social and Cultural Rights.[35]

In the separation of rape, as a method of war and as prohibited by international humanitarian law, from torture, the human rights law provisions of the UN Convention against Torture must necessarily be resorted to.[36]

(3)   International humanitarian law brings human rights law into effect by spelling out, for example, the duties regarding missing persons. Even though 'disappearances' undoubtedly represent a serious human rights violation, the relevant law regarding the obligations of States in such cases is very underdeveloped. In times of armed conflict, the occupying power is obliged by the Third and Fourth Geneva Convention to provide information about detained persons, including notification of the death of detained persons and the possible causes thereof, and to search for persons whose fate is unknown.[37]

In a report to the Security Council entitled 'On the Protection of Civilians in Armed Conflict',[38] the UN Secretary-General voiced his opinion on the cumulative application of all norms which protect the individual, at least those civilians as defined in the Geneva Conventions and their Protocols. He recommended States to ratify equally the relevant instruments of international humanitarian law, international human rights law and refugee law, as all three are 'essential tools for the legal protection of civilians in armed conflicts'.[39] From a practical point of view the growing recourse to international humanitarian law protection is, of course, also a result of the increased occurrence of civil conflicts, which often take place in a grey zone in terms of that law, owing to its relatively few rules governing such situations. Its practical importance for parties to the conflict has been convincingly pointed out in legal literature.[40] Therefore the cooperation of the three main actors in the field (the ICRC, UNHCR and the Human Rights organs of the UN), without compromising their respective mandates, was welcomed in the literature. Meron considers the readiness of the UN human rights rapporteurs to include as yardsticks for compliance not only human rights but also humanitarian law standards as one of the most useful developments and as an example of the convergence.[41]

2.3   Application by the ICJ

The cumulative application of human rights law and international humanitarian law inevitably raises the question of the reciprocal relationship. The ICJ had to answer this question in the Nuclear Weapons Advisory Opinion[42] because the advocates of the illegality of the use of nuclear weapons had argued that such use violated the right to life laid down in Article 6 of the ICCPR.[43] Article 6 of the ICCPR stipulates that: 'No one shall be arbitrarily deprived of his life'. The ICJ established in its Opinion that Article 6 is a non-derogable right and consequently also applies in armed conflict, and that even during hostilities it is prohibited to 'arbitrarily' deprive someone of his life. In the same Opinion, the ICJ recognizes the primacy of international humanitarian law over human rights law in armed conflicts, thereby designating the former as *lex specialis*. The term 'arbitrarily' is, therefore, to be defined according to international humanitarian law.

The 2004 Advisory Opinion concerning the wall in the occupied Palestinian territory tends to show even more clearly that the right to life in times of armed conflict is only to be interpreted according to international humanitarian law.[44] The Human Rights Committee, too, stresses in its General Comment on Article 2 that the ICCPR applies also in situations of armed conflicts to which the rules of international humanitarian law are applicable. However, the Human Rights Committee is not as crystal clear as the ICJ because it avoids touching on the *lex specialis* issue: 'While, in respect of certain Covenant rights, more specific rules of international humanitarian law may be especially relevant for the interpretation of Covenant rights, both spheres of law are complementary, not mutually exclusive.'[45] The *lex specialis* character of international humanitarian law is nevertheless essential. In certain circumstances human rights law cannot be considered. For example, a combatant who, within the scope of a lawful act during an armed conflict, kills an enemy combatant, cannot, according to *jus in bello*, be charged with a criminal offence.[46]

The evaluation given in the ICJ Opinion has been welcomed by academics, mainly for its clarification that the norms developed for peacetime, that is, human rights law, cannot be applied 'in an unqualified manner' to armed conflicts. Human rights have instead to be inserted into the structure of international humanitarian law in a sensitive manner.[47] The primacy of international humanitarian law is herewith emphasized. It must, however, be noted that the provisions of human rights law as a whole remain valid as prescribed in Article 4 of the ICCPR (and the analogous regional treaties), and are consequently of importance. The ICJ in its Advisory Opinions therefore supports the need to regard the protection granted by international humanitarian law and human rights law as a single unit and to harmonize the two sets of international rules.

Admittedly, such a viewpoint inevitably raises the *lex specialis derogat legi generali* objection. It can be refuted by reference to the Martens Clause, which is accepted both in international treaties and in customary international law. This clause confirms that the rules of the laws pertaining to armed conflicts cannot be regarded as the final regulation of the protection of human beings, but can be supplemented with human rights law protection.[48]

The interpretation of the right to life by human rights law in times of armed conflicts becomes more obvious in regional human rights instruments than in the ICCPR. In Article 15 of the ECHR, for instance, it is made clear that cases of death as a result of legal acts of war are not to be regarded as a violation of the right to life spelled out in Article 2 of the ECHR.

2.4 Practical Consequences

Armed conflict does not occur in isolation. It has to be governed according to human rights norms and to international humanitarian law. Both bodies of law contribute to establishing a secure environment for the enjoyment of fundamental rights. The incorporation of human rights principles of accountability, especially, 'can have a positive impact on the regulation of the use of force during armed conflict'.[49] However, in line with the complementarity theory the author claims that the mechanisms of accountability developed to regulate human rights domestically cannot simply be transferred to the international humanitarian law context. This underlines once more the differences between the two bodies of law.

3.   INTEGRATION THEORY

The Convention on the Rights of the Child (CRC) adopted in 1989 impressively corroborates the view of the integration of IHL in the broader concept of human rights law. Here the substantial overlap between international human rights protection and international humanitarian law becomes obvious. Article 38(1) of that Convention obliges the States Parties to undertake to respect and ensure respect for rules of international humanitarian law that deal with the protection of children. Thus, a human rights treaty, normally applicable in peacetime, contains provisions that are not only applicable in armed conflicts, but are also enshrined in the law regulating armed conflicts.

The regulations are even more detailed because Article 38(2), (3) and (4) repeat the standards laid down in Article 77 of Additional Protocol I to the Geneva Conventions which restricts the recruitment and participation of children in armed conflicts. Those standards, adopted in 1977, permit the recruitment and direct participation of children from the age of 15 onwards.

This undoubtedly unsatisfying standard in the CRC of 1989 runs counter both to the progressive codification of international public law and to the goal of the Convention, which, according to Article 3, is to ensure that the 'best interests' of the child (defined in Article 1 as a person below the age of 18 years) are protected. It is most unlikely that it is in the interest of a child aged 15 to take direct part in hostilities.

This contradiction has been severely criticized in legal literature.[50] Particularly at issue is why the 1989 Convention on the Rights of the Child, which was drawn up more than a decade after the adoption of the Additional Protocols to the Geneva Convention and marks considerable progress in codification of the protection of the individual, contains no protection exceeding that of Article 77 of Additional Protocol I. This failure is all the more regrettable because, when the CRC was being negotiated, the opponents of the relevant improvement in child protection (in particular the USA, Iran and Iraq) had not put forward a very sturdy legal argument. As a matter of fact, the USA was of the opinion that neither the General Assembly nor the Human Rights Commission was a suitable forum for the revision of existing international humanitarian law.[51]

However, the American argument, which is based on the aforementioned traditional separation of the law of peace and the law of war, is not convincing, for the CRC was intended to be a new, independent treaty and not a revision or amendment of international humanitarian law. It can, moreover, also be argued that obligations over and above the general standards should have been laid down for the States party to the new instrument, as is definitely possible in treaty law. Since many feared a lowering of standards, the American argument was not further discussed. The USA later departed from its (untenable) position, when, in 1992, it signed the Optional Protocol on the involvement of children in armed conflict to the CRC. This Protocol, adopted in 2000 through Resolution 54/263 of the UN General Assembly, obliges the States Parties to take all feasible measures to ensure that children under the age of 18 do not take a direct part in hostilities. It entered into force on 12 February 2002 and has to date been ratified by 52 States. This means that, at least where these States are concerned, the standard of protection is higher than that propounded in international humanitarian law.[52]

The example of the CRC demonstrates not only that the law of peace and the law of war overlap, but also that, when examining which duties are incumbent on a State in times of armed conflict, it is not possible to avoid taking international human rights law into consideration. This situation alone justifies speaking of a convergence of both bodies of law which is more far-reaching than only 'a natural convergence of humanitarian principle underlying these two bodies of law'.[53] Convergence here means an overlap in terms of the scope of protection. However, the distinction between the two areas of law, which is primarily procedural, must be borne in mind.[54] The convergence approach opens the possibility for the cumulative application of both bodies of law.

The consequence of the convergence approach was the establishment of a human rights law for armed conflict situations. The implementation mechanisms of the treaty bodies of human rights treaties are nowadays obliged to consider the application of human rights treaties in contexts of armed conflicts. Against the background of the lack of effective enforcement mechanisms of international humanitarian law this is doubtless a very positive development and a success story of the integration theory.

NOTES

* Hans-Joachim Heintze is Professor of International Law at the University of Ruhr University Bochum, Germany.
1. R. Kolb, 'Human Rights and Humanitarian Law', *Max Planck Encyclopedia of Public International Law*, (2010), para. 3, available at http://www.mpepil.com (accessed 8 February 2012).
2. *Legality of the Threat or Use of Nuclear Weapons*, Advisory Opinion, I.C.J. Reports 1996, para. 25.
3. N. Lubell, 'Challenges in Applying Human Rights Law to Armed Conflicts', *International Review of the Red Cross* 87 (2005): 737.
4. S. Vöneky, *Die Fortgeltung des Umweltvölkerrechts in Internationalen Bewaffneten Konflikten* (Berlin: Springer, 2001), 286.
5. J. von Bernstorf, 'Martens Clause', *Max Planck Encyclopedia of Public International Law* (2009), available at http://www.mpepil.com (accessed 8 February 2012).
6. This approach is in line with the ICRC's *Avenir* statement, which stresses that 'the relationship between humanitarian law and human rights law must be strengthened'. See D. Forsythe, '1949 and 1999: Making the Geneva Conventions relevant after the Cold War,' *International Review of the Red Cross* 81, No. 834 (1999): 271.
7. C. Tomuschat, 'Obligations Arising for States Without or Against Their Will', *Recueil des Cours* 241, No. 4 (1993): 195.
8. S. Sayapin, 'The International Committee of the Red Cross and International Human Rights Law', *Human Rights Law Review* 9 (2009): 96.
9. H. Meyrowitz, 'Le droit de la guerre et les droits de l'homme,' *Revue de Droit Militaire et de Droit de la Guerre* 88 (1972): 1095.
10. UN Doc. A/C.3/SR. 152, 22 November 1948, 639.
11. R. Kolb, 'The Relationship between International Humanitarian Law and Human Rights Law: A Brief History of the 1948 Universal Declaration of Human Rights and the 1949 Geneva Conventions', *International Review of the Red Cross* 38, No. 324 (1998).

12. A. H. Robertson, 'Humanitarian Law and Human Rights', in *Studies and Essays on International Humanitarian Law and Red Cross Principles in Honour of Jean Pictet*, ed. C. Swinarski (Geneva: International Committee of the Red Cross, 1984), 794.

13. O. Kimminich, *Schutz der Menschen in bewaffneten Konflikten* (Munich: Beck, 1979), 28.

14. G.I.A.D. Draper, 'Humanitarian Law and Human Rights', *Acta Juridica* (Cape Town) (1979): 193, at 199.

15. D. Stephens, 'Human Rights and Armed Conflict – the Advisory Opinion of the International Court of Justice in the Nuclear Weapons Case', *Yale Human Rights and Development Law Journal* 4 (2001): 10.

16. J.C. Bluntschli, *Das moderne Völkerrecht der civilisierten Staaten* (Nördlingen: Beck, 1878), para. 529.

17. Preamble, Convention (IV) respecting the Laws and Customs of War on Land, signed at The Hague, 18 October 1907, in *The Law of Armed Conflicts: A Collection of Conventions, Resolutions and Other Documents*, ed. D. Schindler and J. Toman (Leiden: Martinus Nijhoff, 2004), 55.

18. D.G. Stephens and M.D. Fitzpatrick, 'Legal Aspects of the Contemporary Naval Mine Warfare', *Loyola of Los Angeles International and Comparative Law Journal* 21(1999): 553.

19. G.S. Corn, 'Humanity, Principle of', *Max Planck Encyclopedia of Public International Law*, available at http://www.mpepil.com (accessed 8 February 2012).

20. Kolb, *supra* note 1.

21. W.H. von Heinegg, 'The Rule of Law in Conflict and Post Conflict Situations: Factors in War and Peace Transitions', *Harvard Journal of Law and Public Policy* 27 (2004): 869.

22. *Legality of the Threat or Use of Nuclear Weapons*, *supra* note 2.

23. UN Doc. E/CN.4/Sub.2/1991/55.

24. See A. Rosas and T. Meron, 'Combating Lawlessness in Grey Zone Conflicts through Minimum Humanitarian Standards', *American Journal of International Law*, 89, No. 2 (1995): 215.

25. C.M. Cerna, 'Human rights in Armed Conflict: Implementation of International Humanitarian Law Norms by Regional Intergovernmental Human Rights Bodies', in *Implementation of International Humanitarian Law*, ed. F. Kalshoven and Y. Sandoz (Geneva: International Committee of the Red Cross, 1989), 39.

26. D. Schindler, 'Human Rights and Humanitarian Law', *American University Law Review* 31 (1982): 935.

27. H.-P. Gasser, 'International Humanitarian Law and Human Rights Law in Non-international Armed Conflict: Joint Venture or Mutual Exclusion?', *German Yearbook of International Law* (Berlin) 45 (2002): 162.

28. See, e.g., Forsythe, *supra* note 6, at 271. The Human Rights Sub-Commission of the UN Commission on Human Rights also refers in its Resolution 1989/26 to 'Convergence'.

29. UN Doc. E/CN.4/2000/94, para. 9.

30. J.-M. Henckaerts and L. Doswald-Beck, ed., *Customary International Humanitarian Law*, Vol. I: Rules (Cambridge: Cambridge University Press, 2005), 299.

31. D. Stephens, 'Human Rights and Armed Conflict: The Advisory Opinion of the International Court of Justice in the Nuclear Weapons Case', *Yale Human Rights and Development Law Journal* 4, No. 1 (2001): 2.

32. M.H. Sperber, 'John Walker Lindh and Yaser Esam Hamdi: Closing the Loophole in International Humanitarian Law for American Nationals Captured Abroad while Fighting with Enemy Forces', *American Criminal Law Review* 40 (Winter 2003): 239.

33. T. Meron, *Human Rights in Internal Strife: Their International Protection* (Cambridge: Cambridge University Press, 1987), 28.

34. W. Kälin, ed., *Human Rights in Times of Occupation: The Case of Kuwait* (Bern: Stämpfli, 1994), 27.

35. UN Treaty Series 993: 3.

36. UN Treaty Series 1465: 85. See D. Blatt, 'Recognizing Rape as a Method of Torture', *New York University Review of Law and Social Change* 19, No. 4 (1994): 821.

37. Kälin, *supra* note 34, at 27.

38. UN Doc. S/1999/957.

39. Ibid., para. 36.

40. D. Fleck, 'Humanitarian Protection against Non-State Actors', in *Verhandeln für den Frieden, Liber Amicorum Tono Eitel*, ed. J.A. Frowein et al. (Berlin: Springer, 2003), 78.

41. T. Meron, 'Convergence of International Humanitarian Law and Human Rights Law', in *Human Rights and Humanitarian Law*, ed. D. Warner (The Hague: Martinus Nijhoff, 1997), 102.

42.   Kolb, *supra* note 1, at 26.
43.   According to Greenwood this viewpoint was taken by Malaysia, the Solomon Islands and Egypt. See C.J. Greenwood, '*Jus bellum* and *jus in bello* in the *Nuclear Weapons* Advisory Opinion', in *International Law, the International Court of Justice and Nuclear Weapons*, ed. L. Boisson de Chazournes and P. Sands (Cambridge: Cambridge University Press, 1999), 253.
44.   *Legal Consequences of the Construction of a Wall in the Occupied Palestinian Territory*, Advisory Opinion, I.C.J. Reports 2004, para. 101.
45.   UN Doc. CCPR/C/74/CPR.4/Rev.6.
46.   Boisson de Chazournes and Sands, *supra* note 43, at 253.
47.   M.J. Matheson, 'The Opinions of the International Court of Justice on the Threat or Use of Nuclear Weapons', *American Journal of International Law* 91 (1997): 423.
48.   See H.B. Reimann, 'Menschenrechtsstandards in bewaffneten Konflikten', in *Studies and Essays on International Humanitarian Law and Red Cross Principles in Honour of Jean Pictet*, ed. C. Swinarski (Geneva and The Hague: International Committee of the Red Cross and Martinus Nijhoff, 1984), 773.
49.   K. Watkin, 'Controlling the Use of Force: A Role for Human Rights Norms in Contemporary Armed Conflict', *American Journal of International Law* 98 (2004): 34.
50.   H.-J. Heintze, 'Children Need More Protection under International Humanitarian Law – Recent Developments Concerning Article 38 of the UN Child Convention as a Challenge to the International Red Cross and Red Crescent Movement', *Humanitäres Völkerrecht – Informationsschriften* 8 (1995): 200.
51.   UN Doc. E/CN.4/1989, at 55, Add.1, at 6.
52.   This aspect was not taken into consideration by M. Happold, 'The Optional Protocol to the Convention on the Rights of the Child on the Involvement of Children in Armed Conflict', in *Yearbook of International Humanitarian Law*, ed. H. Fischer, Vol. 3 (2000), (The Hague, 2002), 242.
53.   Stephens, *supra* note 31, at 2.
54.   Sperber et al., *supra* note 32, at 239.

4. The position of individuals in public international law through the lens of diplomatic protection: the principle and its transfiguration

Giovanni Distefano*

In this contribution we endeavour to examine the legal status of individuals from the perspective of diplomatic protection, with the purpose of ascertaining whether the asserted evolution of the latter has had any impact on the international personality of the former. To this end, we will firstly sketch two different definitions of the international personality, and then the main features of diplomatic protection, in its traditional construction as well as in its 'transfigured' form, will be scrutinized.

1. GENERAL REMARKS

Generally speaking, the individual is seen by international law in two different, yet complementary, perspectives. In the first, which can be labelled 'traditional', the individual is taken into consideration as an 'object', that is, an extension of States' jurisdiction; viewed from this angle, they can be the source of a dispute between States as they crystallize the collision between their sovereignties. Therefore, international law is not at all concerned with individuals outside this specific situation; indeed, the regime which applies to them is governed by the national jurisdiction of the State of which they are nationals; in other words, the relationship between a national and its State belongs to the latter's *domaine réservé*.

The second approach, which can be termed the new approach, or *nouvelle vague*, since it came chronologically after the first one, is tacked on to it, without, though, replacing it. We are talking of the widely known – and highly publicized – law related to human rights. According to this perspective – which encompasses the wide and deeply specialized body of rules related to the human rights – a person is protected not as an appendix of a State's sovereignty, but as a holder of human dignity vis-à-vis any State, including, most importantly, the one of which he (or she) is a national.

The two approaches underline, beyond their fundamental differences, the emergence of the individual on the stage of International Law, whose status evolved from that of an 'object' (a mere accessory of his/her own State) to 'subject'. From the diplomatic protection – which best highlights the first approach – through the protection of minorities, up to the international protection of human rights, this legal development shows the penetration of international law into the State's own national jurisdiction, and, at the same time, the latter's shrinking.[1] What was once governed by the State's national jurisdiction is from then onwards determined by International Law, the rules of which are created – directly and indirectly – by States that have then willingly given up their exclusive legal regulation with regard to individuals to International Law.

2.   INTERNATIONAL LEGAL PERSONALITY: A FICTION, YET AN INDISPENSABLE ONE

Sir Robert Jennings wrote wisely that attempts that have been made in the past to define this hazy concept have left 'room for dubiety'.[2] Still, we do need this concept, and, in its wake, a list of subjects must be established. It goes without saying that this list varies according to the definition, so that we can have as many lists as concepts. Therefore, it is safe to say that this question relates to the dogmatics of Law, since its resolution depends upon the dogma that has been chosen. Of course, this does not mean that the dogma of the definition can be arbitrarily selected and construed – there are several axioms that exist in the scientific literature. Without going into technicalities, we can offer two of them here, in the light of which we will examine the international legal personality of the individual as it appears in the mechanisms of diplomatic protection. The first axiom can be labelled as 'democratic' (or extensive), since it allows a large number of candidates to be admitted onto the international legal scene, whilst the other can be named as 'elitist' (or restrictive), as it involves meeting higher requirements. Before reviewing each of these, we should remind ourselves, in the wake of the ICJ's famous 1949 advisory opinion, that firstly, '[t]he subjects of law in any legal system are not necessarily identical in their nature or in the extent of their rights, and their nature depends upon the needs of the community', and, secondly, 'the development of international law... and the requirements of international life [have] already given rise to instances of action upon the international plan by certain entities which are not States'.[3] Therefore, even if we adopt a fixed axiom of definition of international personality, the list which flows from it is not correspondingly mummified, but on the contrary will vary according to the needs of the international community.

3.   THE EXTENSIVE DEFINITION OF INTERNATIONAL PERSONALITY

As for this axiom, to 'possess international personality' amounts – according to the famous ICJ's *ratio decidendi* – to enjoying the 'capacity ... [to]bring an international claim against ... another direct subject of international law'.[4] This legal capacity is thus recognized by a customary law rule and vested with all unchallenged subjects of the international order. This formulation flows from an analogy with the municipal order; even though it contains a slight hint of tautology, it is widely resorted to, in order precisely to distinguish, within the context of the legal position of the individual, between the beneficiary of a right and its (true?) holder. In the *Lac Lanoux Case*, the Arbitral Tribunal correctly stresses this distinction:

L'Accord du 27 mars 1972 est un traité conclu entre deux Etats souverains qui crée des droits et des obligations réciproques dans le chef de ces deux Etats. S'il est vrai que, selon la terminologie utilisée par l'Accord, le droit de 'continuer à pêcher' est destiné à profiter à des 'bâtiments de pêche' (article 3), à des 'embarcations de pêche' (article 4, a) et à des 'chalutiers' (article 4, b), les Etats signataires de l'Accord n'en sont pas moins les seuls titulaires de ces droits de pêche au plan du droit international public et les seuls sujets de droit habilités à en exiger le respect au bénéfice de leurs ressortissants respectifs.[5]

Therefore, the acid test of the international personality resides in the actual and universal (i.e. *erga omnes*) 'capacity to maintain its own rights by bringing international claims'.[6] This capacity must then be embodied in a general rule of international law, or alternatively enshrined in an international treaty so widely ratified and adhered to that it has yielded a corresponding general norm.

4. THE RESTRICTIVE DEFINITION OF INTERNATIONAL PERSONALITY

It has been suggested that there are three capacities[7] which have to be possessed by a legal entity for it to be considered as a subject of international law – the capacity to: (a) make a treaty;[8] (b) establish diplomatic relations;[9] and (c) bring an international claim on a general (and not exclusively treaty) basis.[10] One of the main reasons which leads us to define these three requirements flows from the empirical observation that all the actual (and undisputed) subjects of international law – be they States, international organizations, national liberation movements, insurgents, the ICRC, Vatican, etc. – possess at least, regardless of their differences in nature, origin and the 'extent of their rights',[11] the aforementioned capacities. They could not play on the international legal stage without them. Hence, the fulfilling of these three qualities reveals their independence vis-à-vis other subjects of international law; the (actual) horizontal structure of the international order make these capacities the true test of their real international legal personality. For example, whilst the State has an original independence in its sovereign status, international organizations are independent because this quality is recognized by a customary international law rule (generated by treaty-practice), and so on for the other subjects. Independence is, then, for all subjects of international law what sovereignty is for the State: the measure and the essence of international personality.

5. INTERNATIONAL LEGAL ORDER AND THE INDIVIDUAL: SYSTEMIC PREMISES

International Law remains, even today, fundamentally an inter-State legal order deeply rooted in territorial obsession. The legal position of individuals, notwithstanding recent and epochal developments, cannot be scrutinized but on this historical and empirical determination. From a historical standpoint, modern international law has emerged as a *ius inter potestates* (i.e. law between sovereign entities). One of the main features – if not the principal one (see Art. 2(1) of the UN Charter) – is 'the right to exercise therein [in regard of a portion of territory], to the exclusion of any other State, [all] the functions of a State'.[12] Accordingly, States are recognized by International Law to be vested with the legal power to regulate the social phenomena within their boundaries and to respect reciprocally such a right vis-à-vis other sovereign States. Therefore, International Law does not take into account the individual by him/herself, but as an object entirely submitted to the sovereign power of its State. However, when an individual finds him/herself in the territory of a State of which he/she is not a national (and is thus an alien), their legal position falls within the province of international law. Indeed, the law must resolve a paramount conflict between two different, yet flowing from the same source (i.e. sovereignty), State jurisdictions, namely the territorial and personal. Thus, the mere presence of an individual in a foreign territory engenders a divorce between these two jurisdictions (which are then no longer united with respect to the rights held by an alien). Hence, both States are bound, each on its own side, to exercise their power, leading thus to a conflict of sovereignties: a typical conflict of competing exercise of jurisdictions. This legal puzzle has been solved by a set of customary international law rules, largely determined by a voluminous jurisprudence, which has established respective rights and obligations for both States, as well as by a highly sophisticated mechanism called 'diplomatic protection'. Broadly speaking, the national State has on one hand the right to require, in its own interest, that the other States respect their international duties (related to aliens), but on the other, it must refrain from directly protecting its own nationals on other States' territory, especially if such measures involve the use of force. The foreign State must, on one hand, abide by the aforementioned international legal obligations, yet on the other it has the right to submit any alien to its territorial jurisdiction. By way of consequence, it has the right to require that the other States do not intervene in order to rescue their nationals.

Therefore, the traditional approach amounts to a conflict of sovereignties, and the individual barely plays any role in it. Hence, traditional International Law does not protect technically the individual as such, but the State's interest or right infringed *through* its own national. In other words, the individual legal position is regulated by International Law only if he or she is an alien, that is, an object belonging to the State. To sum up, States are under the obligation to respect and ensure respect of aliens – be they persons or corporations – which are under its jurisdiction vis-à-vis any violation of rights pertaining to that specific set of rules called the 'droit des étrangers'. In the oft-quoted *Island of Palmas Case*, the sole arbiter declares:

> Territorial Sovereignty ... involves the exclusive right to display the activities of a State. This right has a corollary duty: the obligation to protect within the territory the rights of other States, in particular the right to integrity and inviolability in peace and in war, together with the rights each State may claim for its nationals in foreign territory.[13]

The general and paramount duty of the State – as delineated by this excerpt – clearly supports the functional character of sovereignty, its social aim being the Empire of Law on any parcel of a State's territory. Hence, due to its fundamentally horizontal structure, International Law appears to be like a legal system obsessed by the recognition of territorial jurisdictions.

6. DIPLOMATIC PROTECTION: THE PRINCIPLE

The mechanism of diplomatic protection applies each time a person – but not an organ of a State nor any other person in this official capacity – suffers damage on a foreign territory. If the individual cannot get appropriate satisfaction through the exhaustion of local remedies (tribunals or other organs of the foreign State), then this mechanism allows the State of which the person is a national to 'take up the case of its subject'. At first glance, then, by resorting to diplomatic protection, the national State 'is in reality asserting its own right – its right to ensure, in the person of its subjects, respect for the rules of international law'.[14]

Since the authoritative statement of Vattel,[15] it was (is it still?) considered that a State suffers from the injury caused to its national abroad; this conclusion is founded on a 'fiction'. This 'fiction' in fact allows the State to seek reparation for this injury through the mechanism of diplomatic protection, for it cannot – by virtue of the equality of States – either intervene on foreign territory or interfere with the administration of justice of the other State. Indeed, the exclusiveness of State functions – attached to the very principle of sovereignty – prevent the State from acting in such a way, lest it violate the paramount principle enshrined in Art. 2(1) of the United Nations Charter (*supra* section 5).

The *opinion iuris commune* in this regard has not undergone dramatic changes, as the ICJ has reiterated in a well-known *dictum* the distinction between 'the obligations of a State towards the international community as a whole [such as, for instance, those related to human rights], and those arising vis-à-vis another State in the *field of diplomatic protection*'.[16]

Thence no duty – in the international legal order – compels the State to exercise diplomatic protection at the request of its nationals.[17] Conversely, the mainstream doctrine and jurisprudence – confirmed by the practice of States – consider that any renunciation by an individual (through a contract or similar bargain with a foreign State) of diplomatic protection is void, since the State can override it and take up their national's case, albeit against their will[18] (the so-called 'Calvo Clause'). Diplomatic protection has become through the ages – replacing notably the ancient and more intrusive mechanism of 'reprisals' – the main tool by which States protect their (nationals') interests, without thus resorting to the use of force. This mechanism represents then a 'civilized' way of settling disputes through diplomatic channels by way of the engagement of State responsibility. According to the prevailing view, the admissibility of a claim under diplomatic protection is subject to the fulfilment of three conditions: (a) a link of nationality between the person injured and the claimant State; (b) the exhaustion of local remedies; and (c) the alleged wrongful act arising out of the violation of any right related to aliens (or any other specific obligation thereto).[19] An abundant jurisprudence has, since the end of the 19th century, helped to consolidate the body of rules in the matter of diplomatic protection.

7.   THE 'TRANSFIGURED' DIPLOMATIC PROTECTION

One can hardly rebut that only recently has the ICJ nuanced its construction of diplomatic protection. The first breach took place in the *LaGrand Case* when the Court declared, with regard to Article 36 (1)(b) of the 1963 Vienna Convention on Consular Relations, that this provision manifestly 'creates *individual rights*, which ... may be *invoked* in this Court *by the national State* of the detained person'.[20] The definitive interpretation of the aforementioned provision would ultimately be given by this same Court three years later in the oft-cited *Avena Case*. The ICJ, after having recalled the previous case, affirmed that Mexico (the Applicant) not only had 'contend[ed] that *it had itself suffered, directly and through its nationals*', but likewise, that it had '*espouse[d]* the individual claims of its nationals through the procedure of diplomatic protection'.[21] This was due to the specificity of this provision, that, at the same time, clearly embodies the individual's rights ('The said authorities shall inform the person concerned without delay of *his rights* under this subparagraph'),[22] as well as those of the Contracting Party – namely (under Article 36 (1)(c)) the right of the sending State to provide consular assistance to its detained national. The Court then added that in these 'special circumstances of interdependence of the rights of the State and of individual rights',[23] we are faced with a claim to guarantee these distinct rights, albeit they are infringed by the same acts. In one case, Mexico 'espouses' its nationals' claims while in the other it submits to the Court its own claim for the USA had allegedly violated its *own rights* enshrined in Article 36(1)(c) of the 1963 Vienna Convention. Furthermore, the Court underlined that this interdependence means that 'violations of rights of individuals under Article 36 may entail a violation of the rights of the sending State, and that violations of the rights of the latter may entail a violation of the rights of the individual'.[24] The State's representation on the international level of its own nationals' rights resembles that of parents with regard to a minor, a *pupillus*.

It has already been submitted that diplomatic protection is traditionally built upon a fiction – that is, the suffering of a State through its injured national – yet the ILC itself has underlined that, even in the past, this fiction

> was no more than a means to an end, the end being the protection of the rights of an injured national. Today the situation has changed dramatically. The individual is the subject of many primary rules of international law, both under custom and treaty, which protect him at home, against his own Government, and abroad, against foreign Governments.[25]

The ICJ reflected this (new) enlarged conception of diplomatic protection in the recent *Ahmadou SadioDiallo Case*, where it was stated that 'the scope *ratione materiae* of diplomatic protection, originally limited to alleged violations of the minimum standard of treatment of aliens, has subsequently widened to include, *inter alia*, internationally guaranteed human rights'.[26]

Be that as it may, the widening of the scope of diplomatic protection has not transfigured its essence, as it still remains today a tool in the hands of the national State. Borrowing the wording of the ILC in this respect, this '*means*' – moreover an imperfect one (for the discretionary power of the State to avail itself of) – does not in any way constitute an enforceable right for the individual, and certainly not in the international terms. Even the ILC cannot but confess that it 'recommends to States that they should exercise that right [i.e. to bring a claim through diplomatic protection] in appropriate cases'.[27]

8. THE INDIVIDUAL'S POSITION IN THE LIGHT OF THE 'EXTENSIVE DEFINITION' OF THE INTERNATIONAL LEGAL PERSONALITY

It appears obvious that individuals cannot by any means be considered as subjects of international law in the light of the 'restrictive definition' of international personality (*supra* section 4). No demonstration is needed to say that the individual does not possess the three legal capacities, except, maybe, the last one, namely the capacity to 'bring an international claim', but only on a regional level and thanks to a treaty.[28] This feature is precisely the 'only' requirement that must be met by any candidate according to the 'extensive definition' of international personality (*supra* section 3). We will then examine if under this angle *and* taking into account the 'transfigured' signification of diplomatic protection, the individual can be considered as a subject, albeit in a limited way, of public international law.

First of all, it is undisputed – since at least the beginning of the 20th century – that international treaties can create international 'rights and obligations enforceable by national courts',[29] as the PCIJ had affirmed in an oft-quoted case. In this vein, the ILC rightly maintained that the 'State's responsibility for the breach of an obligation under a treaty concerning the protection of human rights may exist towards all the other parties to the treaty, but the individuals concerned should be regarded as the ultimate beneficiaries and in that sense as the holders of the relevant rights'.[30]

Furthermore, the ICJ's recent statements in the *LaGrand* and (notably) *Avena Cases* have revealed that, in addition to human rights, other treaty rights[31] – such as for instance consular rights – can be conferred in such a way as to consider the individual their ultimate beneficiary. The lack of such an International Court of Human Rights, before which any individual would enjoy a *ius standi*, explains why diplomatic protection has come to play the role of guaranteeing human rights. In this connection, while the International Criminal Court allows the international community to judge and punish those individuals who have committed specific international crimes, implicitly recognizing the individual a *ius standi* for international duties; nothing, on the contrary, exists on the universal plan for the individual rights. This discrepancy engenders some unfairness as to the legal position of the individual: States can bring international claims against them, while they cannot avail themselves of the same *locus standi* when their (human) rights are at stake.

As the ICJ had said in the aforementioned *Barcelona Traction Case*: 'Should the natural or legal persons on whose behalf it [i.e. the State] is acting consider that *their rights* are not adequately protected, *they have no remedy in international law*.'[32]

Yet, this does not entail, either logically or legally, the titularity of these rights upon the individuals, as they still have to 'beg' the diplomatic protection of their own State. Indeed, even if we admit that the State 'takes up the case' of its national with the purpose of protecting the latter's infringed rights – and not its own – one can hardly sustain that the individual has a full legal personality, as it lacks *ultimately* the 'capacity to act', which is indisputably the acid test of legal personality. Even the PCIJ, in the aforementioned case (*Jurisdiction of the Courts of Danzig*), fell short of asserting that individuals – in the quite specific circumstances of the Free City of Danzig – could avail themselves of these treaty rights in the international terrain. In this respect, the ILC rightly distinguishes – in the wake of the ICJ's findings in the *Avena case* – between 'direct' and 'indirect' claims, the former relating directly to the State's rights, the latter pertaining to the individual's rights. In addition, the ILC stresses that in some cases, as for example in the *ELSI Case*, one can be faced with a 'mixed claim', thus calling for a determination on 'whether the direct or the indirect element is preponderant'. To this end, the criteria will range from 'the subject of the dispute, the nature of the claim and the remedy claimed'.[33] For instance, if the injured person is an organ of the State, the claim will be direct, but, on the contrary, if the State 'takes up its national's claim', the claim will be considered as an indirect one. This is of course instrumental in assessing whether the claim's admissibility is subject to the rule requesting the exhaustion of local remedies. Furthermore, the latter obligation is hardly compatible with its asserted full international personality, as the *par in parem non habet iurisdictionem* principle clearly shows. In fact, this requirement reveals the individual's lack of independence in relation to the offending State, thus submitting him or her to the State's territorial jurisdiction. Likewise, it stresses the fundamental principle of the equality of States that crushes the individual. All the foregoing clearly shows that diplomatic protection has been transfigured, not in its essence but in its aims,[34] as it has become a powerful, though still *discretionary* tool at the disposal of the States purporting to protect human rights 'in the person of its subjects' … only! This discretionary power (*supra* section 6) of which the national's State is vested for the exercise of diplomatic protection hinders the true titularity of rights, of which the State is nonetheless the real beneficiary.

Therefore, it is not risky to maintain that diplomatic protection has become a tool allowing the State to: (a) protect its own rights whenever one of its nationals has suffered any injury abroad; and (b) protect *its national rights* since the individual national has no international capacity.

At the end of this concise, and, in many respects, fragmentary overview of the international personality of the individual from the angle of diplomatic protection, we can hardly maintain that the individual is a full subject of international law. In fact, while we have observed a tremendous change in the array of rights directly created by treaties (and other sources of international rules) of which the individual is a beneficiary, nothing, or almost nothing, has changed with regard to the instruments at his or her disposal to enforce them at the international level. Indeed, the very fact that diplomatic protection has been given the function of protecting the individual's human rights represents, paradoxically, the proof that no other true judicial means exist (on the universal plan) that can be implemented *autonomously* by the person.

NOTES

* Giovanni Distefano is Professor of International Law at the University of Neuchâtel, Switzerland.
1. *Nationality Decrees Issued in Tunisia and Morocco*, Permanent Court of International Justice (PCIJ), Advisory Opinion, Series B, No. 4 (1923), 24.
2. 'General Course on Principles of International Law', RCADI 121 (1967-II): 346.
3. *Reparations for Injuries Suffered in the Service of the United Nations*, Advisory Opinion, I.C.J. Reports 1949: 178.
4. Ibid., at 177, 178.
5. 'Case concerning filleting within the Gulf of St. Lawrence between Canada and France, Decision, 17 July 1986', *RIAA* XIX, sect. 26: 240. 'Agreement dated 27 March 1972 is a treaty concluded between two sovereign States which creates reciprocal rights and obligations for both States. Should it hold true that, according to the wording used in the agreement, the right to "pursue fishing activities" is meant for the benefit of "fishing buildings" (article 3), "fishing boats" (article 4a) and "trawler men" (article 4b), the signatory States are nonetheless the only holders of these rights and able to request the respect of the agreement for the benefit of their respective nationals.'
6. *Supra* note 3, at 179.
7. See C. Dominice, 'La personnalité juridique dans le système du droit des gens' (1996), *L'ordre juridique international entre tradition et innovation. Recueil d'études* (1997): 70; G. Distefano, 'Observations éparses sur les caractères de la personnalité juridique internationale', *Annuaire français de droit international* LIII (2007): 117–124.
8. '... Through the capacity to conclude treaties with States on a level of parity an international organization receives a valid entry ticket to the world of international relations at the level of international law', C. Tomuschat, 'International Law: Ensuring the Survival of Mankind on the Eve of a New Century: General Course on Public International Law', *RCADI* 281 (1999): 131; 'Strunsky-Mergé Case (United States of America v. Italy), Decision of the Arbitral Commission (10 June 1955)', *RGDIP* 63 (1959-I): 131.
9. Sir R. Phillimore, *Commentaries upon International Law* (London: Butterworth, 1879), Vol. II, Part I, sect. 114, 157.
10. *Supra* note 3, at 177.
11. Ibid., at 178.
12. 'Island of Palmas Case (Netherlands and United States), Arbitral Award of 4 April 1928', RIAA II: 838 (emphasis added).
13. Ibid., at 839.
14. *Mavrommatis Palestine Concessions (Greece v. Great Britain)*, PCIJ, Judgment, Series A, No. 2 (1924), 12.
15. E. De Vattel, *The Law of Nations*, translated from French (1758), Book 2, Chapter VII, 84.
16. *Barcelona Traction (Belgium v. Spain*; 2nd phase), Judgment, I.C.J. Reports 1970: sect. 33, 32 (emphasis added).
17. See Article 2 of the ILC Draft Articles on Diplomatic Protection, UN Doc. A/61/10. Article 19(b), the chapeau of which ('Recommended Practice') clearly suggests that it represents 'an exercise in progressive development', and affirms that the State 'should' in the exercise of diplomatic protection, 'take into account, wherever feasible, the views of injured persons with regard to resort to diplomatic protection and the reparation to be sought'. See in this vein *Barcelona Traction*, ibid., note 18, sect. 78, 45, where the Court, well aware of the deficiencies of the universal judicial system of protection of individual's rights, be they human rights or any others, stresses the persistent discretionary power of the State.
18. However, this will pose some technical problems at the stage of the exhaustion of local remedies, since the national is not (and cannot be) bound to solicit them, thus finally preventing its own State from filing a diplomatic protection against the foreign State.
19. It is worth noting that the ILC has not, quite correctly, considered that the so-called 'clean hands' condition (propounded by a small minority of authors) is required by customary international law.
20. *LaGrand (Germany v. United States)*, Judgment, I.C.J. Reports 2001: § 77, 494 (emphasis added).
21. *Case Concerning Avena and Other Mexican Nationals (Mexico v. United States of America)*, Judgment, I.C.J. Reports 2004: § 40, 35–36 (original emphases).
22. Article 36(1)(b) (emphasis added).

23. *Supra* note 21, at § 40, 36. See likewise (in the lapse of time between the *LaGrand* and *Avena* cases), *Arrest of Warrant of 11 April 2000 (D.R. Congo v. Belgium)*, Judgment, I.C.J. Reports 2002: § 40, 19.
24. *Supra* note 21, at § 40, 36.
25. *Supra* note 17, at 25–26.
26. *Ahmadou Sadio Diallo (Republic of Guinea v. D.R. Congo)*, Judgment, (Preliminary Objections), I.C.J. Reports 2007: § 39.
27. *Supra* note 17, at 30.
28. We are obviously referring to the system of protection of human rights established by the European Convention on Human Rights, allowing for individuals to bring a claim before the Court of Strasbourg against any State party to it, including their own State. Within this context, the individual is freed from control by any State (provided that it is party to the Convention) with regard to an important, albeit limited, set of rights immediately enforceable before a jurisdictional body, thus obtaining a reparation from the wrongful State. In this respect, it is not incorrect to maintain that the individual is a limited (and derived) subject of regional international law.
29. *Jurisdiction of the Courts of Danzig*, PCIJ, Advisory Opinion, Series B, No. 15 (1928), 18.
30. *ILC's Commentary on State Responsibility Draft Articles*, Article 33, UN Doc. A/56/10, 95.
31. The Arbitral Tribunal (Tax regime governing pensions paid to retired UNESCO officials residing in France) (France – UNESCO), Decision, 14 January 2003, *RIAA* XXV: § 82, 261, so said: 'La règle selon laquelle les dispositions d'un traité peuvent créer des droits subjectifs dans le chef des particuliers. Les Parties ont toutes deux reconnu l'existence de cette règle. Cette règle appartient au droit international contemporain. Elle a été souvent appliquée par la Cour internationale de Justice.' ('The rule according to which treaty provisions can create (subjective) rights for the private individuals. Both Parties have recognized the existence of this rule. The latter belongs to contemporary international law. It has often been applied by the International Court of Justice.')
32. *Supra* note 16, at § 78, 45 (emphasis added).
33. *Supra* note 17, at 74–76. See in this respect, *Factory at Chorzów (Germany v. Poland)*, PCIJ, Judgment (Merits), Series A, No. 17 (1928), 28.
34. In this respect, yet with a more radical conclusion, see the thorough and in-depth analysis of S. Touzé, *La protection des droits des nationaux à l'étranger. Recherches sur la protection diplomatique* (Paris: Pedone, 2007).

PART II

COMMON ISSUES

5. The relationship between international human rights and humanitarian law: an overview

Vera Gowlland-Debbas and Gloria Gaggioli*

1. INTRODUCTION

The trend towards fragmentation and compartmentalization of particular sectoral and functional fields of international law is but a reflection of the diversification of globalized society; such fields of law have become purportedly self-contained, whether in substantive, procedural or institutional terms, which raises the problem of fragmentation of international law. A major debate today, therefore, revolves around whether one can still refer to a comprehensive and uniform system of general international law in the face of the development of various subsets of norms.

Yet alongside fragmentation, there is a very visible process of reconciliation – and paradoxically the greater the degree of specialization and the more claims to self-containment, the greater is the trend towards permeability between different fields of law. Thus we find a considerable literature on the links which are being forged, not only between human rights and humanitarian law, but also with refugee law, disarmament or arms control, environmental law and international peace and security – all areas which in the past were hermetically sealed off from one another. In part, this is due to the creation of a general or public interest domain – an international public policy or *ordre public* – which includes protection of the individual, hence requiring coherent, across-the-board, holistic responses. This leads us to the need not only for conflict rules but also for the application of underlying substantive rules to bridge these different areas, including notions of legitimacy, finalities and essential values. There are of course important collisions and tensions between public order norms, as for example between international human rights law and IHL, but these are being fought and gradually ironed out in practice and in the courts.

In this chapter, we will address some of the legal reasons and developments in the international legal system and environment that have led to a convergence between human rights law and IHL. We will then address the difficult and important issue of the interplay between human rights law and humanitarian law at the level of norm conflicts as well as regarding cross-fertilization through the case law of human rights bodies. Finally, we will explore the response of human rights bodies to violations committed in situations of armed conflict in order to assess the contribution of these bodies for providing remedies to victims of armed conflicts.

2. THE CONVERGENCE OF INTERNATIONAL HUMAN RIGHTS AND HUMANITARIAN LAW

2.1   Separate Origins and Development

The interplay between human rights and humanitarian law has been debated at length.[1] It was usual to point out that international human rights law and IHL have separate historical origins and different underlying philosophies, and that they have pursued different trajectories.[2] Generally speaking, they were said to be distinct *ratione personae*, *materiae* and *loci*, to have different objectives, scopes of application, substantive norms and implementing mechanisms, as well as a different ethos. It was commonly argued that human rights law has traditionally largely been concerned with the relationship between States and individuals under their jurisdiction, while IHL has concentrated on the treatment of both combatants and non-combatants by their opponents in wartime – the emergence of an armed conflict being a *sine qua non* condition for its applicability – on the basis of nationality or other status. It was stated that the beneficiaries are different: in the former all individuals are covered without distinction, in the latter, only protected persons as defined by the various instruments, thus, with some exceptions, excluding a State's own nationals, nationals of co-belligerents, and those of neutral third states with whom normal diplomatic relations are maintained; in short, protection is directed to some but not to others. It was also argued that whereas the one grants subjective enforceable rights to individuals, the other constitutes a system of inter-state rights; that while one offsets the rights of individuals against the maintenance of public order, the other seeks to balance military necessity and the principle of humanity.

2.2   Normative Convergence

These were, of course, from the start broad generalizations with a number of exceptions, and increasingly it became evident that strict compartmentalization was no longer tenable, for in the words of T. Meron: 'they now have a shared basis in the fundamental principle of humanity'.[3]

2.2.1   The 'humanization' of IHL
On the one hand, the penetration of human rights law into IHL has led to its normative transformation: the humanitarian character of both the Geneva Conventions of 1949 and the Additional Protocols of 1977 has been largely the result of influence from human rights instruments or standards, beginning with the Universal Declaration of Human Rights.

This is clearly evidenced by the express references to human rights law that can be found in the Additional Protocols to the Geneva Conventions. Additional Protocol II recalls in a preambular paragraph 'that international instruments relating to human rights offer a basic protection to the human person', thereby providing human rights law as an additional framework for the relations between a State and its citizens in an internal armed conflict.[4] Article 72 of Additional Protocol I stresses that 'the provisions of … Section [III dealing with the treatment of persons in the power of a party to the conflict] are additional to … other applicable rules of international law relating to the protection of fundamental human rights during international armed conflict'. By introducing such references, States recognized the applicability and relevance of human rights law in non-international as well as in international armed conflicts.

In addition to these explicit references to international human rights law, IHL treaties integrate fundamental human rights guarantees such as the prohibition of arbitrary killings,[5] the prohibition of torture and other inhuman or degrading treatments, the prohibition of slavery, the right to a fair trial, etc. A first example of this is Common Article 3, which reflects a minimum human rights core identified by the Court in the *Nicaragua* case as the minimum yardstick constituting 'fundamental general principles of humanitarian law' applicable in all circumstances, including international armed conflicts.[6] Articles 4–6 of Additional Protocol II and 75 of Additional Protocol I are further examples of the influence of human rights law on IHL, as evidenced by the preparatory works[7] and the Commentaries to the Additional Protocols.[8]

IHL also contains concepts the interpretation of which needs to include a reference to human rights law, for example, the provision that no one may be convicted of a crime other than by a regularly constituted court 'affording all the judicial guarantees which are recognized as indispensable by civilized peoples' (Common Article 3 (1d) to the Geneva Conventions).

This widening of the protection of the individual in time of armed conflict is also reflected in the evolving norms of international criminal law, as for example Article 8 of the ICC Statute which expands the notion of war crimes to include those committed against *any* civilian, thus going beyond the notion of protected person, as well as in the case-law of the international criminal tribunals.[9]

2.2.2 The 'conflictualization' of human rights law

Although human rights law was initially meant to apply in peacetime,[10] it has increasingly expanded its purview to armed conflict situations at home and abroad.

2.2.2.1 Applicability of human rights in time of armed conflict The continuing applicability of human rights in time of armed conflict (with the exception of lawful derogations) has now been fully accepted by judicial decisions, state practice (although with some notable exceptions), and the practice of international organizations, human rights bodies and NGOs.

Even the United States of America – traditionally reluctant to recognize the relevance of human rights law in armed conflicts – admitted in its Fourth Periodic Report (2011) to the UN Human Rights Committee that

> indeed, a time of war does not suspend the operation of the Covenant [i.e. the International Covenant on Civil and Political Rights] to matters within its scope of application. … In this context, it is important to bear in mind that international human rights law and the law of armed conflict are in many respects complementary and mutually reinforcing.[11]

This has not always been so self-evident.[12] In the context of the *Nuclear Weapons* Advisory Opinion, the ICJ had then been faced with two opposing arguments arising from the pleadings, the one maintaining that the use of nuclear weapons would violate the right to life under the ICCPR, the other that the Covenant was irrelevant since directed to the protection of human rights in peacetime. The Court accepted the continuing applicability of the Covenant in time of armed conflict. This meant that '[i]n principle, the right not arbitrarily to be deprived of one's life applies also in hostilities'.[13]

The Court also had to examine the contention that nuclear weapons violated the prohibition on genocide which has been considered to be one form of arbitrary deprivation of life. In the *Case concerning Application of the Convention on the Prevention and Punishment of the Crime of Genocide*[14] it had recalled the applicability of the Genocide Convention *both in time of peace and in time of war*, as stated in Article I of the Convention. Here then is one particular form of arbitrary deprivation of life which lies at the intersection of human rights and humanitarian law. The Court had also underlined the fact that the rights and obligations enshrined by the Convention are rights and obligations *erga omnes* which are not limited territorially.[15]

The ICJ has thus pointed to certain core guarantees applicable in all circumstances, including peremptory norms and obligations *erga omnes*, such as the 'elementary considerations of humanity' recalled by the ICJ in the *Corfu Channel* case to be respected both in time of war and in time of peace.[16]

However, it is not because human rights provisions are non-derogable or because they codify *jus cogens* norms that 'must be honoured notwithstanding the outbreak of armed conflict'.[17] In the *Wall* case, the Court affirmed that it was the Covenant as a whole, and not just the non-derogable rights, that continues to operate in armed conflict, to the extent that it had not been formally derogated from in accordance with Article 4 which operates 'in time of public emergency which threatens the life of the nation'. The Court had then noted that Israel had only derogated from Article 9 of the ICCPR dealing with the right to liberty and security of person and that therefore the other Articles of the Covenant remained applicable not only to Israeli territory, but also in the Occupied Palestinian Territory. Moreover, the Court re-affirmed the applicability in time of armed conflict not only of the ICCPR but also of all human rights instruments, including the Covenant on Economic, Social and Cultural Rights and the Convention on the Rights of the Child.[18] This was further confirmed by the ICJ in its 2005 judgment in the *DRC v. Uganda* case.[19]

This affirmation of the indivisibility of human rights contributes to providing a greater and more effective protection through one unified complex of human rights. The ICJ's pronouncements in this respect have been reflected in the jurisprudence of international criminal tribunals, as well as the regional courts to which we will return below.

2.2.2.2 The extraterritorial scope of human rights law   The extraterritorial scope of the application of human rights obligations has become widely recognized through a liberal interpretation, extending States' obligations to persons beyond their borders but subject to their jurisdiction.[20] That means acceptance that extraterritorial jurisdiction would apply wherever the State exercises all or some of the public powers it normally exercises over its own territory. There are however differences of views and conflicting jurisprudence as to what triggers such extraterritorial application.[21]

Although limits were set to extraterritorial application by the European Court of Human Rights in the case of *Bankovic* in the very particular circumstances of the NATO bombing of a radio/television station in Belgrade[22] in which the Court determined that air power was not tantamount to effective control over territory, this is considered not to have undermined its previous jurisprudence nor to detract from the wide acceptance of the extraterritorial scope of human rights instruments in the circumstances of effective control or authority exercised over another territory, particularly in situations of occupation.[23]

More difficult has been the case of a State's exercise of control or authority over individuals outside its territory, through the acts of State agents, although this has been confirmed also in the jurisprudence of human rights bodies, including the European Court of Human Rights.[24]

In its recent judgment in the *Al-Skeini* case, concerning killings in the context of the occupation by the United Kingdom of Iraq, the European Court of Human Rights summed up and clarified its position regarding the extraterritorial scope of the European Convention on Human Rights by confirming that there are exceptions to the principle that jurisdiction under Article 1 of the European Convention on Human Rights is limited to a State's own territory.[25] These are notably: (1) 'whenever the State through its agents exercises control and authority over an individual'; and (2) 'when, as a consequence of lawful or unlawful military action, a Contracting State exercises effective control of an area outside that national territory'.[26]

In the *Wall* case, the International Court of Justice also accepted the extraterritorial effects of human rights conventions. It concluded that international human rights instruments are applicable 'in respect of acts done by a State in the exercise of its jurisdiction outside its own territory', particularly in the regime relating to occupied territories.[27]

Although the issue of the extraterritorial application of human rights law goes far beyond situations of armed conflicts, it has the effect of increasing the relevance and applicability of human rights law in cross-border armed conflicts.

2.3 Convergence Resulting from Developments in the International Legal System

2.3.1 The proliferation of non-international armed conflicts and the blurring of the distinction between international and non-international armed conflicts

One of the main developments in international relations having led to a convergence between human rights law and IHL has been a diversification and complexification of the nature of armed conflicts. In fact, contemporary armed conflicts do not resemble traditional wars opposing horizontally regular armies of two belligerent States.

There has been a proliferation of intra-state conflicts of various intensities opposing a State's armed forces to non-state organized armed groups such as those which flourished during the Cold War, or those which erupted in the recent past in Russia (opposing the Government to the Chechen rebel forces) or in Turkey (opposing the Government to the PKK). In such situations, the opposing parties are in a vertical relationship (the Government having to face rebels among its own population) where human rights law typically applies alongside IHL for non-international armed conflicts.

The convergence between IHL and human rights law is quite evident in non-international armed conflict as demonstrated by article 3 common to the Geneva Conventions, which can be qualified as the *sedes materiae* of human rights law in armed conflicts.[28]

Nowadays, the convergence and interplay between IHL and human rights law in non-international armed conflicts also become relevant and especially crucial in so-called 'transnational armed conflicts', that is, armed conflicts opposing a government to a non-State organized armed group and taking place on the territory of several States[29] or where the non-State organized armed group is located in a foreign territory.

In this type of conflict, common article 3 and customary IHL rules applicable to non-international armed conflicts apply alongside human rights law rules (to the extent of their extraterritorial application).[30] In the context of the international fight against terrorism, the question of the parallel applicability of human rights law and IHL has moreover arisen regarding extraterritorial targeted killings[31] taking place outside the territory of belligerent States, leading to an intense debate as to the applicability of IHL and/or HRL to such killings, although it can be argued that the customary prohibition of the arbitrary deprivation of life under HRL continues to apply.[32] Under IHL, the question of extraterritorial targeted killings has revolved around the geographical scope of IHL and the targetability of such suspected terrorists.[33] In this latter respect, the question is whether such suspected terrorists can be targeted abroad – even outside the territory of the belligerent State(s) – as legitimate targets, or whether they are protected by IHL as civilians 'unless and for such time as they take a direct part in hostilities'.[34] Although human rights practice is not well developed regarding extraterritorial targeted killings, the Human Rights Committee addressed the issue in the context of the Occupied Territories.[35] It rejected the possibility of resorting to targeted killings 'as a deterrent or punishment' and stated furthermore that '(b)efore resorting to the use of deadly force, all measures to arrest a person suspected of being in the process of committing acts of terror must be exhausted'. In the famous so-called 'targeted killing case', the Israeli Supreme Court considered that suspected terrorists were not combatants but civilians who could be targeted and killed under IHL only when directly participating in hostilities[36] (although it adopted an expansive view of the IHL condition of 'a civilian taking a direct part in hostilities').[37] It nevertheless also affirmed the conditions laid down by human rights law to the deprivation of life: that is, the consideration of employing less harmful means, such as arrest, interrogation and trial, as well as a thorough retroactive investigation should lethal force be employed, referring in its conclusions, *inter alia*, to the *McCann* case.[38] As L. Doswald-Beck points out, '[i]n effect it therefore used human rights law, although it did not refer to the UN Human Rights Committee'.[39]

Another development in the international legal system that has contributed to the convergence between IHL and human rights law is that the borders between internal and international armed conflicts have become increasingly fuzzy following on the *Tadić* decision, which noted that

> the impetuous development and propagation in the international community of human rights doctrines ... has brought about significant changes in international law, notably in the approach to problems besetting the world community. A State-sovereignty-oriented approach

has been gradually supplanted by a human-being-oriented approach. Gradually the maxim of Roman law *hominum causa omne jus constitutum est* (all law is created for the benefit of human beings) has gained a firm foothold in the international community as well. It follows that in the area of armed conflict the distinction between interstate wars and civil wars is losing its value as far as human beings are concerned. Why protect civilians from belligerent violence, or ban rape, torture or the wanton destruction of hospitals, churches, museums or private property, as well as proscribe weapons causing unnecessary suffering when two sovereign States are engaged in war, and yet refrain from enacting the same bans or providing the same protection when armed violence has erupted 'only' within the territory of a sovereign State? If international law, while of course duly safeguarding the legitimate interests of States, must gradually turn to the protection of human beings, it is only natural that the aforementioned dichotomy should gradually lose its weight.[40]

The fact that the distinction between international and non-international armed conflicts progressively fades away in some areas contributes to enhancing the similarities between IHL and human rights law whose protection remains the same independently of the situation (subject to possible derogations in time of public emergency which threatens the life of the nation).

2.3.2   The birth of human rights instruments bridging the two fields of law and the development of common rules through customary law

Another factor favouring convergence between human rights law and IHL is the contemporary trend towards the creation of human rights instruments bridging the two fields of law. The most relevant example is the Convention on the Rights of the Child. Its article 38 not only refers to the applicability of humanitarian law provisions to children, but also prescribes its own rules in the event of armed conflict (reflecting the standards laid down in article 77 of Additional Protocol I), restricting recruitment and participation of children in armed conflicts. In addition, the Convention on the Rights of the Child is complemented by an Optional Protocol which is entirely devoted to the involvement of children in armed conflict, and which raises the standards provided by IHL by asking States to take all feasible measures to ensure that members of their armed forces who have not attained the age of 18 years old (instead of 15 years old in Additional Protocol I) do not take a direct part in hostilities. Another example worth mentioning is the 2006 UN Convention on Disappearances, which incorporates both human rights and IHL standards.[41] Several other human rights treaties also incorporate an express reference to IHL.[42]

In terms of soft law instruments, the 1990 *Turku Declaration of Minimum Human-itarian Standards*[43] has attempted to paper over the cracks in the protection system by dealing with situations of internal violence, disturbances, tensions and public emergency, and the 2005 *Basic Principles and Guidelines on the Rights to Reparation for Victims of Gross Violations of Human Rights and Humanitarian Law*,[44] treat IHL and international human rights law as identical normative frameworks for the provision of remedies.

An additional reason for the convergence of human rights and IHL is the incorporation of both into customary international law. In a convincing article, M. Sassòli highlighted that in customary law there are no boundaries separating customary IHL rules from customary rules of human rights law.[45] They are both based on the same

State practice and *opinio juris*. Indeed, the ICRC study on customary IHL does recognize specific areas of overlap between IHL and international human rights law.[46]

2.3.3   The practice of international organizations, human rights bodies and non-governmental organizations

There is extensive practice also by international organizations. The convergence of human rights and humanitarian law has been demonstrated by the complementary use of both human rights law and humanitarian law by the political organs of the United Nations, including the former Human Rights Commission,[47] Human Rights Council,[48] General Assembly[49] and Security Council,[50] which have at times invoked in one and the same provision all the relevant guarantees of international law for the protection of individuals. The UN Secretary-General, notably in his Report on the Protection of Civilians in Armed Conflict, has also called for the cumulative application of all norms which protect civilians in such situations.[51] Many UN Special Rapporteurs have also referred to both IHL and HRL in their reports.[52]

There has, however, been extensive criticism from some sources, notably concerning the competence of the Human Rights Council in relation to armed conflicts. For example, some disapproved of the Human Rights Council's resolutions on Israel addressing breaches of both human rights law and IHL in the Occupied Palestinian Territory, which emphasized that 'human rights law and international humanitarian law are complementary and mutually reinforcing'.[53] The extension of the mandate of the Special Rapporteur on Extrajudicial Executions in the 'War on Terror' to cover armed conflicts has also been criticized.[54]

Finally, a number of human rights treaty bodies have referred explicitly or implicitly to IHL.[55] There are also increasing references to both human rights law and IHL in reports of human rights non-governmental organizations such as Human Rights Watch or Amnesty International. The International Red Cross and Red Crescent Movement has also recognized the complementarity of human rights law and IHL in armed conflict situations.[56]

Even though the parallel applicability of human rights law and humanitarian law in armed conflicts, as well as the ensuing convergence between these two bodies of law, is now established, more difficult is the question of the manner in which IHL applies in relation to human rights law: as *lex specialis*, aid to interpretation, or complementarily both by virtue of its scope of application and by virtue of the norms to be applied, as well as its applicability in practical concrete situations.

3.   THE INTERPLAY BETWEEN HUMAN RIGHTS LAW AND INTERNATIONAL HUMANITARIAN LAW

3.1   The Concept of *Lex Specialis* as Interpretative Aid and Exclusionary Principle

In the *Nuclear Weapons* Advisory Opinion the Court utilized the concept of *lex specialis* in concluding that while the Covenant continued to operate in time of armed conflict, humanitarian law exclusively determines what is an arbitrary deprivation of life in armed conflict situations under the conduct of hostilities:

> The test of what is an arbitrary deprivation of life, however, then falls to be determined by the applicable *lex specialis*, namely, the law applicable in armed conflict which is designed to regulate the conduct of hostilities. Thus whether a particular loss of life, through the use of a certain weapon in warfare, is to be considered an arbitrary deprivation of life contrary to Article 6 of the Covenant, can only be decided by reference to the law applicable in armed conflict and not deduced from the terms of the Covenant itself.[57]

The Court thus turned to the concept of *lex specialis* in order to dismiss the relevance of human rights law altogether in regard to the legality of nuclear weapons.

Yet surely the notion of what is 'arbitrary' deprivation of life under the Covenant should also have been interpreted in the context of the treaty as a whole, in the light of its object and purpose, and against constantly evolving standards, for the Covenant has been acknowledged as a living instrument. The International Court of Justice has stated, for example, that the meaning of certain generic terms was 'intended to follow the evolution of the law and to correspond with the meaning attached to the expression by the law in force at any given time'.[58] Such developments have taken place, for example, under the European Convention on Human Rights where it has been pointed out that what is involved in the evolution of human rights concepts is 'a reinterpretation – an evolution – of an already existing obligation, not the incrustation, or impact, upon the Convention of a new obligation that had arisen through the emergence of a new rule of customary or treaty law'.[59] This evolution includes the trend towards the promotion of the right to life beyond the usual legal protection, for example positive obligations on the part of States to preserve it, such as the duty of States to 'prevent war', which would introduce (presumably) the *jus ad bellum* yardstick in determining what is 'arbitrary killing' in time of armed conflict.[60] In short, while the right to life as expressed in the various instruments must be presumed to except from its scope deaths resulting from lawful acts of war, it must also be presumed to include the new standards which are being forged in the framework of human rights bodies.

Moreover, the maxim of *lex specialis derogat generali*, was traditionally applied only as a discretionary aid in interpreting conflicting, but potentially applicable, treaty rules.

> [W]hile international law permits recourse to many principles and maxims it does not always require recourse to them. The appropriateness of applying many of them depends on a variety of considerations which will determine whether, although they are accepted in international law as potentially relevant, they are also suitable for application in all the circumstances of the particular case.[61]

In this context, other rules of resolution of conflict may be relevant, such as the *lex posterior*[62] or the most favourable to the individual rule.[63]

Nor is the maxim of *lex specialis* relevant in determining the incremental nature of treaty rules, unless it is applied not as a conflict rule, but as an interpretative aid. At any rate, a view of the law of armed conflict as *lex specialis*, totally pre-empting the *lex generalis* of the rest of international law, including human rights law, could only be tenable when strict compartmentalization between conditions of peace and conditions of war were possible.[64]

It has been pointed out, moreover, that a body of law as such cannot be considered as a *lex specialis*.[65] The latter applies to conflicts between rules and not between bodies of international law. At the level of the rules, an IHL rule may (in many cases) represent the *lex specialis* regarding a human rights rule. For example, the IHL rule according to which prisoners of war can be interned until the end of hostilities has been interpreted as prevailing over the obligation to provide *habeas corpus* to every person deprived of his/her liberty under human rights law. However, in certain circumstances, the *lex specialis* may well be a human rights law,[66] for example in order to shed light on the general substantive judicial guarantees provided by common Article 3 (1d) to the Geneva Conventions. Here the *lex specialis* nature of the human rights rule does not properly derogate from IHL, but rather complements it. In other cases, a human rights rule may also derogate from IHL. For example, if a prisoner of war contests his status of combatant, he shall have the right to *habeas corpus* in order to contest his internment, even though IHL does not expressly provide for this.[67]

3.2   The Principle of Complementarity

It may also be, however, that the ICJ arrived at its conclusions only in the very specific context of the right to life. For in its Advisory Opinion on the *Legal Consequences of the Construction of a Wall in the Occupied Palestinian Territory*, the Court took a leap forward in stating:

> As regards the relationship between international humanitarian law and human rights law, there are thus three possible situations: some rights may be exclusively matters of international humanitarian law; others may be exclusively matters of human rights law; yet others may be matters of both these branches of international law. In order to answer the question put to it, the Court will have to take into consideration both these branches of international law, namely human rights law and, as *lex specialis*, international humanitarian law.[68]

There was a clear implication, therefore, that the complementarity principle continued to operate alongside the *lex specialis* test.[69] This passage was reiterated in the *DRC v. Uganda* case,[70] not only in the Court's reasoning but in the very *dispositif* of the judgment, thus demonstrating conclusively that IHL and human rights operate side by side during an armed conflict.[71]

Similarly, the Human Rights Committee has moved away from the *lex specialis* articulation of the relationship between international human rights law and IHL; in its General Comment no. 31 it affirmed that 'While in respect of certain Covenant rights, more specific rules of international humanitarian law may be especially relevant for the purposes of the interpretation of Covenant rights, both spheres of law are complementary, not mutually exclusive'.

The ICTY has also pointed out that human rights law and humanitarian law are mutually complementary and have similarities 'in terms of goals, values and terminology'. It was therefore necessary to have recourse to human rights law which 'is generally a welcome and needed assistance to determine the content of customary international law in the field of humanitarian law. With regard to certain of its aspects, international humanitarian law can be said to have fused with human rights law'. However, it pointed out that 'notions developed in the field of human rights can be transposed in international humanitarian law only if they take into consideration the specificities of the latter body of law'.[72]

As revealed by the practice of international courts, tribunals and human rights bodies, IHL does not displace human rights law, but rather adds further specific protections in armed conflicts, and, as such, complements human rights law.

3.3 The Theory of Harmonization

In its report on fragmentation, the ILC examined a series of treaty conflict rules, such as *lex specialis* and the rules relating to successive treaties, as well as hierarchical norms such as *jus cogens* and Article 103 of the Charter.

These rules could have ended up being rather reductionist, were it not for its view that these legal techniques must be placed within the confines of a general 'system' of international law, that they are context-specific and that '[a] weighing of different considerations must take place ... [which] must seek reference from ... the systemic objectives of the law'.[73]

The report therefore placed the problem of the relationship between various areas of law within the context of treaty interpretation by recalling the provisions of Article 31(3) of the Vienna Convention on the Law Treaties which states that treaties are to be interpreted within the context of 'any relevant rules of international law applicable in the relations between the parties'.[74] This rule leads to harmonization rather than to exclusion based on relationships of priority. The ILC approaching international law as a system, thus expressed what could be called a principle of 'systemic integration'. As the ILC stressed, '... law is also about protecting rights and enforcing obligations, above all rights and obligations that have a backing in something like a general, public interest. Without the principle of "systemic integration" it would be impossible to give expression to and to keep alive, any sense of the common good of humankind, not reducible to the good of any particular institution or "regime"'.[75]

This rule of interpretation has been resorted to by a variety of bodies from the WTO to the International Court of Justice.[76] But it has also been referred to by the human rights treaty bodies.[77]

4. THE APPROACH OF HUMAN RIGHTS BODIES TOWARDS INTERNATIONAL HUMANITARIAN LAW: A COMPARISON

The acceptance that human rights law does not disappear in time of armed conflict with the exception of lawful derogations leads to the logical consequence that its implementing mechanisms continue also to operate. That States are bound by all their obligations under both human rights and humanitarian law is one thing; a Court's jurisdiction is of course another matter altogether. But it is evident from the practice of human rights judicial and quasi-judicial treaty bodies that they have not hesitated to assert their competence in individual cases arising in armed conflict situations. However, the solutions they have brought to the interplay of human rights law and IHL have been context-specific. Generally speaking, there has been an acceptance that in accordance with the rules of interpretation of Article 31(3) of the Vienna Convention on the Law of

Treaties, human rights bodies are bound to take into account 'any relevant rules of international law applicable in the relations between the parties', including IHL, and they have relied on the ICJ's pronouncement in the *Namibia* Opinion that '[a]n international instrument must be interpreted and applied within the overall framework of the juridical system in force at the time of the interpretation'.[78] They have also been concerned that invocation of their respective instruments should not be used as justification for violations of IHL or peremptory norms.[79]

As stated above, the interpretation of IHL by human rights treaty bodies has to be made under their respective treaties as a guide to the provisions contained therein and within the bounds of their mandate or jurisdiction. In such cases, the *lex specialis* of humanitarian law would have to act as a test to determine the conformity of State conduct with the *jus in bello*, but only as a prelude to determining conformity with the respective provisions of the instruments concerned.

The different human rights bodies have not, however, demonstrated the same degree of openness towards IHL. While the Inter-American Commission and Court of Human Rights make frequent references to IHL, the European Court of Human Rights tends to adopt a more cautious approach.

4.1   The Open Approach of the Inter-American Commission and Court of Human Rights

The Inter-American Commission on Human Rights stated in the *Las Palmeras* case in connection with the right to life under Article 4 of the Convention which prohibits the intentional deprivation of life, that the case had to be decided *in the light of* 'the norms embodied in both the American Convention and in customary IHL applicable to internal armed conflicts and enshrined in Article 3, common to all the 1949 Geneva Conventions'.[80] In other cases, the Commission referred to the norms of IHL as 'sources of inspiration', or looked to the American Declaration of the Rights and Duties of Man 'as understood with reference to' IHL.[81]

In some cases, the Commission went as far as applying IHL; thus acting more boldly than the Court. In the *Tablada* case[82] it resorted to direct applicability of IHL in assuming the competence to characterize the battle between an armed group and Argentine armed forces as an internal armed conflict and stated that 'it is, moreover, during situations of internal armed conflict that these two branches of international law [i.e. human rights law and IHL] most converge and reinforce each other'.[83] In subsequent reports it determined that there had been violations of the right to life under the Convention *together with* or *in conjunction with* the principles codified in common Article 3 of the Geneva Conventions.[84]

The Commission considered that it was not enough to refer to Article 4 of the American Convention alone because it did not contain provisions stating when deaths are the legitimate consequences of military operations. Therefore, the Commission contended that it must necessarily *look to and apply* definitional standards and relevant rules of humanitarian law contained in Common Article 3 of the Geneva Conventions and other relevant rules, as sources of authoritative guidance and as *lex specialis*.

One of the arguments of the Commission was that the American Convention itself authorized the Commission to address questions of humanitarian law by virtue of

Article 29(b) which provides that no provision of the American Convention shall be interpreted as 'restricting the enjoyment or exercise of any right or freedom recognized by virtue of the laws of any State Party or by virtue of another convention to which one of the said states is a party'. In this case, the higher standard that the Commission had to apply was a rule of humanitarian law.[85]

Although in the case of *Las Palmeras* the Commission requested the Inter-American Court, *inter alia*, to declare that Colombia was responsible for the violation of the right to life under Article 4 of the American Convention *and* Article 3 common to the Geneva Conventions,[86] the Inter-American Court of Human Rights has refused to consider that it has the competence to apply IHL, referring to humanitarian law provisions only as an interpretative tool. It was on this basis that it rejected the *application* as opposed to the *interpretation* of IHL by the Commission in the *Las Palmeras* case when it admitted the second preliminary exception of Colombia, alleging lack of competence *ratione materiae* to apply any other rights than those embodied in the American Convention.[87] The Court concluded that the deprivation of life in this case contravened Article 4 of the American Convention.[88]

In following cases, the Inter-American Court referred occasionally to IHL as an interpretative tool. For example, in the case *Ituango Massacres v. Columbia*, the Court held that it is

> useful and appropriate, in keeping with Article 29 … [of the American Convention], to use international treaties other than the American Convention, such as Protocol II of the Geneva Conventions … to interpret its provisions in accordance with the evolution of the inter-American system, taking into account corresponding developments in international humanitarian law.[89]

4.2   The 'Ivory Tower' Approach of the European Court of Human Rights[90]

The European Court of Human Rights jurisprudence on the right to life, particularly in relation to the cases emerging from the conflict in Chechnya, has directly applied the provisions of Article 2 of the Convention to situations of internal armed conflict rather than turn to humanitarian law as *lex specialis*. On the one hand the Court has appeared to resort to the vocabulary of humanitarian law – 'incidental loss of civilian life', 'choice of means and methods', 'legitimate military targets', 'disproportionality in the weapons used' – and its cardinal principles: limitations of means and methods of combat, principle of distinction and principle of proportionality, for example in the *Ergi* case concerning the armed conflict between the PKK and the Turkish army.[91] On the other hand, it has been pointed out that it has applied its own instrument's human rights provisions to clear cases of fully-fledged internal armed conflict normally regulated by common Article 3 of the Geneva Conventions, Protocol II, and applicable customary IHL. It should be said that the States concerned have been reluctant to acknowledge that such situations had reached the required threshold for application of humanitarian law, nor have they derogated in accordance with Article 15, paragraph 2, of the Convention 'in respect of deaths resulting from lawful acts of war'. The European Court determined that where a State did not officially derogate from the Convention, the military operations had to be 'judged against a normal legal background'.[92]

The Court has thus approached such conflicts more as law enforcement operations than armed conflict, including in cases relating to terrorism. This departure from the *lex specialis* approach in reconciling human rights law and IHL in internal armed conflicts is particularly evident in the Chechen cases involving large-scale attacks, including aerial bombardment, in which the Court dealt squarely with the conduct of hostilities.[93] In these cases, the Court decided that the Russian Federation had violated its obligations under the Convention, in particular its positive obligation to protect the life of the applicants and in respect of its failure to conduct an effective investigation.

This exclusive resort to human rights law has a significant impact on the applicable rules, for the provisions relating to the right to life under Article 2 differ significantly from those of IHL. First, the Convention does not require a threshold to come into operation, but provides a single body of law that covers every gradation of the use of force. Second, there is no principle of distinction, since the protection is extended to both civilians and 'combatants/fighters' alike, with the use of lethal force to be used only where capture is too risky, on the grounds that Article 2 covers also situations where the deprivation of life may be an unintended outcome of legal uses of force.[94] Third, it raises questions of the legitimacy of the use of force, by assessing the conditions and means used in the framework of the justifications under Article 2 for the use of lethal force. Fourth, the condition of proportionality inferred by the Court from Article 2 is very differently assessed in IHL. The one consists in an assessment and balance of military advantage with potential loss of civilian life,[95] injury to civilians and/or damage to civilian objects expressly stated under the rules relating to inter-national armed conflicts, the other permits no more use of force 'than absolutely necessary' to achieve the permitted aim of protecting lives from unlawful violence (Article 2(2)), hence proportionality between pursued aim set out in sub-paragraphs 2 a–c, and loss of life, this being stated by the Court to be a stricter and more compelling test of necessity than under other provisions of the Convention. Most significantly, the test of proportionality also applies to 'combatants/fighters', and not only in respect of civilian collateral damage.[96]

Finally, the direct application of the Convention to armed conflict situations has led the European Court of Human Rights to read the right to life under Article 2 in the light of Article 1 which provides an affirmative obligation on States to secure these rights. Thus Article 2 has been interpreted as imposing a positive obligation on States to take all feasible precautions in the choice of means and methods of a military operation and to

> subject deprivations of life to the most careful scrutiny, particularly where deliberate lethal force is used, taking into consideration not only the actions of the agents of the State who actually administer the force but also all the surrounding circumstances, including such matters as the planning and control of the actions under examination.[97]

It found also that there was a continuing violation of Article 2 on account of the failure of the authorities of the respondent State to conduct an effective investigation.[98]

Commentators are divided as to the adequacy of such an 'ivory tower approach' which ignores IHL, or does not take it explicitly into account, in contexts of unacknowledged non-international armed conflicts. Some consider this approach positive. For example, W. Abresch states: 'the ECtHR has begun to develop an approach that may prove both better protective of victims and more politically viable than that of humanitarian law'.[99] Such an application of the rules under international human rights law to situations of internal armed conflict may be seen as helping to fill the gaps and to strengthen the rules covering internal armed conflicts; particularly in cases where the respondent State refuses to admit the existence of a non-international armed conflict on its soil. Others might consider such an approach as disappointing and dangerous.[100] In fact, by doing so, the European Court of Human Rights has missed an opportunity to provide an impartial legal qualification of the situation. It has not dared to contradict the State by refusing to acknowledge the existence of a non-international armed conflict on its soil. It has also missed the opportunity to elaborate on the interplay between human rights law and IHL in the context of the use of lethal force; a domain which crucially needs clarification.

It is true that in the above-mentioned cases, the Court reached conclusions that were not at odds with IHL. In other words, although the reasoning of the Court was different from an IHL reasoning, the conclusion reached was fairly similar to what an IHL analysis would have led to. However, this might not always be the case. By ignoring IHL, the Court might reach conclusions that are problematic from an IHL perspective. This already happened in the recent *Finogenov v. Russia* case.[101] This case dealt with the Moscow theatre hostage crisis of October 2002 (also known as the 'Nord-Ost siege') in the context of the Chechen conflict.[102] In order to conduct a rescue operation after a siege of two and a half days by Chechen rebels, Russia pumped an unknown chemical gas into the building's ventilation system, which made the hostage takers as well as the hostages fall asleep. Russian forces then raided the building. All the hostage-takers were killed. Moreover, approximately 130 hostages died (out of approximately 730 hostages) because of the effects of the gas employed. If one considers that IHL applied to such a situation given that this event had a clear nexus with the Second Chechen War, then the use of a gas in this situation would have been considered unlawful under IHL, because, first, it was an indiscriminate mean of warfare, and,[103] second, because the use of chemical weapons is prohibited as such in armed conflicts (except for gas such as riot control agents when they are used for law enforcement purposes).[104] The European Court of Human Rights did not reach this conclusion. It adopted a less stringent test of necessity regarding the use of force than usual,[105] and concluded, that, although the gas was dangerous and potentially lethal, it 'was not used "indiscriminately" as it left the hostages a high chance of survival',[106] and thus did not breach Article 2 of the European Convention.[107] Even though the Court still found a violation of the right to life because Russia did not take all necessary precautions to minimize the effects of the gas on the hostages, to evacuate them quickly, to provide them with necessary medical assistance and to investigate the events,[108] its decision remains problematic. In that case, the lack of reference to IHL did not allow affording a better protection to individuals in a situation of armed conflict. Russia was of course in an extremely difficult situation and the decision to use such a gas might have been considered as a 'lesser evil'. This, however, should not have dispensed the European Court from referring to existing legal standards or to apply article 2 in light of them.

The extent to which the European Court of Human Rights will adopt a similar approach for the use of force in situations of international armed conflict remains to be seen.[109] In that regard, the pending cases relating to the 2008 armed conflict between Georgia and Russia will be of critical importance.[110]

It is to be hoped that in these cases of acknowledged international armed conflicts, the Court will take into account IHL in order to produce a convincing and appropriate case law. Taking into account IHL in such cases is not only crucial in order to maintain the credibility of the European system of protection of human rights but also to ensure the consistency of the international legal system as a whole. As aptly highlighted by the Court itself in its admissibility decision in the *Georgia v. Russia* case when addressing the interplay between human rights law and IHL, 'generally speaking, the Convention should so far as possible be interpreted in harmony with other rules of international law of which it forms part'.[111]

Outside of the conduct of hostilities, the Court already referred to IHL as a tool of interpretation in order to corroborate its analysis of article 2 of the European Convention on Human Rights in the context of an international armed conflict.[112] For example, in the *Varnava v. Turkey* case, dealing with the disappearance of Cypriot combatants following the 1974 international armed conflict between Turkey and Cyprus, the Court held: 'Article 2 must be interpreted in so far as possible in light of the general principles of international law, including the rules of international human-itarian law which play an indispensable and universally-accepted role in mitigating the savagery and inhumanity of armed conflict'.[113] On this basis, the Court held that in a zone of international armed conflict, States are under an obligation to protect the lives of those not, or no longer, engaged in hostilities. They must provide medical assistance to the wounded, collect the dead, and provide information about their identity and fate, or allow humanitarian organizations such as the ICRC to do so.[114] The Court then concluded that, by virtue of article 2 of the European Convention, Turkey had a continuing obligation to account for, and thus investigate, the whereabouts and fate of the missing who disappeared in life-threatening circumstances where the conduct of military operations was accompanied by widespread arrests and killings.[115] This case seems to indicate a greater readiness of the Court to refer to IHL in situations related to acknowledged international armed conflicts than in cases of unacknowledged non-international armed conflicts.

In the recent *Al Jedda v. The United Kingdom* case dealing with, this time, the right to liberty regarding the internment of persons in the context of the United Kingdom's occupation of Iraq and its aftermath, the Court took also IHL into account but adopted a different approach than in the *Varnava* case.[116] Instead of building upon IHL, it contradicted it.

In fact, the Court considered that internments by the United Kingdom in Iraq constituted a violation of article 5 of the European Convention on Human Rights, since the United Kingdom did not enter a derogation to the right to liberty, which does not admit administrative detention.[117] Even though the Court acknowledged that IHL allows for the internment of civilians for 'imperative reasons of security', it considered that this would not displace the obligations derived from article 5 of the European Convention since IHL did not 'oblige' the Occupying Power to intern people for imperative reasons of security. According to the Court, internment is merely allowed by

IHL as a 'measure of last resort'.[118] This reasoning is, however, flawed, since, as demonstrated by the International Law Commission in its study on the fragmentation of international law, a conflict between two rules may exist even if there is no opposition between them.[119] The real question the Court should have answered was whether, in that case, the IHL rule constitutes a *lex specialis*. The answer to this question should have been 'yes': IHL does derogate from article 5 of the European Convention on Human Rights (at least in the context of international armed conflicts) in so far as it allows internment because of the specific circumstances of the armed conflict; a practice which would otherwise be prohibited unless Contracting States entered a derogation.[120]

It can therefore be said that, even if the Court looked at IHL in the *Al Jedda* case, it still adopted a kind of 'ivory tower approach' because it refrained from acknowledging that IHL may, in certain circumstances, allow practices which are in conflict with the European Convention on Human Rights.

Finally, the cases where the Court seemed the most willing to take into account IHL are cases dealing with the principle of legality and where the Court had to decide whether the Defending States had violated the principle *nullum crimen sine lege* by prosecuting the applicants for international crimes.[121] The references to IHL in the context of article 7 of the European Convention on Human Rights are, however, particular in the sense that this article allows somehow an indirect application of IHL. In fact, in order to determine whether this article had been violated in the above-mentioned cases, the Court had necessarily to examine whether the acts/omissions committed amounted to international crimes as defined by IHL treaty and customary rules at the time.

In brief, although the European Court of Human Rights has finally admitted that it can refer to IHL, it still adopts a precautionary approach. In matters relating to Turkish and Russian internal armed conflicts (which were not recognized by the States concerned), the Court does not explicitly refer to IHL.

5. CONCLUDING REMARKS

This availability of human rights treaty bodies which may be seized in respect of violations committed during armed conflicts is certainly important, for, unlike the situation under humanitarian law, these do not depend on the case-by-case consent of the State party, and a decision rendered by such bodies incites or requires States to change their internal system in order to conform to their obligations. Moreover, their importance as remedies is enhanced in the face of the reluctance of and limitations on States to pursue grave breaches within domestic courts, and the notable lack of success of IHL-specific mechanisms – the International Fact-Finding Commission, created pursuant to Article 90 of Additional Protocol I to facilitate respect for IHL has never been seized and fact-finding bodies such as the ones established following on the Israeli military operations against Lebanon and Gaza have been established on an *ad hoc* and disparate basis through, for example, the United Nations and human rights bodies. Moreover, apart from the ICC, international criminal tribunals have so far been context specific.

Human rights treaty bodies, as has been seen, have brought different answers to the question of whether and in what manner human rights law applies in armed conflict situations, and whether and how to turn to IHL as *lex specialis* applied as an exclusionary or interpretative principle. It is undisputed that in so doing they have contributed to the evolution of IHL more in keeping with contemporary mores.

But there are obvious problems in the turn to human rights mechanisms, for human rights bodies move IHL along specific paths within the framework of their constituent instruments and their respective jurisdictions. As R. Provost has pointed out there is a risk of fragmentation and cultural relativization of a body of law that has so far been at least promoted as universal.[122]

Moreover, human rights bodies do not provide the only input into IHL. While not a human rights court, the ICJ, as has been seen, has been solicited in a growing number of cases involving both serious violations of human rights and of humanitarian law such as the *Wall* Opinion and the *DRC v. Uganda* case, thus providing its own version of the articulation between international human rights law and IHL. The links between IHL, international peace and security and international criminal law have also led to new input into IHL. The Security Council has in 'legislative' mode, contributed in its resolutions to the development of substantive issues relating to protection of individuals in armed conflicts (see e.g. Security Council resolution 1820 on violence against women and children in armed conflict).

The international criminal tribunals, all linked in their establishment with international peace and security, have likewise made a major input into IHL, redefining its content through their Statutes and contributing to its substantive development, as for example blurring the lines between international and internal armed conflicts.

As T. Meron observes in connection with the applicability of human rights law in armed conflict situations, 'we are talking of areas of law which are subject to very rapid development and evolution. There are certain things which at the beginning might appear to be progressive development, and yet very quickly after that, events take place which grant *lex lata* character to this development'.[123]

While norm conflicts may and certainly will arise, with States confronted with the problem of implementation of competing obligations, this is left to be ironed out in practice within the framework of particular regimes. Nevertheless, the question of the complementarity of human rights and humanitarian law should be examined within a new conceptual legal framework which has seen the juxtaposition of community interests alongside interstate interests, emphasizing the need for teleological and systemic approaches to treaty interpretation.

Rules do not allow of just one result, and in most cases the judge has to choose between alternative meanings or rival interpretations. In relation to the right to life, as Judge R. Higgins in the *Nuclear Weapons* Advisory Opinion points out, 'the judicial lodestar ... in resolving claimed tensions between competing norms must be those values that international law seeks to promote and protect. In the present case, it is the physical survival of peoples that we must have constantly in view'.[124]

NOTES

* Vera Gowlland-Debbas is Emeritus Professor of Public International Law, Graduate Institute of International and Development Studies, Geneva; Gloria Gaggioli is Doctor in International Law and Researcher at the University of Geneva, law faculty. This contribution is in part drawn from Vera Gowlland-Debbas, 'The Relationship between IHL and Human Rights Law: the Right to Life', in C. Tomuschat, E. Lagrange and S. Oeter (eds), *The Right to Life* (Leiden: Martinus Nijhoff Publishers, 2010), 123–150.

1. There is a voluminous literature which we will not cite here, but for the 'pioneers', see D. Schindler, 'Human Rights and Humanitarian Law', *American University Law Review* 31 (1981–1982): 935–977; L. Doswald-Beck and S. Vité, 'International Humanitarian Law and Human Rights Law', *International Review of the Red Cross* 293 (1993): 94–119; F. Hampson, 'Using International Human Rights Machinery to Enforce the International Law of Armed Conflicts', *Revue de droit militaire et de droit de la guerre* 31 (1992): 119–142. See also, generally, R. Provost, *International Human Rights and Humanitarian Law* (Cambridge: Cambridge University Press, 2002), 350; H.-J. Heintze, 'On the Relationship between Human Rights Law Protection and International Humanitarian Law', *International Review of the Red Cross* 86, No. 856 (2004): 789–813; G. Gaggioli, 'L'influence mutuelle entre les droits de l'homme et le droit international humanitaire à la lumière du droit à la vie', (Paris: Pedone, forthcoming); N. Quénivet et al. (ed.), *International Law and Armed Conflict: Challenges in the 21st Century* (The Hague: TMC Asser Press, 2010), 434; R. Arnold and N. Quévinet (eds), *International Humanitarian Law and Human Rights Law* (Leiden and Boston: Martinus Nijhoff, 2008), 596; F.F. Martin, S.J. Schnably, R. Wilson, J. Simon and M. Tushnet, *International Human Rights and Humanitarian Law: Treaties, Cases and Analysis* (Cambridge: Cambridge University Press, 2006), 990; O. Ben Naftali (ed.), *International Humanitarian Law and International Human Rights Law*, Collected courses of the Academy of European Law, XIX: 1 (Oxford: Oxford University Press, 2011), 424; O. Ben Naftali (ed.), *International Humanitarian Law and International Human Rights Law: pas de deux* (Oxford: Oxford University Press, 2011), 388.

2. See, in this volume, the contribution of R. Kolb entitled 'Human Rights Law and International Humanitarian Law between 1945 and the Aftermath of the Teheran Conference of 1968' as well as the contribution of Maya Hertig Randall entitled 'The History of International Human Rights Law'.

3. T. Meron, 'Human Rights in Time of Peace and in Time of Armed Strife: Selected Problems', in T. Buergenthal (ed.), *Contemporary Issues in International Law: Essays in Honor of Louis B. Sohn* (Kehl, Strasbourg, Arlington: N.P. Engel, 1984), 6.

4. See also Article 4 which offers certain fundamental guarantees and Article 13(2) of Additional Protocol II to the Geneva Conventions of 12 August 1949 relating to the Protection of Victims of Non-International Armed Conflicts.

5. Paradoxical as it may sound, the right to life has also been incorporated in a law whose objective has been described by G. Draper as: 'How to kill your fellow human beings in a nice way'. See G.I.A.D. Draper, 'The Relationship between the Human Rights Regime and the Law of Armed Conflict', *Israeli Yearbook of Human Rights* 1 (1971): 191–207, reprinted in *Reflections on Law and Armed Conflicts: The Selected Works on the Laws of War by the Late Professor Colonel G.I.A.D. Draper, OBE*, eds M.A. Meyer and H. McCoubrey (Hague, Boston, London: Kluwer Law International, 1998), 128.

6. *Case Concerning Military and Paramilitary Activities in and against Nicaragua* (Nicaragua v. United States), Merits, Judgment, I.C.J. Reports 1986, 113–114, 218.

7. See, e.g., the *Travaux préparatoires of the 1977 Additional Protocols*, 324 (ICRC), 326 (Mexico), 329 (Ukrainian Soviet Socialist Republic), 330 (Federal Republic of Germany).

8. See, e.g., Y. Sandoz et al. (ed.), *Commentary on the Additional Protocols of 8 June 1977 to the Geneva Conventions of 12 August 1949* (Geneva: ICRC and Martinus Nijhoff, 1987), Commentary of Article 4 APII (4515, 4541) and of Article 6 APII (4597, 4604, 4606–4609, 4613, 4614); M. Bothe et al., *New Rules for Victims of Armed Conflicts* (The Hague, Boston, London: Martinus Nijhoff, 1982), 635–636 (Protocol II, Part II, Introduction).

9. R. Provost, 'The International Committee of the Red Widget? The Diversity Debate and International Humanitarian Law', *Israel Law Review* 40 (2007): 633 *et seq.*

10. Typically, the Universal Declaration of Human Rights does not refer to the concept of war or armed conflict and its drafters did not seem to have other situations than peace in mind when conceiving the declaration. See H. Meyrowitz, 'Le droit de la guerre et les droits de l'homme', *Revue de droit public et de la science politique en France et à l'étranger* 5 (1972): 1082: 'Parce que les auteurs de la déclaration ont considéré le respect des droits de l'homme à l'intérieur de chaque Etat comme une

condition capitale de la sauvegarde de la paix, c'est dans le seul cadre de la paix qu'ils ont envisagé ces droits et qu'ils se sont attachés à les définir'. See also M. El Kouhene, *Les garanties fondamentales de la personne en droit humanitaire et droits de l'homme* (Dordrecht, Boston and Lancaster: Martinus Nijhoff, 1986), 8; K.J. Partsch, 'Human Rights and Humanitarian Law', in *Encyclopedia of Public International Law*, Volume 8 (Amsterdam, New York and Oxford: North-Holland Publishing Company, 1989), 292; R. Kolb, *Ius in bello: Le droit international des conflits armés. Précis* (Basel, Geneva and Munich: Helbing and Lichtenhahn; Brussels: Bruylant, 2003), 551.

11. Paragraphs 506–507. Available at http://www.state.gov/j/drl/rls/179781.htm (accessed 15 February 2012).

12. See V. Gowlland-Debbas, 'The Right to Life and Genocide: the Court and an International Public Policy', in *International Law, the International Court of Justice and Nuclear Weapons*, eds P. Sands and L. Boisson de Chazournes (Cambridge: Cambridge University Press, 1999), 315–337. See also V. Gowlland-Debbas, 'Human Rights and Humanitarian Law: Are There Some Individuals Bereft of all Legal Protection? The Relevance of Paragraph 25 of the I.C.J.'s Advisory Opinion on Nuclear Weapons', *ASIL Proceedings* 98 (2004): 358–363.

13. *Legality of the Threat or Use of Nuclear Weapons*, Advisory Opinion, I.C.J. Reports 1996, 240, 25. Several countries had advanced similar arguments in their written submissions to the Court – the United States, the Russian Federation and France had tacitly accepted the application of human rights law in armed conflict in their written submissions of June 1995, pages 43, 9 and 38, respectively, available at www.icj-cij.org (accessed 15 February 2012).

14. *Application of the Convention on the Prevention and Punishment of the Crime of Genocide* (Bosnia and Herzegovina v. Yugoslavia (Serbia and Montenegro)), Provisional Measures, Order of 8 April 1993, I.C.J. Reports (1993), 22, 45, and in its Judgment on Preliminary Objections, 11 July 1996, I.C.J. Reports (1996), 615, 31.

15. Ibid., I.C.J. Reports (1996), 31. While the Court in the *Nuclear Weapons* Advisory Opinion, rejected the relevance of genocide in relation to nuclear weapons on the grounds that such use would have to entail an element of intent and be directed against one of the groups falling under Article II (*supra* note 13, at 240, 26), Judge Weeramantry had declared in his Dissenting Opinion that '[I]f the killing of human beings, in numbers ranging from a million to a billion, does not fall within the definition of genocide, one may well ask what will', ibid., 517.

16. *Corfu Channel Case* (United Kingdom of Great Britain and Northern Ireland v. Albania), Judgment, I.C.J. Reports (1949), 22; *Nicaragua Case*, *supra* note 6, at 112, 215 and 218; see also P. Tavernier, 'Sécurité internationale, droit international humanitaire et droits de l'homme: quelques réflexions sur le rôle des juridictions internationales', in *La sécurité internationale entre rupture et continuité. Mélanges en l'honneur de professeur Jean-François Guildhaudis* (Bruxelles: Bruylant, 2007), 545–546: 'viser tant le droit humanitaire que les droits de l'homme par delà le droit humanitaire: – on part des préoccupations de sécurité pour arriver aux principes généraux du droit humanitaire en passant par les considérations élémentaires d'humanité'.

17. As stated in *The effect of armed conflict on treaties: an examination of practice and doctrine*, Memorandum by the Secretariat, International Law Commission, UN Doc. A/CN.4/550, 1 February 2005, 23, 32.

18. *Legal Consequences of the Construction of a Wall in the Occupied Palestinian Territory*, Advisory Opinion, I.C.J. Reports (2004), 178, 106.

19. *Case Concerning Armed Activities on the Territory of the Congo* (Democratic Republic of Congo v. Uganda), Judgment, I.C.J. Reports (2005), 168 *et seq.*

20. In this respect, the views of the Human Rights Committee, the European Court of Human Rights and the Inter-American Commission coincide (see respectively, as non-exhaustive examples: *Lilian Celiberti de Casariego v. Uruguay*, HRC, 29 July 1981 (UN Doc. CCPR/C/13/D/56/1979), paras10.2–10.3; *Loizidou v. Turkey*, ECtHR, Application No. 15318/89, Preliminary Objections, Judgment of 23 March 1995, paras 61–64; *Coard et al. v. United States*, IACommHR, Case 10.951, Report No. 109/99, 29 September 1999, 37). Specifically in the case of the detainees at Guantanamo Bay, see, *inter alia*, the communication of 12 March 2002 addressed by the Inter-American Commission on Human Rights to the United States Government, 'Pertinent Parts of Decision on the Request for Precautionary Measures'. For a narrow view of extraterritoriality, however, see *Al Skeini v. Secretary of State for Defence*, House of Lords, Judgment of 13 June 2007, [2007] UKHL 26, [2007] 3 All E.R. 865. In *Ilascu and others v. Moldova and Russia*, ECtHR, Application No. 48787/99, Judgment of 8 July 2004, paras 392–394, the ECtHR found in fact that Russia was responsible for human rights violations in the separatist territory despite the fact that its presence fell short of occupation. In the

Al-Saadoon case, the ECtHR admitted that persons detained by the UK in Iraq were under the jurisdiction of the UK. See *Al-Saadoon and Mufdhi v. United Kingdom*, ECtHR, Application No. 61498/08, Decision on Admissibility, 30 June 2009.

21. On these differences of views and conflicting jurisprudence, see, in this volume, the chapter of R. Goldman entitled 'Extraterritorial Application of the Human Rights to Life and Personal Liberty, Including *Habeas Corpus*, During Situations of Armed Conflict'.

22. *Bankovic v. Belgium and 16 Other Contracting States*, ECtHR, Application No. 52207/99, Grand Chamber, Decision on Admissibility, 12 December 2001, paras 67 *et seq.*

23. This has been the position of the Human Rights Committee in the case of the Occupied Palestinian Territory (UN Doc. CCPR/C/79/Add.93, 18 August 1998, para. 10; UN Doc. CCPR/CO/78/ISR, 21 August 2003, para. 11), and the ECtHR in regard to Turkey's effective control over Northern Cyprus; see *Loizidou, supra* note 20. D. McGoldrick, who points out that *Bankovic* should be read in the light of the political conundrum facing the Court, does not consider that the term 'legal space' used by the Court as limiting the extraterritorial ambit of the ECHR to the territories of signatory States was intended to have general application; see D. McGoldrick, 'Extraterritorial Application of the International Covenant on Civil and Political Rights', in V.F. Coomans and M.T. Kamminga (eds), *Extraterritorial Application of Human Rights Treaties* (Antwerp and Oxford: Intersentia, 2004), 71. See also R. Wilde, 'The "Legal Space" or "Espace Juridique" of the European Convention on Human Rights: Is it Relevant to Extraterritorial State Action?', *European Human Rights Law Review* 2 (2005): 115–124. The Inter-American Commission has also considered admissible a petition regarding the death of four persons belonging to an anti-Castro organization caused by the shooting down by a Cuban aircraft of two civilian aircraft in international space because the victims were considered to be subject to the authority and control of Cuban agents; *Armando Alejandre Jr. and others v. Republic of Cuba ('Brothers to the Rescue')*, IACommHR, Case 11.589, Report No. 86/99, 29 September 1999, quoted in C. Cerna, 'Extraterritorial Application of the Human Rights Instruments of the Inter-American System', in V.F. Coomans and M.T. Kamminga (eds), *Extraterritorial Application of Human Rights Treaties* (Antwerp and Oxford: Intersentia, 2004), 156–158.

24. E.g., *Lilian Celiberti de Casariego, supra* note 20; *Lopez Burgos v. Uruguay*, HRC, 29 July 1981 (UN Doc. CCPR/C/13/D/52/1979); *Öcalan v. Turkey*, ECtHR, Application No. 46221/99, Judgment of 12 May 2005. In *Issa and others v. Turkey*, ECtHR, Application No. 31821/96, Judgment of 16 November 2004, 71, the ECtHR accepted that a State could be held accountable for a violation of Convention rights extraterritorially if the complainants were found to be under the state's authority and control through its agents operating in the other state. In the *Al-Saadoon* case, the ECtHR admitted that persons detained by the UK in Iraq were under the jurisdiction of the UK. See *Al-Saadoon and Mufdhi, supra* note 20.

25. *Al Skeini v. United Kingdom*, ECtHR, Application No. 55721/07, Judgment of 7 July 2011.

26. Ibid., 37–38.

27. *Wall, supra* note 18, at 178–181, 107–113. See also: *Application of the International Convention on the Elimination of All Forms of Racial Discrimination* (Georgia v. Russian Federation), Provisional Measures, I.C.J. Reports 2008, at 353, para. 109, in which the Court found that the provisions of the ICERD 'generally appear to apply, like other provisions of instruments of that nature, to the actions of a State party *when it acts beyond its territory*' (emphasis added).

28. R. Kolb, 'Aspects historiques de la relation entre le droit international humanitaire et les droits de l'homme', *Canadian Yearbook of International Law* 37 (1999), at 78.

29. See S. Vité, 'Typology of Armed Conflicts in International Humanitarian Law: Legal Concepts and Actual Situations', *International Review of the Red Cross* 91, No. 873 (2009): 88. See also *Hamdan v. Rumsfeld*, US Supreme Court, 29 June 2006 (548 U.S. 557).

30. On the applicability of IHL for non-international armed conflicts to such situations, see *Hamdan v. Rumsfeld*, US Supreme Court, 29 June 2006 (548 U.S. 557). See also Vité, *supra* note 29, at 88–93. *Contra*: R.S. Schöndorf, 'Extra-State Armed Conflicts : Is there a Need for a New Legal Regime?', *New York University Journal of International Law and Politics* 37, No.1 (2004):61–75; G.S. Corn, 'Hamdan, Lebanon, and the Regulation of Armed Conflict: The Need to Recognize a Hybrid Category of Armed Conflict', *Vanderbilt Journal of Transnational Law* 40, No. 2 (2007).

31. According to Nils Melzer, targeted killings can be defined as 'the use of lethal force attributable to a subject of international law with the intent, premeditation and deliberation to kill individually selected persons who are not in the physical custody of those targeting them'. See N. Melzer, *Targeted Killing in International Law* (Oxford: Oxford University Press, 2008), at 3.

32.   'International Humanitarian Law and the Challenges of Contemporary Armed Conflicts', Document prepared by the International Committee of the Red Cross, 31st International Conference of the Red Cross and Red Crescent, Geneva, 28 November–1 December 2011, at 22 (31IC/11/5.1.2). Available at: http://www.icrc.org/eng/assets/files/red-cross-crescent-movement/31st-international-conference/31-int-conference-ihl-challenges-report-11-5-1-2-en.pdf (accessed 12 February 2012).

33.   On the issue of extraterritorial targeted killings, see: N. Melzer, *supra* note 31; N. Lubell, *Extraterritorial Use of Force against Non-State Actors* (Oxford: Oxford University Press, 2010); D. Kretzmer, 'Targeted Killing of Suspected Terrorists: Extra-Judicial Executions or Legitimate Means of Defence?', *European Journal of International Law* 16, No. 2 (2005): 171–212.

34.   See Art. 3 common to the Geneva Conventions; art. 51(3) of Additional Protocol I; art. 13(3) of APII. For the ICRC interpretation of what 'direct participation in hostilities' means under IHL, see: N. Melzer, *Interpretative Guidance on the Notion of Direct Participation in Hostilities under International Humanitarian Law* (Geneva: International Committee of the Red Cross, 2009).

35.   Concluding Observations on Israel, HRC, 21 August 2003 (UN Doc. CCPR/CO/78/ISR), 15.

36.   *The Public Committee against Torture in Israel v. The Government of Israel*, High Court of Justice of Israel, 11 December 2005: paras 26–28.

37.   Ibid., para. 39: 'On the one hand, a civilian taking a direct part in hostilities one single time, or sporadically, who later detaches himself from that activity, is a civilian who, starting from the time he detached himself from that activity, is entitled to protection from attack. He is not to be attacked for the hostilities which he committed in the past. On the other hand, a civilian who has joined a terrorist organization which has become his "home", and in the framework of his role in that organization he commits a chain of hostilities, with short periods of rest between them, loses his immunity from attack "for such time" as he is committing the chain of acts. Indeed, regarding such a civilian, the rest between hostilities is nothing other than preparation for the next hostility.'

38.   Ibid., para. 40.

39.   L. Doswald-Beck, 'The Right to Life in Armed Conflict: Does International Humanitarian Law Provide All the Answers?', *International Review of the Red Cross* 88, No.864 (2006): 896.

40.   *Prosecutor v. Dusko Tadic a.k.a 'Dule'*, ICTY, Appeals Chamber, Decision on the Defense Motion for Interlocutory Appeal on Jurisdiction, 2 October 1995 (Case No. IT-94-1AR72), para. 97.

41.   See, in this volume: G. Gaggioli, 'The Prohibition of Enforced Disappearances: a Meaningful Example of a Partial Merger between Human Rights Law and International Humanitarian Law'.

42.   Protocol to the African Charter on Human and Peoples' Rights on the Rights of Women in Africa, Maputo, 2003, Article 11; African Charter on the Rights and Welfare of the Child, Addis-Ababa, 1990, Article 22; Convention on the Rights of Persons with Disabilities, 13 December 2006, Article 11.

43.   Declaration of Minimum Humanitarian Standards, reprinted in Report of the Sub-Commission on Prevention of Discrimination and Protection of Minorities on its Forty-sixth Session, Commission on Human Rights, 51st Session, Provisional Agenda Item 19, at 4, UN Doc. E/CN.4/1995/116 (1995).

44.   A/RES/60/147, 16 December 2005.

45.   M. Sassòli, 'Le droit international humanitaire, une *lex specialis* par rapport aux droits humains?', in A. Auer, A. Flückiger and M. Hottelier (eds) *Les droits de l'homme et la constitution, Études en l'honneur du Professeur Giorgio Malinverni* (Geneva: Schulthess, 2007), 385: 'Par rapport au même problème, il ne peut pas y avoir une coutume "droits humains" et une coutume "droit humanitaire". On s'oriente toujours vers la pratique et l'*opinio juris* manifestées par rapport à des problèmes aussi similaires que possible à celui qu'on doit résoudre.' See also M. Sassòli and L. Olson, 'The Relationship Between International Humanitarian Law and Human Rights Law Where it Matters: Admissible Killing and Internment of Fighters in Non-international Armed Conflicts', *International Review of the Red Cross* 90, No. 871 (2008): 605.

46.   J.-M. Henkaerts and L. Doswald-Beck, *Customary International Humanitarian Law, Volume 1: Rules* (Cambridge: Cambridge University Press, 2005).

47.   Resolution 1991/67 of the Human Rights Commission on Kuwait; Resolution 1995/91 of the Human Rights Commission on Rwanda; Resolution 1995/89 of the Human Rights Commission on Bosnia-Herzegovina. See also the *Working paper on the relationship between human rights law and international humanitarian law* by F. Hampson and I. Salama, Human Rights Commission, 57th session, 21 June 2005 (Doc. NU E/CN.4/Sub.2/2005/14).

48.   See, among many others, Resolution S-9/1: *The grave violations of human rights in the Occupied Palestinian Territory, particularly due to the recent Israeli military attacks against the occupied Gaza Strip*, Human Rights Council, 12 January 2009 (UN Doc. A/HRC/S-9/L.1). The Human Rights Council has also been given the competence, in the context of the universal periodic review, to take

into account IHL. See Resolution 5/1: *Institution-building of the United Nations Human Rights Council*, Human Rights Council, 18 June 2007 (UN Doc. A/HRC/RES/5/1), para. 2: 'In addition to the above and given the complementary and mutually interrelated nature of international human rights law and international humanitarian law, the review shall take into account applicable international humanitarian law.'

49. See, e.g., A/RES/48/157, 20 December 1993, para. 2 on the protection of children affected by armed conflicts. See also the numerous condemnations of Israel for the IHL and HRL violations in the occupied territories. See, e.g., A/RES/2443 (XXIII) of 19 December 1968.

50. See e.g. the series of Security Council resolutions relating to the application of human rights in occupied Iraq, such as S/RES/1483, 22 May 2003. See also the thematic resolutions of the Security Council on the protection of civilians in armed conflicts: S/RES/1265, 17 September 1999, para. 7 and 8 of the Preamble, 4, 5; S/RES/1296, 19 April 2000, para. 7 of the Preamble; S/RES/1314, 11 August 2000, 5 of the Preamble.

51. Report of the Secretary-General to the Security Council on the Protection of Civilians in Armed Conflict, UN Doc. S/1999/957, 8 September 1999, para. 36.

52. See, e.g., W. Kälin, Special Rapporteur, *Report on the situation of human rights in Kuwait under Iraqi occupation*, UN Doc. E/CN.4/1992/26, 16 January 1992.

53. Resolution S-9/1: *The grave violations of human rights in the Occupied Palestinian Territory, particularly due to the recent Israeli military attacks against the occupied Gaza Strip*, Human Rights Council, 12 January 2009 (UN Doc. A/HRC/S-9/L.1), preamble.

54. P. Alston, J. Morgan-Foster and W. Abresch, 'The Competence of the UN Human Rights Council and its Special Procedures in Relation to Armed Conflicts: Extrajudicial Executions in the "War on Terror"', *EJIL* 19 (2008): 183–209.

55. See, e.g., General Comment No. 31: *Nature of the General Legal Obligation Imposed on States Parties to the Covenant*, HRC, 26 May 2004 (UN Doc. CCPR/C/21/Rev.1/Add.13), para. 11. See also below the section entitled 'The approach of human rights bodies towards international humanitarian law: a comparison' (section 4). See also in this volume, Part IV on monitoring mechanisms.

56. Resolution 7 of the Council of Delegates, Geneva, 1999: 'recognising that human rights law is complementary to international humanitarian law in certain action oriented work in the field'; Resolution 3 of the *30th International Conference of the Red Cross and Red Crescent*, Geneva, 26–30 November 2007, preamble: '*underlining*, in this regard, that the protection offered by human rights law does not cease in the event of armed conflict, save through the effect of provisions for derogation, *recalling* that while some rights may be exclusively matters of international humanitarian law, others may be exclusively matters of human rights law and yet others may be matters of both these branches of international law, and *emphasizing* that human rights law, international humanitarian law and refugee law provide protection to victims of armed conflict, within their respective spheres of application'.

57. *Nuclear Weapons*, *supra* note 13, at 25. The French text is even more explicit in this respect: 'c'est *uniquement* au regard du droit applicable dans les conflits armés, et non au regard des dispositions du pacte lui-même, que l'on pourra dire si tel cas de décès provoqué par l'emploi d'un certain type d'armes au cours d'un conflit armé doit être considéré comme une privation arbitraire de la vie contraire à l'article 6 du pacte' (emphasis added).

58. *Aegean Sea Continental Shelf* (Greece v. Turkey), Judgment, I.C.J. Reports (1978), 32, 77, with reference to the concept of 'territorial status'; see also *Legal Consequences for States of the Continued Presence of South Africa in Namibia (South West Africa) notwithstanding Security Council resolution 276 (1970)*, Advisory Opinion, I.C.J. Reports (1971), 31, 53, in regard to the concept of 'sacred trust'.

59. H. Waldock, 'The Evolution of Human Rights Concepts and the Application of the European Convention on Human Rights', in *Mélanges offerts à Paul Reuter. Le droit international: unité et diversité*, (Paris: Pedone, 1981), 535; J.G. Merrills, *The Development of International Law by the European Court of Human Rights* (Manchester: Manchester University Press, 1995), 78–81. For examples of the ECtHR case-law where the Court adopts a dynamic interpretation of some human rights stating that the Convention is a living instrument which must be interpreted in the light of present-day conditions, see: *Tyrer v. The United Kingdom*, ECtHR, Application No. 5856/72, Judgment of 25 April 1978, para. 31; *Loizidou v. Turkey*, ECtHR, Application No. 15318/89, Judgment (Preliminary Objections) of 23 March 1995, para. 71; *Selmouni v. Turkey*, ECtHR, Application No. 25803/94, Judgment of 28 July 1999, para. 101; *Öcalan v. Turkey*, ECtHR, Application No. 46221/99, Judgment of 12 May 2005, para. 163; *Demir and Baykara v. Turkey*, ECtHR, Application No.

34503/97, Judgment of 12 November 2008, para. 146; *Rantsev v. Cyprus and Russia*, ECtHR, Application No. 25965/04, Judgment of 7 January 2010, para. 277.

60. See the link which was made between the right to life and the corresponding duty of states to prevent war, genocide and other forms of mass violence by the Human Rights Committee in its General Comment No. 6: *Right to Life* (article 6), 30 April 1982 (UN Doc. HRI/GEN/1/Rev.8) and that between the right to life and nuclear weapons in its General Comment No.14: *Nuclear Weapons and the Right to Life (article 6)*, HRC, 9 November 1984 (Doc. NU HRI/GEN/1/Rev.8).

61. L. Oppenheim, Sir R. Jennings and Sir A. Watts (eds), *Oppenheim's International Law. Volume 1: Peace*, 9th edition (Oxford: Oxford University Press, 2008), parts 2–4, 1270 and 1280. For an example of the I.C.J.'s resort to the maxim, see *Case Concerning Right of Passage over Indian Territory Case* (Portugal v. India), (Merits), Judgment, I.C.J. Reports (1960), 44. It is interesting to note that the 1969 Vienna Convention on the Law of Treaties does not retain this principle.

62. For example, the Optional Protocol on the Convention on the Rights of the Child mentioned earlier, and which raises the age of members of armed forces who can directly participate in hostilities to 18 years old, can be considered as a *lex posterior* which prevails over Additional Protocol I (where the age foreseen is 15 years old) for States having ratified both of these treaties.

63. On the potential relevance of the most favourable to the individual rule, see, in this book, the chapter of A.-L. Graf-Brugère, 'A *Lex Favorabilis*? Resolving Norm Conflicts between Human Rights Law and Humanitarian Law'.

64. See H.H.G. Post, 'Some Curiosities in the Sources of the Law of Armed Conflict', in L.A.N.M. Barnhoorn and K.C. Wellens (eds) *Diversity in Secondary Rules and the Unity of International Law* (The Hague, Boston and London: Martinus Nijhoff, 1995), 90–91.

65. See A. Lindroos, 'Addressing Norm Conflicts in a Fragmented Legal System: The Doctrine of *Lex Specialis*', *Nordic Journal of International Law* 74, No 1 (2005): 44. See also G. Hafner, 'Risks Ensuing from Fragmentation of International Law', in *Report of the International Law Commission*, annex 321, U.N. GAOR, 55th Sess., Supp. N° 10, U.N. Doc. A/55/10 (Sept. 27, 2000): 'Whereas conflicts of primary norms could perhaps be attempted to be solved by recourse to the general secondary norms of *lex specialis* and *lex posterior*, this remedy is not always helpful in dealing with subsystems: each subsystem always claims for itself to be the *lex specialis* and applies its own rules irrespective of the other subsystem.'

66. See G. Gaggioli and R. Kolb, 'A Right to Life in Armed Conflicts? The Contribution of the European Court of Human Rights', *Israel Yearbook on Human Rights* 37 (2007): 124; Sassòli, *supra* note 45, at 389ff.

67. See Gaggioli, *supra* note 1.

68. *Wall*, *supra* note 18, at 106 (emphasis added).

69. Alston, Morgan-Foster and Abresch, *supra* note 54, at 193–194.

70. *Armed Activities on the Territory of the Congo*, *supra* note 19, at 216, in which the Court found that both massive human rights violations and grave breaches of international humanitarian law had been committed by Ugandan military forces on the territory of the DRC.

71. It is also interesting to note that in the latter case, the I.C.J. no longer referred to the *lex specialis* character of IHL.

72. *Kunarac*, ICTY, Judgment, 22 February 2001 (Case No. IT.96.23.T), paras 467 and 471, cited in A. Orakhelashvili, 'The Interaction between Human Rights and Humanitarian Law: Fragmentation, Conflict, Parallelism, or Convergence?', *EJIL* 19 (2008): 164.

73. *Fragmentation of International Law: Difficulties Arising from the Diversification and Expansion of International Law*, Report of the Study Group of the International Law Commission finalized by Martti Koskenniemi, UN Doc. A/CN.4/L.682, 13 April 2006, at 59, §107.

74. Vienna Convention on the Law of Treaties, Vienna, 1969.

75. Ibid., at 244, 480. See, generally, C. McLachlan, 'The Principle of Systemic Integration and Article 31(3)(c) of the Vienna Convention', *ICLQ* 54 (2005): 279–320; A.E. Cassimatis, 'International Humanitarian Law, International Human Rights Law, and Fragmentation of International Law', *ICLQ* 56 (2007): 623–640.

76. For example, WTO, European Communities – *Measures Affecting the Approval and Marketing of Biotech Products, Reports of the Panel*, 29 September 2006 (WT/DS291/R, WT/DS292/R WT/DS 293/R), and *Oil Platforms* (Iran v. United States), Judgement, I.C.J. Reports 2003.

77. *Banković and others v. Belgium and 16 other contracting States*, ECtHR, Decision on admissibility, Application No. 52207/99, 12 December 2001, para. 57: '… Article 31 § 3 (c) [of the Vienna Convention on the Law of Treaties] indicates that account is to be taken of "any relevant rules of

international law applicable in the relations between the parties". More generally, the Court recalls that the principles underlying the Convention cannot be interpreted and applied in a vacuum. The Court must also take into account any relevant rules of international law... The Convention should be interpreted as far as possible in harmony with other principles of international law of which it forms part.' See also *Loizidou v. Turkey*, ECtHR, Application No. 15318/89, Judgment of 18 December 1996, para. 43: 'the principles underlying the Convention cannot be interpreted and applied in a vacuum. Mindful of the Convention's special character as a human rights treaty, it must also take into account any relevant rules of international law when deciding on disputes concerning its jurisdiction pursuant to Article 49 of the Convention'.

78. See *Coard et al., supra* note 20, at 40; *Loizidou, supra* note 77, para. 43.

79. General Comment No. 29: *States of Emergency (Article 4)*, HRC, 31 August 2001 (UN Doc. CCPR/C/21/Rev.1/Add.11), 9–10.

80. *Las Palmeras v. Colombia*, IACommHR, Case 11.237, Report No. 10/98, 20 February 1998, para. 29.

81. *Coard et al., supra* note 20, at 57.

82. *Juan Carlos Abella v. Argentina* (*La Tablada* case), IACommHR, Case 11.137, Report No. 55/97, 18 November 1997, paras 161–177.

83. Ibid., para. 160. For detailed analysis, see F. Martin, 'Application du droit international humanitaire par la Cour interaméricaine des droits de l'homme', *International Review of the Red Cross* 83, no. 844 (2001): 1037–1066; Provost, *supra* note 9, at 334–336.

84. E.J. Buis, 'The Implementation of International Humanitarian Law by Human Rights Courts: The Example of the Inter-American Human Rights System', in R. Arnold and N. Quénivet (eds), *International Humanitarian Law and Human Rights Law: Towards A New Merger in International Law* (Leiden and Boston: Martinus Nijhoff, 2008), 282–283.

85. *La Tablada* case, *supra* note 82, at 164; Buis, *supra* note 84, at 278–279.

86. *Las Palmeras v. Colombia*, IACtHR, Preliminary Objections, Judgment of 4 February 2000, para. 28.

87. On the difference between interpreting and applying IHL, see: *Bámaca-Velásquez v. Guatemala*, IACtHR, Merits, Judgment of 25 November 2000, para. 208: 'Although the Court lacks competence to declare that a State is internationally responsible for the violation of international treaties that do not grant it such competence, it can observe that certain acts or omissions that violate human rights, pursuant to the treaties that they do have competence to apply, also violate other international instruments for the protection of the individual, such as the 1949 Geneva Conventions and, in particular, common Article 3.'

88. *Las Palmeras v. Colombia*, IACtHR, Preliminary Objections, Judgment of 4 February 2000, paras 33–34.

89. *Ituango Massacres v. Colombia*, IACtHR, Merits, Reparations and Costs, Judgment of 1 July 2006, paras 179–183. See also: *Bámaca-Velásquez v. Guatemala*, IACtHR, Merits, Judgment of 25 November 2000, para. 207; *Mapiripán Massacre v. Columbia*, IACtHR, Merits, Reparations and Costs, Judgment of 15 September 2005, para. 114.

90. Gaggioli and Kolb, supra note 66, at 124.

91. *Ergi v. Turkey*, ECtHR, Application No. 23818/94, Judgment of 28 July 1998, para. 79; see W. Abresch, 'A Human Rights Law of Internal Armed Conflict: The European Court of Human Rights in Chechnya', *EJIL* 16 (2005): 746.

92. *Isayeva v. Russia*, ECtHR, Application No. 57950/00, Judgment of 24 February 2005, para. 91.

93. *Khashiyev and Akayeva v. Russia*, ECtHR, Application Nos 57942/00 and 57945/00, Judgment of 24 February 2005; *Isayeva v. Russia, supra* note 92; *Isayeva, Yusupova and Bazayeva v. Russia*, ECtHR, Application Nos 57947/00, 57948/00 and 57949/00, Judgment of 24 February 2005. See also: *Abuyeva v. Russia*, ECtHR, Application No 27065/05, Judgment of 2 December 2010; *Esmukhambetov and others v. Russia*, ECtHR, Application No 23445/03, Judgment of 29 March 2011; *Khamzayev and others v. Russia*, ECtHR, Application No 1503/02 , Judgment of 3 May 2011; *Kerimova v. Russia*, ECtHR, Application No 17170/04, Judgment of 3 May 2011.

94. *Isayeva and others, supra* note 93, at 169. Abresch, *supra* note 91, at 742–743.

95. Article 51(5)(b), Article 57(2)(a) (iii) and Article 57(b) of Additional Protocol I to the Geneva Conventions.

96. *Isayeva v. Russia, supra* note 92, para. 173; *Isayeva and others, supra* note 93, 169.

97. *McCann and others v. United Kingdom*, ECtHR, Application No 18984/91, Judgment of 27 September 1995, paras 148–150. The ECtHR has repeated this passage in subsequent cases concerning armed conflicts; see, e.g., *Ergi, supra* note 91, at 79, *Isayeva and others, supra* note 93, para. 69, *Isayeva v. Russia, supra* note 92, at 173; Abresch, *supra* note 91, at 752, 762–764. On the precautionary

principle, see G. Gaggioli and R. Kolb, 'L'apport de la Cour européenne des droits de l'homme au droit international humanitaire en matière de droit à la vie', *Revue suisse de droit international et européen* No.1 (2007): 3; N. Quénivet, 'The Right to Life in International Humanitarian Law and Human Rights Law', in R. Arnold and N. Quénivet (eds) *International Humanitarian Law and Human Rights Law: Towards A New Merger in International Law* (Leiden, Boston: Martinus Nijhoff, 2008), 344–351.

98. For example, *Isayeva and others*, *supra* note 93, para. 224.
99. Abresch, *supra* note 91, at 767.
100. G. Gaggioli, *supra* note 1; A. Gioia, 'The Role of the European Court of Human Rights in Monitoring Compliance with Humanitarian Law in Armed Conflict', in O. Ben-Naftali (ed.), *International Humanitarian Law and International Human Rights Law* (Oxford: Oxford University Press, 2011), at 217–218: 'In my opinion, resort to IHL would undoubtedly help in this respect and would, indeed, contribute to giving greater coherence to international law, thus avoiding its future fragmentation.'
101. *Finogenov v. Russia*, ECtHR, Application Nos. 18299/03 and 27311/03, Judgment of 20 December 2011.
102. Around 40 to 50 armed rebel Chechens claiming allegiance to the 'Islamist militant separatist movement in Chechnya' took 850 hostages in the Dubrovka Theatre on 23 October 2002. They demanded the withdrawal of Russian forces from Chechnya and an end to the Second Chechen War.
103. J.-M. Henckaerts and L. Doswald-Beck, *Customary International Humanitarian Law* (Cambridge: Cambridge University Press, 2009), Rule 71.
104. Ibid., Rule 74. See also Convention on the prohibition of the development, production, stockpiling and use of chemical weapons and on their destruction, Paris 13 January 1993, article 1: '1. Each State Party to this Convention undertakes never under any circumstances: ... (b) To use chemical weapons.' This Convention was binding at the time of this event upon Russia, which ratified it on 5 November 1997. The question whether the exception of the use of chemical weapons for law enforcement purposes (see article 2(9 d)) would have applied in such a circumstance is open to debate.
105. *Finogenov v. Russia*, *supra* note 101, paras. 210–216. The Court held that it: 'may occasionally depart from that rigorous standard of "absolute necessity" ... In such a situation the Court accepts that difficult and agonising decisions had to be made by the domestic authorities. It is prepared to grant them a margin of appreciation, at least in so far as the military and technical aspects of the situation are concerned, even if now, with hindsight, some of the decisions taken by the authorities may appear open to doubt. ... What the Court intends to do is to ... apply different degrees of scrutiny to different aspects of the situation under examination.' It is quite worrying to see that the European Court is ready to lessen the standard of necessity for the use of force in situations which are considered as particularly difficult for the authorities without even trying to better circumscribe such kinds of situation.
106. Ibid., para. 232. It should be noted that, under IHL at least, the indiscriminate character of a means or method of warfare does not depend on whether it leaves a chance of survival to civilians. See art. 51, para. 4, API.
107. Ibid., paras 227–236.
108. Ibid., paras 237–282.
109. In the *Al Skeini v. The United Kingdom* case (ECtHR, Application No. 55721/07, Judgment of 7 July 2011), the Court had to deal with the use of force in the context of the UK occupation of Iraq. However, the applicants did not complain before the Court of any substantive breach of the right to life under Article 2. They merely complained that the United Kingdom had not fulfilled its procedural duty to carry out an effective investigation into the killings. The Court held that the UK had violated the right to life in its procedural aspect because of the ineffectiveness of the investigations on the use of lethal force by British soldiers against civilians (mistakenly believed to be individuals being about to commit a hostile act). In the section on relevant international law, the ECtHR had noted that IHL contains provisions imposing a duty to investigate. However, the Court did not analyse whether either of these provisions applied to the case at stake. In our opinion, the Court's conclusion that there is a duty to investigate when civilians are allegedly mistakenly killed is correct under human rights law as well as under IHL since the wilful killing of civilians can amount to a war crime.
110. The Court considered the application 38263/08 of Georgia against Russia regarding the 2008 armed conflict admissible. See *Georgia v. Russia*, ECtHR, Application No. 38263/08, Decision on

Admissibility, 13 December 2011. The Court refused to conclude, as requested by Russia, that the application was inadmissible, notably because (1) jurisdiction was not established, and (2) international humanitarian law was the *lex specialis* regarding international armed conflicts and thus the European Convention on Human Rights did not apply. In fact, the Court considered that these issues – including 'the question of the interplay of the provisions of the Convention with the rules of international humanitarian law in the context of an armed conflict' should be decided when the case is examined on the merits.

111.   *Georgia v. Russia, supra* note 110, para. 72. *See* also: *mutatis mutandis, Al-Adsani v. the United Kingdom,* ECtHR, Application no. 35763/97, Judgment of 21 November 2001, para. 55.

112.   *Varnava and others v. Turkey,* ECtHR, Applications No 16064/90, 16065/90, 16066/90, 16068/90, 16069/90, 16070/90, 16071/90, 16072/90 et 16073/90, Judgment of 18 September 2009.

113.   Ibid., para. 185.

114.   Ibid., para. 185. See also: *Varnava and others v. Turkey,* ECtHR, 10.1.08, §130: 'International treaties, which have attained the status of customary law, impose obligations on combatant States as regards care of wounded, prisoners of war and civilians [in footnote: reference to the four Geneva Conventions and their additional Protocols]. Article 2 of the Convention certainly extends so far as to require Contracting States to take such steps as may be reasonably available to them to protect the lives of those not, or no longer, engaged in hostilities.'

115.   Ibid., para. 186.

116.   *Al Jedda v. The United Kingdom,* ECtHR, Application No 27021/08, Judgment of 7 July 2011.

117.   The European human rights bodies have always refused to invoke derogations *proprio motu.* Already in the case *Cyprus v. Turkey,* which dealt notably with the detention by Turkey of prisoners of war in the context of the 1974 international armed conflict, the Commission refused to analyse a derogation from article 5 of the European Convention on Human Rights. However, it did not find a violation of this article since the ICRC had visited the prisoners of war. This can be interpreted as indicating, implicitly, the *lex specialis* character of IHL regarding the internment of prisoners of war. *Cyprus v. Turkey,* European Commission of Human Rights, Applications n° 6780/74 et 6950/75, Report of the Commission adopted on 10 July 1976. See also the dissenting opinions of judges Sperduti and Trechsel who considered that the mere existence of an occupation would automatically entail a derogation to some of the rights of the ECHR.

118.   *Al Jedda v. The United Kingdom, supra* note 116, para. 107: 'In the Court's view it would appear from the provisions of the Fourth Geneva Convention that under international humanitarian law internment is to be viewed not as an obligation on the Occupying Power but as a measure of last resort.' For a criticism of this decision, see also: J. Pejic, 'The European Court of Human Rights' *Al-Jedda* Judgment: The Oversight of International Humanitarian Law', *International Review of the Red Cross* 93, no. 883 (2011): 837–851.

119.   *Fragmentation of International Law: Difficulties Arising from the Diversification and Expansion of International Law, supra* note 73, paras 24–25.

120.   Pejic, *supra* note 118.

121.   *Kononov v. Latvia,* ECtHR, Application No. 36376/04, Judgment of 24 July 2008; *Kononov v. Latvia,* ECtHR (GC), Application No. 36376/04, Judgment of 17 May 2010; *Korbely v. Hungary,* ECtHR, Application No. 9174/02, Judgment of 19 September 2008. The case *Kononov v. Latvia* dealt with the conviction of a former member of the Red Army for war crimes by Latvian courts in 2004. Mr Kononov was punished for having led a commando unit, which carried out a punitive operation against Latvian villagers who collaborated with Nazi Germany during the Second World War. The case *Korbely v. Hungary* concerned the conviction of a former Hungarian captain in 2001 for crimes against humanity (as a violation of Article 3 common according to Hungarian Courts), mainly for having killed an (armed) insurgent, but also for having ordered his men to shoot at other unarmed insurgents during the 1956 Hungarian Revolution. In each case, the ECtHR has found it necessary to refer to IHL to determine whether the applicant's conviction for international crimes was consistent with Article 7 of the ECHR.

122.   Provost, *supra* note 9.

123.   Comments, in L. Condorelli, A.-M. La Rosa, S. Scherrer, ed., *Les Nations Unies et le droit international humanitaire/The United Nations and International Humanitarian Law.* Université de Genève, Actes du Colloque international (Paris: Pedone, 1996), 198–199.

124.   Dissenting Opinion of Judge Higgins, p. 592.

6. Extraterritorial application of the human rights to life and personal liberty, including *habeas corpus*, during situations of armed conflict

*Robert K. Goldman**

1. INTRODUCTION

In the wake of the September 11, 2001 attacks in the United States, the US, with the assistance of its coalition partners – all parties to various human rights instruments – initiated the so-called 'war on terror' by invading Afghanistan, where their armed forces killed or captured hundreds of 'terrorist suspects'. Some of those detained were taken to the US military facility at Guantanamo Bay, Cuba, while others have languished in US custody in Afghanistan. These actions raise the question whether a State is bound by its human rights obligations when its agents operate outside of national territory. And, if so, how do those obligations interrelate with the State's other obligations under international humanitarian law when its counter-terrorism operations coincide with situations of armed conflict.

This chapter addresses these questions. In particular, it examines the extraterritorial reach of two fundamental human rights during two situations recognized in international law. These rights are the right to life and the right to liberty and the related procedural safeguard of *habeas corpus*. The two situations examined are: (1) international armed conflicts, including occupation; and (2) non-international armed conflicts. The paper surveys the jurisprudence on the extraterritorial application of the International Covenant on Civil and Political Rights (ICCPR), the American Convention on Human Rights (American Convention) and American Declaration of the Rights and Duties of Man (American Declaration), and the European Convention on Human Rights (European Convention), and the extent to which rights in these instruments can be derogated from. It also examines how the treaty bodies supervising these instruments view the relationship between international human rights law (HRL) and international humanitarian law (IHL) in situations of armed conflict. Relevant decisions of the International Court of Justice are also referenced in this connection. The chapter also identifies certain gaps in legal protection.

2. DEROGATION FROM HUMAN RIGHTS TREATIES

As a preliminary matter, it is worth recalling that the UN Security Council in 2001 made clear that any measure taken by States to combat terrorism must comply with all their obligations under international law, including HRL and IHL.[1] This injunction unambiguously requires that States respect both bodies of law while countering terrorism, *whether at home or abroad*, and implicitly recognizes that upholding human rights and protecting the public from terrorist acts are not antithetical, but complementary, responsibilities of States.

When drafting the International Covenant on Civil and Political Rights (ICCPR) and various regional human rights instruments, States were aware of the need to strike a realistic balance between the requirements of national security and the protection of human rights. Accordingly, States included in these instruments provisions that permit them, when confronting an emergency situation – which may include actual or imminent terrorist violence, or armed conflict – to derogate from (suspend) certain rights in these instruments.

The ability of States to derogate from rights under these instruments, however, is *not* automatic in the face of such imminent terrorist violence or outbreak of armed conflict. Rather, it is governed by several conditions which are in turn regulated by the generally recognized principles of proportionality, necessity and non-discrimination. For example, Article 4 of the ICCPR sets forth the following procedural and substantive safeguards regarding the declaration and implementation of a state of emergency: the nature of the emergency must threaten the life of the nation; the existence of the emergency must be officially proclaimed; the measures adopted are strictly required by the exigencies of the situation; derogations cannot be incompatible with the derogating State's other obligations under international law; the derogation must not be discriminatory; and the derogating State must notify other State Parties through the UN Secretary-General of the provisions it has derogated from and the reasons for such derogation, as well as of the date the derogation has ceased to apply. Thus, a State that has not declared an emergency may not derogate from its human rights obligations, which remain fully in effect save for permissible limitations imposed on certain rights.

The key ground for derogation, that the emergency threatens the life of the nation, is especially relevant to some issues explored later in this chapter. That ground might well be satisfied by the existence of a large-scale internal armed conflict within or invasion of national territory by foreign armed forces, since these situations could entail a real threat to the political independence, territorial integrity and/or population of the country. It is questionable, however, whether this ground could be invoked by a State that is engaged in military operations, whatever their nature or origin, that occur exclusively in the territory of another State, particularly if that State's military cannot respond in kind.

While conceding States' ample discretion in adopting anti-terrorism measures, the ICCPR and other instruments also specify certain rights that may not be derogated from even during emergency situations. The list of non-derogable rights in the ICCPR is contained in article 4(2). These are, namely, right to life (article 6); prohibition of torture or cruel, inhuman or degrading treatment or punishment (article 7); prohibition of slavery, slave-trade and servitude (article 8 paragraphs 1 and 2); prohibition of retroactive criminal laws (article 15); the recognition of everyone as a person before the law (article 16); and freedom of thought, conscience and religion (article 18). Moreover, in 2001 the Human Rights Committee in its General Comment No. 29[2] indicated that the following provisions in the Covenant were not lawfully derogable during emergencies: the prohibition of hostage taking, abductions or unacknowledged detentions; and the prohibition of unlawful deportation or transfer of populations.

The jurisprudence of the Human Rights Committee and regional supervisory bodies indicates that derogations are always exceptional and temporary measures. Accordingly, such measures should be lifted as soon as the emergency which justified their imposition no longer exists or can be managed by less intrusive means under the relevant instrument.

3.   EXTRATERRITORIAL APPLICATION OF HUMAN RIGHTS LAW

The Human Rights Committee (HRC), the European Court of Human Rights (ECtHR) and the former European Commission on Human Rights (ECHR), as well as the Inter-American Commission on Human Rights (IACommHR), have all found their respective instruments to apply extraterritorially, even in situations governed by IHL. These treaty bodies seem to agree that extraterritorial jurisdiction attaches in principle when a State exercises effective control over territory and/or persons.

3.1   International Covenant on Civil and Political Rights

The Committee's case law has long given extraterritorial effect to the ICCPR. In 1981, it found that Uruguay had violated the Covenant when its agents abducted in Argentina and Brazil several Uruguayan citizens who opposed that country's military regime.[3] The Committee reasoned that 'it would be unconscionable to so interpret the [state's] responsibility under article 2 of the Covenant as to permit a state party to perpetrate violations of the Covenant on the territory of another state, which violations it could not perpetrate in its own territory'.[4]

The HRC's most complete statement of its views on the extraterritorial reach of the Covenant is found in its General Comment 31.[5] It observed therein that a State Party's duty to respect and ensure rights to all persons within their territory and subject to their jurisdiction includes

> … anyone within the power or effective control of the State Party, even if not situated in the territory of the State Party… This Principle also applies to those within the power or effective control of the forces of the State Party acting outside its territory, regardless of the circumstances in which such power or effective control was obtained, such as forces constituting a national contingent of a State Party assigned to an international peacekeeping or peace-enforcement operation.[6]

Additionally, the HRC has specifically affirmed the ICCPR's extraterritorial application to military and peacekeeping operations outside of the territory of the State concerned.[7]

Several States, most particularly Israel and the United States, have disputed the Committee's position on the Covenant's extraterritorial reach. However, the International Court of Justice in its 2004 Advisory Opinion on *the Legal Consequences of the Construction of a Wall in Occupied Palestinian Territory*,[8] confirmed the Committee's views. After examining the Covenant's *travaux preparatoires* and the Committee's practice, the Court rejected the argument that the Covenant was not applicable outside of a State's territorial borders, and, more particularly, in occupied territory. While recognizing that a State's jurisdiction is primarily territorial, the Court concluded that the Covenant's reach extends to 'acts done by a State in the exercise of its jurisdiction outside its own territory'.[9]

Accordingly, it would appear well settled that the ICCPR has a truly global reach, extending to any territory or person within the power or effective control of a party to that treaty.

3.2   The European Convention on Human Rights

The Strasbourg organs also have considerable case law affirming the extraterritorial scope of the European Convention. In 1975, the former ECHR addressed this issue in *Cyprus v. Turkey*,[10] in which Cyprus charged Turkey with violations of the Convention in that part of Cypriot territory invaded by Turkish armed forces. Turkey claimed that the Commission's competence was limited to the examination of acts committed by a contracting party in its own national territory, and that it had not extended its jurisdiction to any part of Cyprus. The Commission rejected this argument stating:

> In Article 1 of the Convention, the High Contracting Parties undertake to Secure the rights and freedoms defined in Section 1 to everyone 'within their jurisdiction' ... The Commission finds that this term is not ... equivalent to or limited to the national territory of the High Contracting Party concerned. It is clear from the language ... and the object of this article, and from the purpose of the Convention as a whole that *the High contracting parties are bound to secure the said rights and freedoms to all persons under their actual authority and responsibility, whether that authority is exercised within their own territory or abroad* ...[11]

This understanding of jurisdiction as a notion linked to authority and effective control, and not merely to territorial boundaries, has been confirmed in other cases decided by the former Commission and the ECtHR. In *Loizidou v. Turkey*,[12] the Court reaffirmed that the term jurisdiction in Article 1 was not limited to national territory, noting that 'responsibility of Contracting Parties can be involved because of acts of their authorities, whether performed within or outside national boundaries, which produce effects outside their own territory'.[13] The Court added that based on the Convention's object and purpose

> the responsibility of a Contracting Party may also arise when as a consequence of military action – whether lawful or unlawful – it exercises effective control of an area outside its national territory. The obligation to secure, in such an area, the rights and freedoms set out in the Convention derives from the fact of such control whether it be exercised directly, through its armed forces or through a subordinate local administration.[14]

The Court has explained that any other finding

> would result in a regrettable vacuum in the system of human-rights protection in the territory in question by removing from individuals there the benefit of the Convention's fundamental safeguards and their right to call a High Contracting Party to account for violations of their rights in proceedings before the Court.[15]

In the *Bankovic*[16] case, the European Court appeared to depart from its previous case law. This case was brought against 17 European members of NATO for an air strike in 1999 which hit a communications facility in Belgrade, resulting in the deaths of applicants' relatives. In contrast to a situation of occupation, where a State can be regarded as exercising jurisdiction extraterritorially by virtue of its effective control over territory, the Court found no such jurisdictional link between the victims of the extraterritorial bombardment in question and the respondent States in this case. The Court noted that jurisdiction under Article 1 is primarily territorial and that it had only exceptionally recognized extraterritorial acts as constituting an exercise of jurisdiction.[17] Regarding whether its finding would defeat the '*ordre public* mission of the Convention and leave a regrettable vacuum in the Convention system of human rights protection', the Court indicated that the Convention was meant to operate in an essentially regional context, that is, within the Council of Europe (COE), and not throughout the world, 'even in respect of the conduct of contracting states'.[18]

If the Court in *Bankovic* meant to limit jurisdiction under the Convention to the geographical confines of the COE, its subsequent judgments in the *Öcalan* and *Issa* cases appear to retreat from this view. In *Öcalan*,[19] the applicant was arrested by Turkish agents while he was aboard an aircraft in Kenya. The Court found that once the Kenyan authorities delivered Öcalan to Turkish officials he 'was under effective Turkish authority and therefore was brought within the "jurisdiction" of that state for the purpose of Article 1 of the Convention, even though Turkey exercised its authority outside its territory'.[20] The court distinguished the circumstances in this case from those in *Bankovic*, noting that Öcalan 'was physically forced to return to Turkey by Turkish officials and was subject to their authority and control following his arrest and return to Turkey'.[21]

The Court in *Issa*[22] again dealt with events taking place outside of the 'legal space' of the COE. The case was lodged by Iraqi nationals who charged that Turkish forces murdered their relatives during military operations in northern Iraq. While referring to *Bankovic*, the Court made clear that Contracting States 'may also be held accountable for violations of the Convention rights and freedoms of persons who are in the territory of another State but who are found to be under the former State's authority and control through its agents operating – whether lawfully of unlawfully – in the latter State'.[23] Then, citing decisions of the HRC and the IACtHR, the Court added: 'Accountability in such situations stems from the fact that Article 1 of the Convention cannot be interpreted so as to allow a State party to perpetrate violations of the Convention on the territory of another State, which it could not perpetrate in its own territory'.[24] The Court then seemed to posit a new test at odds with *Bankovic* by stating that it did not exclude 'the possibility that, as a consequence of this military action, the respondent State could be considered to have exercised, temporarily, effective overall control of a particular portion of the territory of northern Iraq'.[25] However, because the applicants failed to establish that Turkish troops were in the area where the victims were killed, the Court found that the victims were not within the 'jurisdiction' of Turkey.

More recently, the Court in the *Al-Skeini*[26] case further clarified its views on the extraterritorial reach of the European Convention. *Al-Skeini* involved the killing of five Iraqis by British troops in Basrah in Southern Iraq. The Law Lords, while acknowledging that the United Kingdom was an Occupying Power in Southern Iraq, nonetheless, found that the Iraqi victims were not within the jurisdiction of the UK for purposes of the European Convention because British troops did not effectively control the area where the killings occurred. The European Court disagreed, holding that the UK had exercised jurisdiction over the victims at the time of their deaths. Referring to the general principle in its case law that a State's jurisdiction under Article 1 is primarily territorial, the Court reiterated in *Al-Skeini* that whenever a State's agents, including its military, exercise physical control and authority over an individual outside its territory, it is obliged under Article 1 to secure to that individual '... the rights and freedoms under Section 1 of the Convention that are relevant to the situation of that individual'.[27] The Court also reaffirmed that another exception to the territorial principle occurs when a State, whether by lawful or unlawful military action, exercises effective control over an area outside of its national territory.[28] Importantly, the Court, citing *Issa, Öcalan* and *Al-Saadoon and Mufdhi v. the United Kingdom*,[29] made clear that jurisdiction under Article 1 of the Convention could exist outside the territory covered by COE Member States. Applying these principles, the Court pointedly noted that when the Iraqi victims were killed, the UK was an Occupying Power within the meaning of the Hague Regulations and had thereby 'assumed authority and responsibility for the maintenance of security in South East Iraq'. Accordingly, the Court found that in these 'exceptional circumstances', the UK had, through its soldiers' engagement in security operations in Basrah during the relevant period, 'exercised authority and control over the individuals killed in the course of such security operations, so as to establish a jurisdictional link between the deceased and the United Kingdom for purposes of Article 1 of the Convention'.[30]

Although the Court's jurisprudence on the extraterritorial reach of the European Convention is somewhat confusing, if not contradictory, it would appear, nonetheless, that a contracting party would be exercising jurisdiction when its agents (a) detain or exercise physical power and control over a person anywhere in the world, or (b) occupy or otherwise effectively control the territory of another COE Member State, or perhaps, as indicated in *Issa* and *Al-Skeini*, that of a non-Member State.

A contracting party, however, would incur no responsibility if its agents targeted and killed a person in another State whose territory, at the time, was not subject to its effective control. Unlike a detainee who is killed in custody, the person so attacked would be remediless under the Convention. This result creates a glaring and unseemly gap in legal protection. One remedy, proposed by Françoise Hampson, would be for the ECtHR not to look to control of territory as the test for determining whether the victim comes within the jurisdiction of the State launching the attack, but rather to 'control over the effects said to constitute a violation, subject to a foreseeable victim being foreseeably affected by the act'.[31] As she notes, such an approach would only go to the admissibility, not the merits of the complaint. Another solution would be to posit that the right to life's negative dimension, that is, the duty of States to refrain from violating that right, has acquired the status of customary international law and, as such, is binding on all States and their agents in all circumstances. Thus, overseas killings by State agents that are unlawful under IHL would violate customary HRL. Both approaches are plausible and merit further study.

3.3   The Inter-American Human Rights Instruments

The Inter-American Commission on Human Rights has similarly found that persons falling within a State's authority and control outside of national territory are effectively within that State's jurisdiction, and holders of enforceable rights under applicable instruments. Interestingly, virtually all of the case law to date on the subject has been made by the Commission and not by the Inter-American Court. This is because most cases have involved the United States, which has not ratified the American Convention and thus is bound by the American Declaration by virtue of its membership in the Organization of American States (OAS). Furthermore, most of these cases have involved claims arising from US military operations within the region.

The Commission's most complete statement concerning the American Declaration's extraterritorial reach is found in *Coard et al. v. United States*,[32] which involved the detention of 17 persons by US forces immediately following the US invasion of Grenada in October 1983. The Commission stated that:

> ... under certain circumstances, the exercise of jurisdiction over acts with an extraterritorial locus will not only be consistent with but required by the norms which pertain ... Given that individual rights inhere simply by virtue of a person's humanity, each American State is obliged to uphold the protected rights of any person subject to its jurisdiction.[33]

It added:

> While this most commonly refers to persons within a state's territory, it may, under given circumstances, refer to conduct with an extraterritorial locus where the person concerned is present in the territory of one state, but subject to the control of another state – usually through acts of the latter's agents abroad. In principle, the inquiry turns not on the presumed victim's nationality or presence within a particular geographic area, but on whether, under the specific circumstances, the State observed the rights of the person subject to its authority and control.[34]

The Commission similarly gave extraterritorial application to the American Convention in its recent admissibility decision[35] in the interstate complaint filed by Ecuador against Colombia for the killing of one of its citizens during a military operation by Colombian security forces against FARC rebels on Ecuadorian soil. Citing its own case law and the jurisprudence of other treaty bodies, the Commission concluded that Colombia had exercised jurisdiction over the area attacked and the victim in question. It specifically found the following factors essential for establishing jurisdiction:

> the exercise of authority over persons by agents of a State even if not acting within their territory, without necessarily requiring the existence of a formal, structured and prolonged legal relation in terms of time to raise the responsibility of a State for acts committed by its agents abroad. At the time of examining the scope of the American Convention's jurisdiction, it is necessary to determine whether there is a causal nexus between the extraterritorial conduct of the State and the alleged violation of the rights and freedoms of an individual.[36]

The Commission also noted that during such time as its agents exercise such authority over persons abroad, the State is obliged to respect those persons' rights, particularly, the right to life and humane treatment.[37]

The Commission has also found a State extending its jurisdiction extraterritorially in circumstances not entailing its physical control of territory or custody of persons. Specifically, in *Alejandre et al.*[38] it held that Cuba had violated the right to life of four persons resulting from its agent's shooting down of two unarmed civilian aircraft in international airspace. The Commission found that, unlike the victims in *Bankovic*, the pilots of the doomed planes were under Cuba's 'authority' when its air force attacked them.[39] The Commission also relied on this notion of authority and control when in 2003 it adopted precautionary measures[40] requesting that the United States have a competent tribunal determine the legal status of the detainees at Guantanamo Bay, Cuba. The Commission in 1993 also declared admissible a case[41] arising out of the US invasion of Panama in 1989. In so doing, it simply stated:

> where it is asserted that a use of military force has resulted in non-combatant deaths, personal injury and property loss, the human rights of non-combatants are implicated ... The case sets forth allegations cognizable within the framework of the [American] Declaration. Thus, the Commission is authorized to consider the subject matter of the case.[42]

A merits decision in the matter is still pending.

The Commission's case law to date suggests that it views the region's human rights system as applying solely within the geographic boundaries of the Western Hemisphere. This may explain why it has never opened a case or issued precautionary measures based on the petitions it has received since 2002 concerning the detention of persons in Iraq and Afghanistan who are under the control of US agents. As previously discussed, such detentions abroad by a party to the European Convention would constitute an exercise of jurisdiction, entitling the detainee(s) to the Convention's protections. However, in the *Saldaño* case,[43] in which it interpreted the scope of Article 1(1) of the American Convention, that treaty's jurisdictional clause, the Commission recognized that '... nationals of a state party to the American Convention are subject to that state's jurisdiction in certain respects when domiciled abroad or otherwise temporarily outside of their country or state and that state party must accord them when abroad the exercise of certain convention based rights'.[44] Thus, an OAS Member State whose agents kill or abduct one of its nationals outside of the hemisphere would be exercising jurisdiction over that person and incur responsibility under the American Convention for those illicit acts. The Commission's reasoning would apply equally to those OAS Member States bound only by the American Declaration. If the victim, however, were a non-national, the Commission could not entertain a claim based upon these same acts – which bespeaks of a clear gap in legal protection.

4. THE RELATIONSHIP BETWEEN INTERNATIONAL HUMAN RIGHTS LAW AND INTERNATIONAL HUMANITARIAN LAW

Before examining how the various treaty bodies view the relationship between HRL and IHL, it is instructive to consider the views of the International Court of Justice (ICJ) on this subject. The ICJ has made clear that HRL does not cease to apply during armed conflict. In its advisory opinion on the *Legality of the Threat or Use of Nuclear Weapons*[45] the Court stated the following regarding the right to life in the ICCPR:

> In principle, the right not arbitrarily to be deprived of one's life also applies in hostilities. The test of what is an arbitrary deprivation of life, however, then falls to be determined by the applicable *lex specialis*, namely, the law applicable in armed conflict which is designed to regulate the conduct of hostilities.[46]

The Court in its 2004 Advisory Opinion on the *Legal Consequences of the Construction of a Wall in the Occupied Palestinian Territory*[47] confirmed this view, stating that it: '... considers that the protections offered by human rights conventions does not cease in case of armed conflict, save through the effect of provisions for derogation of the kind to be found in Article 4 of the [ICCPR] ...'.[48] Concerning the relationship between human rights and humanitarian law, it added: '... there are thus three possible situations: some rights may be exclusively matters of international humanitarian law; others may be exclusively matters of human rights law; yet others may be matters of both these branches of international law'.[49] The Court, however, provided no guidance on how this *lex specialis* doctrine should apply in practice.

Human rights treaty bodies have no common approach on how HRL and IHL interrelate when State Parties are engaged in situations of armed conflict within their *own* territory, much less in hostilities *abroad*. For its part, the Human Rights Committee has yet to fashion a comprehensive theory on the subject. However, in its General Comment No. 31, the Committee stated:

> As implied in general comment 29, the Covenant applies to situations of armed conflict to which the rules of international humanitarian law are applicable, While, in respect of certain Covenant rights, more specific rules of international humanitarian law may be specially relevant for purposes of the interpretation of Covenant rights, both spheres of law are complementary, not mutually exclusive.[50]

This would suggest that where a rule of IHL is *lex specialis*, it does not as such derogate from the Covenant right, but rather must be consulted to determine whether that right has been violated.

The Inter-American Commission's case law most closely tracks the views of the ICJ. The Commission[51] has stated that human rights law is not displaced by IHL during armed conflicts and remains fully applicable save for permissible derogations. It has recognized, however, that the test for evaluating the observance of a particular human right during armed conflict may be distinct from that applicable in peacetime. The Commission, therefore, has looked to IHL rules as sources of authoritative guidance, or as the *lex specialis* in interpreting the American Convention and Declaration to resolve claimed violations of those instruments in combat situations.

In contrast, the European Court of Human Rights has to date not expressed an opinion on the relationship between these two bodies of law. Moreover, its consistent jurisprudence, applying essentially law enforcement rules to killings during armed conflicts, suggests that it does not regard IHL as *lex specialis* in such situations.

5. THE RIGHT TO LIFE

The right to life is the most fundamental right guaranteed in human rights law. Articles 6 and 4 of the ICCPR and the American Convention, respectively, prohibit the 'arbitrary' deprivation of life. This right, moreover, is not subject to derogation or limitations under either instrument. In contrast, Article 2 of the European Convention guarantees this right by prohibiting 'intentional' deprivations of life and stipulates the only circumstances when lethal force can lawfully be employed by State agents. Article 15 of the treaty provides an additional ground for use of deadly force in situations of armed conflict by permitting derogation from Article 2 for deaths resulting from 'lawful acts of war'.

This section examines the protection of this right in the following situations: (a) an extraterritorial situation of international armed conflict, including occupation, such as when the United States and its coalition partners invaded and subsequently occupied Iraq; and (b) an extraterritorial situation of non-international armed conflict, such as the current involvement of various NATO Member States in the ongoing internal hostilities in Afghanistan at the invitation of the Afghan government.

5.1   Situations of International Armed Conflict

Human rights treaty bodies have developed an extensive and basically similar jurisprudence on the duty of States to uphold the right to life by essentially employing a law enforcement paradigm that places limits on the use of lethal force by State agents. In principle, State agents may use lethal force only in situations where it is strictly unavoidable to protect themselves or others from imminent threat of death or serious injury, or to maintain law and order where strictly necessary and proportionate. In addition, the case law indicates that State agents should attempt to arrest rather than kill persons posing a threat, and should plan their operations accordingly.

In contrast, IHL, while placing restraints on the conduct of hostilities, permits deadly force to be used directly against combatants at all times until they have been captured or rendered *hors de combat*. Similarly, civilians lose their immunity from direct attack for such time as they directly participate in hostilities.[52] And, unlike HRL, IHL also does *not* require that an attempt be made to arrest or capture these persons before they are attacked.

If enemy combatants and civilians directly participating in hostilities may be lawfully attacked under IHL during international conflicts, how should their deaths be treated under human rights law? The answer might well turn on the particular treaty body's views on the interrelationship of HRL and IHL. Before addressing this issue, the treaty body would have to determine whether the invading State's human rights obligations apply in the country where the hostilities are underway. As previously noted, if the invaded country is outside of the geographic boundaries of the OAS or the COE, these regional bodies' respective instruments would not apply, and any complaint based on these deaths would be inadmissible. If, however, the invaded country were within one of these regions, the question then becomes whether the victims at the time they were killed were within the jurisdiction of the invading State.

The Inter-American Commission's case law would suggest that persons targeted and killed by the invading States' forces were subject to that State's authority.[53] On the merits, the Commission, which regards IHL as the *lex specialis*, should find that killings sanctioned by IHL would not constitute arbitrary deprivations of life under the American Declaration or Convention.[54]

Given the ICCPR's global reach, the location of the event is not critical; but, the Committee would have to decide whether the victims when attacked were within 'the power or effective control' of the invading State's forces. If it so determined, the thrust of General Comment 31 would suggest that the Committee would reach the same conclusion as the IACommHR, finding no violation of the right to life.

Resolution of these issues is more complicated under the European Convention for a variety of reasons. For example, assuming that the invaded country were a COE member, it is doubtful under the ECtHR's jurisprudence that the victims would be found subject to the jurisdiction of the invading State if that State's forces did not exercise effective control over the territory or the victims at the time of their deaths. And, even assuming that jurisdiction did attach, none of the grounds specified in Article 2 of the European Convention authorizing the use of deadly force, which are based on a law enforcement paradigm, could plausibly be invoked by the invading State. These deaths, for instance, could hardly be justified for the purpose of quelling a riot or insurrection. Because these deaths do not come within any of Article 2's exceptions, the invading State could derogate from Article 2 in respect of 'deaths resulting from lawful acts of war.' But, no European State has ever filed such a derogation under Article 15 based on its involvement in an extraterritorial international armed conflict. Moreover, as noted previously, it is questionable whether a State could claim that its engagement in a wholly extraterritorial armed conflict would constitute the kind of emergency that would justify its derogating from the European Convention. Furthermore, if such a derogation were invalid, then the only remaining option for the ECtHR would be to use IHL to interpret Article 2 so as to find that deaths resulting from lawful acts of war do not violate the right to life – something that the Court has shown little inclination to do.

5.2   Occupation

The jurisprudence of the treaty bodies surveyed indicates that human rights law applies during a situation of occupation, which is also governed by IHL rules. As the State Party to the treaty is obliged to respect the right to life in occupied territory, it is crucial to know when territory is occupied and what body of law – IHL or HRL – controls that determination. Professor Hampson notes that human rights treaty bodies have not had to 'define occupation or to determine whether the definition under human rights law is the same as that under IHL'.[55] She correctly states that 'If IHL is the *lex specialis* but human rights law remains applicable, a human rights body should presumably apply IHL to determine whether the situation is one of occupation'.[56]

In this regard, territory is considered occupied under IHL when it is actually placed under the authority of the hostile army, that is, organized resistance must have been overcome and the invading power has substituted its own authority for that of the legitimate government. Additionally, the occupation extends only to territory where such authority has been established and can be exercised. As indicated, extraterritorial application of human rights treaties requires the State to exercise effective control over territory, which may well be coextensive with belligerent occupation. However, as one commentator observes,[57] the effective control test under human rights law may be broader and at times have a lower threshold than that for occupation under IHL. One example would be the *Illascu v. Moldova* case[58] where the ECtHR found Russia responsible for human rights violations in territory it controlled, but could not be said to occupy under IHL. Similarly, the IACommHR in *Coard*[59] found violations of the American Declaration, and actually invoked occupation law when the United States legally was not occupying Grenada.

Another important question is whether IHL or HRL rules govern the use of lethal force by the Occupying Power in occupied territory. The answer should depend on the nature of the occupation. In a relatively 'calm' occupation, the Occupying Power, consistent with its duty under IHL to ensure public order and safety, should operate under a law enforcement paradigm. Thus, its armed forces would have to attempt to arrest or capture criminal suspects before using deadly force against them, which would preclude, in principle, 'targeted killings' of suspected terrorists.[60]

If, however, there is an outbreak or resumption of hostilities in the occupied territory entailing military operations by the Occupying Power's forces against an organized resistance movement and/or the armed forced of the ousted government, then IHL rules should fully apply to the conduct of hostilities with opposing combatants being directly targetable on sight. The killing of civilians in the process of committing terrorist or other hostile acts, amounting to direct participation in hostilities, should also be deemed lawful under both IHL and HRL. Law enforcement rules, however, should continue to apply in connection with ordinary criminal activity not linked to the hostilities.

5.3   Situations of Non-international Armed Conflict

It is important to note that under this scenario State X's armed forces are *not* engaged in a non-international armed conflict (NIAC) within State X, but rather are assisting State Y's military to suppress an insurrection within State Y. While there is considerable case law on the application of human rights law in the former situation, there is virtually no jurisprudence, at least from human rights treaty bodies, on the extra-territorial application of human rights law in the latter situation. Moreover, many of the same threshold issues discussed in the international hostilities section would similarly be posed by State X's extraterritorial involvement in State Y's NIAC.

For example, neither the European Convention nor the Inter-American instruments would be applicable if the State Party were involved in a NIAC outside of the respective region's geographical boundaries. Thus, unlawful killings by State X's forces would not engage its responsibility under these instruments. And, even if State X's forces were fighting within another State Party's territory, the treaty body would still have to determine whether the victims, when killed, were within State X's jurisdiction. In addition, extraterritorial killings in a NIAC would not easily satisfy any of the grounds in Article 2 of the European Convention authorizing the use of deadly force. The permissible ground to quell an insurrection most certainly refers to actions taken by the State Party within its *own* territory, not within that of another State involved in a NIAC. Furthermore, State X's involvement in State Y's NIAC arguably would provide no more justification for derogating from the European Convention than would its engagement in an overseas international armed conflict.

Assuming that the treaty body were seized with the matter, how should it treat killings that are lawful under IHL rules applicable in NIACs? More particularly, which law – IHL or HRL – should determine whether the use of deadly force was permissible? If the treaty bodies apply the same standards to determine the lawfulness of these extraterritorial killings as they would to killings by State agents in a NIAC at home, then they would probably reach different results.

The Inter-American Commission, based on its practice, would likely treat members of government armed forces and of organized armed groups as combatants and, as such, directly targetable, whether they are *on or away* from the battlefield. Moreover, it would apply IHL as *lex specialis* to determine the lawfulness of the killings under the American Declaration or Convention. In contrast, the Human Rights Committee[61] and especially the European Court[62] have applied law enforcement and not IHL rules to find violations of the right to life where State agents have directly targeted members of armed opposition groups *off* the battlefield. However, the Committee would probably find combat-related deaths that are lawful under IHL to not violate the ICCPR.

Whether the European Court would reach this same conclusion is unclear. The Court has taken into account various IHL principles in some recent Turkish[63] and Russian[64] cases involving clashes between governmental and armed opposition forces. However, it has never relied on IHL as *lex specialis* in assessing the legality of deaths arising out of such clashes, but instead has effectively applied HRL to make such determinations. By so doing, the Court risks finding killings that are lawful under IHL as violating the European Convention – a result which, it is submitted, could significantly undermine confidence in both IHL and HRL.

6.   THE RIGHT TO LIBERTY AND *HABEAS CORPUS*

Articles 9 and 7 of the ICCPR and the American Convention, respectively, address the protection of personal liberty by prohibiting arbitrary arrest or detention. Article 5 of the European Convention takes a different approach by exhaustively listing the grounds for lawful arrest or detention. This section examines the protection of this basic right in (a) extraterritorial situations of international armed conflict, including occupation, and in (b) extraterritorial situations of non-international armed conflict.

6.1   Situations of International Armed Conflict

Human rights jurisprudence requires, *inter alia*, that any deprivation of liberty be based upon grounds and procedures established by law, that detainees be informed of the reasons for the detention and promptly notified of the charges against them in case of criminal detention, and that they be provided access to legal counsel. Prompt and effective oversight of detention by a judge or other officer authorized by law to exercise judicial power must be ensured to verify the legality of detention and to protect other fundamental rights of the detainee.

The right to personal liberty applies during armed conflicts, except to the extent that it may be subject to lawful derogation. In this regard, the right to liberty is not included among the non-derogable rights in the ICCPR or the European or American Conventions. However, a State's ability to suspend this right has been strictly and narrowly defined by the treaty bodies. The Human Rights Committee, for instance, has indicated that in order to protect non-derogable rights, the right to *habeas corpus* must not be diminished by a State's decision to derogate from the Covenant.[65] The Inter-American Court has similarly found that *habeas corpus* and *amparo* cannot be derogated from during emergencies.[66] While never finding *habeas corpus* to be non-derogable, the ECtHR has ruled that deprivations of liberty without *habeas corpus* proceedings to review the decision to detain an individual violates article 5(4) of the European Convention.[67]

International Humanitarian Law permits the capture and detention of adversaries as a lawful incidence of war. During international armed conflicts, the Third and Fourth Geneva Conventions of 1949 contain provisions addressing the circumstances under which Prisoners of War (POWs) and civilians, respectively, may be interned or detained and the manner in which their internment/detention must be monitored, including access by the International Committee of the Red Cross (ICRC). The Third Convention (GC III) permits the internment of combatants as POWs until their repatriation at the cessation of active hostilities or the completion of any criminal proceedings or punishment for an indictable offense pending against a POW. The Fourth Convention (GC IV) permits the internment of civilians either in a party's own territory,[68] as well as in occupied territory (see below) provided certain conditions are met. Among them is that the person represents a serious security threat, that he or she has the right to request review of the internment decision, that such review is to be carried out by a court or administrative board and that it must be periodic (every six months).

In addition, persons detained/interned by a party to an international armed conflict and who do not benefit from more favorable treatment under the Geneva Conventions or Additional Protocol I (API) are entitled to certain *minimum* protections under Article 75, AP I, which reflects customary international law. Such persons would include civilians who directly participate in the hostilities, but who do not qualify as POWs under GC III or for protection under GC IV because of the nationality criteria stipulated therein.

Article 75 contains no provisions on permissible grounds for, or review of the lawfulness of detention. However, it stipulates that affected persons must be promptly informed of the reasons for their detention/internment and requires that they 'shall be released with the minimum delay possible and in any event as soon as the circumstances justifying the arrest, detention or internment have ceased to exist'. Article 75's text thus suggests that detention/internment is an exceptional measure which should never be prolonged or indefinite. Moreover, Article 72, AP I makes clear that Article 75's minimum guarantees are supplemented by HRL.

Since IHL authorizes the detention of combatants during international armed conflicts, how should such detentions be treated under HRL? Must a State derogate from the right to personal liberty in order to lawfully detain persons in such conflicts?

And, do wartime detainees have a right to *habeas corpus*? There is little or no human rights jurisprudence on most of these questions. The Inter-American Commission more than any other treaty body has addressed or dealt with some of these issues.

The Commission has said that during international hostilities consideration must be given to IHL rules as the applicable *lex specialis* in interpreting and applying the right to personal liberty, 'with due regard to the overarching principles of necessity, proportionality, humanity and non-discrimination'.[69] Thus, the Commission would look to IHL to determine which grounds of deprivation of liberty are lawful during international hostilities. Since IHL permits the detention of enemy combatants in such hostilities, the Commission would find that such detentions do not constitute 'arbitrary' deprivations of liberty under the American Convention (or Declaration). Accordingly, there would be no need to derogate from Article 7 of the American Convention. Indeed, no OAS Member State has ever derogated from the Convention based on its involvement, whether at home or abroad, in an international armed conflict. Further, as noted in the previous section, any such derogation would be problematic in terms of satisfying the condition that there be an emergency threatening the life of the nation. And, due to the limited geographical reach of the American Convention and Declaration, detention of persons, other than of nationals, by a Member State outside of the Western hemisphere would not generate any State responsibility under either instrument.

As POWs are interned for reasons of military necessity, that is, to prevent them from returning to the battlefield, and not as criminal suspects, GC III does not afford them the procedural protections, including judicial review, that HRL provides to criminal suspects in peacetime. Thus, the IACommHR recognizes that POWs are not entitled 'to be informed of the reasons for their detention, to challenge the legality of their detention, or, in the absence of disciplinary or criminal proceedings, to be provided with access to legal counsel'.[70] While carving out this exception to regional doctrine on *habeas corpus*, the Commission has indicated that in uncertain or protracted situations of armed conflict and occupation, IHL rules and procedures governing detention/ internment might prove 'inadequate' to safeguard the minimum human rights of detainees, including the right to personal liberty.[71] In which case, the Commission has indicated that the supervisory mechanisms and judicial guarantees under HRL and domestic law, including *habeas corpus*, 'may necessarily supercede international humanitarian law'.[72] This was precisely the rationale underlying the Commission's issuance of precautionary measures on behalf of the Guantanamo Bay detainees – all of whom were captured in the 2002 Afghan hostilities and disqualified, without individual status determinations, by the United States from protection under the Geneva Conventions.

In 2004, the US Supreme Court ruled in *Rasul v. Bush*[73] and again in 2008 in *Boumediene v. Bush*[74] that Guantanamo detainees only had the right to challenge the lawfulness of their detention in federal court through a *habeas corpus* petition based on the fact that the naval base is under legal and effective US control. Although the court never expressly referenced human rights law in either case, its rulings are broadly consistent with human rights jurisprudence concerning the non-suspendability of *habeas* relief during emergencies.

The Human Rights Committee has found that extraterritorial detentions constitute an exercise of jurisdiction under the ICCPR. However, it has never decided a case based on the applicability of IHL to wartime detentions under the Covenant. Walter Kälin, a former Committee member, does provide some insight into how the Committee might deal with this issue. He states that during armed conflicts 'IHL determines what is "arbitrary" in terms of Covenant rights protecting against arbitrary deprivations of a specific right' and concludes that a detention would not be arbitrary under Article 9 'if it is permitted by IHL which, as *lex specialis*, determines which grounds for deprivation of liberty are lawful in times of armed conflict'.[75] Accordingly, the Committee would likely reach this decision without regard to the question of derogation under the Covenant. Moreover, a derogation from Article 9 based on the State's involvement in a wholly extraterritorial armed conflict may not pass muster, for reasons previously explained.

Presumably, the Committee, like the IACommHR, would also find that POWs were not entitled to *habeas* relief, at least when IHL supervisory mechanisms were adequately functioning. Professor Kälin does, however, suggest that a right to periodic review of detention 'would seem possible and required to interpret a provision of Article 75, paragraph 3 [of] Additional Protocol I on the guarantees for persons detained for acts in relation to the armed conflict in light of Article 9 of the Covenant and to apply both provisions cumulatively'.[76] It is also arguable that such security detainees, by analogy to civilian internees under GC IV, should have a right to periodic review of the lawfulness of continued detention as a matter of customary international law.

The ECtHR in *Öcalan* also made clear that extraterritorial detentions entail the exercise of authority and control by the State over the detainee. Such detentions during *overseas* international armed conflicts pose many of the same problems as discussed previously. Again, none of the grounds listed in Article 5 of the European Convention could justify detaining combatants or civilians in such situations. Yet, the former European Commission found in *Cyprus v. Turkey* that since Turkey had not derogated from Article 5, its detention of Cypriot troops as POWs violated the Convention.[77] Professor Hampson terms this result 'absurd'.[78] She suggests that such a result could be avoided by the State's derogating to introduce additional grounds for detention permitted by IHL or by the Court's use of IHL as a matter of law.[79] Whether the State should or could derogate in these circumstances requires further study and analysis.

6.2 Occupation

Article 78, GC IV permits, as an exceptional measure, an Occupying Power 'for imperative reasons of security' to intern or place civilians in assigned residences. Such decisions must be made according to a 'regular procedure' which includes the right of detainees to have the decision appealed with the least possible delay, and, if upheld, subject to review 'if possible' every six months 'by a competent body' established by the Occupying Power. Jelena Pejic suggests that this appeal is essentially akin to a *habeas* action since its purpose '... is to enable the competent body to determine whether the person was deprived of liberty for valid reasons and to order his or her release if that was not the case'.[80] She also mentions that 'the authority that initially deprived the person of liberty and the body authorized to conduct the review on appeal must not be the same if the right to petition is to be effective'.[81] Further, citing the Commentary to GC IV's requirement that the reviewing authority be independent and impartial, she argues that such a body must have authority to render final decisions on internment or release.[82] On a related issue, the International Tribunal for the Former Yugoslavia has determined that an initially lawful internment becomes unlawful if the detaining power does not respect a detainee's basic procedural rights and does not establish an appropriate review mechanism as required by Article 43 of GC IV.[83] The Tribunal's reasoning should similarly apply to detainees in occupied territory under Article 78.

The Inter-American Commission's decision in the *Coard* case essentially echoes these views. Although the United States did not legally occupy Grenada after it invaded the island in 2003, the IACommHR, nonetheless, invoked parts of occupation law in its analysis of the case. Specifically, it found Article 78, GC IV applicable and noted that it was generally consistent with the supervisory control required by the American Declaration's prohibition of arbitrary arrest.[84] While affirming that valid security reasons initially justified the United States' detention of petitioners, the Commission indicated that the same IHL rules which authorized this 'as an exceptional security measure' also required a regular procedure which permitted the detainees to be heard and to promptly appeal the decision. Such a procedure, which it suggested could be undertaken by a judicial or quasi-judicial body, 'ensures that the decision to maintain a person in detention does not rest with the agents who effectuated the deprivation of liberty, and ensures a minimal level of oversight by an entity with the authority to order release if warranted'.[85] It noted, moreover, that such supervisory control over detention is an 'essential rationale of the right of *habeas corpus*, a protection which is not susceptible to abrogation'.[86] Because petitioners were held for six to nine days after the end of hostilities without any such review, it found their detention violated the Declaration 'as understood with reference to Article 78 of the Fourth Geneva Convention'.[87]

The Human Rights Committee has dealt with detentions during a situation of occupation. For example, it has addressed Israel's detention of Palestinians from the Occupied Territories in connection with its derogation from Article 9 of the ICPR. In its Concluding Observations on Israel's second periodic report, the Committee recognized Israel's 'serious security concerns in the context of the present conflict', including suicide bombings associated with the second intifada, which led it to declare a state of emergency and derogate from Article 9 of the ICCPR.[88] Nonetheless, it expressed concern about Israel's use of various forms of administrative detention, restricting access to counsel and disclosure of full reasons for detentions. The Committee stated 'these features limit the effectiveness of judicial review, thus endangering the protection against torture and other inhuman treatment prohibited under article 7 and derogating from article 9 more extensively than what in the Committee's view is permissible pursuant to article 4'.[89] Presumably, the European Court would also find persons detained during an occupation entitled to a *habeas* or equivalent proceeding.

6.3   Situations of Non-international Armed Conflict

Although IHL applicable to NIACs envisions the detention of fighters and civilians for reasons related to the conflict, it contains no rules authorizing or regulating such detentions.[90] These are matters governed exclusively by domestic law and HRL. Thus, a State engaged in a NIAC can detain, try and punish insurgents consistent with its human rights obligations. If it instead wants to administratively detain or intern them, then it would have to derogate from the right to personal liberty, which would entail declaring an emergency. However, human rights jurisprudence, as indicated, would preclude it from suspending *habeas corpus* in such situations.

If that State requests other States to help it quell the insurrection within its territory, those States' legal authority to detain insurgents and other persons, unless stipulated otherwise in a legal arrangement, would not be based on their *domestic* laws, but that of the host State. Moreover, any such extraterritorial detentions would also constitute an exercise of jurisdiction under the ICCPR, the European Convention, and the American Convention or Declaration (if carried out in an OAS Member State). No human rights treaty body has yet ruled on the lawfulness of extraterritorial detentions in these particular circumstances. The Human Rights Committee and the IACommHR arguably would not find such detentions to be 'arbitrary' if they were lawful under the law of, and duly authorized by, the host State. However, such detentions do not on the surface satisfy any of the grounds for deprivation of liberty in Article 5 of the European Convention. And, any attempt by a COE State to derogate from that article based on its involvement in a purely extraterritorial NIAC would be questionable for reasons previously explained. Finally, any person detained, administratively or otherwise, by agents of the invited States should be entitled to file *habeas* or equivalent actions before the courts of the *host* State. US case law also suggests that the courts of the *detaining* country might also entertain such petitions.

7.   CONCLUSION

In examining the extraterritorial application of two 'preferred' human rights, this paper has identified serious gaps in legal protection of the right to life under the European and Inter-American human rights systems, which should be remedied. It also has noted potentially significant problems with derogations from these rights based on a State's involvement in purely overseas armed conflicts. Its exploration of how treaty bodies deal with the relationship between IHL and HRL during armed conflicts has revealed major differences in approach, particularly the European Court's failure to use IHL to assess the legality of combat-related killings during armed conflicts. The chapter also points out the need to clarify whether human rights bodies should apply IHL or HRL to determine when territory is occupied, and which body of law should govern the use of deadly force in such situations. Finally, it notes that, with the exception of POWs and civilian internees under GC IV, all other persons deprived of liberty during emergency situations, including armed conflicts, should have, in principle, a right to challenge the lawfulness of his/her detention.

NOTES

*   Robert K. Goldman is Professor of Law and Louis C. James Scholar; Co-Director, Center for Human Rights and Humanitarian Law, American University, Washington College of Law. This chapter is largely based on a paper that was originally prepared by the author for the Working Group on International Humanitarian and Human Rights Law of the Counter-terrorism Project, organized by the Grotius Centre for International Legal Studies, Leiden University and Campus the Hague, and which will appear as a chapter in L.J. van den Herik and N.J. Schrijver (eds), *Counter-terrorism and International Law; Meeting the Challenges* (forthcoming).

1.   S/RES/1373, 28 September 2001.
2.   General Comment No. 29: *States of Emergency (Article 4)*, HRC, 31 August 2000 (UN Doc. CCPR/C/21/Rev.1/Add.11).
3.   *Lopez Burgos v. Uruguay*, HRC, 29 July 1981 (UN Doc. CCPR/C/13/D/52/1979) [hereinafter *Lopez Burgos* case]; *Celiberti v. Uruguay*, HRC, 29 July 1981 (UN Doc. CCPR/C/13/D/56/1979).
4.   *Lopez Burgos* case, *supra* note 3, para. 12.3.
5.   General Comment No. 31: *Nature of the General Legal Obligation Imposed on States Parties to the Covenant*, HRC, 26 May 2004 (UN Doc. CCPR/C/21/Rev.1/Add.13).
6.   Ibid., para. 10.
7.   See Concluding Observations on Israel, HRC, 21 August 2003 (UN Doc. CCPR/CO/78/ISR), para. 178 [hereinafter Concluding Observations on Israel].
8.   *Legal Consequences of the Construction of a Wall in the Occupied Palestinian Territory*, Advisory Opinion, I.C.J. Reports 2004 [hereinafter *Wall* opinion].
9.   Ibid., para. 111.
10.   *Cyprus v. Turkey*, ECtHR, Application No. 6780/74 and 6950/75, Report of the ECHR adopted on 10 July 1976 [hereinafter *Cyprus v. Turkey*].
11.   Ibid. (emphasis added).
12.   *Loizidou v. Turkey*, ECtHR, Preliminary Objections, Judgment of 23 March 1995 [hereinafter *Loizidou* case].
13.   Ibid., para. 62.
14.   Ibid. (emphasis added).
15.   *Cyprus v. Turkey*, *supra* note 10, para. 78.
16.   *Bankovic and others v. Belgium and others*, ECtHR, Application No. 52207/99, Decision on Admissibility, 12 December 2001 [hereinafter *Bankovic* case].
17.   Ibid., paras 61, 67.
18.   Ibid., para. 80
19.   *Öcalan v. Turkey*, ECtHR, Application No. 46221/99, Judgment of 12 March 2003 [hereinafter *Öcalan* case].
20.   Ibid., para. 93.
21.   Ibid.
22.   *Issa and others v. Turkey*, ECtHR, Application No. 31821/96, Judgment of 16 November 2004 [hereinafter *Issa* case].
23.   Ibid., para. 71.
24.   Ibid.
25.   Ibid., para. 74.
26.   *Al-Skeini and Others v. United Kingdom*, ECtHR, Application No. 55721/07, Judgment of 7 July 2011.
27.   The Court also noted that '[i]n this sense, therefore, the Convention rights can be "divided and tailored"'. Compare with *Bankovic and others v. Belgium and others*, ECtHR, Application No.52207/99, Decision on Admissibility, 12 December 2001.
28.   Citing to *Cyprus v. Turkey*, the Court indicated that the controlling State has the responsibility 'under Article 1 to secure, within the area under its control, the entire range of substantive rights set out in the Convention and those additional Protocols which it has ratified', *Cyprus v. Turkey*, ECommHR, Application No. 25781/94, ECHR 2001-IV, paras. 76–77.
29.   *Al-Saadoon and Mufdhi v. the United Kingdom*, ECtHR, Application No. 61498/08, decision of 30 June 2009.
30.   *Al-Skeini* case, *supra* note 26, para. 149.

31. F. Hampson, 'The Relationship between International Humanitarian Law and Human Rights Law from the Perspective of a Human Rights Treaty Body', *International Review of the Red Cross* 90 (2008): 594, at 570 [hereinafter *Hampson*].

32. *Coard et al. v. United States*, IACommHR, Case 10.951, Report No. 109/99, 29 September 1999 [hereinafter *Coard* case].

33. Ibid., para. 37.

34. Ibid.

35. *Franklin Guillermo Aisalla Molina, Ecuador v. Colombia*, IACommHR, Admissibility, Case IP-02, Report No. 112/10, 21 October 2010.

36. Ibid., para. 99.

37. Ibid., para. 100.

38. *Alejandre et al. v. Cuba*, IACommHR, Case 11.589, Report No. 86/99, 29 September 1999.

39. Ibid., para. 25.

40. *Request for Precautionary Measures Concerning the Detainees at Guantanamo Bay, Cuba*, IAComm HR, Decision, 12 March 2002, International Legal Materials 41 (2002): 532.

41. *Salas v. United States*, IACommHR, Case 10.573, Report No. 31/93, 14 October 1993 [hereinafter *Salas* case].

42. Ibid., para. 6.

43. *Victor Saldaño v. Argentina*, IACommHR, Case 12.254, Report No. 38/99, 11 March 1999.

44. Ibid., para. 20.

45. *Legality of the Threat or Use of Nuclear Weapons*, Advisory Opinion, I.C.J. Reports 1996.

46. Ibid., para. 25.

47. *Wall* opinion, *supra* note 8.

48. Ibid., para. 106.

49. Ibid., The Court confirmed this approach in *Case Concerning Armed Activities on the Territory of the Congo* (D.R. Congo v. Uganda), Judgment, I.C.J Reports 2005.

50. General Comment No. 31, *supra* note 5, para. 11.

51. See *Report on Terrorism and Human Rights* (2002), paras 57–62 [hereinafter *Terrorism* report].

52. See International Committee of the Red Cross, 'Interpretive Guidance on The Notion of Direct Participation in Hostilities under International Humanitarian Law' (2009), available at http://www.icrc.org/eng/resources/documents/article/review/review-872-p991.htm

53. See *Salas* case, *supra* note 41.

54. *Juan Carlos Abella v. Argentina*, IACommHR, Case 11.137, Report No. 355/97, 18 November 1997.

55. Hampson, *supra* note 31, at 567.

56. Ibid.

57. C. Droege, 'The Interplay Between International Humanitarian Law and International Human Rights Law in Situations of Armed Conflict', *Israel Law Review* 40 (2007): 310, 325.

58. *Illascu and others v. Russia, Moldova*, ECtHR, Application No. 48787/99, Judgment of 8 July 2004.

59. *Coard* case, *supra* note 32.

60. See Concluding Observations on Israel, *supra* note 7, at para. 15, in which the HRC expressed concern about Israel's targeted killings of suspected terrorists in the Occupied Territories. See also *The Public Committee against Torture in Israel et al. v. the Prime Minister of Israel et al.*, the Supreme Court of Israel sitting as High Court of Justice, Judgment of 14 December 2006.

61. *Guerrero v. Colombia*, HRC, 31 March 1982 (UN Doc. Supp. No. 40 (A/37/40)).

62. See, e.g., *Gül v. Turkey*, ECtHR, Application No. 22676/93, Judgment of 14 December 2000; *Ogur v. Turkey*, ECtHR, Application No. 21594/93, Judgment of 20 May 1999; *Güleç v. Turkey*, ECtHR, Application No. 21593/93, Judgment of 27 July 1998; *McCann and others v. United Kingdom*, ECtHR, Application No. 18984/91, Judgment of 27 September 1995.

63. See *Ahmet Özkan and others v. Turkey*, ECtHR, Application No. 21689/93, Judgment of April 2004; *Ergi v. Turkey*, ECtHR, Application No. 23818/94, Judgment of 28 July 1998.

64. See *Isayeva, Yusupova and Bazayeva v. Russia*, ECtHR, Application No. 57947/00, Judgment of 24 February 2004.

65. General Comment No. 29, *supra* note 2, para. 16.

66. *Judicial Guarantees in States of Emergency, Articles 27(2), 25 and 8 of the American Convention on Human Rights*, IACtHR, Advisory Opinion, 6 October 1987.

67. *Chahal v. United Kingdom*, ECtHR, Application No. 22414/93, Judgment of 15 November 1996.

68. See Fourth Geneva Convention, Articles 41–43.

69. *Terrorism* Report, *supra* note 51, para. 141.

70. Ibid., para. 142.
71. Ibid., para. 146.
72. Ibid.
73. *Rasul v. Bush*, 542 US 466 (2004).
74. *Boumedienne v. Bush*, 553 US 723 (2008).
75. W. Kälin, 'The Covenant on Civil and Political Rights and its Relationship with International Humanitarian Law' in University Center for International Humanitarian Law, Expert Meeting on the Supervision of the Lawfulness of Detention During Armed Conflict, available at http://www.ruig-gian.org/ressources/communication_colloque_rapport04.pdf?ID=256&FILE=/ressources/communication_colloque_rapport04.pdf (accessed 9 February 2012).
76. Ibid.
77. *Cyprus v. Turkey, supra* note 10.
78. Hampson, *supra* note 31, 565.
79. Ibid., 566.
80. J. Pejic, 'Procedural Principles and Safeguards for Internment/Administrative Detention in Armed Conflict and Other Situations of Violence', *International Review of the Red Cross* 87 (2005): 375, 386.
81. Ibid.
82. Ibid., 387.
83. *Prosecutor v. Zejnil Delalic and others*, ICTY, Appeals Chamber, Judgment, 20 February 2001 (Case No. IT-96-21-A, para. 22).
84. *Coard* case, *supra* note 32, para. 55.
85. Ibid., para. 58.
86. Ibid., para. 55.
87. Ibid., para. 57.
88. Concluding Observations on Israel, *supra* note 7, para. 3.
89. Ibid., para.12.
90. But see J. Pejic and C. Droege's article in L.J. van den Herik and N.J. Schrijver (ed.), *Counterterrorism and International Law; Meeting the Challenges* (forthcoming), indicating that 'both customary and treaty IHL contain an inherent power to intern and may thus be said to provide a legal basis for internment in NIAC'.

7. Proportionality in the European Convention on Human Rights

*Enzo Cannizzaro and Francesca De Vittor**

1. INTRODUCTION

In the classical conception, international human rights law constitutes a set of rules which establish limits to sovereign powers. From this perspective, proportionality has the function of determining a reasonable balance between States' and individuals' interests. A different conception is gradually emerging which tends to regard human rights as part of the basic collective values of the international community. In this conception, proportionality is gradually assuming the function of determining the contents of human rights through a constant process of interests- and values-balancing. In this process, individuals' interests are balanced not only with States' interests but also with other individual and collective values of the international community.

The current chapter will focus on the process of transformation of proportionality, from a tool designed to operate in the State–individual relationship, to one which applies to the overall process of values-balancing underlying the dynamics of human rights in contemporary international law. This process will be observed through a study of proportionality in the European Convention on Human Rights, probably the most integrated system of human rights protection established thus far, and one which can serve as a model for the development of a more comprehensive system of protection.[1]

2. PROPORTIONALITY AND DEROGATION IN THE ECHR

Derogation represents the clearest example of how proportionality can be used in order to balance human rights and prerogatives of State sovereignty – in particular, the most evident prerogative, which is typically the power, or even the duty, to safeguard the life of the nation in time of war or of other public emergency.

2.1 European Court of Human Rights' Case Law

Article 15 of the ECHR authorises 'in time of war or other public emergency threatening the life of the nation' any contracting party, to 'take measures derogating from its obligations under [the] Convention to the extent strictly required by the exigencies of the situation'.[2]

On the basis of purely textual interpretation, the role of proportionality appears very limited indeed. Article 15 establishes a certain threshold of gravity, below which no derogation is allowed and above which any derogation measure is allowed, which is necessary or even indispensable to the threat.

A different approach was taken by the Court. The Court granted to States a wide margin of appreciation in the assessment of the existence of a 'public emergency threatening the life of the nation'.[3] In other words, the 'threshold of severity' was lowered[4] and, as a result, the existence of a public emergency for the purposes of Article 15 was ascertained even in situations in which the 'life of the nation' was not under imminent threat.[5] So the Court condoned the prolonged derogation in Northern Ireland despite the principle that the emergency must be temporary in nature.[6] In the more recent case law concerning the aftermath of the 9/11 terrorist emergency, the Court did not consider conclusive the circumstance that only one State among all the parties to the convention decided to derogate the Convention:

> While it is striking that the United Kingdom was the only Convention State to have lodged a derogation in response to the danger from al Qaeda, although other States were also the subject of threats, the Court accepts that it was for each Government, as the guardian of their own people's safety, to make their own assessment on the basis of the facts known to them.[7]

Such a wide margin of appreciation granted to States was, however, balanced by a strict European supervision in the light of the proportionality test, in which a significant role was played by 'the nature of the rights affected by the derogation and the circumstances leading to, and the duration of, the emergency situation'.[8]

Beginning with the *Lawless* case, the Court established some paradigmatic standards of legitimate measures of derogation, 'reasonably necessary' in democratic societies. Formally using the concept of necessity rather than that of proportionality,[9] the Court analysed detention without trial measures in depth, taking into account the inadequacy of less intrusive measures to face cross-border terrorism and the effects of other possible measures, such as the sealing of the border, on the whole population.[10] Moreover, the Court considered the establishment of a number of safeguards and quasi-judicial remedies designed to prevent abuses in the operation of the system of administrative detention.[11]

The proportionality test has been consistently used in the following case law, even though the deferential attitude towards national authorities in ascertaining the existence of a state of emergency was progressively extended also to the nature and scope of the measures adopted to match it.[12] In *Ireland v. United Kingdom*, the Court established a test of proportionality between the gravity of the situation and the measures taken: such a serious derogation from fundamental rights as in, for example, the arrest of innocent persons for the sole purpose of obtaining information about others was justifiable 'only in a very exceptional situation, but the circumstances prevailing in Northern Ireland did fall into such a category'.[13] It is relevant to note that the proportionality and adequacy test is a retrospective examination, done by the Court *a priori*, on the basis of the knowledge the national authority had at the time of the implementation of the measures, without considering, *a posteriori*, the results actually achieved.[14]

In the *Brannigan* case the enlargement of the State discretion seems to be the consequence of the methodology adopted for the proportionality test. Rather than evoking the possibility of adopting different measures which would be less intrusive in respect of fundamental rights, the Court limits itself to reviewing the overall balance between the State's interest in achieving a reasonable standard of security and the need to comply with the individual rights protected by the ECHR.[15]

This approach, combining deference towards national authorities and international control, was maintained and even enhanced in the most recent case law. In *A. and Others v. United Kingdom*, establishing that the detention of foreign nationals under the Anti-terrorism, Crime and Security Act 2001 was a disproportionate limitation of the right granted by Article 5, the Court said:

> the domestic courts are part of the 'national authorities' to which the Court affords a wide margin of appreciation under Article 15. In the unusual circumstances of the present case, where the highest domestic court has examined the issues relating to the State's derogation and concluded that there was a public emergency threatening the life of the nation but that the measures taken in response were not strictly required by the exigencies of the situation, the Court considers that it would be justified in reaching a contrary conclusion only if satisfied that the national court had misinterpreted or misapplied Article 15 or the Court's jurisprudence under that Article or reached a conclusion which was manifestly unreasonable.[16]

A stricter approach was taken in the context of grave and reiterated violations of human rights. The existence of an overall context of violations of 'ordinary' obligations of the Convention seems to have been considered as a concurring factor for assessing the proportionality of derogation measures.[17]

2.2 The Structure of the Proportionality Argument

From the analysis of the preceding paragraph, a particular structure of the proportionality test seems to emerge. Necessity is a fundamental premise of this test, but by no means exhausts it. A derogation measure is necessary if no other measures are at hand of equivalent efficacy but which impinge to a lesser degree on the Conventional rights. Necessity, however, implies that the State's interests prevail over individual interests, if indispensable to attain the level of security sought. By stressing the importance of international supervision on the proportionality of the derogation measures, the Court seems to have implicitly pointed out that, in the system of the Convention, States' interests do not prevail over individual interests, but the various competing interests must be combined together, using as guidance the test of proportionality.

As a result, this test was articulated into two logically distinct steps. The first concerns the reasonableness of the level of security sought by the State. The second concerns the existence of a link of proportionality between such a level and the degree of curtailment that is entailed for individual rights. Even a reasonable degree of security must be lowered if its attainment entails a disproportionate compression of individual rights. By so doing, the Court seems to have forged a conceptual model based on proportionality. Even if the case law reveals the tendency of the Court to rely on the assessment made by the State concerned to restrain the scope of the international supervision and, correspondingly, to recognise a wide margin of appreciation to the State concerned, this model appears of great theoretical interest, as it seems to apply in every situations in which a balance among competing interests and values is at stake.

3. PROPORTIONALITY AND LIMITATION CLAUSES

3.1 The Early Case Law

The proportionality test was constructed, in its main features, from the case law related to the limitation clauses established by Articles 8 to 11, para. 2, of the Convention, by Article 1, para. 1 of Protocol I, by Article 2, paras 3 and 4 of Protocol IV, and by Articles 1, paras 2 and 5 of Protocol VII.

These provisions have analogous formal structure. They list collective interests capable of interfering with individual rights protected by the Convention and establish conditions of the interference. The collective interests are mostly common, such as public order and security; others refer specifically to the limitation of some rights, as, for example, the interest to maintain the authority and impartiality of the judiciary, listed in Article 10, para. 2. An open set of interests capable of interfering with conventional rights is established by Article 1, para.1, of Protocol I, protecting the peaceful enjoyment of private property.

The existence of limitation clauses makes clear that the individual rights concerned do not enjoy absolute protection. These provisions seem rather to identify a plurality of competing interests, individual and collective, whose appropriate balance must be struck on a case-by-case basis using the guidance offered by the proportionality principle. Theoretically, this structure is of the utmost interest, since it marks off these rules from those which rely on a predetermined balance of interests, designed to remain stable over time. The limitation clauses of the ECHR embody an unresolved conflict between competing interests, none of which takes overall priority over the others. The conflict therefore cannot be solved in the *abstracto*, but rather on the basis of the concrete weight to be given to any of these competing interests in the light of the circumstances of every particular situation. The settlement of the conflict thus entails a sophisticated factual and legal analysis aimed at identifying the most appropriate combination of the various interests at stake.

The basic elements of such a proportionality test have been identified by the Court in its early case law. In the *Belgian Linguistic case* the Court declared that the Convention 'implies a just balance between the protection of the general interest of the Community and the respect due to fundamental human rights while attaching particular importance to the latter'; nevertheless the domestic regulation 'must never injure the substance of the right' (in that particular case the right to education granted by Article 2 of Protocol I), 'nor conflict with other rights enshrined in the Convention'.[18]

Handyside supplied the Court with the occasion to render the leading case on the principle of proportionality. The Court noted that the adjective 'necessary', within the meaning of Article 10, para. 2, is not synonymous with 'indispensable' or 'strictly necessary', neither has it the flexibility of such expressions as 'useful', 'reasonable', or 'desirable'; the adjective 'necessary' describes something that is in between absolute necessity and reasonableness, and supposes the existence of a 'pressing social need', the assessment of which is in the competence of national authorities.[19] Nevertheless, the margin of appreciation of national authorities is not unlimited; the Court 'is empowered to give the final ruling on whether a "restriction" or "penalty" is reconcilable with freedom of expression as protected by Article 10 ... This means, amongst other things, that every "formality", "condition", "restriction" or "penalty" imposed in this sphere must be proportionate to the legitimate aim pursued'.[20]

As can be seen in the passages from *Handyside* cited above, in the early case law the proportionality test, based on the concept of necessity in a democratic society, is confused with the analysis concerning the legitimacy of the aim pursued. In the subsequent case law this conceptual ambiguity disappears. The Court has first identified the interests which, in a democratic society, could justify a certain degree of interference and then moved on to determine whether the interference was necessary, appropriate and not excessively impinging upon the individual rights at stake. In this approach, the need to protect collective values, even if set at a reasonable standard according to the model of a democratic society, was not sufficient to conclude the analysis. The proportionality test still requires determining that the satisfaction of collective needs does not entail a disproportionate curtailment in the enjoyment of individual rights. Thus proportionality not only prohibits interference in human rights which are not necessary to protect collective interests in a democratic society, it also determines the level of the protection of these collective interests, taking into account the level of interference they entail upon individual rights.

A clear application of this methodology is the *Sunday Times* case, where the Court observes that

> [i]t is not sufficient that the interference involved belongs to that class of the exceptions listed in Article 10 §2 which has been invoked; neither is it sufficient that the interference was imposed because its subject-matter fell within a particular category or was caught by a legal rule formulated in general or absolute terms: the Court has to be satisfied that the interference was necessary having regard to the facts and circumstances prevailing in the specific case before it.[21]

3.2   The Following Case Law

This logical structure also inspired the subsequent case law. A brief account of this case law, covering the main, but not all,[22] fields in which proportionality was used in the context of limitation clauses, will be given in the forthcoming sections.

3.2.1   Limitations to the right of respect for private and family life (Article 8, para. 2)

The proportionality test has been used by the Court in a great number of cases concerning limitation to the right of respect for private and family life.

The case law concerning the criminal repression of homosexual activities – and other forms of regulation of private sexual and identity choices – acquires paradigmatic value. In *Dudgeon*, the Court clarifies the scope of the margin of appreciation of States, but also its limits where the protection of morals is at issue. In the absence of a uniform European conception of morals, the Court recognises to States an extremely wide margin of appreciation in defining legitimate aims of restriction;[23] however, this is balanced by a strict evaluation of proportionality when the intimate aspects of private life are at stake:[24] the more the restriction impinges on the intimate life of the individual, the less the interference is justified. Conversely, a wider margin of appreciation is recognised to States when the restrictions are aimed at the protection of health. So the Court considered legitimate the prosecution and convictions for assault and wounding in the course of consensual sadomasochistic activities between adults,[25] and the prohibition of assisted suicide.[26]

A significant progress in the proportionality argument was marked in *Odièvre*, where the Court was confronted with the difficult task of balancing competing individual interests, equally protected by Article 8; namely the right of the child to know his own origins, and the right of the mother to anonymously give birth in appropriate health conditions.[27] Even though the French legal order is the only European one providing for anonymous delivery dispositions, the Court considered that

> [t]he French legislation ... seeks to strike a balance and to ensure sufficient proportion between the competing interests. The Court observed in that connection that the States must be allowed to determine the means which they consider the best to reconcile those interests. Overall, the Court considers that France has not overstepped the margin of appreciation which it must be afforded in view of the complex and sensitive nature of the issue of access to information about one's origins, an issue that concerns the right to know one's personal history, the choices of the natural parents, the existing family ties and the adoptive parents.[28]

The Court also uses the proportionality test under Article 8, para. 2, to syndicate welfare choices of the State. In *Wallova and Walla*, the State's decision to separate five children from their parents and place them under public care because the family was unable to find a convenient place to live was disproportionate. The Court recognised that the measure taken by the State pursued the legitimate aim of protecting children, however

> [l]a Cour estime que, pour respecter en l'espèce l'exigence de proportionnalité, les autorités tchèques auraient dû envisager d'autres mesures moins radicales que la prise en charge des enfants. En effet, la Cour considère que le rôle des autorités de la protection sociale est précisément d'aider les personnes en difficultés qui n'ont pas les connaissances nécessaires du système, de les guider dans leurs démarches et de les conseiller, entre autres, quant aux différents types d'allocations sociales, aux possibilités d'obtenir un logement social ou quant aux autres moyens de surmonter leurs difficultés.[29]

This proportionality test was also applied in a line of cases in which the Court assessed the proportionality of expulsion of aliens in the light of the obligation to respect private and family life guaranteed by Article 8 of the Convention. In these cases the Court proceeded to a case-by-case balance between the relevant interests, namely the individual's right to respect for his family life, on the one hand, and the prevention of disorder or crime, on the other.[30] Moreover, the principle of proportionality as defined in the case law concerning Article 8, para. 2, has been applied for the interpretation of Article 1, para. 2, of Protocol VII.[31]

3.2.2 Proportionality in the case law concerning Article 9 and Article 2, of Protocol I

The case law concerning the freedom of thought, conscience and religion provides other interesting examples of the criteria adopted by the Court to balance conflicting interests. In the *Leyla Şahin* case the Court evaluated the legitimacy of the Turkish regulation prohibiting the wearing of the Islamic headscarf at university. It is interesting to note that the Court analysed the Turkish context in order to ascertain that secularism in Turkey was the guarantor of democratic values in a country where the majority of the population are Muslims. In that particular context upholding secularism, even by prohibiting the wearing of the Islamic headscarf at university could be considered necessary to protect the democratic system.[32] The relevance recognised by the Court to the political and social context in Turkey might give the impression that a different decision might be taken in a different context.

Nevertheless, the case law concerning the Islamic headscarf shows the tendency of the Court to accept limitations to the right to manifest one's own religious beliefs in order to safeguard the secularism of institutions, and particularly of educational institutions.[33] The reasons for this attitude are clearly manifested in the *Dahlab* decision, where the Court considered manifestly ill-founded the complaint of a teacher who had been banned from wearing the headscarf at school, on the basis that 'the interference with the applicant's freedom to manifest her religion was justified by the need, in a democratic society, to protect the right of State school pupils to be taught in a *context of denominational neutrality*'.[34] It appears clear from the case law mentioned above that secularism embodies one of the fundamental principles of democratic societies, as a guarantee for pluralism and equality. The high value afforded to secularism seems to justify ultimately the pre-eminence of this collective interest on the individual right protected by Article 9.

The principle of the neutrality of public education has been also the object of some cases under the second sentence of Article 2, Protocol I, considered by the Court as *lex specialis* in respect of Article 9. In the *Folgerø* case the Court established that compulsory participation in 'Christianity, Religion and Philosophy' classes in public schools in Norway was an infringement of the right of parents to ensure education and teaching in conformity with their own religious and philosophical convictions granted by Article 2, Protocol I, and that even the possibility of a partial exoneration was not sufficient to grant the neutrality and pluralism of public teaching.[35] In this case the Court applied, in favour of the individual, the principle, previously established in *Young, James and Webster*, according to which 'democracy does not simply mean that the views of a majority must always prevail: a balance must be achieved which ensures the fair and proper treatment of minorities and avoids any abuse of a dominant position'.[36]

The same criteria had been applied by the Second Section of the Court in the *Lautsi* case. The Court chamber considered that the 'State has a duty to uphold confessional neutrality in public education'. As a consequence, the display of the crucifix in Italian classrooms infringed the right of parents to educate their children in conformity with their convictions, and the right of schoolchildren to believe or not believe.[37] Although this decision was in line with the relevant case law, the Grand Chamber reversed it. It considered that 'a crucifix on a wall is an essentially passive symbol' that 'cannot be deemed to have an influence on pupils comparable to that of didactic speech or participation in religious activities'.[38] Secondly, the Grand Chamber accepted the contextualisation of 'the greater visibility which the presence of the crucifix gives to Christianity in schools'. In particular the Court took into account the circumstance that 'Italy opens up the school environment in parallel to other religions', particularly by authorizing pupils to wear Islamic headscarves or other religious symbols.[39]

A comprehensive analysis of the most recent case law testifies that, *in the absence of a European consensus* on the question of relationship between States and religion, a wide margin of appreciation is accorded to States concerning the place they accord to religion, the only real limitation being that those decisions do not lead to a form of indoctrination. The proportionality test seems thus replaced by the determination of a fixed limit to the discretion of the State.

3.2.3   Proportionality argument in the application of Article 10, para. 2 and Article 11, para. 2

Equally interesting is the case law which applies proportionality to determine the limits to freedom of thought protected by Article 10. In the reasoning of the Court, freedom of thought emerges as one of the most important articulations of the individual rights protected by the Convention, and as an essential corollary of the model of democratic society underlying it. The search for appropriate limitations aimed at protecting collective rights thus appears to be the most interesting exercise of interests-balancing ever attempted by the Court.[40] In the context of effective political democracy, freedom of expression is not only important in itself, but also plays a role in the protection of other rights under the Convention.[41] Indeed, the search for appropriate limitation seems to point to a case-by-case assessment of the relative importance of the exercise of the competing rights at stake: the importance for individuals and for the collectivity to exercise their freedom of expression and to receive information on the one hand, and the necessity to limit these activities to protect other interests, on the other.

The fundamental principles of such a case-by-case factual analysis are well established in the case law, and have been summarised by the Grand Chamber in the *Lindon, Otchakovsky-Laurens and July* case:

> the supervision is [not] limited to ascertaining whether the respondent State exercised its discretion reasonably, carefully and in good faith; what the Court has to do is to look at the interference complained of in the light of the case as a whole and determine whether the reasons adduced by the national authorities to justify it are 'relevant and sufficient' and whether it was 'proportionate to the legitimate aim pursued'. In doing so, the Court has to satisfy itself that the national authorities applied standards which were in conformity with the principles embodied in Article 10 and, moreover, that they relied on an acceptable assessment of the relevant facts.[42]

A case exemplifying this logical exercise is *Barfod*, where the Court found that the interest of the State to maintain the authority and impartiality of the judiciary has to bow to the interest of starting a public debate on the efficiency of certain judicial remedies.[43] In *Informationsverein Lentia and Others*, the Court found that the legitimate purpose of controlling broadcasting activities did not justify a complete ban of private broadcasting activities.[44] In *Piermont*, the Court found that the interest of holding a democratic debate on the French nuclear policy in Polynesia prevailed over the interest of security and public order.[45] In *Goodwin* the Court found that the interest of a company to stop the dissemination of confidential news prevailed over the interest of a journalist not to disclose their confidential sources.[46] In the famous *Open Door and Dublin Well Woman* the Court engaged in what was to remain one of the most notable exercises of identification and balancing of the various individual and collective interests underlying the opposing claims.[47] The issue of freedom of information concerning abortion and family planning, and the limitations the State could impose with respect to national legislation in that field has also been the object of the recent case *Women On Waves*, in which the Court ascertained that the decision of the administrative authorities to prohibit the ship *Borndiep*, which had been chartered with a view to staging activities promoting the de-criminalisation of abortion, from entering Portuguese territorial waters was in breach of Article 10.[48] In the last decade of case law, proportionality was also used to establish the duty of the State to adopt positive measures to grant the effective exercise of freedom of expression, even in the sphere of relations between individuals.[49]

Of great interest is the case law in which the Court has attempted to balance the freedom of information with the right to respect for private life, particularly the right to have one's own reputation protected, granted by Article 8. The Court has tended to give priority to the right granted by Article 10 over that granted by Article 8, especially in the context of public debate on matters of general interest.[50] Conversely, a higher consideration is given to the aim of protecting individuals' privacy and reputation when a verbal attack does not 'form part of an open discussion of matters of public concern'.[51] Moreover, the Court considers that where the sole purpose of a publication is 'to satisfy the curiosity of a particular readership regarding the details of a public figure's private life', such publication 'cannot be deemed to contribute to any debate of general interest to society'; in such cases 'freedom of expression calls for a narrower interpretation', and a fair balance between the public interest in the publication and the need to protect private life should probably give prevalence to the latter.[52]

Not surprisingly, the question of freedom of expression is often closely related to that of freedom of association. In a number of cases the Court reiterated that the protection of personal opinions, as secured by Article 10, is one of the objectives of freedom of assembly and association, as enshrined in Article 11.[53] Even in this context, the Court seems to have frequently reverted to a case-by-case interests analysis. Nevertheless, the Court identified at least one fixed general parameter by establishing that 'freedom of association is of such importance that it cannot be restricted in any way ... so long as the person concerned does not himself commit any reprehensible act by reason of his membership of the association'.[54]

In most cases, the proportionality test was used to pierce the veil separating legal from factual analysis, and to appreciate the proper weight to be given in a democratic society to the exercise of this right. This tendency is well epitomised by the case law concerning the obligation to be part of a trade union,[55] and by the case law concerning the legality of measures for the dissolution of political parties and associations having aims inconsistent with the values underlying a democratic society.[56]

3.3   Qualitative Proportionality and Quantitative Proportionality: Towards a Unitary Paradigm?

The idea of a European supervision underlying the adoption of a proportionality test is fully consistent with the doctrine of the margin of appreciation developed from the early case law of the Court,[57] indeed the two doctrines seem rather to constitute two articulations of one and the same conceptual system.[58] Whereas the margin of discretion doctrine relates to the freedom of the State Party to determine autonomously the standard of protection of certain collective, indeterminate legal values,[59] proportionality entails that each of these standards, although reflecting the pressing social needs of each national environment, must be consistent with the notion of democratic society which constitutes, in the view of the Court, the common turf and a pre-legal condition of the partnership to the Convention. Thus, the standard of protection of collective interests cannot be established independently from the concern for human rights: '[s]uch are the demands of that pluralism, tolerance and broadmindedness without which there is no democratic society'.[60]

In this context, proportionality comes into being in its purely qualitative dimension. Human rights are mainly considered, in this first step, as purely abstract legal values, which must be taken into account in order to determine the standard of reasonableness of State measures, in the light of the pressing social need appropriate to a democratic society.

Once the reasonableness of the collective interests which justify interferences with human rights is determined, however, one must proceed to ascertain whether the interference is proportionate. This logical operation entails the balancing of heterogeneous values such as, on the one hand, collective interests underlying a pressing social need, and, on the other, the individual rights protected by the Convention. In this second phase, proportionality is generally measured in quantitative terms. The Court tends to determine quantitatively the interests of individuals to exercise their rights, and to balance such interests with the competing collective interests. In the words of the Commission in the *Gillow* case: 'the Commission retains a limited review of the legitimacy of the aim of the interference and a fuller review of the proportionality of the actual interference with the applicant's rights'.[61]

In this second logical operation, the competing rights and interests are, in other words, not measured by the abstract legal value but rather through the determination of the concrete interest to exercise them in a specific situation. Paradigmatically, in *Young, James and Webster* the Court went so far as to compare the damage caused to the cohesion of a trade union by the lack of adhesion of a few workers with the prejudice suffered by these workers in case of loss of employment. In the cases concerning the consistency of expulsion measures with the right to private and family life, the Court conducted a close scrutiny on the ties of the person concerned and of his family with the social environment which would have been severed in consequence of the expulsion.[62]

Three further remarks are in order to evidence how proportionality has been applied in the judicial practice to better reflect the specific circumstance of each particular case.

First, as stated above, the Court has consistently tended to consider each of the competing legal values as having a specific weight in the concrete circumstances of the situation in which they collided.

Second, in the case law, individual rights are not considered by themselves, as rights which pertain to a socially isolated monad, but rather as the reflex of the collective interest of a democratic society to their preservation and to their further development. This argumentative technique circumvents the logical apory of combining heterogeneous values such as individual and collective interests.[63] Also individual, and not only collective interests, have been appreciated through the comparative assessment of the social consequences entailed in their exercise.[64]

Lastly, the assessment of proportionality was completed with the consideration of the possible remedies attached to normative measures of interference aimed at minimising the prejudice for individuals and to prevent abuses. In *Klass*, concerning the consistency with the Convention of a system of secret surveillance, the Court said: 'the Court must be satisfied that, whatever system of surveillance is adopted, there exist adequate and effective guarantees against abuses'.[65]

4. PROPORTIONALITY AND THE DETERMINATION OF THE SCOPE OF CONVENTIONAL RIGHTS

By no means has the scope of the proportionality test remained confined to the derogation clause and to the limitation clauses. Quite the contrary, it has spilled over its natural fields of application and emerged as a general principle of interests- and values-balancing within the system of the Convention.

A brief account of how proportionality was employed by the Court even outside these two typical fields can be useful to evidence its emerging nature as a general principle. We will thus examine, in turn, two different but logically related fields of application of proportionality, concerning, respectively, the power of States to regulate the exercise of conventional rights, and the power of States to regulate situations occasionally interfering with the exercise of these rights.

4.1 Regulating the Exercise of Conventional Rights

The first, and to an extent still quite obvious, employment of the proportionality test was to gauge the appropriateness of States' measures designed to regulate the exercise of individual rights protected by the Convention for requirements in the public interest.

The best example of this use of proportionality is to be found in the *Belgian Linguistic case*. The Court found that the right to education, unqualifiedly protected by Article 2 Protocol I,

> by its very nature calls for regulation by the State, regulation which may vary in time and place according to the needs and resources of the community and of the individuals. ... The Convention therefore implies a just balance between the protection of the general interest of the community and the respect due to fundamental human rights while attaching particular importance to the latter.[66]

This scheme was henceforth applied in a number of other situations in which the Court recognised the power of the States to regulate the exercise of conventional rights subject to a condition of proportionality between the aim pursued and the degree of interference with these rights.

In *Golder* the Court pointed out that States can regulate the exercise of non-absolute rights without, however, unduly impairing the very essence of the right.[67] This negative limit was gradually transformed in a positive limit imposed on the power to regulate, in a way quite similar to that used for limitation. Indeed regulation must pursue a legitimate aim and there must be a reasonable relationship of proportionality between the means employed and the aim sought to be achieved.[68]

This scheme was subsequently applied in a variety of situations including the power to regulate the right to access to justice,[69] the right to marry,[70] and the right to vote established by Article 3, Protocol 1. In *Hirst*, concerning the limitation of the right to vote of detainees, the Court clearly established guidelines for a proportionality test in this matter, and explicitly asserted that the proportionality of the restriction on the exercise of the right must be evaluated case-by-case on factual bases.[71] The Court observed that 'there is no evidence that the legislature in the United Kingdom has ever sought to weigh the competing interests or to assess the proportionality of the ban as it affects convicted prisoners'; and on that basis decided that the automatic blanket ban imposed on all convicted prisoners in the United Kingdom violated Article 3 of Protocol I.[72]

Particularly interesting is also the case law concerning the balancing of the right of access to court with jurisdictional immunities granted by international law. In every case the Court confirmed the principle that 'a limitation will not be compatible with Article 6 § 1 if it does not pursue a legitimate aim and if there is no reasonable relationship of proportionality between the means employed and the aim sought to be achieved'.[73] In applying this principle, in cases in which the jurisdictional immunity of international organizations was at issue, the Court assessed the proportionality of the limitation in the light of the circumstances of the case, taking particularly into account the fact that 'the applicants had available to them reasonable *alternative* means to protect effectively their rights under the Convention'.[74] Conversely, in cases concerning State immunity, the Court seems to be satisfied by the circumstance that immunity is provided by customary international law; in consequence, the legitimate aim of respecting customary international law also covers the proportionality of the adopted measure.[75]

4.2   Producing Occasional Interference through Regulation of Situations Falling Outside the Scope of the Conventional Rights

Finally, proportionality was employed in a highly interesting line of cases concerning indirect collisions between conventional rights and States' measures regulating situations falling plainly outside the scope of the Convention. In turn, this category of cases can be divided into two subgroups. In the first the Court used proportionality for determining the scope of the States' competence, unaffected by the Convention. In the second, the Court used proportionality for dealing with issues of indirect conflict in the proper sense, flowing from States' measures enacted in the public interest but occasionally colliding with individual rights protected by the Convention.

The case which best epitomises the first subgroup is probably *Van der Mussele*. Here, proportionality was used to delimit the notion of forced labour, prohibited by Article 4, para. 2, of the Convention, and other situations in which a service not exceeding the normal course of affairs might be imposed by the State as a form of social solidarity.

This would be the case, in particular, where the service is required in order to meet a compelling social need and does not amount to an intolerable or disproportionate burden.[76]

The best example of situations belonging to the second subgroup comes from States' measures in social and economic fields designed to meet general interests and only indirectly colliding with the exercise of the individual right to property.

In the case law of the Court, proportionality was paradigmatically used to determine the scope of general measures of the State in the general interest, producing occasional interference with the right to property. This conceptual scheme was first developed in *Sporrong and Lönnroth*,[77] and was further applied in a variety of other cases concerning, *inter alia*, town planning, protection of the environment[78] and forested areas,[79] securing the payment of taxes,[80] regulation of immigration,[81] controlling illegal trafficking of art objects,[82] regulating the renting of immovable property,[83] forcible eviction for security purposes,[84] and regulation of time limits in actions to recover property in case of adverse possession.[85]

5. CONCLUDING REMARKS

Both quantitatively and qualitatively, proportionality has played a decisive role in the development of the system of protection set up by the European Convention on Human Rights, and has also represented a model for other conventional systems. The way in which the Court has fashioned the proportionality test has, moreover, a general theoretical significance and constitutes an instrument of general application in the relationship between States' sovereign powers and the limitations entailed in external obligations.

An attempt at categorising the infinite variety of the uses of proportionality falls well beyond the scope of the present chapter and also amounts to a temerarious endeavour. By way of conclusion, a few remarks might be in order.

First, from its original turf of the derogation and limitations clauses, proportionality has expanded to potentially cover the whole field of the conflicts between States' powers and conventional rights, and even between conventional rights themselves and with other individual and collective rights. Thus proportionality can be truly considered as a general technique of conflict-settling throughout the scope of the European Convention.

Second, in this process of expansion, proportionality, while maintaining its general end-means relationship structure, has also adapted its content to the particular features of every single conflict. This is quite evident if one compares proportionality in limitation clauses, in which the Convention determines a *numerus clausus* of the interests capable of interfering with individual rights, with the analogous test in the context of open-ended collisions, in which conventional rights might be interfered with by a potentially infinite variety of States' interests.

In the first group of conflicts, the Court has required the existence of a pressing social need which makes it necessary to interfere with the conventional rights. This quite high standard of necessity was set off by the prohibition to touch upon the 'core content' of the individual right at stake. A logically reversed situation occurs in the second category, where an interference with conventional rights is permitted by States' measures in the general interest, without regard to the intensity of the social need underlying such measures. However, this quite loose standard of necessity is set off by the requirement that the interference must not touch upon the 'normal' exercise of the individual right.

Third, proportionality also assumes diverse features with regard to the relative importance of the various elements of the balancing test.

In derogation and limitation clauses, the Convention identifies the States' interests capable of interfering with the individual rights protected by the Convention. In this context, proportionality has the classical structure of a limit to a functional power to interfere with legally protected interest for the achievement of pre-determined goals. A different structure features proportionality in conflicts among a plurality of individual or collective rights entitled to equal protection, where there is, normally, not a controlling interest. In situations of this kind, proportionality reveals itself to be more akin to a bilateral test of reasonableness. The Court is requested first to determine the concrete interest underlying the exercise of each competing right, and, second, to balance these various interests against each other.

NOTES

*   Enzo Cannizzaro is Professor of International and European Law at the University of Roma ('La Sapienza'). Francesca De Vittor is Researcher in International Law at the University of Macerata.
1.   In spite of the importance of the principle of proportionality in the ECtHR case law (Judge Pettiti defined it as 'Règle d'or de la jurisprudence européenne des droits de l'homme', in 'Réflexions sur les principes et les mécanismes de la Convention. De l'idéal de 1950 à l'humble réalité d'aujourd'hui', in L.-E. Pettiti, E. Decaux and P.-H. Imbert (eds) *La convention européenne des droits de l'homme: commentaire article par article* (Paris: Economica, 1995), 33), there are not many studies specifically devoted to this methodology. Among others, see S. van Drooghenbroeck, *La proportionnalité dans le droit de la Convention européenne des droits de l'homme: prendre l'idée simple au sérieux* (Brussels: Bruylant, 2001), and J. Christoffersen, *Fair Balance: Proportionality, Subsidiarity and Primarity in the European Convention on Human Rights* (Leiden: Martinus Nijhoff, 2009).
2.   Article 15(3), provides for a procedural guarantee establishing that 'Any High Contracting Party availing itself of this right of derogation shall keep the Secretary General of the Council of Europe fully informed of the measures which it has taken and the reasons therefore. It shall also inform the Secretary General of the Council of Europe when such measures have ceased to operate and the provisions of the Convention are again being fully executed.' In the absence of a formal communication, the Court considers that even measures adopted to face emergency situations have to be evaluated according to the parameters of interference and restriction established by single articles of the Convention (see *Brogan and Others v. United Kingdom*, ECtHR, Application Nos 11209/84, 11234/84, 11266/84 and 11386/85, Judgment of 29 November 1988, para. 48). Moreover, the territorial scope of the derogation cannot be extended beyond the territories explicitly named in the notice of derogation: *Sakik and Others v. Turkey*, ECtHR, Application Nos 23878/94, 23879/94 and 23880/94, Judgment of 26 November 1997, para. 39; *Abdülsamet Yaman v. Turkey*, ECtHR, Application No. 32446/96, Judgment of 2 November 2004, para. 69; *Sadak v. Turkey*, ECtHR, Application Nos 25142/94 and 27099/95, Judgment of 8 April 2004, para. 56.
3.   See R. Higgins, 'Derogations under Human Rights Treaties', *British Yearbook of International Law* 48 (1976–1977): 281ff. The purpose of Article 15 was firstly enlarged to cover almost every severe crisis in a democratic society in *Lawless v. Ireland (No. 3)*, ECtHR, Application No. 332/57, Judgment of 1 July 1961, where the emergency was defined as an 'exceptional situation of crisis or emergency which affects the whole population and constitutes a threat to the organised life of the community of which the State is composed' (para. 28). The reasons for that enlargement were then clearly established in

Ireland v. United Kingdom and maintained in the following case law: 'By reason of their direct and continuous contact with the pressing needs of the moment, the national authorities are in principle better placed than the international judge to decide both on the presence of such an emergency and on the nature and scope of the derogations necessary to avert it' (*Ireland v. United Kingdom*, ECtHR, Application No. 5310/71, Judgment of 18 January 1978, para. 207. See also, *Case of A. and Others v. United Kingdom* [GC], ECtHR, Application No. 3455/05, Judgment of 19 February 2009, para. 173; *Brannigan and McBride v. United Kingdom*, ECtHR, Application Nos 14553/89 and 14554/89, Judgment of 25 May 1993, para. 43; *Aksoy v. Turkey*, ECtHR, Application No. 21987/93, Judgment of 18 December 1996, para. 68; *Demir and Others v. Turkey*, ECtHR, Application Nos 21380/93, 21381/93 and 21383/93, Judgment of 23 September 1998, para. 43; *Marshall v. United Kingdom*, ECtHR, Application No. 41571/98, Decision on Admissibility of 10 July 2001; *Nuray Şen v. Turkey*, ECtHR, Application No. 41478/98, Judgment of 17 June 2003, para. 25).

4. See J. Fitzpatrick, 'Protection Against Abuse of the Concept of "Emergency"', *Studies in Transnational Legal Policy* 26 (1994): 203.
5. R. Ergec, *Les droits de l'homme à l'épreuve des circonstances exceptionnelles: étude sur l'article 15 de la Convention européenne des droits de l'homme* (Brussels: Bruylant, 1987), 150ff.
6. Still in 2001, the Court accepted that as there had been 'no return to normality' in Northern Ireland, British authorities were entitled to adopt derogation measures (*Marshall v. United Kingdom*, ECtHR, Application No. 41571/98, Decision on Admissibility of 10 July 2001).
7. *A. and Others*, *supra* note 3, at 180. For a critical analysis of the wide margin of appreciation conceded to States, see O. Gross and F. Ní Aoláin, 'From Discretion to Scrutiny: Revisiting the Application of the Margin of Appreciation Doctrine in the Context of Article 15 of the European Convention on Human Rights', *Human Rights Quarterly* 23 (2001): 625–649; J.-P. Loof, 'Crisis Situations, Counter Terrorism and Derogation from the European Convention on Human Rights: a Threat Analysis', in A. Buyse (ed.), *Margins of Conflict: the ECHR and Transitions to and from Armed Conflict* (Antwerp/Portland: Intersentia, 2011), 35–56; see also E. Bates, 'A "Public Emergency Threatening the Life of the Nation"?: the United Kingdom's Derogation from the European Convention on Human Rights of 18 December 2001 and the "A" Case, *British Yearbook of International Law* 76 (2005): 245–335, particularly 291–319. So far the only case in which Strasbourg institutions concluded that there was no public emergency has been the Greek case, see the Report of the Commission of 5 November 1969, 124, 125.
8. *A. and Others*, *supra* note 3, at 173; *Ireland*, *supra* note 3, at 207; *Brannigan and McBride*, *supra* note 3, at 43; *Aksoy*, *supra* note 3, at 68.
9. The proportionality principle seems to be inherent to the principle of necessity, as Professor Higgins observed 'derogation to human rights obligations are acceptable only if events make them necessary and if they are proportionate to the danger that those events represent', *supra* note 3, at 282ff.; see also M.M. El Zeidy, 'The ECHR and States of Emergency: Article 15 – A Domestic Power of Derogation from Human Rights Obligations', *San Diego International Law Journal* No. 4 (2002): 277.
10. *Lawless*, *supra* note 3, at 36. The reference to the freedom of movement of the whole population shows how the Court intended the proportionality test to be not limited to the balance between the particular right in cause and the necessity to face the emergency, but rather as a comprehensive test taking into account the whole system of fundamental rights and the rule of law in the country.
11. Ibid., at 37. The existence of safeguards and remedies plays a very important role in all the following case law (see *Ireland*, *supra* note 3, at 218; *Brannigan and McBride*, *supra* note 3, at 62–64).
12. This attitude has been severely criticized by scholars, see Gross and Ní Aoláin, *supra* note 7, at 628, defining it as 'judicial attitude of undue deference to the concerns of states over individuals', and the doctrine they cite.
13. *Ireland*, *supra* note 3, at 212.
14. Ibid., at 214: 'the Court must arrive at its decision in the light, not of a purely retrospective examination of the efficacy of those measures, but of the conditions and circumstances reigning when they were originally taken and subsequently applied'.
15. *Brannigan and McBride*, *supra* note 3, at 59: '[i]t is not the Court's role to substitute its view as to what measures were most appropriate or expedient at the relevant time in dealing with an emergency situation for that of the Government which have direct responsibility for establishing the balance between the taking of effective measures to combat terrorism on the one hand, and respecting individual rights on the other'.
16. *A. and Others*, *supra* note 3, at 174, referring to House of Lords, *A and Others v. Secretary of State for the Home Department*, 16 December 2004, [2004] UKHL 56.

17. In *Aksoy, supra* note 3, the plaintiff had been detained for 14 days without any judicial control, nor any possibility of contacting a lawyer, a doctor or his family; during that time he was also tortured (see paras 78 and 83 of the Judgment, see also the Commission Decision, para. 181). After the *Aksoy* Judgment, the Court reached the same conclusion in a number of cases: see *Demir and Others v. Turkey*, ECtHR, Application Nos 21380/93, 21381/93 and 21383/93, Judgment of 23 September 1998, para. 57: 'the Court is not convinced that the applicants' incommunicado detention for at least sixteen or twenty-three days, without any possibility of seeing a judge or other judicial officer, was strictly required by the crisis relied on by the Government'; *Bilen v. Turkey*, ECtHR, Application No. 34482/97, Judgment of 21 February 2006, para. 49; *Nuray Şen v. Turkey*, ECtHR, Application No. 41478/98, Judgment of 17 June 2003, para. 28.

18. *Belgian Linguistic case*, ECtHR, Application Nos 1474/62, 1677/62, 1691/62, 1769/63, 1994/63 and 2126/64, Judgment of 23 July1968, para. B.5. See also *Golder v. United Kingdom*, ECtHR, Application No. 4451/70, Judgment of 21 February 1975, para. 45, concerning the right of a detainee to respect for private correspondence under Article 8.

19. *Handyside v. United Kingdom*, ECtHR, Application No. 5493/72, Judgment of 7 December 1976, para. 48.

20. Ibid., at 49.

21. *The Sunday Times v. United Kingdom*, ECtHR, Application No. 6538/74, Judgment of 26 April 1979, para. 65. The case concerned the injunction restraining publication of an article concerning the thalidomide disaster with the aim of maintaining the authority and impartiality of the judiciary dealing with the case.

22. As clearly illustrated by van Drooghenbroeck, *supra* note 1.

23. *Dudgeon v. United Kingdom*, ECtHR, Application No. 7525/76, Judgment of 22 October 1981, para. 52; *Norris v. Ireland*, ECtHR, Application No. 10581/83, Judgment of 26 October 1988, para. 46. The concept was yet developed in case law concerning Article 10, see *Handyside, supra* note 19, at 48.

24. In *Dudgeon, supra* note 23, the Court pointed out that: 'not only the nature of the aim of the restriction but also the nature of the activities involved will affect the scope of the margin of appreciation. The present case concerns a most intimate aspect of private life. Accordingly, there must exist particularly serious reasons before interferences on the part of the public authorities can be legitimate for the purposes of paragraph 2 of Article 8' (at 52; see also *Norris, supra* note 23, at 46).

25. *Laskey, Jaggard and Brown v. United Kingdom*, ECtHR, Application Nos 21627/93, 21628/93 and 21974/93, Judgment of 19 February 1997, para. 44: 'The determination of the level of harm that should be tolerated by the law in situations where the victim consents is in the first instance a matter for the State concerned since what is at stake is related, on the one hand, to public health considerations and to the general deterrent effect of the criminal law, and, on the other, to the personal autonomy of the individual.'

26. *Pretty v. United Kingdom*, ECtHR, Application No. 2346/02, Judgment of 29 April 2002, paras 68–78.

27. A similar balancing was previously done by the Court in cases concerning the determination of paternity by means of DNA test. In *Mikulić v. Croatia*, ECtHR, Application No. 53176/99, Judgment of 7 February 2002, the Court identified the opposite interests as follows: 'persons in the applicant's situation have a vital interest, protected by the Convention, in receiving the information necessary to uncover the truth about an important aspect of their personal identity. On the other hand, it must be borne in mind that the protection of third persons may preclude their being compelled to make themselves available for medical testing of any kind, including DNA testing' (para. 64). In contrast, in *Odièvre, infra* note 28, the Court gave precedence to the child's interest (see also, *mutatis mutandis, Jäggi v. Switzerland*, ECtHR, Application No. 58757/00, Judgment of 13 July 2006, para. 38).

28. *Odièvre v. France*, ECtHR, Application No. 42326/98, Judgment of 13 February 2003, para. 49. For another example of balancing between conflicting private interests under Article 8, see *Evans v. United Kingdom*, ECtHR, Application No. 6339/05, Judgment of 10 April 2007.

29. *Wallová and Walla v. Czech Republic*, ECtHR, Application No. 23848/04, Judgment of 26 October 2006, para. 74 (only French original published) ('The Court considers that, in this case, to meet the requirement of proportionality, the Czech authorities should have considered other measures, less drastic than public child care. Indeed, the Court considers that the role of social welfare is precisely to help people in need, who do not have the necessary knowledge of the system, guiding them in their efforts and advising them, in particular with regard to the different types of social benefits, opportunities to obtain housing, or other ways to overcome their difficulties'); see also *Havelka and Others v. Czech Republic*, ECtHR, Application No. 23499/06, Judgment of 21 June 2007, paras 52–63.

30. In *Boultif v. Switzerland*, ECtHR, Application No. 54273/00, Judgment of 2 August 2001, para. 48, the Court laid down some 'guiding principles' in order to examine whether a measure of expulsion was necessary in a democratic society: 'In assessing the relevant criteria in such a case, the Court will consider the nature and seriousness of the offence committed by the applicant; the duration of the applicant's stay in the country from which he is going to be expelled; the time which has elapsed since the commission of the offence and the applicant's conduct during that period; the nationalities of the various persons concerned; the applicant's family situation, such as the length of the marriage; other factors revealing whether the couple lead a real and genuine family life; whether the spouse knew about the offence at the time when he or she entered into a family relationship; and whether there are children in the marriage and, if so, their age. Not least, the Court will also consider the seriousness of the difficulties which the spouse would be likely to encounter in the applicant's country of origin, although the mere fact that a person might face certain difficulties in accompanying her or his spouse cannot in itself preclude expulsion.' What seems particularly interesting in this passage is the fact that the Court explicitly took into account the situation of the wife who was not an applicant in the case. See also *Moustaquim v. Belgium*, ECtHR, Application No. 12313/86, Judgment of 18 February 1991; *Beldjoudi v. France*, ECtHR, Application No. 12083/86, Judgment of 26 March 1992; *Amrollahi v. Denmark*, ECtHR, Application No. 56811/00, Judgment of 11 July 2002; *Yilmaz v. Germany*, ECtHR, Application No. 52853/99, Judgment of 17 April 2003, where the Court considered that the expulsion was not disproportionate in itself, but that the indefinite exclusion from German territory was (para. 48); *Keles v. Germany*, ECtHR, Application No. 32231/02, Judgment of 27 October 2005; *Üner v. Netherlands*, ECtHR, Application No. 46410/99, Judgment of 18 October 2006. In some recent cases the Court balanced the interest of the State to control immigration and the family links developed by an irregular migrant in the territory and considered that in exceptional cases, characterised by a particularly strong family link such as the parental relationship, the interest of individuals prevails over the sovereign right of the State to control the entry of aliens into its territory and their residence there (*Şen v. Netherlands*, ECtHR, Application No. 31465/96, Judgment of 21 December 2001; *Rodrigues da Silva and Hoogkamer v. Netherlands*, ECtHR, Application No. 50435/99, Judgment of 31 January 2006; *Nunez v. Norway*, ECtHR, Application No. 55597/09, Judgment of 28 June 2011).

31. See Explanatory Report to Protocol No. 7 (ETS No. 117), para. 15; *C.G. and Others v. Bulgaria*, ECtHR, Application No. 1365/07, Judgment of 24 April 2008, para. 78.

32. *Leyla Şahin v. Turkey* [GC], ECtHR, Application No. 44774/98, Judgment of 10 November 2005, para. 114 (the Grand Chamber confirmed the Conclusion reached by the Chamber on 29 June 2004); see also *Köse and 93 Others v. Turkey*, ECtHR, Application No. 26625/02, Decision on Admissibility of 24 January 2006.

33. The prohibition on wearing the Islamic headscarf for secondary students has been considered legitimate also in respect of the French secular model (*Dogru v. France*, ECtHR, Application No. 27058/05, Judgment of 4 December 2008; in that case the restriction was limited to PE classes, but the motivation of the Judgment would probably be applicable also against a more general measure). Among cases in which the individual right has been considered pre-eminent and the interference not proportionate, see *Kokkinakis v. Greece*, ECtHR, Application No. 14307/88, Judgment of 25 May 1993, concerning repression of proselytism.

34. *Dahlab v. Switzerland*, ECtHR, Application No. 42393/98, Decision on Admissibility of 15 February 2001 (emphasis added).

35. *Folgerø and Others v. Norway*, ECtHR, Application No. 15472/02, Judgment of 29 June 2007. See also *Zengin v. Turkey*, ECtHR, Application No. 1448/04, Judgment of 9 October 2007.

36. *Folgerø, supra* note 35, at 84; *Young, James and Webster v. United Kingdom*, ECtHR, Application Nos 7601/76 and 7806/77, Judgment of 13 August 1981, para. 63 (the case concerned the right not to be compelled to join a union under Article 11).

37. *Lautsi v. Italy* [Second Section], ECtHR, Application No. 30814/06, Judgment of 3 November 2009, paras 56 and 57.

38. *Lautsi v. Italy* [GC], ECtHR, Application No. 30814/06, Judgment of 18 March 2011, para. 72.

39. Ibid., at 74.

40. The characteristic of domain is the fact that concepts and issues are reciprocally defined. This is the reason why in freedom of expression cases the concepts of necessity in a democratic society and of proportionality tend to overlap. See the leading cases *Handyside, supra* note 19, and *The Sunday Times, supra* note 21, but also, among numerous Judgments, *Barthold v. Germany*, ECtHR, Application No. 8734/79, Judgment of 25 March 1985, *The Observer and The Guardian v. United*

Kingdom, ECtHR, Application No. 13585/88, Judgment of 26 November 1991, *Women On Waves and Others v. Portugal*, ECtHR, Application No. 31276/05, Judgment of 3 February 2009.

41. Defined as the 'public-watchdog' of democracy since the *Goodwin v. United Kingdom* case (ECtHR, Application No. 17488/90, Judgment of 27 March 1996, para. 39), the press and other media contributing to public information and debate have been given a privileged status and enjoy a high level of protection (for a quite extreme example, see *Jersild v. Denmark*, ECtHR, Application No. 15890/89, Judgment of 23 September 1994). Not surprisingly, artistic and commercial expression receives a lower level of protection (*Otto-Preminger-Institut v. Austria*, ECtHR, Application No. 13470/87, Judgment of 20 September 1994; *Wingrove v. United Kingdom*, ECtHR, Application No. 17419/90, Judgment of 25 November 1996, para. 58; *Markt Intern Verlag Gmbh and Klaus Beermann v. Germany*, ECtHR, Application No. 10572/83, Judgment of 20 November 1989. For an overview of categories of expression in the Court case law, see D.J. Harris, M. O'Boyle and C. Warbrick, *Law of the European Convention on Human Rights*, 2nd edn (London: Butterworths, 2009), 455–465.

42. *Lindon, Otchakovsky-Laurens and July v. France*, ECtHR, Application Nos 21279/02 and 36448/02, Judgment of 22 October 2007, para. 45.

43. *Barfod v. Denmark*, ECtHR, Application No. 11508/85, Judgment of 22 February 1989, para. 31: 'the general interest in allowing public debate about the functioning of the judiciary weighed more heavily than the interest of the two lay judges in being protected against criticism'. Nevertheless, in the circumstance of the case, the Court finds no violation of Article 10. See also *Worm v. Austria*, ECtHR, Application No. 22714/93, Judgment of 29 August 1997.

44. *Informationsverein Lentia and Others v. Austria*, ECtHR, Application Nos 13914/88, 15041/89, 15717/89, 15779/89 and 17207/90, Judgment of 24 November 1993.

45. *Piermont v. France*, ECtHR, Application Nos 15773/89 and 15774/89, Judgment of 27 April 1995.

46. *Goodwin v. United Kingdom*, ECtHR, Application No. 17488/90, Judgment of 27 March 1996, para. 45: 'the Court cannot find that Tetre's interests in eliminating … the residual threat of damage through dissemination of confidential information otherwise than by the press, in obtaining compensation and in unmasking a disloyal employee or collaborator were, even if considered cumulatively, sufficient to outweigh the vital public interest in the protection of the applicant journalist's source'.

47. *Open Door and Dublin Well Woman v. Ireland*, ECtHR, Application Nos 14234/88 and 14235/88, Judgment of 29 October 1992.

48. *Women On Waves*, *supra* note 40. It is interesting to note that the Court considered that, in seeking to prevent disorder and protect health, the Portuguese authorities could have resorted to other means, less restrictive of the applicants' freedom of expression (para. 41).

49. *Özgür Gündem v. Turkey*, ECtHR, Application No. 23144/93, Judgment of 16 March 2000, para. 43; *Fuentes Bobo v. Spain*, ECtHR, Application No. 39293/98, Judgment of 29 February 2000, para. 38. See also *Khurshid Mustafa and Tarzibachi v. Sweden*, ECtHR, Application No. 23883/06, Judgment of 16 December 2008, where the Court established that the right to receive information included the right of an Iraqi family living in Stockholm to have a satellite dish in order to receive television programmes in Arabic and Farsi, which were otherwise unavailable, even though it was forbidden by the tenancy agreement.

50. See *Mamère v. France*, ECtHR, Application No. 12697/03, Judgment of 7 November 2006, paras 27–30. Nevertheless, freedom of expression is not above any limit, journalists have indeed 'duties and responsibilities' and are expected to act in good faith in order to provide accurate and reliable information in accordance with the ethics of journalism (see *Radio France and Others v. France*, ECtHR, Application No. 53984/00, Judgment of 30 March 2004, paras 37–39).

51. *Janowski v. Poland*, ECtHR, Application No. 25716/94, Judgment of 21 January 1999, para. 32.

52. See, among the most recent cases, *MGN Limited v. United Kingdom*, ECtHR, Application No. 39401/04, Judgment of 18 January 2011, paras 142, 143.

53. See *Ezelin v. France*, ECtHR, Application No. 11800/85, Judgment of 26 April 1991, para. 37; *Djavit An v. Turkey*, ECtHR, Application No. 20652/92, Judgment of 20 February 2003, para. 39; *Barraco v. France*, ECtHR, Application No. 31684/05, Judgment of 5 March 2009, para. 27. In *Palomo Sánchez and Others v. Spain* [GC], ECtHR, Application Nos 28955/06, 28957/06, 28959/06 and 28964/06, Judgment of 12 September 2011, the Court examined the facts under Article 10, interpreting it in the light of Article 11 (para. 52; see also *Women On Waves*, *supra* note 40, at 28).

54. *Ezelin v. France*, *supra* note 53, at 53; *Grande Oriente d'Italia di Palazzo Giustiniani v. Italy*, ECtHR, Application No. 35972/97, Judgment of 2 August 2001, para. 26; *Ashughyan v. Armenia*, ECtHR, Application No. 33268/03, Judgment of 17 July 2008, para. 90; *Galstyan v. Armenia*, ECtHR, Application No. 26986/03, Judgment of 15 November 2007, para. 115.

55. *Young, James and Webster, supra* note 36, at 65: 'the detriment suffered by Mr. Young, Mr. James and Mr. Webster went further than was required to achieve a proper balance between the conflicting interests of those involved and cannot be regarded as proportionate to the aims being pursued'. See also *Sigurdur A. Sigurjónsson v. Iceland*, ECtHR, Application No. 16130/90, Judgment of 30 June 1993. In *Sørensen and Rasmussen v. Denmark*, ECtHR, Application Nos 52562/99 and 52620/99, Judgment of 11 January 2006, para. 58, the Court reiterates that 'in the area of trade union freedom and in view of the sensitive character of the social and political issues involved in achieving a proper balance between the respective interests of labour and management, and given the wide degree of divergence between the domestic systems in this field, the Contracting States enjoy a wide margin of appreciation'.

56. See *Refah Partisi (The Welfare Party) and Others v. Turkey*, ECtHR, Application Nos 41340/98, 41342/98, 41343/98 and 41344/98, Judgment of 13 February 2003, in which the court considered that the dissolution of a party whose purpose was to establish Sharia may be regarded as 'necessary in a democratic society'. This conclusion followed 'a rigorous review to verify that there were convincing and compelling reasons justifying Refah's dissolution and the temporary forfeiture of certain political rights imposed on the other applicants' (para. 135).

57. See R. Sapienza, 'Sul margine di apprezzamento nel sistema della Convenzione europa dei diritti dell'uomo', *Rivista di Diritto Internazionale* (1991): 571ff., specifically 611ff.; L. Adamovich, 'Marge d'appréciation du législateur et principe de proportionnalité dans l'appréciation des "restrictions prévues par la loi" au regard de la Convention européenne des droits de l'homme', *R.T.D.H.* (1991): 291ff.; P. Lambert, 'Marge nationale d'appréciation et contrôle de proportionnalité', in F. Sudre (ed.), *L'interprétation de la Convention européenne des droits de l'homme* (Brussels: Bruylant, 1998), 63ff.; E. Brems, 'The Margin of Appreciation Doctrine of the European Court of Human Rights: Accommodating Diversity Within Europe', in D.P. Forsythe and P.C. McMahon (eds), *Human Rights and Diversity* (Lincoln: University of Nebraska Press, 2003), 81–110.

58. Y. Arai-Takahashi, *The Margin of Appreciation Doctrine and the Principle of Proportionality in the Jurisprudence of the ECHR* (Oxford: Intersentia, 2002), 14, defines the proportionality principle as 'the other side of the margin of appreciation'.

59. On the application of the margin of appreciation doctrine in limitation clauses issues see, among a number of scholars, C. Morrison, 'Margin of Appreciation in European Human Rights Law', *R.D.H.* (1973): 263ff.; A. Bleckmann, 'Der Beurteilungsspielraum im Europa – und im Völkerrecht', E.G.Z. (1979): 485ff.; R. Bernhardt, 'Internationaler Menschenrechtsschutz und nationaler Gestaltungsspielraum', in *Völkerrecht als Rechtsordnung – Internationale Gerichtsbarkeit – Menschenrechte. Festschrift für Hermann Mosler* (Berlin, Heidelberg and New York: Springer, 1983), 75ff.; W.J. Ganshof van der Meersch, 'Réflexions sur les restrictions à l'exercice des droits de l'homme dans la jurisprudence de la Cour européenne de Strasbourg', ibid., 263ff.; Heilbronner, 'Die Einschränkung von Grundrechten in einer demokratischen Gesellschaft', ibid., 359ff.; MacDonald, 'The Margin of Appreciation in the Jurisprudence of the European Court of Human Rights', in *Il diritto internazionale al tempo della sua codificazione. Studi in onore di Roberto Ago* (Milan: Giuffrè, 1987), III, 187ff.; Sapienza, *supra* note 57, at 571ff.; H.C. Yourow, *The Margin of Appreciation Doctrine in the Dynamics of European Human Rights Jurisprudence* (The Hague, Boston and London: Martinus Nijhoff Publisher, 1996); Rasilla del Moral, 'The Increasingly Marginal Appreciation of the Margin-of-Appreciation', German Law Journal 7 (2006).

60. See, among cases already cited, *Handyside, supra* note 19, at 49; *Open Door, supra* note 47, at 71; *Palomo Sánchez, supra* note 53, at 53.

61. *Gillow v. United Kingdom*, ECtHR, Application No. 9063/80, Report of the Commission of 3 October 1984, para. 147.

62. See cases under note 30 above.

63. As pointed out by Judge Lagergren in his Dissenting Opinion in *Margareta and Roger Andersson v. Sweden*, ECtHR, Application No. 12963/87, Judgment of 25 February 1992: '[a]nother difficulty is to balance conflicting private interests and public obligations'.

64. In *Handyside, supra* note 19, the Court said that 'the freedom of expression constitutes one of the essential foundations of a democratic society, one of the basic conditions for its progress'. In *The Sunday Times, supra* note 21, the assessment of proportionality was conducted taking into account 'any public interest aspect of the case' (para. 65). In *Barfod, supra* note 43, the Court pointed out that 'the pursuit of the aims mentioned in Article 10(2) must be weighed against the value of open discussion of topics of public concern', and concluded that 'the public interests in allowing public debate about the functioning of the judiciary weighed more heavily that the interest of the two lay

judges in being protected against criticism'. Conversely, in *MGN Limited, supra* note 52, the Court considered that when a publication 'cannot be deemed to contribute to any debate of general interest to society', 'freedom of expression calls for a narrower interpretation'.

65. *Klass and Others v. Germany*, ECtHR, Application No. 5029/71, Judgment of 6 September 1978, para. 50; the Court added: 'This assessment has only a relative character: it depends on all the circumstances of the case, such as the nature, scope and duration of the possible measures, the grounds required for ordering such measures, the authorities competent to permit, carry out and supervise such measures, and the kind of remedy provided by the national law.' This principle is constantly applied in the following case law (see among numerous examples, *Lambert v. France*, ECtHR, Application No. 23618/94, Judgment of 24 August 1998, *Weber and Saravia v. Germany*, ECtHR, Application No. 54934/00, Decision on Admissibility of 29 June 2006). The same principle is also applied in cases concerning the storage of personal information such as fingerprints, photographs or DNA, see *S. and Marper v. United Kingdom*, ECtHR, Application Nos 30562/04 and 30566/04, Judgment of 4 December 2008.

66. *Belgian Linguistic case, supra* note 18, at B.5.

67. *Golder, supra* note 18, at 38. See also *Winterwerp v. Netherlands*, ECtHR, Application No. 6301/73, Judgment of 24 October 1979, concerning the application of Article 5, para. 4, at 60, the Court said: '[m]ental illness may entail restricting or modifying the manner of exercise of such a right ... but it cannot justify impairing the very essence of the right'; moreover, in relation to Article 6, para. 1, at 76, the Court reiterated that '[w]hile mental illness may render legitimate certain limitations upon the exercise of the "right to a court", it cannot warrant the total absence of that right'.

68. This requirement was firstly established in *Ashingdane v. United Kingdom*, ECtHR, Application No. 8225/78, Judgment of 28 May 1985, para. 57, and maintained in subsequent case law.

69. In the particular field of the right of access to court, see, among the most famous or recent cases, *Waite and Kennedy v. Germany* [GC], ECtHR, Application No. 26083/94, Judgment of 18 February 1999, para. 59; *Fogarty v. United Kingdom* [GC], ECtHR, Application No. 37112/97, Judgment of 21 November 2001, para. 33; *Cudak v. Lithuania*, ECtHR, Application No. 15869/02, Judgment of 23 March 2010, para. 55; *Sabeh El Leil v. France*, ECtHR, Application No. 34869/05, Judgment of 29 June 2011; *Woś v. Poland*, ECtHR, Application No. 22860/02, Judgment of 8 June 2006, para. 98. See also, concerning the immunity of members of Parliament, *A. v. United Kingdom*, ECtHR, Application No. 35373/97, Judgment of 17 December 2002, para. 74.

70. Particularly interesting is the case law concerning the regulation of marriage with foreign migrants. In that case the Court balanced the right of the couple to get married and the State's interest to prevent marriages of convenience. In *O'Donoghue and Others v. United Kingdom*, ECtHR, Application No. 34848/07, Judgment of 14 December 2010, the Court pointed out that 'in examining a case under Article 12 the Court would not apply the tests of "necessity" or "pressing social need" which are used in the context of Article 8 but would have to determine whether, regard being had to the State's margin of appreciation, the impugned interference has been arbitrary or disproportionate' (para. 84; see also *Frasik v. Poland*, ECtHR, Application No. 22933/02, para. 90, and *Jaremowicz v. Poland*, ECtHR, Application No. 24023/03, para. 50, Judgments of 5 January 2010 concerning the right to marriage of detainees).

71. *Hirst v. United Kingdom (No. 2)*, ECtHR, Application No. 74025/01, Fourth Section's Judgment of 30 March 2004, para. 50: 'The Court accepts that this is an area in which a wide margin of appreciation should be granted to the national legislature in determining whether restrictions on prisoners' right to vote can still be justified in modern times and if so how a fair balance is to be struck. In particular, it should be for the legislature to decide whether any restriction on the right to vote should be tailored to particular offences, or offences of a particular gravity or whether, for instance, the sentencing court should be left with an overriding discretion to deprive a convicted person of his right to vote.'

72. The Judgment of the Fourth Section in *Hirst*, ibid., has been confirmed by the Grand Chamber of the Court, on 6 October 2005. Previously, proportionality text was used in *Mathieu-Mohin and Clerfayt v. Belgium*, ECtHR, Application No. 9267/81, Judgment of 2 March 1987, *Matthews v. United Kingdom*, ECtHR, Application No. 24833/94, Judgment of 18 February 1999, paras 63–64.

73. *Waite and Kennedy, supra* note 69, at 59; *Al-Adsani v. United Kingdom* [GC], ECtHR, Application No. 35763/97, Judgment of 21 November 2001, para. 53; *McElhinney v. Ireland*, ECtHR, Application No. 31253/96, Judgment of 21 November 2001, para. 34; *Fogarty, supra* note 69, at 33; *Cudak, supra* note 69, at 55; *Sabeh El Leil, supra* note 69.

74. *Waite and Kennedy, supra* note 69, at 68–70, emphasis added; *Beer and Regan v. Germany*, ECtHR, Application No. 28934/95, Judgment of 18 February 1999, para. 55.

75. See *Al-Adsani, supra* note 73; *McElhinney, supra* note 73; *Fogarty, supra* note 69; *Cudak, supra* note 69; *Sabeh El Leil, supra* note 69.

76. *Van der Mussele v. Belgium,* ECtHR, Application No. 8919/80, Judgment of 23 November 1983. The Court observed that '[t]he structure of Article 4 is informative on this point. Paragraph 3 is not intended to "limit" the exercise of the right guaranteed by paragraph 2, but to "delimit" the very content of this right' (para. 38); then the Court noted that 'the obligation ... constituted a means of securing ... the benefit of Article 6(3)(c) of the Convention. To this extent, it was founded on a conception of social solidarity and cannot be regarded as unreasonable. ... Finally, the burden imposed on the applicant was not disproportionate' (para. 39). See also *Zarb Adami v. Malta,* ECtHR, Application No. 17209/02, Judgment of 20 June 2006, para. 47; *Steindel v. Germany,* ECtHR, Application No. 29878/07, Decision on Admissibility of 14 September 2010.

77. *Sporrong and Lönnroth v. Sweden,* ECtHR, Application Nos 7151/75 and 7152/75, Judgment of 23 September 1982, para. 69: 'The fact that the permits fell within the ambit neither of the second sentence of the first paragraph nor of the second paragraph does not mean that the interference with the said right violated the rule contained in the first sentence of the first paragraph. For the purposes of the latter provision, the Court must determine whether a fair balance was struck between the demands of the general interest of the community and the requirements of the protection of the individual's fundamental rights ... The search for this balance is inherent in the whole of the Convention and is also reflected in the structure of Article 1 (P1-1).'

78. See *Matos e Silva, LDA., and Others v. Portugal,* ECtHR, Application No. 15777/89, Judgment of 16 September 1996.

79. *Hamer v. Belgium,* ECtHR, Application No. 21861/03, Judgment of 27 November 2007. In this case, the Court specifically considered that no measure other than restoration of the site – by demolition of the applicant's house – 'appeared appropriate in the particular circumstances of the case, which concerned an undeniable interference with the integrity of a forested area in which no building was permitted' (para. 86). Consequently, the Court concluded that the applicant had not suffered disproportionate interference with her property rights (para. 88).

80. See *Gasus Dosier- und Fördertechnik GmbH v. Netherlands,* ECtHR, Application No. 15375/89, Judgement of 23 February 1995.

81. See the Commision's Report in *Gillow, supra* note 61, specifically at para. 154ff.

82. See *Beyeler v. Italy,* ECtHR, Application No. 33202/96, Judgment of 5 January 2000.

83. See *Immobiliare Saffi v. Italy,* ECtHR, Application No. 22774/93, Judgment of 28 July 1999.

84. *Doğan and Others v. Turkey,* ECtHR, Application Nos 8803–8811/02, 8813/02 and 8815-8819/02, Judgment of 29 June 2004, paras 153–156.

85. *J.A. Pye (Oxford) Ltd v. United Kingdom,* ECtHR, Application No. 44302/02, Judgment of 30 August 2007.

8. Human rights obligations of non-state armed groups: a possible contribution from customary international law?

*Jean-Marie Henckaerts and Cornelius Wiesener**

1. INTRODUCTION

This chapter examines whether and to what extent non-state armed groups can be considered bound by human rights law. First, it will discuss, as a preliminary consideration, the applicability of international humanitarian law to armed groups. It will contrast this with the applicability of international human rights, both treaty law and customary law, to such groups. In so doing, it will present arguments in favour of and against extending human rights obligations to armed groups. It tries to match these arguments with examples from the practice of UN bodies and experts, including the UN Security Council. On this basis, it will examine whether armed groups can now be considered bound by human rights law as a matter of customary international law. This chapter only addresses this question as a matter of principle and does not examine the practical interaction between humanitarian and human rights law obligations of armed groups, should they be considered to exist.

2. APPLICABILITY OF INTERNATIONAL HUMANITARIAN LAW TO ARMED GROUPS

International humanitarian law is premised, generally speaking, on the principle of equality of the parties to the conflict. This implies that the rules of international humanitarian law are binding on both parties to the conflict, whether state parties or non-state parties. This principle applies under both treaty and customary humanitarian law.

Under humanitarian treaty law, Article 3, common to the four Geneva Conventions of 1949, explicitly states that it is binding on 'each Party' to a conflict not of an international character, including non-state armed groups. The approach adopted in common Article 3 is to apply a minimum of basic rules to all conflicts, which are 'not of an international character'. This 'minimal' approach is supplemented by the encouragement for the parties to conclude 'special agreements' that extend some or all parts of the Geneva Conventions to the conflict. Another important element is the explicit recognition that the application of common Article 3 does not affect the legal status of the parties to the conflict.[1] The model of common Article 3 is followed in the Hague Convention for the protection of cultural property.[2] In addition, several recent humanitarian law treaties explicitly state that they apply to all parties in situations of non-international armed conflict,[3] or simply that they apply to situations of non-international armed conflict while including obligations for all parties.[4] These recent treaties also include a statement to the effect that their application does not affect the legal status of the parties to the conflict.[5]

In Additional Protocol II all references to 'parties to the conflict' were deleted in the last days of the negotiations as part of a simplification process aimed at getting the Protocol adopted. Nevertheless, it is clear that the Protocol does not alter the basic premise of humanitarian law. The ICRC Commentary on the Protocol asserts this to be the case:

> The deletion from the text of all mention of 'parties to the conflict' only affects the drafting of the instrument, and does not change its structure from a legal point of view. All the rules are based on the existence of two or more parties confronting each other. These rules grant the same rights and impose the same duties on both the established government and the insurgent party, and all such rights and duties have a purely humanitarian character.[6]

A textual reading of the Protocol also makes it clear that it applies to all parties to the conflict, including armed groups because it requires such groups to 'exercise such control over a part of [a High Contracting Party's] territory as to enable them to carry out sustained and concerted military operations and to implement this Protocol'.[7] The requirement that armed groups be able to implement the Protocol presupposes or implies that such groups are bound by it.

Different approaches have been advanced to explain the binding effect of humanitarian law on armed groups. All these explanations have merit, although none of them seems capable of providing a full and unique answer to the question.[8] The main arguments have been summarized by Ryngaert:

> 1. it was the intention of the parties to the treaty to impose obligations on armed groups (obligations which become binding if the armed groups assent) [Cassese]; 2. armed groups are active on the territory of the State that has ratified the relevant humanitarian law treaty, and are bound by the rules applicable in the State [Zegveld]; 3. armed groups act as de facto authorities and may thus be considered as representing the State as much as the government does [Pictet].[9]

With respect to customary law, a 2005 study under the auspices of the ICRC identified 161 rules of customary international law and found that most customary rules applicable in non-international armed conflicts bind all parties to the conflict.[10] There are a few exceptions related to state responsibility and reparation, compliance and enforcement where the rules applicable in non-international armed conflict were found, on the basis of current practice, to be binding on states only.[11] A question that remains open is whether and to what extent armed groups can contribute to the formation of customary international humanitarian law applicable to them.[12]

In conclusion, today it is generally accepted that non-state armed groups, parties to an armed conflict, are bound by international humanitarian law, both treaty law and customary law. For example, in 2004, the Appeals Chamber of the Sierra Leone Special Court stated that 'it is well settled that all parties to an armed conflict, whether states or non-state actors, are bound by international humanitarian law, even though only states may become parties to international treaties'.[13] Similarly, the 2000 Protocol on the involvement of children in armed conflict explicitly recalls 'the obligation of each party to an armed conflict to abide by the provisions of international humanitarian law'.[14]

3.   APPLICABILITY OF HUMAN RIGHTS LAW TO ARMED GROUPS

Unlike several major humanitarian law treaties, the main human rights treaties only address states as duty holders. This is true for both the universal,[15] and the regional treaties.[16] One possible exception is the Optional Protocol to the Convention on the Rights of the Child on the Involvement of Children in Armed Conflict where it provides that 'armed groups that are distinct from the armed forces of a State should not, under any circumstances, recruit or use in hostilities persons under the age of 18 years'.[17] It has been noted, however, that the use of the term 'should' in the context of this provision suggests that the article does not impose a hard legal duty on armed groups.[18] The legal duty seems rather addressed to States Parties which are enjoined to 'take all feasible measures to prevent such recruitment and use, including the adoption of legal measures necessary to prohibit and criminalize such practices'.[19] At any rate, the Optional Protocol is a *sui generis* human rights treaty and not illustrative for human rights treaty law in general. It deals specifically with the involvement of children in armed conflict and builds upon the earlier incorporation of humanitarian law into the Convention on the Rights of the Child.[20] Another possible exception is the African Union Convention for the Protection and Assistance of Internationally Displaced Persons in Africa (Kampala Convention), which addresses the obligations of 'members of armed groups', but not the group itself.[21] The Convention defines armed groups as 'dissident armed forces or other organized armed forces that are distinct from the armed forces of the state'.[22]

Because the universal and regional human rights treaties are framed to address states' obligations, their monitoring bodies have not looked beyond states' obligations. As a result, they have only addressed the responsibility of states for acts of armed groups that violate human rights, but not the responsibility of the groups themselves.[23] There is, however, some limited practice from the monitoring bodies to consider a non-state entity bound by human rights treaty law of the territorial state. When the Human Rights Committee discussed the situation in Bosnia-Herzegovina in the early 1990s, one of its members stated that the Bosnian Serb authorities were bound by the International Covenant on Civil and Political Rights: 'Thus [they] might be asked to explain how they complied with the Covenant, not as a successor State, but as *an authority in control of a territory*' (emphasis added).[24]

In General Comment 26, the Human Rights Committee developed this idea further:

> The rights enshrined in the Covenant belong to the people living in the territory of the State party. The Human Rights Committee has consistently taken the view, as evidenced by its long-standing practice, that once the people are accorded the protection of the rights under the Covenant, such protection devolves with territory and continues to belong to them, notwithstanding change in government of the State party, including dismemberment in more

than one State or State succession or any subsequent action of the State party designed to divest them of the rights guaranteed by the Covenant.[25]

According to Hessbruegge, 'as an insurrectionary movement takes control over territory and establishes an administration, it therefore automatically assumes the human rights obligations resting on the territory'.[26] However, even if the Human Rights Committee considered that the protection devolved with territory, notwithstanding change in government, the examples given – dismemberment in more than one state, state succession or any subsequent action of the state party – remain limited to *state* action.

On the other hand, there is practice from the monitoring bodies denying the applicability of human rights treaties to armed groups.[27] In 1990, the Inter-American Commission on Human Rights explicitly rejected the possibility that armed groups could violate the American Convention on Human Rights. The Inter-American Commission considered:

> The American Convention concerns the duties of States vis-à-vis the rights and freedoms of persons, the full and free exercise of which they must not only respect but also guarantee. The entire system for protecting human rights is designed on the basis of the State's acknowledgement of itself as a party to a fundamental legal contract on the matter of human rights and it is against the State that complaints alleging violations of the rights upheld in the Convention are brought.[28]

The Commission affirmed this position in a later report on Colombia.[29]

At this point, we can conclude that international human rights treaty law is structured fundamentally different than international humanitarian law. This explains the traditional view, as expressed by Lindsay Moir:

> the humanitarian laws of internal armed conflict are equally binding upon the government and insurgents, and can also … apply to a conflict between two parties, neither of which is the government of the State concerned. There is therefore a degree of reciprocity as far as the application of humanitarian law is concerned. By contrast, human rights obligations are binding on governments only, and the law has not yet reached the stage whereby, during internal armed conflict, insurgents are bound to observe the human rights of government forces, let alone those of opposing insurgents.[30]

However, this traditional view still leaves open the question of whether the insurgents could have an obligation to respect the human rights of the populations living under their control.

We will now turn to a more detailed examination of the arguments against and in favour of applying human rights law to armed groups.

3.1 Arguments Against the Applicability of Human Rights Law to Armed Groups

The main reason for rejecting any expansion of human rights obligations to actors other than states stems from the fact that, unlike humanitarian law, human rights law is based on a vertical relationship between the state and the individual. Although non-state armed groups may negatively affect the enjoyment of human rights of other individuals, such acts would only amount to 'abuses' of human rights as opposed to 'violations' of human rights law. Only states can commit human rights violations, either through their own acts or by failing to fulfil their due diligence obligations with regard to abuses by armed groups. It is the state's responsibility and prerogative to prevent and remedy such abuses. This view is premised on the assumption that state authorities are always powerful enough to enforce the law everywhere on the state's territory. Examples from failed states and countries affected by armed conflict, however, show that this may not always be the case.[31]

An example of the traditional, state-centred concept of human rights law, whereby only states are deemed responsible for human rights 'violations', can be found in a 1996 report of a meeting of Special Rapporteurs and other experts of the Commission on Human Rights. This report stressed that with regard to actions of terrorist groups, a 'distinction should be made between citing [terrorist] groups as human rights violators and the adverse effects their action might have on the enjoyment of human rights'.[32]

The UN Security Council has also sometimes used the term 'abuse' rather than 'violation' of human rights law. For instance in a resolution on Sierra Leone in 2001, it condemned 'human rights abuses committed by the Revolutionary United Front (RUF) and others'.[33] Similarly, in a resolution in 2006 on the situation in Sudan, the Council strongly condemned 'the activities of militias and armed groups such as the Lord's Resistance Army (LRA), which continue to attack civilians and commit human rights abuses in the Sudan'.[34] However, in more recent resolutions the Council has used both terms side by side, for example, in a 2010 resolution on the situation in Somalia, the Security Council strongly condemned:

> all acts of violence, abuses and human rights violations committed against civilians, including women and children, and humanitarian personnel, in violation of international humanitarian law and human rights law, stressing the responsibility of all parties in Somalia to comply fully with their obligations in this regard and reaffirming the importance of the fight against impunity.[35]

Similarly, in 2011, regarding the situation in the Democratic Republic of Congo, the Council used both terms seemingly in a synonymous manner:

> 13. Demands that all armed groups, in particular Forces Démocratiques de Libération du Rwanda (FDLR) and the Lord's Resistance Army (LRA), immediately cease all forms of violence and *human rights abuses* against the civilian population in the Democratic Republic of the Congo, in particular against women and children, including rape and other forms of sexual abuse, and demobilize;
>
> ...
>
> 18. ... encourages the Congolese authorities to promote lasting reconciliation in the Democratic Republic of the Congo by pursuing these efforts to combat impunity against all perpetrators of *human rights and international humanitarian law violations*, including those committed by any illegal armed groups or elements of the Congolese security forces.[36] (emphasis added)

It has also been argued that extending human rights obligations beyond states might dilute states' own responsibilities.[37] The 2006 Report of the Working Group on

Enforced or Involuntary Disappearances relating to the situation in Colombia, for example, reflects this concern. The Report considered the question whether the concept of enforced disappearance could be applied to actions of non-state armed groups:

> 48. Although the inclusion of non-State actors acting without the support or consent of the Government may at first glance look like an advancement of the law, in the sense that it protects more than the limited definition of the Declaration, it is the opinion of the Working Group that enforced disappearance is a 'State crime' (as opposed to kidnapping). Although in other cases of violations of human rights the inclusion of non-State actors indeed offers more protection to the victims (i.e. in the case of discrimination or labour or environmental human rights), in the case of enforced disappearance such inclusion dilutes the responsibility of the State.

> 49. For that same reason, the Working Group resists accepting the official Colombian attitude to 'disappearances', linking the definition of the phenomenon to or even equating it with 'kidnappings'. To accept this definition would amount to diluting or even ousting State responsibility for acts of 'disappearances'. The Working Group made it a point to emphasize that 'disappearances' are a State responsibility, while 'kidnappings' are things one attributes to non-State individuals, gangs or criminal networks. The Working Group also took pains to condemn both acts of 'disappearances' and 'kidnappings', irrespective of their perpetrators, as reprehensible.[38]

However, the extension of human rights obligations to actors other than the territorial state does not necessarily displace or dilute the state's responsibility under human rights law. The responsibility of different actors for violations of human rights law is not mutually exclusive, but can be complementary. The European Court of Human Rights has confirmed this in the *Ilaşcu* case, concerning the responsibility of Moldova under the European Convention on Human Rights with regard to acts of the separatist authorities of Transnistria, a non-state actor. The finding that the conduct of the latter was attributable to Russia did not prevent the Court from holding that Moldova continued to have positive obligations under the Convention.[39] Hence, *a fortiori*, where no third state is involved, the responsibility of a non-state actor would equally not displace or dilute the territorial state's responsibility under human rights law.

One reason why states have been reluctant to acknowledge the existence of obligations under human rights law for armed groups is the concern that this could be seen as granting such groups legitimacy, recognition or status under international law, and would therefore undermine the sovereignty of the state. This concern runs parallel to a similar concern about the application of international humanitarian law to armed groups. However, legitimacy plays maybe an even greater role in human rights law, for example with regard to permissible limitations of rights. In humanitarian law, this concern has been addressed by formally acknowledging, starting in common Article 3 of the Geneva Conventions, that the application of humanitarian law does not affect the status of the parties to the conflict.[40] The Optional Protocol to the Convention of the Rights of the Child on Children in Armed Conflict has adopted the same approach.[41] The more recent Kampala Convention on internally displaced persons has again taken this approach where it states that the application of the relevant provision (Art. 7) 'shall not, in any way whatsoever, be construed as affording legal status or legitimizing or recognizing armed groups'.[42] This recent practice shows that it continues to be possible to overcome this issue and to regulate the obligations of armed groups in treaty law, while recognizing that this does not affect their status.[43]

3.2   Arguments in Favour of the Applicability of Human Rights Law to Armed Groups

A number of arguments have been advanced and used in practice to consider armed groups bound by human rights law. First, it has been argued that if only state forces had to observe – possibly more restrictive – human rights law in the course of a non-international armed conflict, there would be an imbalance between the state and the armed group, running counter to the principle of equality. This principle, however, formally only applies to humanitarian law, and the question is whether and to what extent it can apply to human rights obligations in armed conflict. Nevertheless, the 'equality argument' led the Guatemalan Commission on Historical Clarification to apply humanitarian law and human rights law to both government and rebel forces:

> The Commission also applied the common principles of international human rights law and international humanitarian law to the violent acts committed by the guerrillas, in order to give equal treatment to the Parties, since the dominant trend today is to consider that human dignity is equally offended against, whoever commits the acts that violate it.[44] (authors' translation)

Another argument in favour of imposing human rights obligations on non-state armed groups pertains to the fact that humanitarian law does not govern all of their activities. When there is an armed conflict, many acts or omissions of armed groups are materially not covered by humanitarian law, or even international criminal law, for example some civil and political rights (freedom of assembly, expression and movement), certain economic, social and cultural rights (right to work, food and education), gender equality and minority rights.[45] This is particularly the case, as no humanitarian law of 'occupation' exists for non-international armed conflicts. Hence, issues related to education, food, work, property or security in territory controlled by an armed group are not regulated under humanitarian law governing non-international armed conflicts; as they are in the law of belligerent occupation.[46] It has been pointed out that most conflicts last for years or decades and that 'international humanitarian law was not meant to regulate the everyday life of people living in areas under the control of ANSAs [armed non-state actors] over such an extended period of time'.[47] This may lead to gaps in the legal protection for the populations concerned. These gaps can be closed by recourse to human rights law as an additional set of obligations binding armed groups, at least those meeting certain requirements, in particular control over territory.

Thus, since the early 1990s numerous resolutions, especially from the UN Security Council, have addressed human rights violations committed by non-state armed groups and these groups' obligations under human rights law.[48] This has been done, either by calling directly on such groups, even naming them explicitly, or indirectly by addressing 'all parties'. When calling on armed groups to respect their obligations under international law, the UN Security Council has usually combined references to humanitarian law and human rights law. Even if certain safeguards are similar under both legal regimes, the Council has nonetheless gone beyond what is required under humanitarian law as such. For instance, it called on all parties to the conflict in Côte d'Ivoire to 'ensure freedom of the press and unlimited access to information'[49] and to 'guarantee the security and freedom of movement of all Ivorian nationals'.[50]

With regard to gender equality in Afghanistan when the Taliban were in power, the Council demanded 'that the Afghan factions put an end to discrimination against girls and women'.[51] In 2000, the Council expressed its concern at the 'continued restrictions on their access to health care, to education and to employment outside the home, and about restrictions on their freedom of movement and freedom from intimidation, harassment and violence'.[52]

In addition, in some circumstances, humanitarian law may not, or no longer, govern the acts of armed groups at all, namely where the situation at hand does not qualify as an armed conflict. This may be the case when the requirements of organization and intensity are not yet met, or when those requirements are no longer fulfilled, for example because a peaceful settlement has been reached. In case armed groups continue to control territory after the end of the conflict, their actions would not be governed by humanitarian law.[53] In such a situation, the territorial state might not have any means to prevent the perpetration of human rights abuses by armed groups. The populations concerned would not legally be able to enjoy their human rights if the groups controlling that territory did not have a legal obligation to respect them. In respect of internal disturbances and tensions short of armed conflict, the *Institut de Droit International* resolved in 1999: 'To the extent that certain aspects of internal disturbances and tensions may not be covered by international humanitarian law, individuals remain under the protection of international law guaranteeing fundamental human rights. All parties are bound to respect fundamental rights under the scrutiny of the international community'.[54]

An example from practice where humanitarian law did not apply can be found in the work of the Guatemalan Commission on Historical Clarification. The Chair of the Commission, Professor Tomuschat, explains:

> Not to subject insurgent movements to any obligation owed to the international community *before an armed conflict may be found to exist* would leave them exclusively under the authority of domestic law, favouring them, but also discriminating against them at the same time. It was one of the great challenges of the Guatemalan Historical Clarification Commission to determine the legal yardstick by which conduct of the different guerrilla groups could be measured *even in times when one could hardly speak of an armed conflict.*[55] (emphasis added)

Another example from practice involving a situation where humanitarian law no longer applied can be found in the work of the UN Secretary-General's Panel of Experts on Accountability in Sri Lanka. The Panel considered that '[s]ince the conclusion of the war on 19 May 2009, international human rights law became the sole body of applicable law. Thus, the Panel addresses only human rights violations that are materially or temporally outside the conduct of the war.'[56]

The application of human rights law to armed groups in situations outside armed conflict has been linked to the development of international criminal law, which imposes criminal responsibility on members of groups, and also for crimes committed outside situations of armed conflict, notably for the crime of genocide and crimes against humanity.[57] In this respect, it can be asserted that the fact that armed groups can have human rights obligations can be deduced from international criminal law. Indeed, while war crimes are linked to obligations under humanitarian law applicable in armed conflict, the ability for members of armed groups to commit crimes against humanity presupposes the existence of human rights obligations on the part of such groups.[58]

3.3   Human Rights Obligations of Armed Groups in Areas Under their Control

Another important argument to consider human rights applicable to armed groups – and at the same time a possible criterion for such applicability – is that they may act as a de facto government in areas under their control. This argument has gained increasing support in the practice of UN bodies and experts. Already in 1993, the UN Truth Commission on El Salvador held that an armed group – in this case the FMLN (Frente Farabundo Martí para la Liberación Nacional) – could have obligations under human rights law in areas under their control. In this respect, the Commission stated: 'However, it must be recognized that when insurgents assume government powers in territories under their control, they too can be required to observe certain human rights obligations that are binding on the State under international law. This would make them responsible for breaches of those obligations.'[59]

Control over territory as a criterion for binding armed groups to human rights law is also implicit in some of the resolutions of the UN Security Council, given that most, if not all, groups addressed in such resolutions were arguably in control of some territory. Moreover, some of the resolutions specifically spell out this fact. For instance, in 2000 the Council condemned 'the continuing grave violations of the human rights of women and girls, including all forms of discrimination against them, in all areas of Afghanistan, particularly in areas under the control of the Taliban'.[60] The Council further stressed 'the responsibility of the Taliban for the well-being of the population in the areas of Afghanistan under its control'.[61]

The emphasis on the control of territory is even more obvious in numerous resolutions issued with regard to the situation in the Democratic Republic of the Congo (DRC). In 2001, the Council expressed 'its grave concern at the repeated human rights violations throughout the Democratic Republic of the Congo in particular in the territories under the control of the rebel groups'.[62] In 2002, the Council reminded all parties 'in Uvira and in the area that they must abide by international humanitarian standards and ensure respect for human rights in the sectors they control'.[63] In a resolution adopted in 2002, the Council also stressed the fact that the groups acted as the de facto authority:

> 4. [the Council] … *reiterates* that it holds the Rassemblement Congolais pour la Democratie-Goma, as the de facto authority, responsible to bring to an end all extrajudicial executions, human rights violations and arbitrary harassment of civilians in Kisangani, and all other areas under RCD-Goma's control … ;
>
> 5. *Condemns* the exploitation of ethnic differences in order to incite or carry out violence or human rights violations, *deplores* the humanitarian impact of such abuse, and in this regard *expresses particular concern* at the situation in the Ituri region and in South Kivu, in

particular in the Hauts Plateaux, and *calls on* the de facto authorities in the regions affected to ensure the protection of civilians and the rule of law.[64] (italics in original)

Other UN bodies have also stressed the importance of territorial control for triggering obligations under human rights law on the part of armed groups. For instance, in its 2007 report to the Security Council, the Panel of Experts on the Sudan came to the following conclusions:

> Although it is the primary responsibility of the Government of the Sudan to guarantee the human rights of its citizens and to protect them from any transgression, the different armed opposition movements also bear responsibility in areas under their control. ... Members of the SLA/MM armed groups have consistently committed grave violations of human rights in areas where the armed group has a presence.[65]

Another UN body, the Committee on the Rights of the Child, also seems to support the applicability of human rights law to armed groups in control of territory. Thus, for example, in its Concluding Observations on the DRC in 2001, the Committee noted:

> grave violations of the Convention within territory outside of the control of the Government of the State party and where armed elements, including armed forces under the jurisdiction of other States parties to the Convention, have been active ... In this context, in addition to the responsibility of the State party, the Committee also emphasizes the responsibilities of several other States and certain other actors for the negative impact of the armed conflict upon children and for violations of some provisions of the Convention and international human-itarian law within areas of the State party.[66]

The same is true for the UN Committee Against Torture. In the case of *Elmi v. Australia*, involving allegations of torture in Somalia, the findings of the Committee were implicitly based on the exercise of control over territory by armed groups:

> The Committee notes that for a number of years Somalia has been without a central government, that the international community negotiates with the warring factions and that some of the factions operating in Mogadishu have set up quasi-governmental institutions and are negotiating the establishment of a common administration. It follows then that, de facto, those factions exercise certain prerogatives that are comparable to those normally exercised by legitimate governments. Accordingly, the members of those factions can fall, for the purposes of the application of the Convention, within the phrase 'public officials or other persons acting in an official capacity' contained in article 1.[67]

UN Special Rapporteurs and experts also support the idea that human rights can bind armed groups when they are in control of territory. In his report on the situation of human rights in the Sudan in 2002, the Special Rapporteur noted that he 'urged the SPLM to actively take responsibility to meet the needs of the people living in areas under its control, including in terms of health and education, particularly where peace has been established'.[68]

The 2004 report of the Special Rapporteur on extrajudicial, summary or arbitrary executions stressed the requirement of territorial control for applying human rights law obligations to armed groups:

The traditional approach of international law is that only Governments can violate human rights and thus, such armed groups are simply committing criminal acts. And indeed this may be an accurate characterization. In reality, however, that is often not the end of the matter and in some contexts it may be desirable to address the activities of such groups within some part of the human rights equation. This could mean addressing complaints to them about executions and calling for respect of the relevant norms. This may be both appropriate and feasible where the group exercises significant control over territory and population and has an identifiable political structure (which is often not the case for classic 'terrorist groups').[69]

The 2010 report of the independent expert on the situation of human rights in Somalia dealt specifically with 'human rights abuses by armed groups [Al–Shabaab and Hizbul Islam] in areas under their control' and with the human rights situation in Puntland and Somaliland, which are equally not under the control of the Transitional Federal Government of Somalia.[70]

A number of recent reports of international commissions and combined reports of Special Rapporteurs and Representatives also support the application of human rights to armed groups who have control over territory. A report by several Special Rapporteurs of the UN Human Rights Council and the Representative of the Secretary-General on Internally Displaced Persons on their mission to Lebanon and Israel in the wake of the 2006 conflict considered the exercise of territorial control a key requirement for human rights obligations on the part of Hezbollah:

> Although Hezbollah, a non-State actor, cannot become a party to these human rights treaties, it remains subject to the demand of the international community, first expressed in the Universal Declaration of Human Rights, that every organ of society respect and promote human rights. The Security Council has long called upon various groups which Member States do not recognize as having the capacity to do so to formally assume international obligations to respect human rights. It is especially appropriate and feasible to call for an armed group to respect human rights norms when it 'exercises significant control over territory and population and has an identifiable political structure'.[71]

A subsequent report by the Commission of Inquiry on Lebanon did not explicitly discuss whether Hezbollah had control over territory, although it confirmed that it had obligations under human rights law.[72]

In 2009, the combined report of nine Special Rapporteurs and Representatives on the situation in Gaza concluded, with respect to Hamas, that 'non-State actors that exercise government-like functions and control over a territory are obliged to respect human rights norms when their conduct affects the human rights of the individuals under their control'.[73] Similarly, the 2009 Goldstone report on the conflict in Gaza also emphasized the relevance of territorial control:

> 304. A second issue relates to the human rights obligations of the Palestinian Authority, the de facto authority in the Gaza Strip and other political and military actors. As non-State actors, the question of their human rights obligations must be addressed. It should be noted that the same issue does not arise with regard to IHL obligations, the question being settled some time ago …

> 305. The relationship between IHL and HRL is rapidly evolving, in particular in relation to non-State actors' obligations, with the ultimate goal of enhancing the protection of people and to enable them to enjoy their human rights in all circumstances. In the context of the matter

within the Mission's mandate, it is clear that non-State actors that exercise government-like functions over a territory have a duty to respect human rights.[74]

The issue of territorial control of the armed group also played a central role in the 2011 report of the Panel of Experts on Accountability in Sri Lanka. In its report, the panel stated:

> With respect to the LTTE [Liberation Tigers of Tamil Eelam], although non-state actors cannot formally become party to a human rights treaty, it is now increasingly accepted that non-state groups exercising de facto control over a part of a State's territory must respect fundamental human rights of persons in that territory. Various organs of the United Nations, including the Security Council, have repeatedly demanded that such actors respect human rights law. Although the Panel recognizes that there remains some difference of views on the subject among international actors, it proceeds on the assumption that, at a minimum, the LTTE was bound to respect the most basic human rights of persons within its power, including the rights to life and physical security and integrity of the person, and freedom from torture and cruel, inhuman or degrading treatment and punishment.[75]

The work of the Commission of Inquiry on Libya provides another prominent example. In its report in 2011, the Commission stated:

> Although the extent to which international human rights law binds non-state actors remains contested as a matter of international law, it is increasingly accepted that where non-state groups exercise de facto control over territory, they must respect fundamental human rights of persons in that territory. The Commission has taken the approach that since the NTC has been exercising de facto control over territory akin to that of a Governmental authority, it will examine also allegations of human rights violations committed by its forces.[76]

Most recently, in a 2012 report, the Commission of Inquiry on Syria has taken the same approach where it stated that although non-state actors cannot formally become parties to international human rights treaties, they must nevertheless 'respect the fundamental human rights of persons forming customary international law (CIL), in areas where such actors exercise de facto control'.[77]

This account of international practice shows that non-state armed groups are increasingly considered by UN bodies and experts to have human rights obligations in areas which are under their control enabling them to perform quasi-governmental functions. It may be argued that this practice has given rise to a customary international law norm to the effect that human rights law binds armed groups with such control. According to Constantinides, 'it would not be an overstatement to assert that a customary rule has emerged that extends human rights obligations to AOGs [armed opposition groups] in control of territory. The relevant Security Council practice corroborates this rule.'[78] As indicated above, the Security Council practice is further supported by practice from other UN bodies. However, it would still be necessary to collect further evidence from a larger variety of practice, in particular from States, in order to conclude that such a customary rule has emerged.

Another, related, view advanced by Philip Alston, then UN Special Rapporteur on extrajudicial, summary or arbitrary executions, and supported by some authors, contends that there exists – at least – a legitimate expectation of the international community that armed groups respect human rights law.[79] In his report on his mission to Sri Lanka in 2006, Alston stated:

> 25. Human rights law affirms that both the Government and the LTTE must respect the rights of every person in Sri Lanka. Human rights norms operate on three levels – as the rights of individuals, as obligations assumed by States, and as legitimate expectations of the international community. The Government has assumed the binding legal obligation to respect and ensure the rights recognized in the International Covenant on Civil and Political Rights (ICCPR). As a non-State actor, the LTTE does not have legal obligations under ICCPR, but it remains subject to the demand of the international community, first expressed in the Universal Declaration of Human Rights, that every organ of society respect and promote human rights.
>
> 26. I have previously noted that it is especially appropriate and feasible to call for an armed group to respect human rights norms when it 'exercises significant control over territory and population and has an identifiable political structure'. This visit clarified both the complexity and the necessity of applying human rights norms to armed groups. The LTTE plays a dual role. On the one hand, it is an organization with effective control over a significant stretch of territory, engaged in civil planning and administration, maintaining its own form of police force and judiciary. On the other hand, it is an armed group that has been subject to proscription, travel bans, and financial sanctions in various Member States. The tension between these two roles is at the root of the international community's hesitation to address the LTTE and other armed groups in the terms of human rights law. The international community does have human rights expectations to which it will hold the LTTE, but it has long been reluctant to press these demands directly if doing so would be to 'treat it like a State'.
>
> 27. It is increasingly understood, however, that the human rights expectations of the international community operate to protect people, while not thereby affecting the legitimacy of the actors to whom they are addressed. The Security Council has long called upon various groups that Member States do not recognize as having the capacity to formally assume international obligations to respect human rights. The LTTE and other armed groups must accept that insofar as they aspire to represent a people before the world, the international community will evaluate their conduct according to the Universal Declaration's 'common standard of achievement'.[80]

The question of whether such a legitimate expectation exists is closely related to the existence of a rule of customary international law. It may be argued that the existence of a legitimate expectation that armed groups respect human rights law supports or forms the basis of a customary law rule to the effect that human rights law binds armed groups.[81]

Under both hypotheses, whether a customary rule or a legitimate expectation exists, a further question would still require clarification, namely exactly what level of control over territory would be required for an armed group to incur human rights obligations? The answer may be the same or similar as the level of control required for Additional Protocol II to apply in case of armed conflict.[82] However, a different (customary) standard may apply. Additional Protocol II requires 'control over a part of its territory as to enable them [organized armed groups] to carry out sustained and concerted military operations and to implement this Protocol'. By contrast, from the UN practice, it appears that armed groups are considered to have human rights obligations in areas which are under their control enabling them to perform quasi-governmental functions. Whether this is the same standard or not remains to be clarified.

The above discussion also leaves open the question whether armed groups can have human rights obligations in areas not under their control, to which we turn now.

3.4 Human Rights Obligations of Armed Groups in Areas Not Under their Control

The above practice from UN bodies and experts does not allow to draw a conclusion with regard to whether armed groups may have human rights obligations in areas not under their control. Nonetheless, where armed groups have control over territory (thereby arguably triggering the applicability of human rights obligations in this territory) but perform acts outside such territory, a parallel can be drawn with situations where states act outside their own territory. It is increasingly accepted that such acts of states may engage their responsibility under their respective human rights treaty obligations, that is, the extra-territorial application of human rights law.[83] The same reasoning could be applied to armed groups acting outside the areas under their control, although the Panel of Experts on Accountability in Sri Lanka did not consider this possibility 'because of the uncertainty surrounding whether non-state actors have human rights obligations beyond the territories they control'.[84]

In situations where armed groups do not exercise control over any territory, it is even less clear whether they have any human rights obligations at all. It could be argued that they should at least observe those human rights obligations that would apply to persons in their power (e.g. the prohibition of torture) similar to operations of state agents in areas not under their control.[85] A related possibility is that armed groups should be considered to be bound by peremptory human rights norms (*jus cogens*) regardless of whether or not they have any territorial control.[86] Recently in a report on Non-State Actors in International Law in 2010, the International Law Association's Committee on Non-State Actors stated:

> The consensus appears to be that currently NSAs [non-State actors] do *not* incur direct human rights obligations enforceable under international law. Exceptions include violations of *jus cogens* norms, the duty of insurgents to comply with international humanitarian law, and perhaps, 'legitimate expectations' of the international community that NSAs comply with certain norms, such as for organised armed groups to refrain from committing human rights abuses.[87]

One difficulty with the concept of *jus cogens* is that there is no definitive list of human rights that constitute peremptory norms of international law. The International Law Commission has identified the prohibitions of genocide, slavery, racial discrimination, crimes against humanity and torture as examples of 'clearly accepted and recognized' peremptory norms of international law.[88] The UN Human Rights Committee has identified – indirectly – the following acts in violation of peremptory norms of international (human rights) law: arbitrary deprivations of life, torture and inhuman or degrading treatment, taking of hostages, imposing collective punishments, arbitrary deprivations of liberty, and deviating from fundamental principles of fair trial, including the presumption of innocence.[89] As can be seen from this list, these peremptory norms of international (human) rights law are also part of humanitarian law. In this respect, the extension of peremptory human rights norms to armed groups would not add anything substantially new to the rules of humanitarian law that already apply to them in situations of armed conflict. The situation would of course be different in situations outside armed conflict, where international humanitarian law does not apply. Hence, the importance of the application of peremptory norms of international (human) rights law would lie primarily outside situations of armed conflict.[90]

The considerations on peremptory norms are also related to the content of any possible human rights obligations of armed groups, which is briefly addressed in the next section.

3.5   Content of Human Rights Obligations of Armed Groups

Provided human rights law were to apply to armed groups, a crucial question remains unanswered, namely *which* human rights would apply to armed groups. Based on the practice described in this chapter, several general answers can be formulated. First, it could be that customary human rights law, as reflected largely in the Universal Declaration of Human Rights, would apply.[91] The UN Special Rapporteur on extrajudicial, summary or arbitrary executions, for example, refers to this as the Universal Declaration's 'common standard of achievement'.[92] This may also correspond to what other bodies have considered applicable to armed groups such as 'general principles common to international human rights law',[93] or the 'most basic human rights of persons'.[94] It may also correspond largely to what the *Institut de Droit International* considered applicable, namely 'the principles and rules of international law guaranteeing fundamental human rights'.[95] Another possibility is that only peremptory norms of international (human rights) law apply, as discussed above. But whether customary or peremptory, the exact contours of the human rights obligations incurred by armed groups remains to be clarified.

Another, more flexible, approach has been suggested by Clapham who considers it 'preferable to stress that the obligations apply to the extent appropriate to the context'.[96] According to him, it would depend on the capacity of the group concerned to bear specific obligations.[97] This approach allows taking into account the wide variety of armed groups, as well as the issue of whether they have territorial control or not. In this respect, Sivakumaran underlines that the term armed groups 'captures a wide array of actors, from those in control of a sizeable tract of territory and which act as *de facto* states, to those which barely meet the international humanitarian law requirement of organization'.[98]

The uncertainties as to the scope of the human rights obligations incurred by armed groups can be overcome, in large part, when such groups make explicit commitments to abide by specific standards. Such commitments may also have an impact on the development of customary law in this regard.[99] They can also be seen as creating legally binding obligations for armed groups (and as providing an explanation for the binding nature of those obligations).[100] These commitments may be part of peace agreements concluded between one or more armed groups and the government. The United Nations and/or third states often witness such peace agreements.[101]

Commitments by armed groups have also been made unilaterally, for instance in the framework of the process of 'deeds of commitment' under the auspices of Geneva Call, an organization 'dedicated to engaging armed non-State actors towards compliance with international humanitarian law and human right law'.[102] Moreover, in the follow-up process of a number of thematic Security Council resolutions, for example on children in armed conflict, armed groups have committed themselves to certain rules and to implementing action plans for the protection of specific vulnerable groups. Furthermore, some reports of international bodies have documented such unilateral commitments, for instance in two recent reports on the situation in Libya and in Gaza.[103]

Nevertheless, it is clear that further research into the exact scope of human rights applicable to armed groups would be necessary. This could be done by examining in detail the practice of UN bodies and experts in this regard, as well as by examining the commitments made by armed groups.

4.   CONCLUSION

The analysis in this chapter reveals that it is increasingly accepted by UN bodies and experts that armed groups have obligations under human rights law when they have control over territory, allowing them to exercise de facto government functions. Because human rights treaty law generally does not impose obligations on non-state armed groups, such a development could only have taken place as part of an evolution under customary international law. However, further evidence from a larger variety of practice, in particular from States, would be necessary in order to reach a firm conclusion in this respect. Another view is that respect for human rights by armed groups in control of territory reflects the legitimate expectation of the international community. It may be argued that the existence of such a legitimate expectation further supports the existence of a customary rule.

Whether human rights law also binds armed groups when performing acts outside areas under their control, is far from clear. Drawing an analogy between such acts and extra-territorial acts of states could lead to an affirmative answer. However, neither international practice, nor most doctrine seems to support the claim that human rights law binds armed groups without any control over territory. Another view is to consider armed groups bound by peremptory norms of international (human rights) law, regardless of territorial control. The application of these peremptory norms does not, however, seem to provide additional protection beyond humanitarian law, unless the armed groups in question are acting outside a situation of armed conflict.

Nevertheless, the protection gap that exists by excluding the application of human rights law to armed groups in all circumstances would be reduced by extending human rights obligations to armed groups in control of territory where they exercise de facto government functions. This is particularly the case with regard to activities not covered by humanitarian law and with regard to situations outside armed conflict where humanitarian law does not apply, or no longer applies. However, determining the exact content of the rules of human rights law that might apply to armed groups in such situations would demand further research and maybe a further development of practice in this area.

NOTES

* Jean-Marie Henckaerts, LLM, SJD, is a Legal Adviser in the Legal Division of the International Committee of the Red Cross (ICRC). He was head of the ICRC's project on customary international humanitarian law (2000–2010) and is currently heading the ICRC's project to update the commentaries on the 1949 Geneva Conventions and their Additional Protocols of 1977. Cornelius Wiesener, LLM, is a PhD candidate at the European University Institute in Florence, Italy. He was an intern in the ICRC Legal Division from July to September 2011 and carried out a large part of the research for this chapter. The views in this chapter are those of the authors alone. They do not necessarily reflect those of the ICRC.

1. For more detailed commentary on common Article 3, see J. Pejic, 'The Protective Scope of Common Article 3: More Than Meets the Eye', *International Review of the Red Cross* 881 (2011): 189–225; E. La Haye, 'Common Article 3', in *The Oxford Companion to International Criminal Justice*, ed. A. Cassese (Oxford: Oxford University Press, 2009), 274; L. Moir, *The Law of Internal Armed Conflict* (Cambridge: Cambridge University Press, 2002), 30–88; D. Momtaz, 'Le droit international humanitaire applicable aux conflits armés non internationaux', *Recueil des cours* 292 (2001): 9–146.

2. Convention for the Protection of Cultural Property in the Event of Armed Conflict, The Hague, 14 May 1954, Article 19.

3. Protocol on Prohibitions or Restrictions on the Use of Mines, Booby-Traps and Other Devices, as Amended, Geneva, 3 May 1996, Article 1(3) ('In case of armed conflicts not of an international character occurring in the territory of one of the High Contracting Parties, each party to the conflict shall be bound to apply the prohibitions and restrictions of this Protocol'); Convention on Prohibitions or Restrictions on the Use of Certain Conventional Weapons Which May be Deemed to be Excessively Injurious or to Have Indiscriminate Effects, Geneva, 10 October 1980, Amendment Article 1, 21 December 2001, Article 1(3) ('In case of armed conflicts not of an international character occurring in the territory of one of the High Contracting Parties, each party to the conflict shall be bound to apply the prohibitions and restrictions of this Convention and its annexed Protocols'); Protocol on Explosive Remnants of War (Protocol V to the 1980 Convention), Geneva, 28 November 2003, Article 1(3) which refers back to Amended Article 1 of the Convention. In addition, the Statute of the International Criminal Court, Rome, 17 July 1998, Article 8(2)(c) and (e) applies to war crimes committed in non-international armed conflicts.

4. Second Protocol to the Hague Convention of 1954 for the Protection of Cultural Property in the Event of Armed Conflict, The Hague, 26 March 1999, Article 22(1) ('This Protocol shall apply in the event of an armed conflict not of an international character, occurring within the territory of one of the Parties'). For further details, see J.-M. Henckaerts, 'The Protection of Cultural Property in Non-International Armed Conflicts', in *Protecting Cultural Property in Armed Conflict: An Insight into the 1999 Second Protocol to the Hague Convention of 1954 for the Protection of Cultural Property in the Event of Armed Conflict*, eds L. Lijnzaad and N. van Woudenberg (Leiden: Martinus Nijhoff, 2010), 81–93.

5. See Protocol on Prohibitions or Restrictions on the Use of Mines, Booby-Traps and Other Devices, as Amended, Geneva, 3 May 1996, Article 1(6) ('The application of the provisions of this Protocol to parties to a conflict, which are not High Contracting Parties that have accepted this Protocol, shall not change their legal status or the legal status of a disputed territory, either explicitly or implicitly'); Second Protocol to the Hague Convention of 1954 for the Protection of Cultural Property in the Event of Armed Conflict, The Hague, 26 March 1999, Article 22(6) ('The application of this Protocol to the situation referred to in paragraph 1 shall not affect the legal status of the parties to the conflict'); Convention on Prohibitions or Restrictions on the Use of Certain Conventional Weapons Which May be Deemed to be Excessively Injurious or to Have Indiscriminate Effects, Geneva, 10 October 1980, Amendment Article 1, 21 December 2001, Article 1(6) ('The application of the provisions of this Convention and its annexed Protocols to parties to a conflict which are not High Contracting Parties that have accepted this Convention or its annexed Protocols, shall not change their legal status or the legal status of a disputed territory, either explicitly or implicitly'); Protocol on Explosive Remnants of

War (Protocol V to the 1980 Convention), Geneva, 28 November 2003, Article 1(3) which refers back to Amended Article 1 of the Convention.

6.   Y. Sandoz, C. Swinarski and B. Zimmermann, *Commentary on the Additional Protocols of 8 June 1977 to the Geneva Conventions of 12 August 1949* (Geneva: International Committee of the Red Cross and Martinus Nijhoff, 1987), para. 4442. See also S. Sivakumaran, 'Re-envisaging the International Law of Internal Armed Conflict', *European Journal of International Law* 22 (2011): 219–264, at 248.

7.   Protocol Additional to the Geneva Conventions of 12 August 1949, and relating to the Protection of Victims of Non-International Armed Conflicts (Protocol II), Geneva, 8 June 1977, Article 1(1) (hereinafter 'Additional Protocol II').

8.   For an overview see S. Sivakumaran, 'Binding Armed Opposition Groups', *International and Comparative Law Quarterly* 55 (2006): 369–394.

9.   C. Ryngaert, 'Human Rights Obligations of Armed Groups', *Revue belge de droit international* 41 (2008): 357 (referring to Cassese, 'The Status of Rebels under the 1977 Geneva Protocol on Non-International Armed Conflicts', *International and Comparative Law Quarterly* 30 (1981): 423–429; L. Zegveld, *The Accountability of Armed Opposition Groups under International Law* (Cambridge: Cambridge University Press, 2002), 109, and *Commentary on the First Geneva Convention of 1949*, ed. J.S. Pictet (Geneva: International Committee of the Red Cross, 1960), 51. See also M. Sassòli, 'Transnational Armed Groups and International Humanitarian Law', *HPCR Occasional Paper Series* 6 (Winter 2006): 12 ('Either there is a rule of customary international law according to which [non-State armed groups] are bound by obligations accepted by the government of the state where they fight, or the principle of effectiveness implies that any effective power in the territory of a state is bound by the state's obligations, or they are bound via the implementation or transformation of international rules into national legislation or by the direct applicability of self-executing international rules').

10.   J.-M. Henckaerts and L. Doswald-Beck, *Customary International Humanitarian Law, Volume I: Rules* (Cambridge: Cambridge University Press, 2005). Of the 161 rules identified as customary, 13 apply in international armed conflicts only (Rules 3, 4, 41, 49, 51, 106–108, 114, 130, 145–147), two rules apply in non-international armed conflicts only (Rules 148 and 159) and the remaining 146 rules apply in any type of armed conflict. Among the latter category 138 apply to all parties to the conflicts, leaving eight rules applicable to States only (Rules 141, 143, 144, 149, 150, 157, 158 and 161).

11.   Ibid., Rules 141 (legal advisers), 143 (teaching to civilian population), 144 (ensuring respect *erga omnes*), 149 (state responsibility), 150 (reparation), 157 (universal jurisdiction), 158 (investigation and prosecution of war crimes), and 161 (cooperation in the investigation and prosecution of war crimes).

12.   Ibid., at xlii. For a more elaborate analysis, see, e.g., Hui Han Lie, *The Influence of Armed Opposition Groups on the Formation of Customary Rules of International Humanitarian Law*, unpublished Master's thesis, University of Amsterdam, November 2003.

13.   *Prosecutor v. Sam Hinga Norman* (Case No. SCSL-2004-14-AR72(E)), Decision on preliminary Motion Based on Lack of Jurisdiction (Child Recruitment), Decision, 31 May 2004, para. 22.

14.   Optional Protocol to the Convention of the Rights of the Child on Children in Armed Conflict, 25 May 2000, Article 4(1).

15.   Convention on the Elimination of All Forms of Racial Discrimination, New York, 21 December 1965, Articles 2–7 (addressed to 'States Parties'); International Covenant on Civil and Political Rights, New York, 16 December 1966, Article 2(1) ('Each State Party to the present Covenant undertakes to respect and to ensure to all individuals within its territory and subject to its jurisdiction the rights recognized in the present Covenant'); International Covenant on Economic, Social and Cultural Rights, New York, 16 December 1966, Article 2(1) ('Each State Party to the present Covenant undertakes to take steps … with a view to achieving progressively the full realization of the rights recognized in the present Covenant'); Convention on the Elimination of All Forms of Discrimination Against Women, New York, 18 December 1979, Articles 2–16 (addressed to 'States Parties'); Convention against Torture and Other Cruel, Inhuman or Degrading Treatment or Punishment, New York, 10 December 1984, Articles 2–16 (addressed to 'each State Party' or to 'States Parties'); Convention on the Rights of the Child, New York, 20 November 1989, Article 2(1) ('States Parties shall respect and ensure the rights set forth in the present Convention to each child within their jurisdiction'); Convention on the Protection of the Rights of All Migrant Workers and Members of Their Families, New York, 18 December 1990, Article 7 ('States Parties undertake, in accordance with the international instruments concerning human rights, to respect and to ensure to all migrant workers and members of their families within their territory or subject to their jurisdiction the rights provided for in the present Convention'); Convention on the Rights of Persons with Disabilities, New York, 30 March 2007, Article 4(1) ('States Parties undertake

to ensure and promote the full realization of all human rights and fundamental freedoms for all persons with disabilities without discrimination of any kind on the basis of disability'), and the following regional treaties (*infra* note 16).

16. European Convention for the Protection of Human Rights and Fundamental Freedoms, Rome, 4 November 1950, Article 1 ('The High Contracting Parties shall secure to everyone within their jurisdiction the rights and freedoms defined in Section 1 of this Convention'); American Convention on Human Rights, San José, 22 November 1969, Article 1(1) ('The States Parties to this Convention undertake to respect the rights and freedoms recognized herein and to ensure to all persons subject to their jurisdiction the free and full exercise of those rights and freedoms'); African Charter on Human and Peoples' Rights, Banjul, 26 June 1981, Article 1 ('The Member States of the Organization of African Unity parties to the present Charter shall recognize the rights, duties and freedoms enshrined in this Charter and shall undertake to adopt legislative or other measures to give effect to them').

17. Optional Protocol to the Convention of the Rights of the Child on Children in Armed Conflict, New York, 25 May 2000, Article 4(1). See also Preamble: 'Condemning with the gravest concern the recruitment, training and use within and across national borders of children in hostilities by armed groups distinct from the armed forces of a State, and recognizing the responsibility of those who recruit, train and use children in this regard.'

18. See Ryngaert, *supra* note 9, at 364–365 (who also finds support in the travaux préparatoires) and Sivakumaran, *supra* note 6, at 249 ('Views on the question are mixed, but the majority (and, it is suggested, better) view is that the provision is binding on states alone and does not purport to bind armed groups'). But see A. Clapham, 'Human Rights Obligations of Organized Armed Groups' in *Non-State Actors and International Humanitarian Law. Organized Armed Groups: a Challenge for the 21st Century*, eds M. Odello and G.L. Beruto (Milan: FrancoAngeli, 2010), 102–103. Cf. A. Bellal, G. Giacca, and S. Casey-Maslen, 'International Law and Armed Non-state Actors in Afghanistan', *International Review of the Red Cross* 881 (2011): 65 ('Looking at the wording of that article [4], it appears that the direct legal obligation is imposed, through paragraph 2, on *states* parties and not on armed groups. That argument should, though, be considered in the light of the recent practice of the UN Security Council in relation to the situations of children in armed conflict') (emphasis in original).

19. Option Protocol to the Convention of the Rights of the Child on Children in Armed Conflict, *supra* note 17, Article 4(2).

20. Convention on the Rights of the Child, *supra* note 15, Article 38 (still entirely addressed to 'States Parties').

21. African Union Convention for the Protection and Assistance of Internationally Displaced Persons in Africa (Kampala Convention), Kampala, 22 October 2009, Article 7. See also Bellal, Giacca and Casey-Maslen, *supra* note 18, at 66–67 ('One should be cautious, however, before drawing sweeping conclusions about the impact of Article 7 on the issue of the human rights obligations of non-state armed groups. First, the second paragraph of Article 7 recalls the importance of state responsibility in this context and, second, it covers the obligations of individual *members* of armed groups and not those of the group itself') (emphasis in original).

22. Kampala Convention, *supra* note 21, Article 1(e).

23. This subject is beyond the scope of this chapter. For further information, see in particular L. Zegveld, *The Accountability of Armed Opposition Groups under International Law* (Cambridge: Cambridge University Press, 2002), Chapter 5, 'Accountability of the State for Acts of Armed Opposition Groups', 164–219; see also Ryngaert, *supra* note 9, at 358–362.

24. Decision on State Succession to the Obligations of the Former Yugoslavia under the International Covenant on Civil and Political Rights (separate opinion Mullerson), Human Rights Committee, reprinted in *European Human Rights Reports* 15 (1993): 233, 236.

25. Human Rights Committee, General Comment No. 26: *General Comment on Issues Relating to the Continuity of Obligations to the International Covenant on Civil and Political Rights*, HRC, 8 December 1997 (UN Doc. CPR/C/21/Rev.1/Add.8/Rev.1), para. 4.

26. J.A. Hessbruegge, 'Human Rights Violations Arising from the Conduct of Non-State Actors', *Buffalo Human Rights Law Review* 11 (2005): 40–41. Hessbruegge further notes: 'A similar assumption underlies a 1989 report of the Special Rapporteur in Afghanistan that submitted: "The territorial sovereignty of the Afghan Government is not fully effective since some provinces of Afghanistan are totally or partly in the hands of traditional forces. The responsibility for the respect of human rights is therefore divided".' Report on the Situation of Human Rights in Afghanistan Prepared by the Special Rapporteur, Mr Felix Ermacora, in Accordance with Commission on Human Rights Resolution 1988/67, UN Doc. E/CN.4/1989, 16 February 1989, para. 68.

27. See Liesbeth Zegveld, *supra* note 23, at 39–42 (referring to the Inter-American Commission on Human Rights, *infra* note 28 and 29, and to the UN Commission on Human Rights, Report of the Meeting of Special Rapporteurs/Representatives, Experts and Chairpersons of Working Groups of the Special Procedures of the Commission on Human Rights and of the Advisory Services Programme, Geneva, 28–30 May 1996, UN Doc. E/CN.4/1997/3, 30 September 1996, Annex, paras 46–47 and Analytical Report of the Secretary-General on Minimum Humanitarian Standards, UN Doc. E/CN.4/1998/87, paras 59–64).

28. *Inter-American Yearbook on Human Rights 1990*, at 358. The Inter-American Commission examined this question pursuant to a resolution of the General Assembly of the Organization of American States, AG/Res.1043 (XX-0/90), para. 3, reprinted in *Inter-American Yearbook on Human Rights 1990*, at 354 (recommending that 'in reporting on the status of human rights in the American states, [the Inter-American Commission] include reference to the action of irregular armed groups in such states').

29. Third Report on the Situation of Human Rights in Colombia, OEA/Ser.L/V/II.102, Doc. 9, Rev. 1, at 75–76, paras 13–14; see also *Juan Carlos Abella v. Argentina* (known as the *La Tablada case*), IACommHR, Case 11.137, Report No. 55/97, 30 October 1997, para. 174

30. Moir, *supra* note 1, at 194.

31. A. Constantinides, 'Human Rights Obligations and Accountability of Armed Opposition Groups: The Practice of the UN Security Council', *Human Rights and International Legal Discourse* 4 (2010): 93.

32. UN Commission on Human Rights, Report of the Meeting of Special Rapporteurs/Representatives, Experts and Chairpersons of Working Groups of the Special Procedures of the Commission on Human Rights and of the Advisory Services Programme, Geneva, 28–30 May 1996, UN Doc. E/CN.4/1997/3, 30 September 1996, Annex, para. 44.

33. S/RES/1346, 30 March 2001, para. 6.

34. S/RES/1663, 24 March 2006, para. 7.

35. S/RES/1964, 16 September 2010.

36. S/RES/1991, 28 June 2011.

37. See, e.g., Ryngaert, *supra* note 9, at 376–377.

38. Report of the Working Group on Enforced or Involuntary Disappearances, Mission to Colombia, E/CN.4/2006/56/Add.1, 17 January 2006.

39. *Ilaşcu et al. v. Moldova and the Russian Federation*, ECtHR, Application No. 48787/99, Judgment of 8 July 2004. Given that the Court attributed the conduct of the authorities of Transnistria to Russia, it did not have to examine whether the separatist regime was itself bound by human rights law.

40. See also Convention for the Protection of Cultural Property in the Event of Armed Conflict, The Hague, 14 May 1954, Article 19(4); Protocol on Prohibitions or Restrictions on the Use of Mines, Booby-Traps and Other Devices, as Amended, Geneva, 3 May 1996, Article 1(6); Second Protocol to the Hague Convention of 1954 for the Protection of Cultural Property in the Event of Armed Conflict, The Hague, 26 March 1999, Article 22(6); Convention on Prohibitions or Restrictions on the Use of Certain Conventional Weapons Which May be Deemed to be Excessively Injurious or to Have Indiscriminate Effects, Geneva, 10 October 1980, Amendment Article 1, 21 December 2001, Article 1(6) as amended; Protocol on Explosive Remnants of War (Protocol V to the 1980 Convention), Geneva, 28 November 2003, Article 1(3).

41. Optional Protocol to the Convention on the Rights of the Child, *supra* note 17, Article 4(3) ('the application of the present article shall not affect the legal status of any party to an armed conflict').

42. Kampala Convention, *supra* note 21, Article 7(1).

43. See also Institut de Droit International, The Application of International Humanitarian Law and Fundamental Human Rights in Armed Conflicts in which Non-State Entities are Parties, Session of Berlin, 1999, Resolution of 25 August 1999, available at http://www.idi-iil.org/idiE/resolutionsE/1999_ber_03_en.PDF, para. II (accessed 9 October 2011) ('All parties to armed conflicts in which non-State entities are parties, irrespective of their legal status, as well as the United Nations, and competent regional and other international organizations have the obligation to respect international humanitarian law as well as fundamental human rights. The application of such principles and rules does not affect the legal status of the parties to the conflict and is not dependent on their recognition as belligerents or insurgents').

44. Informe de la Comisión para el Esclarecimiento Histórico, Guatemala Memoria del Silencio, Vol. I, 1999, 46, para. 20 ('Además, la Comisión aplicó a los hechos de violencia cometidos por la guerrilla los principios comunes al Derecho Internacional de los Derechos Humanos y al Derecho Internacional humanitario, *a fin de dar un trato igualitario a las Partes*, tomando en cuenta que la tendencia predominante en la actualidad es considerar que la dignidad de la persona humana se ve igualmente

ofendida quienquiera sea el autor de hechos que la atropellan o la conculcan') (emphasis added), available at: http://shr.aaas.org/guatemala/ceh/mds/spanish/toc.html (accessed 7 October 2011)

45.   Constantinides, *supra* note 31, at 94.
46.   See also Sivakumaran, *supra* note 6, at 243–244 ('Nevertheless, it is difficult to comprehend that, once territory falls under the control of a non-state armed group, international humanitarian law has little or nothing to offer').
47.   Bellal, Giacca and Casey-Maslen, *supra* note 18, at 74.
48.   For an overview, see C. Tomuschat, 'The Applicability of Human Rights Law to Insurgent Movements', in *Krisensicherung und Humanitärer Schutz – Crisis Management and Humanitarian Protection. Festschrift für Dieter Fleck*, eds Horst, Fischer et al. (Berlin: Berliner Wissenschafts-Verlag, 2004), 573–591 and Constantinides, *supra* note 31, at 89–110.
49.   S/PRST/2004/48, 16 December 2004.
50.   S/RES/1721, 1 November 2006, para. 27.
51.   S/RES/1214, 8 December 1998, para. 12.
52.   S/PRST/2000/12, 7 April 2000.
53.   Apart from a number of continuing obligations with regard to persons deprived of their liberty for example. See Additional Protocol II, *supra* note 7, Article 2(2) referring to the continued applicability of Articles 5 and 6.
54.   Institut de Droit International, The Application of International Humanitarian Law and Fundamental Human Rights in Armed Conflicts in which Non-State Entities are Parties, *supra* note 43, para. X.
55.   C. Tomuschat, *Human Rights: Between Idealism and Realism* (Oxford: Oxford University Press, 2003), 261.
56.   Report of the Secretary-General's Panel of Experts on Accountability in Sri Lanka, 31 March 2011, para. 185, available at: http://www.un.org/News/dh/infocus/Sri_Lanka/POE_Report_Full.pdf (accessed 7 October 2011).
57.   Bellal, Giacca and Casey-Maslen, *supra* note 18, at 73 ('Holding non-state armed groups accountable for the violation of core human rights norms also seems to be in line with the development of international criminal law, which assesses the criminal responsibility of individual members of armed groups when international crimes not necessarily committed in relation to an armed conflict (and thus outside the ambit of international humanitarian law) have been perpetrated. This is the case regarding the crime of genocide and crimes against humanity, situations in which human rights violations are criminalized').
58.   See C. Kress, 'Transnational violence' in *Non-State Actors and International Humanitarian Law. Organized Armed Groups: A Challenge for the 21st Century*, eds M. Odello and G.L. Beruto (Milan: FrancoAngeli, 2010), 162–163 (arguing that crimes against humanity can be committed by armed groups using 'a somewhat broader' interpretation of the term 'organizational' in Article 7(2)(a) of the ICC Statute which provides that: 'Attack directed against any civilian population' means a course of conduct involving the multiple commission of acts referred to in paragraph 1 against any civilian population, pursuant to or in furtherance of a State or organizational policy to commit such attack) and Clapham, *supra* note 18, at 103 (stating that the Rome Statute clearly envisaged genocide and crimes against humanity being committed by non-state actors as it requires a State or 'organizational policy').
59.   UN Commission on Truth in El Salvador, Report, UN Doc. S/25500, 1 April 1993, Annex, 20.
60.   S/PRST/2000/12, 7 April 2000.
61.   S/RES/1333, 19 December 2000, Preamble.
62.   S/RES/1376, 9 November 2001, para. 5.
63.   S/PRST/2002/27, 18 October 2002.
64.   S/RES/1417, 14 June 2002, paras 4–5; see also S/PRST/2002/19, 5 June 2002 and S/PRST/2002/22, 23 July 2002 ('that the RCD-GOMA must ensure an end to all violations of human rights and to impunity in all areas under its control').
65.   Report of the Panel of Experts on the Sudan, UN Doc. S/2007/584, 3 October 2007, paras 282 and 330. Compare with the earlier Report of the International Commission of Inquiry on Darfur to the United Nations Secretary-General, UN Doc. S/2005/60, 25 January 2005, paras 172–174 (mentioning the human rights obligations of the Sudanese government, while addressing the obligations of the insurgents in Darfur solely in terms of international humanitarian law).
66.   Committee on the Rights of the Child, Report on the twenty-seventh session, 23 July 2001 (UN Doc. CRC/C/108), para. 155.
67.   *Elmi v. Australia*, Committee against Torture, Communication No. 120/1998, UN Doc. CAT/C/22/D/120/1998, 14 May 1999, para. 6.5.

68. Commission on Human Rights, Situation of Human Rights in the Sudan, Report of the Special Rapporteur, Gerhart Baum, UN Doc. E/CN.4/2002/46, 23 January 2002, para. 91.

69. Report of the Special Rapporteur, extrajudicial, summary or arbitrary executions, Philip Alston, UN Doc. E/CN.4/2005/7, 22 December 2004, para. 76.

70. Report of the independent expert on the situation of human rights in Somalia, Shamsul Bari, Human Rights Council, 16 September 2010 (UN Doc. A/HRC/15/48), paras. 19–22 and 37–50.

71. Report of the Special Rapporteur on extrajudicial, summary or arbitrary executions, Philip Alston; the Special Rapporteur on the right of everyone to the enjoyment of the highest attainable standard of physical and mental health, Paul Hunt; the Representative of the Secretary-General on human rights of internally displaced persons, Walter Kälin; and the Special Rapporteur on adequate housing as a component of the right to an adequate standard of living, Miloon Kothari, Mission to Lebanon and Israel (7–14 September 2006), UN Doc. A/HRC/2/7, 2 October 2006, para. 19.

72. Report of the Commission of Inquiry on Lebanon, A/HRC/3/2, 23 November 2006, para. 67.

73. Combined report, under Resolution S-9/1, of the Special Rapporteur on the right of everyone to the enjoyment of the highest attainable standard of physical and mental health, the Special Representative of the Secretary-General for Children and Armed Conflict, the Special Rapporteur on violence against women, its causes and consequences, the Representative of the Secretary-General on the human rights of internally displaced persons, the Special Rapporteur on adequate housing as a component of the right to an adequate standard of living, and on the right to non-discrimination in this context, the Special Rapporteur on the right to food, the Special Rapporteur on extrajudicial, arbitrary or summary executions, the Special Rapporteur on the right to education, and the Independent Expert on the question of human rights and extreme poverty, UN Doc. A/HRC/10/22, 20 March 2009, para. 22.

74. The Report of the United Nations Fact-Finding Mission on the Gaza Conflict, UN Doc. A/HRC/12/48, 25 September 2009.

75. Report of the Secretary-General's Panel of Experts on Accountability in Sri Lanka, *supra* note 56, para. 188.

76. Report of the International Commission of Inquiry to investigate all alleged violations of international human rights law in the Libyan Arab Jamahiriya, UN Doc. A/HRC/17/44, 1 June 2011, para. 72.

77. Report of the independent international commission of inquiry on the Syrian Arab Republic, UN Doc.A/HRC/21/50, 16 August 2012, p. 47, Annex II, para. 10.

78. See Constantinides, *supra* note 31, at 102–103. See also Hessbruegge, *supra* note 26, at 40–41.

79. For support, see Ryngaert, *supra* note 9, at 374–377.

80. Report of the Special Rapporteur on extrajudicial, summary or arbitrary executions, Philip Alston, Mission to Sri Lanka, UN Doc. E/CN.4/2006/53/Add.5, 27 March 2006, paras 25–27. See also the Report of the Special Rapporteur on extrajudicial, summary or arbitrary executions, Philip Alston, Mission to Philippines, 2008, UN Doc. A/HRC/8/3/Add.2, 16 April 2008, para. 5 ('All parties to the armed conflicts are bound by customary and conventional international humanitarian law and are subject to the demand of the international community that every organ of society respect and promote human rights. In addition, some of the parties have made other formal commitments to respect human rights. Within this legal framework, both state and non-state actors can commit extrajudicial executions'). In his more recent reports, the Special Rapporteur did not explicitly discuss the question of whether armed groups have obligations under human rights law, but merely stated that (most of the) killings perpetrated by such groups violated human rights law. See the Report of the Special Rapporteur on extrajudicial, summary or arbitrary executions, Philip Alston, Mission to Afghanistan, UN Doc. A/HRC/8/3/Add.6, 29 May 2008, paras 27–29; Report of the Special Rapporteur on extrajudicial, summary or arbitrary executions, Philip Alston, Mission to Philippines, Follow-up, UN Doc. A/HRC/11/2/Add.8, 29 April 2009, paras 26–27; Report of the Special Rapporteur on extrajudicial, summary or arbitrary executions, Philip Alston, Mission to Colombia, UN Doc. A/HRC/14/24/Add.2, 31 March 2010, paras 43–48. The current Special Rapporteur, Christof Heyns, has taken a more cautious approach, using the term human rights 'abuse' rather than 'violation'. See the Report of the Special Rapporteur on extrajudicial, summary or arbitrary executions, Christof Heyns, Mission to Afghanistan, Follow-up, UN Doc. A/HRC/17/28/Add.6, 27 May 2011, para. 46 ('In 2010, the Taliban and other armed groups (some anti-Government, and others ostensibly supporting the Government) targeted, abducted, indiscriminately attacked and unlawfully killed civilians, committing human rights abuses and gross violations of international humanitarian law').

81. See International Law Association, Final Report of the Committee on the Formation of Customary (General) International Law, Statement of Principles Applicable to the Formation of General Customary International Law, Report of the Sixty-Ninth Conference, London, 2000, Principle 1(i) ('a

rule of customary international law is one which is created and sustained by the constant and uniform practice of States and other subjects of international law in or impinging upon their international legal relations, in circumstances which give rise to a legitimate expectation of similar conduct in the future'). For a more in-depth discussion of this issue, see M.H. Mendelson, 'The Formation of Customary International Law', *Collected Courses of the Hague Academy of International Law*, 272 (1998): 183–186 (with references to other publications by the same author and to O. Lissitzyn, *International Law Today and Tomorrow* (New York: Oceana Publications, 1965), 35–36.

82.   Additional Protocol II, *supra* note 7, Article 1(1).

83.   See, generally, M. Milanovic, *Extraterritorial Application of Human Rights Treaties* (Oxford: Oxford University Press, 2011). For a recent Decision of the European Court of Human Rights on this issue, see *Al-Skeini and others v. United Kingdom*, ECtHR, Application No. 55721/07, Judgment of 7 July 2011. For more analysis, see in this volume R. Goldman, 'Extraterritorial Application of the Human Rights to Life and Personal Liberty, including *Habeas Corpus* During Situations of Armed Conflict'.

84.   Report of the Secretary-General's Panel of Experts on Accountability in Sri Lanka, *supra* note 56, para. 243 ('The Panel has not considered LTTE abuses outside the conflict zone under international human rights law because of the uncertainty surrounding whether non-state actors have human rights obligations beyond the territories they control').

85.   See, e.g., *Lopez Burgos v. Uruguay*, HRC, 29 July 1981 (UN Doc. CCPR/C/13/D/52/1979), para. 12.3, and *Lilian Celiberti de Casariego v Uruguay*, HRC, 29 July 1981 (UN Doc. CCPR/C/13/D/56/1979); *Coard et al. v. United States*, IACommHR, Case 10.951, Report No. 109/99, 29 September 1999, para. 37; *Öcalan v. Turkey*, ECtHR, Application No. 46221/99, Judgment of 12 May 2005, para. 91.

86.   See Bellal, Giacca and Casey-Maslen, *supra* note 18, at 72–74 ('That appears to be the principle lying behind the practice of the Security Council with regard to children in situations of armed conflict. The Security Council and the Special Representative for Children in Armed Conflict do not distinguish as to the type or structure of an armed group when it comes to its listing in the Annex of the Secretary-General's Reports on Children in Armed Conflict. All that is required for its inclusion is that the group has committed one of the six grave violations mentioned in Security Council Resolution 1612').

87.   International Law Association, Committee on Non-State Actors, First Report of the Committee, *Non-State Actors in International Law: Aims, Approach and Scope of Project and Legal Issues*, The Hague Conference, 2010, para. 3.2., 17, available at: http//www.ila-hq.org/en/committees/index.cfm/cid/1023 (accessed 9 October 2011).

88.   International Law Commission, Draft Articles on Responsibility of States for Internationally Wrongful Acts, with commentaries, Commentary on Article 26, *Yearbook of the International Law Commission*, 2001, Vol. 2, Part Two, 85, para. 5.

89.   General Comment No. 29: *States of Emergency (Article 4)*, HRC, 31 August 2001 (UN Doc. CCPR/C/21/Rev.1/Add.11), para. 11 ('The proclamation of certain provisions of the Covenant as being of a non-derogable nature, in article 4, paragraph 2, is to be seen partly as recognition of the peremptory nature of some fundamental rights ensured in treaty form in the Covenant (e.g., Article 6 and 7). … Furthermore, the category of peremptory norms extends beyond the list of non-derogable provisions as given in article 4, paragraph 2. States parties may in no circumstances invoke article 4 of the Covenant as justification for acting in violation of humanitarian law or peremptory norms of international law, for instance by taking hostages, by imposing collective punishments, through arbitrary deprivations of liberty or by deviating from fundamental principles of fair trial, including the presumption of innocence.')

90.   See also, Declaration of Minimum Humanitarian Standards (Turku Declaration), UN Doc. E/CN.4/1995/116, 2 December 1990. As a follow-up to this document, the UN Secretary-General issued reports seeking to identify fundamental standards of humanity applicable in times of peace and armed conflict, see Report of the Secretary-General, UN Doc. A/HRC/8/14, 3 June 2008.

91.   For a discussion of whether the Universal Declaration of Human Rights (1948) has attained the status of customary law or general principles, see H. Hannum, 'The Status of the Universal Declaration of Human Rights in National and International Law', *Georgia Journal of International and Comparative Law* 25 (1995–1996): 287–395; B. Simma and P. Alston, 'The Sources of Human Rights Law: Custom, Jus Cogens, and General Principles', *Australian Yearbook of International Law* 12 (1992): 82–108.

92.   Report of the Special Rapporteur on extrajudicial, summary or arbitrary executions, Philip Alston, Mission to Sri Lanka, *supra* note 79, para. 27.

93. Guatemala Memory of Silence, Executive Summary Conclusions and Recommendations, UN Doc. A/53/928 Annex, 27 April 1999, para. 127 ('The armed insurgent groups that participated in the internal armed confrontation had an obligation to respect the minimum standards of international humanitarian law that apply to armed conflicts, as well as the general principles common to international human rights law. Their high command had the obligation to instruct subordinates to respect these norms and principles.') For the relevant part of the Spanish full report, see Informe de la Comisión para el Esclarecimiento Histórico, Guatemala Memoria del Silencio, Vol. II, 1999, paras 1699–1700.

94. Report of the Secretary-General's Panel of Experts on Accountability in Sri Lanka, *supra* note 56, para. 188.

95. Institut de Droit International, The Application of International Humanitarian Law and Fundamental Human Rights in Armed Conflicts in which Non-State Entities are Parties, *supra* note 43, para. IV.

96. A. Clapham, 'Human Rights Obligations of Non-state Actors in Conflict Situations', *International Review of the Red Cross* 863 (2006): 502 ('Rather than focusing on the obligations that insurgents cannot fulfil (fair trial with legal aid and interpretation, progressive implementation of access to university education), it is preferable to stress that the obligations apply to the extent appropriate to the context. Even conventional human rights law demands that a state take steps "to the maximum of its available resources" to fulfil progressively its human rights obligations in the context of economic and social rights.').

97. A. Clapham, *Human Rights Obligations of Non-State Actors* (Oxford: Oxford University Press, 2006), 68–69.

98. Sivakumaran, *supra* note 6, at 256.

99. But the issue of the role of the practice of armed groups in the formation of customary law, identified in the area of international humanitarian law would apply *a fortiori* in this area, see *supra* note 12 and accompanying text.

100. See, e.g., Zegveld, *supra* note 23, at 49–51 ('there appears to be no legal rule which would prevent the representatives of an armed opposition group ... from making agreements [in which they agree to be bound by human rights norms] with the established government that are valid on the international plane') and Ryngaert, *supra* note 9, at 372–374.

101. Constantinides, *supra* note 31, at 109. These peace agreements have been well documented, although not all of them contain human rights commitments. See C. Bell, *Peace Agreements and Human Rights* (Oxford: Oxford University Press, 2000): 323–374. See also Zegveld, *supra* note 23, at 149–151.

102. For more information on Geneva Call, see http://www.genevacall.org/ (accessed 7 October 2011).

103. Report of the International Commission of Inquiry to investigate all alleged violations of international human rights law in the Libyan Arab Jamahiriya, *supra* note 76, para. 72; Report of the United Nations Fact-Finding Mission on the Gaza Conflict, *supra* note 74, paras 306–307.

9. Positive obligations in human rights law during armed conflicts

Sandra Krähenmann*

Civil and political rights were originally conceived to protect individuals against the abusive exercise of state authority by their own government[1] during times of peace.[2] Hence, in contrast to economic, social and cultural rights, civil and political rights were perceived to be negative in nature, merely requiring states to abstain from interfering with individuals' rights in times of peace.[3] Both premises proved to be erroneous. The application of human rights law during times of armed conflicts is nowadays widely accepted,[4] although the modalities of the interplay between human rights law and international humanitarian law remain subject to controversy.[5] This development easily fits with texts of the various human rights treaties that do not exclude their application during times of armed conflict[6] and indeed provide for the possibility to derogate during a 'public emergency threatening the life of the nation',[7] which can include situations of armed conflict.[8] In contrast, the texts of the general human rights treaties on civil and political rights reflect their perceived negative nature.[9] With the exception of a few explicit positive obligations,[10] the majority of civil and political rights are framed in terms of prohibitions[11] and a duty to respect.[12] Nonetheless, the various human rights bodies overseeing the implementation of their respective treaties implied so-called positive obligations:[13] in order to secure the effective enjoyment of civil and political rights, states are required 'not only to refrain from an active infringement by its representatives of the rights in question, but also to take appropriate steps to provide protection against an interference with those rights either by State agents or by private parties'.[14]

Thus civil and political rights entail both negative and positive obligations that are often inextricably linked.[15] The duty to plan law enforcement operations in order to minimise the risk for both the target and innocent bystanders[16] exemplarily illustrates the difficulty in disentangling interferences from a failure to act. On the one hand, the obligation to plan can be subsumed in the general assessment of the proportionality of the use of force.[17] On the other hand, if framed differently, the obligation to plan can be analysed separately as a positive obligation.[18] In addition, states are required to put in place an adequate legal framework[19] and to train and instruct their forces accordingly.[20] In other words, the prohibition of the arbitrary use of force by state agents entails a series of positive obligations, enhancing the effective protection against arbitrary use of force.[21] Rather than providing an overview of positive obligations in general,[22] the present chapter proposes to focus on a series of obligations that are particularly relevant in the context of armed conflicts. First, states have to take measures to protect individuals from the effects of hostilities. Second, states have a duty to account for the fate of persons during times of armed conflicts. Third, states have to take measures to protect individuals against both rebels and paramilitary forces.

1. THE OBLIGATION TO PROTECT FROM THE EFFECTS OF HOSTILITIES

The European Court and the Inter-American Court dealt with three issues concerning the protection of the civilian population against the effects of hostilities. First, they confirmed the applicability of the duty to plan and control operations involving the use of force during times of armed conflicts. Second, states have to take measures to protect the population from unexploded war remnants. And finally, all regional human rights bodies are paying increasing attention to the obligations owed to internally displaced people.

1.1 Planning and Control of Operations Involving the Use of Force

It is a well established principle in human rights law that state authorities have an obligation to plan operations involving the use of force with a view to minimise the risk to life of both the lawful target of the operation and innocent bystanders.[23] The same principle applies during times of armed conflict,[24] which entails three important consequences. First, state authorities have to plan their operations with a view to minimising the risk to the civilian population, which, in turn, limits their options with respect to the means used. For example, the European Court held the 'deployment of military aviation equipped with heavy weapons to be, in itself, grossly disproportionate to the purpose of effecting the lawful arrest of a person'[25] or to protect persons from unlawful violence.[26] In the case of *Kerimova v. Russia* arising out of the aerial bombing of the town of Urus-Martan at a time when the town was in the hands of the rebels, the European Court went as far as to require the state to attempt to negotiate the safe passage of the villagers before attacking the town.[27] Second, state authorities need to take into account the potential risk to life originating from the violent reaction of the lawful target.[28] In other words, states have to take precautionary measures to protect civilians from the use of force by the opposing forces.[29] From this, we can infer that the conduct of hostilities close to inhabited areas must be avoided.[30] Finally, and most controversially,[31] the European Court recently confirmed that the obligation to plan with a view to minimising the threat to life arises both in respect of civilians and the lawful target, namely the armed rebels.[32] However, it remains to be seen whether the same obligation would apply in respect of combatants during an international armed conflict. Before turning to the duty to protect the civilian population from unexploded war remnants, one further element arising out of the case *Giuliani and Gaggio v. Italy*[33] concerning the death of a student during the demonstrations against the G8 in Genoa, needs to be highlighted, Rather surprisingly, the Grand Chamber of the European Court distinguished between planned law enforcement operations against a specific target and public order operations where the eruption of violence is unforeseeable,[34] an element hitherto unknown in the jurisprudence of the European Court on the policing of demonstrations, including unauthorized and violent ones.[35] Since the chain of events was unforeseeable, the majority dismissed the serious shortcomings in the planning of the operation, both in general and for the particular operation immediately preceding the fatal shooting.[36] Arguably, the same reasoning could be applied during times of armed conflict.

1.2   Protection from Unexploded War Remnants

The positive obligation 'to take appropriate steps to safeguard the lives of those within its jurisdiction'[37] includes a duty to protect the civilian population against the dangers of landmines and booby traps, whether placed by state agents[38] or rebels.[39] Therefore, the authorities have to mark and fence off known mined areas, warn the local population, and locate and destroy mines.[40] In substance, these positive obligations correspond to the undertakings enshrined in the 1997 Landmine Ban Convention and the 1996 Amended Protocol II to the 1980 Convention on Certain Conventional Weapons. As the European Court expressly confirmed in a different context,[41] the reliance on other international treaties[42] for the purposes of interpretation is not contingent upon whether the Respondent State is bound by these treaties. For example, in the case of *Albekov*,[43] the European Court found that Russia had failed to discharge its positive obligations, although Russia was neither a party to the 1997 Ottawa Convention nor the 1996 Amended Protocol II at the time of the facts of the case. In other words, by resorting to the doctrine of positive obligations, the European Court imports other international treaty obligations and in fact renders them binding for the Respondent State under the European Convention, regardless of the state's consent to be bound by the relevant treaty. Such an approach minimizing state consent might constitute a shocking infringement on state sovereignty.[44] However, in the context of human rights treaties, any other solution seems inconceivable because it would result in a differentiated standard of protection, hinging on the Respondent State's other treaty undertakings. Moreover, states' positive obligations under the European Convention might be more far reaching than under the relevant international treaty, as illustrated by the case of *Paşa et Erkan Erol*:[45] Turkey had violated its positive obligations with respect to the serious injuries suffered by a then nine-year old boy who had stepped on a landmine after entering a marked and fenced off mined perimeter around the village gendarmerie post. The European Court highlighted that the landmines had been placed by the local authorities, although the use of landmines was widely condemned and their dangers to small children well known.[46] Moreover, the marking and fencing in itself was insufficient to prevent children from entering the mined area.[47] Two conclusions can be drawn from this case. First, since the state was responsible for the mining of the area, its positive obligations seem particularly stringent. Indeed, the European Court seems to suggest that landmines are not to be used as a matter of principle, or, at the very least, not to be placed for defensive purposes in the proximity of villages.[48] Second, under human rights law, the measures provided for under the Ottawa Convention and the 1996 Protocol do not suffice to protect children[49] from the dangers of mines in the light of their particular vulnerability.[50]

1.3   Internal Displacement

The reliance on other international law standards is further illustrated by the practice of the African Commission, the European Court and the Inter-American Court in cases concerning the destitute living conditions[51] of internally displaced people as a result of an armed conflict. Relying on the UN Guiding Principles on Internal Displacement, they all confirmed, albeit under different treaty provisions,[52] that states either have to enable internally displaced people to return in safety to their homes or provide them with the necessary means to resettle in dignity.[53] Interestingly enough, against the background of internal displacement following the massacre of villagers by para-military forces, the Inter-American Court highlighted that the return in safety is only possible if the massacres were investigated and those responsible have been identified and prosecuted.[54] In other words, the positive obligations owed to internally displaced people include the obligation to investigate and punish, not simply as a procedural obligation under the right to life but also as a means to enable the safe return of the internally displaced.

2. THE DUTY TO ACCOUNT

It is a well established principle in human rights law that states have to account for the fate of individuals in custody on the basis of their special responsibility for the life and physical integrity of detainees,[55] which entails that the burden of proof shifts to the state. During times of armed conflicts, this duty to account plays a particularly important role in two sets of circumstances. First, all human rights bodies have relied on the duty to account to hold states responsible for the fate of forcibly disappeared persons. Second, a series of cases suggests that human rights bodies have extended the duty to account, and its corollary, the reversed burden of proof, to the use of force in general, including in times of armed conflict.

2.1   The Duty to Account for the Fate of Forcibly Disappeared Individuals

In light of the evidentiary difficulties to prove state involvement[56] in individual cases of enforced disappearances,[57] characterised by an unacknowledged detention,[58] human rights bodies require states to account for the fate of a forcibly disappeared person.[59] As we shall see, the duty to account fulfils a double purpose: on the one hand, it is used to hold the state accountable for the forced disappearance; on the other hand, human rights bodies rely on the failure to account to find a violation of the right to life in cases where no corpse was ever found.

   If allegations of an enforced disappearance are sufficiently substantiated,[60] the Human Rights Committee accepts them as true unless the state provides a satisfactory explanation for the whereabouts of the disappeared person,[61] because such information lies exclusively in the hand of the state.[62] If a corpse has not been found, the Human Rights Committee then proceeds to find that the state failed to protect the life of the forcibly disappeared person on account of its failure to prevent and investigate the enforced disappearance,[63] unless the relatives hope that the victim is still alive,[64] since such a finding arguably implies[65] that the disappeared person is to be presumed dead. The Inter-American Court presumes the state responsible for an individual case of an enforced disappearance if it can be linked[66] to an established practice of enforced disappearances.[67] Since 'the practice of disappearances frequently involves secret executions without trial, followed by concealment of the body to eliminate all material evidence of the crime',[68] the Inter-American Court presumes[69] that the disappeared person was executed[70] in violation of the right to life.[71] After its initially hesitant approach,[72] the European Court aligned itself with the practice of both the Human Rights Committee and the Inter-American Court.[73] First, the European Court extended the presumptions of facts and reversed burden of proof to include instances where the victims were last seen in 'places',[74] 'locations'[75] and 'areas under the control'[76] of the authorities, although it could not be established that they were taken into custody.[77] Second, the European Court accepted that the unacknowledged detention of individuals by unidentified security forces was 'life threatening'[78] in the particular context of south-east Turkey[79] and Chechnya.[80] Therefore, the 'inability of the Government to provide a satisfactory and plausible explanation as to what happened to them [the disappeared]',[81] resulted in a presumption of a death[82] not justifiable under the right to life.[83] It is noteworthy that with respect to enforced disappearances in Chechnya, the European Court adopted this approach from the early cases onwards.[84] Arguably, this indicates a shift in its approach[85] to enforced disappearances to take into account the general context[86] of allegations of widespread enforced disappearances, rather than simply relying on previous case law establishing such enforced disappearances.[87]

2.2   An Emerging Duty to Account for the Use of Force

It is notoriously difficult for the applicants to prove their allegations that state forces resorted to excessive force,[88] in particular before the European Court which has adopted the high standard of 'proof beyond reasonable doubt'.[89] However, the recent practice of the European Court indicates an emerging duty to account for the use of force, accommodating to some extent the criticism with respect to its high burden of proof in such cases.[90] On the one hand, by analogy with the situation of individuals in custody, the European Court shifted the burden of proof to the state[91] in cases where individuals died or were injured in the area of military operations,[92] but the state denied any involvement and blamed rebels if the applicants could make a prima facie case[93] that military operations took place.[94] On the other hand, in cases where it is not contested that individuals died or were injured by state agents, the European Court is increasingly stringent with its assessment of the facts and the justification for the use of force. Hence the European Court not only started to draw negative inferences from both the failure to investigate[95] and the failure to submit documentary evidence[96] but also required the state 'to account for the use of force' and 'to demonstrate that the force was used in pursuit of one of the aims set out in paragraph 2 of Article 2 of the convention and that it was absolutely necessary and therefore strictly proportionate to the achievement of one of those aims'.[97] Therefore, states have to submit operations reports on the planning and execution of an operation.[98] Arguably, the burden of proof to account for the 'absolute necessity' of the use of force is thus shifted to the state.[99] Although not against the background of an armed conflict, both the Human Rights Committee[100] and the Inter-American Court[101] seem to have adopted a similar approach. These cases indicate that the duty to account might be more extensively relied upon in other situations than detention where it is equally difficult for the applicants to prove their allegations. Moreover, it provides an incentive for states to take the duty to investigate seriously.[102]

3. THE PROTECTION FROM ARMED GROUPS

Positive obligations are instrumental[103] in addressing human rights abuses committed by non-state actors before international human rights bodies with their jurisdictional limitation to claims brought against states. Although normally a state is not responsible for human rights abuses committed by private individuals, its responsibility may be engaged if it failed to discharge its positive obligations. Since no 'impossible or disproportionate burden'[104] is imposed on the state authorities, there is no general obligation to take operational measures in reaction to every alleged threat. For a positive obligation to take preventive measures to arise, the threat must be 'immediate and real'[105] and the authorities are aware, or ought to be aware,[106] of the threat. Under those circumstances, the authorities have to 'take measures within the scope of their powers which, judged reasonably, might have been expected to avoid that risk'.[107] All these elements convey the idea that the obligation to take operational steps is not an absolute obligation, but an obligation of due diligence.[108] The assessment of these criteria is obviously context-dependent, but, as we shall see, hinges to a significant extent on the degree of control a state exercises over the alleged offender, which implies the capacity to influence the course of the events.[109] Hence, it is necessary to distinguish between the protection from rebel forces and the protection from paramilitary forces with links, including unofficial ones, to the state forces.

3.1 Protection from Rebel Groups

The threshold to hold states accountable for abuses committed by rebel forces is high since under normal circumstances the state authorities were neither aware nor should have been aware of a 'real and immediate' risk against particular individuals[110] despite the increased risk due to a general situation of violence.[111] However, we can infer from the practice of the European Court and the Inter-American Court that states have to avoid directing hostile forces to inhabited areas and warn the local population of the arrival of hostile forces.[112] Moreover, state forces have a duty to intervene in cases of ongoing violence by private actors,[113] which entails that the failure to take any protective measures during an armed conflict, including the complete breakdown of the state's law enforcement machinery,[114] would most likely result in a violation of the state's positive obligation. The very general assertions of the African Commission in its earlier practice[115] that a state is responsible for the killings by rebels during times of armed conflict because it 'failed to provide security and stability'[116] can be construed in this sense: The state is responsible not because it failed to exercise due diligence to prevent the killings, which would impose an undue burden on the state,[117] but on account of the inefficiency, if not breaking down, of the state's police and security apparatus during the armed conflict. Finally, the European Court confirmed that if the state lost control over part of its territory during an armed conflict, the state 'must endeavour, with all the legal and diplomatic means available to it vis-à-vis foreign states and international organizations, to continue to guarantee the enjoyment of the rights and freedoms guaranteed by the Convention'[118] on behalf of the individuals living in this territory.

3.2   Protection from Paramilitary Groups

Rather than attempting to attribute the conduct of paramilitary forces on account of the traditionally recognised bases of attribution under international law, human rights bodies resort to the doctrine of positive obligations to hold states responsible for the acts committed by such groups. Hence, in its very first cases dealing with enforced disappearances in Honduras,[119] the Inter-American Court relied on a combination of the duty to respect and the duty to ensure,[120] namely the well established failure of the various branches of the Honduran government to take both preventive and remedial measures against the practice of enforced disappearances in general and the individual cases at hand,[121] to hold the state accountable.[122] More recently, the Inter-American Court used a similar approach in a series of cases[123] against Colombia involving human rights abuses committed by the then outlawed[124] paramilitary groups in order to attribute their acts as such[125] to the Colombian government regardless of the direct participation of state agents.[126] According to the Inter-American Court, Colombia incurred special duties of protection and prevention of abuses committed by such groups on account of the government's role in their creation.[127] Similarly, the European Court resorted to a broad application of the duty to protect in cases against Turkey where individuals were killed by unknown perpetrators, allegedly with the connivance of state agents.[128] The European Court rejected the Turkish argument that in light of the security situation in south-east Turkey, every individual was equally at risk, and highlighted that the victims were at a particular risk on account of their association with Kurdish separatism, which rendered them a likely target for paramilitary groups.[129] The European Court then went on to find that the Turkish authorities had failed to protect the life of the victims not only on account of the lack of protective measures but also due to the systematic failure to investigate and punish those responsible.[130] While its practice with respect to the phenomenon of killings and enforced disappearances by unknown perpetrators in south-east Turkey is not always consistent in this respect,[131] the European Court took this approach one step further when addressing enforced disappearances and extrajudicial killings by unknown perpetrators in Chechnya. In this case, the military equipment and vehicles used, information on military activities and the Russian control over the area concerned[132] pointed to the involvement of Russian forces, which, at the very least, failed to prevent these crimes. Hence, in combination with an increasingly stringent duty to account,[133] the European Court routinely established that Russia was responsible for the abductions and killings. In other words, despite the frequently scarce evidence,[134] the European Court holds Russia accountable by mixing the doctrine of positive obligations with the assessment of the contested facts.

4.   CONCLUSION

As we have seen, the doctrine of positive obligations plays an increasingly important role in the protection of the victims of armed conflict. First, the doctrine of positive obligations requires states to take measures to protect their people against the effects of the conduct of hostilities, not only when planning their own operations, but also to protect them from the danger of unexploded war remnants and to alleviate the hardship accompanying internal displacement. Second, human rights bodies increasingly require states to account not only for the fate of disappeared persons during armed conflict but more generally to account for the use of force. Finally, the doctrine of positive obligations is instrumental to hold the state accountable for human rights abuses committed by both rebel forces and paramilitary groups. Such a focus on the active prevention of threats to human rights highlights that states ultimately remain responsible for the effective protection of human rights even during times of armed conflict. Moreover, many of the cases discussed in the present contribution are rather recent and, in light of the incremental expansion of the doctrine of positive obligations, further developments are to be expected in the near future.

NOTES

* Sandra Krähenmann is Doctor in International Law (Graduate Institute of International Studies) and was teaching and research assistant at the University of Geneva (law faculty) at the time of the writing of this chapter.

1. C. Scott, 'The Interdependence and Permeability of Human Rights Norms: Towards a Partial Fusion of the International Covenants on Human Rights', *Osgoode Hall Law Journal* 27 (1989): 792–798; C. Tomuschat, 'Social Rights under the European Convention on Human Rights', in *Human Rights, Democracy and the Rule of Law*, eds S. Breitenmoser et al. (Zurich: Dike, 2007), 838.

2. M. Sassòli, 'La Cour européenne des droits de l'homme et les conflits armés', in *Human Rights, Democracy and the Rule of Law*, eds S. Breitenmoser et al. (Zurich: Dike, 2007), 710.

3. For views emphasising such a distinction, see M. Bossuyt, 'La distinction juridique entre les droits civils et politiques et les droits économiques, sociaux et culturels', *Revue des droits de l'homme: droit international et droit comparé* 8 (1975): 783ff.; E.W. Vierdag, 'The Legal Nature of the Rights Granted by the International Covenant on Economic, Social and Cultural Rights', *Netherlands Yearbook of International Law* 9 (1978): 69. For views challenging such a distinction, see Scott, *supra* note 1, at 769–878; F. Van Hoof, 'The Legal Nature of Economic, Social and Cultural Rights: A Rebuttal of Some Traditonal Views', in *The Right to Food*, eds P. Alston and K. Tomaševski (The Hague: Martinus Nijhoff, 1984), 97–110; M.M. Sepúlveda, *The Nature of the Obligations under the International Covenant on Economic, Social and Cultural Rights* (Antwerp: Intersentia, 2003), 122–156.

4. G. Gaggioli and R. Kolb, 'A Right to Life in Armed Conflicts? The Contribution of the European Court of Human Rights', *Israel Yearbook of Human Rights* 37 (2007): 115–117.

5. For an overview, see, e.g., Gaggioli and Kolb, *supra* note 4, at 118–123; W. Abresch, 'A Human Rights Law of Internal Armed Conflict: The European Court of Human Rights in Chechnya', *European Journal of International Law* 16-4 (2005): 741; F. Hampson, 'The Relationship between International Humanitarian Law and Human Rights Law from the Perspective of a Human Rights Treaty Body', *International Review of the Red Cross* 871 (2008): 558–562; H.-J. Heintze, 'On the Relationship Between Human Rights Law Protection and International Humanitarian Law', *International Review of the Red Cross* 856 (2004): 789–798; M. Sassòli and L.M. Olson, 'The Relationship Between International Humanitarian and Human Rights Law Where it Matters: Admissible Killing and Internment of Fighters in Non-International Armed Conflicts', *International Review of the Red Cross* 871 (2008): 600–609.

6. L. Doswald-Beck, *Human Rights in Times of Conflict and Terrorism* (Oxford: Oxford University Press, 2011), 5.

7. Article 15 of the ECHR. See also Article 4(1) of the ICCPR and Article 27 of the IACHR.

8. General Comment No. 29: *States of Emergency (Article 4)*, HRC, 31 August 2001 (UN Doc. CCPR/C/21/Rev.1/Add.11), para. 3. For an overview of the practice of human rights bodies in respect of derogations during armed conflict, see, e.g., Doswald-Beck, *supra* note 6, at 79–104; Hampson, *supra* note 5, at 562–566.

9. The perceived difference in nature led to the adoption of separate treaties on economic, social and cultural rights such as the International Covenant on Economic, Social and Cultural Rights, see Scott, *supra* note 1, at 791–825. In contrast, the most recent general human rights treaty, the African Charter on Human and Peoples' Rights, includes both civil and political rights as well as economic, social and cultural rights. Moreover, human rights treaties covering a particularly vulnerable group or a specific issue often include express positive obligations, such as the duty to investigate or the duty to take measures to prevent abuses, see, e.g., Article 12 of the 1984 UN Convention Against Torture and Other Cruel, Inhuman and Degrading Treatment: Duty to investigate allegations of torture, and Article 2 of the 1979 UN Convention on the Elimination of All Forms of Discrimination Against Women: Measures to eliminate discrimination against women.

10. In particular, under the right to a fair trial where states have to provide certain minimum services, such as legal aid and, if necessary, an interpreter, see, e.g., Article 14(3) of the ICCPR. Furthermore, all general human rights treaties contain an explicit positive obligation to provide an effective remedy for alleged human rights violations, see, e.g., Article 2(3) of the ICCPR.

11. See, e.g., Article 6(1) of the ICCPR: 'No one shall be arbitrarily deprived of his right to life', or Article 7 of the ICCPR: 'No one shall be subjected to torture or to cruel, inhuman or degrading treatment or punishment'.

12. See, in particular, 'the freedoms', i.e. the right to freedom of expression, freedom of assembly and association and freedom of thought and religion and the right to respect for private and family life. All those rights are framed in similar terms: a general obligation to respect the right followed by a restriction clause that defines the circumstances under which restrictions are possible.

13. F. Sudre, 'Les "obligations positives" dans la jurisprudence européenne des droits de l'homme', in *Protection des droits de l'homme: la perspective européenne. Mélanges à la mémoire de Rolv Ryssdal*, ed. P. Mahoney et al. (Köln/Berlin/Bonn: Carl Heymanns, 2000), 1360; P. Van Dijk, '"Positive Obligations" Implied in the European Convention on Human Rights: Are the States Still The "Masters" of the Convention?', in *The Role of the Nation-State in the 21st Century*, eds M. Castermans-Holleman, F. Van Hoof and J. Smith (The Hague/Boston: Kluwer Law, 1998), 17–33.

14. *Storck v. Germany*, ECtHR, Application No. 61603/00, Judgment of 16 June 2005, para. 101. See also General Comment No. 31: *The Nature of the General Legal Obligation Imposed on States*, HRC, 29 March 2004 (UN Doc. CCPR/C/21/Rev.1/Add.13), para. 8; *Velásquez-Rodríguez v. Honduras* IACtHR, Merits, Judgment of 29 July 1988, para. 166; *Association of Victims of Post Electoral Violence and Interights v. Cameroon*, African Commission of Human and Peoples' Rights, Communication No 272/2003 (2010), paras 88–92.

15. Tomuschat, *supra* note 1, at 841.

16. See *infra* section 1.1. 'Planning and Control of Operations Involving the Use of Force'.

17. When establishing the obligation to plan in *McCann and others v. United Kingdom*, ECtHR, Application No. 18984/91, Judgment of 5 September 1995, the European Court analysed the planning separately from the actual use of force but linked it to the proportionality assessment, not the obligation to protect life, see para. 156; for a further example for the same approach, see *Andronicou and Constantinou v. Cyprus*, ECtHR, Application No. 25052/94, Judgment of 9 October 1997. In other cases, the European Court does not distinguish between the planning of an operation and the actual use of force, but takes into account the planning when analysing the proportionality of the use of force, see, e.g., *Oğur v. Turkey*, ECtHR, Application No. 215494/23, Judgment of 20 May 1999, paras 79–84.

18. In the case of *Ergi v. Turkey*, ECtHR, Application No. 23818/94, Judgment of 28 July 1998, the European Court expressly linked the obligation to plan to the obligation to secure human rights in Article 1, see para. 79. For a further, recent, example, see *Giuliani and Gaggio v. Italy*, ECtHR, Application No 23458/02, Grand Chamber, Judgment of 24 March 2011, paras 244–262. The case of *Isayeva, Yusupova and Bazayeva v. Russia*, ECtHR, Application Nos 57947/00 et al., Judgment of 24 February 2005, probably reveals best the ambiguity of the European Court's approach. Under the heading 'failure to protect life', paras 182–200, the European Court included both the means used and the planning of the operation in its analysis of the proportionality of the air strikes. The Inter-American Court distinguishes between the obligation to plan and the proportionality assessment without expressly qualifying the obligation to plan as a positive obligation, see, e.g., *Montero-Aranguren et al. ('Detention Center of Catia') v. Venezuela*, IACtHR, Preliminary exceptions, merits, reparations and costs, Judgment of 5 July 2006, paras 67–71, and *Zambrano-Vélez et al. v. Ecuador*, IACtHR, Merits, Reparations and Costs, Judgment of 4 July 2007, paras 87–109. Not surprisingly, in legal scholarship the obligation to plan has not consistently been included under the heading of

'positive obligations'. For authors including the obligation to plan, see A.R. Mowbray, *The Development of Positive Obligations under the European Convention on Human Rights by the European Court of Human Rights* (Oxford: Hart Publishing, 2004), 7–15, and R. Pisillo Mazzeschi, 'Responsabilité de l'état pour violation des obligations positives relatives aux droits de l'homme', *Recueil des cours* 333 (2008): 397–401. For authors who do not include the obligation to plan, see K. Starmer, 'Positive Obligations under the Convention', in *Understanding Human Rights Principles*, eds J. Jowell and J. Cooper (Oxford: Hart Publishing, 2001); Sudre, *supra* note 13.

19. *Nachova and others v. Bulgaria*, ECtHR, Application Nos 43577/98 and 43579/98, Grand Chamber, Judgment of 6 July 2005, para. 102; *Soare and others v. Romania*, ECtHR, Application No. 24329/02, Judgment of 22 February 2011, paras 132–137; *Giuliani and Gaggio*, *supra* note 18, at paras 211–215. In recent cases against Russia concerning the use of force against the background of the conflict in Chechnya, the European Court criticised Russia for its failure to submit information on the relevant legal framework, which prevented the Court from assessing whether it complied with the requirements of Article 2, see, e.g., *Suleymanova v. Russia*, ECtHR, Application No. 9191/06, Judgment of 12 May 2010, para. 83, and *Esmukhambetov and others v. Russia*, ECtHR, Application No. 23445/03, Judgment of 29 March 2011, paras 142–143. See also, *Guerrero v. Colombia*, HRC, 31 March 1982 (UN Doc. CCPR/C/15/D/45/1979), para. 13.3, and *Detention Center of Catia*, *supra* note 18, at paras 75–76.

20. *Makaratzis v. Greece*, ECtHR, Application No. 50385/99, Grand Chamber, Judgment of 20 December 2004, para. 70; *Hamiyet Kaplan and others v. Turkey*, ECtHR, Application No. 36749/97, Judgment of 13 September 2005, para. 51; *Giuliani and Gaggio*, *supra* note 18, at paras 254–256. For examples from the Inter-American Court, see, *Detention Center of Catia*, *supra* note 18, at para. 77; *Zambrano Vélez*, *supra* note 18, at para. 87. In addition, the Inter-American Court routinely includes the obligation to train under the reparations ordered, see, e.g., *Bámaca-Velásquez v. Guatemala*, IACtHR, Judgment of 22 February 2002, para. 86, and *Rochela Massacre v. Colombia*, IACtHR, Judgment of 11 May 2007, para. 303. The HRC criticised the lack of training of law enforcement in several Concluding Observations, see,e.g., Concluding Observations on Paraguay, HRC, 24 April 2006 (UN Doc. CCPR/C/PRY/CO/2), para. 11, and Concluding Observations on Portugal, HRC, 17 September 2007, UN Doc. CCPR/CO/78/PRT, para. 9.

21. E. Klein, 'The Duty to Protect and to Ensure Human Rights Under the International Covenant on Civil and Political Rights', in *The Duty to Protect and to Ensure Human Rights*, ed. E. Klein (Berlin: Verlag A. Spitz, 2000), 295.

22. For such general studies, see, e.g., Mowbray, *supra* note 18; Starmer, *supra* note 18; Sudre, *supra* note 13, and Pisillo Mazzeschi, *supra* note 18.

23. See, e.g., *McCann*, *supra* note 17, at para. 192; *Detention Center of Catia*, *supra* note 18, at paras 67–68; *Sudan Human Rights Organisation and The Sudan Centre on Housing Rights and Evictions v. Sudan*, African Commission on Human and Peoples' Rights, Communication Nos 279/03 and 296/05 (2009), para. 147.

24. *Isayeva, Yusupova and Bazayeva*, *supra* note 18, at para. 171.

25. *Esmukhambetov and others*, *supra* note 19, at para. 173. See also *Isayeva, Yusupova and Bazayeva*, *supra* note 18, at paras 181–200.

26. *Esmukhambetov and others*, *supra* note 19, para. 172.

27. *Kerimova and others v. Russia*, ECtHR, Application Nos 17170/04 et al., Judgment of 3 May 2011, para. 252.

28. *Ergi*, *supra* note 18, at para. 79, and *Abdurashidova v. Russia*, ECtHR, Application No. 32968/05, Judgment of 8 April 2010, paras 75–80. In the latter case, the European Court unequivocally established that the victim, a six-year old girl, died from a grenade launched by the two suspects during the raid. Russia was responsible for her death because its forces failed to take protective measures to minimise the risk to her life.

29. Gaggioli and Kolb, *supra* note 4, at 141, and Sassòli, *supra* note 2, at 724.

30. Gaggioli and Kolb, *supra* note 4, at 141. See also *infra* section 3.1 'Protection from Rebel Groups'.

31. See, e.g., Sassòli, *supra* note 2, at 721–722 (against), and Abresch, *supra* note 5, at 741 (in favour).

32. *Esmukhambetov and others*, *supra* note 19, at para. 146, and *Kerimova and others*, *supra* note 27, at para. 248.

33. *Giuliani and Gaggio*, *supra* note 18.

34. Ibid., at paras 216 and 255.

35. See, e.g., *Güleç v. Turkey*, ECtHR, Application No. 54/1997/838/1044, Judgment of 27 July 1998; *Şimşek and others v. Turkey*, ECtHR, Application Nos 35072/97 and 37194/97, Judgment of 26 July 2005; *Muradova v. Azerbaijan*, ECtHR, Application No. 22684/05, Judgment of 2 April 2009.

36. But see the Joint Dissenting Opinion of Judges Rozakis, Tulkens, Zupančič, Gyulumyan, Ziemele, Kalaydjieva and Karakas to the Grand Chamber Judgment. They relied on two main elements to find a violation on this account: (a) the officers were not appropriately trained; and (b) the officer, who had fired the fatal shot, was exhausted and under stress, thus he should have been replaced.

37. *Osman v. United Kingdom*, ECtHR, Application No. 23452/94, Grand Chamber, Judgment of 28 October 1998, para. 115.

38. *Paşa and Erkan Erol v. Turkey*, ECtHR, Application No. 51358/99, Judgment of 12 December 2006, paras 31–32.

39. *Amaç and Okkan v. Turkey*, Application Nos 54179/00 and 54176/00, Judgment of 20 November 2007, paras 41–43, and *Albekov and others v. Russia*, Application No. 68216/01, Judgment of 9 October 2008, para. 86.

40. *Amaç and Okkan*, *supra* note 39, at para. 45; *Paşa and Erkan Erol*, *supra* note 38, at para. 36; *Albekov and others*, *supra* note 39, at paras 87–88.

41. *Demir and Baykara v. Turkey*, ECtHR, Application No. 34503/97, Grand Chamber, Judgment of 12 November 2008, paras 85–88.

42. Generally on the use of international law by the European Court, see M. Forowicz, *The Reception of International Law in the European Court of Human Rights* (Oxford University Press, 2010), 313–351, in particular, on international humanitarian law.

43. *Albekov and others*, *supra* note 39, at paras 87–88. See also *Paşa and Erkan Erol*, *supra* note 38: at the time of the proceedings, Turkey had ratified the 1997 Landmine Ban Convention and the 1996 Amended Protocol II (in 2005), but the facts of the case took place in 1995.

44. See the criticism by J.G. Merrills, *The Development of International Law by the European Court of Human Rights* (Manchester: Manchester University Press, 1993), 225.

45. *Paşa and Erkan Erol*, *supra* note 38.

46. Ibid., at para. 32.

47. Ibid., at para. 37.

48. Ibid., at para. 32.

49. In contrast, the claim of the first applicant, the father of the boy, was rejected as ill-founded.

50. Under the doctrine of positive obligations, children are a particularly vulnerable category of persons entitled to special protection, see, e.g., *Z. and others v. United Kingdom*, ECtHR, Application No. 29392/95, Grand Chamber, Judgment of 10 May 2001, para. 73; *'Street Children' (Villagran-Morales et al.) v. Guatemala*, IACtHR, Judgment of 19 November 1999, para. 146. On the particular vulnerability of children during armed conflict, see, e.g., *Gómez-Paquiyauri Brothers v. Peru*, IACtHR, Judgment of 8 July 2004, paras 170–172, and *Mapiripán Massacre v. Colombia*, IACtHR, Judgment of 15 September 2005, para. 56.

51. In the practice of the Inter-American Court, the right to life is interpreted broadly and includes access to a decent life, see, e.g., *Yakye Axa Indigenous Community v. Paraguay*, IACtHR, Judgment of 17 June 2005, paras 161–162, and *Sawhoyamaxa Indigenous Community v. Paraguay*, Judgment of 29 March 2006, paras 153–154. For an overview of the Inter-American Court's practice in this respect, see L. Burgorgue-Larsen, 'Le droit au respect de la vie dans la jurisprudence de la Cour inter-américaine des droits de l'homme', in *Le droit au respect de la vie au sens de la Convention européenne des droits de l'homme*, ed. M. Leviner (Bruxelles: Bruylant, 2010), 153.

52. See, e.g., *Sudan Human Rights Organisation and The Sudan Centre on Housing Rights and Evictions*, *supra* note 23, at paras 177–178 and paras 201–203: Right to security, freedom of movement and right to property; *Doğan and others v. Turkey*, ECtHR, Application Nos 8803/03 et al., Judgment of 29 June 2004, paras 134–160: Right to private and family life and right to property. Pursuant to its integrated approach, the Inter-American Court addressed such claims under the right to freedom of movement in combination with the right to life and the prohibition of inhuman and degrading treatment, see, e.g., *Mapiripán Massacre*, *supra* note 50, at paras 167–186.

53. *Sudan Human Rights Organisation and The Sudan Centre on Housing Rights and Evictions*, *supra* note 23, at paras 178 and 205; *Doğan and others*, *supra* note 52, at para. 154; *Mapiripán Massacre*, *supra* note 50, at paras 179–180 and 182.

54. *Mapiripán Massacre*, *supra* note 50, at paras 181 and 186. See also *Ituango Massacre v. Colombia*, IACtHR, Judgment of 1 July 2006, paras 221–222.

55. See, e.g., *Zheikov v. Russia*, HRC, 31 March 2006 (UN Doc. CCPR/C/86/D/889/1999), para. 7.2; *Salman v. Turkey*, ECtHR, Application No. 21986/93, Judgment of 26 June 2000, paras 99–100; *Baldéon-García v. Peru*, IACtHR, Judgment of 6 April 2006, para. 120.

56. L. Burgorgue-Larsen and A. Úbeda de Torres, *The Inter-American Court of Human Rights: Case Law and Commentary* (Oxford: Oxford University Press, 2010), 300; T. Buergenthal, 'Remembering the Early Years of the Inter-American Court of Human Rights', *New York University Journal of International Law and Politics* 37 (2005): 271.

57. The African Commission so far has only dealt with cases involving large-scale disappearances.

58. See, e.g., Article 2 of the Inter-American Convention on Forced Disappearances and Article 2 of the UN Convention for the Protection of All Persons from Enforced Disappearances. On the problem of defining 'enforced disappearances', see N. Rodley and M. Pollard, *The Treatment of Prisoners under International Law* (Oxford: Oxford University Press, 2009), 327–337, and Burgorgue-Larsen and Úbeda de Torres, *supra* note 56, at 301ff.

59. See also Sassòli, *supra* note 2, at 718. He points out that the obligation to account for the fate of the forcibly disappeared arises also under international humanitarian law.

60. Such as eyewitness testimony of the arrest or the person in custody, see, e.g., *Almeida de Quinteros v. Uruguay*, HRC, 21 July 1983 (UN Doc. CCPR/C/19/D/107/1981); *Boucherf v. Algeria*, HRC, 27 April 2006 (UN Doc. CCPR/C/86/D/1196/2003); *Edriss El Hassy v. Libya*, HRC, 2 November 2007 (UN Doc. CCPR/C/91/1422/2005); *Grioua v. Algeria*, HRC, 16 August 2007 (UN Doc. CCPR/C/90/D/1327/2004); or previous threats by state agents, see,e.g., *Mojica v. Dominican Republic*, HRC, 10 August 1994 (UN Doc. CCPR/C/51/D/449/91).

61. For examples of unsatisfactory explanations, see *Celis Laureano v. Peru*, HRC, 4 July 1994 (UN Doc. CCPR/C/51/D/540/1993), para. 84, and *Bousroual v. Algeria* HRC, 24 April 2006 (UN Doc. CCPR/C/86/992/2001), para. 9.3: Abduction by unidentified armed group; *Zhora Madoui v. Algeria*, HRC, 1 December 2008 (UN Doc. CCPR/C/94/D/1495/2006), para. 7.4: The victim was suffering from a mental illness and allgedly ran away; *Sharma v. Nepal*, HRC, 6 November 2008 (UN Doc. CCPR/C/94/D/1469/2006): The victim escaped and drowned. For the same reason, a general denial does not suffice, see, e.g., *Boucherf*, *supra* note 60, at para. 9.3.

62. See *Bousroual*, *supra* note 61, at para. 9.4; *Boucherf*, *supra* note 60, at para. 9.4; *Grioua*, *supra* note 60, at para. 7.4; *Zhora Madoui*, *supra* note 61, at para. 7.3; *Sharma*, *supra* note 61, at para. 7.5.

63. See, e.g., *Celis Laureano*, *supra* note 61, at para. 8.4; *Mojica*, *supra* note 60, at para. 5.6; *Bousroual*, *supra* note 61, at para. 9.11. See also the discussion in Rodley and Pollard, *supra* note 58, at 357.

64. *Edriss El Hassy*, *supra* note 60, at para. 6.10; *Sharma*, *supra* note 61, at para. 7.8; *Sarma v. Sri Lanka*, HRC, 16 July 2003 (UN Doc. C/78/D/950/2000), para. 9.6.

65. Doswald-Beck, *supra* note 6, at 231.

66. For example, with respect to (1) the identity of the victims, see *Velásquez-Rodríguez*, *supra* note 14, at para. 147(g)(i): Student leader; *Godínez-Cruz v. Honduras*, IACtHR, Judgment of 21 July 1989, para. 154: Trade union leader; *Bámaca Velásquez*, *supra* note 20, at para. 21: guerillero; and (2) the modus operandi of the abduction, see in particular the case of the *'White Van' (Paniagua Morales et al.) v. Guatemala*, IACtHR, Judgment of 8 March 1998, para. 93: Use of a white van. In a later case, the Inter-American Court relied on the same pattern to hold the state responsible for the detention and torture of the applicant, see *Martiza Urrutia v. Guatemala*, IACtHR, Judgment of 27 November 2003, paras 58–63.

67. In recent years, the Inter-American Court qualified an official practice of enforced disappearances as a crime against humanity, see, e.g., *Almonacid-Arellano et al. v. Chile*, IACtHR, Judgment of 26 September 2006, paras 102–104, with respect to the repression during the Pinochet regime. For a thorough analysis, see F. Megret, 'La notion de crime d'Etat devant la Cour interaméricaine des droits de l'homme', in *Le particularisme interaméricain des droits de l'homme*, eds L. Hennebel and H. Tigroudja (Paris: Pedone, 2009), 313

68. *Velásquez-Rodríguez*, *supra* note 14, at para. 157. See also *Godínez-Cruz*, *supra* note 66, at para. 165; *Bámaca Velásquez*, *supra* note 20, at para. 130.

69. As for the Human Rights Committee, this is indeed a presumption and not a formal finding that the disappeared person is dead, see the discussion in Buergenthal, *supra* note 56, at 272–273.

70. With the exception of cases concerning the abduction of children during internal armed conflicts followed by their de jure or de facto adoption, see *Serrano-Cruz Sisters v. El Salvador*, Judgment of 23 November 2004, paras 130–132. More recently, the Inter-American Court confirmed that the enforced disappearance of children under such circumstances violated the state's duty to protect their right to life, interpreted in the light of the UN Convention on the Rights of the Child as including the

right to development, see *Gelman v. Uruguay*, Judgment of 24 February 2011, para. 130, and *Contreras et al. v. El Salvador*, Judgment of 31 August 2011, para. 90.

71.   See, in particular, *Castillo-Páez v. Peru*, Judgment of 3 November 1997, para. 197, where the Inter-American Court forcefully rejected the Peruvian argument that in the absence of a body no violation of the right to life could be established. See also *Bámaca Velásquez, supra* note 20, at paras 172–173; *Anzualdo Castro v. Peru*, Judgment of 22 September 2009, at paras 85–86.

72.   Hence, the European Court initially abstained from finding a violation of the right to life in the absence of a body or other 'concrete' or 'circumstantial' evidence indicating the death of the person, see *Kurt v. Turkey*, ECtHR, Application No. 15/1997/799/1002, Judgment of 25 May 1998, para. 107; *Çakici v. Turkey*, ECtHR, Application No. 23657/94, Judgment of 8 July 1999, para. 85; *Ertak v. Turkey*, ECtHR, Application No. 20764/92, Judgment of 5 May 2000, paras 131–133. For a critical discussion of the European Court's practice in this respect, see J. Chevalier-Watts, 'The Phenomenon of Enforced Disappearances in Turkey and Chechnya: Strasbourg's Noble Cause?', *Human Rights Review* 11 (2010): 469; Doswald-Beck, *supra* note 6, at 231; Rodley and Pollard, *supra* note 58, at 356–357.

73.   J. Benzimar-Hazan, 'En marge de l'arrêt Timurtas contre la Turquie: vers l'homogénéisation des approches du phénomène des disparitions forcées de personnes', *Revue Trimestrielle des Droits de l'Homme* 43(2001): 983.

74.   *Imakayeva v. Russia*, ECtHR, Application No. 7615/02, Judgment of 9 November 2006, para. 115.

75.   *Tanis v. Turkey*, ECtHR, Application No. 65899/01, Judgment of 8 August 2005, para. 160 and paras 206–210: Victims disappeared after voluntarily entering police station; *Yusupova and Zaurbekov v. Russia*, ECtHR, Application No. 22057/02, Judgment of 9 October 2008, para. 55: Disappearances after entering police station; *Abayeva and others v. Russia*, ECtHR, Application No. 37542/05, Judgment of 8 April 2010, paras 91–94: Disappearance at a checkpoint.

76.   *Luluyev and others v. Russia*, ECtHR, Application No. 6948/01, Judgment of 9 November 2006, paras 80–85; *Mutayeva v. Russia*, ECtHR, Application No. 43418/06, Judgment of 22 April 2010, paras 73–78; *Gelayevy v. Russia*, ECtHR, Application No. 20216/07, Judgment of 15 July 2010, paras 99–103; *Tupchiyeva v. Russia*, ECtHR, Application No. 37461/05, Judgment of 22 April 2010, paras 57–63; *Khantiyeva and others v. Russia*, ECtHR, Application No. 43398/06, Judgment of 29 October 2009, paras 99–105; *Seriyevy v. Russia*, ECtHR, Application No. 20201/05, Judgment of 8 April 2010, para. 79. See also *Varnava and others v. Turkey*, ECtHR, Application Nos 16064/90 et al., Grand Chamber, Judgment of 18 September 2009, paras 181–186: Disappearance of nine men during the armed conflict in Cyprus in an area under the control of the Turkish forces.

77.   Conversely, the burden of proof did not shift in cases where individuals disappeared in places outside the control of the government, such as, for example, when travelling on the roads, see, e.g., *Zakriyeva and others v. Russia*, ECtHR, Application No. 20583/04, Judgment of 8 January 2009, paras 60–70, and in particular *Shakhgiriyeva and others v. Russia*, ECtHR, Application No. 27251/03, Judgment of 8 January 2009, paras 145–147 and 155–159.

78.   *Timurtaş v. Turkey*, ECtHR, Application No. 23531/94, Judgment of 13 June 2000, para. 85.

79.   Initially, the European Court stressed the passage of time to justify its departure from earlier practice, see *Timurtaş, supra* note 78, at paras 81–86: 6.5 years, but in later cases the focus shifted to the 'life threatening circumstances', see, e.g., *Taş v. Turkey*, ECtHR, Application No. 24396/94, Judgment of 14 November 2000, para. 66, in the light of its previous case law and the Dissenting Opinion of Judge Gölcüklü in this respect. The reliance on the simple passage of time as a decisive factor was often criticised in legal scholarship, see, e.g., Chevalier-Watts, *supra* note 72, at 482–484.

80.   *Imakayeva, supra* note 74, at para. 141; *Magomadov and Magomadov v. Russia*, ECtHR, Application No. 68004/01, Judgment of 12 July 2007, para. 98; *Baysayeva v. Russia*, ECtHR, Application No. 74237/01, Judgment of 5 April 2007, para. 119; *Satabayeva v. Russia*, ECtHR, Application No. 21486/06, Judgment of 29 October 2009, para. 91; *Yusupova and Zaurbekov, supra* note 75, at para. 55.

81.   *Taş, supra* note 79, at para. 67.

82.   Unless the applicants object to such a presumption, see *Varnava and others, supra* note 76, at paras 141–156.

83.   See, for example, *Timurtaş, supra* note 78, at para. 86; *Magomadov and Magomadov, supra* note 80, at para. 99.

84.   In the first Chechen disappearance case, *Bazorkina v. Russia*, ECtHR, Application No. 69481/01, 27 July 2006, Russia had acknowledged that the victim had been detained, but claimed that he had absconded. Furthermore, there was strong evidence in the form of video footage showing a Russian

general threatening to kill the applicant's son who was being held by servicemen. However, already in the second and third case, *Luluyev, supra* note 76, at paras 85–87, and *Imakayeva, supra* note 74, at paras 111–115, the European Court held Russia responsible for the disappearance, although there was no direct evidence that Russian servicemen had apprehended the victims. With respect to the presumption of death, the European Court confirmed that the applicant's husband in *Imakayeva, supra* note 74, at paras 155–157 could be presumed dead after almost four years, which is less time than in the case of *Kurt, supra* note 72.

85. For a thorough analysis of the different steps in the evolution of the European Court's practice on enforced disappearances, and a comparison of the Turkish cases with the Chechen cases, see Chevalier-Watts, *supra* note 72, and J. Barrett, 'Chechnya's Last Hope? Enforced Disappearances and the European Court of Human Rights', *Harvard Human Rights Law Journal* 22 (2008): 133.

86. See, e.g., the reference to the general information on enforced disappearances in *Imakayeva, supra* note 74, at para. 141. For a critical assessment of this 'contextualisation', see Chevalier-Watts, *supra* note 72, at 484.

87. However, in later cases, the European Court routinely referred back to its own case law, see, e.g. *Magomadov and Magomadov, supra* note 80, at para. 98; *Khantiyeva and others, supra* note 76, at para. 107.

88. E. Van Nuffel, 'L'appréciation des faits et leur preuve par la Cour européenne des droits de l'homme dans les affaires mettant en cause les forces de sécurité accusées d'homicides et d'actes de torture: le doute raisonnable et l'inhumain,' *Revue Trimestrielle des Droits de l'Homme* 46 (2001): 857–859; R. Wolfrum, 'The Taking and Assessment of Evidence by the European Court of Human Rights', in *Human Rights, Democracy and the Rule of Law*, eds S. Breitenmoser et al. (Zurich: Dike, 2007), 922; L. Dutheil-Warolin, 'La Cour européenne des droits de l'homme aux prises avec la preuve de violations du droit à la vie ou de l'interdiction de la torture: entre théorie classique aménagée et innovation européenne', *Revue Trimestrielle des Droits de l'Homme* 26 (2005): 339–344.

89. See, e.g., *Tanli v. Turkey*, ECtHR, Application No. 26129/95, Judgment of 10 April 2001, para. 109; *Tahsin Acar v. Turkey*, ECtHR, Application No. 26307/95, Grand Chamber, Judgment of 8 April 2004, para. 216; *Buldan v. Turkey*, ECtHR, Application No. 28298/95, Judgment of 20 April 2004, para. 78.

90. For its critics, the standard is too stringent, in particular in the context of widespread human rights violations, see T. Thienel, 'The Burden and Standard of Proof in the European Court of Human Rights', *German Yearbook of International Law* 50 (2007): 544; U. Erdal, 'Burden and Standard of Proof in Proceedings under the European Convention', *European Law Review (Supplement)* 26 (2001): 77–79; H. Tigroudja, 'La Cour européenne des droits de l'homme face au conflit en Tchétchénie', *Revue Trimestrielle des Droits de l'Homme* 65 (2006): 112. See also the criticism from within in the Court: *Labita v. Italy*, ECtHR, Application No. 26772/95, Grand Chamber, Judgment of 6 April 2000, Joint Partly Dissenting Opinion of Judges Pastor Ridrujo, Bonello, Makarczyk, Tulkens, Strážnická, Butkevych, Casadevall and Zupančič; *Ağdaş v. Turkey*, ECtHR, Application No. 34592/97, Judgment of 27 July 2004, Partly Dissenting Opinion of Judge Bratza; *Anguelova v. Bulgaria*, Application No. 38361/97, Judgment of 13 June 2002, Partly Dissenting Opinion of Judge Bonello; *Şirin Yilmaz v. Turkey*, ECtHR, Application No. 35875/97, Judgment of 29 July 2004, Partly Dissenting Opinion of Judge Bonello and Partly Dissenting Opinion of Judge Tulkens; *Tahsin Acar, supra* note 89, Concurring Opinion of Judge Bonello; *Zubayrayev v. Russia*, ECtHR, Application No. 67797/01, Judgment of 10 January 2008, Dissenting Opinion of Judge Loucaides joined by Judge Spielmann.

91. *Akkum and others v. Turkey*, ECtHR, Application No. 21894/93, Judgment of 23 March 2005, para. 211: Individuals found dead in an area of military operations.

92. See, e.g., *Taysumov and others v. Russia*, ECtHR, Application No. 21810/03, Judgment of 14 May 2005, paras 86–91: Artillery shelling, the state claimed that the applicants were injured by self-made explosives: *Mezhidov v. Russia*, ECtHR, Application No. 67326/01, Judgment of 25 September 2009, paras 59–62: Artillery shelling, disputed whether by rebel or government forces; *Musayev and others v. Russia*, ECtHR, Application No. 57941/00, Judgment of 26 July 2007, para. 140: Executions by unknown perpetrators; *Umayeva v. Russia*, ECtHR, Application No. 1200/03, Judgment of 4 December 2008, paras 79–81: Wounding by shelling in Grozny at a time when the Russian forces controlled the town.

93. For examples where the applicants failed to discharge their burden, see *Udayeva and Yusupova v. Russia*, ECtHR, Application No. 36542/05, Judgment of 21 December 2010; *Nakayev v. Russia*, ECtHR, Application No. 29846/05, Judgment of 21 June 2011; *Wolf-Sorg v. Turkey*, ECtHR, Application No. 6458/03, Judgment of 8 June 2010.

94.   Most significantly, the European Court applied this principle in a series of cases concerning massacres in Grozny at a time when the town was under the control of the government forces, but there were no direct eyewitnesses, see, e.g., *Estamirov and others v. Russia*, ECtHR, Application No. 60272/00, Judgment of 12 October 2006, paras 107–113; *Tangiyeva v. Russia*, ECtHR, Application No. 57935/00, Judgment of 29 November 2007, paras 81–83; *Goygova v. Russia*, ECtHR, Application No. 74240/01, Judgment of 4 October 2007, paras 93–96. See also K. Koroteev, 'Legal Remedies for Human Rights Violations in the Armed Conflict in Chechnya: The Approach of the European Court of Human Rights in Context', *Journal of International Humanitarian Legal Studies* 2 (2010): 281–283.

95.   See, e.g., *Erdoğan and others v. Turkey*, ECtHR, Application No. 19807/92, Judgment of 25 April 2006, para. 80; *Stoica v. Romania*, ECtHR, Application No. 42722/02, Judgment of 4 March 2008, para. 67.

96.   See, e.g., *Mansuroğlu v. Turkey*, ECtHR, Application No. 43443/98, Judgment of 26 February 2008, paras 79–80: Killing of an alleged member of the PKK during an armed confrontation; *Arzu Akhmadova and others v. Russia*, ECtHR, Application No. 13670/03, Judgment of 8 January 2009, paras 154–157 and paras 165–170: Security forces staged a fight to cover up that they had apprehended and executed the victims.

97.   See, e.g., the following cases relating to aerial bombings: *Esmukhambetov and others, supra* note 19, at paras 140–141; *Kerimova and others, supra* note 27, at para. 242; *Khamzayev and others v. Russia*, ECtHR, Application No. 1503/02, Judgment of 3 May 2011, para. 175. See also *Arzu Akhmadova and others, supra* note 96, at para. 161: Extra-judicial execution; *Mansuroğlu, supra* note 96, at para. 82: Anti-terrorist operation.

98.   See, e.g., *Mansuroğlu, supra* note 96, at para. 88; *Esmukhambetov and others, supra* note 19, at paras 142–144; *Kerimova and others, supra* note 27, at para. 244; *Khamzayev and others, supra* note 96, at para. 176; *Arzu Akhmadova and others, supra* note 96, at para. 165.

99.   Expressly confirmed by the majority in *Mansuroğlu, supra* note 96, at paras 77–78. In his Concurring Opinion Judge Türmen criticised the majority for departing from its established approach and highlighted that such a reversed burden of proof is normally only used in cases where it is contested whether individuals were killed by government forces. Moreover, the reversed burden of proof follows implicitly from the emphasis on the duty to account, see, e.g., *Esmukhambetov and others, supra* note 19, at para. 145, where the European Court discarded the justification by the Russian government as 'inadequate and unconvincing'. In contrast, in the earlier case of *McKerr v. United Kingdom*, ECtHR, Application No. 28883/95, Judgment of 4 May 2001, para. 119, the European Court rejected the applicant's argument in this direction since 'the situation cannot be equated to a death in custody where the burden may be regarded as resting on the State to provide a satisfactory and plausible explanation'.

100.   *Umetaliev et al. v. Kyrgyzstan*, HRC, 20 November 2008 (UN Doc. CCPR/C/94/D/1275/2004), para. 9.5: Use of force to disperse demonstration.

101.   See, e.g., *Zambrano-Vélez, supra* note 18, at para. 158. In contrast, in the earlier case of *Las Palmeras*, IACtHR, Merits, Judgment of 6 December 2001, the Inter-American Court rejected the argument of the Commission that the burden of proof should be shifted to the Respondent State.

102.   The positive obligation to investigate allegations of human rights violations during armed conflict as such is outside the scope of the present contribution.

103.   A. Clapham, *Human Rights Obligations of Non-State Actors* (Oxford: Oxford University Press, 2006), 349.

104.   *Osman v. United Kingdom*, ECtHR, Application No. 23452/94, Grand Chamber, Judgment of 28 October 1998, para. 115. See also *González et al. ('Cotton Field') v. Mexico*, IACtHR, Preliminary Objections, Merits, Reparations and Costs, Judgment of 16 November 2009, para. 280; *Zimbabwe Human Rights NGO Forum v. Zimbabwe*, African Commission on Human and Peoples' Rights, Communication No. 245/2002 (2006), para. 158.

105.   *Osman, supra* note 104, at para. 116; *Cotton Field, supra* note 104, at paras 282–283.

106.   *Osman, supra* note 104, at para. 116; *Cotton Field, supra* note 104, at paras 282–283; *Post Electoral Violence, supra* note 14, at para. 158.

107.   *Osman, supra* note 104, at para. 116; *Cotton Field, supra* note 104, at para. 284; *Post Electoral Violence, supra* note 14, at para. 158.

108.   J. Künzli, *Zwischen Rigidität und Flexibilität: Der Verpflichtungsgrad internationaler Menschenrechte* (Berlin: Duncker & Humblot, 2001), 249ff; Pisillo Mazzeschi, *supra* note 18, at 390ff.

109. M. Hakimi, 'State Bystander Responsibility', *European Journal of International Law* 21 (2010): 354–355.

110. From the practice of the European Court in respect of private individuals, we can infer that unless there is a previous history of bodily assault or death threats against a previously identified individual, the authorities are not required to have known that there was a real and immediate risk, see, e.g., *Osman, supra* note 104, at paras 120–122: The authorities were not aware nor ought to have been aware of the risk since the schoolteacher who had been harassing the family had never been violent, but see the Partly Dissenting, Partly Concurring Opinion of Judge de Meyer joined by Judges Lopes Rocha and Casadevall. See also *Kontrová v. Slovakia*, ECtHR, Application No. 7510/04, Judgment of 31 May 2007: Domestic proceedings established negligence of the police authorities; *Branko Tomašić v. Croatia*, ECtHR, Application No. 46598/06, Judgment of 15 January 2009: Credible death threats were known to the authorities; *Opuz v. Turkey*, ECtHR, Application No. 33401/01, Judgment of 9 June 2009: The authorities were well aware of the physical abuse suffered by the applicant and her mother from the applicant's husband. Moreover, crimes committed by rebel forces normally are not directed against specific, previously identified individuals. Such cases are more akin to the general positive obligations states have to protect society at large against violent criminals where the threshold is even higher, as two cases against Italy concerning crimes committed by prisoners on conditional leave confirm, see *Mastromatteo v. Italy*, ECtHR, Application No. 37703/97, Grand Chamber, Judgment of 24 October 2002, and *Maiorano and others v. Italy*, ECtHR, Application No. 28634/06, Judgment of 15 December 2009.

Similarly, the Inter-American Court confirmed in *Cotton Field, supra* note 104, at paras 258–282, that the authorities were not aware of a risk to the victims in the present case although it was well aware of the general risk for women in Ciudad Juárez, sadly famous for the phenomenon of unresolved abductions and killings of women. However, the inadequate response of the authorities after being informed of the abductions resulted in a violation of their due diligence obligation, see paras 283–286. For the African Commission, see, in particular, *Post Electoral Violence, supra* note 14, at paras 115–124: The violence erupting after the announcement of the election results was not unforeseeable in light of the country's previous experience. Moreover, the authorities intervened only after four days to try to quell the violence.

111. *Belikza Kaya and others v. Turkey*, ECtHR, Application Nos 33420/96 and 36206/97, Judgment of 22 November 2005, paras 81–82 with respect of the deadly attack on a civilian transport of detainees by terrorists; *Cotton Field, supra* note 104, at para. 282.

112. *Isayeva, supra* note 18, at para. 187. Similarly, see the Inter-American Court in respect of paramilitary forces in *Pueblo Bello Massacre v. Colombia*, IACtHR, Judgment of 31 January 2006, paras 135–139. See also Gaggioli and Kolb, *supra* note 4, at 143.

113. For the European Court of Human Rights see *97 Members of the Gldani Congregation of Jehovah's Witnesses and 4 Others v. Georgia*, ECtHR, Application No. 71156/01, Judgment of 3 May 2007 and *Ouranio Toxo and others v. Greece*, ECtHR, Application No. 74989/01, Judgment of 20 October 2005: Failure to intervene against ongoing mob violence. For the Inter-American Court, see *Ríos et al. v. Venezuela*, IACtHR, Judgment of 28 January 2009, and *Perozo et al. v. Venezuela*, IACtHR, Judgment of 28 January 2009: Duty to protect journalists against mob violence. For the African Commission, see *Post Electoral Violence, supra* note 14, at paras 115–124: Protection from post-electoral violence.

114. Under the doctrine of positive obligations, states need to possess an effective law enforcement machinery for the implementation of its criminal laws, see, e.g., *Koku v. Turkey*, ECtHR, Application No. 27305/95, Judgment of 31 May 2005; *Myrna Mack Chang v. Guatemala*, IACtHR, Judgment of 25 November 2003, para. 153; *Sudan Human Rights Organisation & The Sudan Centre on Housing Rights and Evictions, supra* note 23, at para. 147. See also Pisillo Mazzeschi, *supra* note 18, at 335, and Tomuschat, *supra* note 1, at 854.

115. Moreover, in later cases the Commission adopted a much more nuanced approach, see *Zimbabwe Human Rights NGO Forum, supra* note 104; *Post Electoral Violence, supra* note 14.

116. *Commission Nationale des Droits de l'Homme et des Libertés v. Chad*, African Commission on Human and Peoples' Rights, Communication No. 74/92 (1995), para. 22; *Amnesty International and Others v. Sudan*, African Commission on Human and Peoples' Rights, Communication Nos. 48/90 et al. (1999), para. 50; *Malawi African Association and Others v. Mauritania*, African Commission on Human and Peoples' Rights, Communication Nos. 54/91 et al. (2000), para. 140.

117. See the criticism by Künzli, *supra* note 108, at 251–252.

118.   *Ilaşcu and others v. Moldova and Russia*, ECtHR, Application No. 48787/99, Grand Chamber, Judgment of 8 July 2004, para. 333. On this account, Moldova was found in violation of the European Convention with respect to the detention of Mr Ilaşcu and others in the break-away republic of Transnistria. When the applicants again brought a claim against Moldova and Russia for a continuing failure to secure the release of the detainees, the European Court confirmed that Moldova had discharged its positive obligations in light of the diplomatic measures undertaken by Moldova since the first judgment, see *Ivantoc and others v. Moldova and Russia*, ECtHR, Application No. 23687/05, Judgment of 15 November 2011. For a critical evaluation of the European Court's approach, see S. Karagiannis, 'Le Territoire d'Application de la Convention Européenne des Droits de l'Homme. *Vaetera et Nova*,' *Revue Trimestrielle des Droits de l'Homme* 61 (2005): 33.

119.   *Velásquez-Rodríguez, supra* note 14, and *Godínez-Cruz, supra* note 66.

120.   On a first glance, the Inter-American Court's reliance on the obligation to ensure seems superfluous since the Inter-American Court found in both cases that the disappearances were 'carried out by agents who acted under the cover of public authority', *Velásquez-Rodríguez, supra* note 14, at para. 182, and *Godínez-Cruz, supra* note 66, at para. 192. But a closer look reveals that the Inter-American Court remained quite ambiguous about both the identity and status of the perpetrators, describing their relationship with state security forces as 'connected with', and in terms of 'direction', 'acquiescence' or 'tolerance'.

121.   *Velásquez-Rodríguez, supra* note 14, at paras 178–182; *Godínez-Cruz, supra* note 66, at paras 189–192.

122.   Not surprisingly, in legal scholarship these cases are either taken as an authority for the duty to protect against abuses commited by private actors, see, e.g., Clapham, *supra* note 103, at 425ff., and J. Kokott, 'The Duty to Protect and to Ensure Human Rights Under the Inter-American System of Human Rights', in *The Duty to Protect and To Ensure Human Rights*, ed. E. Klein (Berlin: Verlag A. Spitz, 2000), 260ff; or as an authority for the claim that human rights bodies have started to attribute the acts of paramilitaries to the state in cases of complicity, see J. Cerone, 'Human Rights on the Battlefield', in *Human Rights in Turmoil. Facing Threats, Consolidating Achievements*, ed. S. Lagoutte et al. (Leiden/Boston: Martinus Nijhoff, 2007), 106, footnote 37.

123.   *Mapiripán Massacre, supra* note 50; *Pueblo Bello Massacre, supra* note 112; *Rochela Massacre, supra* note 20; *Ituango Massacre, supra* note 54; *Valle Jaramillo et al. v. Colombia*, IACtHR, Judgment of 27 November 2008; *Manuel Cepeda Vargas v. Colombia*, IACtHR, Judgment of 6 May 2010.

124.   In contrast, in the earlier case of *19 Merchants v. Colombia*, IACtHR, Judgment of 5 July 2004, the paramilitary forces were not yet outlawed at the material time (para. 124). Nonetheless, when establishing the responsibility of the Colombian state for the abduction of the merchants, the Inter-American Court, relied heavily on the duty to ensure rather than simply finding that their acts could be attributed to Colombia since they were entitled by law to exercise governmental functions, as it had done in previous cases with respect to the so-called self-defence patrols in Guatemala, see, e.g., *Blake v. Guatemala*, IACtHR, Judgment of 24 January 1998, paras 73–74, and J.M. Pasqualucci, 'The Application of International Principles of State Responsibility by the Inter-American Court of Human Rights', *Liber amicorum Héctor Fix-Zamudio*, ed. C. Gaviria (Secretaría de la Corte Interamericana de Derechos Humanos, 1998): 1217. At the time of the proceedings, the paramilitary groups had already been outlawed, but their criminal activities continued with similar cases pending. Hence, if the Inter-American Court had exclusively relied on the legal authorization, it would have prejudiced its later cases.

125.   See, in particular, the case of *Mapiripán Massacre, supra* note 50, at para. 97ff., where the Colombian government had accepted its responsibility for the failure to guarantee, but challenged the Commission's attribution of the acts of the paramilitaries as such.

126.   *Pueblo Bello Massacre, supra* note 112, at para. 126; *Ituango Massacre, supra* note 54, at paras 132–133. See also *Manuel Cepeda Vargas, supra* note 123, at paras 101ff., where the Inter-American Court expressly held Colombia responsible for both a violation of the obligation to guarantee and to respect the life of the Colombian senator, Cepeda Vargas, on account of the failure to take any measures to prevent his assassination, despite credible allegations of a plan to execute him and other politicians, and the collusion of security forces with paramilitary forces to carry out the execution.

127.   *Pueblo Bello Massacre, supra* note 112, at para. 126; *Ituango Massacre, supra* note 54, at paras 134–137; *Rochela Massacre, supra* note 20, at para. 102; *Manuel Cepeda Vargas, supra* note 123; *Valle Jaramillo, supra* note 123, at paras 75–80.

128. For the first time, in *Kiliç v. Turkey*, ECtHR, Application No. 22492/93, Judgment of 28 March 2000, and *Mahmut Kaya v. Turkey*, ECtHR, Application No. 22535/93, Judgment of 28 March 2000.
129. *Kiliç, supra* note 128, at paras 66–68, and *Mahmut Kaya, supra* note 128, at paras 87–90.
130. *Kiliç, supra* note 128, at paras 70–76, and *Mahmut Kaya, supra* note 128, at paras 93–98.
131. In the following cases, the European Court confirmed that the applicants belonged to a category of persons at a particular risk and that the state failed to take any protective measures, see *Akkoç v. Turkey*, ECtHR, Application Nos 22947/93 and 229448/93, Judgment of 10 October 2000, para. 81; *Koku, supra* note 114, at para. 31. In contrast, in other cases the European Court either did not address the question of whether the state failed to protect the life of the applicants or discarded it summarily, see, e.g., *Ülkü Ekinci v. Turkey*, ECtHR, Application No. 27602/95, Judgment of 16 July 2002; *Buldan v. Turkey*, ECtHR, Application No. 28298/95, Judgment of 20 April 2004.
132. See, e.g., *Arzu Akhmadova and others, supra* note 96, at para.155; *Mutayeva, supra* note 76, at para. 75; *Khantiyeva and others, supra* note 76, at para. 100; *Khashiyev and Akayeva v. Russia*, ECtHR, Application Nos 57942/00 and 57945/00, Judgment of 24 February 2005, para. 100ff.; *Shaipova and others v. Russia*, ECtHR, Application No. 10796/04, Judgment of 6 November 2008, para. 85.
133. See also *supra*, section 2 'The Duty to Account'.
134. For a critical analysis of the European Court's assessment of facts, see Koroteev, *supra* note 94.

10. Some reflections on the principle of humanity in its wide dimension

Antônio Augusto Cançado Trindade*

1. INTRODUCTION

In the brief reflections that follow, the principle of humanity will be addressed in its wide dimension, encompassing the whole *corpus juris* of international protection of the human person, in any circumstances, and particularly in those of great adversity. The principle of humanity, in line with the longstanding thinking of natural law, will then be considered as an emanation of human conscience, projecting itself into conventional as well as customary international law. Attention will then be turned to its presence in the framework of the Law of the United Nations, as well as to its judicial recognition in the case law of contemporary international tribunals. The way will thus be paved for the presentation of my concluding observations on the matter.

2. THE PRINCIPLE OF HUMANITY: ITS WIDE DIMENSION

When one evokes the principle of humanity, there is a tendency to consider it in the framework of International Humanitarian Law. It is beyond doubt that, in this framework, for example, civilians and persons *hors de combat* are to be treated with humanity. The principle of humane treatment of civilians and persons *hors de combat* is provided for in the 1949 Geneva Conventions on International Humanitarian Law (common Article 3, and Articles 12(1)/12(1)/13/5 and 27(1)), and their Additional Protocols I (Article 75(1)) and II (Article 4(1)). This principle, moreover, is generally regarded as one of customary International Humanitarian Law.

My own understanding is in the sense that the principle of humanity is endowed with an even wider dimension:[1] it applies in the most distinct circumstances, in times both of armed conflict and of peace, in the relations between public power and all persons subject to the jurisdiction of the State concerned. That principle has a notorious incidence when these latter are in a situation of vulnerability or great adversity, or even *defencelessness*, as evidenced by relevant provisions of distinct treaties integrating the International Law of Human Rights.

Thus, for example, at the UN level, the 1990 International Convention on the Protection of the Rights of All Migrant Workers and Members of Their Families provides, *inter alia*, in its Article 17(1), that '[m]igrant workers and members of their families who are deprived of their liberty shall be treated with humanity and with respect for the inherent dignity of the human person and for their cultural identity'. Likewise, the 1989 UN Convention on the Rights of the Child stipulates that 'States

Parties shall ensure that [e]very child deprived of liberty shall be treated with humanity and respect for the inherent dignity of the human person, and in a manner which takes into account the needs of persons of his or her age ...' (Article 37(b)). Provisions of the kind can also be found in human rights treaties at regional level.

To recall but a couple of examples, the 1969 American Convention on Human Rights, in providing for the right to humane treatment (Article 5), determines *inter alia* that '[a]ll persons deprived of their liberty shall be treated with respect for the inherent dignity of the human person' (para. 2). Likewise, the 1981 African Charter on Human and Peoples' Rights disposes *inter alia* that '[e]very individual shall have the right to the respect of the dignity inherent in a human being and to the recognition of his legal status' (Article 5). And the 1969 Convention on the Specific Aspects of Refugee Problems in Africa sets forth, *inter alia*, that '[t]he grant of asylum to refugees is a peaceful and humanitarian act ...' (Article II(2)). And the examples to the same effect multiply.

3. THE PRINCIPLE OF HUMANITY IN THE WHOLE *CORPUS JURIS* OF INTERNATIONAL PROTECTION OF THE HUMAN PERSON

The treatment dispensed to human beings, in any circumstances, ought to abide by the *principle of humanity*, which permeates the whole *corpus juris* of the international protection of the rights of the human person (encompassing International Humanitarian Law, the International Law of Human Rights, and International Refugee Law), conventional as well as customary, at global (UN) and regional levels. The principle of humanity, in effect, underlies the two *general comments*, n. 9 (of 1982, para. 3) and n. 21 (of 1992, para. 4) of the UN Human Rights Committee, on Article 10 of the UN Covenant on Civil and Political Rights (humane treatment of persons deprived of their liberty).[2] The principle of humanity, usually invoked in the domain of International Humanitarian Law, thus extends itself also to that of International Human Rights Law. And, as the Human Rights Committee rightly stated in its *general comment* n. 31 (of 2004), 'both spheres of Law are complementary, not mutually exclusive' (para. 11).

International law is not at all insensitive to the pressing need of humane treatment of persons, and the principle at issue applies in any circumstances, so as to prohibit inhuman treatment, by reference to humanity as a whole, in order to secure protection to all, including those in a situation of great vulnerability (paras. 17–20). *Humaneness* is to condition human behaviour in all circumstances, in times of peace as well as of disturbances and armed conflict. The principle of humanity permeates the whole *corpus juris* of protection of the human person, providing one of the illustrations of the approximations or convergences between its distinct and complementary branches (International Humanitarian Law, the International Law of Human Rights, and International Refugee Law), at the hermeneutic level, and is also manifested at the normative and the operational levels.[3]

In faithfulness to my own conception, I have, in recent decisions of the International Court of Justice (and, earlier on, of the Inter-American Court of Human Rights as well), deemed it fit to develop some reflections on the basis of the principle of humanity *lato sensu*. I have lately done so, for example in my Dissenting Opinion[4] in the case of the *Obligation to Prosecute or Extradite* (Belgium *versus* Senegal, Request for Provisional Measures, Order of 28.05.2009), and in my Dissenting Opinion[5] in the case of *Jurisdictional Immunities of the State* (Counter-Claim, Germany *versus* Italy, Order of 06.07.2010), as well as in my Separate Opinion in the Court's Advisory Opinion on *Accordance with International Law of the Declaration of Independence of Kosovo* (of 22.07.2010).[6]

4. THE PRINCIPLE OF HUMANITY IN THE HERITAGE OF NATURAL LAW THINKING

It should not pass unnoticed that the principle of humanity is in line with natural law thinking. It underlies classic thinking on humane treatment and the maintenance of sociable relationships, also at international level. Humaneness came to the fore even more forcefully in the treatment of persons in situation of vulnerability, or even defencelessness, such as those deprived of their personal freedom, for whatever reason. The *jus gentium*, when it began to correspond to the law of nations, came then to be conceived by its 'founding fathers' (F. de Vitoria, A. Gentili, F. Suárez, H. Grotius, S. Pufendorf, C. Wolff) as regulating the international community constituted by human beings socially organized in the (emerging) States and co-extensive with humankind, thus conforming to the *necessary* law of the *societas gentium*. This latter prevailed over the will of individual States, respectful of the human person, to the benefit of the common good.[7]

The precious legacy of natural law thinking, evoking the natural law of the right human reason (*recta ratio*), has never faded away, and this should be stressed time and time again, particularly in the face of the indifference and pragmatism of the 'strategic' *droit d'étatistes*, so numerous in the legal profession in our days. In so far as the International Law of Human Rights is concerned, it may further be recalled that, in the aftermath of World War II, the 1948 Universal Declaration of Human Rights proclaimed that '[a]ll human beings are born free and equal in dignity and rights' (Article 1). The fundamental principle of equality and non-discrimination, according to the Advisory Opinion n. 18 of the Inter-American Court of Human Rights (IACtHR) on the *Juridical Condition and Rights of Undocumented Migrants* (of 17 September 2003), belongs to the domain of *jus cogens*.

In that transcendental Advisory Opinion of 2003, the IACtHR, in line with the humanist teachings of the 'founding fathers' of the *droit des gens* (*jus gentium*), pointed out that, under that fundamental principle, the element of equality can hardly be separated from non-discrimination, and equality is to be guaranteed without discrimination of any kind. This is closely linked to the essential dignity of the human person, ensuing from the unity of the human kind. The basic principle of equality before the law and non-discrimination permeates the whole operation of the State power, having nowadays entered the domain of *jus cogens*.[8]

5. PRINCIPLES OF HUMANITY AND THE DICTATES OF PUBLIC CONSCIENCE: THE MARTENS CLAUSE

In so far as International Humanitarian Law is concerned, one may recall that, as early as 1907, the IV Hague Convention contained, in its preamble, the *célèbre Martens clause*, whereby in cases not included in the adopted Regulations annexed to it, 'the inhabitants and the belligerents remain under the protection and the rule of the principles of the law of nations, as they result from the usages established among civilized peoples, from the principles of humanity, and the dictates of the public conscience' (para. 8). The Martens Clause, inserted into the preamble of the IV Hague Convention of 1907 – and, even before that, also in the preamble of the II Hague Convention of 1899 (para. 9),[9] both Conventions pertaining to the laws and customs of land warfare – invoked the 'principles of the law of nations' derived from 'established' custom, as well as the 'principles of humanity' and the 'dictates of the public conscience'.

Subsequently, the Martens Clause was again to appear in the common provision, concerning denunciation, of the four Geneva Conventions of International Humanitarian Law of 1949 (Articles 62/63/142/158), as well as in the Additional Protocol I (of 1977) to those Conventions (Article 1(2)), to refer to a couple of the main Conventions of International Humanitarian Law.[10] The fact that, throughout more than a century, the draftsmen of the Conventions of 1899, 1907 and 1949, and of Protocol I of 1977, have repeatedly asserted the elements of the Martens Clause in those international instruments indicates that the Clause is an emanation of human conscience as the ultimate material source of International Humanitarian Law and of International Law in general.

In this way, it exerts a continuous influence in the spontaneous formation of the contents of new rules of International Humanitarian Law. By intertwining the principles of humanity and the dictates of public conscience, the Martens Clause establishes an 'organic interdependence' of the legality of protection with its legitimacy, to the benefit of all human beings.[11] The legacy of Martens is also related to the primacy of Law in the settlement of disputes and in the search for peace.

Contemporary juridical doctrine has also characterized the Martens clause as a source of general international law itself;[12] and no one would dare today to deny that the 'principles of humanity' and the 'dictates of the public conscience' invoked by the Martens Clause belong to the domain of *jus cogens*.[13] The aforementioned Clause, as a whole, has been conceived and repeatedly affirmed, ultimately, to the benefit of humankind as a whole, thus maintaining its topicality. The Clause may be considered as an expression of the *raison d'humanité* imposing limits on the *raison d'État*.[14]

6. THE FUNDAMENTAL PRINCIPLE OF HUMANITY IN THE FRAMEWORK OF THE LAW OF THE UNITED NATIONS

In my lengthy Separate Opinion in the recent Advisory Opinion of the ICJ on the *Accordance with International Law of the Declaration of Independence of Kosovo* (of 22.07.2010), I dwelt, *inter alia*, upon the fundamental principle of humanity in the framework of the law of international organizations, and in particular of the Law of the United Nations (paras 196–211). I recalled therein that the experiments of international organizations of *mandates, minorities* protection, *trust* territories, and, nowadays, *international administration* of territory, have not only turned closer attention to the 'people' or the 'population' concerned, to the fulfillment of the needs, and the empowerment, of the inhabitants, but have also fostered – each one in its own way – their access to justice at international level (para. 90).

Such access to justice is understood *lato sensu*, that is, as encompassing the *realization of justice*. Those experiments of international organizations (rendered possible by the contemporary expansion of the international legal personality, no longer a monopoly of States) have contributed to the vindication by individuals of their own rights, emanating directly from the *droit des gens*, from the law of nations itself (para. 196). In my perception, this is one of the basic features of the new *jus gentium* of our times. After all, every human being is an end in him or herself, and, individually or collectively, is entitled to enjoy freedom of belief and 'freedom from fear and want', as proclaimed in the preamble of the Universal Declaration of Human Rights (para. 2).

Every human person has the right to respect for his or her dignity, as part of human kind.[15] The recognition of this fundamental *principle of humanity* – I added in my aforementioned Separate Opinion – is one of the great and irreversible achievements of the *jus gentium* of our times (para. 197). At the passing of this first decade of the twenty-first century, the time has come to derive the consequences of the manifest non-compliance with this fundamental principle of humanity.[16] States, created by human beings gathered in their social *milieu*, are bound to protect, and not at all to oppress, all those who are under their respective jurisdictions (para. 199).

This corresponds to the minimum ethical, universally reckoned by the international community of our times. States are bound to safeguard the integrity of the human person from repression and systematic violence, from discriminatory and arbitrary treatment. The conception of fundamental and inalienable human rights is deeply engraved in the universal juridical conscience; in spite of variations in their enunciation or formulation, their conception marks presence in all cultures, and in the history of the thinking of all peoples.[17]

It should be kept in mind that the acknowledgement of the principle of respect for human dignity was introduced by the 1948 Universal Declaration, and is at the core of its basic outlook. It firmly asserts: 'All human beings are born free and equal in dignity and rights' (Article 1). And it recalls that 'disregard and contempt for human rights have resulted in barbarous acts which have outraged the conscience of mankind' (preamble, para. 2). The Universal Declaration warns that 'it is essential, if man is not compelled to have recourse, as a last resort, to rebellion against tyranny and oppression, that human rights should be protected by the rule of law' (preamble, para. 3). And it further acknowledges that 'recognition of the inherent dignity and of the equal and inalienable rights of all members of the human family is the foundation of freedom, justice and peace in the world' (preamble, para. 1).

Since the adoption of the Universal Declaration in 1948, one could hardly anticipate that a historical process of generalization of the international protection of human rights was being launched, on a truly universal scale.[18] Throughout more than six decades of remarkable historical projection, the Declaration has gradually acquired an authority which its draftsmen could not have foreseen. This happened mainly because successive generations of human beings, from distinct cultures and all over the world, recognized in it a 'common standard of achievement' (as originally proclaimed), which corresponded to their deepest and most legitimate aspirations.

7. THE FUNDAMENTAL PRINCIPLE OF HUMANITY IN THE CASE LAW OF CONTEMPORARY INTERNATIONAL TRIBUNALS

Last but not least, the fundamental principle of humanity has been asserted also in the case law of contemporary international tribunals. It has met with full judicial recognition.[19] May I recall, on the basis of my own experience, the *jurisprudence constante* of the Inter-American Court of Human Rights (IACtHR) in this respect, which has properly warned – during the period I had the honour to preside over the IACtHR – that the principle of humanity, inspiring the right to humane treatment (Article 5 of the American Convention on Human Rights), applies even more forcefully when a person is unlawfully detained, and kept in an '*exacerbated situation of vulnerability*'.[20]

In my Separate Opinion in the Judgment of the IACtHR in the case of the *Massacre of Plan de Sánchez* (of 29.04.2004), concerning Guatemala, I devoted a whole section (III, paras 9–23) to the judicial acknowledgement of the principle of humanity in the recent case law of that Court, as well as of the *ad hoc* International Criminal Tribunal for the Former Yugoslavia. Furthermore, I expressed therein my understanding that the principle of humanity, orienting the way one treats others (*el trato humano*), 'encompasses all forms of human behaviour and the totality of the condition of the vulnerable human existence' (para. 9).

In the case of the *Massacre of Plan de Sánchez* (Judgment of 29.04.2004), at a certain stage of the proceedings before the IACtHR, the Respondent State accepted its international responsibility for violations of rights guaranteed under the American Convention on Human Rights, and, in particular, for 'not guaranteeing the right of the relatives of the ... victims and members of the community to express their religious, spiritual and cultural beliefs' (para. 36). In my Separate Opinion in that case, I pondered that the primacy of the principle of humanity is identified with the very end or ultimate goal of the Law, of the whole legal order, both domestic and international, in recognizing the inalienability of all rights inherent to the human person (para. 17).

That principle marks its presence – I added – not only in the International Law of Human Rights, but also in International Humanitarian Law, being applied in all circumstances. Whether it is regarded as underlying the prohibition of inhuman treatment (established by Article 3 common to the four Geneva Conventions on International Humanitarian Law of 1949), or as referring to humankind as a whole, or as qualifying a given quality of human behaviour (*humaneness*), the principle of humanity is always and ineluctably present (paras 18–20). The same principle of humanity – I concluded in the aforementioned Separate Opinion in the case of the *Massacre of Plan de Sánchez* – also occurs in the domain of International Refugee

Law, as disclosed by the facts of the *cas d'espèce*, involving massacres and the State policy of *tierra arrasada*, that is, the destruction and burning of homes, which generated a massive forced displacement of persons (para. 23).

Cruelties of this kind unfortunately occur in different latitudes, and in distinct regions of the world – human nature being what it is. The point to be here made – may I insist upon it – is that the principle of humanity operates, in my view, in a way that fosters the convergences among the three trends of the international protection of the rights inherent to the human person (International Law of Human Rights, International Humanitarian Law and International Refugee Law – cf. *supra*).

Likewise, the *ad hoc* International Criminal Tribunal for the Former Yugoslavia (ICTFY) devoted attention to the principle of humanity in its Judgments in, for example, the cases of *Mucic et al.* (2001) and of *Celebici* (1998). The ICTFY (Appeals Chamber), in the *Mucic et al.* case (Judgment of 20.02.2001), pondered that both International Humanitarian Law and the International Law of Human Rights take as a 'starting point' their common concern to safeguard human dignity, which forms the basis of their minimum standards of humanity.[21] In fact, the principle of humanity can be understood in distinct ways. Firstly, it can be conceived as a principle underlying the prohibition of inhuman treatment, established by Article 3 common to the four Geneva Conventions of 1949. Secondly, the principle referred to can be invoked by reference to humankind as a whole, in relation to matters of common, general and direct interest to it. And thirdly, the same principle can be employed to qualify a given quality of human behaviour (humaneness).

Earlier on, in the *Celebici* case (Judgment of 16.11.1998), the ICTFY (Trial Chamber) qualified as *inhuman treatment* an intentional or deliberate act or omission which causes serious suffering (or mental or physical damage), or constitutes a serious attack on human dignity; thus – the Tribunal added – 'inhuman treatment is intentional treatment which does not conform with the fundamental principle of humanity, and forms the umbrella under which the remainder of the listed "grave breaches" in the Conventions fall'.[22] Subsequently, in the *T. Blaskic* case (Judgment of 03.03.2000), the same Tribunal (Trial Chamber) reiterated this position.[23]

For its part, the *ad hoc* International Criminal Tribunal for Rwanda (ICTR) rightly pondered, in the case of *J.-P. Akayesu* (Judgment of 02.09.1998), that the concept of crimes against humanity had already been recognized well before the Nuremberg Tribunal itself (1945–1946). The Martens Clause contributed to that effect (cf. *supra*); in fact, expressions similar to that of those crimes, invoking victimized humanity, appeared much earlier in human history.[24] The same ICTR pointed out, in the case *J. Kambanda* (Judgment of 04.09.1998), that in all periods of human history genocide has inflicted great losses on humankind, the victims being not only the persons slaughtered but humanity itself (in acts of genocide as well as in crimes against humanity).[25]

8.   CONCLUDING OBSERVATIONS

Contemporary (conventional and general) international law has been characterized to a large extent by the emergence and evolution of its peremptory norms (the *jus cogens*), and a greater consciousness, in a virtually universal scale, of the principle of humanity.

Grave violations of human rights, acts of genocide, crimes against humanity, among other atrocities, are in breach of absolute prohibitions of *jus cogens*. The feeling of *humaneness* – proper of a new *jus gentium* of the twenty-first century – comes to permeate the whole *corpus juris* of contemporary International Law. I have called this development – *inter alia* in my Concurring Opinion in the Advisory Opinion n. 16 (of 01.10.1999), of the IACtHR, on the *Right to Information on Consular Assistance in the Framework of the Guarantees of the Due Process of Law* – a historical process of a true *humanization* of International Law.[26]

The prevalence of the principle of respect for the dignity of the human person is identified with the ultimate aim itself of Law, of the legal order, both national and international. By virtue of this fundamental principle, every person ought to be respected (in her honour and in her beliefs) by the simple fact of belonging to humankind, irrespective of any circumstance. The principle of the inalienability of the rights inherent to the human being, in its turn, is identified with a basic assumption of the construction of the whole *corpus juris* of the International Law of Human Rights.

In its application in any circumstances (in times both of armed conflict and of peace), in the relations between public power and human beings subject to the jurisdiction of the State concerned, the principle of humanity permeates the whole *corpus juris* of the international protection of the rights of the human person (encompassing International Humanitarian Law, the International Law of Human Rights, and International Refugee Law), conventional as well as customary. The principle, emanating from human conscience, in the line of natural law thinking, has further projected itself into the law of international organizations (and in particular into the Law of the United Nations), and has met with judicial recognition on the part of contemporary international tribunals. It has given expression to the *raison d'humanité*, imposing limits on the *raison d'État*.

NOTES

* Antônio Augusto Cançado Trindade is former President of the Inter-American Court of Human Rights (IACtHR); Judge of the International Court of Justice; Emeritus Professor of International Law of the University of Brasilia; Honorary Professor of Utrecht University; Doctor *Honoris Causa* at various Latin American Universities; Member of the *Curatorium* of the Hague Academy of International Law, and of the Institut de Droit International.

1. This is the position I upheld in my lengthy Separate Opinion in the recent Decision of the International Court of Justice in the case *A.S. Diallo* (Guinea v. D.R. Congo), Merits, Judgment, I.C.J Reports 2010. I devoted part V of my Separate Opinion specifically to the principle of humanity in its wide dimension (paras 93–106), and further considerations related thereto permeated part VI of my Separate Opinion, on the prohibition of *arbitrariness* in the International Law of Human Rights (paras 107–142).

2. In respect of the recent case *A.S. Diallo*, ibid., resolved by the I.C.J., I saw fit to point out, in my Separate Opinion, *inter alia*, that the principle of humanity underlies, e.g., Article 7 of the UN Covenant on Civil and Political Rights, which protects the individual's personal integrity against mistreatment, as well as Article 10 of the Covenant (concerning persons under detention), which begins by stating that '[a]ll persons deprived of their liberty shall be treated with humanity and with respect for the inherent dignity of the human person' (para. 1). This comprises not only the negative obligation not to mistreat (Article 7), but also the positive obligation to ensure that a detainee, under the custody of the State, is treated with humanity and due respect for his inherent dignity as a human person (para. 98).

3.   See, on this particular point, e.g., A.A. Cançado Trindade, *Derecho Internacional de los Derechos Humanos, Derecho Internacional de los Refugiados y Derecho Internacional Humanitario – Aproximaciones y Convergencias* (Geneva: International Committee of the Red Cross, 2000), 1–66.

4.   Paras 24–25 and 61.

5.   Paras 116, 118, 125, 136–139 and 179. In this lengthy Dissenting Opinion, my reflections relating to the principle of humanity are found particularly in part XII, on human beings as the true bearers (titulaires) of the originally violated rights and the pitfalls of State voluntarism (paras 112 –123), as well as in part XIII, on the incidence of *jus cogens* (paras 126–146), besides the Conclusions (mainly paras 178–179).

6.   In the Court's recent Advisory Opinion on *Accordance with International Law of the Unilateral Declaration of Independence in Respect of Kosovo* (22 July 2010), I devoted one entire section (XIII(4)) of my lengthy Separate Opinion expressly to the 'fundamental principle of humanity' (paras 196–211) in the framework of the law of nations itself. I recalled that the 'founding fathers' of international law (F. de Vitoria, A. Gentili, F. Suárez, H. Grotius, S. Pufendorf, C. Wolff) propounded a *jus gentium* inspired by the principle of humanity *lato sensu* (paras 73–74). My aforementioned Separate Opinion is permeated with my personal reflections on basic considerations of humanity in the treatment of peoples under the law of nations (paras 67–74); part VI is centred on the contemporaneity of the '*droit des gens*', with particular attention to the humanist vision of the international legal order (paras 75–96); part XII is focused on the people-centred outlook in contemporary International Law (paras 169–176), part XIV on a comprehensive conception of the incidence of *jus cogens* (paras 212–217); and part XIII, on principles of international law, the Law of the United Nations and the humane ends of the State (paras 177–211), wherein I address specifically the fundamental principle of humanity in the framework of the Law of the United Nations (paras 196–211, and see *infra*).

7.   A.A. Cançado Trindade, *A Humanização do Direito Internacional* (Belo Horizonte Brazil: Editora Del Rey, 2006), 9–14, 172, 318–319, 393 and 408.

8.   Inter-American Court of Human Rights, Advisory Opinion No. 18, 17 September 2003, on the Juridical Condition and Rights of Undocumented Migrants, Series A, No. 18, paras 83, 97–99 and 100–101. In my Concurring Opinion, I stressed that the fundamental principle of equality and non-discrimination permeates the whole *corpus juris* of the International Law of Human Rights, has an impact in Public International Law, and projects itself onto general or customary international law itself, as well as integrating nowadays the expanding material content of *jus cogens* (paras 59–64 and 65–73). In recent years, the Inter-American Court of Human Rights, together with the *ad hoc* International Criminal Tribunal for the Former Yugoslavia, have been the contemporary international tribunals which have most contributed, in their case law, to the conceptual evolution of *jus cogens* (well beyond the law of treaties), and to the gradual expansion of its material content; see A.A. Cançado Trindade, '*Jus Cogens*: The Determination and the Gradual Expansion of its Material Content in Contemporary International Case-Law', *XXXV Curso de Derecho Internacional Organizado por el Comité Jurídico Interamericano* (Washington DC: Organization of American States, 2008): 3–29.

9.   It was originally presented by the Delegate of Russia (Friedrich von Martens) to the I Hague Peace Conference (of 1899).

10. The Martens Clause has thus been endowed, over more than a century, with continuing validity in its invocation of public conscience, and it continues to warn against the assumption that whatever is not expressly prohibited by the Conventions on International Humanitarian Law would be allowed; quite the contrary, the Martens clause sustains the continued applicability of the principles of the law of nations, the principles of humanity, and the dictates of the public conscience, independently of the emergence of new situations. The Martens clause impedes, thus, the *non liquet*, and exerts an important role in the hermeneutics and the application of humanitarian norms.

11. C. Swinarski, 'Préface', in V.V. Pustogarov, *Fedor Fedorovitch Martens – Jurist i Diplomat*, ed. Mezdunarodinye Otnoscheniya (Moscow: Meždunarodnyie Otnošenija, 1999), XI. And see also, e.g., B. Zimmermann, 'Protocol I – Article 1', in *Commentary on the Additional Protocols of 1977 to the Geneva Conventions of 1949*, eds Y. Sandoz, C. Swinarski and B. Zimmermann (Geneva: International Committee of the Red Cross and Martinus Nijhoff, 1987), 39; H. Meyrowitz, 'Réflexions sur le fondement du droit de la guerre', in *Études et essais sur le Droit international humanitaire et sur les principes de la Croix-Rouge en l'honneur de Jean Pictet*, ed. C. Swinarski (Geneva and the Hague: ICRC and Martinus Nijhoff, 1984), 423–424; and see H. Strebel, 'Martens Clause', in *Encyclopedia of Public International Law*, ed. R. Bernhardt, Vol. 3 (Amsterdam: North-Holland, 1982), 252–253.

12. F. Münch, 'Le rôle du droit spontané', in *Pensamiento Jurídico y Sociedad Internacional – Libro-Homenaje al Prof. D. A. Truyol y Serra*, Vol. II (Madrid: Universidad Complutense, 1986), 836.

13. S. Miyazaki, 'The Martens Clause and International Humanitarian Law', in *Études et essais sur le droit international humanitaire et sur les principes de la Croix-Rouge en l'honneur de J. Pictet*, ed. C. Swinarski (Geneva and The Hague: ICRC and Martinus Nijhoff, 1984), 438 and 440.

14. A.A. Cançado Trindade, *International Law for Humankind – Towards a New Jus Gentium* (Leiden: Martinus Nijhoff, 2010), 150–152 and 275–285.

15. B. Maurer, *Le principe de respect de la dignité humaine et la Convention Européenne des Droits de l'Homme* (Paris: CERIC and Université d'Aix-Marseille, 1999), 18.

16. I further added that: 'Rights inherent to the human person are endowed with universality (the unity of the human kind) and timelessness, in the sense that, rather than being "conceded" by the public power, they truly precede the formation of the society and of the State. Those rights are independent of any forms of socio-political organization, including the State created by society. The rights inherent to the human person precede, and are superior to, the State. All human beings are to enjoy the rights inherent to them, for belonging to humankind. As a corollary of this, the safeguarding of such rights is not exhausted – it cannot be exhausted – in the action of States. By the same token, States are not to avail themselves of their entitlement to territorial integrity to violate systematically the personal integrity of human beings subject to their respective jurisdictions' (para. 198).

17. See, e.g., [Various Authors], *Universality of Human Rights in a Pluralistic World (Proceedings of the 1989 Strasbourg Colloquy)* (Strasbourg and Kehl: N.P. Engel Verlag, 1990), 45, 57, 103, 138, 143 and 155.

18. Already throughout the *travaux préparatoires* of the Universal Declaration (particularly in the 13 months between May 1947 and June 1948), the holistic view of all rights to be proclaimed promptly prevailed. Such an outlook was espoused in the official preparatory work of the Declaration, i.e., the debates and drafting in the former UN Commission on Human Rights (Rapporteur, René Cassin) and subsequently in the Third Committee of the General Assembly. In addition, in 1947, in a contribution to the work then in preparation in the UN Commission on Human Rights, UNESCO undertook an examination of the main theoretical problems raised by the elaboration of the Universal Declaration; it circulated, to some of the most influential thinkers of the time around the world, a questionnaire on the relations between the rights of individuals and groups in societies of different kinds and in distinct historical circumstances, as well as on the relations between individual freedoms and social or collective responsibilities. For the answers provided, see *Los Derechos del Hombre – Estudios y Comentarios en torno a la Nueva Declaración Universal Reunidos por la UNESCO* (Mexico and Buenos Aires: Fondo de Cultura Económica, 1949), 97–98 (T. de Chardin); 181–185 (A. Huxley); 14–22 and 69–74 (J. Maritain); 24–27 (E.H. Carr); 129–136 (Q. Wright); 160–164 (L. Carneiro); 90–96 (J. Haesaert); 75–87 (H. Laski); 143–159 (B. Tchechko); 169–172 (Chung-Shu Lo); 23 (M.K. Gandhi); 177–180 (S.V. Puntambekar), and 173–176 (H. Kabir). The two UN World Conferences on Human Rights (Teheran, 1968, and Vienna, 1993) have given concrete expression to the interdependence of all human rights and to their universality, enriched by cultural diversity.

19. See A.A. Cançado Trindade, 'Le déracinement et la protection des migrants dans le droit international des droits de l'homme', *Revue trimestrielle des droits de l'homme* 19 (Brussels, 2008): 289–328, especially 295 and 308–316.

20. *Maritza Urrutia v. Guatemala*, IACtHR, Judgment of 27 November 2003, para. 87; *Juan Humberto Sánchez v. Honduras*, IACtHR, Judgment of 7 June 2003, para. 96; *Cantoral Benavides v. Peru*, IACtHR, Judgment of 18 August 2000, para. 90; and see *Bámaca Velásquez v. Guatemala*, IACtHR, Judgment of 25 November 2000, para. 150.

21. *Mucic et al.*, ICTFY, Appeals Chamber, Judgment, 20 February 2001 (Case No. IT-96-21-A), para. 149.

22. *Celebici*, ICTFY, Trial Chamber, Judgment, 16 November 1998 (Case No. IT-96-21), para. 543.

23. Paragraph 154 of that Judgment.

24. Paragraphs 565–566 of that Judgment.

25. Paragraphs 15–16 of that Judgment. An equal reasoning is found in the Judgments of the same Tribunal in the aforementioned case *J.P. Akayesu*, as well as in the case *O. Serushago*, ICTR, Judgment, 5 February 1999, para. 15.

26. Paragraph 35 of the Concurring Opinion.

11. Specificities of human rights law and international humanitarian law regarding state responsibility

*Christian Tomuschat**

1. INTRODUCTION

Both international humanitarian law (hereinafter: IHL) and human rights law (herein-after: HRL) are constituent elements of present-day international law. Thus, one might assume that they are naturally governed by the general principles and rules which make up the conceptual framework of the system of international law as a whole.[1] Yet, regarding the secondary rules that come into play if and when a primary rule of conduct has been breached, it turns out that the modern extension of international law, both *ratione personae* and *ratione materiae*, cannot easily be accommodated. All of a sudden, it becomes apparent that international law grew up as inter-State law and that its mechanisms of enforcement were originally framed – or evolved – with a view to accommodating States. Consequently, not only are adjustments necessary; in some instances, the inference cannot be escaped that some of the classic rules are entirely inappropriate in the fields of IHL and HRL.

International responsibility is a case in point. Traditionally, it was understood as inter-State responsibility. Accordingly, the rules drawn up by the International Law Commission (hereinafter: ILC) on Responsibility of States for internationally wrongful acts (hereinafter: ARS), taken note of by General Assembly resolution 56/83 of 12 December 2001, dealt exclusively with the international responsibility which a State incurs through unlawful conduct. At that time, a decade ago, it was already a matter of common knowledge that International Organizations (hereinafter: IOs) may also become liable to make reparation if they violate their obligations under international law. Indeed, since the advisory opinion of the International Court of Justice (herein-after: ICJ) in the *Bernadotte* case,[2] where the rights of the United Nations resulting from an internationally wrongful act were in issue, the general network of rights and duties under general international law has been progressively extended to IOs. Yet the ILC felt that rules governing the responsibility of IOs would have to take account of the specific features of IOs so that such a legal regime could not simply be a copy of the rules applicable to States. Most of the available materials concerned cases in which States were involved. Regarding IOs, the documentary basis was somewhat fragmen-tary. Accordingly, a second project was launched which ended with the adoption of a draft on first reading in 2009.[3] At the end of the day it turned out that the differences were not enormous – a result which had not been foreseen at the inception of the work.

While the inclusion of IOs in the regime of international responsibility could be managed without any major frictions, IHL and HRL both diverge from the usual pattern of international law in that the individual plays a pivotal role. International HRL confers on the individual true entitlements which he/she may in many instances directly enforce against the obligated States. It is indeed the peculiar gist of HRL that human beings are provided with legal weapons which they can use even against their own State. IHL is more State-oriented. It mainly directs its commands to governments, instructing them as to the conduct of their armed forces during armed hostilities. However, many of the commands of IHL at the same time directly address the individual, surrounding him or her with legal defences and providing that serious violations must lead to criminal prosecution. Thus, IHL is also, together with HRL, symptomatic of the advent of a stage of international law where legal relationships are no longer exclusively confined to States.

Many of the special problems that arise in connection with breaches of IHL and HRL are fairly similar to one another. However, the intellectual premises are characterized by wide discrepancies. IHL has evolved from the basic concept of hostilities between two nations; by contrast, the ideal type of human rights protection provides for defences of the individual human being against his/her own State. Therefore, the following discussion will be split into two parts.

2.   INTERNATIONAL HUMANITARIAN LAW

The bulk of the rules of IHL define the rights and duties of the parties to an armed conflict. In this regard, the model set by the 1907 Hague Regulations Respecting the Laws and Customs of War on Land is still applicable today, notwithstanding the comprehensive overhaul of IHL that was effected in 1949 and 1977, and has progressively accentuated the role played by individual human beings involved in hostilities. Accordingly, the main legal consequence of a breach of a rule of international law is that secondary rights of reparation arise for the victim State in consonance with the ARS. In this regard, IHL does not display any structural specificities.

2.1   Responsibility for Breaches of International Humanitarian Law in Practice

In practice, a breach of IHL entails in much fewer instances than within the framework of the rules applicable in time of peace, actual remedial measures according to the reparation model espoused by the ILC (Art. 31 ARS) following the famous *Chorzów* judgments of the Permanent Court of International Justice.[4] First, IHL, whether conventional or customary in nature, is not supported by any general mechanism for the settlement of disputes. The only innovation in this field is the International Fact-Finding Mission which the Protocol Additional to the Geneva Conventions of 12 August 1949, and Relating to the Protection of Victims of International Armed Conflicts (Protocol I) (hereinafter: AP I) (Art. 90) introduced in 1977. Today this procedural device, which is not automatically binding on the parties to AP I, has been accepted by 71 parties – but it has not yet been set into operation in a single case. This lack of adequate dispute settlement procedures is explained by the specific nature of armed conflict. States are generally reluctant to submit *ex ante* to regulatory mechanisms for the settlement of the injurious consequences arising from military confrontations since the dimensions of interests possibly in issue in such instances can never be anticipated with any degree of reliability. Breaches of IHL may touch upon the very existence of a State.[5] The fears which States nurture in this respect are also reflected in the many reservations in the declarations of acceptance of the jurisdiction of the ICJ which exclude from the review of the Court any disputes relating to armed activities.[6] Thus, armed conflict is very rarely the subject-matter of proceedings before the ICJ. One may ascribe it to the lack of diplomatic experience of the Congolese Government and the Government of Uganda that they both accepted the jurisdiction of the ICJ without any reservations by declarations in accordance with Art. 36(2) of the ICJ Statute so that the dispute resulting from the invasion of Congolese territory by Ugandan troops in 1997 could be adjudicated by the ICJ.[7] On the other hand, the parallel application filed against Rwanda was unsuccessful since Rwanda had refrained from submitting to the jurisdiction of the Court by virtue of a unilateral declaration, and was not bound by any conventional clause on jurisdiction either.[8] When in the recent past Germany accepted the Court's jurisdiction in accordance with Art. 36(2), it also explicitly excluded from the scope of its acceptance any dispute that 'relates to, arises from or is connected with the deployment of armed forces abroad, involvement in such deployments or decisions thereon'.[9] As a consequence, the interpretation of IHL has received little support from judicial proceedings the subject-matter of which was (civil) State responsibility. Essentially, its development has been driven by proceedings before the current international criminal courts. In a little number of cases the European Court of Human Rights (hereinafter: ECtHR) has reviewed applications originating from armed conflict by resorting to the legal yardstick available to it, namely HRL.[10] The Inter-American Court of Human Rights has declined its jurisdiction for such disputes.[11]

Another feature characteristic of the way IHL is being handled in practice is the fact that financial settlements of war damages tend to lump together all the damages caused by an armed conflict, without identifying in detail each and every breach of IHL.[12] This is partly due to the fact that after months or years of fighting it becomes normally rather difficult if not outright impossible to clarify occurrences alleged to constitute violations of IHL.[13] Pursuant to proper standards, investigations should be initiated as soon as the first suspicions arise that a war crime has been committed. If this is not done, the evidence becomes generally unreliable and fades away. What remains is a general impression that violations did occur. Such general conclusions do not easily lend themselves to forming bases for reparation claims. Therefore, it then seems advisable to settle the issue of war damages by global payments that are not related to specific incidents.

Lastly, more often than not, *jus ad bellum* and *jus in bello* are simply brushed aside when an international armed conflict has ended by a clear victory of one of the parties. The victor then dictates his conditions for peace, which the vanquished nation must accept.[14] The most famous example of this approach is the 1919 Versailles Treaty[15] which burdened Germany with comprehensive responsibility for all loss and damage caused by World War I (Article 231).[16] The question whether the victor has, on his part, complied with the rules of IHL is then simply not put. IHL may thus retroactively become a pure chimera without any real substance. After World War II, given the horrendous nature of the atrocities perpetrated by the Nazi authorities of the Third Reich, the issue of whether the victorious Allied Powers had at all times respected IHL on their part, was not raised at the inter-State level. Since the establishment of the United Nations such developments of imbalance have decreased in numbers. But even the Security Council may not always act in a true spirit of impartiality, given the preponderance of the five nations occupying permanent seats in that body.

2.2 Monitoring Compliance with International Humanitarian Law

Over and above the scarcity of classic inter-State remedies of judicial settlement, IHL has not followed the modern trend to confer procedural devices on individual victims of unlawful conduct in armed conflict. Consequently, IHL remains under the discrete but determinative influence of the International Committee of the Red Cross (hereinafter: ICRC). The ICRC has kept its leading role as the institution which promotes and secures IHL. The great conferences for the development of IHL (in particular, 1949 and 1977) were initiated and organized by its 'patron'. Still, it has maintained an edge over the United Nations which has also sought to stamp its hallmark on IHL, but has respected its special character as a province entrusted traditionally to the ICRC.[17] Likewise, the ICRC is the key element in guaranteeing the effective implementation of the relevant rules in armed conflict. More than any diplomatic representations, visits to places of detention help ensure compliance with GC III, in particular. State responsibility is therefore not reduced to a bilateral relationship between a wrong-doing State and a victim State. The ICRC, thanks to its explicit mentioning in the Geneva Conventions, is legally omnipresent in armed conflict. Its neutral role makes it an ideal guardian of IHL.[18]

On the other hand, only the Security Council, the body entrusted with overall responsibility for international peace and security and therefore also for seeing to it that IHL be respected, has at its disposal enforcement machinery. Unfortunately, more often than not the Security Council is reluctant to call upon the parties to abide by the legal rules that must be respected, particularly in a situation of armed conflict. Language that appeals instead to the goodwill of the parties is mostly preferred. Generally, the Security Council wishes to increase its chances of success by using soft language. Thus, its intervention is many times confined to recommendatory appeals. However, one also finds clear examples where it unequivocally addresses the parties to an armed conflict by urging them to ensure that all members of their armed forces – and even of the rebel forces opposing them – comply with IHL.[19] As appropriate, it may also 'condemn' violations of HRL and IHL.[20] But not even its binding resolutions under Chapter VII of the UN Charter are always implemented by the parties concerned. In any event, however, the ICRC and the Security Council act together in a symbiotic relationship. Both seek to uphold and enforce IHL. The conventions produced under the aegis of the ICRC provide the legal yardsticks; the ICRC also provides actual assistance to victims of armed activities. The Security Council, for its part, holds the real power of threat and deterrence through which it may activate IHL as it sees fit. Both institutions have therefore contributed a great deal to making IHL a real factor that considerably impacts governmental decisions.

2.3   Third States as Guardians of International Humanitarian Law

It is the leading role of the ICRC and the Security Council which has to date prevented Article 48 ARS from deploying its effects in actual practice. According to this rule, States have a right to intervene with a view to securing respect for obligations established for the protection of 'a collective interest' and obligations 'owed to the international community as a whole', a mechanism founded on the *erga omnes* jurisprudence of the ICJ.[21] The core elements of IHL belong to this class of rules.[22] Through the Geneva Conventions of 1949 and the Additional Protocols of 1977 the States parties have undertaken to 'respect and to ensure' the relevant instruments 'in all circumstances' (common Article 1). Thus, they are obligated towards all the other States parties, which means almost the entire international community, to abide by their commitments in the field of IHL.[23] However, third States do not lightly assume functions of a monitor or mediator.[24] If such an initiative is to be undertaken, a great amount of political energy must be put into its actual operation. A failure can harm the political prestige of a government that has sought to act as go-between but has not been able to achieve any concrete results.

2.4   International Organizations as Addressees of International Humanitarian Law

Although IHL generally addresses State action, hostilities in which International Organizations (IOs) are involved may also come within its purview. Indeed, there is a clear need to evaluate military operations conducted by IOs by the yardstick of IHL. IOs cannot have more rights than States.[25] Conversely, States should not be allowed to escape the requirements of IHL by establishing an IO as a joint enterprise. The humanitarian purpose of IHL must not be frustrated by opening loopholes that lend themselves to abuse. NATO must respect the same limitations on its power of action as every one of its member States. However, in case of an alleged breach of its obligations the question inevitably arises to whom the acts alleged to amount to violations of IHL are to be attributed. Military contingents remain always to some extent under the jurisdiction of the sending States. Other issues are determined by the collective command structure. No general propositions about attribution can be formulated in this connection. In each case, it must be ascertained, as suggested by the draft articles of the ILC on the responsibility of IOs,[26] who exercised effective control over the contro-versial actions.[27] Since in our time States organize their national defence if possible within the framework of alliances with partner nations, the necessity to disentangle individual and collective responsibility has become a structural feature of IHL.[28]

The question also arises of whether an IO is actually in a position to honour all of its commitments under IHL, in particular to redress any damage it may have caused by a breach of these commitments. This is, however, not an issue specifically related to IHL but raises the general questions of the reliability and trustworthiness of IOs as debtors. International practice does not substantiate the suspicion that IOs are formed by States just as a cloak to hide and dismiss their own responsibility. It may even be true that as a rule the actions of military alliances are more respectful of the law than the actions of individual States, given the collective decision-making process which generally pre-cedes them, preventing any kind of rash decisions.

The United Nations was for a long time reluctant to recognize that its operations were governed by IHL. In fact, this reluctance is understandable since in particular peacekeeping operations, in terms of their object and purpose, do not constitute combat activities in an armed conflict. When conducting peacekeeping operations, the UN acts initially as a police force and not as a military force. However, as soon as hostilities emerge and as the threshold from internal disturbances to organized massive fighting is reached, the UN must be considered bound by the customary rules as they are reflected in the relevant conventional instruments. Again, the humanitarian purpose takes precedence. In this regard, it is regrettable that the relevant instruction of the Secretary-General of 12 August 1999[29] does not simply recognize the applicability of IHL to armed conflicts in which UN troops are involved, but has reserved its position by confining the accepted commitments to the 'fundamental principles and rules' of IHL (section 1.1).[30]

2.5 Amorphous Entities as Addressees of International Humanitarian Law

IHL is the legal discipline where entities normally not recognized as subjects of international law are subjected to duties. It is well known that the 'mini-code' enunciated in common Article 3 of the four 1949 Geneva Conventions enjoins each party to an armed conflict of non-international character to comply with a number of basic guarantees which are intended to protect a minimum of human dignity. Additional Protocol II of 1977 follows the same logic, although at the Diplomatic Conference all references to 'parties to the conflict' were removed from the text.[31] The requirement that armed groups must respect IHL has also been set forth in the Hague Convention for the Protection of Cultural Property[32] and its Second Protocol[33] as well as in Amended Protocol II to the Convention on Certain Conventional Weapons.[34] This legal construction is based on the assumption that rebel groups fighting their governments shall be legally bound without their consent – which at first glance seems to be an anomaly within a system where consent is otherwise a precondition for the emergence of a legal obligation.[35] However, one simply has to acknowledge that international law has been shaped and is still being shaped by States who, in a certain sense, are the masters of this branch of the law.[36] It is true that more than just a few governments lack any democratic legitimacy. Yet through the interaction among 193 States international law has established itself at a balanced mid-point between excessive demands on either side. On the whole, this equilibrium reflects the values shared by the entire inter-national community as a whole. It is neither arrogant nor illusory to subject any groups existing within the States that make up the international community to a discipline established by common consent. Thus, the legitimacy of the extension of common Article 3 and Additional Protocol II to rebel groups seems to be unchallengeable, quite apart from the fact that the rules set out in these instruments are today also recognized as customary law. Obviously, the enforcement problem is not resolved by this legal construction.[37]

The question is, however, whether the usual sequence of primary and secondary rules can have the same automaticity with regard to armed groups as in the mutual relationship between States. Article 1 ARS provides: 'Every internationally wrongful act of a State entails the international responsibility of that State.'

Likewise, the draft articles adopted by the ILC on the responsibility of International Organizations[38] state in almost identical language (Article 3): 'Every internationally wrongful act of an international organization entails the international responsibility of that organization.'

IOs are consolidated entities which do not disappear into thin air as soon as they are held accountable. Accordingly, to treat them in the same vein as States can be welcomed without any reservations.

With regard to armed groups, the link between the rules of conduct and a possible duty or right to reparation becomes more problematic. In civil wars and other non-international conflicts, it may well be that an armed group opposing the government in place can be accurately identified.[39] This, however, would rather seem to be an exception. Mostly, such groups have no definite contours. Their membership changes swiftly, the leadership is generally characterized by a high degree of instability, and the names may also vary according to political tastes and preferences in a rhythm of volatility. Thus, armed groups cannot really be gotten hold of as collective entities. Lastly, as long as they are involved in combat against their governments, they generally lack any assets that might be attached to satisfy a claim for compensation.

It is for this reason that Art. 10 ARS deals with insurrectional movements only after they have succeeded in toppling the existing government or in establishing a new secessionist State. It stands to reason that once that threshold has been passed an armed group fits easily within the framework of the traditional system of State responsibility. The question is, however, whether armed groups engaged in armed conflict can become bound to repair damage they have caused in violation of rules of IHL, or whether a right to reparation may accrue to them, irrespective of the outcome of the struggle they are involved in, if the governmental forces of their adversary have breached IHL to their detriment.

In the ICRC publication on *Customary International Humanitarian Law*, edited by J.-M. Henckaerts and L. Doswald-Beck, a few observations are devoted to the possibility of holding to account an armed movement. It is openly admitted that 'the consequences of such responsibility are not clear'.[40] But the reference to a Sudanese case[41] or to a more telling example from the Philippines[42] does not support the conclusion that indeed an insurrectional movement becomes liable under international law to make reparation. It is clear that such groups may infringe their obligations. Time and again, the General Assembly and the Security Council have called upon rebel groups to respect the duties incumbent upon them.[43] But this does not mean that such infringements bring into being a genuine right to reparation against them under international law.

There are two possible ways to tackle the issue. On the one hand, one can argue that indeed the logic of the international system of responsibility requires that every breach of an international obligation be followed by a duty of reparation, and that the vacuum which any such title holder would have to face up to is just a practical problem: the entitlement exists, but it cannot be enforced because the debtor, on account of its lack of a clearly defined identity, can hardly ever be made accountable in actual terms. Or else, one can take the view that the logic of the system reaches here its outer limits. In order to be operative, to make the decisive leap from wishful thinking to genuine hard law, international law requires firm foundations. Actors that cannot be 'nailed down' are not suitable as subjects of international law.

Obviously, a distinction is necessary. Insurrectional movements can be addressed without any major difficulties as to their actual conduct in armed conflict. The leadership will generally know that certain rules must be complied with, and it can also impart instructions to its members. But the fact remains that such groups, given their loose structure, are devoid of all the requisite features of a collective entity that can sustain collective responsibility. Since international law is largely made up of practice and less so of juridical constructions one may have to opt for the second strand of argument. It is telling that even the ICRC has not been able to adduce a single case where a reparation claim was asserted against an insurrectional movement. Furthermore, before civil courts, groups lacking juridical personality have no standing. Of course, much can be achieved through informal methods or even through the conclusion of specific treaties.[44] Obviously, the door is not closed. Should practice develop, a customary rule could arise on that basis.

One would be on even less safe ground by speculating about reparation claims which an armed group might direct against its adversary, the government of its own State. Here, too, abstract logic may seem to require that in case of non-respect of common Article 3 or of Additional Protocol II the victim of a violation must be able to claim reparation. However, given the actual context of non-international armed conflict such a claim would appear to have contradictory features. In principle, any rebellion against governmental power entails criminal responsibility. Since every member of an insurgent group is thus exposed to criminal sanctions, the group as such also operates in unlawful territory. Given these circumstances, governments would never acknowledge a duty of reparation – which would mean that through financial compensation they would support an insurrection prohibited by law. They certainly do not consent to digging their own graves. It should also borne in mind that common Article 3 goes to the outer limits of what governments were prepared to accept back in 1949, fearing that humanitarian generosity might undermine their sovereign powers within the national territory. The world of legal logic may become the real world as soon as a rebellion wins the upper hand. Then a new government will see to it that damage sustained by its fighting members will be compensated. But this is a different configuration. Regarding the issue under review, practice is absolutely lacking.

2.6 Criminal Responsibility

Notwithstanding these sceptical observations, the impression would be erroneous that the duties set forth in common Article 3 and in Additional Protocol II have no teeth, and should be considered as negligible. The inference drawn in the preceding sections only sheds a light on the inappropriateness of the regime of civil responsibility with regard to armed groups operating in non-international conflict. However, nothing stands in the way of activating the criminal responsibility of members of armed opposition groups if they infringe the rules of IHL which are binding on them. An individual cannot simply disappear (although he/she may attempt to hide). This is the only practical way the duties under common Article 3 of the four Geneva Conventions and of Additional Protocol II can be effectuated.

2.7   Civil Responsibility: Individual Reparation Claims?

2.7.1   General international law

The 1907 Hague Regulations establish implicit prohibitions for members of the armed forces (e.g. Articles 23, 47), and they protect the members of the civilian population (e.g. Article 46), but essentially they refrain from directly addressing individuals.[45] Accordingly, Hague Convention IV set up a traditional rule on State responsibility (Article 3) which provides that a 'belligerent party' shall be liable for any violation of the Regulations committed by its armed forces. This provision does not specify to whom the rights deriving from such violations shall accrue. Within the context of the general conception of international law as it was prevalent in 1907 there can be no doubt that indeed injured States were considered as being the holders of the relevant rights of reparation. In 1907, it was almost unthinkable that individuals might be provided, at the level of international law, with rights of reparation against States. Some authors have claimed that the *travaux préparatoires* point to an intention of the drafters to grant to persons having sustained the harmful consequences of an infringement of IHL such entitlements.[46] However, the drafting history does not permit any unequivocal conclusions.

It is true that the German Government, which had introduced some amendments in one of the Commissions of the Peace Conference, spoke in one of these amendments of compensation for 'persons'. This proposed rule, however, was confined to 'neutral persons', that is, citizens of neutral countries, an exception in the course of warfare. The other proposed rule said in a very unspecific manner that in case of prejudice to the adverse party 'the *question* of indemnity will be settled at the conclusion of peace'.[47] In other words, no suggestion was made that generally individual war victims should be compensated, just the contrary: the German proposal proceeded from the assumption that the traditional pattern of making reparation for war damages to the 'adverse party' by way of inter-State treaties should be maintained. In the ensuing debate, a controversy arose concerning the possibility of distinguishing between neutral persons and nationals of the opponent party. It cannot be denied that on this occasion the speakers referred mostly to *persons* having sustained injury. But the British delegate, Lord Reay, also said that indemnification of members of the hostile party 'depends upon the conditions which will be inserted in the treaty of peace and which will be the result of negotiations between the belligerents'.[48]

Eventually the texts were merged and assumed their final shape – where the beneficiary of the proposed reparation claim is not mentioned. A sober assessment of the materials referred to yields no real clue that eventually, at the end of their deliberations, the drafters intended to set forth individual entitlements. Instead, the conclusion seems to be warranted that they renounced setting forth a special rule in favour of nationals of neutral countries.[49]

Furthermore, one must note that international practice simply does not support the conclusions drawn from a somewhat hasty perusal of the *travaux préparatoires*.[50] After the two great European wars of 1914 to 1918 and 1939 to 1945 the settlement was consistently brought about on the basis of the assumption that it was the responsible States that had to shoulder the financial responsibility for the injuries caused by them. As already mentioned, in the Treaty of Versailles Germany had to agree to a clause

(Article 231) according to which it was responsible to the Allied and Associated Governments for 'all the loss and damage' caused by it. No additional supplementary rights of the persons directly harmed during the war by non-respect of IHL were foreseen. The ECtHR has stated quite unequivocally that persons harmed by violations of IHL during World War II could not be considered as holders of individual rights accruing to them under the regime of the 1907 rules.[51]

A similar configuration of reparation in classic terms at inter-State level was present when the victorious Allied Powers made determinations, by way of the Potsdam Accord, on how Germany was to redress the vast amount of damages it had produced by unleashing the horrors of World War II. In Chapter IV of that Accord it was stated that 'Germany' had to compensate 'to the greatest possible extent for the loss and suffering that she has caused to the United Nations'. Specific measures of compensation were agreed upon – like removal of industrial goods or confiscation of German external assets – to the benefit of the countries of the victorious alliance. Again, no mention can be found to the effect that, over and above these compensatory measures, injured individuals should receive specific payments. Thus, international practice militates quite definitely against the theses articulated by Frits Kalshoven.

When after the experiences of World War II in 1949 IHL was reviewed and reformed with a view to ensuring more effectively the victims of war, not only details were amended, but also the general conceptual bases changed. The new class of 'protected persons' was introduced. While the first three conventions do not mention this notion explicitly, although they are of course designed to protect everyone within the scope of application of the relevant instrument, Article 4 of GC IV speaks indeed explicitly of 'protected persons'.[52] One might have deduced from these stipulations that any violation of the new regime to the detriment of such 'protected persons' would bring into being an individual right to compensation of the victims. However, according to the ICRC, such a conclusion was not justified. In a commentary on the common article dealing with 'Responsibilities of the Contracting Parties',[53] it stated quite categorically that it was 'inconceivable, at least as the law stands today, that claimants should be able to bring a direct action for damages against the State in whose service the persons committing the breach was working'.[54]

AP I of 1977 contains again a provision on responsibility for violations of its provisions. It is worded as follows: 'A Party to the conflict which violates the provisions of the Conventions or of this Protocol shall, if the case demands, be liable to pay compensation. It shall be responsible for all acts committed by persons forming part of its armed forces.' This text reproduces, with only minor modifications, the text of Article 3 of Hague Convention IV of 1907. No significant change of the wording can be perceived as far as the holder of rights entailed by a breach is concerned. The ICRC Commentary acknowledges that at the Geneva Diplomatic Conference, which drew up AP I, no intention was manifested to depart from the classical framework of inter-State relationships since the reproduction of the text of Article 3 of Hague Convention IV of 1907 was decided by consensus. Nonetheless, the ICRC states somewhat vaguely that '[t]hose entitled to compensation will normally be Parties to the conflict or their nationals'.[55] And it continues with visible hesitation:

Apart from exceptional cases, persons with a foreign nationality who have been wronged by the unlawful conduct of a Party to the conflict should address themselves to their own government, which will submit their complaints to the Party or Parties which committed the violation. However, since 1945 a tendency has emerged to recognize the exercise of rights by individuals.[56]

No concrete details are given as to the factual circumstances of this 'tendency'. It stands to reason that precedents have to be carefully distinguished as to their legal foundations. Compensation to individuals that has been agreed upon by the parties concerned under a conventional instrument cannot be equated with remedial measures taken without any such legal basis. There does not seem to exist a general practice indicating that violations of IHL should be made good by providing reparation directly to the persons adversely affected by the relevant breaches, except on an *ex gratia* basis.

2.7.2   Special mechanisms

Under special conventional arrangements, the individual may be given a more prominent role in the reparation process.[57] Recent examples include the UNCC, entrusted by virtue of Security Council resolution 687 (1991), para. 18, with providing redress to victims of the armed conflict commenced by the Iraqi invasion of Kuwait, where the intention was pursued to provide reparation to everyone having suffered damage exactly to the extent of this damage. Thus, individual reparation claims were recognized, but the claims had to be submitted by the governments concerned.[58] Another case in point is the Eritrea–Ethiopia Claims Commission established under Article 5 of the Agreement between the two States of 12 December 2000.[59] The Agreement acknowledged that private claims may arise from violations of IHL (Article 5(1)); however, all claims had to be filed by the respective governments (Article 5(8)).[60] In many instances, the Claims Commission found indeed that violations of IHL, including rape, had been committed.[61] However, in consonance with the general mandate of the Commission the findings were made as between the two parties, the State of Eritrea and the Federal Democratic Republic of Ethiopia. The victims appeared only as witnesses.

A judicial pronouncement which does not easily fit into the legal structure outlined above is the advisory opinion of the ICJ in the *Wall* case. The Court pointed out that Israel had the obligation to 'make reparation for the damage caused to all the natural or legal persons concerned' on account of the 'requisition and destruction of homes, businesses and agricultural holdings'.[62] This passage may be read in two different ways. It can be interpreted as meaning that Israel is under an obligation to take measures directly in favour of the individual victims; the word 'to' would then be linked to 'reparation'. On the other hand, the word 'to' can also be viewed as being connected to the two preceding words so that it only serves to identify those who have sustained damage. The first construction is contradicted by the operative part of the opinion where the ICJ confines itself to stating that 'Israel is under an obligation to make reparation for all damage caused',[63] without mentioning the specific victims as beneficiaries. As it appears, the Court left deliberately open the question as to how the injuries should be made good. In fact, the situation in Palestine has atypical features in that Israel faces up not to a State, but to a people under occupation with an 'Authority' that lacks the status of a State government.

2.7.3   A dynamic process?

For those who view international law evolving in a dynamic process under the impact of HRL the balance sheet established hitherto appears entirely unsatisfactory and not corresponding to the new teleology of international law as focusing on the basic needs of the individual. These tendencies have found a reflection in the Basic Principles and Guidelines on the Right to a Remedy and Reparation for Victims of Gross Violations of International Human Rights Law and Serious Violations of International Humanitarian Law (hereinafter: BPG) adopted by the UN General Assembly in 2005 as a set of rules designed progressively to develop the law.[64] In para. 18 of this declaration, one finds the proposition that every victim of a serious breach of IHL – and also of HRL – should be provided with full and effective reparation. Generally, the resolution attempts to transpose the ARS, the body of rules governing international responsibility in an inter-State relationship, to the relationship between individual victims of a breach of IHL and States authors of such breaches. Almost the same remedies as those listed by Article 34 ARS – namely restitution, compensation, and rehabilitation instead of satisfaction – are also mentioned by the BPG (para. 18). This endeavour to strengthen the rights of victims of armed hostilities stems from deep moral convictions. At first glance, it seems absolutely plausible that nothing is more justified for an individual victim than to claim full reparation for unlawful harm suffered. However, no real study of the issue as to whether such an extension of the scope *ratione personae* of the BPG had taken place before the adoption of the relevant resolution.[65] There was a broad consensus that the rights of the victims required to be strengthened.

Many weighty objections militate against the solution propagated by the BPG. First of all, it should be recalled that there is almost no supporting practice, apart from treaties that deal with very specific situations. Also, the advisory opinion of the ICJ in the *Wall* case relates to circumstances that do not correspond to the typical pattern of a case governed by IHL, where armed activities are to be assessed. The ICJ was confronted with the building of a separation wall where the fate of almost every square foot could be accurately established. To deal squarely with the horrendous consequences of true armed activities is infinitely more complex. In very few cases only will it be possible to find a direct link between an alleged breach of IHL and a specific injury suffered by an individual. This is not only a practical problem that could be resolved by sharper analysis and more intensive reflection, but a genuinely structural problem that has led the practice of historical peace settlements to opt for global settlements with lump-sum payments, as already pointed out.

2.7.4   The interrelationship between individual and collective reparations

This practice raises the determinative question as to how the relationship between collective reparation – between the States concerned – and individual reparation – through remedial measures directly to the affected individual victims – should be conceived of. A wrong-doing State cannot be held to account twice, once according to the traditional method of settlement, a second time pursuant to the method advocated by the BPG. Lastly, no real benefit would result for the victims of armed conflict from attributing to them individual claims against a foreign State having infringed IHL to their detriment: they would not find an appropriate forum to vindicate such rights. To date, the traditional rule stands unaffected that no private individual can bring suits before its own courts against a foreign State on account of acts *jure imperii* of that foreign State. The ruling of the Greek Areios Pagos in the *Distomo* case,[66] which departed from that rule, was delegitimized a few years later by the Special Court under Article 100 of the Greek Constitution,[67] while the *Ferrini* judgment of the Italian Corte di Cassazione[68] has not found any followers in the world, and is currently being challenged by Germany in a proceeding before the ICJ.[69] In other words, postulating an individual right to reparation would amount to an advantage for the victims only in theory. It would not really improve their situation. On the other hand, such independent individual rights would make peace settlements after a major conflict almost impossible. Thousands or even millions of claims would have to be processed and decided – with the obvious result that the respondent State would simply refuse to get involved in such proceedings.

2.7.5   Special forms of reparation – moral satisfaction

The above considerations apply primarily to financial compensation. Other forms of reparation can be realized without encountering major difficulties. Restitution of property unlawfully confiscated or looted has often been regulated by particular agreements.[70] Symbolic acts of satisfaction can never impose an excessive burden on the obligated State. Hence, it would appear that there is a much room for differentiation. All of this, however, requires regulation by way of conventional instruments. The actual examples do not yet provide a sufficient basis for the emergence of a new rule of customary law.

3.   HUMAN RIGHTS LAW

In the case of HRL, the double-edged nature of its scope *ratione personae* is even more clearly visible than in the case of IHL. On the one hand, human rights treaties, which have instilled much of their substance into IHL, are international treaties which bring into existence rights and duties in the mutual relationships between the contracting parties. On the other hand, such treaties also establish rights for individuals, namely all the members of the population under the jurisdiction of the contracting parties. In the case of customary rules, the beneficiaries are all human beings on a world-wide scale.

3.1   The Peculiar Logic of Human Rights Treaties

As opposed to classical international treaties, human rights treaties establish primarily rights of the citizens of each State party against their own State. States do not seek, in the first place, advantages for their nationals who live abroad, who in any event enjoy the protection of aliens' law; instead, they pledge themselves to treat their own citizens in the manner specified by the relevant treaty. Thus, foreign States are given a 'droit de regard' in respect of matters which originally were seen as essentially domestic, not to be interfered with from abroad. This role of international monitors is explained by the common realization that under an authoritarian regime or an outright dictatorship the guarantees contained in ordinary legislation or even in constitutions may evaporate fairly quickly. By contrast, no government can unilaterally do away with international commitments. The proposition '*pacta sunt servanda*' does not permit arbitrary rejection of treaty obligations. Thus, international law becomes a subsidiary or parallel constitution that, in theory at least, is proof against the vagaries of political turmoil at national level. Similarly, States are not the masters of customary law. As long as a customary rule exists, they are bound by it and cannot shed it.

Of course, human rights treaties have, additionally, the side-effect of protecting nationals with transboundary activities. Thus, they assume the functions of aliens' law, too. Yet, the main effect of human rights is that they operate as a check against the arbitrary exercise of sovereign powers by a State vis-à-vis its own citizens. Long since, resolutions of the UN General Assembly have determined that in today's world human rights is a matter of international concern, and is not shielded from international interference by the defence of domestic jurisdiction.[71]

The particular structure of human rights treaties gives rise to particular difficulties in instances of breaches. If a State violates the legal entitlements of its citizens, international law cannot operate pursuant to its traditional concept. In such instances, which provide the main bulk of applicable cases, there is no other State which is directly affected. Third States suffer no actual harm. The inherent logic of State responsibility assumes that through its self-interest a State will be motivated to vindicate compensation for the losses it or its citizens have sustained. By contrast, its interest in the well-being of the citizens of another country is generally much weaker. Governments have embraced the dignity of the human person as a core value of the international community. But they consider that as a rule every nation should take care of its own matters. Only if major disturbances become visible even to the outside world will they feel encouraged to take appropriate peaceful action for the protection of people in other countries. Such initiatives are today also supported by the realization that the well-being of my neighbours is at the same time my own well-being because of the world-wide links which every liberal nation entertains today with other nations.

3.2   Individual Remedies

Accordingly, there was almost an institutional pressure to provide for individual remedies to make sure that breaches of human rights obligations entail real and tangible sanctions. Indeed, the most conspicuous feature of human rights treaties is that, as a rule, victims are vested with an individual right of petition, whatever its name (complaint, application, communication). Whereas in the international legal order initially the right of individual petition was generally dependent on specific declarations of acceptance, the European Convention on Human Rights took the intellectual leadership in 1989 by making the application compulsory for every State party through Protocol No. 11.[72] This can be regarded as a revolution within the traditional system of international dispute settlement where specific consent was the basic rule, either with regard to individual cases or to groups of disputes narrowly defined. On the American continent, the requirement of acceptance of the jurisdiction of the Inter-American Court of Human Rights has been upheld,[73] and the same is true of Africa where the individual application is still a rare phenomenon.[74] Most of the universal human rights treaties also provide for complaint mechanisms that can be set into motion by individuals.[75] However, none of these mechanisms is capable of producing binding decisions. All of the views handed down by the relevant expert bodies have the nature of recommendations. This institutional weakness does not detract from the fact that such views carry considerable political weight.

3.3   Monitoring by the International Community

In the current human rights treaties, the rights of third States in the case of a breach of their commitments by other States parties are generally not well defined. The International Covenant on Civil and Political Rights (ICCPR) provides for a mechanism of inter-State communications (Article 41) which is highly unsatisfactory. First, this mechanism has to be specifically accepted. To date (March 2012), only 48 States have made the relevant declaration. Moreover, the mechanism provides only for recommendations as its final outcome. Inevitably, the question has therefore arisen of whether bringing a complaint under Art. 41 ICCPR is the only remedy available or whether the general rules of international responsibility, in particular those on countermeasures, can be resorted to. The answer must be yes. The drafters of the ICCPR wished to strengthen the protection of human rights through Art. 41, not to weaken it. To present the mechanism under Art. 41 ICCPR as an exclusive procedure would, however, produce the contrary result.

Under the European Convention on Human Rights (ECHR), the inter-State application was provided for from the very outset (originally: Article 24, now Article 33). Quite deliberately, the framers wished to set up a system of effective guarantees for the human beings that were meant to be the beneficiaries of the rights freedoms set out by the ECHR. Indeed, the ECHR was established in the aftermath of World War II when it had become obvious that the community of civilized States had to assume a monitoring function in order to make those rights and freedoms a living reality. Many other treaties in the field of human rights provide also for such a collective enforcement mechanism. The usual logic of international law finds itself reversed. Normally, States take action through instituting international proceedings with a view to vindicating their own tangible interests. The concept of the inter-State application, by contrast, is designed from the very outset to protect the rights and interests of citizens of another country. Only on a higher level of abstraction can the interests pursued by such procedural steps be equated with genuine proper interests of a State that comes to the rescue of oppressed individuals abroad.

The ARS have generalized the system of remedies which was originally a specificity of some treaties in the field of human rights. According to Article 48 ARS, States shall have the right to call for respect for rules that serve a general interest of the international community. This has been standard practice in the international community for many years. Beyond individual States, international organizations also avail themselves of that opportunity. The European Union has taken a leading role in calling for respect of HRL in all parts of the world, irrespective of any specific individual interest. Thus, for instance, on 16 September 2010 the European Council at its meeting in Brussels stated with regard to the occupied Palestinian territories: 'The European Union recalls that settlements are illegal under international law and calls for an extension of the moratorium decided by Israel. It continues to call for a complete stop to all violence, in particular rocket fire and terrorist attacks'.[76]

Unfortunately, the draft Articles on the responsibility of international organizations remain stuck in rigid purity by not acknowledging this important function of international organizations – which generally enjoy a greater degree of legitimacy than individual States, being commonly free from the bias which often characterizes the expression of views by individual States. Art. 48 of the draft authorizes international organizations not deemed to be injured only to invoke the responsibility of another international organization, but does not allow it to assert the right to reparation of injured States.[77] Here, an opportunity has been missed to combine the classical system of responsibility with the developments which have been going on within the international system for many decades, where the United Nations and the European Union have paved the way, setting patterns of conduct which are not seriously challenged and thus would seem to be supported by a firm *opinio juris*.

3.4 Individual Reparation Claims

As in the case of IHL, the most important question under HRL is whether individual victims of a violation of human rights are provided with an entitlement to reparation under international law. There is a growing tendency to postulate such a right.[78] This tendency has found its clearest expression in the BPG.[79] According to this instrument victims should have a full right to reparation, including all the remedies listed in the ARS in respect of inter-State relations. One cannot fail to note that the key provision of the BPG, namely para. 18, deliberately uses the word 'should', specifying furthermore that reparation should be effected 'in accordance with domestic law and international law'.[80] Thus, according to the arrangement of the two references, priority shall be given to domestic law. This is a strong argument against the existence of a true right to reparation under international law.

To find the right answer is not easy. It must be recognized that the law is in some kind of development. However, some elements can be indicated that in any event must be taken into account when attempting to formulate a proposition that fits into the general structure of international law. It is laudable that generally human rights lawyers are driven by a profound inclination to mete out justice to the victims of grave breaches. However, international law cannot be conceived solely from the perspective of the individual, its architects must also ask themselves what solutions are best suited for the common good.

In trying to elucidate this issue, the student must first draw a distinction between the level of primary law, the principles and rules intended to govern the conduct of subjects of international law, and the level of secondary law, where determinations are made on the remedies entailed by a breach of human rights law. There can be no doubt that nowadays most human rights bring into being true individual entitlements. In the case of customary law, this occurs independently of the will of any single State. Regarding human rights, no State can oppose itself to the emergence of basic rights that the international community views as essential foundations of a civilized state of coexistence in the international community. The doctrine of persistent objection has long since become moot as it has been overtaken by practice to the contrary;[81] it has (almost) never been acknowledged in the field of human rights[82] and IHL.[83] As far as treaties are concerned, their applicability depends of course on being accepted by States pursuant to the ordinary rules governing their entry into force. But once such a treaty has been ratified, it will engender rights which, as from that moment, do not depend any longer on the consent of the State concerned. In other words, the protected human beings become holders of rights directly under international law. This becomes particularly manifest if and when a human rights treaty provides for a settlement procedure under which anyone believing that his/her rights have been encroached upon may file a complaint, application or communication.

It is not self-evident, however, that entitlements at the level of primary law, human rights and fundamental freedoms, translate into entitlements to reparation in the same manner as this occurs in the case of rights and duties in relationships between States. Most States have built their own specific systems of responsibility for governmental wrongdoing. The notion that 'The King can do no wrong' pertains to the historical past. Under the rule of law, it has been widely acknowledged that persons who have suffered harm at the hands of public authorities must be provided with remedies. However, it would be difficult to find a single country where a general clause provides that any harm inflicted on citizens must be redressed. Mostly, a fairly differentiated system has emerged, according to the specific circumstances in which the injury has been caused. Thus, for instance, in many countries no claims can be directed against the State on account of military activities. In the United States, the Federal Tort Claims Act (1948) establishes that no claim may be brought that arises 'out of the combatant activities of the military or naval forces'.[84] Additionally, the Act denies access to U.S. courts to 'any claim arising in a foreign country'.[85] In Germany, according to the jurisprudence of the Supreme Court, the provisions on governmental responsibility do not encompass claims derived from situations of armed conflict. In a leading judgment of 26 June 2003,[86] the Court held that:

> According to the understanding and the overall system of the German law in force at the time the act was committed (1944) the military acts during war in a foreign State, which are attributable under international law to the German Reich, did not fall within the scope of state liability for official acts as enshrined [in the legislation at that time in force].[87]

This holding was slightly modified in the later case of the *Bridge of Varvarin* where the Court observed that it could be left open whether a doctrine that was applicable in 1944 could be maintained after the entry into force of the Basic Law, since the action brought by the claimants was to be rejected on other grounds.[88]

It would be necessary to proceed to careful stock-taking in order to establish a balance sheet that would evince a complete picture. Even in the absence of such a comprehensive overview, however, it can be said that within the framework of a nation reparation for injuries actually suffered pertains to those internal matters where first of all decisions are required at national level. It is not the same thing to impose, on the one hand, codes of conduct for governments, embodied in human rights instruments, and to prescribe how redress should be effected. Within an international community placed under the duty to respect human rights and fundamental freedoms, every member can and must be expected to refrain from torturing and killing human beings; but no easy advice can be given as to the most suitable remedies once such violations have been perpetrated. No government in a State which is a real State and not just a fictitious entity like Somalia will have any difficulties in repairing harm that has been caused in a single case. However, mass injustices need to be addressed from a different perspective. After the end of an armed conflict or of a dictatorship that has suppressed an entire people for years or even decades, almost everyone, except those belonging to the former ruling clique, might be considered to be victims. In such a situation, it would make little sense to launch comprehensive reparation programmes according to which everyone would obtain a claim to reparation payments – to be financed from his own pocket through taxes levied on all the members of the national community. A national community has quite naturally only a limited capacity to pay, and every member of this community has to content him/herself with the amount of wealth domestically available for distribution. It stands to reason that in such a situation a selection must take place. According to principles of common sense and reasonable-ness, only the persons hardest hit will then be chosen as beneficiaries of adequate measures of reparation. Within a national community, it is the principle of mutual solidarity that supports the conception and implementation of reparation programmes. To design and particularize such a programme pertains in the first place to the realm of national self-determination. It would amount to arrogant interference to dictate to a nation how it should proceed to make good the tangible and immaterial destructions caused in the past, which affected the people in its entirety.

In this regard, relationships inside a nation and relationships between nations are fundamentally different. An injured State is not compelled to take into account the weight of the burden which the wrong-doing State has to grapple with in endeavouring to make good the harm it has caused. The relevant clause which figured in the first draft of the ARS[89] was deleted on second reading – although political wisdom would require taking into consideration what can be reasonably expected of a tortfeasing State, all the more so since it is generally a different generation that has to shoulder the financial consequences. The unfortunate consequences of the Treaty of Versailles have imparted a lesson to the international community which, hopefully, will never be forgotten.

It should not be overlooked that the reparation clauses in the international treaties for the protection of human rights are framed in fairly cautious terms. The European Convention on Human Rights (Art. 41) leaves it in the first place to the individual domestic legal orders to grant reparation in case of a violation of one of the guarantees established under its provisions. The Court is authorized to afford 'just satisfaction' to an injured party 'if necessary'. In this regard, a considerable amount of discretion is left to the Court. It may conclude that the finding of a breach may constitute a sufficient form of reparation, notwithstanding the fact of considerable tangible harm.[90] Although it has by now developed its jurisprudence to a point where in almost all cases it grants financial compensation, it has also clearly stated that with regard to war damages or damages caused by a former regime States may take exceptional measures that under conditions of peace would be unacceptable.[91] On the other hand, the Court is extremely cautious in ordering restitution, the primary remedy in inter-State relationships. For decades, it relied on an understanding of the relevant treaty clause (Article 50, now Article 41) that its role was confined to granting financial compensation. Only a number of hard cases, where unlawful detention was in issue,[92] have changed its mind.

It would obviously amount to a mockery if a person under unlawful detention had to satisfy him/herself with financial compensation without being released.

The Inter-American Court of Human Rights has since its very first substantive judgment in the case of *Velásquez Rodríguez v. Honduras* observed that in every breach of one of the guarantees set forth in the American Convention on Human Rights the State concerned is bound to make full reparation.[93] It has maintained this jurisprudence ever since. However, it has never seriously considered the special circumstances of mass injustices, where full reparation to the benefit of all victims would clearly exceed the capacity of a wrong-doing State. This was clearly visible in the few cases from Guatemala addressed by the Court. Whereas in those cases a meticulous counting of all items of loss and injury was carried out,[94] with considerable amounts of money being awarded to the victims, hundreds of thousands of other Guatemalans, victims of the civil war, remained without any compensatory benefits. A national reparation programme came into existence more than six years after the end of the civil war in April 2003, and then only in rudimentary form. On the other hand, cases arrive at the Inter-American Court somewhat at random. For whoever succeeds in seeing his/her case placed on the agenda of the Court, this is seen as close to a win on a lottery. Such discrepancies can hardly be reconciled with the principles of equality and non-discrimination.

The Human Rights Committee under the International Covenant on Civil and Political Rights (hereinafter: Covenant) has also established a jurisprudence according to which individuals having suffered a breach of one of the rights under the Covenant have a right to claim a remedy. However, the Human Rights Committee has never had to tackle the consequences of widespread injustice, with all the attendant injuries; in any event, it has never done so openly, consistently reiterating instead its standard formulation that

> by becoming a Party to the Optional Protocol, the State party has recognized the competence of the Committee to determine whether there has been a violation of the Covenant or not, and that, pursuant to article 2 of the Covenant, the State party has undertaken to ensure to all individuals within its territory or subject to its jurisdiction the rights recognised in the Covenant and to provide an effective and enforceable remedy in case a violation has been established.[95]

The balance sheet of compliance looks gloomy.[96] In many instances, the respondent State does not even respond to the views conveyed to it.[97] This is a way for governments to make incorrectly clear their correct understanding that the views of the Human Rights Committee under the ICCPR are no more than recommendations. States are not legally bound to abide by such views. However, in any event they would have to set out the reasons why they consider that the Human Rights Committee has come to a wrong conclusion of the case concerned. Irrespective of this issue, one must note that the inconsistent practice of compliance does not provide a firm basis for a customary rule.

In sum, it would seem to be almost impossible and even inappropriate to establish a general rule of reparation for individual victims of a breach of their human rights by their national State. Without any doubt, reparation is desirable. But it must remain within the boundaries of what is feasible and acceptable within a national community.

It is erroneous to translate *tels quels* the principles of State responsibility to violations committed by the governmental apparatus of a State against its own citizens. The *Chórzow*[98] rule is not an iron rule suitable for any set of circumstances.

4. CONCLUDING OBSERVATIONS

IHL and HRL both have as their distinguishing feature the prominent role of the individual human being, which sets them apart from the typical norms of inter-State law. However, the reasons why the regime of State responsibility cannot be extended to breaches of IHL or HRL without major adjustments are fairly different. In the case of armed conflict, a model of settlement must be found which is suitable as a basis for lasting peace between former adversaries. Private mass claims before the civil courts of one of the two (or more) countries would render global settlements impossible and are prone to becoming a permanent source of enmity and unrest. Litigation over breaches of HRL encompasses essentially domestic conflicts, evaluated by international yard-sticks or even international bodies of adjudication. No structural problems arise as long as isolated incidents require to be addressed. However, here again mass claims require a high degree of caution. Regarding these types of dispute, the key element is that every citizen of a given country must share the fate and vicissitudes of his/her national community. Nobody can escape from history, and in a situation of national emergency the burdens as well as the available assets must be shared in equity. In this regard, many nations have their specific individual experiences and remedies. International law is unable to provide the differentiated parameters required to provide appropriate answers.

NOTES

* Christian Tomuschat is Emeritus Professor of Public International Law and European Law at the Humboldt University in Berlin. He is also a former member of the UN Human Rights Committee and the UN's International Law Commission.
1. See C. Tomuschat, 'What is "General International Law"?', in *Guerra y Paz: 1945–2009. Obra homenaje al Dr. Santiago Torres Bernárdez* (Lejona, Vizcaya: Universidad del País Vasco, Servicio editorial, 2010), 329, 340–347.
2. *Reparation for injuries suffered in the service of the United Nations*, Advisory Opinion, I.C.J. Reports 1949, 174.
3. See Report of the ILC on the work of its 61st session, GAOR, Supp. No. 10 (A/64/10), 19. The draft was finalized on second reading in 2011, Report of the ILC on the work of its 63rd session, GAOR, Supp. No. 10 (A/66/10), 54.
4. *Factory at Chorzów*, Permanent Court of International Justice (PCIJ), Jurisdiction, Series A, No. 9 (1927), 21; Merits, Series A, No. 17 (1928), 47.
5. See, in this connection, *Legality of the Threat or Use of Nuclear Weapons*, Advisory Opinion, I.C.J. Reports 1996, 226, at 266, para. 105 E.
6. See references given by C. Tomuschat, comments on Article 36, in *The Statute of the International Court of Justice: A Commentary*, eds A. Zimmermann, C. Tomuschat, K. Oellers-Frahm and C. Tams (Oxford: Oxford University Press, 2nd ed. 2012), 690, footnote 344.
7. *Armed Activities on the Territory of the Congo* (D.R. Congo v. Uganda), Judgment, I.C.J. Reports 2005, 168.

8.   *Armed Activities on the Territory of the Congo, New Application: 2002* (D.R. Congo v. Rwanda), Jurisdiction and Admissibility, I.C.J. Reports 2006, 6.

9.   Declaration of 30 April 2008, http://www.icj-cij.org/jurisdiction/index.php?p1=5&p2=1&p3=3& code=DE (accessed 10 February 2012).

10.   See *Isayeva v. Russia*, ECtHR, Application No. 57950/00, Judgment of 24 February 2005; for a more recent example, see *Taysumov and others v. Russia*, ECtHR, Application No. 21810/03, Judgment of 14 May 2009, paras 93–95; *Suleymanova v. Russia*, ECtHR, Application No. 9191/06, Judgment of 12 May 2010, paras 76–87.

11.   *Las Palmeras v. Colombia*, Preliminary Objections, Judgment of 4 February 2000, para. 33.

12.   See, e.g., F. Kalshoven, 'State Responsibility for Warlike Acts of the Armed Forces', *ICLQ* 40 (1991): 827, at 836; idem, 'Individual Right to Claim Damages under Article 3 of Hague Convention IV: Expert Opinion, 1997', in *Reflections on the Law of War; Collected Essays* (Leiden and Boston: Martinus Nijhoff, 2007), 631, at 647.

13.   S/RES/687, 8 April 1991, however, which determined the conditions for the restoration of international peace and security after Iraq's invasion of Kuwait, singled out 'environmental damage' (para. 16) that had been caused in clear violation of IHL.

14.   See, e.g., R. Wolfrum, 'Enforcement of IHL', in *The Handbook of Humanitarian Law in Armed Conflict*, ed. D. Fleck (Oxford: Oxford University Press, 1995) 517, at 543, margin number 1214.

15.   Reproduced in W.G. Grewe, ed., *Fontes Historiae Iuris Gentium*, Vol. 3/2 (Berlin and New York: Walter de Gruyter, 1992), 683.

16.   Commented upon by P. d'Argent, *Les réparations de guerre en droit international public* (Brussels and Paris: Bruylant and Librairie générale de droit et de jurisprudence, 2002), 77 *et seq.*

17.   Only the agreements on prohibited arms and disarmament are routinely negotiated within the United Nations.

18.   However, it may de facto be prevented by the parties from discharging its role. In practice, governments contend quite often that armed hostilities have not yet reached the threshold of an armed conflict, but remain at the level of 'internal disturbances and tensions' (Article 1(2) AP II).

19.   See, e.g., S/RES/1564, 18 September 2004, para. 10, and S/RES/1574, 19 November 2004, para. 11, both dealing with Sudan.

20.   See, e.g., S/RES/1464, 4 February 2003, para. 7, dealing with Ivory Coast.

21.   *Barcelona Traction* (Belgium v. Spain), Judgment, I.C.J. Reports 1970, 3, 32.

22.   *Legal Consequences of the Construction of a Wall in the Occupied Palestinian Territory*, Advisory Opinion, I.C.J. Reports 2004, 136, 199, para. 155; see also C. Focarelli, 'Common Article 1 of the 1949 Geneva Conventions: A Soap Bubble?', *EJIL* 21 (2010): 125, at 164–170; F. Kalshoven, 'Implementation and Enforcement of IHL', in *Reflections on the Law of War:Collected Essays* (Leiden and Boston: Martinus Nijhoff, 2007), 595, at 618; D. Schindler, 'Die erga omnes – Wirkung des humanitären Völkerrechts', in *Recht zwischen Umbruch und Bewahrung. Festschrift für Rudolf Bernhardt*, U. Beyerlin et al. (Berlin et al.: Springer, 1995), 199 *et seq.* The official commentary of the ILC on the Articles on State Responsibility does not mention IHL as a class of rules under Article 48(1)(a) ARS.

23.   At the same time, the core elements of IHL constitute international customary law, as observed by the I.C.J. in *Military and Paramilitary Activities in and against Nicaragua* (Nicaragua v. United States), Merits, Judgment, I.C.J. Reports 1986, 14, 114, para. 218.

24.   Recalled by S. Villalpando, 'The Legal Dimension of the International Community: How Community Interests are Protected in International Law', *EJIL* 21 (2010): 387, at 396.

25.   *Interpretation of the Agreement of 25 March 1951 between the WHO and Egypt*, Advisory Opinion, I.C.J. Reports 1980, 73, 89, para. 37.

26.   ILC Report 2011, *supra* note 3.

27.   Article 7: 'The conduct of an organ of a State or an organ or agent of an international organization that is placed at the disposal of another international organization shall be considered under international law an act of the latter organization if the organization exercises effective control over that conduct.' In *Behrami v. France* and *Saramati v. France, Germany and Norway* and *Saramati*, ECtHR, Application Nos 71412/01 and 78166/01, Judgment of 2 May 2007, the European Court of Human Rights applied a different standard, namely 'ultimate authority and control' (para. 133). For a critical appraisal, see A. Breitegger, 'Sacrificing the Effectiveness of the European Convention on Human Rights on the Altar of the Effective Functioning of Peace Support Operations', *International Community Law Review* 11 (2009): 155, at 163–175; P. Klein, 'Responsabilité pour les faits commis

dans le cadre d'opérations de paix et étendue des pouvoirs de contrôle de la Cour européenne des droits de l'homme', *AFDI* 53 (2007): 43, at 50–56.

28. This was already emphasized by M. Pérez González, 'Les organisations internationales et le droit de la responsabilité', *RGDIP* 92 (1988): 63, at 69.

29. Bulletin on the Observance by United Nations Forces of International Humanitarian Law, reprinted in *Documents on the Laws of War*, eds A. Roberts and R. Guelff, 3rd edition (Oxford: Oxford University Press, 2000), 725.

30. See D. Shraga, 'The Secretary-General's Bulletin on the Observance by United Nations Forces of IHL: a Decade Later', *Israel Yearbook on Human Rights* 39 (2009): 357–377.

31. See J.-M. Henckaerts and L. Doswald-Beck, eds, *ICRC: Customary International Humanitarian Law*, Vol. I (Cambridge: Cambridge University Press, 2005), 497, Rule 139, 497.

32. Convention for the Protection of Cultural Property in the Event of Armed Conflict, 14 May 1954, Article 19(1).

33. Second Protocol to the Hague Convention of 1954 for the Protection of Cultural Property in the Event of Armed Conflict, 26 March 1999, Art 22.

34. Amended Protocol II to the Convention on Certain Conventional Weapons, 3 May 1996, Art 1(3).

35. However, there is also a practice of unilateral renunciation by armed groups of certain prohibited weapons; on the 'Deed of Commitment for Adherence to a Total Ban on Anti-Personnel Mines and for Cooperation in Mine Action', see S. Herr, 'Vom Regelbruch zu politischer Verantwortung. Die Anerkennung völkerrechtlicher Normen durch nichtstaatliche Gewaltakteure im Sudan', Peace Research Institute Frankfurt, Report No. 5/2010.

36. For a detailed discussion, see L. Zegveld, *The Accountability of Armed Opposition Groups in International Law* (Cambridge: Cambridge University Press, 2002), 14–18.

37. Instructive empirical materials are produced by C. Ewumbue-Monono, 'Respect for International Humanitarian Law by Armed Non-state Actors in Africa', *International Review of the Red Cross* 88, No. 864 (2006): 905, at 920–922.

38. ILC Report 2011, *supra* note 3.

39. In some rare instances, such groups have even established criminal courts, see S. Sivakumaran, 'Courts of Armed Opposition Groups', *JICJ* 7 (2009): 489–513.

40. International Committee of the Red Cross, *supra* note 31, 536, at 550.

41. Ibid., 536.

42. Ibid., 549.

43. See, e.g., C. Tomuschat, 'The Applicability of Human Rights Law to Insurgent Movements', in *Crisis Management and Humanitarian Protection. Festschrift für Dieter Fleck*, eds Horst Fischer et al. (Berlin: Berliner Wissenschafts-Verlag, 2004), 573–591.

44. See International Committee of the Red Cross, *supra* note 31, at Rule 150, 549 *et seq.*

45. But see Articles 3, 13, 32.

46. The main advocate of this reading of Article 3 of Hague Convention IV is Kalshoven, *supra* note 12, *passim*. He has defended his views in two later opinions submitted to Japanese courts in the case of the comfort women: 'Individual Right to Claim Damages under Article 3 of Hague Convention IV: Expert Opinion, 1997', *supra* note 12, 631, at 634; idem, 'Individual Right to Claim Damages under Article 3 of Hague Convention IV: Supplementary Expert Opinion, 1999', ibid., 651, *passim*. Other writers distance themselves to some extent from Kalshoven, stating that his contentions are 'arguable', see Zegveld, *supra* note 36, 497, at 507; at 512 she speaks of 'the possibility of private rights to compensation'. C. Greenwood, 'International Humanitarian Law (Laws of War)', in *The Centennial of the First International Peace Conference*, ed. F. Kalshoven (The Hague: Kluwer Law International, 2000), 161, at 250, just refers to Kalshoven without taking a stance of his own.

47. The relevant texts are reproduced in the original French version by M. Frulli, 'When Are States Liable Towards Individuals for Serious Violations of Humanitarian Law? The Markovic Case', *IJCJ* 1 (2003): 406, at 417. For the English version, see *The Proceedings of the Hague Peace Conferences. The Conference of 1907. Acts and Documents, Vol. III* (New York: Oxford University Press, 1921), 139.

48. *The Proceedings of the Hague Peace Conferences. The Conference of 1907. Acts and Documents, Vol. III* (New York: Oxford University Press, 1921), at 142.

49. W.H. von Heinegg, 'Entschädigung für Verletzungen des humanitären Völkerrechts', *Berichte der Deutschen Gesellschaft für Völkerrecht* 40 (2003): 1, at 31 *et seq.* See also the careful assessment of the drafting history by the Tokyo District Court in the Judgment of 7 December 1963, *ILR* 32: 627; *JAIL* 8: 212, at 246.

50. See also d'Argent, *supra* note 16, at 784–786.

51. *Associazione Nazionale Reduci dalla Prigionia, dall'Internamento e dalla Guerra di Liberazione and 275 Others v. Germany*, ECtHR, Application No. 45563/04, decision as to the admissibility 4 September 2007: 'Whatever sufferings the applicants' forced labour brought about, none of the Conventions referred to by the applicants establishes any individual claims for compensation. When the Foundation Law entered into force there was no legal provision, whether of an international or of a domestic character, supporting the applicants' claims against the Federal Republic of Germany. Furthermore, the applicants have been unable to point to any case-law in their favour.'
52. UK Ministry of Defence, ed., *The Manual of the Law of Armed Conflict* (Oxford: Oxford University Press, 2004), 223, margin number 9.17.
53. Geneva Conventions I, Article 51; Geneva Conventions II, Article 52; Geneva Conventions III, Article 131; Geneva Conventions IV, Article 148.
54. See, e.g., J. Pictet, ed., *Commentary. IV Geneva Convention Relative to the Protection of Civilian Persons in Time of War* (Geneva: ICRC, 1958), 603.
55. Y. Sandoz et al., eds, *Commentary on the Additional Protocols of 8 June 1977 to the Geneva Conventions of 12 August 1949* (Geneva: Martinus Nijhoff/ICRC, 1987), 1056, margin number 3656.
56. Ibid., 1056, margin number 3657.
57. For a comprehensive overview see H.M. Holtzmann and E. Kristjánsdottir, eds, *International Mass Claims Processes: Legal and Practical Perspectives* (Oxford: Oxford University Press, 2007).
58. For a detailed commentary, see d'Argent, *supra* note 16, at 352–418; N. Wühler, 'The United Nations Compensation Commission', in *State Responsibility and the Individual: Reparation in Instances of Grave Violations of Human Rights*, eds A. Randelzhofer and C. Tomuschat (The Hague: Martinus Nijhoff, 1999), 213–229.
59. UN Doc. S/2000/1183, 13 December 2000.
60. For a summary account of the activity of the Claims Commission, which terminated its work in 2009, see the note produced by the Permanent Court of Arbitration, http://www.pca-cpa.org/showpage.asp?pag_id=1151 (accessed 10 February 2012).
61. See 'award of 19 December 2005', *ILM* 45 (2006): 396, at 412.
62. *Supra*, note 22, 198, para. 152.
63. Ibid., 202, para. 163 C.
64. A/RES/60/147, 16 December 2005.
65. For a critical comment on the Basic Principles and Guidelines on the Right to a Remedy and Reparation for Victims of Gross Violations of International Human Rights Law and Serious Violations of International Humanitarian Law (BPG) see, C. Tomuschat, 'Reparation in Favour of Individual Victims of Gross Violations of Human Rights and International Humanitarian Law', in *Promoting Justice, Human Rights and Conflict Resolution Through International Law*. Liber Amicorum *Lucius Caflisch*, ed. M.G. Kohen (Leiden: Martinus Nijhoff, 2007), 569–590; for a positive assessment, see T. Van Boven, 'Victims' Rights to a Remedy and Reparation: The United Nations Principles and Guidelines', in *Reparation for Victims of Genocide, War Crimes and Crimes against Humanity*, ed. C. Ferstman et al. (Leiden and Boston: Martinus Nijhoff, 2009), 19–40.
66. Of 4 May 2000, *ILR* 129: 514.
67. *Margellos* case, 17 September 2002, *ILR* 129: 526.
68. Of 11 March 2004, *Rivista di Diritto internazionale* 87 (2004): 539; *ILR* 128: 569.
69. See now the judgment of the ICJ in *Jurisdictional Immunities of the State* (Germany v. Italy: Greece Intervening), 3 February 2012.
70. Under Annex 7 to the Dayton Peace Agreement for Bosnia and Herzegovina, *ILM* 35 (1996): 136, a Commission for Real Property Claims of Refugees and Displaced Persons was set up, which settled successfully more than 200,000 claims for restitution, see R.C. Williams, 'Post-Conflict Property Restitution and Refugee Return in Bosnia and Herzegovina: Implications for International Standard-Setting and Procedure', *International Law and Politics* 37 2005): 441–553.
71. See, e.g., the World Summit Outcome, A/RES/60/1, 16 September 2005, paras 119–121, 138–139.
72. Of 11 May 1994, in force since 1 November 1998, CETS No. 155.
73. American Convention on Human Rights, Article 62. Of the 35 Member States of the Organization of American States, 23 have accepted the Convention and 21 have submitted to the jurisdiction of the Court.
74. Under Article 34(6) of the Protocol to the African Charter on Human and Peoples' Rights on the Establishment of an African Court on Human and Peoples' Rights, 1998, reproduced in *Basic Documents on Human Rights*, eds I. Brownlie and G.S. Goodwin-Gill, 4th edition (Oxford: Oxford University Press, 2002), 741, States can declare that they accept individual petitions to be considered

by the Court. Little is known about the number of such declarations. However, the African Commission has an impressive record of Decisions on Communications, see http://www.achpr.org/ english/_info/List_Decision_Communications.html (accessed 10 February 2012), and F. Viljoen, *International Human Rights Law in Africa* (Oxford: Oxford University Press, 2007), 319 *et seq.*

75. See C. Tomuschat, *Human Rights – Between Idealism and Realism*, 2nd edition (Oxford: Oxford University Press, 2008), 194–199.

76. Doc. EUCO 21/10, http://www.consilium.europa.eu/uedocs/cms_data/docs/pressdata/en/ec/116547.pdf (accessed 10 February 2012).

77. '1. A State or an international organization other than an injured State or international organization is entitled to invoke the responsibility of another international organization in accordance with paragraph 4 if the obligation breached is owed to a group of States or international organizations, including the State or organization that invokes responsibility, and is established for the protection of a collective interest of the group.
2. A State other than an injured State is entitled to invoke the responsibility of an international organization in accordance with paragraph 4 if the obligation breached is owed to the international community as a whole', Report of the ILC on its 61st session (2009), UN Doc. A/64/10, 19.

78. Thus, Ferstman et al., *supra* note 65, at 7, write in their introduction that the right to reparation already exists, and that currently the only question is what it entails.

79. *Supra* note 64.

80. '18. In accordance with domestic law and international law, and taking account of individual circumstances, victims of gross violations of international human rights law and serious violations of international humanitarian law should, as appropriate and proportional to the gravity of the violation and the circumstances of each case, be provided with full and effective reparation, as laid out in principles 19 to 23, which include the following forms: restitution, compensation, rehabilitation, satisfaction and guarantees of non-repetition.'

81. See J.I. Charney, 'Universal International Law', *AJIL* 87 (1993): 529, 538–542; P. Dumbarry, 'Incoherent and Ineffective: The Concept of Persistent Objector Revisited', *ICLQ* 59 (2010): 779–802; C. Tomuschat, 'Obligations Arising for States Without or Against Their Will', *Recueil des cours* 241 (1993-IV): 195, at 284–290.

82. But see Report of the Inter-American Commission on Human Rights in the case of *Domingues v. United States*, IACommHR, Case 12.285, Report No. 62/02, Merits, 22 October 2002, http:// www.cidh.org/annualrep/2002eng/USA.12285.htm, para. 48 (accessed 10 February 2012). However, the defence raised by the United States was eventually rejected since the Commission held the prohibition on executing minors to constitute *jus cogens*. On this case see L. Holning, 'Rethinking the Persistent Objector Doctrine in International Human Rights Law', *Chicago Journal of International Law* 6 (2005): 495–510.

83. See also the careful and cautious study by C.C. Guldahl, 'The Role of Persistent Objection in International Humanitarian Law', *Nordic Journal of International Law* 77 (2008): 51–86. Henckaerts and Doswald-Beck, the authors of the International Committee of the Red Cross study on customary IHL, avoid taking a stand on the issue, *supra* note 31, at xxxix.

84. 28 USC, para. 2680 (j).

85. 28 USC, para. 2680 (k).

86. *BGHZ*: 155, 279, English translation in *ILM* 42 (2003): 1030.

87. Ibid., 1039.

88. Federal Supreme Court, 2 November 2006, *Juristenzeitung* 62 (2007): 532. http://juris. bundesgerichtshof.de/cgi-bin/rechtsprechung/document.py?Gericht=bgh&Art=en&Datum=2006-11& Sort=1&nr=38105&pos=2&anz=288 (accessed 10 February 2012), with critical note by S. Baufeld, 'Die schadensersatzrechtliche Stellung ziviler Opfer von militärischen Operationen', ibid., 502–509. The Court of Appeals in Cologne, 28 July 2005, *Neue Juristische Wochenzeitschrift* (2005): 2861, at 2862 s., had previously argued that the denial of an individual reparation claim in instances of war operations could not be maintained under the auspices of the Basic Law, which had introduced a new philosophy based on human dignity. The case is currently pending before the Federal Constitutional Court.

89. Article 42(3): 'In no case shall reparation result in depriving the population of a State of its own means of subsistence', *YILC* (1996), Vol. II, Part 2: 63.

90. Famous is the *McCann* case, where notwithstanding a violation of the right to life any tangible pecuniary compensation was denied, *McCann v. United Kingdom*, ECtHT, Application No. 18984/91, Judgment of 27 September 1995, para. 219.

91. See *Kopecký v. Slovakia*, ECtHR, Application No. 44912/98, Judgment of 28 September 2004, paras 36–38; *von Maltzan and others v. Germany*, ECtHR, Application Nos 71916/01, 71917/01 and 102/60/02, Judgment of 2 March 2005, paras 110, 111: 'by choosing to make good injustices or damage resulting from acts committed at the instigation of a foreign occupying force or by another sovereign State, the German legislature had to make certain choices in the light of the public interest. In that connection, by enacting legislation governing issues of property and rehabilitation after German reunification, it had regard, among other things, to the concepts of "socially acceptable balance between conflicting interests," "legal certainty and clarity," "right of ownership" and "legal peace" contained in the Joint Declaration. Similarly, in examining the compatibility of that legislation with the Basic Law, the Federal Constitutional Court referred to the principles of "social justice and the rule of law" and that of the "prohibition of arbitrariness". As the Court has stated above ... where a State elects to redress the consequences of certain acts that are incompatible with the principles of a democratic regime but for which it is not responsible, it has a wide margin of appreciation in the implementation of that policy'; *Szal v. Poland*, ECtHR, Application No. 41285/02, Judgment of 18 May 2010, para. 26.

92. *Assanidze v. Georgia*, ECtHR, Application No. 71503/01, Judgment of 8 April 2004, operative part, para. 14(a); *Ilascu and others v. Moldova and Russia*, ECtHR, Application No. 48787/99, Judgment of 8 July 2004, operative part, para. 22; see also *Al-Sadoon and Mufdhi v. United Kingdom*, ECtHR, Application No. 61498/08, Judgment of 2 March 2010, para. 171 (not in the operative part).

93. *Velásquez Rodríguez v. Honduras*, IACtHR, Merits, Judgment of 29 July 1988, 21 July 1989, paras. 25, 26.

94. See, in particular, the case of *Myrna Mack Chang v. Guatemala*, IACtHR, Judgment of 25 November 2003.

95. See, e.g., the recent case of *Bohuslav Zavrel v. Czech Republic*, HRC, 27 July 2010 (UN Doc. CCPR/C/99/D/1615/2007), para. 12.

96. [2008/2009] Report of the Human Rights Committee, UN Doc. A/64/40, 125 *et seq.*, paras. 230 *et seq.*

97. Regarding Algeria, for instance, the Human Rights Committee has to date found ten violations. Algeria has not responded in a single case, ibid., 126.

98. *Factory at Chorzów*, *supra* note 4.

12. The quest for a non-conflictual coexistence of international human rights law and humanitarian law: which role for the *lex specialis* principle?

*Jean d'Aspremont and Elodie Tranchez**

1. INTRODUCTION

For a long time, international law suffered from a dearth of rules and was deemed particularly underdeveloped in some fields. Nowadays, in some areas, international law is beset by the exact opposite curse, that is, of being awash with 'too many rules'. The protection of individuals is very symptomatic of this phenomenon, for individuals now come under the protection of several sets of rules. Surely, overabundance is not better than a dearth of rules. In both situations, predictability as well as the Rule of Law are put at risk, as is the – equally fundamental – requirement of some elementary *effectivité*, without which there can hardly be a legal system properly so called.[1]

This chapter zeroes in on the simultaneous application of different sets of rules meant to ensure the protection of individuals, and, more particularly, on the frictions that may arise between International Humanitarian Law (hereafter IHL) and International Human Rights Law (hereafter HRL). For a long time such frictions have remained the object of debates exclusively restricted to academic circles when their respective scope of application was considered not to overlap. Yet, the articulation between HRL and IHL has nowadays turned into a matter of great controversy, especially following the unprecedented extension of the scope of application *ratione loci*, *ratione temporis* and *ratione materiae* of HRL, which came to embrace situations previously regulated by only IHL. Indeed, the existence of an armed conflict or hostilities, that is, the classical obstacle to the application of HRL in situations regulated by IHL, has ceased to preclude the application of HRL.[2] Likewise, it has become commonly accepted that States remain bound by HRL in their extra-territorial activities provided they exert an effective control of the territory or the institution concerned.[3] Originally conducted by human rights monitoring bodies, such an extension of the scope of application of HRL has been endorsed by the ICJ.[4] Stretching the ambit of HRL in this manner has added another layer of rules to the applicable IHL in situations of armed conflict, and it is now well recognized that 'the two systems have become increasingly permeable'.[5] The debates about the emergence of multi-layered protections of individuals have not only been the result of an academic craving for consistency and systematization,[6] they also arose out of a practical need for clarity on the legal regime applicable in situation of conflicts.[7]

It is in this context that this chapter seeks to appraise the tools to which international lawyers and judges have resorted to alleviate the frictions between IHL and HRL. After making the argument that the relationships between IHL and HRL should not be seen in terms of conflict but rather in terms of competition, the chapter provides some critical views on the principle *lex specialis non derogat generali*, which is so commonly used by international lawyers and judges when confronted with possible frictions between IHL and HRL and then revaluates its relevance in situations of competition of rules short of any real conflict.

2. INTERNATIONAL HUMANITARIAN LAW AND HUMAN RIGHTS LAW: OSCILLATING BETWEEN KINSHIP AND CONFLICT

After a few observations on the kinship between IHL and IHR (section 2.1), the following paragraphs examine the possibility of conflicting relationships between them (section 2.2) before concluding that it is through the concept of competition, rather than that of conflict, that the relationship between IHL and HRL must be envisaged (section 2.3).

2.1 A Long Ignored Kinship

It has become uncontested among international legal scholars that international humanitarian law and human rights law share some kinship as to their respective object and objectives,[8] Yet, despite their resemblance, these two branches of international law have long lived side by side ignoring one another.[9] It is no coincidence that the humanitarian dimension of IHL, notwithstanding its existence since the advent of the laws of wars – was long overlooked, for the emphasis was put on the protection of those engaged in hostilities *stricto sensu*. It is only since the radical reinforcement of its humanitarian aspect in the aftermath of the second World War – which brought about the embrace of a new denomination[10] – that the relationships between these two bodies of rules grew more apparent.[11] Nowadays, this kinship between IHL and HRL is not the source of much controversy and does not need to be further discussed.

2.2 IHL and HRL as Conflicting Sets of Norms?

For the sake of the argument made here, it is of the utmost relevance to note that, many legal experts construe the articulation between these two branches of international law along the lines of the principle *lex specialis derogat generali*. In a traditional conception of articulation between valid norms, the principles *lex superior derogat legi inferiori*, *lex specialis derogat generali* and *lex posterior derogat legi priori* are secondary rules found in most legal systems, domestic or international, and are used to resolve conflicting normative relationships. They have sometimes been construed as 'logical principles'.[12] While it is possible to raise serious doubts about the so-called 'logical' nature of these devices, their function is hardly disputed: they are meant to resolve relations of conflict between norms. This section focuses on the conflict of the norm-solving mechanism based on the *lex specialis* – the so-called *lex specialis derogat generali*, for it has constituted the traditional linchpin of the contemporary understanding by international judges and lawyers of the articulation between IHL and HRL (section 2.2.1). It will be explained here that the use of the principle *lex specialis derogat generali* presupposes that IHL and HRL are part of the same legal system and legal regime and that their rules conflict with one another (section 2.2.2). It will subsequently be demonstrated that not all these conditions are met in the case of the simultaneous application of IHL and HRL and that this finding must lead us to construe their articulation in terms of competition, rather than conflict (section 2.3).

2.2.1 The use of *lex specialis derogat generali* to articulate IHL and HRL

As has just been indicated, the great majority of international legal experts construe the articulation between IHL and HRL along the lines of the principle *lex specialis derogat generali*. In doing so, most of them concur with the International Court of Justice (hereafter the ICJ)'s use of that principle in its famous 1996 advisory opinion on *Legality of the Threat or Use of Nuclear Weapons*[13] and reiterated in its 2004 advisory opinion in the case of the *Legal Consequences of the Construction of a Wall in the Occupied Palestinian Territory*.[14] It is fair to say that both in case law and legal scholarship, the principle *lex specialis derogat generali* has been elevated to the cornerstone of the articulation of IHL and HRL.

In international law, the principle *lex specialis derogat generali*, inspired by similar mechanism in domestic legal systems,[15] has traditionally been construed as a mechanism to solve conflict of norms.[16] In that sense, the principle operates only after interpretation of the applicable rule has not been capable of solving a conflict between some of its rules.[17] In other words, it is only after the rules have been interpreted as conflicting that a law-applying authority will resort to the principle *lex specialis derogat generali*. By the same token, if the principle *lex specialis derogat generali* is understood as a mechanism for conflict of norms resolution, its application presupposes a conflict between two norms which deal with the same subject matter differently[18] and which provide for diverging standards of behavior.[19] Indeed, there can only be a conflict between two rules whose scopes of application (*ratione materiae, ratione loci, ratione temporis, ratione personae*) overlap in a given situation,[20] but which provide for diverging directives or standards.[21] Likewise, rules with a soft content (*soft negotium*) as well as rules of a soft nature (*soft instrumentum*)[22] cannot generate conflicts to which the principle would apply. In sum, for a conflict of norms to exist, the two rules must regulate the same subject matter and must do so differently, thereby creating diverging directives or standards. Such conditions will be further discussed below with respect to IHL and HRL (cf. section 2.2).

If applied, the principle *lex specialis derogat generali* will endow the rule considered more 'special' with a trumping effect over the rule considered more 'general'. Yet, this does not terminate the *lex generalis*, which does not cease to exist.[23] The application of that principle only allows the *lex specialis* to prevail over the *lex generalis* to the extent of the *lex specialis*.[24] This means that the *lex generalis* continues to apply as far as it does not contradict the *lex specialis*.[25]

The rationale of the principle *lex specialis derogat generali* is generally seen as multifold. Most of the time, the principle is upheld because special law is said to regulate the subject matter more effectively.[26] Alternatively, the priority bestowed upon the special rule is perceived to be more in line with the actual will of the parties.[27]

The application of the principle *lex specialis derogat generali* is not restricted to conflicts between conventional rules.[28] It equally applies to conflict between customary rules and treaty rules[29] or between two rules of customary law, as is illustrated by the famous decision of the ICJ in the *Case concerning the Right of Passage over Indian Territory*.[30] Even though the principle applies to conflicts of norms irrespective of their actual sources, it must be acknowledged that it is mostly in connection with conflict of norms between treaty law and customary law that the principle has been resorted to, thereby allowing the former to override the latter.[31] Such an application of the principle *lex specialis derogat generali* permeates numerous decisions of international tribunals, including the Iran-US Claims Tribunal[32] or the European Court of Human Rights.[33] For its part, the ICJ has repeatedly contended that customary international law only applies (and ought to be ascertained) as long as there is no conventional regime applicable between the parties.[34] In all these judgments, the principle *lex specialis derogat generali* was used to allow the rules of the treaty to prevail over custom. This traditional use of this principle to exclude the application of the contradictory commands of customary international law has led some authors to talk about an 'informal hierarchy' between the two.[35] It should, however, be made clear that the priority bestowed upon treaty law in these cases is not *directly* a consequence of its narrower scope of application *ratione personae*.[36] The trumping effect of treaty law through the principle of *lex specialis derogat generali* remains an attribute inherent in the special subject matter of the treaty, which often regulates a more specific situation, directed at a limited number of States.[37] This being said, it is important to point out that nothing precludes this principle equally from permitting customary law to prevail over treaty law. In other words, there is no reason why treaty law is necessarily *lex specialis* when it clashes with custom.[38] The opposite would mean that there is a hierarchy between treaty law and custom, a conclusion which is unanimously rejected by commentators. Which rule is to be considered *lex specialis* is a case-by-case matter of interpretation, for conventional rules are not, in principle, more special than customary law.

It will not come as a surprise that the determination of those rules that are to be elevated to a *lex specialis* remains the source of much controversy, not only as regards conflicts between treaty rules and customary rules, but also in connection to conflicts between customary rules, or conflicts between treaty rules themselves. As already alluded to, the special character of a rule – being customary or conventional – does not rest in it having a more limited numbers of addressees.[39] Yet, a more limited number of addressees of a rule often means that it regulates a more specific situation.[40] The special character of a rule also depends on the manner in which it regulates the subject matter at stake compared to the other applicable rule. It also seems uncontested that if the special character cannot be established *in abstracto* and hinges on the specific circumstances where the conflict arises, a determination *in concreto* can be carried out.[41]

The abovementioned examples show that the *lex specialis derogat generali* has most of the time been used to solve conflicts between contradictory primary norms of conducts enshrined either in treaty or customary law. Yet, the principle of *lex specialis derogat generali* does not purport to settle only conflicts of *primary* norms. It also allows a *secondary* norm seen as *lex specialis* to prevail over a more general one. This is well illustrated by the famous controversy that broke out between the ICJ and the ICTY regarding the standards of attribution in situations where non-State actors fall under the control of a foreign State.[42] The rebuke of the ICTY by the ICJ rested precisely in the attempt of the ICTY to revamp the general rule of attribution established by the ICJ.[43] Had the ICTY simply – and more modestly – contended that the standard that it uses constitutes a yardstick alien to any question of attribution, there would not have been any controversy.[44] The same would be true if the ICTY had contended that its standard boiled down to a special standard of attribution (*lex specialis*) for the sake of the law of armed conflicts or the criminal responsibility of individuals.

2.2.2 Appraising the application of a conflict of norms solving mechanism to IHL and HRL

The brief outline of the key features of the mainstream understanding of the principle *lex specialis non derogat generali* in the previous section shows that the application of that principle to situations of simultaneous applications of IHL and HRL presupposes that a number of conditions are met. The following paragraphs expound on three of them in particular, namely, membership of the same legal system (a), of the same legal regime (b), and, most importantly, the existence of a conflict of norms (c).

  (a) Prerequisite 1: Are IHL and HRL part of the same legal system? In the famous case *Union des étudiants Juifs de France v. Yahoo! Inc,*[45] a French judge decided that the Californian company *Yahoo!* had the obligation of banning from its website 'auctions' where it was possible to buy memorabilia of the Nazi period. The French decision has been globally criticized since such a ban, based on the French penal code article R.645-1 was said to conflict with the first Amendment of the US Constitution. Most authors considered that such a conflict between norms should have been resolved with the help of the famous device *lex superior derogat legi inferiori*, which functions in the same way as the *lex specialis* and *lex posterior* mechanisms. In that case, the hierarchically superior rule was supposed to trump the hierarchically inferior one; that is to say that the French judge should not have banned *Yahoo!* from welcoming sellers of Nazi literature onto its website – the first Amendment of the US constitution trumping the article R.645-1 of the French penal code. However, as Joost Pauwelyn and Ralf Michaels notably pointed out, 'such reasoning would be perfectly adequate if the conflict had arisen within one legal system, either between the French Constitution and a French Statute, or between the US Constitution and a US Statute'.[46] It is actually a matter of logic that normative relationships of specialty, hierarchy or time can only occur in a same system. That is to say that the conflict of two norms belonging to different systems, for instance one moral system and one legal system, or two legal systems but ultimately based on two different fundamental norms, could never be resolved with *lex superior, lex specialis* or *lex posterior*. As a consequence, examining IHL and HRL under the auspices the *lex specialis non derogat generali* principle presupposes that the two sets of norms belong to one united system.

  Interestingly, without much consideration, the International Law Commission assumed, considering the question of fragmentation of international law, that international law is a legal system.[47] Such an assertion is not without its problems. Indeed, in the age where 'legal pluralism' has become the new mantra,[48] it is more and more common to claim that the quest for legal unity in international law is vain.[49] Likewise, there are more and more observers challenging the presupposition of the systemic character of international law, underlining diversity and chaos in the international law legal system rather than its unity.[50] Surely, deconstructing the contemporary need for systemic unity can be carried out without much difficulty. Since the beginning of the history of thought, unity appeared as a myth, a metaphysical concept, built first as an intuition, by pre-Socratics such as Parmenides, then by Plato himself, deeply by neo-Platonists such as Plotin, and globally by Christian doctrine. Leibnitz, one of the last and most brilliant representatives of metaphysical thought, is famous for having said '*ce qui n'est pas véritablement* un *être, n'est pas non plus* véritablement *un* être'.[51] This was ultimately a very comforting feeling since the argument presupposed a *cosmos* – a global plan ('*le meilleur des mondes possible*' for Leibnitz) – that was the idea of one and only one being. In modern times, notably after the Copernican revolution in science, the argument was not conceivable anymore. Without doubt, this has been a very difficult turn for human thought, as witnessed by John Donne's verses: 'And new Philosophy calls all in doubt/ The Element of fire is quite put out;/ The Sunne is lost, and th'earth, and no mans wit/ Can well direct him where to looke for it … /'Tis all in pieces, all coherence gone;/All just supply, and all Relation.'[52] This corresponds to the discovery that hierarchical and harmonious relationships between elements do not exist *a priori*; as Gaston Bachelard used to say, order is not any more '*donné*' (given), it falls to scientists to create order and unity.

As a consequence, unity is neither an objective truth nor a reality. Eventually if unity exists, it can only be in the 'eye' of the observer. It is up to the observer to see *one* body or two legs, two arms, two feet, two hands … to see *one* army or one thousand soldiers, to see *one* hand or five fingers … It belongs to the observer to find or even create the objective links of causality[53] between elements in order to examine them jointly or separately, thus clearing away the hazard argument. This is eventually the definition of a system that can be raised: a united set from which elements constitute an order since elements are linked both to each other and to the set; so that it would be impossible to analyze each element separately.[54] The main task of the scientist is to establish that he or she is faced with one system when he or she can ascertain that elements interact upon each other and eventually result in one single final element: for instance, it is possible to talk about *one* body rather than two arms plus two legs … since finally, all elements are based on the same last element, the brain. This is the same with the illustration of *one* army; of course there are numerous stages of command, more or less autonomous, numerous entities (marine forces, air forces …) but, at least, the final decision belongs to one decisional body. Obviously, there can be objective systemic unities, as in the case of the human body, or 'conceptual' or 'social' systemic unities, as for instance *one* family, *one* married couple.

It would certainly be overly simplistic to conceive *in asbstracto* what a united system is and then to mechanically apply such a conception to international law. But there is probably no need to demonstrate the existence of international law as a united legal system. Indeed, analyzing international law as a system or not results in more of a methodological point rather than an objective fact. It is a question of choice;[55] it is possible to examine international law by searching out all its inconsistencies, proving chaos and disorder; or, on the contrary, it is possible to search for consistencies, order, and mutual links between elements of international law. One simply has to accept the relativity of that finding and its originating in a – more or less political[56] – choice. That it is relative and somewhat the outcome of a political choice does not prevent international lawyers from construing international law as a unitary system.

In the light of the above, and provided that we remain critical as to the relativity of our own construction, it is argued here that nothing precludes us from construing IHL and HRL as being part of the same legal system.

(b) Prerequisite 2: Are IHL and HRL part of the same legal regime? It should be made clear that unity does not *per se* exclude diversity. If international law can be analyzed as a united system, indubitably there is diversity within this one system. This is what the main part of the doctrine calls legal regimes. In that same perspective, and even if analogies with domestic law are generally fruitless, it seems that an analogy with a 'federal' structure could be pertinent to the extent of its explanatory virtues. The federal law system, in as much as we can compare it to international law, contains the secondary norms of organization, which could be seen as the game's rules. *A contrario* 'federative entities of international law', that is to say international legal regimes, would keep the residual liberty of organizing primary rules of behavior. It is clear that the model must be adapted to apply to the international law system, taking into account the numerous specificities of the latter.[57] If territorial space cannot obviously be the basis of these international federative entities, no doubt the basis could be axiological. It is now quite common to read about the 'secessionist' attempts of the sub-entities through the concept of 'self-contained regimes'. Most of the time, these 'secessionist pretentions' are supposed to illustrate the loss or, worse, the original absence of international law unity. However, rarely can we read about the 'pretention's' origins. The totally uncontrolled creation of primary norms after World War II produced, and still yields, a worrying phenomenon of 'non-absorption'. Of course, or at least, it is better to hope that the intention behind this increasing proliferation was ultimately human development through international law. Yet, the secondary norms of the central system – that is the federal system to pursue the abovementioned federal analogy – were and are still not able to absorb this primary norms abundance, thus forcing 'federative entities' to fill the gaps and to create their own secondary norms.

Obviously, the abovementioned phenomenon creates real issues concerning the conflict or competition resolution of norms belonging to different special legal regimes. In that case, the tools to resolve the competition or conflict between valid norms can definitely not anymore be the *lex superior, lex posterior* or *lex specialis* mechanisms. Even if the two norms belong to the same central or 'federal' system, the question raised is more that of a conflict of laws.[58] Then methods to resolve a conflict of laws, even within a same general system, cannot be based on the idea that one norm should trump another one, since, at least, this would lead to one legal regime trumping another one, which is just unthinkable in international law.

As a consequence thereof, the main question to be asked is: do IHL and HRL belong to the same sub-system, to the same special legal regime? On that point, a general consensus has appeared to emerge in doctrine over recent years recognizing the axiological congruence between IHL and HRL. Thus, as was already alluded to above, a general agreement on the idea that IHL and HRL belong to the same sub-system can be found without too many difficulties. Once again, the fact that the international judges interpret the IHL and HRL articulation issue under the auspices of the *lex specialis* paradigm seems to constitute another and convincing underpinning.

But this surely is not sufficient. More is needed to butress that contention. This is why it is interesting to recall that, with respect to one of the most famous HRL instruments, that is, the ICCPR, not a single State, intervening extra-territorially, 'has indicated, by making a derogation from those rights as provided for under Article 4 of the Covenant, a belief that its actions abroad constituted an exercise of jurisdiction under the Covenant. All derogations under Article 4 have been introduced with respect to internal laws only'.[59] Further, States asked by the HRC to provide information about their extra-territorial interventions did not hesitate to challenge the HRC view. In the context of NATO's intervention in ex-Yugoslavia, the USA declared that the 'Covenant was not regarded as having extraterritorial application' because of the 'dual requirement' of Article 2(1);[60] the Netherlands replied that

> [the] Government disagree[d] with the Committee's suggestion that the provisions of the International Covenant on Civil and Political Rights are applicable to the conduct of Dutch blue helmets in Srebrenica. Article 2 of the Covenant clearly states that each State Party undertakes to respect and to ensure to all individuals 'within its territory and subject to its jurisdiction' the rights recognized in the Covenant, including the right to life enshrined in article 6. It goes without saying that the citizens of Srebrenica, vis-à-vis the Netherlands, do not come within the scope of that provision.[61]

It is not unreasonable to interpret the foregoing as meaning that States tend to favor the option of IHL and HRL as two separate sub-systems, despite their similar axiological roots.

Some other insights could be found in the 1977 Protocols. Indeed, the Additional Protocols contain some of the ICCPR derogable or non derogable rights, while excluding some of them, and some of their special guarantees anticipated in the Covenant. If IHL and HRL are part of one and the same sub-system, it would make no sense to repeat the HRL norms or to exclude some of the fundamental guaranties of HRL. In that sense, it is fair to say that 'the adoption of the two 1977 Protocols additional to the Geneva Conventions is a proof that a separate set of rules for armed conflict is in fact what States want'.[62]

In the light of the above, it can be argued that, despite them sharing some deep axiological roots, IHL and HRL could still be construed as separate sub-systems. However, pursuing the international law analogy previously used as a federal structure – only to the extent of its explanatory virtues – if the 'sub-system HRL' had to develop its own secondary norms because of the primary norms explosion, the 'sub-system IHL' did not witness this phenomenon, remaining a sub-system of primary norms, thus depending on general/federal system secondary norms and on the general/federal judge's protection. One of the main advantages of HRL is indubitably the fact of its benefiting its own judge, whose jurisdiction is often mandatory. It is interesting to note that those judges would generally estimate that IHL and HRL belong the same regime,[63] in contrast to States which, as was indicated earlier, traditionally deem that IHL and HRL are separate. The debate surely remains open-ended, and it would be of no avail to try to settle it here. Yet, the previous paragraphs have tried to show that membership of the same regime is another prerequisite for a possible conflict arising between IHL and HRL.

(c) *Prerequisite 3: Are IHL and HRL in conflict?* As far as the international legal system is concerned, its special nature, highly decentralized character and under-developed hierarchical configuration, has led a great part of the international legal scholarship to embrace a presumption of non-conflict between international legal rules. Such a position was partly premised on the idea that recognizing the existence of too many conflicts of norms could jeopardize the consistency of the system. Such a finding could possibly be lethal to the international legal system itself, for coherence has often been understood as an ontological condition of any system. Such a presumption – whose virtues cannot be denied – nonetheless brings about a very strict and narrow definition of what we should identify as a situation of conflict of norms.

To illustrate this scholarly aversion to conflicts of norms, it suffices here to recall Professor Jenks's famous paper, presented in 1953, in which he shed light on the condition of direct incompatibility between norms, and, as a consequence, on the impossibility for parties to comply with the obligation under both norms to ascertain the existence of a conflict of norms.[64] The influence of this traditional conception remains rife among many scholars' understanding of problems of conflicts.[65] It is also noteworthy that such a position seemed to have been espoused by some international judicial bodies. For instance one of the WTO panels developed the idea that 'in international law for a conflict to exist between two treaties [their] provisions must conflict, in the sense that the provisions must impose mutually exclusive obligations ... Technically speaking, there is conflict when two [or more] treaty instruments contain obligations which cannot be complied with simultaneously.'[66]

This very narrow understanding of conflict of norms somehow finds its roots in deontic logic, which, tries to conceptualize normative articulation in terms of logical relationships, and to develop a formal and representative language of norms. Norms are supposed to be modalized in formulas; while it is not really useful here to describe all the 'symbols' used to conceptualize norms in deontic logic,[67] it is important to clarify the main points.[68] Norms are expressed with mainly four elements. A first variable is supposed to represent the recipient of the norm, then there is one deontic operator that permits the expression of the normative function (O for the notion of *ought* and P for the notion of *may*), then one connective that indicates the normative function (for instance '¬' to express the negation, or '&' to express the addition), and finally, one last variable that expresses the action required. For instance, the norm 'Simon has to close the windows and the door' would be expressed as follows in terms of deontic logic: 's O (p & r)' and inversely, 's O ¬ (p & r)' would means 'Simon should not close the windows and the door'. The main goal of deontic logic is to discover normative *lacunae* and normative inconsistencies, transforming norms in terms of abstract sentences in order to discover their feasible character. In terms of logic, in a same valid system, both the norms 's O p' and 's O ¬ p' cannot simultaneously exist; in this very abstract construction, the two norms are deemed to be conflicting, since with the exact same variables (recipient and action required), the results of the implementation of the norm cannot be simultaneously true: the door cannot be at the same time opened and closed. As a consequence, the norms 's O p' and 's O ¬ q' are not deemed to be conflicting since the objects of the commandment are not the same. Thus deontic logic is used to discover contradiction between norms.

This is ultimately the exact position supported by Gabrielle Marceau – one of the leading proponents of a narrow and classical approach to the conflict of norms – who argues that three main conditions should be present in order to identify a conflict of norms: 'first, two States must be bound by two different treaties, or two different obligations. Second, the treaties (or the obligations) must cover the same substantive subject matter. Third the provisions must conflict, in the sense that the provisions must impose mutually exclusive obligations.'[69] In that sense, hypotheses of conflicting norms are quite rare in all legal systems, especially as this strict approach is also based on the idea that only prescriptive norms could conflict.

It can hardly be disputed that two permissive norms can conflict,[70] since, in such a situation, the legislator has not clearly indicated their preference for a particular behavior and the norms do not provide for contradictory directives of behavior. While it is not possible to deny the impossibility of conflicting relationships between permissive norms, it is quite doubtful to claim that no conflict could occur between prescriptive norms and permissive norms, since eventually it would lead to a nonsense, denying the existence and the effect of the permissive norm.[71]

In this context, it can be concluded that IHL and HRL cannot, strictly speaking, be construed as being in conflict.

2.3 IHL and HRL as Competing Sets of Norms?

The common use of the principle *lex specialis non derogat generali* witnessed in case law and international legal scholarship thus conveys the idea that IHL and HRL are conflicting sets of rules. If we espouse the very narrow definition of conflict of norms defended here (cf. *supra* section 2.1), it can be concluded that IHL and HRL hardly conflict. Although such frictions are not as likely as is sometimes contended,[72] there certainly are *a priori* tensions between IHL and HRL in connection to arbitrary deprivation of life, detention in situations of conflict, protection of privacy under occupation[73] or medical experimentation.[74] However, direct and strict conflicts between IHL and HRL norms hardly exist. Indeed, as was explained above, there can be no conflict of norms short of direct and strict incompatibilities. There is no such direct incompatibility between prescriptive and permissive norms.[75] It is predominantly so in the case of IHL and HRL. If we focus on the often discussed issue of the right to life, in that case IHL and HRL are not conflicting sets of norms since only HRL imposes obligations: IHL does not prescribe killing, it 'just' permits the fact of killing in time of wars.

It is argued here that IHL and HRL should be seen as competitive sets of norms rather than conflicting sets of norms. After a few general observations on the concept of competition of norms (section 2.3.1), the follow paragraphs elaborate on the specific competition between IHL and HRL (section 2.3.2)

2.3.1 The concept of competition of norms

With a view to capturing the concept of competition of norms, it is not irrelevant to start (again) with a – slightly mundane – analogy of a believer and an atheist. If one takes the two hypothetic norms 'all men have to be believers' and 'all men have to be atheists', obviously, there is a conflict of norms since one and the same person cannot simultaneously be both. But it is also possible to witness situations in which there is not necessarily a conflict. If the hypothetic norms are the following: 'all men have to be believers'/'all men have to be agnostic', the two norms are not necessarily in a situation of conflict, since the fact of being agnostic could be, but is not necessarily, opposite to the fact of being a believer. Eventually, we can face situations that would not be qualified as conflict in terms of deontic logic or in the light of the strict approach of the conflict of norms. If the two hypothetic norms are 'all men have to be Christian' and 'all men have to be Muslim', strictly speaking, the two norms are not clashing since, contrary to the instance of a believer and an atheist, being Muslim is not the contrary of being Christian. But eventually, except if we accept the fact of creating a new religion mixing Islam and Christianity, one and the same person cannot be both Muslim and Christian: thus strictly speaking, the two norms are not 'clashing' or 'conflicting', but lead to divergence and, at the end of the day, it appears necessary to choose which one of the two norms should prevail. We can call this a situation of competition of norms: two norms or normative sets are supposed to apply to the same situations and the same recipients, leading to diverging positions.

It is true that the question of competition of norms could seem far less anxiogenic than the one of conflict of norms, since competition of norms does not strictly underline the logical inconsistency of the system as conflicts of norms do. However, at the end of the day, it remains a serious issue, and analyzing normative relationships in terms of logic, as the partisans of the strict approach to conflict of norms mentioned above do, could be appealing in theory but quite fruitless in practice. This is why it is argued here that highlighting normative relationships under the concept of competition of norms, that is to vindicate a larger conception of conflict of norms, is far more useful, for it permits us to embrace situations of real contradictions between norms (that correspond to a narrow approach of conflict of norms), situations of potential conflict between prescriptive and permissive norms, but also cases of norms pointing in different directions without being necessarily conflicting. This is what the following section will try to demonstrate.

2.3.2   The actual competition between IHL and IHR

As was explained above (cf. *supra* section 2.1), the scopes of HRL and IHL are now competing *ratione loci, ratione personae* and *ratione temporis*. *Ratione loci* since from now HRL is not held to bind States only in their territory but also in territories which come under their effective control; *ratione temporis* since HRL is no longer confined to times of peace but also extends to times of war; and *ratione personae* as a result of the application of HRL to intrastate conflict situations. In this context, following the conception of competition of norms that has just been spelled out, we are of the opinion that IHL and HRL should nowadays be seen as competing set of norms rather than conflicting ones. Despite some – incrementally diminishing – divergences as to their scope of application *ratione materiae, ratione loci, ratione temporis* and *ratione personae*, IHL and HRL are primarily meant to protect a similar 'object', that is a human being. It is against the backdrop of this competition that the use of the *lex specialis* principles must now be evaluated.

3. REGULATING THE COMPETITION BETWEEN IHL AND IHR: WHICH USE FOR THE PRINCIPLE OF *LEX SPECIALIS NO DEROGAT GENERALI*?

If the relation between IHL and HRL is to be seen as one of competition rather than conflict, as we have argued in the above, one may wonder what role the principle of *lex specialis no derogat generali* is then to play, if it is not as a conflict of norms solving principle. This question is of particular relevance since, as was explained above (cf. *supra* 2.2.1), international legal scholars and judges, confronted with possible frictions between IHL and HRL, have been inclined to resort to the principle of *lex specialis derogat generali*.

Surely, the conflict of norms solving effect of the principle of *lex specialis derogat generali* is not the exclusive understanding of this principle. This is why this section starts by outlining some of the understandings of the principle *lex specialis derogat generali* which depart from its conflict of norms solving role as depicted above and focuses more particularly on one of its alternative roles – that employed by the ICJ, according to which the principle *lex specialis derogat generali* is a tool that helps calibrate the systemic integration of IHL and HRL. After exposing this very specific use of the principle of *lex specialis derogat generali*, this section will question this alternative understanding for rules like IHL and HRL which are not, as was demonstrated in the above, in conflict but in competition.

3.1 Alternative Conceptions of the Principle *Lex Specialis No Derogat Generali*: from Conflict Solving Back to Norm Interpretation

The understanding of the principle *lex specialis derogat generali* that has been spelled out in section 2.2.1 corresponds with its traditional conceptualization in the legal scholarship as a mechanism to solve conflict of norms. Nonetheless, the principle *lex specialis derogat generali* is occasionally construed in the literature, not as a conflict of norms solving mechanism, but, rather, as a principle of interpretation.[76] Mention must be made of the dominant understanding of the principle in the case law of the European Court of Human Rights. It is interesting to note that the ECHR has most commonly[77] referred to the concept of *lex specialis* with a view to restricting the provisions of the Convention on the basis of which it ought to appraise the conformity therewith of a given act or behavior. In that sense, the concept of *lex specialis* has been resorted to by the European Court as a tool to select *within the Convention* which provisions ought to be the yardstick to appraise the conformity with the Convention of the act or behavior submitted to it.[78]

This chapter is however not concerned with this alternative understanding of the principle *lex specialis derogat generali*, for it seems to be restricted to the ECHR legal order. Rather, it is another conception that will draw the attention here and whose relevance will be tested against the backdrop of the competition between IHL and HRL. The following paragraphs zero in on the use of the principle of *lex specialis derogat generali* as a principle of interpretation rather than conflict of norm solving mechanism with a view to evaluating whether such a conception makes sense in situations of competition of norms.

The use of the principle of *lex specialis derogat generali* as a principle of interpretation is not entirely outlandish. This was mentioned by the ILC, in its report over fragmentation[79] and had also been briefly envisaged during the work of the ILC on the Law of Treaties, but did not find its way into the final text.[80] Yet, this remains a very peculiar understanding of this principle, for, according to the mainstream conception presented above (cf. *supra* 2.2.1) the principle *lex specialis derogat generali* is meant to operate only after interpretation of the applicable rule has not been capable of solving a conflict between some its rules.[81] According to the understanding discussed in this section, the principle is turned into a principle operating at the level of interpretation, that is at a moment where conflicts of norms have not been unearthed, thereby making such a conception of particular relevance for situations of competition of norms.

This section exclusively focuses on the use of the principle *lex specialis derogat generali* to articulate HRL and IHL as a principle of interpretation of international law to calibrate another principle of interpretation of international law, that is the principle of systemic integration. Such a conception permeates the case law of the ICJ and most authors' accounts of the problems of articulation between IHL and HRL. Exposing this specific use of the principle *lex specialis derogat generali* necessitates a few preliminary reminders. This is why this section starts by a brief overview of the principle of interpretation of systemic integration (section 3.1.1). This will subsequently help to show how, in the case of the simultaneous application of IHL and IHL, the principle *lex specialis derogat generali* has been applied, especially by the ICJ to calibrate the systemic integration of international law (section 3.1.2).

3.1.1 The principle of interpretation of systemic integration: a sketch

Interpretation is the very first technique to which an international judge can resort in order to ensure the consistency of the rules which it applies.[82] Although 'it is a fallacy to assume that the existence of [rules of interpretation of international law] is a secure safeguard against arbitrariness and impartiality'[83] because interpretation of law continues to take place in a context to which judges are not completely insensitive,[84] the Vienna Convention on the Law of Treaties[85] has attempted to formalize interpretation of international legal rules by devising principles of interpretation of international law which international judges – and domestic judges[86] – ought to make use of when they apply international law. In particular, Article 31 (3) (c) of the Vienna Convention on the Law of Treaties – which had grown more ambitious than the principle of contemporaneity to which it was originally equated[87] – provides for an interpretation of treaties in which 'any relevant rules of international law applicable in relations between the parties' must be 'taken into account'. Interestingly, among the principles designed by the Vienna Convention on the Law of Treaties, this principle of systemic integration is probably the one that has recently attracted the most attention.[88]

The principle of systemic integration finally enshrined in the Vienna Convention is premised on the *fiction* that, despite international lawmaking being fragmented and decentralized, any new rule has been made with the awareness of other existing rules. In that sense, the principle of systemic integration presupposes the formal unity of the legal system.[89] The principle of systemic integration accordingly prescribes that a treaty be interpreted by reference to its 'normative environment', which includes all sources of international law. That means that when several norms bear on a single issue they should, to the greatest extent possible, be interpreted so as to give rise to a single set of compatible obligations.

If this principle is so construed, its application undoubtedly turns delicate. It requires that the status of the 'normative environment' of the norm be clarified, and that the status of rule to which it is referred – especially its character of *lex lata*[90] – be established. It is only after the scope and the applicability of this other rule of international law are properly ascertained that it can be 'taken into account' in the interpretation of the rule being interpreted. In this context, it should not come as a surprise that the principle of systemic integration leaves great room for maneuver to law-applying bodies and interpreters, as it behooves them to determine the normative environment of the interpreted norm, and in particular, its center of gravity.[91]

Because of this leeway left to the law-applying body or the interpreter, systemic integration of international law can yield very diverging interpretative outcomes. Among the various interpretations that can be achieved through systemic integration, there may well be – as one of these authors explained elsewhere[92] – interpretations that do provide a restrictive conception of international law. In other words, interconnections between international rules which are called upon by the principle of systemic integration can potentially provide very restrictive readings of them.[93] The practice of international tribunals does not offer any such example but such a use of the principle of systemic integration is utterly conceivable.[94] And even if it is used in a manner favorable to the greater development of international law, there are various degrees of integration that can be achieved through the principle of systemic integration. A whole range of integrationist uses of the principle can also be envisaged. In particular, the extent to which the principle of systemic integration can be used to reinforce the integration of the international legal order can go as far as the promotion of an international legal order endowed with all the features of a constitutional order that rests on hierarchy in procedures and substantive standards.[95] In that sense, the principle of systemic integration can be wielded as a tool that enhances not only the formal but also the substantive unity of international law.[96]

Interestingly, this difficulty in applying consistently the principle of systemic integration has been amplified by international judges themselves. In particular, it is noteworthy that the use of that principle that was made by the ICJ has not helped clarify, not only what the 'normative environment' of a rule is but also what 'taken into account' really means. In what probably constitutes one of the least convincing decisions of the ICJ from the standpoint of legal logic, the principle of systemic integration was expressly relied upon by the Court for the very first time in its decision in the *Oil Platform* case. On that occasion, the Court resorted to Article 31 (3) (c) to apply general rules of international law, including rules pertaining to the use of force, to examine whether the measures taken by the United States were necessary under the Treaty of Navigation and Commerce on the basis of which the Court had jurisdiction.[97] In that particular case, the principle of systemic integration allowed the Court to extend its jurisdiction *ratione materiae* in order to judge the behavior of the United States in the light of rules for which the Court, strictly speaking, had no jurisdiction. It is not surprising that the decision of the Court stirred some unease, not only among legal scholars,[98] but also among judges themselves.[99] This 'bold use'[100] of the principle of systemic integration led the Court to change the applicable law.[101] It proved a makeshift tool to create an opportunity for the Court to say a word about the use of force in the Gulf. It can reasonably be contended that the principle of systemic integration cannot go as far as displacing the applicable law. 'Taking into account' other rules of international law applicable between the parties does not mean that the 'normative environment' of the rule being interpreted can displace the latter, especially before a judge who does not have jurisdiction regarding the former. This decision of the ICJ has certainly fuelled some suspicions as to the possible praetorial manipulations to which the rule enshrined in Article 31 (3) (c) of the Vienna Convention can be subject. The more reasonable use of Article 31 (3) (c) in the case *Djibouti v. France*[102] has done little to expunge this suspect use of that provision in the *Oil Platform* case. Leaving these cases aside, the case-law of the Court pertaining to Article 31 (3) (c) remains difficult to evaluate, for the Court has not always been willing to expressly invoke that principle while carrying out an interpretation of the same nature. For instance, the Court impliedly applied a principle of systemic integration in its *Namibia* advisory opinion where it deemed that 'an international instrument has to be interpreted and applied within the framework of the entire legal system prevailing at the time of the interpretation'.[103] Yet, it is difficult to infer any clear lesson from it in the absence of express reference to the principle.

The ICJ is obviously not the only international judicial body to have resorted to the principle of systemic integration. The principle has also been expressly referred to by regional courts[104] or by international Arbitral tribunals – as is illustrated by the 2005 arbitral award in the Iron Rhine Railway (*Ijzeren Rijn*).[105] The WTO appellate body also applied it in the *EC – Measures Affecting the Approval and Marketing of Biotech Products*.[106] While a wide variety of international and regional tribunals have thus made use of the principle of systemic integration, it is worthy of mention that in all these cases, the normative environment upon which interpretation has been based according to the principle of systemic integration has not always been construed in the same manner, especially regarding the similarity that must exist between the respective memberships to the two instruments at stake.[107] In the same vein, it is also interesting to note that some of these judicial bodies have been seesawing between different uses of the principle of systemic integration.

It is ultimately interesting to note that the International Law Commission as well as a significant number of scholars have recently come to appreciate the 'anti-fragmenting potential' of the principle of systemic integration – which, despite its use by international courts, had long remained in oblivion[108] – and, as a result, endowed that principle with an almost constitutionalist character.[109] This understanding of the principle directly stems from its abovementioned use to promote a greater integration of the international legal order and shore up the substantive unity of the latter. This surely is not the place to delve into the debate about the place of the principle of systemic integration in the international legal order as a whole and its possible constitutional qualities.[110] The matter is far too controversial to be taken on here.[111] It only matters, in this context, that, whatever its ultimate nature, the principle of systemic integration primarily boils down to a useful and handy interpretative tool. It is therefore no surprise that it has been resorted to by international judicial bodies, and especially by the ICJ when confronted with situations of simultaneous application of HRL and IHL. Yet, as is explained in the following section, the ICJ has deemed it necessary to wield that principle of interpretation on the basis – and behind the veil – of the principle *lex specialis derogat generali*, remolded, for the occasion, on a principle of interpretation.

3.1.2 The ICJ: calibrating systemic integration of international law through the principle *lex specialis derogat generali*

In this section, it is argued that legal experts and judges, confronted with problems of simultaneous application of IHL and HRL and resorting to the *lex specialis derogat generali* do not actually articulate HRL and IHL along the lines of that principle, but rather engage in a *systemic integration* of these two sets of rules. More specifically, it is submitted here that, under the guise of the principle *lex specialis derogat generali*, most judges and experts apply a principle of interpretation of international law, that is the principle of systemic integration of international law. The ambition of this chapter is accordingly to shed some light on the actual manner in which HRL and IHL have been articulated, and dispel the impressions that are conveyed by the professed use of conflict resolution mechanisms.

Nothing is more illustrative than the ICJ's take on that matter. Indeed, the Court, when confronted with questions of articulation between IHL and HRL in an interpretation of the protection of the rights of individuals that reconciles human rights law and international humanitarian law,[112] resorted to the principle of *lex specialis* less to solve a conflict of norms than to determine the norm of reference of the normative environment of the obligations at stake.[113] Although oft-quoted, the famous passages where the Court expressed its position are worthy of reproduction.

In its 1996 advisory opinion on the Legality of the threat or use of Nuclear Weapons, the Court expressed its opinion for the very first time:

> The Court observes that the protection of the International Covenant of Civil and Political Rights does not cease in times of war, except by operation of Article 4 of the Covenant whereby certain provisions may be derogated from in a time of national emergency. Respect for the right to life is not, however, such a provision. In principle, the right not arbitrarily to be deprived of one's life applies also in hostilities. The test of what is an arbitrary deprivation of life, however, then falls to be determined by the applicable *lex specialis*, namely, the law applicable in armed conflict which is designed to regulate the conduct of hostilities. Thus whether a particular loss of life, through the use of a certain weapon in warfare, is to be considered an arbitrary deprivation of life contrary to Article 6 of the Covenant, can only be decided by reference to the law applicable in armed conflict and not deduced from the terms of the Covenant itself.[114]

In its 2004 advisory opinion on the *Legal Consequences of the Construction of a Wall in the Occupied Palestinian Territory*, after recalling its finding in its abovementioned 1996 advisory opinion, the Court stated that:

> The Court considers that the protection offered by human rights conventions does not cease in case of armed conflict, Save through the effect of provisions for derogation of the kind to be found in Article 4 of the International Covenant on Civil and Political Rights. As regards

the relationship between international humanitarian law and human rights law, there are thus three possible situations: some rights may be exclusively matters of international human-itarian law; others may be exclusively matters of human rights law; yet others may be matters of both these branches of international law. In order to answer the question put to it, the Court will have to take into consideration both these branches of international law, namely human rights law and, as *lex specialis*, international humanitarian law.[115]

The abovementioned passages usefully show that the Court, confronted with the simultaneous application of HRL and IHL, engaged in a *conciliatory interpretation* of the two sets of rules. That means that the Court, by endorsing an interpretation that reconciles them, stopped short of finding a conflict of norms which would have called for the application of a conflict of norms solving mechanism. In other words, the Court did not make one set of rules prevail over the other – that is settling a conflict of rules – but carried out an interpretation that prevents a conflict between them to arise. Yet, the Court referred to the principle *lex specialis derogat generali* which, as was explained above, is classically a conflict of norms solving principle. This use of the principle of *lex specialis derogat generali* by the Court was, however, not meant to solve a conflict of norms – for there was none, given the conciliatory interpretation in which the Court engaged – but rather to elect which rules should constitute the primary interpretative standard.

The conciliatory interpretation on which the Court embarked is clearly reminiscent of the principle of systemic integration. The Court interpreted one set of rules in the light of another sets of rules with a view to harmonizing the possible contradictory commands that each of them could provide for. More precisely, the Court, when interpreting HRL, took into account IHL as a set of 'relevant rules of international law applicable in the relations between the parties' in accordance with Article 31 (3) (c) of the Vienna Convention on the Law of Treaties – whose application, as has been explained above, is not restricted to the rules of treaties. The Court's interpretation of the applicable law was thus meant to harmonize HRL and IHL to the extent prescribed by the principle of systemic integration.

It is important to point out that the Court, when confronted with the simultaneous applications of IHL and HRL, can, as a matter of principle, operate a conciliatory interpretation by interpreting each of them in the light of the other. In other words, the interpretative standard of its conciliatory interpretation could be either IHL or HRL. As the abovementioned paragraphs show, it is IHL which constituted the standard of reference for the conciliatory interpretation carried out by the Court. The Court thus chose IHL, instead of HRL, as being the primary interpretative standard, on the basis of which to carry out its conciliatory interpretation.

The choice between IHL and HRL as the interpretative standard for the sake of systemic integration is precisely the point where the principle *lex specialis derogat generali* comes into play. Indeed, it is that principle on which the Court relied to determine whether IHL or HRL is the standard of reference of its conciliatory interpretation. As is demonstrated by the abovementioned paragraphs, IHL was considered by the ICJ as having an object that makes it the *lex specialis*, HRL being seen as a set of rules of a more general application. According to the Court's reasoning, the 'speciality' of IHL stems from its application being restricted to situations of conflict, and its object being the regulation of the conduct of hostilities.[116]

Because it elected IHL as the *lex specialis*, the Court interpreted applicable HRL in the light of IHL. This means that the Court used IHL to redraw the contours of the obligations enshrined in HRL and provide an interpretation of HRL rules which dovetails with IHL rules. Such a systemic integration of HRL and IHL that rests on the latter being the primary standard of reference has been portrayed as a *humanitarization* of human rights[117] because it leads to an interpretation of HRL on the basis of IHL which is elevated in the primary interpretative standard. The ICJ certainly is not the only judicial body which carried out such a humanitarization of HRL. Confronted with the application of HRL in situations of conflict, human rights monitoring bodies have not balked at interpreting human rights for which they have jurisdiction in the light of IHL. This is, for instance, the case in the European Court of Human Rights,[118] the Inter-American Court of Human Rights[119] or the Human Rights Committee.[120]

Yet, as was said above, the ICJ could well have decided to carry out its conciliatory interpretation of IHL and HRL the other way around in electing HRL as the primary interpretative standard on the basis of which IHL ought to be interpreted. This opposite conciliatory interpretation – which corresponds to a *humanization* of humanitarian law – is not unknown in the practice. Indeed, the international case law also witnesses a tendency by some judges to interpret IHL in the light of HRL, thereby carrying out a systemic integration of HRL and IHL that rests on the former being the primary standard of reference. This is well illustrated by some famous – and sometimes controversial – judgments of the International Tribunal for the Former Yugoslavia[121] or the American Commission of Human Rights.[122] This humanization of IHL – that is a systemic integration of HRL and IHL on the basis of the former – is certainly not idiosyncratic given the uncontested kinship between IHL and HRL.[123]

International case law thus shows interesting oscillations between IHL and HRL as the central interpretative standards in cases of attempted conciliatory interpretations of two different sets of rules. It is true that these oscillations may simply be the result of institutional constraints, including the restrictions pertaining to the law applicable by the judicial body concerned. These oscillations are sufficient to show that when it comes to determining which of IHL or HRL must be the central standard in the light of which the other should be interpreted, judges enjoy some comfortable leeway, which, as has been argued here, the principle *lex specialis derogat generali* has hardly curtailed.

It must nonetheless be noted that there are a few good reasons why, in the context of a systemic integration of IHL and IHL conducted on the basis of the principle *lex specialis derogat generali*, elevating IHL in the *lex specialis* is a more likely solution. It suffices here to mention two of them. First, if HRL were to be elected the central interpretative yardstick for systemic integration of HRL and IHL, this would render IHL totally irrelevant. Indeed, because of the growing scope of application of HRL and, in particular, its application to situations of hostilities, this would curb the amount of situations where IHL is the only applicable set of rules aimed at ensuring the protection of individuals. If, in these situations, HRL is systematically made the interpretative standard upon which systemic integration is carried out, IHL – especially rules of IHL applicable to non-international armed conflicts – would become increasingly irrelevant and decorative. Second, conducting systemic integration along the lines drawn by HRL would also yield directives of behavior that do not correspond with the reality of armed conflicts or situations of hostilities where States generally feel less constrained in their use of coercive means. There are thus reasons why judges have been more inclined to consider that IHL, and not HRL, should form the interpretative standards in the light of which systemic integration of these two sets of rules ought to be carried out. These pragmatic considerations do not, however, bar the theoretical possibility of swaps between interpretative standards in the context of systemic integration of international legal rules, even when calibrated by the principle *lex specialis non derogat generali*.

The – at least theoretical – possibility that a systemic integration of IHL and HRL be conducted either on the basis of the former or the latter, albeit with different results, suffices to show that the central role which the principle *lex specialis derogat generali* could play in determining the interpretative standard of any systemic integration remains rather open-ended. Such a use of the principle *lex specialis derogat generali* leaves the determination of the interpretative standard of systemic integration indeterminate, for it hinges on which rule is elected to the *lex specialis*. While in the abovementioned case law IHL was considered to be so, elevating HRL to that position would have been equally justifiable.

3.2 Calibrating Systemic Integration of International Law through the Principle *Lex Specialis Derogat Generali* in a Situation of Competition of Norms?

As was explained above, interpretation classically precedes conflict of norm resolution. There only is a conflict if norms are interpreted as conflicting, that is, if no conciliatory interpretation can be reached. The abovementioned case law shows, however, that, in the context of the simultaneous application of IHL and HRL, the principle of systemic integration and the principle *lex specialis derogat generali* have been used in tandem to conduct a conciliatory interpretation of IHL and HRL when each of these sets of rules provides for different standards of behavior. This is especially true as far as the ICJ is concerned, for the Court has applied a principle of conflict of norm resolution, that is, the principle *lex specialis derogat generali*, to calibrate its systemic integration of IHL and HRL.

After all, such a use of the principle *Lex specialis derogat generali* is not entirely surprising. Indeed, as has been shown above, IHL and HRL should be seen as being in competition rather than conflict. In this context, the use of *lex specialis derogat generali* to calibrate the systemic integration of IHL and HRL could, at first glance, be welcome, and constitute an appropriate alternative to the traditional conflict-solving understanding of that principle.

Yet, it is argued here that the subtle constructions found in the case law of the ICJ, whereby the standard of reference of conciliatory interpretation is determined by virtue of the principle *lex specialis derogat generali* should nonetheless be critically appraised in the context of competing norms like those of IHL and HRL, for such an understanding yields no more certainty than an entirely deformalized process of interpretation.[124] Because, at least theoretically, HRL could be equally elevated to a *lex specialis*, the calibration of the principle of systemic integration through the principle of *lex specialis derogat generali* leaves almost intact the leeway of judges when carrying out conciliatory interpretations of international legal rules. In that sense, the simultaneous use of a principle of conflict of norms solving and a principle of conciliatory interpretation does not curb the indeterminacy inherent in the interpretative powers of law-applying authorities, and does not help further articulate these two competing sets of norms. In other words, the use of the *lex specialis derogat generali* to calibrate the systemic integration of IHL and HRL does not contribute to the domestification of the competition and thus proves somewhat vain. It could even be argued that such a construction, is not only pointless, but also comes at the cost of the integrity and the clarity of the principle *lex specialis derogat generali*.

4. CONCLUDING REMARKS

IHL and HRL undoubtedly share some kinship. Yet, most international lawyers and judges, confronted with the simultaneous application of these two sets of norms have made a resort to the principle *lex specialis derogat generali*. Their use of that principle has presupposed that norms of IHL and HRL belong to the same legal order and the same legal regime and are, at the surface, in conflict with one another. This chapter has tried to rebut these presuppositions and showed that the relations between IHL and HRL ought to be construed in terms of competition rather than conflict. Drawing on the idea of competition between these two sets of rules, this chapter has subsequently sought to evaluate the contemporary uses of the principle *lex specialis derogat generali* – particularly witnessed in the case-law of the ICJ – to calibrate the systemic integration of international law. It has concluded that such an unorthodox use of that principle does little to alleviate the uncertainty inherent in the competitive character of the relationship between IHL and HRL.

NOTES

*   Jean d'Aspremont is Professor of Public International Law, University of Manchester, UK. Elodie Tranchez is A.T.E.R. at the University of Maine and a PhD candidate at the University Paul Cézanne, CERIC, France.
1.   See H.L.A. Hart, *The Concept of Law* (Oxford: Clarendon, 1997), 56–57, 116–117 and 254–255. The same argument is made as regards the international legal order by G. Fitzmaurice, 'The General Principles of International Law Considered from the Standpoint of the Rule of Law', *Collected Courses* 92 (1957-III): 36–47; or I. Brownlie, *The Rule of Law in International Affairs* (The Hague: Martinus Nijhoff, 1998), 12–13.
2.   In the case law of the European Court of Human Rights, see, e.g., *McCann v. United Kingdom*, ECtHR, Application No. 18984/91, Judgment of 21 September 1995; *Gül v. Turkey*, ECtHR, Application No. 22676/93, Judgment of 14 December 2000; *Güleç v. Turkey*, ECtHR, Application No. 21593/93, Judgment of 27 July 1998, Rec. 1998-IV; *Ogur v. Turkey*, ECtHR, Application No. 21594/93, Judgment of 20 May 1999, Rec. 1999-III; *Hamiyet Kaplan v. Turkey*, ECtHR, Application No. 36749/97, Judgment of 13 September 2005; *Ergi v. Turkey*, ECtHR, Application No. 23818/94, Judgment of 28 July 1998; *Isayeva I and II v. Russia*, ECtHR, Application No. 57950/00 and 57947/00, Judgment of 24 February 2005.
3.   In the case law of the European Court of Human Rights see, e.g., *Loizidou v. Turkey*, ECtHR, Application No. 15318/89, Judgment of 23 March 1995, Series A, No. 310; *Bankovic v. Belgium and 16 Other States*, ECtHR, Application No. 52207/99, Decision of 12 December 2001, ECHR 2001-XII; *Cyprus v. Turkey*, ECtHR, Application No. 25781/94, Judgment of 10 May 2001, ECHR 2001-IV, para. 136. In the same vein, see the Inter-American Commission of Human Rights, *Coard v. United States*, IACommHR, Case 10.951, Report No. 109/99, 29 September 1999, paras 24–25; or the case *Disabled*

People's International et al. v. United States, IACommHR, Case 9213, admissibility decision, 22 September 1987. The Human Rights Committee has adopted a similar approach. See *Lopez Burgos v. Uruguay*, HRC, 29 July 1981 (UN Doc. CCPR/C/13/D/52/1979). See also the Human Rights Committee General Comment No. 31, HRC, 26 May 2004 (UN Doc. CCPR/C/21/Rev.1/Add.13), para. 10. For an appraisal of these various positions and that of their consistency, see R. Wilde, 'Human Rights Without Borders? The Extraterritorial Application of International Human Rights Law' (forthcoming), or R. Wilde, 'Triggering State Obligations Extraterritorially: The Spatial Test in Certain Human Rights Treaties', *Israel Law Review* 40–42 (2007): 503–526.

4. See *Legality of the Threat or Use of Nuclear Weapons*, Advisory Opinion, I.C.J. Reports 1996, para. 25; *Legal Consequences of the Construction of a Wall in the Occupied Palestinian Territory*, Advisory Opinion, I.C.J. Reports 2004, paras 105 *et seq.*; *Armed Activities on the Territory of the Congo* (D.R. Congo v. Uganda), Judgment, I.C.J. Reports 2005, paras 178 and 220.

5. V. Gowlland-Debas, 'The Relevance of Paragraph 25 of the ICJ's Opinion on Nuclear Weapons', *ASILPROC* 98 (2004): 360.

6. Among others, see, e.g., (in alphabetical order): R. Arnold and N. Quénivet, *International Humanitarian Law and Human Rights Law: Towards a New Merger in International Law* (The Hague: Martinus Nijhoff, 2008); C. Byron, 'A Blurring of the Boundaries: the Application of International Humanitarian Law by Human Rights Bodies', *Virginia Journal of International Law* (2007): 839–896; A.-S. Calogeropoulos-Stratis, 'Droit humanitaire et droits de l'homme', *Yearbook of International Humanitarian Law – La protection de la personne en période de conflit armé* (Geneva: IUHEI, 1980); A.-S. Calogeropoulos-Stratis, 'Droit humanitaire. Droits de l'homme et victimes des conflits armés', in *Mélanges Pictet* (Geneva and The Hague: ICRC and Martinus Nijhoff, 1984), 655–663; A.E. Cassimatis, 'International Humanitarian Law, International Human Rights Law, and Fragmentation of International Law', *ICLQ* (2007): 623–639; E. David, 'Droit de l'homme et droit humanitaire,' in *Mélanges Dehousse* (Paris: Nathan-Labor, 1979), 169–181; L. Doswald-Beck, 'The Right to Life in Armed Conflict: Does International Humanitarian Law Provide all the Answers?', *Revue internationale de la Croix-Rouge* (2006): 881–904; L. Doswald-Beck and S. Vité, 'International Humanitarian Law and Human Rights Law', *Revue internationale de la Croix-Rouge* (1993): 94 *et seq.*; C. Droege, 'Elective Affinities? Human Rights and Humanitarian Law', *Revue internationale de la Croix-Rouge* (2008): 501–548; J. Dugard, 'Bridging the gap between human rights and humanitarian law: the punishment of offenders', *Revue internationale de la Croix-Rouge* (1998): 445 *et seq.*; V. Gowlland-Debbas, 'The Right to Life and Genocide: The Court and International Public Policy', in *International Law, the International Court of Justice and Nuclear Weapons*, eds L. Boisson de Chazournes and P. Sands (Cambridge: Cambridge University Press, 1999), 315 *et seq.*; F. Hampson, 'The Relationship Between International Humanitarian Law and Human Rights Law from the Perspective of a Human Rights Treaty Body', *Revue internationale de la Croix-Rouge* (2008): 549–572; H. Krieger, 'A Conflict of Norms: the Relationship Between Humanitarian Law and Human Rights Law in the ICRC Customary Law Study', *Journal of Conflict and Security Law* (2006): 265–291; F. Martin, 'Application du droit international humanitaire par la Cour interaméricaine des droits de l'homme', *Revue internationale de la Croix-Rouge* (2001): 1037–1065; J. Meurant, 'Droit humanitaire et droits de l'homme: spécificités et convergences', *Revue internationale de la Croix-Rouge* (1993): 93–98; R. Provost, *International Human Rights and Humanitarian Law* (Cambridge: Cambridge University Press, 2002); M. Sassòli and L. Olson, 'The Relationship between International Humanitarian Law and Human Rights Law Where it Matters: Admissible Killing and Internment of Fighters in Non-international Armed Conflicts', *Revue internationale de la Croix-Rouge* (2008): 599–627; S. Sayapin, 'The International Committee of the Red Cross and International Human Rights Law', *Human Rights Law Review* (2009): 95–126; D. Schindler, 'Le CICR et les droits de l'homme', *Revue internationale de la Croix-Rouge* (1979): 3–15; H. Tigroudja, 'La Cour Interaméricaine des Droits de l'Homme au service de "L'Humanisation du Droit International Public" propos autour des récents arrêts et avis', *Annuaire Français de Droit International* (2006): 617–640; R.E. Vinuesa, 'Interface, Correspondence and Convergence of Human Rights and International Humanitarian Law', *Yearbook of International Humanitarian Law* (1998): 69–110.

7. A. Carswell, 'Classification des conflits: le dilemne du soldat', *Revue internationale de la Croix-Rouge* (2009): 146.

8. These common objectives were recognized as early as the 1968 Teheran Human Rights Conference, Final Act of the International Conference on Human Rights, Teheran, 22 April to 13 May 1968, UN Doc. A/CONF.32/41 (1968), 3. See also the UN General Assembly Resolution A/RES/2444 (XXIII), 19 December 1968, entitled 'Respect of Human Rights in Armed Conflicts'. On the similarities of the object and objectives of IHL and HRL, see Provost, *supra* note 6, at 133–140.

9. R. Kolb, '*Aperçu de l'histoire de la Déclaration universelle des droits de l'homme et des Conventions de Genève*', *Revue internationale de la Croix-Rouge* (1998): 437.

10. On these terminological questions, see generally R. Kolb, *Ius in Bello* (Geneva: Helbing and Lichtenhahn, and Brussels: Bruylant, 2003), 9–12.

11. D. Schindler, 'Human Rights and Humanitarian Law: Interrelationships of the Laws', *American University Law Review* 31 (1982): 935.

12. See, e.g., J. Pauwelyn, *Conflict of Norms in Public International Law* (Cambridge: Cambridge University Press, 2003), 388.

13. *Legality of the Threat or Use of Nuclear Weapons*, Advisory Opinion, I.C.J. Reports 1996, para. 25

14. *Legal Consequences of the Construction of a Wall in the Occupied Palestinian Territory*, Advisory Opinion, I.C.J. Reports 2004, para. 107 *et seq.*

15. See ILC Study on Fragmentation, A/CN.4/L.682, 34, footnote 57. See also H. Mosler, 'The International Society as a Legal Community', *Collected Courses* 140 (1974-IV): 137.

16. A. Peczenik, *Juridikens metodproblem* (Stockholm: Gebers, 1980), 106. For a clear illustration, see also Appellate Body Report, Guatemala – Anti-Dumping Investigation Regarding Portland Cement from Mexico, WT/DS60/AB/R, adopted 25 November 1998, DSR 1998: IX, 3767.

17. ILC Study on Fragmentation, A/CN.4/L.682, 31, para. 48.

18. ILC Study on Fragmentation, A/CN.4/L.682, 30, para. 46. See also Pauwelyn, *supra* note 12, at 389.

19. For a looser conception of conflicts of norms, see M. Milanovic, 'Norm Conflict in International Law: Whither Human Rights?,' *Duke Journal of Comparative and International Law* 69 (2009): 72–73. For a more flexible conception of a conflict of norms, see also Pauwelyn, *supra* note 12, at 184–188.

20. See ILC, Commentary, about Article 55, Articles SR.

21. G. Fitzmaurice, 'The Law and Procedure of the International Court of Justice 1951–1954: Treaty Interpretation and Other Treaty Points', *British Yearbook of International Law* 33 (1957): 237.

22. On the distinction between rules with a soft negotium and rules with a soft instrumentum, see J. d'Aspremont, 'Softness in International Law: A Self-Serving Quest for New Legal Materials', *EJIL* 19 (2008): 1075–1093.

23. ILC Study on Fragmentation, A/CN.4/L.682, 46, para. 82.

24. S. Sur, *L'interpretation en droit international public* (Paris: Librairie générale de droit et de jurisprudence, 1974), 164.

25. ILC Study on Fragmentation, A/CN.4/L.682, 57, para. 104.

26. ILC Study on Fragmentation, A/CN.4/L.682, 36, para. 60. See also Pauwelyn, *supra* note 12, at 387.

27. ILC Study on Fragmentation, A/CN.4/L.682, 37, para. 60. See also Pauwelyn, *supra* note 12, at 388; C. Rousseau, 'De la compatibilité des normes juridiques contradictoires dans l'ordre international', *RGDIP* (1932): 177; D. Anzilotti, *Cours de droit international*, trans. G. Gidel, Vol. I (Paris: Sirey, 1929), 103.

28. For a traditional example, see Mavrommatis Palestine Concessions case, Permanent Court of International Justice (PCIJ), Series A, No. 2 (1924): 31.

29. See generally, M.E. Villiger, *Customary International Law and Treaties: a Study of their Interactions and Interrelations with Special Consideration of the 1969 Vienna Convention on the Law of Treaties* (Dordrecht: Martinus Nijhoff, 1985). More recently, see the insightful study of A. Tardieu, *Relations entre normes conventionnelles et normes coutumières à la lumière de l'adage* Lex specialis derogat generali (Doctoral thesis, Université Paris 1 Panthéon-Sorbonne, 2009).

30. *Case concerning the Right of Passage over Indian Territory* (Portugal v. India), Merits, Judgment, I.C.J. Reports 1960, 44.

31. H. Thirlway, 'The Law and Procedure of the International Court of Justice', *British Yearbook of International Law* 60 (1989): 147; see, e.g., A. Verdross, '*Règles Générales du Droit international de la Paix*', *Collected Courses* 30 (1929-V): 304. See also the 1995 Resolution of the Institut de Droit international regarding the *Problems Arising from a Succession of Codification Conventions on a Particular Subject*, available at http://www.idi-iil.org/idiE/resolutionsE/1995_lis_01_en.pdf (accessed 9 February 2012), conclusion No. 11: 'There is no a priori hierarchy between treaty and custom as sources of international law. However, in the application of international law, relevant norms deriving from a treaty will prevail between the parties over norms deriving from customary law.'

32. See, in particular, the Iran-US Claims Tribunal, *INA Corporation v. The Islamic Republic of Iran*, award of 12 August 1985, No. 184-161-1, Iran-US Claims Tribunal Reports, Vol. 8, 378–379. See, however, the ambiguity between treaty interpretation and conflict of norms resolution in Case No. A/2, Iran-US Claims Tribunal Reports, Vol. 1 (1981–1982), 104; for an outline of the case law, see ILC Study on Fragmentation, A/CN.4/L.682, 40 *et seq.*

33. ECtHR has commonly referred to the concept of *lex specialis* with a view to restricting the provisions of the Convention on the basis of which it ought to appraise the conformity therewith of a given act or behavior. This will be discussed below. Yet, among the few cases where the Court made a rather orthodox use of the concept of *lex specialis*, that is as expressing the principle *lex specialis derogat generali*, is probably the case *Islamic Republic of Iran Shipping Lines v. Turkey*, where the Court, having regard to the relevant rules of international law to appraise the lawfulness of the interference with the property right of the applicant under Article 1 of Protocol No. 1, considered that the applicable international law among the parties governing transit passage through the Bosphorus was the Montreux Convention, to the exclusion of customary international law (*Islamic Republic of Iran Shipping Lines v. Turkey*, ECtHR, Application No. 40998/98, Judgment of 13 December 2007, para. 92).

34. See, e.g., *North Sea Continental Shelf case* (Federal Republic of Germany v. Netherlands), Judgment, I.C.J. Reports 1969, para. 25: 'The Court now turns to the legal position regarding the equidistance method. The first question to be considered is whether the 1958 Geneva Convention on the Continental Shelf is binding for all the Parties in this case – that is to say whether, as contended by Denmark and the Netherlands, the use of this method is rendered obligatory for the present delimitations by virtue of the delimitations provision (Article 6) of that instrument, according to the conditions laid down in it. Clearly, if this is so, then the provisions of the Convention will prevail in the relations between the Parties, and would take precedence of any rules having a more general character, or derived from another source.' See also *Continental Shelf* (Tunisia v. Libyan Arab Jamahiriya), Judgment, I.C.J. Reports 1982, 38, para. 24: 'it would no doubt have been possible for the Parties to identify in the Special Agreement certain specific developments in the law of the sea … and to have declared that in their bilateral relations in the particular case such rules should be binding as lex specialis'. See *Military and Paramilitary Activities in and against Nicaragua* (Nicaragua v. United States of America), Judgment, I.C.J. Reports 1986, para. 274: 'In general, treaty rules being lex specialis, it would not be appropriate that a State should bring a claim based on a customary-law rule if it has by treaty already provided means for settlement of such a claim.' See, more recently, *Dispute regarding Navigational and Related Rights* (Costa Rica v. Nicaragua), Judgment, I.C.J. Reports 2009, paras 34–35: 'The Court does not consider that it is required to take a position in this case on whether and to what extent there exists, in customary international law, a régime applicable to navigation on "international rivers," either of universal scope or of a regional nature covering the geographical area in which the San Juan is situated. Nor does it consider, as a result, that it is required to settle the question of whether the San Juan falls into the category of "international rivers," as Costa Rica maintains, or is a national river which includes an international element, that being the argument of Nicaragua. … Indeed, even if categorization as an "international river" would be legally relevant in respect of navigation, in that it would entail the application of rules of customary international law to that question, such rules could only be operative, at the very most, in the absence of any treaty provisions that had the effect of excluding them, in particular because those provisions were intended to define completely the regime applicable to navigation, by the riparian States on a specific river or a section of it.'

35. See ILC Study on Fragmentation, A/CN.4/L.682, 47.

36. On this question, see the interesting insights of Tardieu, *supra* note 29, at 45 *et seq.*

37. This has been artfully explained by the I.C.J. in the *Delimitation of the Maritime Boundary in the Gulf of Maine Area* (Canada v. United States of America), Judgment, I.C.J. Reports 1984, paras 81–82, 111; In the same vein, see C. de Visscher, 'Cours général de principes de droit international public', *Collected Courses* 86 (1954-II): 476. It is sometimes argued that treaty law is commonly more detailed than customary international law, which is seen as having a necessarily poorer normative content. See P. Weil, 'Le droit international en quête de son identité', *Collected Courses* 237 (1992-VI): 160.

38. M. Akehurst, 'The hierarchy of sources of international law', *British Yearbook of International Law* 47 (1974–1975): 275.

39. Regarding a conflict between two treaties, see Pauwelyn, *supra* note 12, at 390. Regarding a conflict between two customs, see S. Sur, *La Coutume internationale* (Paris: LITEC, 1990), at 14.

40. ILC Study on Fragmentation, A/CN.4/L.682, 61–62, paras 113–115.
41. Ibid., para. 106.
42. Ibid., para. 4 *et seq.*
43. *Application of the Convention on the Prevention and Punishment of the Crime of Genocide* (Bosnia and Herzegovina v. Serbia and Montenegro), Judgment, I.C.J. Reports 2007, paras 403–406. Compare *Prosecutor v. Dusko Tadić*, ICTY, Judgment, 15 July 1999 (Case No. IT-94-1-A), paras 115, 116–145.
44. ILC Study on Fragmentation, A/CN.4/L.682, para. 49 *et seq.* In the same vein, see J. d'Aspremont and J. de Hemptinne, *Questions spéciales de droit international humanitaire* (Paris: Pedone, forthcoming).
45. T.G.I. (Tribunal de Grande Instance) Paris, 22 May 2000, reproduced in *La semaine juridique* (20 November 2000): 2219.
46. R. Michaels and J. Pauwelyn, 'Conflict of Norms or Conflict of Laws? Different Techniques in the Fragmentation of International Law', *Duke Law Scholarship Repository* (2010): 8.
47. See 'Conclusions of the Work of the Study Group on the Fragmentation of International Law: Difficulties Arising from the Diversification and Expansion of International Law, A/61/10', *Yearbook of the International Law Commission* (2006), Vol. II, Part Two, para. 1.
48. On the multiple meaning of legal pluralism, see N. Krisch, *Beyond Constitutionalism – The Pluralist Structure of Postnational Law* (Oxford: Oxford University Press, 2010), 71–78.
49. G. Teubner and A. Fischer-Lescano, 'Regime-Collisions: The Vain Search for Legal Unity in the Fragmentation of Global Law', *Michigan Journal of International Law* 25(4) (2004): 999–1046.
50. See generally M. Prost, *The Concept of Unity in Public International Law* (Oxford: Hart Publishing, forthcoming).
51. We translate: what is not really *one* being, is not *really* one *being.*
52. *The First Anniversary*, 1611, lines 205–213. See generally on this point A. Koyré, *Du monde clos à l'univers infini* (Paris: Presses Universitaires de France, 1962).
53. The term objective link of causality does not presuppose a 'pre given' order but means a link that is valid and comprehensible universally.
54. J. Combacau, 'Le droit international: bric-à-brac ou système?', *Archives de Philosophie du Droit*, 'Le système juridique' 31 (1986): 86.
55. L. Murphy, 'Better to See Law this Way', *New York University Law Review* 83 (2008): 1104; L. Murphy, 'The Political Question of the Concept of Law', in *Hart's Postcript: Essays on the Postscript to 'The Concept of Law'*, ed. J. Coleman (Oxford: Oxford University Press, 2001), 371.
56. Murphy, *supra* note 55.
57. Except the special case of regional law.
58. On this point see, generally, Michaels and Pauwelyn, *supra* note 46.
59. M. Dennis, 'Application of Human Rights Treaties Extraterritorially in Times of Armed Conflict and Military Occupation', *American Journal of International Law* 99 (2005): 119–141, at 125–126; on this point see also 134 ff.
60. UN Doc. CCPR/C/SR. 1405, para. 20.
61. UN Doc. CCPR/CO/72/NET/Add.1, para. 19.
62. Schindler, *supra* note 11, at 14.
63. With a few exceptions, see, e.g., *Bankovic v. Belgium*, ECtHR, Application No. 52207/99, Decision on Admissibility, 12 December 2001.
64. W. Jenks 'The Conflict of Law-Making Treaties', *British Yearbook of International Law* 30 (1953): 426–427.
65. See, e.g., W. Karl, 'Conflict Between Treaties', in *Encyclopedia of Public International Law* (Amsterdam: Elsevier, 1992), 935; and, generally on this point, E. Vranes, 'The Definition of "Norm Conflict" in International Law and Legal Theory', *EJIL* 17-2 (2006): 395–418.
66. WTO Panel Report, *Indonesia – Certain Measures Affecting the Automobile Industry*, WT/DS54/R, WT/DS59/R, WT/DS64/R, adopted on 23 July 1998, footnote 649.
67. For instance, '↔' means 'implies', '&' means 'and', 'y' means 'or' …
68. See on these points, G.H. Von Right, *Norm and Action* (London: Routledge and Kegan Paul, 1963); G. Kalinowski, *La logique des normes* (Paris: Presses Universitaires de France, 1972).
69. G. Marceau, 'Conflicts of Norms and Conflicts of Jurisdictions: The Relationship between the WTO Agreement and MEAs and other Treaties', *Journal of World Trade* 35 (2001): 1084.
70. See, for a diverging point of view, Stephen Munzer who builds a strong distinction between two questions that lead to different positions of conflict of norms: 'what is it for two rules to conflict in themselves' and 'what is it for two rules to conflict on a particular occasion by virtue of an act or

omission by a norm-subject?'. In the second case, the author indicates that two permissive norms could conflict, S. Munzer, 'Validity and Legal Conflicts', *Yale Law Journal* 82 (1973): 1144–1145.

71. See, on this point, Vranes, *supra* note 65, at 404.

72. See Sassòli and Olson, *supra* note 6, at 599–627.

73. See S. Vité, 'The Interrelation of the Law of Occupation and Economic, Social and Cultural Rights: the Examples of Food, Health and Property', *International Review of the Red Cross* no. 871 (2008): 646.

74. See Y. Dinstein, *The Conduct of Hostilities under the Law of International Armed Conflict* (Cambridge: Cambridge University Press, 2004), 24.

75. Marceau, *supra* note 69.

76. Akehurst, *supra* note 38, at 273; Fitzmaurice, *supra* note 21, at 236; J.B. Mus, 'Conflicts between Treaties in International Law', *Netherlands International Law Review* (1998): 218.

77. It should be noted, however, that the European Court has also used the concept of *lex specialis* to determine the domestic law whose legality ought to be evaluated on the basis of the Convention (see, e.g., *Strain and others v. Romania*, ECtHR, Application No. 57001/00, Judgment of 21 July 2005, para. 48). It is also interesting to note that in *Kononov v. Latvia*, the Court – curiously – referred to the *lex specialis* character of an IHL obligation to assert, for the sake of Article 7 of the Convention, that a military officer should have foreseen that the impugned acts risked being counter to the laws and customs of war as understood at that time (*Kononov v. Latvia*, ECtHR, Application No. 36376/04, Judgment of 17 May 2010, paras 237–238). For a more traditional understanding of the principle by the European Court of Human Rights, see *Islamic Republic of Iran Shipping Lines v. Turkey*, ECtHR, Application No. 40998/98, Judgment of 13 December 2007.

78. As regards Article 6 being a *lex specialis* in relation to Article 13, see, e.g., *Kudla v. Poland*, ECtHR, Application No. 30210/96, Judgment of 26 October 2000, para. 146; *Vasilescu v. Romania*, ECtHR, Appication No. 53/1997/837/1043, Judgment of 22 May 1998, para. 43; *Yankov v. Bulgaria*, ECtHR, Application No. 39084/97, Judgment of 11 December 2003, para. 150. As regards Article 5 being a *lex specialis* in the matter of detention, see, e.g., *Shamayev and others v. Georgia and Russia*, ECtHR, Application No. 36378/02, Judgment of 12 April 2005, para. 435; *Storck v. Germany*, ECtHR, Application No. 61603/00, Judgment of 16 June 2005, para. 142. As regards more specifically Article 5, sect. 4 being a *lex specialis* in relation to the more general requirements of Article 13, see, e.g., *A. and others v. United Kingdom*, ECtHR, Application No. 3455/05, Judgment of 19 February 2009, para. 202; see *Chahal v. United Kingdom*, *European Human Rights Report* 23 (1996): 413, para. 126; *Nikolova v. Bulgaria*, ECtHR, Application No. 31195/96, Judgment of 25 March 1999, para. 69; *Brannigan and McBride v. United Kingdom*, ECtHR, Application Nos 14553/89 and 14554/89, Judgment of 25 May 1993, para. 76; *H.L. v. United Kingdom*, ECtHR, Application No. 45508/99, Judgment of 5 October 2004, para. 139. As regards Article 8 being a *lex specialis* in its relation to Article 12, see, e.g., *P., C. and S. v. United Kingdom*, ECtHR, Application No. 56547/00, Judgment of 16 July 2002, para. 142. As regards, Article 11 being a *lex specialis* in its relation to Article 10, see, e.g., *Djavit An v. Turkey*, ECtHR, Application No. 20652/92, Judgment of 20 February 2003, para. 39. As regards Article 3 of Protocol No. 1 being the *lex specialis* in relation to Article 11, see, e.g., *Zdanoka v. Latvia*, ECtHR, Application No. 58278/00, Judgment of 16 March 2006, para. 141; *Folgero and others v. Norway*, ECtHR, Application No. 15472/02, Judgment of 29 June 2007, para. 54; *Ezelin v. France*, ECtHR, Application No. 11800/85, Judgment of 26 April 1991, para. 35.

79. ILC Study on Fragmentation, A/CN.4/L.682, 34–35, para. 56.

80. See United Nations Conference on the Law of Treaties, Second Session, Vienna, 9 April to 22 May 1969, *Official Records* (New York: United Nations, 1970), 270; also cited by the ILC Report on Fragmentation, A/CN.4/L.682, 39, para. 65.

81. ILC Study on Fragmentation, A/CN.4/L.682, 31, para. 48.

82. Pauwelyn, *supra* note 12, at 237–274 (however, for Pauwelyn, treaty interpretation can only solve apparent conflicts, not genuine conflicts, 272).

83. H. Lauterpacht, 'Restrictive Interpretation and the Principle of Effectiveness in the Interpretation of Treaties', *British Yearbook of International Law* 26 (1949): 53

84. See generally G. Schwarzenberger, 'Myths and Realities of Treaty Interpretations: Articles 25–29 of the Vienna Draft Convention on the Law of Treaties', *VA Journal of International Law* 9 (1968): 15.

85. See, generally, M. Fitzmaurice, O. Elias and P. Merkouris, ed., *Treaty Interpretation and the Vienna Convention on the Law of Treaties: 30 Years On* (The Hague: Martinus Nijhoff, 2010).

86. A. Nollkaemper, 'The Power of Secondary Rules of International Law to Connect the International and the National Legal Orders, Amsterdam Center for International Law Working Paper', available at

http://papers.ssrn.com/sol3/papers.cfm?abstract_id=1515771 (accessed 9 February 2012); see also J. d'Aspremont, 'The Systemic Integration of International Law by Domestic Courts: Domestic Judges as Architects of the Consistency of the International Legal Order', in *Unity or Fragmentation of International Law: The Role of International and National Tribunals*, eds A. Nollkaemper and O.K. Fauchald (forthcoming), available at http://papers.ssrn.com/sol3/cf_dev/AbsByAuth.cfm?per_id=736 816 (accessed 9 February 2012). The same argument can be made as far as the interpretation of foreign domestic law is concerned which ought to be subject to the principles of interpretation of that foreign legal order. See on this point, *Brazilian Loans (France v. United States)*, PCIJ, Judgment, Series A, No. 21 (1929), para. 72 ('Once the Court has arrived at the conclusion that it is necessary to apply the municipal law of a particular country, there seems no doubt that it must seek to apply it as it would be applied in that country. It would not be applying the municipal law of a country if it were to apply it in a manner different from that in which that law would be applied in the country in which it is in force').

87.   On the drafting history of Article 31(3)(c), see P. Merkouris, 'Debating the Ouroboros of International Law: The Drafting History of 31(3)(c)', *International Community Law Review* 9 (2007). It is interesting to note that when this provision was included in the Vienna Convention on the Law of Treaties, it echoed the previous teaching of some scholars. See, e.g., A.D. McNair, *The Law of Treaties* (Oxford: Clarendon Press, 1961), 466; see also the *P. Verzijl, G. Pinson case* (1927–1928), AD No. 292, cited by C. McLachlan, 'The Principle of Systemic Integration and Article 31(3)(c) of the Vienna Convention', *International and Comparative Law Quarterly* 279 54 (2005): 279. This provision also reflected the position of the *Institut de droit international*; see *Yearbook of the Institut de droit international* (1956): 364–365. See also http://www.idi-iil.org/ (accessed 9 February 2012).

88.   On the extent to which Article 31(3)(c) has long been overlooked, see H. Thirlway, 'The Law and Procedure of the International Court of Justice 1960–1989, Part Three', *British Yearbook of International Law* 62 (1991): 58.

89.   See P. Sands, 'Treaty, Custom and the Cross-Fertilization of International Law', *Yale Human Rights and Development Law Journal* 1 (1998): 95; see also J. Combacau and S. Sur, *Droit international public*, 5th edition (Paris: Montchrestien, 2001), 175. On the unity of the legal system, see generally H. Kelsen, 'Les Rapport de système entre le droit interne et le droit international', and 'Les rapports de système entre le droit interne et le droit international public', *Collected Courses* 14 (1926-IV): 264 (who argues that the unity of the system rests on the same principle of validity on which all the constitutive elements of the system rest). Compare P.-M. Dupuy, 'L'unité de l'ordre juridique international, Cours général de droit international public', *Collected Courses* 297 (2002): 9–490.

90.   In the same vein, see A. Orakhelashvili, *The Interpretation of Acts and Rules in Public International Law* (Oxford: Oxford University Press, 2008), 366. See *contra*, *Demir and Baykara v. Turkey*, ECtHR, Application No. 34503/97, Judgment of 12 November 2008, paras 65–67.

91.   In the same sense, see I. Van Damme, 'Some Observations about the ILC Study Group Report on the Fragmentation of International Law: WTO Treaty Interpretation Against the Background of Other International Law', *Finnish Yearbook of International Law* 21 (2006): 38; see also V. Tzevelekos, 'The Use of Article 31(3)(c) of the VCLT in the Case Law of the European Court of Human Rights: An Effective Anti-Fragmentation Tool or a Selective Loophole for the Reinforcement of Human Rights Teleology? Between Evolution and Systemic Integration', *Michigan Journal of International Law* 31 (2010): 688; Orakhelashvili, *supra* note 90, at 366–369.

92.   d'Aspremont, *supra* note 86.

93.   While not formally applying the principle of systemic integration, the US Supreme Court, in *Alvarez Machain* gave a very narrow understanding of the Extradition Treaty between Mexico and the United States, resorting to other rules of international law to back its contention. For a criticism, see M.A. Rogoff, 'Interpretation of international agreements by domestic courts and the politics of international treaty relations: reflections on some recent decisions of the United States Supreme Court', *American University Journal of International Law and Policy* (1996): 559–685.

94.   While not providing a clear example of restrictive interpretation of international law, the practice of international tribunals shows that the principle of systemic integration has been applied in a manner that further fragments international law. This has been argued with respect to the *Loizidou* Decision of the European Court of Human Rights. See *Loizidou v. Turkey*, ECtHR, Application No. 15318/89, Judgment of 18 December 1996, Report (1996-VI), 2216, 2221 *et seq.* See also *Behrami* and *Saramati v. France, Germany and Norway*, ECtHR, Application Nos 71412/01 and 78166/01, Decision on Admissibility, 2 May 2007, para. 129 *et seq.* On this particular use of systemic integration, see Tzevelekos, *supra* note 91, at 671–672 or 677.

95. Such a use of the principle of systemic integration permeates the case law of the European Court of Human Rights. See the examples cited by Tzevelekos, *supra* note 91, at 625. On that use of the principle of systemic integration by domestic courts, see d'Aspremont, *supra* note 86.
96. On the distinction between formal and substantive unity, see, generally, Dupuy, *supra* note 89, at 9–490.
97. *Oil Platforms* (Islamic Republic of Iran v. United States of America), Judgment, I.C.J. Reports 2003, para. 78.
98. See the remarks of P. d'Argent, 'Du commerce à l'emploi de la force: l'affaire des plates-formes pétrolières (arrêt sur le fond)', *Annuaire français de droit international* (2003): 655–678.
99. See the Opinion of Judge Buergenthal, Judge Higgins, or the Opinion of Judge Kooijmans.
100. See McLachlan, *supra* note 87, at 309.
101. Ibid.
102. *Certain Questions of Mutual Assistance in Criminal Matters* (Djibouti v. France), Judgment, I.C.J. Reports 2008, paras 113–114 ('The provisions of the 1977 Treaty of Friendship and Co-operation are "relevant rules" within the meaning of Article 31(3)(c), of the Vienna Convention. That is so even though they are formulated in a broad and general manner, having an aspirational character. According to the most fundamental of these rules, equality and mutual respect are to govern relations between the two countries; co-operation and friendship are to be preserved and strengthened. While this does not provide specific operational guidance as to the practical application of the Convention of 1986, that Convention must nevertheless be interpreted and applied in a manner which takes into account the friendship and co-operation which France and Djibouti posited as the basis of their mutual relations in the Treaty of 1977 … The Court thus accepts that the Treaty of Friendship and Co-operation of 1977 does have a certain bearing on the interpretation and application of the Convention on Mutual Assistance in Criminal Matters of 1986. But this is as far as the relationship between the two instruments can be explained in legal terms. An interpretation of the 1986 Convention duly taking into account the spirit of friendship and co-operation stipulated in the 1977 Treaty cannot possibly stand in the way of a party to that Convention relying on a clause contained in it which allows for non-performance of a conventional obligation under certain circumstances. The Court can thus not accede to the far-reaching conclusions on the impact of the Treaty of 1977 upon the Convention of 1986 put forward by the Applicant').
103. Legal Consequences for States of the Continued Presence of South Africa in Namibia (South West Africa) notwithstanding S/RES/276, 21 June 1971, para. 53.
104. See, e.g., *Golder v. United Kingdom*, ECtHR, Application No. 4451/70, Judgment of 21 February 1975, Series A, No. 18, 13–14; see also *Loizidou v. Turkey*, *supra* note 94, at para. 44. More recently, see *Al-Adsani v. United Kingdom*, ECtHR, Application No. 35763/97, Judgment of 21 November 2001, 79; *Fogarty v. United Kingdom*, ECtHR, Application No. 37112/97 Judgment of 21 November 2001, 157; *McElhinney v. Ireland*, ECtHR, Application No. 31253/96, Judgment of 21 November 2001, 37; *Bankovic v. Belgium and others*, Application No. 52207/99, decision of 12 December 2001, 351.
105. Arbitration regarding the *Iron Rhine Railway, Kingdom of Belgium v. Kingdom of the Netherlands*, 24 May 2005, paras 58 and 79, available at http://www.pca-cpa.org (accessed 10 February 2012). See the remarks of Orakhelashvili, *supra* note 90, at 380–381; see also P. d'Argent, 'De la fragmentation à la cohésion systémique: la sentence arbitrale du 24 mai 2005 relative au Rhin de fer (Ijzeren Rijn)', in *Droit du pouvoir, pouvoir du droit, Liber amicorum Jean Salmon* (Brussels: Bruylant, 2007), 1113–1137.
106. WT/DS291/R; WT/DS292/R; WT/DS293/R, 29 September 2006, para. 7.68. See also WT/DS58/ AB/R, 12 October 1998, para. 158. On the use of Article 31(3)(c) by the Appellate Body, see generally Marceau, *supra* note 69, at 1087
107. See the very restrictive interpretation by the WTO Appellate Body in the *EC – Measures Affecting the Approval and Marketing of Biotech Products* WT/DS291/R; WT/DS292/R; WT/DS293/R, 29 September 2006, para. 7.68 ('Indeed, it is not apparent why a sovereign State would agree to a mandatory rule of treaty interpretation which could have as a consequence that the interpretation of a treaty to which that State is a party is affected by others of international law which that State has decided not to accept'). On this point, see the remarks of B. Simma, 'Universality of International Law from the Perspective of a Practitioner', *EJIL* 20 (2009): 276–277.
108. See Thirlway, *supra* note 88, at 58.
109. See, e.g., the International Law Commission which, in its compilation of studies over the substantive fragmentation of international law, devoted an entire chapter to it. Conclusion No. 4 of the ILC Study

Group on the Fragmentation of International Law, A/CN.4/L.682, *Yearbook of the International Law Commission*, Vol. II, Part 2, paras 4 and 42. For a criticism of that approach, see B. Conforti, 'Unité et fragmentation du droit international', *Revue générale de droit international public* (2007): 16. See also M. Koskenniemi, 'Constitutionalism as Mindset: Reflections on Kantian Themes About International Law and Globalization', *Theoretical Inquiries in Law* 8 (2007). For a criticism about the contradictions in the perspectives endorsed by the ILC, see M. del Mar, 'System Values and Understanding Legal Language', *Leiden Journal of International Law* 21 (2008): 29–61.

110. For an analysis of the possible features that make a legal order a constitutional order, see B. Fassbender, *The United Nations Charter as the constitution of the international community* (The Hague: Martinus Nijhoff, 2009); B. Fassbender, 'The United Nations Charter as constitution of the international community', *Columbia Journal of Transnational Law* 36 (1998); compare with G. Arangio-Ruiz, 'The "Federal Analogy" and UN Charter Interpretation: a crucial issue', *EJIL* 8 (1997).

111. For some critical remarks on constitutionalism in international legal scholarship, see J. d'Aspremont, 'The Foundations of the International Legal Order', *Finnish Yearbook of International Law* 18 (2007): 219–255.

112. See, in particular, *Legality of the Threat or Use of Nuclear Weapons*, Advisory Opinion, I.C.J. Reports 1996, para. 25.

113. See Gowlland-Debbas, *supra* note 6, at 315.

114. Para. 25.

115. Paras 105–106.

116. See *Legality of the Threat or Use of Nuclear Weapons*, *supra* note 112.

117. We owe this argument to conversations with V. Gowlland-Debbas. For further insights on that matter, see J. d'Aspremont and J. de Hemptinne, *Droit international humanitaire* (Paris: Pedone, forthcoming).

118. See, e.g., *Ergi v. Turkey*, ECtHR, Application No. 23818/94, Judgment of 28 July 1998; *Özkan and others v. Turkey*, ECtHR, Application No. 21689/93, Judgment of 6 April 2004; *Isayeva, Yusupova and Bazayeva v. Russia*, ECtHR, Application Nos 57947/00, 57948/00 and 57949/00, Judgment of 24 February 2005, available at http://echr.coe.int/echr/en/hudoc (accessed 9 February 2012).

119. See *Bamaca Velasquez*, IACtHR, Judgment of 25 November 2000.

120. General Comment No. 31, *supra* note 3, at para. 11.

121. See International Criminal Tribunal for the former Yugoslavia, *Furundzija*, ICTY, Trial Chamber, Judgment, 10 December 1998 (Case No. IT-95-17/1-T), paras 134 *et seq.*; *Delalic*, ICTY, Trial Chamber, Judgment, 16 November 1998 (Case No. IT-96-21-T), paras 452 *et seq.*

122. See the controversial Decisions of the Inter-American Commission of Human Rights where it has directly applied IHL but interpreted it in the light of the applicable human rights law. See *Juan Carlos Abella v. Argentina*, known as *La Tablada case*, IACommHR, Case 11.137, Report No. 55/97, 18 November 1997; see also *Third Report on the Human Rights Situation in Colombia*, 26 February 1999, OAS/Ser.L/V/II.102, Doc. 9, Rev.1. This approach sharply contrasts with the approach of the Inter-American Court of Human Rights, *Las Palmeras v. Colombia*, IACtHR, Preliminary Objections, Judgment of 4 February 2000.

123. Regarding links between crimes against humanity and human rights law, see L. Doswald-Beck and Vité, *supra* note 6, at 94. See also P. Akhavan, 'Reconciling Crimes Against Humanity with the Laws of War: Human Rights, Armed Conflict, and the Limits of Progressive Jurisprudence', *Journal of International Criminal Justice* (2008): 26.

124. On various conceptions of formalism in the theory of international law, see J. d'Aspremont, *Formalism in the Sources of International Law – A Theory of the Ascertainment of Legal Rules* (Oxford: Oxford University Press, 2011).

13. A *lex favorabilis*? Resolving norm conflicts between human rights law and humanitarian law

*Anne-Laurence Graf-Brugère**

The purpose of this chapter is to examine the relevance of the 'principle of the most favourable' in the relationship between international humanitarian law (IHL) and human rights law (HRL), especially when IHL and HRL norms conflict with one another. In other words, this chapter seeks to answer the question of whether the conflicts of norms between IHL and HRL can (or must) be solved in the way that is *the most favourable to the individual*. This solution has been put forward, in varying ways, by several authors and international human rights institutions.[1] However, the principle of the primacy of the most favourable norm is still generally considered to be a rule of norm conflict confined to HRL. Accordingly, even though there is a debate in doctrine as to which norm prevails when HRL and IHL are applied simultaneously (that is, in time of armed conflict), the 'principle of the most favourable' is largely ignored in this respect. A study on the meaning and implications of the principle in international law was thus needed to assess its effect on conflicting obligations flowing from HRL and IHL.

Since the 'principle of the most favourable' is usually considered to be specific to HRL, this article first examines the purpose of the principle in HRL (section 2). Then, it addresses the question of whether such a principle exists in IHL (section 3). Finally, the article considers the extent to which the principle could be taken as a rule of norm conflict (as far as States are concerned) between HRL and IHL norms (section 4). As we shall see by outlining the current state of discussions in legal literature (section 1), the answer differs depending on whether HRL and IHL are considered as *two* distinct bodies of law or as *one* body of law designed to serve human beings.

1. CONTRASTING APPROACHES IN LEGAL LITERATURE

G. Gaggioli and R. Kolb include 'the degree of protection [a rule] offers' as an element in the process of determining the *lex specialis*, which, according to mainstream scholarship,[2] can be defined not in abstract terms of bodies of law (HRL *versus* IHL) but rather in concrete terms of normative obligations in HRL and IHL: 'in determining the 'speciality' of a rule, many elements will concur: the precision/clarity of the rule, its adaptation to the particular circumstances of the case and *the degree of protection it offers*'.[3]

By '*lex specialis*', G. Gaggioli and R. Kolb mean the rule that ought to be given priority in case of conflict, 'not necessarily by derogation' but also 'by complementation'.[4] Thus, the *lex specialis* would, depending on the circumstances of the case, either *prevail* over, or *inform* the content of, the other norm. In this view, the 'degree of protection a rule offers to the individual' is part of the dynamic process whereby it is decided, in an individual case, which rule between IHL and HRL prevails over the other.[5] But the importance of the 'degree of protection' criterion in G. Gaggioli and R. Kolb's doctrine is diminished in two ways. Firstly, this criterion co-exists with others. In fact, the authors seem to place equal importance on all three criteria: 'the maxim *lex specialis* requires deciding which rule is more appropriate, protective or adapted to the circumstances of the case'.[6] Thus, the element of 'degree of protection' is thinned down in the general process of determining the *lex specialis*. Secondly, G. Gaggioli and R. Kolb wrote that 'the "degree of protection criterion" is not absolute, insofar as the less protective rule may have been intended to derogate from the rule which is the most favourable to the individual'.[7]

In her doctoral thesis, G. Gaggioli noted the incompatibility between Article 5 of the European Convention for the Protection of Human Rights and Fundamental Freedoms (ECHR)[8] and the right by belligerent States to take prisoners of war, implied by Article 12 of the Third Geneva Convention (GCIII).[9] Article 5(1) ECHR provides that 'no one shall be deprived of his liberty save in the following cases and in accordance with a procedure prescribed by law'. None of the cases enumerated in letters (a) and (f) mention the detention of prisoners of war during an international armed conflict. Does this mean that a prisoner of war cannot be deprived of his/her liberty by a State party to the ECHR? Article 5 of ECHR is certainly more favourable to the combatant having fallen into the hands of the enemy than IHL. Indeed, under the GCIII, a party to the conflict can intern prisoners of war until the end of active hostilities.[10] However, we do agree with G. Gaggioli that the idea that Article 5 of ECHR would prevent a State engaged in an international armed conflict from detaining prisoners of war, is unthinkable.[11] In the case of the detention of prisoners of war, IHL *intends to* derogate from human rights standards.[12] The same is true for the internment of protected civilians under the GCIV.[13] Thus, in certain cases, an IHL norm turns out to be the *lex specialis* even when HRL lays down more favourable provisions. These cases are those where the intention of States to derogate from HRL supersedes the criterion of the 'most protective rule'.

For M. Sassòli, the above-mentioned examples do not merely show the limits of the criterion but, above all, render it irrelevant when IHL and HRL norms are conflicting. His explanation is that IHL already achieves a compromise between military exigencies and those of humanity.[14] The protection of the individual figures among these 'exigencies of humanity'. The criterion of the 'most protective rule' would imbalance it unnecessarily.

By contrast, one author would be inclined to give full impact to the theory of the 'most-favourable-to-the-individual clause'[15] as applies to the relationship between IHL and HRL. In his separate opinion in the case *Caesar versus Trinidad and Tobago* (2005) before the Inter-American Court of Human Rights, Judge A.A. Cançado Trindade wrote that international law was undergoing a process of 'humanization'.[16] He pondered that basic considerations of humanity had permeated areas of international law which were traditionally approached 'from the angle of the "will" of States'.[17] A new mentality emerged, 'centred rather on the ultimate addressees of international norms, the human beings'.[18] Accordingly, there has been a 'constant search for an expansion of the ambit of protection (for the safeguard of an increasingly wider circle of individuals, in any circumstances), *for achieving a higher degree of protection due*, and for the gradual strengthening of the mechanisms of supervision, in the defense of common superior values'.[19]

A.A. Cançado Trindade states that the 'humanization of the law of treaties', implies that human rights treaties are to be interpreted and applied 'so as to ensure an effective protection (*effet utile*) of the guaranteed rights'.[20] Moreover, 'treaties of a humanitarian character' cannot be denunciated, suspended or terminated under the same conditions as other treaties. Their specificity lies in the 'essentially objective character of the obligations' contracted by States.[21] In his general course at The Hague (2005), A.A. Cançado Trindade considered that HRL, IHL and international refugee law were interlinked by this humanising process of international law. They shared, indeed, an identity of purpose: 'the protection of the human person in all and any circumstances'.[22] Therefore, it seems that nothing opposes the application of the most favourable-to-the-individual norm in the case of conflicting or concurrent interpretations when A.A. Cançado Trindade claims that 'one has evolved towards the interaction between norms and institutions of the three regimes, *to the benefit of the protected human beings*'.[23]

For A.A. Cançado Trindade, the *three* regimes that are HRL, IHL and international refugee law, form *one and the same* framework of protection of the human person.[24] With this premise in mind, the 'principle of the most favourable', used first as a means of resolving conflicts between human rights standards (as we shall see), may apply to conflicts between HRL, IHL and international refugee law norms.

The first part of this chapter has briefly presented three ways of considering the issue at stake, that is: *may the 'principle of the most favourable' be of some relevance when it comes to norm conflicts between HRL and IHL?* This study does not aim to come to a decision between these opinions, but to present and analyse the various legal sub-questions that we can infer from the main question. As stated in the introduction, three questions will then be addressed:

(1)   What does the 'principle of the most favourable' in HRL mean? To what extent does it require the 'most favourable norm' to be applied? What are the implications of the principle for States and for the supranational monitoring organs?
(2)   Is there any principle such as the 'principle of the most favourable' in IHL?
(3)   To what extent is the 'principle of the most favourable' applicable to the relationship between HRL and IHL? As a means of resolving norm conflicts? As a means of interpretation?

2.   THE 'PRINCIPLE OF THE MOST FAVOURABLE' IN HUMAN RIGHTS LAW

Most of the authors writing on HRL acknowledge the principle according to which, in the event of conflict between human rights standards, the most favourable to the individual must prevail.[25] These standards can be of a conventional, customary or domestic nature. The 'principle of the most favourable' has not been given much attention in legal doctrine, mostly because it has very little practical importance in the case law of monitoring organs for human rights.[26] This principle is, however, an interesting subject of study. It expresses an idea that underpins the whole philosophy of human rights, that is, human rights are to be applied and interpreted *to the benefit of the individual*. With this in mind, the 'principle of the most favourable' becomes a paramount principle of HRL – a key to understanding the whole discipline. Clearly, the 'principle of the most favourable' requires closer scrutiny.

The first question to emerge pertains to the legal basis of the principle. In this respect, reference is systematically made to the so-called 'saving clauses' or 'safeguard clauses' of the human rights treaties. These include notably:[27]

Article 5(2) of both Covenants,[28]

> There shall be no restriction upon or derogation from any of the fundamental human rights recognised or existing in any State Party to the present Covenant pursuant to law, conventions, regulations or custom on the pretext that the present Covenant does not recognise such rights or that it recognises them to a lesser extent.

Article 53 (former article 60) of ECHR,

> Nothing in this Convention shall be construed as limiting or derogating from any of the human rights and fundamental freedoms which may be ensured under the laws of any High Contracting Party or under any other agreement to which it is a Party.

Article 29(b) of the American Convention on Human Rights (ACHR),[29]

> No provision of this Convention shall be interpreted as … restricting the enjoyment or exercise of any right or freedom recognized by virtue of the laws of any State Party or by virtue of another convention to which one of the said states is a party.

Article 41 of the Convention on the Rights of the Child,[30]

> Nothing in the present Convention shall affect any provisions which are more conducive to the realization of the rights of the child and which may be contained in:
>
> (a) The law of a State party; or
> (b) International law in force for that State.

In fact, these clauses do not clearly postulate a rule of norm conflict whereby the most favourable standard would prevail over the lower one. Formulated negatively, they state that when the treaty comes into force, it *does not affect* the rights recognised to a greater extent in domestic or international law. As a result, treaty *x* safeguards those rights which are 'more favourably recognised' in treaty, custom or domestic law *y*. This explains the term of 'saving clause' referred to in the *travaux preparatoires* of 'Article 5 of both draft covenants'[31] and in legal scholarship.[32] Similarly, the subheading of Article 53 of ECHR spells out 'safeguard for existing human rights'.

The purpose of these clauses has therefore first been presented negatively, that is, 'to preclude the scope of one instrument from being limited by the provisions of one another'.[33] Expressed negatively, the 'saving clauses' do not allow States to plead that a right is less favourably recognised in one instrument to justify an infringement of the right more favourably recognised in another or in domestic law. It follows logically that States are bound to apply the most favourable (to the individual) of their obligations.[34] This was noted by G. Gaggioli and R. Kolb:

> the fact of not offering the greater degree of protection would automatically mean that the State violates one of its legal commitments, that which is enshrined in norm X, the norm that offers the greater degree of protection. By doing so, the State would violate norm X and therefore incur international responsibility.[35]

One could have objected to this argument by retorting that, according to the *lex posterior derogate priori* maxim, preference should be given to the most recent rule. However, in HRL, one does not think in terms of contractual relations between States – the last statement of will prevailing over previous engagements[36] – but in terms of strengthening the protection afforded to the individual. In this regard, the 'saving clauses' underpin the principle that human rights treaties constitute a *minimum standard*.[37] The protection of the individual must be improved perpetually. This idea might be based on the assumption that the recognition of human rights in positive law may never be entirely satisfying,[38] for positive law is the product of men, who are imperfect by nature.

The characteristic of the 'minimum standard' lies at the very heart of the 'principle of the most favourable'. Indeed, such a clause was inserted in the International Labour Organization (ILO) Constitution (Part XIII of the Treaty of Peace of Versailles, 1919)[39] to underline the fact that 'international labour standards, which are designed to improve the conditions of the workers, [were] minimum standards'.[40] Article 405 of the Versailles Treaty provides *in fine* that: 'In no case shall any Member be asked or required, as a result of the adoption of the recommendation or draft convention by the Conference, to lessen the protection afforded by its existing legislation to the workers concerned.' In 1946, the text was modified and became paragraph 8 of Article 19 of the ILO Constitution. It has not changed since. It reads:

> In no case shall the adoption of any Convention or Recommendation by the Conference, or the ratification of any Convention by any Member, be deemed to affect any law, award, custom or agreement which ensures more favourable conditions to the workers concerned than those provided for in the Convention or Recommendation.

This principle is also found in other specific conventions elaborated under the auspices of the ILO.[41] Then, *the 'principle of the most favourable' is not specific to HRL*.[42] In truth, the principle is used to resolve norm conflicts that cannot be solved by reference to formal criteria. Conflicts between human rights standards are not the only concerns. As noticed by N. Valticos, 'the decisive factor should be the substantive criterion deriving from the purpose and the content of the standard'.[43] International labour standards, whose purpose is to protect workers, are to be considered in the same way as human rights standards in the case of conflict. Given the progressive nature of international labour law, 'preference must be given in principle to the standard which is the most favourable to the workers'.[44]

In short, the 'principle of the most favourable' applies (or may be relied upon) in relation to standards that have to be applied or interpreted in accordance with their aims and purpose. In the case of human rights and labour law standards, this purpose is the protection of the individual. The principle dictates that States[45] should apply the 'most favourable to the individual' norm amongst the standards that are concurrently applicable in a given situation while providing for 'the same right for the same person'.[46] This rule applies even if there is no clause providing for this, according notably to E. Roucounas.[47] Indeed, the 'principle of the most favourable' has become a general method of resolving conflicts between concurrent applicable standards that are designed for human beings. Consequently, later in this article attention will be drawn to the case of conflicting HRL/IHL norms.

One last point is worthy of further development. Does the 'principle of the most favourable' have the same implications for supranational monitoring organs as for States? Should there be two concurrent applicable norms, and are treaty bodies required to apply the most favourable norm even if the right in question has not been recognised to this extent (or not recognised at all) by the treaty establishing their jurisdiction? Reasoning in terms of dialectic, two elements are in contradiction: the principle of jurisdiction and the primacy of the most favourable norm when this norm comes from another system of protection (be it in domestic or international law). The experts of the Committee of Ministers, having considered the problems arising from the co-existence of the United Nations Covenants and the ECHR, dwelled on the former Article 60 (new Art. 53) ECHR and stated that this article '[did] not mean that the more favourable provisions of one instrument are automatically incorporated in the system of protection established by the other'.[48] According to this statement, the European Court of Human Rights has not to examine whether there is a breach of the most favourably recognised right.[49] It may nevertheless be suggested that, when a State fails to apply the most favourable to the individual norm of those which are applicable, the treaty body would find an *autonomous* violation of the saving clause[50] (or of the general principle).

The practice of the main human rights monitoring organs differs noticeably from this approach. Three trends can be distinguished in giving (or not giving) effect to the duty of States to apply the most favourable to the individual rule. The case law related to the saving clauses provides a good framework of analysis.

At one extreme, the Human Rights Committee (in charge of monitoring that the ICCPR be respected) and the European Court of Human Rights afford very little attention to the principle as enshrined in the saving clauses,[51] respectively Article 5(2) ICCPR and Article 53 ECHR. Individual applicants have rarely alleged a violation of those articles before the Committee or the Court. In the rare cases where they did, often claiming that their rights under domestic law or other treaties had been violated, the Committee or the Court rejected this part of the application.[52] As stated by the Human Rights Committee, the requirements under Article 5 ICCPR 'were general undertakings by States and cannot be invoked by individuals under the Optional Protocol, without reference to other specific articles of the Covenant'.[53] We believe that this statement is not in accordance with the literal meaning of Article 5(2) which refers to rights which are recognised or exist 'pursuant to law, conventions, regulations or custom … that the present Covenant *does not recognise* …'.[54] Indeed, if Article 5(2) of ICCPR is solely to be invoked in relation to another provision of the Covenant, the rights not recognised by the Covenant would be excluded from the scope of the saving clause. That being said, individual opinions by members of the Human Rights Committee suggest that

Article 5(2) could play a more substantial role in interpreting the Covenant. An abolitionist State should not be authorised to extradite a person to the State having condemned him/her to capital death. In his dissenting opinion in the *Kindler v. Canada* case, R. Lallah argued that: 'Article 5(2) would, even if article 6 of the Covenant were given a minimal interpretation, have prevented Canada from invoking that minimal interpretation to restrict or give lesser protection to that right by an executive act of extradition though, in principle, permissible under Canadian extradition law'.[55]

In a similar case, *Chitat Ng v. Canada*, F.J. Aguilar Urbina held the same view:

> In so far as the misinterpretation of article 6, paragraph 2, has led Canada to consider that the Covenant recognizes the right to life in a lesser degree than its domestic legislation and has used that as a pretext to extradite the author to a jurisdiction where he will certainly be executed, Canada has also violated article 5, paragraph 2, of the Covenant.[56]

They both read Article 6 of ICCPR in light of Article 5(2) and found that Canada could not escape its obligations under Canadian law which was more protective of the right to life than the Covenant.[57] The Human Rights Committee did not uphold these views. The European Court of Human Rights, though, in one remarkable case (*Okyay and others v. Turkey*), shed light on Article 53 of ECHR in a comparable way. Though not directly invoked by applicants, Article 53 of ECHR played a prominent role in determining that the 'right to live in a healthy and balanced environment' – protected under the Turkish constitution – was a 'civil right' in the sense of Article 6 ECHR: 'the concept of "civil right" under Article 6 par. 1 [could] not be construed as limiting an enforceable right in domestic law within the meaning of Article 53 of the Convention'.[58] The European Court interpreted Article 6 in light of Article 53, so that the individual is *not less protected* than on the domestic level. This protection pertained not directly to a substantial right but to the applicability of Article 6 of ECHR that provides for the right to a fair trial. This is the only case that effectively brought Article 53 ECHR into play.[59]

At the other extreme, the Inter-American Commission of Human Rights stated, in the case of *La Tablada*, that in the event of conflict between 'legal standards governing the same or comparable rights in the American Convention' and 'a humanitarian law instrument', it has authority under Article 29(b) of the ACHR to *apply* the 'higher standard(s) applicable to the right(s) or freedom(s) in question',[60] even if this standard is not that of the ACHR. Thus, the Commission affirmed that it has jurisdiction to control the respect of all rights more favourably recognised in domestic and international law than in the ACHR, which has been criticised in doctrine.[61] But what is more interesting for our purposes is the Commission's justification for applying Article 29(b) to conflicting HRL *and* IHL obligations: 'Properly viewed, *the close inter-relationship between human rights law and humanitarian law* also supports the Commission's authority under Article 29 (b) to apply humanitarian law, where it is relevant'.[62] In this regard, the Commission made explicit reference to a point made in legal doctrine,[63] according to which the reciprocal relationship between Part II 'Humane Treatment' of Protocol II to the Geneva Conventions[64] and the ICCPR should be regulated by the same rule as for the application of concurrent human rights treaties, that is, the higher standard prevails over the lower one. This argument will be assessed in the last part of the article. The Inter-American Commission reaffirmed its view in the *Report on Human Rights and Terrorism* (2002).[65]

In between the two, the Inter-American Court of Human Rights has adopted a medium view between the minimalist view of the Human Rights Committee and the European Court and the maximalist view taken by the Inter-American Commission. The Inter-American Court uses Article 29(b) of ACHR as *a means of interpreting the Convention in the way most favourable to the individual*. This process of interpretation is twofold. The Inter-American Court first 'compare[s] the American Convention with the provisions of other international instruments in order to stress certain aspects concerning the manner in which a certain right has been formulated'.[66] This first step in the process of interpretation has been characterised as 'interpretative inter-action between distinct international instruments of protection of the rights of the human person' by A.A. Cançado Trindade.[67] Importantly, this process of 'interpretative interaction' is warranted by Article 29(b) itself.[68] However, as a second step, 'that approach should never be used to read into the Convention restrictions that are not grounded in its text. ... The foregoing conclusion clearly follows from the language of Article 29, which sets out the relevant rules for the interpretation of the Convention'.[69]

Then, the process of 'interpretative interaction' can only be favourable to the individual: 'When interpreting the Convention it is always necessary to choose the alternative that is most favorable to protection of the rights enshrined in said treaty, based on *the principle of the rule most favorable to the human being*'.[70]

Nevertheless, there is a difference between *applying* the most favourable norm (as the Inter-American Commission does) and *interpreting* the Convention in light of the most favourable to the individual rule. In the case of *Ricardo Canese v. Paraguay*, the Inter-American Court made a clear distinction between the duty of States to '*apply* the most favourable norm for the protection of human rights' and the application by the Court of 'the principle of the most favourable norm to *interpret* the American Convention'.[71] We are of the opinion that the Inter-American Court's doctrine reflects at best the meaning, purposes and implications of the 'principle of the most favourable' in HRL.

Much has been said about the principle in HRL, but does such a principle exist in IHL? Is the 'principle of the most favourable' a common paradigm to HRL and IHL?

3. IS THERE A 'PRINCIPLE OF THE MOST FAVOURABLE' IN INTERNATIONAL HUMANITARIAN LAW?

The 'principle of the most favourable' can be said to exist in IHL in *several* (a) but *distinctive* (b) and *limited* aspects (c).

(a) *Several* provisions in IHL treaties are without prejudice to any 'more favourable treatment under the Conventions or the Protocol',[72] 'more favourable treatment' or 'more favourable measures' than may have been used regarding protected persons by one or other of the Parties to the conflict,[73] and even regarding 'any other more favourable provision granting greater protection, under any applicable rules of inter-national law'.[74] These provisions are the expression of the principle that the Convention or the Protocol is a 'minimum standard',[75] meaning that it allows States to go beyond the protection granted to the individual,[76] and, as a consequence, ensures that States remain bound by this 'more favourable to the individual' law.[77] So the essential feature of the 'principle of the most favourable' reappears.

(b) Nonetheless, the principle bears *distinctive* aspects in IHL as compared to HRL. Article 75 of Additional Protocol I to the Geneva Conventions (API),[78] which set forth 'fundamental guarantees in favour of human beings',[79] constitutes a 'minimum standard'[80] *par excellence*. Art. 75(1) is applicable in so far as a person who is in the power of a Party to the conflict does not benefit from 'more favourable treatment under the Conventions or under this Protocol'. This is the case when the person is not a protected civilian under GCIV nor considered as wounded, sick or shipwrecked under GCI and II, nor entitled to a prisoner-of-war status under GCIII or API. In fact, a person is considered to not benefit from more favourable treatment under the Convention or under the Protocol I when he or she falls outside the legal categories that confer full protection under IHL. As stated by Mr Surbeck (ICRC) at the 1974–7 Diplomatic Conference on the Reaffirmation and Development of International Humanitarian Law Applicable in Armed Conflicts, Article 75 'was designed first of all to fill the gaps in treaty law in respect of persons not covered by such law'.[81] According to the ICRC Commentary, they are, first, the persons that cannot lay claim to the full application of the Conventions or Protocol, notably those affected by the derogations provided for in Article 5 of GCIV. Then, there are those that were denied prisoner-of-war status or the status of protected civilian: mercenaries,[82] spies, persons who have participated in hostilities without fulfilling the conditions for prisoner-of-war status, nationals of co-belligerent States or States not Parties to the conflict 'if the State of their nationality does not have normal diplomatic representation in the State in the power they find themselves'.[83] Moreover, the *travaux préparatoires* of API confirm that Article 75 applies to nationals of the Parties to the conflict[84] to the extent that they do not benefit from more favourable treatment afforded by the State of their nationality. What sets Article 75(1) apart from the saving clauses in HRL, is that it has first and foremost a 'gap-filling effect' in the application of IHL, whereas the saving clauses intend to avoid norm conflicts with existing and future treaties. In sum, the saving clauses can better be described as 'compatibility clauses' between concurrent human rights treaties and Article 75(1) as a clause granting 'the minimum level of humane treatment'[85] to any person who is under the power of a Party to the conflict. The saving clauses are open on 'other law', whereas Article 75(1) refers to the law 'under the Conventions and this Protocol'. Conversely, paragraph 8 of Article 75 of API has been clearly drafted, modelled on the clauses contained in HRL treaties.[86] It provides that: 'No provision of this Article may be construed as limiting or infringing any other more favourable provision granting greater protection, under any other rules of international law, *to person covered by paragraph 1*'.[87]

It is pointed out that paragraph 8 must not be read in isolation, but with paragraph 1. Thus, Article 75(8) cannot be taken as a general saving clause for Protocol I or even for IHL. Its personal and material scope is limited.

(c) The scope of Article 75(8) is *limited* in two ways. First, it explicitly refers to 'persons covered by paragraph 1', namely those who do not or only partially enjoy protection under IHL. Therefore, Article 78(5) does not apply to prisoners of war, sick, wounded, shipwrecked or protected civilians. Its personal scope is limited in this way.

Second, Art. 75(8) is strongly connected to the rights and guarantees enunciated in paragraphs 2–7 of the article. These guarantees deal exclusively with the *treatment* of the person being in the power of a Party to the conflict. A doctrinal distinction has been made between the *Law of Geneva* as the body of rules which protect victims of war, and the *Law of The Hague* as provisions which affect the conduct of hostilities. These are no longer considered to be two distinct sources of law, but a distinction is still made between the conduct of hostilities and the rules of IHL governing human treatment, namely for didactic purposes.[88] Article 75(8) and aforementioned provisions of IHL[89] are concerned with a 'minimum standard of human treatment'. Thus, Art. 75(8) is to be understood as restricted, in its material scope, to any other more favourable provision granting *greater human treatment*, under international law, to the individuals concerned. Thus the added value of paragraph 8 of Article 75 (with regard to paragraph 1) lies in the fact that the most favourable norm can be found in 'any other rules of international law', whereas paragraph 1 refers to the more favourable treatment under the Geneva Conventions and Protocol I. According to the ICRC Commentary on Art. 75(8), the persons that may benefit from greater protection under 'any other rules of international law' are the nationals of neutral States who may invoke the Hague Convention V of 1907 Respecting the Rights and Duties of Neutral Powers and Persons, as well as diplomats of enemy or neutral States who may enjoy greater protection under the Vienna Convention on Diplomatic Relations (1961). The ICRC Commentary does not make mention of HRL. Can 'any other rules of international law' be one of *Human Rights Law*? This hypothesis will now be assessed keeping in mind the framework suggested in this article, notably with regard to the limited scope of Article 75 API. Nonetheless, our analysis should be grounded in the reciprocal relationship between HRL and IHL at large with an aim of understanding whether the 'principle of the most favourable' is a general principle transcending HRL and IHL.

4. THE PRINCIPLE IN ACTION: IN THE EVENT OF CONFLICT BETWEEN HUMAN RIGHTS AND INTERNATIONAL HUMANITARIAN LAW NORMS

As quoted by the Inter-American Commission in *La Tablada* case, the authors of the *New Rules* stated that:

> when Protocol II in its more detailed provisions establishes a higher standard than the Covenant, this higher standard prevails, on the basis of the fact that the Protocol is 'lex specialis' in relation to the Covenant. On the other hand, provisions of the Covenant which have not been reproduced in the Protocol or which provide for a higher standard of protection than the Protocol should be regarded as applicable irrespective of the relative times at which the two instruments came into force for the respective State. It is a general rule for the application of concurrent instruments of Human Rights – and Part II 'Humane Treatment' is such an instrument – that they implement and complete each other instead of forming a basis for limitations.[90]

It may be noted that this statement concerns the relationship between the ICCPR and Protocol II to the Geneva Conventions relating to the protection of victims of non-international armed conflicts, which contains no provision similar to that of Article 75(8) of API.[91] Instead, the authors invoke the 'principle of the most favourable' as a general rule of HRL. The argument that follows is that Articles 4–6 of APII (Part II: Humane Treatment) are considered as constituting an instrument of human rights *within IHL. A contrario*, the authors of the New Rules do not consider that the 'principle of the most favourable' governs (or should govern) the reciprocal relationship between HRL and IHL, but merely the relationship between HRL and *IHL provisions having the character of human rights*. In this respect, it is interesting to ask whether these latter provisions become part of HRL or whether these remain part of IHL. We shall also consider Article 75 API in examining this question since it bears the same characteristics.

During the Diplomatic Conference, Art. 75 was characterised by Belgium as a '"mini-convention" concerned with the respect and protection of the human person'[92] and considered by other States as setting forth 'fundamental guarantees in favour of human beings'[93] or 'fundamental human rights'.[94] However, pointing out the formal nature of the elaborated instrument (being that of IHL), Austria stated that: '[Draft] article 65, as adopted, constitutes a body of rules of human rights which, while belonging within the context of the Universal Declaration of Human Rights and the International Covenant on Civil and Political Rights, establishes *special rules applicable in cases of armed conflict.*'[95]

Likewise, Canada recalled that 'the purpose of the Conference was not to draft a Convention on Human Rights'.[96] L. Condorelli, not only a leading scholar of international law but also representative of Italy at the Diplomatic Conference, said that '[draft] Article 65 was one of the most important developments of *international humanitarian law*'.[97] The ICRC Commentary adopts a similar view with regard to the Part II 'Humane Treatment' (arts 4–6) of APII, that is, even though

> Protocol II contains virtually all irreducible rights of the Covenant on Civil and Political Rights ... [t]he Conventions and their additional Protocols have the same purpose as international instruments relating to human rights, i.e. the protection of the human person. However, these are two distinct legal systems, each with its own foundations and mechanisms.[98]

In truth, Articles 75 API and 4–6 APII can either be said to belong to IHL if emphasis is put on the *instrumentum*, or to form a common law affecting rights of the individuals. In the latter, the formal distinction between HRL and IHL is fading away in favour of a material criterion: the protection of the individual. This was the reasoning adopted by the Inter-American Commission of Human Rights in *La Tablada* Case. HRL and IHL share a 'common purpose of protecting human life and dignity'.[99] It appears that the more the authors insist on the convergence of HRL and IHL, the more they are inclined to invoke the 'principle of the most favourable' with regard to their reciprocal relationship. However, the majority of the legal literature maintains that HRL and IHL should remain two distinct bodies of law that can, at best, complement each other.[100] According to this view, in case of conflict, no principle such as 'the most favourable to the individual rule' can be acceptable, *except when there is no fundamental incompatibility between the scopes of material application of HRL and IHL.*

Indeed, we come to the conclusion that the 'principle of the most favourable' can be relied upon as a norm conflict tool with regard to the standards of humane treatment. Since the convergence between HRL and IHL is patent in this field,[101] there is nothing that would contradict the following statement: *in case of armed conflict, States are obliged to apply the rule which guarantees the most favourable treatment to the individuals, standards of HRL and IHL being merged.* Regarding the implications of this duty for the HRL monitoring organs,[102] it follows that these have to interpret HRL in light of the most favourable treatment in IHL (if IHL provides for a more favourable humane treatment). But, we have seen that Article 75(8) has a very limited personal scope since it does not concern the persons who are fully protected by IHL, that is, the protected persons, by referral to paragraph 1. In this respect, we think that a new interpretation of paragraph 8 is needed. Indeed, Article 75 was drafted in 1976. At that time, it may have been thought that the status of protected persons in IHL could not afford better protection to those concerned. Nevertheless, HRL has since then been seen as contributing to the protection of victims of armed conflicts, even in the conduct of hostilities. The argument that Article 75(8) closes the door to greater standards of humane treatment for 'protected persons' (in the sense of IHL) is not sustainable nowadays. In fact, paragraph 1, to which paragraph 8 refers, does not explicitly exclude the protected persons but those who do not benefit from 'more favourable treatment under the Geneva Conventions and this Protocol'. This expression is subject to interpretation and can be intended to mean: 'so long as protected persons do not benefit from more favourable treatment under international law, paragraph 8 does not concern them'. This interpretation would be in accordance with the idea that the fundamental guarantees enunciated in IHL are minimum standards.[103] Yet, paragraph 8 of Art. 75 could not be used to confer the right of *habeas corpus* (through HRL) to prisoners of war. If paragraph 3 of Article 75 is not applicable to prisoners of war,[104] paragraph 8 cannot be used as a means of imposing a right that IHL intended to deny to prisoners of war.

To conclude, HRL, like 'any other rules of international law', is likely to grant greater protection (treatment) to *any* person who is in the power of a Party to the conflict, regardless of its status. As such, HRL may be considered as the most favourable norm, depending on the case. Conversely, IHL may guarantee 'human rights to a greater extent than is done by a non-derogeable human right under the Covenant'.[105] Article 7 of ICCPR states that 'no one shall be subjected without his free consent to medical or scientific experimentation'. As noted by Y. Dinstein, the Geneva Conventions go beyond the issue of consent.[106] Under Article 13 of GCIII ('Humane treatment of prisoners'), 'no prisoner of war may be subjected to physical mutilation or to medical or scientific experiments of any kind which are not justified by the medical, dental or hospital treatment of the prisoner concerned and carried out in his interest'.

Combined with Article 7 of GCIII ('Non-renunciation of rights'),[107] prisoners of war cannot renounce in part or in entirety the rights secured to them by the Convention or by any special agreement between the Parties. It follows that the prisoner's consent to a medical experimentation is void. The 'principle of the most favourable' dictates that States apply *the most favourable standard of treatment.*

However, there remain limits to the application of the 'principle of the most favourable': first, when the contradiction of norms between HRL and IHL has been *intended* to result in the prevalence of IHL even though IHL would not be the most favourable rule in the relevant case; second, when the case relates to the conduct of hostilities, it may be presumed that IHL constitutes the *lex specialis* (by derogation or by complementation)[108] since there is a lack of convergence between HRL and IHL in this field.[109]

In sum, the 'principle of the most favourable' applies to the reciprocal relationship between HRL and IHL when they converge on a point: the treatment of the human being who is in the hands and at the mercy of the enemy.

NOTES

*   Anne-Laurence Graf-Brugère is a PhD candidate and teaching assistant at the University of Geneva (Law Faculty), Switzerland.

1.   Most clearly by the Office of the High Commissioner for Human Rights, *Training Manual on Human Rights Monitoring*, Series 7 (New York and Geneva: OHCHR Professional Training, 2001), 38: 'Since there are inconsistencies and gaps between the protections afforded by various human rights and humanitarian law instruments, as well as by national and local laws, the individual should be entitled to *the most protective provisions of applicable international, national, or local laws*. Accordingly, if humanitarian law affords better rights protections than human rights law, humanitarian law should be applied – and vice versa' (emphasis added).

2.   See *inter alia* C.J. Greenwood, 'Scope of Application of Humanitarian Law', in *The Handbook of International Humanitarian Law*, ed. D. Fleck (Oxford: Oxford University Press, 2008), 75; M. Sassòli, 'The International Legal Framework for Stability Operations: When May International Forces Attack or Detain Someone in Afghanistan?', *Israel Yearbook on Human Rights* 39 (2009): 204.

3.   G. Gaggioli and R. Kolb, 'A Right to Life in Armed Conflicts? The Contribution of the European Court of Human Rights', *Israel Yearbook on Human Rights* 37 (2007): 122 (emphasis added).

4.   Ibid., 123. On the complementation feature (rather than the conflict-solving aspect) of the *lex specialis* doctrine, see A. Lindroos, 'Addressing Norm Conflicts in a Fragmented Legal System: The Doctrine of Lex Specialis', *Nordic Journal of International Law* 74 (2005): 46 ('the special rule must either supplement or displace one of the characteristics of the general rule'); J. Pauwelyn, *Conflict of Norms in Public International Law: How WTO Law Relates to Other Rules of International Law* (New York: Cambridge University Press, 2003), 410. For *contra*, see M. Koskenniemi, 'Study on the Function and Scope of the Lex Specialis and the Question of "Self-Contained Regimes"', International Law Commission, UN Doc. ILC(LVI)/SG/FIL/CRD.1 (2004): 4.

5.   In the same line of reasoning, see N. Prud'homme, 'Lex Specialis: Oversimplifying a More Complex and Multifaceted Relationship?', *Israel Law Review* 40 (2007): 391 (arguing in favour of the application of HRL or 'the most protective rule available' in a non-international armed conflict, where fewer members of armed forces are involved); L. Doswald-Beck, 'Background Paper', Proceedings of the Expert Meeting on the Supervision of the Lawfulness of Detention During Armed Conflict (24–25 July 2004), University Centre for International Humanitarian Law, http://www.adh-geneve.ch/pdfs/4rapport_detention.pdf (accessed 30 September 2010): 9 ('Rather than being locked in sterile arguments over whether humanitarian law is the *lex specialis* for armed conflict, a more constructive approach is to examine the way to ensure the proper balance between security/military needs and individual liberty in the light of modern standards').

6.   Gaggioli and Kolb, *supra* note 3, at 163.

7.   Ibid., 123.

8.   Signed on 4 November 1950 (entered into force on 3 September 1953).

9.   Convention (III) relative to the Treatment of Prisoners of War. Geneva, 12 August 1949 (entered into force on 21 October 1950).

10. Article 118 GCIII.

11. G. Gaggioli, *L'influence mutuelle entre les droits de l'homme et le droit international humanitaire à la lumière du droit à la vie* (Paris: Pedone, forthcoming).

12. Ibid.: 'Il ne faut pas oublier que parfois, les règles de DIH constituent une exception à la protection générale offerte aux individus en temps de paix, et constituent une *lex specialis* dérogatoire. Le

principe du plus favorable ne peut donc pas être considéré comme la solution miracle aux conflits de normes entre règles de droits de l'homme et de droit international humanitaire dans une situation donnée'; Inter-American Commission on Human Rights, *Report on Terrorism and Human Rights –* Executive Summary, OEA/Ser.L/V/II.116, 22 October 2002, para. 26: 'Where terrorist acts may trigger or otherwise take place in the context of an armed conflict, the detailed *lex specialis* of presumptions and mechanisms prescribed under international humanitarian law must inform the manner in which states give effect to the right to personal liberty.'

13. J. Frowein, 'The Relationship between Human Rights Regimes and Regimes of Belligerent Occupation', *Israel Yearbook on Human Rights* 28 (1998): 9.

14. M. Sassòli, 'Le droit international humanitaire, une *lex specialis* par rapport aux droits humains?', in *Les droits de l'homme et la Constitution, Etudes en l'honneur du Professeur Giorgio Malinverni*, ed. A. Auer et al. (Geneva: Schulthess, 2007), 380.

15. The expression comes from T. Buergenthal, 'To Respect and to Ensure: State Obligations and Permissible Derogations', in *The International Bill of Rights. The Covenant on Civil and Political Rights*, ed. L. Henkin (New York: Columbia University Press, 1981), 89. In French, authors speak of 'la primauté de la clause la plus favourable', G. Cohen-Jonathan, 'Les rapports entre la Convention européenne des droits de l'homme et le Pacte des Nations Unies sur les droits civils et politiques', in *Régionalisme et universalisme dans le droit international contemporain*, ed. Société Française de Droit International (Paris: Pedone, 1977), 321.

16. *Caesar v. Trinidad and Tobago*, IACtHR, A.A. Cançado Trindade, Separate Opinion (Merits, Reparation and Costs), Judgment of 11 March 2005, paras 2, 38 and 65.

17. Ibid., paras 2 and 64.

18. Ibid., para. 2; for a similar appraisal, see C. Tomuschat, 'International Law: Ensuring the Survival of Mankind on the Eve of a New Century: General Course on public international law', *Collected Courses* 281 (1999): 23 (emphasising that international law was not to be taken as an end in and of itself but that it has 'a general function to fulfill, namely to safeguard international peace, security and justice in relations between States, and human rights as well as the rule of law domestically inside States *for the benefit of human beings, who, in substance, are the ultimate addressees of international law*' (emphasis added)).

19. Cançado Trindade, *supra* note 16, at para. 60 (emphasis added).

20. Ibid., para. 4.

21. Ibid., para. 5.

22. A.A. Cançado Trindade, 'International Law for Humankind: Towards a New *jus gentium* (II): General Course on Public International Law', *Collected Courses* 317 (2005): 150, see also 151: 'it is undeniable that *basic considerations of humanity* underlie International Humanitarian Law as well as Human Rights Law and International Refugee Law' (emphasis in the original).

23. Ibid., 151 (emphasis added).

24. Ibid.

25. The principle turns out to be of very little importance for generalists writing on the law of treaties or conflicts between treaties. Seyed-Ali Sadat-Akhavi is a notable exception. Chapter 7 of his general study on the *Methods of Resolving Conflicts between Treaties* devotes a substantial part to 'the principle of the "more favourable" provision in the field of Human Rights', Vol. 3 (Leiden: Brill Academic Publishers, Graduate Institute of International Studies (Series), 2003), 213–231.

26. E. Klein, 'Reflections on Article 5 of the International Covenant on Civil and Political Rights' in *Towards Implementing Universal Human Rights – Festschrift for the Twenty-Fifth Anniversary of the Human Rights Committee*, ed. N. Ando (Leiden and Boston: Martinus Nijhoff, 2004), 127–129.

27. Many human rights treaties contain such a clause, see *inter alia* Article 32 of the European Social Charter (1961): 'The provisions of this Charter shall not prejudice the provisions of domestic law or of any bilateral or multilateral treaties, conventions or agreements which are already in force, or may come into force, under which more favourable treatment would be accorded to the persons protected'; Article 23 of the Convention on the Elimination of All Forms of Discrimination against Women (1979): 'Nothing in the present Convention shall affect any provisions that are more conducive to the achievement of equality between men and women which may be contained: (a) In the legislation of a State Party; or (b) In any other international convention, treaty or agreement in force for that State'; Article 5 of the Convention relating to the Status of Refugee (1951): 'Nothing in this Convention shall be deemed to impair any rights and benefits granted by a Contracting State to refugees apart from this Convention'; Article 21 of the Convention on International Access to Justice (1980): '... nothing in this Convention shall be construed as limiting any rights in respect of matters governed by this

Convention which may be conferred upon a person under the law of any Contracting State or under any other convention to which it is, or becomes, a party'; Article 1(2) of the Convention against Torture and Other Cruel, Inhuman or Degrading Treatment of Punishment (1984): 'This article is without prejudice to any international instrument or national legislation which does or may contain provisions of wider application'; Article 22 of the Framework Convention for the Protection of National Minorities (1994): 'Nothing in the present framework Convention shall be construed as limiting or derogating from any of the human rights and fundamental freedoms which may be ensured under the laws of any Contracting Party or under any other agreement to which it is a Party'; and Article 10 of the Rome Statute of the International Criminal Court (1998): 'Nothing in this Part shall be interpreted as limiting or prejudicing in any way existing or developing rules of international law for purposes other than this Statute.' For the similar clauses found in the International Labour Organization (ILO) Constitution and IHL instruments, see *infra* notes 40–41 and 74.

28. International Covenant on Civil and Political Rights (ICCPR) and International Covenant on Economic, Social and Cultural Rights (ICESCR) signed on 16 December 1966 (entered into force respectively on 23 March 1976 and 3 January 1976).

29. Signed on 22 November 1969 (entered into force on 18 July 1978).

30. Signed on 20 November 1989 (entered into force on 2 September 1990).

31. UN Doc. A/2929, Annotations on the text of the draft International Covenants on Human Rights, General Assembly 10th session, Agenda item 28, Part II (1 July 1955), 26.

32. M. Nowak, *U.N. Covenant on Civil and Political Rights: CCPR Commentary* (Kehl am Rhein: Engel, 2005), 111 and 117; M. Sepúlveda, *The Nature of the Obligations under the International Covenant on Economic, Social and Cultural Rights* (Antwerp: Intersentia, 2003), 306; S. Detrick, *A Commentary on the United Nations Convention on the Rights of the Child* (The Hague: Martinus Nijhoff, 1999), 712.

33. Venice Commission (Council of Europe), Opinion on the Legal Problems Arising From the Co-existence of the Convention on Human Rights and Fundamental Freedoms of the Commonwealth of Independent States and the European Convention on Human Rights (adopted 6–7 March 1998), on the basis of the report by G. Malinverni, http://www.venice.coe.int/docs/1998/CDL-INF(1998)008-e.asp (accessed 30 September 2010); this was the conclusion reached by the Committee of Experts on Human Rights in the Report relating to *Problems arising from the co-existence of the United Nations Covenants on Human Rights and the European Convention on Human Rights*, Doc H (70) 7 (September 1970), para. 85: 'restrictions provided for in one instrument may not be invoked to limit the rights set out in the other', http://www.echr.coe.int/library/digdoc/DG2/HDOCS/COE-1970-EN-H(70)7.pdf (accessed 30 September 2010); E. Decaux, 'Article 60', in *La Convention européenne des droits de l'homme, commentaire article par article*, eds L.-E. Pettiti et al. (Paris: Economica, 1999), 901; Nowak, *supra* note 32, at 118.

34. This is confirmed by the *Travaux préparatoires* of the UN Covenants, UN Doc. A/2929, Agenda item 28, Part II, 27, para. 61.

35. Gaggioli and Kolb, *supra* note 3, at 123.

36. P.-M. Dupuy, 'L'unité de l'ordre juridique international: cours général de droit international public (2000)', *Collected Courses* 297 (2002): 30 ('le primat mécanique de la volonté la plus récente sur la plus ancienne', P.-M. Dupuy describes the classical positivist approach to international law).

37. This has been unanimously acknowledged in legal scholarship, Nowak, *supra* note 32, at 118; K. Vasak, 'Les principes d'interprétation et d'application des droits de l'homme', in *Boutros Boutros-Ghali Amicorum Discipulorumque Liber. Paix, développement et démocratie* (Brussels: Bruylant, 1998), 1422.

38. In the same line of reasoning, J. De Meyer, 'Brèves réflexions à propos de l'article 60 de la Convention européenne des droits de l'homme', in *Protecting Human Rights: The European Dimension, Studies in Honour of Gérard J. Wiarda*, eds F. Matscher et al. (Cologne and Berlin: C. Heymann, 1988), 128.

39. The Versailles Treaty, 28 June 1919, *Avalon Project, Documents in Law, History and Diplomacy*, Yale Law School, http://avalon.law.yale.edu/subject_menus/versailles_menu.asp (accessed on 30 September 2010).

40. N. Valticos, *International Labour Law* (Deventer and The Netherlands: Kluwer Law International, 1979), 232, see also at 73: 'the ILO provides (Article 19, para. 8) that an international standard represents a minimum standard in relation to national legislation, and that the latter may ensure more favourable conditions to the workers. The same principle should logically apply in regard to the relationship between different international labour standards.'

41.   Article 20 of the *Hours of Work and Manning (Sea) Convention* (1936): 'Nothing in this Convention shall affect any law, award, custom or agreement between shipowners and seamen which ensures more favourable conditions than those provided by this Convention'; Article 9 of the *Draft Convention [51] concerning the reduction of hours of work on public works*, Official Bulletin ILO, Vol. XXI (1936), 126; Article 10 of the *Draft Convention [54] concerning annual holidays with pay for seamen*, ibid., 186; Article 12 of the *Draft Convention [55] concerning the liability of the ship-owner in case of sickness, injury or death of seamen*, ibid., 192.

42.   This was argued by G. Cohen-Jonathan in his 'conclusions' in *La protection des droits de l'homme par le Comité des droits de l'homme des Nations Unies: les communications individuelles. Actes du colloque de Montpellier, 6–7 mars 1995*, eds F. Sudre et al. (Montpellier: Institut de droit européen des droits de l'homme, 1995), unless he understood 'human rights' in a broader sense (as encompassing all norms conferring protection to the human being).

43.   Valticos, *supra* note 40, at 73.

44.   Ibid. According to N. Valticos, the principle is more a norm conflict *avoidance* rule than a norm conflict *resolution* rule since the implementation of the higher standard automatically entails the implementation of the lower one. There are no conflicting rules but one subordinated to the other. The expressions of norm conflict 'avoidance' or 'resolution' rule are taken from M. Milanovic, 'A norm conflict perspective on the relationship between international humanitarian law and human rights law', *Journal of Conflict and Security Law* 14 (2010), 466–470.

45.   This rule also addresses national judges. In the event of conflict between a domestic norm and a norm of international law directly applicable to domestic law, the national judge must give preference to the most favourable one. In fact, if the domestic norm better protects the individual, domestic law will be given primacy to international law, which, subsequently, will give way to domestic law on the ground that it is more favourable to the individual, J. Velu and R. Ergec, *La Convention européenne des droits de l'homme* (Brussels: Bruylant, 1990), 60.

46.   This point has been made by Sadat-Akhavi, *supra* note 25, at 219. The 'principle of the most favourable' cannot be applicable in the case of conflict between 'different rights of two different persons'. Indeed, what would be more favourable to one person would not be the most favourable to the other. However, in the case *Open Door and Dublin Well v. Ireland*, ECtHR, Application No. 14234/88, 29 October 1992, Dissenting Opinion of the Judges Pettiti, Russo and Lopes Rocha have argued, on the basis of Article 60 ECHR (new Article 53), that the right to life of a foetus was better protected in Irish domestic law than in the ECHR, and that, in assessing whether Ireland has violated Article 10 ECHR (the right to impart information) for having forbidden the non-profit organizations Open Door and Dublin Well to counsel pregnant women to travel abroad to obtain an abortion, 'the Court has failed to take sufficient account of the reference to "the rights of others" in Article 10 of the Convention and of Article 60 in relation to the provisions in the Irish legislation which afford a broader protection of rights than the Convention' (Dissenting Opinion). But, in agreement with Sadat-Akhavi, the 'principle of the most favourable' cannot be used to reconcile two conflicting liberties. In the *Open Door and Dublin Well* case, the issue was more ideological than legal.

47.   E. Roucounas, 'Engagements parallèles et contradictoires', *Collected Courses* 206 (1987): 200. The author considers that the 'principle of the most favourable' is the fairest and most natural way of resolving conflicts between concurrent applicable human rights treaties. The fact that the existence of the rule has been attested in some federal States (for Switzerland, see M. Hottelier, 'Le principe de faveur, arbitre des droits fondamentaux et des droits de l'homme,' in *Les droits de l'homme et la Constitution, Etudes en l'honneur du Professeur Giorgio Malinverni*, eds A. Auer et al. (Geneva: Schulthess, 2007), 171–196) supports the argument made by Roucounas.

48.   Doc H (70) 7, para. 85; Decaux, *supra* note 33, at 901; Nowak, *supra* note 32, at 118.

49.   See *Markopoulou v. Greece* and *F.V. v. Greece*, European Commission of Human Rights, 6 April 1994, para. 4 (only in French). The applicant invoked Article 60 (new Article 53) to support her allegations of violations of the European Social Charter, the European Code of Social Security and the ICCPR. The Commission declined its jurisdiction for this part of the application on the grounds that it has no jurisdiction for finding violations of other instruments than the ECHR.

50.   S.K. Martens pleads for a similar autonomous violation of former Article 53 of ECHR which required from States parties that they abide by judgments of the Court. According to the author, a breach of (the former) Article 53 ECHR should be invoked by complainants as a 'right of procedural nature' when a State fails to implement a Decision of the Court. The breach would not have to be combined with a substantial right of the ECHR, 'Individual Complaints under Article 53 of the European Convention on Human Rights', *Essays in Honour of Henry S.G. Schermers. Volume 3: The Dynamics*

of the Protection of Human Rights in Europe (Dordrecht, Boston and London: Martinus Nijhoff, 1994), 253–292.

51. Mention must nevertheless be made of the General Comment No. 29: *States of Emergency, Article 4*, HRC, 31 August 2001 (UN Doc. CCPR/C/21/Rev.1/Add.11), para. 9: dwelling on Article 4(1) of ICCPR, which requires that no measure derogating from the provisions of the Covenant may be inconsistent with the State's party's other obligations under international law, the Committee noted that this principle (known as 'the principle of consistency') was reflected in Article 5(2) of ICCPR.

52. As for the Human Rights Committee, see *Wackenheim v. France* (known as the *Dwarf Tossing case*), HRC, 8–26 July 2002, UN Doc. CCPR/C/75/D/854/1999, para. 4.5; *Strik v. Netherlands*, HRC, 1 November 2001, UN Doc. CCPR/C/76/D/1001/2001, para. 7.4; *Arutyunyan v. Uzbekistan*, HRC, 29 March 2004, UN Doc. CCPR/C/80/D/917/2000, paras 5.4 and 5.5. The European Court of Human Rights rejected the part of the application related to Article 53 ECHR as being manifestly ill-founded in cases *Dumitrascu v. Romania and Turkey*, ECtHR, Application No. 43007/02, Decision on Admissibility, 9 June 2005, only in French, para. 2; *Volosyuk v. Ukraine*, ECtHR, Application No. 1291/03, Partial Decision on Admissibility, 22 May 2007; *Martinov v. Ukraine*, ECtHR, Application No. 36202/03, Judgment, 14 December 2006, paras 16–17; or found that the requirements of Article 53 were absorbed by another provision of ECHR in cases *Ocone v. Italy*, ECtHR, Application No. 48889/99, Decision on Admissibility, 19 February 2004, only in French, para. 5; *Pisacane v. Italy*, ECtHR, Application No. 70573/01, Decision on Admissibility, 9 December 2004, only in French, para. 3; *Gasparini v. Italy*, ECtHR, Application No. 7206/02, Decision on Admissibility, 15 March 2005, only in French, para. 4.

53. *A.M. v. Finland*, HRC, 14 August 1992, UN Doc. CCPR/C/45/D/398/1990, para. 4.2; *M.G.B. and S.P. v. Trinidad and Tobago*, HRC, 3 November 1989, UN Doc. CCPR/C/37/D/268/1987, para. 6.2.

54. Emphasis added.

55. *Joseph Kindler v. Canada*, HRC, 30 July 1993, UN Doc. CCPR/C/OP/5, pp. 113–133, para. 6 of the Dissenting Opinion of R. Lallah.

56. *Charles Chitat Ng v. Canada*, HRC, 5 November 1993, UN Doc. CCPR/C/OP/5, pp. 94-113, para. 9 of the Dissenting Opinion of F.J. Aguilar Urbina.

57. Still, there are differences between the two views submitted. Lallah, in his Conclusions, found a breach of Article 6 interpreted in the light of Article 5(2) whilst Aguilar Urbina found a violation of Article 6 and, foremost, of Article 5(2).

58. *Okyay and others v. Turkey*, ECtHR, Application No. 36220/97, Judgment of 12 July 2005, para. 68.

59. The other cases involving Article 53 of ECHR were less convincing. In the case *Leempoel and S.A. Ed. Ciné Revue v. Belgium*, ECtHR, Application No. 64772/01, Judgment of 9 November 2006, the applicants complained that the withdrawal from sale and ban on distribution of the magazine *Ciné Télé Revue* infringed Article 10 of ECHR. They further maintained that Article 25 of the Belgian Constitution afforded a greater protection than Article 10 and that its application should have been safeguarded by virtue of Article 53 ECHR. In its Judgment on 9 November 2006, the Court brushed aside the alleged violation of Article 53 on the grounds that the interference in Article 10(1) was 'prescribed by law' (sects 86–87). In the case of *Handyside v. United Kingdom*, ECtHR, Application No. 5493/72, Judgment of 7 December 1976, para. 54, the Court mentioned Article 60 (new Article 53) in order to state that the Convention 'never puts the various organs of the Contracting States under an obligation to limit the rights and freedoms it guarantees. In particular, in no case does Article 10 para. 2 (Article 10-2) compel them to impose 'restrictions' or 'penalties' in the field of freedom of expression'.

60. *Juan Carlos Abella v. Argentina*, IACommHR, Case 11.137, Report No. 55/97, 18 November 1997, para. 165 (known as the '*La Tablada case*').

61. According to L. Zegveld, the Commission could solely have found a breach of Article 29(b), 'The Inter-American Commission on Human Rights and International Humanitarian Law: A Comment on the Tablada Case', *International Review of the Red Cross* 324 (1998): 509.

62. *La Tablada case*, *supra* note 60, at para. 166 (emphasis added).

63. Ibid., referring to M. Bothe et al., eds, *New Rules for Victims of Armed Conflicts, Commentary on the Two 1977 Protocols Additional to the Geneva Conventions of 1949* (The Hague, Boston and London: Martinus Nijhoff, 1982), 636.

64. Protocol Additional to the Geneva Conventions of 12 August 1949, and relating to the Protection of Victims of Non-International Armed Conflicts (Protocol II), signed on 8 June 1977 (entered into force on 7 December 1978).

65. *Report on Human Rights and Terrorism*, Executive Summary, Inter-American Commission on Human Rights, OEA/Ser.L/V/II.116, 22 October 2002, para. 8.
66. Compulsory membership in an association prescribed by law for the practice of journalism (Articles 13 and 29 of the American Convention on Human Rights), IACtHR, Advisory Opinion, No. OC-5/85, 13 November 1985, para. 51.
67. *Las Palmeras v. Colombia*, IACtHR, Preliminary Objections, Judgment of 4 February 2000, para. 4 of the Separate Opinion of Judge Cançado Trindade.
68. 'Other treaties' subjected to the consultative jurisdiction of the Court (Article 64 of the American Convention on Human Rights), IACtHR, Advisory Opinion, No. OC-1/82, 24 September 1982, para. 42: 'The Court is of the view, therefore, that to exclude, a priori, from its advisory jurisdiction international human rights treaties that are binding on American States would weaken the full guarantee of the rights proclaimed in those treaties and, in turn, conflict with the rules enunciated in Article 29(b) of the Convention.'
69. Compulsory membership, paras 51–52. See also para. 50 regarding freedom of expression.
70. *The Mapiripán Massacre v. Colombia*, IACtHR, Merits, Reparations and Costs, Judgment of 15 September 2005, para. 106 (emphasis added). See also *Ricardo Canese v. Paraguay*, IACtHR, Judgment of 31 August 2004, para. 181; *Herrera Ulloa v. Costa Rica*, IACtHR, Judgment, 2 July 2004, para. 184; *Baena Ricardo et al.*, IACtHR, Preliminary Objections, Judgment of 18 November 1999, para. 37; and Certain Attributes of the Inter-American Commission on Human Rights (Articles 41, 42, 44, 46, 47, 50 and 51, American Convention on Human Rights), Advisory Opinion, No. OC-13/93, 16 July 1993, para. 50.
71. Ricardo Canese, respectively paras 180 and 181 (emphasis added).
72. Article 75(1) API, which sets forth fundamental guarantees, applies to persons 'in so far as they are affected by [an international armed conflict in the sense of Article 1 of Protocol I], who are in the power of a Party to the conflict and who do not benefit from *more favourable treatment under the Conventions or under this Protocol*', see also paragraph 7(b) of the same Article, concerning the trial and prosecution of persons accused of war crimes and crimes of humanity 'who do not benefit from *more favourable treatment under the Conventions or this Protocol*'; Article 33(2) API ('In order to facilitate the gathering of information [in the search for persons reported missing], each Party to the conflict shall, with respect to persons who would not receive *more favourable consideration under the Conventions and this Protocol* ...'), in this respect see Article 34(1) API ('... where their remains or gravesites would not receive more favourable consideration under the Conventions and this Protocol'); Article 45(3) API ('Any person who has taken part in hostilities, who is not entitled to prisoner-of-war status and who does not benefit from *more favourable treatment in accordance with the Fourth Convention* shall have the right at all times to the protection of Article 75 of this Protocol' (emphasis added)).
73. Articles 6(2) of GCI, GCII and GCIII; Article 4(B)(2) GCIII; Article 7(2) GCIV; Article 83(2) of the Convention relative to the Treatment of Prisoners of War, 27 July 1929; Article 2 of the Convention for the Amelioration of the Condition of the Wounded and Sick in Armies in the Field, 27 July 1929 (*in fine*: 'Belligerents shall, however, be free to prescribe, for the benefit of wounded or sick prisoners such *arrangements as they may think fit beyond the limits of the existing obligations*') and Article 2 of the same Convention but adopted on 6 July 1906 ('The belligerents remain free ... to mutually agree upon such clauses, by way of exception or *favor*, in relation to the wounded or sick as they may deem proper'). Emphasis added.
74. Article 75(8) API ('No provision of this Article [75] may be construed as limiting or infringing any other more favourable provision granting greater protection, under any applicable rules of international law, to persons covered by paragraph 1'). See also Article 165(d) of the San Remo *Manual on International Law Applicable to Armed Conflicts at Sea* ('Nationals of an enemy State ... are entitled to prisoner-of-war status and may be made prisoners of war if they are ... d) crew members of enemy merchant vessels or civil aircraft not exempt from capture, unless they benefit from *more favourable treatment under other provisions of international law*' (emphasis added)), similar in this respect to Article 13(5) GCI and II and Article 4(A)(5) GCIII.
75. By referral to those 'minimum standard': Articles 49(4) GCI, 50(4) GCII, 129(4) GCIII and 146(4) GCIV (' ... the accused persons shall benefit by safeguards of proper trial and defence, which shall *not be less favourable* than those provided by Article 105 [GCIII] and those following of the [GCIII]'); Article 46(2) GCIII ('conditions [of transfer] *no less favourable* than those under which the forces of the Detaining Power are transferred') (emphasis added).

76. 'In general, the Geneva Conventions represent minimum standards to be accorded to war victims, and the Powers are invited to act more generously', *Commentary to the Geneva Convention (II) for the Amelioration of the Condition of Wounded, Sick and Shipwrecked Members of Armed Forces at Sea*, J. Pictet, ed. (Geneva: ICRC, 1960), 45.

77. D. De Stoop, 'New Guarantees for Human Rights in Armed Conflicts – a Major Result of the Geneva Conference 1974–1977', *Australian Yearbook of International Law* 6 (1978): 75.

78. Additional Protocol to the Geneva Conventions of 12 August 1949, and Relating to the Protection of Victims of International Armed Conflicts (Protocol I), signed on 8 June 1977 (entered into force on 7 December 1978).

79. Mr Reimann (Switzerland), CCDH/III/SR.44, 3 May 1976, in *Protection of War Victims: Protocol 1 to the 1949 Geneva Conventions*, ed. H.S. Levie, Vol. IV (Dobbs Ferry New York: Oceana Publications, 1981), 52.

80. Reimann, ibid.; Report to the third committee on the work of the working group, CCDH/III/369, 28 April 1977, ibid., 62: 'minimum standards of humane treatment'; Austria, CCDH/SR.43: Annex IV, 27 May 1977, ibid., 78; *Commentary on the Additional Protocols of 8 June 1977 to the Geneva Conventions of 12 August 1949*, Y. Sandoz et al., eds (Geneva: Martinus Nijhoff, 1987), 868 at para. 3016.

81. Mr Surbeck (ICRC), CCDH/III/SR.43, 30 April 1976, ibid., 38; see also *inter alia* Mr Fissenko (Byelorussian Soviet Socialist Republic), CCDH/III/SR.44, 3 May 1976, ibid., 55; Mrs Mantzoulinos (Greece), ibid., 57; Bothe et al. *supra* note 63, at 457.

82. CCDH/III/366, ibid., 64–65, notably Mr Miles (United States of America) stating at 65 that: 'a person who would qualify as a mercenary ... was none the less a human being entitled to the basic guarantees of [draft] Article 65'.

83. Y. Sandoz et al., eds, *Commentary on the Additional Protocols of 8 June 1977 to the Geneva Conventions of 12 August 1949* (Geneva: Martinus Nijhoff, 1987), 866.

84. There were great controversies regarding 'the question of whether the protections of the article were to be extended to a Party's own nationals', *Report to the third committee*, 62.

85. Surbeck, CCDH/III/SR.43, *supra* note 81, at 39.

86. In this respect, Bothe et al. mention former Article 60 ECHR (new Article 53) but consider that Article 60 'is limited to safeguarding conventional international law but not customary law, which *is* included in para. 8', *supra* note 63, at 466 (emphasis in the original). On the other hand, they note that paragraph 8 does not relate to national legislation of States (as does the ECHR) whereby rights could be more favourably recognised to individuals: 'it would be left to the internal legal order of State Parties to determine the relationship between the provisions of Article 75 and national law'. Contrary to this opinion, we assume that it was clear to the drafters of Article 75 (draft Article 65) that national legislation of State parties could go beyond the minimum standard established by the Protocol (see *supra*, note 76).

87. Emphasis added.

88. See International Committee of the Red Cross, *Interpretative Guidance on the Notion of Direct Participation in Hostilities Under International Humanitarian Law* (Geneva: International Committee of the Red Cross, May 2009), 7. It raises the question of whether what is stated as regards the law governing the conduct of hostilities *ipso facto* affects the status and treatment of the persons finding themselves in the adversary's hands, or whether these two aspects can be dissociated.

89. *Supra* notes 72–75.

90. Bothe et al., *supra* note 63, at 636.

91. Article 5(1) APII should nevertheless be mentioned since it provides for provisions which 'shall be respected *as a minimum* with regard to persons deprived of their liberty for reasons related to the armed conflict' (emphasis added), as well as paragraph 2 of Preamble APII 'Recalling ... that international instruments relating to human rights offer a basic protection to the human person'.

92. Mr de Breucker (Belgium), CCDH/III/SR.43, *supra* note 79, at 43.

93. Reimann, CCDH/III/SR.44, *supra* note 79, at 52.

94. Mgr Luoni (Holy See), CCDH/III/SR.57, *supra* note 79, at 64.

95. Austria, CCDH/SR.43, Annex: VI *supra* note 79, at 78.

96. Mr Wolfe (Canada), CDDH/III/SR.44, *supra* note 79, at 55 (not agreeing with the application of Article 75 to a State's nationals).

97. Mr Condorelli (Italy), CDDH/III/SR.43, *supra* note 79, at 48 (emphasis added).

98. Sandoz et al., eds, *Commentary on the Additional Protocols of 8 June 1977 to the Geneva Conventions of 12 August 1949* (Geneva: Martinus Nijhoff, 1987), 1340 at para. 4429.

99.   *La Tablada case, supra* note 60, at para. 158.
100. Illustrated by the paradigm of 'belt and suspenders' by W.A. Schabas, '*Lex Specialis?* Belt and Suspenders? The Parallel Operation of Human Rights Law and the Law of Armed Conflict, and the Conundrum of *Jus ad Bellum*', *Israel Law Review* 40 (2007): 593.
101. R. Kolb, 'Human Rights and Humanitarian Law', in *Max Planck Encyclopedia of Public International Law* (Heidelberg: Max Planck Institute for Comparative Public Law and International Law and Oxford University Press, 2010), para. 2.
102. See *supra* section 2.
103. Sandoz et al., eds, *Commentary on the Additional Protocols of 8 June 1977 to the Geneva Conventions of 12 August 1949* (Geneva: Martinus Nijhoff, 1987), 875 at para. 3060
104. Ibid.
105. Y. Dinstein, *The Conduct of Hostilities under the Law of International Armed Conflict* (Cambridge: Cambridge University Press, 2008), 24.
106. Ibid.
107. Articles 7/7/7/8 GCI/II/III/IV.
108. See *supra* note 4.
109. Schabas considers that HRL and IHL have a 'fundamental incompatibility, rooted in their differing attitudes to the *jus ad bellum*', *supra* note 100, at 612.

PART III

THE NEED FOR A COMBINED APPROACH

14. The law of occupation and human rights law: some selected issues

*Tristan Ferraro**

1. INTRODUCTION

Human rights law can certainly play an important role in delimiting the occupying power's rights and duties, notably in relation to the occupied population. Indeed, the creation of a robust human rights law (hereafter HRL) regime has significantly altered international expectations with regard to the treatment of inhabitants of occupied territory, in particular since this body of law has been, over time, widely recognized as applicable in situations of occupation.[1] Therefore, HRL may arguably impose formal obligations on the occupant in the course of its administration of the occupied territory.[2]

Recently, the International Court of Justice underlined the relevance of HRL in times of occupation and the occupant's legal obligation to take it into account in the actions it carries out and the policies it develops in the occupied territory.[3] As a result, it has been argued that HRL might serve as a basis for changing existing local laws[4] or even be used to justify transformative objectives.[5] This illustrates that nowadays one cannot consider contemporary occupation contexts without addressing the issue of HRL application. As A. Roberts put it nicely, 'it is neither desirable nor possible to view the laws of war as necessarily and in all cases providing a complete framework, such that human rights law is of little relevance. On the contrary, human rights law enters in to such situations in numerous ways and its role should be accepted'.[6] Undoubtedly, actions of the occupant must be examined not only through the lens of International Humanitarian Law (hereafter IHL) but also through that of HRL. Consequently, the question at stake is not anymore whether HRL applies or not in occupied territory but rather to identify how, and to what extent, this body of law applies in such circumstances.[7]

Public international law has evolved significantly since the instruments of occupation law were drafted. As E. Benvenisti wrote, more recent fundamental concepts of public international law, such as HRL, have not been duly reflected in occupation law.[8] In this respect, it has been submitted that these changes in international law should have required the law of occupation to revise its approach, in particular by taking into account the advent of human rights instruments.[9] In addition, the application of HRL to occupation has been interpreted as a primary cause of the fundamental shift in the policy goals of modern occupations because the need to protect human rights would oblige occupiers to engage in nation building. According to some writings, modern occupiers would even be expected to meet modern human rights standards and to put in place state structures and a representative form of government to fulfil human rights obligations during occupation.[10]

Promoters of such a position also underline that the increasing inadequacy of the basic premise underlying the law of occupation – namely that the exercise of provisional authority to which the occupant is entitled under occupation law – does not permit the introduction of wholesale changes in the legal, political, institutional and economical structure of the territory in question. Thus, it has been contended that the static nature of occupation law places an undue emphasis on preserving the socio-political *continuum* of the occupied territory, especially in light of the general acceptance within the international community of the applicability of certain universal standards of human rights and good governance. The transformation of an oppressive governmental system or the redress of society in complete collapse by means of occupation would be in the interests of the international community and possibly necessary for the maintenance or restoration of international peace as well as for the implementation of HRL.[11] These requested far-reaching political and institutional changes have consequently entailed an element of tension between the occupation law requirement to respect the laws and institutions in place and the perceived necessity to fundamentally alter the society of the occupied territory under certain circumstances in the name of the universality of HRL.

All this demonstrates that occupation is at the core of the interaction between IHL and HRL. Still, the legal interplay between the two bodies of law needs to be carefully examined. This is particularly important for subject matters where IHL is silent or vague or where it contains unclear definitions, such as the right to education, the right to adequate housing or the right to health, to name but a few examples. While the International Court of Justice (hereafter ICJ) has already proposed some guidance on the issue,[12] the exact nature of the relationship between the law of occupation and HRL – bodies of law which certainly have important differences[13] – still deserves more elaboration.

On the question surrounding the very fact of co-application, it appears that the dominant view now supports the co-applicability of the two legal regimes.[14] Indeed, the current direction of international law is to apply human rights norms to situations of armed conflict in general and to situations of belligerent occupation in particular, as evident in the interpretation of human rights treaties, in the decisions of treaty bodies, and in the rulings of the courts that interpreted them, including the European Court of Human Rights (ECHR).[15] The two recent ICJ decisions, then, have marked the victory of the convergence thesis.[16]

Beyond such convergence, it has been recognized that these two bodies of law could even complement each other with the view to enhancing the protection of those affected by armed conflicts.[17] The complementary approach of the relationship between human rights law and IHL would effectively increase the set of the legal protection afforded by international law to individuals living under occupation in so far as these two legal regimes provide rules that attribute obligations and responsibilities for the welfare and dignity of the occupied population.

In so far as complementarity seems to be the buzz word, the delineation of this notion becomes essential for the purposes of examining the relationship between occupation law and HRL. As C. Droege specified:

complementarity means that human rights law and humanitarian law do not contradict each other but, being based on the same principles and values, can influence and reinforce each other mutually. In this sense, complementarity reflects a method of interpretation enshrined in Article 31(3)(c) of the Vienna Convention on the Law of Treaties, which stipulates that, in interpreting a norm, 'any relevant rules of international law applicable in the relations between the parties' shall be taken into account. This principle, in a sense, enshrines the idea of international law understood as a coherent system. It sees international law as a regime in which different sets of rules cohabit in harmony. Thus human rights can be interpreted in the light of international humanitarian law and vice versa.[18]

In this respect, it is clear that complementarity also means that HRL and IHL, in particular the law of occupation, are mutually influencing. In this respect, one could well support an approach to the interaction between IHL and human rights law based on complementarity and cross-interpretation. It can be argued that the two bodies of law have to be interpreted in light of each other; such an interpretation working in both ways. Not only could human rights law be interpreted in light of IHL, as the ICJ jurisprudence highlighted, but IHL could also be interpreted in light of human rights law. In this regard, it is advocated that the *lex specialis derogat legi generali* principle be turned into a *lex specialis compleat legi generali* principle.[19] In light of the latter position, the *lex specialis derogate legi generali* principle would not disappear entirely but would only intervene when a clear conflict between two norms of occupation law and human rights law materialized.

While generally sharing those views, I nonetheless nuance them a bit and uphold that, despite the advent of the complementary thesis, the law of occupation still constitutes the *lex specialis*.[20] Occupation law is indeed the body of law specifically dealing with occupation and, therefore, has taken the specific characteristics of this situation for all its norms. As such, it should obtain an interpretive dominance and shape the application of the other applicable bodies of law as well, in particular HRL. The *lex specialis* argument does not mean that IHL definitively precludes human rights law. One logical consequence of the establishment of IHL as the specific body of law in situations of armed conflict and occupation is that HRL could not be applied in an unqualified manner in such circumstances. Rather, HRL would need to adjust to the specific situation of occupation. Consequently, HRL should be applicable in international armed conflict, including occupation, alongside IHL but in a manner respecting the proper balance set by the *lex specialis* between humanitarian considerations and military necessities. Thus, one should avoid the conclusion according to which HRL steps in automatically and unfettered as soon as IHL is not as specific with respect to certain subject matters. Rather, HRL must be integrated in a sensible way into the structure of IHL, in particular the law of occupation.

Overall, one has to recognize the importance of HRL in situations of occupation in so far as this body of law may well redefine the precise scope of the occupying power's obligations and serve as a benchmark for assessing the lawfulness of the measures it may take in occupied territory. While the effect of HRL in situations of occupation is to be nuanced by the specific norms of IHL, it may, however, still serve useful purposes in so far as it may influence the interpretation of IHL or fill normative gaps with a view to affording an enhanced protection to the occupied population.

The limited scope of this contribution does not allow for a comprehensive analysis of the interactions between occupation law and HRL. Rather, it will address the issue of the co-application of HRL and the law of occupation through the lens of three specific themes, namely transformative occupation, prolonged occupation and the use of force in occupied territory.

2.   CAN THE IMPLEMENTATION OF HUMAN RIGHTS LAW BE USED AS A JUSTIFICATION FOR THE OCCUPYING POWER'S 'TRANSFORMATIVE' AGENDA?

The recent occupation of Iraq has shown that HRL could well serve as a basis for pursuing transformative goals[21] and for departing from the conservationist principle underpinning the law of occupation.[22] Indeed, some authors have justified certain transformative policies on the basis that these are the best way to meet certain goals and principles enshrined in HRL, including the principle of self-determination.[23]

Before addressing in a more detailed fashion the issue at stake, one should first agree upon a definition of the concept of transformative occupation. In this respect, at the occasion of an expert meeting convened by the ICRC within the framework of a project on occupation and other forms of administration of foreign territory, the participants described transformative occupation as an operation whose main objective was an overhaul of the institutional and political structures of the occupied territory, often to make them accord with the occupying power's own perspectives.[24]

In this respect, the concept of transformative occupation appears to be completely at odds with occupation law's basic premises.[25] Consequently, it is submitted here that the concept of transformative occupation as defined above has no legal basis and does not find any justification whatsoever under current IHL. In so far as the occupying power does not acquire any sovereign rights over the occupied territory, it is not entitled to bring about changes in the occupied territory or to undertake reforms that could not be reversed by the legitimate government once the occupation is over. The transitory character of the rights and duties incumbent upon the foreign administrator thus precludes bringing definitive and large-scale changes into the institutional structures of the occupied territory, even when those changes are made in the name of HRL implementation.

Thus, one has to recall the importance of the conservationist principle whose continuous integrity shall be respected and promoted. This principle also reflects the dictates of prudence and the basic legal premises on which the international community was built, according to which, fundamental decisions about a territory's institutional structures should be made by the legitimate sovereign institutions and not by outsiders such as occupying powers under the guise of respect for HRL. Indeed, the transformative occupation legitimized on the grounds that it is supported by HRL would upset the balance of conflicting policies inherent in reconciling human rights imperatives with the conservationist principle. Applying HRL obligations *in extenso* could even oblige the occupying power to go so far as to impose a new constitution, new political institutions or new civil or criminal laws. It is therefore of the utmost importance to recall that, in the absence of an explicit Security Council resolution, transformative occupation cannot be justified in any case, including under the guise of HRL compliance.

However, it is submitted here that this principled position's emphasis on the necessity to respect the conservationist principle should not be interpreted as precluding any kind of changes in occupied territory. The nuance is slight but is of the utmost importance. Indeed, it is important to differentiate fully-fledged transformative projects entailing disruptions of sovereignty from smoother changes aimed at getting the basic infrastructure of the occupied society to work in accordance with the relevant occupation law norms. It is underscored that the illegality of the transformative occupation concept under IHL should not be confused with a general prohibition on effecting changes in occupied territory. On the contrary, compliance with the obligation to restore and maintain public order and civil life in occupied territory as set forth in Article 43 of The Hague Regulations could even call for some changes and oblige the occupant to engage in important reforms, some of which were justified or even required by HRL. Circumstances warranting such changes would notably include situations in which the local laws in force are contrary to IHL and HRL provisions, or prevented the occupying power from fulfilling its duties under occupation law or other relevant bodies of law such as HRL.

As a matter of fact, Article 43 of The Hague Regulations and Article 64 of the Geneva Convention IV (hereafter GCIV) impose the suspension or abrogation of oppressive local laws if the latter hindered the occupying power from discharging its duties under the GCIV and – by way of an evolutive interpretation of this obligation – to implement any other obligations derived from international law, in particular human rights law.[26] Indeed, it is almost unanimously agreed nowadays that HRL lays down obligations that occupying powers are bound to respect vis-à-vis the occupied population.

Human rights obligations to which States have committed generally include three components: the obligation to respect, to protect and to fulfil. Applied to situations of occupation, this triptych signifies that the obligation to respect means that occupying powers should refrain from interfering with or curtailing the enjoyment of human rights unless authorized by occupation law. The obligation to protect requires that the occupying powers defend individuals and groups against human rights violations. Eventually, the obligation to fulfil means that occupying powers should take positive action to facilitate the enjoyment of basic human rights.

Nowadays an occupying power has a strong argument that the combined application of Articles 43 of The Hague Regulations and 64 of the GCIV oblige it not only to disregard local laws contrary to HRL but also to take measures with the view to implementing HRL in occupied territory. Nevertheless, one should have to set outer limits to the leeway actually accorded to the foreign forces enforcing effective control. Indeed, the difficulty of setting limits to the transformations required by human rights law could render almost void the conservationist principle. Since HRL is essentially an agenda for social reform, the contradiction between the conservationist principle and the implementation of this body of law in occupied territory could become quite problematic.

If some changes can be effected by the occupying power in the name of HRL, they cannot in any case lead to transformative occupation as defined above. One has to recognize, however, that the line separating lawful changes from others affiliated to transformative occupation is very thin. Consequently, it might be difficult to find ways of permitting the fundamental conservationist principle and the necessary HRL implementation to coexist in situations of occupation.

In this respect, it could be argued that the outer limits to the occupant's legislative measures taken in occupied territory are set to a certain extent by the principle of self-determination taken in its internal meaning. As M. Sassòli specified in has seminal article on Article 43 of The Hague Regulations, the right to self-determination normally bars an occupying power from taking decisions in relation to the political, economic and social system. However, when wondering whether an occupying power would be authorized to exert the latitude granted to States on how they implement HRL, Sassòli specified that:

> while such exercise of discretion is contrary to the right to self-determination and to the principle that legislation must be based upon the will of the people, it is inherent in the situation of occupation and must therefore be accepted until the local population can exercise their right to self-determination. An occupying power must however take into account, while exercising such discretion, that it is not the sovereign and may only introduce as many changes as absolutely necessary under its human rights obligations and must stay as close as possible to similar local standards and the local cultural, legal and economic traditions.[27]

Such a position is attractive but still provides a great leeway to the occupying power. In this respect, one should wonder whether a position according to which HRL implementation be confined to limited reforms should be considered. In this respect, G. Fox recently wrote:

> at its core, the conservationist principle seeks to preserve this decision-making capacity by preventing, as McDougal and Feliciano put it, 'the active transformation and remodelling of the power and other value processes of the occupied country.' This is not to support the continuation of laws that clearly violate core human rights. But at a certain point, an occupier's reforms may become so sweeping and far-reaching that inhabitants lose the opportunity to make important choices about the nature of their own society. Deferring sweeping reforms until the return of an indigenous government allows both objectives to be served: core human rights obligations would be respected through narrowly-tailored reforms enacted during occupation, while self-determination would remain meaningful for the post-occupation society by prohibiting overbroad systemic changes.[28]

3.   THE ROLE OF HUMAN RIGHTS LAW IN SITUATIONS OF PROLONGED OCCUPATION: AN EXTENSION OF THE OCCUPYING POWER'S AUTHORITY IN OCCUPIED TERRITORY?

Articles 43 of The Hague Regulations and 64 of the GCIV constitute the most essential rules defining and delimiting the occupying power's authority in occupied territory. These provisions address the obligation of an occupier to restore and ensure public order and safety in occupied territory, and the extent to which the occupier may change local laws and initiate new legislation. As such, those provisions play a central role in circumscribing the occupying power's ability to take measures with the view to administering the occupied territory in compliance with IHL and other bodies of law, including HRL. In this respect, it is clearly admitted that the occupying power can take measures in order to fulfil its obligations under the GCIV but also in order to enhance civil life in occupied territory,[29] in particular when the occupation is characterized by its duration.

Indeed, prolonged occupation clearly affects the implementation of the occupying power's obligations under the law of occupation and calls for special measures. The duration element might lead to changes in the occupied territory that would normally not be necessary during short-term occupation. In that regard, it is submitted that the occupation law should be interpreted with flexibility when an occupation endures. It is a given that there would be a need for changes on a far greater scale during protracted occupation, simply because public policies should be adjusted in order to keep up with the passing of the time. Under such a framework, HRL may play an increasing role in so far as the changing needs of the occupied population would become even more compelling over time. Decisions notably in relation to the social and economic spheres cannot be indefinitely postponed and would need to be taken into account in order to maintain as normal a life as possible in occupied territory, as required by Article 43 of The Hague Regulations. In this respect, the welfare of the local population should be established as the main principle guiding the measures and policies undertaken by the occupying power in the administration of the occupied territory.

If the notion of the welfare of the occupied population is of the utmost importance in particular in situations of prolonged occupation, it is also characterized by its vagueness. None of the occupation law obligations describe in detail what the concept of the welfare of the occupied population consists of, as implied by certain IHL norms. In this respect, it could be appropriate to refer to HRL in order to flesh out the notion and to analyse how it impinges upon the occupying power's duties under occupation law. It is thus suggested that HRL could play an important role in substantiating the meaning of the concept of the welfare of the population. In this respect, it may be a great support in shaping the so-called 'obligation to administer the occupied territory for the benefit of the occupied population', as suggested in certain writings[30] and national judicial decisions.[31]

Consequently, it can be contended that HRL plays a key role and becomes, in situations of prolonged occupation, an integral component of the obligation to ensure that the occupied population lives as normal a life as possible, as derived from Article 43 of The Hague Regulations. In other words, the implementation of HRL in occupied territory happens to be a kind of precondition to make the occupying power comply with its obligations under IHL, specifically when the occupation endures.

Eventually, the reasoning according to which HRL would be applicable through the prism of Article 43 of The Hague Regulations was used by the ICJ in the *DRC v. Uganda* case. In its decision, the ICJ stated:

> The Court thus concludes that Uganda was the occupying Power in Ituri at the relevant time. As such it was under an obligation, according to Article 43 of the Hague Regulations of

1907, to take all the measures in its power to restore, and ensure, as far as possible, public order and safety in the occupied area, while respecting, unless absolutely prevented, the laws in force in the DRC. *This obligation comprised the duty to secure respect for the applicable rules of international human rights law* and international humanitarian law, to protect the inhabitants of the occupied territory against acts of violence, and not to tolerate such violence by any third party. (emphasis added)[32]

Thus, in situations in which HRL may influence the interpretation of IHL, the importance of HRL increases in proportion to the length of occupation, so that the IHL obligations are construed in light of the HRL obligations as set forth in the relevant HRL instruments.[33] In this respect, the International Covenant on Economic, Social and Cultural Rights (hereafter ICESCR) is of a particular importance.

Indeed, discussions on the relationship between IHL and HRL have tended to focus on civil and political rights, in particular those dealing with the use of force and deprivation of liberty. Less attention has been paid to economic, social and cultural rights. It has often been argued that IHL would always prevail over economic, social and cultural rights, in particular when it comes to positive obligations.[34] Indeed, it has been argued that obligations derived from ICESCR cannot be implemented by the occupant because of the latter's limited power to legislate under the law of occupation. In this respect, the ICJ in the Wall advisory opinion decided that the OP would be bound by the rules of the ICESCR, but only 'in the exercise available to it'.[35]

However, as underlined by Sassòli, 'tout ceci ne signifie évidemment nullement que les droits humains ne s'appliquent pas dans un territoire occupé partout où la lex specialis que constitue le dih ne les contredit pas'.[36] The content and scope of the powers referred to by the ICJ can only be determined with reference to the law of occupation. Thus, the occupying power is only authorized to make use of the leeway allowed with regard to economic, social and cultural rights within the limits set by IHL. However, one can obviously challenge the view according to which the occupant's powers in occupied territory are rather limited in this respect. If such a line had prevailed in the wake of The Hague Regulations of 1907 which reflected the theory of 'laissez-faire' implying a minimal intervention of the authorities in social and economic life and which envisioned the law of occupation against the background of a peaceful coexistence between the occupant and the local population, contemporary forms of occupation would have outdated such a vision of occupation. The evolution of the central government's role and the ever-increasing regulation of markets and other social activities have turned Article 43 of The Hague Regulations into a very broad grant of authority allowing the occupying power to intervene in almost every aspect of the occupied territory's life. In this respect, an evolutive interpretation of the law of occupation has transformed the occupant from a disinterested watchdog into a fully-fledged administrator. Thus, the so-called limited legislative power assigned to the occupying power under the law of occupation is no longer an excuse in order not to implement obligations deriving from HRL, in particular the ICESCR.

In addition, one can be tempted to refer to the conservationist principle[37] in order to discard any occupying power's responsibility vis-à-vis the implementation of human rights obligations derived from the ICESCR. Indeed, the application of the Covenant implies a long-term perspective and the existence of a sovereign power to effect far-reaching transformations of societies. The realization of some rights listed in the

ICESCR would thus oblige the occupying power to devise development strategies which would commit the occupied territory's economy for a long time and could clash with the conservationist principle underpinning the law of occupation, which would offer some resistance to changes of that kind. Consequently, a very strict interpretation of occupation law would restrain considerably the implementation of the ICESCR.

However, as mentioned above, occupation law should be subject to a more evolutive interpretation taking into account the changes in the role played by an occupying power whose responsibility obliges it to be involved in almost all aspect of the social and economic life in the occupied territory. Moreover, the realization of economic, social and cultural rights does not necessarily imply reforms that are so radical that they would be at odds with the basic premises of the law of occupation.

Eventually, it has to be admitted, as described above, that the duration of the occupation could play an important role in relaxing those restraints and in admitting that HRL and the ICESCR in particular are of a certain relevance in order to delimit the legal framework governing protracted occupation.

In many respect, prolonged occupation would favour the application of the ICESCR in so far as the application of the Covenant implies a long-term perspective and the existence of a stable authority ready to effect the transformations it requires.[38]

Indeed, the nature of the obligations set forth in the ICESCR and their flexibility as regards their implementation, facilitate the application of this treaty during occupation, in particular in the context of enduring occupations. The ICESCR recognizes that its rules are to be applied over time and that their application could go through different stages by virtue of the very nature of the prescribed obligations. This flexibility is particularly important during a period of occupation since it would permit the implementation of the ICESCR to be adjusted to the realities of the situation on the ground. For instance, once the situation in an occupied territory is stabilized over time, the normative content of the occupying power's obligations would become more extensive. The ICESCR's flexibility permits those variations in the factual situation in the field to be taken into account and accordingly makes it very practical for the occupying power.

Nevertheless, this flexibility should not be misinterpreted and misused. The progressive realization of economic, social and cultural rights does not mean that the occupying power has a right to wait for the most favourable circumstances before meeting its obligations under the Covenant. Such an interpretation would deprive the instrument of its normative content, as the occupying State would be free to decide the extent of its undertakings vis-à-vis the occupied population. Thus, during periods of occupation, the authorities in place should therefore not refer to the temporary nature of their presence on foreign territory in order to evade these obligations. In this respect, the position of the United Nations Committee on Social, Economic and Cultural Rights has shown that States implementing the ICESCR should adhere to a basic normative threshold, whatever the circumstances, including those prevailing in the occupied territory.[39]

Consequently, it has been argued that, despite its intrinsic flexibility, the ICESCR would oblige the occupying power to implement immediately some core rights. Thus, the Covenant distinguishes between two normative levels: (a) provisions establishing obligations of immediate effect; and (b) provisions establishing obligations to be realized progressively. As a result, an occupying power bound by that instrument would not be able to refer to its programmatic nature in order to delay its application as a whole in the occupied territory.[40]

In light of the above, it is submitted that some of the obligations flowing from the ICESCR appear to be a very useful complement to some rather basic obligations set forth in the law of occupation, for instance the right to health, the right to education or the right to food.

From the perspective of HRL, the right to an adequate standard of living implies that each person has access to the conditions necessary for his or her individual livelihood. According to the terms of the ICESCR, this essential minimum standard includes, in particular, adequate food, clothing and housing as well as the continuous improvement of living conditions. The Covenant also recognizes 'the right of everyone to the enjoyment of the highest attainable standard of physical and mental health'. Defining the core of each of those rights, applicable under all circumstances, would consequently clarify the rules applicable during occupation.

For instance, the right to adequate food under the ICESCR includes as an essential element the fundamental right of everyone to be free from hunger. That rule constitutes the core of the right to food, which could be violated, for example, if the occupation forces destroyed the civilian population's food stocks or affected the means of production (for example, by placing mines in agricultural areas, displacing farming or fishing communities, immobilizing the transport network or blocking access to certain basic services). This right would also be violated if the occupying power failed to adopt necessary measures to prevent third parties from carrying out similar practices.[41]

The right to food also requires the occupant to adopt certain positive measures facilitating the realization of the right. The occupying power would therefore be required to set up an effective relief distribution system and take account of the needs of the most vulnerable persons, particularly children, the elderly and the handicapped.[42]

Thus, economic, social and cultural rights complement even more efficiently the law of occupation when the occupation is prolonged[43] in so far as this latter body of law might be a bit general for defining a long-term normative framework. HRL and the ICESCR in particular appear all the more helpful when the occupation stabilizes and tends to persist. If certain immediate measures can be adopted to cover the essential content of the right to food for instance, the ICESCR also calls for a long-term approach to achieve its full realization progressively. Once the emergency period is over, it is no longer sufficient for the occupying power to distribute food to the civilian population. The system of human rights provides for civilians to have access to the resources and means to enable them to ensure their own livelihood. To that end, the foreign administration should establish measures in regard to all aspects of the food system, including the production, processing, distribution, marketing and consumption of safe food, as well as parallel measures in the fields of health, education, employment and social security. That obligation means, in particular, that the administration would be obliged to ensure the sustainable management of the natural resources used to produce food.[44]

In the field of the right to health, human rights law would require the authorities to look to the future if the occupation persists. For example, these authorities need to devise a public health strategy and plan of action in order to meet its obligation under the ICESCR.

Consequently, in the area of the right to health and the right to food, economic, social and cultural rights make explicit reference to matters that are merely touched on by the law of occupation. This evidences the necessary complementarity between human rights law and IHL, which ultimately would result in the enhanced protection of the occupied population. Such examples thus show that the occupant's obligations are not limited to the minimum defined by IHL, but are larger and should be viewed from a perspective which encompasses the complementary contribution made by human rights law.

In order to illustrate this essential interaction between HRL and IHL in the field of the right to health, N. Lubell wrote recently:

> what would the obligations be, for instance, of an occupying power towards the inhabitants of the occupied territory in terms of the right to health? As noted earlier, it would seem that human rights law obligations, including ESC rights, do apply to occupied territories. The need for these rights can be even more acute when dealing with prolonged occupation spanning decades. It might not, however, be practicable to apply the same standards and obligations to the occupied territory as those expected with regard to the right to health in the State's own territory, besides being debatable whether this is required by law. A three-tiered approach is sometimes used when analysing the human rights obligations of a State to 'respect, protect, and fulfil.' While the existing IHL rules may cover many of the 'respect' and 'protect' aspects of the right to health (e.g. protection of medical facilities), the 'fulfil' aspect is not as clear. Under IHL, aliens in the territory of a party to a conflict are generally entitled to the same level of health care as is provided to the State's own nationals. There is no equivalent IHL obligation concerning inhabitants of an occupied territory. But if the human right to health is considered to be equally applicable in the State's own territory and in the occupied territory, then it might be argued that the inhabitants of the latter are entitled to the same health care as the State provides for its own nationals. Yet occupation is envisaged as a temporary situation, and although the Fourth Geneva Convention allows for the adoption of health measures, the ability of the occupying power to establish an elaborate health system can be restricted in practical terms. Also, should the occupying power be able to provide a higher standard of health care than was previously available, then ending the occupation could potentially amount to a problematic regressive measure that would cause the health situation to deteriorate by reverting to the responsibilities of a sovereign State unable to provide the same level of care. The case for equal or almost equal health care might arguably be viable when dealing with prolonged occupation, especially if the occupying power is providing a high level of health care to its own citizens residing in the occupied territory. In general, however, when it comes to implementing ESC human rights obligations in situations to which IHL is applicable, for instance in occupied territory, there are obviously difficulties as regards derogation and level of fulfilment which need to be addressed.[45]

4. HUMAN RIGHTS LAW AND THE ISSUE OF THE USE OF FORCE IN OCCUPIED TERRITORY[46]

One of the most important challenges in contemporary occupations is to determine how and when law enforcement rules as well as conduct of hostilities rules apply in relation to the use of force by the occupying power.[47] Under Article 43 of The Hague Regulations, the occupying power has an obligation to provide – as far as possible – security in occupied territory through maintaining public order and quelling riots and disturbances, as well as enforcing the law against criminal acts. Thus, besides the enforcement of the occupying power's military authority over enemy forces, the law of occupation places upon the latter the duty to exercise police powers in the territory under its effective control.[48]

As recent occupations have shown, the regulation of the use of force vis-à-vis civil unrest and ongoing armed opposition is not so clear-cut.[49] Although the occupier is supposed to ensure security by means of law enforcement, uncertainty persists with regard to the applicable legal regimes, in particular in relation to situations where it is difficult to distinguish hostilities from civil unrest or where the occupying power is confronted by both at the same time in the entire, or parts of, the occupied territory.[50]

If the law of occupation places an important duty upon the occupying power with regard to the maintenance of public order and safety, and also recognizes that it can carry out military operations in parallel, The Hague Regulations and the GCIV do not spell out when and how force may be used in occupied territory. On the contrary, the law of occupation is silent as to the separation or interaction between law enforcement measures and the use of military force under the conduct of hostilities model. Nor does it give any concrete direction as to how to confront resistance movements and other armed opposition militarily. In this respect, the law of occupation leaves a significant degree of uncertainty as to the identification of the legal regime(s) governing the use of force in occupied territory. This situation inevitably opens the door to different interpretations on how the use of force may be resorted to in occupied territory, under what circumstances and according to which body of law. This inevitably calls into question the application of HRL in relation to the use of force in occupied territory.

In light of past practice, it appears clear that the use of force by the occupying power can be based on two alternative models. The first relates to law enforcement activities carried out within the framework of Article 43 of The Hague Regulations. This law enforcement paradigm presupposes a relatively secure hold by the foreign authority over the occupied territory, in which it seeks to ensure that the rule of law is upheld. The second model, which applies exclusively to the conduct of hostilities, is based on the premise that violent actions carried out by organized armed groups or by the remaining occupied forces still endure or have resumed.

Based on the fundamental distinction between these two models, it may be argued that their correlative rules and standards governing the use of force are also inherently dissimilar. Within the framework of the law enforcement paradigm, stricter standards apply as a consequence of the prohibition for the occupying power to deprive arbitrarily individuals of their right to life. This means that the use of lethal force by the occupying power while assuming its policing functions is only authorized under very strict circumstances characterizing the law enforcement paradigm. Indeed, under this paradigm, the occupying power may only use lethal force when this is strictly unavoidable in order to protect life and when less extreme means are insufficient to achieve that objective. As such, this law enforcement model suggests that HRL would be the more appropriate legal framework of reference.[51]

The second paradigm – which relates to the conduct of hostilities – allows more leeway to the occupying power when involved in the use of force. In the case of hostilities, the occupying forces are normally authorized to attack enemy combatants as well as civilians directly participating in the hostilities. The law of armed conflict also allows – albeit under strictly pre-established conditions – a certain level of civilian losses, often referred to in a generic way as 'collateral damage'.[52] As such, this second model constitutes the realm of IHL as the *lex specialis*.

The key challenge concerning situations of occupation lies in the fact that the above theoretical construct does not provide any further guidance in order to determine when a factual situation falls into one or other of these paradigms, nor does it explain how to switch from one paradigm to the other.[53] Still, such a determination is essential when it comes to the use of force in occupied territory since the two paradigms may apply concurrently or simultaneously and end up with quite distinct results. Moreover, the determination of the applicable model will also be of the utmost importance for the identification of the legal framework governing the occupying power's resort to force.[54]

Indeed, the occupying power may well be engaged in the conduct of hostilities (for instance against remaining enemy armed forces or other organized armed groups) but may also carry out, at the same time, law enforcement tasks as required by the law of occupation (such as quelling spontaneous demonstrations by the civilian population). In such circumstances, the challenge ahead will be to identify when each model applies and when it becomes necessary to switch from one to the other in light of the situation prevailing in the occupied territory. One would also have to wonder whether in occupied territory the occupying power is able, or even obliged, to take law enforcement measures against members of organized armed groups instead of directly using deadly force under the conduct of hostilities paradigm.

An additional challenge posed by the issue at stake arises from the necessity to identify the exact content of the rules governing law enforcement in a situation of occupation. In this respect, one would have to determine whether the rules and standards governing the use of force in law enforcement operations derive from HRL as applicable in peacetime, IHL, or from a complementary combination of these two bodies of law.

The description of the issues at stake thus shows the necessity of finding ways and methods to designate the paradigm – and its correlative rules – with exactness that would govern the use of force in occupied territory.

4.1 Can Human Rights Law Be Interpreted as the Exclusive Framework Governing the Use of Force in Occupied Territory?

Indeed, it has been argued that a HRL regime would be relevant, not to say prevalent in light of its ability to govern the use of force in all circumstances. The starting point for this position lies in the fact that while IHL and HRL apply simultaneously in occupied territory, the former should not necessarily be considered as the *lex specialis* derogating from the latter in its entirety. On the contrary, it has been contended that IHL should only be considered as a complementary body of law since HRL would generally provide adequate and sometimes more precise answers to issues linked with the use of force in occupied territory.[55]

The supporters of such a theory stress that a comparison between IHL and HRL would demonstrate that the difference in tools and reasoning would not result in substantially different outcomes. Although the HRL regime would generally go a bit further in terms of protection – as it is based on a peacetime paradigm – the variations between the two *corpuses juris* would only be a matter of degree. Furthermore, these slight differences would even tend to disappear progressively under the decisions of the human rights bodies, in particular the European Court on Human Rights, which has developed a set of human rights applicable in situations of armed conflict, adjusted to the specificities of that type of situation. It is thus argued that the HRL regime would apply also to belligerent relationships.

This prevalence of HRL is deemed all the more justified in so far as this legal regime could govern simultaneously the activities of law enforcement and military operations, both being generally conducted by the occupying power while enforcing its effective control of the foreign territory. According to the supporters of the HRL's prevalence in situation of occupation, the latter is mainly due to the flexibility of this *corpus juris*, whose rules and standards could be easily adjusted to the large variety of situations faced by the occupying power.[56] This flexibility is notably characterized by the fact that the resort to force under human rights law is assessed in light of the level of control exerted by the occupying forces over a specific situation and the level of threat they faced. Resort to HRL would thus prove particularly useful when the occupying forces were not in a position to establish with certainty whether a hostile act or intent threatening them presented – or not – a nexus with the armed conflict.

In this respect, it was deemed important to counter the misconception that HRL would only apply to law enforcement operations as its standards would be too strict to realistically govern the conduct of hostilities. This assertion is considered wrong by the promoters of HRL prevalence, since standards such as necessity or immediacy could be interpreted more leniently in light of the factual situation prevailing in armed conflict, leading to a use of force whose consequences were similar to those resulting from the application of the conduct of hostilities paradigm. It has thus been said that the interesting aspects of HRL in relation to a situation of occupation is that the use of force under this legal regime would not depend upon the status of those against whom the force could be used. This would assist in overcoming the difficultly relating to the distinction between fighters and civilians required under the conduct of hostilities model; a distinction always difficult to make in situations of occupation.

4.2 The Unrealistic Character of an Approach Solely Based on the Application of Human Rights Law

Despite the efforts made by some for promoting the central role of HRL in situations of occupation, the arguments put forward in relation to the use of force are not really convincing. On the contrary, I am of the view that this model is simply inadequate to deal with a scale of violence characterizing hostilities between the occupying power to the occupied armed forces and/or affiliated armed groups, such a situation being governed more efficiently by the conduct of hostilities model and its looser rules on the use of force.

In addition, the emphasis previously placed by the promoters of the HRL's prevalence in relation to the use of force on the similarities between human rights and IHL regimes, not only in terms of governing principles but also in terms of practical results is misplaced. In this respect, it can be convincingly argued that IHL and HRL still present sharp differences, be they at the level of their general rationale or at the level of their core rules. In particular, it is submitted here that the logic governing the use of force under a HRL-based law enforcement paradigm could not be compared to that of the conduct of hostilities paradigm as they differ significantly due to the different realities the respective norms were intended to address: armed conflicts for IHL and peacetime for HRL. The two regimes also significantly vary as to the way to address the issue of the use of force. While HRL considers the use of force from an individualized perspective, IHL's starting point lies in a broader and collective approach to the use of force linked to the opposition of two organized armed groups.

Furthermore, some important divergences still exist between the rules and standards governing the two paradigms and legal regimes. On the one hand, the use of force appears to be more limited in application of the well-proscribed law enforcement paradigm, which placed an important emphasis on limiting the use of force to situations of absolute necessity. Thus, lethal force could be intentionally employed only in circumstances where it is strictly unavoidable. As a consequence, the use of force under this paradigm could never be regarded as necessary unless it was clear that there were no feasible possibility of protecting the prospective victim by apprehending the suspected perpetrator. On the other hand, under IHL, the use of lethal force is inherent to waging war and aims to avoid or limit death, particularly of persons protected against direct attack, while acknowledging that the very nature of armed conflict is such that loss of life could not be eliminated.

As a matter of example, the issue of proportionality illustrates the differences between the two available paradigms. The aim of the IHL principle of proportionality is to limit incidental damage to protected persons and objects, while nevertheless recognizing that an operation could be carried out even if such damage was likely, provided that it would not be excessive in relation to the concrete and direct military advantage anticipated. In contrast, the aim of the principle of proportionality under HRL is to prevent harm from happening to anyone else except to the person against whom force was being used. Even such a person should be spared lethal force if there was another, non-lethal way of achieving the aim of the law enforcement operation.

In light of the above, I refute the thesis according to which the law enforcement regime would provide adequate rules and standards in order to quell threats stemming from insurgent groups in occupied territory and submits that the legal test as proposed in the *McCann* or *Issayeva* jurisprudence of the European Court on Human Rights would not prove sufficient to allow the occupier to undertake efficient military operations.[57] In this respect, it seems very likely that States exerting effective control over a foreign territory would probably never consider embarking on military operations against the enemy in occupied territory under the law enforcement regime since the latter would always be more constraining in terms of preparation, execution and *ex post facto* assessment than IHL in relation to the targeting of individuals. Thus, the HRL regime would certainly not provide all the answers on the issue of the use of force in occupied territory.

On the contrary, it is submitted here that HRL could only fit with the kind of activities falling strictly under the occupier's duty to ensure public order and safety in the occupied territory (policing activities). Furthermore, one should have also to examine whether occupation law would not provide for any detailed rule permitting the delineation of when and how the occupying power would use force during law enforcement activities.

4.3   The Role of the Law of Occupation as a Framework of Reference for the Regulation of the Use of Force in Law Enforcement Operations

The position according to which HRL is the only referral body of law for law enforcement operations carried out within the framework of the occupying power's obligation to restore and maintain public order and safety as reflected in Article 43 of The Hague Regulations is clearly not justified, in particular because it does not give enough credit to IHL. In this regard, there is an essential need to refute the misconception that occupation law *per se* could not provide a valuable legal framework regulating the use of force in law enforcement operations. Indeed, it is clear that the law enforcement paradigm can be applied in occupied territory not as a matter of HRL but as a matter of the law of occupation as stipulated in key provisions of The Hague Regulations and the GCIV. It is thus suggested here that the combination of Article 43 of The Hague Regulations, and Articles 27 and 64 of the GCIV forms the backbone of the law enforcement role of the occupier and constitutes quite a precise legal framework permitting the regulation of the use of force in occupied territory. Yet, while maintaining that standards governing the use of force in law enforcement is occupation law based, one should also recognize that these standards could be effectively supplemented by those stemming from HRL. In this respect, such an approach would illustrate perfectly the materialization of the concept of *lex specialis compleat legi generali* consecrating the complementarity between IHL and HRL. IHL, and occupation law in particular, would thus provide the main legal framework, while HRL would operate as a complement with additional standards such as precaution and proportionality. Such an approach to law enforcement in occupied territory would be more acceptable to States, in so far as rooting law enforcement rules in IHL would permit them to get around the difficulties relating to the contentious issue of the extraterritorial application of HRL.

This leads us to the interpretation and application of law enforcement standards in occupied territory. Indeed, it can be argued that these standards, stemming from the HRL or occupation law regimes, should be interpreted and applied more liberally when the occupying forces resort to force during police operations. This position is based in particular on the fact that law enforcement standards as applied in situations of occupation would differ from those applied in peacetime. Consequently, one could wonder whether the standards on the use of force drawn from HRL could be transposed as such to police operations undertaken by the occupying power in occupied territory. Indeed, the belligerency inherent in situations of occupation could also justify an adjustment to the precaution, proportionality and necessity standards in order to enable the occupying power to achieve what it was required to do under occupation law: the maintenance of public order and safety in a volatile and hostile environment.

Thus, it may be argued that the context of armed conflict in which the occupier's law enforcement activities are carried out could, in certain circumstances, authorize the occupying power to use force with more leeway than it would have had in police operations carried out on its own territory. Indeed, Article 27§4 of the GCIV (forming part of the occupation law-based law enforcement paradigm) authorizes the occupying power to take security measures 'as may be necessary' as a result of the occupation. Since the use of force during police operations would necessarily fall under the said provision, it could be considered that this clause opens the door to substantial flexibility under the law enforcement paradigm in situations of occupation. Thus, security measures, including the use of force, within the meaning of Article 27§4 of the GCIV seems not to be based on the standard of 'strict' or 'absolute necessity' required under a human rights law regime, but rather on the more generous concept of military necessity underlying IHL as a whole.

Albeit seducing, this position errs notably on the side of lack of protection for the occupied population. For protection purposes, one should favour a position according to which any use of force by the occupying power in situations other than the conduct of hostilities remains subject to the law enforcement standards of precaution, proportionality and necessity similar to those deriving from HRL. Therefore, it could be concluded that the lawfulness of any deprivation of life unrelated to the conduct of hostilities in occupied territory has to be analysed in light of the same criteria and conditions as in peacetime, ultimately sanctioning a parallel content between HRL and IHL in relation to the use of force in law enforcement operations. Furthermore, it has to be recognized also that the application of the above standards in occupied territory would probably end up with different results than in peacetime but that this variation is not because of an increased flexibility in the standards, but because of the self-evident factual differences surrounding the use of force in situations of occupation.

5. CONCLUSION

Today, the majority view supports HRL applicability/application in situations of occupation. As a result, the issue of co-application and the correlative interrelations between IHL and HRL have definitely broadened and enriched the normative framework governing occupation. Ultimately, this newly recognized complementarity will benefit the occupied population and enhance the set of protections accorded to the latter by international law. This is particularly the case when HRL norms come into play in order to substantiate certain provisions of the law of occupation and thus specify more effectively the obligations incumbent upon the occupying power.

Nevertheless, the interaction between the occupation law and HRL is still evolving and still needs further work. In terms of delimiting with more exactness the normative system regulating occupation, some challenges still exist, notably when addressing issues such as prolonged occupation or the use of force in occupied territory.

In this respect, one should note that the ICRC has since 2007 embarked on a Project aimed at addressing some specific legal challenges raised by occupation and other forms of administration of foreign territory. After extensive internal research and a phase of external consultation, the Project culminates with the publication (in the second half of 2011) of a comprehensive report reflecting the discussions held during three expert meetings organized during 2008–2009. Among other issues, the report tackles the legal challenges arising from the interaction between the law of occupation and HRL. As such, the report will contribute to clarifying the law of occupation and will represent a useful tool for all those interested in this evolving area of public international law.

NOTES

* Tristan Ferraro, PhD, is Legal Adviser at the International Committee of the Red Cross (ICRC). The opinions expressed in this chapter are those of the author and do not necessarily reflect those of the ICRC.

1. However, divergent views still exist and continue to support the idea that HRL is not applicable in occupied territory. See, for instance, M.J. Dennis, 'Application of Human Rights Treaties Extra-territorially in Times of Armed Conflict and Military Occupation', *American Journal of International Law* 99:1 (2005): 119–141. The State of Israel still considers that HRL has no extraterritorial application and therefore is not binding upon an occupying power, see, O. Ben Naftali and Y. Shany, 'Living in Denial: The Application of Human Rights in Occupied Territories', *Israel Law Review* 37:1 (2003–2004): 25–40.

2. One should notice that a proposal aimed at giving the occupier the right to repeal local legislation contrary to HRL was rejected during the negotiation of the fourth Geneva Convention of 1949. The rejection of this Mexican proposal was mainly due to the embryonic character of human rights law at the time of the negotiations.

3. *Legal Consequences of the Construction of a Wall in the Occupied Palestinian Territory*, Advisory Opinion, I.C.J. Reports 2004, section 102 *et seq. Armed Activities on the Territory of the Congo* (D.R. Congo v. Uganda), Decision, I.C.J. Reports 2005, section 178.

4. M. Sassòli, 'Legislation and Maintenance of Public Order and Civil Life by Occupying Powers', *European Journal of International Law* 16 (2005): 673–675.

5. A. Roberts, 'Transformative Military Occupation: Applying the Laws of War and Human Rights', *American Journal of International Law* 100 (2006): 580–622.

6. A. Roberts, 'Human Rights Obligations of External Military Forces', excerpt of a keynote discussion on 'The extraterritorial application of human rights obligations', 18 May 2006, International Society for Military Law and the Law of War, XVIIth Congress, Scheveningen, 16–21 May 2006.

7. I hold the view that HRL obligations apply in territory or parts thereof over which foreign forces have effective control within the meaning of IHL. In this respect, it is submitted here that effective control under IHL is of a higher threshold than effective control for the purposes of HRL. Therefore, when foreign forces enforce effective control over foreign territory within the meaning of IHL, this suffices to trigger HRL obligations incumbent upon the occupying power.

8. E. Benvenisti, *The International Law of Occupation* (Princeton: Princeton University Press, 2004), Preface for the paperback edition, ix–x.

9. H. Zahawi, 'Redefining the Laws of Occupation in the Wake of Operation Iraqi Freedom', 95 *California Law Review* (2008): 2295–2352; D.P. Goodman, 'The Need for Fundamental Change in the Law of Belligerent Occupation', *Stanford Law Review* 37:6 (1985): 1573 *et seq.*; D.J. Scheffer, 'Beyond Occupation Law', *American Journal of International Law* 97:4 (2003): 842–860; D.B. Rivkin Jr. and D.R. Bartram, 'Military Occupation: Legally Ensuring a Lasting Peace', *The Washington Quarterly* 26:3 (2003): 87–103; M. Patterson, 'Who's Got the Title? or, the Remnants of Debellatio in Post-Invasion Iraq', *Harvard International Law Journal* 47:2 (2006): 469: 'occupation law is unsuitable for nation building... an inherently unsuitable body of international law that ostensibly places undue restrictions on the occupiers'.

10. G.T. Harris, 'The Era of Multilateral Occupation,' *Berkeley Journal of International Law* 24:1 (2006): 1–78

11. C. Garraway, 'The Duties of the Occupying Power: an Overview of the Recent Developments in the Law of Occupation', in *Facets and Practices of State-Building*, ed. J. Raue and P. Sutter (Leiden and Boston: Martinus Nijhoff, 2009), 190 *et seq.*

12. In particular, *Legal Consequences of the Construction of a Wall in the Occupied Palestinian Territory*, Advisory Opinion, I.C.J. Reports 2004, section 106. See also N. Prud'homme, 'Lex Specialis: Oversimplifying a More Complex and Multifaceted Relationship?,' *Israel Law Review* 40:2 (2007): 355–395; D. Stephens, 'Human Rights and Armed Conflict: the Advisory Opinion of the ICJ in the Nuclear Weapons Case', *The Yale Human Rights and Development Law Journal* IV (2001): 1–24.

13. If these branches of international law share similarities – in purpose and content to a certain extent – they are, however, dissimilar in method, character, scope and in the addressees of the norms, for example. Occupation law articulates the obligations of a belligerent for the welfare of the population of the enemy, while HRL normally provides obligations to the State with regard to the welfare of its own citizens. The role and responsibilities of States as well as means to enforce those rules are also inherently different. This difference might have important consequences when the two regimes apply side by side in a particular situation, as is often the case in occupied territory. This overlap generates a certain confusion which is not conducive to bringing about the necessary legal clarity.

14. N. Lubell, 'Parallel Application of IHL and International Human Rights Law: an Examination of the Debate', *Israel Law Review* 40:2 (2007): 648–660.

15. For a discussion of recent European cases on human rights in armed conflict, see W. Abresch, 'A Human Rights Law of Internal Armed Conflict: The European Court of Human Rights in Chechnya', *European Journal of International Law* 16:4 (2005): 741–767.

16. *Supra* note 2. See also C. Droege, 'Elective Affinities? Human Rights and Humanitarian Law', *International Review of the Red Cross* 90:871 (2008): 507 *et seq.*

17. H.J. Heintze, 'On the Relationship Between Human Rights Law Protection and IHL', *International Review of the Red Cross* 86:856 (2004): 789–814.

18. Droege, *supra* note 16, at 521–522.

19. Lubell, *supra* note 14, at 655; see also R. Kolb and G. Gaggioli, 'A Right to Life in Armed Conflicts? The Contribution of the European Court of Human Rights', *Israel Yearbook on Human Rights* 37 (2007): 118 *et seq.*

20. While supported by some important writers such as Y. Dinstein, *The International Law of Belligerent Occupation* (Cambridge: Cambridge University Press, 2009), 85–88, this position is not necessarily shared by other authors; see, for instance, M. Sassòli, 'Le droit international humanitaire, une lex specialis par rapport aux droits humains?', in *Les droits de l'Homme et la Constitution, Etudes en l'honneur du Professeur G. Malinverni*, eds A. Auer, A. Flückiger and M. Hottelier (Geneva, Zurich and Bâle: Schultess, 2007), 375–395.

21. Roberts, *supra* note 5.

22. G. Fox, 'The Occupation of Iraq', *Georgetown Journal of International Law* 36 (2005): 195–297. In this article, the author denies the fact that HRL would be a sufficient legal basis for justifying transformative occupation under *lex lata*.

23. Harris, *supra* note 10.

24. ICRC Report, 'Occupation and Other Forms of Administration of Foreign Territory', prepared and edited by Tristan Ferraro, April 2012, p. 67. For a different definition, see Roberts, *supra* note 5, 580, which describes the concept as an occupation 'whose stated purpose (whether or not actually achieved) is to change states that have failed, or have been under tyrannical rule'. Another author specifies that 'l'expression "occupation transformative" a été utilisée par la doctrine pour décrire des formes d'occupation dont la caractéristique essentielle est de réorganiser le système administratif du territoire occupé, dans des proportions telles que cette réorganisation s'apparente à un changement de régime', V. Koutroulis, 'Mythes et réalités de l'application du droit international humanitaire aux occupations dites "transformatives"', *Revue Belge de Droit International* XL No 2 (2007): 371.

25. As traditionally understood, occupation law requires occupiers to leave the legal and political structures of the occupied territory intact. Indeed, Article 43 of The Hague Regulations obliges occupiers to respect laws in force 'unless absolutely prevented' from doing so. Article 64 of GCIV focuses specifically on the continuity of penal laws and provides that the penal laws of the occupied territory shall remain in force, with the exception that they may be repealed or suspended by the Occupying Power in cases where they constitute a threat to its security or an obstacle to the application of IHL. This obligation has been referred to as the 'conservationist principle'. The conservationist principle was fundamental to the traditional understanding of an occupier's legal position. An occupation is not an annexation, but a temporary and limited form of control falling short of *de jure* sovereignty. Thus, the powers of the occupier are limited precisely by the presumed temporary nature of the occupation regime and in particular by the need to avert creeping annexation through the imposition of the legal regime and administrative structure of the enemy power. The occupier thus assumes only as much of the displaced sovereign's authority as is necessary to administer the territory, but no more. General legislative competence remains with the displaced regime as the continuing *de jure* authority over the territory. The legitimate sphere of an occupier's concern, in other words, is limited to pragmatic tasks of orderly administration. The conservationist principle may be seen as an allocation of decision-making competence between the occupier and the

ousted sovereign. This allocation rests on the contrast between the fullness and permanence of sovereign power and the temporary and precarious position of the occupier. The occupying power is competent to legislate to maintain security and to fulfil the obligations under occupation law that secure basic rights for the local population. But the occupier possesses no local legitimacy or necessary stake in the welfare of the territory after it departs and it is not competent to enact reforms that fundamentally alter governing structures in the territory or create long-term consequences for the local population. See Fox, *supra* note 22, at 234–236.

26.   Y. Dinstein, 'Legislation Under Article 43 of the Hague Regulations: Belligerent Occupation and Peace Building', *HPCR, Occasional Paper Series, Harvard University* (2004), 6. See also Sassòli, *supra* note 4, at 673–674.

27.   Sassòli, *supra* note 4, at 674.

28.   Fox, *supra* note 22, at 276. On the relationship between the law of occupation and the principle of self-determination, see J.L. Cohen, 'The Role of International Law in Post-Conflict Constitution-Making: Towards a Jus Post Bellum for "Interim Occupation"?', *New York Law School Law Review* 51 (2006–2007): 496–532. This position is also very interesting in so far as it permits the avoidance of applying HRL in occupied territory being perceived as imposing a form of imperialism, in particular if HRL implementation leads to the imposition of culturally inappropriate norms in occupied territory. See, R. Wilde, 'Complementing Occupation Law? Selective Judicial Treatment of the Suitability of Human Rights Norms', *Israel Law Review* 42 (2009): 80–100.

29.   Sassòli, *supra* note 4, at 675.

30.   G. Von Glahn, *The Occupation of Enemy Territory: a Commentary on the Law and Practice of Belligerent Occupation* (Minneapolis: University of Minnesota Press, 1957), 97; E.H. Schwenk, 'Legislative Power of the Military Occupant under Article 43, Hague Regulations', *Yale Law Journal* 54 (1945): 400–401; M.J. Kelly, 'Iraq and the Law of Occupation: New Test for an Old Law', *Yearbook on International Humanitarian Law* 6 (2003): 155; A. Cassese, 'Powers and Duties of an Occupant in Relation to Land and Natural Resources', in *International Law and the Administration of Occupied Territories, Two Decades of Israeli Occupation of the West Bank and the Gaza Strip*, ed. E. Playfair (Oxford: Clarendon Press, 1992), 423–424.

31.   See, for instance, *The Jerusalem District Electricity Company Inc. v. The Minister of Energy*, summarized in *Israel Yearbook on Human Rights*, Supreme Court of Israel, Judgment, HC 351/80, (1981): 354 *et seq.*

32.   *Armed Activities on the Territory of the Congo* (D.R. Congo v. Uganda), Decision, I.C.J. Reports 2005, section 178.

33.   Ben Naftali and Shany, *supra* note 1, at 89.

34.   Sassòli, *supra* note 20, at 388.

35.   *Legal Consequences of the Construction of a Wall in the Occupied Palestinian Territory*, Advisory Opinion, I.C.J Reports 2004, para. 112.

36.   Sassòli, *supra* note 20, 388.

37.   *Supra* section 1.

38.   S. Vité, 'The Interrelation of the Law of Occupation and Economic, Social and Cultural Rights: the Examples of Food, Health and Property', *International Review of the Red Cross* 90:871 (2008): 629–651.

39.   General Comment No. 3: *The Nature of States Parties' Obligations (Article 2, para. 1, of the Covenant)*, CESCR, 14 December 1990 (UN Doc. E/1991/23), para. 9, 10. See also The Maastricht Guidelines on Violations of Economic, Social and Cultural Rights, UN Doc. E/C.12/2000/13, 2 October 2000, No. 8.

40.   Vité, *supra* note 38. Despite their inherent flexibility, each of the economic, social and cultural rights have an irreducible normative content that has to be respected in all circumstances, irrespective of the country's economic level, its political situation or its institutional structure. An occupying power would have a core obligation to ensure the satisfaction of at least the minimum essential levels of each of the rights, even in the earliest stage of the occupation. The flexibility allowed by virtue of Article 2(1) of the ICESCR therefore has some limits.

41.   Vité, *supra* note 38.

42.   Vité, *supra* note 38.

43.   T. Ruys and S. Verhoeven, 'DRC v. Uganda: the Applicability of International Humanitarian Law and Human Rights Law in Occupied Territories', in *International Humanitarian Law and Human Rights Law: Towards a New Merger in International Law*, eds R. Arnold and N. Quenivet (Leiden: Martinus Nijhoff, 2008), 186–189.

44. Vité, *supra* note 38.

45. N. Lubell, 'Challenges in Applying Human Rights Law to Armed Conflict', *International Review of the Red Cross* 87:860 (2005): 752–753.

46. Application of human rights law to law enforcement operations in occupied territories also raises the question whether this body of law applies at all in situations of occupation. This question has been already briefly addressed in the preliminary section of this contribution and will not be reiterated here. Nonetheless, human rights applicability to police operations also brings up the question as to whether an occupying power might derogate from certain human rights obligations if necessary to restore and maintain public order and safety in an occupied territory. As Marco Sassòli put it, 'even a serious disruption of civil life in an occupied territory could sometimes be considered as "threatening the life of the [occupied] nation"', see Sassòli, supra note 4, at 665.

47. R. Kolb and S. Vité, *Le droit de l'occupation militaire, perspectives historiques et enjeux juridiques actuels* (Brussels: Bruylant, 2009), 347 *et seq.*

48. Y. Dinstein, 'The Israel Supreme Court and the Law of Occupation: Article 43 of The Hague Regulations', *Israel Yearbook on Human Rights* 29 (1995): 1–20.

49. Dinstein, *supra* note 20, at 94–105.

50. K. Watkin, 'Controlling the Use of Force: a Role for Human Rights Norms in Contemporary Armed Conflict', *American Journal of International Law* 98:1 (2004): 1–34.

51. Droege, *supra* note 16, at 537–539.

52. See, for instance, Article 57(2)(b) of Additional Protocol I: 'an attack shall be cancelled or suspended if it becomes apparent that the objective is not a military one or is subject to special protection or *that the attack may be expected to cause incidental loss of civilian life, injury to civilian objects, or a combination thereof, which would be excessive in relation to the concrete and direct military advantage anticipated*' (emphasis added).

53. The limited character of this contribution does not allow for an analysis on the interaction between the two paradigms and the identification of criteria determining when and how to swap between the law enforcement model and the conduct of hostilities paradigm. This question is examined in detail in the ICRC Report, 'Occupation and Other Forms of Administration of Foreign Territory', prepared and edited by Tristan Ferraro, April 2012, pp. 109–110.

54. University Center for IHL, Report, Expert Meeting on the Right to Life in Armed Conflict and Situations of Occupation, 2005, 20–29. Available at http://www.adh-geneve.ch/docs/expert-meetings/2005/3rapport_droit_vie.pdf (accessed 12 February 2012).

55. ICRC Report, 'Occupation and Other Forms of Administration of Foreign Territory', prepared and edited by Tristan Ferraro, April 2012, pp. 116–119.

56. The flexibility of the human rights law rules pertaining to the use of force would permit their application in almost all factual situations faced by the occupying power, ranging from the enforcement of the law against criminal acts such as robbery or drug trafficking to open hostilities pitting the occupying forces against insurgent armed groups. This benefit would in itself justify considering the human rights law regime as the central piece of the legal framework governing the use of force in occupied territory.

57. *McCann v. United Kingdom*, ECtHR, Application No. 18984/91, Judgment of 27 September 1995; *Isayeva, Yusupova*, and *Bazayeva v. Russia*, ECtHR, Application Nos 57947/00, 57948/00 and 57949/00, Judgment of 24 February 2005.

15. Humanitarian assistance to protect human rights and international humanitarian law

Roberto Giuffrida*

(1) Humanitarian assistance plays a crucial role in the International Community and a strong debate currently revolves around many of its facets: funding sources, adequacy of means, and the solutions adopted to grant universal access to victims.[1]

In case of humanitarian emergency, contrasts among the States often arise, as well as conflicts among, or inside, the main International Organizations.

Public opinion plays a key role too, by facilitating the achievement of the defined goals as well as by monitoring the development of humanitarian activities to make sure they follow clear and transparent procedures. The search for this transparency is assigned to the media, which are frequently accused of arbitrarily putting forward some emergencies while ignoring others. Or, also, of creating the illusion of a prompt response from the International Community even when this is lacking.[2]

The aforementioned debate is amplified by natural disasters and armed conflicts, particularly asymmetric conflicts, where, unfortunately, we witness an increase in civil victims and the killing of humanitarian operators.[3] In situations of conflict, the presence of humanitarian assistance operations are nowadays considered to be not only an important condition for the calling of a truce, but a necessary element to reach, in the words of the UN Secretary General, 'Global Peace', which requires the solution of social, economic, cultural and humanitarian problems.[4] Therefore, any obstacle to the delivery of aid is correctly considered as a danger to international peace and security.[5]

But this integrated approach is often criticized as it would interfere with the independence of humanitarian operations. In brief, actions of solidarity might be mistaken as a way of defending the interests of financing countries.[6]

Besides, when military forces are employed to ensure the distribution of supplies, the coexistence of civil and military elements in the same humanitarian operation is criticized.[7]

Anyway, these concerns, as important as they may be, did not affect the regulatory decisions of the UN concerning humanitarian assistance. It is stated that humanitarian assistance comprises 'all acts, activities and human and material resources for the provision of goods and services of an exclusively humanitarian character, indispensable for the survival and fulfillment of the essential needs of the victims of disasters'.[8]

Humanitarian assistance is provided, by definition, by third parties or private operators when the sovereign entity in a given territory is 'unable or unwilling' to provide for the basic needs of the population. Its undisputable premise is, under Art. 10 of the IV Geneva Convention, the consent of the subjects capable of exercising power over the territory subject to humanitarian assistance.[9]

Of course, the aforementioned consent may be obtained through a 'coercive inducement', as the International Community cannot ignore dramatic situations without trying, through consensus, to help the victims.[10]

Now, it has to be stressed that the relationship between, on the one hand, fundamental human rights and international humanitarian law, and, on the other, the factual provision of humanitarian assistance, has a double meaning.

Firstly, humanitarian assistance can only be properly offered, by all the subjects involved, their being rescuers or entities exerting control over a given territory, if in full compliance with the fundamental human rights and with some international humanitarian rules.

Secondly, at the same time, it is thanks to humanitarian aid that the proper application of the aforementioned rules can be ensured, and the goals defined therein can be reached.

This double meaning allows us to understand how fundamental the respect of some basic international rules might be to the provision of humanitarian assistance.[11] Eventually, it is thanks to humanitarian aid that the rights to life and health can be secured.[12]

(2) It is our duty now to investigate what the 'juridical status' is of both the State in whose territory it is necessary to carry out assistance, and the other States involved, as well as, lastly, of international organizations, either national or non-governmental. Practically, then, we should investigate if there are any so-called *primary* rules providing for a right to humanitarian assistance, and who are the subjects that can invoke this right and who are bound to the corresponding obligations.[13] Moreover, the investigation should be extended to the existence of so-called *secondary* rules capable of ensuring the application of primary ones by bestowing certain rights.

Furthermore, in the light of the current development of International Law, we should assess if it is possible, through interpretation, to construe a right for individuals, victims of an emergency situation, to obtain humanitarian assistance, as per the declaration of the Council of the Institute of Humanitarian Law, held in San Remo in April 1993.[14]

In essence, the right to obtain humanitarian assistance is implicitly included in the right to survive, which is in turn an expression of the right to live under art. 6 of the Covenant on Civil and Political Rights of 1966 and art. 3 of the Universal Declaration of Human Rights. The right to survive will be addressed below. However, we may briefly outline that the latter could be autonomously ensured both by HR and IHL, as a system, or, by convenience, by the interaction of both. In particular, according to recent theories, the right to survive in general would find specific ground on some disposition of the Covenant on Economic Social and Cultural Rights.[15] In this regard, the International Court of Justice, in the case concerning the construction of the wall in Palestine, has recognized that some of these 'second generation' rights are directly applicable and do provide both negative obligations to respect certain 'juridical status', and positive obligations to adopt protection and prevention measures and to ensure the provision of essential goods for survival such as food, accommodation, medical care and a healthy environment.

The Court has also recognized extraterritorial effects to these categories of obligations and affirmed that the same should be observed, without exceptions, in any circumstances.

To ensure long-term survival, a specific right should be recognized to individuals, which we may call a *third generation* right, to attain a constant development of their general economic conditions.[16]

On the contrary, the self-standing right to obtain humanitarian assistance may find its basis in the most recent doctrines of International Law. On the one side, the attention on the cooperation process between States, within the context of international organization, has noticeably increased, and the same has happened with the consequential definition of a new juridical scale of values at the head of which is the enforcement of human rights.[17] On the other side, we are still contributing to a trend where the different categories of HR will be more and more specified in order to better shape, improve and update them. Accordingly, the right to obtain humanitarian assistance might be considered an autonomous right, in respect to other well-established and extensively recognized rights, with the aim of justifying the adoption of specific regulations that shall identify the subjects to whom the same rights are granted and the general recognition thereof.[18]

For sure, human beings are already specifically protected in their 'passive status' by some important international rules. These rules, rather than referring to the interests of States, apply directly to each and every human being, no matter which State they belong to, and they protect inalienable rights that cannot be waived by the States.[19]

This approach is opposed to another one that sees individuals as being granted a number of rights and obligations before the whole International Community, therefore allowing them, under certain circumstances, to act directly for the protection of their interests.[20] Consequently, individuals are recognized as active participants in the international regulatory system, this role being particularly relevant in order to assess the responsibility of States in cases of the violation of fundamental human rights.[21]

In any case, the right of the individual to obtain humanitarian assistance, or protection (as you may call it), implies the recognition of the direct responsibility of States to provide the required assistance. Briefly, it cannot be doubted that there is a general recognition of the assistance obligations of States in case of emergency.[22]

In the end, we do believe that the right of individuals to humanitarian assistance is recognized as such by International Law. This, no doubt, provides for some related assistance and protection obligations, also before the International Community, to be observed by the States through adapting their internal rules to ensure that individuals may be adequately protected.

(3) When an emergency occurs, humanitarian assistance should be considered the most important evidence of both international solidarity and a spirit of mutual cooperation, which, most of the time, exist among States.

We now wish to examine if, and within which limits, international cooperation subsists as a duty in cases of emergency, and what are the juridical consequences arising from the recognition of such a duty.

This duty of cooperation, imposed upon national bodies that have authority over a territory affected by an emergency, should be considered as something different from the expression of consent given by the same bodies to the offer of relief assistance made by other States or humanitarian organizations. Indeed, the duty of cooperation implies the fulfilment of a series of obligations concerning both conduct and results that a simple expression of consent cannot guarantee.[23]

The cooperation may have different characters: either 'institutional', for instance when an humanitarian body like the International Committee of the Red Cross is charged with coordinating aid provided by the transnational movement that acts under its symbol; or multilateral, when the task of coordination is assigned to an International Organization.[24] Obviously, cooperation may be also bilateral and this is a trend that deserves to be stressed: the general acceptance, inside the International Community, of the values manifested through cooperation on behalf of the preservation of human society and civilization.[25]

Some dispositions of the UN Charter have certainly opened the way to acknowledging cooperation as mandatory in the promotion of respect for human rights.[26] This interpretation is challenged by those scholars who consider the character of the same dispositions to be too vague and thus incapable of specifying a concrete commitment that can be honoured in certain fields; or, they consider them capable of producing effects within the UN itself and not beyond.[27]

However, if we view the UN Charter as a living instrument that evolves over the years, we must rely, according to its Article 13, on a progressive development of international law by supporting the efforts of the General Assembly to make recommendations that promote cooperation in the political, economic, social, cultural, educational and health spheres.[28]

In this respect, special weight should be given to the 1970 Declaration of Principles of International Law concerning Friendly Relations of Cooperation among States, adopted unanimously by the General Assembly, and to the 1974 Charter of Economic Rights and Duties of States (Article 7). In light of these, we may affirm that there is a strong evidence of the existence of an '*opinio juris*' that allows for a general obligation to cooperate as a fundamental principle of international law.[29]

The increased acceptance of this duty brings with it some important consequences. The players in the International Community should act in conformity with one another, through a process of negotiation and coordination, taking into account their interest in common problems. If we now turn our attention to the field of the protection of human rights, we may ascertain the basis of this said duty to cooperate in some specific provisions of the UN Charter.

In the Preamble we read, 'The peoples of the United Nations ... reaffirm faith in fundamental human rights'; in Article 1, which contains the fundamental purposes of the organization, there is a specific reference to cooperation 'in promoting and encouraging respect for human rights and for fundamental freedoms'. We can apply this expression also to human rights in armed conflicts and IHL.[30]

According to Articles 55 and 56 the States have to cooperate jointly and separately with the UN to promote the same goals.[31] Hence the States must adopt a cooperative attitude and act, in good faith, positively for the achievement of the aforementioned fundamental purposes.[32]

While we are tempted to view the text of the UN Charter as a rigid fence, we should assign greater weight, by following a teleological method of interpretation, to the dispositions promoting the respect of human rights.[33]

Moreover, a general peremptory goal of solidarity is acknowledged in common Article 1 of the Geneva Conventions that links States with a common goal of safeguarding universal values.[34] Article 1 calls for collective protection in order 'to ensure respect' of the Geneva Conventions via significant collaboration among States parties, especially when involved in an emergency situation.[35]

The general duty to cooperate may provide, as already noted, the basis for more concrete rights and obligations that imply specific activities. The distinction commonly drawn between obligations of conduct and obligations of result may assist in ascertaining when a State fails to meet the general duty to cooperate.[36] Some scholars point out that, according to this duty, a State has an obligation of conduct to prevent and to minimize the effects of any emergency situation and an obligation of result to disclose and share all the information necessary to deal with such a situation. This must be done taking into account that the success of the humanitarian assistance will largely depend on the information received within a framework of fair collaboration.[37]

The necessity to respect the aforementioned obligations is strongly recommended by the International Law Commission in its 2001 Draft Articles on Prevention of Trans-boundary Harm from Hazardous Activities.[38]

In light of the above, we may affirm that International Law should recognize a duty to cooperate in order to enforce the individual right to humanitarian assistance.

(4) A new conceptual approach, mentioned in various UN documents, has given broader importance to life-supporting protection and assistance to populations at risk.[39] This concept is based on a not entirely new reading of sovereignty as responsibility, and implies, first, that all States are responsible for protecting the safety and lives of their citizens; secondly, that States can be relied upon to assume this position of responsibility towards their own citizens and the International Community as a whole; and thirdly, that particular prominence should be given to the accountability of national authorities for their actions.

According to this concept, States have the primary responsibility to protect their own citizens from avoidable humanitarian catastrophes, and when they are unwilling or unable to do so, that responsibility must be borne, in a subsidiary way, by the International Community.[40] The primary responsibility, as a guiding principle, is obviously justified by the fact that the State is the agent most likely to be in a position to best secure respect for human rights.[41]

Under customary International Law a State has the primary responsibility to take any measure, within its spectrum of available resources, to ensure the material welfare and survival of its citizens.[42]

The territorial sovereign's primary responsibility has been endorsed by a series of conventional provisions and by some important resolutions of the UN General Assembly.[43]

According to these instruments, it is up to each State or any other authority, for example rebels, which has control over a territory, even if not within its formal claimed jurisdiction, to take care of the victims of any emergency situation occurring therein.[44]

The primary responsibility to protect implies a commitment to prevention, according to which, three essential conditions have to be met: first, the so-called 'early warning', that is, knowledge of the situation's degree of fragility and the risk associated with it; second, understanding of the policy measures available; and third, willingness to apply those measures.[45]

In any emergency the most important aim of the authority that has control over a territory shall be the satisfaction of survival requirements of the population living therein.[46]

Some scholars have tried to determine a list of goods and services to be considered as the fundamental relief supplies essential to meet the humanitarian needs arising from emergency situations.[47] In this respect, the UN General Assembly has declared that women and children 'shall not be deprived of shelter, food, medical aid or other inalienable rights'.[48] The satisfaction of certain basic needs may help in ascertaining the goods and services to be included in such a list of fundamental relief supplies – so we may consider food, water, basic clothing, emergency shelter, heating, medicine and, in general, medical and social services.[49]

However, even though some dispositions of the Geneva Conventions and their additional Protocols provide for fixed lists of goods and services to meet basic needs, it would be useless to predetermine their content for different categories of emergencies, as these situation are in constant flux.

So once we have recognized that the victims of any disaster have a fundamental right to life, which implies the right to survive, we must include in the aforementioned lists all goods and services deemed consistent and necessary to enforce the said rights.

There is no doubt that the right to survive, or to have access to a minimum standards of living and health, is formally expressed in Articles 3, 5 and 25 of the Universal Declaration of Human Rights, and is subsequently expanded and clarified in Articles 6 and 7 of the 1966 International Covenant on Civil and Political Rights and in Articles 11 and 12 of the 1966 International Covenant on Economics, Social and Cultural Rights.[50]

The right to survive is provided for by other important regional agreements like the 1950 European Convention on Human Rights, the 1969 American Convention on Human Rights and the 1981 African Charter on Human Rights.[51] Moreover, the most essential part of IHL deals with the right to survive, which shall be guaranteed in any circumstances by the State or by the authority that has occupied or has taken control over a territory.

Specifically, we may mention Article 46 of the Regulation attached to the Fourth Hague Convention, common Article 3 and Article 55 of the Fourth Geneva Convention. The First Protocol, especially in Article 69, in addition to the duties specified by the said Article 55 concerning food and medical supplies, determines a list of basic needs in occupied territories: 'clothing, bedding, means of shelter, other supplies essential to the survival of the civilian population (and objects necessary for religious worship)'. The subsequent Article 70 calls for relief actions when a territory 'under the control of a Party' is not adequately provided via the supplies mentioned in Article 69. The right to survive is also expressed in Articles 54 and 75 of the same Protocol.[52]

Similarly, the Second Protocol, in its Articles 4, 5 and 14, formally recognize the right to survive.[53]

An offhand remark deserves our attention. The ICJ has clearly endorsed the concept that 'elementary considerations of humanity' are an integral element of the international legal order. There are, according to the Court, 'intransgressible principles of human-itarian law' which should be applied at any time and in any circumstance. These principles are stated in the Martens Clause and thoroughly endorsed by common Article 3 and other dispositions of the Geneva Conventions.[54] So, any failure to recognize the right to survive, abandoning the victims without humanitarian assistance, shall be deemed an offence to human dignity and finally a serious breach of the said intransgressible principles.

(5) As already noted, the right to humanitarian assistance may be implemented only through the International Community's full observance of the duty to cooperate.

According to this duty, in case of an emergency, States can no long disregard the universally accepted standards of human rights protection by invoking sovereignty.[55] This question deserves further attention.

The principle of non-intervention involves the right of every sovereign State to have its territorial integrity respected.[56] The General Assembly, in its fundamental resolution 46/182 adopting the guiding principles of humanitarian assistance, has once again stressed that the sovereignty, territorial integrity, and natural unity of States must be fully respected, in accordance with the Charter of the UN.[57] But, we may add that this principle shall be interpreted in accordance with the duty to cooperate. In this respect, the same resolution 46/182 states that humanitarian assistance should be provided with the consent of the affected country and 'in principle' on the basis of its appeal.[58] The rationale of this statement clearly conceives this consent as mandatory, and we may have no doubt that to arbitrarily refuse international assistance, when essential humanitarian needs are not met, shall be deemed a breach of the duty to cooperate.[59] Even a consent not given within a reasonable time may increase the entity of a humanitarian disaster,[60] when, for example, a territorial State does not desire to recognize its vulnerability in the face of such an event in time. In this case the consequences of the delays may entail certain responsibilities, which should be assessed by the International Community through adequate means.[61]

As regards the means of control, we shall point out that the States in conflict, when abiding by Article 1 common of the Geneva Conventions, are required not to hinder the presence of third States in a territory where there are populations in need. This presence should not be considered as an unfriendly or an unlawful interference in the internal affairs of the territorial States, but as controls in order to achieve, concretely, the enforcement of IHL.[62]

Examining dispositions of the IHL, we see there is evidence that 'the occupying Power' or any 'Party to the conflict' that has control over a territory, has the duty to demand humanitarian assistance when all local possibilities have been exhausted. We refer to Articles 23 and 59 of the fourth Geneva Convention, and to Articles 69 and 70 of the first Protocol, and, as for non-international armed conflicts, to Article 18 of the second Protocol[63] to support this affirmation.

In light of the above, humanitarian assistance shall be requested as soon as the population of a territory is not able to face its basic needs, according to the criteria provided for by the aforementioned Articles 69 and 70 of the first Protocol and Articles

18 of the second Protocol. To these articles we may add Articles 54 of the first Protocol and 14 of the second Protocol providing the prohibition against starving civilians.[64]

Obviously, there are circumstances in which the request of assistance may not be made due to the lack of an authority capable of performing any State function whatsoever. As many scholars have pointed out, a failed State, despite its incapability, remains a sovereign State. However in this case, there is no room for waiting for a formal request of humanitarian assistance.[65] The consent of the failed State must be presumed 'in view of the fact that the assistance is of paramount importance and should not suffer any delay'.[66]

(6) The request for humanitarian assistance implies the rising of some obligations to which all the actors with a role in an emergency situation are beholden.

First of all, the territorial State shall ensure access to the victims by allowing the transit of goods, materials and personnel bringing relief. Moreover, the same State shall do its best to grant the facilities necessary for the assistance to be provided and to ensure the protection of personnel engaged.[67]

Secondly, all States are under an *obligatio de contrahendo*, according to which they have to agree how to carry out their relief actions.[68] Most of the time, at the outset, consent for humanitarian access is given in an informal way by the territorial State.[69] However, all the actors involved shall, as soon as possible, reach an arrangement on the rules to be followed to ensure the coordination of their actions. The task of coordination, in accordance with principle 4 of the Resolution 46/182, should be assigned, to the extent possible, to the State affected by the emergency.[70]

Thirdly, all States in proximity to the populations in need shall facilitate the transit of humanitarian assistance.[71]

The fulfilment of these obligations shall be logically consistent with the full observance of the duty of cooperation and with the enforcement of the individual right to humanitarian assistance, as defined above.

The free passage of goods and support services is provided for by some precise dispositions of the fourth Geneva Convention and its additional Protocols. At the same time, only when the populations in need are reached by the humanitarian relief, may we affirm that the aims of some dispositions of HIL and HRL are definitively met.

In particular, during an international armed conflict, the free passage to a controlled or occupied territory, or to a besieged area, is affirmed respectively by Articles 23, 59 and 17 of the fourth Geneva Convention.[72] In any case, the protected persons, according to Article 38 of the same Convention 'shall be enabled to receive the individual or collective relief that may be sent to them'. Furthermore, it is important to remember that the distribution of relief consignments shall be carried out, according to Article 61, 'with the cooperation and under the supervision' of the Protecting Power, and, if so agreed, this task may be assigned to a Neutral Power or to the International Committee of the Red Cross, or to any other impartial humanitarian body.[73]

The first additional Protocol develops the above-mentioned dispositions by couching them in a more advanced and complete statement.[74]

Articles 69 and 70 strengthen the juridical regime of relief actions respectively in favour of the population of any occupied or controlled territory. The relief personnel engaged therein are protected by Articles 70 and 71 of the same Protocol.[75]

Article 3 common of the Geneva Conventions deserves special attention. This article is the first to recognize the international character of relief actions offered by impartial humanitarian bodies.[76] In the same vein, Article 18 of the second additional Protocol affirms that the territorial State shall give its consent to relief actions 'which are of an exclusively humanitarian and impartial nature and which are conducted without any adverse distinction'.[77] If the humanitarian action takes place exclusively in a territory controlled by rebels, their consent shall be considered sufficient to legitimate the free passage.[78]

If we now turn our attention to the Security Council and the General Assembly of the UN, we may note that their role has been always consistent with the aforementioned rules of IHL. The General Assembly has adopted Resolutions 43/131 and 45/100 on 'the humanitarian assistance to victims of natural disasters and similar emergency situations' and 46/182 on the 'coordination of humanitarian emergency assistance of the UN'. In these fundamental acts the General Assembly reaffirms the duty to cooperate and calls upon the States to facilitate and protect, in any circumstance, those who have the task to implement humanitarian assistance; in particular by ensuring the prompt and smooth distribution of medical and good care and by establishing, on a temporary basis, relief corridors.[79]

Evidence of the importance the Security Council gives to the establishing of a free passage may be found in most of its resolutions concerning humanitarian emergencies. The Security Council, in a peremptory way, has requested all concerned parties to guarantee free, unhindered, effective access to humanitarian aid, by also stressing the urgent character of the delivery.[80] The same Council, acting in most cases under Chapter VII of the UN Charter, has considered any hindrance made to full, unimpeded access to the civilians in need, and to the protection of the safety, security and freedom of movement of the humanitarian personnel involved to be a serious threat to peace and security.[81]

Likewise, the attitude of some non-governmental organizations (NGOs), like MSF, which, with the aim of assessing and enforcing, in any circumstances, the individual right to humanitarian assistance, have refused 'to wait for the approval of all parties before acting', has been stressed.[82] However this attitude has not been followed by the majority of NGOs, which, for the sake of clarity, always seek a strong collaboration with and protection from the territorial States.

In this respect we should remember that the States party to the New York December 1994 Convention have undertaken to take all appropriate measures to ensure the safety of UN associated personnel 'carrying out activities in support of the fulfilment of the mandate of the UN operations', in particular when, according to Article 2 of the December 2005 Optional Protocol, these operations are concerned with 'delivering humanitarian, political or development assistance in peace building or delivering emergency humanitarian assistance'.[83]

(7) Examining the position of third actors in order to determine what actions can be undertaken by them to deal with emergencies, we must admit that the general international law now recognizes their right to offer humanitarian assistance.[84] The offer of relief by national authorities, national and international organizations or NGOs ought not to be regarded as an unfriendly act.[85] Moreover, some fundamental

provisions of IHL – common Article 3, Article 9 of the first, second and third Geneva Conventions, Articles 10 and 59 of the fourth Geneva Convention, Article 12 of the first Additional Protocol and Article 18 of the second Additional Protocol – clearly acknowledge, in favour of the ICRC and other impartial humanitarian organizations, the right to take the initiative in offering supplies and services essential for the persons in need.[86]

The role played by all States and NGOs in responding to the effects of any emergency has been stressed by the General Assembly of the UN in Resolutions 43/131, 45/100 and 46/182. According to the latter, humanitarian assistance should be provided with the consent and 'in principle on the basis of an appeal of the affected country'. The phrase 'in principle' may, in practice, mean that the consent should be subordinate to the said right of third actors to offer the same assistance.[87] In the case of Nicaragua/United States, the ICJ has stated that the humanitarian assistance cannot be considered an unlawful interference in the internal affairs of a State, provided that, it is 'limited to the purposes, allowed in practice, namely to prevent and alleviate human suffering, and to protect life and health and to ensure respect for the human being, without discrimination to all in need'.[88] We may conclude that the offer of help should not be seen as incompatible with State sovereignty, but rather as affirming it.[89]

We must now turn our attention to another critical aspect of the legal condition of third States receiving a request for help. Do they have an obligation to assist the population in need whether or not they are in position to do so?

This question has given rise to much controversy. Most scholars do not recognize such an obligation as anything more than a moral duty to act without endangering the vital interests of their own populations.[90] The same doctrine highlights the fact that even in cases of environmental disasters, the general international law doesn't seem to impose a commitment to provide relief actions.[91] We may disagree with this opinion because it seems inconsistent with the recognition, in the international law, of a duty to cooperate, as already defined.

We may summarize by saying that all States shall have a duty to cooperate in order to enforce the individual right to receive humanitarian assistance when the territorial State is unable or unwilling to fulfil its primary obligation to guarantee the right of survival of its populations. And this duty shall be included in the categories of obligations *erga omnes* owed to the International Community as a whole, especially when there is a request of assistance because all local possibilities have been exhausted.[92]

(8) After having examined the consequences of a request for assistance made by the territorial State in emergency situations, we may now turn our investigation to the behaviour that should be maintained by the UN and other main regional organizations to meet such a request.

Inside these organizations, on many occasions, their principal organs have highlighted the real importance of abiding by the duty to cooperate in order to address emergency situations and to strengthen the response capacity of affected countries.[93] And the cooperation should always allow for the carrying out of concrete actions. In this respect, the UN Secretary General and the Security Council have tried to determine which actions can be undertaken to face and deal with emergencies, and, in response to a new approach, to 'do something'.[94]

In particular, the role of the Secretary General has been developed in order to secure assistance by deploying only civilian personnel with adequate means, in a context in which all the parties involved have already reached an agreement, most of the time through the friendly good offices of the same Secretary General.[95] In this view, States must rely on a new notion of domestic interest based upon some fundamental values like democracy, pluralism and protection of human rights. For this reason, States shall accept all the necessary limitations on their sovereignty in order to guarantee fundamental human rights. Ultimately, the Secretary General established the principle of integration according to which the UN must place people at the centre of everything it does, by integrating human rights into every aspect of the work of the same organization.[96]

Likewise, the Secretary General has, on several occasions, called for the creation of a 'culture of protection' in dealing with situations of armed conflicts.[97] In his opinion, when there is evidence of gross and systematic violations of human rights, the Security Council has a moral duty to act on behalf of the International Community.[98]

We have already examined the broader importance given to the new concept called, in various UN documents, the 'responsibility to protect'. All States have undertaken to collaborate with the UN to secure humanitarian assistance. And accordingly, the UN has committed itself to carrying out prompt and effective actions to protect populations at risk. Any inactivity of the main bodies of the UN will not be justified. The existence of a general *opinio juris* on this commitment may not be challenged; we need merely consider its recognition in various reports made by various panels of experts set up by the Secretary General or approved by the General Assembly.[99]

We all are aware of the important role played by the Security Council in securing the right of access to populations in need.[100] In this respect we may note that the same organ relies on a more flexible notion of threat to peace and security by including therein, as a further meaning, humanitarian tragedies. When these events occur, even if the use of armed force has not been ascertained, the Security Council may automatically determine, without any other justification, the existence of a threat to peace and security and act according to Chapter VII of the UN Charter.[101]

As we know, the Security Council has established, with the consent of all the parties involved, several peacekeeping missions, most of them with a mandate to protect civilians and to facilitate the provision of humanitarian assistance.[102]

However, as regards these missions, the Security Council has not behaved in a linear way. Sometimes, by considering the consent of all the parties involved as the prevailing aspect, the Security Council has exercised the powers granted to it by Chapter VI of the UN Charter. On other occasions, however, when in its opinion the prevailing aspect has been to impose some obligations on the parties, the same Council has acted in accordance with Chapter VII of the UN Charter. For instance, in Albania, where there was a formal request for help sent by the Government of that country, the Security Council established a peacekeeping mission by considering the existing dire humanitarian crisis a situation to which Article 39 of the UN Charter should be applied.[103]

Obviously, it is possible that consent given to a peacekeeping mission at the beginning of a humanitarian crisis, is later withdrawn by some of the actors involved (for instance rebels or political party), because of overriding political or economic reasons. In this event, the Security Council, acting under the Chapter VII of the UN Charter, authorizes a peace-enforcing operation, which has specific characteristics: its mandate, though with exclusively humanitarian aims, may imply the use of armed force in order to avoid hindrances to the fulfilment of the specific tasks assigned therein. According to some scholars, and following the experiences in Somalia and Rwanda, peace-enforcing operations should be characterized by the fact that their mandate extends to the possibility of exercising the right of self-defence against armed attacks for the protection of security zones and relief corridors.[104]

It is evident that the debate is still open over the need for armed protection. However, even the International Committee of the Red Cross has admitted a certain degree of coercion when humanitarian assistance encounters serious difficulties.[105] On this issue, let us insist on the fact that all kinds of peacekeeping operations need, from the moment of their approval by the Security Council, the consent and the cooperation of all parties involved. And once begun on these grounds, the delivery of humanitarian supply cannot be hindered or interrupted without seeking a proper reaction by the International Community and thus by the Security Council.[106] There is an increasing consensus among scholars that supports 'multilateral interventions in situations of extreme human rights deprivations and suffering'.[107]

For these purposes, the Security Council has often established safety zones that do not entirely meet the criteria set for such zones in IHL. The likely reason for this is that the Security Council has deemed that the realities of a given situation are unique and possessed of a particular nature that may not allow them to be governed by dispositions of the Geneva Conventions and their additional Protocols.[108]

As we know, in these Conventions there are detailed dispositions that allow the parties, by mutual consent, to establish, in time of peace or after the outbreak of hostilities, hospitals and safety or neutralized zones. In particular, Article 23 of the first Convention, and Articles 14 and 15 of the fourth Convention indicate who may legitimately enter such a zones. Thus, the said areas may be created in order to receive, separately, different categories of persons.[109]

Yet with the adoption of the 1977 first additional Protocol, we have evidence of an initial change of view over the legal regime to be applied to safety zones. According to Articles 59 and 60 of the said Protocol the parties, by mutual consent, may establish non-defended localities or demilitarized zones to protect places where a group of persons is already gathered. Furthermore, the first Protocol tends to remove the distinction between wounded or sick military personnel and civilians.[110]

So, the said Article 60 makes provisions for zones in which, in times of conflict, individuals may be sheltered from hostilities in an organized manner, on the basis of specific agreements which may even be concluded in peacetime, in places as far away as possible from the fighting.

However, the above-mentioned dispositions have seldom been applied, and there is now a different approach on the matter. We can see that the legal regime of the safety zones has changed considerably if we compare the detailed provisions of the Geneva Conventions and their additional Protocols with the decisions of the Security Council that established several recent safety areas whose unique aim is to separate groups of individuals in territories where a serious humanitarian crisis already exists. In other words, most of the time, in order to prevent clashes between communities, the security zones are now set up not in order to receive or to shelter populations in need, but rather to exclude some categories of individuals which may represent a danger for the achievement of the peace or the supply of humanitarian assistance.[111] Unfortunately, the Security Council has never specified the legal regime to be applied to these security zones, nor has it accompanied their creation with clear information concerning their potential beneficiaries.[112]

The situation is particularly uncertain when the Security Council makes decisions under Chapter VII of the UN Charter. In this case, according to Article 43 of the Regulations of the fourth Hague Convention, and Article 64 of the fourth Geneva Convention, the organs of the States, or those under their control, that establish a security zone, shall be responsible for securing public order and an adequate level of protection for the populations living therein or outside, without any form of discrimination and in the most effective manner.[113]

Obviously, we realize that because of these zones of separation we are now facing a dangerous lack of certitude concerning some critical elements; this may hinder and undermine the general recognition and acceptance of a normative evolution in favour of institutional humanitarian action. But, in this respect, we cannot underestimate the important role played by the Secretary General and the Security Council in meeting the requests for aid in an emergency situation.

The same attitude has been held by the most important regional organizations that now formally recognize the duty to cooperate. The most important evidence of this recognition may be found in Article 3(h) of the African Union, in Article 37 of the Organization of American States Charter, and in a series of EU dispositions.[114] In particular, according to Article 21(2)(g) of the Treaty on European Union and to Article 214 of the Treaty on the functioning of the European Union, that organization shall 'provide ad hoc assistance and relief protection for people in third countries who are victims of natural or man-made disasters, in order to meet humanitarian needs resulting from these different situations'.

(9) By way of conclusion, we may admit the existence of some specific elements that characterize actions linked to humanitarian assistance. There are some autonomous grounds on which such actions shall rest, grounds that should be justified according a specific logic.

First of all, the actions in question should be seen as the most proper response that the International Community might give in order to foster the general acceptance of an individual right to humanitarian assistance. Moreover, the proposed humanitarian assistance should always be legitimated by explicit reference to the duty to cooperate, which now receives universal recognition from general international law.

The humanitarian assistance, as already noted, is strictly linked to respect for HIL and HRL: on one hand, the relief actions may be effective only when the actors involved utterly abide by HIL and HRL; on the other hand, the actions are the sole means through which it is possible to enforce some fundamental dispositions of IHL and HRL.

The aim of humanitarian assistance is to guarantee and, at the same time, to actuate, in all circumstances, respect for 'elementary considerations of humanity', which, in the opinion of the ICJ, should be defined as 'intrangressible principles belonging to the international legal order'.[115]

These considerations, deriving 'from dictates of public conscience', and as such reflecting the fundamental values of the International Community, are proclaimed by the Martens Clause, as endorsed in some dispositions of the Geneva Conventions and in their common Article 3.[116]

The system of protection set forth therein shall apply at any time, in any place, and in any situation due either to material disasters or riots and national or international armed conflict.[117] In this respect it is useless or unnecessary to determine the threshold beyond which a conflict moves from a situation in which only domestic law applies, to one where International Law should also be taken into consideration.[118]

The interdependence between the two different fields of IHL and HRL has been confirmed by the ICJ, and it cannot be denied that humanitarian assistance is now ruled by a unique system or, if you prefer, by a network of complementary bodies of law that share a common goal – the protection of individuals.[119] And obviously all actors involved in relief actions shall respect this system.

As regards the UN peacekeeping operations, we may stress the role played by the Security Council and the Secretary General in demanding, though using language that is not always legally accurate, that all participant fully respect, in any and all circumstances, IHL and HRL.[120]

(10) There is still one vital question that deserves a satisfactory answer: how can we strengthen the enforcement of IHL and HRL so that human beings are effectively protected?

In this respect there are some real issues at stake that have been highlighted in order to improve the existing system of protection.

Undoubtedly, this system is now confronting new situations that it is no longer entirely able to deal with. Some scholars have pointed out the lack of rules, or their inadequacy in facing some important aspects of contemporary conflicts. The fact that some conflicts, through their very nature, entail a great number of violations of IHL is a challenge that deserves a prompt reply from the International Community as a whole. The first problem arises from the fact that it is hard to identify the nature of a great number of armed conflicts – so-called asymmetric wars, where regular armies and irregular forces with different legal standings are involved, or when an authoritarian regime organizes a savage repression of the right to peaceful association.[121] In this or similar cases, the debate remains open on who should be considered a belligerent, or when a conflict of this nature should be said to end.[122] Some scholars, in this respect, have suggested the evolution of the existing rules of IHL to address the issue of non-State entities as new actors in armed conflicts.[123] Even the functions of the Security Council should be better understood because of the risk of confusion between *jus in bello* and *jus ad bellum*:[124] any derogation made by this organ of the content of IHL must be explicit and its resolutions must be interpreted, wherever possible, in a manner compatible with this content.[125]

However, we take the view that a normative development of IHL is not desirable or necessary, since the existing rules offer an appropriate system of protection even where contemporary conflicts are concerned. Any development could even weaken the general recognition on the mandatory effects of the same rules.[126] The task of the International Community is rather to enhance the implementation of the said system of protection by increasing the extent to which the system is respected. The general opinion is that the violation of rules pertaining to humanitarian assistance is not due to their inadequacy but rather to an unwillingness to respect those rules.

We all know that human rights issues have already become imperative in current international relations. There is a real concern about how to improve humanitarian assistance in the case of an emergency.[127] So, as already noted, it is important to develop, at all levels, a culture of protection.[128] Surely there is 'a trend towards the accomplishment of a true human security based on the effective protection of human beings'.[129] In a system lacking a central institution, any element producing an acceptable standard of observance of the rules and providing effective protection should be adopted at various levels and entail 'the action of many subjects as possible of the International Community, working together'.[130]

And this aim may be reached only by the full observance of the duty to cooperate on which humanitarian assistance, in the end, shall rest.

All the actors involved in an emergency situation shall undertake to cooperate by upholding and respecting the binding humanitarian principles of humanity, neutrality and impartiality; principles that, moreover, reflect the practice and the experience in the field of the Red Cross.[131] In the opinion of the ICJ, humanitarian assistance must be 'limited to the purposes allowed in the practice of the Red Cross, namely: to prevent and alleviate human suffering; to protect life and health; and, to ensure respect for the human being', and above all, 'without discrimination'.[132] According to the Court, within those limits, humanitarian assistance shall be always considered lawful.[133]

The general observance of the principles of humanity, neutrality and impartiality can never be compromised, especially when there is not full cooperation among all the parties involved.[134] We must not underestimate the role played by these same principles in cases of emergency in which it is impossible to predict an ever-changing situation. They need to be considered as guiding principles when interpreting the relevant rules to be applied, in any circumstance, by relief personnel.

The importance of having universally recognized general principles may not be forgotten because they are founded upon simple rules that may be easily identified and interpreted. Furthermore, these principles are appropriate for diverse and changing circumstances that cannot be easily mapped by the guidelines, policy papers, and other standards for coordination, adopted, at a multilateral level, to carry out humanitarian assistance.[135]

NOTES

*   Roberto Giuffrida is Associate Professor of International Law at the University for Foreigners, Perugia, Italy.
1.   On this point, see P. Micheletti, 'Les humanitaires victimes des logiques d'Etat', in *Le Monde Diplomatique*, June, 2007, and 'L'humanitaire, du tsunami à Haiti', in *Le Monde Diplomatique*, March, 2010.
2.   We may share the perplexities of J. Patrnogic who recalls that 'another element which should be taken into account is public opinion. Humanitarian action constitutes a new type of interference in a country's

internal affairs and other countries cannot engage in this type of action without the support of their public. In practice, however, this support comes in the main from national media which may be extremely partial in their presentation of information. Modern technical means, television in particular, are able to create public opinion by emphasizing the suffering of some victims and neglecting those of others. They can therefore present a completely false picture of the real suffering of a population to justify the action of their government and there are several examples of this', in *Proceedings of the Qatar International Law Conference, International Legal Issues Arising under the UN Decade of International Law* (The Hague, London, Boston: Brill, 1995), 1029. In this sense, according to the International Commission on Intervention and State Sovereignty, a Commission co-chaired by G. Evans and M. Sahnoun: 'Television is thus something of a double-edged sword with regard to the protection of civilians in armed conflict. The media do not like to depict misery without also showing that someone is doing something about it. The presence of outside aid workers in zones of deadly conflict mitigates the horror, by suggesting that help is at hand, and affords the illusion that major powers are doing something', International Commission on Intervention and State Sovereignty, *Responsibility to Protect: Report of the International Commission on Intervention and State Sovereignty* (Ottawa: International Development Research Centre, 2001), 191.

3. Among others this view is held by E. Decaux when he notes that 'it is very difficult to qualify the nature of the armed conflict, with a mixture of international and non-international conflicts, regular armies and irregular forces on the turf', *International Peace Operations and International Humanitarian Law* (San Remo: International Institute of Humanitarian Law, 2008), 79.

4. On the new concepts of peace and security which imply in every conflict the search for solutions to all social, economic, cultural and humanitarian problems at stake, see the Opinion of Boutros Boutros-Ghali in his report, *An Agenda for Peace, Preventive Diplomacy, Peacemaking and Peacekeeping, Report of the Secretary-General pursuant to the Statement Adopted by the Summit Meeting of the Security Council on 31 January 1992*, 17 June 1992. According to D. Montaz ,'l'assistance humanitaire doit être considérée comme l'un des éléments constitutifs de la paix', 'Les actions de secours au cours d'un conflit armé', in *Studi di diritto internazionale in onore di Gaetano Arangio-Ruiz* (Naples: Ed. scientifica, 2004), 2074. On the role played by the UN in taking into account human rights issues when dealing with international peace and security, see J. Al-Sabah, 'The Reform of the UN and the Establishment of a Mechanism to Implement IHL', in *Protection of Human Beings in Disaster Situations* (Milan: International Institute of Humanitarian Law, 2006), 109. On the principle expressed by the Secretary General of integrating human rights even more fully into every aspect of the work of UN, see B.G. Ramcharan, *The Security Council and the Protection of Human Rights* (The Hague, London, New York: Kluwer Law International, 2002), 12.

5. As regards the attitude of the Security Council, see, among others, its Resolution 794 of 3 December 1992. According to Montaz, it is clear that 'd'après cet organe, les obstacles mis à l'acheminement de l'aide humanitaire constituent une menace contre la paix et la sécurité internationale', *supra* note 4, at 2074.

6. The only ground for refusing a humanitarian action is the failure to comply with the principles of humanity, impartiality and neutrality, see Y. Sandoz, C. Swinarski and B. Zimmermann, eds, *Commentary on the Additional Protocols of 8 June 1977 to the Geneva Conventions of 12 August 1949* (Geneva: International Committee of the Red Cross and Martinus Nijhoff, 1987), Article 70, and the Supplementary Volume to *Responsibility to Protect*, *supra* note 2, at 180. However, when the principles indicated above are met in the field, humanitarian organizations shall not prove their independence, because this element becomes less conclusive. In this sense, see Sandoz, Swinarski and Zimmermann, 'traditional links, or even the geographical situation, may prompt a State to undertake (such) relief actions, and it would be stupid to wish to force such a State to abandon the action', at para. 2803. *Contra* Micheletti, 'Les humanitaires victimes', *supra* note 1.

7. On this point, D. Caillaux notes 'there is a vast literature about the evolution of humanitarian response since the end of the cold war. In the past, things were simple: the military and civilian sides were evolving in their separate realms. This parallel universe was guaranteeing the sanctity of the humanitarian space', 'Civil-Military Cooperation: Common Sense or Pandora's Box?', in *International Peace Operations and International Humanitarian Law* (San Remo: International Institute of Humanitarian Law, 2008), 101. According to the Supplementary Volume to *Responsibility to Protect*, *supra* note 2, at 188: 'the coming together of the more hierarchical and disciplined military and the more horizontal humanitarian cultures was not without its problems. The mantra resulting from recent complex emergencies is for improved collaboration and perhaps integration among the intervention trio

of the military, political-diplomatic elements, and humanitarian agencies'. For a critical approach, see Micheletti, 'l'humanitaire, du tsunami à Haiti', *supra* note 1.

8. This definition has been adopted by the XVIth Commission of the Institute of International Law, in its Resolution on Humanitarian Assistance, 2 September 2003.

9. On the necessity of the consent of the territorial State, see E.W. Petit, 'Les actions d'urgence dans les catastrophes: évolution des activités des Organisations interétatiques et des ONG', in *The International Aspects of Natural and Industrial Catastrophes*, eds D.D. Caron and C. Leben (The Hague, Boston, London: Martinus Nijhoff Publishers, 2001), 552.

10. On the various terms like 'unqualified consent, coerced consent, coercive inducement', which have been coined to justify a military intervention to pursue humanitarian objectives, see D.C.F. Daniel, B.C. Hayes and C. De Lange Oudraat, *Coercive Inducement and the Containment of International Crises* (Washington DC: US Institute of Peace, 1999), and Supplementary Volume, *Responsibility to Protect*, *supra* note 2, at 16.

11. In this sense, see P. Benvenuti, *Ensuring Observance of IHL. Functions, Extent and Limits of the Obligations of Third States to Ensure Respect of IHL. 15th Round Table of Current Problems of IHL* (San Remo: International Institute of Humanitarian Law, 1989–1990), 27–55.

12. According to the 'Résolution sur la reconnaissance du droit d'assistance humanitaire et du droit à cette assistance', adopted by the Conférence internationale de droit et morale humanitaire, held in Paris on 28 January 1987 and organized by M. Bettati and Médecins du Monde: 'l'assistance humanitaire constitue une des contributions essentielles au respect et à l'exercise du droit à la vie et du droit à la santé'; on this aspect, see M. Bettati and B. Kouchner, *Le devoir d'ingérence* (Paris: Denoël, 1987), 291–292 ; F. Zorzi-Giustiniani, *Le Nazioni Unite e l'assistenza umanitaria* (Naples: Ed. scientifica, 2008), 24.

13. On the recognition of the right to humanitarian assistance in favour of internally displaced persons, see L. Franco, 'An Examination of Safety Zones for Internally Displaced Persons as a Contribution Toward Prevention and Solution of Refugee Problems', in *Proceedings of the Qatar International Law Conference*, *supra* note 2, 887.

14. The individual right to assistance is recognized by the Guiding Principles on the Right to Humanitarian Assistance, recommended by the Council of the International Institute of Humanitarian Law, held in San Remo, in April 1993. In particular, according to its Article 1: 'Every human being has the right to humanitarian assistance in order to ensure respect for the human rights to life, health, protection against cruel and degrading treatment and other human rights which are essential to survival, well-being and protection in public emergencies.'

15. On the right of survival as a natural consequence of the right to life provided for by Article 6 of the Covenant on Civil and Political Rights, see F. Menghistu, 'The Satisfaction of Survival Requirements', in *The Right to Life in International Law*, ed. B.G. Ramcharan (Dordrecht: Martinus Nijhoff Publishers, 1985), 68 ff. As regards the role played by the Covenant on Economic, Social and Cultural Rights, its disposition is considered less precise but proper to meet survival requirements especially in the long term. We may agree with Ramcharan, 'in its modern sense, the right to life encompasses not merely protection against international or arbitrary deprivation of life, but also places a duty on the part of each government to pursue policies which are designed to ensure access to the means of survival for every individual within its country', in 'The Right to Life,' *Netherlands International Law Review* 30 (1983): 302.

16. See *Legal Consequences of the Construction of a Wall in the Occupied Palestinian Territory*, Advisory Opinion, I.C.J. Reports 2004, paras 106 and 112. On the recognition of a positive obligation to take measures in order to ensure the right of survival, the Inter-American Court of Human Rights states: 'One of the obligations that the State must inescapably undertake as guarantor to protect and ensure the right of life, is that of generating minimum living conditions that are compatible with the dignity of the human person and of not creating conditions that hinder or impede it. In this regard the State has the duty to take positive, concrete measures geared toward fulfilment of the right to a decent life, especially in the case of persons who are vulnerable and at risk, whose care becomes a high priority', *Indigenous Community Yakye Axa v. Paraguay*, IACtHR, Merits, Reparations and Costs, Judgment of 17 June 2005, para. 161. On the right to a progressive development, see M. Nowak, 'Article 6, The Right to Life, Survival and Development', in *A Commentary on the UN Convention on the Right of the Child*, ed. M. Nowak (Leiden and Boston: Martinus Nijhoff Publishers, 2005), 5 and 6.

17. On this evolution, see T. Buergenthal, 'The Evolution of International Human Rights in an Historical Perspective', in *Human Rights: Concepts and Standards*, ed. J. Symonides (Dartmouth: Ashgate, 2000), 3 ff.

18. In the view of some scholars we are witnessing a strong trend of specification of human rights in order to continuously improve and to update their content; in this sense, see N. Bobbio, *L'età dei diritti* (Turin: Einaudi, 1990), 61; A. Cassese, *I diritti umani nel mondo contemporaneo* (Rome and Bari: Laterza, 1994), 74.

19. G. Barile, 'Obligationes Erga Omnes e individui nel diritto internazionale umanitario', *Rivista di diritto internazionale* LXVIII (1985): 7 and 17.

20. In the Commentary to Article 33 of the Draft Articles on Responsibility of States for Internationally Wrongful Acts, we may read: 'When an obligation of reparation exists toward a State, reparation does not necessarily accrue to that State's benefit. For instance, a State's responsibility for the breach of an obligation under a treaty concerning the protection of human rights may exist towards all the other parties to the treaty, but the individuals concerned should be regarded as the ultimate beneficiaries and in that sense as the holders of the relevant rights. Individual rights under international law may also arise outside the framework of human rights. The range of possibilities is demonstrated from the Judgment of the International Court in the *La Grand* case (Germany v. United States), Judgment, I.C.J. Reports 2001, 494, where the Court held that Article 36 of the Vienna Convention on Consular Relations creates individuals rights, which by virtue of Article 1 of the Optional Protocol, may be invoked in this Court by the national State of the detained person', in Report of the International Law Commission, November 2001, 234. According to C. Tomuschat, 'it is today almost uncontroversial that the rights of the so-called first generation set forth in human rights treaties or laid down in customary law encapsulate indeed subjective rights that qualify as true individual entitlements', 'Reparation in Favour of Individual Victims of Gross Violation of HR and IHL', in *Promoting Justice, Human Rights and Conflict Resolution through International Law*, Liber Amicorum, *Lucius Caflisch*, ed. M. Kohen (Leiden: Martinus Nijhoff Publishers, 2007), 577.

21. Most of the scholars take the view that individuals shall be considered as participants in the international legal order, by exercising their rights under human rights treaties or bilateral investment agreements. In this sense, see R. Higgins, *Problems and Process, International Law and How We Use It* (Oxford: Clarendon Press, 1995), 49; R. Pisillo Mazzeschi, *La Codificazione della Responsabilità internazionale degli Stati alla prova dei fatti* (Milan: Giuffrè, 2006), 419; G. Bartolini, *Riparazione per violazione dei diritti umani e ordinamento internazionale* (Naples: Jovene, 2009), 53.

22. The better approach is to complement the perspective of an individual's right to protection with the nature of the responsibility that others may have to provide that protection. In this respect, we may read that, 'State authorities carry the primary burden for delivering relief, as for the protection of rights. Yet, humanitarian organizations argue that people have a right to receive assistance, and if this cannot be fulfilled by the State, outsiders have a right of access to fill the gap. The programme of action from the 1993 Vienna World Conference on Human Rights most directly supported this approach by reaffirming in Article 1.29 the right of victims to be assisted by humanitarian organizations, as set forth in the Geneva Convention and calls for the safe and timely access for such assistance', Supplementary Volume, *Responsibility to Protect, supra* note 2, at 145.

23. On the existence of a general duty to cooperate as a general principle of international law, see F.X. Perez, *Cooperative Sovereignty* (The Hague, London, Boston: Kluwer Law International, 2000), 264 ff.

24. On the task of institutionalized coordination assigned to the International Committee of the Red Cross, see P. Benvenuti, 'Lineamenti e natura della Croce Rossa internazionale e delle sue componenti', in *Scritti in onore di Giuseppe Auletta*, (Milan: Giuffrè, 1989), 407.

25. On this point, see A. Von Bogdandy, 'Democrazia, globalizzazione e futuro del diritto internazionale', in *Rivista di diritto internazionale* 87 (2004): 337. We may also recall that according to the Preamble of the Statute of the Council of Europe 'the pursuit of peace based upon justice and international cooperation is vital for the preservation of human society and civilization'.

26. We may share the view of F. Lattanzi on the effects of Articles 1, para. 3, 55 and 56 of the UN Charter, in *Garanzie dei diritti dell'uomo nel diritto internazionale generale* (Milan: Giuffrè, 1983), 15.

27. In this sense, see H. Kelsen, *Principles of International Law* (New York: Rinehart, 1952), 226; R. Wolfrum, 'Article 56', in *The Charter of the UN: A Commentary*, ed. B. Simma (Oxford: Oxford University Press, 1994), 794. *Contra* G. Arangio-Ruiz, 'Human Rights and Non Intervention in the Helsinki Final Act', *Recueil des Cours de l'Academie de droit international* 157:IV (1977): 238. The duty to cooperate provided for by the UN Charter is also underlined by the Committee on Economic, Social and Cultural Rights: 'States have a joint and individual responsibility, in accordance with the Charter of the United Nations, to cooperate in providing disaster relief and humanitarian assistance in

times of emergency, including assistance to refugees and internally displaced persons.' General Comment No. 12: *The right to adequate food (Article 11)*, CESCR, 12 May 1999 (UN Doc. E/C.12/1999/5), para. 38. The same Committee has always considered that some economic, social and cultural rights shall have an immediate effect, and as such shall be applied by courts and similar judicial bodies. See, in particular, its General Comment No. 3: *The Nature of States Parties Obligations*, CESCR, 14 December 1990 (UN Doc. E/1991/23). On this aspect, see A. Eide, 'Economic, Social and Cultural Rights as Human Rights', in *Economic, Social and Cultural Rights*, A. Eide, C. Krause and A. Rosas (Dordrecht, Boston, London: Martinus Nijhoff Publishers, 2001), 10; and M.D. Stewart, 'Justiciability of Economic, Social and Cultural Rights: Should there be an International Complaints Mechanism to Adjudicate the Rights to Food, Water, Housing and Health?,' *American Journal of International Law* 98 (2004): 462.

28. 'UN Charter as living instrument' are the words of C. Tomuschat, 'Peace Enforcement and Law Enforcement: Two Separate Chapters of International Law?', in *Studi di diritto internazionale in onore di Gaetano Arangio-Ruiz* (Naples: Ed. scientifica, 2004), 1753. In the same sense, see Supplementary Volume, *Responsibility to Protect*, *supra* note 2, at 163.

29. On this point, we share the view of Perez, *supra* note 23, at 268 and 269.

30. In this sense, see *supra* note 16. There is no doubt that the UN Charter's notion of human rights and fundamental freedoms for all also includes what the UN itself has called human rights in armed conflict and International Humanitarian Law. On this aspect, see the General Comment No. 29: *States of Emergency (Article 4)*, HRC, 31 August 2001 (UN Doc. CCPR/C/21/Rev.1/Add.11).

31. On the role played by the General Assembly and the interpretation of Articles 55 and 56, see G. Arangio-Ruiz, 'The Normative Role of the General Assembly of the UN and the Declaration of Principles of Friendly Relations', *Recueil des Cours de l'Academie de droit international de la Haye* 137:III (1972), 419 and 614.

32. According to Article 2.2 of the UN Charter 'all members shall fulfil in good faith the obligations assumed by them'. On this aspect, see S. Marchisio, *L'ONU. Il diritto delle Nazioni Unite* (Bologna: il Mulino, 2000), 58. The same view is held by P.R. Romano, who points out 'Comme l'a établi la CIJ dans l'affaire du Nicaragua les principaux principes établis par la Charte des NU ont acquis de nos jours une valeur coutumière', in 'L'obligation de prévéntion des catastrophes industrielles et naturelles', in *The International Aspects of Natural and Industrial Catastrophes*, eds D.D. Caron and C. Leben (The Hague, Boston, London: Martinus Nijhoff Publishers, 2001), 397.

33. In this sense, see Tomuschat, *supra* note 28, at 1751; and S. Zappalà, 'Nuovi sviluppi in tema di uso della forza armata in relazione alle vicende del Kosovo', *Rivista di diritto internazionale* (1999): 990.

34. According to Benvenuti: 'most of the rules of IHL weave a net of joint and complementary duties binding on all States in conflict and third States together in the aim of achieving a peremptory goal of solidarity, that is the safeguarding of universal values and fundamental interests in favour of protected persons also in such a difficult period as that of international armed conflict', in 'Ensuring Observance of IHL: Function, Extent and Limits of the Obligations of Third States to Ensure Respect of IHL,' Benvenuti, *supra* note 11, at 530.

35. In this sense, see Barile, *supra* note 19, at 16.

36. In this sense, see Perez, *supra* note 23, at 260 ff. On the distinction commonly drawn between obligations of conduct and obligations of result, see R. Ago, *Le fait internationalement illicite de l'État, source de responsabilité internationale, Scritti sulla responsabilità degli Stati*, Vol. II, 2, eds A. Di Blase and S. Marchisio (Naples: Jovene, 1986), 905.

37. On this aspect, see Romano, *supra* note 32, at 429. On the duty to inform as customary international law, see N. Nordstrom, 'Managing Transboundary Environmental Accidents: The State Duty to Inform', in *The International Aspects of Natural and Industrial Catastrophes*, ed. D.D. Caron and C. Leben (The Hague, Boston and London: Martinus Nijhoff Publishers, 2001), 350 *et seq.*

38. This draft was enacted on 30 November 2001.

39. The first relevant document to be considered is the Report on the *Responsibility to Protect*, *supra* note 2. This Report has opened a wide debate on the idea of sovereignty as responsibility instead of as control. This new reading of sovereignty has been recognized in various UN documents. See, in this sense, the Report of the High-level Panel on Threats, Challenges and Change, *A More Secure World: Our Shared Responsibility*, published by the United Nations in 2004. This Panel was appointed by the Secretary General in September 2003; The UN Secretary General's Report titled *In Larger Freedom: Towards Development, Security and Human Rights for All*, issued on 21 March 2005; the document was adopted on 24 October 2005 by the UN General Assembly, named the 'World Summit Outcome'. On this point, see C. Focarelli, 'La dottrina della responsabilità di proteggere e l'intervento

umanitario', *Rivista di diritto internazionale* 91:2 (2008): 327 ff.; and E. Greppi, *The Responsibility to Protect: an Introduction* (San Remo: International Institute of Humanitarian Law, 2009).

40. On this aspect, see Ramcharan, *supra* note 4, at 4; L. Condorelli and L. Boisson de Chazournes, 'De la responsabilité de protéger, ou d'une nouvelle parure pour une notion déjà bien établie en droit international', *Revue Générale du droit international public* 110:1 (2006): 11; T.G. Weiss, *Humanitarian Intervention* (Cambridge: Polity Press, 2007), 98; C. Stahn, 'Responsibility to Protect: Political Rhetoric or Emerging Legal Norm?', *American Journal of International Law* 101:1 (2007): 99 ff.

41. According to Article 4 of the Guiding Principles on the Right to Humanitarian Assistance, 'The primary responsibility to protect and assist the victims of emergencies is that of the authorities of the territory in which the emerging causing urgent humanitarian needs occurs', *supra* note 14. On this aspect, see K. Bennoune, 'Sovereignty vs Suffering? Re-examining Sovereignty and Human Rights through the Lens of Iraq', *European Journal of International Law* 13:1 (2008): 259. We may, however, share the view of A. Bianchi who stresses that 'While it is in principle true that the State, by exercising its sovereign prerogatives, may indeed be in a better position to secure respect for human rights… it is also undeniably true that external scrutiny of State conduct by international law has been fundamental in fostering human rights and in promoting worldwide the idea that States can no longer disregard universally accepted standards of human rights protection by invoking sovereignty'. See A. Bianchi, 'Ad-hocism and the Rule of Law', *European Journal of International Law* 13:1 (2008): 264. In the same sense, see *Tadić*, ICTJ, Appeals Chamber, Judgment, 2 October 1995.

42. In this sense, see Franco, *supra* note 13, at 874.

43. The primary responsibility of the territorial State has been endorsed in three important Resolutions adopted by the UN General Assembly ('Humanitarian Assistance to Victims of Natural Disaster and Similar Emergency Situations', A/RES/43/131, 8 December 1988, and A/RES/45/100, 14 December 1990, and 'Strengthening of the Coordination of Humanitarian Emergency Assistance of the UN,' A/RES/46/182, 19 December 1991). Moreover, on this aspect, see paragraphs 138 and 139 of the document named 'Word Summit Outcome', *supra* note 39.

44. On the duty of any authority which has de facto control over the victims of an emergency to provide them with the necessary humanitarian assistance, see also Article 3 of the 'Resolution on Humanitarian Assistance', adopted by the XVIth Commission of the International Institute of Humanitarian Law, Bruges, 2 September 2003.

45. In this sense, see *Responsibility to Protect supra* note 2, at 20. The responsibility to protect, according to some scholars implies the recognition of a right to survive which shall be ensured through the observance by the States of some specific obligations: the obligation to respect and to protect basic needs, and the obligation to facilitate access to all the necessary goods and services to meet these needs.

46. According to H. Shue, to recognize the subsistence rights of the population, the State shall have an obligation to avoid deprivation, to protect from deprivation and to aid the deprived, *Basic Rights: Subsistence, Affluence and US Foreign Policy* (Princeton: Princeton University Press, 1980), 25. In the view of some scholars, the occupying power should guarantee even the progressive development of the economic, social and cultural rights in case of prolonged occupation. According to M. Sassòli, 'As the legislative function is a continuous, necessary function of every State on which the evolution of civil life depends, a legislative vacuum created by the disruption of the legitimate sovereign must at a certain point in time be filled by the occupying power', in 'Legislation and Maintenance of Public Order and Civil Life by Occupying Powers', *European Journal of International Law* 16:4 (2005): 679.

47. On this aspect, see F.K. Abiew, *The Evolution of the Doctrine and Practice of Humanitarian Intervention* (The Hague, London, Boston: Martinus Nijhoff Publishers, 1999), 273.

48. See the 'Declaration on the Protection of Women and Children in Emergency and Armed Conflicts', A/RES/318 (XXIX), 14 December 1974, paragraph 6.

49. In this sense, see Patrnogic, *supra* note 2, at 1026.

50. On this point, see *supra* notes 15 and 16.

51. In other words the right to survive shall be included in the catalogue of fundamental human rights, considered as an intrangressible '*noyau-dur*' (hard core) by all the important regional agreements. In this sense, see G. Cohen-Jonathan, 'La responsabilité internationale pour atteinte aux droits de l'homme: sur quelques tendances recentes', in *Studi di diritto internazionale in onore di Gaetano Arangio-Ruiz* (Naples: Ed scientifica, 2004), 680.

52. The limit of such dispositions is that, in principle, they may not force a belligerent party to guarantee the right to survive to its own population.

53. According to Montaz: 'l'expression utilisée par le Protocol II additionnel pour déterminer l'object des actions de secours est suffisamment souple pour pouvoir englober tout vivre ou matériel dont l'envoi s'avérerait nécessaire à la survie d'une population civile prise dans la tourmente d'un conflit armé non international', *supra* note 4, at 2070.

54. In the view of the Court the elementary considerations of humanity shall be respected in any circumstance as an intransgressible principle of the customary international law. See the cases, *Corfu Channel* (United Kingdom v. Albania), Judgment, I.C.J. Reports 1949, 22; *Military and Paramilitary Activities in and against Nicaragua* (Nicaragua v. United States), Judgment, I.C.J. Reports 1986, 113; and *Legal Consequences of the Construction of a Wall in Palestinian Territory*, Advisory Opinion, I.C.J. Reports 1996, 257. On this aspect, see R. Abi-Saab, 'Les Principes généraux du droit humanitaire selon la Cour internationale de Justice', *Revue internationale de la Croix-Rouge* 69 (1987): 384.

55. On this point, we may share the opinion of Bianchi who underlines that 'the human rights doctrine, despite its Western connotations, has enormously contributed to laying the foundations of an international public order based on a commonality of core values which most people, despite their government's view, would regard as fundamental', *supra* note 41, at 265.

56. In this respect we may read, 'On two occasions the International Court of Justice ruled on cases that involved assessing the legality of interventions for which humanitarian purposes had been declared: the United Kingdom in the Corfu Channel and the United States in Nicaragua. In both cases, the ICJ adhered to the position that the principles of non intervention involves the right of every sovereign State to conduct its affairs without outside interference and that international law requires territorial integrity to be respected', Supplementary Volume, *Responsibility to Protect*, *supra* note 2, at 18.

57. These are the words of the Guiding Principle No. 3 of A/RES/46/182, 19 December 1991. See on this point, Romano, *supra* note 32, at 424.

58. In this sense, see Supplementary Volume, *Responsibility to Protect*, *supra* note 2, at 19. On this point, see the remarks of M. Bettati, *Le droit d'ingerence. Mutation de l'ordre international* (Paris: Odile Jacob, 1996), 104.

59. In this sense, see L. Condorelli, 'Intervention humanitaire et/ou assistance humanitaire. Quelques certitudes et beaucoup d'interrogations', in *Proceedings of the Qatar International Law Conference*, *supra* note 2, 2005.

60. As regards the consequences of the earthquake, see Zorzi-Giustiniani, *supra* note 12, at 25.

61. On this aspect, see F. Kalshoven who notes that the national authorities 'may not wish to recognize the vulnerability of their societies in the face of an unforeseen natural disaster and, indeed, their own inability effectively to cope with the effects thereof', in 'Assistance to the Victims of Armed Conflicts and other Disasters. Introduction to the Conference Theme', in *Assisting the Victims of Armed Conflicts*, ed. F. Kalshoven (Dordrecht: Martinus Nijhoff Publishers, 1989), 22.

62. In this sense, see Benvenuti, *supra* note 11, at 18.

63. On the importance of the first and second Protocols to developing and completing the dispositions of the fourth Geneva Convention, see Montaz, *supra* note 4, at 2066.

64. On this aspect, according to A. Eide, a State has always the burden of proving that 'it has unsuccessfully sought to obtain international support to ensure the availability and accessibility of the food', in 'Economic, Social and Cultural Rights as Human Rights', in Eide, *supra* note 27, at 27. In the Commentary on Article 14 of the second Protocol we may read 'If the survival of the population is threatened and a humanitarian organization fulfilling the required conditions of impartiality and non-discrimination is able to remedy this situation, relief action must take place.... A refusal would be equivalent to a violation of the rule prohibiting the use of starvation as a method of combat', Sandoz, Swinarski and Zimmermann, *supra* note 6, at para. 4885. This approach is followed by F. Bugnion, 'Le Comité international de la Croix-Rouge et la protection des victimes de la guerre', *International Review of the Red Cross* 839 (2000), 994.

65. On this aspect, see the Report of the first Commission, in *Armed Conflicts and Disintegration of States, Humanitarian Challenge, 21st Round Table on Current Problems of International Humanitarian Law* (San Remo: International Institute of Humanitarian Law, 1996), 62. On the debate over the definition of a failed State, see D. Thurer, 'The Failed State and International Law', *International Review of the Red Cross* 836 (1999): 731; and A. Tancredi, 'Di pirati e Stati falliti: il Consiglio di Sicurezza autorizza il ricorso alla forza nelle acque territoriali in Somalia', *Rivista di diritto internazionale* 91:4 (2008): 943.

66. These are the words of Sandoz, Swinarski and Zimmermann, *supra* note 6, at para. 4884.

67. In this sense, see Articles 6, 11 and 12, *supra* note 14. On the relevance of the application of Articles 16 and 17 of the Covenant on Economic, Social and Cultural Rights, the Committee, in its Concluding Observations regarding Israel stated: 'The Committee is particularly concerned that on frequent occasions, the State party's closure policy has prevented civilians from reaching medical services and that emergency situations have ended at times in death at checkpoints. The Committee is alarmed over reports that Israeli security forces have turned back supply missions of the ICRC and the UN Relief and Work Agency for Palestine Refugees in the Near East attempting to deliver food, water and medical relief to affected areas', UN Doc. E/C.12/1/Add.69, 31 August 2001, para. 13.

68. Most of the time the access is negotiated and the territorial State agrees to respect standard rules, codes of conduct or memoranda of understanding. In this respect, see the Report of the Secretary General of 12 January 2001 on the 'Fundamental Standards of Humanity', paragraphs 42–45.

69. In this sense, see Zorzi-Giustiniani, *supra* note 12, at 94.

70. According to Article 4 of the Guiding Principles of A/RES/46/182, 19 December 1991 'the affected State has the primary role in the initiation, organization, coordination, and implementation of humanitarian assistance within its territory'.

71. These are the words of Article 7 of the Guiding Principles of A/RES/46/182, 19 December 1991. Some scholars do not recognize that third States have a general duty to facilitate the transit of humanitarian assistance, in this sense, see D. Bindschedler-Robert, 'Actions of Assistance in Non-International Conflicts, Article 18 of Protocol II', in *European Seminar on Humanitarian Law* (Krakow: ICRC, 1979), 77.

72. On the debate over the interpretation of Article 23 of the IV Geneva Convention, see P. MacAlister Smith, *International Humanitarian Assistance. Disaster Relief Actions in International Law and Organization* (Dordrecht, Boston, Lancaster: Henri Dunant Institute, 1985), 28.

73. According to the Commentary of Article 38: 'the right of protected persons to receive relief implies an obligation of the country of residence to allow the consignment to enter its territory and to pass them on intact to the addressee', *Commentary, IV Geneva Convention*, eds O. Uhler and H. Coursier (Geneva: ICRC, 1958).

74. In this sense, see Montaz, *supra* note 4, at 2066.

75. The rule provided for by Article 69 shall be considered as customary law, in this sense, see J.M. Henckaerts and L. Doswald-Beck, *Customary International Humanitarian Law* (Cambridge: Cambridge University Press, 2005), 263. According to C.A. Allen 'The language of Article 70 ... suggests both a weighty duty to permit relief and an acknowledgement that details must be agreed upon', in 'Civilian Starvation and Relief during Armed Conflict: the Modern Humanitarian Law,' *Georgia Journal of International and Comparative Law* 19:1 (1989): 72.

76. In the view of L. Condorelli: '(A) l'article 3 commun aux quatre Conventions de 1949, est due une véritable révolution juridique: celle consistant à soumettre à des normes internationales les conflicts se déroulant à l'intérieur d'un Etat entre le gouvernement de celui-ci et une partie de sa population. Il faut souligner, en particulier, que l'article commun codifie le droit des organismes humanitaires d'offrir leurs services, ce qui implique clairement la reconnaissance que les besoins humanitaires causés par ce type de conflit relèvent de la competence internationale, et non pas du domaine réservé des Etats', *supra* note 59, at 1007. On the same aspect, see F. Bougnion, ed., *Le Comité international de la Croix-Rouge et la protection des victimes de la guerre* (Geneva: International Committee of the Red Cross, 2000), 519.

77. In the view of L. Condorelli, 'Le IIème Protocole proclame explicitement pour la première fois, à l'art, 18, par. 2, même si d'une façon embryonnaire et par un langage prudent, le principe suivant lequel les actions impartiales de secours humanitaire seront entreprises avec le consentement de la Haute Partie contractante concernée, en cas de privations excessives endurées par la population civile', in 'Intervention humanitaire et/ou assistance humanitaire? Quelques certitudes et beaucoup d'interrogations', *Proceedings of the Qatar International Law Conference, supra* note 2, 1007.

78. On this aspect, see M. Bothe, 'Relief Actions: the Position of the Recipient State', in *Assisting the Victims of Armed Conflict and Other Disasters*, ed. F. Kalshoven (Dordrecht: Martinus Nijhoff Publishers, 1989), 91 ff.

79. On the role played by the Resolutions of the General Assembly in assessing the duty to cooperate to ensure the prompt and smooth delivery of relief assistance, see M. Bettati, 'Ingérence, intervention ou assistance humanitaire?' in *Proceedings of the Qatar International Law Conference, supra* note 2, 942.

80. As regards the attitude of the Security Council, see, as first examples, S/RES/733, 23 January 1992; S/RES/758, 8 June 1992; S/RES/794, 3 December 1992; S/RES/813, 26 March 1993. In this respect,

the role played by the Secretary General has been fundamental – in his view 'it is the obligation of States to ensure that affected populations have access to the assistance they require for their survival', See 'Report of the Secretary General to the Security Council on the Protection of Civilians in Armed Conflicts', 8 September 1999, para. 51.

81. On this point, see the S/RES/1674, 28 April 2006, on the 'Protection of Civilians in Armed Conflicts'.

82. See the Charter of Médecins sans frontières. In particular in the MSF International Activity Report 2000 one may read that the organization 'refuses to wait for the approval of all parties before acting. It insists on the right to speak out in the face of human rights violations. Putting populations in danger first, above political considerations, is engrained as a core to our mission, and in this MSF has helped shape the humanitarian movement world-wide.'

83. In the same sense, see the Convention on Special Missions adopted by the UN General Assembly on 8 December 1969.

84. On this point, see J.A. Carrillo Salcedo, 'Le droit à l'assistance humanitaire: à la recherche d'un équilibre entre les devoirs des autorités territoriales et les obligations des donateurs des secours humanitaires', in *European Commission, Law in Humanitarian Crises, Volume II. Access to Victims: Right to Intervene or Right to Receive Humanitarian Assistance* (Luxembourg: Office for Official Publications of the European Communities, 1995), 100.

85. According to the International Committee of the Red Cross 'the offer of disaster relief by an impartial international humanitarian organization ought not to be regarded as an unfriendly act', in 'Declaration of Principles for International Humanitarian Relief to the Civilian Population in Disaster Situations'. This Declaration was adopted by the XXIth International Conference of the Red Cross, Resolution XXVI, Istanbul, September 1969. In the same sense, see the 'Declaration of Principles for International Humanitarian Relief to the Civilian Population in Disaster Situations', adopted by the UN General Assembly in A/RES/2675 (XXV), 9 December 1970, and the Guiding Principles on the Right to Humanitarian Assistance adopted in San Remo, 1993, where we may read in its Article 5: 'National authorities, national and international organizations whose statutory mandate provides for the possibility of rendering humanitarian assistance, such as ICRC, UNHCR, other organizations of the UN system, and professional humanitarian organizations, have the right to offer such assistance when the conditions laid down in the present Principles are fulfilled'.

86. The right to take the initiative may not be confused with the right to offer humanitarian assistance at the request of the recipient government.

87. The phrase in principle may, in practice, mean that consent may be subordinate to the necessity to provide assistance in the face of an overwhelming human tragedy, or indeed that consent should come from citizens, rather than governments', Supplementary Volume, *Responsibility to Protect, supra* note 2, at 19. On the debate over the text of the A/RES/4/131, see Bettati, *supra* note 58, at 104.

88. In particular, see *Military and Paramilitary Activities in and against Nicaragua, supra* note 54, paras 267, 268 and 243.

89. In this sense, see Abiew, *supra* note 47, at 255.

90. In this sense, see Carrillo Salcedo, *supra* note 84, at 100; R.M. Giles Carnero, *De la asistencia a la injerencia humanitaria: la práctica reciente del Consejo de Seguridad* (Seville: Universidad de Huelva, 1997), 32. *Contra*, L. Boisson de Chazournes and L. Condorelli underline the importance of common Article 1 in assessing international solidarity, 'Common Article 1 of the Geneva Conventions Revisited: Protecting Collective Interests', in *International Review of the Red Cross* 837 (2000): 67.

91. According to P.R. Romano 'l'on peut affirmer que dans l'état actuel du droit international coutumier un Etat n'assume aucune obligation de fournir son assistance à un autre Etat frappé par une catastrophe ... A tout le moins peut-on affirmer que les Etats faisant object d'une demande d'aide d'urgence ont le devoir d'évaluer cette demande de bonne foi, de déterminer leur volonté d'intervention sur la base de leur capacité matérielle plutôt qu'en fonction de considérations politiques et enfin de justifier leur refus éventuel', Romano, *supra* note 32, at 421.

92. In other words, the State has a positive obligation to secure the basic needs indispensable for the survival of its population. On the recognition of the individual right to survive, see *supra* paragraphs 2 and 4. On the recognition of a positive obligation, see also *Indigenous Community Sawhoyamaxa v. Paraguay*, IACtHR, Judgment of 29 March 2006, paragraph 176.

93. In this sense, see Ramcharan, *supra* note 4, at 35. In this respect once again we may stress the important role played by A/RES/43/171; A/RES/45/100; and A/RES/46/182.

94. The so-called 'do something' approach is strongly sustained by the Commission on Intervention and State Sovereignty, Supplementary Volume, *Responsibility to Protect, supra* note 2, at 203.

95. In this respect, we may recall that the consent of all the parties involved is necessary because, according to the Supplement to the Agenda for Peace of the Secretary General, an enforcement action 'at present is beyond the capacity of the UN except on a very limited scale', in 'Supplement to an Agenda for Peace: Position Paper of the Security General on the Occasion of the 50th Anniversary of the UN', 3 January 1995. The Secretary General has stated the same principle in many other documents, such as the 'Secretary General's Report to the UN Security Council on the Protection of Civilians in Armed Conflicts', 26 November 2002.

96. In this sense, the Secretary General has affirmed, before the UN General Assembly, 'I am determined to integrate human rights even more fully into every aspect of our work', 10 November 2001, available at http://www.un.org/webcast/ga/56/statements/011110sgE.htm (last accessed 13 February 2012).

97. On the development of a culture of protection, see the 'Report of the Secretary General to the Security Council on the Protection of Civilians in Armed Conflicts', 30 March 2001. On this point, we may read: 'Civilians now constitute the majority of war casualties, an atrocious and alarming trend that has moved the UN Secretary General to call for the creation of a culture of protection in dealing with situations of armed conflict', Supplementary Volume, *Responsibility to Protect, supra* note 2, at 191.

98. According to the Secretary General: 'Surely no legal principle, not even sovereignty, can ever shield crimes against humanity. Where such crimes occur and peaceful attempts to halt them have been exhausted, the Security Council has a moral duty to act on behalf of the international community. The fact that we cannot protect people everywhere is no reason for doing nothing when we can', in K. Annan, *We the Peoples. The Role of the United Nations in the 21st Century* (New York: United Nations, 2000), 48.

99. See *supra*, paragraph 4. *Contra* the recognition of a general 'opinion juris' on this commitment, see C. Focarelli who underlines that according to the United States 'the Charter has never been interpreted as creating a legal obligation for Security Council members to support enforcement action in various cases involving serious breach of international peace', *supra* note 39, at 335. In this respect, see the *American Journal of International Law* 2 (2006): 463.

100. In this sense, see Montaz, *supra* note 4, at 2074.

101. In this sense, see M. Iovane, *Il divieto dell'uso della forza armata tra obblighi degli Stati e diritto dei popoli alla pace* (Naples: Ed. Scientifica, 2000), 109.

102. In this respect, S/RES/1674, 28 April 2006, deserves our attention. Indeed this Resolution set out a non-exhaustive list of the types of activities for the protection of civilians which could be endorsed by multinational forces: protecting civilians in imminent threat of physical danger; taking all feasible measures to ensure the security in and around camps of refugees and internally displaced persons and that of their inhabitants; facilitating the provision of humanitarian assistance; creating conditions conducive to the voluntary, safe, sustainable return of the refugees and internally displaced persons. On this point, see E.C. Gillard, *UN-OCHA Perspective in International Peace Operation and International Humanitarian Law*, in Contributions presented at the Seminar on 'International Peace Operations and International Humanitarian Law' organized by the International Institute of Human-itarian Law, San Remo, in cooperation with Centro Alti Studi per la Difesa, Roma and Società Italiana per l'Organizzazione Internazionale, Roma with the support of the Italian Ministry of Foreign Affairs, Rome, 27 March 2008, at 48.

103. See S/RES/1101, 28 May 1997.

104. In this sense, see Marchisio, *supra* note 32, at 268; P. Benvenuti, 'Le Forze multinazionali e diritto internazionale umanitario, in Comando e Controllo nelle forze di pace e nelle coalizioni militari', in *Contributo alla riforma della Carta delle Nazioni Unite*, ed. N. Ronzitti (Milan: Franco Angeli, 1999), 237.

105. On this aspect, see C. Sommaruga, 'Action humanitaire et opération de maintien de la paix', *International Review of the Red Cross* 824 (1993): 267. We may note that according to the Guiding Principles on the Right to Humanitarian Assistance: 'The competent UN organs and regional organizations may undertake necessary measures, including coercion in accordance with their respective mandate, in cases of severe, prolonged and mass suffering of populations, which could be alleviated by humanitarian assistance ...' *supra* note 14, at Principle 7.

106. In this sense, on the US policy of assertive multilateralism supporting the delivery of humanitarian assistance, see M.K. Albright, 'The Use of Force in a Post- Cold War World', in *US Department of State Dispatch* 4.2 (1993), 665.

107. These are the words of Abiew, *supra* note 47, at 246.

108. On this aspect, see R. Giuffrida, *La Costituzione di zone e corridoi di sicurezza quale contenuto dell'intervento umanitario* (Turin: Giappichelli, 2008), 164.
109. On the evolution of the concept of Safety Zone, see B.S. Chimni, 'The Incarceration of Victims: Deconstructing Safety Zones', in *Proceedings of the Quatar International Law Conference, supra* note 2, 828.
110. On the first change of view over the legal regime of the Safety Zone, see Franco, *supra* note 13, at 913; Giuffrida, *supra* note 108, at 161.
111. Even the changing terminology employed by the Security Council to define the zones, as 'zones of separation, temporary security zones, zones of operation, regroupment camps, protected zones, demilitarized zones, security zones of the UN', are not allowed to specify their legal regime.
112. In this sense, see Y. Sandoz, 'The Establishment of Safety Zones for Persons Displaced within their Country of Origin', in *Proceedings of the Qatar International Law Conference, supra* note 2, 926.
113. According to M. Sassòli, Article 64 shall be interpreted in the sense that the occupying power shall secure the respect of international humanitarian law and human rights, in particular those rights which are economic and social, *supra* note 46, 667. On the possibility of the occupying power changing the legislation of the occupied territory in order to preserve fundamental human rights the debate is still open, see M. Starita, 'L'occupation de l'Iraq, le Conseil de Securité, le droit de la guerre et le droit des peuples à disposer d'eux même', *Revue générale de droit international public* 108:4 (2004): 889.
114. On this point, see Supplementary Volume, *Responsibility to Protect, supra* note 2, at 168.
115. As regards the Decisions of the I.C.J., see *supra*, at paragraph 4. According to C. Tomuschat, 'The ICJ has already endorsed the notion that elementary considerations of morality are included, as integral elements, in the international legal order', in 'Obligations Arising for States Without or Against their Will', in *Academie de droit international, Recueil des cours* 241 (1993): IV, 304.
116. In this sense, see Barile, *supra* note 19, at 11; P. Benvenuti, 'Riflessioni sul carattere nazionale del DIU e del movimento della Croce Rossa e Mezzaluna Rossa', in *Assistenza umanitaria e DIU* (Naples, 2001). In particular, the I.C.J. has clearly affirmed that common Article 3 shall be applied as customary law under all circumstances in all kinds of conflict, see the case *Military and Paramilitary Activities in and against Nicaragua, supra* note 54, para. 218.
117. In this sense, see P. Benvenuti, 'Movimenti insurrezionali e protocolli aggiuntivi alle Convenzioni di Ginevra del 1949', in *Studi in onore di Cesare Sanfilippo* (Milan: Giuffrè, 1983), 72.
118. These are the words of E. Eide, 'The New Humanitarian Law in Non-International Armed Conflicts', in *Proceedings of the 1976 and 1977 Conferences, Vol. II*, ed. A. Cassese (Naples: Editoriale Scientifica, 1979), 120. On this aspect, see M. Sassòli, 'La première décision de la Chambre d'appel du Tribunal international pour l'ex-Yougoslavie: Tadić (compétence)', *Revue Générale de droit international public* 100 (1966): 101.
119. Even though the dispositions of IHL are always considered more precise and predictable than those of HR. On the interdependence of the two systems, see J. Kellenberger, 'Protection of Humanitarian Beings in Disaster Situations', International Institute of Humanitarian Law, 23; A. Guellali, 'Lex specialis, droit international humanitaire et droits de l'homme: leur interaction dans les nouveaux conflicts armés', *Revue générale de droit international public* 111:3 (2007): 541. We may note that the interdependence between the two systems can be explained by their common goal: the protection of human dignity. This interdependence has positive effects especially when we look at the influence of human rights over the interpretation of international humanitarian law in order to assess the priority of the principle of humanity over the principle of necessity.
120. According to R. Kolb, 'la qualification ou les missions d'une opération n'ont que peu de pertinence pour l'applicabilité du droit international humanitaire. L'application de celui-ci repose sur le simple fait de l'existence d'un conflit armé, c'est-à-dire d'hostilités d'une certaine qualité. La nature, la qualification et les tâches des opérations n'indiquent qu'un degré de probabilité factuelle qu'une Force soit entraînée dans un conflit armé', in *Droit humanitaire et opérations de paix internationales*, 2nd edition (Geneva, Bâle, Munich: Helbing & Lichtenhahn/Bruylant, 2006), 43. In the same sense, see the 'UN Secretary General Bulletin', 6 August 1999. In a general way we share the view that IHL shall be considered as customary law. In this sense, see L. Condorelli, 'Le Statut des forces de l'ONU et le droit international humanitaire', *Rivista di diritto internazionale* 78 (1995): 901. On the relevance of the *'opinio juris'* to justify the existence of a general rule even when the *usus* has not been ascertained, see R. Kolb, 'Selected Problems in the Theory of Customary International Law', *Netherlands International Law Review* 50 (2003): 124.

121. In this sense, see S. Lazzarotto, 'Current Challenges of International Humanitarian Law', International Peace Operations and International Humanitarian Law, in Contributions presented at the Seminar on 'International Peace Operations and International Humanitarian Law' organized by the International Institute of Humanitarian Law, San Remo in cooperation with Centro Alti Studi per la Difesa, Roma and Società Italiana per l'Organizzazione Internazionale, Roma with the support of the Italian Ministry of Foreign Affairs, Rome, 27 March 2008, at 97.

122. It is very difficult to qualify the nature of the contemporary armed conflict because most are non-international armed conflicts with an international dimension. On this aspect of the problem, see Decaux, *supra* note 3, at 79.

123. On this issue, see E. Greppi, 'Some Reflections on the Challenges which International Humanitarian Law has to Face in Contemporary Armed Conflict,' in Contributions presented at the Seminar on 'International Peace Operations and International Humanitarian Law' organized by the International Institute of Humanitarian Law, San Remo in cooperation with Centro Alti Studi per la Difesa, Roma and Società Italiana per l'Organizzazione Internazionale, Roma with the support of the Italian Ministry of Foreign Affairs, Rome, 27 March 2008, at 84.

124. On this aspect, see M. Nabot, 'Le rôle du Conseil de Securité dans le mise en oeuvre du droit international humanitaire (notamment au travers de son pouvoir coercitif)', in Proceedings of the International Conference of the International Institute of Humanitarian Law, *Application of International Humanitarian Law, Human Rights and Refugee Law: UN Security Council, Peacekeeping Forces, Protection of Human Beings in Disaster Situations*, San Remo, 8–10 September 2005, 134.

125. In this sense, see M. Sassòli, who underlines that the field of IHL, in which the Security Council has in recent years played an interesting role between interpretation and change, is the extent of the legislative powers of an occupying power by giving a reinterpretation of Article 43 of the 1907 Hague Convention, 'Interpretation of International Humanitarian Law by the Security Council', in Proceedings of the International Conference of the International Institute of Humanitarian Law, *Application of International Humanitarian Law, Human Rights and Refugee Law: UN Security Council, Peacekeeping Forces, Protection of Human Beings in Disaster Situations*, San Remo, 8–10 September 2005, 105.

126. And this because any kind of new convention will only bind States.

127. In this sense we already note the role played by the Security Council and the UN Secretary General.

128. On the so-called 'do something' approach and the development of the culture of protection, see Supplementary Volume, *Responsibility to Protect*, *supra* note 2, at 193.

129. These are the words of Greppi, *supra* note 123, p. 85.

130. This is the view of Benvenuti, *supra* note 11, at 55.

131. In this sense, see the S/RES/1296, 19 April 2000; S/RES/1341, 22 February 2001; and S/RES/1502, 26 August 2003. On the relevance of the said principles, see Montaz, *supra* note 4, at 2068.

132. This is the opinion of the Court in the case *Military Activities in and against Nicaragua*, *supra* note 54, paras 242 and 243.

133. In particular, according to the Court 'there can be no doubt that the provision of strictly humanitarian aid to persons or forces in another country, whatever their political affiliation or objectives, cannot be regarded as unlawful intervention, or in any other way contrary to international law'. This sentence reproduces the content of Article 70 of the first Protocol.

134. In this sense, the Security Council underlines 'the importance for the humanitarian organizations to uphold the principles of neutrality, impartiality and humanity in their humanitarian activities', S/RES/1052, 26 August 2003. In its Resolution 'World Summit Outcome', the UN General Assembly declares that member States undertake to 'uphold and respect the humanitarian principles of humanity, neutrality, impartiality and independence and ensure that humanitarian actors have safe and unhindered access to populations in need in conformity with the relevant provisions of international law and national law', *supra* note 39, at paragraph 38.

135. In other words, in the face of legal ambiguity the respect of some fundamental principles assume an increasing importance. The establishment of a set of principles, generally recognized, is the only way to mitigate any potential abuse.

16. The prohibition of enforced disappearances: a meaningful example of a partial merger between human rights law and international humanitarian law

*Gloria Gaggioli**

1. INTRODUCTION

The phenomenon of enforced disappearances is not new. It is generally claimed that Hitler's *Nacht und Nebel* decree, which provided for enforced disappearance of 'undesirable elements',[1] was one of its first formulation. Enforced disappearances have been practised on a large scale in Latin America.[2] This phenomenon has not yet been eradicated, as evidenced by the Reports of the Working Group on Enforced or Involuntary Disappearances.[3] The practice of secret detentions by the United States of America in the context of the 'war on terror' is just one of many recent examples.[4]

The first international treaties addressing the problem of disappearances in a broad sense were the 1949 Geneva Conventions. They include a range of preventive obligations in this regard, without however embracing the concept of 'enforced disappearance'.[5] This latter concept was developed subsequently by the case law and practice of human rights monitoring bodies as well as by human rights treaties and soft law instruments. Meanwhile, the case law of international criminal tribunals has recognized that this practice, when widespread or systematic, may constitute a crime against humanity.

From these various elements, was born the 2006 *Convention for the Protection of All Persons against Enforced Disappearance* (hereinafter Convention against Enforced Disappearance).[6] It provides the latest (but not necessarily the most complete) definition of this phenomenon, namely:

> [T]he arrest, detention, abduction or any other form of deprivation of liberty by agents of the State or by persons or groups of persons acting with the authorization, support or acquiescence of the State, followed by a refusal to acknowledge the deprivation of liberty or by concealment of the fate or whereabouts of the disappeared person, which place such a person outside the protection of the law.[7]

In practice, the phenomenon of disappearances consists most often in the abduction, by a State or a 'political organization', of persons considered a 'security-threat', their torture and killing, and finally the hiding of their bodies so that the guilty go unpunished.[8]

This chapter will present successively how IHL, HRL and international criminal law contributed, in their own way, to the prohibition and criminalization of enforced disappearances. It will show that these bodies of law are complementary and that their mutual influence allowed a progressive enhancement of the legal protection of persons against enforced disappearances. Finally, it will show how the merger of the rules belonging to these different bodies of law into the Convention against Enforced Disappearances contributed to strengthen the prohibition of enforced disappearances in international law.

2. PREVENTING DISAPPEARANCES: THE CONTRIBUTION OF IHL

While IHL does not deal *a priori* with the phenomenon of enforced disappearances, it still contains a number of provisions designed to prevent them. If warring parties scrupulously respected their IHL obligations in times of armed conflict, the issue of enforced disappearances would not materialize. In fact, enforced disappearances violate a variety of IHL obligations, such as the prohibition of arbitrary detention, the prohibition of torture and the prohibition of arbitrary killings.[9]

Moreover, IHL treaties applicable in international armed conflicts contain numerous provisions aimed at preventing that combatants or civilians go missing during armed conflicts. Among these provisions, there are:

(1) *IHL provisions relating to the dead.* Belligerent parties must take all possible measures, particularly after an engagement, to search for the dead.[10] They must identify the dead, transmit relevant information (including death certificates) and repatriate personal effects.[11] They must honourably bury the dead and mark the graves so that they can always be found.[12] They shall organize at the commencement of hostilities an Official Graves Registration Service, to allow subsequent exhumations and to ensure the identification of bodies, whatever the site of the graves, and the possible transportation to the home country.[13] Additional Protocol I also provides that the High Contracting Parties shall conclude agreements to facilitate access to the gravesites by relatives of the deceased and by representatives of official graves registration services, to protect and maintain such gravesites permanently and facilitate the return of remains of the deceased and of personal effects to the home country upon its request or, unless that country objects, upon the request of the next of kin.[14]

(2) *IHL provisions regarding detainees/internees.* The third and fourth Geneva Conventions provide for an obligation to establish a capture card and to provide information on the transfers, releases, repatriations, escapes, hospitalization, health status, births and deaths of detainees/internees.[15] Prisoners of war and civilian internees are also entitled to correspond with relatives.[16] States are required to investigate when prisoners of war or civilian internees died in special circumstances.[17] Belligerent states shall develop national Information Bureaux which will collaborate with the Central Tracing Agency of the ICRC for transmitting said information to the warring parties involved.[18] The warring parties must also provide access to places of internment and detention to the ICRC,[19] whose role is crucial in clarifying the fate of missing persons in armed conflict.[20]

(3) *IHL provisions regarding the missing.* Additional Protocol I has complemented the Geneva Conventions by adding specific provisions for war missing.[21] The relevant

section of Additional Protocol I starts with the recognition of a new fundamental right:[22] the right of families to know the fate of their relatives.[23] This is quite odd since Additional Protocol I seems to recognize a new 'human right',[24] whose existence had never been acknowledged in the human rights law sphere.[25] This IHL right of families to know the fate of their relatives is however different from the rights stemming from HRL. On the one hand, it does not grant an individual right that can be legally claimed by 'families'.[26] On the other hand, it imposes no obligation on a State towards its own citizens, which would be unthinkable in the logic of HRL.[27] So this 'right of families to know the fate of their relatives' is more akin to a guiding principle than to an individual human right.[28] Although HRL is probably not the source of this 'right', its influence remains palpable in the formulation of this IHL principle. Several specific obligations derive from this IHL 'right of families to know the fate of their relatives'. These include the obligation to search for persons reported missing by an adverse Party and to provide all relevant information concerning such persons, in particular to the Central Tracing Agency;[29] the obligation, to the fullest extent possible, to facilitate and, if need be, to carry out the search and the recording of information concerning persons who have died as a result of hostilities or occupation;[30] the obligation for the Parties to the conflict to agree on arrangements for teams to search for, identify and recover the dead from battlefield areas.[31]

IHL treaty provisions relating to non-international armed conflicts contain only the obligation to search for the dead.[32] However, many of the provisions cited above can be said as belonging to customary international humanitarian law and applicable to both international and non-international armed conflicts.

Finally, it is worth noting that, according to the *ICRC Study on Customary International Humanitarian Law*, the prohibition of enforced disappearances as such belongs to customary IHL for international and non-international armed conflicts.[33] In fact, the ICRC study considers that the 'cumulative effect' of the IHL provisions cited above is tantamount to a prohibition of enforced disappearances in IHL.[34] The ICRC study then cites some military manuals and the national laws of many states mentioning the prohibition of enforced disappearances;[35] resolutions adopted at the International Conferences of the Red Cross and Red Crescent in 1981,[36] 1986,[37] and 1999[38] dealing with the prohibition of enforced disappearances.[39] It notes, moreover, the absence of contrary official practice and the existence of international condemnations (especially from the United Nations).[40] It notes that the ICC Statute, following the ICTY, describes the systematic practice of enforced disappearances as a crime against humanity.[41] Last but not least, the ICRC study cites the extensive human rights practice banning enforced disappearances.[42] On this basis, the study concludes that '... although it is the widespread or systematic practice of enforced disappearance that constitutes a crime against humanity, any enforced disappearance is a violation of international humanitarian law and human rights law'.[43]

Human rights treaties and jurisprudence prohibiting enforced disappearances constitute, in fact, the real foundation for the formation of a customary international humanitarian law rule on the matter (at least in the context of non-international armed conflicts).[44] This human rights practice then influenced military manuals, national legislation, resolutions of the International Conferences of the Red Cross and Red Crescent, the practice of the United Nations, the work of the ICTY and the drafting of the ICC Statute.

In the context of enforced disappearances, the influence of HRL on the formation of customary international humanitarian law appears very clearly and provides a fine example of the dynamic interplay between HRL and IHL.

3. ENFORCED DISAPPEARANCES: A MULTIPLE AND CONTINUING VIOLATION OF HUMAN RIGHTS LAW

Although enforced disappearances were initially not prohibited as such in general human rights treaties, human rights case law developed this concept of enforced disappearances configuring it as a multiple (or complex) and continuing violation of HRL.[45]

The rights that may be considered as primarily (but not exclusively) violated in case of enforced disappearances are the following:[46]

(1) *The right to liberty and security.* By definition, a person may be considered as a victim of an enforced disappearance if he or she disappeared after having been captured, or deprived in any other way of his/her liberty, by the State or with its connivance.[47] The demonstration of the capture of the disappeared can be based on circumstantial evidence.[48] Most human rights bodies tend to agree that enforced disappearances violate the right to liberty and security.[49] In fact, very often victims of enforced disappearances have been deprived of their liberty without legal justification,[50] because of their political opinions for example. Moreover, independently of whether the initial detention was justified (because for example the disappeared had committed a crime), the right of liberty and security will be violated because of the fact that the detention is incommunicado,[51] unacknowledged,[52] because the disappeared did not have access to a *habeas corpus* procedure,[53] because no charges have been brought against the disappeared,[54] etc. In brief, the right to liberty and security will be violated because of the absence of legitimate grounds (under domestic and international law) for the deprivation of liberty and/or because the disappeared did not benefit from the procedural and judicial safeguards he/she was entitled to. The right to liberty and security may also be violated because the State party failed to prevent the disappearance and protect the victims[55] or failed to adequately investigate the alleged disappearance.[56] Moreover, the Human Rights Committee held that the right to security may also be violated in cases where State authorities threatened the personal liberty and security of individuals who subsequently disappeared.[57]

(2) *The prohibition of inhuman and degrading treatment.* First, most human rights bodies consider the disappeared person as having suffered an inhuman and degrading treatment as a result of his/her incommunicado detention.[58] Moreover, as the case may be, victims of enforced disappearances have often been subjected to acts of torture before their execution.[59] Finally, enforced disappearances give rise to inhuman and degrading treatment of the family because of the anxiety provoked by the disappearance of their next-of-kin and also because of the authorities' attitude towards them and/or in respect of the disappeared.[60]

(3) *The right to life*. Human rights supervisory bodies generally admit the existence of a breach of the right to life, even in situations where the corpse of the disappeared has not been found or where there are no direct evidences attesting of the death of the disappeared. The finding of a violation is based very often on circumstantial evidences or on mere presumption of facts. For the Inter-American Court of Human Rights, the violation of the right to life will be assumed on the basis of elements such as the general context revealing a systematic practice of disappearances often leading to the assassination of the disappeared,[61] the identity of the deceased (a person suspected by the State of being a 'security-threat') and the importance of time that has elapsed since the disappearance.[62] Moreover, the Court will generally find a violation by the State of its positive obligations to prevent such disappearances, to ensure compliance with human rights and to investigate and prosecute those responsible.[63] After some reluctance,[64] the European Court of Human Rights progressively admitted to presume a violation of the right to life taking into account circumstantial evidences in the same way as the Inter-American Court of Human Rights.[65] It did so mainly in the context of the non-international armed conflicts in Turkey[66] and Russia.[67] In the Russian cases, the Court even recognized the existence of the 'phenomenon' of disappearances in Chechnya, a euphemism for the systematic or administrative practice of enforced disappearances.[68] This led the Court to readily admit that unacknowledged detention by unidentified soldiers was likely to put the inmate's life in danger.[69] In all cases involving enforced disappearances, the Court also found a violation of the obligation to investigate. In some Russian cases, the European Court even held that the passivity of the authorities and/or the fact that the investigation does not produce any results or, in other words, the total lack of *due diligence*, proved indirectly the responsibility of the State for the disappearance, or at least its acquiescence to its happening, and involved a violation of Article 2 in its substantial limb.[70] The Human Rights Committee adopts an approach slightly different from the Inter-American and European Court of Human Rights. Instead of trying to prove through circumstantial evidence a violation of the negative obligation not to arbitrarily deprive a prisoner of his life, the Committee bases its analysis on the positive obligation stated in its *General Comment No. 6* to 'prevent the disappearance of individuals' and to 'investigate thoroughly cases of missing and disappeared persons in circumstances which may involve a violation of the right to life'.[71] In some cases where the applicant had not lost hope of finding the disappeared alive, the Committee even renounced making any finding in respect of the right to life, in order not to appear to presume the death of the disappeared.[72] The African Commission on Human and People's Rights did not have the opportunity to analyse thoroughly the phenomenon of enforced disappearances. In one case, the African Commission simply referred to the 1992 *Declaration on the Protection of All Persons against Enforced Disappearance*, whose Article 1 (2) states that '[a]ny act of enforced disappearance... violates or constitutes a grave threat to the right to life'.[73]

(4) *The right to recognition of a person before the law*. This right can be found in several human rights instruments.[74] It aims at guaranteeing the legal subjectivity of individuals, which is a prerequisite for the enjoyment of other rights.[75] It has not been systematically resorted to in human rights case law and its exact scope remains therefore unclear.[76] Commentators are divided as to whether enforced disappearances violate that right.[77] In particular, it is unclear whether 'intentionally removing a person

from the protection of the law for a prolonged period of time' – as provided in the definition of enforced disappearances under the UN Convention against Enforced Disappearances – implies a violation of the right to recognition of a person before the law.[78] In light of recent case law, it seems that enforced disappearances do violate this right since 'disappeared persons are in practice deprived of their capacity to exercise entitlements under law, including all their other rights..., and of access to any possible remedy as a direct consequence of the actions of the State, which must be interpreted as a refusal to recognize such victims as persons before the law.'[79]

(5) *The 'right to know' or 'right to truth'.* This right has sometimes been invoked before human rights bodies.[80] It draws its inspiration from the IHL 'right of families to know the fate of their relatives'.[81] As highlighted by B. Taxil:

> Les prémisses de ce droit figuraient dans l'article 32 du premier protocole aux conventions de Genève. Depuis, il était en voie d'extension, du droit humanitaire vers les droits de l'homme, par le biais notamment des instruments relatifs aux disparitions forcées, et surtout par une affirmation plus générale contenue dans les 'principes' que l'on peut qualifier de soft law.[82]

In human rights jurisprudence, this 'right' has gradually been recognized as a right in itself,[83] or as incorporated into other rights.[84]

Finally, the prohibition of enforced disappearances is considered as an obligation having a continuing character. This means that States have an obligation to investigate until the circumstances of the disappearance have been elucidated.[85]

Beside human rights case law, a number of human rights instruments have been adopted – before the UN Convention against Enforced Disappearance (to be discussed below) – in order to complement the prohibition of enforced disappearances. These include mainly the 1992 *United Nations Declaration on the Protection of All Persons from Enforced Disappearance* and the 1994 *Inter-American Convention on Forced Disappearance of Persons*.[86]

In summary, it can be said that HRL has developed, although not always systematically or consistently, a complex legal system in order to address the issue of enforced disappearances.

The prohibition of enforced disappearances has been applied to situations of internal disturbances, non-international armed conflicts and, less clearly, however, to international armed conflicts. This prohibition is non-derogable. Better, in the case *Goiburú et al. v. Paraguay*,[87] the Inter-American Court of Human Rights held that the prohibition of enforced disappearance of persons and its corresponding obligation to investigate and punish perpetrators has attained the status of *jus cogens*.[88]

By creating a non-derogable right and giving birth to customary rules applicable in armed conflicts, HRL has been able to influence IHL, as highlighted previously.[89] Conversely, IHL has also influenced HRL in the context of enforced disappearances. This influence goes beyond the mere suggestion of a new 'right to know' as mentioned earlier.

First, human rights bodies have used IHL to corroborate their human rights analysis. For example, in the case *Bámaca-Velásquez v. Guatemala,* concerning the enforced disappearance of a guerrilla commander (of the Luis Ixmatá Front) captured by the

Guatemalan army in the context of a non-international armed conflict, the Inter-American Court of Human Rights recalled that even IHL and Article 3 common to the Geneva Conventions prohibit attempts against the life and personal integrity of persons who are not participating directly in the hostilities or who have been placed *hors de combat* for whatever reason.[90] The Court noted that although it lacks competence to declare that a State is internationally responsible for the violation of international humanitarian law treaties (that do not grant it such a competence), it can observe that certain acts or omissions that violate the American Convention on Human Rights, also violate IHL.[91]

Second, IHL obligations aiming at preventing disappearances can be turned into positive obligations under HRL. In fact, the vast majority of IHL obligations presented above (for example, the requirement to identify the dead before burial, the obligation to search for the dead after an engagement, the right of prisoners of war and civilian internees to correspond with their relatives, etc.) are eligible for transposition into HRL through the development of positive obligations. For example, in the *Varnava v. Turkey* case, concerning disappearances in the context of the 1974 international armed conflict having opposed Turkey to Cyprus, the European Court of Human Rights held that:

> Article 2 must be interpreted in so far as possible in light of the general principles of international law, including the rules of international humanitarian law which play an indispensable and universally-accepted role in mitigating the savagery and inhumanity of armed conflict. ... The Court therefore concurs with the reasoning of the Chamber in holding that in a zone of international conflict Contracting States are under obligation to protect the lives of those not, or no longer, engaged in hostilities. This would also extend to the provision of medical assistance to the wounded; where combatants have died, or succumbed to wounds, the need for accountability would necessitate proper disposal of remains and require the authorities to collect and provide information about the identity and fate of those concerned, or permit bodies such as the ICRC to do so.[92]

In other words, IHL obligations (to care for the wounded, to collect remains and provide information about the identity and fate of the deceased etc.) were seen as incorporated in the obligation to protect life under article 2 of the European Convention. Moreover, these obligations indicated that article 2 implies a continuing obligation on the respondent Government to account for the whereabouts and fate of the missing, and thus to provide a proper investigation, even in the absence of evidence that the missing person had been captured.[93] This obligation can be compared with the IHL obligation to trace missing persons.[94]

Thus, far from contradicting each other, HRL and IHL each bring their contribution to the prohibition of the practice of enforced disappearances. Despite their differences in approach, they influenced each other significantly.

4.   ENFORCED DISAPPEARANCES AS AN INTERNATIONAL CRIME

Enforced disappearances are not only serious violations of IHL and HRL entailing State responsibility, but they can also constitute international crimes entailing the responsibility of individuals.

The first person having been prosecuted by an international tribunal for having participated in enforced disappearances was the German field marshal Wilhelm Keitel, who had implemented the sadly famous decree 'Nacht und Nebel'.[95] The Nuremberg International Military Tribunal sentenced him for war crimes.[96] It can thus be said that the first criminalization of enforced disappearances was based on IHL violations.

Since then, however, enforced disappearances have no longer been qualified as war crimes, but rather as crimes against humanity, that is to say, as serious violations of human rights law primarily.[97] As explained by P. Currat, '… ce crime contre l'humanité est typique d'une violation massive et systématique des droits de l'homme. Il est d'ailleurs symptomatique que la définition des disparitions forcées soit une construction jurisprudentielle, notamment développée par la Cour interaméricaine des droits de l'homme dans son arrêt rendu en l'affaire *Velásquez Rodríguez.*'[98]

In fact, following several developments in the human rights law sphere,[99] the 1996 *Draft Code of Crimes against the Peace and Security of Mankind* included among the examples of crimes against humanity the act of committing forced disappearance of person in a systematic manner or on a large scale and instigated or directed by a Government or by any organization or group.[100] Then, although the ICTY Statute did not mention such an offense, the ICTY considered that forced disappearance of persons fall under the category of 'other inhuman acts' as crimes against humanity. In the *Kupreskic* case, indeed, the ICTY considered that:

> Less broad parameters for the interpretation of 'other inhumane acts' can instead be identified in international standards on human rights such as those laid down in the Universal Declaration on Human Rights of 1948 and the two United Nations Covenants on Human Rights of 1966. Drawing upon the various provisions of these texts, it is possible to identify a set of basic rights appertaining to human beings, the infringement of which may amount, depending on the accompanying circumstances, to a crime against humanity. … the expression at issue undoubtedly embraces … the enforced disappearance of persons (prohibited by General Assembly Resolution 47/133 of 18 December 1992 and the Inter-American Convention of 9 June 1994).[101]

Finally, the ICC Statute has codified the customary international law rule resulting from the foregoing practice and recognizing that the systematic practice of enforced disappearances constitutes a crime against humanity.[102]

5. THE CONVENTION FOR THE PROTECTION OF ALL PERSONS AGAINST ENFORCED DISAPPEARANCES

After several months of negotiations,[103] the *Convention for the Protection of All Persons against Enforced Disappearance* was adopted by the UN General Assembly on 20 December 2006.[104] It entered into force four years later on 23 December 2010. It is a human rights Convention adopted under the aegis of United Nations, following the model of the *Convention against Torture and Other Cruel, Inhuman or Degrading Treatment or Punishment* of 1984.[105] It also creates a treaty body to monitor its implementation called the 'Committee on Enforced Disappearances'.[106]

The peculiarity of this human rights treaty is that it incorporates rules coming from different branches of international law, and primarily from HRL, IHL, international criminal law and refugee law.[107] It performs a kind of compendium of rules derived from these various branches of international law in order to address the multifaceted issue of enforced disappearances.[108] The preamble of the Convention sets the tone when it recalls the relevance of related international instruments belonging to HRL, IHL and international criminal law.[109]

Based on the different contributions of these branches, it creates, or rather acknowledges, the birth of a new right: the 'right of everyone not to be subjected to enforced disappearance'.[110] This right or, from the perspective of the State obligation, the prohibition of enforced disappearances,[111] is considered non-derogable.[112] No exceptional circumstances whatsoever, whether a war or any other circumstances, may be invoked to justify enforced disappearance.[113]

The definition of enforced disappearance in the Convention[114] (quoted above in the introduction) is based on the definitions provided in previous human rights instruments relating to disappearances[115] and on the ICC Statute.[116] There are four elements in this definition.

(1)   Enforced disappearance is characterized by a deprivation of liberty, arbitrary or not;
(2)   The deprivation of liberty must be the consequence of actions by 'agents of the State or by persons or groups of persons acting with the authorization, support or acquiescence of the State';
(3)   The deprivation of liberty must be followed by a refusal to acknowledge the deprivation of liberty or by concealment of the fate or whereabouts of the disappeared person; and
(4)   The deprivation of liberty must place the disappeared person outside the protection of the law.

Although the definition could be criticized under several aspects, it will suffice here to note that it is quite disappointing to see that the Convention adopts a traditional human rights approach, since the violation must necessarily involve the State directly or by complicity.[117] Yet, in practice, it is not rare that non-state actors (and in particular non-state organized armed groups) perpetrate enforced disappearances without any State support. The Convention does not address this phenomenon directly. It only provides in article 3 that States parties shall investigate enforced disappearances committed by non state actors acting without the authorization, support or acquiescence of the State and bring those responsible to justice.[118] This is a step backwards compared to the definition of the ICC Statute, including enforced disappearances by a 'political organization'.[119] In the words of B. Taxil:

> Ce faisant, la cohésion entre branche 'humaine' et branches humanitaire et pénale du droit international atteint ici ses limites, inhérentes aux finalités distinctes des domaines. En effet, la convention demeure ici dans une approche faisant primer la logique des droits de l'homme, destinée à responsabiliser l'Etat pour qu'il répare les préjudices individuels.[120]

In our view, it would have been better to take IHL (which binds both state and non-state organized armed groups) as a model and admit that enforced disappearances can also be committed by non-state actors, while, at the same time, recalling that the State must take steps internally to criminalize and prevent such acts.[121]

Leaving aside the issues relating to the definition of enforced disappearances, the Convention, in addition to creating a new right at the crossroads of HRL, IHL and international criminal law, is remarkable for its complexity and the multitude of issues it covers. The Convention includes obligations ranging from prevention to investigation, prosecution and sentences. It incorporates rules on extradition and mutual legal assistance in criminal matters. It provides a broad definition of victims and recognizes a right to reparation. It offers increased protection to children who are directly or indirectly victims of enforced disappearances etc.[122]

In the perspective of the interplay between HRL and IHL, the Convention draws heavily on IHL, which is quite exceptional for a human rights treaty. In fact, the Convention includes many IHL obligations or, at least, IHL-like obligations. For example, the Convention includes the right of any victim to know the truth,[123] in which case, similarities with the right of families to know the fate of their relatives has already been pointed out earlier.[124] It includes also a State obligation to take appropriate steps to research, locate and release disappeared persons and, in case of death, to locate their remains, respect them and return them.[125] Similar obligation can be found in IHL (with the exception of the obligation to release the disappeared and return the remains).[126]

The obligation to cooperate and to afford mutual assistance to assist victims of enforced disappearance and to search for, locate and release disappeared persons and, in the event of death, to exhume, identify and return the remains under Article 15 of the Convention, can also partially be found in Additional Protocol I of 1977.[127] Regarding persons deprived of their liberty, the Convention provides an obligation to keep official registers and/or records of persons deprived of liberty and to guarantee access to places of detention,[128] as provided in IHL treaties.[129] In this regard, the Convention establishes a kind of 'habeas data'[130] requiring States to guarantee to any person with a legitimate interest in this information, such as relatives of the person deprived of liberty, their representatives or their counsel, access to a certain amount of information, such as the authority that ordered the deprivation of liberty, the whereabouts of the person deprived of liberty, facts relating to the state of health of the person deprived of liberty, etc.[131] This requirement is similar to that provided by IHL to make available this information to the Protecting Powers or the Central Tracing Agency of the ICRC.[132] Finally, the requirement of training of military personnel or civilians[133] is modelled on the well-known obligation to disseminate IHL.[134]

Moreover, in many respects, the Convention seems to take IHL as an inspiration. For example, the Committee on Enforced Disappearances has a kind of 'humanitarian' mandate because relatives of the disappeared person or their legal representatives, their counsel or any person authorized by them can submit a request for urgent action to the Committee to ask that a disappeared person is sought and found.[135] This mandate was modelled on the work of the UN Working Group on Enforced Disappearance,[136] which was itself inspired by the ICRC's humanitarian work on enforced disappearances in times of armed conflict.[137] It is however disappointing to note that article 26, paragraph 1, of the Convention provides that the Committee on Enforced Disappearances shall be comprised of experts in the field of human rights, without mentioning the necessity to include experts in IHL.[138]

IHL is also taken into account explicitly in article 16 dealing with the principle of non-refoulement in cases of 'a consistent pattern of gross, flagrant or mass violations of human rights or of serious violations of international humanitarian law'.[139]

Finally, the Convention against Enforced Disappearance includes a clause of non-prejudice in relation to IHL (article 43). It reads as follows:

> This Convention is without prejudice to the provisions of international humanitarian law, including the obligations of the High Contracting Parties to the four Geneva Conventions of 12 August 1949 and the two Additional Protocols thereto of 8 June 1977, or to the opportunity available to any State Party to authorize the International Committee of the Red Cross to visit places of detention in situations not covered by international humanitarian law.[140]

Some States, like the United States of America and the United Kingdom,[141] as well as some authors[142] have interpreted this provision as a reaffirmation of the *lex specialis* character of IHL in armed conflict situations.

This interpretation is not convincing. Article 43 does not provide for the primacy of IHL rules in case of conflict with the Convention. It merely states that the Convention is without prejudice to IHL provisions or to the possibility for the ICRC to continue to visit places of detention outside armed conflict situations with the authorization of the State Party concerned. S. McCrory also argues in this sense when she writes:

> This provision is probably included to ensure States Parties are not discouraged from authorising the ICRC to carry out visits to places of detention out of concern that their responsibility under the Convention might be thus engaged. Such visits may continue to take place on the same basis they have done to date without the Convention having any impact.[143]

A contextual interpretation shows that article 43 is not either a most-favourable-to-the-individual clause as provided in Article 37 of the Convention.[144] Article 43 offers rather an interpretative indication that the Convention does not conflict with IHL and the ICRC activities and should be interpreted in harmony with IHL provisions.[145]

In any case, it is unclear how the Convention against Enforced Disappearance could 'prejudice' IHL provisions. The only provision that seems to come into direct conflict with IHL is Article 17, par. 2, letter d) of the Convention which 'Guarantee[s] that any person deprived of liberty shall be authorized to communicate with and be visited by his or her family, counsel or any other person of his or her choice, subject only to the conditions established by law ... '.[146] On the contrary, Article 5 of the Fourth Geneva Convention provides that a civilian internee suspected of engaging in activities hostile to the security of the State, may be deprived of his rights of communication.[147] In this case, it would not be impossible to refer to Article 43 of the Convention to state that the right of belligerent States to deprive a person of his rights of communication under Article 5 of the Fourth Geneva Convention remains intact, notwithstanding section 17, para. 2, letter d) of the Convention against Enforced Disappearance. However, interpreting Article 43 as creating an absolute primacy of IHL concerning enforced disappearances – thus designing IHL as a *lex specialis* derogating from the Convention on Enforced Disappearances as a whole – would seriously undermine the contribution of this Convention in times of armed conflict. It would also be clearly contrary to the object and purpose of the Convention against Enforced Disappearance, which is to render non-derogable the prohibition of enforced disappearances and to provide precise positive obligations – complementing those already existing under IHL – in order to ensure such a prohibition.

6. CONCLUSION

The prohibition of enforced disappearances took place gradually, and mainly through the practice of human rights bodies and the development of certain specific human rights treaties.

While IHL is silent on the practice of enforced disappearances as such, it prohibits arbitrary detentions, torture, arbitrary killings even in times of armed conflicts. It thus indirectly prohibits enforced disappearances, which often violate all these IHL prohibitions. In addition, IHL provides for a range of specific provisions to prevent that combatants or civilians go missing during armed conflicts.

Human rights law and IHL thus complement each other on this matter. Better, they have influenced each other. The practice of human rights bodies has influenced the development of the prohibition of enforced disappearances under customary IHL. Human rights bodies have borrowed specific IHL obligations aiming at preventing disappearances to interpret human rights treaties that they do have competence to apply.

The ban of enforced disappearances through human rights law and IHL has led to the criminalization of the widespread or systematic practice of enforced disappearance as a crime against humanity.

Finally, the separate and specific contributions of these different branches of international law were merged and systematized in the UN Convention against Enforced Disappearance, which also added some innovations, some inspired from IHL.

The Convention on Enforced Disappearances is thus a fine example of partial merger between human rights law and IHL. In this way, the Convention has significantly strengthened the absolute prohibition of enforced disappearances. This proves, or at least indicates that, although human rights law and IHL are – and must remain – two distinct bodies of international law, a merger in some specific areas is possible and can be meaningful. This is particularly the case in areas where, as for enforced disappearances, these two branches of international law provide different, but complementary, legal protections.

The definitive success of such a merger in the context of enforced disappearances, however, still depends on the implementation of this Convention by States Parties and by the newly constituted Committee on Enforced Disappearances.

NOTES

* Gloria Gaggioli is doctor in international law and researcher at the University of Geneva (Switzerland).
1. *Report submitted by Mr. Manfred Nowak, independent expert charged with examining the existing international criminal and human rights Framework for the protection of persons from enforced or involuntary disappearances, pursuant to paragraph 11 of Commission resolution 2001/46*, 8 January 2002 (UN Doc. E/CN.4/2002/71), para. 7; T Scovazzi and G. Citroni, *The Struggle against Enforced Disappearance and the 2007 United Nations Convention* (Leiden, Boston: Martinus Nijhoff Publishers, 2007), 4.
2. Nowak, ibid., paras 8–9.
3. See for example: *Report of the Working Group on enforced or involuntary disappearances*, Human Rights Council, 10th session, 25 February 2009 (UN Doc. A/HRC/10/9); *Report of the Working Group on enforced or involuntary disappearances*, Human Rights Council, 16th session, 26 January 2011 (UN Doc. A/HRC/16/48); *Report of the Working Group on enforced or involuntary disappearances*, Human Rights Council, 19th session, 2 March 2012 (UN Doc. A/HRC/19/58/Rev.1).
4. See, for example, the report by Human Rights Watch, *Ghost Prisoner: Two Years in Secret CIA Detention*, February 2007, vol. 19, no.1 (G.): http://www.hrw.org/reports/2007/02/26/ghost-prisoner-0.
5. These prohibitions are part of conventional and customary IHL for international and non-international armed conflicts. See J.-M. Henckaerts and L. Doswald-Beck, *Customary International Humanitarian Law* (Cambridge: Cambridge University Press, 2009), Vol. I, Rule 98.
6. The Convention was adopted on 20 December 2006 during the sixty-first session of the General Assembly by resolution A/RES/61/177. The Convention was opened for signature on 6 February 2007. In accordance with its article 39, para. 1, the Convention entered into force on 23 December 2010.
7. Art. 2 of the 2006 *Convention for the Protection of All Persons against Enforced Disappearance* (hereinafter Convention against Enforced Disappearance).
8. *Velásquez-Rodríguez v. Honduras*, IACtHR, Merits, Judgment of 29 July 1988, para. 157; *Godínez-Cruz v. Honduras*, IACtHR, Merits, Judgment of 20 January 1989, para. 165; *Bámaca-Velásquez v. Guatemala*, IACtHR, Merits, Judgment of 25 November 2000, para. 130: '[enforced disappearance] frequently involves secret execution [of those detained], without trial, following by concealment of the corpse in order to eliminate any material evidence of the crime and to ensure the impunity of those responsible'.
9. Henckaerts and Doswald-Beck, *supra* note 5, Rule 98, at 340 *et seq.*
10. The wording is slightly different in the first and second Geneva Conventions. According to article 15 of the First Geneva Convention, the search must be done 'at all times, and particularly after an engagement'. Instead, article 18 of the Second Geneva Convention provides that the search must be done only 'after each engagement'.
11. Articles 16–17 of the First Geneva Convention, 19–20 of the Second Geneva Convention; article 120, para.3, of the Third Geneva Convention. However, IHL does not provide for the obligation to undertake detailed identification measures of the dead (such as DNA) nor that of giving back the remains to the families of the disappeared. M. Sassòli and M.-L. Tougas, 'The ICRC and the missing', *International Review of the Red Cross* 84, No. 848 (2002): 731 and 743.
12. Art. 17 GCI; Art. 20(4-5) GCIII; Art. 130 GCIV. See also Art. 34 API. At sea, this requirement shall not apply unless the dead are landed, in which case art. 17 GCI applies. See art. 20(2) GCII.
13. Art.17 GCI and 120 GCIII.
14. Art. 34 (2–4) of API.
15. Art. 122 (4–5) GCIII and 136–138 GCIV. See also art. 70 CGIII (capture card) and 120(1-2) CGIII (will and death certificate); 106 GCIV (internment card) and 129 GC IV (will and death certificate), 33(2, a) API (extension *ratione personae* of the obligation to provide information).
16. Art. 71 GCIII and 107 GCIV.
17. Art. 121 GCIII and 131 GCIV.
18. Art.122-123 GCIII and 136-137 GCIV.
19. Art. 125(3) GCIII and 142 GCIV.
20. For details on the work of the ICRC on disappearances, see: Sassòli and Tougas, *supra* note 11, at 727–750.
21. Part II, Section III of API.

22. See ICRC Commentary of article 32 API, in *Commentary on the Additional Protocols of 8 June 1977 to the Geneva Conventions of 12 August 1949*, Y. Sandoz et al., eds (Geneva: Martinus Nijhoff, 1987), para. 1197.

23. Art. 32 API. See *Commentary on the Additional Protocols of 8 June 1977 to the Geneva Conventions of 12 August 1949*, ibid., para. 1200: 'The Rapporteur of the Working Group ... , recognized that "it was unusual to state the premises on which an article was based", but emphasized the fact that the general principle had been incorporated "in response to a strong feeling of many delegations and institutions that it was important to express in the Protocol the idea that families had a right to know what had happened to their relatives"'.

24. It is interesting to note that the Director of the United Nations Human Rights Division, in his speech following the adoption by consensus of the section containing the right of families to know the fate of their relatives, made the following statement: 'The text which had just been adopted by consensus was an important step forward in the field of international efforts to protect human rights. The Conference would emphasize the "right" of families to be informed of the fate of their next-of-kin involved in armed conflicts.' See Acts XII of the 1977 Diplomatic Conference, p. 265, CDDH/II/SR.78 by.46. Quoted in: *Commentary on the Additional Protocols of 8 June 1977 to the Geneva Conventions of 12 August 1949*, ibid., para. 1211.

25. See the *Study by the Office of United Nations High Commissioner for Human Rights on the right to the truth*, 8 February 2006, at 4–5. (UN Doc. E/CN.4/2006/91). Note, however, Resolution 3220 (XXIX) of the General Assembly of 6 November 1974 whose preamble underlines that 'the desire to know the fate of loved ones lost in armed conflicts is a basic human need ...'.

26. *Commentary on the Additional Protocols of 8 June 1977 to the Geneva Conventions of 12 August 1949, supra* note 22, para. 1212.

27. Ibid.

28. Article 32 of API is *interestingly* entitled 'general principle'.

29. Art. 33(1 and 3) *API*.

30. Art. 33(2 b) API.

31. Art. 33(4) API.

32. Art. 8 APII.

33. Henckaerts and Doswald-Beck, *supra* note 5, Rule 98.

34. Ibid., at 340–341.

35. Ibid.

36. *XXIV International Conference of the Red Cross and Red Crescent*, 1981, Manila: Resolution II: '[enforced disappearances] imply violations of fundamental human rights such as the right to life, freedom and personal safety, the right not to be subjected to torture or cruel, inhuman or degrading treatment, the right not to be arbitrarily arrested or detained, and the right to a just and public trial'.

37. *XXV International Conference of the Red Cross and Red Crescent Societies*, 1986, Geneva: Resolution XIII: '[condemns] any act leading to the forced or involuntary disappearance of individuals or groups of individuals'.

38. *XXVII International Conference of the Red Cross and Red Crescent Societies*, 1999, Geneva: Action Plan for the years 2000 to 2003: requests the warring parties to take effective measures to ensure that 'strict orders are given to prevent all serious violations of international humanitarian law, including ... enforced disappearances'.

39. Henckaerts and Doswald-Beck, *supra* note 5, Rule 98, at 341.

40. Ibid.

41. Ibid., at 342.

42. Ibid., at 342–343.

43. Ibid., at 343.

44. It is true that the practice of HR supervisory bodies focuses on enforced disappearances in the context of non-international armed conflicts and almost never in the context of international armed conflicts. Article XV of the *Inter-American Convention on Forced Disappearance of Persons* states: 'This Convention shall not apply to the international armed conflicts governed by the 1949 Geneva Conventions and their Protocols, concerning protection of wounded, sick, and shipwrecked members of the armed forces; and prisoners of war and civilians in time of war.'

   Similarly, the Working Group of the United Nations on Enforced Disappearances has no mandate to deal with this phenomenon in international armed conflicts. (See Rule 5 'International armed conflicts' of the Revised methods of work of the Working Group. For the doctrine, see F. Andreu-Guzman, 'Le Groupe de Travail sur les Disparitions Forcées des Nations Unies', *Revue internationale de la Croix-Rouge* 84:848 (2002): 807.) Finally, the United Nations Convention against Enforced Disappearance of 2006 also contains a non-prejudice clause regarding IHL whose significance is controversial (see *infra*). However, these same human rights instruments relating to enforced disappearances, and some human rights supervisory bodies have asserted the non-derogable nature of the prohibition of enforced disappearance. See *Declaration on the Protection of All Persons against Enforced Disappearance*, art.7, *Inter-American Convention on Forced Disappearance of Persons*, Preamble; *International Convention for the Protection of All Persons against Enforced Disappearance*, art. 1(2). For the case law, see e.g. *Goiburú et al. v. Paraguay*, IACtHR, Merits, Reparations and Costs, Judgment of 22 September 2006, para. 84. It is not absurd to consider these elements as relevant practice for the emergence of a customary norm prohibiting enforced disappearances in international armed conflicts as well.

45. See, for example, *Velásquez-Rodríguez v. Honduras*, *supra* note 8, para. 155; *Godínez-Cruz v. Honduras*, *supra* note 8, para. 158; *Blake v. Guatemala*, IACtHR, Merits, Judgment of 24 January 1998, para. 35; *Bámaca-Velásquez v. Guatemala*, *supra* note 8, para. 128; *The 19 Merchants v. Colombia* IACtHR, Merits, Reparations and Costs, Judgment of 7 May 2004, para. 142; *Goiburú et al. v. Paraguay*, *supra* note 44, paras 80 ff.

46. For an extensive analysis of the human rights that are violated by enforced disappearances, see L. Ott, *Enforced Disappearances in International Law* (Cambridge, Antwerp, Portland: Intersentia, 2011).

47. See below the definition provided for enforced disappearances under the title '5. The Convention for the Protection of All Persons against Enforced Disappearances'.

48. *Bámaca-Velásquez v. Guatemala*, *supra* note 8, para. 132 and paras 136 et seq. See also *Velásquez-Rodríguez v. Honduras*, *supra* note 8, para. 155; *Godínez-Cruz v. Honduras*, *supra* note 8, para. 163; *Castillo-Páez v. Peru*, IACtHR, Merits, Judgment of 3 November 1997, para. 46, *The 19 Merchants v. Colombia*, *supra* note 45, paras 144 et seq.

49. See, for example: *Velásquez-Rodríguez v. Honduras*, *supra* note 8, para. 155; *Bámaca-Velásquez v. Guatemala*, *supra* note 8, paras 136 et seq.; *Kurt v. Turkey*, ECtHR, Application No. 24276/94, Judgment of 25 May 1998, para. 129; *Timurtaş v. Turkey*, ECtHR, Application No. 23531/94, Judgment of 13 June 2000, para. 106; *Bazorkina v. Russia*, ECtHR, Application No. 69481/01, Judgment of 27 July 2006, para. 149; *Bleier v. Uruguay*, HRC, 29 March 1982 (UN Doc. CCPR/C/15/D/30/1978), para. 14; *Mouvement burkinabé des droits de l'homme et des peuples v. Burkina Faso*, AfCommHPR, Communication No. 204/97 (2001), para. 44.

50. *Velásquez-Rodríguez v. Honduras*, *supra* note 8, para. 186.

51. *Boucherf v. Algeria*, HRC, 27 April 2006 (UN Doc. CCPR/C/86/D/1196/2003), para. 9.5; *Grioua v. Algeria*, HRC, 10 July 2007 (CCPR/C/90/D/1327/2004), para. 7.5; *Kimouche v. Algeria*, HRC, 10 July 2007 (CCPR/C/90/D/1328/2004), para. 7.5; *El Alwani v. Libya*, HRC, 11 July 2006 (UN Doc. CCPR/C/90/D/1295/2004), para. 6.4.

52. *Kurt v. Turkey*, *supra* note 49, para. 124; *Çakici v. Turkey*, ECtHR, Application No. 23657/94, Judgment of 8 July 1999, para. 104: *Timurtaş v. Turkey*, *supra* note 49, para. 103 ; *Bazorkina v. Russia*, *supra* note 49, para. 146 ; *Luluyev v. Russia*, ECtHR, Application No. 69480/01, Judgment of 9 November 2006, para. 122 ; *Imakayeva v. Russia*, ECtHR, Application No. 7615/02, Judgment of 9 November 2006, para. 171.

53. *Velásquez-Rodríguez v. Honduras*, *supra* note 8, para. 186 ; IACtHR, *Godínez-Cruz v. Honduras*, *supra* note 8, para. 163 ; *Bámaca-Velásquez v. Guatemala*, *supra* note 8, para.142.

54. *Bautista de Arellana v. Colombia*, HRC, 27 October 1995 (UN Doc. CCPR/C/55/D/563/1993), para. 8.5; *Laureano Atachahua v. Peru*, HRC, 25 March 1996 (UN Doc. CCPR/C/56/D/540/1993), para. 8.6; *Jegatheeswara Sarma*, HRC, 6 July 1993 (UN Doc. CCPR/C/78/D/950/2000), para. 9.4; *Bousroual v. Algeria*, HRC, 30 March 2006 (Doc. NU CCPR/C/86/D/992/2001), para. 9.5; *El Alwani v. Lybia*, *supra* note 51, para. 6.4.

55. *Pueblo Bello Massacre v. Colombia*, IACtHR, Merits, Reparations and Costs, Judgment of 31 January 2006, para. 140.

56. See for example: *Kurt v. Turkey*, *supra* note 49, para. 128 ; *Çakici v. Turkey*, *supra* note 52, para. 107; *Timurtaş v. Turkey*, *supra* note 49, para. 106 ; *Bazorkina v. Russia*, *supra* note 49, para. 149; *Luluyev v. Russia*, *supra* note 52, para. 125; *Imakayeva v. Russia*, *supra* note 52, para. 178.

57. *Mojica v. Dominican Republic*, HRC, 15 July 1994 (UN Doc. CCPR/C/51/D/449/1991), para. 5.4; *N'Goya v. Zaire*, HRC, 25 March 1996, (UN Doc. CCPR/C/56/D/542/1993), para. 5.3.

58. See for example: *Velásquez-Rodríguez v. Honduras*, *supra* note 8, paras 156 and 187; *Bámaca-Velásquez v. Guatemala*, *supra* note 8, para. 150; *Mojica v. Dominican Republic*, *supra* note 57, para. 5.7; *Zegveld and Ephrem v. Eritrea*, AfCommHPR, Communication No. 250/2002 (2003), para. 55.

By contrast, the ECtHR refuses to find a violation of Article 3 in respect of the disappeared in the absence of evidence of abuse. See for example: *Taş v. Turkey*, ECtHR, Application No. 24396/94, 14 November 2000, para. 76.

59. For example, in the case *Bámaca-Velásquez v. Guatemala*, the disappeared had been seen in custody and co-detainees testified that he had been tortured before disappearing.

60. See for example: *Blake v. Guatemala*, *supra* note 45, paras 114–116; *Bámaca-Velásquez v. Guatemala*, *supra* note 8, para. 165; *Almeida de Quinteros et al. v. Uruguay*, HRC, 21 July 1983 (UN Doc. CCPR/C/19/D/107/1981, para. 14; *Amnesty International et al. v. Sudan* CommAfDHP, Communication No. 48/90, 50/91, 52/91, 89/93 (1999), para. 54. Here again, the ECtHR appears to be more restrictive than the other HR monitoring bodies since it raises a number of conditions for a relative to be considered a victim of Article 3 of the ECHR. See *Çakici v. Turkey*, *supra* note 52, paras 98–99. According to the ECtHR, there is no 'general principle that a family member of a "disappeared person" is thereby a victim of treatment contrary to Article 3. Whether a family member is such a victim will depend on the existence of special factors which gives the suffering of the applicant a dimension and character distinct from the emotional distress which may be regarded as inevitably caused to relatives of a victim of a serious human rights violation. Relevant elements will include the proximity of the family tie – in that context, a certain weight will attach to the parent-child bond –, the particular circumstances of the relationship, the extent to which the family member witnessed the events in question, the involvement of the family member in the attempts to obtain information about the disappeared person and the way in which the authorities responded to those enquiries. The Court would further emphasise that the essence of such a violation does not so much lie in the fact of the "disappearance" of the family member but rather concerns the authorities' reactions and attitudes to the situation when it is brought to their attention. It is especially in respect of the latter that a relative may claim directly to be a victim of the authorities' conduct.' Based on these explanations, the ECtHR has refused, in this case, to find a violation of Article 3 ECHR in respect of the applicant's disappeared brother.

61. Note: The existence of a systematic practice of enforced disappearances is invoked by the Inter-American Court of Human Rights, first, to assume that a person has been subjected to enforced disappearance, and second, to presume that the person is dead. As shown by the *Bámaca-Velásquez* case, it is not necessary to provide direct evidence that a person has been subjected to enforced disappearance. It is sufficient to prove that the State in question practised enforced disappearances at that time and to be able to link the disappearance of a particular individual with this practice through circumstantial evidence. *Bámaca-Velásquez v. Guatemala*, *supra* note 8, para. 130. See also: *Velásquez-Rodríguez v. Honduras*, *supra* note 8, paras 124 et seq.; *Godínez-Cruz v. Honduras*, *supra* note 8, para. 132. See also *Fairén Garbi and Solís Corrales v. Honduras*, IACtHR, Merits, Judgment of 15 March 1989.

62. *Bámaca-Velásquez v. Guatemala*, *supra* note 8, para. 173. See also: *Velásquez-Rodríguez v. Honduras*, *supra* note 8, para. 147e), 157 and 188; *Godínez-Cruz v. Honduras*, *supra* note 8, paras 165 and 198; *Castillo-Páez v. Peru*, *supra* note 48, paras 71–74. See also for the case law of the Inter-American Commission on Human Rights among many others: *Rojas Ccorahua v. Peru*, IACommHR, Case 9802, Report No. 10/89, 14 April 1989; *Huayhua v. Peru*, IACommHR, Case 10.203, Report No. 77/90, 22 February 1991; *Vásquez Juárez v. Salvador*, IACommHR, Case 10.517, Report No. 4/94, 1 February 1994; *Escobar Jurado v. Peru*, IACommHR, Case 10.251, Report No. 42/97, 19 February 1998; *Palomino Morales et al. v. Peru*, IACommHR, Case 10.551, Report No. 53/99, 13 April 1999; *Tordecilla Trujillo v. Colombia* IACommHR, Case 10.337, Report No. 7/00, 24 February 2000; *Gramajo López v. Guatemala*, IACommHR, Case 9207, Report No. 58/01, 4 April 2001; *Catalán Lincoleo v. Chile*, IACommHR, Case 11.771, Report No. 66/01, 16 April 2001.

63. *Bámaca-Velásquez v. Guatemala*, *supra* note 8, para. 129 and 172. See also: *Velásquez-Rodríguez v. Honduras*, *supra* note 8, paras 161 et seq.; *Godínez-Cruz v. Honduras*, *supra* note 8, paras 166 et seq.; *The 19 Merchants v. Colombia*, *supra* note 45, paras 142 and 153; *Goiburú et al. v. Paraguay*, *supra* note 44, paras 66 et seq.

64. *Kurt v. Turkey*, *supra* note 49, paras 107–108. In the case of the *Kurt v. Turkey* case in 1998, concerning the disappearance of a young Kurdish man seen for the last time in the hands of Turkish forces, the ECtHR refused to comment on the alleged violation of the right to life, as there was no concrete evidence proving beyond reasonable doubt that the applicant's son had been killed by the authorities.

65. *Çakici v. Turkey*, *supra* note 52, paras 85–87; *Timurtaş v. Turkey*, *supra* note 49, paras 82–85. In the *Timurtaş v. Turkey* case in 2000, the Court admitted that the death of the disappeared, who had been

captured by the authorities (or at least with their connivance), could be 'presumed on the basis of circumstantial evidence'. In order to do so, the Court took into account the period of time elapsed since his capture (six and a half years); the identity of the deceased (an alleged member of the PKK); and the general situation in South-East Turkey in 1993, which did not exclude that the unacknowledged detention of such a person was likely to be life-threatening.

66.   *Ertak v. Turkey*, ECtHR, Application No 20764/92, Judgment of 9 May 2000; *Taş v. Turkey*, *supra* note 58; *Çiçek v. Turkey*, ECtHR, Application No 25704/94, Judgment of 27 February 2001; *Akdeniz et al. v. Turkey*, ECtHR, Application No 23954/94, Judgment of 31 May 2001; *Orhan v. Turkey*, ECtHR, Application No 25656/94, Judgment of 18 June 2002; *İpek v. Turkey*, ECtHR, Application No 25760/94, Judgment of 17 February 2004; *Akdeniz v. Turkey*, ECtHR, Application No 25165/94, Judgment of 31 May 2005; *Tanış et al. v. Turkey*, ECtHR, Application No 65899/01, Judgment of 2 August 2005. Instead, if there is no evidence that the person was captured, the ECtHR does not find a violation of the right to life. *Tekdağ v. Turkey*, ECtHR, Application No 27699/95, Judgment of 15 January 2004; *Tahsin Acar v. Turkey*, ECtHR, Application No 26307/95, Judgment of 8 April 2004; *Erkek v. Turkey*, ECtHR, Application No 28637/95, Judgment of 13 July 2004; *Seyhan v. Turkey*, ECtHR, Application No 33384/96, Judgment of 2 November 2004; *Türkoğlu v. Turkey*, ECtHR, Application No 34506/97, Judgment of 17 March 2005; *Toğcu v. Turkey*, ECtHR, Application No 27601/95, Judgment of 31 May 2005; *Özgen et al. v. Turkey*, ECtHR, Application No 38607/97, Judgment of 20 September 2005.

67.   See *infra*, note 69.

68.   *Contra:* J. Barrett, 'Chechnya's Last Hope? Enforced Disappearances and the European Court of Human Rights', *Harvard Human Rights Journal* 22 (2009): 142: 'The ECtHR's jurisprudence has recognized that unacknowledged detention by unidentified persons in Chechnya may mean that a victim's life is threatened, and has expressed concern about the volume and similar fact patterns of the enforced disappearance cases emanating from the region. In contrast, however, to certain human rights tribunals addressing cases in other jurisdictions, it has not held that enforced disappearances in Chechnya constitute an administrative practice.' It is true that the ECtHR does not use the term 'administrative practice', but it goes further than in the Turkish cases where it clearly denies the existence of a 'practice'. In the Russian cases, on the contrary, it recognizes the existence of the phenomenon of disappearances in Chechnya. In our view, it is a diplomatic way to say that there is indeed an administrative practice of enforced disappearances in Russia in the context of the Chechen conflict.

69.   *Imakayeva v. Russia*, *supra* note 52, para. 141: 'The Court also notes the applicant's reference to the available information about the phenomenon of "disappearances" in Chechnya and agrees that, in the context of the conflict in Chechnya, when a person is detained by unidentified servicemen without any subsequent acknowledgement of detention, this can be regarded as life-threatening.' See also: *Baysayeva v. Russia*, ECtHR, Application No. 74237/01, Judgment of 5 April 2007, para. 119; *Alikhadzhiyeva v. Russia*, ECtHR, Application No. 68007/01, Judgment of 5 July 2007, para. 61; *Khamila Isayeva v. Russia*, ECtHR, Application No. 6846/02 Judgment of 15 November 2007, para. 122; *Betayev and Betayeva v. Russia*, ECtHR, Application No. 37315/03, Judgment of 29 May 2008, para. 72; *Gekhayeva et al. v. Russia*, ECtHR, Application No. 1755/04, Judgment of 29 May 2008, para. 90; *Ibraguimov et al. v. Russia*, ECtHR, Application No. 34561/03, Judgment of 29 May 2008, para. 84; *Sangarieva et al. v. Russia*, ECtHR, Application No. 1839/04, Judgment of 29 May 2008, para. 66; *Utsayeva et al. v. Russia*, ECtHR, Application No. 29133/03, Judgment of 29 May 2008, para. 162; *Takhayeva et al. v. Russia*, ECtHR, Application No. 23286/04, Judgment of 18 September 2008, para. 79; *Akhmadova et al. v. Russia*, ECtHR, Application No. 20755/04, Judgment of 25 September 08, para. 66; *Lyanova and Aliyeva v. Russia*, ECtHR, Applications Nos 12713/02 and 28440/03, Judgment of 2 October 2008, para. 94. Note that in the Russian cases, the Court has often dealt with situations where there was no direct evidence that the perpetrators were agents of the State. The ECtHR, however, still recognizes the version of the applicants which accuses the State, either arguing that the State did not allege that the perpetrators were the rebels (see *Baysayeva v. Russia*, ibid. *Alikhadzhiyeva v. Russia*, ibid.) or assuming the responsibility of the State because it refused to submit certain documents that would clarify the situation (see *Khamila Isayeva v. Russia*, ibid.; *Lyanova and Aliyeva*, ibid.; *Gekhayeva et al. v. Russia*, ibid.; *Ibraguimov et al. v. Russia*, ibid.; *Utsayeva et al. v. Russia*, ibid.; *Takhayeva et al. v. Russia*, ibid.). On the latter issue, see: Barrett, *supra* note 68, pp. 133–143.

70.   *Imakayeva v. Russia*, *supra* note 52, para. 155: '... the stance of the prosecutor's office and other law-enforcement authorities after the news of his detention had been communicated to them by the

applicant significantly contributed to the possibility of disappearance, because no necessary actions were taken in the crucial first days or weeks after the detention. Their behaviour in the face of the applicant's well-established complaints gives a strong presumption of at least acquiescence in the situation and raises strong doubts as to the objectivity of the investigation.' See also: *Baysayeva v. Russia*, supra note 69, para. 119; *Alikhadzhiyeva v. Russia* , supra note 69, para. 61; *Betayev and Betayeva v. Russia*, supra note 69, para. 74; *Gekhayeva et al. v. Russia*, supra note 69, para. 92; *Ibraguimov et al. v. Russia*, supra note 69, para. 86; *Sangarieva et al. v. Russia*, supra note 69, para. 68; *Utsayeva et al. v. Russia*, supra note 69, para. 164.

71. *General Comment No. 6: Right to life (Article 6)*, HRC, 30 April 1982, (UN Doc. HRI/GEN/1/Rev.8), para. 4. For the case law, see: *Herrera Rubio et al. v. Colombia*, HRC, 2 November 1987 (UN Doc. CCPR/C/31/D/161/1983), para. 11; *Arevalo Perez et al. v. Colombia (Sanjuan Brothers)*, HRC, 3 November 1989 (UN Doc. CCPR/C/37/D/181/1984), para. 10; *Mojica v. Dominican Republic*, supra note 57, para. 5.5; *Laureano Atachahua*, supra note 54, para. 8.3.

72. *Jegatheeswara Sarma*, supra note 54, para. 9.6; *El Alwani v. Libyan Arab Jamahiriya*, HRC, 11 July 2007 (UN Doc. CCPR/C/90/D/1295/2004), para. 6.2.

73. *Mouvement burkinabé des droits de l'homme et des peuples v. Burkina Faso*, supra note 49, para. 44.

74. Art. 16 ICCPR; art. 3 IACHR; art. 5 AfCHPR; art. 18 Arab Charter on Human Rights. The right to recognition of a person before the law is also considered as non-derogable. See art. 4(2), ICCPR, 27(2) ACHR; 4(2) Arab Charter. The ECHR does not guarantee this right as such. The right to recognition of a person before the law is also explicitly mentioned in art. 2 of the *United Nations Declaration on the Protection of All Persons from Enforced Disappearance*. It is not mentioned in the *Inter-American Convention on Forced Disappearance of Persons* or in the *UN Convention against Enforced Disappearances*.

75. Ott, *supra* note 46, at 83.

76. Ibid.

77. For authors considering that enforced disappearances violate the right to recognition of a person before the law, see Ott, *supra* note 46, at 88; M. F. Perez Solla, *Enforced Disappearances in International Human Rights* (Jefferson, NC, London: McFarland & Company, 2006), at 90. *Contra:* M. Nowak, *CCPR Commentary* (Kehl: N.P. Engel, 2005), at 374.

78. Nowak, *supra* note 77.

79. *Grioua v. Algeria*, supra note 51, para. 7.8. See also: *Kimouche v. Algeria*, supra note 51, para.7.8 and 7.9; *Madoui v. Algeria*, HRC, 28 October 2008 (UN Doc. CCPR/C/94/D/1495/2006), paras 7.7 and 7.8; *El Abani v. Lybia*, HRC, 26 July 2010 (UN Doc. CCPR/C/99/D/1640/2007), para. 7.9; *Benaziza v. Algeria*, HRC, 26 July 2010 (UN Doc. CCPR/C/99/D/1588/2007), para. 9.8; *Aboussedra v. Lybia*, HRC, 25 October 2010 (UN Doc. CCPR/C/100/D/1751/2008), para. 7.9. For the Inter-American Commission of HR, see *Medina Charri v. Colombia*, IACommHR, Case 11.211, Report No. 3/98, 7 April 1998, paras 123 et seq.; *Cruz Gomez v. Guatemala*, IACommHR, Case 10.606, Report No. 11/98, 7 April 1998, para. 57. For the Inter-American Court of Human Rights, see *Anzualdo-Castro v. Peru*, IACtHR, Preliminary Objections, Merits, Reparations and Costs, Judgment of 22 September 2009, para. 101; *Radilla-Pacheco v. Mexico*, IACtHR, Preliminary Objections, Merits, Reparations and Costs, Judgment of 23 November 2009, para. 157; *Chitay Nech v. Guatemala*, IACtHR, Preliminary Objections, Merits, Reparations and Costs, Judgment of 25 May 2010, paras 97 et seq.; *Ibsen-Cárdenas and Ibsen-Peña v. Bolivia*, IACtHR, Merits, Reparations and Costs, Judgment of 1 September 2010, paras 102 and 118; *Gomes Lund v. Brazil*, IACtHR, Preliminary Objections, Merits, Reparations and Costs, Judgment of 24 November 2010, para. 125.

80. See the *Study on the right to the truth of the UN Office of the High Commissioner for Human Rights to the attention of the Human Rights Commission*, 8 February 2006 (UN Doc. E/CN.4/2006/91).

81. See Art. 32 of API discussed earlier. On the distinction between the right of families to know the fate of their relatives and the right to the truth, see *Study on the right to the truth of the UN Office of the High Commissioner for Human Rights to the attention of the Human Rights Commission*, 8 February 2006 (*supra* note 80). See also: 'Legal Brief Amicus Curiae, presented by the International Commission of Jurists, before the Inter-American Court of Human Rights in the Case of Efraín Bámaca Velásquez v. Guatemala', in L. Doswald-Beck (ed.), *Impunity, Crimes Against Humanity and Forced Disappearance*, Geneva, International Commission of Jurists, The Review No. 62–63, 2001, at 130–145. In short, we can say that the right to truth, as conceived today, is wider than the right of families to know the fate of their relatives. It is not only relevant in the cases of enforced disappearances but also in cases of other serious violations of HRL; it belongs not only to 'family', but to society as a whole.

82. B. Taxil, 'A la confluence des droits: la Convention internationale pour la protection de toutes les personnes contre les disparitions forcées', *Annuaire français de droit international* LIII (2007) 139. See also: Scovazzi and Citroni, *supra* note 1, 347.

83. See A. Seibert-Fohr, *Prosecuting Serious Human Rights Violations* (Oxford: Oxford University Press, 2009), 68–70. It was explicitly recognized by the IACommHR and after some hesitation, by the IACtHR as well. See *Parada Cea et al. v. El Salvador*, IACommHR, Case 10.480, Report No. 1/99, 27 January 1999, paras 153 et seq.; *Bámaca-Velásquez v. Guatemala*, IACtHR, Reparations and Costs, Judgment of 22 February 2002, para. 77.

84. *Study on the right to the truth of the UN Office of the High Commissioner for Human Rights to the attention of the Human Rights Commission*, *supra* note 80, para. 42: 'The right to the truth is closely linked to the right to an effective remedy; the right to legal and judicial protection; the right to family life; the right to an effective investigation; the right to a hearing by a competent, independent, and impartial tribunal; and the right to obtain reparation. The Human Rights Committee, the ECtHR, IACommHR and the African Commission on Human and Peoples' Rights have all considered that the failure to give information about the fate and whereabouts of disappeared persons or of the circumstances of an execution and the exact place of burial of the executed persons can amount to torture or ill-treatment. Nonetheless, the right to the truth remains an autonomous right with its own legal basis.'

85. *Velásquez-Rodríguez v. Honduras*, *supra* note 8, para. 181. The continuing character of the prohibition of enforced disappearances has procedural consequences for human rights bodies. The latter will consider themselves as competent to hear cases dealing with enforced disappearances having been committed at a time where the State did not yet recognize their competence to hear individual complaints. See for example: *Blake v. Guatemala*, *supra* note 45, para. 97; *Varnava and others v. Turkey*, ECtHR [GC], Judgment of 18 September 2009, para. 148. It should be noted, however, that human rights bodies do then only analyse whether the State failed to investigate enforced disappearances. They will not address the substantial aspects of the violation because they lack competence to do so.

86. *United Nations Declaration on the Protection of All Persons from Enforced Disappearance*, in A/RES/47/133 of 18 December 1992; *Inter-American Convention on Forced Disappearance of Persons*, 9 June 1994.

87. This was a case involving several cross-border enforced disappearances as part of the so-called 'Operation Condor', a collaboration between several dictatorships in the region to fight against leftist movements.

88. *Goiburú et al. v. Paraguay*, *supra* note 44, para. 84: 'In brief, the Court finds that, as may be deduced from the preamble to the aforesaid Inter-American Convention, faced with the particular gravity of such offenses and the nature of the rights harmed, the prohibition of the forced disappearance of persons and the corresponding obligation to investigate and punish those responsible has attained the status of *jus cogens*.' *The Cantuta v. Peru*, IACtHR, Merits, Reparations and Costs, Judgment of 29 November 2006, para. 160. See also the opinion of Judge A.A. Cançado-Trindade (para. 15) in the case of *Blake v. Guatemala*, *supra* note 45.

89. See *supra* in section 2 entitled 'Preventing Disappearances: the Contribution of IHL'.

90. *Bámaca-Velásquez v. Guatemala*, *supra* note 8, paras 206 et seq.

91. Ibid., para. 208.

92. *Varnava and others v. Turkey*, *supra* note 85, para.185. See also *Varnava and others v. Turkey*, ECtHR, Judgment of 10 January 2008, para. 130.

93. *Varnava and others v. Turkey*, ECtHR [GC], Judgment of 18 September 2009, para.186. See also *Varnava and others v. Turkey*, ECtHR, Judgment of 10 January 2008, para. 130.

94. Art. 33, para. 1, of API.

95. Nowak, *supra* note 1, para. 65.

96. Ibid.

97. Ibid. See also: R.S. Lee (ed.), *The ICC: Elements of Crimes and Rules of Procedure and Evidence* (New York: Transnational Publishers Inc., 2001), 99.

98. P. Currat, *Les crimes contre l'humanité dans le statut de la Cour pénale internationale*, (Bruxelles: Bruylant; Genève, Zürich, Bâle: Schulthess, 2006), 467.

99. Resolution 666 (XIII-0/83) of the General Assembly of the OAS, in Annual Report 1984, Chapter II, para. 4: '... the practice of forced disappearance of persons in the Americas is an affront to the conscience of the hemisphere and constitutes a crime against humanity'; *Velásquez-Rodríguez v. Honduras, supra* note 8, para. 153 and *Godínez-Cruz v. Honduras, supra* note 8, para. 161. In these cases, the Court noted that: 'International practice and doctrine have often categorized disappearances as a crime against humanity, although there is no treaty in force which is applicable to the States Parties to the Convention and which uses this terminology. ... The General Assembly of the OAS has resolved that it "is an affront to the conscience of the hemisphere and constitutes a crime against humanity" ... and that "this practice is cruel and inhuman, mocks the rule of law, and undermines those norms which guarantee protection against arbitrary detention and the right to personal security and safety" ... .' See also, *United Nations Declaration on the Protection of All Persons from Enforced Disappearance*, in A/RES/47/133 of 18 December 1992, Preamble: '*Considering that* enforced disappearance undermines the deepest values of any society committed to respect for the rule of law, human rights and fundamental freedoms, and that the systematic practice of such acts is of the nature of a crime against humanity'; *Inter-American Convention on Forced Disappearance of Persons*, 9 June 1994, preamble: 'reaffirming that the systematic practice of the forced disappearance of persons constitutes a crime against humanity'.

100. *Draft Code of Crimes against the Peace and Security of Mankind*, Geneva, 5 July 96, article 18 i).

101. *Kupreskic et al.*, ICTY, Trial Chamber, Decision of 14 January 2000 (Case No. IT-95-16), para. 566. See also: *Kvocka*, ICTY, Trial Chamber, Judgment, 2 November 2001 (Case No. IT-98-30/1-T), para. 208.

102. Art. 7, para. 1 i), ICC Statute: 'For the purpose of this Statute, "crime against humanity" means any of the following acts when committed as part of a widespread or systematic attack directed against any civilian population, with knowledge of the attack: ... i) Enforced disappearance of persons... .' Enforced disappearance is defined as 'the arrest, detention or abduction of persons by, or with the authorization, support or acquiescence of, a State or a political organization, followed by a refusal to acknowledge that deprivation of freedom or to give information on the fate or whereabouts of those persons, with the intention of removing them from the protection of the law for a prolonged period of time'. The definition of this crime in the ICC Statute can be criticized. It seems to require the demonstration of a certain *mens rea*, i.e. the intention of removing the missing from the protection of the law for a prolonged period of time. This intention will often be very difficult to prove. This may drastically reduce the scope of the criminalization. See O. Triffterer, *Commentary on the Rome Statute of the ICC: Observers' notes, article by article* (München, C.H. Beck, 2008), paras 132–133; Scovazzi and Citroni, *supra* note 1, at 273 et seq.; Nowak, *supra* note 1, para. 74.

103. For a brief history of the negotiations, see O. de Frouville, 'La Convention des Nations Unies pour la protection de toutes les personnes contre les disparitions forcées: les enjeux juridiques d'une négociation exemplaire', *Droits fondamentaux* 6 (2006): 1–13.

104. The Convention was adopted at the 61st session of the UN General Assembly in its resolution 61/177.

105. Taxil, *supra* note 82, at 131.

106. Art. 26 of the *Convention against Enforced Disappearances*.

107. Taxil, *supra* note 82, at 132: '... c'est bien là que se situe toute l'originalité d'un traité résolument moderne: il se situe à la confluence de plusieurs droits, établissant des passerelles entre les trois branches composant un "droit international de la personne humaine" bâtissant des ponts entre prévention et répression de la disparition forcée, entre responsabilité de l'Etat et de l'individu, entre droit international et droit interne. Il rassemble des éléments jusque-là épars.'

108. Ibid.

109. *Convention against Enforced Disappearances*, Preamble, para. 3: '*Recalling* the International Covenant on Economic, Social and Cultural Rights, the International Covenant on Civil and Political Rights and the other relevant international instruments in the fields of human rights, humanitarian law and international criminal law.'

110. *Convention against Enforced Disappearances*, Preamble, para. 7 and art.1 para. 1.

111. Art.1 para. 1: 'No one shall be subjected to enforced disappearance.'

112. Art.1 para. 2.

113. Art.1, para. 2. The non-derogable character of the prohibition of enforced disappearances was already recognized in article 7 of the *United Nations Declaration on the Protection of All Persons from Enforced Disappearances*, and in article 10 of the *Inter-American Convention on Forced Disappearance of Persons*.

114. Art. 2 of the *Convention against Enforced Disappearances*.
115. *United Nations Declaration on the Protection of All Persons from Enforced Disappearances*, Preamble, para. 3: 'Deeply concerned that in many countries, often in a persistent manner, enforced disappearances occur, in the sense that persons are arrested, detained or abducted against their will or otherwise deprived of their liberty by officials of different branches or levels of Government, or by organized groups or private individuals acting on behalf of, or with the support, direct or indirect, consent or acquiescence of the Government, followed by a refusal to disclose the fate or whereabouts of the persons concerned or a refusal to acknowledge the deprivation of their liberty, which places such persons outside the protection of the law.' *Inter-American Convention on Forced Disappearance of Persons*, art. 2: 'For the purposes of this Convention, forced disappearance is considered to be the act of depriving a person or persons of his or their freedom, in whatever way, perpetrated by agents of the state or by persons or groups of persons acting with the authorization, support, or acquiescence of the state, followed by an absence of information or a refusal to acknowledge that deprivation of freedom or to give information on the whereabouts of that person, thereby impeding his or her recourse to the applicable legal remedies and procedural guarantees.'
116. Art. 7, para. 2 i) of the ICC Statute, '"Enforced disappearance of persons" means the arrest, detention or abduction of persons by, or with the authorization, support or acquiescence of, a State or a political organization, followed by a refusal to acknowledge that deprivation of freedom or to give information on the fate or whereabouts of those persons, with the intention of removing them from the protection of the law for a prolonged period of time'.
117. For a traditionalist approach to HRL in this regard and its justification, see Scovazzi and Citroni, *supra* note 1, at 278–279.
118. Art. 3 of the *Convention against Enforced Disappearances*: 'Each State Party shall take appropriate measures to investigate acts defined in article 2 committed by persons or groups of persons acting without the authorization, support or acquiescence of the State and to bring those responsible to justice.'
119. Art. 7, para. 2 i), of the ICC Statute.
120. Taxil, *supra* note 82, at 136. See also: de Frouville, *supra* note 103, at 23: 'Les obligations mentionnées pèsent exclusivement sur l'Etat, à l'exclusion de toute entité privée. On demeure ainsi sans conteste dans le cadre conceptuel des droits de l'Homme, sans déborder sur le territoire du droit international humanitaire: seuls les Etats sont ici redevables des obligations posées par la Convention.'
121. See in this sense the recommendations of M. Nowak, independent expert appointed to examine the existing international framework for the protection of persons against enforced disappearances, to the drafting committee of the UN Convention against enforced disappearances. See Nowak, *supra* note 1, para. 73.
122. On these issues, see articles by: de Frouville, *supra* note 103, 1–92; Taxil, *supra* note 82, at 129–156; S. McCrory, 'The International Convention for the Protection of all Persons from Enforced Disappearance', *Human Rights Law Review* 7:3 (2007): 545–566.
123. *Convention against Enforced Disappearances*, Preamble, para. 8: 'Affirming the right of any victim to know the truth about the circumstances of an enforced disappearance and the fate of the disappeared person, and the right to freedom to seek, receive and impart information to this end'; Art. 24, para. 2: 'Each victim has the right to know the truth regarding the circumstances of the enforced disappearance, the progress and results of the investigation and the fate of the disappeared person. Each State Party shall take appropriate measures in this regard.'
124. Art. 32 of API. See also *supra*.
125. Art. 24, para. 3, of the *Convention against Enforced Disappearances*.
126. Arts 33 and 34 of API. See also: arts 15–17 GCI, 18-20 GCII; 120 para. 3 and 6 GCIII.
127. de Frouville, *supra* note 103, at 60: '... les inspirateurs non gouvernementaux de la Convention ont voulu innover, en instaurant une forme d'entraide plus spécifique d'assistance aux victimes de disparitions forcées en vue de la recherche des personnes disparues. L'idée était présente dans l'article 8 du projet de convention. Elle s'inspirait de toute évidence du droit international humanitaire et en particulier des articles 136 à 141 de la Convention IV relative à la protection des civils, relatifs à l'Agence centrale de renseignement et aux bureaux de renseignements des Parties au conflit, mais aussi et surtout des articles 32, 33 et 34 du Protocole I consacré aux "personnes disparues et décédées". Ces dispositions mettent en place un régime qui permet, pour celles de la Convention IV, de "pister" et de faciliter la transmission d'informations relative à des "personnes protégées" se trouvant au pouvoir d'une des parties au conflit et, pour celles du Protocole,

d'organiser la recherche par chaque Partie au conflit des personnes dont la disparition a été signalée par une Partie adverse, y compris l'identification de ces personnes et la gestion des restes des personnes décédées sur le territoire d'une des parties.'

128.   Art. 17 para. 1 e) and 17 para. 3 of the *Convention against Enforced Disappearances.*

129.   Registration: Arts.70, 122, para. 4, GCIII, 106, 136, 138, 140 GC IV, 33 API. Access to places of detention: Art.125, para. 3 GCIII and 142 GCIV. See de Frouville, *supra* note 103, at 69.

130.   de Frouville, *supra* note 103, at 72.

131.   Art. 18 para. 1 of the *Convention against Enforced Disappearances.*

132.   Art. 70 and 122 GCIII, 106, 136, 138, 140 GC IV, 33, para. 3, API.

133.   Art. 23 of the *Convention against Enforced Disappearances.*

134.   Arts 47/48/127/144 of the GC; 83 and 87, para. 2, API; 19 APII.

135.   Art. 30, para. 1, of the *Convention against Enforced Disappearances.*

136.   Taxil, *supra* note 82, at 153. She stressed that the Committee on Enforced Disappearances has a mandate that goes beyond that of the Working Group because, notably, it may request provisional measures.

137.   Andreu-Guzman, *supra* note 44, at 804: 'Le Groupe a ainsi vu le jour avec pour mandat de "faciliter la communication entre les familles des personnes disparues et les gouvernements intéressés afin de faire en sorte que les cas suffisamment circonstanciés et clairement identifiés fassent l'objet d'enquêtes et que la lumière soit faite sur le sort des personnes disparues".' This mandate was described as a 'humanitarian mandate'. For the ICRC's work regarding the missing: See, *The Missing: ICRC Progress Report*, ICRC Publication 2006, 46 pages.

138.   Art. 26, para. 1, of the *Convention against Enforced Disappearances*. See Taxil, *supra* note 82, at 152.

139.   Art. 16 of the *Convention against Enforced Disappearances*: '1. No State Party shall expel, return ("refouler"), surrender or extradite a person to another State where there are substantial grounds for believing that he or she would be in danger of being subjected to enforced disappearance. 2. For the purpose of determining whether there are such grounds, the competent authorities shall take into account all relevant considerations, including, where applicable, the existence in the State concerned of a consistent pattern of gross, flagrant or mass violations of human rights or of serious violations of international humanitarian law.'

140.   Article 43 of the *Convention against Enforced Disappearances.*

141.   See the statements of the United Kingdom: 'It was understood that article 43 operated as a "savings clause" in order to ensure that the relevant provisions of international humanitarian law took precedence over any other provisions contained in the Convention.' United Nations, General Assembly, *Third Committee Approves Draft Resolution Concerning Convention on Enforced Disappearances*, GA/SHC/3872, 13.11.06. Available at: http://www.un.org/News/Press/docs/2006/gash c3872.doc.htm

   For the position of the United States of America, see United Nations, General Assembly, Note verbale dated 20 June 2006 from the Permanent Mission of the United States of America to the United Nations Office at Geneva addressed to the secretariat of the Human Rights Council, 27 June 2006 (UN Doc. A/HRC/1/G/1): 'The United States wishes to place on record our understanding of Article 43 of the draft convention. We understand this provision to confirm that the provisions of the law of armed conflict, also called international humanitarian law, remain the *lex specialis* in situations of armed conflicts and other situations to which international humanitarian law applies. The United States understands Article 43 to operate as a "savings clause" in order to ensure that the relevant provisions of international humanitarian law take precedence over any other provisions contained in this Convention.'

142.   Taxil, *supra* note 82, at 132.

143.   McCrory, *supra* note 122, at 561. See also: Scovazzi and Citroni, *supra* note 1, at 266: 'As provided for in Article 43, the 2007 Convention does not prejudice the provisions of international humanitarian law. ... This means that the specific rules applying to certain forms of deprivation of liberty which are typical in time of war ... are not modified by the 2007 Convention. However, it is also clearly understood that acts of enforced disappearance are not allowed against prisoners of war and the civilian population, either in a belligerent country or in territories occupied by it. Such acts, which are also in conflict with international humanitarian law, fall under the scope of the 2007 Convention.'

144.   Article 37 of the *Convention against Enforced Disappearances* reads as follows: 'Nothing in this Convention shall affect any provisions which are more conducive to the protection of all persons

from enforced disappearance and which may be contained in: (a) The law of a State Party; (b) International law in force for that State.'

145. Section 37 of the *Convention against Enforced Disappearances* can be compared, as to its formulation, with Article 21 of the *Declaration on the Protection of All Persons from Enforced Disappearances*: 'The provisions of the present Declaration are without prejudice to the provisions enunciated in the Universal Declaration of Human Rights or in any other international instrument, and shall not be construed as restricting or derogating from any of those provisions.'

146. It was the ICRC that proposed to introduce a provision guaranteeing the rights of communication of prisoners. See de Frouville, *supra* note 103, at 68.

147. Art. 5 GCIV.

17. 'Humanitarian rights': how to ensure respect for human rights and humanitarian law in armed conflicts

Dan Kuwali*

1. INTRODUCTION

Today's wars have no frontiers. Villages are the battlefronts. Cities have become scenes of unfathomable atrocities. Civilians are deliberate targets. Children are warlords as well as victims. Rape is a weapon of war such that it is now even more dangerous to be a woman than a soldier in contemporary armed conflicts. Human rights and humanitarian law violations are committed in armed conflicts by insurgents as well as government troops. For example, in the Democratic Republic of the Congo (DRC), the most visible threat to the human rights of civilians are the government soldiers. The inevitable trend is that battlefields have been increasingly imposed on civilians in contemporary warfare. Yet, the principle of the protection of civilians and non-combatants in armed conflicts is the centrepiece of the 1949 Geneva Conventions and the 1977 Additional Protocols. The challenge is how to ensure respect of human rights and humanitarian norms by belligerents in an on-going armed conflict.

Humanitarian aid workers and peacekeepers have also been abducted and murdered by unscrupulous belligerents in conflict situations such as Darfur. Peacekeepers, who are supposed to be protecting civilians, often find themselves in these precarious situations without capacity and capability to protect civilians, which sends the wrong signal to warring factions as well as the populations they are supposed to protect. This growing trend also raises disturbing questions about the political will, capability and capacity of the military forces in the protection of civilians in armed conflicts. The question, therefore, is how to compel States and non-state armed groups to comply with obligations under human rights and humanitarian law, especially in an on-going armed conflict?[1] Therefore, from a practitioner's perspective, this chapter intends to explore the challenges in the implementation of human rights and international humanitarian law (IHL) in peace support operations (PSOs) in order to suggest legal approaches to ensure compliance of the law by belligerents.

The implementation mechanisms of human rights and humanitarian law can be classified into three groups, that is, preventive measures to be taken in peacetime; mechanisms to ensure respect during armed conflicts; and mechanisms to repress violations *post facto*.[2] Although, the twenty-first century is the century of prevention, the regime for the protection of human rights and IHL has largely been reactive and event driven in the face of specific threats or acts of repression, yet prevention is more effective and cheaper than reacting after the fact.[3] Given that observance of the law in prospect is more worthwhile for the victims than punishment of perpetrators in retrospect, this discussion will examine the following issues: (a) how to ensure compliance of human rights and humanitarian law by the belligerents in an armed conflict; and (b) how to protect civilians in an on-going armed conflict by deterring potential perpetrators of violations. Since the challenges revolve around the implementation and enforcement of human rights and humanitarian law in the current legal regime, it is necessary to contextualize the problems at the outset.

1.1   Challenges of Implementation of Human Rights and International Humanitarian Law in Conflicts

Most of the belligerents in contemporary armed conflicts are non-State armed groups. While the protection of civilians is a responsibility of States, often it is the government itself that perpetrates abuses. Both governments and non-State actors are, and can be, violators of human rights and IHL obligations. For example, M. Sassòli has noted that some of the inherent challenges for implementation of IHL are:

> Because [IHL] applies to such violent situations as are armed conflicts; because it is not sufficiently understood, or conversely, it is well understood but manipulated; because a situation must be classified as armed conflict before it can be applied; because the implementation mechanisms either do not function, or, if they do function (such as the ICRC and criminal prosecution) nevertheless have their limits; and finally, because the structures of authority necessary to enforce any legal order are lacking.[4]

One of the most important means of ensuring compliance with IHL is scrutiny by, and pressure from, third parties.[5] In this case, the major responsibility and burden for preventing violations of IHL may be on the neighbouring States of countries at war, who presumably, have the most interest in the crises. The diminishing impact of the 'protecting power' system has shifted the burden to the International Committee of the Red Cross (ICRC) to assume the humanitarian functions. While it is true that the ICRC has been successful in its private persuasion where it detected violations, it is also clear that the ICRC may not openly pressure perpetrators to refrain from violations as it operates strictly on a confidentiality basis.[6] At the same time, human rights NGOs have problems of access to victims in armed conflicts, and even where they do, they are unable to effectively mobilize public opinion and pressurize errant parties to comply with the law. In addition, although Article 90 of Protocol I provides for the establishment of an International Fact-Finding Commission to inquire into alleged violations of the Geneva Conventions and Protocols, the International Fact-Finding Commission's jurisdiction is limited and it has no power to impose any kind of penalty.[7] According to C. Greenwood:

> The most difficult question to answer about the laws of armed conflict is how States can be brought to comply with them. There can be no denying that the enforcement machinery of international law in general is comparatively weak and that it lacks most of the features found in national law. There is no international police and no network of courts with compulsory jurisdiction. Moreover, it is probably true to say that there is no area of international law in which the deficiencies of enforcement are so apparent as the laws of armed conflict.[8]

The problems are exacerbated by the fact that the enforcement mechanism of human rights and humanitarian law are not only parallel but also fragmented. How can one ever explain the fact that the 1949 Geneva Conventions and the 1977 Additional Protocols thereto have been universally ratified, only to find them dishonoured in breach? How can one explain that laws against mass atrocity crimes and laws that embody universal jurisdiction are still not part of the legislative fabric of the several countries at the epicentre of the maelstrom of armed conflicts? How can one ever explain the dilemma in application of IHL in internationalized armed conflicts and the obstacles in the implementation of IHL by non-State actors who make up more than half of the protagonists in these conflicts? What, if at all, is the justification for killing innocent civilians who are at the heart of the protection regime of the Geneva Conventions? These concerns underscore the need to find a workable solution to the implementation of human rights and humanitarian law to prevent violations in order to enhance the protection of civilians in armed conflict.

1.2 Problems of Protection of Civilians in Contemporary Armed Conflicts

Today, civilians constitute the bulk of casualties in armed conflicts, often deliberately targeted rather than merely caught up in the fighting. Women and children constitute the majority of victims of contemporary armed conflicts and are exposed to high rates of sexual violence. Violence against women, especially sexual violence, is increasingly used as a tactic during armed conflicts. For example, in the Rwandan genocide in 1994, an estimated 500 000 women and children were raped by marauding militias and soldiers. About 85 per cent of the refugees, asylum-seekers and internally displaced persons (IDPs) who are victims of conflicts are women and children. More than 2 million children worldwide have been killed in situations of armed conflicts, at least 6 million have been permanently disabled or injured, and over 14 million children have been displaced within their home countries due to armed conflicts. Given their limited mobility and vulnerability, the elderly and people with disabilities are even more exposed to the brutalities of warfare.

Protection of civilians is more difficult in a situation of war or 'public emergency which threatens the life of the nation' by allowing States to 'derogate' from, or suspend, some human rights commitments during such situations. Further, certain core principles of international law evidently clash when it comes to the issue of internally displaced persons who are invariably entangled in armed conflicts, especially those of state sovereignty on the one hand, and the contemporary interpretation of the justifiable role of the international community, particularly as regards international protection of human rights, on the other hand. At the same time, the absence of a consistent legal framework or useful reporting mechanisms can dissuade victims from reporting abuses, and, therefore, render the norm of protection mere rhetoric.

While the protection of civilians is a responsibility of States, often it is the government itself that perpetrates abuses. However, States have a responsibility to protect populations at risk and prevent violations by non-state actors against civilians. In resolution 1674 of 2006 on the protection of civilians in armed conflict, the UN Security Council reaffirmed the political commitment of responsibility to protect (R2P), which is rooted in the notion of 'sovereignty as a responsibility'. As with the broader notion of human security, the ultimate focus of R2P is on the safety and well-being of the people themselves. The protection of civilians is a human, political and legal imperative that recognizes the inherent dignity and worth of every human being. The challenge is how to move away from fragmented, *ad hoc* approach into the direction of a more comprehensive and effective approach to protect civilians from abuse, to mitigate the impact of warfare and to alleviate their suffering.

Clearly, there is an urgent need for a comprehensive doctrine to guide the protection of civilians in armed conflicts. While the UN has recently been working to develop doctrines and operational capacities to meet such challenges, the actual protection of civilians on the ground is stalled by lack of political will to 'save strangers'. Although UN Security Council Resolution 1325 (2000) provides an opportunity to recognize gender concerns within the conflict management, it has been civil society rather than national governments that has been the principal proponent of its implementation. Further, ensuring an effective protection regime is another matter. Hence, there is need for policymakers to take steps towards filling the gap that exists between reporting situations of the plight of civilians in armed conflicts and the necessary action of bringing appropriate responses to the information documented. Forward planning is needed for a comprehensive doctrine, rules of engagement, and better training of troops to protect civilians on the ground. The massive violations against civilians show that there is a 'capacity gap' for peacekeepers in the protection of civilians in armed conflicts.

1.3 Impunity for Serious Violations of Human Rights and Humanitarian Law

In the past, due to the absence of effective international mechanisms of justice, dictators and warlords committed violations of human rights and humanitarian law with impunity.[9] The national judicial systems in post-conflict societies cannot immediately handle wide-scale prosecutions for mass atrocity crimes in accordance with inter-national standards of due process. The failure to punish those responsible for mass atrocity crimes perpetuates a cycle of disrespect for justice. 'Impunity' means the impossibility, *de jure* or *de facto*, of bringing the perpetrators of violations to account – whether in criminal, civil, administrative or disciplinary proceedings – since they are not subject to any inquiry that might lead to their being accused, arrested, tried, and, if found guilty, sentenced to appropriate penalties, and to making reparations to their victims.[10] Thus, impunity can be understood as the absence or inadequacy of penalties and/or compensation for massive and grave violations of human rights as well as humanitarian law.

Impunity arises from

> a failure by States to meet their obligations to investigate violations, to take appropriate measures in respect of the perpetrators, particularly in the area of justice, by ensuring that they are prosecuted, tried and duly punished, to provide victims with effective remedies and reparation for the injuries suffered, and to take steps to prevent any recurrence of such violations.[11]

There is a distinction between amnesty, which immunizes the perpetrators from domestic prosecution, and exile and asylum in a foreign country, which puts the perpetrator out of the jurisdictional reach of domestic prosecution.[12] In this version, M.O. Scharf elaborates the downside of amnesty as regards impunity thus:

> While prosecution and punishments can reinforce the value of law by displacing personal revenge, failure to punish former leaders responsible for widespread human rights abuses encourages cynicism about the rule of law and distrust toward the political system. To the victims of human rights crimes, amnesty or exile represents the ultimate in hypocrisy: While they struggle to put their suffering behind them, those responsible are allowed to enjoy a comfortable retirement. When those with power are seen to be above the law as a fundamental necessity in a society transitioning to democracy.[13]

It is noticeable that amnesties may facilitate suspension of ongoing violations but then amnesties may also undermine deterrence, the law of state responsibility, and human rights.[14] Prospective violators may conclude that if they do not prevail, they can negotiate an amnesty. However, for every crime there must be a legal punishment. For example, all States Parties to the Geneva Conventions have a duty to search for perpetrators of war crimes and bring them to justice. Similarly, Article 8 of the Universal Declaration of Human rights provides for a remedy for violations of human rights. Therefore, impunity denies the right to an effective remedy. An important part of this includes victim's fundamental rights, known as 'the Joinet Principles', which, broadly, include the victim's right to know, the victim's right to justice, and the victim's right to compensation. Accountability is the antithesis of impunity, which occurs either *de facto* or through amnesties.[15] This entails that impunity poses a serious threat to human rights and humanitarian law and compromises the international obligation of States to guarantee as well as to respect human rights and IHL and to punish perpetrators thereof. It also puts to question the essence of proclaiming human rights and IHL if they can be violated with impunity. The daunting task for the international community, therefore, is how to ensure that all perpetrators of gross violations of human rights and IHL, be it States or non-State actors, do not slip away with impunity.

2.   WHY HUMANITARIAN RIGHTS?

Traditionally, human rights law has been applicable in times of peace and has protected individuals from their own governments, whereas IHL governs the conduct of belligerents in time of war and protects individuals from enemy powers.[16] With the shift in the nature of most contemporary armed conflicts, from international to non-international and mixed conflicts, IHL 'has been pulled in the direction of human rights'.[17] In this case, common Article 3 is a textbook example of the convergence of international human rights and humanitarian law as it contains the most universally recognized humanitarian principles buttressed by fundamental guarantees in humanitarian law that are 'applicable at all times, in all circumstances and to all parties and from which no derogation is permitted'.[18] Further, human rights institutions have been faced with situations where IHL is central and have thus been impelled to apply IHL.[19] Following the increasing convergence between international human rights and IHL, it is generally accepted that although human rights law is applicable in armed conflicts, IHL takes precedence as *lex specialis*.

However, since IHL is based on completely different historical roots from human rights law, it has been considered mutually exclusive. According to the *Nuclear Weapons* Advisory Opinion, IHL is tailored for extraordinary situations of armed conflict and for the protection of the respective interests of the (State) parties, while human rights deal with limitations on regular governmental activities vis-à-vis the individual.[20] The normative separation of human rights and IHL has also been driven by the institutional divergence in implementation. For example, the ICRC acting on its mandate as a guardian of IHL has focused on *jus in bello*. In carrying out its mandate, the ICRC has traditionally endeavoured to keep its neutrality and, therefore, inadvertently distanced itself from questions of human rights, which seemed as an emanation of political agendas in the UN. On its part, as an organization for world peace and security, the UN concentrated on *jus contra bellum* and refrained from dealing with the 'laws of war'.[21] This was punctuated by the International Law Commission (ILC) which excluded the law of war among the subjects with which it concerns itself.[22]

However, in view of more than 250 armed conflicts that have occurred, and more than 40 ongoing, the argument would lose its relevance and credibility. It can also be argued that IHL would be politicized if the UN had direct responsibility. However, while this argument seems correct, it should be seen as an argument in favour, because IHL is also a political issue.[23] Usually, conflict has its origins in patterns of human rights abuse.[24] No doubt, IHL regulates and contributes to the containment of violence and the preservation of fundamental standards of humanity in the midst of conflicts. IHL is an important component in maintaining peace and its very nature shatters the dangerous illusion of unlimited force or total war, creates areas of peace in the midst of conflict, imposes the principle of a common humanity and calls for dialogue.[25] This explains why IHL is increasingly becoming part of global thinking on security issues at the national, regional and international levels. The inclusion of IHL complements the current concept of human security that the implementation of IHL should form part of a culture of conflict prevention for the twenty-first century.

Humanitarian instruments in force form part of international law and are interlinked with the system of international security, whether for arms control or for peaceful settlement of conflicts. In *Legal Consequences of the Construction of a Wall in the Occupied Palestinian Territory (Israel Wall* case), even the International Court of Justice (ICJ) confirmed that human rights law continues to apply in situations to which IHL is applicable.[26] The Human Rights Committee has also affirmed that in situations of armed conflict 'both spheres of the law are complimentary, not mutually exclusive'.[27] This underscores the suggestion that IHL should be highlighted in the general context of international peace and security. Thus, in so far as human rights violations may occur during armed conflicts and that violations of humanitarian law may also be human rights violations, the two branches of international law are interlinked and complementary. This view is buttressed by the 'Brahimi Report' that reaffirmed the centrality of human rights to UN conflict prevention, peacemaking and peace operations.[28] The link between human rights and IHL is also confirmed by the recent approach of the Human Rights Council initiating its Special Procedures to investigate, monitor and publicly report on violations of human rights and humanitarian law in situations such as Darfur and Gaza. The scope of application of human rights is extended to wartimes in Article 4(1) of the International Covenant on Civil and Political Rights (ICCPR).[29]

Protection of civilians in armed conflicts is the confluence between international human rights and humanitarian law and the broader human security agenda. International human rights and humanitarian law prohibits all means and methods of warfare that fail to discriminate between armed parties and non-combatants. The co-existence of human rights and international humanitarian law provides windows of opportunity for the effective protection of civilians in armed conflicts. This helps explain why the Brahimi Report observed that peace support operations should engage in both human rights monitoring and capacity building.[30] To the extent that human rights law applies in armed conflicts, it covers much the same ground as IHL. It is now settled that human rights and international humanitarian law are complementary and mutually reinforcing.[31] As a result of the 'constructive complementarity' of international human rights and humanitarian law, this chapter terms 'humanitarian rights' as the symbiotic doctrine and methodology regarding the protection of fundamental human rights and humanitarian norms in order to enhance the protection of civilians in armed conflicts.[32] Humanitarianism in this sense refers to the non-Statist, de-politicized and neutral duty of care pioneered by Henry Dunant in 1859.[33]

As to the question why a 'humanitarian rights' approach, the simple reason is that since violations of human rights and IHL occur simultaneously during armed conflicts, therefore, prevention of such violations should focus on the protection of the civilian population and not necessarily on when and who should monitor what legal regime.[34] The protection of the human rights of civilians against violations is better served when the constructive complementarity between international human rights and humanitarian law is duly recognized.[35] The premise is that parties to the conflict, including non-State actors, have legally binding obligations concerning the rights of persons affected by the conflict and that State Parties to the 1949 Geneva Conventions have undertaken to respect and ensure respect for the Geneva Conventions in all circumstances in terms of common Article 1 of the Conventions.[36]

Further, human rights and IHL are complementary and mutually reinforcing, and all human rights require protection equally; and the protection provided by human rights law continues in armed conflict situations, taking into account when IHL applies as *lex specialis*.[37] Furthermore, fundamental human rights are non-derogable in all circumstances, and any measures derogating from the provisions of the ICCPR must be in accordance with Article 4 of the ICCPR in all cases, and ought to be exceptional and temporary.[38] Given the principle of *lex specialis derogat legi generali*, it follows that the combined application of international human rights law and IHL does not necessarily mean two norms are to be applied simultaneously, but rather that 'one should seek to identify the norm that provides the most specific answer for each particular situation'.[39]

If IHL is applied as the *lex specialis*, it means that there will be a violation of human rights only if the act in question constitutes a violation of IHL.[40] As to protection of civilians, a humanitarian rights approach entails a vertical relationship between the general regime and *lex specialis*. It does not necessarily mean that *lex specialis* prevails over the general legal regime nor that the former displaces the latter but rather that if there are gaps in the latter regime, they will be filled in with the generally applicable rule relating to the question at stake. In this case, the 'general is at the bottom and is the default position.' In this way, *lex specialis* is a subdivision of the general and is above it.[41]

The constructive complementarity of human rights and IHL is necessary, given that human rights law applies in armed conflicts subject to derogations. This means that where there is no derogation, human rights law is applicable in its entirety, 'which could result in acts lawful under applicable rules of IHL being found unlawful under human rights law'.[42] According to common Article 2 of the Geneva Conventions, IHL is, or is not, applicable as a matter of law, and not because a state recognizes its applicability.[43] Although human rights law has a preventive element, it is principally designed to be applied after the event and has inherent mechanisms to be situation-specific.[44] Likewise, although IHL can be enforced *post facto*, it is principally designed to be applied at the time a decision is taken and has to provide a general rule applicable in a given situation.[45] Given the constructive complementarity of human rights and IHL, there is need to develop coherent principles – a human rights approach – to determine the simultaneous application of international human rights and IHL in an armed conflict in order to protect civilians as outlined below.

3.   HUMANITARIAN RIGHTS: PROTECTING CIVILIANS IN ARMED CONFLICTS

The principle of distinction lies at the heart of IHL and aims to protect civilians and non-combatants in armed conflicts. Similarly, human rights law is an essential basis for the protection of civilians in armed conflicts. The ICRC defines protection as 'encompass[ing] all activities aimed at ensuring full respect for the rights of the individual in accordance with the letter and spirit of the relevant bodies of law, i.e., human rights law, international humanitarian law and refugee law'.[46] In light of this, a protection activity is viewed as an activity which

> prevents or puts a stop to specific pattern of abuse and/or alleviates its immediate effects (responsive action); restores people's dignity and ensures adequate living conditions through reparation, restitutions and rehabilitation (remedial action); fosters an environment conducive to respect for the rights of individuals in accordance with the relevant bodies of law (environment building).[47]

This definition locates the importance of activities for the protection of human rights and humanitarian norms such as monitoring, reporting, analysis, dissemination and intervention.

For these reasons, the UN Office of the High Commissioner for Human Rights (OHCHR) and the UN Department of Peacekeeping Operations (DPKO) have established a formal relationship between them to enhance the protection of civilians in peace support operations.[48] As stated above, civilians constitute the vast majority of victims of armed conflicts. In line with principles of IHL and peacekeeping, a humanitarian rights-based approach to protection should be impartial and non-discriminatory. This entails that protection of civilians should, therefore, aim at addressing the plight of the most victimized and most vulnerable groups in conflict situations. In particular, internally displaced persons, women and children, abductees, the elderly and persons with a disability demand priority attention.

Although non-State armed groups are not formally bound by human rights treaty law, it is possible to bring them into compliance with the law as individuals, be they government or non-State actors, and they may be held accountable under international criminal law for gross violations of human rights and IHL. It is in this regard that this chapter builds on the jurisprudential developments in human rights, humanitarian law and international criminal law to expose legal approaches that may be employed to deter potential violators in order to protect civilians in armed conflicts. The premise is that implementation of human rights and IHL through permanent, preventive and corrective scrutiny in the field is more appropriate preventive action than *a posteriori* penalization of violations after the fact.[49]

3.1 Just Peace: Accountability for Grave Violations of Human Rights and Humanitarian Law

Debates abound over prosecution versus amnesty for perpetrators of heinous crimes in countries emerging from civil wars. The goal of most political leaders who seek to end conflicts or facilitate transitions is trading justice for political gains, albeit in the pursuit of peace.[50] The grim reality is that in order to obtain peace, negotiations must be held with the very leaders who are frequently the ones who committed, ordered, or allowed terrible crimes to be committed. Thus, the choice presented to negotiators is whether to have peace or justice.[51] M.C. Bassiouni rightly submits that 'no one can argue that peace is unnecessary and preferable to a state of violence. But the attainment of peace is not necessarily to the exclusion of justice, because justice is frequently necessary to attain peace'.[52] In agreement with M.C. Bassiouni, F.A. Nielssen has noted that:

> Peace and justice is no longer seen as alternatives but as complementary objectives. 'No peace without justice' is no longer regarded as an empty slogan but as a recognised truth and a legitimate and achievable policy aim for societies in transition. The concept of just peace is developing not only in international law but also in international relations.[53]

In the same vein, K. Annan has noted that:

> There are times when we are told that justice must be set aside in the interests of peace. It is true that justice can only be dispensed when the peaceful order of society is secure. But we have come to understand that the reverse is also true: without justice, there can be no lasting peace.[54]

It is obvious that durable peace and reconciliation cannot be built on a foundation of impunity.[55] To state the obvious, both peace and justice are of fundamental importance. However, the fact is that when it comes to ending conflicts they cannot always be reconciled in full, at least in the short term. The so-called peace and justice dilemma is more apparent during peace talks, as it is often at this stage that the parties find their thoughts turning to justice and accountability issues. It is easy to notice the reason for this that 'they do not want their hard won peace to result in them being tried and imprisoned for atrocities they may have committed during the conflict'.[56] According to N. Grono:

> [a] more useful way of approaching this question is to say that justice serves a number of critically important public policy goals. Framed that way, we can then examine those goals, and compare them with other public policy objectives, such as those that might be served by an immediate end to conflict. By so doing we can then attempt to somehow determine which particular policy course will serve the greater good … at very least, an objective examination of the range of competing policy goals should lead to better informed decision making.[57]

On the one hand, the public policy served by peace is straightforward – an end to violence which is an obstacle to development. On the other hand, however, justice tends to serve a complex and diverse range of purposes especially in the context of peace negotiations. This means that the case for justice is not always as clear-cut as that for peace, rendering it difficult to accept the claim that justice must always be pursued, even at the cost of continued conflict.[58] The strongest argument for preferring justice, and the most common claim on its behalf in peace negotiations, is a functional one – that peace is not sustainable in the absence of justice. Yet the evidence for this is far from unequivocal.[59] In this connection, S. Landsman has articulated policies that might justify forgoing prosecution thus:

> [I]t may be the overwhelming majority's view that prosecutions will not serve the best interests of society. When this conclusion is expressed at the ballot box, either through a plebiscite or the election of representatives who have campaigned on such a platform, it is questionable whether a democratic government can ignore popular political sentiment. The very essence of a democracy is that it openly discusses and decides such monumental questions as the nature of justice and the proper course to be pursued by government.[60]

If follows therefore that where the concerned populations have legitimately opted for prosecution, the international community should be cautious about condemning that option. 'This is not to say that every criminal case ought to be put to a vote, but rather that when a transformative event occurs in a society, the majority of its members ought to have a critically influential voice in deciding the new direction to be taken'.[61] Whatever the choice, the decision can never be made by the international community without consulting the community involved. Not the least because it is that community that paid the price in the past and will have to live with the immediate and long-term consequences of the decisions made. Therefore, when setting up transitional justice mechanisms, they should enhance reconciliation in post-conflict settings while not compromising justice and the peace process. The accountability mechanisms may undermine the campaign to protect civilians in armed conflicts if they are perceived to give in to the demands of those who have committed mass atrocity crimes. This would send a wrong signal to perpetrators.[62] Conventional wisdom is that peace and justice are mutually exclusive, but complementary such that if you want peace, you must work for justice.[63] The fact is that accountability forms the cornerstone of any just and sustainable peace.

While trading justice for peace may be politically expedient at a given time, it circumvents international law, undermines the fight against impunity, and may perpetuate what could be an underlying cause of the conflict. As such, political trade-offs between peace and justice should be the rare exception and not the rule since there cannot be real peace without justice. Therefore, policies for combating impunity should be informed by public consultations, including in particular the views of victims. However, analysts have advised eschewing one-size-fits-all formulas and the importation of foreign models, recommending, instead, base support on national assessments, national participation and national needs and aspirations.[64]

Safeguarding a principle of international human rights is more important than attaining a peace settlement. However, in conflict situations, the price for maintaining the moral and rhetorical high ground will be paid in additional lives lost from continuation of the conflict, often with no possibility of further progress being made with regard to the issue at stake. Where there are important questions of timing, or trade-offs to be made between peace and justice, the answers are better given by the concerned societies, not imposed from the outside.[65] Building on the foregoing arguments and emerging jurisprudence, the focus should not be on the question whether peace or justice, but rather on bringing peace and justice given that the two can co-exist, as elaborated below.

Admittedly, under classic formulations of international law and humanitarian law, no legal obligation exists to prosecute individual human rights violators upon the conclusion of a peace treaty.[66] Yet, serious international crimes are insulated from the statute of limitations. Increasingly, therefore, practitioners are deriving such an obligation to prosecute perpetrators after cessation of hostilities out of various international human rights and humanitarian law treaty instruments. Almost invariably, this disposition has been tied, implicitly or explicitly, to a bias favouring Western-liberal legal models of human rights enforcement with its attendant requirement of formal legal proceedings against indicted suspects.[67]

There are at least five goals that can be achieved through accountability for mass atrocity crimes: firstly, accountability gives the victims a sense of justice and closure as prosecutions signal the return to the rule of law in post-conflict societies. Secondly, in transitional regimes, accountability tends to repair the damage done to a society traumatized by atrocities and promoting national reconciliation. Thus, prosecutions facilitate reconciliation by creating a public record of violations, to help institutionalize mechanisms for punishing past violations, thereby minimizing vigilant justice. Thirdly, by assigning individual responsibility for criminal acts, it may deter future violations through the prospect of punishment for such offences. Fourthly, it serves to rehabilitate the offender. Fifthly, it affords retribution for wrongdoing and it is a moral condemnation of heinous offences.[68] However, considering that sometimes these goals cannot actually be served through the prosecutorial mechanisms alone, civil accountability can also give rise to reparations and compensation to the victims.[69] The common denominator of all of these goals should be to protect, re-establish, or create a public order characterized by low expectations of violence and a heightened respect for human rights.[70] However, the downside of prosecution is that:

Closely linked to adjudicator bias is the charge that 'prosecutions are nothing more than victors' justice,' a settling of scores by those who have won the contest. This sort of prosecution sets the stage for revanchism rather than democracy and casts doubt upon the wisdom of proceeding, at least in some cases. Prosecution also raises a very difficult set of questions concerning the selection of defendants. It is likely to be impossible to prosecute all human rights violations. Therefore, some subset of possible cases will have to be selected. That subset may include a few powerful defendants and/or a group of malefactors whose deeds are particularly visible or egregious.[71]

In the long run, international criminal prosecutions may serve to deter violations in future cases, but may increase the costs of suspending ongoing violations if violators conclude that continued resistance is preferable to facing a judgment by a penal institution.[72] In cases of transitional societies, the compelling arguments in favour of accountability are reconciled with the tensions that some forms of accountability may engender. Attempts to crack the bastion of impunity enjoyed by the erstwhile regime might threaten the functioning of the new political system.[73] Trials closest to the affected society, victim, perpetrators and evidence clearly advance the purposes of accountability best. There is also need for the affected society, possibly in conjunction with the international actors, to determine the number of targets involved in the accountability process.

Hence, it is a superficial conclusion to say that accountability for mass atrocity crimes would undermine efforts towards building lasting peace. It is rather by bringing perpetrators of crimes to justice through fair trial that there can be justice, reconciliation and sustained peace. Admittedly, there can be no single model for addressing mass atrocity crimes. Rather, the political, social and historical conditions in a country will govern the weights of the competing considerations, and thus the means for approaching accountability. In short, however, any peace agreement between the target government and rebel groups should reiterate the obligation of all parties to the conflict to respect human rights and abide by IHL. This requires the creative drafting of peace agreements by leaving no obvious room for impunity. Thus, accountability for mass atrocity crimes may deter potential perpetrators, and thereby protect civilians in armed conflicts.

3.2 No Amnesty for Serious Violations for Human Rights and Humanitarian Law

Article 6(5) of the Additional Protocol II crystallized an approach to transitional justice or post-conflict justice that set peace and reconciliation as the fundamental objective.[74] Although this provision is viewed as encouraging the granting of amnesties with respect to internal armed conflicts commentators submit that the object of this sub-paragraph is to encourage gestures of reconciliation which can contribute to re-establishing normal relations in the life of a nation which has been divided.[75] While amnesties for gross human rights offences granted to individuals may, in certain cases, be politically expedient, such amnesties are generally incompatible with international law and do not have any effect outside the borders of the country in which they are granted; nor do they absolve other States of their responsibility and their duty to prosecute or to transfer such individuals for trial. It is one thing to suggest that in a given case the decision not to prosecute violators represents a poor policy judgment, it is quite another to conclude that such a decision violated international law. Where such a conclusion is possible, the decision to forego prosecution could be challenged before a competent court.

While recognizing that amnesty is an accepted legal concept and a gesture of peace and reconciliation at the end of a non-international armed conflict, the UN has recommended rejecting amnesties which purport to award impunity for war crimes, genocide and crimes against humanity, including those relating to ethnic, gender and sexually based international crimes.[76] As a general rule, therefore, the UN Secretary-General has recommended that peace agreements and Security Council resolutions and mandates should reject amnesties.[77] Thus, the question is not really whether and how to deal with the past, but rather how best to ensure that the past is dealt with in a way that is legitimate and effective.

Indeed, in *Prosecutor v. Kallon and Kamara*, the Special Court for Sierra Leone confirmed that domestic amnesties for crimes against humanity and war crimes committed in an internal armed conflict were not unlawful under international law.[78] Similarly, the *Furundžija* case reaffirmed the incompatibility of amnesties that lead to impunity with respect to the duty of States to punish serious crimes under international law, and that such amnesties 'would not be accorded international legal recognition'.[79] In the *Barrios Altos* case, the Inter-American Commission decided that:

> all amnesty provisions on prescription and the establishment of measures designed to eliminate responsibility are inadmissible, because they are intended to prevent the investigation and punishment of those responsible for serious human rights violations such as torture, extra-judicial, summary or arbitrary execution and forced disappearance, all of them prohibited because they violate non-derogable human rights.[80]

Therefore, the general principle is that amnesty cannot apply to mass atrocity crimes. It is on this basis that human rights groups have reiterated the need to ensure that there is no amnesty from prosecution for persons implicated in serious violations of international human rights and humanitarian law in any peace agreement with the rebel groups.[81] However, at present only a handful of States have ratified the 1968 UN Convention on the Non-Applicability of Statutory Limitations to War Crimes and Crimes against Humanity.[82] This indicates that there is still reluctance on the part of several States to support the proposition that no time prescriptions should apply to these crimes, thus making it difficult to prosecute the perpetrators of such crimes.[83] In comparison, the Council of Europe adopted the 1974 European Convention on the Non-Applicability of Statutory Limitations to Crimes against Humanity and War Crimes (Inter-European). Surprisingly, Africa does not have such a treaty at the regional level. Yet, it is a continent that has been infested by such egregious crimes, if the current cases before the ICC are to be a yardstick. To ensure the protection of civilians in armed conflicts, there is need to institutionalize the imprescriptibility of mass atrocity crimes along the lines of the 1968 UN Convention and the 1974 Inter-European Convention.

3.3   The Duty to Cooperate with the International Criminal Court

Specifically, Article 93 of the Rome Statute requires States Parties to assist the International Criminal Court (ICC) by cooperating in relation to investigations and prosecutions that are underway before the ICC.

The duty to cooperate comes to the fore here considering that although the ICC has issued indictments for the leadership of the Lord's Resistance Army that wages war on civilians in northern Uganda, the ICC Prosecutor continues to seek the cooperation of the international community for the arrest and surrender of the suspects. The same is true with the three or so indictments in Darfur. When the Security Council referred the situation in Darfur to the Chief Prosecutor of the ICC under Chapter VII of the UN Charter on 31 March 2005, Resolution 1593 (2005) explicitly directed the Sudanese Government and all other parties to the Conflict to 'cooperate fully with, and provide any necessary assistance to, the [ICC] and the Prosecutor'.

In this vein, Principle 4 of the Princeton Principle on Universal Jurisdiction stipulates that:

> A state shall comply with all international obligations that are applicable to: prosecuting or extraditing persons accused or convicted of crimes under international law in accordance with a legal process that complies with international due process norms, providing other states in investigating or prosecuting such crimes with all available means of administrative and judicial assistance, and undertaking such other necessary and appropriate measures as are consistent with international norms and standards.[84]

Hence, State Parties to the Rome Statute have a duty to cooperate with the ICC in order to protect civilians subjected to crimes under the jurisdiction of the ICC, such as war crimes, genocide and crimes against humanity.[85] More so, the UN General Assembly adopted Resolution 2840 (1971) on War Criminals,[86] which affirmed that a State's refusal 'to cooperate in the arrest, extradition, trial, and punishment' of persons accused or convicted of war crimes and crimes against humanity is 'contrary to the [UN Charter] and to generally recognized norms of international law'.[87] In addition, in 1973 the General Assembly adopted Resolution 3074 on 'Principles of International Co-operation in the Detention, Arrest, Extradition, and Punishment of Persons Guilty of War Crimes and Crimes Against Humanity'.[88] In the same vein, Article 48(2) of the UN Charter requires UN members to carry out the decisions of the Security Council under Chapter VII of the Charter directly and through their action in the appropriate international agencies of which they are members. This means that any factual circumvention by States entail breaches of obligation, since UN members have agreed to accept and carry out decisions of the Security Council in Article 25 of the UN Charter.[89]

The obligation to cooperate entails that the international community must ensure that the Security Council resolutions should be enforced and punitive measures applied. It also entails that States should bear a responsibility to participate in the provision of such assistance and cooperation in overcoming political constraints on accountability of perpetrators of war crimes, genocide and crimes against humanity.[90] This requires institutionalization of the principles of cooperation as outlined in General Assembly Resolution 2840(1971) and 3074 (1973) and also the universal ratification of the 1949

Geneva Conventions and the 1977 Additional Protocols, the Genocide Convention and the Rome Statute.[91]

On its part, the Organization of American States (OAS) has developed impressive jurisprudence, especially in the fight against impunity, from which other regional organizations can learn. For instance, the OAS General Assembly adopted its Resolution on the Promotion of the ICC that calls on States to ratify and implement the Rome Statute as well as to cooperate with the ICC in, *inter alia*, investigation, prosecution, and punishment of the perpetrators of war crimes, crimes against humanity, genocide, and crimes against the administration of justice of the ICC.[92] States should also establish national and regional mechanisms to ensure accountability in order to end impunity, prevent mass atrocity crimes and protect civilians in situations of human rights and IHL violations.[93] Importantly, there is need for a multifaceted institutional and legal framework for reporting and monitoring compliance with IHL and human rights obligations, if the prevention of human rights and IHL violations against civilians in armed conflicts is to be proactive.

3.4 Defend the Defenceless: the Need for a Capability to Protect

As the 'eyes and ears' of the UN, monitoring by peacekeepers constitutes a preventive function in that the presence of peacekeepers can deter human rights and IHL violations.[94] However, the peacekeepers, who are supposed to be protecting civilians, often find themselves in untenable situations without proper strategy, training, doctrine or equipment to protect civilians. The failure to protect civilians in armed conflicts under the watch of peacekeepers may encourage perpetrators to commit violations and discourage the victims whom they are supposed to protect. This growing trend also raises disturbing questions about mandate and the political will, as well as capability and capacity of the military forces in the protection of civilians in armed conflicts. While some missions have explicit 'civilian protection' mandates, other UN peace operations have implicit goals of protection.[95] Although the UN Security Council is increasingly using language that explicitly provides for UN-led operation to protect civilians 'under imminent threat of physical violence', it is not clear if peacekeepers deployed in these operations view the defence of civilians as a primary mission or task.[96] Additional factors such as actual capacity, perceived capacity and location determine whether protection of civilians can actually be carried out.

Further, the interpretation of phrases such as 'protect civilians under imminent threat of physical violence' varies in practice, as does the preparation of peacekeepers, commanders, and the political leadership for such operations. The gaps in peacekeeping forces' institutional capacity also present challenges in recruiting and deploying personnel, meeting logistical requirements, managing mission operations, and sustaining forces on the ground. Aside from this, there are difficulties in developing doctrine and matching mandates to mission tasks. Therefore, the challenge is how to move away from fragmented, *ad hoc* approaches towards a more comprehensive and effective approach to protect civilians from abuse, to mitigate the impact of warfare and to alleviate their suffering. This shows that there is an urgent need for a comprehensive doctrine to guide the protection of civilians in armed conflicts. While there have been efforts to develop doctrines and operational capacities to meet such challenges, the protection of civilians on the ground remains a matter of political will and much more work needs to be done. Additional mechanisms should be explored to enhance the observance of IHL and incorporate a 'Code of Conduct' on human rights and IHL into the training of all armed forces involved in the campaign to protect civilians.

The idea is for peacekeepers to have military superiority over opposing forces in an armed conflict because of the presumption of armed opposition and the need to deter opposition. More often than not, the rag-tag perpetrators of mass atrocities are killers but not fighters and usually know nothing about the laws of war. Typical among the perpetrators are children, abducted and forced to commit despicable acts of barbarity. This explains why they find civilians soft targets. Peacekeepers should have the 'capability to protect' in order to effectively conduct the campaign to protect civilians.[97] The challenge of protecting civilians from the scourges of war requires considerable military deployment capacity. There is a saying that guns do not kill people, people kill people. As such, where appropriate and within their mandates, peacekeepers should have a credible deterrent capacity. The NATO Response Force (NRF) and the EU Battlegroups are good models for the formation of a doctrine for the protection of civilians in conflict zones.

The uncontrolled spread of small arms and light weapons as well as the problem of landmines constitute a threat to peace and security to civilians, women and children. Therefore, to better protect civilians, it will be essential to further address the menace and supply of small arms which have largely contributed to the commission of violations of human rights and humanitarian law.[98] Therefore, a comprehensive disarmament and enforcement of arms embargo by peacekeepers should be part and parcel of the campaign to protect civilians in armed conflicts. There is need for policymakers to take steps towards filling the gap that exists between reporting situations of the plight of civilians in armed conflicts and the necessary action of bringing appropriate responses. Forward planning is needed for a comprehensive doctrine, rules of engagement, and better training of troops to protect civilians. A timely decision by relevant authorities would enable peacekeepers to protect civilians with an appropriate mandate and adequate resources.

4. THE FUTURE OF HUMANITARIAN RIGHTS

In order to enhance the mechanism for the protection of civilians in armed conflicts it is necessary to consider the following jurisprudential developments. The idea is to construct a regime that is able to prevent atrocities against civilians before they occur, by deterring potential perpetrators.

4.1 The Evolving Role of the United Nations' Human Rights Council

In March 2006, the UN General Assembly established a new and more authoritative human rights body, the Human Rights Council, to replace the Commission on Human Rights as the principal human rights body of the UN. The UN General Assembly established the Human Rights Council as its subsidiary and stipulated that the work of the Council shall be 'guided by the principles of universality, impartiality, objectivity and non-selectivity, constructive international dialogue and cooperation, with a view to enhancing the promotion and protection of all human rights'.[99] International humanitarian law is one of the basis for consideration of the human rights record of member states in the universal periodic review (UPR), which is the most innovative mechanism of the Council. Nevertheless, others argue that it might not be fully appropriate that the Human Rights Council, as a body with a specific mandate in the field of human rights, extend its action to the related but well differentiated sector of humanitarian law.[100] The argument goes that if the Human Rights Council does not meet the requisite conditions to address international humanitarian law situations, it may 'run the risk of losing its authority and credibility'.[101]

On the other hand, however, the counterargument is that 'given the complementary and mutually interrelated nature of international human rights law and international humanitarian law, the reference to "applicable international humanitarian law" as a basis when undertaking the universal periodic review is a correct one and does not cause any confusion'.[102] In this way, the recourse to IHL is necessary 'to ensure that a government cannot escape scrutiny by announcing a state of emergency'.[103] One reason to use IHL is the fact that IHL is the *lex specialis* in armed conflicts. In this way, it would be possible for human rights bodies to constructively use IHL to determine whether there was a violation of human rights law, without regard to the question of derogation.[104] The Council may make a finding based on IHL and expressed in the language of human rights law.[105] Importantly, the Council can engage with all relevant actors, both States and non-State actors for the purposes of ensuring the observance of relevant international human rights and humanitarian law.

Protection of civilians has been one of the subjects of specific recommendations of the Council.[106] It is possible for the Council to apply both human rights and IHL, for example, since the manner in which investigations for violations are conducted is more or less similar for all mechanisms, irrespective of whether they are humanitarian law or human rights law violations.[107] The simultaneous application of international human rights and IHL by the Human Rights Council reflect the complimentary nature of the two regimes and may lead to the benefit of the civilians that need protection. The Council may need to train its internal expertise in IHL or to use external IHL experts when faced with situations relating to protection of civilians in armed conflicts. On their part, states need to recognize their obligation, stemming from the UN charter, to cooperate with all appropriate organs of the UN, including the Human Rights Council as well as its special procedures, in their efforts to promote and protect the rights of civilians in armed conflicts.[108]

4.2 Adoption of Universal Jurisdiction

Under the Geneva Conventions, any State has the jurisdiction to try perpetrators of war crimes, irrespective of where the crime was committed and whether the State exercising jurisdiction was a party to the armed conflict in which it occurred. All States Parties to the Geneva Conventions have a duty to search for perpetrators of war crimes and bring them to justice.[109] Further, jurisdiction over other types of war crimes is by customary international law and it is also universal in that any State may exercise jurisdiction.[110] Therefore, universal jurisdiction is a useful tool that is available to ensure compliance with human rights and IHL and bring the perpetrators to justice regardless of where the offence was committed. In principle, the prospect that one may be prosecuted anywhere on the planet in respect of a violation of IHL or for mass atrocity crimes should act as a serious deterrent to potential perpetrators.

Gross violations of human rights and IHL are of legitimate concern to the international community, and give rise to prosecution under the principle of universal jurisdiction.[111] The principle of universal jurisdiction recognizes that certain acts are so heinous and widely condemned that any State may prosecute an offender once custody is obtained. The principle of universal jurisdiction does not require establishment of any link between the criminal and the prosecuting State. All that is required is universal condemnation of the offence. Universal jurisdiction is a useful tool that is available for the international community to ensure compliance with human rights and IHL treaties and bring the perpetrators of mass atrocities to justice regardless of where the offence was committed. Therefore, one viable means to enhance the protection of civilians is to promote widespread adoption of the principle of universality as the legal basis for prosecutorial jurisdiction. The grave human rights situation in conflict regions deserves international scrutiny and accountability within multilateral processes.

Most States have accepted the principle of universal jurisdiction by becoming parties to instruments which provide for universal jurisdiction over war crimes, genocide and crimes against humanity. These crimes are also espoused in the 1949 Geneva Conventions, the 1948 Genocide Convention and the 1984 Convention against Torture. However, many States have not ensured that their courts can exercise jurisdiction in respect of mass atrocity crimes on the basis of universal jurisdiction. To ensure that perpetrators of serious violations of human rights and IHL are brought to justice, States need to 'adopt measures, including legislative and administrative, that will ensure that their national courts can exercise universal jurisdiction over gross human rights offences, including, but not limited to, those contained in the Rome Statute'.[112] This is echoed in Principle 11 of the Princeton Principles on Universal Jurisdiction, which holds that States should enact national legislation to enable the exercise of universal jurisdiction.[113]

However, there are problems relating to the normative content of universal jurisdiction. Firstly, universal jurisdiction merely authorizes rather than obliges States to prosecute and punish offenders. International law does not import a mandatory obligation upon States to undertake prosecution. Secondly, there exists no systematic or general rule of law conferring an obligation, or even a right, upon States to prosecute and punish perpetrators of war crimes, genocide and crimes against humanity, in general. Apart from the problems in the normative content of universal jurisdiction, the legal status of universal jurisdiction as a norm of international law is still questionable. State practice regarding the application of universal jurisdiction has been neither general nor consistent; thus universal jurisdiction is far from universal.[114] This leaves room for perpetrators to escape prosecution and punishment because some States may be willing to provide safe haven to a fugitive of justice. The questionable status of universal jurisdiction in international law exposes the need for systematic extradition, prosecution and punishment of perpetrators of mass atrocities.

While not all States recognize the application of the theory of universality, few states have enacted the national legislation needed to prosecute perpetrators of mass atrocity crimes. Surely, if more States would recognize and apply this theory of universal jurisdiction, national criminal justice systems would have the competence to exercise their jurisdiction for such crimes. The fact that the mass atrocity crimes such as genocide, war crimes and crimes against humanity are subject to universal jurisdiction indicates that such crimes 'are universally repulsive, uniformly condemned, and subject to universal prosecution by any government, anywhere, at any time'.[115] As such, universal jurisdiction is an important tool to end impunity and prevent violations of human rights and IHL in order to protect civilians.

States should ensure the effectiveness of the assumption of universal jurisdiction through reforms in criminal justice, prosecutions and collection of evidence. States must ensure that they fully satisfy their legal obligations in respect of international and internationalized criminal tribunals. This requires States to enact domestic legislation that enables States to fulfil obligations that arise through their adherence to the ICC Statute and other binding instruments, including implementation of applicable obligations to apprehend and surrender suspects and to cooperate in respect of evidence. Institutionalizing universal jurisdiction will spread the web of jurisdiction to fill any jurisdictional vacuum and diminish safe havens for perpetrators of mass atrocities. The legitimacy of international justice, coupled with the greater accessibility of domestic justice, can facilitate the internalization of accountability in the political culture.[116]

The crimes in Article 5(1) of the Rome Statute are highly political crimes which often involve government machinery. As such there is a great possibility that a territorial state may not be capable of effectively prosecuting and punishing such crimes. As such, there is need for a legal framework that attributes a right and, even more so, an obligation upon states to exercise universal jurisdiction over mass atrocity crimes, if authors of atrocities are to be deterred from committing such heinous crimes. While there is a growing recognition for the exercise of universal jurisdiction for mass atrocity crimes, in the absence of treaty law or an authoritative judicial decision, the basis for a national court to exercise universal jurisdiction may be contested. Hence States should enact legislation unequivocally providing for universal jurisdiction.

It is, therefore, recommended that States should review their laws and policies to ensure arrest, extradition and prosecution of suspected perpetrators of mass atrocities. Through a concerted effort to facilitate the extradition and trial of perpetrators of mass atrocities, the international community can take positive steps towards ending the culture of impunity. There has been a gap in the practice of some States in deporting or denying entry to foreign nationals who are suspected of having committed atrocities, where they have not acted to ensure that these individuals are prosecuted abroad. The European Union has narrowed this gap through decisions establishing a 'European Network of Contact Points' in respect of persons responsible for genocide, crimes against humanity and war crimes, and requiring mutual assistance in the investigation of such crimes. This is a model that can be emulated to ensure that there is no safe haven for perpetrators of violations of human rights and humanitarian norms. This view is supported by Principle 12 of the Princeton Principles on Universal Jurisdiction which urges that in all future treaties, and in protocols to existing treaties, concerned with mass atrocity crimes, states shall include provisions for universal jurisdiction.[117]

4.3   The Potential Role of the African Court of Justice and Human Rights

The African Union (AU) has established the African Court of Justice and Human Rights (ACtJHR or the 'African Court'). An important catalyst for recourse to the African Court is, *inter alia*, Article 28(d) of the ACtJHR Statute which provides that actions may be brought before the Court on the basis of any question of international law. An obvious example would be the interpretation of the often politico-legal penumbra issue of whether or not genocide has been committed in a given situation, as in the Darfur scenario. Further, according to Article 53(1) of the ACtJHR Statute, the African Court may give an advisory opinion on any legal question at the request of any of the organs of the AU or any other body as may be authorized by the AU Assembly.

Although not yet operational, the generous jurisdiction of the African Court provides wide latitude to the African Court to deal with cases of mass atrocity crimes, with the potential to change the behaviour of repressive States and individual perpetrators.[118] The African Court can also provide legal clarity, for instance, on the dilemma in cases of trade-off between peace and justice in post-conflict settings and the often one-sided victor's justice for war crimes. Furthermore, according to Article 31 of the ACtJHR Statute, the African Court is mandated to apply as sources of law any relevant human rights instrument ratified by the State in question, including the general principles of law recognized universally or by African States. In other words, the African Court could become the judicial arm of a panoply of human rights agreements to which AU States are parties, as well as the Geneva Conventions and Additional Protocol thereto and the ICC Statute.[119]

Experience has shown that mass atrocity crimes are committed under the hand of the State or those who wield State-like power.[120] This fact begs the difficult question of who will try the perpetrators of war crimes, genocide or crimes against humanity. Apart from the ICC and *ad hoc* penal institutions, the African Court may also be a possible forum for bringing such cases. Although the African Court cannot actually prosecute perpetrators of human rights violations, its involvement in cases relating to them can serve far-reaching goals. Given the inter-State complaint procedure and the limited NGO access to the African Court, its judgment can put pressure on governments to comply with extraterritorial obligations such as the *aut dedere aut judicare* principle and duty to cooperate with efforts to bring perpetrators of atrocities to justice. The African Court can also establish an authoritative factual record and adjudicate state responsibility for violations of fundamental human rights and IHL, which may provide psychological support to victims. The African Court may provide an opportunity for parties to initiate cases relatively quickly and inexpensively since its work will not require apprehension of offenders.

To this end, the African Court may serve the most useful purpose as an adjunct to other mechanisms of individual accountability. Such legal suits may clarify international obligations concerning arrest, prosecution, extradition, or judicial assistance and encourage recalcitrant States to comply with them. For example, if a State has custody of an 'indictee' and refuses requests for extradition to a competent national or international tribunal, a case may be brought to induce that State to extradite the indictee.[121] By the same token, if a State refuses to investigate abuses or grants an amnesty to perpetrators in violation of its international law obligations to prosecute them, a suit might be brought against that State to restrain it from doing so.

The African Court has potential to be the single most powerful engine for the enforcement of human rights and IHL commitments by AU States and the prevention of mass atrocity crimes against civilians. Given that the 'Single Protocol', which established the African Court, allows African governments and inter-governmental organizations (IGOs) as well as the African Commission to bring cases before the African Court, these institutions should closely coordinate in pursuing delinquent States beyond borders and bring them to justice through the African Court. It is, thus, important that African judicial institutions need to be strengthened, and an emphasis placed on the creation of credible enforcement mechanisms that will back up the judgments of the African Court.[122] Therefore, the stakeholder community, AU States, civil society, the AU, and indeed the international community, should intensify their efforts to urge States to ratify the 'Single Protocol', and AU States should make the declaration allowing for individual petitions.[123]

4.4   The Case for Regional International Humanitarian Law Institutions

The most important means of ensuring compliance with IHL is scrutiny by, and pressure from, third parties. A State engaged in an armed conflict will often be heavily dependent upon the goodwill of neutral States, which may well be put in jeopardy by allegations of atrocities. Such allegations can also have a major effect upon public opinion in the belligerent States themselves. Pressure of this kind operates outside the law itself, since the law makes no express provision for it.[124] It is in such areas where 'pressure operates outside the law' that regional organizations need to intervene to fill the compliance gap. This argument is validated by the fact that the diminishing impact of the 'protecting power' system has shifted the burden to the ICRC to assume the humanitarian functions.[125]

Given the fact that armed conflicts are the major contributors to the suffering of civilians, to protect civilians in armed conflicts, regional organizations may need to establish a committee at a regional level to oversee the compliance with IHL to complement the ICRC – to do at regional level what the ICRC does on the international plane. Such a regional IHL committee should ensure that States in the region should make a declaration pursuant to Article 90 of Additional Protocol I recognizing the competence of the International Fact-finding Commission, and that countries at war declare a state of emergency pursuant to Article 4 of the ICCPR or else there can be no derogations of fundamental human rights. The recommendations of such a committee should be binding on States in the region. The idea of establishing regional IHL committees is not to overlook the important role of the ICRC but rather to complement it, since monitoring the implementation of IHL cannot be the sole role or the exclusive domain of the ICRC.

It is necessary to emphasize reporting and monitoring compliance with IHL and human rights by non-State armed groups. Nonetheless, due to the traditional confidential approach of the ICRC, there may be a need to establish a distinct body providing comments with regard to the IHL and human rights performance of an armed group and publishing the group's allegations about its performance. It is on this basis that a regional organization should consider establishing a legal framework that should include a mechanism for enforcing the compliance of international human rights and humanitarian law by belligerents including armed non-State groups.

In the same vein, there has been no 'treaty body' or committee charged with ensuring the Genocide Convention's implementation and helping to define its content. Schabas states that the Genocide Convention 'most certainly suffered from the absence of a monitoring organ' similar to the other UN treaty bodies. A suggestion that this weakness be corrected was made but has not been taken up. For Schabas, a 'Committee on Genocide' would be 'the logical forum to provoke debate on and ultimately spell out the details of the obligation to prevent genocide'.[126] This is a suggestion that regional organizations can pick up extending the monitoring to extend to war crimes and crimes against humanity. Target States must provide to such an institution timely reports of steps they have taken towards implementing international obligations to prevent mass atrocity crimes. The monitoring body, in turn, should be directed to publish the target State's report as well as its own assessments of the State's efforts.[127] The crucial point would be to provide a mechanism where recommendation of such a committee would be binding on States.

In armed conflicts, redress to the victims is central such that regional organizations may need to develop appeal mechanisms for the redress of victims' grievances and ensure punishment of violators. Enforcement of IHL in non-international armed conflicts is difficult under the current legal regime, such that regional mechanisms may need to formulate a comprehensive legal framework for all armed conflicts without distinction. As initiated by the ICRC, regional organizations may need to harness the customary laws applicable to armed conflicts which should bind both State and non-State armed groups. On their part, States should also develop appeal mechanisms at national and regional levels for the redress of grievances relating to failures to protect civilians in armed conflict. This will help to enhance the protection of civilians in armed conflicts, ensure punishment of violators and lay a solid foundation for containment and prevention of conflict and mass atrocity crimes. To this end, human rights and humanitarian NGOs within the regional framework should encourage and support governments to review all international instruments and agreements relevant to the protection of civilians in armed conflicts and reform national legislation to be in accord with the regional arrangements.

5.   CONCLUSION

In situations of armed conflict, human rights and IHL 'are complementary, not mutually exclusive'.[128] This underscores the significance of a 'humanitarian rights' approach by way of highlighting both human rights and IHL in the general context of protection of civilians in armed conflicts. The protection of civilians in armed conflict touches not only the war-torn countries directly, but the region and the international community at large. At the same time, the responsibility for ensuring civilian protection should be respected by both state and non-state actors. Implementation of human rights and IHL through permanent, preventive, and corrective scrutiny in the field is more appropriate than *a posteriori* prosecution of violators.[129]

Given the limited functions of the present implementation regime of human rights and IHL in armed conflicts, there is need for regional bodies to fill in the gaps. For example, regional organizations should establish a committee within its machinery to oversee the implementation of IHL in their respective regions as complementary to the ICRC. To this end, the UN Special Representative for the Promotion of Protection of Civilians in Armed Conflicts has a monumental task to play in encouraging States to make declarations pursuant to Article 90 of the Additional Protocol I recognizing the competence of the International Fact-finding Commission. The Special Representative should also ensure that countries at war declare a state of emergency pursuant to Article 4 of the ICCPR to prevent derogations of fundamental human rights. More so, there should be no amnesty for mass atrocity crimes against civilians. On their part, States should domesticate the principle of universal jurisdiction in order to offer violators of human rights and IHL no safe haven. The prospect that one may be prosecuted by any State worldwide, in respect of serious human rights and IHL violations may be a serious deterrent to potential perpetrators.[130] States that have not yet ratified the Rome Statute should be encouraged to do so and those that have ratified should not only implement the Rome Statute but also cooperate with the ICC to arrest and prosecute offenders. Needless to say, peacekeepers should not only have a capability to protect but also a coherent strategy to protect civilians in armed conflicts.

While IHL is the *lex specialis* during hostilities, human rights law continues to apply in time of armed conflict, subject only to derogations.[131] The ICCPR requires that even during an armed conflict, measures derogating from the ICCPR are allowed only if, and to the extent that, the situation constitutes a threat to the life of the nation, after a careful analysis of its justification and why such measures are necessary and legitimate in the circumstances.[132] It follows that no measure derogating from the ICCPR should be inconsistent with the State party's obligations under international law, particularly the rules of IHL.[133] Thus, there are situations where some issues may be exclusively matters of IHL, and other situations which are exclusively matters of human rights, and yet other matters which may be matters of both legal regimes. International human rights law and IHL are not mutually exclusive but complementary. The fact that two bodies of law are applicable in an armed conflict situation should not be seen as a dilemma but rather as an opportunity.[134] Those suffering from violations do not distinguish whether those violations are violations of international human rights or international humanitarian law. What they need is protection. Hence, humanitarian rights imply the cross-fertilization of international human rights and humanitarian law to protect civilians in armed conflicts. In this case, a humanitarian approach may help to guide how the constructive complementarity of international human rights and IHL ensures better protection of the rights of civilians.

NOTES

*   Dan Kuwali, Dr. iuris, is Post Doctoral Fellow at the Centre for Human Rights, Faculty of Law, University of Pretoria; Fellow, Harvard Kennedy School of Government's Carr Centre for Human Rights Policy, Harvard University; and Associate Professor, Centre for Security Studies, Mzuzu University, Malawi.

1. C. Greenwood, 'The Law of War (International Humanitarian Law)', in *International Law*, ed. M.D. Evans (Oxford: Oxford University Press, 2003), 817.
2. M. Sassòli, 'The Implementation of International Humanitarian Law: Current and Inherent Challenges', in *Yearbook of International Humanitarian Law* 10 (2007): 46.
3. M. Nowak, *An Introduction to Human Rights Regime* (Leiden: Martinus Nijhoff, 2003), 2.
4. Sassòli, *supra* note 2, at 48.
5. Greenwood, *supra* note 1, at 820.
6. Ibid., 820–821.
7. Ibid., 821.
8. Greenwood, *supra* note 1, at 817.
9. For example, Uganda's Idi Amin and Ethiopia's Mengistu Haile Mariam.
10. Definitions, Updated Principles on Impunity for the protection and promotion of human rights through action to combat impunity, Updated Principles on Impunity, E/CN.4/2005/102/Add.1, 8 February 2005.
11. Principle 18 of the Updated Principles on Impunity, ibid.
12. M.O. Scharf, 'Trading Justice for Peace: The Contemporary Law and Policy Debate', in *Atrocities and International Accountability – Beyond Transitional Justice*, ed. E. Hughes et al. (Tokyo: United Nations University Press, 2007), 248.
13. Ibid., 252.
14. P. Akhavan, 'Beyond Impunity: Can International Criminal Justice Prevent Future Atrocities?', *American Journal of International Law* 95 (7) (2001): 28.
15. M.C. Bassiouni, 'Searching for Peace and Achieving Justice. The Need for Accountability', *Law and Contemporary Problems* 59 (9) (1996): 19 (Bassiouni, 1996b).
16. T. Meron, 'Human Rights Law Marches into New Territory: The Enforcement of International Human Rights in International Criminal Tribunals', in *The Making of International Criminal Justice*, (Oxford: Oxford University Press, 2011): 181.
17. Ibid., 3.
18. See *Prosecutor v. Ćelebici*, ICTY, Appeal Chamber, Judgment, 20 February 2001 (Case No. IT 96-21-A), para. 143; see also Meron, *supra* note 16, at 33.
19. Meron, *supra* note 16, at 3.
20. *Legality of the Threat or Use of Nuclear Weapons*, Advisory Opinion, I.C.J. Reports 1996, (i), para. 24.
21. But see United Nations, A/RES/2444 (XXIII), 19 December 1968, Respect for human rights in armed conflicts; A/RES/2675 (XXV), 9 December 1970; S/RES/794, 3 December 1992; S/RES/993, 12 May 1995; S/RES/1564, 18 September 2004; S/RES/1574, 19 November 2004; S/RES/1593, 31 March 2005; Commission on Human Rights, Report of the United Nations High Commissioner for Human Rights and Follow-Up to the World Conference on Human Rights, Situation of Human Rights in the Darfur Region of the Sudan, E/CN.4/2005/3, 7 May 2004; General Comment No. 31: *Nature of the General Legal Obligation Imposed on States Parties to the Covenant*, HRC, 26 May 2004 (UN Doc. CCPR/C/21/Rev.1/Add.13).
22. The International Law Commission decided at its first meeting in 1949 not to include the law of war on its agenda.
23. G. Melander, *The Relationship between Human Rights, Humanitarian Law and Refugee Law* (Lund: Raoul Wallenberg Institute [Undated]), 33.
24. M. O'Flaherty, 'Human Rights Monitoring and Armed Conflict: Challenges for the UN', *Disarmament Forum* (2004): 51.
25. See the Preamble to the 1977 Protocol Additional to the Geneva Conventions of 12 August 1949 Relating to the Protection of Victims of International Armed Conflicts (hereafter Additional Protocol I); see also M. Veuthey, 'International Humanitarian Law and the Restoration and Maintenance of Peace', available at: http://www.iss.co.za/Pubs/ASR/7No5/InternationalHumanitarian.html (accessed 15 February 2003).
26. *Legal Consequences of the Construction of a Wall in the Occupied Palestinian Territory*, Advisory Opinion, I.C.J. Reports 2004, General List No. 131, paras 107–112.
27. General Comment No. 31: *The Nature of the General Legal Obligation on the States Parties to the International Covenant on Civil and Political Rights*, HRC, 26 May 2004 (UN Doc. CCPR/C/21/Rev.1/Add.13), para. 11.
28. Report of the Panel on the United Nations Peace Operations, *Brahimi Report*, United Nations, 21 August 2000 (UN Doc. A/55/305S/2000/809).

29. H. Krieger, 'A Conflict of Norms: The Relationship between Humanitarian Law and Human Rights Law in the ICRC Customary Law Study', *Journal of Conflict and Security* 11(2) (2006): 266–267; see also Article 15(2) of the European Convention for the Protection of Human Rights and Fundamental Freedoms, Strasbourg, 1950.

30. *Brahimi Report, supra* note 28.

31. Resolution 9/9, *Protection of the Human Rights of Civilians in Armed Conflicts*, Human Rights Council, in UN Doc. A/HRC/9/28, 2 December 2008, fifth recital.

32. Meron, *supra* note 16, at 2.

33. Human Rights Council Resolution 9/9, *supra* note 31, eighth recital.

34. O' Flaherty, *supra* note 24, at 50.

35. Ibid., 4.

36. United Nations, Report of the Office of the High Commissioner on the outcome of the expert consultation on the issue of protecting the human rights of civilians in armed conflict, para. 7, 3 (Report of the UN High Commissioner for Human Rights).

37. Ibid., para. 7, 4; see also Human Rights Council, Resolution 9/9, *supra* note 31, ninth recital.

38. Human Rights Council Resolution 9/9, *supra* note 31, tenth recital.

39. Ibid., para. 14, 5.

40. F. Hampson, 'The Relationship Between International Humanitarian Law and Human Rights Law from the Perspective of a Human Rights Treaty Body', *International Review of the Red Cross*, Vol. 90 (871) (2008): 570.

41. Ibid., 549–572.

42. Ibid., 566; see, for example, *Isayeva and others v. Russia*, ECtHR, Application No. 57947-9/100, Judgment of 24 February 2005.

43. Hampson, *supra* note 40, 556.

44. Ibid., 561.

45. For a detailed analysis, see Hampson, *supra* note 40.

46. International Committee of the Red Cross, *Strengthening Protection in War* (Geneva: International Committee of the Red Cross, 2001).

47. Ibid.

48. United Nations, Memorandum of Understanding between the Office of the High Commissioner for Human Rights (OHCHR) and the UN Department of Peacekeeping Operations (DPKO), Geneva, 2002.

49. M. Sassòli, 'Possible Legal Mechanisms to Improve Compliance by Armed Groups with International Humanitarian Law and International Human Rights Law', Centre of International Relations, Liu Institute for Global Issues, University of British Columbia, Vancouver, 14–15 November 2003: 15–17.

50. Bassiouni, *supra* note 15, at 12.

51. Ibid.

52. Ibid.

53. F.A. Nielssen, *From Peace to Justice* (The Hague: Hague Academic Press, 2004), 5.

54. Quoted in Amnesty International, 'Nigeria: No Impunity for Charles Taylor', AI Index: AFR 44/024/2003.

55. A. Aderinwale, 'The Conference on Security, Stability, Development and Cooperation in Africa: Framework and the Role of the Regional', in *Peace, Human Security and Conflict Prevention in Africa, Proceedings of the UNESCO-ISS Expert Meeting, Pretoria, South Africa, 23–24 July 2001* (available at: http://www.iss.co.za/Pubs/Books/Unesco/Aderinwale.html (accessed 2 May 2008), 67.

56. N. Grono, 'The Role of Deterrence and Accountability in the Darfur and Northern Uganda Peace Process', lecture, TMC Asser Institute, 12 March 2008.

57. Ibid., 2.

58. Ibid., 6.

59. Ibid.

60. S. Landsman, 'Alternative Responses to Serious Human Rights Abuses: Of Prosecution and Truth Commissions', *Law and Contemporary Problems* 59(9) (1996): 86.

61. Ibid.

62. N. Grono and A. O'Brien, 'Exorcising the Ghost of the ICC', *The Monitor*, 31 October 2006; N. Boustany, 'For Ugandan Rebel, a Question of Justice', *The Washington Post*, 12 July 2007.

63. M.C. Bassiouni, 'Introduction, A Review of Accountability Mechanisms for Mass Violations of Human Rights', *Law and Contemporary Problems* 59 (4) (1996): 5 (Bassiouni 1996a).

64. A.R. Lamin, 'Truth, Justice and Reconciliation: Analysis of the Prospects and Challenges of the Truth and Reconciliation Commission in Liberia', in *A Tortuous Road to Peace*, eds F.B. Aboagye and A.M.S. Bah (Pretoria: The African Book Publishing Record, 2005), 243.

65. T.L. Putnam, 'Human Rights and Sustainable Peace', in *Ending Civil Wars: The Implementation of Peace Agreements*, eds S.J. Stedman et al. (London, Boulder: Lynne Rienner Publishers, 2002), 239–241.

66. Lamin, *supra* note 64, at 229–247.

67. Putnam, *supra* note 65, at 251–252.

68. Ibid., 249, 250–251; S.R. Ratner and J.S. Abrams, *Accountability for Human Rights Atrocities in International Law – Beyond the Nuremberg Legacy*, 2nd edition (Oxford: Oxford University Press, 2001), 155.

69. Landsman, *supra* note 60, at 83.

70. M.W. Reisman, 'Legal Responses to Genocide and Other Massive Violations of Human Rights', *Law and Contemporary Problems* 59(9) (1996): 76.

71. Landsman, *supra* note 60, at 85.

72. Reisman, *supra* note 70, at 77.

73. Ratner and Abrams, *supra* note 68, at 151–159.

74. W.A. Schabas and R. Thakur, in *Atrocities and International Accountability – Beyond Transitional Justice*, eds E. Hughes, W.A. Schabas and R. Thakur (Tokyo: United Nations University Press, 2007), 277.

75. Article 6(5) of the 1977 Additional Protocol II to the Geneva Conventions provides that '[a]t the end of hostilities, the authorities in power shall endeavour to grant the broadest possible amnesty to persons who have participated in the armed conflict, or those deprived of their liberty for reasons related to the armed conflict, whether they are interned or detained'; see C. Pilloud et al., *Commentary on the Additional Protocols of 8 June 1977 to the Geneva Conventions of 12 August 1949* (Geneva: International Committee of the Red Cross, 1987), 1402.

76. Report of the UN Secretary-General on the establishment of a Special Court for Sierra Leone: UN Doc. S/2000/915, 4 October 2000, para. 22.

77. Report of the UN Secretary-General on the Rule of Law and Transitional Justice in Conflict and Post-conflict Societies, UN Doc. S/2004/616, 3 August 2004.

78. *Prosecutor v. Kallon and Kamara* 1, 75. Case No. SCSL-2004-15-AR72 (E), SCSL-2004-16-AR72 (E), para. 7(13).

79. *Furundžija* case, ICTY, Trial Chamber, Judgment, 10 December 1998 (Case No. IT-95-17/1-T), para. 155.

80. *Barrios Altos v. Peru*, IACtHR, Merits, Judgment of 14 March 2001, paras. 39–41.

81. Principle 24 of the Updated Principles on Impunity, *supra* note 10.

82. The Non-Applicability of Statutory Limitations to War Crimes and Crimes against Humanity, United Nations, UN Treaty Series, Vol. 754: 73.

83. Bassiouni (1996a), *supra* note 63, at 16.

84. See *Principle 4 of the Princeton Principles on Universal Jurisdiction*; see *Princeton Principles on Universal Jurisdiction* (Princeton University Press, 2001) ('Princeton Principles'), available at: http://lapa.princeton.edu/hosteddocs/unive_jur.pdf

85. M. Banda, *The Responsibility to Protect: Moving the Agenda Forward* (Ottawa: United Nations Association in Canada, 2007), 38.

86. A/RES/2840 (XXVI), 18 December 1971.

87. M.C. Bassiouni, *Crimes against Humanity in International Law* (Dordrecht: Martinus Nijhoff, 1992), 499–527; see also M.C. Bassiouni, 'Searching for Peace and Achieving Justice: The Need for Accountability', *Law and Contemporary Problems* 59 (4) (1996): 16, footnote 30.

88. A/RES/3074 (XXVIII), 3 December 1973.

89. Article 25 of the UN Charter states that the UN Member States 'agree to accept and carry out the decisions of the Security Council in accordance with' the Charter; United Nations, S/RES/216, 12 November 1965.

90. M.H. Morris, 'International Guidelines against Impunity: Facilitating Accountability', *Law and Contemporary Problems* 59 (4) (1996): 35.

91. See H. Krieger, 'A Conflict of Norms: The Relationship between Humanitarian Law and Human Rights Law in the ICRC Customary Law Study', *Journal of Conflict and Security* 11(2) (2006): 266–267.

92. Organization of American States, The XXVI OAS General Assembly Resolution AG/RES. 2176 (XXXVI-O/06) on the Promotion of the International Criminal Court.

93. See General obligations of States to take effective action to combat impunity, Principle 1 of the Updated Principles on Impunity, *supra* note 10.

94. O'Flaherty, *supra* note 24, at 50.

95. Missions with explicit protection mandates include MONUC (S/RES/1291, 24 February 2000 and S/RES/1493, 28 July 2003) and Sierra Leone (S/RES/1270, 22 October 1999); and an example of a mission with implicit mandate is International Assistance Force (ISAF).

96. V.K. Holt, 'The Responsibility to Protect: Considering the Operational Capacity for Civilian Protection', Discussion Paper, Washington DC: The Henry L. Stimson Center, January 2005, 5.

97. C. Hinote, 'Campaigning to Protect: Using Military Force to Stop Genocide and Mass Atrocities', Paper presented at the Carr Center for Human Rights Policy, Cambridge, Massachusetts, 15 May 2008; C. Gompert, 'For a Capability to Protect: Mass Killing, the African Union and the NATO', *Survival* 48(1) (2006): 8.

98. See Organization for Security and Co-operation in Europe, Charter for European Security, Istanbul, 1999, available at: www.fas.org/nuke/control/osce/text/charter_for_european_security.htm (accessed 7 March 2007); the ECOWAS Moratorium on the Import, Export and Manufacture of Light Weapons in West Africa, 31 October 1998, available at: http://www.fas.org/nuke/control/pcased/text/ ecowas.htm (accessed 8 October 2012); The Southern Africa Development Community (SADC) Protocol on Firearms, Ammunition and Other Related Materials, available at: http://www.sadc.int/ english/key-documents/protocols/protocol-on-control-of-firearms/ (accessed 8 October 2012); the Bamako Declaration on an African Common Position on the Illicit Proliferation, Circulation and Trafficking of Small Arms and Light Weapons, available at: http://www.armsnetafrica.org/ content/bamako-declaration-african-common-position-illicit-proliferation-circulation-and-trafficking (accessed 8 October 2012); see United Nations, The World Summit Outcome, UN Doc. A/60/L.1 (15 September 2005), paras 92–96.

99. K. Kemileva et al., 'Expertise in the Human Rights Council: a policy paper prepared under the auspices of the Geneva Academy of International Humanitarian Law and Human Rights', Geneva, June 2010, 5, available at: http://www.adh-geneva.ch/docs/expertise.pdf (accessed 12 February 2012).

100. M. Lempinen and M. Scheinin, *The New Human Rights Council: The First Two Years* (Åbo: Åbo Akademi University, Institute for Human Rights, 2007), 5.

101. Ibid., 5.

102. Ibid.

103. Ibid.

104. See, for example, *Abella v. Argentina*, IACommHR, Case 11.137, Report No. 55/97, 18 November 1997; *Bámaca Velásquez* Case, IACtHR, Judgment of 25 November 2000.

105. Hampson, *supra* note 40, at 559.

106. See, for example, Report of the Office of the High Commissioner, *supra* note 36, at 14.

107. Lempinen and Scheinin, *supra* note 100, at 5.

108. Lempinen and Scheinin, *supra* note 100, at 29.

109. Four Geneva Conventions: articles 49(2) GCI; 50(2) GCII; 129(2) GCIII; 146(2) GCIV.

110. See Greenwood, *supra* note 1, at 817.

111. Africa Legal Aid, *Cairo-Arusha Principles on Universal Jurisdiction in Respect of Gross Human Rights Offences: An African Perspective*, 20 October 2002, Principle 6.

112. Ibid., Principle 3.

113. Principle 11 of the Princeton Principles on Universal Jurisdiction, *supra* note 84.

114. L.S. Sunga, *International Responsibility in International Law for Serious Human Rights Violations* (Dordrecht: Martinus Nijhoff, 1992), 114.

115. C.C. Joyner, 'Arresting Impunity: The Case for Universal Jurisdiction in Bringing War Criminals to Accountability', *Accountability for International Crimes and Serious Violations of Fundamental Human Rights* 59(4) (1996): 169.

116. Akhavan, *supra* note 14, at 22.

117. Principle 12 of the Princeton Principles on Universal Jurisdiction, *supra* note 84.

118. A. de Hoogh, *Obligations Erga Omnes and International Crimes: A Theoretical Inquiry into the Implementation and Enforcement of the International Responsibility of States* (The Hague: Kluwer Law International, 1996), 404.

119. Project on International Courts and Tribunals, African Court of Human and Peoples' Rights, available at: http://www.pict-pcti.org/courts/ACHPR.html (accessed 12 July 2009).

120. W.A. Schabas, *Genocide Convention at Fifty*, Special Report (Washington DC: United States Institute of Peace, 1999), 4.
121. Ratner and Abrams, *supra* note 68, at 225–227.
122. D. Mepham and S. Ramsbotham, *Safeguarding Civilians: Delivering on the Responsibility to Protect in Africa* (London: Institute of Policy Research, 2007), 33.
123. According to Article 30(f) of the ACtJHR Statute, individuals and NGOs accredited to the AU or to its organs can only submit cases against States if the State concerned has made a declaration accepting the competence of the African Court to do so under Article 8 of the 'Single Protocol'. Article 8 of the 'Single Protocol' as read with Article 30(f) of the ACtJHR Statute provides for an Additional Declaration to be signed by a State Party upon ratification of the 'Single Protocol', accepting the competence of the African Court to hear cases from NGOs and individuals.
124. Greenwood, *supra* note 1, at 820.
125. Ibid., at 820–821.
126. The suggestion was made by the UN Sub-Commission on the Prevention of Discrimination and the Protection of Minorities; Schabas, *supra* note 120, at 7.
127. 'Fundamental Standards of Humanity', Report of the UN Secretary-General submitted pursuant to Commission on Human Rights Decision 2001/112, E/CN.4/2002/103, paras 26–30.
128. General Comment No. 31: *The Nature of the General Legal Obligation on the States Parties to the International Covenant on Civil and Political Rights*, HRC, 26 May 2004 (UN Doc. CCPR/C/21/Rev.1/Add.13), para. 11.
129. Sassòli, *supra* note 49, at 15–17.
130. Greenwood, *supra* note 1, at 821.
131. *Nuclear Weapons* Advisory Opinion, *supra* note 20, at para. 25; *Israel Wall* Advisory Opinion, *supra* note 26, at para. 106.
132. Report of the UN High Commissioner for Human Rights, *supra* note 36, at para. 27, 8.
133. Ibid., para. 27, 8.
134. Ibid., para. 17, 5.

18. Human rights law and international humanitarian law as limits for Security Council action

*Michael Bothe**

1. THE PROBLEM: THE DEVELOPMENT OF ACTIVITIES OF THE UNITED NATIONS BEYOND THE IMAGINATION OF THE AUTHORS

The activities of the Security Council in the maintaining or restoring of international peace and security have expanded enormously since the end of the Cold War.[1] The breakthrough for Security Council action was the Kuwait crisis – the invasion of Kuwait by Iraq, and the ensuing successful military action to repel it. On this occasion, the Security Council showed considerable creativity in designing measures to cope with the situation, and not all of them corresponded exactly to what could be anticipated by just reading the relevant texts of the UN Charter.[2] This fact and further developments have fomented a debate which existed already during earlier decades, namely a discourse on the legal basis of the powers of the Security Council and their limitations. The question whether and to what extent the norms of international human rights law and international humanitarian law limit the freedom of action, or the creativity of the Security Council in designing action, is a major part of that debate. The political developments and the ensuing legal debate highlight legal uncertainties. Organs of the United Nations exercise public authority in relation to individuals – which raises the question whether they have to apply human rights in doing so, and whether human rights, thus, limit the freedom of action of UN organs, including the Security Council. Armed forces of the United Nations are involved in military hostilities – which raises the question whether the rules of international law relating to such hostilities if conducted by States apply as well to the military operations conducted by the UN. The United Nations are brought into factual situations which were not foreseen by the drafters of the Charter, or were at least not clear in their minds. Whether or not the exercise of public authority by the UN, or the UN becoming a party to an armed conflict, could have been foreseen, it was at least beyond the scope of the imagination of the drafters.

As to the first problem – the application of human rights by the United Nations – there is at least one precedent for the League of Nations exercising public authority in relation to individuals, namely the administration of the Saar. But apparently, no need was felt in 1945 to spell out the law applicable in such a situation. The administration of the Saar had worked smoothly. As to the application of international human rights law, it must however be remembered that this area of international law was only *in statu nascendi* at the time the Charter was negotiated.

As to the application of international humanitarian law, one could have thought that the establishment of a system of military enforcement measures would trigger at least some debate concerning the law applicable to such operations. But the very concept of these operations is not clearly regulated.[3] Sometimes it appears that the troupes engaged in such operations would remain organs of the States placing them at the disposal of the Security Council, sometimes it would seem that they are organs of the United Nations.[4] Both options were used in later practice.

Both questions are different, but on the other hand they belong together in a special way. The question of whether the United Nations are bound by human rights is part of a mega-problem of the current shape of the international order, namely the rules governing the exercise of public power by international institutions, which has become a characteristic aspect of that order.[5] The norms governing the exercise of public power by States are contained in their constitutional and administrative law. Is there a similar body of law for international institutions, in particular the United Nations?

The question of the application of international humanitarian law is of a different nature.[6] That law applies in the relationship between parties to an armed conflict, which is a relationship of legal equality, at least in principle, that is to say the contrary of the exercise of a legally constituted authority. Yet within the body of international humanitarian law, there are many rules for situations where a party exercises some kind of power over protected persons – which is a typical situation for the application of human rights. For this reason, there is, in situations of armed conflict, a parallel application of human rights law and international humanitarian law.[7] To that extent, the questions whether the United Nations are bound by either body of international law belong together.

In regard to both questions, different perspectives have to be distinguished. There are, first, the legal obligations of the United Nations which an organ of the Organization has to respect, and second, the possible powers of the Security Council to set aside or to modify these obligations. This is a problem of the interpretation of the United Nations Charter and of the interplay between the law of the Charter and general international law. But the more extensive the exercise of powers by the UN becomes, the more there is a political problem of the justification or legitimacy of such action. This is a matter of successful policy, or, in its scientific aspect, of political theory.

2. THE BASIS OF ATTRIBUTION OF SECURITY COUNCIL POWERS

If the Security Council were bound by human rights law and international humanitarian law, this would indeed mean a limitation of its powers. Thus, the *fons et origo* of these powers has to be considered. The UN Charter, this is the basic point of departure, establishes a system of 'enumerated powers' in the sense the term is used in constitutional law. The organs of the United Nations have only those powers which are granted to them by the Charter.[8] These powers are defined in a very general way, yet they are not unlimited.[9]

Since the Advisory Opinion '*Reparation for Injuries*',[10] the ICJ has recognized that these powers have to be interpreted in the sense that they include implied powers, that is, powers that are not expressly mentioned, but are granted by necessary implication for the effective performance of the powers expressly granted.

According to the same logic, there exist implied limitations of these powers. These implied limitations derive from a systematic interpretation of the Charter. The Charter is to be interpreted as a whole. This means in particular that the goals of the Organization, which are formulated in the Preamble, in Art. 1 and in a number of other provisions dealing with specific activities of the Organization, have to be taken into account. The powers of UN organs, including the Security Council, cannot be understood as permitting the violation of principles the protection of which is the very purpose of the UN.

This line of reasoning adopted by the Court clearly indicates that the Security Council is bound at least by the principles of human rights law.

The most fundamental formulation of the UN's adherence to human rights is the 2nd paragraph of the Preamble which expresses the determination of the United Nations 'to reaffirm faith in fundamental human rights, the dignity and worth of the human person, in the equal rights of men and women …'.

As to the operational parts of the Charter, both Art. 1 (3) and Art. 55 (c) stipulate a duty of the Organization to further human rights. The UN shall promote 'universal respect for, and observance of, human rights and fundamental freedoms for all without distinction as to race, sex, language, or religion'. Although the drafters of the Charter may not have foreseen that the UN would itself be in a factual position to violate such rights in the relationship between the Organization and an individual, it would be illogical if the UN were entitled not to respect those rights the observance of which it is obligated to promote.

Thus, as a first step in the argument, one can conclude that there is an implied limitation of the powers of the Security Council requiring that the Council, in the exercise of its functions, respects fundamental human rights.

As to the second part of the question, international humanitarian law, one must recall that it has an important human rights aspect. To that extent at least, one must conclude that the Security Council must respect international humanitarian law at least as it contains human rights principles. This is in particular the case for all those provisions which protect persons in the power of a party to the conflict, such as detainees, nationals of a party to the conflict in the territory of the other party, and the population of occupied territory. In relation to other parts of international humanitarian law, in particular the rules on the conduct of hostilities, a similar line of argument has also been used: the rules on the conduct of hostilities, too, enshrine fundamental principles of humanity which the Organization is bound to protect.[11] Yet more generally, one must ask whether and to what extent the United Nations are bound by customary international law, including international humanitarian law.

3. THE UNITED NATIONS AND CUSTOMARY INTERNATIONAL LAW

3.1   General Considerations

In order to ascertain whether and to what extent the United Nations and in particular the Security Council are bound by customary law, one has to turn once more to the Advisory Opinion *'Reparation for Injuries Suffered in the Service of the United Nations'*. The question to be answered by the Court was this:

> [H]as the United Nations, as an Organization, the capacity to bring an international claim against the responsible *de jure* or *de facto* government with a view to obtaining the reparation due in respect of the damage caused (*a*) to the United Nations, (*b*) to the victim and to persons entitled through him?[12]

In other words, the General Assembly asked whether the rules of customary international law applicable to States in a comparable situation applied to the United Nations as well, and with what modifications, if any. In its preliminary observations the Court indeed refers to the rules on State responsibility.[13] The Court then asks whether the Organization possesses a competence which a State possesses where the responsibility of another State is at stake, namely the capacity to bring a claim: 'Competence to bring an international claim is, for those possessing it, the capacity to resort to the customary methods recognized by international law for the establishment, the presentation and the settlement of claims ... This capacity certainly belongs to the State ... '.

But does it also belong to the Organization? The affirmative answer to this question is based on the argument that the parties to the Charter must have endowed the Organization with those capacities which are necessary to enable it to perform its functions:

> Accordingly, the Court has come to the conclusion that the Organization is an international person. That is not the same thing as saying that it is a State ... What it does mean is that it is a subject of international law and capable of possessing international rights and duties, and that it has capacity to maintain its rights by bringing international claims.[14]

A first lesson has to be drawn from the last phrase: the reasoning of the Court does not only relate to rights of the Organization, but also to duties. These duties of the Organization mean limitations of the freedom of action of the Organization.

What are these rights and duties? According to the Court, they are derived from customary international law, but are not necessarily identical with the rights and duties of States:

> Whereas a State possesses the totality of international rights and duties recognized by international law [an expression which must be understood as to the totality of rights and duties under *customary* international law], the rights and duties of an entity such as the Organization must depend upon its purposes and functions as specified or implied in its constituent documents and developed in practice.[15]

The question of whether the United Nations has the rights and duties recognized by customary international humanitarian law has thus to be answered by a conditional phrase: yes, if and to the extent that this is necessary for the performance of the functions entrusted to the Organization by the Charter. If that condition is fulfilled, the duties of the Organization under international humanitarian law would have to be respected by all its organs, including the Security Council.

It does not follow from this reasoning that the customary law rights and duties of States and of international organizations must be exactly the same. Quite to the contrary, the reference to the functions entrusted to the organization as the basis for applying international customary law to it may imply some adaptation of the rule which applies to States. This is what the ICJ has recognized in the *Reparation for injuries* opinion: it substituted the functional protection which the Organization exercises in favour of its agents for the traditional diplomatic protection exercised by States.

Nevertheless, the essential point of departure for the application of customary international law is the meaning of that law as it applies to States. That kind of transfer of applicable rules from States to organizations corresponds to a fundamental method of legal reasoning: where the lawyer encounters a new problem (e.g. the rule of behaviour of international organizations), he or she will seek advice from rules which are traditionally applied in a similar situation and will then decide whether this similarity justifies the application of the rule (by analogy) to the new problem, *mutatis mutandis* as the case may be. This is essentially what the Court did in the *Reparation for injuries* opinion.

In addressing this problem, the particular characteristics of the area of law in question must also be considered. In this connection, a trend must be noted that international humanitarian law as a whole applies to all kinds of armed conflicts between entities having a status under international law, not only to armed conflicts to which States are parties.[16]

But before addressing the problem as to what these considerations have meant and may mean in practice in relation to human rights and international humanitarian law, two preliminary questions have to be answered: First, are the above considerations also valid for the Security Council in the light of its central position in the system of the Charter? And secondly, could the Security Council set aside these customary law obligations by way of a decision which is binding pursuant to Art. 25 UN Charter?

3.2 Discretionary Powers of the Security Council?

The Security Council certainly is a 'political' organ. This means, in practice and in theory, that its activities are rather prompted by political considerations, not by legal ones. But this does not mean that the Council is not bound by international law, that it is not limited by the rule of enumerated powers. The powers may be defined broadly, the Charter may grant the Security Council a very broad discretion, but they are still powers based on, and limited by, the Charter of the United Nations and those rules of international law which bind the United Nations.[17] This principle is expressed by Art. 24 of the Charter.

This principle has been formulated very clearly by the Appeals Chamber of the ICTY in the *Tadić* case:[18]

It is clear from [the text of Art. 39] that the Security Council plays a pivotal role and exercises a very wide discretion under this Article. But this does not mean that its powers are unlimited. The Security Council is an organ of an international organization, established by a treaty which serves as a constitutional framework for that organization. The Security Council is thus subjected to certain constitutional limitations, however broad its powers under the constitution may be. ... [N]either the text nor the spirit of the Charter conceives of the Security Council as *legibus solutus* (unbound by law).

The specific impact of this rule on Security Council activities for the maintenance of international peace and security under Ch. VII is as follows. First, there is a basic condition for the exercise of these powers, namely that there is a situation as described in Art. 39, that is, a 'threat to the peace, breach of the peace, or act of aggression'. As the Security Council 'shall determine the existence of' such a situation, the question arises whether the Security Council may only make this determination where such a situation objectively exists as a matter of law or whether the Council has a discretion or margin of appreciation in making this determination. This is controversial.[19] The Council has shown, to say the least, a great degree of creativity in interpreting Art. 39. For the purpose of the present study, this question is only of indirect relevance, as will be shown.[20]

Once the Security Council has determined that there is a situation as defined in Art. 39, four types of measures may be taken by the Council:

- recommendations;
- provisional measures (Art. 40);
- enforcement measures not involving the use of military force;
- enforcement measures involving the use of military force.

The Council has a discretion whether to take any measure at all (subject to a responsibility to protect),[21] and as to the type of measure it wants to take as well as to the content and shape of the measure. But as to the last mentioned discretion, it is at least limited[22] by two considerations: It must be a measure for the purpose of maintaining or restoring peace and security (which does not mean that it must effectively achieve that purpose),[23] and it must respect any other rule binding the United Nations, subject, however, to the power of the Council to change the applicable rules by a binding decision.

Another legal construction which gives a certain freedom to the Security Council in designing its activities is what in other contexts is called 'margin of appreciation'.[24] It relates to indeterminate legal concepts, giving the body or institution enjoying such a margin the freedom to evaluate facts in relation to the applicable norm. A court would not substitute its own judgement for that of the other decision-making body. That construction is, thus, a question of the relationship between a decision-making and a reviewing body, in constitutional terms a question of separation of powers. Notions like 'necessity' and 'proportionality' lend themselves to such construction.

As a matter of principle, this is a sound construction, but the question has to be asked how far it goes. If it is construed in the sense of an 'authoritative concret-ization'[25] of its powers by the Security Council which puts its decisions beyond any legal challenge, it would go too far.[26] The borderline, however, is difficult to draw.

3.3 Customary Law Versus Article 25 of the United Nations' Charter

The power of the Security Council to take decisions binding the member States mainly relates to measures taken under Ch. VII, that is measures taken for the maintenance or restoration of international peace and security. It lies in the very nature of those measures that they restrict the freedom of action States would otherwise possess under customary international law. Therefore, rules of international customary law do not necessarily bar Security Council action.[27] The essential limitation of the powers of the Security Council is derived from the principle of attribution:[28] a decision which is not justified by the purpose of maintaining peace and security would be *ultra vires*, and thus, as a matter of principle, not binding. This entails, however, a difficult problem, namely whether and under what conditions States may pass a judgement on the legality or otherwise of a Security Council decision and may refuse to respect a decision if they consider it to be *ultra vires*.[29]

The question of whether the Security Council could set aside international humanitarian law or human rights law can only be answered in the affirmative if such action were a valid contribution to the maintenance of international peace and security. This is barely conceivable, but not impossible.

There is yet another fundamental limitation to the power of the Security Council to take a binding decision, namely the respect of *ius cogens*.[30] It lies in the very nature of *ius cogens* that it can only be changed by a norm having the same character (Art. 53 VCLoT), which excludes a modification by any other actor.[31] This also bars any modification by the Security Council. This shields the core of human rights law and of international humanitarian law against any infringement by the Security Council.

3.4 Control of the Legality of Security Council Action

The somewhat uncertain limits of Security Council powers which have been explained entail the problem of the final arbiter of the issue of legality, or rather of the lack thereof. The procedural variety of the doctrine of self-concretization[32] means that it is the Council itself which is the final judge of its powers. The question was addressed in a somewhat controversial way by the ICJ in the *Certain Expenses* case. The Court said that each organ must, 'in the first place at least', determine its own jurisdiction.[33] The addition of the words 'in the first place' indicates that this determination is not final. It can be challenged.

On the other hand, the judicial review of Security Council action is underdeveloped.[34] The ICJ is not a kind of constitutional court empowered to control the legality of other UN organs. That question may, however, arise as an incidental question in court proceeding at the national or regional level[35] or even before the ICJ, as it did in the *Lockerbie* case.[36] In that case, the Court did not say that it was bound to respect the determination made by the Council, it only accepted that determination on a *prima facie* basis for the purpose of the indication of provisional measures. A clear and explicit example of incidental control is the decision of the Appeals Chamber of the ICTY in the *Tadić* case,[37] which, in contradistinction to the Trial Chamber, held that it was entitled to review the constitutionality of the Security Council decision to establish the Tribunal.

The relative weakness of judicial control must not be misunderstood as a proof of a lack of legal obligations. There is a legal discourse around the activities of UN organs which is clearly based on the assumption that they are indeed subject to legal obligations.

4.   THE DEBATE ABOUT THE APPLICATION OF INTERNATIONAL HUMANITARIAN LAW

On the basis of the aforementioned considerations, we can address the question of whether the United Nations, by implication, has rights and duties under international humanitarian law, and duties under international human rights law. What is relevant in this respect is not only the interpretation of the Charter, but also, as the ICJ put it, the development of UN practice. First, the development of the practice relating to international humanitarian law will be considered, as this practice is older than the one concerning human rights.

The question of whether the UN was bound by international humanitarian law came up soon after armed forces which were organs of the UN were established, even before they became involved in armed hostilities. At the centre of this debate was an exchange of views between the ICRC and the United Nations,[38] which, however, somewhat distorted the fundamental issues as it only related to the respect of the Geneva Conventions to which the United Nations obviously are not a party and by which they therefore cannot be bound as a matter of treaty law.[39] Since the establishment of the first UN peacekeeping force, UNEF I in 1956, the ICRC emphasized the need that these forces comply with the Geneva Conventions.[40] The United Nations reacted with a compromise formula which is contained in the internal Regulations for UNEF I,[41] and later in those for ONUC[42] and UNFICYP:[43] 'The Force shall observe and respect the principles and spirit of the general international Conventions applicable to the conduct of military personnel.'

This provision is referred to in the Agreement between the United Nations and participating States and explained as follows:

> 11. The international Conventions referred to in these Regulations include, *inter alia*, the Geneva (Red Cross) Conventions of 12 August 1949 to which your Government is a party and the UNESCO Convention on the Protection of Cultural Property in the Event of Armed Conflict, signed at The Hague on 14 May 1954. In this connection, and particularly with respect to the humanitarian provisions of these Conventions, it is requested that the Governments of the participating States ensure that the members of their contingents serving with the Force be fully acquainted with the obligations arising under these Conventions and that appropriate steps be taken to ensure their enforcement.[44]

These texts clearly suggest that the obligations to respect the norms in question are obligations of the United Nations, not of the contributing States. Otherwise, it could not be explained that the text does not differentiate between parties and non-parties to the Conventions, which is a practical problem regarding the Cultural Property Convention, to which not all contributing States were parties.[45] Consequently, the obligations envisaged by these texts must be obligations under customary law. Then, what is meant by 'spirit and principles' must be the customary law element contained in those Conventions. So far, this is a matter of legal logic. But the texts do not answer the question whether this customary law of armed conflict applicable to the United Nations is the same as that applicable to States in a similar situation. That question is left open, and it remained open for a considerable period.

When the ICRC approached the UN during the Congo crisis concerning the application of the Geneva Conventions, the Secretary-General used the same 'spirit and principles' formula.[46]

Some voices in the doctrinal debate held that the law of armed conflict could not apply to UN Forces because they were 'soldiers without enemies'.[47] This is simply an illusion. From time to time, UN peacekeepers indeed have enemies and they have to fight them like any army fights an enemy army.[48] The thesis is also wrong because it confuses two questions which have to be distinguished: namely first, whether the United Nations are generally capable of being a subject of the law of armed conflict; and second, whether there is a situation where the law of armed conflict applies, or rather, where it would apply if armed forces of States were in the same situation in which the peacekeepers find themselves.

All these questions were finally clarified by two interrelated instruments, namely by the Convention on the Safety of United Nations and Associated Personnel,[49] on the one hand, and the Secretary-General's 'Bulletin' on 'Observance by United Nations Forces of International Humanitarian Law' of 6 August 1999.[50]

The Bulletin defines its scope of application:

> 1.1 The fundamental principles and rules of international humanitarian law set out in the present bulletin are applicable to United Nations forces when in situations of armed conflict they are actively engaged therein as combatants ... .

On the other hand:

> 1.2 The promulgation of this bulletin does not affect the protected status of members of peacekeeping operations under the 1994 Convention on the Safety of United Nations and Associated Personnel or their status as non-combatants, as long as they are entitled to the protection given to civilians under the international law of armed conflict.

This mirrors indeed the provision on the scope of application contained in the said Convention:[51]

> This Convention shall not apply to a United Nations operation authorized by the Security Council as an enforcement action under Chapter VII of the Charter of the United Nations in which any of the personnel are engaged as combatants against organized armed forces and to which the law of international armed conflict applies.

These texts recognize that there are situations during UN military operations which have to be characterized as armed conflict and to which, therefore, the law of armed conflict applies. It is for these situations only that the bulletin formulates a set of rules which indeed reflect the current state of the customary law of armed conflict without going into too many details. If that situation does not exist, then the peacekeepers are indeed soldiers without enemies, and the law of peace, as concretized in the Convention, applies.

Thus, the practice of the United Nations has developed in the sense that the United Nations possesses rights and duties under international humanitarian law similar to those of States in similar situations. This is a legal situation which the Security Council may only modify within the limits explained above. Until now, it has never done so.

5. THE UNITED NATIONS AND HUMAN RIGHTS

5.1 General

The question of whether the United Nations are bound by international human rights law has a number of different practical aspects. As has been pointed out above, the question arises in all those situations where the Organization takes a decision having a direct impact on individuals. Therefore, a major example is the presence of peace-keeping forces in a given territory as those forces by necessity have an impact, *de facto* or *de jure*, on the situation of individuals. The problem of human rights obligations involves a broad range of issues, duties of abstention, that is, a duty not to interfere with individual rights, and affirmative duties, that is, duties to take positive action to enhance the situation of individuals. Two examples of both aspects will be discussed below.

Before doing so, a general remark must be made: No human right is absolute. Therefore, international human rights treaties provide for limitations of these rights (e.g. Arts 12 para. 3, 19 para. 3 ICCPR, 10 para. 2 ECHR), in particular in the case of emergencies (Arts 4 ICCPR, 15 ECHR). But these possibilities of limitation are themselves subject to limitations. These limitations of limitations may be substantive ('necessary in a democratic society', Art. 19 ICCPR, principle of proportionality), they may be procedural ('prescribed by law'). An important limitation of deprivation of personal liberty is the requirement that 'anyone arrested or detained on a criminal charge shall be brought promptly before a judge or other officer authorized by law to exercise judicial power' (Art. 9 para. 3 ICCPR). As these limitations of limitations frequently refer to institutions which are typical for States (courts, legislation), their application by international organizations presents a difficulty. The argument that international organizations could not be bound by these human rights because they do not possess the institutions needed to implement these rights or their limitations is not acceptable. It is a countersense to assume that a UN police force could detain a person indefinitely without bringing him or her before a judge because the UN does not have such a judge. On the other hand, it would jeopardize the efficiency of a UN operation to maintain order if it were unable to detain persons for that very reason. The solution of the problem lies in a logical extension of the argument already used by the ICJ in the *Reparation for Injuries* case.[52] Human rights apply to the UN *mutatis mutandis*. If the UN does not possess institutions needed to implement the rights and to administer their limitations, it must create equivalent institutions.

5.2 A Particular Example: Listing and De-listing Decisions

A relevant development of international practice which sheds light on the questions treated in this chapter is the debate about so-called targeted sanctions, that is sanctions directly and explicitly subjecting individual persons or enterprises to restrictions designed to enforce Security Council decisions.[53] This raises the problem as to how the United Nations must respect the individual rights of the persons thus targeted. The list of these resolutions is quite long.[54] One has to distinguish between resolutions obliging States to execute such sanctions against individuals fulfilling certain criteria and decisions explicitly and directly addressing certain individuals. Whether in the latter case the Security Council decisions have direct effect in the law of the Member States is a question which may be answered differently from State to State. But even where there is no such direct effect, the resolution which is binding pursuant to Art. 25 of the UN Charter obliges the Member State to deprive a particular individual of fundamental freedoms, the freedom to enjoy one's property and the freedom of movement. Thus, putting a particular individual on a sanctions list (listing) amounts to an exercise of public authority by the Security Council vis-à-vis the individual in question. Whatever measures implementing the lists are taken at the national or EU level, the listing or de-listing decision of the Security Council directly affects fundamental rights of the targeted individuals. Therefore, the question arises whether those individuals enjoy the same or similar procedural guarantees which individuals could claim if a similar decision were taken by a State authority.

If the decision to freeze assets or to deny access to a country were taken by a State, certain basic procedural human rights would have to be observed: during the administrative procedure, a right to be informed of that procedure and to be heard as well as a right to be informed of the decision would apply. Once the decision is taken, there is a right to judicial review in a procedure which respects procedural justice. In the case of Security Council listing decisions, all these human rights guarantees are absent.

This has led to reactions on the national and EU levels in a number of judgements concerning listing decisions. These decisions were implemented by the EC/EU by regulations transposing the listing decisions of the Security Council listing decisions into an EC/EU regulation without giving the persons so listed any additional means of defence. The Court of First Instance held that the EC was bound by the decisions of the Security Council except in decisions violating a norm of *ius cogens*.[55] The Court, furthermore, considered the establishment of the 'focal point' as a protection which respected the *ius cogens* core of the right to judicial protection and that the decision was thus binding.[56] Therefore, it upheld the regulation. The Court of Justice of the European Union, however, reversed that judgement using a completely different reasoning. It held, on the one hand, that the Court was not entitled to review the conformity of Security Council decisions with the Charter or other relevant legal norms.[57] But under EU law the individual was entitled to fundamental human rights, which are part of the EU constitutional order. The constitutional principles of EU law have in the Community (now Union) legal order a rank which is higher than that of an international agreement.[58] They could thus not be set aside by an international treaty, even not by the UN Charter. The restrictions imposed on the plaintiffs in that case amounted to a deprivation of property without due process of law. This was the essential point which led the Court to annul the Regulation.[59] It was immaterial for that result whether the Security Council decision in question was or was not in conformity with UN law. The Court does not indicate whether it would have reached a different result if the Security Council had provided for a fully fledged review of its decision at the UN level, a way of argument which is suggested by the Advocate General in his conclusions.[60]

Whatever the exact legal construction, the practical result is that Security Council decisions disregarding fundamental procedural requirements are not implemented automatically without further scrutiny. In other words, the said procedural human rights requirements constitute a limitation, be it *de facto* or *de iure*, of the powers of the Security Council.

Even before the Court of Justice of the European Communities reached that decision, the cases had not only triggered a considerable doctrinal debate, but also initiatives to improve the Security Council procedure in order to render Security Council decisions less vulnerable against such human rights challenges. Critiques of the Security Council practice came from national governments,[61] NGO position papers[62] and from the Council of Europe.[63] The UN General Assembly dealt with the issue and addressed the Security Council as follows:

> We also call on the Security Council, with the support of the Secretary-General, to ensure that fair and clear procedures exist for placing individuals and entities on sanctions lists and for removing them, as well as granting humanitarian exceptions.[64]

So far, the reactions of the Security Council have not really lived up to the relevant human rights requirements. On an abstract level, the Security Council seems to recognize the problem. In a Presidential Statement, it is declared:

> The Council is committed to ensuring that fair and clear procedures exist for placing individuals and entities on sanctions lists and for removing them … .[65]

More concretely, the Security Council adopted a number of resolutions providing for a review of listing decisions and for a de-listing procedure, in particular resolutions 1617 (2005), 1730 (2006), 1735 (2006), 1822 (2008), 1904 (2009), 1988 (2011) and 1989 (2011). Sanctions committees have developed guidelines for this purpose. At a closer look, however, the practical reaction of the Security Council is still far from meeting human rights requirements, although some progress has been made in this direction. Resolution 1720 (2006) requests the Secretary-General to establish within the Secretariat a so-called Focal Point, a kind of revamped letter box where a listed individual can indeed submit a request for de-listing. This triggers a consultation process with the 'designating government(s)', that is the governments which had taken the initiative to have the individual in question listed, and the government(s) of citizenship and residence. If none of those governments recommends a de-listing, the person remains on the list. If one of those governments recommends de-listing, the Sanctions Committee will take the request on its agenda. The individual is informed about the result. To call this procedure a 'remedy' for the individual would really be an exaggeration. The Advocate General of the Court of Justice of the European Communities comments on this procedure:[66]

The existence of a de-listing procedure at the level of the United Nations offers no consolation in this regard. That procedure allows petitioners to submit a request to the Sanctions Committee or to their government for removal from the list. Yet the processing of that request is purely a matter of intergovernmental consultation. There is no obligation on the Sanctions Committee actually to take the views of the petitioner into account. Moreover, the delisting procedure does not provide even minimal access to the information on which the decision was based to include the petitioner in the list. In fact, access to such information is denied regardless of any substantiated claim as to the need to protect its confidentiality. One of the crucial reasons for which the right to be heard must be respected is to enable the parties concerned to defend their rights effectively, particularly in legal proceedings which might be brought after the administrative control procedure has come to a close.

Yet further progress has been made in the meantime. The Security Council is aware of the challenges and has asked Member States and 'relevant international organizations' (which certainly alludes to the EU) 'to inform the Committee of any relevant court decisions'.[67] By the same resolution, certain responsibilities for de-listing relating to an important sanctions list, namely the Al Qaida and Taliban list, are entrusted to an Ombudsperson. The positive aspect of the new procedure is that the Ombudsperson has to engage in a dialogue with the listed person.[68] But the information which the Ombudsperson must give to the petitioner still is restricted to procedural questions.[69] As to substance, the Ombudsperson is bound to respect 'the confidentiality of Committee deliberations and confidential communications between the Ombudsperson and Member States'.[70] This still falls short of the requirement to obtain the information needed for an effective defence. The Ombudsperson reports to the Committee on the information he or she has collected and on 'the principal arguments concerning the delisting request'. The Committee is obliged to place the request submitted through the Ombudsperson on the agenda, but is otherwise completely free concerning how to deal with it. This is still a far cry from an independent and impartial review of a listing decision. The situation has improved, yet still not decisively, by the recent resolution directing 'the Committee to remove expeditiously individuals and entities on a case-by-case basis that no longer meet the listing criteria'.[71]

Although the respect for human rights by the Security Council, thus, still leaves something to be desired, the following conclusion is important for the present paper: At least on an abstract level, there is a recognition that the Security Council has to abide by fundamental requirements of procedural justice. If the Security Council is reluctant to fully meet these requirements in practice, it has made some concessions to these requirements and it is aware of the consequence of not respecting them – the listing decision in question will not be implemented without an additional procedure at the national or EU level providing the human rights guarantees the Council refuses to grant. The legal logic of this position is somewhat complex: the Security Council seems to recognize that it is obliged to respect human rights, but prefers to forgo the obligatory character of its resolution instead of granting to the persons targeted by it the rights it would be required to grant if it wanted the resolution to be binding and effective.

5.3   R2P and Human Rights

Another issue involving human rights obligations of the Security Council is the 'Responsibility to Protect' (R2P).[72] This responsibility is derived from a construction of human rights, especially the right to life, which involves an affirmative duty to protect such rights.[73] This responsibility is understood to impose certain duties on States to act to prevent massive violations of human rights, but the concept must not be misunderstood as legally justifying unilateral action of a State claiming to protect a population by the use of military force against human rights abuses.[74] Where, however, military means to protect a population against human rights violations committed by its own government are considered necessary, it can only be the Security Council which would legitimize that use of force.

During recent years, a lot of lip service has been paid to the concept of R2P. Two questions have to be distinguished: Has R2P developed into a norm of positive international law? Is the Security Council bound by that rule?

As to the first question, it can be recognized that the alleged rule has some political impact. R2P has been evoked in cases where the Security Council did act. Yet it is difficult to ascertain whether this political trend has really led to the establishment of a rule of positive international law. Too many are the cases of inactivity of States and of the United Nations in cases of human rights violations. To mention only a few: Rwanda, Srebrenica. It is probably more correct to speak of the R2P as an emerging norm or principle.[75] But the recent resolution concerning Libya[76] is interpreted as being an implementation of R2P by the Security Council. The relevant resolution expressly reiterates 'the responsibility of the Libyan authorities to protect the Libyan population', and the failure of the Libyan authorities to fulfil this responsibility is the basis for Security Council action. This is an element of UN practice which can be understood as confirming the character of R2P as a norm of positive international law.

What is important for the purposes of the present paper is the fact that it seems to be taken for granted that if R2P were a legal norm, it would not only be addressed to States, but also to the United Nations.[77]

6.   HUMAN RIGHTS AND HUMANITARIAN LAW COMBINED – HUMANITARIAN EXCEPTIONS TO SANCTIONS REGIMES

A traditional type of sanction imposed by the Security Council is the embargo, that is, a mandatory interruption of trade relations. This has resulted in serious deprivations of the civilian population, that is of persons who bear no responsibility for the wrongs which triggered the sanction decisions. This has been the object of severe criticism.

In terms of human rights law and international humanitarian law, the question can be formulated as follows. If the embargo relates to an armed conflict, the provisions concerning relief for the civilian apply: Art. 23, 59 GC IV, Art. 69, 70 AP I. The essential content of these norms constitutes customary law and requires that relief actions take place. As a norm of customary law, it could bind the United Nations if they were a Party to a conflict and, as the case may be, an occupying power.

In terms of human rights law, systematically depriving a civilian population of its means of subsistence constitutes a violation of the right to life and the right to the protection of a private sphere of life (Art. 6, 17 ICCPR), of the right to a decent standard of living and the right to health (Art. 11, 12 ICESCR).[78]

Against this legal background, demands have been made, especially by the ICRC, that the Security Council should admit humanitarian exceptions to sanctions regimes.[79] These demands have generally been heeded. The most elaborate example is the 'Oil for Food' programme in the framework of the sanctions against Iraq during the 1990s.[80] Another example is the sanctions regime imposed upon Haiti.[81] It is significant that the recognition of 'humanitarian exceptions' by the Security Council is formulated in resolutions dealing also with another human rights issue, namely listing and de-listing persons on sanctions lists.[82] This practice clearly indicates that the Council considers itself bound by a humanitarian principle according to which economic sanctions may not lead to a massive deprivation of the civilian population.[83]

7.   TOWARDS AN INTERNATIONAL CONSTITUTIONAL AND ADMINISTRATIVE LAW

It was said at the outset that the question as to whether the United Nations, including the Security Council as an organ of the United Nations, is bound by human rights is part of the problem of the increasing exercise of public authority by international institutions. These are new forms of international governance which involve what is called a 'public law approach'.[84] This means that the rules of international governance increasingly resemble similar rules applying to State activities, which holds true despite warnings against overstating these similarities.[85] There is an international constitutional law[86] and an international administrative law.[87] The exercise of public authority by the Security Council is part of this phenomenon. General principles of (State) constitutional law are applied to its actions.[88] It entails an obligation to respect human rights.[89]

8.   INTERNATIONAL ORGANIZATIONS AND THE RULE OF LAW

International organizations are creations of the international legal system. Therefore, they must be subject to the fundamental rules of that system. Also the United Nations are subject to, not above, international law. Therefore, the question whether the United Nations including the Security Council is bound by human rights and international humanitarian law is part of another related discourse, namely that on the rule of law at both the national and the international level.

The Secretary-General has submitted various reports on the rule of law activities of the United Nations. They essentially address support for the rule of law at the national level, especially in post-conflict situations.[90] Yet the Secretary-General defines the concept of rule of law in very general terms which could well be applied to the United Nations themselves:[91]

> The 'rule of law' is a concept *at the very heart of the Organization's mission*. It refers to a principle of governance in which all persons, institutions and entities, public and private, including the State itself, are accountable to laws that are publicly promulgated, equally enforced and independently adjudicated, and which are consistent with international human rights norms and standards. It requires, as well, measures to ensure adherence to the principles of supremacy of law, equality before the law, accountability to the law, fairness in the application of the law, separation of powers, participation in decision-making, legal certainty, avoidance of arbitrariness and procedural and legal transparency.

The idea that these principles should apply to the United Nations themselves is rarely expressed in United Nations debates. A laudable formulation is found in the statement made by Liechtenstein in the VIth Committee of the General Assembly during the debate on 'The Rule of Law at the National and International Levels' on 13 October 2008:[92]

> Another disconnect that should be remedied step by step exists between the organization's role as a legislative forum and its own application of relevant rules of international law. We acknowledge that the rule of law at the 'institutional' level is a conceptually challenging notion. It requires United Nations organs to examine the extent to which they are bound not just by the United Nations Charter, but also by applicable rules of customary international law. Given the ever increasing scope of the United Nations' activities, however, improving adherence to international law internally is indispensable to uphold the organization's legitimacy and credibility.

The last sentence takes up an important point which has already been mentioned in the introduction, namely that of the legitimacy of the action of international organizations.[93] The more these activities have a direct or indirect impact on the fate of individuals, the more there is a need for such legitimacy. As democratic legitimacy is not available to international organizations in the same way as it is for States, respect for the rule of law plays a decisive role for such legitimacy.

Respect for human rights is at the heart of the requirements imposed by the rule of law.

Another related discourse leads to the same result, namely the accountability of international organizations,[94] to which the Report of the Secretary-General quoted above refers, too.[95] This discourse has been convincingly formulated by the Committee of the International Law Association on 'Accountability of International Organisations'.[96] This accountability has procedural aspects both as to decision-making (in particular transparency) and as to review mechanisms. It has also a substantive side, namely the requirement that the organization respects human rights and international humanitarian law.[97]

9.   CONCLUSION

This chapter has tried to show that the Security Council in its activities is indeed bound by the international law of human rights and international humanitarian law. Various strands of legal reasoning coincide in that result. They are both theoretical and practical. There is no denying the fact, however, that a certain tension exists between the pure legal argument and political practice. The five permanent members of the Security Council are rather loath to accept legal control of their political action. Yet there are enough political forces at work which prevent this political unwillingness from turning into an obsolescence of the applicable law.

NOTES

*   Michael Bothe is Professor emeritus of Public Law, Goethe University Frankfurt/Main, Germany.

1.   T. Sato, 'The Legitimacy of Security Council Activities under Chapter VII of the UN Charter since the End of the Cold War', in *The Legitimacy of International Organizations*, eds J.-M. Coicaud and V. Heiskanen (Tokyo: United Nations University Press, 2001), 309 *et seq.*

2.   S. Lamb, 'Legal Limits to United Nations Security Council Powers', in *The Reality of International Law: Essays in Honour of Ian Brownlie*, eds G.S. Goodwin-Gill and S. Talmon (Oxford: Oxford University Press, 1999), 362. For critical comments on the resolution regarding military action against Iraq 1990, see M. Bothe, 'Die Golfkrise und die Vereinten Nationen – Rückkehr zur kollektiven Sicherheit?', *Demokratie und Recht* 19 (1991): 2–10; see also the discussion by D. Sarooshi, *The United Nations and the Development of Collective Security: The Delegation by the Security Council of its Chaper VII Powers* (Oxford: Oxford University Press, 1999), 174 *et seq.*; for the armistice regime, see B. Graefrath, 'Iraqi Reparations and the Security Council', *ZaöRV* 55 (1995): 1–68, in particular at 11 *et seq.*

3.   Already H. Kelsen, *The Law of the United Nations* (London: The Lawbook Exchange, 1950), 748 *et seq.*, points to a lack of clarity of the provisions on military enforcement measures in many respects.

4.   Kelsen, *supra* note 3, at 756, regards both options as being covered by Articles 42 and 48.

5.   A. von Bogdandy, R. Wolfrum, J. von Bernstorff, P. Dann and M. Goldmann, eds, *The Exercise of Public Authority by International Institutions: Advancing International Institutional Law* (Heidelberg: Springer, 2010).

6.   R. Provost, *International Human Rights and Humanitarian Law* (Cambridge and New York: Cambridge University Press, 2002), *passim.*

7.   *Legal Consequences of the Construction of a Wall in the Occupied Palestinian Territories*, Advisory Opinion, I.C.J. Reports 2004, 136, paragraph 106.

8.   M. Bothe, 'Les limites de pouvoirs du Conseil de Sécurité,' in *Le développement du rôle du Conseil de Sécurité, Colloque, La Haye, 21–23 juillet 1992*, ed. R.-J. Dupuy (Dordrecht: Martinus Nijhoff Publishers, 1992), 67–81.

9.   J. Delbrück, Article 24, margin note 10, in *The Charter of the United Nations: A Commentary*, ed. B. Simma, 2nd edition (Oxford: Oxford University Press, 2002); further discussion *infra* section 3.2.

10.   *Reparation for injuries suffered in the service of the United Nations*, Advisory Opinion, I.C.J. Reports 1949, 174.

11.   T.D. Gill, 'Legal and Some Political Limitations on the Power of the UN Security Council to Exercise its Enforcement Powers under Chapter VII of the Charter', *Netherlands Yearbook of International Law* 26 (1995): 82.

12.   *Supra* note 10, at 175.

13.   *Supra* note 10, at 177.

14.   *Supra* note 10, at 179.

15.   *Supra* note 10, at 180.

16.   J.G. Gardam, 'Legal Restraints on Security Council Military Enforcement Action', *Michigan Journal of International Law* 17 (1996): 318.

17.   Lamb, *supra* note 2, at 365.

18.   *Prosecutor v. Tadić*, ICTY, Appeals Chamber, Decision, 2 October 1995 (Case No. IT-94-1-A), para. 28.

19.   Lamb, *supra* note 2, at 374 *et seq.*; E. de Wet, *The Chapter VII Powers of the United Nations Security Council* (Oxford and Portland: Hart Publishing, 2004), 133 *et seq.*; A. Stein, *Der Sicherheitsrat der Vereinten Nationen und die Rule of Law* (Baden-Baden: Nomos, 1999), 14 *et seq.*

20.   *Infra* section 3.3.

21.   *Infra* section 5.3.

22.   *Tadić*, *supra* note 18, at para. 32

23. *Tadić, supra* note 18, at para. 39.
24. B. Martenczuk, *Rechtsbindung und Rechtskontrolle des Weltsicherheitsrats* (Berlin: Duncker & Humblot, 1996), 240 *et seq.*
25. M.J. Herdegen, 'The "Constitutionalization" of the UN Security System', *Vanderbilt Journal of Transnational Law* 27 (1994): 152.
26. Martenczuk, *supra* note 24, at 143 *et seq.*, 150.
27. See Gardam, *supra* note 16, at 313; Lamb, *supra* note 2 at 369.
28. Lamb, *supra* note 2, at 366 *et seq.*
29. Delbrück, Article 25, margin note 18, in Simma, *supra* note 9. This has been an issue regarding the European Community (now Union), see the Judgments discussed *infra* section 5.2.
30. Herdegen, *supra* note 25, at 156; Lamb, *supra* note 2, at 372 *et seq.*; De Wet, *supra* note 19, at 187 *et seq.*
31. Court of First Instance of the European Communities, *Kadi v. Council and Commission*, Judgment, 21 September 2005 (Case T-315/01), para. 226.
32. *Supra* section 3.2., in particular the text accompanying note 25.
33. *Certain Expenses of the United Nations*, Advisory Opinion, I.C.J. Reports 1962, 168.
34. Martenczuk, *supra* note 24, at 73 *et seq.*; Stein, *supra* note 19, at 347 *et seq.*; Lamb, *supra* note 2, at 363; Gill, *supra* note 11, at 106 *et seq.*
35. *Infra* section 5.2.
36. *Case concerning questions of interpretation and application of the 1971 Montreal Convention arising from the aerial incident at Lockerbie, Libya v. United States of America*, Preliminary Objections, I.C.J. Reports 1998, 115; on that case see De Wet, *supra* note 19, at 2 *et seq.*; see also Stein, *supra* note 19, at 347 *et seq.*, in particular at 365 *et seq.* on the *Lockerbie case*.
37. *Tadić, supra* note 18, at para. 22.
38. U. Palwankar, 'Applicabilité du droit international humanitaire aux Forces des Nations Unies pour le maintien de la paix', *Revue internationale de la Croix-Rouge* 75 (1993): 245–259; see also D. Schindler, 'United Nations forces and international humanitarian Law', in *Studies and essays on international humanitarian law and Red Cross principles in honour of Jean Pictet* (The Hague: Martinus Nijhoff Publishers,1984), 521–530.
39. As early as 1971, the Institut de droit international adopted a much broader approach to the question and declared (Conditions of Application of Humanitarian Rules of Armed Conflict to Hostilities in which United Nations Forces May be Engaged, Resolution adopted at the session of Zagreb): 'The humanitarian rules of armed conflict apply to the United Nations as of right, and they must be complied with in all circumstances by United Nations Forces which are engaged in hostilities.'
40. See 'Memorandum of the International Committee of the Red Cross, 10 November 1961', *Revue internationale de la Croix-Rouge* 43 (1961): 592.
41. UN Treaty Series 271: 168, Article 44
42. UN Doc. ST/SGB/ONUC/1: Article 43.
43. UN Treaty Series 555: 132, Article 40.
44. Text as in the Exchange of letters constituting an agreement between the United Nations and Canada concerning the service with the United Nations Peace-Keeping Force of the national contingent provided by the Government of Canada, 21 February 1966, UN Treaty Series 555: 120.
45. Canada, for instance, ratified the Convention only in 1998.
46. *Revue internationale de la Croix-Rouge* 44 (1962): 28.
47. L.L. Fabian, *Soldiers without Enemies. Preparing the United Nations for Peace-keeping* (Washington DC: Brookings Institution, 1971).
48. Palwankar, *supra* note 38, at 247, 254; Schindler, *supra* note 38, at 523; this is also the basis for the Resolution adopted by the Institut de droit international, *supra* note 39.
49. A/RES/49/59, 9 December 1994.
50. UN Doc. ST/SBG/1999/13.
51. Article 2(2).
52. *Supra* section 3.1.
53. M. Bothe, 'Security Council's Targeted Sanctions against Presumed Terrorists,' *Journal of International Criminal Justice* 6 (2008): 541–555; C.A. Feinäugle, 'The UN Security Council Al-Qaida and Taliban Sanctions Committee: Emerging Principles of International Institutional Law for the Protection of the Individual?', in von Bogdandy et al., *supra* note 5, at 101–131.
54. The latest examples are S/RES/1973, 17 March 2011, and S/RES/1970, 26 February 2011 concerning Libya.

55. *Kadi v. Council and Commission, supra* note 31, at para. 226.
56. *Ibid.*, para. 262 *et seq.*
57. Court of Justice of the European Union, *Kadi and Al Barakaat International Foundation v. Council and Commission*, Judgment of the Court (Grand Chamber), 3 September 2008 (Cases C-402/05 P and C-415/05 P), para. 287.
58. *Ibid.*, para. 289.
59. *Ibid.*, para. 369 *et seq.*
60. *Kadi v. Council and Commission*, Case C-402/05 P. Conclusions of Advocate General Maduro, 16 January 2008, para. 54: 'Had there been a genuine and effective mechanism of judicial control by an independent tribunal at the level of the United Nations then this might have released the Community from the obligation to provide for judicial control of implementing measures that apply within the Community legal order. However, no such mechanism currently exists.'
61. Letter dated 19 May 2006 from the Permanent Representatives of Germany, Sweden and Switzerland to the United Nations addressed to the President of the Security Council, UN Doc. A/60/887-S/2006/331.
62. Human Rights Watch, *UN: Sanctions Rules Must Protect Due Process*, 4 March 2002. Available at: http://www.hrw.org/es/news/2002/03/03/un-sanctions-rules-must-protect-due-process
63. Council of Europe, Parliamentary Assembly, Resolution 1597 (2008) and Recommendation 1824 (2008), both adopted 23 January 2008.
64. 2005 World Summit Outcome, A/RES/60/1, 24 October 2005.
65. UN Doc. S/PRST/2006/28, 22 June 2006.
66. *Supra* note 60, at para. 51.
67. S/RES/1904, 17 December 2009, para. 15.
68. S/RES/1904, 17 December 2009, Annex II, paragraphs 5 and 6.
69. S/RES/1904, 17 December 2009, Annex II, para. 1(b) and (c).
70. S/RES/1904, 17 December 2009, Annex II, para. 14.
71. S/RES/1988, 17 June 2011, para. 18.
72. International Commission on Intervention and State Sovereignty, *Responsibility to Protect, Report of the International Commission on Intervention and State Sovereignty* (Ottawa: International Development Research Centre, 2001).
73. *Ibid.*, at 14 *et seq.*
74. *Ibid.*, at 54 *et seq.*
75. *Ibid.*, at 16.
76. S/RES/1973, 17 March 2011.
77. *Ibid.*, at 16.
78. De Wet, *supra* note 19, at 219 *et seq.*
79. H.-P. Gasser, 'Collective Economic Sanctions and International Humanitarian Law', *Zeitschrift für ausländisches öffentliches Recht und Völkerrecht* 56 (1996): 880 *et seq.*; De Wet, *supra* note 19, at 226 *et seq.*
80. S/RES/986, 14 April 1995, which provides humanitarian exceptions to the embargo decided by S/RES/661, 6 August 1990.
81. S/RES/841, 16 June 1993, and S/RES/917, 6 May 1994.
82. *Supra* note 54.
83. Herdegen, *supra* note 30, at 156.
84. A. von Bogdandy, P. Dann and M. Goldmann, 'Developing the Publicness of Public International Law: Towards a Legal Framework for Global Governance Activities', in Bogdandy et al., *supra* note 5, at 3–32; S. Kadelbach, 'From Public International law to International Public Law: A Comment on the "Public Authority" and the "Publicness" of their Law', *ibid.*, 33–49.
85. M. Herdegen, *supra* note 30, at 150 *et seq.*; for a balanced analysis, see Sato, *supra* note 1, at 325 *et seq.*
86. This goes beyond the long-standing debate as to whether the constituent instruments of international organizations can rightly be called 'constitution', see T. Sato, *Evolving Constitutions of International Organizations* (The Hague: Martinus Nijhoff Publishers, 1996), 229 *et seq.*; see also P.-M. Dupuy, 'The Constitutional Dimension of the Charter of the United Nations Revisited', *Max Planck Yearbook on United Nations Law* (1997), 1–33, in particular at 19.
87. Kadelbach, *supra* note 84, at 41 *et seq.*
88. Sarooshi, *supra* note 2, at 20 *et seq.*
89. Kadelbach, *supra* note 84, at 46 *et seq.*; see also Feinäugle, *supra* note 53.

90. See, e.g., the SG Report 'The rule of law and transitional justice in conflict and post-conflict societies', UN Doc. S/2004/616, 23 August 2004.
91. UN Doc. S/2004/616, para. 6 (emphasis added).
92. Available at http://www.regierung.li/index.php?id=387 (accessed 12 February 2012).
93. See the volume edited by Coicaud and Heiskanen, *supra* note 1, on the Security Council in particular, see, Sato, *supra* note 1; see also Dupuy, *supra* note 86, at 32; D.D. Caron, 'The Legitimacy of the Collective Authority of the Security Council', *AJIL* 87 (1993): 556 *et seq.*
94. E. de Wet, 'Holding International Institutions Accountable: The Complementary Role of Non-Judicial Oversight Mechanisms and Judicial Review', in von Bogdandy et al., *supra* note 5, at 855–882. Feinäugle, *supra* note 53, at 130 *et seq.*
95. *Supra* note 91.
96. International Law Association, *Report of the Seventy-First Conference*, Berlin 2004, 164–234.
97. *Ibid.*, Part Two, section four, at 193–196.

19. UN territorial administrations: between international humanitarian law and human rights law

*Ivan Ingravallo**

1. DEFINITION OF TERRITORIAL ADMINISTRATION

The international administration of territories is the performance by an international organization of government functions in a territory, both when it involves all the sectors that comprise the State government (executive, legislative, judicial) and when it involves only a part of them. The key element is given by the fact that the 'last word' is up to the international organization rather than to the sovereign territorial or local government institutions, if any. As a result, an international territorial administration is not realized when an international organization does not exercise powers of government over a territory, but has only the tasks of supervision, assistance or support to the functioning of public institutions of a State or territory.[1]

The international administration of territories had gained new momentum at the end of the 1990s, when the United Nations (UN) created some operations with such a mandate. On 15 January 1996 the UN Security Council established the United Nations Transitional Administration for Eastern Slavonia, Baranja and Western Sirmium (UNTAES) by Resolution 1037 as a result of the Peace Agreement signed between the Government of Croatia and the representative of the local Serb minority.[2] In the Agreement the parties asked the Security Council to establish a territorial administration with a mandate to 'govern' that area for a transitional period and to promote the peaceful return of these territories under the authority of the Croatian Government.[3] UNTAES had a civilian and a military component, both placed under the 'overall authority' of a Transitional Administrator, entrusted with legislative powers.[4] Resolution 1037 qualified UNTAES as a peace-keeping operation. It operated for two years and completed its mandate in 1998.

Another Transitional Administration was established in Kosovo, a province of Serbia inhabited mostly by people of Albanian origin, progressively discriminated against by the Yugoslav and Serbian authorities. On 10 June 1999, at the end of a unilateral armed attack realized by numerous NATO States against the Federal Republic of Yugoslavia (FRY), the Security Council adopted Resolution 1244. By this Resolution the Council authorized the deployment in Kosovo of two international presences, a civil one (United Nations Interim Administration Mission in Kosovo, UNMIK),[5] and a military one (Kosovo force, KFOR).[6] The former was led by a Special Representative nominated by the UN Secretary-General, while the latter was under NATO command, but included also troops from non-NATO States, and was independent from the civilian presence,[7] with obvious risks of insufficient coordination and overlap in some areas of *expertise*.[8] UNMIK was vested with the task of administering Kosovo *ad interim*, in order to provide a substantial autonomy within FRY (FRY in the meantime became Serbia-Montenegro and, since May 2006, Serbia) and to 'provide transitional administration while establishing and overseeing the development of provisional democratic self-governing institutions to ensure conditions for a peaceful and normal life for all inhabitants of Kosovo'.[9] Despite the lack of clarity of Resolution 1244, the Secretary-General, in the report by which he proposed to the Security Council the structure and the powers of UNMIK, affirmed: 'All legislative and executive authority with respect to Kosovo, including the administration of the judiciary, is vested in UNMIK and is exercised by the Special Representative of the Secretary-General.'[10] This very big amount of powers was confirmed by the first Regulation enacted by the Special Representative.[11] UNMIK administered Kosovo for nine years, until the declaration of independence of Provisional Institutions of Kosovo (17 February 2008), that questioned the authority of UNMIK. On 4 February 2008 the European Union established a mission, called EULEX Kosovo, with the task of monitoring, mentoring and advising the Institutions of Kosovo on all areas related to the wider rule of law (including a customs service), whilst retaining certain executive responsibilities.[12] The Secretary-General, given the inability of the Security Council to act, decided to reconfigure UNMIK, and on 26 November 2008 the Security Council accepted the proposal of the Secretary-General[13] to place EULEX Kosovo under the UN 'umbrella'.[14] The limited mandate of EULEX Kosovo leads to the negation of its qualification as a territorial administration.

In 1999 the Security Council decided to establish another territorial administration, on the territory of East Timor, an old Portuguese colony until the mid-1970s, then occupied by Indonesia. On 5 May 1999 Portugal and Indonesia concluded an Agreement on East Timor and two more Agreements with the UN Secretary-General.[15] Article 6 of the first Agreement provided for the institution of a territorial administration for the future independent State of East Timor. UNTAET (United Nations Transitional Administration in East Timor) was decided by the Security Council Resolution 1272 of 25 October 1999.[16] Unlike UNMIK, that does not control the military component, UNTAET included a civilian and a military component. It was 'endowed with overall responsibility for the administration of East Timor' and 'empowered to exercise all legislative and executive authority, including the administration of justice', and authorized to take 'all necessary measures to fulfil its mandate'. UNTAET was led by a Transitional Administrator nominated by the Secretary-General and administered that territory until its independence, which took place on 20 May 2002 under the new name of Timor-Leste.

The establishment of three territorial administrations in the 1996–1999 period has produced numerous studies devoted to this topic.[17] But, as many scholars have noted, the administration of a territory by an international organization is not a completely new task, considering that it is possible to find examples of similar operations in the practice of the League of Nations (LoN), of the UN and of regional organizations, like the European Union (EU). The LoN administered the Saar Basin (1920–1935)[18] and the Leticia District (1933–1934).[19] The UN administered the West Irian (1962–1963),[20] projected administering the Free Territory of Trieste[21] and the City of Jerusalem,[22] and tried to administer Namibia,[23] Western Sahara[24] and Cambodia.[25] As far as regional organizations are concerned, the practice is very poor; only the EU administered the City of Mostar.[26] However, other regional organizations may have the opportunity to exercise that function in the future, such as the ECOWAS (Economic Community of West African States) or the AU (African Union). In fact, there appears to be no objection in principle (neither of these are in the relevant international practice) to the possibility that the UN – which does not have a territorial character and does not exercise, as a rule, the powers of a State – can perform the tasks of territorial administration.[27] As for the UN, its competence to administer a territory is generally accepted, even in the absence of a precise reference in the UN Charter; the exercise of this competence was not contested by the Member States or in the legal doctrine;[28] the debate concerns, rather, the different models of territorial administration, its legal basis and the appropriateness of its use.[29]

The territorial administrations that have been implemented, or have been planned, over the years do not have all the same characteristics and the same legal basis, but they all share a common feature: the final authority to administer is vested in the operation, through an organ of the organization which created it (that's why it is not possible to consider the international administration of Bosnia and Herzegovina a territorial administration).[30] Moreover, the executive, legislative and judiciary powers of the sovereign and/or of the population on the territory are temporarily greatly limited, if not suspended,[31] but the organization does not have 'complete' sovereignty over the administered territory, because it cannot determine autonomously the destiny of that territory.[32]

The exercise of governmental powers by the territorial administrations is limited by the mandate received, and by the rules of international law. The purpose of this study is precisely to determine whether the rules of IHL and those of HRL are applicable in respect of the territorial administrations. Hence it will be necessary to consider also if the control mechanisms included in some international agreements on human rights protection are able to operate with respect to violations that have been carried out within the territorial administrations.

2.   WHAT ROLE FOR INTERNATIONAL HUMANITARIAN LAW IN THE CONTEXT OF TERRITORIAL ADMINISTRATIONS?

As mentioned above, the territorial administrations are responsible for the exercise of executive, legislative and judicial powers in the territories in which they are deployed. On some occasions, the territorial administrations have had also military and police functions. Some authors argue that it is mandatory to apply them for the international law rules of IHL on the belligerent occupation,[33] which are enshrined mainly in the Regulations annexed to the Hague Convention IV of 18 October 1907, concerning the Laws and Customs of War on Land,[34] in the IV Geneva Convention of 12 August 1949 on the Protection of Civilian Persons in Time of War[35] and in the I Additional Protocol of 8 June 1977 to the Geneva Conventions of 12 August 1949, relating to the protection of Victims of International Armed Conflicts.[36] It is true, in fact, that the occupation and the administration of territories are similar – in both cases there is a subject different from the sovereign that exercises for a certain period ample powers on a certain territory – and it is also true that the UN, as an international subject, is bound by the rules of IHL, that have progressively taken on a customary character.

But most scholars (and I agree with them) do not share the above mentioned opinion, because the differences between the territorial administrations and occupation are greater than the similarities.[37] First of all, the territorial administrations do not create a situation of armed conflict or war; they do not intend to produce the *debellatio* of a certain State or to occupy its territory, but are directed to maintaining or re-establishing international and domestic peace and security.[38] Moreover, while the occupier administers the territory mainly for its interest, the territorial administrations are established both for the general interest for the maintenance of peace and security and for the particular interest of the well-being of the territorial community which they administer.[39] That is why the legal discipline of occupation is directed to limiting the powers of the occupier (Article 43 of the Hague Regulations and Article 64 of the IV Geneva Convention), but this limitation is not convincing in relation to the territorial administrations.

However, as many authors maintain, the fact that it is not possible to apply *de jure* the discipline of occupation to the territorial administrations does not prevent applying this discipline *de facto*,[40] or by analogy.[41] In fact, their detailed nature and their universal acceptance are useful in order to solve practical matters that can emerge in the day-to-day administration activity. For instance, the rules of occupation may provide a useful inspiration concerning the maintenance of public order and civil life in the administered territory. In practice, in the administration of Kosovo and East Timor principles analogous to those of the laws of occupation have been applied with reference to the respect of local law (Article 43 of the Hague Regulations) and to the administration of state and socially-owned property (Articles 53 and 55 of the Hague Regulations).[42]

The territorial administration may also take a unilateral commitment regarding the application of the rules of IHL, as happened in Kosovo, where the UN, though declaring that the situation in place is neither one of armed conflict nor one of occupation, added that UNMIK is willing to apply the relevant provisions of the Hague Convention for the protection of cultural property in the event of armed conflict of 14 May 1954, and, as a consequence of this willingness, UNMIK is bound to apply the relevant provisions of the Convention with the necessary modifications flowing from the nature of UNMIK and the legal status of Kosovo. For the UN, the obligation to preserve and protect cultural and religious property is part of a more general obligation binding upon UNMIK; while its implementation may be delegated to domestic institutions, but the international responsibility, in case of failure, lies ultimately with UNMIK.[43]

Apart from the military occupation, if we consider more generally IHL, when the territorial administrations include a military component, this component is obliged to respect the relevant rules of IHL under customary international law, which binds both the UN and its Member States.[44] Such a conclusion derives also from a well-founded practice of the peace-keeping operations. Article X of the Model agreement between the UN and Member States contributing personnel and equipment to UN peace-keeping operations, in fact, provides that the forces put at disposal of the UN 'shall observe and respect the spirit and principles of the general international conventions applicable to the conduct of military personnel'.[45] In recent years, moreover, the UN has developed a practice of including such an obligation in the Status of Force Agreements (SOFAs) concluded between the UN and the State (or the States) in which the operations are deployed. Furthermore, the mentioned obligation derives from the well-known Secretary-General Bulletin of 1999 on the observance by the United Nations forces of the fundamental principles and rules of IHL.[46] The Bulletin, however, does not contain a complete discipline and does not make reference to the occupation, and this means that, for the matters not covered by the Bulletin, the national contingents must observe their pertinent national obligations regarding the IHL, not least because of the duty to respect and 'ensure respect' for Geneva Conventions and Additional Protocol I, contained in their common Article 1. Undoubtedly, an element of clarity may result from the approval by the Security Council of a more explicit mandate as regards the application of IHL by the military component of the territorial administrations.[47]

A related problem concerns what happens when a breach of an IHL obligation occurs in the context of a territorial administration. In order to determine if the responsibility is borne by the UN or its Member States (or both) it must be considered who has effective control. The problem of attribution will be discussed later, since it is also linked to the second part of this study, which is dedicated to the applicability of the rules of HRL to the territorial administrations. As we shall see shortly, the main problem is not the obligation to respect these rules, an obligation that is quite certain, but rather that of the possibility of utilizing the domestic and the international remedies against the relevant acts or the omissions in the context of a territorial administration. The attribution of the conduct, to the UN or to the States, is, again, crucial in order to carry a reflection on the consequences of breaches of IHL and HRL.

3. WHAT ROLE FOR HUMAN RIGHTS LAW IN THE CONTEXT OF A TERRITORIAL ADMINISTRATION?

The protection of human rights has been one of the tasks generally included in the mandate of territorial administrations. Moreover, the territorial administrations have adopted, or have been tasked to adopt, numerous acts which have declared the applicability of many international rules on human rights in the territory under administration. As regards the Free Territory of Trieste, such obligations derived from Articles 4 and 17 of the Permanent Statute,[48] while in the case of the project of international administration for Jerusalem it is possible to recall Article 9 of the Statute approved by the Trusteeship Council.[49] In the administration of West Irian, UNTEA and Indonesia agreed to guarantee and protect many human rights of the inhabitants of that territory.[50]

In the 1990s, the Security Council gave the territorial administrations various tasks related to human rights protection. In para. 12 of Resolution 1037 it commissioned UNTAES to monitor the parties' compliance with their commitment under the Erdut Agreement to respect the highest standards of human rights and fundamental freedoms. In the case of Kosovo the Council, in para. 11(j) of Resolution 1224, decided that one of the main responsibilities of UNMIK shall be to protect and promote human rights.[51] Sec. 1.3 of UNMIK Regulation 1999/24 imposes on all persons undertaking public duties or holding public office in Kosovo the duty to 'observe internationally recognized human rights standards',[52] recalling, as an example, the Universal Declaration on human rights as well as many universal and regional agreements on human rights.[53] The same approach is followed in the Constitutional framework for provisional self-government adopted in 2001, that provides that all persons in Kosovo shall enjoy human rights and fundamental freedoms and commits the Provisional Institutions of Self-Government to observe and ensure internationally recognized human rights and fundamental freedoms.[54] The international and regional treaties recalled in the Constitutional framework correspond only partly to those included in UNMIK Regulation 1999/24, but this does not seem relevant, because the two lists are only a sample.

UNTAET's mandate, for its part, was not well focused on human rights protection. In Resolution 1272 there is only a reference to the development of a human rights institution in East Timor (para. 8), and to the importance of including in UNTAET personnel with appropriate training in humanitarian law, human rights and refugee law (para. 15).[55] In spite of this, in its first Regulation UNTAET decided that, in exercising their functions, 'all persons undertaking public duties or holding public office in East Timor shall observe internationally recognized human rights standards', recalling a list identical to that contained in UNMIK Regulation 1999/24, except for the European Convention on Human Rights.[56]

As a result of the above mentioned acts, in the administered territories many international rules on human rights protection (of customary or conventional type) have been applied on the basis of a decision adopted by the territorial administrations in the exercise of their power to legislate. It is now necessary to consider whether the international rules on human rights protection bind also the territorial administrations during their administration. It is a very peculiar problem, since, as a rule, the UN do not exercise a power over human beings that involves the obligation to respect human rights. The situation changes dramatically in the cases considered here, as it is the UN that establishes and manages a territorial administration and therefore exerts significant legislative, executive and judiciary powers over a local community, being involved in numerous situations which are relevant to possible human rights violations.[57] In recent years, the territorial administrations have been accused of violating those rights in the administered territories.[58] They have also been criticized for their lack of respect for democratic principles,[59] for the 'inherent contradiction' between the principles of the rule of law and democratic government, regarded as preconditions for effective protection of human rights, and the nature of the administration and the centralization of power exercised on the part of the Special Representative.[60]

The UN, as a subject under international law, is obliged to comply with the rules on human rights protection that are part of the *ius cogens*,[61] and, under the same conditions as other international actors, the UN must also meet the customary rules.[62] Furthermore, it is bound by its own Statute, including the human rights commitments included in it,[63] and the territorial administrations must act within the limits of their mandate.[64] Hence, the main problem is to apply to the territorial administrations the rules on human rights protection contained in international agreements that can be ratified only by the States, and not by the UN.[65]

Some scholars argue that the territorial administrations shall have the same conventional human rights commitments as the UN Member States.[66] This argument is not convincing, because it seems to ignore the separate international legal personality of the UN, and there is also the practical problem that the Member States do not have all the same conventional obligations.[67] Many scholars believe instead (and I agree with them) that the reference to international agreements on human rights in acts of the territorial administrations is to be considered as a unilateral manifestation of their commitment to ensure the implementation of these agreements in the administered territory. The recall of these international agreements in acts adopted by the territorial administrations does not imply the participation of the territorial administrations in those agreements, but the fact that the territorial administration decides what the human rights standards are in the administered territory implies that it accepts unilaterally a binding self-commitment to respect these standards and to protect the rights contained therein.[68]

This is to say with reference to the substantive obligations imposed by these agreements, while the related issue of the usability of the remedies provided by some of these international agreements turns out to be more complex; in this respect there is the problem of attributing violations to the UN or to the Member States contributing personnel to the territorial administrations, as I will consider in the next paragraph.

It should also be considered that the personnel of the territorial administrations shall respect the law of the host country, including the rules on human rights protection. This is an essential obligation of all personnel involved in a peace operation, as provided for in the SOFAs.[69] In these territories the international human rights commitments accepted by the territorial sovereign also continue to operate. Such a conclusion is supported by the General Comment 26 adopted by the UN Human Rights Committee in 1997.[70] The Committee, in fact, affirmed that the rights enshrined in the UN Covenant on Civil and Political Rights belong to the people living in the territory of a State Party and that 'once the people are accorded the protection of the rights under the Covenant, such protection devolves with territory and continues to belong to them, notwithstanding change in Government of the State Party'.[71] The territorial administrations are not a new territorial sovereign, but perform extended public functions in the administered territory and control over it, and this implies that they shall continue to offer to the population the protection provided for in the human rights conventions previously applied in that territory. Moreover, it is undeniable that the same criterion cannot be used in cases in which sovereignty is disputed, for example in relation to the situation in East Timor.[72]

4.   THE JUDICIAL AND QUASI-JUDICIAL CONTROL OVER THE TERRITORIAL ADMINISTRATIONS: THE ATTRIBUTION OF CONDUCT AS THE PROPER CRITERION TO FIND OUT WHO IS THE OBLIGED SUBJECT

If, as just considered, territorial administrations are obliged to respect HRL in the administered territories, we must now investigate what are the legal means used by those who consider themselves victims of a violation committed by a territorial administration.

First of all, the judicial control of the local judges in the administered territory is essentially non-existent, not only because of the centralization of powers in the hands of the territorial administrations, but mostly because of the immunities enjoyed by the territorial administrations and by their personnel. In fact, as in general for peace operations,[73] even those with territorial administration functions enjoy substantial privileges and immunities; with reference to the territorial administrations established by the UN, the applicable rules derive from the Convention of 13 February 1946 on the Privileges and Immunities of the UN,[74] while in the case of the EU Administration in Mostar the rules of the Vienna Convention on Diplomatic Relations of 18 April 1961 were applied.[75]

But, whereas the usual system of immunities is justified by the need to protect the operations from any interference of the territorial sovereign, this justification cannot extend to the territorial administrations. The latter, in fact, have relevant governmental powers over the territories where they are deployed, and the corresponding powers of the territorial sovereign are highly reduced, as well as its possibility to hamper the activities of the territorial administrations.[76]

This broad immunity may appear as a guarantee of impunity in favour of the territorial administrations[77] and does not help to affirm the principles of justice and accountability in the administered territories.[78] Moreover, the provision of para. 51 of the 'UN Model SOFA' was not implemented; it provided for the establishment, in the context of the UN peace-keeping operations, of standing claims commissions to decide over any dispute or claim of a private law character to which the operation or any member thereof is a party and over which the domestic courts of the host country do not have jurisdiction because of the immunity. Usually, third party claims of private law type have been settled through a local claims review board, a UN administrative body operating in the host country, which cannot be considered a proper tribunal.

At any rate, the immunity of the staff involved in peace operations is not absolute and there is a tendency, within the UN, to limit it further,[79] and it should also be noted that the Secretary-General may (and, some say, must) waive the immunity in the presence of serious breaches. Following this trend and considering what we have just noted above, I think that the Security Council, when deciding to establish a territorial administration, should adopt a more restrictive approach regarding the immunity; and the Secretary-General should follow the same approach when he has to decide to waive an immunity.[80]

Given this broad limitation for the national judges, can the alleged victim utilize the control mechanisms included in international agreements declared applicable in the administered territories by virtue of an act adopted by the territorial administrations, against the territorial administrations? Is it possible to appeal to the UN Human Rights Committee, or to the European Court of Human Rights, against a violation of the UN Covenant on Civil and Political Rights, or a violation of the European Convention on Human Rights which occurred in the context of a territorial administration? To answer these questions it is necessary to identify who is responsible for the act or omission which caused the breach.

The proper criterion for the attribution of a conduct to a State or to the UN appears to be that of 'effective control', which is generally used in international law to allocate the international responsibility.[81] This criterion is also used by the International Law

Commission in Article 6 of the Draft Articles on Responsibility of international organizations, adopted at first reading on 6 July 2009.[82] In order to impute the act or the omission it is necessary to distinguish between personnel belonging to the organization, or otherwise placed under its effective control, as it is generally for the civilian component of the territorial administrations, from the staff which belongs to the States and is under their effective control, as it is usually for the military component of the territorial administrations. The attribution must be considered on a case-by-case basis, because in the practice often also the civilian and police personnel of peace operations is 'associated' or 'seconded' to the organization, and, as a consequence, effective responsibility for its activities is to be attributed to the organization or to the contributing States on the basis of the effective control exercised.[83]

If the violations can be attributed directly to the UN, the victim cannot appeal, because there is no jurisdiction *ratione personae*, as the UN has a juridical subjectivity distinct from that of its Member States and is not, as such, a Contracting Party to the aforementioned agreements. This seems to be the most correct solution, despite its paradoxical nature: those who are in the territory shall enjoy the rights posed by international agreements on human rights, also depending on the choices contained in acts of the territorial administrations, but against the latter the control mechanisms governed by the same agreements cannot be used.[84] In order to avoid, at least partly, that paradox, the approach centred on the concept of 'functional duality' of the International Administrations, chosen by the General Assembly with regard to the Council for Namibia,[85] and, in recent times, by the Constitutional Court of Bosnia and Herzegovina considering the powers exercised by the High Representative for that State,[86] could be followed. The latter, in fact, while acknowledging that it cannot control the powers of the High Representative, which derive from international instruments, however asserts that when such an institution acts in place of an institution of the Bosnian State and takes legislative measures, given that the Bosnian Constitution provides that such measures are subject to review by this Court, the same will occur when such measures are adopted by the High Representative.[87] This approach seems to have been accepted by the High Representative[88] and, in my opinion, should be applied also to the territorial administrations,[89] considering separately the activities carried out by the territorial administrations as subsidiary organs of the UN, and those carried out as the administrators of the territory. Hence, it will be necessary to identify from time to time both the benchmark to be considered in order to evaluate the measures adopted by the territorial administrations, and the court responsible for making this assessment, and its powers.

On the contrary, if the breach is attributable to a State Party, as caused by the action or omission of a subject on which that State has effective control, the injured parties can use against that State the remedies provided for by the above mentioned international agreements on human rights by which that State is bound. It is possible to derive this obligation by reason of the exercise of its jurisdiction in the administered territory (and with regard to personnel through which the jurisdiction is exercised).[90]

In this regard it is worth recalling the wording of the General Comment 31 adopted by the UN Human Rights Committee in 2004, which claims not only that 'a State Party must respect and ensure the rights laid down in the Covenant to anyone within the power or effective control of that State Party, even if not situated within the territory of the State Party', but also:

> This principle also applies to those within the power or effective control of the forces of a State Party acting outside its territory, regardless of the circumstances in which such power or effective control was obtained, such as forces constituting a national contingent of a State Party assigned to an international peace-keeping or peace-enforcement operation.[91]

Depending on the circumstances, there may also be a shared responsibility between the UN and a State,[92] or another international organization. This shared responsibility may derive from the difficulty to identify with clarity the chain of command in that peculiar situation or precisely the subject responsible for the violation.[93] It may also enhance the level of the protection offered to the victims of the violations, because it can be difficult for them to ascertain, with reference to a specific situation, to whom the violation is attributable, and because the interest of the victim is to have justice and a reparation, and it is secondary if these are given by the UN or by a State or another international organization.

I do not think that an obstacle to the use of international legal remedies by those who complain about violations of their human rights committed by a State in the context of a territorial administration may derive from the criterion of territorial application of the international agreements on human rights.[94] Rather, the extraterritorial application of the Covenant of 1966 has been authoritatively established not only by the same Committee, in its rulings on individual cases as well as in the aforementioned General Comment 31, but also by the International Court of Justice in its advisory opinion of 9 July 2004 on the *Legal Consequences of the Construction of a Wall in the Occupied Palestinian Territory*, together with the Covenant on Economic, Social and Cultural Rights, and with the UN Convention on the Rights of the Child of 20 November 1989.[95]

There is an extensive jurisprudence also on the extraterritorial application of some regional agreements on human rights protection. The extraterritorial application of the American Convention on Human Rights has been affirmed by the Inter-American Commission on Human Rights in the well known decision of 29 September 1999 in the case *Coard et al.* v. *United States*.[96] With regard to the European Convention on Human Rights, for many years the concept of 'jurisdiction' contained in its Article 1[97] has not been interpreted as strictly territorial, but also personal and functional, through the notion of 'effective control'.[98] The European Court chose a different approach in the decision of inadmissibility in the *Banković* case,[99] when, in order to deny its competence for the bombing of a Serbian radio and television station by aircraft of several NATO States, it interpreted the concept of jurisdiction as 'essentially territorial'. In the later case law, however, the Court has returned to interpreting the concept of jurisdiction as an effective control, so reaffirming the extraterritorial application of the European Convention.[100]

In the situation now under consideration, given that the territorial administrations undoubtedly exert a direct power over human beings, it seems possible to utilize against the States Parties of international agreements on human rights protection the remedies included in some of these agreements for the violations committed by individuals on which these States exercise an effective control.

A related problem, also resulting from the *Banković* case law, could arise from the possibility, affirmed by the Court, of considering only offences committed in the 'legal space' of the Convention, namely in the territory of one of its States Parties.[101] This criterion does not seem correct, nor acceptable.[102] Moreover, the Court itself has not reaffirmed that criterion in its subsequent judgments, and this leads us to consider it only an *obiter dictum* related to that case.[103]

The problems just discussed were not considered by the UN Human Rights Committee,[104] while they were the subject of a controversial ruling by the European Court of Human Rights, which on 2 May 2007 adopted the first decision on cases involving alleged breaches of human rights committed in Kosovo under direct UN administration.[105] The Grand Chamber decided, by majority vote, that the applications brought against certain States Parties were inadmissable, as the Court is not competent *ratione personae*. That ruling, by virtue of the considerations above, was correct in so far as the Court says it had no jurisdiction *ratione personae* to judge the acts attributable to UNMIK, as this is placed under the UN control, even if the Court could utilize the aforementioned theory of 'functional duality' developed by the Constitutional Court of Bosnia and Herzegovina in case U 9/00.

On the contrary, the reasoning of the Grand Chamber is absolutely not acceptable when it denies the attribution to States Parties of the acts committed by their organs participating in KFOR, on the assumption that the Security Council retains 'ultimate authority and control' over military presence, placed under the unified command of NATO, and that the UN is also responsible for the acts of the multinational force authorized.[106] This reconstruction of the Grand Chamber is incorrect in describing the KFOR, as it does not consider the difference between UN peace operations and forces authorized by the Security Council.[107] Indeed, as also noted in the Commentary to Draft Articles on Responsibility of international organizations previously mentioned, in considering the effective control it is not appropriate to refer to the criterion of 'ultimate control', as the European Court does, but rather to that of 'operational control'.[108]

Another concern stems from the fact that the Court has confirmed this approach in subsequent cases, both with regard to Kosovo,[109] and by applying the *Behrami* case law to cases that occurred in Bosnia and Herzegovina.[110]

However, there is still a major problem. In fact, a violation could be brought to the attention of the European Court or to the UN Human Rights Committee if it is committed by a person controlled by a State Party to the European Convention or to the Optional Protocol to the Covenant on Civil and Political Rights, or otherwise attributable to it, but this could not happen if the same violation is committed by a body belonging to a State not Party to these agreements. Therefore, there is a risk of causing a 'jeopardization' of the human rights protection in the context of the territorial administrations, because the rights shall be guaranteed to all, but only some may make an appeal if there is a breach of the same rights.

5. THE NON-JUDICIAL MECHANISMS FOR MONITORING COMPLIANCE WITH HUMAN RIGHTS BY THE TERRITORIAL ADMINISTRATIONS

With particular reference to respect for human rights by the territorial administrations, in addition to the judicial and quasi-judicial mechanisms of control above mentioned, the non-judicial mechanisms must also be considered, in particular the Ombudsperson institutions created by the territorial administrations in the 1990s.

The Administration for Mostar included an EU Ombudsman, provided for in Article 7A of the memorandum of understanding of 5 July 1994, and established by the EU Council.[111] The EU Ombudsman for Mostar was competent to receive any complaint from any natural person residing in the city and any legal person operating in it, directly and individually concerned, who claims that his or her rights have been violated by a decision of the European Union Administration in Mostar (EUAM), when all other legal remedies have been exhausted. The EU Ombudsman for Mostar may address recommendations concerning those claims to the EU Administrator and, in a serious matter, if the Administrator does not agree with the Ombudsman's recommendations, the latter may refer the matter to the EU Council.

In Kosovo the Ombudsperson Institution was established in 2000, with the task of promoting and protecting the rights and freedoms of everyone who lives and operates in that territory, ensuring that every natural or legal person can enjoy effectively the human rights conferred on it by the rules of international law, in particular by the European Convention on Human Rights and the UN Covenant on Civil and Political Rights.[112] The Ombudsperson has both tasks of preventive action, and subsequent action, since it is competent to receive and investigate complaints from any person in Kosovo concerning human rights violations and acts which constitute an abuse of authority by UNMIK or local institutions. The powers of this Institution, however, are limited when compared to the objective that it is called upon to pursue. In fact, it can only make recommendations or requests to the competent authorities and has no jurisdiction in respect of KFOR; it cannot access all detainees and documents; it must carry out its investigations with reference only to cases that occurred after 30 June 2000; and, if the authorities or public officials involved do not take the necessary measures within a period of time reasonable, or do not properly justify their refusal to meet the requirements of the Ombudsperson, the Institution can only bring this to the attention of the Special Representative, in addition to making public the circumstances of the case and its findings and recommendations.

Also UNTAET established an Ombudsperson Institution for East Timor. In 1999 the Secretary-General tasked its Special Representative to facilitate the creation of an independent East Timorese human rights institution, whose functions include the investigation of alleged violations of human rights.[113] That Institution was created informally in September 2000 and appointed in May 2001, being operational by that date. But UNTAET has not determined precisely its mandate in a regulation, nor has provided much information relating to its establishment, which has made the Ombudsperson for East Timor unimportant and rarely used.[114]

The creation of these institutions is to be welcomed, because it shows the commitment of the territorial administrations to ensure respect for human rights in carrying out their activities. These institutions, or similar mechanisms, should be used more widely within the territorial administrations.[115] Nonetheless, it is questionable that the Ombudsperson institutions have the power to cancel or amend the acts of the territorial administrations which are contrary to HRL. They, therefore, do not constitute an 'effective remedy' for the protection of human rights, having only limited powers, and they are thus a 'toothless' form of control that cannot be compared to a judicial authority. Plus, there is the issue of their independence in all cases where the territorial administration appoints the Ombudsperson, as well as replaces it, without the involvement of the representatives of the administered population. The greatest contribution made by the Ombudsperson lies in making public and accessible information and criticism on human rights protection in the territories placed under territorial administration.[116]

A change of some importance in relation to monitoring compliance with human rights in Kosovo by UNMIK was made in 2006 by establishing the Human Rights Advisory Panel, created under Regulation 2006/12.[117] The Advisory Panel is a non-judicial mechanism composed of three foreign experts appointed by the Special Representative on the proposal of the President of the European Court of Human Rights, and it has jurisdiction to consider petitions from individuals or groups of individuals about the violation of human rights posed by some international acts,[118] committed by UNMIK. The Panel carries out its activities at the request of an injured party or *ex officio* and can only deal with alleged violations which occurred on the territory of Kosovo after 23 April 2005 and those started earlier and continued after that date. It is, therefore, an authority of last resort, because it can take action within six months following the final decision on the issue and only after determining 'that all other available avenues for review of the alleged violations have been pursued'.

The Advisory Panel has the task of determining whether there has been a violation of human rights by UNMIK and to make such recommendations as it deems appropriate, which must be given wide publicity. But any final decision rests with the Special Representative, who, according to Regulation 2006/12, 'shall have exclusive authority and discretion to decide whether to act on the findings of the Advisory Panel'.

The establishment of the Advisory Panel is certainly positive, even for its appointment procedure, which is characterized by greater impartiality than a discretionary choice entirely made by the Special Representative. But the Advisory Panel has important limitations: it cannot deal with violations attributed to KFOR, while it has only power of exhortation, and is therefore not comparable to a court.[119] These elements of weakness of the Advisory Panel, together with the above mentioned limitation to its competence *ratione temporis*, raise doubts about the suitability of this mechanism to be an effective tool for sanctioning human rights violations attributable to UNMIK.

Monitoring the human rights situation in the administered territories may also derive from the acceptance of international monitoring mechanisms by the territorial administrations, which can be considered a manifestation of the previously mentioned self-binding commitment. Again the most notable example has concerned the Kosovo. Indeed, on 23 August 2004 UNMIK signed two Agreements with the Council of

Europe, through which it accepted the operation of the control mechanisms under the European Convention for the Prevention of Torture and Inhuman or Degrading Treatment or Punishment of 26 November 1987, and the Framework Convention for the Protection of National Minorities of 1 February 1995.[120] Both Agreements, on the assumption that UNMIK is not (neither could it become) a Party to these two Conventions, are intended to allow the control mechanisms laid down by the latter to carry out their functions with regard to Kosovo.

The first Agreement provides that UNMIK allows visits by the Committee for the Prevention of Torture and Inhuman or Degrading Treatment or Punishment in every place where persons are deprived of their liberty on the basis of an act of UNMIK. The Agreement provides that the Committee delivers a report and recommendations in confidence following the visit and that if UNMIK does not cooperate or refuses to improve the situation according to these recommendations, the Committee may decide by a majority of two-thirds of its members to make public its views on regard; in addition, the Committee must make public its report 'whenever requested to do so by UNMIK'.[121]

Under the second Agreement UNMIK accepted, also on behalf of the Provisional Institutions of Self-Government of Kosovo, to take action in accordance with the principles contained in the Framework Convention and to submit, within six months, a public report on the measures, legislative and other, taken to ensure compliance with those principles, and, thereafter, periodic reports.[122]

UNMIK has also submitted reports on the human rights situation in Kosovo to other international bodies, particularly the two Committees related to the UN Covenants of 1966, the Human Rights Committee and the Committee on Economic, Social and Cultural Rights, stating in both cases its claim to act 'under the authority granted to it' by Resolution 1244.[123]

6. CONCLUSIONS

The Agreements concluded with the Council of Europe and the reports submitted to international bodies just mentioned are positive changes, as they demonstrate the growing awareness and willingness by UNMIK to accept an independent external audit on effective human rights protection in the administered territory. In this perspective, it is necessary not only that this practice be confirmed by the future territorial administrations, but also that the importance granted to the non-judicial mechanisms under international agreements in the administered territories be gradually accompanied by the recognition of the powers – against human rights violations committed by the territorial administrations – of the judicial mechanisms, both domestic to the administered territories, and resulting from international agreements.

NOTES

*   Ivan Ingravallo is Associate Professor of International Law at the University of Bari 'Aldo Moro', Italy.

1. D. Shraga, 'Military Occupation and UN Transitional Administrations – The Analogy and Its Limitations', in *Promoting Justice, Human Rights and Conflict Resolution through International Law. La promotion de la justice, des droits de l'homme et du règlement des conflits par le droit international.* Liber Amicorum *Lucius Caflisch*, eds M. Kohen et al. (Leiden: Martinus Nijhoff, 2007), 483.

2. Basic Agreement on the Region of Eastern Slavonia, Baranja and Western Sirmium, 12 November 1995, known also as Erdut Agreement, see UN Doc. A/50/757-S/1995/951, 15 November 1995.

3. See G. Cellamare, 'Note sull'Amministrazione Transitoria delle Nazioni Unite in Slavonia Orientale (UNTAES)', in *Divenire sociale e adeguamento del diritto. Studi in onore di Francesco Capotorti*, Vol. I (Milan: Giuffrè, 1999), 83; P. Šimunović, 'A Framework for Success: Contextual Factors in the UNTAES Operation in Eastern Slavonia', *International Peacekeeping* 6(1) (1999): 126; J.-P. Klein, 'The United Nations Transitional Administration in Eastern Slavonia (UNTAES)', *ASIL Proceedings* 97 (2003): 205.

4. Resolution 1037, para. 2.

5. See, *ex multis*, E. Lagrange, 'La Mission intérimaire des Nations Unies au Kosovo, nouvel essai d'administration directe d'un territoire', *Annuaire Français de Droit International* 45 (1999): 335; T. Garcia, 'La Mission d'administration intérimaire des Nations Unies au Kosovo (MINUK)', *Revue Générale de Droit International Public* 104 (2001): 61; A. Yannis, 'Kosovo under International Administration', *Survival* 43 (2001–2002): 31; A. Zimmermann and C. Stahn, 'Yugoslav Territory, United Nations Trusteeship or Sovereign State? Reflections on the Current and Future Legal Status of Kosovo', *Nordic Journal of International Law* 70 (2001): 423; J. Friedrich, 'UNMIK in Kosovo: Struggling with Uncertainty', *Max Planck Yearbook of United Nations Law* 9 (2005): 225; G. Serra, 'The International Civil Administration in Kosovo: A Commentary on Some Major Legal Issues', *Italian Yearbook of International Law* 18 (2008): 63.

6. M. Guillaume, G. Marhic and G. Etienne, 'Le cadre juridique de l'action de la KFOR au Kosovo', *Annuaire Français de Droit International* 45 (1999): 308.

7. UNMIK and KFOR are autonomous and do not have a hierarchical relationship, while Resolution 1244 provides only a duty of mutual cooperation.

8. See Guillaume, Marhic and Etienne, *supra* note 6, at 316; Garcia, *supra* note 5, at 63; U. Villani, 'Les rapports entre l'ONU et les organisations régionales dans le domaine du maintien de la paix', *Recueil des Cours de l'Académie de Droit international de La Haye* 290 (2002): 421; Yannis, *supra* note 5, at 32; H. Corell, 'Authorization for State-Building Missions: Legal Issues Related to their Creation and Management', *ASIL Proceedings* 99 (2005): 32; P. Daillier, 'Les opérations multinationales consécutives à des conflits armés en vue du rétablissement de la paix', *Recueil des Cours de l'Académie de Droit international de La Haye* 314 (2005): 342; A. Heinemann-Grüder and I. Grebenschikov, 'Security Governance by Internationals: The Case of Kosovo', *International Peacekeeping* 13 (2006): 43.

9. Resolution 1244, para. 10.

10. UN Doc. S/1999/779, 12 July 1999, para. 35.

11. UNMIK/REG/1999/1, 25 July 1999, section 1.1.

12. Council of the European Union, Joint action 2008/124/CFSP, 4 February 2008, Article 3.

13. Report contained in UN Doc. S/2008/692, of 24 November 2008.

14. EULEX Kosovo will fully respect S/RES/1244, 10 June 1999, and operate under the overall authority and within the status-neutral framework of the United Nations. See UN Doc. S/PRST/2008/44 and, for references and practices, I. Ingravallo, 'Il Kosovo tra l'amministrazione delle Nazioni Unite e le prospettive di ammissione all'Unione europea', *Studi sull'integrazione europea* 5 (2010): 528.

15. UN Doc. A/53/951-S/1999/513, Annexes I–III (Agreement between the Republic of Indonesia and the Portuguese Republic on the question of East Timor; Agreement regarding the modalities for the popular consultation of the East Timorese through a direct ballot; East Timor popular consultation).

16. See, *ex multis*, J. Chopra, 'The UN's Kingdom in East Timor', *Survival* 42 (2003): 27; B. Kondoch, 'The United Nations Administration of East Timor', *Journal of Conflict and Security Law* 6 (2001): 245; S. Chesterman, 'East Timor in Transition: Self-determination, State-Building and the United Nations', *International Peacekeeping* 9(1) (2002): 45; M. Benzing, 'Midwifing a New State: The United Nations in East Timor', *Max Planck Yearbook of United Nations Law* 9 (2005): 295.

17. See, *ex multis*, M. Bothe and T. Marauhn, 'UN Administration of Kosovo and East Timor: Concept, Legality and Limitations of Security Council-Mandated Trusteeship Administration', in *Kosovo and the International Community: A Legal Assessment*, ed. C. Tomuschat (The Hague: Kluwer Law International, 2001), 217; M. Ruffert, 'The Administration of Kosovo and East-Timor by the

International Community', *International and Comparative Law Quarterly* 50 (2001): 613; Y. Daudet, 'L'action des Nations Unies en matière d'administration territoriale', *Cursos euromediterráneos Bancaja de derecho internacional* VI (2002): 459; S. Chesterman, *You, The People. The United Nations, Transitional Administrations, and State-Building* (Oxford: Oxford University Press, 2004); E. de Wet, 'The Direct Administration of Territories by the United Nations and its Member States in the Post-Cold War Era: Legal Bases and Implications for National Law', *Max Planck Yearbook of United Nations Law* 8 (2004): 291; R.D. Caplan, *International Governance of War-Torn Territories: Rule and Reconstruction* (Oxford: Oxford University Press, 2005); K. Ardault, C.-M. Arion, D. Gnamou-Petauton and M. Yetongnon, 'L'administration internationale du territoire à l'epreuve du Kosovo et du Timor Oriental: la pratique à la recherche d'une théorie', *Revue Belge de Droit International* 39 (2006): 300; D.S. Smyrek, *Internationally Administered Territories – International Protectorates? An Analysis of Sovereignty over Internationally Administered Territories with Special Reference to the Legal Status of Post-War Kosovo* (Berlin: Dunker and Humblot, 2006); M.J. Aznar-Gómez, *La administración internacionalizada del territorio* (Barcelona: Atelier, 2008); G.H. Fox, *Humanitarian Occupation* (Cambridge: Cambridge University Press, 2008); I. Ingravallo, *Il Consiglio di sicurezza e l'amministrazione diretta di territori* (Naples: Editoriale Scientifica, 2008); H.F. Kiderlen, *Von Triest nach Osttimor. Der völkerrechtliche Rahmen für die Verwaltung von Krisengebieten durch die Vereinten Nationen* (Berlin: Springer, 2008); B. Knoll, *The Legal Status of Territories Subject to Administration by International Organisations* (Cambridge: Cambridge University Press, 2008); C. Stahn, *The Law and Practice of International Territorial Administration: Versailles to Iraq and Beyond* (Cambridge: Cambridge University Press, 2008); R. Wilde, *International Territorial Administration: How Trusteeship and the Civilizing Mission Never Went Away* (Oxford: Oxford University Press, 2008); E. de Brabandere, *Post-conflict Administrations in International Law. International Territorial Administration, Transitional Authority and Foreign Occupation in Theory and Practice* (Leiden: Martinus Nijhoff, 2009); O. Tansey, *Regime-building: Democratization and International Administration* (Oxford: Oxford University Press, 2009).

18. See paras 16–33 of Annex to Article 50 of the Versailles Treaty, which entrusted the power to administer the Saar Basin to a Commission of the LoN, and the subsequent Resolutions adopted by the Council of the LoN.

19. See the Geneva Agreement concluded between Colombia and Peru (25 May 1933) and the subsequent Resolutions adopted by the Council of the LoN.

20. See the New York Agreement concluded between Indonesia and The Netherlands (15 August 1962), as a result of which the General Assembly adopted the Resolution A/RES/1752 (XVII), 21 September 1962, and decided to deploy UNTEA (United Nations Temporary Executive Authority) in that territory. In October 1962 the Secretary-General made available to UNTEA a military force tasked with peace-keeping (UNSF, United Nations Security Force).

21. See the annexes VI and VII of the Peace Treaty with Italy, concluded in Paris on 10 February 1947, which placed the territory under the authority of the Security Council. The latter approved the Resolution 16 of 10 January 1947, which accepted the responsibilities incumbent on it deriving from the instrument for the provisional regime of the Free Territory and from the Permanent Statute for the Free Territory, but these obligations weren't implemented.

22. On 29 November 1947 the General Assembly adopted Resolution 181 (II), by which it recommended the establishment of Jerusalem as a *corpus separatum*, subject to a peculiar regime of direct UN administration. The UN Trusteeship Council approved the Statute for Jerusalem (see UN Docs T/118/Rev.2, 21 April 1948, and T/592, 4 April 1950), but the administration wasn't realized.

23. On 19 May 1967, the General Assembly adopted Resolution A/RES/2248(S-V) establishing the United Nations Council for Namibia, with the task of administering that territory until its independence. The opposition of South Africa has impeded the Council in the exercise of most of its activities.

24. On 29 April 1991 the Security Council adopted Resolution S/RES/690, establishing MINURSO (United Nations Mission for the Referendum in Western Sahara). MINURSO was tasked with the sole and exclusive authority on every question related to the referendum, including its military component. Morocco did not cooperate with MINURSO and it has fulfilled only a minor part of its broad mandate. The planned referendum in 1988 has not yet taken place and the Security Council has progressively limited the operation's mandate.

25. By the Paris Agreements of 23 October 1991, the Cambodian factions asked the UN to administer many sectors of their State. UNTAC (United Nations Transitional Authority in Cambodia) was established by the Security Council Resolution 745, of 28 February 1992. In practice, UNTAC has exercised only a part of its broad powers, mainly because of the insufficient cooperation of the

factions in achieving the goals set in the Paris Agreements and the choice of the Special Representative of the Secretary-General in an approach characterized by the control and supervision of Cambodian institutions, rather than direct management.

26. EUAM (European Union Administration in Mostar) was established by the EU following a request contained in the agreement concluded in Washington on 18 March 1994 on the creation of the Muslim-Croat Federation of Bosnia and Herzegovina, followed by the memorandum of understanding concluded in Geneva on 5 July 1994 between the EU and WEU Member States and the Republic of Bosnia and Herzegovina, the Federation of Bosnia and Herzegovina, the local administrations of Mostar and the Bosnian Croats. See the Decisions of the Council of the European Union: 94/308/CFSP, 16 May 1994; 94/790/CFSP, 12 December 1994; 95/23/CFSP, 6 February 1995; 95/517/CFSP, 4 December 1995; 95/552/CFSP, 19 December 1995. About EUAM, see F. Pagani, 'L'Administration de Mostar par l'Union européenne', *Annuaire Français de Droit International* 42 (1996): 234; O. Korhonen, 'International Governance in Post-Conflict Situations', *Leiden Journal of International Law* 14 (2001): 520.

27. M. Virally, 'La notion de fonction dans la théorie de l'organisation internationale,' in *Mélanges offerts a Charles Rousseau* (Paris: Pedone, 1974), 292, affirmed: 'le traité constitutif d'une Organisation n'établit plus qu'une structure fondamentale, mais inachevée, appelée à connaître un continuel développement, au fur et à mesure de l'apparition de besoins fonctionnels nouveaux'.

28. F. Seyersted, 'United Nations Forces: Some Legal Problems', *British Yearbook of International Law* 31 (1961): 451. Daudet, *supra* note 17, at 473, affirms that there is a 'véritable *principe d'adaptation constante*' of the purposes contained in Article 1 of the UN Charter. See also the recent analysis carried out by B. Conforti and C. Focarelli, *The Law and Practice of the United Nations*, 4th revised edition (The Hague: Martinus Nijhoff, 2010), 294.

29. J. Crawford, *The Creation of States in International Law*, 2nd edition (Oxford: Oxford University Press, 2006), 564. In the Report of the Panel on the United Nations Peace Operations (*Brahimi Report*, UN Doc. A/55/305-S/2000/809, 21 August 2000), for example, it is written that the territorial administration 'faces challenges and responsibilities that are unique among United Nations field operations'. The Report poses 'the larger question of whether the United Nations should be in this business at all, and if so whether it should be considered an element of peace operations or should be managed by some other structure' (paras 77–78).

30. The Administration for Bosnia and Herzegovina is headed by a High Representative, whose extensive powers come from Article V of Annex X to the Dayton Peace Agreement, signed in Paris on 14 December 1995, and para. 2 of section XI of the Conclusions of the Peace Implementation Council, adopted at the end of the Bonn meeting of 9–10 December 1997. The High Representative is appointed by (and accountable to) the Peace Implementation Council, which includes more than fifty States and intergovernmental organizations and agencies involved in implementing the Dayton Agreement, and is only supported by the UN Security Council. See M. Cox, 'The Dayton Agreement in Bosnia and Herzegovina: A Study of Implementation Strategies', *British Yearbook of International Law* 69 (1998): 201ss.; K. Oellers-Frahm, 'Restructuring Bosnia-Herzegovina: A Model with Pit-Falls', *Max Planck Yearbook of United Nations Law* 9 (2005): 179ss.

31. C. Stahn, 'International Territorial Administration in the former Yugoslavia: Origins, Developments and Challenges ahead', *Zeitschrift für ausländisches öffentliches Recht und Völkerrecht* 61 (2001): 135; A. Yannis, 'The Concept of Suspended Sovereignty in International Law and its Implications in International Politics', *European Journal of International Law* 13 (2002): 1037; B. Knoll, 'United Nations *Imperium*: Horizontal and Vertical Transfer of Effective Control and the Concept of Residual Sovereignty in "Internationalized Territories"', *Austrian Review of International and European Law* 7 (2002): 3; M. Salamun, *Democratic Governance in International Territorial Administration. Institutional Prerequisites for Democratic Governance in the Constitutional Documents of Territories Administered by International Organisations* (Baden-Baden: Nomos, 2005), 31.

32. Zimmermann and Stahn, *supra* note 5, at 423. For a different opinion, see M.J. Matheson, 'United Nations Governance of Postconflict Societies', *American Journal of International Law* 95 (2001): 76; F.L. Kirgis, 'Security Council Governance of Postconflict Societies: A Plea for Good Faith and Informed Decision Making', *American Journal of International Law* 95 (2001): 579. For a critical opinion about the inaction of the UN after the declaration of independence of Kosovo, see I. Ingravallo, 'Kosovo after the ICJ Advisory Opinion: Towards a European Perspective?', *International Community Law Review* 14 (2012): 219.

33. See Bothe and Marauhn, *supra* note 17, at 238; J. Cerone, 'Minding the Gap: Outlining KFOR Accountability in Post-Conflict Kosovo', *European Journal of International Law* 12 (2001): 485; S.S.

Ratner, 'Foreign Occupation and International Territorial Administration: The Challenges of Convergence', *European Journal of International Law* 16 (2005): 695; A. Roberts, 'Transformative Military Occupation: Applying the Laws of War and Human Rights', in *International Law and Armed Conflict: Exploring the Faultlines. Essays in Honour of Yoram Dinstein*, eds M.N. Schmitt and J. Pejic (Leiden: Martinus Nijhoff, 2007), 490; Y. Arai-Takahashi, *The Law of Occupation: Continuity and Change of International Humanitarian Law, and its Interaction with International Human Rights Law* (Leiden: Martinus Nijhoff, 2009), 584. T.H. Irmscher, 'The Legal Framework for the Activities of the United Nations Interim Administration Mission in Kosovo: The Charter, Human Rights, and the Law of Occupation', *German Yearbook of International Law* 44 (2001): 374, affirms that the applicability to UNMIK of the rules on occupation is subordinate to Resolution 1244. For a partially different opinion, see C. Rueger, 'The Law of Military Occupation: Recent Developments of the Law of Military Occupation with Regard to UN Security Council Mandated International Territorial Administrations', *Revue de droit militaire et de droit de la guerre* 45 (2006): 226, that suggests applying to the territorial administrations both the principles and rules on occupation and those deriving from the concept of trusteeship. In a broader perspective, see C. Stahn, '"*Jus ad bellum*", "*jus in bello*"... "*jus post bellum*"? Rethinking the Conception of the Law of Armed Force', *European Journal of International Law* 17 (2007): 921.

34. See Articles 42–56.
35. See Articles 27–33 and 47–78.
36. See Article 72.
37. See F. Mégret and F. Hoffmann, 'The UN as a Human Rights Violator? Some Reflections on the United Nations Changing Human Rights Responsibilities', *Human Rights Quarterly* 25 (2003): 333; de Wet, *supra* note 17, at 323; Daillier, *supra* note 8, at 368; Friedrich, *supra* note 5, at 281; P. Picone, 'Le autorizzazioni all'uso della forza tra sistema delle Nazioni Unite e diritto internazionale generale', *Rivista di diritto internazionale* 88 (2005): 55, footnote 144; Ardault et al., *supra* note 17, at 358; Shraga, *supra* note 1, at 479.
38. Conforti and Focarelli, *supra* note 28, at 298.
39. Bothe and Marauhn, *supra* note 17, at 220; M. Sassòli, 'Droit international pénal et droit pénal interne: le cas des territoires se trouvant sous administration internationale', in *Le droit pénal à l'épreuve de l'internationalisation*, eds R. Roth and M. Henzelin (Paris/Geneva/Bruxelles: L.G.D.J./Georg/Bruylant, 2002), 147; Leopold von Carlowitz, 'UNMIK Lawmaking between Effective Peace Support and Internal Self-determination', *Archiv des Völkerrechts* 41 (2003): 364; de Wet, *supra* note 17, at 330; S. Vité, 'L'applicabilité du droit international de l'occupation militaire aux activités des organisations internationales', *Revue internationale de la Croix-Rouge* 86 No 853 (2004): 19 and 25; Shraga, *supra* note 1, at 493.
40. Sassòli, *supra* note 39, at 143; von Carlowitz, *supra* note 39, at 364 and 374; Friedrich, *supra* note 5, at 281; Ardault et al., *supra* note 17, at 360; Shraga, *supra* note 1, at 496. In the opinion of Ratner, *supra* note 33, at 705, footnote 39, this distinction is 'somewhat baffling'.
41. In the opinion of R. Kolb, G. Porretto and S. Vité, *L'application du droit international humanitaire et des droits de l'homme aux organisations internationales. Forces de paix et administrations civiles transitoires* (Brussels: Bruylant, 2005), 225, in the legal regime of the territorial administration there is 'une adaptation' of the rules of the military occupation, with reference to the rules finalized on the protection of the individuals (not for those related to the prerogatives of the occupier).
42. Rueger, *supra* note 33, at 222; Shraga, *supra* note 1, at 487.
43. See the Note of the Assistant Secretary-General of 5 January 2004, published in *United Nations Juridical Yearbook*, 2004, Part 2, Chapter VI, 350.
44. See, in general, R. Murphy, 'United Nations Military Operations and International Humanitarian Law: What Rules Apply to Peacekeepers?', *Criminal Law Forum* 14 (2003): 189; N. Ronzitti, *Diritto internazionale dei conflitti armati*, 4th edition (Turin: Giappichelli, 2011), 156. See also M. Sassòli, 'Legislation and Maintenance of Public Order and Civil Life by Occupying Powers', *European Journal of International Law* 16 (2005): 686; C. Greenwood, 'Scope of Application of Humanitarian Law', in *The Handbook of International Humanitarian Law*, ed. D. Fleck, 2nd revised edition (Oxford: Oxford University Press, 2008), 51; O. Engdahl, 'Compliance with International Humanitarian Law in Multinational Peace Operations', *Nordic Journal of International Law* 78 (2009): 513; R. Kolb and S. Vité, *Le droit de l'occupation militaire. Perspectives historiques et enjeux juridiques actuels* (Brussels: Bruylant, 2009), 100.
45. UN Doc. A/46/185, 23 May 1991.
46. UN Doc. ST/SGB/1999/13, 6 August 1999.

47. Kolb, Porretto and Vité, *supra* note 41, at 225, affirm that in the future the Security Council should adopt a Resolution on the application *de facto* of the rules on military occupation by the Territorial Administrations. The opinion is shared by Arai-Takahashi, *supra* note 33, at 606.

48. Article 4, Human rights and fundamental freedoms: 'The Constitution of the Free Territory shall ensure to all persons under the jurisdiction of the Free Territory, without distinction as to ethnic origin, sex, language or religion, the enjoyment of human rights and of the fundamental freedoms, including freedom of religious worship, language, speech and publication, education, assembly and association. Citizens of the Free Territory shall be assured of equality of eligibility for public office.' Article 17, Responsibility of the Governor to the Security Council: 'The Governor, as the representative of the Security Council, shall be responsible for supervising the observance of the present Statute including the protection of the basic human rights of the inhabitants … .'

49. Article 9, Human rights and fundamental freedoms: '1. All persons are entitled to all the rights and freedoms set forth in this Statute, without distinction of any kind, such as race, colour, sex, language, religion, political or other opinion, national or social origin, property, birth or other status.… 15. Without prejudice to the provisions of the preceding paragraphs, the Universal Declaration of Human Rights shall be accepted as a standard of achievement for the City.' Article 13, General powers of the Governor: '1. The Governor shall be the representative of the United Nations in the City. 2. The Governor, on behalf of the United Nations, shall exercise executive authority in the City and shall act as the chief administrative officer thereof, subject only to the provisions of this Statute and to the Instructions of the Trusteeship Council.'

50. New York Agreement of 15 August 1962, Article XXII, para. 1: 'The UNTEA and Indonesia will guarantee fully the rights, including the rights of free speech, freedom of movement and of assembly of the inhabitants of the area. These rights will include the existing rights of the inhabitants of the territory at the time of the transfer of administration to the UNTEA.'

51. See also para. 42 of Secretary-General Report S/1999/779: 'In assuming its responsibilities, UNMIK will be guided by internationally recognized standards of human rights as the basis for the exercise of its authority in Kosovo. UNMIK will embed a culture of human rights in all areas of activity, and will adopt human rights policies in respect of its administrative functions.'

52. See also para. 38 of Secretary-General Report S/1999/779.

53. Universal Declaration on Human Rights of 10 December 1948; European Convention for the Protection of Human Rights and Fundamental Freedoms of 4 November 1950 and the Protocols thereto; International Covenant on Civil and Political Rights of 16 December 1966 and the Protocols thereto; International Covenant on Economic, Social and Cultural Rights of 16 December 1966; Convention on the Elimination of All Forms of Racial Discrimination of 21 December 1965; Convention on Elimination of All Forms of Discrimination Against Women of 17 December 1979; Convention Against Torture and Other Cruel, Inhumane or Degrading Treatment or Punishment of 17 December 1984; International Convention on the Rights of the Child of 20 December 1989.

54. UNMIK/REG/2001/9, 15 May 2001, Chapter 3.

55. For a shared critical review, see A. Devereux, 'Searching for Clarity: A Case Study of UNTAET's Application of International Human Rights Norms', in *The UN, Human Rights and Post-Conflict Situations*, eds N.D. White and D. Klaasen (Manchester: Manchester University Press, 2005), 297.

56. UNTAET/REG/1999/1, 27 November 1999.

57. B. Kondoch, 'Human Rights Law and UN Peace Operations in Post-Conflict Situations', in *The UN, Human Rights and Post-Conflict Situations*, eds N.D. White and D. Klaasen (Manchester: Manchester University Press, 2005), 33; J. Cerone, 'Reasonable Measures in Unreasonable Circumstances: A Legal Responsibility Framework for Human Rights Violations in Post-Conflict Territories under UN Administration', in *The UN, Human Rights and Post-Conflict Situations*, eds N.D. White and D. Klaasen (Manchester: Manchester University Press, 2005), 61.

58. C. Bongiorno, 'A Culture of Impunity: Applying International Human Rights Law to the United Nations in East Timor', *Columbia Human Rights Law Review* 33 (2002): 623; E. Abraham, 'The Sins of the Saviour: Holding the United Nations Accountable to International Human Rights Standards for Executive Order Detentions in Its Mission in Kosovo', *American University Law Review* 52 (2003): 1291; Mégret and Hoffmann, *supra* note 37, at 314; I. Ingravallo, 'La tutela dei diritti umani nel Kosovo sotto amministrazione diretta dell'ONU', in *Studi in onore di Vincenzo Starace*, Vol. I (Naples: Editoriale Scientifica, 2008), 447; A. Devereux, 'Selective Universality? Human-Rights Accountability of the UN in post-Conflict Operations', in *The Role of International Law in Rebuilding Societies after Conflict: Great Expectations*, eds B. Bowden, H. Charlesworth and J. Farrall (Cambridge: Cambridge University Press, 2009), 198; P. Klein, 'L'administration internationale de territoire: quelle place pou

l'Etat de droit?', in *L'Etat de droit en droit international* (Paris: Pedone, 2009), 392. As for Kosovo, see the extensive report on the human rights situation after June 1999 presented by UNMIK to the UN Human Rights Committee (UN Doc. CCPR/C/UNK/1, 13 March 2006), that was the subject of several surveys by the same Committee in its Concluding Observation (UN Doc. CCPR/C/UNK/CO/1, 14 August 2006). See also the Opinion 280/2004 of the European Commission for Democracy through Law (Venice Commission) on Human Rights in Kosovo: Possible Establishment of Review Mechanism, 11 October 2004, CDL-AD (2004)033.

59. See J.C. Beauvais, 'Benevolent Despotism: A Critique of U.N. State-Building in East Timor', *New York University Journal of International Law and Politics* 33 (2001): 1169; Bongiorno, *supra* note 58, at 632.

60. M.G. Brand, 'Institution-Building and Human Rights Protection in Kosovo in the Light of UNMIK Legislation', *Nordic Journal of International Law* 70 (2001): 462; Klein, *supra* note 58, at 392. See also von Carlowitz, *supra* note 39, at 347; Chesterman, *supra* note 17, at 127; E. de Wet, *The Chapter VII Powers of the United Nations Security Council* (Oxford: Hart, 2004), 320; Friedrich, *supra* note 5, at 284; Kolb, Porretto and Vité, *supra* note 41, at 259.

61. Bongiorno, *supra* note 58, at 638, and Kolb, Porretto and Vité, *supra* note 41, at 254 and 335, emphasize the difficulty of identifying precisely which rules of IHL and HRL are part of *ius cogens*.

62. S. Marchisio, *L'ONU. Il diritto delle Nazioni Unite* 2nd edition (Bologna: il Mulino, 2012), 75; Benzing, *supra* note 16, at 326.

63. Zimmermann and Stahn, *supra* note 5, at 445. See also J. Werzer, 'The UN Human Rights Obligations and Immunity: An Oxymoron Casting a Shadow on the Transitional Administrations in Kosovo and East Timor', *Nordic Journal of International Law* 77 (2008): 111, who affirms that the Security Council 'is bound by international human rights, not only because of their being part of customary international law, but… also because they are included in the principles and purposes of the UN'.

64. See Bothe and Marauhn, *supra* note 17, at 237: 'if UNMIK is to protect human rights, it cannot itself violate human rights standards'; D. Marshall and S. Inglis, 'The Disempowerment of Human Rights-Based Justice in the United Nations Mission in Kosovo', *Harvard Human Rights Journal* 16 (2003): 104.

65. For a different opinion, see Kolb, Porretto and Vité, *supra* note 41, at 241.

66. Irmscher, *supra* note 33, at 372; Kolb, Porretto and Vité, *supra* note 41, at 241; M. Tondini, 'The "Italian Job": How to Make International Organisations Compliant with Human Rights and Accountable for Their Violations by Targeting Member States', in *Accountability for Human Rights Violations by International Organisations*, eds J. Wouters et al. (Antwerp: Intersentia, 2010), 191.

67. M. Forteau, 'Le droit applicable en matière de droits de l'homme aux administrations territoriales gérées par des organisations internationales', in *La soumission des organisations internationales aux normes internationales relatives aux droits de l'homme*, SFDI (Paris: Pedone, 2009), 24.

68. Bothe and Marauhn, *supra* note 17, at 237; Irmscher, *supra* note 33, at 366; Stahn, *supra* note 31, at 150; Marshall and Inglis, *supra* note 64, at 104; Kolb, Porretto and Vité, *supra* note 41, at 245; Benzing, *supra* note 16, at 324; Friedrich, *supra* note 5, at 270. For a critique to this approach, see Forteau, *supra* note 67, at 19.

69. See the 'UN Model SOFA', contained in the Secretary-General Report of 9 October 1990 (UN Doc. A/45/594). See also the Model memorandum of understanding between the United Nations and [Participating State] contributing resources to [the United Nations Peacekeeping Operation] (UN Doc. A/51/967, 27 August 1997). This Model memorandum of understanding was modified in 2007 to increase the obligations of human rights protection borne by the peacekeepers and their awareness of how to behave, and also to ensure a more effective punishment of those found guilty of wrongdoing: see UN Doc. A/61/19 (Part III), 12 June 2007. See Z. Deen-Racsmány, 'The Amended UN Model Memorandum of Understanding: A New Incentive for States to Discipline and Prosecute Military Members of National Peacekeeping Contingents?', *Journal of Conflict & Security Law* 16 (2011): 321.

70. See, Continuity of Obligations, HRC, 8 December 1997 (UN Doc. CCPR/C/21/Rev.1/Add.8/Rev.1). See Cerone, *supra* note 33, at 474; Irmscher, *supra* note 33, at 371; Benzing, *supra* note 16, at 329; Kolb, Porretto and Vité, *supra* note 41, at 280.

71. As regards Kosovo, on 28 July 2004 this Committee, considering the inability of the State of Serbia and Montenegro to discharge its responsibilities with regard to the human rights situation in Kosovo, and considering also that the Covenant continues to remain applicable in Kosovo, has encouraged UNMIK, in cooperation with the Provisional Institutions of Kosovo, to provide a report on the

situation of human rights in Kosovo since June 1999. See Concluding Observations on Serbia, HRC, 12 August 2004 (UN Doc. CCPR/CO/81/SEMO), para. 3.

72. See Ardault et al., *supra* note 17, at 364, note 337; Forteau, *supra* note 67, at 26.

73. See the 'UN Model SOFA' and the Model agreement between the UN and Member States contributing personnel and equipment to UN peace-keeping operations. See F. Rawski, 'To Waive or Not To Waive: Immunity and Accountability in U.N. Peacekeeping Operations', *Connecticut Journal of International Law* 18 (2002): 111; Werzer, *supra* note 63, at 118.

74. For UNTEA see Article XXVI of the New York Agreement of 1962. For UNTAES see the request of the Security Council to Croatia to extend the territorial application of the previous SOFA of 15 May 1995 (para. 13 of Resolution 1037) and the exchange of letters published in *United Nations Juridical Yearbook*, 1996, Part 1, Chapter II, 14. UNMIK did not conclude a SOFA with FRY and adopted a Regulation on the privileges and immunities of UNMIK and KFOR (UNMIK/REG/2000/47, 18 August 2000). UNTAET did not conclude a SOFA, nor adopt an *ad hoc* Regulation, but in practice has provided large functional immunities for its personnel on the basis of the UN Convention of 1946. See Rawski, *supra* note 73, at 118.

75. See Article 19 of the *memorandum of understanding* of 5 July 1994.

76. See C. Stahn, 'The United Nations Transitional Administrations in Kosovo and East Timor. A First Analysis', *Max Planck Yearbook of United Nations Law* 5 (2001): 160; Daudet, *supra* note 17, at 536; Rawski, *supra* note 73, at 105; Benzing, *supra* note 16, at 342; Friedrich, *supra* note 5, at 277; Kolb, Porretto and Vité, *supra* note 41, at 408; Ardault et al., *supra* note 17, at 365; R. Everly, 'Reviewing Governmental Acts of the United Nations in Kosovo', *German Law Journal* 8 (2007): 21.

77. Rawski, *supra* note 73, at 114. See also Daillier, *supra* note 8, at 417; Marshall and Inglis, *supra* note 64, at 112. In the opinion of Condorelli, 'Conclusions', in *La soumission des organisations internationales aux normes internationales relatives aux droits de l'homme* (Paris: Pedone, 2009), 127: 's'il n'y a pas de juge international habilité à vérifier le respect des droits de l'homme ou, pour mieux dire, si l'organisation internationale n'offre pas de garanties équivalentes, alors l'immunité de l'organisation ne devrait pas pouvoir être invoquée avec succès devant les juges nationaux'. See also T. Dannenbaum, 'Translating the Standard of Effective Control into a System of Effective Accountability: How Liability Should Be Apportioned for Violations of Human Rights by Member State Troop Contingents Serving as United Nations Peacekeepers', *Harvard International Law Journal* 51 (2010): 191.

78. See the Special Report 1 of the Ombudsperson Institution in Kosovo, of 26 April 2001 (On the Compatibility with Recognized International Standards of UNMIK Regulation 2000/47 on the Status, Privileges and Immunities of KFOR and UNMIK and their Personnel in Kosovo): 'The rationale for classical grants of immunity, however, does not apply to the circumstances prevailing in Kosovo, where … UNMIK … in fact acts as a surrogate state. It follows that the underlying purpose of a grant of immunity does not apply as there is no need for a government to be protected against itself … .'

79. See the Report of the Group of experts on recommendations to ensure the accountability of United Nations staff and experts on mission with respect of criminal acts committed in peacekeeping operations (UN Doc. A/60/980, 16 August 2006), and the subsequent Resolutions adopted by *consensus* by the General Assembly (A/RES/62/63, 6 December 2007; A/RES/63/119, 11 December 2008; A/RES/64/110, 16 December 2009; A/RES/65/20, 6 December 2010; and A/RES/66/93, 9 December 2011). See M. Odello, 'Tackling Criminal Acts in Peacekeeping Operations: The Accountability of Peacekeepers', *Journal of Conflict and Security Law* 15 (2010): 347.

80. See the opinion contained in the above mentioned Report of the Group of experts, 11: 'A peacekeeping mission may be given an executive mandate so that it exercises governmental powers in the host State. This enables the United Nations, as the administering authority, to create a legal system that complies with rule-of-law requirements. In these situations, the host State will be the State asserting jurisdiction over serious crimes committed by peacekeeping personnel. In addition, as the United Nations has established a system with respect for human rights as one component, the Secretary-General should have less difficulty waiving any applicable immunity for this purpose.'

81. Kolb, Porretto and Vité, *supra* note 41, at 426; Ingravallo, *supra* note 58, at 447. For a different, not convincing, approach, see M. Forteau, 'La situation juridique des contingents militaires français charges d'assurer le maintien de l'ordre public sur le territoire d'un Etat étranger', *Revue Générale de Droit International Public* 107 (2003): 637.

82. Article 6 of the Draft Articles: 'The conduct of an organ of a State or an organ or agent of an international organization that is placed at the disposal of another international organization shall be considered under international law an act of the latter organization if the organization exercises

effective control over that conduct.' The Draft Articles have been adopted on the basis of the proposals made by the Special Rapporteur Giorgio Gaja. For the text of the Draft Articles and its Commentary see UN Doc. A/64/10, Report of the International Law Commission Sixty-first session (4 May–5 June and 6 July–7 August 2009), 19. See the recent extensive contribution of Dannenbaum, *supra* note 77, at 156.

83. M. Tondini, 'Putting an End to Human Rights Violations by Proxy: Accountability of UN and Member States in the Framework of Jus Post Bellum', in *Jus Post Bellum. Towards a Law of Transition from Conflict to Peace*, eds C. Stahn and J.K. Kleffner (The Hague: TMC Asser Press, 2008), 200. See also Tondini, *supra* note 66, at 185; P.C. Cammaert and B. Klappe, 'Authority, Command, and Control in United Nations-led Peace Operations', in *Handbook of the International Law of Military Operations*, eds T. Gill and D. Fleck (Oxford: Oxford University Press, 2010), 159.

84. M.J. Aznar-Gómez, 'Some Paradoxes on Human Rights Protection in Kosovo', in *Völkerrecht als Wertordnung, Common Values in International Law. Festschrift für Christian Tomuschat, Essays in Honour of Christian Tomuschat*, eds P.M. Dupuy et al. (Kehl: Engel, 2006), 32.

85. See A/RES/32/9F, 4 November 1977, Programme of work of the United Nations Council for Namibia, and the *memorandum* to the Under-Secretary-General of 20 April 1982, on the Legal status of United Nations Council for Namibia in regard to the United Nations Convention on the Law of the Sea, in *United Nations Juridical Yearbook* (1982): Part 2, Chapter VI, 165.

86. See the sentences in cases U 9/00, 3 November 2000, and U 25/00, 23 March 2001, available at http://www.ustavnisud.ba (accessed 12 February 2012). For a comment, see J. Marko, 'Challenging the Authority of the UN High Representative Before the Constitutional Court of Bosnia and Herzegovina', in *Review of the Security Council by Member States*, eds E. de Wet, P.A. Nollkaemper and P. Dijkstra (Antwerp: Intersentia, 2003), 113. In the legal doctrine, the functional duality of the territorial administrations has been recognized by Ruffert, *supra* note 17, at 626; von Carlowitz, *supra* note 39, at 344; B. Knoll, 'From Benchmarking to Final Status? Kosovo and the Problem of an International Administration's Open-ended Mandate', *European Journal of International Law* 16 (2005): 645; Forteau, *supra* note 67, at 11. For a different opinion, see Daudet, *supra* note 17, at 502; Kolb, Porretto and Vité, *supra* note 41, at 112.

87. See Stahn, *supra* note 31, at 166; Oellers-Frahm, *supra* note 30, at 211; Salamun, *supra* note 31, at 160: 'Bosnia and Herzegovina presents the only territory administered by UN, in which the acts of the international administrator are subject to judicial review'; B. Knoll, 'Beyond the Mission Civilisatrice: The Properties of a Normative Order within an Internationalized Territory', *Leiden Journal of International Law* 19 (2006): 295.

88. See Order on the Implementation of the Decision of the Constitutional Court of Bosnia and Herzegovina in the Appeal of Milorad Bilbija et al., NO. AP-953/05, in which the High Representative affirms: '*Considering* that the High Representative intends to continue to consent to the review of certain of his acts within the framework of the above-mentioned domestic theory of functional duality … .' In Article 2 he adds: 'Any step taken by any institution or authority in Bosnia and Herzegovina in order to establish any domestic mechanism to review the Decisions of the High Representative issued pursuant to his international mandate [not the internal one] shall be considered by the High Representative as an attempt to undermine the implementation of the civilian aspects of the General Framework Agreement for Peace in Bosnia and Herzegovina and shall be treated in itself as conduct undermining such implementation.'

89. For a different opinion, see Daudet, *supra* note 17, at 531, who considers the situation of the territorial administrations as different from that of Bosnia and Herzegovina: 'la conception qui sous-tend les opérations d'administration territoriale des Nations Unies vise à réaliser une certaine extériorité de l'administration internationale par rapport au territoire et à ses institutions. … Dès lors, bien qu'ils soient évidemment pris au bénéfice du territoire considéré, les actes adoptés demeurent donc des actes des Nations Unies'.

90. See Cerone, *supra* note 33, at 475; N. Mole, 'Who Guards the Guards – the Rule of Law in Kosovo', *European Human Rights Law Review* 6 (2001): 285; Stahn, *supra* note 31, at 151; Marshall and Inglis, *supra* note 64, at 105; de Wet, *supra* note 60, at 324; Friedrich, *supra* note 5, at 272; Kolb, Porretto and Vité, *supra* note 41, at 288; Knoll, *supra* note 87, at 289; Dannenbaum, *supra* note 77, at 113.

91. See General Comment No. 31: *Nature of the General Legal Obligation Imposed on States Parties to the Covenant*, HRC, 26 May 2004 (UN Doc. CCPR/C/21/Rev.1/Add.13). Kolb, Porretto and Vité, *supra* note 41, at 407, indicate furthermore that the above-mentioned 'UN Model SOFA' does not provide for powers of control or sanction for the shortcomings of the States to punish their officials who have committed crimes. In this regard, the High Court of Justice of the United Kingdom has ruled in the affirmative, recognizing the responsibility of some of the British military of KFOR. See *Bici* and *Bici v. Ministry of Defence*, Decision, 7 April 2004.

92. See L. Condorelli, 'Le statut des forces de l'ONU et le droit international humanitaire', *Rivista di diritto internazionale* 78 (1995): 894 (with reference to IHL); Condorelli, *supra* note 77, at 127 (with reference to HRL). See also Tondini, *supra* note 83, at 196; Dannenbaum, *supra* note 77, at 113.

93. See C. Leck, 'International Responsibility in United Nations Peacekeeping Operations: Command and Control Arrangements and the Attribution of Conduct', *Melbourne Journal of International Law* 10 (2009): 346.

94. On this subject there is a rather extensive bibliography. See, for numerous references and practices, the writings contained in *Extraterritorial Application of Human Rights Treaties*, eds F. Coomans and M.T. Kamminga (Antwerp: Intersentia, 2004); S. Negri, 'L'applicazione extraterritoriale delle convenzioni sui diritti umani nella giurisprudenza internazionale', in *Studi in onore di Vincenzo Buonocore*, Vol. I (Milan: Giuffrè, 2005), 559; S.I. Skogly, *Beyond National Borders: States' Human Rights Obligations in International Cooperation* (Antwerp: Intersentia, 2006); M. Gondek, *The Reach of Human Rights in a Globalizing World: Extraterritorial Application of Human Rights Treaties* (Antwerp: Intersentia, 2009). With special reference to the European Convention, see, *ex multis*, P. De Sena, *La nozione di giurisdizione statale nei trattati sui diritti dell'uomo* (Turin: Giappichelli, 2002); M. Gondek, 'Extraterritorial Application of the European Convention on Human Rights: Territorial Focus in the Age of Globalization?', *Netherlands International Law Review* 52 (2005): 349.

95. See paras 108–113.

96. *Coard et al.* v. *United States*, IACommHR, Case 10.951, Report No. 109/99, 29 September 1999.

97. Article 1: 'The High Contracting Parties shall secure to everyone within their jurisdiction the rights and freedoms defined in Section I of this Convention.'

98. See the well-known Decision in the case *Cyprus v. Turkey*, ECtHR, Application Nos 6780/74 and 6950/75, 26 May 1975, repeatedly confirmed by the supervisory bodies established by the European Convention on subsequent Judgments.

99. See *Banković et al. v. Belgium, Czech Republic, Denmark, France, Germany, Greece, Hungary, Iceland, Italy, Luxembourg, Netherlands, Norway, Poland, Portugal, Spain, Turkey and United Kingdom*, ECtHR, Application No. 52207/99, Decision, 12 December 2001. See, *ex multis*, P. Pustorino, 'Responsabilità degli Stati parti della Convenzione europea dei diritti dell'uomo per il bombardamento NATO alla radio-televisione serba: il caso Banković', *La Comunità Internazionale* 56 (2001): 695; G. Ress, 'Problems of Extraterritorial Human Rights Violations – The Jurisdiction of the European Court of Human Rights: The Banković Case', *Italian Yearbook of International Law* 12 (2002): 51; E. Roxstrom, M. Gibney and T. Einarsen, 'The NATO Bombing Case (Bankovic et al. v. Belgium et al.) and the Limits of Western Human Rights Protection', *Boston University International Law Journal* 23 (2005): 55; L.G. Loucaides, 'Determining the Extra-territorial Effect of the European Convention: Facts, Jurisprudence and the Bankovic Case', *European Human Rights Law Review* 11 (2006): 391.

100. See the Decision in the case *Issa et al. v. Turkey*, ECtHR, Application No. 31821/96, 16 November 2004, para. 69. In para. 71 the Court reiterates the position adopted by the UN Human Rights Committee and by the Inter-American Commission on Human Rights, and affirms furthermore: 'Accountability ... stems from the fact that Article 1 of the Convention cannot be interpreted so as to allow a State Party to perpetrate violations of the Convention on the territory of another State, which it could not perpetrate on its own territory.'

101. See para. 80: 'In short, the Convention is a multi-lateral treaty operating ... in an essentially regional context and notably in the legal space (*espace juridique*) of the Contracting States. The FRY clearly does not fall within this legal space. The Convention was not designed to be applied throughout the world, even in respect of the conduct of Contracting States. Accordingly, the desirability of avoiding a gap or vacuum in human rights' protection has so far been relied on by the Court in favour of establishing jurisdiction only when the territory in question was one that, but for the specific circumstances, would normally be covered by the Convention.'

102. See, *ex multis*, S. Karagiannis, 'Le territoire d'application de la Convention européenne des droits de l'homme. Vaetera et nova', *Revue trimestrielle des droits de l'homme* 16 (2005): 33; R. Wilde, 'The "Legal Space" or "Espace Juridique" of the European Convention on Human Rights: Is it Relevant to Extraterritorial State Action?', *European Human Rights Law Review* 10 (2005): 115; Loucaides, *supra* note 99, at 398.

103. See Gondek, *supra* note 94, at 377.

104. The Committee adopted a Decision of Inadmissibility in the case *Kurbogaj* and *Kurbogaj v. Spain*, HRC, 14 July 2006 (UN Doc. CCPR/C/87/D/1374/2005), motivated by the lack of exhaustion of domestic legal remedies. The victims have denounced an alleged infringement of their rights under Articles 2, para. 3(a), 7 and 17 of the UN Covenant on Civil and Political Rights, committed by a Spanish Police Unit of UNMIK.

105. *Behrami* and *Behrami v. France* and *Saramati v. France, Germany and Norway*, ECtHR, Application No. 71412/01; 78166/01, decision of 2 May 2007. See, for a critical opinion, P. Palchetti, 'Azioni di forze istituite o autorizzate dalle Nazioni Unite davanti alla Corte europea dei diritti dell'uomo: i casi Behrami e Saramati', *Rivista di diritto internazionale* 90 (2007): 681; P. Bodeau-Livinec, G.P. Buzzini and S. Villalpando, 'Agim Behrami and Bekir Behrami v. France; Ruzhdi Saramati v. France, Germany and Norway. Joint Application Nos 71412/01 and 78166/01: European Court of Human Rights (Grand Chamber), 2 May 2007', *American Journal of International Law* 102 (2008): 232; P. Klein, 'Responsabilitée pour les faits commis dans le cadre d'opeérations de paix eétendue du pouvoir de contrôle de la Cour europeéenne des droits de l'homme: quelques consideérations critiques sur l'arrêt Behrami et Saramati', *Annuaire Français de Droit International* 53 (2007): 43; E. Brandolino, 'Amministrazioni ONU e tutela dei diritti umani: osservazioni in margine ai casi Behrami e Saramati', *La Comunità Internazionale* 63 (2008): 279; K. Mujezinovic Larsen, 'Attribution of Conduct in Peace Operations: The "Ultimate Authority and Control" Test', *European Journal of International Law* 19 (2008): 509; P. De Sena and C. Vitucci, 'The European Courts and the Security Council: Between Dédoublement Fonctionnel and Balancing of Values', *European Journal of International Law* 20 (2009): 193; G. Gaja, 'Responsabilité des Etats et/ou des organisations internationales en cas de violation des droits de l'homme: la question de l'attribution', in *La soumission des organisations internationales aux normes internationales relatives aux droits de l'homme*, SFDI (Paris: Pedone, 2009), 99.

106. See paras 133–140, Decision, 2 May 2007.

107. Moreover, the difference has been reported to the Court by the UN, that on 13 October 2006 submitted observations, as *amicus curiae*, in cases *Behrami* and *Saramati*. Extensive extracts of these observations are published in *United Nations Juridical Yearbook* (2006): Part 2, Chapter VI, 510.

108. See UN Doc. A/64/10, 67.

109. See the subsequent Decisions of Inadmissibility in the cases *Kasumaj v. Greece*, ECtHR, Application No. 6974/07, Decision, 5 July 2007, and *Gajic v. Germany*, ECtHR, Application No. 31446/02, Decision, 28 August 2007.

110. *Berić et al. v. Bosnia and Herzegovina*, ECtHR, Application No. 36357, Decision, 16 October 2007.

111. Decision 94/776/EC, 28 November 1994. See Pagani, *supra* note 26, at 247. Also in Bosnia and Herzegovina, in accordance with Annex VI to Dayton Agreements (Articles IV–VI), an Ombudsman has been established, nominated by OSCE, competent to receive complaints, however, only directed against the acts of local institutions, not against those of the High Representative.

112. See UNMIK/REG/2000/38, 30 June 2000. On the Ombudsperson Institution in Kosovo see Brand, *supra* note 60, at 461; C.P.M. Waters, 'Human Rights in an International Protectorate: Kosovo's Ombudsman', *The International Ombudsman Yearbook* 4 (2000): 141; J. Nilsson, 'UNMIK and the Ombudsperson Institution in Kosovo: Human Rights Protection in a United Nations "Surrogate State"', *Netherlands Quarterly of Human Rights* 22 (2004): 389; Everly, *supra* note 76, at 31.

113. See Secretary-General Report S/1999/1024, 4 October 1999, para. 42.

114. Devereux, *supra* note 55, at 315.

115. See Bongiorno, *supra* note 58, at 677; Marshall and Inglis, *supra* note 64, at 145; Friedrich, *supra* note 5, at 286; M. Zwanenburg, *Accountability of Peace Support Operations* (Leiden: Martinus Nijhoff, 2005), 310.

116. With reference to the Ombudsperson Institution in Kosovo, see Marshall and Inglis, *supra* note 64, at 138.

117. See UNMIK/REG/2006/12, 23 March 2006, about which more in B. Knoll and R.-J. Uhl, 'Too Little, Too Late: The Human Rights Advisory Panel in Kosovo', *European Human Rights Law Review* 12

(2007): 534; D. Pacquée and S. Dewulf, 'International Territorial Administrations and the Rule of Law: The Case of Kosovo', *Essex Human Rights Review* 4 (2007): 1.

118. See the list in Section 1.2 of UNMIK/REG/2006/12.

119. G. Nolte, 'Human Rights Protection against International Institutions in Kosovo: The Proposals of the Venice Commission of the Council of Europe and Their Implementation', in *Völkerrecht als Wertordnung, Common Values in International Law. Festschrift für Christian Tomuschat, Essays in Honour of Christian Tomuschat*, eds Dupuy et al. (Kehl: Engel, 2006), 257. See also I. Ingravallo, 'Amministrazione territoriale in Kosovo e tutela dei diritti umani: il parere della Commissione di Venezia', *Diritti umani e diritto internazionale* 5 (2011): 388.

120. The Committee of Ministers of the Council of Europe authorized the stipulation of the Agreement adopting a Decision on 30 June 2004. Knoll, *supra* note 86, at 646, affirms that it is the 'very first measure ever to tie an international territorial administration into a multilateral accountability framework'.

121. See Article 7, para. 2, of the Agreement. The first visit of the Committee in Kosovo took place in March 2007 because it was necessary to await the conclusion of a Treaty between the Council of Europe and NATO, in order to allow the Committee access to KFOR detention centres (see exchange of letters between the Secretaries General of both Organizations on 19 July 2006). The Opinion of the Committee is contained in document CPT/Inf.(2009)3, 25 July 2007, released on 20 January 2009.

122. On the subject, see the two opinions issued by the Advisory Committee of independent experts established under the Framework Convention (ACFC/OP/II(2009)004, 25 November 2005, published on 2 March 2006, and ACFC/OP/I(2005)004, 5 November 2009, published on 31 May 2010), as well as the Resolution adopted by the Committee of Ministers of the Council of Europe on 21 June 2006, ResCMN(2006)9.

123. See UN Docs. CCPR/C/UNK/1, and E/C.12/UNK/1, of 15 January 2008.

20. International humanitarian law and human rights rules in agreements regulating or terminating an internal armed conflict

*Luisa Vierucci**

1. INTRODUCTION

The agreements stipulated between a government and an armed opposition group to regulate the relations that originate from internal armed conflict, numbering in the hundreds,[1] form an outstanding practice that deserves examination under an international law perspective from many different angles.[2] To date, this practice has been largely ignored by international lawyers, with the notable exception of C. Bell, who has devoted two monographs to the analysis of these agreements.[3]

Our chapter focuses on the provisions of the agreements concerning the regulation of the conduct of hostilities and the treatment of persons deprived of their liberty in connection with armed conflict, as well as the protection of human rights. These provisions can be included in the agreements that specifically aim to regulate those very aspects of the relations originating from the conflict or in the agreements having a different object, for example in the pacts establishing a ceasefire. Actually, although the aim of the agreements under examination is twofold, in that they either purport to regulate the conduct of hostilities or to address the causes of the conflict, with a view to terminating it, the object of the agreements is varied and it can be roughly classified into nine distinct categories: the modalities of the conduct of negotiations; the conduct of hostilities; the ceasefire and the cessation of hostilities; the re-settlement of and assistance to refugees and internally displaced persons; the protection of indigenous peoples; the demobilisation, disarmament and reintegration of armed groups; the protection of human rights; the social and economic reforms; and the political and constitutional reforms. The above matters can be regulated either in a single agreement or in several separate agreements, each of which have a distinct material content and is usually signed at different moments but normally produces legal effects only upon the signature of the last agreement. The second modality of stipulation is primarily followed for peace agreements proper,[4] which are complex texts covering a wide range of topics.

The objective of the inquiry is to verify whether the above agreements' provisions amount to international law regulating an armed conflict,[5] namely international humanitarian law (IHL), or guaranteeing internationally protected human rights, namely international human rights law (HRL). Should this be the case, consequences would ensue relating to the application of international law to a field that has traditionally been considered, to a great extent, as the realm of state sovereignty (IHL in internal armed conflict) or as a prerogative of the relationship between the state and the individuals (HRL). Were this not the case, attention should be turned to verify whether those provisions, contained in agreements addressing different conflict situations worldwide, possess a sufficient degree of uniformity so as to possibly indicate the emergence of new international rules.

The question of the qualification of certain agreements' provisions as HRL or as IHL would be easily solved if a clause explicitly identifying, in general terms, the applicable law were present in the agreements. As this is not the case,[6] one is bound to check whether specific parts of the agreements make a referral ('renvoi') to the applicable law, namely, for the purposes of this chapter, to international law.

As we shall see, conflicting parties resort to the legal technique of referral to international law almost exclusively with respect to the human rights field, while the area relating to the conduct of hostilities and the treatment of persons in relation to the armed conflict is mostly carried out through ad hoc agreed upon rules between the parties. The above requires that the analysis of the two bodies of law be conducted at different levels: while for the human rights field the main aspect of research consists in the examination of the modalities of operation of the referral, and the consequences that such a referral entails given that also non-state actors accept this legal technique, with respect to IHL the salient part of the examination is devoted to the identification, if any, of uniform rules among different agreements, with a view to pointing to the possible creation of new international rules. Before getting into the details of the inquiry, a general overview of the main features of the agreements' clauses relating to human rights and the regulation of armed conflict will be given.

2. HUMAN RIGHTS

2.1 Modalities of the Referral to International Law

Human rights rules are usually contained in agreements addressing the causes of the conflict, in particular in agreements dealing with political and constitutional reforms or defining a new social and economic structure of power. At times the agreements are expressly labelled as 'Human Rights Agreements' or as 'Human Rights and International Humanitarian Law Agreements'. Notable examples of such a practice are the Agreement on Human Rights signed on 26 July 1990 by the Government of El Salvador and the Frente Farabundo Martí para la Liberación Nacional;[7] the Comprehensive Agreement on Human Rights signed on 29 March 1994 by the Government of Guatemala and the Unidad Revolucionaria Nacional Guatemalteca;[8] and the Comprehensive Agreement on Respect for Human Rights and International Humanitarian Law between the Government of the Republic of the Philippines and the National Democratic Front of the Philippines signed on 18 March 1998 (henceforth: CARHRIHL).[9]

As is well known, the parties to an agreement are free to decide what is the law applicable to the negotiated text. Our objective is to verify the intention of the parties to have international law applied to some of their relations, without addressing the more complex question of whether the agreements under examination are regulated by international law or national law. Such an intention is manifested by the use of the legal technique known as referral ('renvoi') between different legal orders.[10] The use of such a technique has the effect of incorporating internally the international law rules to which the renvoi is made.

In the human rights agreements addressing the causes of an internal armed conflict or in the agreements containing human rights provisions, international law holds a prominent place, as the referral to the HRL is the most used mechanism to incorporate human rights rules into the agreements.[11] Such a referral can assume three distinct forms, as it can consist of: (i) a simple referral to all the existing international human rights rules or a category thereof (e.g. only the civil and political rights may be referred to); (ii) a general referral to the relevant international rules accompanied by a catalogue where specific human rights are set forth; and (iii) the assumption of the obligation, on the part of the government, to become a party to an international convention on human rights or to incorporate such a convention into the national legal order.

As far as the simple referral to the international rules on human rights is concerned, it must be noticed that this type of renvoi can take place with respect to differing sources of international law. Firstly, the referral can be made to the principles and standards of international law on human rights. This type of referral is expressed in quite general terms. Its advantage consists in its broad *ratione materiae* scope,[12] but it has the disadvantage of not clarifying whether the referral concerns all the international instruments on human rights or only those to which the country is a party. In addition, the simple referral can only be made to treaty law or soft law (in particular, to the resolutions of international organisations). For example, the 1992 Protocol of Agreement between the Government of the Republic of Rwanda and the Rwandese Patriotic Front on the Rule of Law,[13] makes a renvoi to the Universal Declaration on Human Rights and to the African Charter on Human and Peoples' Rights.[14] Lastly, this type of referral may concern only specific rules of international law on human rights, for example only the freedom of association and movement as internationally recognised – as is the case of the 1994 Comprehensive Agreement on Human Rights relating to Guatemala.[15]

Turning to the second type of referral, the renvoi to international law constitutes the chapeau after which specific rights are listed. For instance, in the Protocol between the Government of Sudan and the Sudan People's Liberation Movement on Power Sharing,[16] reference is made to 'the international human rights treaties to which it is or becomes a party'[17] (e.g. the Convention for the Elimination of Any Form of Racial Discrimination; the Convention on the Rights of the Child; the Convention on the Status of Refugees) as well as the African Charter on Human and Peoples' Rights, and a list of the main civil and political rights is then annexed.[18] As to the chapeau, the renvoi therein contained can take place according to the first two modalities of operation of the simple referral,[19] because the third modality makes no sense in the presence of a detailed catalogue of human rights.

It is important to observe that the catalogue of human rights can be taken verbatim from a treaty. In this case, the catalogue constitutes a mere reiteration of the obligation that is already binding on the state, but the reiteration importantly affirms the adherence to this obligation also from the armed opposition group. Alternatively, it can consist of a reformulation of the relevant international rules, with the consequence that it is necessary to analyse each single formula in order to evince consistency with inter-national law standards. One cannot a priori exclude cases in which the reformulation entails a limitation of the scope of some human rights compared to the internationally protected ones or where the list of the human rights included in the agreements is not as comprehensive as the international one,[20] given that the catalogue allows the parties to tailor the content of human rights clauses to their specific needs. However, these occurrences do not subtract relevance to the principle underlying such a practice, namely the willingness of the parties to the agreement to take HRL as the point of reference for the regulation of their future relations. Actually, also states when incorporating a treaty into their domestic legal order through the reformulation technique occasionally distort an international rule.

In the third place, the referral to international rules can take the form of the engagement, contracted by the government, to become a party to one or some specific human rights treaties or to incorporate them into the national legal order.[21] For example, through the Memorandum of Understanding concluded with the Free Aceh Movement, the Government of Indonesia endeavoured to adhere to the two 1966 Covenants on Human Rights,[22] while in the 1993 Agreement the Transitional Rwandan Government undertook the obligation not only to ratify 'all International Conventions, Agreements and Treaties on Human Rights', which the state had signed, but also to 'waive all reservations entered by Rwanda when it adhered to some of those international instruments'.[23]

It may also occur that two or all of the three types of referral to international law are simultaneously adopted in the same agreement. For instance, the 1994 Lusaka Protocol terminating the Angola conflict establishes that:

> The Government and UNITA commit themselves to implement the 'Acordos de Paz par Angola' (Bicesse), the relevant resolutions of the United Nations Security Council and the Lusaka Protocol, respecting the principles of the rule of law, the general principles of internationally human rights, more particularly, the Universal Declaration of Human Rights and the fundamental freedoms of the individual, such as defined by the national legislation in force and the various international legal instruments to which Angola adheres.

The recourse to any or all of the three types of renvoi to HRL provides useful indications concerning the attitude of the parties to the agreement to be bound by international law. Indeed, should one of the parties to the agreement object to international law (or some international rules), no modality of incorporation of international law rules would be chosen.

2.2   The Referral to Substantive International Human Rights Law

In general, the agreements containing a catalogue of human rights distinguish between civil and political rights, on the one hand, and social, economic and cultural rights, on the other. Among the great variety of rights set forth, particularly recurring are, as to the first category of rights, the right to life, the right not to be tortured and arbitrarily deprived of life, the right to a fair trial, the right not to be discriminated against, as well as the right to take part in the governance of one's country.[24] Also the freedom of movement, conscience, expression and association rank high among the human rights protected by the agreements.[25] Civil and political rights are frequently set out in power sharing agreements, where also the new political structure of the country is defined.[26]

At a closer scrutiny, the political rights inserted in the agreements highlight the trend towards adoption of the principles that are typical of the liberal democracy of Western origin. Indeed it is notable that such a trend is manifest also in the agreements concerning countries that do not share such an origin. For instance, the peace agreements concerning Mozambique and Burundi provide not only for the right to vote, but also specify that the elections must be free, fair, regular and funded on a multiparty system. The requisite that needs fulfilling so that these rights can be enjoyed by *any* citizen is the participation of the members of the armed opposition group to the government of the country and the taking into due consideration of the interests that they represent. To this end, the agreements provide for differing modalities of transformation of the group from an entity promoting a political message through violence to a political party that is free to express its ideas through the means that are typical of a system of political pluralism. This process is usually time consuming and is articulated in a variety of steps, consisting in disarmament as well as demobilisation measures to finally achieve integration of the disarmed group into the political arena as a legally recognised political party. Also the modality of performance of the elections is set out in detail; for example, the 1999 Lomè Peace Agreement on Sierra Leone[27] contains a detailed provision aimed at ensuring that the members of the demobilised Revolutionary United Front be enabled to hold public office, whereas a number of agreements set forth rules for the proportional representation of all political groups, including those ensuing from a process of demobilisation.[28] Finally, virtually all peace agreements contain provisions detailing the modalities of participation of the demobilised armed groups to the transitional government.

As far as economic and social rights are concerned, the agreements mainly recognise the right of each citizen to possess private property and to have it protected against expropriation or seizure measures except on specific grounds and conditions; the right to health assistance and unhindered supply of medicines; the right to education and to human working and living conditions as well as special protection for children.[29] The right to intellectual property is less present in the agreements, similarly to the right to form and join trade unions. Also cultural rights hold no prominent place compared to civil and political rights, at least as far as the protection of cultural property and heritage is concerned. Nonetheless, cultural aspects are taken into consideration either in respect of specific rights,[30] or in agreements concluded between a government and an armed opposition group that set forth the protection of indigenous peoples.[31]

2.3   The Referral to Procedural International Human Rights Law[32]

The agreements on human rights addressing the causes of an internal armed conflict not only set out the rights that the parties endeavour to respect but also create or specify the remedy mechanisms in case of violation for both past and future human rights abuses. The analysis of these mechanisms allows us to reflect on the way the dilemma of peace versus justice is dealt with in the agreements at issue and the role that international law plays with respect to this dilemma. However, it should preliminarily be recalled that the procedural branch of HRL is much less developed than the substantive one. Indeed, one can probably only affirm that there exists an obligation under international law to create remedies for serious human rights abuses,[33] yet the type of remedy, for example whether it must be of a criminal or civil nature, is not specified under international law.

The agreements establish a plurality of mechanisms through which the parties consent to come to terms with serious human rights violations. A broad distinction can be made between non-prosecutorial and prosecutorial mechanisms.

As to the remedies of a non-prosecutorial character, they can be quite varied but usually consist in the creation of human rights commissions, truth and reconciliation commissions and forms of reparation. The former ones can be assimilated to inquiry commissions, inasmuch as they can usually perform only fact-finding activities,[34] and their composition can either be international or internal. The commissions created to investigate the infractions of the human rights recognised in the agreements – hence in a *pro futuro* perspective – deserve a special mention because the international community is usually heavily involved in them. Since the establishment of the UN Human Rights Verification Mission for El Salvador in 1992,[35] the peacekeeping missions of the United Nations or regional organisations have often been entrusted with this task in a peace agreement, but it is also common to attribute such a mandate to a commission purposefully created and composed of all the parties to the agreement on an equal footing as well as representatives of the states or international organisations that have acted as mediators between the parties.[36] Normally, the *ratione temporis* competence of these commissions is defined in the agreements as well as their powers, which only exceptionally extend beyond mere fact-finding.

The truth and reconciliation commissions, though differing widely one from another, generally aim to build a historical record of the atrocities committed in the course of the conflict, to create an arena where victims and persecutors can confront each other in a constructive way, and sometimes also to push those responsible to publicly admit their guilt.[37] Also the truth and reconciliation commissions normally feature an international component.

All these newly created non-prosecutorial mechanisms are usually independent from the judicial system of the country and have no power to mete out sanctions or determine reparation measures.

As far as reparation is concerned,[38] in general the measures with a material element are privileged compared to those having a mere symbolic value. In particular, rehabilitation,[39] restitution[40] and compensation[41] are the most recurring reparation initiatives agreed upon between conflicting parties.

There are two common traits of the reparation measures detailed in the agreements that need emphasising. Firstly, new institutions are created in order to meet the victims' reparation claims. These mechanisms are usually of a quasi-judicial nature and can either have exclusive or concurrent jurisdiction with civil tribunals. This practice denotes a tendency that is starting to assume a certain consistency towards the recognition of the right of the victim to a remedy for human rights violations.[42] Indeed, some agreements expressly provide for such a right; for example, the CARHRIHL expressly affirms '[t]he right of the victims and their families to seek justice for violations of human rights, including adequate compensation or indemnification, restitution and rehabilitation, and effective sanctions and guarantees against repetition and impunity'.[43] Furthermore, the individual right to reparation is recognised not only with respect to the victims of IHL violations, but also to any person that has had a damage, loss or prejudice in the course of the war – hence also as a consequence of lawful acts of war.[44]

By contrast, express references to prosecutorial means to investigate human rights violations are exceptional[45] and, where present, they consist in the strengthening of the existing institutions,[46] whereas new international organs competent to adjudicate upon the most serious crimes committed in the course of the armed struggle have never been established by an agreement. Actually, in the 2000 Peace and Reconciliation Agreement for Burundi the parties had agreed on the creation of an ad hoc international criminal tribunal, had the international judicial commission of inquiry determined that acts of genocide, crimes against humanity or war crimes had been allegedly committed in the course of the conflict. However, such a tribunal has never been set up, despite the indications coming from the international commission of inquiry.

This practice might appear surprising in a period of rapid development of international criminal justice, and more so in the light of three additional considerations. Firstly, not only no international or mixed criminal tribunal is created through the type of agreements under examination, but also no reference to international criminal justice is usually contained in these negotiated instruments.[47] Secondly, no reference to international criminal justice is included even in those agreements towards which a special criminal tribunal acts as an application guarantee. We are referring to the Special Court of Sierra Leone, whose jurisdiction, according to the 2002 Statute, extends over the 'persons who bear the greatest responsibility for serious violations of international humanitarian law and Sierra Leonean law committed in the territory of Sierra Leone since 30 November 1996, including those leaders who, in committing such crimes, have threatened. the establishment of and implementation of the peace process in Sierra Leone'.[48] Indeed, the *dies a quo* of the temporal jurisdiction of the Court has been chosen as it represents the date of the signature of the Abidjan peace agreement between the Government of Sierra Leone and the Revolutionary United Front[49] yet neither that agreement nor the one signed on 7 July 1999 makes any reference to the establishment of the special court. Thirdly, international criminal justice is at times perceived as an obstacle to the peace process up to the point of urging the conflicting parties to come to an agreement aimed at evading the reach of the International Criminal Court (ICC).[50]

With respect to international criminal justice, also the amnesty clauses contained in the agreements are relevant. As we shall see in the next paragraph,[51] these clauses are increasingly aimed at avoiding impunity for acts amounting to international crimes.

In brief, by reading the texts of the agreements terminating an internal armed conflict the conclusion is warranted that the criminal response to the human rights abuses committed in the past is not reckoned by the conflicting parties as a measure per se able to lead to national reconciliation. Emphasis is instead put in the agreements on non-prosecutorial means to address human rights violations, in particular on the creation of ad hoc mechanisms of a quasi-judicial nature, such as truth and reconciliation commissions, or recourse to reparation measures, with special regard to rehabilitation programmes and the institution of claims commissions. The reluctance of conflicting parties to take prosecutorial means of redressing atrocities is even clearer with respect to international criminal justice, which is of minimal relevance in the agreements and may even constitute an obstacle to the peace process.[52] However, international criminal law is increasingly playing a role in the case of international crimes inasmuch as the latter constitutes a bar for the concession of amnesty.

At the same time, the scarce consideration for the prosecutorial approach does not mean that human rights abuses are left without remedies. On the contrary, the non-prosecutorial means to address such atrocities are numerous and varied, ranging from human rights commissions, truth and reconciliation commissions to reparation programmes.

2.4   Concluding Remarks on Human Rights

The agreements addressing the causes of internal armed conflicts are a privileged lens through which different aspects of human rights can be observed. Although each agreement presents specific features, a high degree of homogeneity characterizes these negotiated texts as to the very notion of human rights that is adopted and the entities that are bound thereof.

First of all, the human rights included in the agreements are those rooted in international law. Indeed, the parties adopt a variety of modalities, which we have illustrated, to refer to international law when addressing human rights issues.

Secondly, the variety of cultures from which the agreements emanate, the scant references to the regional treaties on human rights compared to the universal treaties, and the rare attempts to reformulate single human rights to accommodate local traditions, tend to corroborate the universality of human rights.

Thirdly, though civil and political rights stand out as the most frequently evoked rights, and the cultural ones as the less present, in general all categories of human rights feature in the agreements. In light of the agreements, one may only conclude that the universality feature is shared, at varying degrees, by all the human rights that are internationally protected.

Fourthly, the agreements prove the acceptance of HRL also on the part of those entities that have not contributed to the elaboration of the law, namely the armed opposition groups that are parties to the negotiated instruments.[53]

By contrast, the mechanisms that are devised in the agreements to remedy past human rights abuses and address those that may occur in the future are very much context-related. Each agreement provides tailored solutions,[54] hence confirming a phenomenon that the doctrine on transitional justice has abundantly explored.[55] Nonetheless, also in the great variety of manifestations of this practice, some broad indications can be inferred. There is no doubt that the non-prosecutorial means of addressing past abuses are by far preferred in the agreements. This may be an expected result, considering that the agreements between conflicting parties are brokered when there is a substantial equality of forces between the adversaries, yet it needs emphasising, since it shows the slight relevance of international criminal justice in the situations at issue. The only means of meting out justice that appears permeable to international criminal justice is amnesty. This measure is increasingly excluded, according to the terms of the agreements, in case of acts of genocide, war crimes and crimes against humanity.

However, it would be wrong to conclude that the prevalence of the non-prosecutorial means to redress past abuses is tantamount to impunity. On the contrary, the agreements exhibit the creativity of the parties as to the accountability forms that are alternatives to criminal justice, such as human rights commissions, truth and reconciliation commissions and reparation measures. Most importantly, reparation measures, such as compensation, are so widely agreed to and display such similar traits as to be able to impact upon the formation of an international law rule concerning the individual right to reparations for serious human rights abuses committed in the course of an internal armed conflict.

3. INTERNATIONAL HUMANITARIAN LAW

3.1 General Overview

A preliminary observation concerns the small number of agreements where the government and armed opposition groups commit themselves simply to respecting IHL, be it by referring generally to this body of law or to specific treaties such as the 1949 Geneva Conventions.[56] This practice is limited especially in view of common art. 3 to the Four Geneva Conventions of 1949 and art. 19, par. 2, of the Convention for the Protection of Cultural Property in the Event of Armed Conflict of 1954, through which the contracting parties have engaged to conclude special agreements bringing into force, in a specific internal armed conflict, the rules applicable to international conflicts.[57] In addition, remarkably lacking is any reference to Protocol II Additional to the Four Geneva Conventions of 1949 and relating to the Protection of Victims of Non-international Armed Conflicts, while only some scant references to art. 3 common to those Conventions, dealing with the protection due to the persons hors de combat in a conflict of a non-international character, can be found in the agreements.

The reluctance of government and/or armed opposition groups to conclude agreements relating to the regulation of internal conflict may be motivated by a number of factors, but it certainly indicates the difficulties of the conflicting parties to get to a common position while armed conflict is in full swing. In this situation it is easier for the parties to have recourse to a unilateral declaration of adherence to IHL rules or to conclude an agreement on IHL with third parties rather than negotiating with the adversary.[58]

The search for the rules addressing specific aspects of the regulation of the conflict, without any explicit reference to IHL, is more fruitful. In particular, such a type of rules can be found in agreements concerning the protection of civilians, the release of prisoners, the delivery of humanitarian assistance, ceasefire and the cessation of hostilities, and the protection of internally displaced persons, as well as peace treaties proper. The comparative analysis of all the agreements shows that an important number of rules possess a high degree of uniformity although they address a variety of conflict situations worldwide.

The humanitarian rules that appear most frequently in the agreements concern the release of persons deprived of their freedom in connection with the armed conflict and the amnesty of certain offences, as well as provisions on the delivery of humanitarian assistance. Given the space available in this chapter, we will only analyse the provisions concerning release and amnesty because they both pertain to the same IHL area, namely the status and treatment of persons deprived of their freedom for reasons connected to the conflict.

Before turning to the analysis of release and amnesty, it should be emphasised that little is contained in the agreements in relation to the means of warfare, and such rules, when present, concern almost exclusively mines and chemical weapons. Notably lacking are the principles of precaution and proportionality in attack, the rules prohibiting the spreading of terror among the civilian population, and the rules on the special protection due to women and children, or property such as historical monuments. All in all, the parties to the agreements regulating an internal armed conflict privilege the protection of persons hors de combat rather than detailing the means and methods of combat that are prohibited – an issue upon which it is understandably difficult to attract the consent of conflicting parties while the armed struggle is ongoing.

3.2 Release of Persons Deprived of their Freedom

While only a few agreements between a government and an armed opposition group are specifically devoted to the release of persons deprived of their freedom for reasons connected to the armed conflict,[59] numerous agreements contain provisions on this matter.[60] Interestingly, these provisions are frequently included in agreements concerning the ceasefire or the cessation of hostilities.[61] As is well known, the latter type of agreements may be stipulated either as a preliminary condition for the peace negotiations[62] or as a part of the comprehensive regulation of the causes of the conflict.[63] However, in both cases a ceasefire agreement does not seek to restore the situation prevailing before the outbreak of the conflict but merely purports 'to paralyse military operations and leave them as they are at the time of its entry into force'.[64] And '[i]n keeping with the same spirit, a cease-fire is accompanied by provision concerning the fate of prisoners of war'.[65] The practice under examination shows that the release of persons deprived of their freedom is one of the first measures agreed upon on occasion of the first contacts or renewed contacts after a stall in the negotiations.

Interestingly, no distinction is made in the agreements between civilian and military persons, on the contrary, the release usually concerns 'all' detained persons, apart from those held on criminal charges, irrespective of whether they have been arrested, have surrendered or have been abducted.[66] Limiting our analysis to the release of fighters,[67] it must be noted that the release appears to rely on a different rationale compared to that inspiring the liberation and repatriation of prisoners of war in an international armed conflict. In the latter type of conflict the release of the prisoners of war seals the end of 'active hostilities'[68] and the restoration of the situation existing before the beginning of the conflict, knowing that the prisoners will not resume fighting because hostilities have ceased.[69] On the contrary, in an internal armed conflict the release of fighters seems to be a preliminary condition for the resolution of the causes of the conflict;[70] indeed, the liberation, especially when it occurs on a mutual basis, often operates as a confidence building measure.[71]

Notwithstanding the different rationale underlying the release of the persons having taken up arms in international and internal armed conflicts, the modalities and conditions for the release appear to be largely similar. The parties to the agreements almost invariably request that the measures necessary for the release and the supervision over the whole operation be undertaken either by the ICRC or a joint committee composed of the parties to the agreement and an international subject.[72] When an international subject is involved in the release operations, the agreements set out the obligation of the parties to cooperate with the monitoring committee.[73]

Few conditions attach to the release as detailed in the agreements at issue and they relate to non-release and the deadline for the release of those held for a crime. As to the timing, the agreements usually provide that the detainees be freed as soon as possible after the entry into force of the negotiated text. At times it is specifically provided that the release shall take effect before a set deadline (usually between five and fifteen days from the entry into force of the agreement).[74] Importantly, some agreements exclude the release of persons detained on charges of threatening state security[75] or international crimes.[76] In particular the Darfur Peace Agreement rules out the liberation of the persons convicted for violations of human rights or international humanitarian law, including incitement to commit such acts.[77] It should be emphasised that limiting the release to the persons not detained on charges related to threat to the security of the state or international crimes seems to have the effect of subtracting the person from the jurisdiction of the detaining power in case he/she has fought in observance of the relevant IHL rules.

The above takes us to a semantic consideration. Under the terms of some agreements the release shall concern both 'prisoners of war' and 'detainees'.[78] The use of both terms in the same agreement seems to indicate that the parties use those terms to refer to different categories of persons. The question of the meaning of the expression 'prisoner of war' is of particular interest because to this well known formula IHL attaches a well defined legal status pertaining to international armed conflicts. Now, the use of such an expression in the agreements under analysis does not seem justified by the existence, on the territory where the agreement applies, of an international armed conflict in parallel to the internal one, nor by the circumstance that the internal conflict has become internationalised, for instance, through the recognition of belligerency.[79] All that can be *prima facie* inferred from the use of the expression 'prisoner of war' is that it refers to a category of persons that do not qualify as 'detainees'. Now, since the 'detainees' are often labelled in the agreements as 'political', one may expect that this term is used with respect to the persons deprived of their freedom who have played a political role in the conflict. If this is so, it would be logical to label as 'prisoners of war' those persons who have taken up arms in connection with the conflict.

If our interpretation is correct, it does not *ipso facto* follow that those who have been labelled as 'prisoners of war' enjoy the legal status or treatment that IHL affords to them in international armed conflict. However, some indications in this direction can be gathered from the analysis of the provisions on amnesty contained in the agreements. We shall therefore now turn to the examination of such provisions.

3.3   Amnesty for Acts Connected with the Armed Conflict[80]

An important number of the agreements contain provisions concerning amnesty for persons detained in connection with the conflict. This type of provision can be limited *ratione personae*[81] or *materiae*. For our purposes only the latter limitation is relevant. Accordingly the agreements can be divided into two distinct groups. In the first group, rank the clauses on unconditional amnesty; in the second group, are placed the clauses that contemplate *ratione materiae* limits to the operation of this legal act.

It is mainly the pre-2000s agreements that fall into the group of unconditional amnesty, such as the 1988 Preliminary Agreement on Nicaragua,[82] the agreement on Colombia of 9 March 1990 (Acuerdo político entre el Gobierno nacional, los partidos políticos, el M-19 y la Iglesia Católica en calidad de tutora moral y espiritual del proceso),[83] the 1993 Cotonou Agreement on Liberia,[84] and the 1997 Peace Agreement between the Government of Sudan and various armed opposition groups.[85]

The second group covers conditional amnesties, in particular those excluding impunity to persons suspected of, or convicted for, internal or international crimes[86] or both.[87] At times the criterion for excluding amnesty is the seriousness of the crime.[88] Only recently has an explicit reference to the crimes coming under the jurisdiction of the International Criminal Court started to appear as an element preventing the concession of the amnesty.[89] In general, clauses on conditional amnesties are contained in the most recent agreements, though this is only a trend and important exceptions should be pointed to.[90]

Two remarks arise with respect to the features of the amnesty clauses contained in the agreements regulating or terminating an internal armed conflict. In the first place, similarly to the provision on the release of the persons deprived of their freedom, also the amnesty clauses play the role of a confidence building measure, when included in agreements brokered at an early stage of the negotiating process and as a preliminary condition to the discussions on the causes of the conflict. Indeed, amnesty is at times considered as a bargaining chip to convince the rebels to lay down their arms. However, although the relevant IHL rule provides that the authorities take into consideration the granting of amnesty 'at the end of the hostilities',[91] the deliberation of amnesty measures when the hostilities are merely suspended does not necessarily contradict the rationale of the rule, which consists in 'encourag[ing] gestures of reconciliation which can contribute to re-establishing normal relations in the life of a nation which has been divided'.[92]

In the second place, the limitations *ratione materiae* that the amnesty clauses are increasingly facing with respect to international crimes arguably produce the indirect effect of assimilating the treatment of the persons that have taken direct part in the armed conflict in compliance with international law with the treatment due to prisoners of war.[93] In this perspective, amnesty may be viewed as a measure aimed at legalising actions that, in an international armed conflict, would qualify as lawful acts of war.[94] Obviously, important differences persist concerning the treatment of a prisoner of war in an international armed conflict compared to an internal one. First of all, in international conflicts prisoners of war not only have the right to a certain treatment but also enjoy an inalienable status, while in internal conflicts the said treatment stems from a legislative measure which is taken *ex post facto*, and, though widely used, there is no international obligation to pass such a measure.[95] Secondly, while in the latter type of conflict a treatment similar to that of prisoner of war is recognised only indirectly by the authorities, in international conflicts the prisoner of war status arises *ipso facto* by virtue of the possession of certain requisites.

3.4   Concluding Remarks on International Humanitarian Law

The agreements stipulated between the government and armed opposition groups regulating the internal conflict stand out for the paramount importance they attribute to the measures pertaining to the release and amnesty of persons for acts having a nexus with the armed struggle.

Concerning release, a body of rules is developing that goes beyond what is established under current IHL treaty rules for internal armed conflicts, namely that safety measures be taken in case of liberation,[96] and resembles the corresponding rules applicable to international armed conflict. In particular, the analogy with the regulation of the latter type of conflict relates to the timing of the liberation, whose close deadline recalls the obligation of the Third Geneva Convention to release and repatriate prisoners of war 'without delay' after the cessation of 'active hostilities'.[97] Most importantly, the rules on release contained in the agreements arguably produce the effect of creating, for certain aspects,[98] a status similar to that afforded to prisoners of war in international armed conflict, inasmuch as they exclude the liberation of persons being detained on charges connected with international crimes. Such an effect is corroborated by those agreements' provisions that grant amnesty to those persons having fought in accordance with the modalities prescribed by international law.

As a matter of fact, it is not surprising that the similarities with the IHL rules relative to international armed conflicts pertain to the status of the persons detained because of their active participation in the conflict. Indeed, by not clearly recognising the international legal status of fighters, current IHL regulating internal armed conflict lacks not only an incentive for the non-state party to the conflict to respect such a body of rules[99] but also to sit at the negotiating table with the government. Remarkably enough, it is the necessities of pacification that are shaping the IHL rules on the status of fighters applicable in internal armed conflict.

4.   GENERAL CONCLUSIONS

The agreements stipulated between a government and an armed opposition group form a body of rules, pertaining to the regulation of an internal armed conflict and to the definition of the new state structure, that is relevant to international law in two respects: firstly, because in the realm of human rights, referral is always made to the relevant international law rules; and secondly, because some aspects of the regulation of internal conflicts are so uniformly treated in different agreements, in particular with respect to the release and amnesty of persons having a nexus with the conflict, so as to suggest that new international law rules may be emerging.[100]

Starting from the human rights rules provided for in the agreements, the prominent role that such rules play should be immediately stressed. Not only a high number of agreements are entirely devoted to human rights, but also agreements regulating specific aspects of the causes of the conflict, for example power sharing agreements, contain provisions on human rights. Indeed, human rights, which, as we have seen, are defined by referral to the relevant international law rules, constitute a common language between the conflicting parties and prove the acceptance of universal rules also on the part of those entities that have not contributed to their elaboration, namely armed opposition groups. The application *erga omnes* of the international law on human rights, in a context where the future structure of the state is being redesigned, shows that this branch of international law acts as a parameter of good governance for the states coming out of an armed confrontation, especially with respect to the values typical of a liberal democracy.

The practice regarding the use made of human rights in the agreements originating from internal armed conflicts is so rich that it deserves further exploration with regard to the impact that it may have on customary international law rules. It is actually to be expected that this abundant practice may contribute to confirming the existence of a certain customary rule, or to specifying its content, or to crystallising the formation of a new rule. This is particularly true for the agreements' provisions concerning reparation for past abuses.

On the contrary, the role played by another branch of international law, that is international criminal justice, with the exception of conditional amnesty, is less relevant than one might expect, since restorative forms of justice are generally preferred in a negotiated settlement aimed at ending an internal armed conflict. Actually, amnesty is a pivotal measure, as it embraces both the IHL and human rights provisions set out in the agreements, though with differing consequences in the two fields. Under IHL, the amnesty granted only to the persons that are not held on charges of international crimes produces the indirect effect of subtracting fighters to the jurisdiction of the detaining power for the lawful acts of war they have committed; in a human rights perspective, instead, the very concession of amnesty shows the preference for the non-prosecutorial means to redress past abuses operated by the parties to the agreements.

Conclusively, the analysed practice shows that the very concept of human rights is undergoing a change, since the latter tends to act as a bulwark against not only the abuses of the state but also of non-state entities.

Turning to IHL, the agreements regulating internal armed conflicts or the IHL provisions included in the agreements terminating such type of conflict deal with specific IHL aspects of what was traditionally labelled as the Geneva law, in particular the release and amnesty for persons deprived of their freedom for acts having a nexus with the conflict. Remarkably few clauses of the agreements are devoted to the so-called Hague law, apart from scant references to the prohibition of using certain means of warfare.

Also notable is the lack of reference to the 1977 Additional Protocol II and the very rare references to common article 3 to the Four Geneva Conventions, considering that the agreements under examination aim at regulating the very category of conflicts for which those treaty rules have been devised. This element of fact seems to suggest the irrelevance, for the agreements *de quo*, of the threshold approach to IHL and the preference for a technique combining HRL and IHL rules.[101] However, the validity of such a conclusion should be verified through the analysis of the other field of IHL rules which is abundant in the agreements, namely the provisions on humanitarian assistance, that we have not made the object of our study.

Although IHL agreements concluded between the government and armed opposition groups in the course of an armed conflict are not the preferred modality to regulate the confrontation while the conflict is ongoing, hence are of little assistance when trying to ascertain the existence of uniform rules, the agreements on ceasefire or cessation of hostilities as well as peace treaties proper that contain IHL clauses point to a direction that deserves scrutiny with respect to the body of rules that conflicting parties agree to apply in internal armed conflicts.

In the first place, it is the necessities of peace, rather than the 'necessities of war',[102] that are shaping the IHL rules regulating internal struggles. After all, 'to humanize war is not to encourage it, but to spread a spirit of peace in the midst of war which can contribute towards its conclusion'.[103] Our analysis, that has focused on the release and amnesty of persons having committed acts related to the conflict, tends to indicate that, even if the rationale behind the concession of release and amnesty as resulting from the agreements is different from that accruing to IHL rules relative to international armed conflicts,[104] the consequences ensuing from the analysed practice are not insignificant, since they show that the shaping analogy between the prisoners of war status typical of international conflict and the status of fighters applicable in internal conflict may be an inescapable factual necessity.

The above developing practice also demonstrates that the current IHL treaty rules relating to the treatment of fighters in internal armed conflict are only partially able to humanise war. Following the avenue opened by the analysed agreements might be the first step in the right direction, since that path has proven rewarding in quite a number of conflict situations.

Furthermore, ways to fill the gaps in the protection that current IHL affords both to the persons hors de combat and to those directly participating in the hostilities should be explored. This inquiry should take as a starting point the fact that in the agreements we have examined the rules on the protection of the civilian population are taken into consideration almost exclusively in a sort of *ius ad bellum* perspective, as they are chiefly included in the agreements concerning a ceasefire or the cessation of hostilities.

Altogether, the analysis of the application of HRL and IHL to the agreements concluded between governments and armed opposition groups invalidates the traditional view whereby these two entities are reluctant, if not openly opposed, to have international law regulating the relations between them, as the government fears that the application of international law to an armed opposition group amounts to the recognition of the international legal status of the group; while opposition groups hold that international law is *res inter alios acta*. This conclusion is susceptible to affecting the question of the legal status of armed opposition groups under international law.[105]

NOTES

* Luisa Vierucci is Doctor in International Law and Researcher in International Law at the University of Florence, Italy.

1. The author has built her own database consisting of around 300 agreements concluded in writing between governments and armed opposition groups, with the exclusion of national liberation movements and those agreements ensuing from international armed conflicts. The vast majority of the collected agreements have been concluded since the end of the Cold War. Where available, the United Nations source for the agreement will be given, otherwise the mere indication 'on file with author' will appear.

2. One of the thorniest issues concerns the qualification of these agreements as treaties, see C. Bell, 'Peace Agreements: their Nature and Legal Status', *American Journal of International Law* 100 (2006): 373–412; and L. Vierucci, '"Special Agreements" between Conflicting Parties in the Case-law of the ICTY', in *The Legacy of the International Criminal Tribunal for the Former Yugoslavia*, eds B. Swart, G. Sluiter and A. Zahar (Oxford: Oxford University Press, 2011), 401–433.

3. C. Bell, *Human Rights and Peace Agreements* (Oxford: Oxford University Press, 2000), and *On the Law of Peace – Peace Agreements and the Lex Pacificatoria* (Oxford: Oxford University Press, 2008). See, also, O. Corten and P. Klein, 'Are Agreements between States and Non-State Entities Rooted in the International Legal Order?', in *The Law of Treaties beyond the Vienna Convention*, ed. E. Cannizzaro (Oxford: Oxford University Press, 2011), 3–24; E. Roucounas, 'Peace Agreements as Instruments for the Resolution of Intrastate Conflicts', in *Conflict Resolution: New Approaches and Methods* (Paris: UNESCO, 2000), 113–140; and R. Goy, 'Quelques accords reécents mettant fin à des guerres civiles', *Annuaire français de droit international* 38 (1993): 112–135.

4. For example, the peace agreement concluded between the Government of Guatemala and the Unidad Revolucionaria Nacional Guatemalteca (Agreement on a Firm and Lasting Peace, UN Doc. A/51/796-S/1997/114, 7 February 1997), 29 December 1996, is formed by the Comprehensive Agreement on Human Rights of 29 March 1994; the Agreement on Resettlement of the Population Groups Uprooted by the Armed Conflict of 17 June 1994; the Agreement on the Establishment of the Commission to Clarify Past Human Rights Violations and Acts of Violence that have caused the Guatemalan Population to Suffer of 23 June 1994; the Agreement on identity and rights of indigenous peoples of 31 March 1995; the Agreement on Social and Economic Aspects and the Agrarian Situation of 6 May 1996; the Agreement on the Strengthening of Civilian Power and on the Role of the Armed Forces in a Democratic Society of 19 September 1996; the Agreement on the Definitive Ceasefire of 4 December 1996; the Agreement on Constitutional Reforms and the Electoral Regime of 7 December 1996; the Agreement on the Basis for the Legal Integration of the Unidad Revolucionaria Nacional Guatemalteca of 12 December 1996; and the Agreement on the Implementation, Compliance and Verification Timetable for the Peace Agreements of 29 December 1996. All these agreements, with the exception of the Comprehensive Agreement on Human Rights, entered into force upon the signature of the peace agreement.

5. This inquiry differs from that aiming at establishing whether the parties intend to have the whole agreement regulated by international law, see, on this point, F.A. Mann, 'The Proper Law of Contracts Concluded by International Persons', *British Yearbook of International Law* 37 (1959): 44; and J. Barberis, 'Le concept de "traité international" et ses limites', *Annuaire français de droit international* 47 (1984): 259.

6. A notable exception is represented by the Peace Treaty and Principles of Interrelation between the Russian Federation and the Chechen Republic of Ichkeria, signed on 12 May 1997 [on file with author], where the parties have expressly agreed 'To develop their relations on generally recognised principles and norms of international law'.

7. UN Doc. A/44/971-S/21541, 16 August 1990.

8. UN Doc. A/48/928-S/1994/448, 19 April 1994.

9. Agreement on file with author.

10. F.A. Mann, 'The Law Governing State Contracts', *British Yearbook of International Law* 21 (1944): 190–191.

11. For the purpose of this chapter the term 'referral' to international law will be used also in those cases where, technically, the reference to international law manifests the intention of the parties to have the agreement regulated by international law. In other words, we do not draw any distinction between an agreement regulated by international law (i.e. a treaty, see Article 2 of the 1969 Vienna Convention on the Law of Treaties) and an agreement regulated by national law that only incorporates some rules of international law through the referral, because the distinction is not relevant to the objective of the chapter.

12. It is not clear whether with the terms 'principles' and 'standards' reference is made to legal rules or also to non-binding rules, for example to soft law instruments.

13. The Agreement was signed on 18 August 1992 and is a component of the peace agreement, UN Doc. A/48/824-S/26915, 23 December 1993.
14. See Article 6 of the Agreement.
15. See Article V(1) of the Agreement.
16. The Agreement is available at http://peacemaker.unlb.org (accessed 22 August 2011).
17. See Article 1, para. 6(1) of the Agreement.
18. See Article 1, para. 6(2) of the Agreement.
19. For example, in the CARHRIHL, the first type of referral is contained in Part III, Article 1, according to which 'In the exercise of their inherent rights, the Parties shall adhere to and be bound by the principles and standards embodied in international instruments on human rights'.
20. For the view that HRL (and IHL) 'in some cases impose more exacting obligations' than those set out in the Ceasefire Agreement between the Government of the Democratic Socialist Republic of Sri Lanka and the Liberation Tigers of Tamil Eelam of 22 February 2002, see the Report of the Special Rapporteur on Civil and Political Rights, including the Question of Disappearances and Summary Executions, on the Mission in Sri Lanka, UN Doc. E/CN.4/2006/53/add.5, 27 March 2006, para. 24.
21. A high number of agreements provide for the submission of a human rights treaty or specific human rights rules to the parliament in order for the latter to incorporate the rules internally. The wording of the agreements is varied: sometimes the government only endeavours to present a certain bill to the parliament, which remains free to adopt it, to amend it or to reject it (see the Agreement on Identity and Rights of Indigenous Peoples concerning Guatemala where the government undertakes to promote in the Congress a bill incorporating the International Labour Organization Convention No. 169 on indigenous peoples, UN Doc. A/49/882-S/1995/256, 10 April 1995); at other times the agreement is couched in terms of the obligation of the parliament to adopt the bill submitted by the government. The latter wording has become the object of a Judgment of the Supreme Court of the Philippines, according to which the Memorandum of Understanding on Ancestral Domain between the Government of the Philippines and the Moro Islamic Liberation Front constitutes a violation of the Constitution, because 'the President – in the course of conducting peace negotiations – may validly consider implementing even those policies that require changes to the Constitution, but she may not unilaterally implement them without the intervention of Congress, or act in any way as if the assent of that body were assumed as a certainty', *The Province of North Cotabato et al. v. the Government of the Republic of the Philippines Peace Panel on Ancestral Domain et al.*, Judgment, 14 October 2008, http://sc.judiciary.gov.ph/jurisprudence/2008/october2008/183591.htm (accessed 1 April 2012).
22. See Article 2(1) of the Memorandum of Agreement between the Government of the Republic of Indonesia and the Free Aceh Movement, signed on 15 August 2005, http://peacemaker.unlb.org (accessed on 22 August 2011).
23. Article 15 of the Protocol of Agreement between the Government of the Republic of Rwanda and the Rwandese Patriotic Front on Miscellaneous and Final Provisions, 3 August 1993. With the 2004 Protocol on Power Sharing concerning Sudan also the government of Sudan engaged to ratify those treaties that it had signed (Article 1, para. 6(1)).
24. E.g., see Article 19 of the Peace Agreement Between the Government of Sierra Leone and the Revolutionary United Front of Sierra Leone signed in Lomè on 7 July 1999, UN Doc. S/1996/1034, 11 December 1996.
25. See Article V of the Comprehensive Agreement on Human Rights concerning Guatemala, see *supra* note 8; Articles 5–8 of the Agreement on Human Rights concerning El Salvador, see *supra* note 7; Articles I, II and III of Protocol III (Principles of the Electoral Act) of the General Peace Agreement for Mozambique, signed on 4 October 1992 by the Government of Mozambique and the Renamo, UN Doc. S/24635, 8 October 1992; and Article 3, paras 13–15, of Protocol II (Democracy and Good Governance) of the Arusha Peace and Reconciliation Agreement for Burundi of 28 August 2000, http://peacemaker.unlb.org (accessed 22 August 2011).
26. See, e.g., the 2004 Protocol on Power Sharing concerning Sudan, *supra* note 16. Power sharing agreements are often crucial to the resolution of armed conflict, as shown by the study of B. Walter, *Committing to Peace: the Successful Settlement of Civil Wars* (Princeton: Princeton University Press, 2002), which examines civil wars that broke out between 1940 and 1992. Power sharing is a particularly delicate issue in disputes relating to self-determination, see M. Weller and B. Metzger, *Settling Self-Determination Disputes: Complex Power-Sharing in Theory and Practice* (Leiden: Martinus Nijhoff, 2008).
27. See *supra* note 24. In particular, Article IV of the agreement establishes a tight deadline for the government to take the necessary steps to amend the relevant laws and regulations that may prevent

the RUF from holding public office. In addition, the article provides that 'within seven days of the removal of any such legal impediments, both parties shall meet to discuss and agree on the appointment of RUF/SL members to positions in parastatals, diplomacy and any other public sector'. On this point, see also the Agreement on the Implementation of the Tripoli Agreement between the Government of the Philippines and the Moro National Liberation Front of 2 September 1996, available at: http://peacemaker.unlb.org (accessed 22 August 2011).

28. See Peace Accords for Angola, Attachment IV, Protocol of Estoril, 1 May 1991, UN Doc. S/22609, 17 May 1991; General Peace Agreement for Mozambique, *supra* note 25; Protocol on Power Sharing concerning Sudan, *supra* note 16.

29. See especially the Darfur Peace Agreement between the Government of the Sudan, the Sudan Liberation Movement/Army and the Justice and Equality Movement, 5 May 2006, available at: http://peacemaker.unlb.org (accessed 22 August 2011); the Peace and Reconciliation Agreement for Burundi, *supra* note 25; and the Comprehensive Peace Agreement held between Government of Nepal and Communist Party of Nepal (Maoist), signed on 21 November 2006, available at: http://peacemaker.unlb.org (accessed 19 August 2011).

30. For example, Article 5 of the Human Right Agreement for El Salvador, *supra* note 7, takes into account the cultural aspects with respect to the right of association.

31. See Article III of the Agreement on Identity and Rights of Indigenous Peoples, signed by the Government of Guatemala and the Unidad Revolucionaria Nacional Guatemalteca on 31 March 1995, UN Doc. A/49/882- S/1995/256, 10 April 1995; and the Joint Declaration of the Government of Mexico and the EZLN of 16 February 1996, available at: http://peacemaker.unlb.org (accessed 18 August 2011).

32. With the expression 'procedural international human rights law' we only refer to the type of institutions, that are established through the agreements, to address human rights violations.

33. Bell, *supra* note 3, at 197.

34. Exceptionally, the human rights commissions are empowered to use the findings of their activity to institute legal proceedings, see Rwanda, Protocol on the Rule of Law, Article 15, *supra* note 13.

35. See Article 10 of the El Salvador Agreement on Human Rights, *supra* note 7.

36. See, e.g., Article 248 of the Darfur Peace Agreement, see *supra* note 29, and Article XII of the Acuerdo Final concluded on 25 January 1991 between the Government of Colombia and the Partido Revolucionario de los Trabajadores, available at: http://peacemaker.unlb.org (accessed 25 July 2011).

37. Generally on truth and reconciliation commissions, see P. Hayner, *Unspeakable Truths: Transitional Justice and the Challenge of Truth Commissions*, 2nd edition (New York: Routledge, 2011); and J. Cockayne, 'Truth and Reconciliation Commissions', in *The Oxford Companion to International Criminal Justice*, eds A. Cassese et al. (Oxford: Oxford University Press, 2009), 543–553.

38. With the term 'reparation' reference is made to a number of measures, e.g., restitution, compensation, rehabilitation and satisfaction.

39. Rehabilitation measures consist in programmes of assistance to the community, see, e.g., Article XXXI of the Comprehensive Peace Agreement Between the Government of Liberia and the Liberians United for Reconciliation and Democracy (LURD) and the Movement for Democracy in Liberia (MODEL) and Political Parties, 18 August 2003, UN Doc. S/2003/850, 29 August 2003, and Article 8 of the Accord de Reforme et de Concorde Civile, between the Government of the Republic of Djibouti and the Front pour la Restauration de l'Unité et de la Démocratie (FRUD-Armé), signed on 21 May 2001 [on file with the author].

40. A case in point are the measures agreed upon in the Memorandum of Understanding on Aceh, see *supra* note 22, Article 3.2, and in the Darfur Peace Agreement, Articles 194–198.

41. Darfur Peace Agreement, Articles 199–213.

42. This tendency started with the Dayton Peace Accords on Bosnia and Herzegovina, UN Doc. A/50/790-S/1995/999, 30 November 1995, which created a Human Rights Chamber competent to issue final and binding Decisions concerning the remedy in case of a breach of the agreement (see Annex 6, Agreement on Human Rights, Art. XI, para. 1), as well as a Commission for Real Property Claims of Displaced Persons and Refugees in Bosnia and Herzegovina, which can order the restitution of property or a 'just compensation' (Agreement on Refugees and Displaced Persons, Article i, para. 1). Those agreements pre-dating the Dayton Peace Accords that contained references to the reparation, such as the Comprehensive Agreement on Human Rights concerning Guatemala (Article VIII, para. 1, see *supra* note 7 for the details of the agreement), acknowledged the existence of a 'humanitarian duty' to compensate and assist the victims of human rights violations, but did not spell out the means through which such a duty had to be discharged.

43.   Similarly, see Article 199 of the Darfur Peace Agreement, where the parties recognise that the war-affected persons in Darfur have an 'inalienable right' 'to have their grievances addressed in a comprehensive manner and to receive compensation'.

44.   However, a link between the loss, injury or prejudice and the conflict is required, see Article 200 of the Darfur Peace Agreement. See principle 31 of the Report of the independent expert to update the set of principles to combat impunity, Diane Orentlicher, Addendum, E/CN.4/2005/102/Add.1, 8 February 2005, according to which 'The right to reparation shall cover *all injuries* suffered by victims' (emphasis added).

45.   The principle of individual criminal responsibility is affirmed in some agreements, such as the Agreement on a Cease-fire and Arrangements to Monitor its Observance, signed by the Government of Georgia and the Abkhaz side of 7 July 1993, UN Doc. S/ S/2625, 6 August 1993.

46.   See Article XXV(1) of the Lomè Agreement concerning Sierra Leone, *supra* note 24.

47.   The exception is constituted by the Dayton Peace Accords, *supra* note 42, containing several references to the International Criminal Tribunal for the Former Yugoslavia, that had been created by the UN Security Council through S/RES/827, 25 May 1993 and partially by the Agreement on Accountability and Reconciliation signed by the Government of Uganda and the Lord's Resistance Army/Movement on 29 June 2007, UN Doc. S/2007/345, 17 July 2007.

48.   See Article 1, para. 1, of the Statute.

49.   The Agreement was signed on 30 November 1996, UN Doc. S/1996/1034, 11 December 1996.

50.   Illustrative is the direction taken by the negotiations between Uganda and the Lord's Resistance Army/Movement following the issuance of the arrest warrants by the International Criminal Court against the leaders of the rebel group. The parties have since then signed the Agreement on Accountability and Reconciliation, aiming at excluding the opening of the trial before the ICC whose compatibility with the obligations accruing to Uganda as a party to the ICC Statute is debatable (Uganda ratified the ICC Statute on 14 June 2002).

51.   See *infra*, section 3.3.

52.   On these issues, recently, J.N. Clark, 'Peace, Justice and the International Criminal Court: Limitations and Possibilities', *Journal of International Criminal Justice* 39 (2011): 521–545.

53.   This practice gives support to that doctrine that has propounded the applicability of international human rights groups also to non-state actors; see A. Clapham, *Human Rights Obligations of Non-state Actors* (Oxford: Oxford University Press, 2006) and M. Pedrazzi, 'The Status of Organised Armed Groups in Contemporary International law', in *Non-state Actors and International Humanitarian Law*, eds M. Odello and G.L. Beruto (Milan: FrancoAngeli, 2010), 79.

54.   For arguments in favour of tailored solutions with respect to transitional justice issues in peace agreements, see C. Bell, 'The "New Law" of Transitional Justice', in *Building a Future on Peace and Justice*, eds K. Ambos et al. (Berlin and Heidelberg: Springer, 2009), 105–125.

55.   See, in particular, the seminal book by R. Teitel, *Transitional Justice* (Oxford: Oxford University Press, 2000), and K. Ambos, 'The Legal Framework of Transitional Justice: A Systematic Study with a Special Focus on the Role of the ICC', in K. Ambos et al., eds, *supra* note 54, 19–86.

56.   Only two agreements contain the expression international humanitarian law in the title, namely the CARHRIHL and the Agreement on the Application and the Implementation of International Humanitarian Law within the Context of the Conflict in Bosnia-Herzegovina, signed under International Committee of the Red Cross Auspices on 22 May 1992 (see *infra*). However, other negotiated texts, though they are not denominated as IHL agreements, do in fact deal with the protection of persons hors de combat and other IHL issues, i.e., the five Agreements Concluded Under International Committee of the Red Cross Auspices between the representatives of the various factions of the conflict in Bosnia-Herzegovina, namely a representative of Alija Izetbegovic (President of the Republic of Bosnia and Herzegovina and the Party of Democratic Action), Radovan Karadzic (President of the Serbian Democratic Party) and Miljenko Brkic (President of the Croatian Democratic Community) [text of the agreement on file with the author] and signed respectively on 22 and 23 May 1992, 6 June 1992 and 1 October 1992; the Agreement between the Government of the Republic of Sudan and the Sudan People's Liberation movement to protect non-combatant civilians and civilian facilities from military attack, 10 March 2002 and the Agreement on the Civilian Protection Component of the International Monitoring Team between the Government of the Philippines and the Moro Islamic Liberation Front, 27 October 2009. All these agreements are on file with the author.

57.   Curiously enough, the Comprehensive Agreement on Human Rights concerning Guatemala, *supra* note 8, explicitly excludes that it constitutes a special agreement in the terms of common Article 3 to the 1949 Geneva Conventions (see Article IX, para. 2). By contrast, the Agreement on the Application

and the Implementation of International Humanitarian Law within the Context of the Conflict in Bosnia-Herzegovina, *supra* note 56, qualifies as a special agreement in the meaning of Article 3 common to the 1949 Geneva Conventions.

58. S. Sivakumaran, 'Binding Armed Opposition Groups', *International Comparative Law Quarterly* 55 (2006): 387–389; and M. Veuthey, 'Learning from History: Accession to the Conventions, Special Agreements, and Unilateral Declarations', in *Relevance of International Humanitarian Law to Non-state actors: Proceedings of the Bruges Colloquium: 25th–26th October 2002* (Bruges [etc.]: College of Europe [etc.], 2003): 139–151.

59. One of the five agreements concluded in 1992 under the International Committee of the Red Cross Auspices during the conflict in Bosnia-Herzegovina treats exclusively with the release of prisoners, namely the Agreement on the Release and Transfer of Prisoners, 1 October 1992, see *supra* note 56. See also the Protocol of the Meeting of the Working Groups, Formed under the Negotiations Commissions, to Locate Missing Persons and to Free Forcibly Detained Persons, signed on 10 June 1996 between the Russian Federation and the Chechen Republic of Ichkeriya [on file with the author].

60. It should be underlined that the release of prisoners often takes place as a unilateral measure taken by the armed opposition group (see BBC News, 'Sri Lanka Rebels Release War Prisoners', 21 January 2002, http://news.bbc.co.uk/2/hi/south_asia/1773652.stm (accessed 1 April 2012); National Democratic Front of the Philippines, 'Prisoners of War Released by NPA are Now Prisoners in their Own Camp', 12 April 2009, http://www.ndfp.net/joom15/index.php/releases-archives-mainmenu-101/617-prisoners-of-war-released-by-npa-are-now-prisoners-in-their-own-camp.html; or by the Government (BBC News, 'Philippines Peace Talks to Resume', 10 March 2001, http://news.bbc.co.uk/2/hi/asia-pacific/1212891.stm (accessed 1 April 2012)).

61. N'Sele Cease-fire Agreement between the Government of the Rwandese Republic and the Rwandese Patriotic Front, 12 July 1992, *supra* note 13; Peace Accords for Angola, Attachment I ('Cease-fire Agreement'), Article II, para. 3, *supra* note 28; Lusaka Protocol, signed on 15 November by the Government of Angola and the UNITA, Annex III 'Military Issues', UN Doc. S/1441/1994, 22 December 1994, Article II, para. 10: 'Release of all civilian and military prisoners detained or withheld as a consequence of the conflict, under the supervision of the ICRC.'

62. This role of the ceasefire agreements has been made explicit in the ceasefire brokered between the Government of Rwanda and the Rwandese Patriotic Front, as a part of the peace agreement see *supra* note 13, according to which 'The present Cease-fire Agreement is the first stage of a peace process which shall culminate in a Peace Agreement to be signed at the conclusion of the political negotiations', Article I, para. 3. See also the Agreement on a Cease-fire, the Cessation of Military Activities and on Measures for a Settlement of the Armed Conflict on the Territory of the Chechen Republic, 27 May 1996, Article 2 [on file with the author]; Accord de Cessez-le-Feu et de Cessation des Hostilités entre le Haut Commandement de la Force Publique et le Haut Commandement des Force d'Autodéfense de la Résistance (FADR) en Republique du Congo Brazzaville, 29 December 1999, Article 5, available at: http://peacemaker.unlb.org (accessed 12 June 2011).

63. Linas-Marcoussis Agreement, signed by a round-table of the Ivorian political forces on 24 January 2003, Article 3, para. 1, UN Doc. S/2003/99, 27 January 2003; Agreement on Permanent Ceasefire and Security Arrangements – Implementation Modalities Between the Government of the Sudan and the Sudan People's Liberation Movement/Army During the Pre-interim and Interim Periods, 31 December 2004, Article 1, para 8, available at: http://peacemaker.unlb.org (accessed 22 August 2011).

64. S. Bastid, 'The Cease-fire,' in *Le Cessez-le-feu, Recueils de la Societé Internationale de Droit Pénal Militaire et de Droit de la Guerre* (Brussels, 1974), 38.

65. Ibid.

66. For example, Article 3(i) of the Linas-Marcoussis Agreement on Ivory Coast, *supra* note 63, sets out the release of military personnel, including soldiers in exile. The 1999 Lomè Peace Agreement on Sierra Leone provides for the liberation of the 'prisoners of war' and 'abductees' by both parties (Article XXI of the Agreement) (this clause takes account of one of the features of the conflict in Sierra Leone which consisted in the abduction of minors in order to compel them to take up arms on behalf of the abducting power). The lack of differentiation between the release of military and civilian persons contrasts with the IHL rules applicable to international armed conflicts, where specific provisions are drawn up for prisoners of war and civilian internees.

67. We use this term in the comprehensive meaning of International Institute of Humanitarian Law, *The Manual on the Law of Non-International Armed Conflict* (San Remo: International Institute of Humanitarian Law, 2006), namely 'fighters are members of armed forces and dissident armed forces or other organized armed groups, or taking an active (direct) part in hostilities', Article 1.1.2 (a).

68. According to Article 118 of the Third Geneva Convention of 1949 Relative to the Treatment of Prisoners of War: 'Prisoners of war shall be released and repatriated without delay after the cessation of active hostilities'; whereas civilian internees shall be released 'as soon as the reasons which necessitated [their] internment no longer exists', Article 132 of the Fourth Geneva Convention of 1949 Relative to the Protection of Civilian Persons in Time of War.
69. See J. Pictet, ed., *Commentary to the Third Geneva Convention of 1949 Relative to the Treatment of Prisoners of War* (Geneva: International Committee of the Red Cross, 1960), 546–547.
70. Indeed, in the case that the agreement on a ceasefire or cessation of hostilities is not followed by the solution of the causes of the conflict, it is likely that the prisoners that have been released take up arms again.
71. Article 214(g) of the Darfur Peace Agreement, *supra* note 29. This conclusion appears to be in contrast with the ICRC evaluation of the existence of an international customary law rule according to which 'Persons deprived of their liberty in relation to a non-international armed conflict must be released as soon as the reasons for the deprivation of their liberty cease to exist', Rule 128C, J.-M. Henckaerts and L. Doswald-Beck, *Customary International Humanitarian Law*, Vol. I (Cambridge: Cambridge University Press, 2005), 451.
72. The International Committee of the Red Cross is often part of the joint commission, see by way of illustration, the Darfur Peace Agreement, Article 365, *supra* note 29.
73. See, e.g., Article X of the Peace Agreement on Liberia, *supra* note 39.
74. For example, the Ceasefire Agreement between the Government of Rwanda and the Rwandese Patriotic Front, see *supra* note 13, provided that the persons arrested because and as a result of the war be released within five days following the entry into force of the agreement.
75. See Article 3(i) of the Linas-Marcoussis Agreement on Ivory Coast, *supra* note 63.
76. This practice corroborates the existence of that part of Rule 128 as identified by the International Committee of the Red Cross study, *Customary International Humanitarian Law*, *supra* note 71, which provides that 'The persons … may continue to be deprived of their liberty if penal proceedings are pending against them or if they are serving a sentence lawfully imposed', 452.
77. See Article 364 of the Agreement. Interestingly, the exception to the release of all persons detained in connection with the armed conflict is formulated as a measure of execution of the UN Security Council Resolution S/RES/1556, 30 July 2004, which, at para. 6, established that 'the Government of the Sudan fulfil its commitments to disarm the Janjaweed militias and apprehend and bring to justice Janjaweed leaders and their associates who have incited and carried out human rights and international humanitarian law violations and other atrocities'.
78. For instance, see Article 2 of the Accord sur la Libération des Prisonniers Civils et Militaires, signed on 1 November 2002 between the Government of Ivory Coast and Le Mouvement patriotique de Côte d'Ivoire; Article 10 of the Accord Accra II (Ghana) sur la crise en Côte d'Ivoire, 7 March 2003; Article 1, para. 11, of Annexure 1 to the Comprehensive Ceasefire Agreement between the Government of the Republic of Burundi and the Palipehutu – FNL, signed on 7 September 2006 (all the agreements are available at http://peacemaker.unlb.org (accessed 20 August 2011)).
79. The circumstance that the Sudan People's Liberation Army/Movement (SPLA/M) has repeatedly stated that it would treat the detainees belonging to the armed forces of the Government of Sudan as prisoners of war and the inclusion of this decision in the Implementation of the Ceasefire Agreement and Security Arrangements, *supra* note 63, Article 1, para. 8, might be considered as the first step of the recognition of belligerency. However, neither the government nor any third state has ever recognised the same treatment to the SPLA/M fighters captured by the government forces.
80. It is worth recalling that while release is a fact, whose operational details may be regulated by normative acts, amnesty is a legal act, usually taking the form of a legislative measure.
81. This issue is addressed, also with respect to the amnesty provisions contained in the agreements originating from internal armed conflicts, in L. Mallinder, 'Exploring the Practice of States Introducing Amnesties', in Ambos et al., *supra* note 54, 144–147.
82. Preliminary Cease-fire Agreement signed by the Government of Nicaragua and the Nicaraguan Resistance on 23 March 1988, text reproduced in *International Legal Materials* (1988): 955–956.
83. See Article 8, para. 3 of the Agreement.
84. Agreement signed on 15 July 1993, which covers all acts carried out 'while in actual combat or on authority of any of the Parties in the course of actual combat'. The peculiar aspect of this amnesty clause consists in the provision of extinction also of all business operations 'legally carried out' by the parties to the agreement with private companies on the basis of domestic law.

85. Article 8(ix) of the Peace Agreement between the Government of Sudan and the South Sudan United Democratic Salvation Front, the Sudan People's Liberation Movement, the Equatoria Defence Force and the South Sudan Independents Group, 21 April 1997, available at: http://peacemaker.unlb.org (accessed 20 August 2011). See also the Memorandum of Understanding between the Government of Angola and UNITA of 4 April 2002, Chapter 2, Article 2, para. 1, UN Doc. S/2002/483, 26 April 2002; Article 1 of the Protocol on Political Issues between the Government of Tajikistan and the United Tajik Opposition, 18 May 1997, UN Doc. S/1997/385, 20 May 1997; Article 10 of the Lincoln Agreement on Peace, Security and Development on Bougainville, signed on 23 January 1998 [on file with the author]; and Article 5 of the Ceasefire Agreement concerning Congo-Brazzaville, *supra* note 62.

86. On the strength of Article 3 of the Accord de Paix entre le Gouvernement de la République du Tchad et le Mouvement National, 25 July 2007 [on file with the author], amnesty cannot be granted to persons having committed common law crimes; Article III (22) of the Lusaka Ceasefire Agreement on the Democratic Republic of the Congo, excludes amnesty for acts of genocide. The Agreement, originally signed on 10 July 1999 by Angola, Namibia, Democratic Republic of the Congo, Rwanda, Uganda and Zimbabwe, was adhered to on 1 August 1999 by the Movement for the Liberation of the Congo and on 31 August 1999, by the Congolese Rally for Democracy.

87. For instance, see Article 3(c) of the Quadripartite Agreement on Voluntary Return of Refugees and Displaced Persons between the Abkhaz and Georgian side, the Russian Federation and the United Nations High Commissioner for Refugees, signed on 4 April 1994, UN Doc. S/1994/397, 5 April 1994; Article 6, para. 3, of the Ouagadougou Political Agreement between the Government of the Republic of Ivory Coast and the Forces Nouvelles, signed on 4 March 2007, UN Doc. S/2007/144, 13 March 2007; and Article 3, para. 1, of the Agreement between the Government of the Democratic Republic of the Congo and the Congrès National pour la Défense du Peuple, 23 March 2009 [on file with the author].

88. For example, according to Article VII, para. 5, of the Linas-Marcoussis Agreement on Ivory Coast, *supra* note 64, 'under no circumstance' shall amnesty be granted to the persons having committed 'serious economic violations and serious violations of human rights and international humanitarian law'.

89. Notably, Article 2 of the Accord de Paix Global, signed on 21 June 2008 by the Government of the Central African Republic, the Armée Populaire pour la Restauration de la Démocratie, the Front Démocratique du Peuple Centrafricain and the Union des Forces Démocratiques pour le Rassemblement, available at: http://peacemaker.unlb.org (accessed 20 August 2011), excludes amnesty for the crimes falling under the jurisdiction of the ICC.

90. For example under Article 3 of the 2005 Memorandum of Understanding on Aceh, *supra* note 22, the Government undertakes to grant an amnesty, which seems to be unconditional because no limits are set as to the categories of crimes that can be extinguished. Similar is the scope of the amnesty provided for in Article 331 of the Bougainville Peace Agreement of 30 August 2001 on Papua New Guinea [on file with the author]. The Lomè Peace Agreement on Sierra Leone, *supra* note 24, is only a partial exception because, though it sets out a blanket amnesty, the declaration released by the UN Secretary General Representative during the ceremony of signature of the agreement specified that the amnesty clause 'shall not apply to the international crimes of genocide, crimes against humanity, war crimes and other serious of international humanitarian law', UN News Release, 5 October 2000, available at: http://un.org./News/briefings (accessed 25 May 2007), has been later implicitly incorporated into the Statute of the Special Court for Sierra Leone.

91. See Article 6, para. 5, of Additional Protocol II, as well as the corresponding customary rule, International Committee of the Red Cross study, *Customary International Humanitarian Law*, *supra* note 71, at 611.

92. Y. Sandoz et al., eds, *Commentary on the Additional Protocols of 8 June 1977 to the Geneva Conventions of 12 August 1949* (Geneva: Martinus Nijhoff, 1987), 1402, para. 4618.

93. This is true for the immunity from prosecution by the detaining authorities for acts of war carried out in observance of IHL. On the contrary, unlike the numerous provisions of the Third Geneva Convention concerning the treatment of prisoners of war, the treatment due to the persons deprived of their freedom can only exceptionally be found in the agreements.

94. By establishing the principles of individual criminal responsibility for the violation of IHL in internal armed conflict, the Appeals Chamber of the ICTY in *Prosecutor v. Tadić*, 2 October 1995 (Case No. IT-94-1-A), para. 128ff., has indirectly affirmed the lawfulness of acts of war, committed in an internal armed conflict, in compliance with IHL.

95. According to Article 6, para. 5, of Additional Protocol I to the Four Geneva Conventions, 'At the end of hostilities, the authorities in power shall endeavour to grant the broadest possible amnesty'. The literal interpretation of this clause indicates the existence of the faculty of the authorities to grant the broadest possible amnesty, but not of an obligation. At most, according to this provision, one may conclude in favour of the procedural obligation to take into consideration the opportunity to grant amnesty measures.

96. The only provision on the release of persons in international armed conflict is contained in Article 5, para. 4, of the 1977 Additional Protocol I, by virtue of which: 'If it is decided to release persons deprived of their liberty, necessary measures to ensure their safety shall be taken by those so deciding.'

97. A Judgment of an international tribunal for the first time has shed light on the meaning of the expression 'without delay' contained in Article 118 of the Third Geneva Convention. In the Partial Award, Prisoners of War, Eritrea's Claim 17, between the State of Eritrea and The Federal Democratic Republic of Ethiopia, The Hague, 1 July 2003, the Eritrea-Ethiopia Claims Commission has determined that 'repatriation should occur at an early time and without unreasonable or unjustifiable restrictions or delays. At the same time, repatriation cannot be instantaneous. Preparing and coordinating adequate arrangements for safe and orderly movement and reception, especially of sick or wounded prisoners, may be time-consuming. Further, there must be adequate procedures to ensure that individuals are not repatriated against their will', para. 147. In the case at issue, the Commission found that a delay of 77 days in the repatriation of Eritrean prisoners of war by Ethiopia was unjustified, para. 13.

98. On the possibility that the prisoner of war regime be de-composed into different categories with respect to internal armed conflicts, see S. Sivakumaran, 'Re-envisaging the International Law of Internal Armed Conflict', *European Journal of International Law* 22 (2011): 247–248.

99. The issue of the incentives for compliance with IHL from armed groups is a complex one, see P. Hayner, 'Creating Incentives for Compliance: between Amnesty and Criminalization', in *Non-state Actors and International Humanitarian Law*, *supra* note 53, 181–186; and M. Sassòli, 'Transnational Armed Groups and International Humanitarian Law', *Program on Humanitarian Policy and Conflict Research, Harvard University, Occasional Paper Series* 6 (Winter 2006): 28–38.

100. M. Sassòli, 'Involving Armed Opposition Groups in the Development of the Law?,' in *Non-state Actors and International Humanitarian Law*, eds M. Odello and G.L. Beruto (Milan: FrancoAngeli, 2010), 213–221.

101. According to the threshold approach, different IHL rules apply to internal armed conflicts of differing intensity, whereas the unification approach advocates the adoption of the same rules regardless of the intensity of the conflict, see Sivakumaran, *supra* note 98, 235–236.

102. See the Preamble to the 1868 Saint Petersburg Declaration Renouncing the Use, in Time of War, of Explosive Projectiles Under 400 Grammes Weight.

103. Y. Sandoz, 'The Red Cross and Peace: Realities and Limits', *Journal of Peace Research* 24 (1987): 287.

104. As we have seen, *supra* section 3.2, these provisions are included in the agreements at a preliminary stage of the negotiations and may also act as an exchange token in the hands of the armed opposition group to sit at the negotiating table.

105. Actually, only a very small number of agreements contain an express provision to the effect that the negotiated regulation does not affect the legal status of the parties, i.e. Uganda Peace Talks Agreement for the Restoration of Peace to the Sovereign State of the Republic of Uganda between the Government of Uganda and the National Resistance Movement, 17 December 1985, Annexure D (it incorporates verbatim common Article 3 to the 1949 Geneva Conventions); Agreement on the application and the implementation of international humanitarian law within the context of the conflict in Bosnia-Herzegovina, Preamble, *supra* note 57; and CARHRIHL, Part VI, Article 3. It should also be noted that it is highly debatable that a clause concerning the status of the parties is sufficient to deny international personality to an armed group, should the group have already acquired personality at the moment of the signature of an agreement. On this point, see G. Abi Saab, 'Les conflits armés non-internationales', in *International Dimensions of Humanitarian Law* (Geneva: UNESCO, 1988) 259; and Barberis, *supra* note 5, at 253.

PART IV

MONITORING MECHANISMS

21. Universal human rights bodies and international humanitarian law

*Walter Kälin**

1. INTRODUCTION

Protecting people in times of armed conflict is the aim of the Geneva Conventions and their Additional Protocols as well as that of international human rights law (HRL). However, unlike human rights law, international humanitarian law (IHL) does not provide for standing mechanisms monitoring the implementation of its provisions by States parties. Since the end of the Cold War, the UN human rights bodies have started to deal regularly, albeit not systematically, with violations of IHL even though their mandate is focused on HRL, and they have developed several approaches in this regard.

This contribution looks at how the UN human rights bodies, in particular the treaty bodies as expert committees monitoring the implementation of the UN human rights conventions, the Human Rights Council as principal intergovernmental body dealing with human rights, and its Special Procedures as independent experts reporting to the Council, presently address IHL and its relationship to HRL. To what extent are the UN human rights bodies ready to explicitly invoke IHL and monitor its implementation? Which are the key IHL issues raised by these bodies? How do they see the relationship between IHL and human rights law? And how can we assess their overall contribution to the monitoring of compliance with IHL?

2. THE ORIGINS: HUMAN RIGHTS IN ARMED CONFLICT

The origin of endeavors of the UN human rights system to look at IHL can be traced back to the late 1960s.[1] In 1967, the Security Council linked HRL and IHL in a resolution on the situation in the Middle East: It considered 'the urgent need to spare the civil populations and the prisoners of the war in the area of conflict in the Middle East additional sufferings', stressed 'that essential and inalienable human rights should be respected even during the vicissitudes of war' and recommended 'to the Governments concerned the scrupulous respect of the humanitarian principles governing the treatment of prisoners of war and the protection of civilian persons in time of war contained in the Geneva Conventions of 12 August 1949'.[2]

One year later, the Final Act of the International Conference on Human Rights, held in Teheran in 1968, included a resolution on 'Human rights in armed conflict' which observed that 'widespread violence ... including massacres, summary executions, torture, inhuman treatment of prisoners, killing of civilians in armed conflicts and the use of chemical and biological means of warfare … eroded human rights', and highlighted 'that even during the periods of armed conflict, humanitarian principles must prevail'. It requested that the UN Secretary-General should:

> after consultation with the International Committee of the Red Cross … draw the attention of States members of the United Nations system to the existing rules of international law on the subject and … urge them to observe that in all armed conflicts, the inhabitants and belligerents are protected in accordance with 'the principles of the law of nations derived from the usages established among civilized peoples, from the laws of humanity and the dictates of the public conscience'.[3]

This reference to the Martens Clause[4] allowed bridging the gap between IHL and HRL at a time when human rights still were thought by many to be applicable in times of peace only.

The UN General Assembly, at its twenty-fifth session, on 9 December 1970, reconfirmed the inviolability of humanitarian and human rights rules and principles in several resolutions regarding the protection of civilians in armed conflicts. It affirmed certain 'basic principles for the protection of civilian populations in armed conflicts', the first of which being that '[f]undamental human rights, as accepted in international law and laid down in international instruments, continue to apply fully in situations of armed conflict'.[5] In another resolution on 'Respect for human rights in armed conflict', the General Assembly urged 'strict compliance with the provisions of the existing international instruments concerning human rights in armed conflicts'.[6]

The Iraqi occupation of Kuwait in 1990/91 provided an important opportunity for the General Assembly and the then UN Human Rights Commission to concomitantly invoke, in their resolutions,[7] HRL and IHL. The Special Rapporteur of the Human Rights Commission on the situation of human rights in Iraqi occupied Kuwait referred in his report[8] to the two bodies of law in a way that, according to R. Kolb, 'IHL and HRL are so interwoven that they can no longer be disentangled'.[9]

In 1993, the Vienna Declaration and Program of Action adopted by the World Conference on Human Rights synthesised these developments by declaring:

> Effective international measures to guarantee and monitor the implementation of human rights standards should be taken in respect of people under foreign occupation, and effective legal protection against the violation of their human rights should be provided, in accordance with human rights norms and international law, particularly the Geneva Convention relative to the Protection of Civilian Persons in Time of War … and other applicable norms of humanitarian law.[10]

With these statements, the international community highlighted the close relationship between HRL and IHL and thus opened the way for overcoming the traditional dichotomy between HRL as a body of law applicable in peace and IHL as a set of rules substituting human rights law in times of armed conflict.

3.   UNITED NATIONS TREATY BODIES: CONCOMITANT APPLICATION OF INTERNATIONAL HUMAN RIGHTS LAW AND HUMANITARIAN LAW

Each of the nine UN core human rights conventions[11] provides for an independent body tasked with monitoring the implementation of the respective instrument. These treaty bodies are committees composed of independent experts elected by States parties to the respective conventions.

All conventions provide for a compulsory State reporting procedure, obliging States parties to periodically submit a report on the implementation of their treaty obligations to the committee concerned. These reports are examined within the framework of a dialogue between the committee and a delegation from the State party concerned. The examination ends with the adoption of recommendations (usually called 'Concluding Observations').[12] Individual communication procedures, which allow victims of alleged human rights violations to initiate a formal procedure against the violating State before the committee, exist for all treaties except the Convention on the Rights of the Child.[13] Such complaint procedures are not available automatically but only when the State party concerned makes a corresponding declaration or ratifies an optional protocol.[14]

Furthermore, in order to assist States to fulfill their obligations, the treaty bodies adopt what most of them call 'General Comments', that is, brief commentaries on specific issues providing guidance on the scope and content of States parties' obligations.[15]

In all these contexts, treaty bodies may have to deal with human rights violations in situations of armed conflict. While the earlier treaties contain derogation clauses indicating not only that without an explicit declaration to derogate from the conventions concerned they continue to apply even in times of armed conflict but also designating certain key rights as non-derogable, later ones either expressly say they cannot be limited during emergency or explicitly highlight the obligation to respect IHL together with relevant human rights.[16]

Concluding Observations provide the richest material in quantitative terms to understand the Committees' positions while General Comments by the Human Rights Committee and other Committees explain the doctrinal underpinnings of their approaches to IHL. In contrast, no references to IHL can be found yet in the views of Committees adopted in the context of examining individual communications.

3.1   General Comments: Stressing the Complementarity of International Human Rights Law and Humanitarian Law

3.1.1   The Human Rights Committee
In their general comments, treaty bodies quite often refer to the relevance of human rights in situations of armed conflict. While as many as five out of the nine[17] existing treaty bodies made explicit references to IHL in their General Comments, only the Human Rights Committee set up under the International Covenant on Civil and Political Rights (ICCPR) has explained the doctrinal underpinnings of the relationship between HRL and IHL.

In its General Comment No. 31, the Human Rights Committee explicitly[18] recognises that, subject to derogations that can be made for certain rights in times of public emergency affecting the life of the nation (Article 4 ICCPR),[19] the Covenant on Civil and Political Rights 'applies also in situations of armed conflict to which the rules of international humanitarian law are applicable'.[20] This concomitant applicability not only rests on the assumption that both bodies of law can be applied at the *same time*, but also in the *same place*,[21] including in areas of armed conflict outside a State party's territory.[22]

While many human rights conventions do not explicitly refer to their territorial scope of application,[23] the issue of extraterritorial applicability is rather complex in the case of the ICCPR. Its Article 2, paragraph 1, requires each State party to respect and ensure Covenant rights 'to all individuals within its territory and subject to its jurisdiction'.[24] Some States, among them the United States of America[25] insist that this wording limits the applicability of the ICCPR to their own territory, while the Human Rights Committee early on underlined that this wording covered different situations including those where a State exercises jurisdiction only and therefore should not be narrowly constructed.[26] In General Comment No. 31 the Human Rights Committee stresses that according to article 2 of the ICCPR, 'a State party must respect and ensure the rights laid down in the Covenant to anyone within the power or effective control of that State Party, even if not situated within the territory of the State Party' and underlined that '[t]his principle also applies to those within the power or effective control of the forces of a State Party acting outside its territory, regardless of the circumstances in which such power or effective control was obtained … '.[27] The Committee thus acknowledges that the wording 'within its territory and subject to its jurisdiction' is ambiguous: the 'and' can be construed as a cumulative requirement[28] or as an 'and/or' alternative.[29] The latter interpretation has been explicitly endorsed by the International Court of Justice in its Advisory Opinion on the *Legal Consequences of the Construction of a Wall in the Occupied Palestinian Territory*[30] but has been criticized by some authors.[31]

The concomitant applicability of HRL and IHL raises the question of the kind of relationship between the two bodies of law. The Committee's answer is as follows: 'While, in respect of certain Covenant rights, more specific rules of international humanitarian law may be especially relevant for the purposes of the interpretation of Covenant rights, both spheres of law are complementary, not mutually exclusive'.[32]

The Committee thus recognizes the *lex specialis* character of IHL,[33] however not in the sense of more specific rules derogating the more general ones of the Covenant but rather as a body of law that with its specific rules for a specific situation – i.e. that of armed conflict – complements the more general and generally applicable human rights guarantees. In its opinion, IHL is what an expert meeting in 2004 called 'lex specialis *complementa* (complementary) and not *derogata* (derogatory) of human rights law'.[34]

The Committee's position is consistent with the ICJ's approach to this issue. In its Advisory Opinion of 8 July 1996 on the *Legality of the Threat or Use of Nuclear Weapons*, the Court affirmed with regard to the right to life:

> In principle, the right not arbitrarily to be deprived of one's life applies also in hostilities. The test of what is an arbitrary deprivation of life, however, then falls to be determined by the

applicable lex specialis, namely, the law applicable in armed conflict which is designed to regulate the conduct of hostilities.[35]

The ICJ, in its Advisory Opinion of 9 July 2004 on the *Legal Consequences of the Construction of a Wall in the Occupied Palestinian Territory*, further stated that three possible situations can be distinguished: '[S]ome rights may be exclusively matters of international humanitarian law; others may be exclusively matters of human rights law; yet others may be matters of both these branches of international law.'[36]

The existence of these three situations is acknowledged by the Human Rights Committee. Guarantees that are exclusively a matter of IHL such as, for example, the role of the ICRC, by their nature cannot be of concern to the Human Rights Committee whose powers are limited to matters covered by the rights enshrined in the ICCPR. Of course, in cases of matters exclusively enshrined in HRL as, for example, the issue of political rights and access to public service guaranteed by Article 25 of the ICCPR, IHL cannot play a role. However, as most rights enshrined in the ICCPR have at least some equivalent in IHL, and as violations of IHL can affect human rights, the areas of potential overlap are rather important when the protection of civilians in armed conflict is at stake.

3.1.2 Other United Nations' treaty bodies

Other UN treaty bodies have not systematically addressed the relationship between international human rights and humanitarian law in their General Comments.

The Committee on Economic, Social and Cultural Rights occasionally refers to the obligations of States to respect IHL guarantees. It stressed that States should refrain from limiting access to health services as a punitive measure during armed conflicts in violation of relevant IHL guarantees;[37] should take steps to ensure that prisoners and detainees are provided with sufficient and safe water for their daily individual requirements in accordance, *inter alia*, with IHL;[38] and refrain from 'limiting access to, or destroying, water services and infrastructure as a punitive measure, for example, during armed conflicts in violation of international humanitarian law'.[39] These statements reflect the Committee's opinion that HRL and IHL have to be applied in parallel during armed conflicts. They also indicate that, according to the Committee, some breaches of IHL may be tantamount to violations of the Covenant, in so far as in situations of armed conflict IHL may determine the content of general human rights clauses. On one occasion, the Committee explicitly noted 'that during armed conflicts ... the right to water embraces those obligations by which States parties are bound under international humanitarian law'.[40] According to this view, obligations elaborated in IHL give more context-specific information to how to protect the relevant human right. Overall, CESCR's approach seems to be rather systematic[41] and similar to that of the Human Rights Committee.

The other UN treaty bodies are less systematic. To the extent that they refer to IHL – and they do so to a lesser extent than do the Human Rights Committee and CESCR in their General Comments – it is done in a rather haphazard manner. The Committee on the Rights of the Child, for example, highlighted that IHL constitutes an important, but all too often neglected, dimension of an education that is directed towards the development of respect for human rights and fundamental freedoms,[42] and stressed that in the case of unaccompanied and separated children outside their country of origin States must fully respect non-refoulement obligations deriving not only from human rights and refugee law but also from IHL.[43] It also stressed that if internment of a child soldier over the age of 15 is unavoidable and in compliance with IHL and HRL, the conditions of such internment should be in conformity with international standards.[44] The Committee on the Elimination of Racial Discrimination called on States to ensure that non-citizens arrested and detained in the context of 'the fight against terrorism are properly protected by domestic law that complies with international human rights, refugee and humanitarian law'.[45] Finally, the Committee on the Elimination of Discrimination against Women noted that gender-based violence which impairs or nullifies the enjoyment by women of the 'right to equal protection according to humanitarian norms in time of international or internal armed conflict' constitutes discrimination.[46]

3.2   Concluding Observations: Reminding States of their Obligations in Times of Armed Conflict

The Human Rights Committee is hesitant to directly refer to IHL as, in the context of the examination of State reports, its own powers are limited to monitoring the ICCPR. Thus, the Committee refrains from invoking IHL where, as in the case of 'targeted killings' or treatment of internally displaced persons during armed conflict[47] such references would be easy. However, in accordance with its General Comments, it regularly insists on the extraterritorial applicability of the Covenant during armed conflict by States parties that do not accept this position.[48] Sometimes, it also stresses that the right to an effective remedy requires not only the investigation, prosecution, and sanctioning of violations of HRL but also of IHL, as well as providing reparation for such violations,[49] a recommendation that is justified by the fact that IHL violations usually also violate a corresponding human rights guarantee.

The Committee on the Rights of the Child has two obvious entry points for such references. First, according to Article 38 of the Convention on the Rights of the Child 'States Parties undertake to respect and to ensure respect for rules of international humanitarian law applicable to them in armed conflict'. This indicates not only that IHL and HRL can co-apply but also that respect for IHL also becomes a human rights issue. Second, the Convention and its Optional Protocol prohibit the recruitment and use of children in armed conflict.[50] It is regularly in these contexts that the Committee raises concerns about the violation of IHL and recommends to States, *inter alia*, that they fully respect IHL, including the rules of distinction and proportionality;[51] refrain from recruiting children or protect them against recruitment by non-state armed groups; take measures to protect child soldiers; and rehabilitate children traumatized by armed conflict.[52] In one case, the Committee dealt with the capture of persons under the age of 18 during military operations abroad, thus recognising the extraterritorial applicability of the Convention on the Rights of the Child.[53]

Like the Convention on the Rights of the Child and its optional protocols, the Convention on the Rights of Persons with Disabilities directly refers to international humanitarian law in its article 11.[54] Reflecting developments under other HRL treaties, situations of armed conflict were not excluded from the application of the Convention on the Rights of Persons with Disabilities. Nor does this Convention contain a restrictive jurisdictional clause or one permitting derogations during times of emergency threatening the life of the nation, as did the earlier human rights treaties adopted at a previous stage of development of the UN system. Thus, there is a solid basis for that Committee to make references to IHL in view of protection of relevant human rights, should these be deemed necessary.

The basis for references to IHL by the Committee against Torture is more elusive but it seems to take the approach of looking at human rights violations within its mandate resulting from the same acts that could also constitute IHL breaches. While it stresses for good reasons the extraterritorial applicability of the Convention against Torture in times of armed conflict and rejects the argument that IHL is a *lex specialis* derogating the Convention against Torture in such situations,[55] it is more difficult to see why violations of humanitarian law in the context of house demolitions[56] or the recruitment of children[57] should fall within the notion of torture or inhuman and degrading treatment as contained in the Convention. However, the link with the recruitment of children and human rights may be justified in so far as (as already recognised by the Convention on the Rights of the Child and its Optional Protocol on child recruitment) psychological manipulation, humiliation, shaming, or physical intimidation, including in the presence of weapons, threats to family, whether explicit or implicit, might be used in recruiting children and ensuring their continued loyalty. This could fall within the realm of inhuman or degrading treatment.

Other Committees only very rarely refer to IHL in their concluding observations.[58] The Committee on Economic, Social and Cultural Rights, has stressed that the International Covenant on Economic, Social and Cultural Rights applies during times of armed conflict and binds States parties even where they act outside their territory.[59] The concomitant and extraterritorial applicability of HRL and IHL was also highlighted by the Committee on the Elimination of Discrimination against Women[60] which, otherwise, does not seem to refer to IHL at all when examining state reports. Similarly, the Committee on the Elimination of Racial Discrimination rejected the position that HRL 'is not applicable to the treatment of foreign detainees held as "enemy combatants", on the basis of the argument that the law of armed conflict is the exclusive *lex specialis* applicable',[61] and held that 'actions that change the demographic composition of the Occupied Palestinian Territories are also of concern as violations of human rights and international humanitarian law'.[62]

3.3   Conclusions: International Humanitarian Law as Relevant Issue Despite Limited Powers of Treaty Bodies

The powers of the UN treaty bodies are limited to monitoring the implementation of their respective conventions. Therefore, it is far from obvious that they can deal with IHL issues.

A key reason for multiple references to IHL in recent years is the position of some countries, in particular the United States of America and Israel,[63] that they are not bound by the UN human rights conventions during armed conflicts outside their own territory. Treaty bodies responded in a unified manner insisting that, subject to possible derogations (permitted but limited in the earlier, but not later human rights treaties), human rights guarantees are applicable during times of armed conflict, including in situations where the country concerned operates outside its territory. This position was crystallised in the more recent treaties indicating that HRL continues to apply in armed conflicts and creating new formal HRL obligations to respect IHL in so far as relevant rights are concerned (and presumably in so far as IHL is consistent with HRL).

Beyond taking the position of continued (and extraterritorial) applicability during armed conflict, treaty bodies seem to be rather reluctant to take up IHL issues and to look into the substance of its provisions. Except, to some limited extent, the Human Rights Committee, these treaty bodies also refrain from exploring what exactly a concomitant application of HRL and IHL actually means.

One reason for this is the fact that, unlike in the case of the European Court of Human Rights,[64] no individual communications have been brought yet to the UN treaty bodies of persons claiming to be victims of violations of their human rights during armed conflict. Such cases would provide the Human Rights Committee and other treaty bodies with an opportunity to explore the relationship between specific human rights and their equivalents in international humanitarian law.

Overall, the treaty bodies have not developed a full theory of the relationship between HRL and IHL in cases where the two bodies of law overlap or where human rights conventions such as the Convention on the Rights of the Child and the Convention on the Rights of Persons with Disabilities formally oblige them to take IHL into account. Their statements in General Comments and Concluding Observations, however, allow concluding that such theory would need to distinguish at least the three following categories:

(1)   Often, IHL is *lex specialis* in so far as its more detailed provisions add specificity to the content of more general human rights clauses. In this sense, the Human Rights Committee also looked at IHL when it had to determine whether and to what extent the fair trial guarantees of Article 14 ICCPR are derogable. It found that no justifications exist to derogate from those 'elements of the right to a fair trial [that] are explicitly guaranteed under international humanitarian law during armed conflict' during other emergency situations.[65] In line with this approach, IHL also adds specificity in situations of armed conflict. For example, it provides indications as to:
   - what, as has been stressed by the Committee on Economic, Social and Cultural Rights, constitutes the content of the right to water in situations of armed conflict;[66]
   - what is 'arbitrary' in terms of Covenant rights protecting against arbitrary deprivations of a specific right.[67] Thus, for example, deprivations of life permissible under applicable IHL would not, according to this view, violate the right to life of the Covenant, and internment of civilians permissible under IHL would not amount to arbitrary deprivation of liberty; or
   - what is a permissible restriction of those freedoms of the Covenant that have limitation clauses.[68] Thus, for example, limitations to Article 12 of the International Covenant on Civil and Political Rights on the liberty of movement may be imposed, in accordance with paragraph 3 of this provision, if, for

example, an Occupying Power is permitted, in accordance with Article 49, paragraph 2, of the Fourth Geneva Convention, to 'undertake total or partial evacuation of a given area if the security of the population or imperative military reasons so demand'.[69]

While this approach helps to reconcile the ideals of HRL with the realistic assumptions of IHL about the nature of armed conflict, it may, unless used cautiously, lower human rights protection, at least in some cases, below the levels that human rights on their own might guarantee.

(2)   Sometimes human rights law may *complement* IHL where this body of law leaves an issue unaddressed or uses open and undefined notions that can be given more concrete meaning in the light of relevant human rights guarantees. Thus, for example, the prohibition of common Article 3(1)(c) to the 1949 Geneva Conventions to pass sentences and to carry out 'executions without previous judgment pronounced by a regularly constituted court, affording all the judicial guarantees which are recognized as indispensable by civilized peoples' needs to be interpreted in the light of the core guarantees of Article 14 of the International Covenant on Civil and Political Rights on fair trial. The same is true for the notion of the 'essential guarantees of independence and impartiality as generally recognized' that courts trying prisoners of war should offer (Article 84, paragraph 2, of the Third Geneva Convention). In this type of situation, it is possible that HRL informs and adds specificity to IHL.

(3)   Finally, there are situations where the general principle that human rights treaties must not be interpreted as impairing the right of individuals guaranteed to them by other applicable treaties[70] requires the *cumulative* application of both bodies of law where both provide protection to individuals concerned by complementing rather than contradicting each other. Due to the non-derogable nature of the right to life, and the related prohibition to exclude any groups of people from its protection explicitly or implicitly, States Parties to the International Covenant on Civil and Political Rights must, for example, respect all the safeguards of Article 6, paragraph 2, of the Covenant when imposing the death penalty on prisoners of war under all circumstances. At the same time, they are under an obligation to respect the six-month waiting period between judgment and execution as provided for in Article 101 of the Third Geneva Convention, although the Covenant does not have such a requirement.

4. THE HUMAN RIGHTS COUNCIL: PROMOTING AND MONITORING INTERNATIONAL HUMANITARIAN LAW

The Human Rights Council, created in 2006[71] to replace the former UN Human Rights Commission, has been assigned multiple tasks, including the protection of victims of human rights violations, in particular to 'address situations of violations of human rights, including gross and systematic violations, and make recommendations thereon'[72] and to 'respond promptly to human rights emergencies';[73] the promotion of human rights not only in general but also in specific countries, in particular through educational, capacity-building and technical assistance activities;[74] and the prevention of human rights violations through proposing measures aimed at ensuring that human rights violations do not occur or re-occur.[75]

Among the instruments provided to the Council by the General Assembly the Universal Periodic Review (UPR) 'of the fulfilment by each State of its human rights obligations and commitments',[76] the system of special procedures, and the possibility to hold special sessions and adopt country specific resolutions are particularly relevant for the topic of this chapter.

4.1   Country Situations: Monitoring International Humanitarian Law in Specific Armed Conflicts

UN General Assembly Resolution 60/251 (2006) creating the Human Rights Council does not refer to IHL but links all tasks and activities of the Council to international human rights law. Nevertheless, the Council, like its predecessor, the Human Rights Commission, regularly invokes IHL when dealing with the situation of countries involved in an armed conflict. While this is not questioned in general, the United States, starting in 2003, repeatedly contested the competence of the Human Rights Commission and Council and its Special Procedures to address issues arising under the law of armed conflict.[77] Recently, however, the United States did not oppose the inclusion of references to IHL in resolutions adopted by the Human Rights Council.[78]

The Council addresses country situations particularly in the context of special sessions. Such sessions are held at the request of one or several members of the Council with the support of one third of the membership of the Council.[79] Out of the 16 Special sessions held between June 2006 and April 2011, all except five[80] concerned serious human rights situations in countries with armed conflict. With one exception,[81] all resolutions on these situations contain explicit references to IHL: The first Special session resolution entitled 'Human rights situation in the Occupied Palestinian Territory'[82] expressed 'deep concern at the breaches by Israel, the occupying Power, of international humanitarian law and human rights law in the Occupied Palestinian Territory, including ... the military attacks against Palestinian ministries, including the office of the Premier, and the destruction of Palestinian infrastructure, including water networks, power plants and bridges' (last preambular paragraph), and demanded that Israel 'abide scrupulously by the provisions of international humanitarian law and human rights law, and refrain from imposing collective punishment on Palestinian civilians' (operative paragraph 2), as well as urging 'all concerned parties to respect the rules of international humanitarian law, to refrain from violence against the civilian population and to treat under all circumstances all detained combatants and civilians in accordance with the Geneva Conventions' (operative paragraph 5).

Resolution S-2/1 on 'The grave situation of human rights in Lebanon caused by Israeli military operations'[83] adopted during the second special session is particularly interesting as the Human Rights Council expressed here its approach to the concomitant application of HRL and IHL by '[e]mphasizing that human rights law and international humanitarian law are complementary and mutually reinforcing'.[84]

This and other resolutions adopted during special sessions[85] or regular meetings[86] regarding armed conflicts involving Israel essentially follow the same pattern.[87] In these resolutions, the Human Rights Council, *inter alia,*

- affirmed the applicability of both HRL and the Fourth Geneva Convention to the Occupied Palestinian Territory;[88]
- qualified as 'grave' or 'gross' violations of HRL and IHL 'Israeli military attacks and incursions into the Occupied Palestinian Territory',[89] 'killings of innocent civilians and the destruction of houses, property and infrastructure in Lebanon',[90] and 'the Israeli willful killing of Palestinian civilians, including women and children';[91]
- stressed that each party to the Fourth Geneva Convention 'is under obligation to take action against persons alleged to have committed or to have ordered the commission of grave breaches of the Convention';[92] and
- urged parties to the conflict to respect IHL and treat protected persons accordingly.[93]

Another interesting case is the Council's approach to the Darfur crisis. While no reference to IHL can be found in the Council's resolution adopted during a special session on this situation,[94] other decisions or resolutions do so. However, the Council in 2006 called 'on all parties to put an immediate end to the ongoing violations of human rights and international humanitarian law, with a special focus on vulnerable groups, including women and children, while not hindering the return of all internally displaced persons to their homes'.[95] Later the same year, it expressed

> its deep concern regarding the seriousness of the ongoing violations of human rights and international humanitarian law in Darfur, including armed attacks on the civilian population and humanitarian workers, widespread destruction of villages, and continued and widespread violence, in particular gender-based violence against women and girls, as well as the lack of accountability of perpetrators of such crimes.[96]

It also expressed its concerns about the prevailing impunity and urged the Government of Sudan to investigate and prosecute all allegations of HRL and IHL violations.[97]

Other country situations where the Human Rights Council referred to IHL include the Democratic Republic of Congo where the Council, *inter alia*, called upon the parties to the conflict 'to comply fully with their obligations under international law, including international humanitarian law, human rights law and refugee law', and underlined the primary responsibility of the government 'to investigate and bring to justice perpetrators of violations of human rights and of international humanitarian law'.[98] The latter point was also made in a more general form in resolutions on the situation in Côte d'Ivoire,[99] Myanmar[100] and Somalia.[101]

Another particular feature of these resolutions is the fact that, in several cases, the Human Rights Council set up commissions of inquiry or tasked a group of special rapporteurs to report to it on the situation. Examples include 'a high-level commission of inquiry comprising of eminent experts on human rights law and international humanitarian law' tasked with investigating the situation in Lebanon during the 2006 armed conflict,[102] a 'high-level fact-finding mission … to travel to Beit Hanoun' in late 2006,[103] 'a High-Level Mission to assess the human rights situation in Darfur' in December of the same year,[104] a group of seven thematic special procedures 'to urgently examine the current situation in the east of the Democratic Republic of the Congo with a view to providing a comprehensive report to the Council',[105] 'an urgent, independent international fact-finding mission ... to investigate all violations of international human rights law and international humanitarian law by the occupying Power, Israel, against the Palestinian people throughout the Occupied Palestinian Territory, particularly in the occupied Gaza Strip' in 2009,[106] and 'an independent, international commission of inquiry ... to investigate all alleged violations of international human rights law in the Libyan Arab Jamahiriya' in 2011.[107] The reports of these bodies[108] without exception examined and assessed the situations in the countries concerned not only from a human rights perspective but also on the basis of applicable humanitarian law instruments. They all concluded that specific violations of HRL and IHL had taken place that had to be qualified as grave or serious. These reports, which cannot be analysed in detail here, provide a wealth of material on the concomitant application of HRL and IHL to situations of armed conflict. In so far as they take IHL into account, these commissions can be said to substitute, at least to some extent, for the underused[109] International Humanitarian Fact-Finding Commission provided for by Article 90 of the 1977 First Protocol Additional to the Geneva Conventions.

4.2   Thematic Issues: Occasional References to International Humanitarian Law

The Human Rights Council occasionally but not systematically refers to IHL in resolutions on thematic issues, too.

In 2009 it urged, for example, States to ensure that measures taken to counter terrorism comply with HRL as well as IHL and to respect, in particular, the right to a fair trial as guaranteed by these two bodies of law,[110] stressed the obligation of States to 'ensure that religious places, sites, shrines and symbols are fully respected and protected' in accordance with HRL and IHL,[111] expressed its concerns regarding 'attacks on religious places, sites and shrines, including any deliberate destruction of relics and monuments, particularly when in violation of international law, in particular human rights and humanitarian law',[112] and encouraged States to ensure that legislation on violence against women 'conforms with relevant international human rights instruments and international humanitarian law'.[113]

Many similar examples could be added. They show that references to IHL in thematic resolutions are usually very general in nature and always made in conjunction with invocations of HRL.

4.3   Special Procedures: Complementary Relationship of International Human Rights Law and Humanitarian Law

Special procedures are mechanisms originally established by the Commission on Human Rights that were kept by the Human Rights Council when it was established.[114] They consist of independent experts either working as individual Special Rapporteurs or as Working Groups with the task of addressing either the human rights situation in a specific country (presently Belarus, Cambodia, Burundi, Côte d'Ivoire, Eritrea, Haiti, Iran, Myanmar, North Korea, occupied Palestinian territories, Somalia, Syria and Sudan),[115] or thematic human rights issues in all parts of the world. Thematic mandates either deal with a particular right (e.g. right to health, prohibition of torture), a particular group of victims or persons in a situation of vulnerability (e.g. minorities, indigenous peoples, internally displaced persons) or a specific problem (e.g. human rights and extreme poverty, human rights and terrorism).[116]

As part of their activities, mandate holders carry out country missions including to countries with (present or past) armed conflicts. In such cases, they often address in their reports IHL issues besides relevant human rights guarantees.[117] While their mandates only mention HRL and not IHL as benchmarks for the mandate holders, the Human Rights Council and member States in general seem to accept this. As noted above,[118] however, the United States of America argued for some time that 'international humanitarian law falls outside the mandate of the Special Rapporteur and of the Human Rights Council'.[119]

Among country mandates, the Independent Expert appointed by the Secretary-General on the situation of human rights in Somalia, the Independent Expert on the situation of human rights in the Sudan and the Special Rapporteur on the situation of human rights in the Palestinian territories occupied since 1967 often refer to IHL. Despite the armed conflict in the east of the country, reports by the former Independent Expert on the situation of human rights in the Democratic Republic of the Congo invoked this body of law only occasionally and always in the context of impunity for war crimes.[120]

Among the thematic mandates, particularly numerous references to IHL can be found in the mission reports of the Representative of the Secretary General on the Human Rights of Internally Displaced Persons and the Special Rapporteur on extrajudicial, summary or arbitrary executions.[121]

Usually, Special Procedures mandate holders do not go into much detail or legal analysis when invoking IHL. However, there are reports that look at the specific meaning of specific IHL guarantees and their relationship to HRL.[122] One particularly illustrative example is a joint report by several mandate holders on the 2006 armed conflict in Lebanon. The report highlights that HRL, 'does not cease to apply in times of war, except in accordance with precise derogation provisions relating to times of emergency',[123] and explains:

> Human rights law and international humanitarian law are not mutually exclusive but exist in a complementary relationship during armed conflict, and a full legal analysis requires consideration of both bodies of law. In respect of certain human rights, more specific rules of international humanitarian law may be relevant for the purposes of their interpretation.[124]

It further explains the principle of distinction, the principle of proportionality, and the obligation to take precautionary measures,[125] highlights the obligations of defenders[126] and assesses the actual conduct of the parties to the conflict in light of this legal framework.[127] The position that the conflict in question was of an asymmetric nature which justified certain measures not compatible with IHL was rejected with the argument that in addition to HRL, 'the principles of humanitarian law are entirely applicable to this conflict and deviations from these principles cannot be justified on the basis of the alleged novelty or distinctiveness of this conflict'.[128]

In the same context, the Special Rapporteur on the right to food provided in his report a thorough analysis of IHL provisions giving content to the right to food in situations of armed conflict and concluded that the right to food and water is protected both under HRL and IHL which create central obligations in time of war essential for the survival of civilian populations.[129]

Besides reports on country missions, Special Rapporteurs may also prepare studies on thematic issues. In this context, a report by the Special Rapporteur on extrajudicial, summary or arbitrary executions about targeted killings is particularly interesting for its in-depth analysis of IHL.[130] Regarding the applicable legal framework to such killings carried out in the context of an armed conflict, the report notes:

> Both IHL and human rights law apply in the context of armed conflict; whether a particular killing is legal is determined by the applicable *lex specialis*. To the extent that IHL does not provide a rule, or the rule is unclear and its meaning cannot be ascertained from the guidance offered by IHL principles, it is appropriate to draw guidance from human rights law.[131]

4.4   Universal Periodic Review: Focusing on Dissemination of International Humanitarian Law

Finally, the Human Rights Council is tasked with undertaking 'a universal periodic review, based on objective and reliable information, of the fulfilment by each State of its human rights obligations and commitments in a manner which ensures universality of coverage and equal treatment with respect to all States'; this review is 'based on an interactive dialogue, with the full involvement of the country concerned and with consideration given to its capacity-building needs'.[132] This mechanism ensures all member States of the UN are periodically reviewed in terms of whether and to what extent they fulfil their human rights obligations. The examination is organised as a peer-review process, that is, as providing other States with an opportunity to express concerns and make recommendations, and the country concerned with the possibility to accept or reject what was recommended by its peers. The process is based on reports prepared by the country concerned as well as by the Office of the High Commissioner for Human Rights which compiles information contained in concluding observations of treaty bodies, reports of special procedures and additional 'credible and reliable' information provided by other stakeholders such as non-governmental organisations and National Human Rights Institutions.

Benchmarks for the review are relevant standards of the UN Charter, the Universal Declaration of Human Rights and human rights instruments to which the State concerned is a party.[133] Interestingly enough, the Human Rights Council decided that, in addition 'and given the complementary and mutually interrelated nature of international human rights law and international humanitarian law, the review shall take into account applicable international humanitarian law'.[134]

While one country, despite this clear wording, did not accept IHL as a basis for the Universal Periodic Review,[135] issues related to IHL are quite regularly taken up by States. In this context, States primarily provide information or are asked about the following issues:

- National Commissions on Humanitarian Law[136] or national action plans and policies on HRL and IHL;[137]

- Measures such as training or investigations to ensure that their security forces respect HRL and IHL in situations of armed conflict;[138]
- Ratification of the 1977 Protocols Additional to the Geneva Conventions of 1949[139] or of the Rome Statute;[140]
- Strict adherence to HRL and IHL in the fight against terrorism;[141]
- Concerns regarding violations of IHL in an on-going armed conflict[142] and impunity for such violations;[143]
- Ending an on-going occupation.[144]

Overall, only relatively few questions and recommendations focus on violations of IHL, and concerns raised are relatively general. The main emphasis of remarks and recommendations is on dissemination of IHL.

5. CONCLUSION: GROWING CONTRIBUTION OF UN HUMAN RIGHTS BODIES TO MONITORING INTERNATIONAL HUMANITARIAN LAW

While the Human Rights Committee and to a lesser extent other treaty bodies address IHL through the lens of HRL, the Human Rights Council and its Special Procedures invoke IHL explicitly together with HRL when dealing with countries involved in an armed conflict where fundamental guarantees for the protection of human persons are particularly at risk and often systematically violated. In these contexts, they often come to the conclusion that both bodies of law have been violated. Like the treaty bodies,[145] they see HRL and IHL as complementary sets of legal obligations that are binding upon States in situations of armed conflict regardless of its location and that reinforce each other, and accept that in certain cases human rights guarantees must be interpreted in light of relevant IHL provisions. Some reports by Special Rapporteurs can even be seen, as highlighted by R. Kolb, as a 'sort of merger by way of shaping new law permeated by both branches'[146] which contribute to the progressive inter-penetration of IHL and HRL and thus the emergence of 'human rights in armed conflict' as a specific branch of law.[147]

This development is of paramount importance in particular in institutional terms. Taking into account that the ICRC can only rarely publicly address violations of IHL and that the international criminal tribunals primarily focus on the behaviour of individuals and not parties to a conflict as such, the Human Rights Council and its mechanisms have become 'the major forum in which governments are most likely to be held to account for abuses committed' in the context of armed conflict where they 'are called upon to justify their conduct publicly and in a systematic manner'.[148] Thus, it has become the main substitute for the lacking monitoring mechanisms under the Geneva Conventions and the Protocols additional to them.

A particular weakness of this arrangement, however, lies in the essential political character of the Human Rights Council as an intergovernmental body. As such, it may approach situations of IHL violations selectively and one-sidedly, and it has been accused of doing so particularly as regards Israel. Selectivity is problematic in so far as the legitimacy and authority of IHL will be undermined in the long run by one-sided criticism. Special procedure mandate holders as independent experts may have opportunities to counterbalance such tendencies, and they have done so.[149] Another weakness is the often superficial invocation and application of IHL by treaty bodies that may not do justice to the detailed content and the conceptual underpinnings of the law of armed conflict.

On the positive side, the proactive role of the Human Rights Council and its mechanisms provides States with an important opportunity not only to show that they respect IHL but also 'to ensure respect' for IHL as provided for by common Article 1 to the 1949 Geneva Conventions, a duty which implies that States parties engage with States that do not respect their obligations.[150] This is not only true for member States of the Human Rights Council but for each and every country participating in the Universal Periodic Review. However, as shown above, the Universal Periodic Review, too, is selectively used to address violations and statements referring to IHL primarily, addressing issues of dissemination of this body of law rather than actual implementation. This hesitation may not be entirely a bad thing if it demonstrates a reluctance to apply rules of IHL that the international community in 1949 hoped would never be needed.[151] To the extent that IHL can be used as a tool to reinforce, without undermining, HRL, and to increase accountability, careful application should be continued.

Overall, however, it is fair to say that the UN human rights bodies because of the proactive stance taken with regard to IHL have become key actors in monitoring the Geneva Conventions and the Protocols Additional to them. It remains to be hoped that, in the long run, all actors participating in the work of these bodies take an objective and principled approach to IHL issues which contribute to, rather than undermine, the authority and credibility of international humanitarian law as well as HRL, or of the bodies applying them.

NOTES

*   Walter Kälin is Professor of International Law at the University of Bern, Switzerland. I would like to thank Irene Grohsmann, MLaw (Bern) and Ellen Walker, M.A.S./LL.M. (Geneva), J.D. (Michigan) for assistance in the preparation of this contribution.
1.   See also R. Kolb, 'Human Rights Law and International Humanitarian Law Between 1945 and the Aftermath of the Teheran Conference of 1968', in this volume.
2.   S/RES/237, 14 June 1967.
3.   Resolution XXIII, Human rights in armed conflict, adopted on 12 May 1968, in Final Act of the International Conference on Human Rights, Teheran, 22 April–13 May 1968, UN Doc. A/CONF.32/41, 18, Preamble and Operational Paragraph 2.
4.   The Martens Clause was first included in the Preamble to The Hague Regulations of 1907 concerning the Laws and Customs of War on Land. It is also part of the four Geneva Conventions: Article 63 of the First, Article 62 of the Second, Article 142 of the Third and Article 158 of the Fourth Geneva Convention.
5.   A/RES/2675 (XXV), 9 December 1970, Basic Principles for the protection of civilian populations in armed conflict.
6.   A/RES/2676 (XXV), 9 December 1970, Respect for human rights in armed conflict, para. 6.
7.   Situation of human rights in Kuwait under Iraqi occupation, A/RES/46/135, 17 December 1991, and UN Commission on Human Rights, The Situation of Human Rights in Kuwait under Iraqi Occupation, Resolution 1991/67, 6 March 1991.

8. Situation of Human Rights in occupied Kuwait, Report on the situation of human rights in Kuwait under Iraqi occupation, prepared by Mr Walter Kälin, Special Rapporteur of the Commission on Human Rights, in accordance with Commission Resolution 1991/67.

9. R. Kolb, 'Human Rights and Humanitarian Law', in *Max Planck Encyclopedia of Public International Law*, ed. R. Wolfrum (Oxford: Oxford University Press, 2008); online edition available at http://www.mpepil.com (accessed 15 June 2011).

10. Vienna Declaration and Programme of Action, adopted by the World Conference on Human Rights on 25 June 1993, UN Doc. A/CONF.157/23, operative paragraph 5.3.

11. International Convention on the Elimination of All Forms of Racial Discrimination of 21 December 1965 (ICERD); International Covenant on Civil and Political Rights of 16 December 1966 (ICCPR); International Covenant on Economic, Social and Cultural Rights of 16 December 1966 (ICESCR); Convention on the Elimination of All Forms of Discrimination against Women of 18 December 1979 (CEDAW); Convention against Torture and Other Cruel, Inhuman or Degrading Treatment or Punishment of 10 December 1984 (CAT); Convention on the Rights of the Child of 20 November 1989 (CRC); International Convention on the Protection of the Rights of All Migrant Workers and Members of Their Families of 18 December 1990 (ICRMW); International Convention for the Protection of All Persons from Enforced Disappearance of 20 December 2006 (CPED); Convention on the Rights of Persons with Disabilities of 13 December 2006 (CRPD).

12. See W. Kälin, 'State Reports', in *The UN Human Rights Treaty Bodies: Law and Legitimacy*, ed. H. Keller and G. Ulfstein (Cambridge: Cambridge University Press, 2012).

13. The Optional Protocol to the Convention on the Rights of the Child on a Communications Procedure of 19 December 2011 had not entered into force at the time of writing.

14. Some treaties further provide for a procedure for interstate communications (compulsory or optional depending on the treaty), which allows States Parties to file a complaint against another State with the committee concerned, irrespective of whether their own interests are at stake or whether they are acting in pursuit of a general interest in the implementation of human rights, but this procedure was never used by a State for UN treaties. Furthermore, the Convention against Torture (CAT), the Convention on the Elimination of All Forms of Discrimination against Women (CEDAW), the Convention for the Protection of All Persons from Enforced Disappearance, and the Optional Protocol to the Convention on the Rights of Persons with Disabilities (CRPD) also have inquiry procedures, which allow the committees concerned to conduct an on-site inquiry under certain circumstances. The most recent types of procedure are the preventive procedure, created by the 2002 Optional Protocol to the Convention against Torture, the similar national monitoring mechanism required in the CRPD, and the possibility for urgent actions in cases of disappearances in accordance with the Convention for the Protection of All Persons from Enforced Disappearances (CPED). These procedures are potentially relevant for IHL issues but have not yet been used in the context of armed conflict.

15. For a compilation of General Comments, see UN Doc. HRI/GEN/1/Rev.9 (Vol. I and Vol. II). The compilation is regularly updated.

16. See ICCPR Articles 4–5 (permitting but limiting derogations on some human rights and prohibiting efforts to destroy rights), and ICESCR Articles 4–5 (restricting limitations on rights and prohibiting their destruction). ICERD, CEDAW and the CRPD contain no derogation clauses. Article 38 CRC, the CRC's optional protocol on children and armed conflict, Article 11 CRPD (requiring protection of persons with disabilities in accordance with HRL and IHL in situations of risk), Article 2(2) CAT (prohibiting using any emergency as justification for torture), and Article 1 CPED, fall into the group of later treaties. See also Articles 80–82 CMW. Conventions also may contain 'without prejudice' clauses indicating that the present treaty cannot reduce greater rights contained in national legislation or other international obligations, e.g., CEDAW Article 23.

17. None of the existing General Comments adopted by the Committee against Torture and the Committee on Migrant Workers mention IHL. The Committee on the Rights of Persons with Disabilities and the Committee on Enforced Disappearance have not yet adopted General Comments.

18. An implicit recognition can be found in General Comment No. 29: *Derogations During a State of Emergency (Article 4)*, HRC, 31 August 2001 (UN Doc. HRI/GEN/1/Rev.9, Vol. I, 235), para. 3.

19. Ibid., 234, para. 2.

20. General Comment No. 31: *The Nature of the General Legal Obligation Imposed on States Parties to the Covenant*, 26 May 2004 (UN Doc. HRI/GEN/1/Rev.9), Vol. I, 245, para. 11.

21. See in this volume, V. Gowlland-Debbas and G. Gaggioli, 'The Relationship between International Human Rights and Humanitarian Law: an Overview'.

22. See in this volume R. Goldman, 'Extraterritorial Application of the Human Rights to Life and Personal Liberty, Including *Habeas Corpus*, During Situations of Armed Conflict'.
23. No references to the territorial scope of application are made, for example, in ICESCR, ICERD, CEDAW and CRPD. Like the ICCPR, the ICESCR explicitly includes States Parties responsible for administering Non-Self-Governing and Trust Territories in its Article 1(3) on self-determination. Article 2 CRC requires States to ensure rights 'to each child within their jurisdiction'.
24. Article 2(1) CAT takes a slightly different approach, making it the duty of each State party to prevent torture 'in any territory under its jurisdiction'.
25. See Comments by the Government of the United States of America on the Concluding Observations of the Human Rights Committee, 12 February 2008 (UN Doc. CCPR/C/USA/CO/3/Rev.1/Add. 1), 2–3.
26. See *López Burgos v. Uruguay*, HRC, 29 July 1981 (UN Doc. CCPR/C/13/D/52/1979), para 12.3; *Celiberti de Casariego v. Uruguay*, HRC, 29 July 1981 (UN Doc. CCPR/C/13/D/56/1979), para 10.3. The two cases concerned Uruguay's responsibility for the torture and killing of opponents of the regime who had been tracked down and arrested abroad by the country's intelligence services. The Committee held that the Covenant had extraterritorial scope, arguing that a literal interpretation of Article 2 would lead to the absurd conclusion that States Parties could perpetrate with impunity abroad human rights violations that were prohibited within their own frontiers. It stressed that the wording of Article 2 was not intended to apply to such cases but to special circumstances in which the State was faced with material problems in exercising its jurisdiction in part of the national territory.
27. *Supra* note 20, at 243, para. 10.
28. I.e., individuals in those parts of the national territory that are subject to the jurisdiction of the State concerned.
29. I.e., individuals within a State's territory and subject to its jurisdiction; and, in addition, individuals who are subject to the jurisdiction of the said State only, i.e., without a direct link to its territory.
30. *Legal Consequences of the Construction of a Wall in the Occupied Palestinian Territory*, Advisory Opinion, I.C.J. Reports 2004, paras 109 and 111. The Court referred to the ambiguity of the word 'and', and held that in light of its object and purpose the ICCPR has to be interpreted as being applicable when a State is exercising jurisdiction outside its territory, and underlined that such interpretation is consistent with the drafting history because the drafters of the Treaty had not intended the wording of Article 2 to allow States to shirk their obligations when they exercised jurisdiction abroad. The I.C.J. confirmed at the same time that the ICESCR and the CRC also have extraterritorial scope of application, stressing, however, that ICESCR rights, by their nature, are essentially territorial, so that a State is bound by obligations outside its territory only if it exercises effective jurisdiction as in the case of occupation (ibid., para. 112). On the extraterritorial application of the ICESCR, see F. Coomans, 'The Extraterritorial Scope of the International Covenant on Economic, Social and Cultural Rights in the Work of the United Nations Committee on Economic, Social and Cultural Rights', *Human Rights Law Review* 11 (2011): 1–35.
31. E.g., M.J. Dennis and A.M. Surena, 'Application of the International Covenant on Civil and Political Rights in Times of Armed Conflict and Military Occupation: The Gap between Legal Theory and State Practice', *European Human Rights Law Review* 6 (2008): 714–731. See the rejoinder by N. Rodley, 'The Extraterritorial Reach and Applicability in Armed Conflict of the International Covenant on Civil and Political Rights: A Rejoinder to Dennis and Surena', *European Human Rights Law Review* 5 (2009): 628–636. See also N.K. Modirzadeh, 'The Dark Side of Convergence: A Pro-Civilian Critique of the Extraterritorial Application of Human Rights Law in Armed Conflict', *U.S. Naval War College International Law Studies* 86 (2010): 349–410.
32. *Supra* note 20, at 245, para. 11.
33. See in this volume J. d'Aspremont and E. Tranchez, 'The Quest for a Non-Conflictual Coexistence of International Human Rights Law and Humanitarian Law: Which Role for the *Lex Specialis* Principle?'
34. The conclusion of an expert meeting held in 2004. See Expert Meeting on the Supervision of the Lawfulness of Detention during Armed Conflict, organised by The University Centre for International Humanitarian Law, Geneva, Convened at The Graduate Institute of International Studies, Geneva 24 – 25 July 2004, 45, http://www.ruig-gian.org/ressources/communication_colloque_rapport04.pdf?ID= 256&FILE=/ressources/communication_colloque_rapport04.pdf (accessed 7 November 2012).
35. I.C.J. Reports 1996-I, 240, para. 25.
36. I.C.J. Reports 2004, 178, para. 106.
37. General Comment No. 14: *Right to the Highest Attainable Standard of Health (Article 12)*, CESCR, 11 August 2000 (UN Doc. HRI/GEN/1/Rev.9), Vol. I, 86, para. 34.

38. General Comment No. 15: *Right to Water (Articles 11 and 12)*, 20 January 2003 (UN Doc. HRI/GEN/1/Rev.9, Vol. I), 101, para. 16(g).

39. Ibid., 102, para. 21.

40. Ibid., para. 22.

41. However, in some General Comments the Committee explicitly addresses situations of armed conflict without referring to IHL. See General Comment No. 7: *The Right to Adequate Housing (Article 11.1): Forced Evictions*, CESCR, 20 May 1997 (UN Doc. HRI/GEN/1/Rev.9), Vol. I, 39, para. 5; and General Comment No. 19: *Right to Social Security (Article 9)*, 4 February 2008 (UN Doc. HRI/GEN/1/Rev.9), Vol. I, 157, para. 27.

42. General Comment No. 1: *The Aims of Education*, Committee on the Rights of the Child, 17 April 2001 (UN Doc. HRI/GEN/1/Rev.9), Vol. II, 388, para. 16.

43. General Comment No. 6: *Treatment of Unaccompanied and Separated Children Outside their Country of Origin*, Committee on the Rights of the Child, 1 September 2005 (UN Doc. HRI/GEN/1/Rev.9), Vol. II, 449, para. 26.

44. Ibid., para. 57.

45. General Recommendation XXX: Discrimination against Non-Citizens, Committee Against Racial Discrimination, 1 October 2002 (UN Doc. HRI/GEN/1/Rev.9), Vol. II, 304, para. 20.

46. General Recommendation No. 19: *Violence against Women*, Committee on the Elimination of All Forms of Discrimination against Women, 1992 (UN Doc. HRI/GEN/1/Rev.9), Vol. II, 332, para. 7(c).

47. See Concluding Observations on Israel, HRC, 21 August 2003 (UN Doc. CCPR/CO/78/ISR), para. 15 ('targeted killings'), or Concluding Observations on Uganda, HRC, 4 May 2004 (UN Doc. CCPR/CO/80/UGA), para. 12 (internally displaced persons).

48. See Concluding Observations on Germany, HRC, 4 May 2004 (UN Doc. CCPR/CO/80/DEU), para. 11; Concluding Observations on Israel, HRC, 21 August 2003 (UN Doc. CCPR/CO/78/ISR), para. 11 and 3 September 2010 (UN Doc. CCPR/C/ISR/CO/3), para. 5; Concluding Observations on Belgium, HRC, 12 August 2004 (UN Doc. CCPR/CO/81/BEL), para. 6; Concluding Observations on United States of America, HRC, 12 February 2008 (UN Doc. CCPR/C/USA/CO/3), para. 10; Concluding Observations on United Kingdom, HRC, 30 July 2008 (UN Doc.CCPR/C/GBR/CO/6), para. 14.

49. See, e.g., Concluding Observations on Central African Republic, HRC, 27 July 2006 (UN Doc. CCPR/C/CAF/CO/2), para. 8; Concluding Observations on Russian Federation, HRC, 24 November 2009 (UN Doc. CCPR/C/RUS/CO/6), para. 13; Concluding Observations on Colombia, HRC, 4 August 2010 (UN Doc. CCPR/C/COL/CO/6), para. 9.

50. Article 38 CRC and Optional Protocol to the Convention on the Rights of the Child on the involvement of children in armed conflict of 25 May 2000.

51. See the International Committee of the Red Cross customary law study, J.-M. Henckaerts and L. Doswald-Beck, eds, *Customary International Humanitarian Law*, Vol. I (Cambridge: Cambridge University Press, 2005) Rule 1: 'The parties to the conflict must at all times distinguish between civilians and combatants. Attacks may only be directed against combatants. Attacks must not be directed against civilians', and Rule 14: 'Launching an attack which may be expected to cause incidental loss of civilian life, injury to civilians, damage to civilian objects, or a combination thereof, which would be excessive in relation to the concrete and direct military advantage anticipated, is prohibited.'

52. See, e.g., Concluding Observations on India, Committee on the Rights of the Child, 23 February 2000 (UN Doc. CRC/C/15/Add.115), paras 63 and 64; Concluding Observations on Burundi, Committee on the Rights of the Child, 16 October 2000 (UN Doc. CRC/C/15/Add.133), para. 71; Concluding Observations on Democratic Republic of the Congo, Committee on the Rights of the Child, 9 July 2001 (UN Doc. CRC/C/15/Add.153), para. 6; Concluding Observations on Israel, Committee on the Rights of the Child, 9 October 2002 (UN Doc. CRC/C/15/Add.195), paras 5, 50, 52. In some of these cases, it is not obvious that IHL actually applied to the country concerned during the period of examination (e.g., Concluding Observations on Uzbekistan, Committee on the Rights of the Child, 7 November 2001 (UN Doc. CRC/C/15/Add. 167), para. 62 referring to military operations outside the context of armed conflict).

53. Concluding Observations on Canada, Committee on the Rights of the Child, 9 June 2006 (UN Doc. CRC/C/OPAC/CAN/CO/1), paras 11 and 12.

54. Article 11, Situations of risk and humanitarian emergencies, provides: 'States Parties shall take, in accordance with their obligations under international law, including international humanitarian law and international human rights law, all necessary measures to ensure the protection and safety of

persons with disabilities in situations of risk, including situations of armed conflict, humanitarian emergencies and the occurrence of natural disasters.'

55. Concluding Observations on Israel, Committee Against Torture, 23 June 2009 (UN Doc. CAT/C/ISR/CO/4), para. 11; Concluding Observations on United States of America, Committee Against Torture, 25 July 2006 (UN Doc. CAT/C/USA/CO/2), para. 14.

56. Concluding Observations on Israel, Committee Against Torture, 23 June 2009 (UN Doc. CAT/C/ISR/CO/4), para. 33.

57. Concluding Observations on Philippines, Committee Against Torture, 14 May 2009 (UN Doc. CAT/C/PHL/CO/2), para. 24. See also Concluding Observations on Chad, Committee Against Torture, 4 June 2009 (UN Doc. CAT/C/TCD/CO/1), para. 34 (however, without reference to IHL).

58. Until now, the Committee on Migrant Workers never mentioned IHL in its Concluding Observations.

59. Concluding Observations on Israel, CESCR, 26 June 2003 (UN Doc. E/C.12/1/Add.90), para. 31. The parallel application of HRL and IHL was also highlighted in the case of Sri Lanka, E/C.12/LKA/CO/2-4, para. 28: '… the prevention of access to humanitarian food aid in internal conflicts constitutes a violation of Article 11 of the Covenant as well as a grave violation of international humanitarian law'.

60. Concluding Observations on Israel, Committee on the Elimination of All Forms of Discrimination against Women, 22 July 2005 (UN Doc. CEDAW/C/ISR/CO/3), para. 23.

61. Concluding Observations on United States of America, Committee on the Elimination of Racial Discrimination, 8 May 2008 (UN Doc. CERD/C/USA/CO/6), para. 24.

62. Concluding Observations on Israel, Committee on the Elimination of Racial Discrimination, 14 June 2007 (UN Doc. CERD/C/ISR/CO/13), para. 14.

63. Regarding the positions of the United States and Israel, see the concerns raised by the Human Rights Committee, see Concluding Observations on United States of America, HRC, 12 February 2008 (UN Doc. CCPR/C/USA/CO/3/Rev.1), para. 10; Concluding Observations on Israel, HRC, 21 August 2003 (UN Doc. CCPR/CO/78/ISR), para. 11, and 3 September 2010 (UN Doc. CCPR/C/ISR/CO/3), para. 5, and the Committee against Torture Concluding Observations on Israel, Committee Against Torture, 23 June 2009 (UN Doc. CAT/C/ISR/CO/4), para. 11; Concluding Observations on United States of America, Committee Against Torture, 25 July 2006 (UN Doc. CAT/C/USA/CO/2), paras 14 and 15.

64. See in this volume L. Moir, 'The European Court of Human Rights and International Humanitarian Law'.

65. General Comment No. 29: *Derogations During a State of Emergency (Article 4)*, HRC, 31 August 2001 (UN Doc. HRI/GEN/1/Rev.9), Vol. I, 236, para. 11.

66. General Comment No. 15: *Right to Water (Articles 11 and 12)*, HRC, 20 January 2003 (UN Doc. HRI/GEN/1/Rev.9), Vol. I, 102, para. 22.

67. Articles 6, 9 and 17, ICCPR.

68. See Articles 12, 18, 19, 21 and 22, ICCPR.

69. Similarly, Article 17, Additional Protocol II.

70. See, e.g., 41 CRC.

71. A/RES/60/251, 3 April 2006. The Council started its work in June 2006.

72. Ibid., para. 3.

73. Ibid., para. 5, sub-paragraph f.

74. Ibid., para. 5, sub-paragraph a.

75. Ibid., para. 5, sub-paragraph f.

76. Ibid., para. 5, sub-paragraph a.

77. For a detailed account see P. Alston, J. Morgan-Foster and W. Abresch, 'The Competence of the UN Human Rights Council and its Special Procedures in Relation to Armed Conflicts: Extrajudicial Executions in the "War on Terror"', *The European Journal of International Law* 1 (2008): 183–209, in particular 185–190, with numerous references.

78. The United States, as a member of the Council, did not oppose the adoption without a vote of Resolution S-14/1: *Situation of human rights in Ivory Coast in relation to the conclusion of the 2010 Presidential Election*, Human Rights Council, 19 January 2010 (UN Doc. A/HRC/S-14/1), 3–4, and Resolution 16/25: *Situation of human rights in Ivory Coast*, Human Rights Council, 13 April 2011 (UN Doc. A/HRC/Res/16/25) which both refer to HRL as well as IHL. In June 2011, the United States co-sponsored Human Rights Council Resolution HRC/17/17 entitled 'Situation of human rights in the Libyan Arab Jamahiriya Libya' in which the Council condemned 'ongoing gross and systematic human rights violations, in particular indiscriminate armed attacks against civilians' (Operational Paragraph 1), and urged 'all parties concerned to respect applicable international law, in particular international human rights law and international humanitarian law' (Operational Paragraph 4).

79. A/RES/60/251, 3 April 2006, para. 10.
80. Special Session 7 held in May 2008 dealt with the food price crisis: see Resolution S-7/1: *The negative impact of the worsening of the world food crisis on the realization of the right to food for all*, Human Rights Council, 17 July 2008 (UN Doc. A/HRC/S-7/2), 3–5. Special Session 10 examined the impact of the financial crisis on human rights: see Resolution S-10/1: *The impact of the global economic and financial crises on the universal realization and effective enjoyment of human rights*, Human Rights Council, 30 March 2009 (UN Doc. A/HRC/S-10/2), 3–6. Regarding country situations outside the context of armed conflict; Resolution S-11/1: *Assistance to Sri Lanka in the promotion and protection of human rights*, Human Rights Council, 26 June 2009 (UN Doc. A/HRC/S-11/2), 3–6; Resolution S-15/1: *Situation of human rights in the Libyan Arab Jamahiriya* (the Special Session was held before armed conflict broke out), Human Rights Council, 25 February 2011 (UN Doc. A/HRC/S-15/1), 3–5; Resolution S-16/1: *The current human rights situation in the Syrian Arab Republic in the context of recent events*, Human Rights Council, 6 May 2011 (UN Doc. A/HRC/S-16/2), 3–4; Resolution S-12/1: *The human rights situation in the Occupied Palestinian Territory, including East Jerusalem*, Human Rights Council, 21 October 2009 (UN Doc. A/HRC/S-12/1), 3–6.
81. Ibid.
82. Resolution S-1/1: *Human rights situation in the Occupied Palestinian Territory*, Human Rights Council, 18 July 2006 (UN Doc. A/HRC/S-1/3), 3–4.
83. Resolution S-2/1: *The grave situation of human rights in Lebanon caused by Israeli military operations*, 17 August 2006 (UN Doc. A/HRC/S-2/2), 3–5.
84. 8th preambular paragraph. The same language is used in Resolution S-9/1: *The grave violations of human rights in the Occupied Palestinian Territory, particularly due to the recent Israeli military attacks against the occupied Gaza Strip*, Human Rights Council, 27 February 2009 (UN Doc. A/HRC/S-9/2), 3–6, 7th preambular paragraph.
85. See Resolution S-3/1: *Human rights violations emanating from Israeli military incursions in the Occupied Palestinian Territory*, including the recent one in northern Gaza and the assault on Beit Hanoun, Human Rights Council, 20 November 2006 (UN Doc. A/HRC/S-3/2), 3–4. Resolution S-9/1, *supra* note 84, 3–6. Resolution S-6/1: *Human rights violations emanating from Israeli military attacks and incursions in the Occupied Palestinian Territory, particularly in the occupied Gaza Strip*, Human Rights Council, 31 March 2008 (UN Doc. A/HRC/S-6/2), 3–4.
86. E.g., Resolution 10/17: *Human rights in the occupied Syrian Golan*, Human Rights Council, 26 March 2009 (UN Doc. A/HRC/RES/10/17), para. 5.
87. No references to IHL can be found in Decision S-4/101, *Situation of human rights in Darfur*, Human Rights Council, 22 January 2007 (UN Doc. A/HRC/S-4/5), 3, and Resolution S-11/1, *Assistance to Sri Lanka in the promotion and protection of human rights*, Human Rights Council, 26 June 2009 (UN Doc. A/HRC/S-11/2), 3–5, even though in both cases they clearly addressed a situation of armed conflict.
88. Resolution S-3/1, *supra* note 85, 1st preambular paragraph. See also resolution S-9/1, *supra* note 84, 6th preambular paragraph.
89. Resolution S-6/1, *supra* note 85, 3rd preambular paragraph.
90. Resolution S-2/1, *supra* note 83, 15th preambular paragraph.
91. Ibid., 5th preambular paragraph.
92. Resolution S-2/1, *supra* note 83, 7th preambular paragraph.
93. E.g., Resolutions S-2/1, *supra* note 83, paras. 4 and 5; S-3/1, *supra* note 85, para. 6; S-6/1, *supra* note 85, paras. 4 and 5; Resolution 10/17, *supra* note 86, para. 5, Resolution 10/21, Follow-up to Council Resolution S-9/1: *The grave violations of human rights in the Occupied Palestinian Territory*, Human Rights Council, 12 January 2009 (UN Doc. A/HRC/S-9/L.1), para. 2.
94. Decision S-4/101, *supra* note 87.
95. Decision 2/115, *Darfur*, Human Rights Council, 22 March 2007 (UN Doc. A/2/53HRC/2/9), 23, para. 2.
96. Resolution 4/8: *Follow-up to decision S-4/101*, Human Rights Council, 13 December 2006, adopted by the Human Rights Council at its fourth Special Session entitled 'Situation of human rights in Darfur', 12 June 2007 (UN Doc. A/HRC/4/123), 18, para. 3.
97. Resolution 6/35: *Human Rights Council Group of Experts on the Situation of human rights in Darfur*, Human Rights Council, 14 April 2008 (UN Doc. A/HRC/6/22), 73, para. 4.
98. Resolution 8, S-8/1: *Situation of human rights in the east of the Democratic Republic of the Congo*, Human Rights Council, 16 January 2009 (UN Doc. A/HRC/S-8/2), 3–5, paras 1 and 6.

99.　Resolution S-14/1: *Situation of human rights in Ivory Coast in relation to the conclusion of the 2010 presidential election*, Human Rights Council, 28 December 2010 (UN Doc. A/HRC/S-14/1), 4, para. 8.
100.　Resolution 7/31: *Situation of human rights in Myanmar*, Human Rights Council, 14 July 2008 (UN Doc. A/HRC/7/78), 95, para. 3(e).
101.　Resolution 7/35: *Assistance to Somalia in the field of human rights*, Human Rights Council, 14 July 2008 (UN Doc. A/HRC/7/78), 103, para. 2.
102.　Resolution S-2/1, *supra* note 83, para. 7.
103.　Resolution S-3/1, *supra* note 85, para. 7.
104.　Decision S-4/101, *supra* note 87, para. 4.
105.　Resolution S-8/1, *supra* note 98, para. 7.
106.　Resolution S-9/1, *supra* note 84, para. 14.
107.　Resolution S-15/1, *supra* note 80, para. 11.
108.　Report of the Commission of Inquiry on Lebanon pursuant to Resolution S-2/1, Human Rights Council, 23 November 2006 (UN Doc. A/HRC/3/2). Report of the High-Level Mission on the situation of human rights in Darfur pursuant to Decision S-4/101, Human Rights Council, 9 March 2007 (UN Doc. A/HRC/4/80); Combined report of seven thematic special procedures on technical assistance to the Government of the Democratic Republic of the Congo and urgent examination of the situation in the east of the country, Human Rights Council, 5 March 2009 (UN Doc. A/HRC/10/59); Report of the United Nations Fact-Finding Mission on the Gaza Conflict, Human Rights Council, 25 September 2009 (UN Doc. A/HRC/12/48); Report of the International Commission of Inquiry to investigate all alleged violations of international human rights law in the Libyan Arab Jamahiriya, Human Rights Council, 1 June 2011 (UN Doc. A/HRC/17/44).
109.　The International Humanitarian Fact-Finding Commission has not yet obtained a mandate to become active. See its annual reports, http://www.ihffc.org/index.asp?page=public_reports&listfilter=off (accessed 7 November 2012). See also F. Kalshoven, 'The International Humanitarian Fact-Finding Commission: A Sleeping Beauty?', *Humanitäres Völkerrecht – Informationsschriften* 4 (2002): 213–216.
110.　Resolution 10/15: *Protection of human rights and fundamental freedoms while countering terrorism*, Human Rights Council, 9 November 2009 (UN Doc. A/HRC/10/29), 39–41, paras 1 and 7.
111.　Resolution 10/22: *Combating defamation of religions*, Human Rights Council, 9 November 2009 (UN Doc. A/HRC/10/29), 52–56, para. 15.
112.　Resolution 10/25: *Discrimination based on religion or belief and its impact on the enjoyment of economic, social and cultural rights*, Human Rights Council, 9 November 2009 (UN Doc. A/HRC/10/29), 61–64, Preambular paragraph.
113.　Resolution 11/2: *Accelerating efforts to eliminate all forms of violence against women*, Human Rights Council, 16 October 2009 (UN Doc. A/HRC/11/37), 6–9, para. 4.
114.　A/RES/60/251, *supra* note 71, para. 6.
115.　See the list of country mandates, http://www.ohchr.org/EN/HRBodies/SP/Pages/Countries.aspx (accessed 7 November 2012).
116.　See the list of thematic mandates, http://www.ohchr.org/EN/HRBodies/SP/Pages/Themes.aspx (accessed 7 November 2012). At the time of this writing there were 33 such mandates.
117.　A search of the http://uhri.ohchr.org/ database shows that during the period 2006–2010 the following mandates have at least once explicitly referred to IHL in their conclusions and recommendations: Independent Expert appointed by the Secretary-General on the situation of human rights in Somalia; Independent Expert on the situation of human rights in Burundi; Independent Expert on the situation of human rights in the Democratic Republic of the Congo; Independent Expert on the situation of human rights in the Sudan; Representative of the Secretary-General on the human rights of internally displaced persons; Special Rapporteur on extrajudicial, summary or arbitrary executions; Special Rapporteur on freedom of religion or belief; Special Rapporteur on the independence of judges and lawyers; Special Rapporteur on the promotion and protection of human rights and fundamental freedoms while countering terrorism; Special Rapporteur on the right to food; Special Rapporteur on the situation of human rights and fundamental freedoms of indigenous people; Special Rapporteur on the situation of human rights defenders; Special Rapporteur on the situation of human rights in Myanmar; Special Rapporteur on the situation of human rights in the Palestinian territories occupied by Israel since 1967; Special Rapporteur on the situation of human rights in the Palestinian territories occupied since 1967; Working Group on the use of mercenaries as a means of impeding the exercise of the right of peoples to self-determination.

118. For the position of the United States, see *supra* note 77 and accompanying text.

119. Report of the Special Rapporteur on extrajudicial, summary or arbitrary executions, Philip Alston, Addendum, Mission to the United States of America, UN Doc. A/HRC/11/2/Add.5, 28 May 2009, 31–32, para. 71.

120. See, e.g., Report of the independent expert on the situation of human rights in the Democratic Republic of the Congo, Mr Titinga Frédéric Pacéré, Un Doc. A/HRC/4/7, 21 February 2007, 11–13, paras 58, 60, 63, 67.

121. The Universal Human Rights Index database summarizing the conclusions and recommendation parts of reports by Special Rapporteurs references ten reports each by the Representative of the Secretary General on the Human Rights of Internally Displaced Persons and the Special Rapporteur on extrajudicial, summary or arbitrary executions that mention IHL during the period 2006–2010, http://www.universalhumanrightsindex.org (accessed 7 November 2012).

122. See, e.g., Situation of detainees at Guantánamo Bay, Report of the Chairperson-Rapporteur of the Working Group on Arbitrary Detention, Leila Zerrougui; the Special Rapporteur on the independence of judges and lawyers, Leandro Despouy; the Special Rapporteur on torture and other cruel, inhuman or degrading treatment or punishment, Manfred Nowak; the Special Rapporteur on freedom of religion or belief, Asma Jahangir; and the Special Rapporteur on the right of everyone to the enjoyment of the highest attainable standard of physical and mental health, Paul Hunt, UN Doc. E/CN.4/2006/120, 27 February 2006.

123. Report of the Special Rapporteur on extrajudicial, summary or arbitrary executions, Philip Alston; the Special Rapporteur on the right of everyone to the enjoyment of the highest attainable standard of physical and mental health, Paul Hunt; the Representative of the Secretary-General on human rights of internally displaced persons, Walter Kälin; and the Special Rapporteur on adequate housing as a component of the right to an adequate standard of living, Miloon Kothari, Mission to Lebanon and Israel, 7–14 September 2006, UN Doc. A/HRC/2/7, 2 October 2006, 6, para. 15 (footnote omitted).

124. Ibid., 7, para. 16 (footnotes omitted).

125. Ibid., 8, paras 24–28.

126. Ibid., 8–9, paras 29–30.

127. Ibid., 9–14, paras 35–58 and 16–17, paras 68–75.

128. Ibid., 21, para. 98.

129. Human rights in Lebanon, Report of the Special Rapporteur on the right to food, Jean Ziegler, on his mission to Lebanon, UN Doc. A/HRC/2/8, 29 September 2006, 7–8, paras 10–13, and 14, para. 31.

130. Report of the Special Rapporteur on extrajudicial, summary or arbitrary executions, Philip Alston, Addendum Study on targeted killings, UN Doc. A/HRC/14/24/Add.6, 28 May 2010.

131. Ibid., 10, para. 29 (footnotes omitted).

132. A/RES/60/251, *supra* note 71, para. 5(e). See also, *Institution Building; Annex to Human Rights Council Resolution 5/1, Part I*, Human Rights Council, 7 August 2007 (UN Doc. A/HRC/5/21), 4–10, paras 1–38. The review is conducted by a working group chaired by the President of the Council and composed of the 47 members of the Council in the form of a three-hour long interactive dialogue between the State under review and Council members. This process is facilitated by a group of three Rapporteurs from different regional groups who are selected by the drawing of lots among the members of the Council. These Rapporteurs are tasked with drafting a report about the dialogue that serves as a basis for the discussion and adoption of an outcome document by the plenary of the Council. This outcome document contains an assessment of the human rights situation in the country concerned, as well as recommendations, including those explicitly accepted by the State concerned.

133. Resolution 5/1: *Institution-building of the United Nations Human Rights Council, Annex, United Nations Human Rights Council: Institutional Building*, Human Rights Council, 7 August 2007 (UN Doc. A/HRC/5/21), 4, para. 1.

134. Ibid., 5, para. 2.

135. United Kingdom, 23 May 2008 (UN Doc. A/HRC/8/25), 10–11, para. 36. However, in the Geneva process of the five-year review of the Council that took place from October 2010 to March 2011, the Council reaffirmed and left untouched IHL as one of the bases of the UPR in the outcome of the Review. The United Kingdom did not voice opposition to this. See *Review of the work and functioning of the Human Rights Council*, 25 March 2011 (UN Doc. A/HRC/16/21).

136. E.g., Ecuador, Human Rights Council, 13 May 2008 (UN Doc. A/HRC/8/20), 3, para. 6; Tunisia, Human Rights Council, 22 May 2008 (UN Doc. A/HRC/8/21), paras, 8, para. 21, and 12, para. 41;

Costa Rica, Human Rights Council, 4 January 2010 (UN Doc. A/HRC/13/15), 6–7, para. 32, and 9, para. 53; Kuwait, Human Rights Council, 16 June 2010 (UN Doc. A/HRC/15/15), 6, para. 26, and 8–9, para. 46.

137. E.g., Colombia, Human Rights Council, 9 January 2009 (UN Doc. A/HRC/10/82), 9, paras 25 and 27, and 14, para. 44.

138. E.g., Philippines, Human Rights Council, 23 May 2008 (UN Doc. A/HRC/8/28), 5, para. 10; Pakistan, Human Rights Council, 4 June 2008 (UN Doc. A/HRC/8/42), 17, para. 104; Burundi, Human Rights Council, 8 January 2009 (UN Doc. A/HRC/8/10/71), 4–5, para. 14; Colombia, Human Rights Council, 9 January 2009 (UN Doc. A/HRC/10/82), 9, para. 26; Canada, Human Rights Council, 5 October 2009 (UN Doc. A/HRC/11/17), 11–12, para. 64; Central African Republic, Human Rights Council, 4 June 2009 (UN Doc. A/HRC/12/2), 5, para. 17, 10, para. 40, 13, paras 57, 58, 59, and 16–17, para. 74 (Recommendations 12, 14, 15, 16, 19); Afghanistan, Human Rights Council, 20 July 2009 (UN Doc. A/HRC/12/9), 18, para. 95 (Recommendation 66); Ivory Coast, Human Rights Council, 4 January 2010 (UN Doc. A/HRC/13/9), 10, para. 99 (Recommendation 65); Gambia, Human Rights Council, 24 March 2010 (UN Doc. A/HRC/14/6), 13, para. 88; El Salvador, Human Rights Council, 18 March 2010 (UN Doc. A/HRC/14/5), 16, para. 81 (Recommendation 55); Bosnia and Herzegovina, Human Rights Council, 17 March 2010 (UN Doc. A/HRC/14/16), 18, para. 90 (Recommendation 75); Guinea, Human Rights Council, 14 June 2010 (UN Doc. A/HRC/15/4), 13, para. 71 (Recommendations 15 and 16).

139. E.g., Pakistan, Human Rights Council, 4 June 2008 (UN Doc. A/HRC/8/42), 8, para. 33.

140. E.g., Mozambique, Human Rights Council, 28 March 2011 (UN Doc. A/HRC/17/16), paras 90.1, 90.5, 90.6 and 90.8.

141. E.g., Pakistan, Human Rights Council, 4 June 2008 (UN Doc. A/HRC/8/42), 19, para. 106 (Recommendation 25); Bhutan, Human Rights Council, 4 January 2010 (UN Doc. A/HRC/13/11), 20, para. 101 (Recommendation 82).

142. E.g., Sri Lanka, Human Rights Council, 5 June 2008 (UN Doc. A/HRC/8/46), 10–11, para. 47; Israel, Human Rights Council, 8 January 2009 (UN Doc. A/HRC/810/76), 6–7, paras 22, 24, 25, 26, 13–14, paras 54, 57, etc.; Colombia, Human Rights Council, 9 January 2009 (UN Doc. A/HRC/10/82), 11, para. 32, and 16, para. 49; Democratic Republic of the Congo, Human Rights Council, 4 January 2010 (UN Doc. A/HRC/13/8), 7, para. 44; Iraq, Human Rights Council, 15 March 2010 (UN Doc. A/HRC/14/14), 13–19, para. 81 (Recommendations 27, 121 and 124).

143. E.g., United Kingdom, Human Rights Council, 23 May 2008 (UN Doc. A/HRC/8/25), 9–10, paras 28 and 36, 14, para. 48, and 17, para. 56 (Recommendations 11 and 12); Sri Lanka, Human Rights Council, 5 June 2008 (UN Doc. A/HRC/8/46), 15, para. 74, and 19, para. 82 (Recommendation 29); Democratic Republic of the Congo, Human Rights Council, 4 January 2010 (UN Doc. A/HRC/13/8), 15–17, para. 94 (Recommendations 48, 77, 87).

144. E.g., Israel, Human Rights Council, 8 January 2009 (UN Doc. A/HRC/10/76), 7, para. 25, and 14, para. 57; Russian Federation, Human Rights Council, 29 May 2009 (UN Doc. A/HRC/11/19), 12, para. 54.

145. *Supra*, section 2.

146. Kolb, *supra* note 9, para. 32.

147. See ibid., paras 38 and 43. This development has been criticized by some authors. Besides Dennis, Surena and Modirzadeh, *supra* note 31, see also G. Corn, 'Mixing Apples and Hand Grenades – The Logical Limit of Applying Human Rights Norms to Armed Conflict', *International Humanitarian Legal Studies* 1 (2010): 52–94; A.M. Gross, 'Human Proportions: Are Human Rights the Emperor's New Clothes of the International Law of Occupation', *The European Journal of International Law* 18 (2007): 1–35; B.A Feinstein, 'The Applicability of the Regime of Human Rights in Times of Armed Conflict and particularly to Occupied Territories: The Case of Israel's Security Barrier', *Northwestern Journal of International Human Rights Law*, 2 (2005), 238–302.

148. Alston et al., *supra* note 77, 184–185.

149. E.g., in Human Rights Council Resolution S-2/1, *supra* note 83, a majority of Council members strongly condemned the grave Israeli violations of human rights and breaches of international humanitarian law in Lebanon in 2006 but did not mention violations by Hezbollah and limited the mandate of the Commission of Inquiry it set up to Israeli violations. However, the joint report of several mandate holders on their 'Mission to Lebanon and Israel (7–14 September 2006)', *supra* note 123, deals with both parties to the conflict. Similarly, the report by the Commission of Inquiry on Lebanon, *supra* note 108, stressed 'that any independent, impartial and objective investigation into a particular conduct during the course of hostilities must of necessity be with reference to all the

belligerents involved. Thus an inquiry into the conformity with international humanitarian law of the specific acts of the Israel Defense Forces (IDF) in Lebanon requires that account also be taken of the conduct of the opponent', para. 6.

150. See, e.g., L. Condorelli and L. Boisson de Chazournes, 'Quelques Remarques à propos de l'obligation des Etats de "respecter et de faire respecter" le droit international "humanitaire en toutes circonstances"', in *Studies and Essays on International Humanitarian Law and Red Cross Principles in Honour of Jean Pictet*, ed. C. Swinarski (Geneva and The Hague: Martinus Nijhoff, 1984), 26–29.

151. See Resolution 8, Pacific Settlement of International Differences, Resolutions of the Diplomatic Conference of Geneva, 1949, reprinted in *International Committee of the Red Cross, The Geneva Conventions of August 12 1949* (2008): 225, 'The Conference wishes to affirm before all nations: that, its work having been inspired solely by humanitarian aims, its earnest hope is that, in the future, Governments may never have to apply the Geneva Conventions for the Protection of War Victims; that its strongest desire is that the Powers, great and small, may always reach a friendly settlement of their differences through cooperation and understanding between nations, so that peace shall reign on earth for ever'.

22. The Inter-American Court of Human Rights and international humanitarian law

Hélène Tigroudja *

The Inter-American Court of Human Rights was established by the American Convention on Human Rights (ACHR) and adopted in November 1969[1] by the Member States of the Organization of American States (OAS).[2] From the end of the 1970s to 2011, the judicial body of the ACHR delivered more or less 200 judgments and 20 advisory opinions,[3] and one of the main features of its practice is that most of the time, it deals with grave and massive violations of Human Rights. Forced disappearances, extra-judicial killings, detentions *in communicado*, torture, rapes and other ill treatments, committed by public agents (police and security forces) or paramilitary groups acting in the name of the States are still denounced before the Inter-American Court. Another feature of the Inter-American situation of Human Rights is that the American States involved in the judicial procedure before the Court are in general very new democratic regimes. Others are still facing non-international armed conflicts such as Colombia, Peru or El Salvador.

The consequence of the concrete political situation of the American Continent is that the Framework of the Inter-American System of Protection of Human Rights is quite different from the European System, born after the Second World War within pacified and democratic States.

Another feature of the Inter-American System rests on the way the Inter-American Court functions. Compared to the Strasbourg Court, the Tribunal of San José has developed very special methods of interpretation of the ACHR and especially, the *holist* interpretation of Human Rights. It can be illustrated with the situation of children or indigenous peoples. When the Court has to interpret the rights of these two vulnerable categories of persons (both in contentious cases or in advisory proceeding), the Tribunal of San José uses *all kinds* of international and domestic instruments, binding or not, to determine the content of the rights. It is remarkable in the significant advisory opinion 17 relative to the Judicial Conditions and Human Rights of Children (2002),[4] the *Moiwana Community* case (2003), and it can be extended to women, migrants, disabled persons, Human Rights defender, etc. In order to interpret the ACHR *pro victim* or *pro homine*, the Inter-American Court uses the so-called '*international corpus juris*' including Universal, European, African, Asian and domestic rules.[5] This element explains the status of International Humanitarian Law within the framework of the Inter-American jurisprudence I am going to develop.

But it is necessary to go further. This *holist* method of interpretation developed by the Court – and criticized by some internationalist lawyers[6] – is based on a special philosophy of International Public Law, as expressed by the Former President of the Tribunal of San José, Antônio Cançado Trindade. To his mind, International Public Law – and the ACHR – is based on the '*juridical conscience*' or '*universal conscience*' that leads '*beyond State legal positivism*'.[7] Accordingly, when a Human Rights Tribunal has to interpret a provision, it can rest on various instruments and norms, even if they are not ratified or accepted by the interested State. One must keep this particular philosophy in mind to understand the way the International Humanitarian Law raises and is used in the Inter-American System.

There are many concrete references to Humanitarian Law in the contentious cases judged by the Tribunal of San José – many more than in the European practice[8] – but its position has evolved from the *Las Palmeras v. Colombia* case (2000) to the more recent, *Prison Miguel Castro Castro v. Péru* (2006). In the former, the Tribunal strongly refused to condemn Colombia for the breach of International Humanitarian Law and in the latter, it interpreted some rights in the light of Humanitarian Law and International Criminal Law. From the mid-2000s, precise and numerous references to the Geneva Conventions, their Protocols or customary humanitarian law are so frequent that one can ask the question whether the differences between International Law of Human Rights and Humanitarian Law still exist.[9]

In order to cast light on the relationship between the ACHR as interpreted by the Court and the Humanitarian Rules, I will look at the different cases where these latter were invoked and used (Part 1). Secondly, I am going to comment on this case-law (Part 2) and I will conclude this chapter with final remarks.

PART 1   THE REFERENCES TO INTERNATIONAL HUMANITARIAN LAW IN THE JURISPRUDENCE OF THE TRIBUNAL OF SAN JOSÉ

As mentioned above, most of the cases adjudicated by the Inter-American Court raise significant questions of grave and massive breaches of Human Rights and especially, the Right to Life (Article 4 of the ACHR),[10] the Prohibition of Torture and other Ill Treatments (Article 5 of the ACHR)[11] and the Right to Justice (Articles 8 and 25 of the ACHR).[12] During the proceedings, the Inter-American Commission or the petitioners do invoke the Humanitarian Law or International Criminal Law as a base for their legal reasoning, and, in general, the Inter-American Court does follow their arguments.

In this part, I am illustrating with concrete cases where Humanitarian Rules or International Criminal Law were referred to.

1.1   *Las Palmeras v. Colombia*[13]

In 1991, six people were killed in the village of *Las Palmeras* during a military operation led by the police. It was not disputed between the parties that the State agents were responsible for the killings. Others died in combat under unclear circumstances. During the proceeding before the Inter-American Court, the Commission did affirm in its conclusions that these murders constituted both a violation of Article 4 of the ACHR (Right to life) and Article 3 common to the Four Geneva Conventions of 1949.[14] The State raised a preliminary objection on the material jurisdiction of the Court and this latter did accept the objection, adopting a strict – and correct – reading of the ACHR:

The American Convention is an international treaty according to which States Parties are obliged to respect the rights and freedoms embodied in it and to guarantee their exercise to all persons subject to their jurisdiction. The Convention provides for the existence of the Inter-American Court to hear 'all cases concerning the interpretation and application' of its provisions (Article 62.3). When a State is a Party to the American Convention and has accepted the contentious jurisdiction of the Court, the Court may examine the conduct of the State to determine whether it conforms to the provisions of the Convention, even when the issue may have been definitively resolved by the domestic legal system. The Court is also competent to determine whether any norm of domestic or international law applied by a State, in times of peace or armed conflict, is compatible or not with the American Convention. In this activity, the Court has no normative limitation: any legal norm may be submitted to this examination of compatibility. 33. In order to carry out this examination, the Court interprets the norm in question and analyzes it in the light of the provisions of the Convention. The result of this operation will always be an opinion in which the Court will say whether or not that norm or that fact is compatible with the American Convention. The latter has only given the Court competence to determine whether the acts or the norms of the States are compatible with the Convention itself, and not with the 1949 Geneva Conventions.[15]

1.2   *Plan de Sanchez Massacre v. Guatemala*[16]

The facts as described in the Judgment of the Inter-American Court reveal the massacre of more than 250 persons from the *Maya* community, at the beginning of 1980. At this time, Guatemala was facing a non-international armed conflict, and before the Tribunal of San José, it recognized its International Responsibility[17] for the grave violations of Human Rights committed by public agents. But the key question raised by the Commission was the legal qualification of the material facts. As far as the Commission was concerned, these murders of hundreds persons from the *Maya* community must be qualified as a genocide prohibited by the International Criminal Law since the Convention of 1948 on the prevention and punishment of genocide.[18] Despite the gravity of the established facts, the Inter-American Court refused to qualify them as genocide, underlying its narrow material jurisdiction.[19]

1.3   *Las Hermanas Serrano Cruz v. El Salvador*[20]

As with many Central or Latin America Countries, El Salvador had to cope with a non-international armed conflict from the beginning of the 1980s and the facts in the case of the *Sisters Serrano Cruz* are deeply linked to this context. Two very young girls were kidnapped by Salvadorian security forces and disappeared in 1982. The family of the two sisters never heard of the whereabouts of the young girls, and no domestic judicial proceedings discovered where they were or who was responsible for the forced disappearance. Before the Inter-American Court, El Salvador raised various preliminary objections, and, especially, the State affirmed that the ACHR was not applicable to the facts. The legal framework of this non-international armed conflict was the International Humanitarian Law and the Court had no jurisdiction to implement this branch of International Law.[21]

The answer of the Court is interesting for two reasons. First, the Tribunal of San José underlined the *complementarity* of IHL and ILHR.[22] The case-law of the ICJ on the same topic is not quoted[23] but the Inter-American Court did adopt a similar position. Second, the Court recalled that the ACHR can be interpreted in the light of other international treaties or rules when needed. There should be *no gap* in the protection provided by the Inter-American System, even if – and above all! – the violations of human rights did occur during times of emergency, non-international or international conflict.[24] For these reasons, the Court rejected the preliminary objection of El Salvador.

1.4   *Mapiripan Massacre v. Colombia*[25]

In this case, the Commission pledged the responsibility of Colombia for the ill-treatments and assassinations of civilians located in the village of Mapiripan which occurred in 1997. Before determining the provisions breached by the State, the Inter-American Court recalled the role played by International Humanitarian Law in its legal reasoning:

> [T]he Court cannot set aside the existence of general and special duties of the State to protect the civilian population, derived from International Humanitarian Law, specifically Article 3 common of the August 12, 1949 Geneva Agreements and the provisions of the additional Protocol to the Geneva Agreements regarding protection of the victims of non-international armed conflicts (Protocol II). Due respect for the individuals protected entails passive obligations (not to kill, not to violate physical safety, etc.), while the protection due entails positive obligations to impede violations against said persons by third parties.
>   ... The obligations derived from said international provisions must be taken into account, according to Article 29.b) of the Convention, because those who are protected by said treaty do not, for that reason, lose the rights they have pursuant to the legislation of the State under whose jurisdiction they are; instead, those rights complement each other or become integrated to specify their scope or their content. While it is clear that this Court cannot attribute international responsibility under International Humanitarian Law, as such, said provisions are useful to interpret the Convention, in the process of establishing the responsibility of the State and other aspects of the violations alleged in the instant case.[26]

1.5   *Vargas Areco v. Paraguay*[27]

This case directly addresses the topic of the recruitment of a minor of 15 years old in the army – the facts occurred at the end of the 1980s. The minor was killed under unclear circumstances and the Court concluded on the responsibility of the State in his death. As far as the recruitment is concerned, the Tribunal of San José expressly referred to International Humanitarian Rules, the Optional Protocol to the Convention on the Rights of the Child on the involvement of children in armed conflict and the Convention No. 182 of the International Labour Organization concerning the prohibition of and immediate action for the elimination of the worst forms of child labour:

> As to international humanitarian law, the Additional Protocols to the Geneva Conventions of August 12, 1949, on the protection of victims of international (Protocol I) or domestic (Protocol II) armed conflict establish the need to provide special protection for children. Protocol I establishes that 'the Parties to the conflict shall take all feasible measures in order that children who have not attained the age of fifteen years do not take a direct part in hostilities and, in particular, they shall refrain from recruiting them into their armed forces. In

recruiting among those persons who have attained the age of fifteen years but who have not attained the age of eighteen years, the Parties to the conflict shall endeavor to give priority to those who are oldest.' As regards to fundamental rights, Article 4 of Protocol II sets forth that '[c]hildren shall be provided with the care and aid they require, and in particular ... children who have not attained the age of fifteen years shall neither be recruited in the armed forces or groups nor allowed to take part in hostilities'.[28]

The Inter-American Court reaffirmed the same principle in a similar case denouncing forced disappearances in *Bamaca Velasquez v. Guatemala*,[29] where the Court did interpret Article 1 of the ACHR in the light of Article 3 of the Four Geneva Conventions,[30] or the grave breaches of Human Rights committed by paramilitary groups supported by the Colombian State in *Ituango Massacres v. Colombia* delivered a few months later. In this case, the Court read the right to property (Article 21 of the ACHR) in the light of Article 13 and Article 14 of the Protocol II of the Geneva Conventions.[31] In another judgment delivered more recently against Guatemala, the Tribunal of San José (Case of the *'Las Dos Erres' Massacre v. Guatemala*) analysed the protection due to children during armed conflict in the light of Article 4(3) of the Protocol II,[32] and, in a concurring opinion, one of the judges pointed out the significance of International Humanitarian Law when the facts revealed such grave and massive violations of Human Rights.[33] One must not forget the significant judgment delivered against Peru in the case *Miguel Castro Castro* concerning the murders and ill-treatments which occurred in 1992 during a police operation conducted by security forces and decided by the former President, A. Fujimori. The real aim of this operation was '*the physical elimination of the inmates accused of Terrorism*' and during the operation, a lot of persons were deprived of their life, were ill-treated, raped and tortured. The Court focused on the violence against women (especially against pregnant women) and recalled that under International Law, such violence was analysed as a crime against humanity.[34]

In other cases, the Inter-American Court takes into account the gravity of the violations of Human Rights and their *qualification as crimes against humanity* to underline the special duty of the State to investigate and to punish. In the afore-mentioned judgment *Miguel Castro Castro v. Peru* of 2006, in the decision *Almonacid Arellano v. Chile*,[35] or in its recent judgment in the *Gomes Lund v. Brazil* case,[36] the Inter-American Court had to cope with domestic legislations of amnesties and other obstacles to the right to justice and the right to truth revealed in the *Bamaca Velasquez v. Guatemala* case. From this *qualification as crime against humanity*, the Court concluded that there had been a violation of the ACHR, and, especially, the judicial guarantees enshrined in Articles 8 and 25 of the Convention.

In the case *Miguel Castro Castro*, the statements made by the Court are the following:

> ... [it] concludes that there is evidence to state that the deaths and tortures committed against the victims of this case by state agents, for the reasons mentioned in the previous paragraphs constitute crimes against humanity. The prohibition to commit these crimes is a norm of the ius cogens, and, therefore, the State has the obligation to not leave these crimes unpunished and therefore it must use the national and international means, instruments, and mechanisms for the effective prosecution of said behaviors and the punishment of their perpetrators, in order to prevent them and avoid that they remain unpunished.

This Tribunal has invariably stated that the State has the duty to avoid and fight impunity, characterized as 'an offense within the obligation to investigation, persecute, capture, prosecute, and sentence those responsible for the violations of the rights protected by the American Convention.' Impunity must be fought through all means available, taking into account the need to make justice in a specific case and that promotes the chronicle repetition of violations to human rights and the total defenselessness of the victims. This Tribunal has also pointed out that the nature and seriousness of the facts within contexts of systematic violations of human rights generates a greater need to eradicate the impunity of the facts.[37]

PART 2: ANALYSIS OF THE REFERENCES TO IHL

The reading and analysis of Inter-American case-law can be understood by keeping in mind three core features of the Inter-American system and the legal reasoning and position adopted by the Court, not only in these cases of armed conflicts but more generally, in adjudicating *all kind of violations* of the ACHR.

2.1 A Dynamic and Broad Interpretation of Article 29 of the ACHR

Compared to the African Charter on Human and Peoples' Rights of 1981, the American Convention on Human Rights does not contain precise provisions concerning the rule of Interpretation of the Treaty. Indeed, Articles 60 and 61 of the African Charter encourage the Commission – and the future Court, when it works – to rest on other International Treaties and legal Instruments to interpret the Charter of 1981,[38] and, in practice, the African Commission does.[39] Accordingly, when the factual context of violations of the African Charter is an armed conflict as in the interstate petition *Democratic Republic of Congo v. Burundi, Rwanda and Uganda*,[40] the Commission reads its Convention in the light of International Humanitarian Law as prescribed in the African Charter.

The position of the Inter-American Court is a little bit different. The rules of interpretation of the American Convention are contained in Article 29, providing the following:

No provision of this Convention shall be interpreted as: 1. permitting any State Party, group, or person to suppress the enjoyment or exercise of the rights and freedoms recognized in this Convention or to restrict them to a greater extent than is provided for herein; 2. restricting the enjoyment or exercise of any right or freedom recognized by virtue of the laws of any State Party or by virtue of another convention to which one of the said states is a party; 3. precluding other rights or guarantees that are inherent in the human personality or derived from representative democracy as a form of government; or 4. excluding or limiting the effect that the American Declaration of the Rights and Duties of Man and other international acts of the same nature may have.

The rules of interpretation of the ACHR are mentioned but in a *negative* manner and no positive encouragement to external references can be found in the Convention, and despite the absence of a clear authorization to quote and use external sources, the Inter-American Court has interpreted Article 29 as the formal admittance by States of such references to other International Rules. Of course, the Court has a clear conscience in its material competence as explained in the *Las Palmeras v. Colombia* case: it has no jurisdiction under International Humanitarian Law. But the Court has interpreted the prohibition under Article 29 – no interpretation restricting the scope of Human Rights – as an *authorization* to enlarge the content of the rights protected by the Convention. This specific case-law is not the sole example of such an broad interpretation of Article 29,[41] and from a *formal and legal* point of view, it could be criticized,[42] but this dynamic approach of the rules of interpretation is justified by the Court itself by the aim and object of the American Convention, that is the protection of *Human* Rights. This is the so-called *pro homine* interpretation of the American Convention.

2.2   From the Refusal of a 'Gap-approach' to the Struggle for Unity of International Law

Another core element must be taken into account to understand and appreciate the references to the IHL in the Inter-American case-law. Indeed, the Court refuses the so-called 'gap approach' or 'legal black hole'[43] in cases where violations of the ACHR occur during armed conflicts. This position is quite similar to the legal reasoning adopted by other International Organs such as the ICJ and the African Commission of Human and Peoples' Rights in the above-mentioned case-law, the Human Rights Committee,[44] and more recently, the European Court of Human Rights.[45]

Further, it seems that the philosophical considerations guiding the interpretation of the ACHR rest on the *fundamental unity of international law* as explained by the former President A.A. Cançado Trindade first in 1987[46] and then in 2005.[47] Accordingly, the International Legal Order is characterized by its deep *material* unity, even it there are various *formal* rules adopted by the States in different fields. And as mentioned in the introduction to this chapter, this *material unity* of the International Legal Order has its roots in a *'universal juridical conscience'* (A.A. Cançado Trindade) and not in the willingness of the States as taught during decades in Western Universities.[48] The Court adopts a *holist* approach towards the rights of persons, and the context in which violations occurred should have no consequences on the material scope of this protection. The formal consideration on the jurisdiction of the Court over Legal Instruments of International Humanitarian Law are taken into account – as seen in the *Las Palmeras* or in the cases versus Guatemala where the Court refused to state the violation of the International Convention on prevention and punishment of genocide – but these effects are minimized by the freedom with which the Court interprets the Convention. It means that even if the Court pays attention to 'classical' International Law (the so-called *'Westphalian model of strictly interstate dimension'*)[49] and, especially, the Vienna Convention on the right of Treaties between States of 1969 and the core principle of consent of States, this attention is conditioned to the *universal juridical conscience* and this conscience can lead the Tribunal to go and search external norms in order to complete its legal order. As stated above, it can be criticized from a formal point of view but the Court legitimizes this holist approach by the aim of the Convention, that is, the protection of the rights of individuals.

As I have explained in another article,[50] the case-law of the Court adds a significant part to the process of *humanization* of International Law.

2.3   The Inter-American Court of Human Rights as the Watchdog of an 'International *Corpus Juris*'

For these reasons, the Inter-American Court has developed a significant case-law based on the principle that it would be the 'watchdog' of an '*international* corpus juris'. It is true in the field of violations of human rights occurring in times of armed conflicts, but, actually, this theory can be applied for all provisions and issues the Court has to cope with (indigenous peoples; rights of migrants;[51] protection of children;[52] protection of disabled persons;[53] displaced persons;[54] protection of economic, cultural and social rights[55] ...). The Former Président of the Inter-American Court, Antônio Cançado Trindade, developed this approach in his separated opinions and especially, under the *Pueblo Bello Massacre v. Colombia* case.[56]

And the reading of the various judgments and advisory opinions of the Inter-American Court illustrates the fact that this international *corpus juris* is not limited to the American Court but is composed of *all kind of norms*, binding or not, regional or universal, international or domestic, related to the provision the Court has to interpret. It means that even if the Inter-American Court was established to control the implementation of a specific treaty, the ACHR, its task is *formally* bound by this regional Convention, but from a *material* point of view the Court perceives itself as a *Human Rights* Tribunal before being a *Regional Body*.[57] The American Convention of Human Rights plays the role of the '*receptacle formel*' of this *international corpus juris*, and the Court, as the organ of implementation of the Convention, is legitimate in referring to this set of rules. Even if the European Court of Human Rights quotes external references as well, it is not so frequent and systematic, and by this way of reasoning, it would be more accurate to compare the Inter-American Court to the African Commission. But as explained above, the significant difference between the two organs – except for the question of their *nature* – is that the African Commission is authorized by its treaty to use external references whereas the Inter-American is not, or not clearly.

From this legal material, I would like to draw some final conclusions. The first conclusion deals with the relationship between the International Law of Human Rights, the International Humanitarian Law and the International Criminal Law. The various decisions of the Inter-American Court illustrate the movement of bridging the gap between these branches of International Law, fed by many other international judicial decisions.[58] Thomas Meron talked about the '*humanization of International Humanitarian Law*'[59] whereas nowadays, we are witnessing the '*humanitarization of the International Law of Human Rights*'. It does not mean that the boundaries between the branches have totally disappeared but it does mean that the Human Rights Bodies have contributed to the bridging of rules that are technically different but aim for the same goal, that is, the protection of private persons.

The second final remark I would like to formulate deals with the influence of the decisions delivered by the Inter-American Court on International Humanitarian Law and International Criminal Law. Especially, this Inter-American practice has influenced decisions delivered by the International Criminal Court on the Right of participation of victims under Article 68 of the Rome Statute[60] or more recently, by the Special Tribunal for Lebanon. In an Order delivered in April 2010 (*El-Sayed* case), the

President of the Tribunal, Antonio Cassese, used the *Goiburu v. Paraguay* case (2006) to affirm that the right to justice has become a norm of *jus cogens*. Actually, this kind of cross-fertilization illustrates the deep unity of International Law as affirmed by the Judges of the Inter-American Court, and from this element, I draw the conclusion that the Court is right when it uses external sources to interpret its Convention. But over and above the formal critiques that some scholars have formulated against the practice of the Court, it seems to me that this pretention of the Inter-American Court to *unity and universality* can be dangerous as potentially a source of legal insecurity. By ratifying the American Convention, a State should be ready to face with obligations described by the Treaty but with a vague content determined by the Court on a case-by-case basis, using all kind of norms, binding or non-binding (!), adopted in the framework of the Organization of American States, the United Nations or anywhere else ...

The third and last conclusion is about the effectiveness of International Humanitarian Law. We all know that one of the most significant weaknesses of this branch of International Law is the lack of effectiveness, and, especially, the lack of a strong mechanism of implementation. By using some rules of Humanitarian Law, and even if these do not formally enter into the material jurisdiction of the Inter-American Court, the Tribunal of San José – as the European Court of Strasbourg or the African Commission – becomes in some cases and indirectly a kind of *Court of Humanitarian Law*. One can criticise this '*Imperialism of Human Rights*' on the battlefield,[61] but to my mind, the *jurisdictionalisation* of armed conflicts is one of the most sensitive developments in the Rule of Law since the mid-twentieth century.[62]

NOTES

*   Hélène Tigroudja is Professor of International Law at the Aix-Marseille University, France.
1.   *American Convention on Human Rights*, San Jose, 1969 (entered into force 27 August 1978).
2.   On the Inter-American system, see generally H. Faundez Ledesma, *The Inter-American System for the Protection of Human Rights: Institutional and Procedural Aspects* (San Jose: Inter-American Institute of Human Rights, 2007); D. Harris and S. Livingstone, eds, *The Inter-American System of Human Rights* (Oxford: Clarendon Press, 1998); S. Davidson, *The Inter-American Human Rights System* (Dartmouth: Aldershot, 1997); A.A. Cançado Trindade, 'El Sistema Interamericano de Protección de los Derechos Humanos (1948–1995): Evolución, Estado Actual y Perspectivas', in *Derecho Internacional y Derechos Humanos*, eds D. Bardonnet and A.A. Cançado Trindade (San Jose: Inter-American Institute of Human Rights, 1996), 47; T. Buergenthal and D. Shelton, *Protecting Human Rights in the Americas: Cases and Materials* (Kehl: Engel, 1995); C. Medina Quiroga, *The Battle of Human Rights: Gross Systematic Violations and the Inter-American System* (The Hague: Kluwer Law International, 1988); T. Buergenthal and R. Norris, *Human Rights: The Inter-American System* (Dobbs Ferry: Oceana, 1982). See also A.A. Cançado Trindade, 'Le système inter-américain de protection des droits de l'homme: état actuel et perspectives d'évolution à l'aube du XXIème siècle', *AFDI* 46 (2000): 547; D. Harris, 'Regional Protection of Human Rights: The Inter-American Achievement', in *The Inter-American System of Human Rights*, eds D. Harris and S. Livingstone (Oxford: Clarendon Press, 1998), 1; A.A. Cançado Trindade, 'Current State and Perspectives of the Inter-American System of Human Rights Protection at the Dawn of the New Century', *Tulane Journal of International and Comparative Law* 8 (2000): 5; A.A. Cançado Trindade, 'The Evolution of the Organization of American States (OAS) System of Human Rights Protection: An Appraisal', *German Yearbook of International Law* 26 (1982): 498. See also the following: T. Buergenthal, D. Shelton and D. Stewart, *International Human Rights in a Nutshell* (St-Paul: Westgroup, 2004), 221; H. Steiner, P. Alston and R. Goodman, *International Human Rights in Context: Law, Politics, Morals* (Oxford University Press, 2007), 1020.

3. On the Inter-American Court, see L. Hennebel, *La Convention américaine des droits de l'homme: mécanismes de protection et étendue des droits et libertés* (Brussels: Bruylant, 2007); J.M. Pasqualucci, *The Practice and Procedure of the Inter-American Court of Human Rights* (Cambridge University Press, 2003); H. Tigroudja and I.K. Panoussis, *La Cour interaméricaine des droits de l'homme: Analyse de la jurisprudence consultative et contentieuse* (Brussels: Bruylant, 2003); A.A. Cançado Trindade, 'The Operation of the Inter-American Court of Human Rights', in *The Inter-American System of Human Rights*, eds D. Harris and S. Livingstone (Oxford: Clarendon Press, 1998), 133; Davidson, *supra* note 2; A.A. Cançado Trindade, 'Formación, Consolidación y Perfeccionamiento del Sistema Interamericano de Protección de los Derechos Humanos', in *XVII Curso de Derecho Internacional Organizado por el Comité Jurídico Interamericano* (Washington, DC: Secretaria General Asuntos Jurídicos OEA, 1990); C. Cerna, 'The Structure and Functioning of the Inter-American Court of Human Rights (1979–1992)', *British Yearbook of International Law* 63 (1992): 135.

4. See also *Chitay Nech et al. v. Guatemala*, IACtHR, Judgment of 25 May 2010, paras 156 et al.

5. In one of its opinions, the Judge Garcia Ramirez summarized the method of the Court: '... the above does not impede the Inter-American Court from invoking elements or references contained in international Law as a whole, when it is appropriate to do so to interpret or integrate the provisions of the aforementioned conventions and protocol, bearing in mind the characteristics of the facts alleged and the text and meaning of the immediately applicable provisions. In this event, other instruments are not directly applied, to decide on violations of the rights or duties set forth in them, but rather they are used as elements of interpretation, assessment or judgment for a better understanding and the immediate application of the principles that explicitly grant it competence; in other words, for the direct application of the provisions contained in the latter' (see *Plan de Sanchez Massacre v. Guatemala*, IACtHR, Judgment of 29 April 2004, Separate Opinion of Judge Garcia Ramirez, para. 19).

6. See, for instance, the *positivist* approach adopted by S. Touzé, 'Les techniques interprétatives des organes de protection des droits de l'homme', *RGDIP* 11:2 (2011–2012): 517 *et seq.*

7. A.A. Cançado Trindade, *International Law for Humankind. Towards a new* Jus Gentium (Leiden and Boston: Martinus Nijhoff, 2010), 141 *et seq.*

8. As far as the African Commission of Human and Peoples' Rights is concerned, the Organ seems to follow the same philosophy as the Inter-American Court and when necessary, the Commission does not keep from quoting and using various humanitarian rules as in the Inter-State case, *D.R. Congo v. Burundi, Rwanda and Uganda*, Communication No. 227/99 (2003).

9. See, for instance, H. Tigroudja, 'Droit international des droits de l'homme, droit international humanitaire, droit international pénal: vers la confusion des branches?', in *Mélanges offerts à Paul Tavernier* (forthcoming).

10. By virtue of Article 4, '1. Every person has the right to have his life respected. This right shall be protected by law and, in general, from the moment of conception. No one shall be arbitrarily deprived of his life. 2. In countries that have not abolished the death penalty, it may be imposed only for the most serious crimes and pursuant to a final judgment rendered by a competent court and in accordance with a law establishing such punishment, enacted prior to the commission of the crime. The application of such punishment shall not be extended to crimes to which it does not presently apply. 3. The death penalty shall not be reestablished in states that have abolished it. 4. In no case shall capital punishment be inflicted for political offenses or related common crimes. 5. Capital punishment shall not be imposed upon persons who, at the time the crime was committed, were under 18 years of age or over 70 years of age; nor shall it be applied to pregnant women. 6. Every person condemned to death shall have the right to apply for amnesty, pardon, or commutation of sentence, which may be granted in all cases. Capital punishment shall not be imposed while such a petition is pending decision by the competent authority.'

11. According to Article 5, '1. Every person has the right to have his physical, mental, and moral integrity respected. 2. No one shall be subjected to torture or to cruel, inhuman, or degrading punishment or treatment. All persons deprived of their liberty shall be treated with respect for the inherent dignity of the human person. 3. Punishment shall not be extended to any person other than the criminal. 4. Accused persons shall, save in exceptional circumstances, be segregated from convicted persons, and shall be subject to separate treatment appropriate to their status as unconvicted persons. 5. Minors while subject to criminal proceedings shall be separated from adults and brought before specialized tribunals, as speedily as possible, so that they may be treated in accordance with their status as minors.

6. Punishments consisting of deprivation of liberty shall have as an essential aim the reform and social readaptation of the prisoners.'

12. Article 8 provides, '1. Every person has the right to a hearing, with due guarantees and within a reasonable time, by a competent, independent, and impartial tribunal, previously established by law, in the substantiation of any accusation of a criminal nature made against him or for the determination of his rights and obligations of a civil, labor, fiscal, or any other nature. 2. Every person accused of a criminal offense has the right to be presumed innocent so long as his guilt has not been proven according to law. During the proceedings, every person is entitled, with full equality, to the following minimum guarantees: a. the right of the accused to be assisted without charge by a translator or interpreter, if he does not understand or does not speak the language of the tribunal or court; b. prior notification in detail to the accused of the charges against him; c. adequate time and means for the preparation of his defense; d. the right of the accused to defend himself personally or to be assisted by legal counsel of his own choosing, and to communicate freely and privately with his counsel; e. the inalienable right to be assisted by counsel provided by the state, paid or not as the domestic law provides, if the accused does not defend himself personally or engage his own counsel within the time period established by law; f. the right of the defense to examine witnesses present in the court and to obtain the appearance, as witnesses, of experts or other persons who may throw light on the facts; g. the right not to be compelled to be a witness against himself or to plead guilty; and h. the right to appeal the judgment to a higher court. 3. A confession of guilt by the accused shall be valid only if it is made without coercion of any kind. 4. An accused person acquitted by a nonappealable judgment shall not be subjected to a new trial for the same cause. 5. Criminal proceedings shall be public, except insofar as may be necessary to protect the interests of justice.'

Article 25 of the ACHR, '1. Everyone has the right to simple and prompt recourse, or any other effective recourse, to a competent court or tribunal for protection against acts that violate his fundamental rights recognized by the constitution or laws of the state concerned or by this Convention, even though such violation may have been committed by persons acting in the course of their official duties. 2. The States Parties undertake: a. to ensure that any person claiming such remedy shall have his rights determined by the competent authority provided for by the legal system of the state; b. to develop the possibilities of judicial remedy; and c. to ensure that the competent authorities shall enforce such remedies when granted.'

13. IACtHR, Preliminary Objections, Judgment of 4 February 2000, Series C, No. 67.

14. Ibid., section 12: 'The Commission respectfully requests that Court: Conclude and declare that the State of Colombia has violated the right to life, embodied in Article 4 of the Convention, and Article 3, common to all the 1949 Geneva Conventions, to the detriment of six persons. ...
Establish the circumstances of the death of a seventh person, who had presumably died in combat ... in order to determine whether the State of Colombia has violated his right to life embodied in Article 4 of the Convention and Article 3, common to all the 1949 Geneva Conventions.'

15. Ibid., paras. 32–33.

16. IACtHR, Merits, Judgment of 29 April 2004.

17. Ibid., paras. 34 et al.

18. Ibid., para. 2.

19. Ibid., para. 51.

20. IACtHR, Preliminary Objections, Judgment of 23 November 2004.

21. Ibid., para. 107.

22. For instance, the Court compared the content of the ACHR to the content of Article 75 of the Protocol II of 1977.

23. Especially, *Legal Consequences of the Construction of a Wall in the Occupied Palestinian Territory*, Advisory Opinion, I.C.J. Reports 2004. On this Opinion and more generally, the case-law of the I.C.J. concerning articulation between IHL and Human Rights, see C. Tomuschat, 'Human Rights and International Humanitarian Law', *European Journal of International Law* 1 (2010): 15–23.

24. IACtHR, Preliminary Objections, Judgment of 23 November 2004, paras. 111 et al.

25. IACtHR, Merits, Reparations and Costs, Judgment of 15 September 2005, Series C, No. 134.

26. Ibid., paras. 114–115.

27. Vargas Areco v. Paraguay, IACtHR, Judgment of 26 September 2006.

28. Ibid., para. 113.

29. IACtHR, Judgment of 25 November 2000, para. 203 *et seq.*

30. Ibid., para. 207: 'The Court considers that it has been proved that, at the time of the facts of this case, an internal conflict was taking place in Guatemala. ... As has previously been stated ... instead of

exonerating the State from its obligations to respect and guarantee human rights, this fact obliged it to act in accordance with such obligations. Therefore, and as established in Article 3 common to the Geneva Conventions of August 12, 1949, confronted with an internal armed conflict, the State should grant those persons who are not participating directly in the hostilities or who have been placed hors de combat for whatever reason, humane treatment, without any unfavorable distinctions. In particular, international humanitarian law prohibits attempts against the life and personal integrity of those mentioned above, at any place and time.'

31. IACtHR, Merits, Reparations and Costs, Judgment of 1 July 2006. See especially para. 179–180: 'When examining the scope of the said Article 21 of the Convention in this case, the Court considers it useful and appropriate, in keeping with Article 29 thereof, to use international treaties other than the American Convention, such as Protocol II of the Geneva Conventions of August 12, 1949, relating to the protection of victims of non-international armed conflicts, to interpret its provisions in accordance with the evolution of the inter-American system, taking into account the corresponding developments in international humanitarian law. Colombia ratified the Geneva Conventions on November 8, 1961. On August 14, 1995, it acceded to the provisions of the Protocol II to the Geneva Conventions 180. It has been proved, and the State has acknowledged, that the paramilitary incursion in El Aro, and also the theft of the livestock, happened with the acquiescence or tolerance of members of the Colombian Army, in the context of the internal armed conflict (supra paras. 63 and 64). In this regard, the Court observes that Articles 13 (Protection of the civilian population) and 14 (Protection of the objects indispensable to the survival of the civilian population) of Protocol II of the Geneva Conventions prohibit, respectively, 'acts or threats of violence the primary purpose of which is to spread terror among the civilian population', and also 'to attack, destroy, remove or render useless, for that purpose, objects indispensable to the survival of the civilian population.'

32. IACtHR, Preliminary Objections, Merits, Reparations and Costs, Judgment of 24 November 2009, para. 191.

33. Concurring Opinion of Ramon Cadena Ramila. In the case, the lack of justice (investigation, prosecution and punishment) was denounced before the Court, over the massacre of more than 200 persons at the beginning of the 1980s. The persons included children and women – and pregnant women raped and beaten until they aborted.

34. IACtHR, Merits, Reparations and Costs, Judgment of 25 November 2006, paras 206, 223–226, 402–404.

35. IACtHR, Merits, Reparations and Costs, Judgment of 26 September 2006.

36. IACtHR, Preliminary Objections, Merits, Reparations and Costs, Judgment of 24 November 2010.

37. IACtHR, Merits, Reparations and Costs, Judgment of 25 November 2006, Series C, No. 160, paras 404–405. In this case, the Court did affirm that Peru had to prosecute the former President Fujimori, even if he had taken refuge in another country at this time and even if he was protected by domestic or international immunities (see para. 406).

38. Article 60: 'The Commission shall draw inspiration from international law on human and peoples' rights, particularly from the provisions of various African instruments on human and peoples' rights, the Charter of the United Nations, the Charter of the Organization of African Unity, the Universal Declaration of Human Rights, other instruments adopted by the United Nations and by African countries in the field of human and peoples' rights as well as from the provisions of various instruments adopted within the Specialized Agencies of the United Nations of which the parties to the present Charter are members.'

Article 61: 'The Commission shall also take into consideration, as subsidiary measures to determine the principles of law, other general or special international conventions, laying down rules expressly recognized by member states of the Organization of African Unity, African practices consistent with international norms on human and peoples' rights, customs generally accepted as law, general principles of law recognized by African states as well as legal precedents and doctrine.'

39. See, for instance, and among many others, *Kenneth Good v. Botswana*, Communication No. 313/05 (2010) (about expulsion; references to the ECHR and the ACHR).

40. *D.R. Congo v. Burundi, Rwanda and Uganda*, Communication No. 227/99, May 2003. This communication was based on Article 49 of the African Charter and the Democratic Republic of the Congo did denounce the grave violations of Human Rights committed by the respondent States on its territory. The Commission referred especially to Article 75 of the Protocol I and to the Fourth Geneva Convention of 1949 on the protection of civilians.

41. See, for instance, the case-law concerning the rights of indigenous peoples; the rights of women; the rights of children; the rights of migrants. For an example taken from the case-law on indigenous

peoples, see *Comunidad Indigena Sawhoyamaxa v. Paraguay*, IACtHR, Judgment of 29 March 2006 (references to the Convention No. 169 adopted in the framework of the International Labour Organization). See also L. Lixinski, 'Treaty Interpretation by the Inter-American Court of Human Rights: Expansionism at the Service of the Unity of International Law', *European Journal of International Law* 3 (2010): 585–604.

42.   See G. Neuman, 'Import, Export and Regional Consent in the Inter-American Court of Human Rights', *European Journal of International Law* 1 (2008): 101 *et seq.*

43.   F. Ni Aolain, 'The No-gaps Approach to Parallel Application in the Context of the War on Terror', *Israel Law Review* 40: No. 2.

44.   D. Weissbrodt, 'The Role of the Human Rights Committee in Interpreting and Developing Humanitarian Law', *University of Pennsylvania Journal of International Law* (2010): 1185 *et seq.*

45.   See *Varnava and others v. Turkey*, ECtHR, Judgment of 18 September 2009, para. 185: 'Article 2 must be interpreted in so far as possible in light of the general principles of international law, including the rules of international humanitarian law which play an indispensable and universally-accepted role in mitigating the savagery and inhumanity of armed conflict. ... The Court therefore concurs with the reasoning of the Chamber in holding that in a zone of international conflict Contracting States are under obligation to protect the lives of those not, or no longer, engaged in hostilities. This would also extend to the provision of medical assistance to the wounded; where combatants have died, or succumbed to wounds, the need for accountability would necessitate proper disposal of remains and require the authorities to collect and provide information about the identity and fate of those concerned, or permit bodies such as the ICRC to do so.' For an analysis, see especially A. Gioia, 'The Role of the European Court of Human Rights in Monitoring Compliance with Humanitarian Law in Armed Conflict', in *International Humanitarian Law and International Human Rights Law*, ed. O. Ben-Naftali (New York: Oxford University Press, 2011), 201–249.

46.   A.A. Cançado Trindade, 'Co-Existence and Co-ordination of Mechanisms of International Protection of Human Rights at Global and Regional Level', *Collected Courses of the Hague Academy of International Law* 202 (1987-II): 435.

47.   Trindade, *supra* note 7, at 726.

48.   On this debate concerning the unity of the International Legal Order, see also R. Huesa Vinaixa and K. Wellens, *L'influence des sources sur l'unité et la fragmentation du droit international* (Brussels: Bruylant, 2006), 280.

49.   Trindade, *supra* note 7, at 399.

50.   H. Tigroudja, 'La Cour interaméricaine des droits de l'homme au service de l'humanisation du droit international', *Annuaire français de droit international* (2006).

51.   *Juridical Condition and Rights of Undocumented Migrants*, Advisory Opinion, IACtHR, 17 September 2003.

52.   *Juridical Condition and Human Rights of Child*, Advisory Opinion, IACtHR, 28 August 2002.

53.   *Ximenes-Lopes v. Brazil*, IACtHR, Judgment of 4 July 2006.

54.   *Ituango Massacre v. Colombia*, IACtHR, Judgment of 1 July 2006.

55.   *Acevedo Buendia v. Peru*, IACtHR, Judgment of 1 July 2009.

56.   IACtHR, Judgment of 31 January 2006.

57.   See L. Hennebel and H. Tigroudja, 'La Convention américaine des droits de l'homme et la protection universelle des droits de l'homme: une filiation retrouvée', *L'Observateur des Nations Unies* 25 (2008/2): 71–96; H. Tigrouja, 'La légitimité du particularisme interaméricain en question', in *Le particularisme interaméricain des droits de l'homme. En l'honneur du 40e anniversaire de la Convention américaine des droits de l'homme*, L. Hennebel and H. Tigroudja (Paris: Pédone, 2009), 383–412.

58.   C. Droege, 'The Interplay between International Humanitarian Law and International Human Rights Law in Situations of Armed Conflicts', *Israel Law Review* 2 (2007): 310 *et seq.*

59.   T. Meron, 'The Humanization of International Humanitarian Law', *American Journal of International Law* 94:2 (2000): 266 *et seq.* See also D. Koller, 'The Moral Imperative: Toward a Human Rights-based Law of War', *Harvard International Law Journal* 46 (2005), 247 *et seq.*

60.   ICC, Preliminary Chapter I, Decision, 17 January 2006, on the request of participation to the proceedings of VPRS1, VPRS2, VPRS3, VPRS4, VPRS5, VPRS6. The ICC quoted the *Villagran Morales v. Paraguay* case delivered in 1999.

61.   R. Wilde, 'Complementing Occupation Law? Selective Judicial Treatment of the Suitability of Human Rights Norms', *Israel Law Review* 1 (2009): 86–89: the author quoted the opinion of one of the Lords of the House of Lords in the significant case *Al-Skeini v. Secretary of State for Defence* of 2005. See

also M.J. Dennis, 'Non-Application of Civil and Political Rights Treaties Extraterritoriality During Times of International Armed Conflicts', *Israel Law Review* 2 (2007): 453–502.

62. On this issue, see Y. Sandoz, 'Les situations de conflits armés ou d'occupation: quelle place pour l'Etat de droit?', in *Société française pour le droit international, L'Etat de droit en droit international* (Paris: Pédone, 2008), 361–383.

23. The European Court of Human Rights and international humanitarian law

*Lindsay Moir**

1. INTRODUCTION

In a sense, it would be possible to dispose of this issue with little or no discussion: the European Court of Human Rights has never applied the rules of international humanitarian law. That is as it should be – its jurisdiction, after all, extends to the enforcement of the European Convention on Human Rights (ECHR) and no further. Nonetheless, there has always been the possibility of its using other international legal rules (including those of international humanitarian law) as a device to assist in the interpretation of the Convention rights, and hence in its enforcement duties. The 1969 Vienna Convention on the Law of Treaties, for example, provides in Article 31(3)(c) that, in interpreting the terms of any treaty, 'any relevant rules of international law applicable in the relations between the parties' shall be taken into account. Similarly, in frequently quoted passages of its *Nuclear Weapons* and *Palestinian Wall* Advisory Opinions, the International Court of Justice has indicated that human rights law continues to be applicable during armed conflict, and that the relationship between human rights and humanitarian law can be characterised in the following way: '… some rights may be exclusively matters of humanitarian law; others may be exclusively matters of human rights law; yet others may be matters of both these branches of international law'.[1] International humanitarian law is thus considered to be *lex specialis* in the context of armed conflicts.

Whilst, historically, it is probably fair to say that the Strasbourg machinery encountered a relatively limited range of cases in which humanitarian law was relevant, even when given the opportunity to use humanitarian law as just such an interpretative device, it has chosen not to do so.[2] This apparent unwillingness to engage with the norms of humanitarian law has been criticised. Indeed, Dame Rosalyn Higgins was perhaps rather charitable in describing the Court's approach to the parameters of its role in relation to the rules of humanitarian law as being a 'work in progress'.[3]

The purpose of this chapter is to examine the extent of this 'progress', by assessing the approach of the Court to those situations where state forces have been engaged in hostilities and where an appreciation of the rules and application of international humanitarian law might therefore be seen to be necessary or, at least, helpful in addressing the existence of human rights violations. Three such categories can be identified: namely, cases arising in the context of internal armed conflicts; cases involving the extra-territorial use of military force; and Article 7 cases, arising from domestic prosecutions for violations of the laws of war, and necessitating an understanding of the state of the law in historical context.

2. INTERNAL ARMED CONFLICTS

Although a relatively recent phenomenon in terms of ECHR enforcement, the European Court of Human Rights has now had ample opportunity to examine the protection of human rights in the context of internal armed conflict. Initial communications arose out of the situation in Northern Ireland – cases that were considered in the context of internal disturbances and tensions, that is, as falling short of the threshold for armed conflict. Yet, to the extent that they concerned the right to life, and the use of lethal force by the organs of the state as regulated by Article 2 of the Convention, these decisions were clearly of potential value and importance in the context of human rights protection during hostilities.[4] By the mid-1990s, however, the security situation in South-East Turkey – characterised by numerous armed clashes between Turkish troops and the Workers Party of Kurdistan (PKK) – had become a fertile source of complaints more squarely placed in the internal armed conflict arena. These hostilities therefore provided a body of relevant case law that has since been built upon by the numerous cases arising out of Russian military activities in Chechnya.

It is important to note at the outset that none of the three states involved accepted their internal difficulties as constituting armed conflicts, and that the UK, Turkey and Russia have all therefore denied the applicability of humanitarian law through the operation of the provisions of common Article 3, Additional Protocol II, or else through the relevant customary rules. This should not be seen as surprising. Perhaps understandably, political considerations mean that states are generally reluctant to concede that an internal armed conflict exists on their territory – an act that tends to be perceived as bestowing some form of official status on the insurgent party. As suggested by Abresch, 'to apply humanitarian law is to tacitly concede that there is another "party" wielding power in the putatively sovereign state'.[5] Practice demonstrates that efforts to allay such fears in the terms of common Article 3 and Additional Protocol II have proved largely futile, and the result is that states seldom accept common Article 3 as being applicable – and Additional Protocol II even less so.[6]

For its part, whilst the Court has always proved willing to consider the general security situation surrounding any given case, at no point did it seem to explicitly accept that the situation of unrest in South-East Turkey constituted an armed conflict, preferring instead to talk in terms of 'significant civil strife', or of 'serious disturbances'.[7] On an objective assessment, however, there would seem to be little doubt that the situation did cross the threshold of common Article 3,[8] and it is interesting to note that, despite its refusal to refer to the existence of an armed conflict, the Court has made reference to frequent loss of life in the area arising from 'the prevalence of violent armed clashes',[9] and to the protection of 'villagers … caught up in the conflict'.[10]

Its approach to the Chechen situation was slightly different. There seems to be general agreement that at least common Article 3 was applicable (indeed, a number of scholars have suggested that the character of hostilities was sufficient to meet the higher threshold of Additional Protocol II),[11] and the Court did refer to the 'conflict' in Chechnya. In *Isayeva*, for example, it accepted that the situation:

... called for exceptional measures by the State in order to regain control over the Republic and to suppress the illegal armed insurgency. Given the context of the conflict in Chechnya at the relevant time, those measures could presumably include the deployment of army units equipped with combat weapons, including military aviation and artillery.[12]

Despite this, the Court's consideration of the complaint was based upon the fact that Russia had neither declared a state of emergency, nor made any derogation under the terms of Article 15 of the Convention. As such, the Court asserted that, 'The [military] operation in question therefore has to be judged against a normal legal background',[13] and saw little role for the rules of humanitarian law.

Granted, there is a degree of substantive overlap as far as the relevant rules of human rights and humanitarian law are concerned, and it has been suggested that common Article 3 is as much a human rights provision as it is a humanitarian law provision.[14] It may well be the case, then, that the application of human rights law and/or humanitarian law would generally lead to a similar outcome:

> The treatment of persons detained or otherwise in the power of a state is prescribed in a very similar way. The judicial guarantees for persons undergoing trial are likewise very similar, but they are better developed in human rights. The jurisprudence of the European Court of Human Rights ... shows that even on such a typical humanitarian law subject as precaution-ary measures, which have to be taken for the benefit of the civilian population when attacking military objectives, human rights can lead to the same result as humanitarian law.[15]

Significantly, however, this congruence of result does not necessarily exist in the context of the right to life, or the killing of enemy forces, during internal armed conflict.

The rules of humanitarian law regulating international hostilities are well developed in this regard. Based on the long-standing legal distinction between clearly defined categories of individuals (i.e., between combatants and civilians), enemy combatants remain a legitimate target at all times. Provided that they have not surrendered, or are otherwise *hors de combat*, they can be lawfully attacked and killed on sight.[16] In other words, 'the combatant trades his right to life for the right to kill'.[17] During internal armed conflict, the legal position is slightly more complex. For obvious reasons, states have never accepted that insurgents have any right to attack and kill government forces. Rather, insurgents are treated as criminals in domestic law, and the very notion of a 'combatant' with rights and obligations is present in neither common Article 3 nor Additional Protocol II.[18] The principle of distinction is not, however, absent from the law of internal armed conflict, and only those individuals who are taking an 'active' or 'direct' part in hostilities may be attacked. Unfortunately, this does not always offer adequate clarification,[19] and whilst Sassòli and Olsen have suggested the alternative possibilities that either direct participation in hostilities 'can be understood as encom-passing the mere fact of remaining a member of [an armed] group, or of retaining a fighting function', or else that 'fighters can be considered not to be "civilians"', neither option manages to avoid practical difficulties entirely.[20]

Human rights law, on the other hand, provides for no legal distinction or categorisa-tion whatsoever, and does not permit the targeting of individuals on the basis of any particular status. Instead, the ECHR provides in Article 2(1) that: 'Everyone's right to life shall be protected by law. No one shall be deprived of the right to life intentionally save in the execution of a sentence of a court following his conviction of a crime for which this penalty is provided by law'. Article 2(2), however, carries special importance for the present discussion, and it provides that:

> Deprivation of life shall not be regarded as inflicted in contravention of this article when it results from the use of force which is no more than absolutely necessary:
>
> (a) in defence of any person from unlawful violence;
> (b) in order to effect a lawful arrest or to prevent the escape of a person lawfully detained;
> (c) in action lawfully taken for the purpose of quelling a riot or insurrection.

Article 15(2) provides that derogation from Article 2 is not permitted – except for those deaths resulting from 'lawful acts of war'. Given that human rights law does not address the conduct of hostilities, it cannot indicate the lawfulness or otherwise of military activity in that context. In order to assess whether any particular death has been the result of such activity, then, the Court would need to have recourse to the relevant rules of international humanitarian law. For the same reason that states are unwilling to accept the existence of an internal armed conflict on their territory, however, they are equally unwilling to seek to derogate from Article 2, and no state party has ever done so.[21] Without doing so, however, they are unable to benefit from the operation of the laws of war and the result is that, even in situations which clearly cross the threshold for an armed conflict, the Court's jurisprudence on Article 2 remains remarkably free of any reference to the provisions of humanitarian law.

Instead, the Court uses a different framework in assessing the conduct of states in the context of Article 2. The approach is generally referred to as the 'law enforcement model', and was set out in the case of *McCann v. UK*.[22] In essence, the Court determines whether the planning and control of an operation was such as to minimise, to the greatest extent possible, recourse to lethal force,[23] and whether any deaths could be justified by reference to the terms of Article 2(2). In other words, the use of lethal force must be: (a) absolutely necessary in the prevailing circumstances; (b) proportionate to the threat posed and to the legitimate aims set out in Article 2(2); and (c) limited to circumstances where arrest or detention is either not possible, or else too dangerous.[24] Clearly, this framework comprises two distinct elements in the context of military operations: the planning phase, and the operational phase. Thus, in *McCann* (a case that involved the killing of three IRA terrorists by British security forces on the – mistaken – assumption that they were about to detonate a car bomb) the UK was held to be responsible for violating Article 2 at the planning stage only, through the dissemination of poor quality intelligence to the soldiers involved. On the basis of the intelligence supplied, the soldiers were thought by the Court to have acted perfectly reasonably in that, in the prevailing circumstances, the use of force did seem 'absolutely necessary'. As such, their operational activities did not violate Article 2.[25]

Unlike international humanitarian law, which varies in terms of applicable rules depending on the particularities of any given situation, the 'law enforcement' framework has been applied by the Court irrespective of the threshold or intensity of the conflict situation. The *McCann* rules have therefore been applied consistently to circumstances ranging from relatively low-intensity operations between rioters and police officers, to large-scale hostilities between government armed forces and organised armed insurgent groups, such as those in Chechnya. This does not mean that the scale and intensity of hostilities is irrelevant or unimportant for Article 2 purposes. Indeed, in the context of large-scale hostilities, the use of lethal force is more likely to be considered lawful because the individual or individuals targeted pose much more of a threat to the state's security forces, and attempting to detain them would be more likely to endanger government soldiers. The underlying rule may remain constant, but its practical application by the Court varies according to the specific risks involved in any given situation and, in contrast to humanitarian law, the Court therefore operates according to a 'single regime of flexible rules'.[26] The point is that there is no rule pursuant to Article 2 whereby even the most organised insurgents can automatically be targeted with lethal force.[27]

Thus, in *Ergi v. Turkey*, the Court examined the death of a civilian during a military operation aimed at capturing Kurdish rebels. It held that the responsibility of Turkish troops was engaged: '... where they fail to take all feasible precautions in the choice of means and methods of a security operation mounted against an opposing group with a view to avoiding or, at least, minimising incidental loss of civilian life'.[28] The same approach was taken in *Güleç v. Turkey*,[29] concerning the death of a 15-year-old schoolboy during the forcible dispersal by Turkish security forces of a large, unauthorised demonstration, and in the two cases involving large-scale military operations undertaken by Russian troops in the Chechen conflict.[30]

In *Güleç* the Court assessed the lawfulness of Turkey's use of force on the basis of its proportionality to the aim and the means used, with a particular focus on how these impacted upon the question of whether the force employed was 'absolutely necessary'. Importantly, it noted that frequent 'violent armed clashes' (which could reasonably be argued to indicate the existence of an internal armed conflict) did not serve to release Turkey from its observance of Article 2.[31] Both Chechen cases revolved around civilian deaths resulting from significant battles between Russian forces and Chechen insurgents, and involving extremely heavy aerial bombardment by Russian troops.[32] In both cases the Court steadfastly stuck with the law enforcement model, preferring to characterise the Chechen rebels as demonstrating 'active resistance to ... law enforcement bodies',[33] and admonishing Russian troops on the basis that:

> ... using this kind of weapon in a populated area, *outside wartime* and without prior evacuation of the civilians is impossible to reconcile with the degree of caution expected from a law-enforcement body in a democratic society. ... Even when faced with a situation where ... the population of the village had been held hostage by a large group of well-equipped and well-trained fighters, the primary aim of the operation should be to protect lives from unlawful violence. The massive use of indiscriminate weapons stands in flagrant contrast with this aim and cannot be considered compatible with the standard of care prerequisite to an operation of this kind involving the use of lethal force by State agents.[34]

The language used by the Court in these cases has been the subject of some controversy, with some commentators perceiving the adoption of what seems to be the vocabulary of international humanitarian law as evidence of the almost surreptitious application of humanitarian law rules or principles. Orakhelashvili, for example, has suggested that the Court's approach to such cases has been based on 'the implicit application of the standards of humanitarian law, albeit cloaked in the Convention-specific categories of legitimacy, necessity and proportionality'.[35] He is not alone.[36] Indeed, it has even been suggested that the Court's approach can be viewed as determining whether the acts in question are actually violations of the laws of war. Thus, Reidy has claimed that, in *Ergi*, the Court resorted directly to humanitarian law in that:

> ... the Convention bodies examined the operation to see, *inter alia*, whether there was a lawful target, whether the attack on the lawful target was proportionate and whether there was a foreseeable risk of death to non-combatants that was disproportionate to the military advantage. The analysis of the operation in these terms illustrates clearly that humanitarian law can be validly enforced through human rights norms.[37]

On closer inspection, this is a difficult argument to sustain. It is true that the Court refers to feasible precautionary measures aimed at avoiding 'incidental loss of civilian life',[38] and that it does so in terms extremely reminiscent of Article 57(2)(a)(ii) of Additional Protocol I, which requires those responsible for planning an attack to 'take all feasible precautions in the choice of means and methods of attack with a view to avoiding, and in any event to minimizing, incidental loss of civilian life, injury to civilians and damage to civilian objects'. It is also true that the Court openly refers in *Isayeva v. Russia* to the use of 'indiscriminate weapons',[39] and in *Isayeva and Others v. Russia* to the concepts of 'legitimate targets' and 'disproportionality in the weapons used'.[40] It must be recalled, however, that in neither situation did the Court accept that an armed conflict was in progress – nor is Turkey party to either of the 1977 Additional Protocols.[41] In addition, as Abresch cautions, none of the language used is necessarily exclusive to humanitarian law, and the real test in any case is not whether the Court has (or has not) borrowed the language and/or principles of international humanitarian law, but whether it has in fact 'adopted the legal rules and standards' contained therein.[42] He concludes that, if the Court really is trying to apply humanitarian law, 'it is doing so in a highly imprecise manner'.[43]

In fact, it is clear from the Court's jurisprudence that it has made no attempt to apply the rules of humanitarian law. Rather, as outlined above, its approach has been to apply the 'law enforcement' model of human rights, even where a situation can be characterised objectively as an armed conflict, in the context of large-scale hostilities, and in a way that is patently inconsistent with the rules of humanitarian law.[44] This is especially clear in terms of its approach to the use of lethal force, where some killings which would be lawful under the criteria of humanitarian law are nonetheless violations of human rights law through the operation of Article 2. It will be recalled that individuals taking a direct part in hostilities are liable to lawful attack under humanitarian law – even in situations where their arrest or detention are possible alternatives. The ECHR, on the other hand, requires that individuals be captured – even during hostilities – unless this poses too great a risk to the security forces.

Nor is the concept of proportionality in the context of humanitarian law analogous to that contained in ECHR Article 2. Humanitarian law is predicated upon the assumption that an armed conflict exists, 'and for that reason expects that there will be civilian casualties when force is used, even if civilians are not directly targeted'.[45] Its provisions are therefore concerned with the issue of proportionality in relation to *the scale of civilian casualties resulting from an attack on a legitimate military objective* – measured in terms of whether or not such incidental losses are 'excessive in relation to the concrete and direct military advantage anticipated'.[46] In contrast, ECHR Article 2 demonstrates human rights law to be based on the 'presumption that the State will take the utmost care to protect the lives of civilians',[47] and considers proportionality in relation to *the protection of the right to life*. The humanitarian law test is therefore 'rather less exacting'.[48] It permits government troops to attack enemy combatants (or, in the context of internal armed conflict, members of enemy armed forces or individuals taking an active part in hostilities), and would prohibit an attack only where the incidental loss of life was considered disproportionate to the anticipated military advantage – not where the loss of life was disproportionate to the aims of ECHR Article 2(2).[49] It is, however, the latter test that has consistently been applied by the European Court of Human Rights, and which can be seen as imposing upon states parties the obligation to protect the lives of all those within their jurisdiction, even in the context of planning and carrying out military operations.[50] As Bowring indicates, 'The outcome could not have been more different than what could have been achieved under IHL'.[51]

Clearly, then, the Court's approach demonstrates a certain degree of conflict between the operation of humanitarian law and human rights in the context of internal armed conflict.[52] In particular, the application of ECHR Article 2 to such situations might be seen to impose what are 'unrealistic expectations of practically eliminating risk to civilian lives'.[53] Abresch, for example, accepts that it may be difficult to apply human rights law to situations of internal armed conflict in a manner that is 'persuasive and realistic'.[54]

In response to such problems, it has been widely suggested that the Court's approach of refusing to permit killings that would be perfectly lawful under humanitarian law is unhelpful, and that humanitarian law ought to be applied to internal armed conflicts as *lex specialis*.[55] The result would be that, even during an internal armed conflict, the Court would need to consider the facts of any given situation in order to determine whether human rights law or humanitarian law was the most appropriate regime – that is, whether the case in question concerned activities that could more accurately be described as law enforcement, or else as hostilities.[56] This is not necessarily easy in the case of internal armed conflict. Nor, indeed, is it necessarily the case that the rules of humanitarian law can be said, without question, to represent *lex specialis* in the context of internal hostilities. As has been outlined above, the rules regulating lawful killing and incidental loss of life are much more developed in the context of international armed conflict than they are for internal armed conflict and, whilst it seems likely that most – if not all – of the relevant provisions can be applied to internal armed conflict as customary law, this position is not universally accepted.[57] In contrast, the European Court of Human Rights' body of jurisprudence (largely mirroring the rules of international armed conflict) is much more developed than the provisions of either common Article 3 or Additional Protocol II.[58]

3. EXTRA-TERRITORIAL MILITARY ACTIVITY

As has been demonstrated, human rights law is an equally valid regulatory regime in the context of internal armed conflict,[59] where military activities are confined to the territory of the state concerned and the relationship tends to be between a state and its nationals. In contrast, it might initially appear that human rights are inapplicable in the context of international armed conflict or other extraterritorial military operations. It should, after all, be recalled that ECHR Article 1 requires states parties to secure the rights set out elsewhere in the Convention to 'everyone within their jurisdiction'. Given that attacks carried out in the context of international armed conflict are likely to be aimed at targets located beyond the territorial limits of the attacking state, it would perhaps seem to be the case that this jurisdictional link is, *prima facie*, missing.[60]

The Strasbourg organs have, however, consistently held that jurisdiction is not necessarily limited geographically, instead turning on the exercise of authority by a state. In the first of the *Cyprus v. Turkey* cases (concerning numerous alleged violations of the Convention arising out of Turkey's 1974 invasion and subsequent occupation of northern Cyprus), for example, the European Commission on Human Rights indicated that the term 'jurisdiction' in Article 1 extended beyond the national territory of contracting parties, and that states parties are accordingly 'bound to secure the said rights and freedoms to all persons under their actual authority and responsibility, whether that authority is exercised within their own territory or abroad'.[61] Continuing to hold that the Turkish armed forces operating in Cyprus were 'authorised agents of Turkey', the Commission stated that they:

> ... bring any other persons or property in Cyprus 'within the jurisdiction' of Turkey, in the sense of Art. 1 of the Convention, to the extent that they exercise control over such persons or property. Therefore, insofar as these armed forces, by their acts or omissions, affect such persons' rights or freedoms under the Convention, the responsibility of Turkey is engaged.[62]

The European Court of Human Rights indicated in even broader terms in *Drozd and Janousek v. France and Spain* that, 'the term "jurisdiction" is not limited to the national territory of the High Contracting Parties; their responsibility can be involved because of acts of their authorities producing effects outside their own territory'.[63]

There can be no doubt that a state's military activities have the capacity to produce extra-territorial effects, or can result in the exercise of authority on the territory of another state. Military occupation is perhaps the clearest example of this, although military attacks on foreign targets can similarly produce significant, and extremely damaging effects beyond the territory of the attacking state. Both types of situation have occurred in a European context in recent years, and it is not surprising, then, that the Court has had occasion to assess the protection of human rights in the context of extra-territorial military activity, bringing into sharp focus thorny questions as to the extent of extra-territorial jurisdiction.

As outlined above, the general approach of the Court has been to require a state party to exercise effective control over another state's territory in order to find a jurisdictional link present for the purposes of ECHR Article 1. Such a level of control is almost inevitably present in the case of military occupation, such as the Turkish occupation of northern Cyprus. Indeed, the 1907 Hague Regulations state in Article 42 that territory is considered to be occupied 'when it is actually placed under the authority of the hostile army', and that 'occupation extends only to the territory where such authority has been established and can be exercised'. This ability to exert authority results in a substantial number of specific obligations, as set out in Geneva Convention IV. It is important to bear in mind, however, that the degree of control exercised by the occupying power is a question of *fact*, and that the obligations imposed by humanitarian law arise out of the effectiveness of the occupation, not its lawfulness.

In light of this, the Court has held Turkey to be legally responsible for the implementation of the ECHR in several cases relating to northern Cyprus. Thus, as outlined in *Loizidou v. Turkey*:

> ... although Article 1 sets limits on the reach of the Convention, the concept of 'jurisdiction' under this provision is not restricted to the national territory of the High Contracting Parties ... the responsibility of Contracting Parties can be involved because of acts of their authorities, whether performed within or outside national boundaries, which produce effects outside their own territory.
>
> Bearing in mind the object and purpose of the Convention, the responsibility of a Contracting Party may also arise when as a consequence of military action – whether lawful or unlawful – it exercises effective control of an area outside its national territory. The obligation to secure, in such an area, the rights and freedoms set out in the Convention derives from the fact of such control whether it be exercised directly, through its armed forces, or through a subordinate local administration.[64]

Having said that, it is noteworthy that in none of the northern Cyprus cases has the Court actually taken a position regarding whether northern Cyprus was occupied territory or not. Hence, there has been no discussion of the extent to which the relevant rules of humanitarian law were relevant. This is perhaps even more striking given a number of the Court's other statements. In *Loizidou*, for example, it asserted it to be 'obvious from the large number of troops engaged in active duties in northern Cyprus that her army exercises effective overall control over that part of the island',[65] and that its responsibility therefore extended to acts of the local 'TRNC' administration, the survival of which was possible only 'by virtue of Turkish military and other support'.[66] The Court also made reference to UN Security Council Resolution 550, expressing its grave concern regarding 'the further secessionist acts in the *occupied* part of the Republic of Cyprus'.[67]

Perhaps most startling, however, was the Court's statement in *Loizidou v. Turkey* (Merits) that the ECHR must be interpreted in light of the rules set out by the 1969 Vienna Convention on the Law of Treaties and that, as such, it 'cannot be interpreted and applied in a vacuum': 'Mindful of the Convention's special character as a human rights treaty, it must also take into account any relevant rules of international law when deciding on disputes concerning its jurisdiction ...'.[68] The Court proceeded, however, to use this only as a means to assess the legitimacy of the TRNC, and not to consider the relevant rules of humanitarian law.[69]

The occupation of northern Cyprus is relatively uncomplicated, however, in that both Turkey and Cyprus are states parties to the ECHR. The Court accordingly found that Turkish responsibility for the application of the Convention necessarily resulted from

Cyprus' inability to ensure the availability of the Convention rights in the portion of its territory occupied by Turkish forces. Any alternative approach would have resulted in: '... a regrettable vacuum in the system of human rights protection in the territory in question by removing from individuals there the benefit of the Convention's fundamental safeguards and their right to call a High Contracting Party to account for violation of their rights in proceedings before the Court'.[70]

More complex is the situation where states parties engage in military operations on the territory of third states who are not parties to the ECHR. A broad reading of the northern Cyprus cases might, after all, suggest that the Convention provides for jurisdiction even when extra-territorial 'effects' result from 'an armed incursion into another State where individuals are captured, tortured, or killed'.[71] Such a role for human rights in the context of actions that are ostensibly subject to the rules of humanitarian law is controversial, and the Court appeared to take a much more restrictive approach to extra-territorial jurisdiction in just such a situation in the *Bankovic* Case.[72]

It will be recalled that *Bankovic* concerned NATO's Operation Allied Force against Serbia in 1999, and, in particular, its aerial attack on the RTS television station in Belgrade. The case was brought by one of the 32 civilian victims of the attack, and by relatives of five others, against the 17 NATO member states also parties to the ECHR.[73] The Court recalled its previous assertions of jurisdiction over extra-territorial acts, but cautioned that these had resulted from 'exceptional' circumstances, where the respondent state: '... through the effective control of the relevant territory and its inhabitants abroad as a consequence of military occupation or through the consent, invitation or acquiescence of the Government of that territory, exercises all or some of the public powers normally ... exercised by that Government'.[74]

The Grand Chamber saw no such jurisdictional link between the NATO states and the victims of the attack in this case, and rejected the application as inadmissible. It asserted that the drafters of the ECHR could have 'adopted a text the same as or similar to the contemporaneous Articles 1 of the four Geneva Conventions' if the intention had been to provide for jurisdiction as wide-ranging as that sought by the applicants,[75] and proceeded to outline a further, geographical justification for its decision; namely, that the attack had taken place on the territory of the former Yugoslavia, which was not a state party to the ECHR, and that the acts complained of were accordingly not within the *espace juridique* of the Convention:

> The Convention was not designed to be applied throughout the world, even in respect of the conduct of Contracting States. Accordingly, the desirability of avoiding a gap or vacuum in human rights protection [as per *Cyprus v. Turkey*] has so far been relied on by the Court in favour of establishing jurisdiction only when the territory in question was one that, but for the specific circumstances, would normally be covered by the Convention.[76]

Not only did this seem inconsistent with a broad reading of the northern Cyprus cases, it was also contrary to the Court's previous admissibility decisions in *Öcalan v. Turkey*,[77] and *Issa and Others v. Turkey*;[78] cases involving the activities of Turkish agents in Kenya and Iraq respectively – neither of which are parties to the ECHR. The Court seemed unconcerned, however, arguing that in neither case had Turkey raised the issue of jurisdiction, and that 'in any event the merits of those cases remain to be decided'.[79] It accordingly avoided passing any comment on the conduct of hostilities by NATO.[80]

The reasoning of the Court has been the subject of intense scrutiny, and not inconsiderable criticism.[81] Some aspects are certainly problematic.[82] And yet, in the context of the role and importance of humanitarian law, the ultimate decision was the right one. Rights and obligations under international humanitarian law derive from factual circumstances. The use of force is prohibited by international law, and yet humanitarian law applies to all armed conflicts. As will be recalled in the context of military occupation, for example, the rights and duties of occupying powers depend on the effectiveness of their occupation – not its lawfulness.

As a matter of *fact*, it is difficult to see the applicants in *Bankovic* as having been subject to the authority of NATO forces. No structured relationship existed for any period of time between the victims and NATO member states, nor had there been any 'assertion or exercise of legal authority, actual or purported, over persons owing some form of allegiance to [those states] or who ha[d] been brought within [their] control'.[83] Rather, the victims were simply located either in, or near, a target.[84] NATO members may well have been responsible in international law for the actions of their armed forces in carrying out the attack, but that does not *per se* imply a relationship between those states and the victims capable of engaging the jurisdiction of the European Court of Human Rights.[85] Nor were the victims left in a legal vacuum:

> A body of law exists which regulates the conduct of hostilities in international armed conflicts: international humanitarian law. Indeed, there existed a Court with jurisdiction over violations of that body of law in the former Yugoslavia at the time of the attack ... That the Prosecutor of the ICTY declined to bring proceedings with regard to the bombing of RTS is not something that can be laid at the door of the European Court of Human Rights, nor should the Court have stepped in to do the Tribunal's work.[86]

The logical consequence is that individuals cannot necessarily complain to the Court regarding alleged violations of the law regulating military (and especially aerial) attacks. *Bankovic* should, however, be construed narrowly, and cannot be taken to mean that jurisdiction does not exist beyond the *espace juridique* of the ECHR.[87] Subsequent jurisprudence confirms this in that, when the Court came to decide *Öcalan* on the merits, it found Turkey responsible for violating ECHR Article 5 in relation to the applicant's detention in Kenya.[88] Clearly beyond the *espace juridique*, the decisive factor for the Court was that the applicant had been detained by agents of Turkey, and was therefore under its jurisdiction in terms of Article 1 from the time of his arrest, by virtue of its physical control over him.[89]

Similarly, *Issa* reiterated that the responsibility of a state could be engaged for actions carried out beyond the geographical limits of the ECHR provided that the requisite level of control could be demonstrated.[90] Despite finding that Turkish troops were not proven to be in the relevant area of northern Iraq at the time of the alleged violation, the Court held that this did not exclude the possibility that, in light of its military operations, Turkey could still be considered to have exercised, 'temporarily, effective overall control of a particular portion of the territory of northern Iraq', and that provided there was:

... sufficient factual basis for holding that, at the relevant time, the victims were within that specific area, it would follow logically that they were within the jurisdiction of Turkey (and not that of Iraq, which is not a Contracting State and clearly does not fall within the legal space ... of the Contracting States ...).[91]

Thus, whilst ultimately the Court did not consider Turkey to have been in effective control of the relevant area, it reaffirmed that:

... a State may also be held accountable for violation of the Convention rights and freedoms of persons who are in the territory of another State, but who are found to be under the former State's authority and control through its agents operating – whether lawfully or unlawfully – in the latter State. Accountability in such situations stems from the fact that Article 1 of the Convention cannot be interpreted so as to allow a State party to perpetrate violations of the Conventions on the territory of another State, which it could not perpetrate on its own territory.[92]

It seems clear, then, that the crucial factor for the Court in assessing human rights protection in the context of extra-territorial military activity is whether the state was exercising effective control over either the territory or the individuals in question, such that they were in a position to ensure respect for the ECHR, and not whether the acts in question occurred within or beyond the geographical limits of the Convention. It also seems clear that the notion of effective control in terms of human rights law does not correspond exactly with that in humanitarian law, and that a lesser degree of control can still result in the imposition of human rights obligations.[93] In *Ilaşcu v. Moldova and Russia*,[94] for example, the applicants were found to come within Russia's jurisdiction on the basis that it had been providing the Transdniestrian separatists with military and political support. As such, the separatist regime had been under 'the effective authority, or at the very least under the decisive influence' of Russia; this despite the presence on Moldovan territory of a relatively small number of troops.[95]

4. CRIMES COMMITTED DURING ARMED CONFLICT

As is clear from the above discussion, the Court has never sought to apply the rules of international humanitarian law in any of its case law, nor has it been willing to use humanitarian law as an interpretative device in the enforcement of the ECHR. Recently, however, it has engaged in some extremely direct and detailed analysis of the laws of war. This can be seen in two particular cases which centred on domestic prosecutions for crimes committed during armed conflicts. The first case, *Korbely v. Hungary*,[96] concerned an applicant who was found by the Hungarian courts to have been responsible for the commission of crimes against humanity – arising from violations of common Article 3 – during the Hungarian Revolution of 1956. The second, *Kononov v. Latvia*,[97] concerned an applicant convicted of war crimes committed during World War II.

In both cases, it was asserted by the applicants that the actions leading to their convictions did not represent crimes at the time they had been committed, and that ECHR Article 7 had therefore been violated. Article 7 provides that:

(1) No one shall be held guilty of any criminal offence on account of any act or omission which did not constitute a criminal offence under national or international law at the time when it was committed …

(2) This article shall not prejudice the trial and punishment of any person for any act or omission which, at the time when it was committed, was criminal according to the general principles of law recognized by civilized nations.

This clearly requires consideration of the way that national or international rules external to the ECHR system have been applied by domestic jurisdictions. As such, although not involving the application of humanitarian law *per se*, both cases did require the Court to assess the state of humanitarian law at the relevant time in order to evaluate whether the actions carried out by the applicants represented criminal offences within that context at the time of their commission or not.

Taking *Korbely* first, the applicant was an officer in the Hungarian military, ordered to overcome a group of armed insurgents and to regain control of the Tata police department. Following what was described as a 'heated dispute' between the applicant and one of the insurgents, the insurgent:

> … reached towards a pocket in his coat and drew his handgun. The applicant responded by resolutely ordering his men to fire. Simultaneously, he fired his submachine gun at [the insurgent in question], who was shot in his chest and abdomen and died immediately. One of the shots fired on the applicant's orders hit another person and three hit yet another person. A further insurgent was shot and subsequently died of his injuries. Two individuals ran out onto the street, where the other platoon of the applicant's men started to shoot at them. One of them suffered a non-lethal injury to his head; the other person was hit by numerous shots and died at the scene.[98]

The Court determined that it was not foreseeable to the applicant at the time (i.e., in 1956) that his actions would constitute a crime against humanity, and that ECHR Article 7 had therefore been violated.[99]

The decision hinged on two factors: (a) the legal requirements of a crime against humanity in 1956; and (b) whether the victim came under the protection of common Article 3 at the time he was shot. It was felt that the Hungarian courts had been preoccupied with the second issue and that, whilst this was important, it had 'no bearing on whether the prohibited actions set out in common Article 3 are to be considered to constitute … crimes against humanity'.[100] Making reference to the Charter of the IMT,[101] and subsequent Statutes of the ICTY,[102] ICTR[103] and ICC,[104] all of which explicitly include murder as a potential crime against humanity, the Court accepted that murder in violation of common Article 3 was, *prima facie*, a possible basis for the commission of a crime against humanity in 1956, but it indicated that certain other elements were also required by international law. Thus, in order for murder to be a crime against humanity, it could not be an isolated act. Rather, the offence in question must result from state policy, in terms of a widespread and systematic attack on the civilian population.[105] According to the Court, whether these constituent elements of a crime against humanity were present in this case was 'open to question'.[106]

As far as the second issue (i.e., the status of the victim) was concerned, the Court was critical of the approach taken by some of the domestic courts regarding the applicability of common Article 3. In particular, it was felt that there had been a degree of mishandling of the question as to the impact of Article 1 of Additional Protocol II on the scope of common Article 3, and thus whether an internal armed conflict could be said to have existed in Hungary at the relevant time. The Supreme Court had, for example, asserted that:

> Having regard to the principle of *nullum crimen sine lege*, the question whether the impugned act constituted a crime prohibited by international law in 1956 will be resolved depending on whether the general conditions set out in the initial clause of common Article 3 were fulfilled.
>
> However, the Conventions did not clarify in common Article 3 or in any other provisions the notion of an 'armed conflict not of an international character occurring in the territory of one of the High Contracting Parties'...
>
> Article 1 of [Additional Protocol II]... provides that the Protocol 'develops and supplements Article 3 common to the Geneva Conventions of 12 August 1949 without modifying its existing conditions of application' ...
>
> Therefore, the Supreme Court has held that the sole authoritative interpretation was the definition set out in Article 1(1-2) of the above Protocol.

On that basis, and unable to determine that the insurgents had operated under a responsible command or controlled substantial territory,[107] it concluded that 'the level of organisation required by the notion of an armed conflict of a non-international character had not been attained'.[108]

Such an approach is problematic. It is certainly true that Additional Protocol II develops and supplements common Article 3, but it does so without affecting the latter's scope of application. In other words, the higher threshold that undoubtedly exists in Article 1 of Additional Protocol II cannot be seen as having limited the scope of common Article 3 in any way. Instead, common Article 3 retains its own independent (and lower) threshold for application.[109] The Court therefore supported the different approach taken by the Hungarian Supreme Court's review bench in June 1999, whereby 'the conditions for the applicability of Additional Protocol II ... are to be applied exclusively to the Protocol itself'.[110] The original scope of common Article 3 is unaffected, so that common Article 3 and Additional Protocol II must not be interpreted 'in conjunction with each other'.[111]

Accordingly, all those not actively participating in hostilities are to receive (and, indeed, received in 1956) the protection of common Article 3, provided that an internal armed conflict existed at the relevant time, as measured by the requirements of common Article 3 itself. The European Court of Human Rights therefore had to determine whether the 'primary' insurgent victim had been actively participating in hostilities, and, if so, whether in the circumstances he could be said to have laid down his arms in conformity with common Article 3. It held that the first question should be answered in the affirmative, on the basis that the victim was the leader of an armed group of insurgents,[112] and the second in the negative, on the basis that he had failed to communicate any intention to surrender 'in a clear and unequivocal way' as required by the relevant rules of humanitarian law.[113] It should perhaps be noted that the authorities provided by the Court in support of this proposition were all subsequent to 1956.

Nonetheless, with some brevity, the Court felt it 'reasonable to assume that the same principles were valid' at the time.[114] The victim was therefore found to have fallen outside the protection of common Article 3, and it was not foreseeable to the applicant that his actions could be construed as a crime against humanity.

The Court's approach to the facts of the case can, perhaps, be called into question. It did explicitly accept that:

> ... it is not its task to substitute itself for the domestic jurisdictions. It is primarily for the national authorities, notably the courts, to resolve problems of interpretation of domestic legislation. This also applies where domestic law refers to rules of general international law or international agreements. The Court's role is confined to ascertaining whether the effects of such an interpretation are compatible with the Convention.[115]

Nonetheless, it chose to interpret the activities – and consequently, the status – of the victim differently from the national courts, who had found that, given the nature of the situation, the applicant 'might have misunderstood [the victim's] motion in reaching into his pocket', but that the victim 'had the intention to hand over the pistol in his possession when the defendant ordered fire'.[116] Leaving this aside, however, its approach to the application of common Article 3 in practice, and the relationship between common Article 3 and Additional Protocol II, was entirely accurate.

An even more detailed exposition of certain humanitarian law rules was provided by the Grand Chamber in *Kononov*,[117] concerning a military operation carried out in the German-occupied village of Mazie Bati by a unit of Soviet Red Partisans, commanded by the applicant, on 27 May 1944. Suspecting six villagers of collaborating with the Nazis, the applicant's unit entered the village wearing Nazi uniforms and searched the homes of the suspects, finding German weapons in each. All of the suspects were shot, killing four of them outright, before two of their houses were set alight, burning one of the wounded suspects plus a further three people (all of whom were women, including the – nine months pregnant – wife of one of the suspects) to death.[118] Kononov was convicted by the Latvian Supreme Court for the killings on the basis that they constituted war crimes, and it fell to the Grand Chamber to determine whether there was a legal basis for the conviction; in particular, whether international law was sufficiently clear and accessible in May 1944 for the applicant to have known at the time that his actions could/would constitute war crimes involving individual criminal responsibility.

The Grand Chamber engaged in a relatively wide-ranging survey of the state of humanitarian law in 1944. Paragraphs 52–142 of the Judgment considered an impressive range of conventional and customary international legal rules, from the 1863 Lieber Code to the 1977 Additional Protocols, alongside examples of war crimes prosecutions ranging from the 1899–1902 US courts-martial regarding its counter-insurgency campaign in the Philippines to the IMT at Nuremburg, and other national prosecutions following World War II. It ultimately held that the applicant's conviction for war crimes did not violate Article 7.

The Court first determined that the applicant and his unit were combatants, although it did also note that they were wearing *Wehrmacht* uniforms, and so not necessarily complying with all of the relevant legal requirements for combatant status (stated to have crystallised in international law before their consolidation in Article 1 of the 1907

Hague Regulations, which itself represented customary law by 1939).[119] The legal status of at least the male villagers was less certain.[120] The Chamber of the European Court of Human Rights had previously found legitimate grounds to consider them collaborators and that, as such (and even if they failed to meet all of the international legal requirements for combatant status) they were not automatically considered to be civilians by the *jus in bello*. It therefore held that their deaths were not '*per se* contrary to the laws and customs of war as codified by the Hague Regulations 1907'.[121]

This was a misapplication of humanitarian law. Even if the villagers had collaborated with the Nazis, they remained civilians – and protected from attack – unless, and only for such time as, their collaboration constituted their direct participation in hostilities. This was not necessarily easy to determine (especially given the substantial period of time between the facts in question and the case itself), and the Grand Chamber therefore elected 'to begin its analysis on the basis of a hypothesis most favourable to the applicant', according to which the villagers could be considered either to have been combatants (through their participation in hostilities in a formal auxiliary capacity), or else civilians having participated in hostilities.[122] In neither situation, however, did the Grand Chamber consider their deaths to have been lawful.

The judgment determined that, by 1944, international law clearly provided: (a) that the distinction between civilians and combatants was 'a cornerstone of the laws and customs of war', whereby civilians could be the subject of lawful attack only for as long as they took a direct part in hostilities;[123] and (b) that combatants who were captured, surrendered or rendered *hors de combat* were entitled to prisoner of war status and humane treatment.[124] Even had their participation in hostilities represented, or involved, violations of the *jus in bello*, they remained subject to arrest, fair trial and – *only then* – subsequent lawful punishment.[125] As such, the Court held that sufficiently clear grounds for the applicant's prosecution existed in that the activities he had been involved in were all widely recognised as war crimes in May 1944,[126] and states were permitted (even if they were not by then legally required) to prosecute individuals for such activities.[127] Thus:

> Given his position as a commanding military officer... [and] having regard to the flagrantly unlawful nature of the ill-treatment and killing of the nine villagers in the established circumstances of the operation on 27 May 1944 ... even the most cursory reflection by the applicant, would have indicated that, at the very least, the impugned acts risked being counter to the laws and customs of war as understood at that time and, notably, risked constituting war crimes for which, as commander, he could be held individually and criminally accountable.[128]

5. CONCLUSIONS

Despite suggestions that the European Court of Human Rights has been remiss in failing to consider the rules of humanitarian law in relation to military activities, its approach has much to commend it. Jurisprudence to date suggests that individuals who are killed or injured by extra-territorial aerial attacks are unlikely to be within the jurisdiction of the attacking state – and that they may not complain to the Court as a result, whereas states are likely to be held to account in terms of ensuring ECHR rights where they exercise effective authority over the territory of a third state – as is the case in military occupation. Both approaches seem correct.

Likewise, the application of human rights law alone to situations of internal armed conflict, achieved through ECHR Article 2 and with no supporting reference to humanitarian law, has been both reasonable and sensible. Whilst it may perhaps seem that the Court has been willing to collude in the fiction that armed conflicts did not exist in south-east Turkey or in Chechnya, the unwillingness of the states in question to accept the relevance and/or application of humanitarian law (and to seek to derogate from its human rights obligations pursuant to Article 15), means that the Court has been right to disregard the leeway that humanitarian law might afford in the use of lethal force and to hold states bound by the stricter obligations imposed by human rights law. The approach also provides the potential for more effective observance of the law by states, in that the acceptance of human rights rules applicable to every conceivable situation is likely to be much easier politically than to admit that the situation is '"out of control", or even out of the ordinary'.[129]

Finally, the Court's willingness to engage in detailed consideration of the rules of humanitarian law, and individual criminal responsibility for their violation, in the context of Article 7 indicates that there is no general antipathy to the regime, and that it is capable of providing a fairly nuanced discussion of the relevant provisions. The 2008 *Kononov* decision does demonstrate that the treatment and (indirect) application of humanitarian law is not always as accurate as might be desirable, but this is not a defect unique to the European Court of Human Rights.

NOTES

* Professor of International Law, University of Hull Law School, United Kingdom.
1. *Legal Consequences of the Construction of a Wall in the Occupied Palestinian Territory*, Advisory Opinion, I.C.J. Reports 2004, para. 106. An example of how the I.C.J. saw this working in practical terms can be seen in *Legality of the Threat or Use of Nuclear Weapons*, Advisory Opinion, I.C.J. Reports 1996, para. 25, where, in the context of the right to life, it stated that, 'The test of what is an arbitrary deprivation of life [under ICCPR Article 6]… can only be decided by reference to the law applicable in armed conflict and not deduced from the terms of the Covenant itself'.
2. See, e.g., A. Reidy, 'The Approach of the European Commission and Court of Human Rights to International Humanitarian Law', *International Review of the Red Cross* 324 (1998): 516.
3. R. Higgins, 'The International Court of Justice and the European Court of Human Rights: Partners for the Protection of Human Rights', in a speech delivered at the ceremony marking the 50th Anniversary of the European Court of Human Rights, 30 January 2009, available at: http://www.echr.coe.int/ NR/rdonlyres/38D1E6A5-DE24-42BD-BC3D-45CCCC8A7F8A/0/30012009PresidentHigginsHearing_ eng_.pdf (accessed 12 February 2012).
4. See, in particular, *McCann and others v. The United Kingdom*, ECtHR, Application No. 18984/91, Grand Chamber Judgment of 27 September 1995.
5. W. Abresch, 'A Human Rights Law of Internal Armed Conflict: The European Court of Human Rights in Chechnya', *European Journal of International Law* 16:4 (2005): 756.
6. Common Article 3 provides that its application 'shall not affect the legal status of the Parties to the conflict', whilst Article 3(1) of Additional Protocol II states that 'Nothing in this Protocol shall be invoked for the purpose of affecting the sovereignty of a State'. See L. Moir, *The Law of Internal Armed Conflict* (Cambridge: Cambridge University Press, 2002), 65–67, 95–96 and 119–120.
7. See, e.g., *Akdivar and others v. Turkey*, ECtHR, Application No. 21893/93, Grand Chamber Judgment of 16 September 1996, paras 13 and 70.

8. For a general discussion of the scope of application of common Article 3 see Moir, *supra* note 6, at 31–45. In relation to categorisation of the situation in South-East Turkey, see Abresch, *supra* note 5, at 755.

9. *Güleç v. Turkey*, ECtHR, Application No. 21593/93, Judgment of 27 July 1998, para. 81.

10. *Ergi v. Turkey*, ECtHR, Application No. 23818/94, Judgment of 28 July 1998, para. 80.

11. See, e.g., Abresch, *supra* note 5, at 754; Moir, *supra* note 6, at 127–128; and Human Rights Watch, 'A Summary of Human Rights Watch Research on Attacks on Fleeing Civilians and Civilian Convoys during the War in Chechnya, Russia, between October 1999 and February 2000' (April 2003), referred to in *Isayeva and others v. Russia*, ECtHR, Application Nos 57947/00, 57948/00 and 57949/00, Judgment of 24 February 2005, paras 102–104, and *Isayeva v. Russia*, ECtHR, Application No. 57950/00, Judgment of 24 February 2005, paras 113–115.

12. *Isayeva v. Russia*, *supra* note 11, para. 180. See also *Isayeva and others v. Russia*, *supra* note 11, para. 181. Later pronouncements seemed even more explicit. See, e.g., *Dzhamayeva and others v. Russia*, ECtHR, Application No. 43170/04, Judgment of 14 September 2009, para. 88, referring to 'an armed conflict, such as that in Chechnya'. The Court nonetheless went on to discuss the case in terms of 'the difficulties in *policing* modern societies' (emphasis added).

13. *Isayeva v. Russia*, *supra* note 11, para. 191.

14. See, e.g., *Juan Carlos Abella v. Argentina*, IACommHR, Case 11.137, 18 November 1997, para. 158, footnote 19, where common Article 3 is described as 'essentially pure human rights law'. See Moir, *supra* note 6, at 197–208; and L. Moir, 'Decommissioned? International Humanitarian Law and the Inter-American Human Rights System', *Human Rights Quarterly* 25 (2003): 193–194.

15. M. Sassòli and L.M. Olsen, 'The Relationship between International Humanitarian Law and Human Rights Law Where it Matters: Admissible Killing and Internment of Fighters in Non-international Armed Conflicts', *International Review of the Red Cross* 871 (2008): 600–601.

16. See, e.g., Y. Dinstein, *The Conduct of Hostilities under the Law of International Armed Conflict*, 2nd edition (Cambridge: Cambridge University Press, 2010), 34: 'Enemy combatants in an international armed conflict can be attacked at all times and in all circumstances.'

17. Abresch, *supra* note 5, at 757.

18. See, e.g., Abresch, *supra* note 5, at 757; Moir, *supra* note 6, at 59–60; UK Ministry of Defence, *The Manual of the Law of Armed Conflict* (Oxford: Oxford University Press, 2004), 389–390. Indeed, neither common Article 3 nor Additional Protocol II seek to regulate hostilities at all – at least beyond the relatively general Article 13 of Additional Protocol II, requiring that the civilian population be immune from attack and protected from the effects of hostilities.

19. The International Committee of the Red Cross has recently published its guidance in the question: see N. Melzer, *Interpretive Guidance on the Notion of Direct Participation in Hostilities under International Humanitarian Law* (Geneva: International Committee of the Red Cross, 2009). For discussion, see D. Akande, 'Clearing the Fog of War? The ICRC's Interpretive Guidance on Direct Participation in Hostilities', *International and Comparative Law Quarterly* 59 (2010): 180.

20. See Sassòli and Olsen, *supra* note 15, at 607–608.

21. Although it has been argued that, 'considering that at the time when the ECHR was drafted, internal armed conflicts were regulated by international law at a very limited level, the term war stated in article 15 should be… understood as international war'. See K. Altiparmak, '*Bankovic*: An Obstacle to the Application of the European Convention on Human Rights in Iraq?,' *Journal of Conflict and Security Law* 9 (2004): 235.

22. *McCann v. The United Kingdom*, *supra* note 4, para. 149.

23. Ibid., para. 194.

24. See C. Droege, 'The Interplay between International Humanitarian Law and International Human Rights Law in Situations of Armed Conflict', *Israel Law Review* 40 (2007): 344.

25. *McCann v. The United Kingdom*, *supra* note 4, paras 200–214.

26. See Abresch, *supra* note 5, at 753, contrasting humanitarian law's 'different regimes of relatively rigid rules'.

27. Abresch, *supra* note 5,759.

28. *Ergi v. Turkey*, *supra* note 10, para. 79. See also *Ahmet Özkan and others v. Turkey*, ECtHR, Application No. 21689/93, Judgment of 6 April 2004, para. 297. The Court took the same approach in *Isayeva v. Russia*, *supra* note 11, para. 176, and *Isayeva and others v. Russia*, *supra* note 11, para. 177, although in slightly different terms.

29. *Güleç v. Turkey*, *supra* note 9.

30. I.e., *Isayeva v. Russia*, and *Isayeva and others v. Russia, supra* note 11.

31.   *Güleç v. Turkey*, *supra* note 9, paras 69–73 and 77–82.
32.   In *Isayeva and others v. Russia*, *supra* note 11, the military had used 12 S-24 non-guided air-to-ground missiles, each creating several thousand pieces of shrapnel, with an impact radius in excess of 300 metres (para. 195), whilst in *Isayeva v. Russia*, *supra* note 11, the military had employed FAB-250 and FAB-500 free-falling high-explosion bombs with a damage radius exceeding 1,000 metres, in addition to other non-guided heavy combat weapons (para. 190).
33.   *Isayeva v. Russia*, *supra* note 11, para. 180. See Abresch, *supra* note 5, at 752, who asks whether this approach represents 'Euphemism? Or paradigm shift?'.
34.   *Isayeva v. Russia*, *supra* note 11, paras 180 and 191 (emphasis added).
35.   A. Orakhelashvili, 'The Interaction Between Human Rights and Humanitarian Law: Fragmentation, Conflict, Parallelism, or Convergence?', *European Journal of International Law* 19 (2008): 174.
36.   A significant body of opinion sees the Court's willingness to apparently borrow phraseology and concepts from humanitarian law as a means of relying on principles close to humanitarian law, whilst 'outwardly only applying the European Convention of Human Rights'. See, e.g., Droege, *supra* note 24, at 346; C. Byron, 'A Blurring of the Boundaries: The Application of International Humanitarian Law by Human Rights Bodies', *Virginia Journal of International Law* 47 (2007): 856.
37.   Reidy, *supra* note 2, at 526–527, an approach she saw as 'encouraging'. See also H.-J. Heintze, 'On the Relationship between Human Rights Law Protection and International Humanitarian Law', *International Review of the Red Cross* 856 (2004): 810. Bowring, on the other hand, was extremely critical of the suggestion, failing to see 'how the use of the alien framework of IHL in such a case would be "encouraging"'. See B. Bowring, 'Fragmentation, *Lex Specialis* and the Tensions in the Jurisprudence of the European Court of Human Rights', *Journal of Conflict and Security Law* 14 (2010): 496.
38.   Para. 79.
39.   Para. 191.
40.   Paras 175 and 197.
41.   Although the precautionary measures as set out in Article 57 of Additional Protocol I can probably be considered to represent customary rules applicable both to international and internal armed conflicts. See J.M. Henckaerts and L. Doswald-Beck, *Customary International Humanitarian Law, Volume I: Rules* (Cambridge: Cambridge University Press, 2005), 51–55; C. Greenwood, 'Customary Law Status of the 1977 Geneva Protocols', in *Humanitarian Law of Armed Conflict: Challenges Ahead*, eds A.J.M. Delissen and G.J. Tanja (Dordrecht: Martinus Nijhoff Publisher, 1991), 111; and Byron, *supra* note 36, at 853.
42.   Abresch, *supra* note 5, at 746.
43.   Ibid. It would, nonetheless, seem to be the case that he believes humanitarian law to be the most appropriate legal regime. See discussion in Bowring, *supra* note 37, at 495–496.
44.   Abresch, *supra* note 5, at 742.
45.   Bowring, *supra* note 37, at 492.
46.   Additional Protocol I, Article 51(5)(b).
47.   Bowring, *supra* note 37, at 493. See also Droege, *supra* note 24, at 345.
48.   Byron, *supra* note 36, at 855.
49.   Although there is at least an element of proportionality in terms of attacks on enemy forces through the customary rule that weapons employed in an attack must not be such as to cause unnecessary suffering. See Henckaerts and Doswald-Beck, *supra* note 41, at 237–244.
50.   Abresch, *supra* note 5, at 762.
51.   Bowring, *supra* note 37, at 493.
52.   As discussed by Abresch, *supra* note 5, at 764–766, there is also tension between human rights and humanitarian law in their approaches to the relationship between *jus ad bellum* and *jus in bello*: humanitarian law is largely concerned with whether the means of attack is proportionate to the ends, whereas human rights law requires further consideration of whether the ends can be justified according to Article 2(2). See, e.g., *Isayeva and others v. Russia*, *supra* note 11, para. 181: 'Given the extent of the conflict in Chechnya at the relevant time, the Court will assume … that the military reasonably considered that there was an attack or a risk of attack from illegal insurgents, and that the air strike was a legitimate response to that attack.' It is, however, doubtful whether a *jus ad bellum* in relation to internal conflict exists, and Abresch sees the Court's approach as 'indistinguishable in its result from an analysis of indiscriminate attacks and precautionary measures' in any case.
53.   Byron, *supra* note 36, at 856.

54. Abresch, *supra* note 5, at 750: 'Human rights law must be realistic in the sense of not categorically forbidding killing in the context of armed conflict or otherwise making compliance with the law and victory in battle impossible to achieve at once.' Unlike the European Court of Human Rights, the Inter-American Commission on Human Rights considered this too difficult, accepting in *Abella v. Argentina, supra* note 14, para. 161, that its 'ability to resolve claimed violations of [the right to life] arising out of an armed conflict may not be possible in many cases by reference to Article 4 of the American Convention alone'.

55. Although see Bowring, *supra* note 37, at 486, who criticises this approach as a 'category error', dismissing the suggestion that human rights law and humanitarian law have *any* relationship with each other as 'Chalk... being compared with, or even substituted by, cheese'.

56. See, e.g., Droege, *supra* note 24, at 346.

57. See Abresch, *supra* note 5, at 749–750. Henckaerts and Doswald-Beck, *supra* note 41, at 3–8 and 51–55, assert that this is the case, but Abresch argues that their position is misleading, in that it 'typically infers that military manuals and declarations by states are (a) intended as statements of international law, rather than domestic law or policy, and (b) apply to internal armed conflicts unless explicitly limited to international armed conflicts. These assumptions appear unwarranted. When ... states are reluctant to acknowledge the applicability of treaty-based humanitarian law, it is difficult to credit that they consider themselves bound under customary humanitarian law.'

58. Abresch, ibid., 747 and 762.

59. At least in terms of the legal obligations and responsibilities placed upon states.

60. See, e.g., Sassòli and Olsen, *supra* note 15, at 600. They continue to point out that the application of human rights law to international hostilities is often moot, in that, 'with regard to many issues, one or other of the branches simply contains no rules. There is nothing in humanitarian law about the freedom of the press in occupied territories, and human rights law says nothing about whether and how combatants have to distinguish themselves from the civilian population.'

61. *Cyprus v. Turkey*, ECtHR, Application Nos 6780/74 and 6950/75, Commission Decision on Admissibility, 26 May 1975, para. 8.

62. Ibid., para. 10.

63. *Drozd and Janousek v. France and Spain*, ECtHR, Application No. 12747/87, Judgment of 26 June 1992, para. 91. The case concerned the activities of French and Spanish judges in an Andorran court, with the Court asserting that, '[t]he question to be decided here is whether the acts complained of ... can be attributed to France or Spain or both, even though they were not performed in the territory of those States'.

64. *Loizidou v. Turkey*, ECtHR, Application No. 15318/89, Preliminary Objections, Grand Chamber Judgment of 23 March 1995, para. 62. The last sentence is aimed at overcoming Turkey's claim that it was not the appropriate respondent, but that this should have been the 'allegedly independent and autonomous' Turkish Republic of Northern Cyprus (TRNC).

65. *Loizidou v. Turkey*, ECtHR, Application No. 15318/89, Merits, Judgment of 18 December 1996, para. 56.

66. *Cyprus v. Turkey*, ECtHR, Application No. 25781/94, Grand Chamber Judgment of 10 May 2001, para. 77.

67. See, e.g., *Loizidou v. Turkey, supra* note 65, para. 42; and *Cyprus v. Turkey*, ibid., para. 14. See S/RES/550, 11 May 1984 (emphasis added), and discussion in Heintze, *supra* note 37, at 806–809.

68. Para. 43.

69. A failure which has been criticised in light of the fact that the case concerned interference with property rights, and that reference to Article 49 of Geneva Convention IV may well have supported the Court's Decision. See Heintze, *supra* note 37, at 807–808.

70. *Cyprus v. Turkey, supra* note 66, para. 78.

71. Byron, *supra* note 36, at 870.

72. *Bankovic and others v. Belgium and others*, ECtHR, Application No. 52207/99, Grand Chamber Decision on Admissibility, 12 December 2001.

73. Belgium, the Czech Republic, Denmark, France, Germany, Greece, Hungary, Iceland, Italy, Luxembourg, the Netherlands, Norway, Poland, Portugal, Spain, Turkey and the United Kingdom.

74. *Bankovic and others v. Belgium and others, supra* note 72, para. 71.

75. Ibid., para. 75.

76. Ibid., para. 80.

77. *Öcalan v. Turkey*, ECtHR, Application No. 46221/99, Decision on Admissibility, 14 December 2000.

78. *Issa and others v. Turkey*, ECtHR, Application No. 31821/96, Decision on Admissibility, 30 May 2000.
79. *Bankovic and others v. Belgium and others*, *supra* note 72, para. 81. Whether this was strictly true in the case of *Öcalan* has been disputed: see Altiparmak, *supra* note 21, at 237. Nonetheless, the clear implication is that, had Turkey objected to jurisdiction under Article 1, 'the Court would have accepted this plea and held the application inadmissible'. See M. Happold, *'Bankovic v. Belgium* and the Territorial Scope of the European Convention on Human Rights', *Human Rights Law Review* 3(2003): 82.
80. A subsequent case also addressed the bombing, in the context of Italy's unwillingness to entertain a claim for compensation arising from an alleged violation of humanitarian law as indicated in Additional Protocol I, Article 91. The applicants were found to have a jurisdictional link, having first brought the case at the domestic level, but the Court determined that Article 91 provided obligations only between states, and did not therefore entail a right to reparation for individuals. See *Markovic and others v. Italy*, ECtHR, Application No. 1398/03, Grand Chamber Judgment of 14 December 2006, and discussion in S. Shah, 'Seeking Remedies for Violations of International Humanitarian Law: *Markovic v. Italy*', *Human Rights Law Review* 7 (2007): 412.
81. See, e.g., Byron, *supra* note 36, at 869–878; Altiparmak, *supra* note 21, at 223–234; Happold, *supra* note 79; R. Wilde, 'Legal "Black Hole"? Extraterritorial State Action and International Treaty Law on Civil and Political Rights', *Michigan Journal of International Law* 26 (2005): 792–801; A. Ruth and M. Trilsch, *'Bankovic v. Belgium* (Admissibility) Application No. 52207/99', *American Journal of International Law* 97 (2003): 168; Droege, *supra* note 24, at 328–329.
82. Perhaps especially the suggestion in para. 71 that what matters is whether extra-territorial jurisdiction is lawful or not, with unlawful exercises of jurisdiction falling outside the Convention. The Decision also leads to an apparent distinction between what a state can do internally and externally, and depending on whether the territory in question is that of a state party or not. For an excellent discussion of these issues, see Happold, *supra* note 79, at 87–88 in particular.
83. The argument made by the respondents in *Bankovic and others v. Belgium and others*, *supra* note 72, para. 36.
84. See Happold, *supra* note 79, at 90. As to whether a television station would be a legitimate military target, see, e.g., W.J. Fenrick, 'Targeting and Proportionality during the NATO Bombing Campaign Against Yugoslavia', *European Journal of International Law* 12 (2001): 489; A.P.V. Rogers, 'What is a Legitimate Military Target?', in *International Conflict and Security Law: Essays in Memory of Hilaire McCoubrey*, eds R. Burchill, N.D. White and J. Morris (Cambridge: Cambridge University Press, 2005), 160.
85. It has been suggested that states retain control over their armed forces acting abroad, and that this imputability should be sufficient to trigger jurisdiction under a broadly-interpreted Article 1. See, e.g., A. Orakhelashvili, 'Restrictive Interpretation of Human Rights Treaties in the Recent Jurisprudence of the European Court of Human Rights,' *European Journal of International Law* 14 (2003): 540; and Altiparmak, *supra* note 21, at 224.
86. Happold, *supra* note 79, at 90.
87. Wilde, *supra* note 81, at 796, suggests that *Bankovic* is best seen as a 'limited response' to a particular case, rather than a general statement of principle; and that nothing in *Bankovic* excludes 'the notion that the language in the *Cyprus v. Turkey* case speaks to a more general policy objective'.
88. *Öcalan v. Turkey*, ECtHR, Application No. 46621/99, Grand Chamber Judgment of 12 May 2005.
89. Ibid., para. 91.
90. *Issa and Others v. Turkey*, ECtHR, Application No. 31821/96, Judgment of 16 November 2004, para. 71.
91. Ibid., para. 74.
92. Ibid., para. 71.
93. That is not to say that, even during a military occupation, the level of control will always be sufficient to engage responsibility in terms of human rights law. See, e.g., the British case of *Al Skeini and others v. Secretary of State for Defence*, *UKHL* 26 (2007), where the deaths of 5 civilians during military operations in Iraqi territory nominally under the control of UK troops were found to have occurred in a context of insufficient effective control. Only in the case of the death of Baha Mousa, who was in the custody of UK troops at the time, was the level of control deemed adequate to invoke jurisdiction. The case provides further confirmation that the obligation to ensure ECHR rights cannot depend solely on whether the occupied state is a party to the Convention or not. Further cases arising

from the occupation of Iraq seems likely. See, e.g., *Al-Saadoon and Mufdhi v. United Kingom*, ECtHR, Application No. 61498/08, Judgment of 2 March 2010.

94. *Ilaşcu and others v. Moldova and Russia*, ECtHR, Application No. 48787/99, Judgment of 8 July 2004.

95. Ibid., para. 392. There had been only 2000 Russian troops in the area, compared to over 30 000 Turkish troops in northern Cyprus (see para. 355). The Court reaffirmed, however, at para. 315, that '[i]t is not necessary to determine whether a Contracting Party actually exercises detailed control over the policies and actions of the authorities in the area situated outside its national territory, since even overall control of the area may engage the responsibility of the Contracting Party concerned'.

96. *Korbely v. Hungary*, ECtHR, Application No. 9174/02, Grand Chamber Judgment of 19 September 2008.

97. *Kononov v. Latvia*, ECtHR, Application No. 36376/04, Grand Chamber Judgment of 17 May 2010.

98. Paras 14–15. The accuracy of this has, however, been criticised. See below.

99. Para. 95.

100. *Korbely v. Hungary*, *supra* note 96, para. 80.

101. Charter of the International Military Tribunal, 8 August 1945, Article 6(c).

102. Statute of the International Criminal Tribunal for the Former Yugoslavia, 1993, Article 5.

103. Statute of the International Criminal Tribunal for Rwanda, 1994, Article 3.

104. Statute of the International Criminal Court, 1998, Article 7.

105. Paras 82–83. See the requirements as set out in the Statutes of the ICTY, ICTR and ICC. The Court stated in paragraph 82 that, even by 1956, the IMT requirement of a nexus between crimes against humanity and armed conflict may no longer have been relevant. This is certainly accepted as true today, as illustrated by Article 7 of the ICC Statute. Note, however, that Article 5 of the ICTY Statute reintroduces the requirement for the purposes of that Tribunal – a step that the ICTY has accepted 'deviates from the development of the doctrine after the Nuremberg Charter' (*Prosecutor v. Tadić*, ICTY, Judgment, 7 May 1997, Case No. IT-94-1-T, para. 627). See Moir, *supra* note 6, at 148–149.

106. Para. 85.

107. At least outside Budapest; insurgents within the capital were found to have 'controlled 3 to 4 square kilometres… [although] the revolutionary groups did not fully close off the area and the government forces could pass through it, though with losses'.

108. Supreme Court Decision, 5 November 1998. See *Korbely*, para. 32, and the earlier Decisions of the Military Bench of the Budapest Regional Court (29 May 1995, and 7 May 1998), outlined at paras 23 and 31.

109. See Moir, *supra* note 6, at 100–103.

110. Hungarian Supreme Court review bench Decision, 28 June 1999, reproduced in *Korbely v. Hungary*, *supra* note 96, para. 34.

111. *Korbely v. Hungary*, *supra* note 96, para. 87.

112. Para. 89.

113. Para. 90. The Court relied upon the International Committee of the Red Cross, *Commentary on the Additional Protocols of 8 June 1977 to the Geneva Conventions of 12 August 1949* (Geneva: ICRC, 1987), paras 1618–1619, where it is stated that, '[i]n general, a soldier who wishes to indicate that he is no longer capable of engaging in combat, or that he intends to cease combat, lays down his arms and raises his hands'. In particular, '*[i]f the intention to surrender is indicated in an absolutely clear manner*, the adversary must cease fire immediately' (emphasis added). Reference was also made to Henckaerts and Doswald-Beck, *supra* note 41, at Rule 47, protecting 'anyone who clearly expresses an intention to surrender'; and the UN Secretary-General's Report, 'Respect for Human Rights in Armed Conflict', UN Doc. A/8052, 18 September 1970, para. 107, indicating the principle that it should be 'prohibited to kill or harm a combatant who has obviously laid down his arms or who has obviously no longer any weapons', and that intent to surrender should be 'clearly conveyed'.

114. Para. 90. It is true that Article 23(c) of the 1907 Hague Regulations declared it forbidden to 'kill or wound an enemy who, having laid down his arms … has surrendered', and that similar provisions were to be found in the Lieber Code of 1863, the Brussels Declaration of 1874 and the Oxford Manual of 1880. None of these, however, discussed or indicated the appropriate method of surrender, and some further discussion by the Court might have been useful.

115. Para. 72.

116. The findings of fact of the Military Bench of the Budapest Regional Court in its Decision of 18 January 2001 are reproduced in para. 42. In its Appeal Judgment of 8 November 2001, the Supreme Court went even further, holding the correct conclusion to be that the defendant 'knew that the victim

intended to hand over the gun, rather than to attack with it'. See para. 44. In the Joint Dissenting Opinion of Judges Lorenzen, Tulkens, Zagrebelsky, Fura-Sanström and Popović, para. 2, the European Court of Human Rights' approach is roundly criticised: '... the majority, without any explanation, head off in a different direction and, on a flimsy, uncertain basis, quite simply substitute their own findings of fact for those of the Hungarian judicial authorities. In view of the complexity of the task of reconstructing the facts of the case more than fifty years after they occurred, we see no reason to place more reliance on the conclusions reached by the Court than on those of the domestic courts. On the contrary, we consider that the national courts were in a better position to assess all the available facts and evidence.'

117. Addressing many of the deficiencies of a Chamber Decision of 24 July 2008, which found (by four votes to three) that there had been a violation of Article 7. Following a request by Latvia, the case was subsequently referred to the Grand Chamber. For criticism of the Chamber's Decision, see G. Pinzauti, 'The European Court of Human Rights' Incidental Application of International Criminal Law and Humanitarian Law', *Journal of International Criminal Justice* 6 (2008): 1043.

118. Paras 15–20.

119. Paras 200–201. The requirements considered were those outlined in Articles 49, 57 and 63–65 of the Lieber Code, Article 9 of the Brussels Declaration, and Article 2 of the Oxford Manual. The 1907 Hague Regulations were found to be declaratory of customary international law, at least by 1939, in the IMT (Nuremberg) Judgment. See also para. 217, where the domestic court was found to have acted reasonably in finding such conduct to be a violation of Article 23(b) of the Hague Regulations, and accordingly the separate crime of treacherous wounding and killing.

120. The Chamber's approach to the female victims was that their situation had either been the same (if they had also assisted the German administration), or else that their deaths had resulted from an 'abuse of authority', which did not violate humanitarian law, and was therefore statute time barred in domestic law. See para. 147.

121. *Kononov v. Latvia*, ECtHR, Application No. 36376/04, Judgment of 24 July 2008, outlined in the Grand Chamber Judgment, para. 146.

122. Para. 194.

123. Para. 203.

124. Para. 202.

125. I.e., in no circumstances could they be liable to summary execution. See para. 204.

126. Paras 214–227.

127. Paras 205–213.

128. Para. 238.

129. Abresch, *supra* note 5, at 757.

24. The African Union and international humanitarian law

*Djacoba Liva Tehindrazanarivelo**

On 11 July 2000 in Lomé, Togo, the leaders of 53 African States adopted the Constitutive Act of the African Union (AU), which abrogates the Charter of the Organization of African Unity (OAU) of 25 May 1963 and organizes the succession of the OAU by the AU.[1] While the OAU Charter insisted on principles and objectives reflecting the African people's struggle for political independence, human dignity and economic emancipation, the AU Constitutive Act added new principles and organs relating to the multifaceted challenges that continue to confront the African continent. These include the issues of socio-economic development, unity, conflict prevention and resolution, the promotion and protection of human and peoples' rights, democratization, good governance and the rule of law.[2] Despite these differences in the OAU and AU core objectives and principles, there is an equal feature of the two successive African continental organisations: on the one hand, neither the OAU Charter nor the AU Constitutive Act expressly mention the words 'International Humanitarian Law' (IHL) while, on the other, the two organisations have each adopted decisions and treaties relating to the promotion of and respect for IHL by African States and non-State armed groups. This singular feature gives an indication of the intriguing connection between the AU and IHL, the object of the present chapter.

Actually, there is no direct reference to IHL in the AU proclaimed objectives and principles, even though one could perceive allusions to humanitarian rules and principles in the AU objective to 'Promote and protect human and peoples' rights in accordance with the African Charter on Human and Peoples' Rights and *other relevant human rights instruments*';[3] in the 'right of the Union to intervene in a Member State pursuant to a decision of the Assembly in respect of grave circumstances, namely war crimes, genocide and crimes against humanity';[4] and in the AU principle on the 'respect for the sanctity of human life, condemnation and rejection of impunity and political assassination, acts of terrorism and subversive activities'.[5] This is to say that notwithstanding the lack of express mention of IHL in the AU Constitutive Act, there is undeniably an AU commitment to promote, respect and ensure respect for IHL. Such a commitment could be seen in the AU instruments relating to human rights and humanitarian concerns (I), in its peace and security instruments and activities (II), and in the AU principles and measures relating to the sanction for the violation of IHL (III). As this chapter comes under the 'Monitoring Mechanisms' part of the Handbook, we will particularly consider in these planned three sections how the 53 AU Member States act through the AU organs[6] to uphold their obligation to respect and ensure respect for IHL in the conflict situations in Africa, as provided for in common Article 1 of the Four Geneva Conventions to which all of them are parties, except the Saharawi Arab Democratic Republic (SADR).[7]

1.   THE COMMITMENT TO RESPECT AND PROMOTE
     INTERNATIONAL HUMANITARIAN LAW IN AFRICAN UNION
     INSTRUMENTS RELATING TO HUMAN RIGHTS AND
     HUMANITARIAN CONCERNS

Inspired by the AU objective and principles mentioned earlier, the AU has adopted decisions and treaties relating to human rights and humanitarian concerns in which express references to IHL are observed. Such references are also present in the findings of the African Commission on Human and Peoples' Rights.

1.1   The References to International Humanitarian Law in African Union Treaties, Solemn Declarations and Decisions

1.1.1   The references in African Union treaties

Adopted under the OAU era, the *African Charter on the Rights and Welfare of the Child*[8] contains, in its Article 22, States' undertaking 'to respect and ensure respect for rules of international humanitarian law applicable in armed conflicts which affect the child' (para. 1), and also an obligation of States Parties to 'take all necessary measures to ensure that no child shall take a direct part in hostilities and refrain in particular, from recruiting any child' (para. 2). Furthermore, States Parties 'shall, in accordance with their obligations under international humanitarian law, protect the civilian population in armed conflicts and shall take all feasible measures to ensure the protection and care of children who are affected by armed conflicts. Such rules shall also apply to children in situations of internal armed conflicts, tension and strife' (para. 3).

Likewise, the AU *Protocol to the African Charter on Human and Peoples' Rights on the Rights of Women in Africa*[9] encompasses in its Article 11 relating to the protection of women in armed conflict two undertakings by States Parties and two specific obligations linked to IHL. First, States Parties undertake 'to respect and ensure respect for the rules of international humanitarian law applicable in armed conflict situations, which affect the population, particularly women' (para. 1) and 'to protect asylum seeking women, refugees, returnees and internally displaced persons, against all forms of violence, rape and other forms of sexual exploitation, and to ensure that such acts are considered war crimes, genocide and/or crimes against humanity and that their perpetrators are brought to justice before a competent criminal jurisdiction' (para. 3). Secondly, States shall, 'in accordance with the obligations incumbent upon them under international humanitarian law, protect civilians including women, irrespective of the population to which they belong, in the event of armed conflict' (para. 2), and 'take all necessary measures to ensure that no child, especially girls under 18 years of age, take a direct part in hostilities and that no child is recruited as a soldier' (para. 4). Hence, in their periodic reports on the national implementation of the Protocol, States shall include information on national measures they have taken on the protection of women in armed conflicts, especially the protection provided for in paragraphs 3 and 4 of Article 11.[10] At its 269th meeting of 28 and 29 March 2011, the Peace and Security Council (PSC) devoted a thematic open session on 'Women and children and other vulnerable groups in armed conflicts', attended by more than 25 representatives of women's organizations. The PSC for the first time heard testimonies from women victims of sexual violence during conflicts, in the presence of all AU representatives and the Commission leadership. These testimonies, held the PSC, 'further highlight the need for a collective and determined effort to effectively address the problem of sexual violence'. The PSC urged Member States that have not yet done so, to ratify the 2003 Protocol on the Rights of Women in Africa, and requested those countries that have ratified the Protocol to domesticate it. At the same time, the PSC

> expressed concern at the situation of women and children in conflict situations and post-conflict contexts, stressing the need to fully investigate cases of crimes committed against women and children, to launch preventive campaigns specifically aimed at the armed forces and the police, and to ensure that perpetrators are brought to justice.

In addition, it emphasized the specific vulnerabilities of women and children who are refugees or internally displaced persons (IDPs).[11]

The most extensive references to IHL in AU treaties adopted so far are seen in the *African Union Convention for the Protection and Assistance of Internally Displaced Persons in Africa*.[12] First, 'the Heads of State and Government of the Member States of the African Union' recognised in the Preamble of the Convention the 'inherent rights of internally displaced persons as provided for and protected in international human rights and humanitarian law'. This is a confirmation by the AU supreme organ of the roots of IDPs' rights in IHL and human rights law (HRL) as mentioned in the United Nations (UN) *Guiding Principles on Internal Displacement*,[13] rights which the AU qualifies as 'inherent'. After this confirmation, the Convention – the first multilateral treaty on IDPs – lays down 'general obligations' and 'specific obligations' for States, which in fact endorse, and develop, the principles declared in the UN document.

Among the 'general obligations', States Parties shall:

> c. Respect and ensure respect for the principles of humanity and human dignity of internally displaced persons; ... e. Respect and ensure respect for international humanitarian law regarding the protection of internally displaced persons; f. Respect and ensure respect for the humanitarian and civilian character of the protection of and assistance to internally displaced persons, including ensuring that such persons do not engage in subversive activities; g. Ensure individual responsibility for acts of arbitrary displacement, in accordance with applicable domestic and international criminal law; h. Ensure the accountability of non-State actors concerned, including multinational companies and private military or security companies, for acts of arbitrary displacement or complicity in such acts.[14]

'Specific obligations' of States address the protection of individuals from internal displacement. They start with a duty of States to 'respect and ensure respect for their obligations under international law, including human rights and humanitarian law, so as to prevent and avoid conditions that might lead to the arbitrary displacement of persons'.[15] In its Article 4(4), the AU Convention recognises 'a right [of all persons] to be protected against arbitrary displacement', and refers to specific IHL rules prohibiting arbitrary displacement, namely:

> b. Individual or mass displacement of civilians in situations of armed conflict, unless the security of the civilians involved or imperative military reasons so demand, in accordance

with international humanitarian law; c. Displacement intentionally used as a method of warfare or due to other violations of international humanitarian law in situations of armed conflict; ... e. Displacement as a result of harmful practices; ... g. Displacement used as a collective punishment; h. Displacement caused by any act, event, factor, or phenomenon of comparable gravity to all of the above and which is not justified under international law, including human rights and international humanitarian law.[16]

Article 4 ends with an obligation vested on States Parties to 'declare as offences punishable by law acts of arbitrary displacement that amount to genocide, war crimes or crimes against humanity' (para. 6). This is to be connected with one of the States' obligations during internal displacement to

protect the rights of internally displaced persons regardless of the cause of displacement by ... preventing ... : Genocide, crimes against humanity, war crimes and other violations of international humanitarian law against internally displaced persons; ... [s]exual and gender based violence in all its forms, notably rape, enforced prostitution, sexual exploitation and harmful practices, slavery, recruitment of children and their use in hostilities, forced labour and human trafficking and smuggling; and [s]tarvation.[17]

On the protection and assistance to IDPs in situations of armed conflict, specified in Article 7, the AU Convention states first that such a protection and assistance 'shall be governed by international law and in particular international humanitarian law' (para. 3). It then goes on to require that 'Members of armed groups shall be prohibited from' various acts provoking arbitrary displacement, or against displaced persons.[18] That provision duly takes into account the asymmetric nature of many conflicts in Africa, which involve non-State armed actors. The AU makes here a call upon African States to undertake, in ratifying the Convention, to ensure respect for IHL and HRL by members of non-State armed groups acting in their territory. This is an obligation of result, leaving to States the means to achieve the goals of the provision by taking the necessary national legislation and measures. In support of this States' undertaking, Article 7(4) of the Convention provides that members of armed groups 'shall be held criminally responsible for their acts which violate the rights of internally displaced persons under international law and national law'. In fact, acts contrary to the prohibition mentioned above may fall under the qualification of war crimes as defined in Article 8 of the Rome Treaty of the International Criminal Court.[19]

Finally, it is to be remembered that under Article 3(1), 'States Parties undertake to respect and ensure respect for the present Convention', including indeed the HRL and IHL principles enshrined in the Convention as implied by the express recall, in the Preamble, of the 1949 Four Conventions, the 1977 Additional Protocols, and the universal and regional instruments on human rights and on the protection of refugees and IDPs.

Besides these treaty provisions, strong IHL undertakings are also observed in AU solemn declarations and decisions.

1.1.2   The references to IHL in AU declarations and decisions

On the eve of the AU's creation, the *Grand Bay (Mauritius) Declaration and Plan of Action* of the First OAU Ministerial Conference on Human Rights[20] made important recommendations regarding various acts inconsistent with IHL perpetrated in Africa. Essentially, the Conference recommended that States

> take the necessary measures to stop the practice of child soldiers and to reinforce the protection of civilian populations, particularly children in conflict situations; ... adopt measures to eradicate violence against women and children, child labour, sexual exploitation of children, trafficking in children and to protect children in conflict with the law as well as refugee children [para. 6]

> ... ensure that ... acts [of genocide, crimes against humanity and other war crimes] are definitively eradicated on the Continent and ... that these serious acts of violation be adequately dealt with [para. 11].

The Conference also reaffirmed the 'commitment of Africa to the promotion, protection and observance of Human Rights obligations'. In this framework, it requested those States which have not yet done so to 'give consideration to the ratification of all major OAU and UN Human Rights Conventions, in particular ... : j) The Four Geneva Conventions governing the Treatment of War Wounded, Prisoners of War and Civilians as well as the Two Additional Protocols; ... m) The Statute of the International Criminal Court'.[21] Similarly, the AU Assembly has invited AU Member States to ratify specific humanitarian treaties, such as the 1980 UN Convention on Banning the Use of Certain Conventional Weapons with a Traumatic Effect or Which Strike Indiscriminately (CCW).[22]

Finally, and as part of the Grand Bay Plan of action, the Conference

> recognizes the necessity for States to give effect to the African Charter, International Humanitarian Law and other major international Human Rights instruments which they have ratified, in their national legislations for wider effect throughout Africa ...
> ... appeals to the Secretary General of the OAU and the African Commission on Human and Peoples' Rights to develop appropriate strategies and take measures to sensitize and raise the awareness of African populations about Human Rights and International Humanitarian Law through formal and non formal educational processes comprising among others, a special module in school curricula.[23]

One could notice in these references the linking of IHL with HRL – namely the inclusion of the Four Geneva Conventions and their Additional Protocols among 'Human Rights Conventions'[24] – and the combination of the two bodies of law in the field of their promotion, protection and observance as well as in their effective implementation in the domestic legal system of States. Such combinations are frequent in the numerous AU texts reported in the present chapter.

One year after the AU launching, a First AU Ministerial Conference on Human Rights in Africa was held in Kigali, Rwanda. Reaffirming the commitments, purposes and principles proclaimed in the 1999 Grand Bay Declaration and Plan of Action, the Conference in its *Kigali Declaration* of 8 May 2003, further:

> Requests the relevant organs of the AU, in the exercise of their peace building and conflict resolution functions, to ensure the inclusion of human rights, humanitarian principles and other legal protection measures in peace agreements [para. 14] ...

Calls upon Member States to fulfill their obligations under international law and, in particular, to take the necessary measures to put an end to the practice of child-soldiers and to ensure the protection of civilian populations, particularly children, women, elderly persons and persons with disability in situations of armed conflict [para. 17]... [and]

Urges Member States which have not yet done so to incorporate in their domestic legislation provisions of the African Charter on Human and Peoples' Rights, its protocols, international humanitarian law in particular the Four (4) Geneva Conventions (1949) and their Additional Protocols (1977) and other major international human rights instruments, which they have ratified, and to honour their obligations thereon, including reporting, where applicable [para. 25].[25]

Besides, it is reported that more decisions relating to IHL have been adopted during the period of transition from OAU to AU, in particular:

OAU Council of Ministers *Decision CM/2264 (LXXVII)* of July 2002 relating to the Implementation and Universality of the Prohibition, Development, and Production of Chemical Weapons; AU Executive Council *Decision EX/CL/Dec.46 (III)* of 4–8 July 2003 on the Situation of Refugees, Returnees, and Displaced Persons, which in paragraph 7 condemned the 'serious acts of violence perpetuated against civilian populations including refugees and displaced persons and urged all parties in the conflict to scrupulously observe International Humanitarian Law'; AU Executive Council *Decision EX/CL/Dec.47 (III)* of 4–8 July 2003 on the Report of the First Ministerial Conference on Human Rights in Africa in Kigali, which specifically referred to the ICRC, UNDP, OHCHR, UNHCR, UNICEF and UNESCO as partners in human rights and IHL in Africa; and AU Executive Council *Decision EX/CL/Dec.63 (III)* of 10–12 July 2003 on the Global Report on Violence and Health, which called on member States to facilitate coordinated access for humanitarian organizations to all victims of armed conflicts and internal violence, and to do so on the basis of IHL, which guarantees respect for the neutrality of medical missions during armed conflicts.[26]

The competence of the AU Executive Council, composed of the Ministers of Foreign Affairs or other relevant Ministers, to take these decisions could be based on the function of the Council to 'co-ordinate and take decisions on policies in areas of common interest to the Member States, including ... environmental protection, humanitarian action and disaster response and relief'.[27]

Another OAU/AU organ that participates a lot in the promotion and implementation of IHL is the African Commission on Human and Peoples' Rights (African Commission), the monitoring organ of the African Charter on Human and Peoples' Rights (ACHPR), which had its first meeting in 1987.[28]

1.2   The Promotion and Application of IHL by the African Commission on Human and Peoples' Rights

1.2.1   The activities of promotion
In its resolutions, the African Commission has expressed the need to disseminate and implement in Africa the provisions of IHL, in view of their close link with human and peoples' rights, which it is assigned to monitor. Hence, the African Commission,

Considering that human rights and international humanitarian law (IHL) have always, even in different situations, aimed at protecting human beings and their fundamental rights ...

1. Invites all African States Parties to the African Charter on Human and Peoples' Rights to adopt appropriate measures at the national level to ensure the promotion of the provisions of international humanitarian law and human and peoples' rights; 2. Stresses the need for specific instruction of military personnel and the training of the forces of law and order in international humanitarian law and human and peoples' rights respectively; 3. Stresses further the importance of regular exchange of information between the African Commission on Human and Peoples' Rights, the International Committee of Red Cross and human rights non-governmental organisations, on teaching and dissemination activities undertaken on the principles of human and peoples' rights and international humanitarian law, in the schools, universities and all other institutions.[29]

In other resolutions which address conflicts in Africa, including the accompanying mines laying, the African Commission,

concerned with the consequences of persistent wars in several African States, on the civilian population, which prevent the realisation of the right to development ... urges all those parties engaged in war on the African continent, to abide by the provisions of International Humanitarian Law, particularly with regard to the protection of civilians and to undertake all efforts to restore peace.[30]

Moreover, 'Considering the significant ravages caused by the indiscriminate use of anti-personnel mines, particularly in Africa where more than 30 million mines are scattered', the African Commission encouraged African States 'to ratify, within the shortest possible time, the 1980 United Nations Convention on prohibition or restriction on the use of certain conventional weapons which may be deemed to be excessively injurious or to have indiscriminate effects'.[31] This promotion of IHL by encouragement to the ratification of relevant instruments was extended to a call

on all States Parties to the African Charter on Human and Peoples' Rights to carry out all the appropriate constitutional procedures to sign and ratify the Rome treaty on the International Criminal Court; ... to take all necessary legislative and administrative steps to bring national laws and policies into conformity with the statute.[32]

Another measure of promotion is the organisation by the African Commission of seminars on IHL for the representatives of States Parties to the ACHPR and NGOs.[33]

In addition to these measures of promotion, the African Commission has also played a role in the application of IHL.

1.2.2 The invocation of international humanitarian law in the findings of the African Commission

The combination of Articles 60 and 61 of the ACHPR allows the African Commission to consider violation of IHL in the fulfilment of its monitoring mandates. Accordingly, the African Commission invoked IHL in the first ever inter-States case brought before it, between Democratic Republic of Congo (D.R. Congo) and three of its neighbouring countries, Burundi, Rwanda and Uganda.[34] D.R. Congo alleged grave and massive violations of human and peoples' rights committed by the armed forces of these States during their military activities in, and occupation of, its eastern provinces, including series of massacres, rapes, mutilations, mass transfers of populations and looting of the peoples' possessions. The African Commission considered that these series of violations fall within the province of IHL, and are therefore covered by the Four Geneva Conventions and their Additional Protocols. It affirmed that it cannot turn a blind eye to such violations attendant to the occupation of the parts of the D.R. Congo's provinces,[35] and asserted its competence to invoke IHL in considering these violations as follows:

> The combined effect of Articles 60 and 61 of the African Charter enables the Commission to draw inspiration from international law on human and peoples' rights, the Charter of the United Nations, the Charter of the Organisation of African Unity [now the AU Constitutive Act] and also to take into consideration, as subsidiary measures to determine the principles of law, other general or special international conventions, laying down rules recognized by Member States of the Organization of African Unity [now the AU], general principles recognized by African States as well as legal precedents and doctrine. *By virtue of Articles 60 and 61 the Commission holds that the Four Geneva Conventions and the two Additional Protocols covering armed conflicts constitute part of the general principles of law recognized by African States, and take them into consideration in the determination of this case.*[36]

As a result, the Commission condemned Burundi, Rwanda and Uganda for violations of IHL in the territory of the D.R. Congo. In so doing, it indicated clearly the specific IHL provisions that were breached, which is quite exceptional for a human rights organ. These include:

> the killings, massacres, rapes, mutilations and other grave human rights abuses committed while the Respondent States' armed forces were still in effective occupation of the eastern provinces of the Complainant State [which are] reprehensible and also inconsistent with their obligations under Part III of the Geneva Convention Relative to the Protection of Civilian Persons in Time of War of 1949 and Protocol 1 of the Geneva Convention [para. 79]; ... the besiege of the hydroelectric dam in Lower Congo province, contrary to Article 56 of the Additional Protocol I and Article 23 of The Hague Convention (II) with Respect to the Laws and Customs of War on Land [paras 83 and 84]; the raping of women and girls, which is inconsistent with Article 76 of the Additional Protocol I and also offends against both the African Charter and the Convention on the Elimination of All Forms of Discrimination Against Women [para. 86]; 'the indiscriminate dumping of and or mass burial of victims of the series of massacres and killings perpetrated against the peoples of the eastern provinces of the Complainant State while the armed forces of the Respondent States were in actual fact occupying the said provinces', contrary to Article 34 of Additional Protocol I which provides for respect for the remains of such peoples and their gravesites [para. 87].[37]

In the above findings, it is interesting to note that the series of acts against women and girls during the military occupation were held as inconsistent with both IHL and HRL. This dual determination was extended to other types of acts, which are generally seen as violations of IHL. Thus:

> The looting, killing, mass and indiscriminate transfers of civilian population, the besiege and damage of the hydro-dam, stopping of essential services in the hospital, leading to deaths of patients and the general disruption of life and state of war that took place while the forces of the Respondent States were occupying and in control of the eastern provinces of the Complainant State are in violation of Article 14 guaranteeing the right to property, articles 16

and 17 (all of the African Charter), which provide for the rights to the best attainable state of physical and mental health and education, respectively [para. 88].[38]

In addition, the African Commission recalled Part III of the 1949 Geneva Convention Relative to the Protection of Civilian Persons in Time of War, particularly Article 27 which 'provides for the humane treatment of protected persons at all times and for protection against all acts of violence or threats and against insults and public curiosity …' as well as 'the protection of women against any attack on their honour, in particular against rape, enforced prostitution, or any form of indecent assault' (para. 89).[39]

Such determinations grounded on both HRL and IHL are facilitated by the specificities of the African system for the protection of human rights where States have a continuing obligation to respect all human and peoples' rights even in time of war and public emergency, due to the absence of derogation clauses in the ACHPR. Actually the African Charter, 'unlike other human rights instruments, does not allow for States Parties to derogate from their treaty obligations during emergency situations. Thus, even a situation of … war … cannot be cited as justification by the State violating or permitting violations of the African Charter'.[40]

These findings are made in the context of international armed conflict and inter-States communications. In individual communication cases arising from situations of internal conflict, the African Commission also invoked IHL, mainly to remind States of their obligation to respect IHL and ensure respect for it by all parties to the conflict. In *Amnesty International et al. v. Sudan* case, relating to the extrajudicial execution of thousands of the civilian population during the civil war in the South of Sudan, the African Commission held:

> In addition to the individuals named in the communications, there are thousands of other executions in Sudan. Even if these are not all the work of forces of the government, the government has a responsibility to protect all people residing under its jurisdiction. … Even if Sudan is going through a civil war, civilians in areas of strife are especially vulnerable and the state must take all possible measures to ensure that they are treated in accordance with international humanitarian law.[41]

On the same lines of extended capacity of the African Commission to consider IHL in its determination of the ACHPR violations, the AU Assembly considered in February 2009 the possibility of granting the AU human rights organs the competence to judge international crimes. It mandated the AU Commission, that is, the AU Secretariat, in consultation with the African Commission and the African Court on Human and Peoples' Rights, 'to examine the implications of the Court being empowered to try international crimes such as genocide, crimes against humanity and war crimes, and report thereon to the Assembly in 2010'.[42] This decision is motivated by the feeling that some non African States are abusing the principle of universal jurisdiction by indicting high officials of African States, and the desire the see these officials judged by African courts and in Africa in line of the AU principles on the fight against impunity.

In its July 2009 session, the Assembly requested the AU Commission to ensure the early implementation of the mentioned decision, 'which would be complementary to national jurisdiction and processes for fighting impunity'.[43] At the time of writing, it seems that such implementation is suspended to the operationalization of the merger of the African Court on HPR and the AU Court of Justice into a single 'African Court of Justice and Human Rights', the Statute of which provides for two Sections: a General Affairs Section and a Human Rights Section.[44] Probably, the contemplated international criminal cases would be considered by the Human Rights Section since the General Affairs Section shall be competent to hear inter-State disputes 'save those concerning human and/or peoples' rights issues', as specified in Article 17 of the ACJHR Statute. Following the practice of the African Commission discussed above, the Human Rights Section also would consider IHL in the determination of the cases brought before it in view of the fact that the new Court in carrying out its functions shall have regard, like the African Commission, to 'general principles of law recognized universally or by African States', and even better to 'Any other law relevant to the determination of the case', among other sources.[45] It remains to be seen whether the victims of the international crimes would have an individual right to make claims before the ACJHR as is the case for the human rights victims, for which one could appreciate the significant broadening of the *locus standi* of the new Court.[46]

This new development is linked to the AU contribution to the sanction and judicial enforcement of IHL. Before looking at such a contribution, let us first see the numerous IHL undertakings in the AU instruments relating to peace and security.

2. THE COMMITMENT TO RESPECT AND ENSURING RESPECT FOR INTERNATIONAL HUMANITARIAN LAW IN THE AFRICAN UNION'S KEY DOCUMENTS RELATING TO PEACE AND SECURITY

The AU has interestingly made express references to IHL in the regulations of the activities of its principal organ for the prevention, management and resolution of conflicts, namely the Peace and Security Council (PSC), a permanent organ composed of 15 Member States. In these references, the AU has shown clear commitment to the respect for IHL in its peace activities, as confirmed in other key documents relating to peace and security in Africa.

2.1   The References to IHL in the PSC Protocol and Subsequent Measures

In the *Protocol relating to the Establishment of the Peace and Security Council of the African Union*,[47] the AU Member States, 'concerned about the continued prevalence of armed conflicts in Africa and the fact that no single internal factor has contributed more to … the suffering of the civilian population than the scourge of conflicts within and between our States', have called on the PSC to 'promote and encourage democratic practices, good governance and the rule of law, protect human rights and fundamental freedoms, respect for the sanctity of human life and international humanitarian law, as part of efforts for preventing conflicts'.[48] Here, the AU includes the respect for IHL among the tools for conflict prevention, thus extending in some way the virtue of IHL beyond strict *jus in bello*, that is, the humanisation of conflicts and the introduction of constraints in waging war.[49] In fulfilling this mandate, the PSC shall be guided by the 'respect for the rule of law, fundamental human rights and freedoms, the sanctity of human life and international humanitarian law'.[50] Moreover, the PSC shall perform functions in 'peace support operations and intervention', which include 'humanitarian action and disaster management'.[51]

Accordingly, the AU peace support operations deployed so far – as many other peacekeeping operations – have been granted a civilian protection mandate, with the ability to take all necessary measures to 'protect civilians under imminent threat of physical violence', to use the typical expression in UN Security Council resolutions authorizing the deployment of AU operations. Thus, while the main mandates of the first AU peacekeeping operation, the African Mission in Burundi (AMIB), were to protect returning political leaders and train an all-Burundian protection force, secure identified assembly and disengagement areas, provide VIP protection for a designated returning leader, and facilitate safe passage for the parties during planned movement to the designed assembly areas, AMIB's Rules of Engagement allowed it to use force to protect civilians 'under imminent threat of physical violence'.[52] For the second operation, the AU Observer Mission in the Darfur region of Sudan (AMIS), the humanitarian mandate had moved from securing the unrestricted humanitarian access and assistance for the protection of IDPs or refugee returnees to the protection of civilians whom the Mission 'encounters under imminent threat'.[53] Specifically, the focus of the military component of the UNAMID, which took over AMIS, is 'the protection of civilians and the provision of security for vulnerable populations', with the assistance of the police component which could conduct joint patrols within and in the immediate vicinity of IDPs camps in the demilitarized and buffer zones.[54]

The AU is also working on the strengthening of the civilian protection mandate of the African Mission in Somalia (AMISOM). The AU Commission, in collaboration with the Australian Government, organised in March 2010 a four-day International Symposium on the Protection of Civilians in Conflict Zones. The Symposium aimed at brainstorming on the AU Draft Guidelines for the Protection of Civilians by Peace Support Missions, which shall reflect the values, principles, laws and conventions of the AU, as well as reviewing the steps that have been taken by peace support operations to provide protection to civilians in the African context. Participants to the Symposium shared views on the contemporary experiences from the AMISOM on the protection of civilians, the responsibilities and expectations for Heads of Missions, the development of a Protection of Civilians Directive and its content, among other issues.[55] Following up on the Symposium outcome, the PSC discussed at its 279th meeting of 18 May 2011 the issue of the protection of civilian populations in armed conflicts, on the basis of the *Progress Report of the Chairperson of the Commission on the Development of Guidelines for the Protection of Civilians in African Union Peace Support Operations* [PSC/PR/2(CCLXXIV)] as well as the statements made by the representatives of the UN and the ICRC. In the press release on the meeting, the PSC emphasized the importance of the protection of civilians, and urged the AU Commission to finalize, as early as possible, the Draft Guidelines, drawing lessons from relevant experiences. It encouraged the Commission to mainstream the protection of civilians into the whole spectrum of the African Peace and Security Architecture. It particularly welcomed the efforts being made to mainstream the Draft Guidelines into the work of AMISOM, and encouraged the Commission to pursue its efforts, notably through the development of:

> (i) an AMISOM approach for the protection of civilians, (ii) a lessons learned report, (iii) protection threats, vulnerabilities and risks indicators for the Continental Early Warning System (CEWS), (iv) a Guidance Note on protection mandates, (v) a Framework for developing mission specific protection strategies, (vi) and drafting of training guidelines, as well as through the conduct of awareness raising and outreach activities.[56]

In line with the PSC recommendations, in August 2011 AMISOM held, in Kigali, a three-day roundtable on enhancing respect for IHL in the implementation of its mandate, which 'was a clear demonstration of AMISOM's and indeed the African Union Commission's commitment towards respect for IHL not only in Somalia but also in all its Peace Support Operations across the continent'.[57] This commitment to respect IHL is reiterated in other AU key documents on peace and security in Africa.

2.2   The References to IHL in other AU Key Documents on Peace and Security

Such references are found in both AU declarations and treaties. In the *Bamako Declaration on an African Common Position on the Illicit Proliferation, Circulation and Trafficking of Small Arms and Light Weapons*,[58] the Ministers of OAU Member States recognised that

> the problem of illicit proliferation, circulation and trafficking of small arms in Africa (i) sustains conflicts, exacerbates violence, contributes to the displacement of innocent populations and threatens international humanitarian law, as well as fuels crime and encourages terrorism; ... (iv) also has devastating consequences on children, a number of whom are victims of armed conflict, while others are forced to become child soldiers.

They therefore agreed that in order to promote peace, security, stability and sustainable development on the continent, it is vital to address this problem in a comprehensive, integrated, and efficient manner through, among others, 'the respect for international humanitarian law' (para. 2(ix)).

In the AU *Solemn Declaration on a Common African Defence and Security Policy*,[59] the existence of grave circumstances, namely war crimes, genocide and crimes against humanity; the lack of respect for the sanctity of human life, impunity, political assassination, acts of terrorism and subversive activities; the use of landmines and unexploded ordinance; and the illicit proliferation, circulations and trafficking in small arms and light weapons' are qualified as common *internal* threats to Africa, which call for common actions by the AU.[60] These are all facts that fall within the province of IHL and their inclusion among the common threats to security in Africa reinforced the idea according to which the Common African Defence and Security Policy (CADSP) 'is based on the notion of human security, rather than the narrower concept of state security, and aims to promote a culture of peace amongst AU Member States'.[61]

In the same vein, the Solemn Declaration qualifies as common *external* threats to Africa international terrorism and terrorist activities, as well as the accumulation, stockpiling, proliferation and manufacturing of weapons of mass destruction, particularly nuclear weapons, chemical and biological weapons, unconventional long-range and ballistic missiles.[62] With regard to terrorism, the *Protocol to the Organization of African Unity (OAU) Convention on the Prevention and Combating of Terrorism* stressed 'the imperative for all Member States of the African Union to take all necessary measures to protect their populations from acts of terrorism and to implement all relevant continental and international humanitarian and human rights instruments'.[63] These are strong statements for the promotion of and respect for IHL as many provisions of IHL treaties prohibit terrorist acts, as such or as means of warfare.[64] Likewise, the International Court of Justice has noted that in view of the unique characteristics of nuclear weapons – and by extension of similar weapons of mass destruction – mainly their destructive capacity, their capacity to cause untold human suffering, and their ability to cause damage to generations to come, the use of such weapons in fact seems scarcely reconcilable with the cardinal principles and rules of IHL.[65]

From an operational point of view, the AU has placed on the African Stand-by Force (ASF) an obligation to respect IHL.[66] The PSC Protocol stipulates that the ASF shall be adequately equipped to undertake humanitarian activities in their mission areas, and shall facilitate the activities of the humanitarian agencies in these areas.[67] The personnel hired to undertake such activities shall receive 'training on International Humanitarian Law and International Human Rights Law, with particular emphasis on the rights of women and children'.[68] Such training courses are to be coordinated by the AU Commission, in collaboration with the ICRC and other competent organisations. In the framework of the operationalization of the ASF, the African Chiefs of Defence Staff (ACDS) recommended that all ASF peace support operations 'should be conducted in a manner consistent with the relevant UN and OAU instruments'.[69] Consequently, while the PSC is the legitimate mandating authority of these operations, it shall act in accordance with Chapter VIII of the UN Charter, by asking the authorization of the UN Security Council and keeping it fully informed of the activities undertaken or in contemplation.[70] In addition, the development of an AU standardised doctrine, required for an effective multinational peace operation according to the ACDS, as well as the training standards and materials, shall both take inspiration from existing UN documents, with the necessary adaptation to suit African conditions. In this regard, the Policy Framework explicitly mentioned the 1999 UN Secretary-General Bulletin on the *Observance by United Nations forces of international humanitarian law*, and the 2003 *Handbook on United Nations Multidimensional Peacekeeping Operations*. It also stated that the UN should be invited to participate in the planning and conduct of all forms of peacekeeping training and exercises.[71] The ACDS further stressed that:

> Troops that participate in peace support operations are placed under particular scrutiny regarding their adherence to the highest standards of international humanitarian law/Law of armed conflict. This subject should be covered in national training as well as by any regional peacekeeping training institutions. Reference could here be made to bulletin issued by the UNSG in 1999 on international humanitarian law. (para. 2.19)

This framework for ASF operations was confirmed in the *Roadmap for the Operationalisation of the African Standby Force*,[72] from the mandating authority and the respect for the UN Charter (para. 10) to the requirement of doctrine and training which emphasize the observance of IHL (para. 20). It was then decided to establish ASF brigades in the five political regions of Africa (Eastern, Northern, Western, Central and Southern Africa), as recommended in the Framework Document. Progress on the implementation of this decision from the relevant sub-regional organisations is presented in the Roadmap.[73]

Interestingly, AU members have echoed their continental commitment to IHL within the sub-regional organisations to which they are parties. Thus, the 15 members of the Economic Community of West African States (ECOWAS) have reaffirmed their 'commitment to the protection of fundamental human rights and freedoms and the rules of international humanitarian laws', including in the activities of the ECOWAS Cease-fire Monitoring Group (ECOMOG), which is a structure composed of several Stand-by multi-purpose modules (civilian and military) in their countries of origin and ready for immediate deployment. They planned a training of civilian and military personnel of ECOMOG stand-by units 'in various fields, particularly in international humanitarian law and human rights'.[74] In 2001, the same group of States indicated that 'The armed forces, the police and other security agencies shall during their training receive instructions on … ECOWAS principles and regulations, human rights, humanitarian law and democratic principles', within their respective territory or in joint training sessions for ECOWAS States.[75]

In the East, an Eastern Africa Standby Brigade (EASBRIG) was established pursuant to a Decision of the AU Summit of July 2004, the doctrine of which 'shall be consistent with the doctrine, procedures and standards of the UN', and 'the training curriculum shall include the African Charter on Human and Peoples Rights (ACHPR), the International Humanitarian Law (IHL), the Human Rights Law (HRL) and the Refugee Law (RL), as well as the UN code of conduct for peacekeepers'.[76]

In the South, States in the region agreed that the *Southern African Development Community Mutual Defence Pact* 'shall not derogate from the State Parties' rights and obligations under the Charter of the United Nations and the Constitutive Act of the African Union and relevant treaties and conventions concerning human rights and international humanitarian law'. The Pact also shall not derogate from the responsibility of the UN Security Council for the maintenance of international peace and security.[77]

Finally, 11 central African States have specified that the international force they created through the Economic Community of Central African States (ECCAS), namely the Central African Multinational Force (FOMAC or *Force Multinationale d'Afrique Centrale*), 'shall be deployed in conformity with the basic rules and principles contained in the conventions which codify the International Humanitarian Law including the Conventions of Geneva of 12 August 1949 and their additional Protocols'.[78] To reinforce that obligation of the FOMAC to respect IHL rules and principles, the ECCAS members added a mechanism for judicial review of the FOMAC conduct: 'Ad hoc courts shall be set up to take cognisance of infractions, which occur in the execution of FOMAC operations, which can be described as war crime or genocide. Ad hoc courts shall be set up at the request of the Chairman of the Conference'.[79] This denotes an African contribution to the sanction and judicial enforcement of IHL.

3.   THE AFRICAN UNION CONTRIBUTION TO THE SANCTION AND JUDICIAL ENFORCEMENT OF INTERNATIONAL HUMANITARIAN LAW

The persistence of conflicts and instabilities in Africa has brought with it lots of atrocities and sufferings for civilian populations and other vulnerable peoples. The AU cannot turn a blind eye to these atrocities; it has proclaimed its commitment to put an end to the culture of impunity in Africa, and condemned violations of IHL and HRL in the conflicts occurring in the continent.

3.1   The African Union Commitment to the Fight Against Impunity

This commitment is grounded on various principles enshrined in the AU Constitutive Act. The first of them is the 'right of the Union to intervene in a Member State pursuant to a decision of the Assembly in respect of grave circumstances, namely war crimes, genocide and crimes against humanity', in accordance with Article 4(h) of the AU Constitutive Act. This is the most cited provision in the decisions in which the Assembly and the PSC reaffirm the AU's commitment to fight against impunity.[80] The AU intervention, decided by the Assembly upon the recommendation of the PSC,[81] could be seen as a sanction for the violation of States' obligation under Article 3 of the *African Union Non-Aggression and Common Defence Pact*[82] 'to prohibit and prevent genocide, other forms of mass murder as well as crimes against humanity'.

To the AU right to intervene, we should add the principle on the 'respect for the sanctity of human life, condemnation and rejection of impunity and political assassination, acts of terrorism and subversive activities'.[83] Likewise, the *African Charter on Democracy, Elections and Governance* proclaims the principle of 'condemnation and rejection of ... impunity', with an obligation vested on States to 'take all necessary measures to strengthen the Organs of the Union that are mandated to promote and protect human rights and to fight impunity and endow them with the necessary resources'.[84] Furthermore, Article 7 of the AU IDPs Convention affirms the individual criminal responsibility of the members of non-State armed groups under domestic or international criminal law for their gross violations of HRL and IHL, and asks States to act accordingly. These principles are at the heart of the AU tools to react to grave violations of both HRL and IHL. The subsequent decisions in application of these principles constitute an important contribution to the sanction of IHL.

The AU commitment to fight against impunity has been reaffirmed and enriched in subsequent treaties, declarations and decisions. Of particular relevance are the three sets of the AU Assembly's decisions in which the African leaders reiterated the AU's 'unflinching commitment to combating impunity', namely the decisions relating to the trial of the former Chadian President Hissène Habré,[85] the ICC arrest warrants for the incumbent President of the Sudan, Omar El-Bashir,[86] and the abuse of universal jurisdiction,[87] which the AU defines as 'a principle of International Law whose purpose is to ensure that individuals who commit grave offences such as war crimes and crimes against humanity do not do so with impunity and are brought to justice, which is in line with Article 4(h) of the Constitutive Act of the African Union'.[88]

In its first decision on Hissène Habré's trial, the Assembly created a Committee of Eminent African Jurists 'to consider all aspects and implications of the ... case as well as the options available for his trial'. In its reaction to the Committee's report,[89] the Assembly affirmed its competence to deal with the question of international crimes and the prosecution of their perpetrators, relying in so doing on specific powers granted in the Constitutive Act, not on implied powers. Essentially, the Assembly 'observes that, according to the terms of Articles 3(h), 4(h) and 4(o) of the Constitutive Act of the African Union, the crimes of which Hissène Habré is accused fall within the competence of the African Union'.[90] It then 'mandate[d] the Republic of Senegal to prosecute and ensure that Hissène Habré is tried, on behalf of Africa, by a competent Senegalese court with guarantees for fair trial'.[91] More generally and in line with that call for prosecution of international crimes by African national courts, the AU Assembly

> encourages Member States to initiate programmes of cooperation and capacity building to enhance the capacity of legal personnel in their respective countries regarding the drafting and security of model legislation dealing with serious crimes of international concern, training of members of the police and the judiciary, and the strengthening of cooperation amongst judicial and investigative agencies.[92]

The two other series of decisions contain also a reaffirmation of the AU commitment to fight against impunity, before expressing reservations on some prosecutions conducted by non-African States and organisations against high African State officials. From a normative point of view, the commitment to put an end to the impunity for grave violations of HRL and IHL is then well rooted in the AU legal order.[93] This is supported by the instances of formal condemnations of such grave violations by AU organs.

3.2   The African Union Condemnations of International Humanitarian Law Violations in Conflict Situations in Africa

Different AU organs have condemned the grave violations of IHL and HRL in internal conflicts in Africa, such as the Assembly, the PSC, the Chairperson of the Commission, the African Commission on HPR, among other organs.

At the time of the OAU, the Assembly already noted with concern that the plight of millions of African children is worsening by the day due to war, their conscription for armed conflicts and their abusive exploitation in many respects.[94] On the recent conflict situations in Africa, the AU Assembly expressed its condemnation of the violations of HRL and IHL in Darfur in the above-mentioned decisions relating to the arrest warrants for El-Bashir. The day after the issuance of the 2009 arrest warrant, the PSC while expressing various concerns over the warrant reiterated the AU's unflinching commitment to combating impunity, its strong condemnation of the gross violations of human rights in Darfur, and called for the immediate prosecution of the perpetrators.[95] This triple expression of commitment to impunity, condemnation of violations, and call for trial of perpetrators was repeated by the PSC in its review of the situation in Darfur pursuant to a report of the Chairperson of the AU Commission.[96] These three elements tend to be thoroughly present in other AU decisions.

On 'the grave humanitarian consequences caused by the deterioration of the security situation in Côte d'Ivoire, resulting from the intensification of military operations following the refusal of Mr. Laurent Gbagbo to cede power', the PSC at its 270th meeting of 5 April 2011

> deplored the loss of many lives, condemned the violation of human rights and other abuses in the context of military conflict, and reiterated the imperative of the protection of the civilian population and the binding responsibility of all sides for the respect of international humanitarian law, including access of humanitarian agencies to civilian populations needing assistance. In this regard, Council stressed the need for an independent investigation into the killings of civilians in Douékoué. Council encouraged UNOCI, within the framework of the relevant resolutions of the Security Council of UN, to vigorously implement its mandate to protect civilians.[97]

In this situation, it is important to note that the call to the respect for IHL is addressed to all parties, not only to the party who refused to cede power, and, because of that, disapproved by the international community.

With regard to Somalia, the PSC 'strongly condemned the attacks and other acts of violence perpetrated by Al Shabaab and other terrorist groups against the TFG, the Somali people and AMISOM', and 'the despicable terrorist attacks claimed by Al Shabaab perpetrated against innocent civilians in Kampala on 11 July 2010'.[98] AMISOM and the AU Special Representative for Somalia condemned too the suicide car bomb in Mogadishu on 18 October 2011, which they described as an 'indiscriminate terror attack' and a 'deliberate targeting [of] civilians'.[99] In their 5th consultative meeting at the AU Headquarters, in Addis Ababa, the AU PSC and the UN Security Council (UNSC) expressed their grave concern at the dire humanitarian situation in Somalia, the continued suffering of the Somali populations, terrorism, and the recruitment and use of child soldiers.[100]

The members of the UNSC and the AUPSC also expressed their deep concern over the continuation of violence in Libya, reaffirmed their commitment to the full implementation of UNSC resolutions 1970 (2011) and 1973 (2011) to ensure protection of civilians in Libya, and demanded the immediate establishment of a ceasefire and a complete end to violence and all attacks against, and abuses of, civilians. They finally 'expressed serious concern over the deteriorating humanitarian situation in the country, and called for full compliance with human rights and International Humanitarian Law and the creation of the required conditions for the delivery of assistance to all needy populations across Libya'.[101] Likewise, the African Commission on HPR, declared itself:

> Deeply concerned about the alarming human rights situation that these events have engendered, characterized by serious and massive human rights violations resulting from the blind and indiscriminate use of force, in particular through aerial bombings, the recourse to mercenaries to suppress peaceful demonstrations and the legitimate protests of the citizens; Concerned by the huge loss of lives and the wanton destruction of buildings and property in violation of the African Charter and other relevant judicial, regional, international human rights instruments and humanitarian law; Further concerned about the massive displacement of the population afraid for their lives, and the humanitarian consequences on women, children and other vulnerable groups; ... [and]

> Strongly condemns the divisionist speeches of the Head of State, Mouammar El Kadhafi
> and the bloody reprisal by the Government of ... Libya against its own population;
> Invites the Government ... to put an immediate end to the acts of violence and to all the
> forms of suppression perpetrated against the population and the destruction of property;
> Calls on the responsibility of the African Union, the Peace and Security Council of the
> African Union, and the International Community to take all the necessary political and
> legal measures for the protection of the Libyan population ...[102]

This is in line with the numerous condemnations by the African Commission of grave
violations of HRL and IHL in conflict situations in Africa, which include calls for the
full respect of these bodies of law by the parties to the conflict and, sometimes, the
sending of a fact-finding mission to the region or State concerned.[103]

Finally, and among other cases of condemnation which cannot be exhaustively listed
in this chapter, it could be added that the Pan-African Parliament (PAP), one of the
organs listed in Article 5 of the Constitutive Act, which is granted the power to
'examine, discuss or express an opinion on any matter ... to respect of human rights,
the consolidation of democratic institutions and the culture of democracy, as well as the
promotion of good governance and the rule of law',[104] has shown its desire to see IHL
respected. For example, and among others, the PAP Permanent Committee on Justice
and Human Rights, upon consideration of the conclusions of a Fact-finding Mission to
Sierra Leone, has stressed the need to 'bring to justice those who bear the greatest
responsibility for serious violations of international humanitarian law ... committed in
the territory of Sierra Leone since November 1996' and called for the full support by
States of the works of the Special Court on Sierra Leone.[105] This is part of the AU
contribution to the judicial enforcement of IHL.

3.3 The African Union Contribution to the Judicial Enforcement of International Humanitarian Law

In the various AU decisions discussed above, we have seen regular AU calls upon
States to bring to justice the perpetrators of the grave violations of human rights and
IHL it has condemned. We also presented the AU Assembly proposal to extend the
jurisdiction of the upcoming African Court of Justice and Human Rights to the
consideration of international crimes. These are quite in line with the AU commitment
to fight against impunity, which led African States to largely ratify the Rome Statute of
the ICC, in response to the calls made by the AU Assembly and the African
Commission on this regard, as mentioned above.[106] Yet, it is a truism to say that the
relationship between the AU and the ICC has deteriorated; following mainly the latter's
indictments of acting African heads of State. Thus, the AU has rejected the arrest
warrants for Omar El-Bashir, of Sudan, and for Colonel Qaddafi, of Libya, and decided
that AU members shall not cooperate with the ICC in the execution of these warrants.
The legal reasons for such rejections are, first, the AU concerns on the negative impacts
of the criminal proceedings on the on-going negotiations for a peaceful solution to the
conflicts at stake. This led the AU to ask the UN Security Council to defer, in
accordance with Article 16 of the Rome Statute, the proceedings against El-Bashir and
Qaddafi as well as the investigations and prosecutions in relation to the 2008
post-election violence in Kenya.[107] The second reason is linked to the plea for the

personal immunity of heads of State with regard to the execution of an international arrest warrant.[108]

Many commentators have criticized the AU position in these cases as undermining the works of the ICC. These critics have their merits but it is outside the scope of this chapter to discuss them here. Our focus is to uncover from the debated AU position some elements of development of the law and practice of the ICC, and more generally the judicial enforcement of IHL. It is important to note to begin with that the AU has used legal arguments in its decisions to not cooperate with the ICC and is consistent in insisting over the years on the proper application of the provisions it invoked. Thus, on the first plea, it could be argued that the AU position put to the fore the issue of the relationship between peace and justice in the fulfilment of the ICC functions, including the role of the UN Security Council in this regard. The drafters of the Rome Statute have taken into account this issue by including Article 16. The Security Council has been facing that issue with the insistent request of deferral under Article 16 by the AU Assembly, since 2008. The Security Council has not yet taken a decision on the matter, despite the repetition of the request in each AU Assembly session. This denotes the difficulty in giving a suitable answer on the matter. The Security Council has a special responsibility for the maintenance of international peace and security and cannot then ignore the plea for conciliating the efforts to achieve peace with the search for justice. On the other hand, it has also considered in the past that the prosecutions of international crimes may be part of the measures to restore peace, as shown in its creation of the international criminal tribunals for the former Yugoslavia and for Rwanda in 1993 and 1994. One could only hope that a clear position of principle will ensue from these AU requests, made in full respect of the letter and spirit of Article 16 of the Rome Statute (contrary to the precedent of Security Council Resolution 1422), and that this will help to clarify the principle on the relationship between peace and justice in the situations before the ICC or other international criminal courts.[109]

Moreover, in its rejection of the arrest warrants for El-Bashir, the AU has initiated a reflection on the relationship between the principle of irrelevance of official capacity in the prosecution of international crimes and the respect of the personal immunity of Heads of State. The said principle, which forfeits the right to immunity of senior State officials, including Heads of State and Government, is now considered as having acquired the status of customary international law.[110] The principle is reaffirmed in Article 27 of the Rome Statute,[111] but the AU Assembly maintains that El-Bashir, being a President of a non-State party, still enjoys his personal immunity. The Assembly invoked on this regard Article 98 of the Rome Statute[112] and requested a 'Clarification on the immunities of officials whose States are not party to the Statute' and a 'Comparative analysis of the implications of the practical application of Articles 27 and 98 of the Rome Statute'.[113] Actually, if Article 27(2) settles the question of immunities of the officials of States parties to the Rome Statute – i.e. lack of immunities – this is not applicable to non-State parties so that a Head of a non-State party like Sudan may invoke his immunity.[114] Because international practice on the exclusion of personal immunities of high State officials is not uniform, customary rules on the immunity from criminal jurisdiction and inviolability of incumbent Heads of State and Government and Ministers of Foreign Affairs remains applicable, except in certain circumstances.[115]

Relating to a waiver of immunity in relation to the prosecution before the ICC, Article 98 bars the ICC from requesting a State to arrest an official if this would involve the requested State to breach the diplomatic immunity of a person from a non-State party to the Rome Statute, unless that third State waives the immunity of the person concerned. There arises a question of coordination between Article 27(2) which enables the ICC to exercise its jurisdiction even over individuals enjoying immunities and Article 98(1) which seems to significantly narrow the scope of Article 27(2).[116] It was said that

> a failure to proceed successfully according to Article 98 may in practice and contrary to the wording of Article 27 'bar the Court from exercising its jurisdiction over such a person', if the Court cannot secure the attendance of the person in any other way, because the Rome Statute does not provide a trial *in abstentia*.[117]

It is this uncertainty on the rule provided by the combined operation of Article 27 and Article 98 of the Rome Statute that the AU brought into play in its rejection of the arrest warrants for El-Bashir. This is supported by the absence so far of a waiver by the Sudan of the El-Bashir's immunity, and the non-existence under international law of an explicit obligation for States to waive the immunities of their officials. For the Assembly, African States Parties to the Rome Statute have the right not to arrest and surrender El-Bashir if he enters their territory, as this would require them to act inconsistently with their customary obligation to respect the un-waived personal immunity of the Sudanese President. The Assembly has thus affirmed that 'by receiving President Bashir, the Republic of Chad, Kenya, and Djibouti were discharging their obligations under Article 23 of the Constitutive Act of the African Union and Article 98 of the Rome Statute as well as acting in pursuit of peace and stability in their respective regions'.[118]

Here again, the AU move may have the merit of inducing the clarification of that rule by the Assembly of States Parties to the Rome Statute or by the Court itself, which will be important for its future works as the nature of the crimes to be judged by the ICC generally involve high State officials. May such clarifications come sooner to improve the relationship between the AU and the ICC, and thus facilitate the works of the Court in Africa in line with the AU commitment to combating impunity.

4. CONCLUDING REMARKS

At the end of this study on the African Union and International Humanitarian Law, one has to admit that the continental African organisation has over years developed and consolidated a valuable framework for the promotion of and respect for IHL, based on AU treaties, declarations, decisions and reports on human and peoples' rights – including the rights of women, children, refugees and IDPs, rule of law, peace and security, and terrorism. These instruments took inspiration from the relevant universal rules and principles, with the necessary adaptation to suit African conditions and shared values. Conclusively, it could be held that the AU framework on IHL meets the five core protection challenges identified by the UN Secretary-General in his report released in 2009, ten years after the first consideration of the civilian protection theme by the UN Security Council.[119] The calls upon States to respect and ensure respect for IHL in conflict situations in Africa, the obligation vested on the members of AU peace support operations to respect IHL in fulfilling their mandates, supported by relevant doctrine and training, the condemnations by different AU organs of violations of IHL and HRL during conflicts occurring in Africa, and the calls to bring to justice the perpetrators of such violations, all these dealings indeed help to enhance compliance with international law by the parties to conflict, enhancing compliance with humanitarian rules and principles by non-State armed groups, strengthening protection of civilians by peace-keeping and other missions, improving humanitarian access to victims, and enhancing accountability for violations of international law, particularly IHL and HRL, the five core protection challenges.

In view of this consolidated legal framework:

> [the] focus for the AU should no longer be the adoption of additional instruments, unless exceptional circumstances so require, but rather the implementation of the existing ones ... renewed efforts from all concerned to address implementation gaps, enhance compliance and live up to the expectations ... from the commitments made by the African leaders.[120]

We fully share this acknowledgment by the AU of both its normative achievement and the limits in the effective implementation of its instruments. Ratifying the promising treaties referred to in the present study, some of them are not yet in force years after their adoption, will be the first step for the AU Member States to live up to the expectations from these treaties, and subsequent declarations, thus turning words to deeds.

NOTES

*   Djacoba Liva Tehindrazanarivelo holds a PhD in International Law (Graduate Institute of International Studies, Geneva), and is a lecturer at Boston University Study Abroad Geneva and at the Institute of Human Rights of the Catholic University of Lyon.

1.   Constitutive Act of the African Union (hereafter AU Constitutive Act), entered into force on 26 May 2001, Article 33(1); which also stipulates the devolution of OAU assets and liabilities to AU. Based on this succession, we will include in our analysis of the AU law and practice the OAU Decisions and achievements, where relevant.

2.   See Preamble of the AU Constitutive Act, and T. Maluwa, 'Reimagining African Unity: Preliminary Reflections on the Constitutive Act of the African Union', *African Yearbook of International Law* 9 (2001): 24.

3.   AU Constitutive Act, Article 3(h), emphasis added. According to AU organs' interpretations, as we will see, these 'other relevant human rights instruments' include IHL instruments. The same AU objective has been recalled in the Preamble of the 2001 Protocol to the Treaty Establishing the African Economic Community relating to the Pan-African Parliament (PAP Protocol).

4.   AU Constitutive Act, Article 4(h). The AU right to intervene is reaffirmed in Articles 4(j), 6(d) and 7(e) of the 2002 Protocol relating to the Establishment of the Peace and Security Council of the African Union (PSC Protocol), as well as in Article 8(1) of the 2009 African Union Convention for the Protection and Assistance of Internally Displaced Persons in Africa (AU IDPs Convention).

5.   AU Constitutive Act, Article 4(o). This principle is reiterated in the *Solemn Declaration on African Defence and Security Policy*, Sirte, 2004, para. 11(l).

6. By AU organs, we mean the organs created by the AU Constitutive Act and subsequent treaties (e.g., the Peace and Security Council, the Panel of the Wise, the Pan African Parliament) as well as those created by the treaties adopted under the former OAU, such as the African Commission on Human and Peoples' Rights or the African Committee of Experts on the Rights and Welfare of the Child.

7. Proclaimed on 27 January 1976, SADR is a State recognised by the OAU/AU, which regroups all African States, except Morocco which has a sovereignty claim over the Western Sahara territory. It was reported that 40 other States from Latin America, Caribbean Islands, Asia and Eastern Europe have also recognized SADR, with some of them cancelling or freezing their recognition from the early 1990s on, at the end of the Cold War; see http://www.arso.org/03-2.htm (accessed 30 September 2011). At the United Nations (UN) website (http://www.un.org/aboutun) (accessed 30 September 2011), SADR is listed neither among UN member States nor as part of the Permanent Observers (Holy See and Palestine).

8. Adopted on 11 July 1990, entered into force on 29 November 1999.

9. Adopted on 11 July 2003, entered into force on 25 November 2005.

10. Guidelines for state reporting under the Protocol to the African Charter on Human and Peoples' Rights on the Rights of Women in Africa, developed by a gender Experts meeting in Pretoria, South Africa, in August 2009 and adopted by the AU Commission in May 2010, in C. Heyns and M. Killander, eds, *Compendium of Key Human Rights Documents of the African Union*, 4th edition (Pretoria University Law Press, 2010), 208.

11. PSC/PR/BR(CCLXIX), 29 March 2011, paras 3, 4 and 5. See also Institute of Security Studies, *Peace and Security Council Report*, No. 22 (May 2011): 14.

12. Hereafter AU IDPs Convention, adopted in Kampala, Uganda, on 23 October 2009, not yet in force. As of 22 August 2011, date of the latest record in the AU treaties website, http://www.au.int/en/treaties (accessed 30 September 2011) at the time of writing, there are 32 signatories and seven ratifications of the treaty, out of the 15 needed for its entry into force.

13. Guiding Principles on Internal Displacement, 1998, para. 3 of the Introduction and Principle 2(2). For further comments, see, among other, W. Kälin, 'Guiding Principles on Internal Displacement – Annotations', in *ASIL Studies in Transnational Legal Policy* 32 (2000), available at http://www.idpguidingprinciples.org/, Brookings-LSE Project on Internal Displacement (accessed 20 October 2011).

14. AU IDPs Convention, Article 3 (1)(c), (e), (f), (g) and (h).

15. Ibid., Article 4 (1).

16. Ibid., Article 4(4), (b), (c), (e), (g) and (h).

17. Ibid., Article 9(1), (b), (d), (e).

18. Such acts as members of armed groups shall be prohibited from include: a. Carrying out arbitrary displacement; b. Hampering the provision of protection and assistance to IDPs under any circumstances; c. Denying IDPs the right to live in satisfactory conditions of dignity, security, sanitation, food, water, health and shelter; and separating members of the same family; e. Recruiting children or requiring or permitting them to take part in hostilities under any circumstances; f. Forcibly recruiting persons, kidnapping, abduction or hostage taking, engaging in sexual slavery and trafficking in persons especially women and children; g. Impeding humanitarian assistance and passage of all relief consignments, equipment and personnel to IDPs; h. Attacking or otherwise harming humanitarian personnel and resources or other materials deployed for the assistance or benefit of IDPs and destroying, confiscating or diverting such materials; and i. Violating the civilian and humanitarian character of the places where IDPs are sheltered and infiltrating such places; ibid., Article 7(5)(a), (b), (c), (e), (f), (g), (h) and (i).

19. Hereafter ICC Rome Statute, adopted on 17 July 1998 and entered into force on 1 July 2002.

20. Hereafter Grand Bay Declaration, adopted on 16 April 1999, http://www.achpr.org/instruments/grandbay/

21. Ibid., paras 13 (j) and (m). The African Commission on Human and Peoples' Rights made the same call.

22. The Assembly 'Invites African States to massively accede to this Convention in order to strengthen their contribution to the building and consolidation of International Humanitarian Law, particularly the formulation of international rules for the control of conventional weapons', Assembly/AU/Dec.321(XV), 27 July 2010, para. 4.

23. Grand Bay Declaration, paras 14 and 20.

24. This actually is not technically correct but could be taken as part of the aspiration not to separate the two bodies of law when it comes to the protection of the civilian population.

25. *Kigali Declaration* of 8 May 2003, available at: http://www.africa-union.org/Structure_of_the_ Commission/Political%20Affairs/x/KIGALI%20DECLARATION%20as%20adopted%20in%20 Kigali.pdf

26. C. Ewumbue-Monono and C. Von Flüe, 'Promotion of International Humanitarian Law through Cooperation between the ICRC and the African Union', *International Review of the Red Cross* 85, No. 852 (2003): 766–767. See also this article for further analysis of the nature, object and achievements of the cooperation between the two organizations, which we cannot develop in the present chapter for reason of space. It suffices to mention that the cooperation has formally started in 1992 in an agreement between the OAU and the ICRC, as part of the ICRC's 'humanitarian diplomacy' aimed at 'spreading knowledge of international humanitarian law, applying and ensuring the application of its provisions, facilitating accomplishment of the institution's mission and promoting independent humanitarian action' (ibid., 750). The ICRC has participated in the elaboration of AU treaties relating to humanitarian issues through its liaison office established in 1993 the AU headquarter, in Addis Ababa, which is now a Permanent Observer.

27. AU Constitutive Act, Article 13(e).

28. The ACHPR was adopted on 27 June 1981 and entered into force on 21 October 1986. The African Commission is mandated, among others, to promote human and people's rights in Africa, review the periodic state reports on the implementation of the ACHPR, and consider individual and inter-State communications on allegations of the violation of the ACHPR.

29. ACHPR/Res.7(XIV)93: Resolution on the Promotion and Respect of International Humanitarian Law and Human and Peoples' Rights (1993), Preamble and paras 1 and 2.

30. ACHPR/Res.14(XVI)94: Resolution on the Situation of Human Rights in Africa (1994), Preamble and para. 6.

31. ACHPR/Res.18(XVII)95: Resolution on Anti-Personnel Land Mines (1995), Preamble and para. 1. See also ACHPR/Res.26(XXIV)98: Resolution on the Ratification of the Convention on Anti-Personnel Mines (1998).

32. ACHPR/Res.26(XXIV)98: Resolution on the Ratification of the Treaty on the International Criminal Court (1998), paras 1 and 2. See also ACHPR/Res.59(XXXI)02: Resolution on the Ratification of the Statute of the International Criminal Court by OAU Member States (2002).

33. On these seminars and other measures of promotion, see G. Gaggioli, *L'influence mutuelle entre les droits de l'homme et le droit international humanitaire à la lumière du droit à la vie* (Paris: Pedone, forthcoming).

34. ACmHPR, Communication No. 227/99, *D.R. Congo v. Burundi, Rwanda and Uganda*, May 2003.

35. Ibid., para. 69.

36. Ibid., para. 70, emphasis added; see also para. 78.

37. Para. 79, African Commission on Human and Peoples Rights, Communication 227/99, *D.R. Congo/Burundi, Rwanda and Uganda*, decided on the 33rd ordinary session, May 2003, *20th Activity Report: Jan 2006–June 2006*, published in French in *Recueil africain des décisions des droits humains 2004* (Pretoria: Pretoria University Law Press – PULP, 2011) p. 99, English text available at http://caselaw.ihrda.org/doc/227.99/view/ (accessed 15 October 2012)

38. Ibid.

39. These grave violations of both HRL and IHL in the Democratic Republic of the Congo are later confirmed in the Report of the Mapping Exercise documenting the most serious violations of human rights and international humanitarian law committed within the territory of the Democratic Republic of the Congo between March 1993 and June 2003, published by the UN Office of the High Commissioner for Human Rights in August 2010, 566. Unsurprisingly, all three neighbouring States mentioned above appended comments to the Mapping Report, contesting parts of the findings on their violations of HRL and IHL. For the report and the three comments, see http://www.ohchr.org/en/ Countries/AfricaRegion/Pages/RDCProjetMapping.aspx (accessed 20 October 2011).

40. African Commission on HPR, *D.R. Congo v. Burundi, Rwanda, Uganda*, para. 65. See also Communication Nos 140/94, 141/94, 145/95, *Constitutional Rights Project, Civil Liberties Organisation and Media Rights Agenda / Nigeria*, para. 41; and Communication Nos 279/03, *Sudan Human Rights v. The Sudan* and 296/05, *Centre on Human Rights and Evictions v. The Sudan*, para. 165.

41. Communication Nos 48/90, 50/91, 89/93, *Amnesty International, Comité Loosli Bachelard, Lawyers' Committee for Human Rights, Association of Members of the Episcopal Conference of East Africa v. Sudan*, para. 50.

42. Assembly/AU/Dec.213(XII), Decision on the Implementation of the Assembly Decision on the Abuse of the Principle of Universal Jurisdiction, February 2009, para. 9.

43. Assembly/AU/Dec.245(XIII), Decision on the meeting of African States Parties to the Rome Statute of the International Criminal Court (ICC), 3 July 2009, para. 5.
44. Protocol on the Statute of the African Court of Justice and Human Rights (ACJHR Statute), Articles 16 and 17; adopted on 1 July 2008, not yet in force. Requiring 15 ratifications to that end, it has been ratified only by five of the 28 signatory States as of 14 August 2012, the date of the latest record at the AU treaties website (by November 2012).
45. Ibid., Article 31(d) and (f).
46. According to Article 30 of the ACJHR Statute: 'The following entities shall also be entitled to submit cases to the Court on any violation of a right guaranteed by the African Charter, by the Charter on the Rights and Welfare of the Child, the Protocol to the African Charter on Human and Peoples' Rights on the Rights of Women in Africa, or any other legal instrument relevant to human rights ratified by the States Parties concerned: a) State Parties to the present Protocol; b) the African Commission on Human and Peoples' Rights; c) the African Committee of Experts on the Rights and Welfare of the Child; d) African Intergovernmental Organizations accredited to the Union or its organs; e) African National Human Rights Institutions; f) Individuals or relevant Non-Governmental Organizations accredited to the African Union or to its organs, subject to the provisions of Article 8 of the Protocol.'
47. Hereafter PSC Protocol, adopted on 9 July 2002, entered into force on 26 December 2003.
48. Ibid., Article 3(f).
49. This idea is also reflected in the AU Assembly Decision on the accession of African countries to the Convention on banning the use of certain conventional weapons with a traumatic effect or which strike indiscriminately, where the Assembly 'Reiterates its determination to promote peace and security in Africa and in the world by contributing to the … maintenance of International Humanitarian Law'; Assembly/AU/Dec.321(XV), 27 July 2010, para. 2.
50. PSC Protocol, Article 4(c).
51. Ibid., Article 6(d) and (f).
52. Henri Boshoff, *Burundi: The African Union's First Mission, African Security Analysis Programme Situation Report* (Pretoria: Institute for Security Studies, 10 June 2003), available at http://www.iss.co.za/AF/current/burundijun03.pdf (accessed 16 November 2004).
53. For the evolution of the mandates of AMIS, AMIS II, AMIS II-Enhanced and then the AU-UN hybrid force in Darfur (UNAMID), see D.L. Tehindrazanarivelo, 'The African Union and Reactions to International Crimes', in *International Law, Conflict and Development: The Emergence of a Holistic Approach in International Affairs. Liber Amicorum Joseph Voyame*, eds W. Kälin, R. Kolb, C.A. Spenlé and M. Voyame (Leiden and Boston: Martinus Nijhoff, 2010), 538–549.
54. Report of the Chairperson of the AU Commission and the Secretary-General of the UN on the Hybrid Operation in Darfur, PSC/PR/2(LXXIX), 22 June 2007, para. 69.
55. AU Commission, Press Release No. 26/2010, 5 March 2010. The Symposium saw the participation of experts from the AU Commission, the Asia-Pacific Civil-Military Centre of Excellence – Australia, UN DPKO, OCHA, UNHCR, ICRC, and key AU troop and police contributing countries.
56. PSC/PR/BR (CCLXXIX), 18 May 2011.
57. Message from Ambassador Boubacar Gaoussou Diarra, Special Representative of the Chairperson of the AU Commission for Somalia, in *AMISOM Bulletin* 30 (August 2011): 2. By its Resolution 2010, the UN Security Council extended until 31 October 2012 its authorization to the deployment of AMISOM and the latter's ability 'to take all necessary measures to carry out its mandate'. It also welcomed the progress made by AMISOM in reducing civilian casualties during its operations and urged AMISOM to continue to undertake its efforts to prevent civilian casualties and to develop an effective approach to the protection of civilians as requested by the AU PSC; S/RES/2010, 30 September 2011, paras 1 and 7.
58. Adopted by the Ministers of OAU Member States on 1 December 2000, in anticipation of the UN Conference on the Illicit Trade in Small Arms and Light Weapons in all its Aspects, held in New York in July 2001.
59. Hereafter Solemn Declaration on CADSP, adopted at the 2nd extraordinary session of the AU Assembly held in Sirte, Libya, from 27 to 28 February 2004.
60. Ibid., para. 8(e), (f), (o) and (p) of the operative part.
61. M. Juma, ed., *Compendium on Key Documents on African Peace and Security* (Pretoria University Law Press, 2006), 83. This concept of human security is developed in paragraph 6 of the operative part of the Solemn Declaration on CADSP.
62. Solemn Declaration on CADSP, para. 9(d) and (f) of the operative part.

63. Preamble, AU Protocol to the OAU Convention on the Prevention and Combating of Terrorism, adopted on 8 July 2004, not yet in force. As of 17 October 2012, it had been signed by 43 States and ratified by 14 out of the 15 required for its entry into force.

64. See, for example, the prohibition of terrorist acts in Article 33 of the 1949 Geneva Convention IV, Article 4(2)(d) of the 1977 Protocol II, reinforced by the incrimination of such acts as violations of common Article 3 of the Four Geneva Conventions and the inclusion of Article 4(d) of Protocol II in the Statute of the ICTR (Annex to S/RES/955, 8 November 1994); the prohibition of acts of terror as means of warfare in Article 52(2) of Protocol I and Article 13(2) of Protocol II, which were qualified as war crimes by the ICTY, *Galic*, Judgment 5 December 2003 (Case No. IT-98-29-T), paras 86–138); see P.-M. Dupuy, 'Les Nations Unies et la lutte contre le terrorisme international', in *La Charte des Nations Unies: commentaire article par article*, eds J.P. Cot, A. Pellet and M. Forteau, 3rd edition (Paris: Economica, 2005), 163ff.; M. Sassòli and A.A. Bouvier, *How Does Law Protect in War?*, 2nd edition, Vol. I (Geneva: International Committee of the Red Cross, 2006), 112–114.

65. *Legality of the Threat or Use of Nuclear Weapons*, Advisory Opinion, I.C.J. Reports 1996, paras 36, 78 and 95. See also para. 105 (2)d.

66. Provided for in Article 13 of the PSC Protocol, the ASF is one of the subsidiary organs of the PSC, composed of standby multidisciplinary contingents, with civilian and military components stationed in their countries of origin and ready for rapid deployment at appropriate notice to perform various types of peace support operations; PSC Protocol, Article 13(3), (b) and (f).

67. Ibid., Article 15(3) and (4).

68. Ibid., Article 13(13).

69. Policy Framework for the Establishment of the African Standby Force and the Military Staff Committee (Part 1), adopted by the African Chiefs of Defence Staff (ACDS) at their 3rd meeting on 14 May 2003 in Addis Ababa, para. 1.4. The Policy Framework was considered, improved and revised by the AU Regional Economic Communities – i.e. the eight sub-regional organisations officially recognized by the AU – and other African and External Partners in Addis Ababa on 14–15 April 2003, and subsequently by a meeting of Government Experts in Addis Ababa from 12–14 May 2003. At its July 2003 Summit, the AU Assembly adopted Decision Assembly/AU/Dec.16(II), which, *inter alia*, took note of the Policy Framework document. The ACDS revised the Policy Framework at their 4th meeting in January 2004.

70. Ibid., para. 2.2. Paragraph 1.6 of the Policy Framework enumerates six typical operations of the ASF (called 'conflict scenarios'), namely: 1) AU/Regional Military advice to a Political mission, 2) AU/Regional Observer mission co-deployed with UN mission, 3) Stand alone AU/Regional Observer mission, 4) AU/Regional Peacekeeping Force for UN Charter Chapter VI and preventive deployment missions, 5) AU Peacekeeping Force for complex multidimensional Peacekeeping mission – low level spoilers (a feature of many current conflicts), and 6) AU intervention – e.g., genocide situations where the international community does not act promptly.

71. See ibid., paras. 2.12, 2.15 and 5.7.

72. Hereafter ASF Roadmap, produced at an Experts meeting on the relationship between the AU and the Regional Mechanisms for Conflict Prevention, Management and Resolution held in Addis Ababa from 22 to 23 March 2005.

73. Ibid., para. 6. For further information, see J. Cilliers, *The African Standby Force: An Update on Progress* (Pretoria: ISS Paper 160, March 2008); J.E. Marshall, *Building an Effective African Standby Force to Promote African Stability, Conflict Resolution and Prosperity* (London: LSE Crisis States Discussion Papers No. 16, April 2009).

74. Protocol Relating to the Mechanism for Conflict Prevention, Management, Resolution, Peace-Keeping and Security, adopted on 10 December 1999, Articles 2(d), 21, and 30. Under Article 22, the ECOMOG is charged, among other things, with the missions of peacekeeping and restoration of peace; humanitarian intervention in support of humanitarian disaster, such as in event of serious and massive violation of human rights and the rule of law; and peacebuilding, disarmament and demobilisation; ibid., Article 22(b), (c) and (f).

75. Protocol on Democracy and Good Governance, adopted on 21 December 2001, Article 23.

76. Policy Framework for the Establishment of the Eastern Africa Standby Brigade (EASBRIG), adopted at the 1st EASBRIG Assembly of Heads of State and Government in Addis Ababa on 11 April 2005, paras 4 and 26. EASBRIG is composed of countries in the region namely Comoros, Djibouti, Eritrea, Ethiopia, Kenya, Madagascar, Mauritius, Rwanda, Seychelles, Somalia, Sudan, Tanzania and Uganda.

77. SADC Mutual Defence Pact, adopted in Dar es Salaam, Tanzania, 27 August 2003, Article 15(3) and (4).

78. Standing Orders of the Central African Multinational Force (FOMAC), adopted at the 10th Ordinary Session of Heads of State and Government of ECCAS in June 2002 in Malabo, Equatorial Guinea, Article 11. Article 27(iii) of the same document added that the FOMAC Commander shall, among other missions, ensure the security of the staff and equipment of humanitarian organisations in the FOMAC mission area.
79. Ibid., Article 15.
80. In the following terms: 'Reiterates its commitment to fight impunity in conformity with the provisions of Article 4(h) of the Constitutive Act of the African Union'; see the list of Decisions *infra* notes 85 to 87.
81. Elsewhere, we argued that this attests the fundamentally collective nature of the AU right to intervene, unlike the controversial 'right or duty of humanitarian intervention'. Building on the I.C.J. interpretation of the conditions of admission to the UN, we concluded that the PSC recommendation is a prerequisite to the Assembly Decision on the intervention; see Tehindrazanarivelo, *supra* note 53, at 533–534.
82. Adopted on 31 January 2005 and entered into force on 18 December 2009. However, the intervention could be decided against any AU member, not only States Parties to the Non-Aggression and Common Defence Pact, based on the collective recognition of such an AU right to intervene in Article 4(h) of the Constitutive Act.
83. AU Constitutive Act, Article 4(o); reiterated in the 2004 Solemn Declaration on ADSP, para. 11(l). We saw earlier that the PSC Protocol, in its Article 3(f), expressly connects the respect for the sanctity of human life with IHL, which the PSC shall 'promote and encourage'.
84. Articles 3(9) and 7 of the African Charter on Democracy, Elections and Governance, 30 January 2007, entered into force on 15 February 2012.
85. Assembly/AU/Dec.103(VI), 24 January 2006, para. 1; Assembly/AU/Dec.127(VII), July 2006, para. 3 (titled Decision on the Hissène Habré Case and the African Union); Assembly/AU/Dec.240(XII), February 2009; Assembly/AU/246(XIII), July 2009; Assembly/AU/Dec.272(XIV), February 2010, para. 2; Assembly/AU/Dec.297(XV), 27 July 2010, para. 2; Assembly/AU/Dec.340(XVI), 31 January 2011, para. 4 (Decision on the Hissène Habré Case). Decisions 240(XII) and 246(XIII) do not reiterate explicitly the commitment to fight impunity but call upon the AU members to contribute to the budget of the Hissène Habré trial, and deplore the lack of positive reaction to that call.
86. These Decisions have different titles: Assembly/AU/Dec.221(XII), Decision on the application by the International Criminal Court (ICC) Prosecutor for the indictment of the President of the Republic of the Sudan, 1–3 February 2009; Assembly/AU/Dec.245(XIII), Decision on the meeting of African States Parties to the Rome Statute of the International Criminal Court (ICC), 3 July 2009; Assembly/AU/Dec.270(XIV), Decision on the Report of the Second Meeting of States Parties to the Rome Statute on the International Criminal Court (ICC), 2 February 2010; Assembly/AU/ Dec.296(XV), Decision on the Progress Report of the Commission on the Implementation of Decision Assembly/AU/DEC.270(XIV) on the Second Ministerial Meeting on the Rome Statute of the International Criminal Court (ICC), 27 July 2010; Assembly/AU/Dec.334(XVI), Decision on the Implementation of the Decisions on the International Criminal Court, 31 January 2011.
87. Assembly/AU/Dec.199 (XI), Decision on the Report of the Commission on the Abuse of the Principle of Universal Jurisdiction, 30 June to 1 July 2008, para. 3; Assembly/AU/Dec.213(XII), Decision on the Implementation of the Assembly Decision on the Abuse of the Principle of Universal Jurisdiction, February 2009, para. 3; Decision(s) on the Abuse of the Principle of Universal Jurisdiction: Assembly/AU/Dec.271(XIV), 2 February 2010, para. 4; Assembly/AU/Dec.292(XV), 27 July 2010, para. 2; Assembly/AU/Dec.335(XVI), January 2011, para. 2.
88. Assembly/AU/Dec.199 (XI), 1 July 2008, para. 3.
89. Report of the Committee of Eminent African Jurists on the case of Hissène Habré (hereafter 'CEAJ Report'), May 2006, paras 29 and 17–19. The document, on file with the author, is undated and unreferenced.
90. Assembly/AU/Dec.127(VII), para. 3. In the same vein, the Committee of Eminent African Jurists while considering the establishment of an African *ad hoc* tribunal as another option indicates that '[t]he power of the Assembly to set up such an ad hoc tribunal is based upon Article 3(h), 4(h) and (o), 9(1)(d), and Article 5(1)(d) of the Constitutive Act of the African Union'; CEAJ Report, para. 23. Article 9(1)(d) gives the Assembly the power to 'establish any organ of the Union' and Article 5(1)(d) refers to the Court of Justice as one of the AU organs. The rest of the mentioned provisions relate to the various principles on the AU commitment to fight against impunity, listed earlier.

91. Assembly/AU/Dec.127(VII), para. 5(ii). Senegal has accepted this 'African mandate', which it seems to see not as a reminder of its obligation under the 1984 Convention against torture, to which it is a party, but as a service given to the AU. At the time of writing, the 'mandate' is not yet fulfilled.
92. Assembly/AU/Dec.245(XIII), 3 July 2009, para. 6.
93. Whether the practice is consistent with this normative evolution is not the point here, as such a discussion goes beyond the scope of the present study. For that discussion, see D.L. Tehindrazanari-velo, 'The African Union Principle on the Fight against Impunity and the Arrest Warrants for Omar Hassan El-Bashir', in *Perspectives of International Law in the 21st Century. Liber Amicorum Professor Christian Dominicé in honour of his 80th birthday*, eds M. Kohen, R. Kolb and D. L. Tehindrazanarivelo (Leiden: Martinus Nijhoff, 2011), 397–442.
94. AHG/Decl.2(XXXVI), 12 July 2000.
95. PSC/PR/Comm(CLXXV), 5 March 2009, paras 9 and 10.
96. PSC/PR/Comm(CXCVIII), 21 July 2009, para. 13. See also PSC/MIN/Comm(CXLII) Rev. 1, 21 July 2008, paras 2, 10 and 11, adopted just after the ICC Prosecutor's application for an arrest warrant for El-Bashir.
97. PSC/PR/BR.1(CCLXX), 5 April 2011, paras 2 and 4.
98. PSC/PR/BR(CCXXXIX), 24 August 2010, last paragraph.
99. AMISOM Press Release of 18 October 2011, http://amisom-au.org/amisom-condemns-deliberate-targeting-of-civilians-in-mogadishu/ (accessed 25 October 2011).
100. Communiqué of the Consultative meeting between members of the Security Council of the United Nations and the Peace and Security Council of the African Union, 21 May 2011, para. 18.
101. Ibid., paras 8, 9 and 11. See also the Statement of the Third Meeting of the International Contact Group on Libya (Abu Dhabi, 9 June 2011), which declared that 'the use of force against civilians by Qadhafi and his followers and mercenaries must cease immediately and unconditionally'; and deplored the severe magnitude of devastation and civilian casualties as a direct result of the Qadhafi regime's actions, and reiterated its firm intention to further pursue the objectives set by UN Security Council Resolutions 1970 and 1973 in order to protect civilians (paras 2 and 3).
102. ACHPR/Res.181(EXT.OS/IX)2011: Resolution on the human rights situation in Libya, 1 March 2011.
103. See, for example, Resolutions ACHPR/Res.8(XV)94 and ACHPR/Res.12(XVI)94 on Rwanda; ACHPR/Res.15(XVII)95 on Sudan; ACHPR/Res.67(XXXV)04 on Ivory Coast; ACHPR/Res.68(XXXV)04 on Darfur; ACHPR/Res.70(XXXV)04 on Nigeria; ACHPR/Res.74(XXXVII)05 on the human rights situation in Darfur; ACHPR/Res.103(XXXX)06 on the Situation of Women in the Democratic Republic of the Congo; ACHPR/Res.129(EXT.OS/IV)08 on the Human Rights Situation in the Republic of Somalia; see Gaggioli, *supra* note 33. The same author remarked, however, that in other Resolutions relating to conflict situations, the African Commission made no reference to IHL, for instance in Resolutions ACHPR/Res.24(XIX)96 on Burundi; ACHPR/Res.20(XIX)96 on Liberia; ACHPR/Res.40(XXVI)99 on the situation of human rights in Africa; ACHPR/Res.50(XXVIII)00 on the respect for and immediate implementation of the Arusha peace agreements on Burundi; ACHPR/Res.49(XXVIII)00 on the situation in Palestine and occupied territories; and ACHPR/Res.44(XXVII)00 on the peace process in the Democratic Republic of the Congo; ibid.
104. Protocol to the Treaty Establishing the African Economic Community relating to the Pan-African Parliament (PAP Protocol) of 2 March 2001, entered into force on 14 December 2003, Article 11(1).
105. Permanent Committee on Justice and Human Rights of the Pan-African Parliament, Resolution on Fact-Finding Mission to Sierra Leone, PAP(2)/P/CJHR/RES(IV), 27 May 2011.
106. African States actually constitute the largest group in the Assembly of States Parties (ASP) to the Rome Statute. Among the five regional groups in the ASP, there are 33 African States, 26 Asia-Pacific States, 18 Eastern European States, 26 Latin-American and Caribbean States, and 26 Western European and other States; see http://www.icc-cpi.int/Menus/ASP/States+Parties/African%20States (accessed 31 October 2011).
107. Assembly/AU/Dec.366(XVII), Decision on the Implementation of the Assembly Decisions on the International Criminal Court, 1 July 2011.
108. See Assembly/AU/Dec.245(XIII), para. 8(iv) and (v).
109. This is actually different from the choice of the mechanisms for transitional or post-conflict justice by a State within its territory, where the decision belongs to the national stakeholders in due consideration of relevant international rules and principles.

110.   A. Cassese, *International Criminal Court* (Oxford: Oxford University Press, 2003), 267–270. The principle was first affirmed in an international text in Article 7 of the Statute of the International Military Tribunal of Nuremberg (London Agreement, 8 August 1945).

111.   '1. This Statute shall apply equally to all persons without any distinction based on official capacity. In particular, official capacity as a Head of State or Government, a member of a Government or parliament, an elected representative or a government official shall in no case exempt a person from criminal responsibility under this Statute, nor shall it, in and of itself, constitute a ground for reduction of sentence. '2. Immunities or special procedural rules which may attach to the official capacity of a person, whether under national or international law, shall not bar the Court from exercising its jurisdiction over such a person.'

112.   Rome Statute, Article 98: Cooperation with respect to waiver of immunity and consent to surrender '1. The Court may not proceed with a request for surrender or assistance which would require the requested State to act inconsistently with its obligations under international law with respect to the State or diplomatic immunity of a person or property of a third State, unless the Court can first obtain the cooperation of that third State for the waiver of the immunity. '2. The Court may not proceed with a request for surrender which would require the requested State to act inconsistently with its obligations under international agreements pursuant to which the consent of a sending State is required to surrender a person of that State to the Court, unless the Court can first obtain the cooperation of the sending State for the giving of consent for the surrender.'

113.   Assembly/AU/Dec.245(XIII), para. 8(iv) and (v).

114.   A. Cassese, 'Guistizia impossibile', *La Repubblica*, 5 March 2009, French translation in *Courrier international*, 5 March 2009, under the title 'Soudan – Un mandat d'arrêt aussi spectaculaire qu'inutile'.

115.   See *Case concerning the Arrest Warrant of 11 April 2000* (D.R. Congo v. Belgium), Judgment, I.C.J. Reports 2002, para. 58. The I.C.J. observed that respect of this customary rule on immunity does not mean impunity, and it identified four circumstances under which criminal prosecution against persons enjoying such immunity is possible: (1) such persons could be tried by their own countries' courts in accordance with the relevant rules of domestic law because they enjoy no criminal immunity under international law in their countries; (2) their States may decide to waive the immunity; (3) they will no longer enjoy all of the immunities accorded by international law after they cease to hold office, and then might be tried by a court of another State which has, under international law, established its jurisdiction to do so; (4) they may be subject to criminal proceedings before certain international criminal courts, if such courts have jurisdiction (ibid., para. 61).

116.   P. Gaeta, 'Official Capacity and Immunities,' in *The Rome Statute of the International Criminal Court: A Commentary*, eds A. Cassese, P. Gaeta and J.R.W.D Jones (Oxford: Oxford University Press, 2002), 992.

117.   O. Triffterer, 'Article 27,' in *Commentary on the Rome Statute of the International Criminal Court – Observers' Notes, Article by Article*, ed. O. Triffterer, 2nd edition (Oxford: Hart Publishing, 2008), 787.

118.   Assembly/AU/Dec.366(XVII), 1 July 2011, para. 5. Article 23(2) of the Constitutive Act provides that 'any Member State that fails to comply with the decisions and policies of the Union may be subjected to … sanctions'.

119.   UN Doc. S/2009/277, Report of the Secretary-General on the protection of civilians in armed conflict, 29 May 2009, Chapter III, paras 26ff.

120.   Second AU High Level Retreat on the Promotion of Peace, Security and Stability in Africa, Cairo Declaration: 'Strengthening Political Governance for Peace, Security and Stability in Africa', HL/Retreat/YoPS.Decl.(II), 5 September 2011, 3.

25. A new World Court of Human Rights: a role for international humanitarian law?

*Manfred Nowak**

1. PROTECTING DIGNITY: AN AGENDA FOR HUMAN RIGHTS

On the occasion of the 60th anniversary of the Universal Declaration of Human Rights, the Swiss Government presented an 'Agenda for Human Rights'.[1] In addition to a number of substantive recommendations for improving the enjoyment and implementation of human rights in the 21st century, the Swiss Agenda includes two institutional proposals: the establishment of a Global Fund for National Human Rights Protection Systems and of a World Court of Human Rights. The Swiss Agenda is based on a report by a 'Panel of Eminent Persons' chaired jointly by Mary Robinson and Paulo Sérgio Pinheiro. This report devotes one chapter to arguing for the need for a World Court of Human Rights.[2] It concludes as follows:

> The World Court of Human Rights should be a permanent court established by a multilateral treaty under the auspices of the United Nations. It should be competent to decide in a final and binding manner on complaints of human rights violations committed by state and non-state actors alike and provide adequate reparation to victims. The United Nations Secretary-General is requested to commission an expert study on ways to advance towards the establishment of a World Court of Human Rights.[3]

The Panel of Eminent Persons has not ceased to exist with the publication and formal promulgation of the Swiss Agenda for Human Rights in December 2008. As the term 'progress report' indicates, the Swiss Agenda itself is an ongoing project aimed at convincing governments around the world, global civil society and the United Nations of the urgent need to act in order to narrow the increasing implementation gap in the field of universal human rights. Within the framework of the Swiss Agenda, the Panel of Eminent Persons selected a number of research projects on various aspects of the Agenda, including two research projects aimed at drafting a Statute for the World Court of Human Rights. In June 2009, two draft Statutes were presented to the Panel, one developed by Martin Scheinin (European University Institute in Florence), the other one by Manfred Nowak and Julia Kozma (University of Vienna).[4] The Panel requested all three authors to join forces and submit a consolidated version of a draft Statute. On the basis of extensive discussions within the Association of Human Rights Institutes (AHRI), the COST project on 'The Role of the EU in UN Human Rights Reform', and with representatives of the Berkeley Project 2048 such a consolidated version was submitted by the three authors to the Panel in June 2010.[5] It forms the basis for the following discussion.

2. THE RATIONALE BEHIND THE FUTURE WORLD COURT OF HUMAN RIGHTS

The idea of a World Court of Human Rights is not new. As early as 1947, the Australian Government strongly argued in the UN Commission for Human Rights for the establishment of an International Court of Human Rights. After all, the proposition that where there is no remedy there is no right is a notion found in most legal systems, and should apply to human rights in the same way as it applies to civil rights and obligations, labour rights, administrative and other domestic rights. This idea behind the early Australian proposal was later confirmed by the UN General Assembly when it adopted in 2005 the Basic Principles and Guidelines on the Right to a Remedy and Reparation for Victims of Gross Violations of International Human Rights Law and Serious Violations of International Humanitarian Law.[6] The term 'human rights' with its corresponding obligations of duty-bearers implies accountability, i.e., the rights-holders should have the legal possibility in case of an alleged violation of such obligation to hold the duty-bearer accountable before an independent national, regional or international court. If the court finds a violation, it must have the power to order adequate reparation, including restitution, rehabilitation, compensation, satisfaction and guarantees of non-repetition. This is the general legal approach to civil wrongs. Why should it be different for violations of the most important of all rights, i.e., human rights? Needless to say, binding judgments of human rights courts need to be enforced by competent law enforcement agencies. On the national level, individuals claiming a violation of their human rights usually enjoy the right to a legal remedy before an independent domestic court. Since World War II, all regional organizations with a more or less functioning system for the protection of human rights, i.e., the Council of Europe, the Organization of American States and the African Union, have established a regional court with the power to decide in a legally binding manner on individual human rights complaints.[7] The European and Inter-American Courts of Human Rights also have the power to order States to provide reparation to the victims of human rights violations.

The United Nations, on the contrary, adopted a total of nine core human rights treaties and established nine different treaty monitoring bodies, most of which are entrusted with the optional mandate to decide on individual human rights complaints. But this function is still phrased in the spirit of the Cold War when only the smallest common denominator between Western and Socialist States could be achieved. In fact, UN treaty monitoring bodies are only quasi-judicial expert bodies which decide, if at all, in a legally non-binding manner by means of 'final views' on 'communications' from individuals. Although the Human Rights Committee and other treaty bodies have done their best to formulate their 'views' similar to court judgments, it is not surprising that only a few individuals have availed themselves during the last four decades of this possibility.[8]

Since the need for a fundamental reform of the UN treaty monitoring system has long been acknowledged,[9] the former UN High Commissioner for Human Rights has advocated for a consolidated treaty body which, however, could only be achieved by means of amendments to all relevant UN human rights treaties. This is not only unrealistic to achieve, it would also be counterproductive as it would continue to deprive individuals at the global level of their rights to hold the duty bearers accountable before an independent court. A World Court of Human Rights, on the other hand, could be created without any treaty amendment by adopting a new treaty, similar to the Rome Statute for an International Criminal Court. States ratifying the Statute of the World Court would only gradually hand over the competence to decide on individual complaints from existing treaty bodies to the World Court, and the treaty bodies consisting of experts from different disciplines and with a specific expertise in children rights, women rights and other areas covered by their specific treaties could concentrate on their main function, namely to examine State reports. As a judicial body, the World Court should be established as a full-time professional court, similar to the European Court of Human Rights, consisting only of highly qualified lawyers deciding by means of binding judgments on individual complaints. In conformity with the principle of shared responsibility in the 21st century, the World Court should also be competent to decide on complaints against other entities than States, such as inter-governmental organizations, transnational corporations and rebel groups willing to voluntarily accept the jurisdiction of the Court.

3. IS THERE A ROLE FOR INTERNATIONAL HUMANITARIAN LAW?

Legally speaking, it is up to the drafters of the Statute for a World Court to decide which treaties shall be subject to the jurisdiction of the Court. Indeed, there are significant differences between the various proposals submitted so far. While the Berkeley Project 2048 suggested establishing the jurisdiction of the Court only in relation to a number of 'fundamental rights',[10] the draft by Martin Scheinin wished to entrust the Court to deal with all core UN human rights treaties, i.e., those treaties which are presently subject to the monitoring of existing treaty bodies.[11] The draft of Nowak and Kozma, on the other hand, went far beyond the core treaties and included a significant number of other human rights treaties of the United Nations and its specialized agencies. It did not include, however, the four Geneva Conventions or other treaties relating to international humanitarian law. Article 5(1) of the consolidated draft Statute contains, as a compromise, a fairly complete list of current UN human rights treaties but neither treaties of UN specialized agencies nor those relating to inter-national humanitarian law. Article 5(2) provides for a simplified procedure to add other treaties to this list: 'On the proposal of a State Party any additional treaty can be included in the list of treaties specified in paragraph 1 by decision of two-thirds of the Assembly of States Parties'. In principle, the Assembly of States Parties could, therefore, also include the Geneva Conventions or other treaties in the field of international humanitarian law or treaties relating to other fields of international law, such as environmental law. In such a case, all States Parties to the Geneva Conventions could in principle accept the jurisdiction of the World Court unless they make a reservation in accordance with Article 50(1). On the other hand, each State Party may declare in accordance with Article 50(4) at any time that it 'recognizes the jurisdiction of the Court also in relation to UN human rights treaties not listed in Article 5(1)'. This 'opting in' clause enables States Parties, for example, to recognize the jurisdiction of the World Court also in relation to certain treaties of specialized agencies, such as the ILO or UNESCO. Whether the jurisdiction of the World Court may be extended to the Geneva Conventions by means of an 'opting in'-declaration in accordance with Article 50(4) depends on whether they can be regarded as 'UN human rights treaties'. Such a decision would ultimately rest with the World Court.

Traditionally, international humanitarian law, which has its roots in the late 19th century and only applies in times of international or non-international armed conflicts, has been strictly separated from international human rights law which, in principle, only developed after World War II. In times of peace, only human rights law applies, whereas in times of war, both types of international law apply in a complementary manner.[12] Over the years, the relationship between human rights law, humanitarian law, refugee law and international criminal law intensified. While international criminal law originally applied primarily to grave breaches of the rules of international humanitarian law during armed conflicts (war crimes),[13] it today also relates to gross and systematic violations of human rights in times of peace (crimes against humanity). While the Statute of the International Criminal Tribunal for the former Yugoslavia (ICTY) still contains the nexus to times of armed conflict,[14] this explicit link no longer appears in the Statute of the International Criminal Court. One may discuss whether genocide can, in principle, be committed in times of 'peace', but the UN Genocide Convention of 1948 was always considered as part of international human rights law and is, therefore, also included in the draft Statute for the World Court. The same applies to the Geneva Refugee Convention of 1951. One might, therefore, argue that international human-itarian law, similar to international refugee law and criminal law, has become part of the broader concept of international human rights law. In fact, international human-itarian law spells out the specific human rights that apply to a particular group of human beings (whether combatants or civilians) during armed conflict, as the Refugee Convention contains specific rights of refugees, the Convention on the Rights of the Child contains specific rights of persons under the age of 18, or the Convention on the Rights of Persons with Disabilities contains specific rights of this vulnerable and discriminated group of human beings. The official 'Compilation of International Human Rights Instruments', published by the Office of the UN High Commissioner for Human Rights, seems to follow this approach, as it includes the Geneva Refugee Convention 1951, the Rome Statute of an International Criminal Court 1998 and the four Geneva Conventions of 1949 among 'human rights instruments'.[15] In the end, this seems to be more a question of a terminological than of a substantive nature relating to the definition of human rights in its traditional narrow sense or in a broader and more generic sense including all treaties that spell out subjective rights of human beings.

One may, nevertheless, raise the question whether there are substantive reasons that would speak in favour or against including the Geneva Conventions and other treaties in the field of international humanitarian law in the list of treaties subject to the jurisdiction of the World Court of Human Rights. One might argue, for example, that *human rights law only creates obligations of States whereas international human-itarian law also applies directly to certain non-State actors*, such as dissident armed forces or other organized armed groups. Although this argument is, in principle, still correct, it has lost much of its pervasive force due to recent developments, both in law and in theory, aimed at holding non-State actors accountable.[16] Already the Slavery

Convention of 1926 dealt primarily with the human rights responsibility of private actors, such as slave holders and slave traders.[17] Article IV of the Genocide Convention 1948 stipulates that persons committing genocide shall be punished, 'whether they are constitutionally responsible rulers, public officials or private individuals'. The International Covenant on Economic, Social and Cultural Rights 1966 repeatedly refers to the obligation of States Parties to take steps, 'individually and through international assistance and co-operation',[18] which implicitly contains a certain responsibility of the international (donor) community to assist poor States in meeting their obligations to fulfil the right to an adequate standard of living and similar rights.[19] The Convention on the Rights of the Child 1989 contains various references to the 'primary responsibility' of parents for the upbringing and development of the child.[20] The Palermo Protocol 2000 aims at preventing and combating trafficking in persons, above all women and children, by private actors of organized crime.[21] In addition to these specific examples, there is a general trend to hold non-State actors accountable for their human rights violations. The Special Representative of the Secretary-General on the issue of human rights and transnational corporations and other business enterprises, John Ruggie, has developed a 'protect, respect and remedy' policy framework, which explicitly includes the 'corporate responsibility to respect human rights, which means to act with due diligence to avoid infringing on the rights of others'.[22] This 'United Nations framework' aimed at holding the corporate sector directly responsible under international human rights standards has been explicitly welcomed by the Human Rights Council, States, the business community and civil society. Similar developments occurred in relation to the direct responsibility of inter-governmental organizations, above all the United Nations, for human rights violations, such as in territories under a transitional UN administration.[23] In the Swiss Agenda for Human Rights, this shared responsibility between States, inter-governmental organizations, the corporate sector, civil society and other non-State actors has been described as 'the 21st Century Approach' to human rights.[24] This means that in respect of the direct applicability of international law to non-State actors, there is no longer any significant difference between international humanitarian law and human rights law. Since the jurisdiction of the World Court should also be extended to inter-governmental organizations and non-State actors, the direct legal obligations of organized armed groups under international humanitarian law would speak in favour of applying the Statute of the World Court to international humanitarian law, most importantly to Article 3 common to the four Geneva Conventions and Protocol II relating to the protection of victims of non-international armed conflicts.

Another argument often used to make a clear distinction between international humanitarian law and human rights law is that humanitarian law forms part of traditional international law, i.e., determining relations amongst sovereign States to be implemented primarily through the *principle of reciprocity*, i.e., the existence of mutual/joint interests. Although international treaties for the protection of human rights are also agreed upon amongst States, the principle of reciprocity usually fails to ensure implementation as States are extremely reluctant to endanger their political or economic relations with other States 'only' because the respective governments violate human rights of their 'own' populations. The lack of any genuine State interest in protecting human rights in other States is the main reason why human rights treaties are in need of special mechanisms of independent expert monitoring and enforcement. If a

State violates the human rights of a person under its jurisdiction, it violates its treaty obligations, which are legal obligations towards all other States parties. In reality, however, the State violates its obligations towards the individuals concerned. On the other hand, if a State violates its obligations under international humanitarian law, it violates, at least in an international armed conflict, equally its obligations towards the individual concerned and the other State party to the conflict. This distinction becomes however, blurred in cases of non-international armed conflicts which today constitute the vast majority of all armed conflicts. It is interesting to note that the Preamble of Protocol II of 1977 establishes a clear link between international humanitarian law and human rights law by recalling that 'international instruments relating to human rights offer a basic protection to the human person', and at the same time emphasizing the 'need to ensure a better protection for the victims of those armed conflicts'. To sum up, although there are still certain differences between the two sets of international law regarding treaty obligations towards other States, and despite the fact that international humanitarian law is more phrased in the language of State obligations than rights of individuals, these differences do not constitute a convincing argument to exclude international humanitarian law from the jurisdiction of the World Court of Human Rights.

Another argument which might be used against the jurisdiction of the World Court is the *special role of the International Committee of the Red Cross* (ICRC) as a guardian of international humanitarian law and its principles of neutrality and absolute confidentiality. In its revised guidelines concerning its action in the event of violations of international humanitarian law of 2005, the ICRC confirmed that its 'preferred mode of action in response to a violation of international humanitarian law committed by a specific party is and remains to carry out representations within the framework of a bilateral confidential dialogue with the authorities responsible for the violation'.[25] Traditionally, the implementation of international humanitarian law rests on three pillars: the principle of reciprocity, the quiet diplomacy of the ICRC and its presence in the field, and the individual criminal responsibility for war crimes. Complaints by victims against violations of their rights under humanitarian law against the States or non-State actors responsible were never part of the implementation mechanisms. Monitoring of State compliance with international human rights law, on the other hand, is based primarily on individual complaints against States before independent committees (most importantly the UN Human Rights Committee), commissions (Inter-American and African Human Rights Commissions) and courts (European and Inter-American Court of Human Rights, African Court of Justice and Human Rights) and on the public State reporting procedure before the UN Human Rights Council (Universal Periodic Review) and independent expert committees (e.g. UN treaty monitoring bodies, African Commission on Human and Peoples' Rights and various expert committees under Council of Europe human rights treaties).[26] Other procedures, such as the ex-officio inquiry procedure (by the UN Committees against Torture and Discrimination against Women) or the inter-State complaints procedure (before the European Court of Human Rights and certain ILO-bodies) only play a comparatively small practical role. A more recent and fairly successful human rights monitoring procedure is, however, modelled on the experience of the ICRC: the system of preventive visits to places of detention for the purpose of preventing torture and improving prison conditions under the European Convention for the Prevention of

Torture and the Optional Protocol to the UN Convention against Torture. Nevertheless, the ICRC could regard individual complaints by victims of violations of international humanitarian law as an interference with its confidential role as guardian of humanitarian law by means of its presence in the field, its access to places of detention and its quiet diplomacy.

In my opinion, these fears would not be justified. As the experience of the ICRC in conducting preventive visits to places of detention has had a positive influence in introducing this method as an additional procedure of implementing international human rights law, the implementation of international humanitarian law might benefit from the experience of the European Court of Human Rights and other bodies in dealing with individual complaints. As many victims of human rights violations have found relief and reparation for the harm suffered by having lodged complaints with regional human rights courts, victims of humanitarian law might benefit from judgments by a future World Court of Human Rights. By deciding on individual complaints by means of legally binding judgments, such courts also interpret and further develop the respective treaties and force States to bring their legal system into conformity with the requirements of international law.

In fact, the ICRC, on the occasion of the 60th anniversary of the Geneva Conventions, has conducted a comprehensive internal research study aimed at addressing the lack of compliance with IHL and at developing proposals on how to move forward, both substantively and procedurally.[27] In a statement to a conference of 9 November 2009, ICRC President Kellenberger concluded that 'existing mechanisms provided for in the Geneva Conventions and the First Additional Protocol – namely the system of protecting powers, the formal enquiry procedure and the International Humanitarian Fact-Finding Commission – have not been effective, principally because they are subject to consent by the parties concerned'. He expressed the hope that participants in this workshop 'will share ideas and suggestions on how to improve existing compliance mechanisms or even to create new ones'.[28] Perhaps a complaint mechanism against States and non-State actors before a future World Court of Human Rights (and Humanitarian Law) might become an innovative feature of holding also those accountable who systematically violate the rights laid down in the Geneva Conventions and other treaties of IHL.

4. CONCLUSIONS

Both international human rights and humanitarian law suffer from an increasingly unacceptable gap between high legal standards and a lack of political will of States and non-State actors to comply with these standards, and implement them in practice. There is an urgent need to address this enormous implementation gap and to hold those who violate human rights and humanitarian law standards accountable by all available means. While international criminal law aims at holding individual perpetrators of the worst violations of human rights and humanitarian law (crimes against humanity, war crimes and genocide) accountable before the ICC and ad hoc international criminal tribunals, there is presently no equivalent at the global level to hold States, intergovernmental organizations and non-State actors accountable before an international civil, human rights or humanitarian law court with the power to hand down legally binding judgments and provide reparation to the victims of such violations. On balance, the reasons for including the Geneva Conventions and other IHL treaties in the list of treaties subject to the jurisdiction of the future World Court of Human Rights (and Humanitarian Law) seem to be stronger than the arguments against. For pragmatic reasons of achieving the necessary support of States and the global civil society for such an endeavour, it might however be more prudent to start with a World Court of Human Rights only. But the door should definitely be left open to also include IHL treaties at a later stage, in particular if the ICRC would consider such an individual complaints mechanism as a useful tool of strengthening compliance with IHL.

NOTES

*   Manfred Nowak is Professor of International Law and Human Rights at the University of Vienna.
1.   Swiss Confederation, Federal Department of Foreign Affairs and Geneva Academy of International Humanitarian Law and Human Rights, ed., *Protecting Dignity: An Agenda for Human Rights* (Geneva, 2008), available at: http://www.UDHR60.ch (accessed 10 September 2011).
2.   Progress Report of the Eminent Persons Panel by Manfred Nowak, Panel member and Rapporteur, Chapter 7.3 in Swiss Confederation, Federal Department of Foreign Affairs and Geneva Academy of International Humanitarian Law and Human Rights, ed., *Protecting Dignity: An Agenda for Human Rights* (Geneva, 2008), available at: http://www.UDHR60.ch (accessed 10 September 2011), 36.
3.   Ibid., 41.
4.   See M. Scheinin, 'Towards a World Court of Human Rights', available at: http://www.udhr60.ch/report/hrCourt_scheinin0609.pdf (accessed 10 September 2011); M. Nowak and J. Kozma, 'A World Court of Human Rights', available at: http://www.udhr60.ch/report/hrCourt-Nowak0609.pdf (accessed 10 September 2011).
5.   See J. Kozma, M. Nowak and M. Scheinin, *A World Court of Human Rights – Consolidated Statute and Commentary* (Vienna: Neuer Wissenschaftlicher Verlag, 2011).
6.   A/RES/60/147, 16 December 2005.
7.   See Article 46 European Convention on Human Rights (ECHR), Article 68 American Convention on Human Rights (ACHR), Article 30 Protocol to the African Charter on Human and Peoples' Rights (AfCHPR) on the establishment of an African Court of Human and Peoples' Rights.
8.   For a more detailed analysis of the rationale behind the World Court, see M. Nowak, 'The Need for a World Court of Human Rights', *Human Rights Law Review* 7(1) (2007): 251; M. Nowak, 'Eight Reasons Why we Need a World Court of Human Rights', in *International Human Rights Monitoring Mechanisms: Essays in Honour of Jakob Th. Möller*, G. Alfredsson et al., 2nd revised edition (Leiden and Boston: Martinus Nijhoff, 2009), 695–706.
9.   See. P. Alston and J. Crawford, *The Future of UN Human Rights Treaty Monitoring* (Cambridge University Press, 2000); UN Commission on Human Rights, Effective Functioning of Human Rights Mechanisms: Treaty Bodies, UN Doc. E/CN.4/2004/98, 11 February 2004; A. Bayefsky, *The UN Human Rights Treaty System. Universality at the Crossroads* (Hague/New York: Kluwer Law International, 2001). M. O'Flaherty and C. O'Brien, 'The Reform of the United Nations Treaty Bodies: a Critique of the High Commissioner's Concept Paper', *Human Rights Law Review* 7(1) (2007): 141; H. Steiner, 'Individual Claims in a World of Massive Violations: What Role for the Human Rights Committee', in *International Human Rights in Context. Law, Politics, Morals*, H. Steiner and P. Alston, 2nd edition (Oxford: Oxford University Press, 2000), 767–770; M. Nowak, *Introduction to the International Human Rights Regime* (Leiden/Boston: Martinus Nijhoff, 2003), 78–81. See also the recent report of UN High Commissioner for Human Rights Naventhem Pillay of June 2012 'Strengthening the United Nations human rights treaty body system' in which she advocates a more simplified State reporting system.
10. See University of California Berkeley School of Law, Project for Human Rights: 2048. The Berkeley 2048 Project has left UK Berkeley's law school and has evolved into the International Bill of Rights. See: http://www.internationalbillofrights.org/.

11. Scheinin, *supra* note 4, Article 7.
12. See, e.g., *Legality of the Threat or Use of Nuclear Weapons*, Advisory Opinion, I.C.J. Reports 1996, para. 25; *Legal Consequences of the Construction of a Wall in the Occupied Palestinian Territory*, Advisory Opinion, I.C.J. Reports 2004, para. 106; General Comment No. 31: *Nature of the General Legal Obligation Imposed on States Parties to the Covenant*, HRC, 26 May 2004, para. 11 (UN Doc. CCPR/C/21/Rev.1/Add.13); UN Commission on Human Rights, *Situation of Detainees at Guantánamo Bay*, Report of the Chairperson-Rapporteur of the Working Group on Arbitrary Detention, the Special Rapporteur on the independence of judges and lawyers, the Special Rapporteur on torture and other cruel, inhuman or degrading treatment or punishment, the Special Rapporteur on freedom of religion or belief, and the Special Rapporteur on the right of everyone to the enjoyment of the highest attainable standard of physical and mental health, 27 February 2006, paras 6–16 (UN Doc. E/CN.4/2006/120); UN Human Rights Council, *Global Practices in Relation to Secret Detention in the Context of Countering Terrorism*, Joint Study of the Special Rapporteur on the promotion and protection of human rights and fundamental freedoms while countering terrorism, the Special Rapporteur on torture and other cruel, inhuman or degrading treatment or punishment, the Working Group on Arbitrary Detention, and the Working Group on Enforced or Involuntary Disappearances, 19 February 2010, paras 17–56 (UN Doc. A/HRC/13/42).
13. See T. Meron, *The Humanization of International Law* (Leiden/Boston: Martinus Nijhoff, 2006), and T. Meron, *International Law in the Age of Human Rights*, in Recueil des cours (Hague Academy of International Law) 301 (2004): 9–490; International Law Commission, Principles of International Law Recognized in the Charter of the Nuremberg Tribunal and in the Judgment of the Tribunal, 1950, Principle 6(b).
14. Statute of the International Tribunal for the Former Yugoslavia, Security Council Resolution 827, 25 May 1993, Article 5; See also Meron, *supra* note 13. See also the Decisions in the case of Dusko Tadić, *Prosecutor v. Tadić*, ICTY, Appeals Chamber, Decision, 2 October 1995 (Case No. IT-94-1-A), where the Tribunal defines armed conflict between states thus: 'armed conflict exists whenever there is a resort to armed force between states' as well as non-international armed conflict as: 'whenever there is … protracted violence between government authorities and organised armed groups or between such groups within the state'.
15. See Office of the United Nations High Commissioner for Human Rights (OHCHR), Human Rights. A Compilation of International Instruments, Volume I (Second Part), 2002, Chapters S, T and U.
16. See, e.g., A. Clapham, *Human Rights Obligations of Non-State Actors* (Oxford: Oxford University Press, 2006); for case studies and further discussion on accountability of non-state actors, see L. Koechlin, T. Förster, G. Fenner Zinkernagel and A. Peters, eds, *Non State Actors as Standard Setters* (Cambridge: Cambridge University Press, 2009); and G. Andrepoulos, Z.F. Kabasakal Arat and P. Juvelier, eds, *Non State Actors in the Human Rights Universe* (Bloomfield: Kumarian Press, 2006).
17. See Slavery Convention of 25 September 1926.
18. See, e.g., Articles 2 (1) and 11 (2) ICESCR.
19. The precise extent of this obligation remains a highly controversial issue: see, e.g., OHCHR, Guidelines and Principles on a Human Rights Based Approach to Poverty Reduction Strategies, Guideline 7, paras 101–105.
20. See, e.g., Articles 5, 18(1) and 27(2) CRC.
21. See the Protocol to Prevent, Suppress and Punish Trafficking in Persons, Especially Women and Children, supplementing the United Nations Convention against Transnational Organized Crime.
22. See, e.g., the report of John Ruggie to the Human Rights Council of 9 April 2010, paras 1 and 54 *et seq.* (UN Doc. A/HRC/14/27). His 'Guiding Principles on Business and Human Rights' were unanimously adopted by the UN Human Rights Council on 16 June 2011 (A/HRC/RES/17/4).
23. See, e.g., the transitional administrations of the UN in East Timor or Kosovo; see also the report submitted by the United Nations Interim Administration in Kosovo to the Human Rights Committee, *Human Rights Situation in Kosovo since June 1999*, HRC, 13 March 2006 (UN Doc. CCPR/C/UNK/1).
24. See Chapter 3, *supra* note 2, at 13.
25. See *International Review of the Red Cross* 858 (June, 2005): 394.
26. See Nowak, *supra* note 9.
27. See. J. Kellenberger, Statement on 12 August 2009 in Geneva on the occasion of the Ceremony to celebrate the 60th anniversary of the Geneva Conventions.
28. See. J. Kellenberger, Statement on 9 November 2009 in Geneva at the Conference on the challenges for IHL posed by new threats, new actors and new means and methods of war, organized by the Swiss Federal Department of Foreign Affairs in cooperation with the ICRC.

26. The International Committee of the Red Cross and human rights law

Godofredo Torreblanca*

The International Committee of the Red Cross (ICRC), founded in 1863 by Henry Dunant in collaboration with four Swiss citizens and originally called International Committee for Relief to the Wounded, is considered the guardian of International Humanitarian Law (IHL) or the law of armed conflicts. In general its main tasks are to bring protection and assistance to the victims of these atrocious events. Nonetheless, IHL is not the only law applicable in this context and, on the other hand, the ICRC mandate also covers situations of internal violence that are under the threshold of an armed conflict.

There is nowadays a common agreement that Human Rights Law (HRL) applies in peace and wartime. In the former case, its scope of application obviously includes situations of internal violence. This chapter attempts to scrutinise how the ICRC deals with this law in fulfilling its international mandate in either armed conflicts or situations of internal violence. More precisely, it looks at whether the ICRC can or should take HRL into account in performing its mandate; and secondly, how the ICRC makes use of this law in its day-to-day work.

The first part of this chapter focuses briefly on the ICRC's legal nature, some of its main features and its international mandate in case of armed conflicts or situations of internal violence. This part ends with a legal analysis of the ICRC's competence in dealing with HRL. The second part presents the ICRC position vis-à-vis HRL from an historical perspective. It finally explores from a practical viewpoint the ways the ICRC uses and applies HRL in its day-to-day work.

1. PRELIMINARY REMARKS

In this endeavour, preventive measures and control mechanisms, in the sense of ensuring respect for the law during armed conflicts or situations of internal violence, are considered from the understanding that both are closely intertwined in order to promote the effective observance of the law in armed conflict or other situations of violence.

This approach responds to the contexts in which the ICRC operates. In armed conflicts and many situations of internal violence there is a presumption that human behaviour is not characterised by strong compliance with the law. In former centuries some even considered that the law presupposed peace and thus in wartime almost no law was applicable. This has changed since the 19th century and especially after the Second World War.[1] Nowadays the law attempts to limit the effects of these events, laying down certain protections for those who are in the middle or even involved in these episodes. Nevertheless, one must distinguish between what the law prescribes (what should be) and the dynamics of armed conflicts and other situations of internal violence in the general framework of international law and its lack of third party adjudication (what actually happens and what monitoring can do).[2] In these scenarios the ICRC presence is absolutely relevant to remind the parties to comply with their legal obligations or to persuade them to cease any transgression of the relevant law. However, notwithstanding the enormous effort of such kind of institutions, the margin of effectiveness may be limited.

Being conscious of these limits, and based on its own experience for more than 100 years, the ICRC puts a strong emphasis on promoting preventive measures, which do not aim to avoid those situations, but to create better conditions to prevent misbehaviours or to persuade the actors to stop them.[3] Because of this, any preventive mechanism is not only as pivotal as any monitoring mechanism in the strict sense, but also concomitant to the latter. These concerns are not only part of ICRC policy-making, but also are enshrined in IHL rules.[4] Therefore, due to the relevance of these measures, this chapter will embrace all ICRC activities that seek the observance of the law in an armed conflict or a situation of internal violence regardless of its preventive or monitoring character.

Secondly, mechanisms of repression are not part of the analysis, in as much as this topic is addressed in other chapters of the handbook. Likewise, this chapter will not deal with the interaction between IHL and HRL, and will only refer to it as long as it is strictly necessary to determine the ICRC role and position vis-à-vis HRL.

2.   THE ICRC'S LEGAL NATURE AND ITS MAIN FEATURES

2.1   ICRC's Legal Nature

The ICRC came into existence through a private initiative, like other private international unions during the second half of the 19th century. All of them had in common that their interests had an international character and required permanent bodies, presence in different states and cooperation with different actors, including states.[5] The relationships between these private unions and governments were of different types. In the case of the ICRC, this relationship ended up in treaties regulations, without changing its structure and composition. Thus regardless of its dynamic evolution, the ICRC has always remained a non-governmental institution.

Despite its origin as an association governed by article 60 of the Swiss Civil Code, the ICRC possesses an international personality due to the particular mandate that the international community has entrusted it with. Many scholars have focused on this institution, concluding that its international legal character is unquestionable at the present time, albeit its *sui generis* legal nature.[6] Indeed, although it is not an inter-governmental organisation, the ICRC does not perceive itself as an NGO.[7] In contrast with NGOs, the ICRC does not only have a special legal status under IHL treaties,[8] but also its statutory law includes the 'Red Cross Law'[9] – the fundamental principles, the statute and resolutions adopted within the International Red Cross and Red Crescent Movement, with the participation of the state parties to the Geneva

Conventions. This gives an exceptional feature to an institution that otherwise could be classified as an NGO with international personality. Therefore the ICRC has a *sui generis* legal nature[10] in as much as it cannot be classified as an international organisation or as an NGO,[11] but its legal personality embraces an international and internal one.[12]

The fact that the ICRC enjoys an international subjectivity means that it is capable of holding rights and obligations laid down and regulated by international law.[13] Certainly, in exercise of its international personality the ICRC can celebrate treaties with states and intergovernmental organisations.[14] It also enjoys privileges and immunities, similar to those granted to intergovernmental organisations. Finally, it has the capacity to bring claims or be held responsible in case of a breach of an international obligation.[15]

In general there is a trend to assimilate these rights and obligations to those held by intergovernmental organisations.[16] This is partially right, but the content of the ICRC rights and obligations are ultimately shaped by its international mandate established in the 1949 four Geneva Conventions (GCs), 1977 Additional Protocols (APs) I and II, its statute, the statute of the International Movement of the Red Cross and Red Crescent and the resolutions adopted within this framework,[17] and the subsequent practice developed by states, other subjects of international law and the ICRC itself.[18] To sum up, at the international scene the ICRC activities and its relationship with other subjects of international are regulated by general international law and the above-mentioned treaties and norms.

2.2   ICRC's Unique Features

It should be remarked that the ICRC has membership to the International Movement of the Red Cross and Red Crescent, together with the International Federation of the Red Cross and Red Crescent Societies and the Red Cross and Red Crescent National Societies. Any good understanding of the ICRC and its activities, in legal and practical terms, must take into account this framework, in particular the seven Fundamental Principles of the Red Cross proclaimed in 1965 during the 20th International Conference of the Red Cross.

Notably the principles of humanity,[19] impartiality,[20] neutrality[21] and independence[22] are the backbone of the ICRC and have a pivotal importance in the way it understands and executes its international mandate. They characterise the ICRC and make its DNA different from other subjects of international law and humanitarian entities. It must be pointed out that:

> Although neutrality defines the attitude of the Red Cross towards belligerents and ideologies, it never determines its behaviour towards the human beings who suffer because, in the first place, the wounded do not fight one another. And, above all, the essential characteristic of the Red Cross is to act and not to remain passive.[23]

The ICRC action is thus victim-oriented. This is the top priority of its mandate and it illuminates its actions even when this may entail perceptions of some specific dilemmas with other key values of the international community.

In day-to-day life, these principles guide the ICRC policies and activities in order to achieve the objects of its international mandate. Throughout its existence this organisation has developed concrete tools in order to carry out this mandate successfully, having as a priority bringing relief to the victims of armed conflicts. One of the most particular and controversial tools that characterised the ICRC is its confidentiality.

In armed conflicts and some situations of internal violence one can presume that external witnesses and scrutiny are not always welcome. Their access would be hampered and moreover any person acting in these roles would be in a situation of potential serious risk. Because of this the ICRC understands confidentiality is an indispensable tool to fulfil its mandate. It enables its staff to have access to people affected by armed conflicts or other situations of violence and to establish a direct and fluent channel of communication with all the actors involved in these events, based on trust and constructive dialogue. In contrast with other organisations – intergovernmental organisations and NGOs – as a general rule the ICRC does not speak out when it finds violations of the relevant laws applicable to armed conflicts or other situations of internal violence. This does not mean the ICRC remains silent. It shares its concerns directly with the authorities or the pertinent party. These may include allegations and recommendations upon specific situations or events which are the object of a continued follow-up.

The relationship set up between the ICRC and its interlocutors is based in a mutual compromise of confidentiality and all must ensure as far as possible that information remains confidential.[24] However, the fact that the ICRC classifies some information as confidential does not imply it must be kept secret and that it cannot be used in order to solve humanitarian concerns or violations of the laws. If the purpose of this information is to stop or correct an illegal behaviour or to prevent similar actions in the future, the ICRC and the concrete authority in possession of the information, acting in good faith, can reasonably share it – in a discrete and confidential manner – with third parties, if this is absolutely necessary to solve or to correct a serious humanitarian concern or violation of the law.[25]

In addition, in some specific – very exceptional – circumstances, the ICRC may disclose confidential information:[26] for instance, if it has exhausted all possible means without any effect on serious violations, and publicity will prevent the party continuing to commit them;[27] or if the authorities make public excerpts of an ICRC confidential report.

Obviously this tool may involve tension with other humanitarian concerns. Recognising the functional need for it and the autonomy of the ICRC to decide on a case-by-case basis when it is opportune to make public some specific confidential information, it would be advisable that based on its own experience and the requirements of the field, the ICRC continues setting more specific criteria in this regard. For its recent experience, it seems that in some specific cases the ICRC has found means to answer to other humanitarian concerns, while preserving the main core of its confidentiality. Nevertheless, it is early to identify a clear trend.[28]

It is also the international community which understands the functional importance of the ICRC confidentiality, and which grants it and its staff absolute functional judicial immunities, thus preventing any court, in judicial or quasi-judicial proceeding, to call its staff for testimony or to request that the ICRC divulge its confidential information.[29]

A second major feature of the ICRC is its neutral intermediary role. Due to the operational needs, the ICRC attempts to establish a fluent dialogue with all the parties or actors involved in an armed conflict or situation of internal violence, as well as with the persons affected by these events regardless of the reasons why these persons are in a particular situation. For this purpose, the ICRC must abstain to judge the underlying reasons for the existence of the conflict and must not take part in any kind of political controversy among the parties to it.[30] The operational importance of this feature may be reflected in the fact that the ICRC developed this role gradually within the humanitarian context, even when it did not have any expressed recognition by the IHL treaties.[31]

3. THE LEGAL BASIS OF ICRC ACTION

Actions implemented by the ICRC may be of different types and can take place in different contexts. In general the set of legal rules applicable to ICRC actions are of conventional and customary,[32] or statutory character.[33] The former includes treaties such as the GCs and APs, and the latter the ICRC Statutes, the Statutes of the International Red Cross and Red Crescent Movement[34] and the International Conference of the Red Cross's (International Conference) resolutions.[35] Their legal basis and the extent of their functions can differ depending on the context in which they are implemented: international armed conflict (IAC), non-international armed conflict (NIAC) or situations of internal violence.

In armed conflict the main role of the ICRC is to promote the observance of IHL by all parties and to bring assistance to the victims of these events.

In IAC the ICRC may have the following tasks:

- to access to all prisoners of war (PoWs) and internees and interview them without witnesses;
- to supply humanitarian relief to prisoners of war (PoWs) and the civilian population;
- to collect information about PoWs and protected persons – in particular internees – (organising a Central Information Agency), and to transmit information to their relatives in order to maintain the family link;
- to exercise its good offices in order to facilitate the creation of hospital zones and neutralised localities; and
- to assume duties incumbent on the Protecting Powers under the agreement of the concerned State.

In addition the ICRC has a right of initiative whereby it can propose a different range of measures in order to improve or ensure the situation or conditions of those affected by an armed conflict.[36] The GCs state it can undertake different activities for the protection of protected persons, subject to the consent of the parties to the conflict concerned. In spite of this, practice has transcended this conventional limit. Indeed the right of initiative has been understood in a broader sense, and due to this flexibility, it emerges as a practical and effective humanitarian tool in different armed conflicts.[37]

In NAIC the ICRC may offer its service to the parties to the conflict. Despite the fact that parties' consent is always needed – in contrast to the case of international armed conflict – there is a large practice with regard to the ICRC action carried out in this context. This shows that in humanitarian terms, with the exception of some specific duties related to specific categories of protected persons, the ICRC action is equally necessary in international or non-international armed conflict.[38]

It must be noted that the ICRC mandate with regard to IHL is not restricted exclusively to wartime. For different reasons, some ICRC actions must be executed in other contexts than armed conflict. Furthermore, some of them ideally should be performed in peacetime. This is the case of the role of the ICRC in promoting the development, dissemination and implementation of IHL.

In addition to these duties, the Statutes of the International Red Cross and the Red Crescent Movement extends the humanitarian action of the ICRC, as neutral institution to 'internal strife – to ensure the protection of and assistance to military and civilian victims of such events and of their direct results'.[39] This statutory basis thus allows the ICRC to deploy its humanitarian services, subject to the consent of the State in the case of internal violence.

4.   HUMAN RIGHTS LAW AS PART OF THE LEGAL FRAMEWORK FOR ICRC ACTION

There is a spreading idea that in executing its humanitarian mandate the ICRC uses IHL as legal framework of reference. Under this assertion, whatever the action is – either humanitarian diplomacy or pointing out to the authorities allegations over detention conditions – this branch of international law becomes the legal standard that illuminates the ICRC action. Being the guardian of IHL and having a specific mandate with regard to this law, it is common sense that the ICRC uses it as the most relevant legal framework, especially when it comes to assessing possible violations of the law during armed conflict.[40] Nevertheless, IHL, as any other law, is not an end in itself. Its main aim is to limit the effects of armed conflicts, protecting people who suffer their consequences. Likewise the ICRC mandate is of a humanitarian character, that is, within its scope, its final aim is to bring a minimum of protection and relief to the human beings who are in the middle of an armed conflict or a situation of internal violence. Secondly, in the path from an international law of co-existence to an international law of cooperation, diverse and sophisticated laws have emerged to regulate different aspects at the international sphere. Some of these laws applicable in all times, such as human rights, are significant for the protection of the human being. Thus, this section attempts to analyse whether the ICRC, in compliance with this mandate, can or must take into account laws other than IHL as part of the legal framework of reference and, if so, how it shall deal with these laws.

4.1   Identifying the International Institutional Law Applicable to the ICRC

Notwithstanding that human rights law is applicable at all times and is a cornerstone of the protection of human beings, no rule, neither in international law nor in the ICRC statutory law, establishes expressly the way the ICRC must or must not deal with it. When this happens to international organisations, international law allows the determination of whether an organisation may hold other implied,[41] attributed[42] or inherent[43] powers necessary to carry out the duties imposed in its constitutive treaty. Despite the fact the ICRC is not an international organisation, there is a trend to grant the ICRC a similar legal treatment. However, to what extent international institutional law – or the international law of international organisations – in particular the theory of implied powers, is applicable to the ICRC by analogy; and, in general, whether the rules on interpretation of treaties, contained in the 1969 and 1986 Vienna Conventions of the Law of Treaties[44] may guide this analysis.

The 1969 and 1986 Vienna Conventions enshrined some provisions upon methods of interpretation applicable not only to treaties but to different legal acts. These provisions have actually been applied to documents others than treaties, such as resolutions of the UN General Assembly. Therefore, as long as these rules are generally accepted in international law as norms of interpretation not exclusively of treaties, it seems logical that they guide the interpretation of all provisions that lay down the ICRC international mandate, including its statutory law, in so far as this contains and develops part of this mandate entrusted by the international community.[45]

The applicability of the international institutional law raises more complexity. Its conception responds to characteristics and dynamics of intergovernmental organisation. Hence some of their provisions, conceived for entities of different origins, compositions and competences, might not suit the particular features of the ICRC. Notwithstanding it is not possible to apply the entire law of international institutions, one can presume that at least the content of core provisions can be adapted and applied to a *sui generis* organisation such as the ICRC that, conversely, also shares some similarities with intergovernmental organisations.

In the case of the theory of implied powers, the main obstacle to its application is related to the fact that this theory relies on the constitutive treaty of the organisation in order to assess whether it holds implied powers 'essential to the performance of its duties'[46] established by its founding fathers. The ICRC does not have a constitutive treaty and, furthermore, its international mandate comes from different sources, that is, treaties and its statutory law. Secondly, its international mandate does not have its origins in the ICRC founders, but in the international community – mainly states. Regardless of these differences, the theory of implied powers may be suitable for finding out whether the ICRC mandate may contain implied powers necessary for the performance of its duties. The ICRC mandate has clear origins in IHL treaties, the Statutes of the International Red Cross and Red Crescent Movement and its own Statutes. The former statutes are imposed exclusively or with the participation of the state parties to the conventions, whereas in the latter case, the GCs and APs, and thus their state parties, through their recognition of the ICRC, implicitly recognise its Statutes. All together this sets up an international legal framework that from the substantive viewpoint is similar to one that could be granted to an intergovernmental organisation by treaty. On the other hand, it would be absurd to hinder the ICRC humanitarian role by constraining it to remain attached to the express wording of the provisions that regulate its mandate. Unlike this narrow view, the ICRC's own mandate – and the provisions' wording that enshrined it – seem to acknowledge the need for great flexibility in contexts where the dynamics of the conflicts and situations of internal violence may require from the ICRC fast changes and adaptations in order to fulfil its pivotal aim, that is, the protection of persons affected by these events.

In fact, the implied power theory's assumptions have been applied to the ICRC in the past. For instance, on the occasion of the killing of its delegate Mr George Olivet and two other collaborators in Congo in a region under the control of the United Nations,[47] the ICRC addressed this institution directly to claim for damages concerning its delegate. Afterwards, an enquiry commission was set up and as a result of it the United Nations gave compensation directly to the ICRC. The grounds that inspired this were none other than the reasoning developed by the ICJ in the *Reparation case.* Likewise legal scholarship has used this theory in order to analyse different legal matters related to the ICRC and even to the International Red Cross and Red Crescent Movement.[48] Consequently in the case of the ICRC the implied power theory seeks to determine, by implication, whether this institution may possess the powers or means necessary to the performance of its duties in the framework of an international mandate that emanates from the community of states.

4.2 ICRC and Human Rights Law

The way the ICRC approaches human rights law may have a twofold view: How does the ICRC deal with this law in executing its mandate? And, how does this law bind the ICRC in a more general manner – for example, vis-à-vis its employees' rights? Only the former is the purpose of this chapter and, any answer must have as its starting point the fact that HRL and IHL are applicable in times of armed conflict in complementary fashion. Second, as part of its functions, the ICRC may need to make legal analysis in order to judge whether there is a violation of the law or an inadequate observance of it.[49] Third, the main role of the ICRC is to promote the compliance of IHL by all parties and to bring assistance to the victims of these events. It should be taken into account that the main purpose of this action is of humanitarian type. It intends to draw the attention of the authorities regarding specific facts in order to put an end to and/or to change certain behaviours or conditions, and to prevent them from happening again. Even though ICRC's activities determining violations of the law are inherent to the ICRC mandate,[50] it does not attempt to exercise this function as a quasi-judicial entity and therefore its action does not have to be narrowed or guided by judicial principles.[51]

The contexts in which the ICRC action is carried out may give rise to different legal reasoning. It should be noted, however, that these differences remain mainly in the legal analysis and in practice their impact is tenuous and almost not relevant. When the ICRC exercises specific functions laid down in IHL treaties, it can validly complement its legal framework of reference including human rights law if it considers that it is relevant to assess a particular situation from a legal perspective. The specific roles established in those treaties do not prevent the ICRC from resorting to human rights law. Moreover if both branches of law, with their own characteristics, share the same philosophical origin and final aim,[52] it seems logical that the ICRC, as the main humanitarian institution in armed conflicts, can use these laws in order to foster and to strengthen the protection of the human being.

Second, the role that the ICRC must carry out in armed conflicts – international and non-international – is not limited to specific duties laid down in IHL treaties. The action that the ICRC may assume, for instance based on its right of initiative, must involve all necessary means to ensure the faithful application of IHL and the protection of and assistance to military and civilian victims, provided that the ICRC keeps its humanitarian, neutral and impartial character. In other words, its legal framework should not be restricted to narrow interpretations of its functions, and, on the contrary, may imply all the necessary means and conditions to exercise its humanitarian role in an efficient manner.[53] Regarding HRL, this assertion is even clearer when the ICRC assumes a role in situations of internal violence. In this case, violence does not reach the threshold of applicability of IHL and the ICRC's general protective and human-itarian role does not emerge from IHL rule but from its right of initiative set up in its statutory law. In addition to national legislation, HRL surfaces as the relevant legal framework of reference to procure the protection of the people affected by these events. Consequently, even when there is no expressed reference to human rights law, it is implied within its humanitarian role. The ICRC may resort to this branch of law as a legal framework of reference whenever it concludes this is necessary to perform the humanitarian mandate that the international community has entrusted it with.[54]

In sum, on one hand, it remains exclusively in ambit of the ICRC to decide when to make use of human rights standards. On the other, it can only resort to human rights as long as they are necessary to perform its mandate. This does not mean there are some rights that could or could not be invoked. In practice, the ICRC can only take a decision – that is mainly of operational and political character – on a case-by-case analysis, in so far as it can assess the benefits or the need to invoke human rights in order to fulfil its humanitarian mandate without jeopardising either its unique identity or main features.

5.   HUMAN RIGHTS LAW AS A LEGAL RESORT WITHIN THE ICRC'S ACTION

5.1   Historical Perspective

5.1.1   Foundation of the ICRC and the first half of 20th century

In general it makes sense to analyse what the ICRC position was regarding HRL or how the ICRC dealt with it after the adoption of the Universal Declaration of Human Rights by the UN General Assembly in 1948.[55] Nonetheless, since its creation the ICRC has played an active and pivotal role in the international sphere regarding the protection of the human being. Even when its role was circumscribed to the perform-ance of its functions, it transcended the framework imposed in the first years of its existence and necessarily influenced the process of consolidation of the idea that international law should regulate the protection of human beings within states' territory. I refer here to the ICRC practice and concerns, expressed in internal discussions or in public, more than to the international legal norms such as the Martens Clause[56] or specific treaties adopted at that time. It is nevertheless evident that the adoption of IHL treaties, with the active participation of the ICRC, constituted a general progress for humankind vis-à-vis states' power.[57]

Soon after its foundation, the ICRC expressed its concerns about humanitarian problems in contexts other than interstate wars. During the *Third Carlist War* in Spain (1872–1876), for the first time the ICRC questioned itself on its rights and duties in case of civil war. It followed the events, with special attention for the situation of detainees and wounded persons, not without internal controversies. Moynier offered to the national society the ICRC's good offices and services. At the end the ICRC supported the Spanish national society and launched an appeal for cooperation. By the end of the war none of the detainees or the wounded was executed.[58] The ICRC held a similar position with regard to the insurrection of 1875 in Herzegovina. In this case, it expressed its concerns in favour of the persons detained in the contexts of internal disturbances. Afterwards, it requested the national societies to act, in particular to help victims who had crossed the border to Montenegro. Finally, the ICRC itself assisted these victims at the request of Montenegro's authorities.[59] Likewise, the ICRC did not remain indifferent to some events of internal violence, and, in fact, expressed its position in the sense that national societies had a duty to assist the victims during the acts of violence in Argentina (1890), Brazil (1894), Venezuela (1894–95) and Macedonia (1903). In the case of Brazil, it went even further and condemned the destruction of a hospital of the insurgents by the governmental authorities.

Therefore, the fact that the ICRC was conceived as an answer to the horror of interstate wars did not prevent the ICRC from expressing its concern about other forms of violence that could cause serious humanitarian problems and affect the population within the territory of a state. Indeed, these concerns were part of discussions and reflections of the ICRC and national societies. During the IXth International Conference in Washington (1912), an intense discussion was held upon possible humanitarian activities within the framework of what is currently classified as non-international armed conflict and internal disturbances. According to the project elaborated for that conference, it would allow the ICRC and national societies to bring relief in cases of civil wars and internal disturbances.[60] Nevertheless many representatives argued that it was a local and specific problem (especially in Latin America) to be part of an International Conference's agenda. The Russian representative qualified the debate as of political character on a topic that, in his view, entailed the fighting against criminals.[61] The project was finally dismissed.

Almost a decade latter,[62] in 1921, during the Xth International Conference in Geneva, the adoption of the resolution XIV recognised that the ICRC might intervene in social disturbances and revolutions.[63] In the aftermath of the conference, the ICRC intervened in some contexts such as in Ireland (1922–23)[64] and Poland (1924),[65] among others. This trend continued and was an important point during the Spanish Civil War, to which the ICRC, in coordination with the League of Nations, brought its relief action.[66] Despite the fact that in all these cases the ICRC's action was based on its characteristics as an international, neutral and impartial organisation, these measures were not taken without internal institutional doubts.[67] This influenced negatively the possibility of adopting a treaty with regard to the ICRC humanitarian relief in case of situations of violence other than interstates wars. In fact, the study for the amendment of the 1929 Convention never considered including situations of internal disturbances, and narrowed the analysis to the possibility to regulate civil wars.[68] This, however, did not hamper the confirmation of the ICRC competences in cases of civil wars and internal disturbances by the XVth International Conference in London (1938).[69]

In sum, the ICRC

> [i]ndependently of the development of international humanitarian law [and the emergence of the international law of human rights] ... has acted also in various other ways to protect the victims of armed conflicts and, as a consequence, to work for the defence of human rights ... [and] has also carried out a wide range of relief operations to bring aid to persons affected by international or non-international conflicts and to the victims of internal strife and tension.[70]

This is perhaps a sort of verification, from practical experiences on the ground, that, albeit having different logics, the philosophical fundaments of the general protection of the human being are the same in IHL as in HRL.[71]

5.1.2   The creation of the United Nations and the second half of 20th century

In the aftermath of the Second World War, different measures were implemented as a reaction to the tragedy of the war. Many of them sought a twofold purpose: to limit the capacity of states to resort to the use of force; and to protect human beings in general from states' power. Based on the experience of the League of Nations, the United Nations was created as a universal international organisation to ensure international peace and security, and the UN Charter forbids the resort of use of force by states. Meanwhile, states, for the first time in history, began to accept that it was essential to legally limit their power in order to guarantee a minimum of protection for human beings within their territories. This took two parallel paths. On one hand, a process of strengthening IHL, led by the ICRC, attempted to adopt a convention to protect civilians in times of international armed conflict and to agree a minimum regulation for non-international conflicts. And, on the other hand, within the UN framework, states adopted a declaration in order to list the rights inherent to all individuals. This division would mark the paths of IHL and human rights as well as of the organisations involved in their promotion in the following decades. It was then understood that the UN only dealt with human rights issues.

The Universal Declaration did not include any provision on armed conflicts. Some general comments were made during the elaboration of the draft, but they did not find any support.[72] In fact, the United Nations decided to avoid any discussion related to armed conflicts and the law of war under the assumption that this would contravene the spirit of the Charter and 'undermine the force of *jus contra bellum*, as proclaimed in the Charter, and would shake confidence in the ability of the world body to maintain peace'.[73] Having as a starting point a 'state of peace', the UN set itself up as the promoter and guardian of human rights law.[74] This attitude was reflected in the International Law Commission that refused to place IHL issues into the agenda of its first session. The commission did not share the arguments in the sense that IHL was there to prevent excesses when the UN failed to prevent the use of force, and some even argued that IHL contravened the new spirit of peace that was inspired by the creation of the UN.[75]

On the other side of the protection of the human being, the ICRC reaffirmed its role regarding IHL, with an active participation in the adoption of the 1949 GCs – and the protection of those individuals who find themselves in the middle of a war (civilians). In this case, the preparatory work of the GCs made few and vague references to human rights.[76] Even though the GCs contained provisions that had some similarity or coincidence with this branch of law, no express mention of the protection of human rights was included.[77]

The ICRC feared jeopardising its fundamental institutional features by getting involved in a process of the development of a body of law that was perceived to have political connotations. On the other hand, the context was not the most favourable for the ICRC and some doubts existed over the validity of IHL in the new scenario of the collective security system in which the unilateral resort to the use of force was banned. Indeed, at that moment, the ICRC was questioned by some states due to its performance during the Second World War,[78] while some questioned the applicability of IHL and the coherence of maintaining it.[79]

Therefore, these two institutions built an invisible wall drawing a line between IHL and HRL as well as limiting their functions to one of these branches.[80] Nonetheless, they held ambivalent positions;[81] perhaps because the line drawn with regard to their functions vis-à-vis IHL and human rights as well as the reasons that motivated this, was in reality somewhat artificial. This characterised the development and application of these laws in the coming years, but did not prevent these institutional policies from beginning to become eroded. In practice, what had started was a gradual approach between these laws, that would keep their autonomy, but share certain overlaps.[82] In fact, as Schindler points out, the adoption of article 3 common to the GCs constituted a milestone in the relationship between states and the persons who stay within their territories 'and, consequently, encroaches upon the traditional sphere of human rights'.[83] The beginning of this approach is somehow confirmed when the drafter of the European Convention on Human Rights (Convention for the Protection of Human Rights and Fundamental Freedoms) promptly took into consideration the reality of armed conflicts, including a provision on derogations in 'time of war' in the draft version of 1950.

In parallel, the ICRC and national societies kept showing their concerns about the humanitarian problems that might come up in the case of non-international armed conflict – in the sense that article 3 common of the GCs only offered a minimum of protection – and other forms of internal violence. In the framework of these concerns some assessments were made regarding the convenience of including expressly human rights law as part of the ICRC activities' legal body. For instance, in 1951 members of the Statutes' Commission of the ICRC suggested that the right of initiative should have included the possibility to intervene in case of flagrant violations of human rights. However, an experts' commission upheld that it was unfeasible in practice and might emphasise the weakness of the ICRC. Moreover, the Commission concluded this could create conflicts of competence with the UN.[84] In 1952 a legal commission adopted an internal document (D 205) whereby it was established that in case of a situation under the threshold of article 3 of the GCs, the ICRC could intervene if the national society would not do so, if the event had a certain degree of emergency, duration, organisation of the parties, and there were a significant number of victims.[85] The adoption of an additional protocol to the GC IV was even suggested and analysed in an internal report (D 252) that pointed out the positive and negative elements, in particular the fact that this would curtail the ICRC's focus on consolidating its classic role worldwide.[86] Likewise during the 1950s the ICRC commentaries on the GCs, edited by Jean Pictet, also included some timid references to human rights. However, it should be noted that most of them were upon provisions that were similarly adopted in human rights law.[87] In the field, the ICRC maintained its disposal to bring its relief actions to different situations of violence; nonetheless, the political context of some events made it problematic. The ICRC faced dilemmas with regards to its rights and duties during the disturbance that took place in Tunis (1952). Even though the ICRC considered the situation had created serious humanitarian problems and had received many requests for intervention from the Tunisian side initially the ICRC decided to contact the French national society – at that time Tunis was under French protectorate – and promote its intervention in order to avoid any negative reaction from the French authorities.[88] Afterwards the ICRC tried to get an authorisation in order to visit detainees (1952–53). But, in the view of French authorities, an (international) organisation such as the ICRC could not intervene in this context.[89] Similarly the ICRC received other requests for intervention in cases of internal disturbance, in many cases in order to visit 'political detainees'. In some cases, like in Venezuela (1952), the ICRC decided not to intervene, assuming that the authorities would not accept its presence, whereas in other cases the ICRC considered it should use its right of initiative, as in Bolivia, Ecuador, Panama, Algeria (previous to the application of IHL), Malaysia, Cyprus, Greece and Poland.[90] The ICRC action often included the visiting of detainees.

In the 1960s ICRC studies continued to focus mainly on NIAC, but they also included some topics regarding its intervention in cases of internal disturbance. An experts' commission (1962) – charged by the ICRC to analyse the problem of humanitarian aid for the victims of NIAC – highlighted that in the case of internal disturbances, the ICRC did not have a reason to invoke IHL, but it had the right of initiative. The commission emphasised the fact the states did not have any legal obligation to accept the ICRC offer; thus the use of this mandate must be prudent.[91] In 1964–65 an ICRC legal advisors' group held a similar position and stated some criteria that the ICRC should consider when deciding whether to intervene in internal disturbances: among others, suspension of judicial guarantees, weak rule of law or declaration of a state of emergency, internment or deportation of people considered dangerous by the state, signs of inhuman treatment of people under detention, and disproportional penalties (Doc. D 851 bis, 1965, revised in 1968).[92] This matter became more relevant with the adoption of resolution XXXI, in the 20th International Conference in Vienna (1965), whereby the conference expressed its concern about the difficulties of ensuring enough protection to the victims of NIAC and internal disturbances, in particular detainees.[93]

The turning point in relation to what has been created since the foundation of the UN and the adoption of the Universal Declaration was seen in the framework of the UN, in the 1968 International Conference on Human Rights in Teheran, with the adoption of resolution XXIII, that recognised that 'armed conflicts continue to plague humanity' and requested the General Assembly and the Secretary-General to take some steps towards the application of IHL norms. Months later the General Assembly adopted resolution 2444 (XXIII) recognising the necessity of applying basic humanitarian principles in all armed conflict and affirming the need to implement the previous resolution. Following this new trend the Secretary-General published a first report on the respect of human rights in armed conflicts (UN Doc A/7720, 1969), and a second one in 1970 (UN Doc A/8052). The reality of the armed conflicts in Africa, in particular the wars of national liberation, in Vietnam and the Arab–Israeli conflict in the Middle East,[94] pulled down the invisible line drawn by the UN during its first five-years of existence.[95] This was also the decade of the adoption of human rights treaties such as the ICCPR and the ACHR whose provisions on derogations contained reference to time of war. In parallel, the 21st International Conference in Istanbul (1969) approved the report of an experts' commission on the reaffirmation and development of the laws and customs of war. Among its conclusions, the experts argued that situations of internal disturbance or internal tension had to be considered as within period of peacetime, and therefore was human rights the relevant law to be applied.[96] However, if in a concrete case human rights instruments were not applicable (mainly because the state involved was not party to the treaties), the ICRC could base its observation on the fundamental principles of the GCs and the content of common article 3.[97] Notwithstanding that the issue of internal disturbances was part of the discussion, it was discarded by the Conference of Government Experts on the Reaffirmation and Development of IHL Applicable to Armed Conflicts (1971).[98]

Thus, despite the development of the international law of human rights, the basis of the ICRC action remained the same. Neutrality, independence and impartiality as well as confidentiality continued being pivotal to fulfilling its international mandate in an efficient manner.[99] It adopted a practical/operational approach, increasing its response to humanitarian needs in NAIC or in situations of internal disturbances,[100] addressing all the parties involved, but maintaining doubts on the convenience of invoking human rights law. In fact, in those days the context was highly politicised due to the Cold War and the process of decolonisation.[101] Second, invoking human rights, attached to this politicised context, might jeopardise the general perception of the ICRC's particularities. Finally, human rights were conceived in a manner that their obligations would bind states exclusively. They did not bind non-state actors such as organised armed groups. This entailed some problems for the ICRC in so far as it should have addressed all the parties in a NIAC on an equal basis. How could the ICRC address the parties to the conflict under different legal bases without affecting their perception over it? Furthermore, at the time, it could make the ICRC face similar problems in cases of IAC, in particular in cases of military occupation, unless it argued for the extra-territorial applicability of human rights treaties. Nowadays there is no discussion on this latter point; whereas it is still controversial to argue that human rights obligations bind organised armed groups, notwithstanding some specific cases in this area,[102] and a scholarly trend towards a broader position that includes non-state actors. Many international bodies have held a different position, for instance: 'particular acts of armed opposition groups as human rights violations must be distinguished from the denunciation of these acts as "abuses" of human rights. International bodies have often condemned acts of armed opposition groups as harming human rights without considering their acts to be breaches of human rights law'.[103]

In the following decades, the complementary between IHL and HRL became clearer and more intense. The adoption of the 1977 APs included norms inspired by developments in human rights and some general reference to them, that somehow would had not been possible in other contexts.[104] The old idea that states are sovereign and thus international law cannot regulate their relationships with the people within their territory started vanishing. In parallel, IHL and human rights remain separated, keeping their own autonomy and different logics, but have become closer operationally speaking. New treaties regulate both branches of international law. Political, quasi-judicial and judicial organs, in the framework of the UN or of regional organisations, refer to IHL or human rights, making little distinction between them.[105]

The ICRC has also contributed to this rapprochement. Always giving priority to IHL's norms and principles and reaffirming its neutrality, impartiality and independence, it seems that, based on its experience on the ground, the ICRC realised that IHL and human rights began to be concomitant and their synergies could not be ignored, especially with regard to common standards.[106] On the other hand, in the last two decades, in particular after the end of the Cold War, HRL has become an essential element of the international legal order and states' international relations. States' authorities, regardless of their political position, recognise its importance, and its use is not perceived as almost 'subversive'. Therefore in a new most favourable context, the ICRC seems to be more open to invoking human rights, especially within its preventive action.

In practice, in all these decades the ICRC has privileged its humanitarian role visiting detainees (sometimes even 'all detainees') or bringing relief to victims that were not necessarily connected with armed conflicts. Its action has strengthened the protection of human rights law,[107] regardless of whether the ICRC expressly invoked or not human rights standards – in many cases it did.

5.2   How Does the ICRC Invoke Human Rights Law?

In general, the current practice listed below confirms that the ICRC perceives itself as an eminently humanitarian organisation. This guides all its activities regardless of the contexts in which they are carried out: an armed conflict, a situation of internal disturbances or tension, or a completely peaceful environment. The main aim of its mission is to bring relief to the victims of armed conflicts and internal violence, to promote the respect of the relevant law and to persuade the parties to observe it. Its vocation is to assist and protect the individuals who are in these situations. Therefore, bringing relief and assistance is its first priority. This is even clearer in situations of internal disturbances.

In all these cases and for all its activities its approach is practical rather than legal. This is even the case when the ICRC action aims to protect human beings affected by armed conflicts, internal disturbances or other forms of internal violence. The law is not an aim in itself, but an important tool that brings objective standards in order to fulfil its mission. Nevertheless it should not be overestimated; the success of any action depends on different factors, and the law's concrete weight may vary case-by-case. A decision to resort to a law other than IHL implies an assessment of these factors as well as the possible political and operational consequences.

When invoking the law, it seems that the ICRC has a natural and logical preference for IHL. It is understandable if one takes into account that it has a specific international mandate with regard to this branch of law and maintains a great expertise in it. Nonetheless, it does not prevent the ICRC from resorting to other branches of international law, in particular HRL, or even national legislation. In fact, in many cases, the lack of instruction of its interlocutors, among other reasons, can turn the whole body of international law – IHL and human rights included – into an ineffective or even useless tool. If a legal standard is needed, national law – if suitable and in accordance with the principles enshrined in IHL and HRL – is the only resource to be used. That is why it is pivotal to promote measures of national implementation. In the invocation of any law other than IHL one of the main concerns of the ICRC is to avoid any negative impact due to a possible politicisation of it. For this reason, it often prefers to use general or indirect references to this branch of law – even though it is clear that underlying to its argumentation, the ICRC is using human rights law standards or principles. In general it seems that the ICRC is more open to invoking and using human rights, and even to giving technical advice on it, within its preventive action.

If in a concrete situation, IHL is not applicable or a party puts in doubt its applicability, the ICRC may tend to invoke first the principles contained in IHL and the content of its basic norms, as well as the movement's principles, while reminding the party of the applicability of IHL to that concrete case. In addition to this, ICRC may resort to using HRL first and foremost if it contributes to achieving the ICRC's mission. It may happen that human rights develop IHL norms or standards, it is considered the appropriate applicable law, or it is the only way to bring some protection to a person in an armed conflict. For example, it is useful when a state denies the existence of a non-international armed conflict and the only way to establish a dialogue with the authorities entails basing legal argumentation in human rights.

Obviously, human rights, applicable at all times, become the legal framework for the ICRC's activities in situations of internal violence.[108] In these cases, the ICRC often limits its action to bringing relief, in coordination with national societies. When its actions – to protect arrested persons or to guarantee access to medical relief – imply the invocation of the law, the ICRC prefers to make general reference to HRL and to principles or standards that are common to IHL and this branch of law.

In sum, the ICRC has gradually included human rights as a legal framework for its actions as a response to the needs that it faces on the field. Even when the ICRC does not have a specific mandate with regard to HRL, it may be a necessary complement to carry out its humanitarian action in armed conflicts or internal disturbances. Nonetheless, the ICRC does not pretend to become a human rights institution nor to adopt human rights institution methods. It only considers the use of HRL for operational reasons. When doing so, it looks for a balance between the possibility of invoking human rights when it is necessary and, on the other side, not to jeopardise its unique characteristics that facilitate its relief action and its access to all parties.

5.2.1 Visits to persons deprived of their freedom
In an armed conflict or situation of internal disturbances,[109] there is a presumption that persons who are in the hands of the enemy or the 'opponent' are in higher risk than

other persons deprived of their freedom. Under different legal bases, the ICRC visits attempt to prevent enforced disappearance, extrajudicial executions, any mistreatment, in particular torture or inhuman treatment, or any other abuse. Similarly, it tries to ensure all detainees' rights to judicial guarantees are respected. Finally the visits are also important to bring medical relief and to maintain family links. Hence the principal aim of the ICRC visits is to ensure human dignity, and most of the time involves legal standards that are common to IHL and human rights.[110]

Perhaps one of the most important contributions to the protection of the human being is the way in which the ICRC carries out its visit. With more than a hundred years of experience visiting persons deprived of their freedom, the ICRC has strict conditions for the visit that always should be observed and are recognised by the international community – full and unimpeded access to all detainees and to all places where they are held, the possibility of having private interviews, the possibility of repeat visits, and the possibility of drawing up lists of persons' names.[111]

When the ICRC decides to bring allegations, in a confidential manner, before authorities, it seems that it makes use of other branches of international law in very different ways. In part, it depends on the context and the category of detainees.[112] In some cases, despite the lack of expressed reference to human rights law, due to the common standards of these two branches, the legal argumentation also strengthens the observance of human rights[113] or is even inspired by human rights developments (UN documents, judicial precedents, etc.). This is the case of the action of the ICRC with regard to the respect of judicial guarantees. In other cases, the ICRC complements its legal argumentation with expressed reference to human rights[114] or soft law that enhances human rights issues.[115] In some others, it refers in general to international law and sometimes even includes the ethics codes of professional organisations.[116]

It should be remarked that in practice when the ICRC visits persons detained in connection with a NIAC,

> [it] is often led by extension to concern itself with other detainees held in the same places of detention, but for ordinary penal offences. ... In such cases, the ICRC considers either that all detainees are affected by the prevailing situation, or that it is contrary to its principles of humanity and impartiality to address the needs of only one category of detainees when others have identical, or sometimes even greater, humanitarian needs.[117]

Furthermore, in some cases the ICRC has wide agreements with states' authorities that allow visiting of all places of detention and all detainees.[118]

In fact, the ICRC has developed a comprehensive approach towards certain recurrent problems that its delegates find in prisons. In these cases, the ICRC action attempts to mobilise the authorities and representatives of the civil society in order to foster the adoption of integral public policies that attack the problems' roots. Obviously, when the authorities, with the technical support of the ICRC, implement successful and efficient policies, the result affects positively the whole prison's population whose rights become more effective. This is the case with the ICRC action that supports authorities to improve detention conditions through the establishment of national standards (in the Philippines),[119] or the ICRC health programmes that support the establishment and implementation of public health policies (Bolivia).[120]

5.2.2   Concerns on the excessive use of force

Another main concern of the ICRC is that the use of force by security forces respects people's life and dignity. It may happen within different contexts: a police operation within an armed conflict, execution of security measures in prison facilities or an operation in case of internal disturbances. In all these cases, HRL is the applicable legal framework.

However the ICRC points out that:

> In addressing the consequences, in humanitarian terms, of the use of force in situations other than armed conflict, the ICRC does not refer to the whole spectrum of international human rights law (HRL) instruments. It refers to a core of fundamental rules that protect human beings in situations of violence. These constitute a small but central and essential part of HRL.[121]

Sometimes the ICRC makes general references to international standards[122] or to human rights[123] governing the use of force. The ICRC also invokes some specific rights that enshrine humanitarian principles such as the right to life.[124]

5.2.3   Missing

One of the main concerns in armed conflicts and internal disturbances is to know the fate of missing people. This situation has the most dramatic consequences not only for the person disappeared, but also for his family. The ICRC has been playing an important role in mobilising states and other actors concerned at international and domestic levels. When dealing with this problem the ICRC directly or indirectly also fosters and strengthens the protection of human rights in so far as both IHL and human rights law share very similar standards. In this context, the ICRC often prefers to make a general reference to 'the protection of human dignity'[125] or 'human rights law'.[126]

5.2.4   Dissemination and training for the police and security forces

The ICRC's actions with regard to the police and security forces have a twofold purpose: to promote and to participate in the training of police officers within the rules and standards of IHL applicable to the police's function, and to promote and advise on the comprehensive integration of human rights standards into the doctrine, instruction and training of police forces.

The programme thus entails the ICRC dealing with human rights treaties and soft law.[127] The ICRC not only promotes this, but directly assists governmental authorities with technical support on human rights issues. Rather than being theoretical, the ICRC proposes a practical approach, in particular in order to prevent unlawful responses of the security forces in cases of internal disturbances or other forms of internal violence.[128] The ICRC has been very active in states such as Indonesia, Brazil, Peru and Ecuador, among others. Their activity is in part explained by the increasing interest that the ICRC has in the humanitarian consequences of internal disturbances or other forms of internal violence (e.g. urban violence, riots, among other).

5.2.5   Dissemination to different publics

In order to build respect for IHL, the ICRC understands that education is a key point. Its programme 'Exploring Humanitarian Law' tries to attract the attention of the young population concerning the respect of human dignity, the protection of IHL in armed conflicts and humanitarian action. Even when it is not a direct aim of the programme, it has a major impact on the fostering of the respect of human rights law values. It is clearer when it deals with the limits of IHL protection and distinguishes armed conflicts from other situations of violence that are under the threshold of IHL's scope of application.

5.2.6   The ICRC study on customary IHL

The study published in 2005[129] proposes 42 international customary rules applicable to IAC and NIAC. Notwithstanding its aim to identify IHL rules, human rights are frequently present throughout the work. Indeed the study takes into account human rights law practice (norms, judgments and decisions of judicial and quasi-judicial organs as well as other relevant human rights law documentation). Accordingly the ICRC resorts to human rights developments as complements of IHL. This is reasonable, especially with regard to common standards.[130] A general assessment of the study suggests that, in contrast to some decades ago, the ICRC feels much more comfortable in dealing with these two branches of law, accepting that they complement each other.

6.   CONCLUSION

The ICRC's mandate transcends IHL and armed conflicts, including also situations of internal violence, such as internal disturbances. In all these contexts, it carries out its activities and functions within a rather flexible legal framework, in which HRL plays a decisive role. This is even clearer in the context of violence other than armed conflicts in which IHL is not applicable. Therefore, the particular features of the ICRC's mandate imply that HRL is an important legal resort within its action, remaining exclusively for the ICRC to decide when to make use of it. Although this institution is mainly recognised and identified as IHL's guardian, it has gradually included HRL as part of its legal framework on which its actions are based as a response to the humanitarian needs that it faces in the field.

NOTES

*   Godofredo Torreblanca is writing a PhD thesis at the University of Geneva (Law Faculty), and working as a Human Rights Officer at the OHCHR. This chapter was written in the author's personal capacity, and does not necessarily reflect the opinions on the organisations/bodies with which he is associated.
1.   J. Pictet, *Développement et Principes du Droit International Humanitaire* (Geneva: Institut Henry-Dunant and Pedone, 1983), 11–71.
2.   See M. Sassòli, 'The Implementation of International Humanitarian Law: Current and Inherent Challenges', *Yearbook of International Humanitarian Law* 10 (2007): 45–73.
3.   International Committee of the Red Cross, 'Prevention Policy' (Geneva: International Committee of the Red Cross, 2010), available at: http://www.icrc.org/eng/assets/files/publications/icrc-002-4019.pdf (accessed 14 January 2011).

4. Y. Sandoz, 'Implementing International Humanitarian Law', in *International Dimensions of Humanitarian Law* (Geneva: Henry Dunant Institute and UNESCO, 1988), 259. D. Schindler, 'The International Committee of the Red Cross and Human Rights', *International Review of the Red Cross* 208 (Jan–Feb 1979): 12.
5. P. Sands and P. Klein, *Bowett's Law of International Institutions*, 5th edition (London: Sweet and Maxwell, 2001), 4–6; C.F. Amerasinghe, *Principles of the Institutional Law of International Organizations* (Cambridge: Cambridge University Press, 1996), 3–4. On this foundation of the ICRC and its international character, see J. Pictet, *Une Institution unique en son genre: Le Comité International de la Croix-Rouge* (Geneva: Institut Henry Dunant and Pédone, 1985), 7–20.
6. M.N. Shaw, *International Law*, 6th edition (Cambridge: Cambridge University Press, 2010), 261–262; R. Portmann, *Legal Personality in International Law* (Cambridge: Cambridge University Press, 2010), 112–113; J. Klabbers, *An Introduction to International Institutional Law*, 2nd edition (Cambridge: Cambridge University Press, 2009), 7; E. David, *Principes de Droit des Conflits Armés*, 4th edition (Brussels: Bruylant, 2008), 641–643; H.G. Schermers and N.M. Blokker, *International Institutional Law: Unity Within Diversity* (The Hague: Martinus Nijhoff, 1995), 33; F. Bugnion, *The International Committee of the Red Cross and the Protection of War Victims* (Geneva: International Committee of the Red Cross and Macmillan, 2003), 954–972; J.A. Barberis, *La Personnalité juridique internationale in RCADI, Vol. I – 1983* (The Hague: Martinus Nihjoff, 1984), 178; M. Sassòli and A.A. Bouvier, 'How Does Law Protect in War?', *Outlines of International Humanitarian Law: Possible Teaching Outlines*, 2nd edition, Vol. I (Geneva: International Committee of the Red Cross, 2006), 356. P. Reuter, 'La Personnalité Juridique Internationale du Comité International de la Croix-Rouge', in *Studies and Essays on International Humanitarian Law and Red Cross Principles in Honour of Jean Pictet*, ed. C. Swinarski (Geneva: International Committee of the Red Cross and Martinus Nijhoff, 1984), 783–791; C. Dominicé, 'La Personnalité Juridique Internationale du CICR', in *Studies and Essays on International Humanitarian Law and Red Cross Principles in Honour of Jean Pictet*, ed. C. Swinarski (Geneva: International Committee of the Red Cross and Martinus Nijhoff, 1984), 663–673. See also *Prosecutor v. B. Simić et al.*, Decision on the Prosecutor Motion under Rule 73 for a Ruling concerning the Testimony of a Witness, Case No. IT-95-9, 27 July 1999, para. 46.
7. A.-K. Lindblom, *Non-Governmental Organisations in International Law* (Cambridge: Cambridge University Press, 2005), 71–72. G. Ronna, 'The ICRC's status: In a class of its own', available at: http://www.icrc.org/eng/resources/documents/misc/5w9fjy.htm (accessed 28 December 2010).
8. Dominicé, *supra* note 6, at 667.
9. Bugnion, *supra* note 6, at 363–388.
10. Some consider the ICRC legal nature as *unique* in international law. There is no doubt that for decades this has been the case and will probably remain so if one takes into account the ICRC within the International Red Cross and Red Crescent Movement. This framework is what makes the ICRC's legal nature unique rather than its international personality itself. In fact, similar subjects of international law might appear in the future due to the increased presence of societies established and governed by municipal law that do not only have significant weight in the international scene, but also include the presence or representation of states in their executive bodies. For instance, the Geneva Centre for the Democratic Control of the Armed Forces (DCAF), an international foundation under the Swiss Civil Code, established on the initiative of the Swiss Confederation, at present comprises 54 states, which are part of its decision-making bodies (Council and Assembly) and participate in its institutional life, e.g., the Director is appointed by the Council upon recommendation of the Swiss Confederation. Three other states have Permanent Observer status on its Council. See http://www.dcaf.ch/About-Us#bylaws (accessed 4 January 2011).
11. Other subjects of international law have not remained indifferent to this particular case. For instance, it should be remarked that, unlike the treatment granted to other entities, it was the United Nations (UN) General Assembly that granted to the ICRC Observer status at the UN in 1990 (UN Doc. A/45/191). See C. Koenig, 'Observer Status for the International Committee of the Red Cross at the United Nations: A Legal Viewpoint', *International Review of the Red Cross* 91, No. 280 (1991): 37–48.
12. David distinguishes four different kinds of legal personalities: a universal one based on the Geneva Conventions and Additional Protocols, a second one based on its observer status in the UN General Assembly, a third one based on its headquarter agreements with different states, and a fourth one based on private law as a private association under Swiss law. David, *supra* note 6, at 643–644. In my opinion it should not be confused with the international legal personality and the extent of it.
13. Reuter, *supra* note 6, at 785.

14. See, for instance, Headquarters Agreement between the ICRC and the Swiss Confederation in *International Review of the Red Cross* 293 (1993): 152–160; ICRC-ICTY agreement throughout exchange of letters of their respective Presidents, available at http://www.icty.org/x/file/ Legal%20Library/Detention/UNDUappointment_of_inspect1995_en.pdf (accessed 16 January 2011); Cooperation Agreement between the Organizations of American States, *International Review of the Red Cross* 313 (Jul–Aug 1996): 443–446.

15. After the death of Georges Olivet, ICRC Delegate, and two other collaborators, in Congo, in 1961, the ICRC addressed the UN in as much as this organisation controlled the zone where the dead bodies were found. Under similar grounds as those laid down by the I.C.J. in the *Reparation* case, both organisations set up an enquiry commission, whose findings made the UN pay compensation to the ICRC and to the deceased's relatives. It must be noted that it was the ICRC which directly brought the issue before the UN. This functional protection was accepted in light of the I.C.J.'s previous Decision in the *Reparation* case as well. J. Barberis 'El Comité Internacional de la Cruz Roja como sujeto de derecho de gentes', in *Studies and Essays on International Humanitarian Law and Red Cross Principles in Honour of Jean Pictet*, ed. C. Swinarski (Geneva: International Committee of the Red Cross and Martinus Nijhoff, 1984), 640; Dominicé, *supra* note 6, at 671; Bugnion, *supra* note 6, at 967–968.

16. Reuter, *supra* note 6, at 784.

17. Regarding the importance of the International Conference of the Red Cross for the ICRC legal framework and the development and interpretation of IHL, see F. Bugnion, 'The International Conference of the Red Cross and Red Crescent: Challenges, Key Issues and Achievements', *International Review of the Red Cross* 91, No. 876 (2009): 675–680, 688–705; M. Meyer, 'The Importance of the International Conference of the Red Cross and Red Crescent to National Societies: Fundamental in Theory and in Practice', *International Review of the Red Cross* 91, No. 876 (2009): 728–731. Also, as an example of the involvement of states in the International Conference, see the Cable of the United States Embassy in Reykjavik, Iceland, commenting on the position of European states for a coming International Conference, Cable 06REYKJAVIK224, 19 June 2006, available at: http://www.cablegatesearch.net/search.php?q=06reykjavik224&qo=65024&qc=0&qto=2010-02-28 (accessed 19 January 2011).

18. Regarding the differences among subjects of law, the I.C.J. held 'The subjects of law in any legal system are not necessarily identical in their nature or in the extent of their rights, and their nature depends upon the needs of the community', *Reparation for Injuries Suffered in the Service of the United Nations*, Advisory Opinion, I.C.J. Reports 1949, 178(8), available at: http://www.icj-cij.org/ docket/files/4/1835.pdf (accessed 28 December 2010).

19. Principle of humanity: 'The Red Cross, born of a desire to bring assistance without discrimination to the wounded on the battlefield, endeavours – in its international and national capacity – to prevent and alleviate human suffering wherever it may be found. Its purpose is to protect life and health and to ensure respect for the human being. It promotes mutual understanding, friendship, co-operation and lasting peace amongst all peoples.'

20. Principle of impartiality: 'It makes no discrimination as to nationality, race, religious beliefs, class or political opinions. It endeavours only to relieve suffering, giving priority to the most urgent cases of distress.'

21. Principle of neutrality: '*In order to continue to enjoy the confidence of all*, the Red Cross may not take sides in hostilities or engage at any time in controversies of a political, racial, religious or ideological nature' (emphasis added).

22. Principle of independence: 'The Red Cross is independent. The National Societies, while auxiliaries in the humanitarian services of their Governments and subject to the laws of their respective countries, must always maintain their autonomy so that they may be able at all times to act in accordance with Red Cross principles.'

23. International Committee of the Red Cross, 'Commentaries of the Fundamental Principles of the Red Cross', available at http://www.icrc.org/eng/resources/documents/misc/fundamental-principles-commentary-010179.htm (accessed 4 January 2010).

24. New technology represents an opportunity and a challenge with regard to ICRC confidentiality. In the last years ICRC confidential reports have been leaked and published all around the world. See for instance, BBC News, 'Israel Jerusalem Policy Condemned. The ICRC has privately accused Israel of reshaping Jerusalem to further its own interest, in violation of international law', 17 May 2007, available at: http://news.bbc.co.uk/2/hi/middle_east/6658799.stm (accessed 18 December 2010). Also see *infra* notes 25, 110 and 114. Notwithstanding, this general problem also affects confidential

information of states in general, they must take all the necessary measures in order to ensure the confidentiality of ICRC's information.

25.   ICRC deputy director says: 'In some instances, we may indeed share general or specific concerns with selected third parties – usually with States. Such exchanges, which are intended to explain the status of our activities, take place in the framework of our efforts to mobilize support for important humanitarian initiatives. Sometimes, the aim may be to indirectly influence the parties concerned so that a given situation can be improved. These exchanges take place on an exclusively bilateral and strictly confidential basis', 'Confidentiality: Key to the ICRC's work but not unconditional. An interview with ICRC deputy director of operations Dominik Stillhart, 20 September 2010', available at: http://www.icrc.org/eng/resources/documents/interview/confidentiality-interview-010608.htm (accessed 8 February 2011). For instance, see the information shared between the ICRC and the US Diplomatic Representatives in India. US Embassy Cable NEW DELHI002606, 6 April 2005, available at: http://www.guardian.co.uk/world/us-embassy-cables-documents/30222 (accessed 25 January 2011). Likewise, it seems reasonable that if an authority receives allegations about unlawful behaviour of persons under his responsibility, this information can be shared with other competent and relevant authorities, if it is necessary to take corrective measures.

26.   The ICRC states 'the confidentiality of the ICRC's dialogue with authorities and other actors is not without limits. It is proportional to the willingness of the authorities to take into account the ICRC's recommendations. The justification for confidentiality thus depends on the quality of the ICRC's dialogue with authorities and other actors and on the humanitarian impact of its bilateral confidential representations. The ICRC reserves the right, should this dialogue not have the desired impact, to resort to other action, including public denunciation', 'ICRC Protection Policy. Institutional Policy', *International Review of the Red Cross* 90, No. 871 (2008): 758–759.

27.   For instance during the genocide in Rwanda in 1994, the ICRC decided to go public in a very decided and strong way. See the interesting assessment of its Head of Delegation at that time: Talk given by Philippe Gaillard, ICRC Head of Delegation in Rwanda from 1993 to 1994, on 18 October 1994 at the International Museum of the Red Cross and Red Crescent, Geneva, entitled 'Rwanda 1994: La vraie vie est absente' (Arthur Rimbaud), available at: http://www.icrc.org/eng/resources/documents/misc/5xkca5.htm (accessed 5 January 2011)'. See also Speech by Philippe Gaillard, head of the ICRC's delegation in Rwanda, 1993–1994, given at the Genocide Prevention Conference, London, January 2002, organised by the Aegis Trust and the UK Foreign Office, available at: http://www.icrc.org/eng/resources/documents/misc/5xfncq.htm (accessed 5 January 2011).

28.   See the ICRC position before the request of cooperation of the Peruvian Truth Commission with regard to information of missing persons. The ICRC decided 'to provide [limited] information that only it possessed to the commission to enable it to solve cases of missing persons'. In contrast, the ICRC denied sharing information with the Rwandese *Gacaca* courts in so far as doing so could be associated with a sort of 'judicial' process. T. Pfanner, 'Cooperation between Truth Commission and the ICRC', *International Review of the Red Cross* 88, No. 862 (2006): 367–368. In a different case the ICRC denied authorisation to use ICRC confidential information in the Eritrea-Ethiopia Claim Commission, even though both parties, at least officially, agreed to use it before the Commission. *Prisoners of War: Ethiopia's Claim 4* (partial Award, 2003), Eritrea Ethiopia Claims Commission, para. 48, available at: http://www.pca-cpa.org/showfile.asp?fil_id=145. See some comments on the limited effects of the ICRC work due to its confidentiality in Sassòli, *supra* note 2, at 53.

29.   See Rule 73 of Rules of Procedure and Evidence of the International Criminal Court (ICC) and Rule 164 of Rules of Procedure and Evidence of the Special Tribunal for Lebanon. *Prosecutor v. B. Simić et al.*, ICTY, Decision on the Prosecutor Motion under Rule 73 for a Ruling concerning the Testimony of a Witness, 27 July 1999 (Case No. IT-95-9), paras 73–74; *Prosecutor v. Muvunyi*, ICTR, Reasons for the Chamber's Decision on the Accused's Motion to Exclude Witness TQ, 15 July 2005 (Case No. ICTR-2000-55A-T), para. 16. G. Distefano, 'Le CICR et l'Immunité de Juridiction en Droit International contemporain: Fragments d'Investigation Autour d'une Notion Centrale de l'Organisation Internationale', *Revue Suisse de Droit International et de Droit Européen* 3 (2002): 355–370.

30.   C. Swinarski, 'La notion d'un organisme neutre et le droit international', in *Studies and Essays on International Humanitarian Law and Red Cross Principles in Honour of Jean Pictet*, ed. C. Swinarski (Geneva: International Committee of the Red Cross and Martinus Nijhoff, 1984), 832; T.C. van Boven, however, notes: 'When the principle of ideological neutrality prescribes not to "engage at any time in controversies of political, racial, religious or ideological nature," this cannot imply an indifference vis-à-vis ideologies and doctrines adhered to by governments that render themselves

guilty of the most heinous acts against persons who are in their power. If the principle of ideological neutrality would imply that no value judgments could be made with regard to the type of ideologies and doctrines mentioned a moment ago, the reasoning behind the principle of neutrality, viz. "in order to continue to enjoy the confidence of all," would lose its meaning and effect. In fact, such ideological neutrality would on the contrary have the effect of largely undermining confidence and credibility', T.C. van Boven, 'Some Reflections on the Principle of Neutrality', in *Studies and Essays on International Humanitarian Law and Red Cross Principles in Honour of Jean Pictet*, ed. C. Swinarski (Geneva: International Committee of the Red Cross and Martinus Nijhoff, 1984), 648. See also 646–647.

31.   D.-D. Junod, *The Imperiled Red Cross and the Palestine-Eretz-Yisrael Conflict 1945–1952. The Influence of Institutional Concerns on a Humanitarian Operation* (London: Kegan Paul International, 1996), 11–12.

32.   Swinarski, *supra* note 30, at 831.

33.   Nevertheless, as Sassòli and Bouvier note, 'The distinction between the legal bases of ICRC action provided by the Conventions and those derived from the Movement's Statutes is important in legal terms. In practical terms, however, it is not essential because the ICRC generally offers its service without specifying the legal basis for its offer, in order to avoid having to make a judgement as to the type of conflict involved', Sassòli and Bouvier, *supra* note 6, at 356.

34.   Swinarski points out 'Adoptés par la Conférence internationale où, à côté des entités composantes de la Croix-Rouge Internationale, siègent, de plein droit, les Etats parties aux Conventions de Genève, les Statuts de la Croix-Rouge Internationale ont une valeur juridique qui dépasse le cadre du "droit interne" de la Croix-Rouge', Swinarski, *supra* note 30, at 833.

35.   On its legal nature, its role in the movement and its contribution to the development of the ICRC mandate and IHL, see the comprehensive study of R. Perruchoud, *Les Résolutions des Conférences Internationales de la Croix-Rouge* (Geneva: Institut Henry-Dunant, 1979); Bugnion, *supra* note 6, at 376–381.

36.   In this sense, Eide holds, 'The right of initiative has been used courageously and has often been used in a pioneering way, evolving in a pragmatic way to cover situations not yet foreseen in the Conventions. To some extent the basis has been laid in Resolutions of the Red Cross Conference', A. Eide, 'The Laws of War and Human Rights – Differences and Convergences', in *Studies and Essays on International Humanitarian Law and Red Cross Principles in Honour of Jean Pictet*, ed. C. Swinarski (Geneva: International Committee of the Red Cross and Martinus Nijhoff, 1984), 694.

37.   It must be stressed that in addition to the Protecting Power, 'The other machinery for supervision and control under the laws of war is that of the ICRC, which to some extent might be performed also by other humanitarian organisations. In the early years, there was no conventional basis for the ICRC role, but it developed in practice as a "right of initiative" which was codified in the *1949 Convention*', Ibid., 694. See also R. Kolb, *Ius in Bello. Le Droit International des Conflits Armés*, 2nd edition (Basel: Helbing Lichtenhahn and Bruylant, 2009), 463–466. Pictet, *supra* note 5, at 58–59.

38.   See E. Crawford, *The Treatment of Combatants and Insurgents Under the Law of Armed Conflict* (Oxford: Oxford University Press, 2010), 97.

39.   Article 4(1)(d), ICRC Statutes and Article 5(2)(d), Statutes of the International Red Cross and Red Crescent Movement. See also the Article 5.3.1., 1997 Seville Agreement.

40.   Dominicé holds, 'La mission propre du CICR le conduit à intervenir auprès des Etats pour défendre les victimes des conflits. Il le fait directement au plan du droit international en sa qualité de gardien des conventions humanitaires et dans l'exercice des responsabilités qui lui sont confiées', Dominicé, *supra* note 6, at 670.

41.   *Reparations for Injuries Suffered in the Service of the United Nations*, Advisory Opinion, I.C.J. Reports 1949: 182–183. See criticism to this theory in Klabbers, *supra* note 6, at 32–64.

42.   Competence of the International Labour Organisation to Regulate, Incidentally, the Personal Work of the Employer, Advisory Opinion (1926), Permanent Court of International Justice (PCIJ), Series B, No. 13, 18; Jurisdiction of the European Commission of the Danube, Advisory Opinion (1927), PCIJ, Series B, No. 14, 25–37; *Legality of the Use by a State of Nuclear Weapons in Armed Conflict*, Advisory Opinion, I.C.J. Reports 1996, para. 20–21. 'The idea behind attribution is, quite simply, that international organizations and their organs, can only do those things for which they are empowered', Klabbers, *supra* note 6, at 56.

43.   *Prosecutor v. Tohomir Blaskić*, ICTY, Judgment on the Request of the Republic of Croatia for Review of the Decision of Trial Chamber II, 18 July 1997, ICTY-Appeal Chamber, 29 October 1997 (Case No. IT-95-14-AR108bis), 15, footnote 27. Klabbers points out that 'Organizations, on this view, once

established, would possess inherent powers to perform all those acts which they need to perform to attain their aims, not due to any specific source of organizational power ... but simply because they inhere in organizationhood. ...

[T]he act must aim to achieve the organization's purpose, and second, it may not be expressly prohibited', Klabbers, *supra* note 6, at 66. On the *Blaskić case*, see J. Verhoeven, *Droti International Public* (Brussels: Larcier, 2000), 220.

44. Articles 31–33 in both conventions.

45. See a different position in David, *supra* note 6, at 643.

46. Reparation case, 182 (12).

47. See *supra* note 15. This theory has also been used to find out whether the ICRC holds International legal personality. Based on this theory, Reuter holds that 'La personnalité internationale du CICR s'affirme en raison de deux données: la nature des fonctions qu'il assume et les caractères spécifiques de certains actes qu'il est amené a poser dans l'exercice de ses fonctions', Reuter, *supra* note 6, at 787.

48. For instance, in determining the binding force of the International Conference Resolutions, Bugnion applies the implicit power theory – principle of effectiveness – to the analysis of the Statutes of the movement. In general he argues these considerations apply to the internal rules of an organization. Bugnion, *supra* note 6, at 377–378.

49. ICRC activities '... comprennent à côté d'activités caritatives (envoi de vivres, de matériel sanitaire, de médecins, d'équipes de secours, etc) toute démarche, intervention, suggestion ou mesure pratique touchant à la protection conventionnelle. Un tel droit devrait entrainer pour le CICR la possibilité de procéder à des constatations de fait et de droit et d'en faire état dans ses relations avec les autorités de l'Etat belligérant concerné', David, *supra* note 6, at 645, see also 647.

50. S. Vité, *Les Procédures Internationales d'Etablissement des Faits dans la Mise en Œuvre du Droit International Humanitaire* (Brussels: Bruylant, 1998), 39–40.

51. See the differences between the ICRC and judicial entities in *Prosecutor v. B. Simić et al.*, ICTY, Decision on the Prosecutor Motion under Rule 73 for a Ruling concerning the Testimony of a Witness, 27 July 1999 (Case No. IT-95-9), para. 79. David notes, commenting on Articles 126 GC III and 143 GC IV, that 'Les activités humanitaires du CICR comportent donc moins des fonctions d'enquête que des pouvoirs de procéder à des constatations de fait', David, *supra* note 6, at 646. In an opposing view, Reuter argues that the ICRC role as a control mechanism that 'amène le CICR à se prononcer sur le respect ou la violation d'une convention internationale, ce qui constitue une fonction quasi-judiciaire internationale', Reuter, *supra* note 6, at 788.

52. David, *supra* note 6, 1026. In this sense, E. Crawford holds, 'To fill those gaps, other international legal principles and dictates can be consulted. The most appropriate of these alternate sources of obligation is international human rights law (HRL). Human rights law includes equivalent rights and protections for persons deprived of their liberty in non-international armed conflicts, and can be drawn on to supplement IHL where it lacks depth or detail. The utility of human rights law lies specifically in the fact the HRL regulates the conduct of a State towards its nationals', Crawford, *supra* note 38, at 118.

53. For instance, notwithstanding the lack of express regulation, regarding family links, Bugnion argues that, 'The ICRC can therefore base its efforts to facilitate the reunion of dispersed families on this provision, on the fundamental principle of humanity expressed by Article 3 of the 1949 Conventions and Article 4, paragraph 1, of Protocol II, and on the inalienable rights of the family enshrined in the Universal Declaration of Human Rights and the International Covenant on Civil and Political Rights', Bugnion, *supra* note 6, at 784, see also his footnote 8. See also Schindler, *supra* note 4, at 14.

54. In determining the set of rules applicable to the ICRC activities, Bugnion deems it must include, among other legal sources, human rights law provisions that might be contained in treaties or other instruments such as UN organs' Resolutions. He holds 'I therefore believe that the Committee should draw up a thorough and detailed catalogue of all general and specific rules relevant to its work, drawn from every formal source of public international law. There is every reason to believe that such a list would open up new perspectives for the ICRC and enable it to strengthen the foundations of its work.' Afterwards, he adds: 'Finally – and perhaps most importantly – there must be a constant awareness that the humanitarian conventions are really no more than the expression of the fundamental humanitarian principles which underlie them.' Whereas, in his conclusions about the ICRC mandate he points out that '[i]ts greatest asset is unquestionably the mandate entrusted to it by the international community, and recognition by public international law of that mandate *together with the competence and prerogatives it needs to discharge it*'. Bugnion, *supra* note 6, 397–399, 1023 (emphasis added).

55. In this sense, regarding the emergence of the international law of human rights and its relationship with IHL, Kolb points out 'Human rights are concerned with the organization of State power vis-à-vis the individual. They are the product of the theories of the Age of Enlightenment and found their natural expression in domestic constitutional law … It was only after the Second World War, as a reaction against the excesses of the Axis forces, that human rights law became part of the body of public international law. The end of the 1940s was when human rights law was first placed beside what was still called the law of war. The question of their mutual relationship within the body of international law can be considered only from that moment', R. Kolb, 'The Relationship Between International Humanitarian Law and Human Rights Law: A Brief History of the 1948 Universal Declaration of Human Rights and the 1949 Geneva Conventions', *International Review of the Red Cross* 324 (September 1998): 410.

56. On the relevance of the Martens Clause David holds 'Nous pensons que cette clause produit un effet proche de celui résultant de certaines clauses générales de sauvegarde des droits fondamentaux que l'on trouve dans les instruments protecteurs des droits de l'homme. Selon ces clauses, des restrictions ou des dérogations aux droits fondamentaux de la personne reconnus dans les Etats parties ne peuvent en aucun cas y être apportées sous prétexte que la convention ne reconnaîtrait pas ces droits ou les reconnaîtrait à un moindre degré … Ce type de clause qui est une illustration de l'intérêt dû aux victimes se retrouve aussi, mais de manière plus limitée, dans le droit des conflits armés (voy. 1er PA, art. 75, § 8). Nous pensons toutefois que la clause Martens joue un rôle analogue à ces dispositions pour l'ensemble du droit des conflits armés', David, *supra* note 6, at 615.

57. See Schindler, *supra* note 4, at 4–5.

58. In 1875 Moynier wrote to Dr Landa, President of the Spanish national society, 'ce triomphe de l'aidée humanitaire dans sa plus complète réalisation, parmi les écueils de la guerre civile et du fanatisme politique et religieux, doit nous encourager à demander toujours la réalisation du mieux, et de ne pas nous contenter du moindre mal', quoted by J. Moreillon, *Le Comité International de la Croix-Rouge et la protection des détenus politiques. Les activités du CICR en faveur des personnes incarcérées dans leur propre pays l'occasion de troubles ou de tensions internes* (Lausanne: L'ade d'Homme, 1973), 26–27.

59. Ibid., 27–29.

60. Ibid., 35.

61. Ibid., 36.

62. In the meantime the ICRC continued holding the same disposition to bring humanitarian relief in these cases, either directly or through national societies. According to Moreillon, during the Russian civil war (1918), the ICRC even visited detainees. Ibid., 44–47.

63. Perruchoud notes, 'Le projet de convention internationale, présenté en 1912 par Clark, prévoit que la CRI est habilitée à porter secours aussi bien dans les guerres civiles que dans les situations de troubles intérieurs, voire de tension internes, mais il n'est pas retenu. En 1921, la résolution XIV, dont nous avons donné de larges extraits, reconnaît expressément que la CRI a le droit et le devoir d'agir en cas de "troubles sociaux et révolutionnaires": jusqu'en 1965, cette résolution constituera la seule base d'action du CICR et des SN', Perruchoud, *supra* note 35, at 275. See also 267–269. Regarding the X International Conference in 1921, Moreillon points out that 'Et c'est ainsi qu'au sortir de la X Conférence International de la Croix-Rouge, le CICR se trouva non seulement muni d'un mandat d'intervention en cas de conflits et de trouves internes, mais encore encouragé d'intervention en cas de conflits et de troubles internes, mais encore encouragé à demander pour les personnes détenues dans ces situations, un traitement analogue à celui des prisonniers de guerre', Ibid., 62.

64. Due to the abstention of the British Red Cross, the ICRC concluded it had the duty of offering its service. Ibid., 76.

65. According to Moreillon this was the first time the ICRC intervened in a situation of internal strife (political tension). Ibid., 94.

66. G. Willemin and R. Heacock, under the direction of J. Freymond, *The International Committee of the Red Cross* (Boston: Martinus Nijhoff and HEI, 1984), 140.

67. In Moreillon's opinion, between 1921 and 1928 the ICRC 's'est montré plus timide devant le problème théorique de son intervention en faveur des détenus politiques que dans les différentes situations pratiques où des individus devaient et pouvaient être secourus', Moreillon, *supra* note 58, at 92.

68. Ibid., 104–105.

69. Ibid., 96–99.

70. Schindler, *supra* note 4, at 5. Due to the lack of legal basis, the ICRC tried to persuade the parties to apply the 1934 draft convention concerning the conditions and the protection of civilians of enemy nationality in international wars (Tokyo, 1934) but with little success. Junod, *supra* note 31, at 17–19.

71. See A. Calogeropoulos-Stratis, 'Droit humanitaire – Droit de l'Homme et victimes des conflits armés', in *Studies and Essays on International Humanitarian Law and Red Cross Principles in Honour of Jean Pictet*, ed. C. Swinarski (Geneva: International Committee of the Red Cross and Martinus Nijhoff, 1984), 655.

72. Kolb comments, 'During the drafting of the Universal Declaration of 1948 the question of the impact of war on human rights was touched on only in exceptional cases. Paragraph 2 of the Preamble describes respect for human rights as a condition for the maintenance of peace. This is *jus contra bellum*. There was a shift towards *jus in bello* when a few delegates indicated in passing, in a very secondary way, that the rights envisaged by the Declaration presuppose a state of peace. In the long debates in the Third Committee of the United Nations, for example, Jimenez de Arechaga expressed the view that human rights have to "govern, in times of peace, an international community based on the principles of the United Nations". Campos Ortiz, the Mexican delegate, made a similar comment in the plenary meetings of the Third Session of the United Nations General Assembly, when he used the expression "in a peaceful world". Only the delegate of Lebanon, Mr Azkoul, explicitly went further. Speaking on Article 26 of the draft, he said that "fundamental human rights, as set out in the Declaration, should also be guaranteed in time of war"', Kolb, *supra* note 55, at 412.

73. Ibid., 410.

74. Ibid., 412–413.

75. Sandoz, *supra* note 4, at 260–261. Schindler, *supra* note 4, at 7.

76. Kolb, *supra* note 55, at 413. In particular regarding the debate of Article 3 common to GCs, Kolb notes: 'Quite naturally, Article 3 common to the four Conventions also gave rise to references to human rights. The Special Committee nominated by Committee II of the Conference had proposed, for the Convention on prisoners of war, a third paragraph containing a kind of Martens clause. It had been said in the Special Committee that even when a person did not benefit under the provision of the Convention, that person would nevertheless remain "safeguarded by the principles of the rights of man as derived from the rules established among civilized nations ...". In the view of the Danish delegate, Cohn, Article 3 should not be interpreted in such a way as to deprive individuals of any rights they may have acquired from other sources, in particular human rights', Kolb, *supra* note 55, at 414. It should be noted that in the 1949 Diplomatic Conference all reference to internal disturbances and possible events attached to this situation was omitted. See Moreillon, *supra* note 58, at 110–111.

77. See Crawford, *supra* note 38, at 122–125.

78. The ICRC, for example, was the object of attacks from the USSR and other communist States. They denounced the ICRC for its performance during the Second World War. Junod, *supra* note 31, at 14–17.

79. After the system of the UN had settled down, this idea was often present, with some slight differences. For instance, some pretended IHL was only applicable to the aggressor, even during the 1974 Conference. Pictet always perceived this as a serious danger; Pictet, *supra* note 1, at 100.

80. Kolb holds 'These institutional factors affected the development of the rules: the United Nations, the guarantor of international human rights, wanted nothing to do with the law of war, while the ICRC, the guarantor of the law of war, did not want to move any closer to an essentially political organization or to human rights law which was supposed to be its expression. The result was a clear separation of the two branches', Kolb, *supra* note 55, at 411.

81. See, for instance, the statement of the President of the 1949 Conference during the signing ceremony upon the Universal Declaration and the GCs texts. In Ibid., 415–416. Also see the Resolution (XX, *Personnes poursuives ou détenues ou des raisons d'ordre politique*) adopted in the 17th International Conference in Stockholm (1948), whereby States were invited to ensure the benefits of humanitarian principles to these persons. According to Moreillon, the legal commission of the Conference held that 'les expériences faites dans ce domaine, au cours de la seconde guerre mondiale, justifiaient pleinement que la Croix-Rouge et les Gouvernements se penchent sur ce problème et s'efforcent, particulièrement à une *époque où l'on reconnaissait les droits fondamentaux de l'homme*, de garantir *les détenus politiques contre un traitement inhumain*', Moreillon, *supra* note 58, at 109 (emphasis added).

82. Schindler, *supra* note 4, at 3.

83. Ibid., 7–8.

84. Moreillon, *supra* note 58, at 118–119.

85. Ibid., 120.
86. Ibid., 119–121.
87. See Kolb, *supra* note 55, at 417–418.
88. Moreillon, *supra* note 58, at 127–128. It should be noted that a few years later, in 1955, the French authorities upheld a different position regarding ICRC visits to places of detention in order to verify the detention regime (Algeria and Morocco 1955); see 140–141.
89. Ibid., 129–130.
90. Ibid., 135–136.
91. Ibid., 159–160.
92. Ibid., 163 and 253–254.
93. Perruchoud, *supra* note 35, at 276; Moreillon, *supra* note 58, at 162 and 265. It must be pointed out that the British delegate proposed to delete the phrase 'internal disturbances', but this was rejected by 73 against 12.
94. According to Calogeropoulos-Stratis, a document on the occupied territories, in the context of the Arab–Israeli war, was the first one in which was included a reference to human rights regarding a situation of armed conflict. Calogeropoulos-Stratis, *supra* note 71, at 658–659.
95. Schindler, *supra* note 4, at 8.
96. Moreillon, *supra* note 58, at 172–173.
97. Ibid., 179.
98. During the debate one expert argued that common article 3 contained, inside some of its provisions, minimum rules applicable to such situations. Report on the Work of Conference of Government Experts on the Reaffirmation and Development of IHL Applicable to Armed Conflicts, 1971, 21 (para. 27).
99. Calogeropoulos-Stratis, *supra* note 71, at 659.
100. A. Aeschlimann, 'Protection of Detainees: ICRC Action Behind Bars', *International Review of the Red Cross* 87, No. 857 (2005): 85.
101. The emergence of new states was, for instance, a matter of Pictet's thoughts and concerns. He held, 'I have moreover arrived at the conclusion that the future of the Red Cross rests in its universality, in the acceptance of humanitarian principles by all men and all nations, but it is unfortunately true that the people of emergent nations who have been in tutelage and who today are acceding to independence, might be inclined to reject the Red Cross idea, in common with everything they thrust aside, because they have received it from their former masters, like any other product imported from Europe. They risk "throwing the child away with the bath water". Now, we know that the entire world can accept the conception of the Red Cross because it is based on motives common to all men, and because it corresponds to the acknowledged interests of mankind', J. Pictet, 'The Doctrine of the Red Cross', *International Review of the Red Cross* 15 (June, 1962): 296.
102. See, for instance, the San José Agreement between El Salvador and the FMLN. UN Doc. A/44/971-S/21541, 16 August 1990, Annex.
103. L. Zegveld, *Accountability of Armed Opposition Groups in International Law* (Cambridge University Press, 2002), 39, in general 38–46. See also Crawford, *supra* note 38, at 126; Sassòli, *supra* note 2, at 63–67; N.S. Rodley, 'Can Armed Opposition Groups Violate Human Rights?', in *Human Rights in the Twenty-first Century: A Global Challenge*, K.E. Mahoney and P. Mahoney, eds, (Dordrecht: Martinus Nijhoff, 1993), 297–302; and the interesting analysis of A. Clapham, 'Human Rights Obligations of Non-State Actors in Conflict Situations', *International Review of the Red Cross* 88, No. 863 (2006): 491–523.
104. Schindler, *supra* note 4, at 9, 13–14. See Articles 72, 75, 76 and 77 API; 4, 5, 6 and the Preamble APII.
105. Dugard holds, 'Since the 1968 Tehran International Conference on Human Rights, the situation has changed dramatically and the two subjects are now considered as different branches of the same discipline. A number of factors have contributed to this merger, including the growing significance of international criminal law and the criminalization of serious violations of human rights', J. Dugard, 'Bridging the Gap Between Human Rights and Humanitarian Law: The Punishment of Offenders', *International Review of the Red Cross* 324 (September, 1998): 445.
106. Pictet, who was previously very reluctant to the idea of merging human rights and IHL, held 'on en vient de plus en plus à considérer qu'une partie du droit international, que l'on pourrait appeler le droit humain, couvrant à la fois le droit des conflits armés et les droits de l'homme, a la vocation d'assurer un minimum de garanties et d'humanité à tous les hommes, que ce soit en temps de paix ou en temps de guerre. On pourrait formuler comme suit le principe du droit humain: les exigences

militaires et le maintien de l'ordre public resteront toujours compatibles avec le respect de la personne humaine', Pictet, *supra* note 1, at 76. Afterwards, he set up a group of fundamental principles common to IHL and human rights that were related to the right to life, the prohibition of torture, inhuman and cruel treatment, the right to a legal personality, the right to honour, rights of family, the right to keep family links (correspondence), and the right not to be deprived of your property and judicial guarantees, at 78–83.

107. In 1979, Schindler pointed out, 'The fact that, since the Second World War and in situations unconnected with armed conflicts, ICRC delegates have been able to visit in over seventy countries some 300,000 detainees unprotected by any Convention is, in the context of the protection of human rights, an achievement of considerable importance. As a result, this protection has been extended to a category of persons who are in a situation very similar to that of prisoners of war or civilian internees but for whom the States are not very eager to sign a convention because in the majority of cases these persons are nationals of the States', Schindler, *supra* note 4, at 5.

108. In fact, it should be noted that the ICRC does not only work in places where an armed conflict has taken place. On the contrary, many of the places in the world, if not most of them, where the ICRC operates or has activities, do not face an armed conflict.

109. See ICRC News Release, 31 January 2011, 'Tunisia: ICRC resumes visits to detainees', available at http://www.icrc.org/eng/resources/documents/news-release/2011/tunisia-news-2011-01-31.htm (accessed 2 February 2011).

110. In the context of the war in Iraq, the ICRC requested the authorities of the Coalition Forces 'to respect at all times the human dignity, physical integrity and cultural sensitivity of the persons deprived of their liberty held under their control', Report of the International Committee of the Red Cross (ICRC) on the Treatment by the Coalition Forces of Prisoners of War and Other Protected Persons by the Geneva Conventions in Iraq During Arrest, Internment and Interrogation, February 2004 (fax copy of a strictly confidential report leaked to the media. Hereinafter 'ICRC Report on Iraq'), para. 8. Also in the exchange of letters between the ICRC's and ICTY's Presidents (Agreement on ICRC's visits), both institutions agreed: Letter from Antonio Cassese, President of the International Criminal Tribunal for the former Yugoslavia, to Cornelio Sommaruga, President of the International Committee of the Red Cross, 28 April 1995: 'The role of the ICRC shall be to inspect and report upon all aspects of conditions of detention, including the treatment of persons held at the Detention Unit, to ensure their compliance with internationally accepted standards of human rights or humanitarian law.' Letter from Cornelio Sommaruga, President of the International Committee of the Red Cross, to Antonio Cassese, President of the International Criminal Tribunal for the former Yugoslavia, 5 May 1995: 'Therefore, the ICRC is ready to carry out visits to detainees held under the authority of the Tribunal in its Detention Unit in accordance with the conditions outlined in your letter of 28 April 1995', 'Agreement between the International Criminal Tribunal for the former Yugoslavia and the ICRC on procedures for visiting persons held on the authority of the Tribunal', *International Review of the Red Cross* 311, (March–April, 1996): 238–242. See in particular 239 and 241–242.

111. 'Respect for the life and dignity of the detainees', available at: http://www.icrc.org/eng/what-we-do/visiting-detainees/overview-visiting-detainees.htm (accessed 20 January 2011).

112. Aeschlimann, *supra* note 100, at 107.

113. 'ICRC Report on Iraq'. See, in general, the legal argumentation of the report.

114. See references to Article 9(1) of 1966 ICCPR and Article 1 of the 1984 CAT in footnotes 18 and 19 of the ICRC 'Report on the Treatment of Fourteen "High Value Detainees" in Custody', February 2007 (strictly confidential report leaked to the media. Hereinafter 'ICRC Report on Guantanamo').

115. See reference to Article 3 of the Code of Conduct for Law Enforcement Officials and Article 9 of the Basic Principles on the Use of Force and Firearms by Law Enforcement Officials in 'ICRC Report on Iraq', para 49; as well as references to Principles 16 and 19 of the 1998 Body of Principles for the Protection of all Persons under any Form of Detention or Imprisonment, Rule 37 of the 1977 Standard Minimum Rules for the Treatment of Prisoners, in footnote 16 of 'ICRC Report on Guantanamo'.

116. For instance in 'ICRC Report on Guantanamo', the ICRC upheld 'As such, the interrogation process is contrary to international law and the participation of health personnel in such a process is contrary to international standards of medical ethics', 23. Later, in a different passage, it added: 'Customary rules of IHL and human rights soft law instruments contain similar explicit provisions on the obligation of registration of detainees and the prohibition of unacknowledged detention, as well as provisions on contacts with family, applicable in situations of non-international armed conflicts and

other situations of violence', 24. See, as examples of ethical code or guidelines, the 1975 Declaration of Tokyo of the World Medical Association (WMA) and the WMA 1991 Declaration of Malta, and ICRC comments on these documents in Hernán Reyes, 'Medical and Ethical Aspects of Hunger Strikes in Custody and the issues of Torture'. Extract from Maltreatment and Torture, available at http://www.icrc.org/eng/resources/documents/article/other/health-article-010198.htm (accessed 15 January 2011). According to Reuters, referring to the hunger strike in Guantanamo Bay prison facilities, in 2005, the 'The ICRC backs a 1975 Tokyo declaration by the World Medical Association stating that doctors should not participate in force-feeding, but keep prisoners informed of the sometimes irreversible consequences of their hunger strike', available at: http://www.redorbit.com/news/general/263964/icrc_says_hunger_strike_at_guantanamo_bay_serious/index.html (accessed 15 January 2011).

117.   Aeschlimann, *supra* note 100, at 88.
118.   For instance, Algeria accepted ICRC visits to all detainees in January 1995. Crawford, *supra* note 38, at 98. The author also says: 'Following the insurgency and eventual overthrow of the Somoza government, the ICRC was allowed access to prisoners held in national prisons and police stations. They also carried out widespread relief actions, including the distribution of food, medical and sanitary supplies, educational materials, and assisted in the training of prison paramedics. The ICRC also established assistance programmes for the families of detainees', 99.
119.   ICRC News Release 10/212, 18 November 2010, 'Philippines: New standards adopted to improve detention conditions', available at: http://www.icrc.org/eng/resources/documents/news-release/2010/philippines-news-2010-11-18.htm (accessed 15 January 2011).
120.   See ICRC Operational Update, 11 March 2010, 'Bolivia: ICRC offers advice and expertise to Bolivia institutions', available at: http://www.icrc.org/eng/resources/documents/update/bolivia-update-090 310.htm (accessed 15 January 2011). ICRC Report on Bolivian prisons conditions. See Comunicado de prensa CICR, 24 October 2007, 'Bolivia: Publicación de informe del CICR sobre la situación carcelaria', available at: http://www.icrc.org/web/spa/sitespa0.nsf/htmlall/bolivia-news-241007?open document (accessed 15 January 2011). On the ICRC support to prevent tuberculosis in Latin American prisons, see also Interview with Dr Alain Vuilleumier, 23 March 2010, 'America Latina: Las cárcerles son bolsones de tuberculosis', available at: http://www.icrc.org/web/spa/sitespa0.nsf/html/peru-interview-220310 (accessed 15 January 2011).
121.   International Committee of the Red Cross, *Violence and the Use of Force* (Geneva: International Committee of the Red Cross, 2008), 51. This publication refers explicitly to different human rights such as right to life, liberty and security of person, right to hold opinions without interference, to freedom of expression, of peaceful assembly, to freedom of association laid down in the Universal Declaration of Human Rights, the ICCPR, ECHR and IACHR, as well as the 1979 UN Code of Conduct for the Law Enforcement Official and the 1990 Basic Principles on the Use of Force and Firearms by Law Enforcement Officials. See 10–11 and 15.
122.   For instance, during the violent events in Cairo, in January 2011, the ICRC Head of Operations for the Middle East said 'Security forces must apply international standards governing the use of force in their efforts to restore law and order. Those arrested and detained must be treated in conformity with the law', ICRC News Release, 29 January 2011, 'Egypt: ICRC calls for human life and dignity to be respected', available at: http://www.icrc.org/eng/resources/documents/news-release/2011/egypt-news-2011-01-29.htm (accessed on 2 February 2011).
123.   During the events in Yemen in March 2011, the Head of the ICRC Delegation in Yemen held, '[t]he ICRC calls upon the authorities, demonstrators and all others involved to respect human life and dignity at all times'. The ICRC News release added 'Security forces must comply with international human rights law and international standards governing the use of force in their efforts to restore law and order. Those arrested and detained must be treated humanely', ICRC News Release 11/62, 18 March 2011, 'Yemen: ICRC calls for respect for human life and dignity', available at: http://www.icrc.org/eng/resources/documents/news-release/2011/yemen-news-2011-03-18.htm (accessed 20 March 2011). There is also general reference to 'human rights norms that protect the human being'. See the information about the visits of persons detained in connection to internal disturbances in Paraguay and Chile during the last bimestrial of 2010. ICRC Bulletin of the ICRC Regional Delegation in *Boletin Janeiro a Março de 2011*. Notícias da Delegação Regional do Comitê International da Cruz Vermelha para Argentina, Brasil, Chile, Paraguai e Uruguai, 1 March 2011, available at: http://www.icrc.org/web/por/sitepor0.nsf/html/southcone-newsletter-1-11 (accessed 20 March 2011).

124. In an interview about the problems of internal disturbance in Latin American states and the ICRC action, the Head of the ICRC Regional Delegation in Buenos Aires pointed out, 'The rules of international human rights law therefore apply, which govern the use of force by agents of the State and provide a series of basic guarantees. These basic rules of international human rights law can also be described as "humanitarian principles," given that the right to life and to human dignity are found in both international human rights law and international humanitarian law', Interview with the Head of the ICRC Regional Delegation in Buenos Aires, on his address to the Committee on Juridical and Political Affairs of the OAS on the subject of internal violence, ICRC Interview, 30 June 2010, 'Latin America and the Caribbean: Protecting people in situations of internal violence', available at: http://www.icrc.org/eng/resources/documents/misc/america-internal-violence-itw-070708.htm (accessed 16 January 2011).

125. See, for instance, Statement by the ICRC in the 59th Annual Session of the United Nations Commission on Human Rights. Agenda item 11, 10 April 2003, available at: http://www.icrc.org/eng/resources/documents/misc/5lgemt.htm (accessed 19 January 2011).

126. ICRC Overview, 29 October 2010, 'Missing persons and International humanitarian law', available at: http://www.icrc.org/eng/war-and-law/protected-persons/missing-persons/overview-missing-persons.htm (accessed 19 January 2011).

127. The ICRC notes that it 'is mandated to promote international humanitarian law, but not international human rights law. Moreover, the ICRC does not refer to international human rights law as a whole. It refers to a set of fundamental rules that protect human beings in situations of violence. The following are of particular relevance in its dialogue with law enforcement officials:
    * the right to life, liberty and security as enshrined in particular in Article 3 of the Universal Declaration of Human Rights of 1948; Articles 6.1, 9.1 and 10.1 of the International Covenant on Civil and Political Rights of 1966, as well as in regional human rights treaties;
    * the guidance provided by both the United Nations Code of Conduct for Law Enforcement Officials of 1979 and the Basic Principles on the Use of Force and Firearms by Law Enforcement Officials of 1990;
    * the prohibition of torture as provided, mainly, by the Convention against Torture and Other Cruel, Inhuman, or Degrading Treatment or Punishment of 1984;
    * all standards regarding imprisonment or detention conditions as well as judicial guarantees; and
    * all standards for victim protection and assistance.'ICRC, ICRC Dialogue with Police Forces, information sheet, 2010. See International Committee of the Red Cross, *To Serve and to Protect* (Geneva: International Committee of the Red Cross, 1997).

128. See International Committee of the Red Cross, 'Human Rights Challenges for the Police in Peru', 2010, video, available at: http://www.icrc.org/eng/resources/documents/audiovisuals/video/01071-peru-human-rights-police-video-2010.htm (accessed 19 January 2011).

129. J.-M. Henckaerts and L. Doswald-Beck, *Customary International Humanitarian Law* (Cambridge: International Committee of the Red Cross, 2005).

130. J.-M. Henckaerts, 'Study on Customary International Humanitarian Law: A Contribution to the Understanding and Respect for the Rule of Law in Armed Conflict', *International Review of the Red Cross* 87 No. 857 (2005): 195–196.

27. The International Humanitarian Fact-Finding Commission and the law of human rights

*Eric David**

The International Humanitarian Fact-finding Commission (IHFFC) established by the 1977 first Protocol Additional (AP 1) to the 1949 Geneva Conventions (GC) became a legal reality on 20 November 1990 when Canada was the 20th State to recognize the jurisdiction of the Commission, pursuant to Art. 90, § 1, b, of the 1st AP, which subordinated its inception to 20 declarations of acceptance of its jurisdiction. At the end of 2010, 72 States among the 168 States parties to the Protocol had recognized its jurisdiction, but after some 20 years of existence, the IHFFC has never received any request for investigation.

This 'technical unemployment' of IHFFC is surprising because, if among the 72 States that have recognized the competence of the Commission, few are, or were confronted with armed conflicts, such conflicts have not disappeared since 1991, and nothing precludes a third State or an international organization to request a fact-finding mission from the Commission.

The object of this short note is not to describe the fact-finding procedure established by the AP but rather whether the Commission could deal with human rights violations. Given the lack of practice of the Commission, the following developments will remain purely theoretical.

The question of the jurisdiction of the Commission with respect to human rights may arise for two reasons: as part of an agreement between two parties to lodge a request with the Commission for an investigation outside the context of an armed conflict (section 1 below); and as part of an armed conflict when an allegation of human rights violation is submitted to the Commission (section 2 below).

This chapter contends that the Commission can exercise its jurisdiction in the second case but not in the first one.

1. THE COMMISSION HAS NO JURISDICTION TO ENTERTAIN AN ALLEGATION OF HUMAN RIGHTS VIOLATION SUBMITTED TO IT OUTSIDE AN ARMED CONFLICT

Art. 90, paragraph 2, of AP I provides that:

> ... (c) The Commission shall be competent to:
>
> > (i) enquire into any facts alleged to be a grave breach as defined in the Conventions and this Protocol or other serious violation of the Conventions or of this Protocol;

(ii)   facilitate, through its good offices, the restoration of an attitude of respect for the Conventions and this Protocol.

(d)   In other situations, the Commission shall institute an enquiry at the request of a Party to the conflict only with the consent of the other Party or Parties concerned ...

The text confers jurisdiction on the Commission to investigate 'grave breaches' under the GC (Art. 50/51/130/147) and AP 1 (Art. 11, § 4, and Art. 85) and other 'serious violations' of the Conventions or the first AP.

Art. 90, paragraph 2, d, however, extends this competence to 'other situations' with the agreement of all parties concerned. These situations are generally regarded as referring to non-international armed conflicts. The Commission itself stated so from its first meeting,[1] without raising any objection from States Parties to AP 1.

It is possible that in such cases, the IHFFC has to consider the facts in the light of human rights, but this issue can also arise in the context of a conventional international conflict, and will be discussed in section 2 below.

The more specific question raised here by the extension of the scope of the jurisdiction of the Commission to 'other situations' is whether it is legally possible that, under the guise of 'other situations' and with the agreement of the parties, the Commission can be requested to preside over matters of human rights violation that arise outside an armed conflict.

The answer seems clearly no. States created the IHFFC in the first AP for investigating any allegations of 'grave breach' or 'serious violation' of the GC or AP 1; States parties to AP 1 who recognized the jurisdiction of the IHFFC pay its administrative expenses (Art. 90, § 7) for this purpose only, not to add a new organ to the existing supervisory bodies of human rights (Committee for Human Rights,[2] Human Rights Council,[3] etc).

Of course it is not forbidden to members of the IHFFC to sit in another organ dedicated to the settlement of issues which would have to deal with respect of human rights or IHL: besides the fact that the IHFFC is, for now, far from drowning in work-finding – a fact that the Commission is the first to complain of – its members are not its full-time agents; if they are subject to a duty of self-restraint (*'devoir de réserve'*),[4] they may nevertheless carry out judicial or quasi-judicial activities outside the Commission. The members of the Commission should, at most, be guided by rules similar to Practice Directions of the ICJ[5] that limit access to the functions of judge and counsel for the parties before the ICJ; thus, according to these rules, they should not be an *ad hoc* judge, a person acting or having acted as agent, counsel or advocate in a case before the ICJ over the past three years; nor should they be agent, counsel or advocate for a party, or a person acting or having acted as a member or high official of the Court in the three years preceding the date of the designation (Practice Directions VII and VIII).

Subject to the observance of these limits, that can easily be transposed *mutatis mutandis* to the IHFFC, nothing should prevent its members from deciding on issues of human rights as stakeholders of other bodies or procedures; however, as members or participants in these organs or other procedures, concerned members of the IHFFC would then act in their personal capacity, not as members of the Commission as such.

2. THE INTERNATIONAL HUMANITARIAN FACT-FINDING COMMISSION CAN ADDRESS HUMAN RIGHTS VIOLATIONS WHICH ARISE IN AN ARMED CONFLICT

The Commission being competent to 'enquire into any facts alleged to be a grave breach as defined in the Conventions and this Protocol or other serious violation of the Conventions or of this Protocol' (AP 1, Art. 90, § 2, c, i), it can take cognizance of a human rights violation in two ways: either because a State having recognized its jurisdiction alleges that provisions of the GC or AP which are the expression of human rights have been violated (section 2.1), or because the Commission has received an allegation of violation of GC and AP, and consideration of this claim requires it to examine the respect for human rights (section 2.2).

2.1 The International Humanitarian Fact-Finding Commission Hears Complaints Alleging Violations of Rules of the Geneva Conventions and their Additional Protocols that Correspond to Rules Designed to Protect Human Rights

Various provisions of the GC and AP provide for rights enshrined in different instruments protecting human rights such as, the right to life and the prohibition of torture, referred to, *inter alia*, in Art. 3 common to the 4 GC, Arts 27–28, 31–32 of the 4th GC, Art. 75 of AP 1 and Arts 4–5 of AP 2; these rights are also set out in Arts 6–7 of the International Covenant on Civil and Political Rights. It follows that any serious violation of human rights provided for by the GC or AP can justify, under the conditions set by Art. 90 of AP 1, the jurisdiction of the IHFFC, and thus its ability to deal with human rights violations.

Of course, these human rights essentially relate to persons who are in the power of the enemy and are without prejudice of the IHL rules applicable to the conduct of hostilities (*infra*).

Practically, this means that the IHFFC is entitled, in such circumstances, to take inspiration from the jurisprudence of human rights organs for solving the legal problems that might arise in cases assigned to it.

2.2 In Considering an Allegation of Violations of the Geneva Conventions and/or their Additional Protocols, the International Humanitarian Fact-Finding Commission may have to Examine the Respect for Human Rights

Human rights apply in an armed conflict for various reasons:

- instruments protecting human rights explicitly provide that States which are parties can never suspend certain rights deemed non-derogable, even in the case of war or serious crisis threatening the existence of a nation (European Convention on Human Rights, Art. 15; Covenant on Civil and Political Rights, Art. 4; Inter-American Convention on Human Rights, Art. 27);
- an armed conflict does not terminate, *ipso facto* or *ipso jure*, international law, which binds the State confronted to the conflict;[6]

- international jurisprudence has recognized that human rights are applicable in an armed conflict: in its Advisory Opinion on the *Legality of the Threat or Use of Nuclear Weapons* (1996), the ICJ observed: 'The protection of the International Covenant on Civil and Political Rights does not cease in times of war, except by operation of Art. 4 of the Covenant whereby certain provisions may be derogated from in a time of national emergency.'[7]

These principles apply, without prejudice, of course, as mentioned above, of the *lex specialis*, being rules specific to the law of armed conflicts.[8] It follows that, as in the case where the GC and the AP merely reflect human rights, the IHFFC is inevitably led to take into account human rights if the situation before it involves these rights and if the circumstances of their alleged violation in an armed conflict do not lead to exclude their application, particularly in the framework of the conduct of hostilities: for example, if the right to life is hardly compatible with combat situations, this does not preclude its applicability to the situation of persons in the power of the enemy.

It should be noted, however, that even in the conduct of hostilities, it is possible to verify whether the means and methods of warfare did not violate certain human rights: thus, it is with regard to only Art. 2 of the European Convention on Human Rights (and not with regard to IHL) that the European Court of Human Rights considered the legality of the manner in which Russian forces had attacked rebel forces in Chechnya and caused significant collateral damages to civilians.[9] It is true that the European Court of Human Rights was acting as custodian of the Convention and not of IHL, while the role of the IHFFC is limited to armed conflicts and IHL.

The fact remains, however, that armed conflicts do not occur in a world completely foreign to human rights. The two categories of rules are closely related to each other. This explains why human rights are part of the rules applicable in an armed conflict and why the IHFFC can rule on their respect or their violation when it must perform a fact-finding mission in the context of an armed conflict.

Just as a surgeon cannot operate by focusing only on the mechanical precision of his gestures and ignoring the overall health of the patient, the IHFFC cannot examine the reality of a fact regardless of the legal context within which the act in question is located. As such, human rights are inextricably part of the legal environment of an armed conflict and when the Commission considers an alleged violation of the GC or the AP, it must take into account the former when it decides on the latter.

NOTES

*　Eric David is Emeritus Professor at the Free University of Brussels. A member of the IHFFC since 2007, he is expressing here his personal views which do not represent the official position of the IHFFC.
1.　First ordinary meeting of the Commission in Bern, 12–13 March 1992, para. 3.59, 7°, et réf.
2.　International Covenant on Civil and Political Rights, Article 41.
3.　A/RES/60/251, 15 March 2006.
4.　Annual meeting of the IHFFC, February 2009.
5.　Practice Directions adopted in 2001 as amended in 2009, available at: http://www.icj-cij.org/documents/ (accessed 10 September 2011).

6. Developments in E. David, *Principes de droit des conflits armés* (Brussels: Bruylant, 2008), paras 1.9 *et seq.*
7. *Legality of the Threat or Use of Nuclear Weapons*, Advisory Opinion, I.C.J. Report 1996, 240, para. 25; also *Legal Consequences of the Construction of a Wall in the Occupied Palestinian Territory*, Advisory Opinion, I.C.J. Reports 2004, para. 105.
8. *Legality of the Threat or Use of Nuclear Weapons*, ibid., para. 25.
9. *Khachiev and Akaïeva v. Russia*, ECtHR, Application No. 57942/00; 57945/00, Judgment of 24 February 2005, paras 136–147; *Isayeva et al. v. Russia*, ECtHR, Application No. 57947/00; 57948/00; 57949/00, Judgment of 24 February 2005, paras 174–200.

28. Human rights in the context of international criminal law: respecting them and ensuring respect for them

*Damien Scalia**

1. INTRODUCTION

In the context of the present chapter, international criminal law, working as a means of implementation of international human rights law,[1] is of particular importance. The motivation of the international community was first to judge those who were responsible for violating international humanitarian law (initially through the condemnation of war crimes)[2] and then developed to a certain extent to the judgement of those responsible for grave violations of human rights.[3] In fact, crimes that are categorized under the title of 'crimes against humanity'[4] in international criminal law essentially correspond to grave violations of human rights.[5]

The links between international criminal law and human rights law are complex, as becomes evident in view of the number of questions raised in this chapter: Are human rights (including the rights of the accused) respected in international criminal law?[6] Are they a source of law for the international criminal courts?[7] What influence do human rights have on international criminal law?[8] Furthermore, to paraphrase the title of the well-known work written on the relationship between human rights law and criminal law: are they the shield or the sword of international criminal law?[9] This chapter does not pretend to give a full oversight of all the links that unify these two branches of international law.[10] The purpose of human rights law is to protect individuals[11] when they are confronted by a superior power (legitimate or not), be it the State, the judicial system or the prison system, etc. The situation should be the same in international criminal law, the superior power being in such instances international criminal jurisdictions. However, as we have already mentioned, international criminal law is also put in place to protect human rights. Consequently, international criminal law must face two prospects: on the one hand, international criminal law must apply human rights law, and on the other hand, it must enforce it.[12] It has to respect human rights law and ensure respect for them. The aim of this chapter is to analyse how this duality of function plays out before the international criminal tribunals.

In international criminal law, human rights are put forward under a number of guises – as a source of international criminal law, in terms of procedural rights and also as a fundamental law. In this instance, I will show that the references to international human rights law by judges of international criminal jurisdictions (case-law from the regional courts concerning human rights, international conventions that focus on human rights and resolutions of the UN General Assembly regarding human rights) reveal the aforementioned duality: the reference to human rights concerns, on the one hand, the rights of the accused during the international criminal procedure (section 3), and on the other hand, the definition of the crimes for which the accused is tried (section 4). The function of human rights law in the international criminal courts is therefore dual.

2. GENERAL COMMENTS

Before analysing the specific issue raised in this chapter, a few general remarks are necessary. First, while the obligation for international criminal tribunals (ICTs) to consider human rights is not explicitly mentioned in their mandate, on many occasions these tribunals make reference to the jurisprudence of regional courts in the area of human rights, or, at the very least, use this branch of international law in the decisions taken.[13] As Professor Cassese has said, qualifying as 'sauvage' (in French) the approach taken by the ICTs when referring to sources of law,

> il est évident que cette approche 'sauvage' tend à mettre le droit 'extérieur' à la juridiction pénale internationale ... sur le même plan que le droit applicable par cette juridiction: le Tribunal pénal international fait référence ou applique les arrêts nationaux ou ceux de la Cour européenne [de sauvegarde des droits de l'Homme] au même titre que d'autres arrêts du Tribunal ou d'autres juridictions pénales internationales.[14]

The International Criminal Court (ICC) Statute explicitly mentions international human rights law in the article that refers to the applicable laws in its Court.[15] Article 21 of the Rome Statute refers to 'internationally recognized human rights' as those that can serve in the interpretation and application of other sources of law that are found in the same article. In this context, they are not referred to as a major applicable law but as a framework for interpreting and applying the law, and to its great potential and its fundamental role.[16] In fact, whatever source of law the Court may refer to, it has to do so in a manner that respects human rights. Thus, Article 21 appears to provide a category of rules that have a superior authority to other norms of international law: internationally recognized human rights.[17] As Professor Pellet remarks, the introduction of this category of rules, backed-up by a special judicial authority, is not an innovation; the international criminal tribunal for the former Yugoslavia (ICTY) makes reference to this category.[18] The principles of human rights law that are internationally recognized must be respected in the context of international criminal law, as is outlined in Article 21(3) of the statute of Rome.[19] However, in the light of the work done by the ICC, this article is hardly ever referred to. This can perhaps easily be explained by the fact that no decision on this basis has ever been taken by the Court. I will return to these references in the next chapters.

Secondly, international human rights law, being a source of international criminal law, occupies a unique place.[20] Even if it is important for judges of the international criminal jurisdictions to refer to this legal corpus, it is not possible to simply transpose every rule of international human rights law. This fact was noted by the Trial Chamber in the *Kunarac* case in reference to the interaction of international humanitarian law and human rights law:

In attempting to define an offence under international humanitarian law, the Trial Chamber must be mindful of the specificity of this body of law. In particular, when referring to definitions which have been given in the context of human rights law, the Trial Chamber will have to consider two crucial structural differences between these two bodies of law: (i) Firstly, the role and position of the state as an actor is completely different in both regimes. Human rights law is essentially born out of the abuses of the state over its citizens and out of the need to protect the latter from state-organised or state-sponsored violence. Humanitarian law aims at placing restraints on the conduct of warfare so as to diminish its effects on the victims of the hostilities. In the human rights context, the state is the ultimate guarantor of the rights protected and has both duties and a responsibility for the observance of those rights. In the event that the State violates those rights or fails in its responsibility to protect the rights, it can be called to account and asked to take appropriate measures to put an end to the infringements. In the field of international humanitarian law, and in particular in the context of international prosecutions, the role of the state is, when it comes to accountability, peripheral. Individual criminal responsibility for violation of international humanitarian law does not depend on the participation of the State and, conversely, its participation in the commission of the offence is no defence to the perpetrator. Moreover, international humanitarian law purports to apply equally to and expressly bind all parties to the armed conflict whereas, in contrast, human rights law generally applies to only one party, namely the State involved, and its agents … (ii) Secondly, that part of international criminal law applied by the Tribunal is a penal law regime. It sets one party, the prosecutor, against another, the defendant. In the field of international human rights, the respondent is the state. Structurally, this has been expressed by the fact that human rights law establishes lists of protected rights whereas international criminal law establishes lists of offences. The Trial Chamber is therefore wary not to embrace too quickly and too easily concepts and notions developed in a different legal context. The Trial Chamber is of the view that notions developed in the field of human rights can be transposed in international humanitarian law only if they take into consideration the specificities of the latter body of law.[21]

As A. Cassese has said, the 'juges de La Haye et d'Arusha ont été conscients des limites du recours à d'autres corpus juridiques imposées par les spécificités du procès pénal international'.[22]

These general remarks were necessary to understand to what extent human rights have been implemented by the criminal jurisdictions in order to ensure they are widely respected.

3. HUMAN RIGHTS AS THE FOUNDATION OF THE RIGHTS OF THE ACCUSED

It is throughout this discussion (on the rights of the accused) that references to international human rights law are to be seen most explicitly.[23] The judges of international criminal jurisdictions make references to human rights law (general principles of law or specific laws) to examine the validity of the procedures established in their Court process. These references concern principally: certain principles of law (section 3.1); the right to liberty (section 3.2); the impartiality of judges or of tribunals (section 3.3); and the right to a fair trial (section 3.4). The recourse to human rights also raises other procedural issues (section 3.5).

3.1   Principles of Law

An important reference is made to human rights law in a number of cases in order to define the principle of legality of crimes and punishments.[24] In this context, the judges of the international criminal jurisdictions use both international conventions and case law from the European Court of Human Rights (ECtHR) and the American Court of Human Rights (ACtHR) to define this principle: 'while the Statute of the International Tribunal lists offences over which the International Tribunal has jurisdiction, the Tribunal may enter convictions only where it is satisfied that the offence is proscribed under customary international law at the time of its commission.[25]

Regardless of whatever references are made, the principle itself does not really appear to have been respected by ICTs – at least in relation to the principle of legality of penalties.[26]

Furthermore, the judges of the ICTY have established the principle of *stare decisis*, in making reference to human rights. In the case of *Aleksovski*, the Appeal Chamber referred to the jurisprudence of the ECtHR and stated that it was 'not strictly bound, [that] it would normally follow its previous decisions and would only depart from them if there were "cogent reasons"'.[27] In this context, cogent reasons will be largely applied.

Regarding the principles of law, it is important to remember what was written by Judge Shahabuddeen, in an individual opinion in 1998:

> The exceptional nature of a criminal procedure that was focused on war crimes that were committed in the course of the Second World War renders inapplicable … the principles formed by the jurisprudence of the Commission and of the European Court of Human Rights having dealt with other breaches of human rights. (unofficial translation)[28]

This was already pronounced in a decision of the First Chamber of Trial Instance in the Tadić case:

> The interpretations of Article 6 of the ECHR [European Convention for Human Rights] by the European Court of Human Rights are meant to apply to ordinary criminal and, for Article 6 (1), civil adjudications. By contrast, the International Tribunal is adjudicating crimes which are considered so horrific as to warrant universal jurisdiction. The International Tribunal is, in certain respects, comparable to a military tribunal, which often has limited rights of due process and more lenient rules of evidence.[29]

Such an application of principles of human rights appears to be a curious concept. Nonetheless, certain rights of the accused are recognized and carried out by judges of the international criminal courts – I will examine this in the next section of this chapter.

3.2   The Right to Liberty

Regarding the right to liberty, ICTY and ICC repeatedly refer to international human rights law (the International Covenant on Civil and Political Rights (ICCPR), ECHR, and jurisprudence of the ECtHR). In the *Dokmanović* case the Trial Chamber of the ICTY uses human rights first to define the terms 'arrest' and 'detention'.[30] They also use ECHR and ICCPR to define what 'ruse' means in the context of arrest.[31] After having interpreted different jurisdictions' decisions on the matter, the judges conclude that no violation of human rights had occurred in the arrest of Mr Dokmanović. He thought at the time of his arrest that he would be meeting with a representative from the ICTY Prosecutor's office to discuss the possibility of standing witness.

Again in connection with the right to liberty, the judges of the ICTY make reference to human rights,[32] stating that pre-trial detention should be the exception and not the rule.[33] They add that the 'detention of an accused on the basis of a reasonable suspicion that the accused committed the crime or crimes charged is in accordance with jurisprudence under the European Convention for the Protection of Human Rights and Fundamental Freedoms'.[34] They define that 'having a "reasonable suspicion" presupposes the existence of facts or information which would satisfy an objective observer that the person concerned may have committed the offence'.[35] They continue in declaring that reasonable suspicion in itself is not sufficient for depriving a person of his liberty. Moreover, they examine the nature of exceptional circumstances that can justify the release of an imprisoned person. On this subject, the judges constantly refer to the jurisprudence of the ECtHR and to the other international texts on human rights.[36]

In two cases, the ICC makes reference to international human rights law in order to define what constitutes a violation of the right to liberty. In the *Bemba* case, the Pre-trial Chamber III refers to the jurisprudence of the ECtHR in order to confirm the rule that 'when dealing with the right to liberty, one should bear in mind the fundamental principle that deprivation of liberty should be an exception and not a rule'.[37] In the *Lubanga* case, the judges of the ICC refer to human rights in order to interpret 'reasonable suspicions'[38] that allow a person to be kept imprisoned prior to the Court's judgment. In all cases, the references made to human rights allowed for imprisonment.

3.3 Impartiality of Judges and Tribunals

On several occasions, ICTY refers to international human rights law regarding the impartiality of judges and tribunals. In the *Delalić* case, for example, the accused persons questioned the independence of the judge, arguing that Judge Odio-Benito

> ceased to meet the qualifications for a Judge of the International Criminal Tribunal for the Former Yugoslavia by virtue of her having taken the oath of office of a Vice-President of the Republic of Costa Rica in accordance with Articles 136 and 137 of the Constitución Política de la República de Costa Rica 1949 (as amended). Further and/or in the alternative, that the Learned Judge, having now become a member of the executive branch of the Government of the Republic of Costa Rica, has ceased to possess the criteria required for an independent judge in international law and has acquired an association which may affect her impartiality.[39]

ICTY referred to the ECHR as well as the jurisprudence of the ECtHR to answer this question. On the one hand, it concluded that the impartiality of a judge is an inalienable right granted to all accused persons (article 6-1 of the ECHR), and on the other hand, it referred to the jurisprudence of the ECtHR in defining what is meant by the term 'impartiality':

> The existence of impartiality for the purposes of article 6(1) must be determined according to a subjective test, that is on the basis of the personal conviction that a particular judge has in a given case, and also according to an objective test, that is ascertaining whether the judge offered guarantees sufficient to exclude any legitimate doubt in this respect. Under the objective component of this test, the court must assess relevant circumstances that may give rise to an 'appearance' of partiality. If there is 'legitimate reason to fear' a lack of impartiality in a judge, he or she must withdraw from the case. The challenge to the Judge's impartiality in this case is linked to the question of her independence as a judge. The test for measuring independence has been set forth thus by the Court in Campbell and Fell v. United Kingdom: 'In determining whether a body can be considered to be independent – notably of the executive and the parties in the case – the Court has had regard to the manner of appointment of its members and the duration of their term of office, the existence of guarantees against outside pressures and the question whether the body presents an appearance of independence'.[40]

Analysing these elements, the judges concluded that the impartiality of Judge Odio Benito is not to be questioned because of her election, seeing as she committed herself not to undertake any political function prior to the end of her mandate as Judge.

In the *Furundžija* case, the judges of the Appeals Chamber of the ICTY had to examine the impartiality of Judge Mumba. Prior to her position as judge, she represented her government in the United Nations Commission on the Status of Women. Some members of this commission had lodged an *amicus curiae* report in the *Furundžija* case. Notably, the judges refer to the jurisprudence of the ECtHR in order to reach their conclusion that

> a Judge should not only be subjectively free from bias, but also that there should be nothing in the surrounding circumstances which objectively gives rise to an appearance of bias. On this basis, the Appeals Chamber considers that the following principles should direct it in interpreting and applying the impartiality requirement of the Statute.[41]

The judges concluded that the simple fact that she had been a member of a Commission did not demonstrate a lack of impartiality.

3.4 The Right to a Fair Trial

Numerous references are made to human rights in connection with an examination of the definition of 'fair trial' and 'due process'. In the *Delalić* case, the judges refer to the ICCPR and the ECHR to decide that the defence would have to inform the prosecutor of the names of the witnesses it intended to call to trial at least seven days before their hearing.[42] In the same case, the judges of the ICTY make reference to the jurisprudence of the European Commission and Court on Human Rights in order to define the power of judges to limit the number of witnesses that are requested by the accused (making reference to Article 6(3) of the ECHR).[43] Another decision in the same case demonstrates the importance of referring to human rights when dealing with fair trial issues. In a decision of 19 September 1997, the judges of the ICTY consider that 'article 42 du Statut énonce les dispositions essentielles du droit à un interrogatoire équitable comme prévu à l'article 6-3)-c) de la CEDH'.[44] In addition, they decide that the absence of a lawyer at police interrogation stage does not respect article 18 of the Statute and article

42 of the Rules of Procedure and Evidence (RPE). They add that this later article 42 is a *mutatis mutandis* adaptation of article 6(3) of the ECHR and of article 14(3) of the International Charter on Civil and Political Rights.[45] The right to protection from self-incrimination is also discussed in the *Delalić* case. Referring to the jurisprudence of the ECtHR, the judges of the ICTY decide that the accused is not obliged to provide a sample of his handwriting, because it could result in a violation of his right not to testify against himself.[46]

In the context of the right to fair trial, the judges in the *Blaškić* case consistently refer to international human rights law when defining the right of the accused to be informed of the charges and the accusations being made against him. The accused requested the rejection of the indictment for 'vice de forme'. And yet, noting that every accused has the right to be informed of the charges that are being brought against him (Article 6(3) of the ECHR and 14(3)(a) of the ICCPR),[47] the judges decide that the indictment requires only some modifications.[48] Regarding the same question, the International Criminal Tribunal for Rwanda (ICTR) also make reference to regional and international conventions on the protection of human rights in the *Semanza* case (ECHR, ICCPR and the American Convention on Human Rights).[49] The ICTR decides, notably, that a delay of 18 days without being informed of the charges brought against the accused is a violation of human rights that would necessitate proportionate redress for the accused.[50]

Without explicitly referring to a body in charge of the protection of human rights, the judges in this same case state that the failure to respect the procedures in habeas corpus (i.e. the impossibility of introducing an appeal regarding the legality of the detention of the accused) also constitutes a violation of human rights. For these violations, the Trial Chamber reduced the sentence of imprisonment of the accused by six months.[51]

In addition, the ICTR and the ICC judges make references to human rights concerning the right of the accused to freely choose his legal counsel. The judges of the ICTR remarked in the *Kambanda* case that

> with respect to the right to choose one's counsel ... in the light of a textual and systematic interpretation of the provisions of the Statute and the Rules, read in conjunction with relevant decisions from the Human Rights Committee and the organs of the European Convention for the Protection of Human Rights and Fundamental Freedoms, that the right to free legal assistance by counsel does not confer the right to choose one's counsel.[52]

A contrario, when they have to decide on whether the accused has the right to freely choose his legal counsel, the ICC judges refer to human rights in general terms and to the right to fair trial in more focused terms.[53]

It is also notable that the ICTY turned to international human rights law when reconciling the rights of the accused with the rights of witnesses. Without detailing the legal reasoning followed by the judges in the *Delalić* case once again, it suffices to note that the judges find that 'ideally, face to face confrontation is the core of the values epitomised in the accused confronting his accuser in each case. It is not a condition sine qua non of the right'.[54]

In parallel, the ICC provides 'that under the jurisprudence of the European Court of Human Rights a guilty verdict may not be founded solely on the evidence of anonymous witnesses'.[55]

3.5 Other Procedural Issues

The ICC also uses human rights to define or clarify other procedural issues. The decision of the Pre-Trial Chamber I of 17 January 2006 makes reference to human rights to define the term 'proceedings', in order to find out when legal proceedings in a criminal process actually begin. Founding their decision on the jurisprudence of the ECtHR and the Inter-American Court of Human Rights, the judges decide that proceedings start from the opening of the investigation. This question is raised in the context of the participation of victims in legal proceedings. Such participation is allowed from the opening of the investigation.[56] In addition to the jurisprudence of the competent courts in the matter of human rights, the judges refer to two other international instruments : the Declaration of Basic Principles of Justice for Victims of Crime and Abuse of Power in 1985 by the UN General Assembly, and the Basic Principles and Guidelines on the Right to a Remedy and Reparation for Victims of Gross Violations of International Human Rights Law and Serious Violations of International Humanitarian Law, adopted by the Human Rights Commission. International human rights law appears to be a subsidiary source, which will be certainly defined more strictly in future jurisprudence from the ICC.

The ICC also refers to human rights (and also Article 21(3) of its Statute) to interpret and apply the expression 'reasonable grounds to believe' (contained in article 58 of the statute of Rome).

> Thus, in interpreting and applying the expression 'reasonable grounds to believe', the Chamber will be guided by the 'reasonable suspicion' standard under article 5(1)(c) of the European Convention on Human Rights and the jurisprudence of the Inter-American Court of Human Rights on the Fundamental right to personal liberty under article 7 of the American Convention on Human Rights.[57]

The ICC opts for the same reasoning as in the decision of 10 February 2006 (§ 12), regarding the situation in the Democratic Republic of Congo.[58]

Thus, making reference to international human rights law allows judges of international criminal law to 'justify', to a certain degree, decisions taken in international criminal law proceedings by respecting the human rights of those who are accused. For example, the ICTR refers to human rights in order to analyse the potential limits that can apply to freedom of expression.[59] However, this justification remains under the control of those same judges, and, even if they have referred to human rights in the past, it does not mean that they favoured the accused.

4. HUMAN RIGHTS AS THE FOUNDATION FOR CERTAIN DEFINITIONS OF CRIMES

In this context of defining crimes, reference to international human rights law appears to be less important than it is regarding the definition of procedural rights. The Statutes of the International Criminal Tribunals are relatively imprecise concerning the definition of crimes. International judges refer to a number of sources of law in order to interpret the provisions included in the constitutive texts of the International Criminal Tribunals.[60] International human rights law is among them. As I will demonstrate, making reference to international human rights law allows Judges of the ICTY to reject the argument challenging the legality of ICTY (section 4.1). In addition, it is able to precisely define specific crimes such as torture or inhuman and degrading treatment (section 4.2). It also contributes to a more precise and complete definition of 'crimes against humanity' (crimes against humanity are closer to human rights violations than they are to other crimes – war crimes or genocide for example) (section 4.3).[61] This section will finally deal with a number of decisions of the ICC which make reference to human rights in order to define crimes (section 4.4).

4.1 The Foundations of the ICTY

One of the first references to human rights law made by the ICTY judges is in the *Tadić* case in 1995. In this decision, the Appeal Chamber judges mention human rights when they are confronted with the argument that State sovereignty is fundamentally in conflict with the competence of the Tribunal. The Judges respond that it

> would be a travesty of law and a betrayal of the universal need for justice, should the concept of State sovereignty be allowed to be raised successfully against human rights. Borders should not be considered as a shield against the reach of the law and as a protection for those who trample underfoot the most elementary rights of humanity.[62]

It is therefore on the basis of human rights that the idea of ICTY is born, allowing the pursuit and condemnation of the authors of international crimes.

In the same decision, the ICTY judges make reference to international human rights law in order to minimize the difference in the applicability of law between international armed conflict (IAC) and non-international armed conflict (NIAC). In this core decision, the Appeal Chamber decides that the protection of human rights has reduced the difference in the law applicable in IAC and NIAC. They make clear what kind of fundamental rights of the person would be protected in both forms of armed conflict.[63] In this context, the ICTY judges decide, in the *Delalić* and *Halilović* cases, that common article 3 to the four Geneva Conventions protects rights in times of NIAC as well as in times of IAC. Human rights applicable in armed conflicts demonstrate this fact.[64]

These decisions demonstrate the level of influence that human rights law has on international criminal law, and, as mentioned by Professor A. Cassese, the necessity to refer to it, at least at the beginning of the activity of the international criminal tribunals.[65]

4.2 Precise Definition of Specific Crimes Such as Torture or Inhuman and Degrading Treatment

The use of human rights law allows for clearer definitions of international crimes. The principle of legality demands that the definition of crimes be clear and precise. Therefore the judges have to define the crimes that are recognized in the Statutes of the international criminal tribunals.

In a number of cases, the ICTY refers to human rights law in order to define 'cruel, inhuman or degrading treatment'.[66] In the *Aleksovski* case, for example, in making reference to the jurisprudence of the ECtHR and to the Convention against torture and other cruel, inhuman and degrading treatment, the judges of the Trial Chamber of the ICTY reaffirm the existing definition in human rights law and transpose it into international criminal law. The judges decide that 'it is also instructive to recount the general definition of the term "inhuman treatment" propounded by the ECHR, which to date is the only human rights monitoring body that defines the term.[67] Here, the reference aids in defining a protected interest as well as defining the essential criteria in determining the objective element of the crime.[68]

From the same perspective, the ICTY judges refer to international human rights law to define 'torture' (which is not defined by the Statute of ICTY or international humanitarian law),[69] and also to consider rape as an act of torture.[70] In this context of rape, the judges interpret the notion of torture to have a broader definition than any existing in international human rights instruments.[71] According to the judges, the definition of this crime had been crystallized in customary law and could consequently be used in international criminal justice.[72] The judges also include the humiliation of someone as an additional criterion in the definition of torture.

4.3   Crimes Against Humanity

Referring to international human rights law also allows for other violations of human rights law to be defined – specifically those that amount to crimes against humanity – even if, as is noted by the ICTY, 'it is not required that each alleged underlying act be regarded as a violation of international law'.[73] In the *Kunarac* case, the ICTY judges refer to a number of international texts relating to human rights law in order to define the abolition of slavery (Universal Declaration of Human Rights of 1948, ICCPR, ECHR, the American Convention on Human Rights of 1968 and the African Charter on Human and Peoples' Rights of 1981).[74] The definition of imprisonment is also sharpened by reference to human rights law[75] and this is the case for further definitions of other acts of inhumanity contained in article 5 of the ICTY.[76]

Thus, the crime of persecution is better defined due to reference to human rights law in the first relevant cases. To determine which behaviour falls within the scope of this definition, the Tribunal decided that 'persecution may encompass acts which are listed in the Statute, as well as acts which are not listed in the Statute'.[77] The ICTR judges decided that:

> it has resulted from international customary law that the crime of persecution can encompass acts that are contained in sub-categories of crimes against humanity – whether they are murder or deportation – as long as they have been motivated by discriminatory reasons. Persecution can also encompass other diverse acts of discrimination that are not enumerated elsewhere in the Statute but which concern grave attacks on the rights of the individual.[78]

In the *Kupreskić* case, the ICTY judges pursued the same reasoning and decided that in

> drawing upon the various provisions of these texts it proves possible to identify a set of fundamental rights appertaining to any human being, the gross infringement of which may

amount, depending on the surrounding circumstances, to a crime against humanity. Persecution consists of a severe attack on those rights, and aims to exclude a person from society on discriminatory grounds. The Trial Chamber therefore defines persecution as the gross or blatant denial, on discriminatory grounds, of a fundamental right, laid down in international customary or treaty law, reaching the same level of gravity as the other acts prohibited in Article 5.[79]

Since then, numerous acts have been considered as falling within the definition of persecution: retaliations,[80] forced labour,[81] destruction of property,[82] illegal arrest, unlawful imprisonment,[83] murder, extermination and torture,[84] terrorization.[85] 'De manière générale, le tribunal a considéré que toute violation grave de droits considérés comme indérogeables par les droits de l'Homme était susceptible d'être qualifiée de persécutions'.[86]

4.4   Reference to Human Rights by the ICC

Few decisions of the ICC involve reference to human rights law for the definition or clarification of an offence. This is mostly due to the fact that the ICC has passed only one judgment so far and that the ICC Statute defines more precisely the crimes it intends to punish. Despite this, the ICC judges refer to human rights law to specify that recruiting children in armed conflict is not only a crime under international criminal law but also a violation of international human rights law.[87] This means that the illegality of the act committed is reinforced.

Thus, references to human rights law allow the different elements of numerous violations of law to be defined with greater precision – these elements being absent from the texts of the ICT or the ICC.

5.   CONCLUSION

Reference to international human rights law appears to be a frequent occurrence in the international criminal courts' decisions. It allows, on the one hand, the establishment of procedures respecting fundamental rights and, on the other hand, the interpretation, specification or confirmation of rights existing at international level and the recognition of them as such. Reference to human rights law also allows the more precise definition of the offences for which accused persons are judged at an international level, and in so doing, contributes to the respect of the principle of legality.[88] However, making reference to human rights law does not necessarily guarantee the respect of human rights. The example of the legality of punishments and sentences illustrates this idea well – this issue has been analysed by the author elsewhere.[89] Likewise, while the rights of the accused have been recognized as applicable in cases, they have not always been respected.[90] As Professor Cassese has remarked, the judges of the international criminal courts have sometimes not referred to human rights in instances where such reference really was necessary.[91]

The duality of the relationship between national criminal law and human rights law can be seen at international level: as both shield and sword, it is imperative that human rights be respected in international criminal law; criminal law can only truly render justice if that is the case.

NOTES

*   Damien Scalia has a PhD in international criminal law. He wrote this chapter during a fellowship in the Irish Centre for Human Rights (Galway, Ireland). The author would like to thank Prof. W. Schabas for his welcome to the ICHR and also Ms D. Bernard and Ms S. Perdiz for their proof-reading and valuable comments. This chapter was written in January 2011.

1.   G. Gaggioli, *L'influence mutuelle entre les droits de l'homme et le droit international humanitaire à la lumière du droit à la vie* (Paris, Pedone, forthcoming); E. David, *Principes de droit des conflits armés*, 4th edition (Brussels: Bruylant, 2008), 645 *et seq.*; R. Kolb, *Jus in bello, Le droit international des conflits armés*, 2nd edition (Bâle: Helbing Lichtenhahn, 2009), sections 588–597.

2.   Report of the Secretary-General pursuant to paragraph 2 of Security Council Resolution 808, 3 May 1993, S/25704, sections 5 *et seq.*; Preamble of ICC Statute.

3.   W. Schabas, 'Droit pénal international et droit international des droits de l'homme: faux frères?', in *Le droit pénal à l'épreuve de l'internationalisation*, eds M. Henzelin and R. Roth (Paris and Brussels: Librairie générale de droit et de jurisprudence and Bruylant, 2002), 166.

4.   Crime against humanity is one of the four crimes in the jurisdiction of international criminal jurisdiction.

5.   P. Currat, *Les crimes contre l'humanité dans le statut de la Cour Pénale Internationale* (Basel: Schultess Medias Juridiques, 2006), 746.

6.   R. Koering-Joulin, 'Droits fondamentaux et droit pénal international', in *Les droits fondamentaux: inventaire et théorie générale: Colloque de Beyrouth, 6 et 7 novembre 2003* (Brussels: Bruylant, 2005), 333–348; Schabas, *supra* note 3, at 165–181; G. Mettraux, 'Using human rights law for the purpose of defining international criminal offences – the practice of the international criminal tribunal for the former Yugoslavia', in *Le droit pénal à l'épreuve de l'internationalisation*, eds M. Henzelin and R. Roth (Paris and Brussels: Librairie générale de droit et de jurisprudence, Bruylant, 2002), 183–216; *Lubanga*, ICC, Appeals Chamber, Judgment on the appeal of the Prosecutor against the decision of Trial Chamber I entitled 'Decision on the consequences of non-disclosure of exculpatory materials covered by Article 54(3)(e) agreements and the application to stay the prosecution of the accused, together with certain other issues raised at the Status Conference on 10 June 2008' (ICC-01/04-01/06 OA 13), 21 October 2008, para. 46; *Bemba*, ICC, Appeals Chamber, Judgment on the appeal of Mr. Jean-Pierre Bemba Gombo against the decision of Pre-Trial Chamber III entitled 'Decision on application for interim release', 16 December 2008 (ICC-01/05-01/08 OA), para. 28.

7.   A. Cassese, 'L'influence de la CEDH sur l'activité des Tribunaux pénaux internationaux', in *Crimes internationaux et Juridictions internationales*, eds A. Cassese and M. Delmas-Marty (Paris: Presses Universitaires de France, 2002), 143–182; S. Trechsel, *Human Rights in Criminal Proceedings* (Oxford: Oxford University Press, 2005); G. Bitti, 'Chapter 16 – Article 21 of the Statute of the International Criminal Court and the treatment of sources of law in the jurisprudence of the ICC', in *The Emerging Practice of the International Criminal Court*, eds C. Stahn and G. Sluiter (Leiden and Boston: Martinus Nijhoff, 2009), 285–304; Mettraux, *supra* note 6.

8.   Cassese, *supra* note 7, at 143–182.

9.   Y. Cartuyvels et al., *Les droits de l'Homme: Bouclier ou épée du droit pénal?* (Brussels: St Louis and Bruylant, 2007).

10.   For an overview on the subject, refer to Cassese, *supra* note 7, at 143–182; Trechsel, *supra* note 7; Bitti, *supra* note 7, at 285–204; I. Caracciolo, 'Applicable Law', in *Essays on the Rome Statute of the International Criminal Court*, eds F. Lattanzi and W. Schabas (Ripa Fagnano Alto (AQ): il Sirente, 1999), 211–232; Mettraux, *supra* note 6.

11.   Cartuyvels et al., *supra* note 9.

12.   Schabas, *supra* note 3, at 172.

13.   *Tadić*, ICTY, Appeal Chamber, Judgment, 2 October 1995 (Case No. IT-94-1-A), section 45; *Furundžija*, ICTY, Trial Chamber, Judgment, 10 December 1998, (Case No. IT-95-17/1-T), section 183; Gaggioli, *supra* note 1.

14.   Cassese, *supra* note 7, at 149.

15. Article 21 of ICC Statute.
16. Caracciolo, *supra* note 10, at 228.
17. A. Pellet, 'Applicable Law', in *The Rome Statute of the International Criminal Court: A Commentary*, eds A. Cassese, P. Gaeta and J.R.W.D. Jones (Oxford: Oxford University Press, 2002), 1079–1080.
18. Ibid., at 1080.
19. According to pre-trial Chamber II, these humans rights are also included in Article 21(2) of ICC the Rome Statute. See. ICC, Bemba (ICC-01/05-01/08), Decision Pursuant to Article 61(7)(a) and (b) of the Rome Statute on the Charges of the Prosecutor Against Jean-Pierre Bemba Gombo, 15 June 2009, para. 39.
20. Gaggioli, *supra* note 1, at 245.
21. *Kunarac*, ICTY, Trial Chamber, Judgment, 22 February 2001 (Case No. IT-96-23 and 23/1), sections 470–471.
22. Cassese, *supra* note 7, at 152 *et seq.*
23. Cassese, *supra* note 7, at 150–151.
24. *Blaškić*, ICTY, Appeal Chamber, Judgment, 29 July 2004 (Case No. IT-95-14), section 141; *Lubanga*, ICC, Trial Chamber I, Judgment pursuant to Article 74 of the Statute, 14 March 2012 (ICC-01/04-01/06), para. 581.
25. Ibid.
26. D. Scalia, 'Constat sur le respect du principe nulla poena sine lege par les Tribunaux Pénaux Internationaux', *Revue internationale de droit comparée* 1 (2006): 185–212.
27. *Aleksovski*, ICTY, Appeals Chamber, Judgment, 24 March 2000 (Case No. IT-95-14/1-A), section 95.
28. *Kovačević*, ICTY, Individual Opinion of Judge Shahabuddeen, 2 July 1998 (Case No. IT-97-24-AR73), 4.
29. *Tadić*, ICTY, Decision on the Prosecutor's Motion requesting Protective Measures for Victims and Witnesses, 10 August 1995 (Case No. IT-94-1), section 28.
30. *Dokmanović*, ICTY, Décision relative à la requête aux fins de mise en liberté déposée par l'accusé Slavko Dokmanović, Trial Chamber, 22 October 1997 (Case No. IT-95-13a), sections 27–28. In this Decision, judges make references to human rights (ECHR and ICCPR) to define the term 'law' (section 60).
31. *Dokmanović*, ibid., at sections 64–67.
32. ICCPR, General Comment of Human Rights Commission, Resolutions of European Council.
33. *Delalić*, ICTY, Trial Chamber, Decision on Motion for Provisional Release Filed by the Accused Zejnil Delalić, 25 September 1996 (Case No. IT-96-21), section 19.
34. Ibid., section 21.
35. Ibid., section 22.
36. Ibid., sections 23–27.
37. *Bemba*, ICC, Pre-Trial Chamber III, Decision on Application for Interim Release, 16 December 2008 (ICC-01/05-01/08), para. 31.
38. ICC, *Lubanga*, Decision on the Prosecutor's Application for a Warrant of Arrest, Article 58, 10 February 2006, Annex I to Decision issued on 24 February 2006, ICC-01/04-01/06-8-Corr, Pre-Trial Chamber I, paras 11–12.
39. *Delalić*, ICTY, Decision of the Bureau on Motion on Judicial Independence (President McDonald, Vice-President Shahabuddeen, Judge Cassese and Judge Jorda), 4 September 1998 (Case No. IT-96-21).
40. Ibid.
41. *Furundžija*, ICTY, Appeal Chamber, Judgment, 21 July 2000 (Case No. IT-95-17/1), para. 189.
42. *Delalić*, ICTY, Decision on the Prosecution's Motion for an Order Requiring Advance Disclosure of Witnesses by the Defence, 4 February 1998 (Case No. IT-96-21), para. 22.
43. *Delalić*, ICTY, Trial Chamber, Decision on the Motion of the Joint Request of the Accused Persons Regarding the Presentation of Evidence Dated 24 May 1998, 12 June 1998 (Case No. IT-96-21), paras 34–48.
44. Cassese, *supra* note 7, at 166–167
45. *Delalić*, ICTY, Trial Chamber, Decision on Zdravko Mucić's Motion for the Exclusion of Evidence, 2 September 1997 (Case No. IT-96-21), paras 48–60.
46. *Delalić*, ICTY, Trial Chamber, Decision on the Prosecution's Oral Requests for the Admission of Exhibit 155 into Evidence and for an Order to Compel the Accused, Zdravko Mucic, to Provide a Handwriting Sample, 19 January 1998 (Case No. IT-96-21), paras 45–46 and Disposition.

47. *Blaskić*, ICTY, Trial Chamber, Decision on the defence Motion to dismiss the Indictment based upon Defects in the Form thereof (Vagueness/Lack of Adequate Notice of Charges), 4 April 1997 (Case No. IT-95-14), paras 12–16.
48. Ibid., Disposition.
49. *Semanza*, ICTR, Appeal Chamber, Decision, 31 May 2000 (Case No. ICTR-97-20-A), para. 78.
50. Ibid., para. 87. In the case of Barayagwiza, the same Tribunal decides, basing their decision on the ECHR, that a maximum period of time of 24 hours before the arrest of the accused and informing them of charges against them does not violate the human rights of the accused (*Barayagwiza*, ICTR, Appeal Chamber, Judgment, 3 November 1999 (Case No. ICTR-97-19-AR72), para. 84).
51. *Semanza*, ICTR, Trial Chamber, Disposition, Judgment and Sentence, 15 May 2005 (Case No. ICTR-97-20-A).
52. *Kambanda*, ICTR, Appeals Chamber, Judgment, 19 October 2000 (ICTR 97-23-A), para. 33. In this Decision, judges quote another Judgment with the same conclusion: *Ntakirutimana*, ICTR, Trial Chamber, Decision on the Motions of the Accused for Replacement of Assigned Counsel, 11 June 1997 (Case Nos ICTR-96-10-T and ICTR-96-17-T), 2 *et seq.*
53. *Lubanga*, ICC, Reasons for 'Decision of the Appeals Chamber on the Defence application "Demande de suspension de toute action ou procédure afin de permettre la désignation d'un nouveau Conseil de la Défense" filed on 20 February 2007', issued on 23 February 2007, Appeal Chamber, 9 March 2007 (ICC-01/04-01/06 OA8), para. 15.
54. *Delalić*, ICTY, Trial Chamber, Decision on the Motions by the Prosecution for Protective Measures for the Prosecution Witnesses Pseudonymed 'B' through to 'M', 28 April 1997 (Case No. IT-96-21), paras 34–55. This Decision answers the argument from the Accusation to protect the witnesses, victims of sexual abuse.
55. *Lubanga*, ICC, Pre-Trial Chamber, Decision on Victims' participation, 18 January 2008 (ICC-01/04-01/06), para. 78.
56. ICC, Décision relative à la requête du Procureur sollicitant l'autorisation d'interjeter appel de la décision de la Chambre du 17 janvier 2006 sur les demandes de participation à la procédure de VPRS 1, VPRS 2, VPRS 3, VPRS 4, VPRS 5 et VPRS 6, Pre-Trial Chamber I, 31 March 2006.
57. Harun, ICC, Decision on the Prosecution Application under Article 58(7) of the Statute, Pre-Trial Chamber I, 27 April 2007 (ICC-02/05-01/07), para. 28.
58. ICC, Situation in the Democratic Republic of the Congo, ICC, Decision on the Prosecutor's Application for Warrants of Arrest, Article 58, Pre-Trial Chamber, 10 February 2006 (ICC-01/04-01/07), para. 12.
59. *Nahimana*, ICTR, Trial Chamber, Judgment and Sentence, 3 December 2003 (Case No. ICTR-96-11), paras 991–1010.
60. Cassese, *supra* note 7, at 151.
61. Currat, *supra* note 5, at 746.
62. *Tadić*, ICTY, Appeal Chamber, Decision on the Defence Motion for Interlocutory Appeal on Jurisdiction, 2 October 1995 (Case No. IT-94-1), para. 58.
63. *Tadić*, ICTY, Appeal Chamber, Decision on the Defence Motion for Interlocutory Appeal on Jurisdiction, 2 October 1995 (Case No. IT-94-1), paras 97 *et seq.*
64. *Delalić*, ICTY, Appeal Chamber, Judgment, 20 February 2001 (Case No. IT-96-21), para. 149; *Halilović*, ICTY, Trial Chamber, Judgment, 16 November 2005 (Case No. IT-01-48), para. 25.
65. Cassese, *supra* note 7.
66. *Delalić*, ICTY, Trial Chamber, Judgment, 16 November 1998 (Case No. IT-96-21), para. 462; *Blagojević*, ICTY, Trial Chamber, Judgment, 17 January 2005 (Case No. IT-02-60), para. 587.
67. *Aleksovski*, ICTY, Trial Chamber, Judgment, 25 June 1999 (Case No. IT-95-14/1), para. 53.
68. Cassese, *supra* note 7, at 162.
69. *Krnojelac*, ICTY, Trial Chamber, Judgment, 15 March 2002 (Case No. IT-97-25), para. 181; *Kvočka*, ICTY, Trial Chamber, Judgment, 2 November 2001 (Case No. IT-98-30/1), para. 142; *Kunarac, supra* note 21, at para. 466.
70. *Furundžija*, ICTY, Trial Chamber, Judgment, 10 December 1998 (Case No. IT-95-17/1), para. 159. This Decision will be reaffirmed in a number of Judgments: *Delalić*, ICTY, Trial Chamber, Judgment, 16 November 1998 (Case No. IT-96-21), paras 481–493; *Kvočka*, ICTY, Trial Chamber, Judgment, 2 November 2001 (Case No. IT-98-30/1), para. 145; *Kunarac, supra* note 21, at para. 437.
71. Cassese, *supra* note 7, at 177–178.

72. *Furundžija*, ICTY, Trial Chamber, Judgment, 10 December 1998 (Case No. IT-95-17/1), paras 160–163. The same reasoning has been followed by the ICTR: *Akayesu*, ICTR, Trial Chamber, Judgment, 2 September 1998 (Case No. TPIR-96-4-T), para. 593.
73. *Simić*, ICTY, Trial Chamber, Judgment, 17 October 2003 (Case No. IT-95-9), para. 48.
74. *Kunarac*, *supra* note 21, at para. 533.
75. *Krnojelac*, ICTY, Trial Chamber, Judgment, 15 March 2002 (Case No. IT-97-25), para. 109.
76. *Simić*, ICTY, Trial Chamber, Judgment, 17 October 2003 (Case No. IT-95-9), para. 48; *Stakić*, ICTY, Trial Chamber, Judgment, 31 July 2003 (Case No. IT-97-24), para. 720.
77. *Simić*, ICTY, Trial Chamber, Judgment, 17 October 2003 (Case No. IT-95-9), para. 48
78. *Semanza*, ICTR, Trial Chamber, Judgment and Sentence, 15 May 2003 (Case No. ICTR-97-20), para. 349.
79. *Kupreskić*, ICTY, Trial Chamber, Judgment, 14 January 2000 (Case No. IT-95-16), paras 619–621.
80. *Kupreskić*, ICTY, Trial Chamber, Judgment, 14 January 2000 (Case No. IT-95-16), para. 529.
81. *Krnojelac*, ICTY, Appeal Chamber, Judgment, 17 September 2003 (Case No. IT-97-25), para. 200; *Simić*, ICTY, Trial Chamber, Judgment, 17 October 2003 (Case No. IT-95-9), para. 84.
82. *Kupreskić*, ICTY, Trial Chamber, Judgment, 14 January 2000 (Case No. IT-95-16), para. 631.
83. *Simić*, ICTY, Trial Chamber, Judgment, 17 October 2003 (Case No. IT-95-9), para. 60.
84. *Kordić and Čerkez*, ICTY, Appeal Chamber, Judgment, 17 December 2004 (Case No. IT-95-14/2), para. 106; *Blaskić*, *supra* note 24, at paras 136 and 143; *Blaskić*, ICTY, Trial Chamber, Judgment, 3 March 2000 (Case No. IT-95-14), para. 220.
85. *Blagojević*, ICTY, Trial Chamber, Judgment, 17 January 2005 (Case No. IT-02-60), para. 592.
86. Gaggioli, *supra* note 1, at 210, quoting *Blaškić*, *supra* note 84.
87. Judges particularly mention the Convention on the rights of children of 1989: *Lubanga*, ICC, Pre-Trial Chamber, Decision on the confirmation of charges, 29 January 2007 (ICC-01/04-01/06), paras 245 and 310.
88. Mettraux, *supra* note 6; D. Scalia, 'A few thoughts on guaranties inherent to the rule of law as applied to sanctions and the prosecution and punishment of war crimes', *International Review of the Red Cross* 870 (2008): 343–357.
89. Scalia, *supra* note 26.
90. S. Zappalà, *Human Rights in International Criminal Proceedings* (Oxford: Oxford University Press, 2003).
91. Cassese, *supra* note 7, at 174–177.

29. Is there a need for new international humanitarian law implementation mechanisms?

Paolo Benvenuti and Giulio Bartolini*

1. INTRODUCTORY REMARKS ABOUT GUARANTEES IN IHL

The contributions contained in this chapter prompt some further remarks about the effectiveness of the traditional means of enforcement envisaged by international humanitarian law (IHL) and about the advisability of reinforcing them, eventually grafting on to them some human rights (HR) implementation approaches. We must look at the means of implementation of IHL with some innovative ideas in order to overcome a situation in which the contemporary realities of armed conflicts are frequently paved with regrettable humanitarian defeats. There can be no doubt about the need to do everything possible in order to reinforce those means of implementation which, if carefully used, could strengthen the weakest section of IHL: namely its observance.

In fact, IHL instruments show special care in setting out many rules specifically devoted to the execution of substantive obligations, rules which give the responsibility of ensuring respect for IHL, both to the Parties in conflict and to third States. In reality, in so far as IHL rules are provided in the interest of protected persons as such, it follows that the obligations envisaged are not bilateral obligations linking the Parties in conflict *inter se* only. On the contrary, we frequently find *erga omnes* obligations. This rationale in guaranteeing IHL is set out clearly in Article 1 common to the Geneva Conventions and to Additional Protocol I: all States Parties 'undertake to respect and to ensure respect' for IHL Conventions 'in all circumstances'.[1] Therefore, while the Parties in conflict primarily bear the responsibility for respecting IHL, all States have some sort or juridical title in this regard. All States are under a duty to abstain from any conduct which could assist the Parties in conflict in disregarding IHL; moreover, they have the right and sometimes even the duty, to interfere positively with the behaviour of the States in conflict.

However, overemphasising such an *erga omnes* character of IHL rules is not a solution to the problem if States do not concretely display interest in making use of the opportunities provided by those legal means of enforcing law inspired by an *erga omnes* approach. Certainly, it is possible, in a logic of common responsibility, to imagine new and advanced concepts working for a better implementation of IHL such as the recent elaboration of the theory of 'Responsibility to protect'; but good concepts not flanked by the real interest of States in translating them into practice and policies result in illusory effectiveness and do not offer great relief to victims of armed conflicts.

Furthermore, the instruments of IHL appropriately accept a wide notion of 'guarantee', that is, a notion which includes, according to a relative but nevertheless useful distinction in dealing with the subject, preventive measures of implementation, as well as measures monitoring the application of IHL during an armed conflicts and measures operating after a violation of IHL has taken place. One could additionally include in a wide notion of 'guarantee' also those measures which third States may carry out in case of grave danger to humanitarian values, such as humanitarian assistance.

Note should also be taken of the fact that a major contribution to ensuring compliance with IHL can also come, independently of the 'legal' measures mentioned above, from the presence of 'de facto' guarantees that are not strictly 'de jure'. We are referring in particular to the role of public opinion today, which can exercise influence on the parties to a conflict to induce them to comply with IHL. IHL has become more receptive to the 'borderless' opinions of NGOs, which bring pressure to ensure a more effective protection of human beings, even in emergencies caused by war.

2. THE APPROACH CHARACTERISING THE PRESENT CONTRIBUTION

After the previous remarks about guarantees in IHL, it is useful to outline briefly the approach characterising this contribution.

First, the study will focus on the specific means provided for by the current system of IHL (sections 3–5). The potentialities of such means will be evaluated alongside their limits, and proposals of amendment will be considered in order to improve their sphere of action. In fact, sometimes they show critical aspects and intrinsic weaknesses which are related to their original field of application circumscribed to inter-State armed conflicts. The great part of contemporary hostilities are non-international armed conflicts (NIACs) and those which are international in character are nowadays crowded by new actors having an active role in the conduct of hostilities: therefore specific attention is needed towards these conflict situations challenging the traditional enforcement of IHL. In such context, the role of private military companies (PMCs) and of international organisations in current conflicts will be evaluated. Furthermore, we observe a further peculiar element: new typologies of actors interested and able to work toward implementation, overcoming the classic inter-State approach: we are referring to the individual as such and to non-governmental organisations (NGOs) which are acquiring an increasing role in the mechanism assuring respect for fundamental human values.

Moreover, in section 6 we will focus on the recent trends aiming at borrowing, for the advantage of IHL, mechanisms alien to it: in particular those means provided by the law of international organisations, human rights law, and customary international law as well as domestic law. In fact, the awareness of the limits encountered by IHL has favoured the resort to complementary instruments outside IHL *stricto sensu* in order to react. We have to explore the limits of these additional instruments, as it is difficult to maintain that they can be considered as a definitive panacea to problems related to the enforcement process of IHL.

Furthermore, as analysed in section 7, while from an abstract point of view, several additional instruments within the IHL system may be proposed, it will be necessary to balance *de lege ferenda* evaluations with concrete realities of the international community and contemporary armed conflicts.

However, it should be maintained that in relation to the nature of some contemporary armed conflicts every possible assessment and proposals of improvement may turn out to be merely theoretical. The analysis which follows must take note also of the fact that the traditional goals of the use of armed force (e.g. acquisition of territories, overthrowing a government) is challenged in some of current conflicts: in fact, sometimes the goal is the very violation of IHL and HRL, as it may happen in ethnic cleansing, or the creation of a predatory system aiming to loot natural resources and humanitarian aid provided by the international community.[2] When something like this happens, some of the traditional means of enforcement dramatically lose effectiveness.

3. PREVENTIVE MEASURES OF ACCOMPLISHING IHL

Coming specifically to legal guarantees, we will start by saying that, according to the Geneva Conventions, States must be prepared to accomplish their tasks adequately when an armed conflict breaks out. In other words, it is necessary for States to adopt all those appropriate measures which are usually referred to as preventive in the implementation of IHL. Such measures must be planned in peacetime, as is clearly indicated by Common Article 2 of the 1949 Conventions, to make it easier to protect humanitarian values in the event of a subsequent armed conflict. These preventive measures, prescribing a particular course of action, work on different levels.

3.1   Adequacy of Domestic Laws to IHL Standards

A first level is that concerning the adequacy of domestic laws of States with respect to IHL standards. The negotiators in Geneva were particularly sensitive to this matter, because the success of IHL is to a large extent dependent upon the level of its recognition in domestic laws. In fact the conformity with IHL of internal laws is an essential condition for the spontaneous respect of humanitarian standards.

Although the above remark is true in general with respect to the various chapters of IHL, it is most appropriate in connection with grave breaches of IHL. According to the Geneva Conventions, all Parties, whether or not they are engaged in an armed conflict, have the duty to enact the necessary legislation for providing effective penal sanctions for persons committing, or ordering others to commit, any grave breaches of the Conventions themselves. In addition, third States must adopt a system of universal criminal jurisdiction with respect to such grave breaches, in order for it to be possible for them to prosecute persons having committed war crimes, whatever their nationality and wherever their unlawful acts have been committed.

A universal system of prosecution can undoubtedly be helpful in dissuading the commission of grave breaches of IHL. Unfortunately, very few States have a national legal order allowing them to abide satisfactorily by these obligations. And this is the very reason for which, recently, the jurisdiction of States has been flanked by criminal jurisdiction in favour of international ad hoc tribunals and the ICC.

3.2 The Adequacy of National Technical and Operative Standards to IHL Rules

Further, the adoption of preventive measures necessary to comply with substantive IHL rules can have a wider meaning. In fact, such measures cannot be considered as limited to the evaluation of conformity of national laws with international legal standards, as they can also include technical and operative assessments. For instance the analysis deserves to be extended to an evaluation of conformity to IHL rules of weapons available to States, to military doctrines, or to preparation of technical equipment suitable for the effective protection of humanitarian values, in a specific circumstance of armed conflict. In this latter regard, it is clear that, in spite of the goodwill of States and individuals, it is impossible for them to abide by duties such as the one according to which wounded, sick and shipwrecked persons shall be protected and shall receive the medical care required by their condition, if they are not equipped with instruments indispensable in affording humanitarian aid. The same applies to the obligations to provide a network of 'civil defence' structures for civilians. Also in relation with these elements we can note several problems.

First, there are notorious cases where States have not complied with the destruction of weapons, as required by disarmament treaties: this phenomenon implies the permanent risk of their future potential use.[3] Second, especially taking into account lessons learned from other war scenarios, States should also review the compatibility of available weapons with IHL provisions, for instance taking into account new and clearer legal limits on their use.[4]

In recent conflicts, for example, some of the alleged violations of IHL, in particular concerning non-compliance with principles of distinction and proportionality arising from the use of cluster weapons, have been attributed to the continued use of munitions which are not technologically advanced. These inconsistencies have implied, in subsequent scenarios, the abandonment of such obsolete weapons and their replacement with more advanced systems in order to make their employment more in keeping with IHL.[5] Similarly, the recent Israeli decision to establish a new strategic doctrine on urban warfare[6] by issuing special directives imposing more stringent requirements which take into account the criticisms raised in the international community as a result of Cast Lead operation, appears in line with the need for States to use non-conflict periods to assess the lawfulness of their past practices.

Concerning the preparation of technical equipment suitable for the effective protection of humanitarian values, it happens that we sometimes find inadequate attention. On the contrary, such measures must be carried out immediately, without delay, in peace-time. The fact of not paying adequate attention to them, by believing that war is a distant event, involves serious consequences in safeguarding humanitarian values.

3.3 Current Limits for the IHL System in Assessing the Adoption of Preventive Measures by States

In relation to the above remarks, we can infer some limitations inherent in the current system of IHL. In particular the adoption of these preventive measures depends essentially on the willingness of States Parties that can delay the fulfilment of their obligations.

For instance, the implementation of national legislation can be considered a non-priority legislative policy. In such cases a positive role can be played by lobbying activities carried out by bodies like the National Committees on IHL, usually made up of representatives of relevant government departments, academic experts and actors more involved in IHL, such as the Red Cross/Red Crescent National Societies. However, these bodies are present in only about half of the States Parties to the Geneva Conventions and, moreover, differences in their effectiveness are notorious, due, in many cases, to their sporadic action. Also, the role played by the International Committee of the Red Cross (ICRC) Advisory service in this area is predominantly dependent on the willingness of States to rely on it. Similarly, if technical and concrete actions are requested, the risk is that they can be evaluated as economically unsustainable or their importance may be underestimated. In contrast, a comprehensive approach to preventive measures, which partly overlaps with the obligation of dissemination of IHL, seems essential to ensure the readiness of States to comply with it.

Moreover, in many cases, a positive interaction with other States Parties to IHL system is lacking in this phase, given the absence of adequate tools to monitor the effective implementation of these obligations by States. In the context of IHL, there is clearly neither a mechanism charged to review periodic reports by States Parties, comparable to mechanisms operating in the field of human rights treaties, nor a body competent to deal with this issue. The proposals made by the ICRC in the mid-1990s of the last century to develop, through a committee of experts, a mechanism 'to examine reports and advise States on any matters regarding the implementation of IHL',[7] has not been accepted. At the same time, doubts may arise about the development and the actual benefit of these potential reporting mechanisms in the framework of IHL, given the well-known difficulties in the management of these control mechanisms in human rights law, characterised by delays and lack of attention by States as to the fulfilment of reporting obligations.

At the moment, the IHL system only disposes of informal monitoring activities carried out by ICRC, through its Advisory Service on IHL, which has developed a database on the implementation of relevant treaties by States Parties. However, this instrument, apart from not being comprehensive, is more an informative tool than one aiming to exercise pressure on States highlighting possible gaps.

Other mechanisms may, however, be employed. For example one could envisage a growing role in monitoring by the International Conferences of the Red Cross and Red Crescent. Before the Conference, States are requested to prepare documents providing information on the implementation of pledges made by them during the previous Conference, including those ones referring to 'National implementation of IHL'. The Conference, in its follow-up activity, could provide a more detailed scrutiny of any deficiencies. However, it seems unlikely that this more incisive role can be effectively exercised in this forum as the International Conference has currently more of a diplomatic nature than a monitoring approach. The practice clearly attests that actors involved in it voluntarily avoid turning this meeting into a possible site of scrutiny, so as to avoid politicisation:[8] it is difficult to imagine a change of behaviour in the coming years. In addition, at present, reasons of time-restraint do not permit any scrutiny. Lastly, if in the future this activity is going to involve a contrast between participants, this possibility itself could be materially affected by the lack of participation of States to pledges on this issue.

Moreover, even in treaties relevant for IHL, such as those on disarmament, which already establish more structured control mechanisms on compliance, for example periodic meetings of States Parties or Review Conferences, we can note that they do not play a decisive role. For instance, even if the overviews highlight deficiencies in compliance, the subsequent action is rather bland, usually limited to the adoption of documents in which other States limit themselves to expressing their 'concern' over the situation, without envisaging additional measures.[9]

In any event, in this field, a growing role in facilitating compliance has now been taken by civil society. It is clear that, especially with reference to certain areas, such as the regulation of weapons or adaptation of national laws to comply with IHL and international criminal law, an important role of putting pressure on governments is carried out by several NGOs.[10] These are constantly engaged in advocacy and lobbying activities in order, primarily, to engage States with these treaties and, secondly, to ensure effective domestic implementation. However, it is obvious that the final result in this context goes beyond the meritorious action taken by these non-state actors (NSAs) and depends, primarily, on the autonomous government's will.

Recently, this growing role for NGOs has also found a clear recognition in some treaties. For example, the Ottawa and Oslo Conventions or the Second Protocol to the 1954 Hague Convention attach relevant functions to NGOs. These entities are specifically mentioned among the actors that States are invited to contact to obtain technical, material and financial assistance to implement pertinent obligations.[11] Moreover, these treaties allow participation of 'relevant NGOs' in review conferences or regular meetings of States Parties, thus recognising not only their role in lobbying, but also their technical expertise in discussing the main practical problems arising from the implementation of these treaties.[12]

Therefore, we are witness to substantial points of evolution in this field, which emphasise the current role of these NSAs in the dynamics of national implementation of IHL. In fact, previous treaties only referred to autonomous activities carried out by States Parties or, under an inter-State approach, at most, an opening was established to support activities undertaken by international organisations.[13]

3.4 The Implementation of International Humanitarian Law in the Internal Order of International Organisations

However, contemporary armed conflicts raise more complex issues with regard to preventive implementation of IHL by other actors actively involved in hostilities, different from the typical scenario provided by governmental armed forces.

An initial reference can be made to international organisations, given the increasing cases in which peace support operations conducted under their command and control may be involved as parties to an armed conflict. Without being able to resume here the broad debate on the legal basis for considering international organisation, per se, as bound by IHL, in such cases these actors ought to address the issue of the implementation of IHL obligations in their internal order, so to dispose of an adequate regulatory system. However, this activity has been carried out with difficulty. In essence, the only relevant example can be identified in the 1999 Bulletin of the UN Secretary General, containing a common IHL standard for national contingents operating under the UN command and control.

This sort of adaptation of international organisations' internal law with the provisions of IHL is therefore still fragmentary. Although many regional organisations are now involved in peace support operations having a 'robust' mandate, we do not find, within their relevant documents, an accurate clarification of IHL standards for troops involved in missions. For example, the main instrument adopted so far by the EU[14] is just intended to draw up measures to monitor respect for IHL by external actors acting in the area of pertinence of the EU mission, without any reference to the nature and extent of the obligations imposed on the EU Force itself.

Of course, unlike the UN missions characterised by the presence of contingents having non-homogeneous legal backgrounds, it is conceivable that this lack of interest by regional organisations to define common IHL regulations is primarily due to the belief that IHL standards are substantially similar among participating States as we must remember that national troops are still binding on IHL obligations pertaining to their States. Therefore, as expressed in some documents, there could be an assumption that these problems have been resolved at the domestic level, without the need to find a common approach.[15]

However, this evaluation does not seem conclusive. On the one hand, national legislations of participating States may be deficient or there could be a non-common background among contributing States, especially having regard to the increasing participation of countries outside the regional system of reference.[16] Second, as a matter of internal policy of legitimacy and commitment to IHL, the international organisation could prefer to increase legal standards of reference, such as the Secretary-General made in elaborating the Bulletin, where he introduced a series of prohibitions translated from the most recent conventions even if several Members States were not parties to these instruments. Moreover, because of the known difficulties in identifying pertinent substantive IHL obligations in relation to conflicts involving international organisations, the creation of self-regulatory standards by them would undoubtedly facilitate a more straightforward application of the law in every possible context, regardless of the actors at issue, legal qualification of the conflict, and so on.

3.5   The Dissemination of International Humanitarian Law by States and Other Actors Involved in Contemporary Armed Conflicts

An additional level of these preventive measures concerns the widest possible dissemination of IHL. Geneva Conventions point out the necessity that IHL should be part of the programmes of military instruction and that also the civilian population should be acquainted with it. Moreover, Protocol I obliges State parties to ensure that legal advisers are available to advise military commanders on the application of IHL.

However, it is clear that the realisation of this obligation depends primarily on the willingness of States, and, consequently, it is not surprising that some aspects, for instance dissemination activities in favour of the civilian population, are particularly weak and sporadic. At the same time, in the training of military personnel particular attention is not always placed on the dissemination of IHL. As recognised by the ICRC, States usually give only a formal significance to that duty, through the mere issuance of formal instruction or providing modest training activities, which raise doubts about the possibility, in cases of conflict, to ensure enforcement of the discipline.[17] On the contrary, prior to an armed conflict, at least members of the armed forces should have already assimilated these rules, according to different levels of responsibility, so that there would be a spontaneous observance of IHL, given the 'internalisation' of legal limits concerning conduct of hostilities. Moreover, the increasing complexity over the decades of IHL results in a strong need for States to have staff structurally embedded in this branch of law to address additional challenges.

In this sector it is therefore fundamental to create a strong synergy among States and institutional actors committed to offering their technical services in this area. The hope is that the relevant experiences arising from the ICRC, through its Advisory Service, or by NGOs specialising in the training of the armed forces, such as the military courses organised for over 40 years by the Sanremo International Institute of Humanitarian Law (IIHL), may find greater development.

This action carried out at the national level can also have a positive impact on the involvement of other actors in armed conflicts, such as international organisations. The possibility that military operations involving these entities comply with IHL depends essentially on the legal background already assimilated by national contingents,[18] as possible subsequent training activities on contingents already deployed are obviously late.

This necessity, among other things, is expressly emphasised by UN documents which recognise the importance of a proper training of personnel under IHL and the duty for contributing States to assure that their personnel are fully acquainted with IHL principles.[19] Moreover, as recently manifested in the practice of the UN, the forces of the international organisation can play a notable active role in the external dissemination of IHL. For instance the Security Council has requested MONUC (United Nations Organization Mission in the Democratic Republic of Congo) to 'Provide in the short term basic training, including in the area of … international humanitarian law … to various members and units of the FARDC integrated brigades'.[20]

Even greater problems arise in relation to dissemination activities in NIACs, where an express obligation to comply with this duty by armed groups is formally recognised.[21] However, the nature of organised armed groups, usually composed of individuals lacking previous military experience, makes the application of IHL difficult, as this body of law is usually unknown to these actors. Especially in these armed conflicts, we can therefore notice the disastrous consequences of a failure by States to disseminate IHL to the civilian population.

Activities devoted to these subjects, although late, are therefore essential, but difficulties appear. Several factors interact in relation to that purpose, such as: the level of internal organisation of the group; the willingness of commanders to develop such activities; resources available; the possibility of relying on external experts from humanitarian organisations; the inability to conduct dissemination activities in the early phases of the conflict. ICRC remains essentially the main actor in this area. Not without difficulties it has been able, taking into account the peculiar characteristics of these groups and past experiences, to develop specific dissemination activities aimed at increasing the awareness on IHL obligations by these groups. This approach takes into account relevant cultural elements, for example through the appropriate simplification and translation of basic IHL principles into local languages.[22]

Even in relation to new actors present in current conflict scenarios, such as PMCs, we can face similar problems regarding the dissemination of IHL within their affiliates. Contrary to common perception, it is impossible to claim a reduced importance of this issue based on the presumption that these individuals necessarily have a military background and, therefore, they have already internalised an adequate knowledge of the discipline. Beyond problems already highlighted on the actual level of knowledge of IHL by State armed forces, a significant percentage of the staff of these PMCs do not have previous experience in regular units.[23]

This need has now been detected in relevant instruments. For example, the Montreux Document explicitly indicates that, in respect of IHL, 'Contracting States have an obligation ... to: a) ensure that PMSCs [private military and security companies] that they contract and their personnel are aware of their obligations and trained accordingly'.[24] This need has been reiterated in relevant State documents. For example, the US DoD Directive 2311.01 requires 'contractors to institute and implement effective programs to prevent violations of the law of war by their employees and subcontractors, including law of war training and dissemination'.[25] However, subsequent analysis has shown major shortcomings in achieving this goal.[26] Moreover, similar provisions have not been proposed by other States. Therefore the need for the development of concrete programs for the dissemination of IHL among these actors would seem to be urgent, as evidenced by the ICRC's first attempts to establish a constructive dialogue on these issues with them.

Among other things, a greater knowledge and, consequently, a greater chance of being able to respect IHL, can have positive effects for the PMCs in terms of legitimacy. No wonder, therefore, that the PMCs are attempting to stress the relevance of dissemination of IHL in their codes of self-regulation. However, so far, these documents, whose effectiveness is doubtful, contain only vague references to IHL and the need for these companies to train their personnel 'on applicable legal framework(s) and ethical conduct'.[27]

4.   MEANS FOR SUPERVISING RESPECT FOR INTERNATIONAL HUMANITARIAN LAW DURING ARMED CONFLICTS

4.1   The Responsibility of Commanders to Supervise the Enforcement of International Humanitarian Law by Subordinates

We will now make some remarks about the current means of supervising respect for IHL which can take a variety of specific forms.

First of all the Parties in a conflict have the important duty of supervising the enforcement of their own humanitarian obligations. Therefore, according to Article 87 of Protocol I, military commanders are required, with respect to members of armed forces under their command and others persons under their control, to prevent and, where necessary, to suppress and report breaches of IHL to competent authorities. Furthermore, commensurate with their level of responsibility, commanders shall ensure that members of the armed forces under their command are aware of their obligations under IHL. The failure to exercise such control may have heavy consequences for the commander, as it entails his personal criminal responsibility, as confirmed in Article 28 of the Statute of the ICC.

We observe that the command responsibility, the origin of which is related to international armed conflict, is considered now – according to the case law of the international criminal ad hoc tribunals[28] – a general principle applicable also in non-international armed conflicts. We may also add that, to some extent, the Bulletin on the applicability of IHL to UN Forces was promulgated in 1999 by the UN Secretary-General, taking into account the command responsibility pertaining to him as the vertex of the administration, when such forces in situations of armed conflicts are actively engaged in combat operations under UN command and control.

The approach of command responsibility appears to be in harmony with the logic of spontaneous observance of international law, which is connatural to a juridical system devoid of a hierarchical structure. Nevertheless, if duties of this kind, incumbent upon the States and armed groups in conflict, may represent a useful defence against violations committed by individuals escaping the control of their organisation, on the contrary these measures of internal supervision are ineffective vis-à-vis those violations of the law of armed conflicts which are – as has been not infrequently the case in many contemporary armed conflicts (e.g. ethnic cleansing, looting, rape) – a 'war policy' of the parties in conflict. Moreover, difficulties may arise from the point of view of the impartiality of self-supervision and there are also situations in which States have failed and the chain of military command appears broken. We have also situations of non-state actors which are characterised by an internal structure too feeble to assure a de facto control in assuring respect of IHL by subordinates. Especially in asymmetric conflicts there are situations where the weaker side often lacks the necessary structure of authority, hierarchy, communication between superiors and subordinates and a process of accountability, all of which are necessary to self-enforce IHL. IHL implementation depends heavily on 'parties' of armed conflicts (States and organised armed groups): they need a minimum of structure and authority. Lacking such a minimum basis of structure and authority, we have to recognise that IHL is not applicable and that such a kind of situation is covered by a different branch of international law: HRL.

4.2 Third Party Supervision: The Role of Protecting Powers

If self-supervision is not always apt, then the importance of a parallel external supervision through monitoring performed by third parties to the conflict or by a technical impartial body is self-evident. Moreover, the fact of being third parties to the conflict tends, at least in principle, to increase the impartiality of the supervision.

A power of supervision in favour of third States flows directly from customary international law. In so far as IHL creates absolute duties in favour of all members of the international community, every State is entitled to monitor the situation. Depending on the result of this supervision, third States should consequently take action. States, however, are often unwilling to perform this task for various reasons, including a sort of 'governmental solidarity' against the protected persons. Furthermore, in practice, a supervision of this kind is not always easy to carry out, because the principle of territorial sovereignty does not allow third States to investigate in the territory controlled by the Parties in conflict without their permission.

Moreover, the Conventions and Protocols regulate specifically the role of supervision entrusted to third States and carried out in the territory of the Parties in conflict. We refer to the role of the Protecting Powers, which, by virtue of a trilateral agreement, third States are called upon by the States in conflict to act out for the implementation of IHL. But the system of Protecting Powers, after 1949, has not worked satisfactorily: it has very rarely been used in practice for various reasons. Moreover, it is a system operating exclusively in international conflicts, intrinsically extraneous to the field of NIACs mostly involving NSAs. The experts convened by the ICRC in 2003 have indicated a number of possible reasons for the failure to designate a Protecting Power: the perception that very few States are considered neutral and either able or willing to carry out the role of the Protecting Power; and the fact that the majority of the current conflicts are NIACs, where Protecting Powers are not foreseen. It happens also that States do not recognise the existence of the armed conflict; and sometimes diplomatic relations are maintained despite the conflict. Maybe it is possible to imagine a number of suggestions to revitalise the role of Protecting Powers, such as those contained in the ICRC Report quoted above,[29] but they do not seem such as to reverse the current crisis of the system of Protecting Powers.

4.3   The Role of the ICRC

As a substitute to the Protecting Power, according to the Geneva Conventions, the ICRC may act in order to supervise respect for IHL. But, apart from acting as a substitute for the Protecting Power, the ICRC enjoys, according to the law of Geneva and to customary law, a very wide humanitarian mandate in favour of the victims of armed conflicts, and exercises a traditional right of humanitarian initiative, as an impartial, neutral and independent institution. The ICRC makes use of a 'proximity' strategy which is, de facto, a kind of 'on the spot' control on the behaviour of the belligerents.

The ICRC has an invaluable function for war victims, but its role has some limits too, part of them consubstantial to the nature of ICRC. We mean the approach of its action characterised by confidentiality and bilaterality. This is a really positive behaviour for those who need protection, but sometimes it creates a perception in public opinion that the respect of humanitarian values is not a question of law, but just of morality. Other limits are proper in the case of NIACs: the consent of the State to its actions is required. It happens also that the action of the ICRC may be restrained by the necessity to grant security to its personnel on the ground.[30]

4.4 Fact-Finding Commissions

Moreover, in so far as means of control are concerned, IHL creates a system of Fact-Finding Commissions. These can be ad hoc Commissions by special compromise, as provided for by the 1949 Conventions.[31] But States never turned to these kind of Enquiry Commissions, which lacked their consent in this regard.

An Enquiry Commission may also be permanent, as in the case of the one provided by Article 90 of Protocol I. But this Commission has also never been used as planned, notwithstanding the efforts of the Commission itself in promoting its role on the occasion of many international conferences and during missions to various countries. States having accepted its competence never requested its enquiry services and, on the other hand, such services are not available to international organisations or NSAs according to the wording of Art. 90.

Maybe some additional efforts could be developed by the International Humanitarian Fact-Finding Commission (IHFFC) in order to use its further power to offer good offices so as to facilitate the restoration of an attitude of respect for IHL, taking account of the fact that, according to Art. 90, para. 2 (c) (ii), such power is not conditioned by the consent of States having recognised its competence and it could be well extended in regard to NIACs.

As analysed in para. 6.2, a role of fact finding and control of IHL has, on the contrary, been entrusted to organs acting within the framework of the United Nations (UN) or other organisations.

4.5 Meetings of the High Contracting Parties to the Geneva Conventions

In this context, we cannot avoid mentioning also Article 7 of AP I, according to which at the request of one or more of the High Contracting Parties (HCPs), and upon the approval of the majority of the said Parties, the depositary shall convene a meeting of the HCPs to consider the general problems concerning the application of the Conventions and Protocols. It may happen that these problems are emphasised when States adopt preventive measures of implementation. The wording of Article 7 excludes the competence of this meeting in respect of specific individual cases, but it is probably true that general problems concerning the application of the Convention are usually highlighted by specific concrete cases and by the concrete application of IHL rules in a given armed conflict. It is evident that these meetings in such cases could be a measure aiming to avoid, at least in the future, the wrongful application of IHL. It may happen also that these meetings lead to a further development of IHL by activating the procedure for amendments according to Article 97 of Protocol I.

Anyway, until now, Article 7 has found a limited application: a meeting of the States Parties was convened in 1998 to discuss, under a general perspective, the items of respect for and security of the personnel of humanitarian organisations and of armed conflicts linked to the disintegration of State structures. Recently, the idea was advanced to make use of Article 7 again following the adoption of the UN General Assembly (GA) Resolution 64/10 concerning the Goldstone Report. Para. 5 of this resolution recommends that the Government of Switzerland, depositary of the fourth GCs, undertake the steps necessary to reconvene a Conference of HCPs on measures to enforce the Convention in the Occupied Palestinian Territories: but up to now we do not have any concrete result.

4.6   Means for Ensuring the Implementation of IHL by Rebels

Lastly, concerning means for ensuring respect for IHL during non-international armed conflict, we can make reference to the need to provide NSAs involved in hostilities with a clear and adequate legal background, as this is a prerequisite for the fulfilment of their IHL obligations. From a strictly formal point of view, the question has no particular legal significance. Several theories can be proposed to maintain that organised armed groups do not have any role in this area as they are formally obliged to respect IHL, both customary or treaty law ratified by governmental authorities of the State concerned, without the need to demonstrate their formal commitment to these rules.[32] However, these doctrinal solutions risk having only a theoretical role, as armed groups tend to refuse IHL rules if they are perceived as the product of external imposition. As highlighted by the ICRC, it is difficult to oblige these groups to respect IHL provisions, claiming that they must comply with obligations arising from treaties ratified by the government they are combating against.[33]

The IHL system already provides such instruments, aiming to ensure that IHL standards are endorsed by organised armed groups,[34] as 'special arrangements' under common Art. 3 to the GCs involving NSAs and the legitimate government. However, only in limited cases have similar agreements been concluded, mainly in the case of substantially symmetrical conflicts in terms of capabilities of forces at issue,[35] while we can record several failures in the negotiation process.[36] Moreover, even if not expressly provided by treaty provisions, practice shows a frequent recourse to 'unilateral declarations' by the leadership of organised armed groups, which can have various contents.[37] Through these different instruments, authorities responsible for these NSAs realise a sort of 'internal implementation', favouring an acceptance and recognition of IHL principles by their subordinates. In addition, these tools can integrate in their contents relevant treaty provisions which, as notorious, have a rudimentary nature. Therefore, any increase in the ownership of these rules by NSAs should be favoured, thus permitting a better compliance.[38]

Even regarding these instruments we can notice recent relevant novelties, which confirm the multi-polar nature of actors involved in the enforcement of IHL. Beyond the main role still played by the ICRC in this area, we should mention relevant functions performed by some NGOs, especially the experience of Geneva Call which has been able to obtain the signature of more than 40 NSAs on the Deed of Commitment on anti-personnel landmines.[39] This instrument has provided, apart from substantive obligations, the possibility to operate an original control mechanism, managed by the same NGO, on alleged violations of this Deed of Commitment by NSAs.[40]

Nonetheless, several doubts have been raised on the effectiveness of these instruments. For instance it has been claimed that unilateral declarations have mainly been issued to create greater legitimacy and support for these armed groups in the international community. However, apart from utilitarian purposes for the leadership of these groups, there is no doubt that these instruments can still be considered as a first step for developing a constructive dialogue with these actors.[41] For example, the ICRC has been able to use these documents to favour humanitarian activities, discussing allegations of non compliance or for offering dissemination activities.[42]

However, the concrete incidence of these instruments as to the enforcement of IHL will depend, ultimately, on the real intention behind their conclusion and by the willingness of these leaders to translate these commitments, in many cases made in vague and general terms, in specific guidelines for commands and members of armed groups.[43]

5. SANCTIONS FOR THE VIOLATION OF IHL

5.1 Reprisals and their Limits

Let us now consider sanctions for the violation of humanitarian rules. Reprisals, which are the measures typically taken to force a country to comply with international law, require some comment. In the law of armed conflict, reprisals have a narrow operating ground in the context of relations among belligerent Parties. Reprisals fall within the operating margin resulting from the observance of humanitarian rules. In fact, Geneva Conventions and other IHL instruments include formal prohibitions of reprisals against protected persons and objects. Moreover, in those cases where they may be considered lawful, reprisals are subject to stringent conditions to be respected: the only purpose is inducing the adversary to comply with the law (reprisals are not a means of revenge, so they have to stop as soon as the adversary complies with the law); they must be a measure of last resort, where no other lawful alternative conduct is available to the belligerents to enforce the law; they must be proportionate to the violations they aim to stop; and more, reprisals have to be preceded by a formal warning; lastly, the decision to resort to reprisals must be taken at the highest level of command. We add that reprisals are perceived as a primitive way of assuring respect for law, because they risk making the 'innocent' pay rather than the 'wrongdoer'. The restrictions to the adoption of reprisals among belligerent parties is also linked to another fact: the usual and effective reprisals that States use in peacetime – that is, the extinction or suspension of treaties – have a marginal function in an armed conflict. Probably, most of the treaties relating to political and economic cooperation between belligerent powers are no longer in force or are suspended.

All this explains the considerable importance which, on the contrary, the actions and sanctions carried out by third States could have in compelling belligerent countries to respect IHL. Third States have access to more effective measures of reprisal (not, of course, in the form of armed force) which they could carry out toward a useful and constructive end, possibly under the coordination of international organisations. Such measures, in case of gross violations of IHL, may also be justified as a form of special responsibility following the commission of an international crime of the State, that is, a serious, widespread breach of an international obligation essential to the interests of the international community. States could act in cooperation through the UN system as envisaged by Art. 89 of AP I. But it is evident to all that UN collective security functions only in some cases and selectively: the UN Security Council (SC) has as its priority putting an end to the fighting and not to violations of IHL.

In concluding these brief remarks on reprisals, it is useful to stress that, according to a general understanding, the related prohibition works also in non-international armed conflicts. Parties to this kind of conflict do not have the right to resort to reprisals whenever the peremptory obligation of basic human treatment is involved.

5.2   Individual Responsibility: the Prosecution of War Crimes

Another form of sanction is connected with individual responsibility for breaches of IHL. The Geneva Conventions and Protocol I, while obliging States to suppress all violations of IHL, specifically include a list of grave breaches which are regarded as war crimes.

However, the Conventions and Protocols do not themselves set out specific penalties, nor do they create a tribunal to try offenders. Instead, they expressly require States to enact any substantive and procedural criminal legislation necessary to provide effective prosecution and punishment of persons committing grave breaches or ordering them to be committed. It has also to be taken into account that the failure by the commander to exercise a proper control over his subordinates entails his personal criminal 'command responsibility', as has been previously pointed out. Under a different perspective, the fact that the defendant acted pursuant to the order of his Government or of a superior shall not relieve him from responsibility, but eventually may be considered in mitigation of punishment.

In addition to the enactment of criminal rules, all States must adopt a system of mandatory and universal jurisdiction. Consequently they are required to search for and punish all those alleged to have committed or to have ordered others to commit grave breaches, whatever their nationality and wherever their unlawful acts have been committed. States are obliged to bring such persons before their own courts. Alternatively, they may also perform their obligation by handing over such persons, in accordance with the provisions of their own legislation, to be tried in another State, provided such a State has made out a *prima facie* case (according to the principle *aut judicare aut dedere*). Therefore, the Geneva instruments make compulsory the right that – according to international customary law – all States have to prosecute grave breaches of IHL by whoever committed, wherever committed.

If traditional war crimes and the universal duty to repress them has been affirmed with regard to the situation of international armed conflict, a recent approach in the reading of the IHL system has led to the affirmation of the innovative idea according to which 'serious and grave breaches' of the Geneva Conventions may occur also in the context of armed conflicts not of an international character. The obligations of States are consequential, including the right/duty to assert a mandatory criminal jurisdiction. The idea has been endorsed by the International Criminal Tribunal for Yugoslavia and by the experience of the International Criminal Tribunal for Rwanda, which is competent explicitly, *inter alia*, to prosecute serious breaches of Article 3 common to the Geneva Convention and of the additional Protocol II. The Statute of the International Criminal Court (ICC) contains a list of breaches of IHL in international conflicts not of an international character constituting war crimes. The right of the State to exercise universal jurisdiction in both international and internal armed conflicts is recognised as a customary rule of IHL by Rule 157 of the *Customary International Humanitarian Law*, edited by the ICRC.

If one looks at the Geneva system and at the network of legal obligations relating to jurisdiction incumbent on all States Parties, one might be led to think that there is no way out for the wrongdoers.

Unfortunately, the system is jeopardised by the fact that most States do not have suitable legislation in so far as substantive penal sanctions and the extension of the tribunal's jurisdiction under the mandatory principle of universality are concerned. Moreover, many difficulties arise in practice as a result of different attitudes, from a lack of cooperation and mutual judicial assistance among States; from a deficiency in coordination of national legal systems in so far as active and passive extradition is concerned; because the legislation of the States contains statutory limitations barring legal actions or the enforcement of the sentence. The recognition of constitutional immunities to the advantage of high-level State organs may be a further limit to the prosecution of war crimes. In addition, prosecution and trials occurring abroad impose particular problems of effectiveness in relation to the gathering of evidence, respect of defendant's rights and protection of witnesses and victims. But, we have also to recognise that often, with regard to many conflict scenarios, it is the political will in prosecuting war crimes that is absent and that this therefore impedes the legal prosecutorial system from working appropriately. One cannot say that the system of repression of violations of IHL through the action of national courts is a success.

As to armed groups, we may affirm that they also have the obligation to prosecute grave breaches, but this obligation does not appear quite realistic because armed groups do not usually have the factual organisation, legal instruments and legislation apt to perform such a role in an appropriate manner and respecting the fundamental rights of those who could be indicted.[44]

All the elements pointed out above constitute the very reason for which as we said before, recently, the criminal jurisdiction of national courts has been flanked by criminal jurisdiction in favour of international ad hoc Tribunals for Rwanda and the former Yugoslavia, and for which the Statute of a Permanent International Criminal Court has been adopted. The ICC has the power to try, *inter alia*, grave or serious violations of IHL, according to the material competence on war crimes provided by the long list contained in Article 8 of the Statute: the principle of complementarity allows the Court to exercise its jurisdiction if national criminal jurisdictions are unwilling or unable genuinely to carry out the investigation or prosecution.

5.3 The Obligation of Reparation

International law obliges the wrong-doing State to provide full reparation for violations of its obligations. State responsibility can be invoked to eliminate harmful consequences for violations of IHL rules and specific treaty provisions deal with this issue. In particular this kind of guarantee was first included in the IV Hague Convention of 1907 and it has been confirmed in Art. 91 I AP. However, even this form of guarantee raises many practical problems.

First, we must underline that, although Article 91 refers specifically to the obligation of compensation, this provision does not affect the possibility that in the case of violations of IHL other measures of reparation provided by international law may also be relevant.[45] Indeed, some measures provided in the system of IHL, such as repressive actions against war criminals or international fact-finding commissions, can play an important role in executing some of the obligations of reparation, especially concerning measures of satisfaction.

However, States have invoked the obligation of reparation for violations of IHL only on a few occasions.[46] On the contrary, in the framework of war reparation, what is more usually raised against States are any sort of prejudices arising from the conflict. Thus, the focus on liability is on breaches of *ius ad bellum* rather than *ius in bello*, as any damage attributed to the recourse to force by the wrong-doing State is considered as a possible title of reparation regardless of their possible compliance with IHL.[47] Moreover, although the obligation of reparation for violations of IHL exists for all States participating in the hostilities, this responsibility has usually been enforced only against the losing party to the conflict, as confirmed by recent practice.[48]

Even if in recent years we can observe a greater emphasis on this theme, it is difficult to assume a definitive change from previous trends. It is easy to recognise that cases in which States fail to respect this obligation are certainly more numerous than other instances, even if such requests come from the international community, as was the case for conflicts in Gaza, Darfur or Georgia.[49] Basically the only recent case which satisfies the spirit of Art. 91 I AP is represented by the experience of the Eritrea-Ethiopia Claims Commission, which has recently issued a significant award concerning compensation for damages arising from violations of IHL and *jus ad bello*.[50]

In any case, it is notorious that today the most debated issue is the possible recognition of an individual right to reparation for violations of *jus in bello*. For a long time such a claim had been regarded as unfounded, given the evaluation of relevant rules, such as Art. 3 of the 1907 IV Hague Convention, as only providing rights for States. However, at present, an increasing number of authors, taking into account relevant case-law, tend to emphasise the existence of such an individual right, usually while holding that this solution is better qualified as a progressive development of international law, as the ILA has also recently recognised.[51]

The actual affirmation of this principle may, however, face several obstacles, particularly of a procedural nature, which, however, appear in character outside the system of IHL. First, if these actions involve a foreign State an obstacle both on the merits and in the execution phase could be the principle of State immunity and in this respect doctrine and case law provide different solution. In addition, domestic courts, even those that explicitly recognise an individual right to reparation, have invoked the theory of the Act of State for refusing individual claims based on alleged violations of IHL once the national State was involved in such proceedings.[52] Finally, the possible existence of individual claims once there has been a peace treaty regulating war damages is still a debated issue.[53]

Moreover, further issues have been raised by current conflict scenarios about this mechanism. First, the actual extent of the obligation to reparation in the context of NIACs must still be assessed. The ICRC's study on Customary IHL affirms the existence of this obligation on States for violations committed during these conflicts too, but cases in which States have actually recognised reparation to victims are unfortunately episodic.[54] Especially in this case, the possibility that an action of reparation be carried out mainly depends on the will of the State concerned and on the possibility for individuals, mainly in post-conflict reconciliation processes, to rely on domestic legislation regulating such liability, which usually provides only partial reparation for victims. Moreover, it is clear that a possible role played by other States in the reparation process for breach of IHL obligations in NIACs, taking into account the *erga omnes* character of these rules, is purely theoretical at the moment.

Furthermore, difficulties in arranging reparation are of course almost insurmountable when dealing with the responsibility of organised armed groups. From an abstract point of view the obligation of reparation appears the necessary corollary of the assumption that these groups are bearers of IHL obligations and are therefore required to repair the effects of violations. However, it is virtually impossible to imagine that such liability may be enforced against them. As affirmed by the study on Customary IHL, 'the consequences of such responsibility are not clear'.[55] Nevertheless, the existence of such an obligation, even in the hands of these NSAs, has been confirmed in recent international practice,[56] and in order to avoid such difficulties it has been suggested resorting to trust funds based on international voluntary contributions aimed at compensating victims of crimes committed by NSAs[57] or, alternatively, such a duty has been fulfilled by the State concerned.[58] In this case, other mechanisms of accountability, largely unrelated to the IHL system, may provide a partial solution, as in relation to legal proceedings brought by victims in third States against organised armed groups and their leaders,[59] or mechanisms of compensation such as those provided by Art. 75 of the ICC Statute.[60]

In addition, the implementation of the obligation to reparation in post-conflict situations faces difficulties for various reasons, which go beyond legal aspects. First we can refer to economic, political and administrative difficulties which can hinder the fulfilment of this obligation. Second, particularly in NIACs, reparation could be considered as an obstacle to any peace process underway, as it necessarily implies the need to establish the facts complained of and to ascertain the responsibility of the individuals and armed groups involved.

However, these obstacles appear to be surreptitious in many cases. On the one hand, we can accept that, especially with regard to compensation, it is difficult to provide a detailed evaluation of any economic loss related to violations of IHL. The vast number of individuals involved and the actual economic difficulties faced by some States could be a relevant element in assessing such claims, as recently maintained by the Eritrea-Ethiopia Claims Commission.[61]

But nothing seems to prevent, for example, that other forms of reparation, in particular measures of satisfaction which do not involve substantial costs for States, may play an important role.[62] With regard to victims of violations and their families, it has been found that a primary purpose underlying their claims is the desire to establish the truth and related responsibilities, rather than obtaining economic benefit.[63] In addition, States could operate in accordance with well established mechanisms related to mass claims, according to positive experiences already provided in other sectors of international law.

Moreover, failure to comply with this obligation necessarily increases the perception of impunity for those responsible, thus causing a significant detriment to the entire IHL system of guarantees and serious repercussions in the development of an effective national reconciliation process. Finally, a potential supplementary role of the international community in this area should not be underestimated. As maintained in some UN documents, once the fulfilment of this obligation raises several difficulties, we can assume a greater involvement of other States or international organisations, for instance through the adoption of positive measures such as voluntary funds for the benefits of victims.[64]

In relation with other scenarios, the implementation of the obligation of reparation by other actors involved in contemporary armed conflicts remains largely unexplored. With regard to international organisations, problems may arise regarding the attribution of responsibility and practical means to implement this responsibility, especially by individuals directly affected by violations of IHL. Regarding these actors, some reference can only be identified in relation to norms regulating responsibility for peace-keeping missions, thus in a context in which the application of IHL is not at issue.[65] However, from a theoretical point of view, nothing seems to prevent that the issue of reparations for violations of *jus in bello* can also be raised in the future against international organisations.[66]

Similarly, the conduct of the PMCs could also introduce additional problems. On the one hand State responsibility could be raised, especially in relation with the contracting State, where we can ascertain that their unlawful activities can be attributed to it. On the other hand, but in this case we are mainly referring to the enforcement of domestic legislation, victims may introduce claims against the PMCs themselves in order to obtain redress. However, individuals face several difficulties in resorting to this mechanism.[67]

In conclusion, we must emphasise that even where this obligation of reparation can be applied it only exists in relation to activities violating IHL. This element implies that lawful acts of war, while also causing extensive damage and civilian casualties, are excluded from the application of this principle. This element may be perceived as an injustice and scholars have sometimes requested an extension in its application to take into account all victims of armed conflict, regardless of the nature of the events that led to injurious effects.[68] However, as correctly maintained by other authors, it is difficult to accept such proposals.[69] Such actions, while unfortunately causing collateral damage, did not violate any IHL rule and, ultimately, that solution would result in a disincentive for parties to the conflict to respect these norms. Indeed, such an approach would have the ultimate effect that almost any military action would raise such an obligation, without drawing the necessary distinction between lawful and unlawful actions as envisaged in Art. 91 I AP.

6. THE POSSIBILITY OF EMPLOYING MECHANISMS EXTERNAL TO THE IHL SYSTEM IN ORDER TO ENFORCE HUMANITARIAN VALUES

Following the analysis of mechanisms currently operating within the IHL system it is necessary to evaluate other opportunities which occur in other areas of international law to ensure enforcement. In particular, taking into account developments of recent decades, these can be traced to: the activities of international and national judicial and quasi-judicial bodies in relation to events related to an armed conflict; functions performed by international organisations; and recourse to customary international law.

6.1 Activities Conducted by International and National Bodies having Judicial or Quasi-judicial Functions

As far as action carried out by bodies having judicial or quasi-judicial functions is concerned, these organs present different characteristics, mainly based on the level, international or national, at which they operate and on the actors involved. Due to their nature, however, it is clear that, unless exceptional circumstances pertain, these mechanisms focus primarily on the ascertainment of alleged violations at the end of a conflict, without the possibility of providing a control while military operations are still in progress.

An initial reference can be made to international disputes involving States on issues relating to IHL. In this case a major role could be played by the International Court of Justice, but in practice this body has been involved only in a few cases.[70] The limited contribution of the ICJ to the enforcement of IHL is obviously related to its arbitral nature, which implies the necessity of recognising an appropriate title of jurisdiction. This element can greatly compress the action of the ICJ with respect to disputes relating to armed conflicts, as emphasised by the recent case of *Georgia v. Russia*. The *erga omnes* nature of IHL obligations has not had any influence over the jurisdiction of the Court, thus limiting the concrete role of this innovative characterisation of international obligations. In addition, enforcement of judgments of the Court, in the few cases relating to armed conflicts, has encountered great difficulty.

The advisory function of the Court presents similar limits. If the Court's contribution to the discipline was somewhat questionable in its opinion on the legality of nuclear weapons, a greater relevance can be attached to the *Wall* opinion in the definition of the law of occupation. However, given the non-binding nature usually recognised to such opinions, they mainly assume a theoretical value, given the difficulty of affecting the conduct of the States concerned.

States may also use ad hoc Claims Commissions to solve disputes concerning the application of IHL. However, this possibility seems exceptional, as in this case too we must first ascertain the willingness of States to submit the conduct of hostilities to a judicial scrutiny. Even if the ad hoc nature of these bodies, with the possibility for Parties to influence the selection of arbitrators, may represent an incentive in comparison with recourse to an external body such as the ICJ, it is not surprising that the only recent experience in this area is the Eritrea-Ethiopia Claims Commissions.

However, it is self-evident that the recent increased involvement of judicial or quasi-judicial bodies in IHL matters has mainly been determined through individual claims, particularly in the context of mechanisms created by human rights treaties.

At the international level this possibility has faced several difficulties. These claims, brought in front of human rights bodies, necessarily imply a reference to a parallel violation of human rights norms, thus raising well-known difficulties in the relationship between this branch and IHL. In addition, other elements peculiar to human rights treaties can add further obstacles in resorting to these mechanisms for introducing complaints related to unlawful events that occurred in an armed conflict. This is especially the case in divergent views within human rights bodies on the possibility of guaranteeing extra-territorial application of human rights treaties.[71] If this element does not assume specific importance in relation to traditional NIACs, its relevance is evident in order to introduce a system of scrutiny over alleged violations related to international armed conflicts or the so-called multi-national NIACs.

A review of armed conflicts involving contracting States could also be carried out through the exam of periodic reports. This mechanism, for its intrinsic characteristics, is certainly a milder instrument than judicial investigation. This evaluation is reflected in the few concluding comments made by some of these bodies, in which we can find, at most, general references to States as to respect for IHL or some specific provisions.[72] However, the presence of such references does not follow a uniform approach, since only a small number of States engaged in armed conflicts have been addressed with these requests and not all human rights bodies have acted in such way. Moreover, even in these cases, doubts could be raised as to the competence of these bodies to make specific references to IHL rules.

In any case, as a significant novelty, we can emphasise that, at least in the Inter-American system, the mechanism of periodic reports has also been used to carry out an analysis with respect to the conduct of organised armed groups involved in NIACs.[73] While this approach is still isolated, it is particularly significant taking into account the current lack of appropriate IHL control mechanisms in relation to that type of armed conflict and those actors. However, while this instrument can bring inter-national attention to such conduct, the implicit risk is a lack of practical impact of this mechanism of control over organised armed groups under review.

The increasing relevance of issues related to armed conflicts within human rights treaty bodies is still not without difficulties. On the one hand, in many cases, there could be claims of a possible lack of competence on the part of these bodies in referring to IHL rules in the analysis conducted, as the legal basis of their activities is usually limited to application of human rights treaties. Secondly, if their monitoring activities are carried out on the basis of human rights standards, it is necessary to find a balance between exigencies and principles of these two branches of international law. In some areas there could be difficulties of interpretation, which can lead to legal uncertainty. Until now, these contrasts have not concretely appeared. Cases examined by human rights bodies were in clear violation both of IHL and human rights standards, but in the future several difficulties in interpretation could arise.

To this end, some have claimed the need to facilitate a better understanding of the paradigms of IHL by members of human rights bodies, which, in many cases, do not have a specific background in this area. If this criticism is probably too severe, this difficulty can still be overcome with innovative approaches, such as joint consultations between these bodies and actors institutionally involved in IHL, such as the ICRC. In any case, apart from some difficulties, it is clear that these monitoring mechanisms may exert a positive influence in promoting the development of a 'judicial process' related to armed conflicts. In addition, these instruments emphasise one of the recent trends in the enforcement of IHL recalled above, that is, the enhanced role of the individual in this area. It is clear that without action taken by individuals before these bodies, it would be hard to ascertain and enforce State responsibility with respect to situations which are not only violations of human rights, but also contrary to basic standards of IHL. In fact States have resorted to human rights mechanism of inter-State complaints in very few occasions related to an armed conflict, mainly in cases in which they were directly involved in the hostilities at issue.[74]

Another possibility to ensure the enforcement of IHL by instruments external to this system can be identified by mechanisms operating at the national level.

First, we can refer to independent monitoring bodies, especially those that can operate on the basis of allegations introduced by individuals, in States involved in an armed conflict. Recently, the most significant experience has been provided by the Afghanistan Independent Human Rights Commission. This body has developed monitoring activities on hostilities carried out in that country through fact-finding missions and, on the basis of conclusions claiming violations of IHL, has established a constructive dialogue with high-level military and legal organs of international missions located in Afghanistan.[75] Despite the fact that this organ does not have a judicial or quasi-judicial function, its activity is still significant, especially since it operates in the context of an NIAC.

In any case, at the domestic level, a greater chance of developing a control on compliance with IHL is provided by the introduction of individual claims before national tribunals challenging State responsibility for wrongful activities that occurred during an armed conflict. Although similar examples could be observed in the past, it is self-evident that in recent years there has been a growing involvement of national courts in the judicial review of war conducts, also through a reference to parallel violations of human rights standards.[76] This phenomenon is strictly linked with the above analysed attempt to affirm an individual right to reparation for violations of IHL. It represents a significant change from the classic framework provided by this system, where the role of national judges was limited to the repression of war crimes.

However, this involvement is not easy to achieve and several difficulties can be observed, such as: the limit of State immunity; the invocation of the doctrine of Act of State for denying a legal review of military operations;[77] the refusal to apply relevant legal principles to the merit of the case, claiming the exhausted relevance of questions at issue due to cessation of hostilities in the area,[78] etc. Finally, the lack of recognition of an individual right to reparation for violations of IHL has prevented consideration on the merits of several cases.

6.2   Activities Performed by International Organisations in this Area and the Residual Role of Customary Law to Enforce IHL

Other ways to ensure the enforcement of IHL are provided by the activities of international organisations. The role of these subjects in this area has grown significantly, overcoming occasional references made to them in IHL treaties, such as Art. 89 I AP, which, moreover, formally implies their involvement only in relation with international armed conflicts. On the contrary, practice developed by international organisations shows their pervasive role in any kind of armed conflict, and through this joint action in international fora, States seem to concretely implement the obligation of ensuring respect for IHL, as provided in common Art. 1 GCs. Beyond possible actions that international organisations can adopt prior to armed conflicts, especially through promotional activities in the respect of IHL, the most significant contributions relate to monitoring activities in ongoing conflicts or repressive measures on violations which have already occurred.

Obviously, the international organisation most involved in this area can be identified in the United Nations through the various functions performed by its bodies. First, the SC has taken several actions, as violations of IHL have been considered as possible causes of further deterioration of international security.[79] In addition to developing mechanisms devoted to monitoring or analysing in-depth specific IHL issues, for example with regard to child soldiers or the protection of civilians in armed conflict, the SC has carried out relevant activities on ongoing hostilities. However, this action has been primarily taken through non-binding resolutions, merely inviting parties to the conflict to respect IHL or to implement specific obligations.[80] In some circumstances, nevertheless, the SC has adopted more concrete actions, providing, for instance, assistance to victims of conflict and access to humanitarian corridors or the creation of protected areas.

The response to violations of IHL has been particularly significant, characterised by the establishment of independent Commissions of inquiry on violations of IHL and human rights during armed conflicts. In some cases these have represented a first step towards the creation of international criminal tribunals[81] or the referral of such situations to the ICC.[82] A recent significant development has occurred on 'smart sanctions' regimes imposed by the SC on military and political elites. In fact, among criteria identified by this organ for the inclusion of individuals in lists elaborated by the Committees for sanctions, we can also record an express reference to serious violations of IHL,[83] even if the workability of these measures faces several obstacles.

These complex initiatives have certainly contributed to the enforcement of IHL, and, moreover, have permitted the development of a particular focus on NIACs, where IHL guarantee mechanisms are less developed. However, even the action of the SC is not free from concern. On the one hand, in relation with non-binding resolutions, the attitude of the parties to the conflict is still crucial to implement requests made by the SC, and, in cases of failure, subsequent actions have only been adopted on a few occasions, and, even in such cases, their realisation involved a close cooperation by Member States. Second, since evaluations of ongoing conflicts made by this organ can also include elements of *jus ad bellum*, there is a risk that the SC would not follow a basic principle of IHL, that is, equality among actors involved in hostilities, while adopting measures bearing on this system.[84] Finally, as a general limit, it is clear that the SC's activities have been selective with respect to conflicts which have arisen in the last decades. This conduct can be explained by the political-diplomatic limits of this body, with the additional consequence that it is essentially paralysed when one of the permanent members is involved in the armed conflict.

Of course, other UN organs have been involved in activities relevant for IHL, although to a lesser extent. For example, the Secretary-General has been asked to collaborate with the SC in this area, and is obviously a primary point of reference for humanitarian activities,[85] while the contribution provided by the ICJ has been examined above. Similarly, the General Assembly (GA) drew attention to compliance with IHL by the end of the 1960s, with periodic resolutions relating to general topics,[86] or through resolutions condemning violations which occurred in specific conflicts.[87] However, the overall limit for the GA lies both in the non-binding value of its resolutions and in political considerations that sometimes dictate its agenda.

Among subsidiary organs of the GA, the main role in the enforcement of IHL is definitely attributed to the Human Rights Council, which has increased the activities performed by the former Commission on this matter. Although the main focus of this body remains human rights law, as IHL assumes a secondary role, the Commission and the Council have significantly increased references to this discipline in recent years. Explicit mentions to IHL are included in several Special Procedures, as numerous thematic[88] or 'country'[89] mandates led to an examination of the IHL issue, also with regard to activities carried out by NSAs. However, thematic mandates meet the limitation of being directed only to specific issues of interest for IHL. Similarly, in the majority of monitoring activities related to a specific State, beyond the selectivity of this choice, we can usually notice generic references to IHL. This activity has also implied a review of specific armed conflicts, both international and non-international, through the establishment of special sessions,[90] independent commissions of inquiry also responsible for monitoring compliance with IHL,[91] and resolutions condemning violations of IHL rules and aiming to obtain respect for these provisions.[92] An important contribution could be provided through the Universal Periodic Review (UPR) mechanism, since the resolution establishing this instrument expressly gives the Council the mandate to examine the State over its obligations concerning IHL.[93]

However, activities of the Commission and Council in relation to IHL face several difficulties. The non-binding action of the Council should be noted as basic, which can ultimately only provide a public denunciation of violations. In many cases, even if findings have emphasised serious violations, there has not been a subsequent appropriate action by other UN bodies, particularly the SC.[94] In addition, specific problems arise about its action in the field of IHL.

First of all, opposition expressed by some States on the possibility of developing specific monitoring activities on IHL are notorious, since references to this area have been considered as going beyond the mandate granted to this body. This trend, already emphasised in the context of some special procedures,[95] has found further expression during the UPR, notwithstanding express reference to IHL in its mandate.[96] Moreover, the nature of the Council, as a body of States, has a significant impact on its activity, since this forum can sometimes appear to be politically oriented, with a specific interest only in certain conflicts, without any consideration for equally serious situations.

This latter limit could perhaps be overcome through a more effective use of the URP, which allows a periodic assessment for all Member States. However, this new instrument shows some limitations in relation with IHL. First, its diplomatic-political nature, aimed at creating a constructive dialogue among States, could affect the possibility to ensure a substantive examination of these issues. This element is reflected in the rather general character of observations proposed by other States during the examination process. These statements are characterised by general invitations to ensure compliance with IHL, without a detailed examination of specific allegations of non compliance.[97] Furthermore, the analysis of a State's situation, which takes place every four years, may not coincide with its involvement in armed conflicts, thus limiting the scope of this control mechanism. In addition, possible action in this area by NGOs does not appear as particularly relevant. While these organisations have been entitled to submit their comments on the State under examination, they have devoted little attention to IHL, preferring to concentrate on violations of human rights law, obviously because of an overriding thematic interest.

Other international organisations, especially having a regional character, have also been involved in the discussion of issues relating to IHL, with a growing interest in recent years.

For example, you can refer to the EU, particularly to its political and diplomatic action towards third States. This activity has resulted in the creation of commissions of inquiry on past conflicts, even being competent to investigate violations of IHL,[98] and the adoption of soft-law documents aiming to develop operational tools for the EU and its institutions in order to favour implementation of IHL by third parties, providing mechanisms of reporting, dissemination and monitoring of IHL.[99] However, even with respect to these instruments, there is still uncertainty as to the actual practical extent of such documents regarding the definition of EU policies. These activities are still embryonic, with the need for greater integration of IHL into the EU system. For instance, the system of special generalised preferences, under Regulation (EC) 732/2008 – which provides favourable tariff concessions to those countries that meet a series of international standards referring to human rights, environment and workers' rights – does not mention IHL. This inclusion would ensure the disposal of an additional pressure mechanism toward third parties, which has already found its first operational applications.[100]

Beyond these activities, more opportunities could be offered by general international law. The *erga omnes* nature of IHL obligations may in fact create more opportunities for States in case of violations. However, as shown by solutions adopted by the ILC on the subject, it is difficult to define actions that States not directly affected by violations may take, especially given the uncertainty about the possibility to resort to unilateral countermeasures.

6.3   An Evaluation of the Effectiveness of these External Mechanisms in Providing Enforcement for IHL

Ultimately, this set of guarantee mechanisms, alien to the IHL system, provides a highly fragmented scenario, with respect to which it is difficult to identify common trends. In many cases these possible developments affect only certain geographic areas, or this action is characterised by a political-diplomatic nature, mainly expressed with soft-law documents with respect to which it is difficult to understand the concrete relevance for parties to the conflict. At the same time, in relation to the more solid opportunities provided by these additional mechanisms, the predominant role of States for the enforcement of IHL reappears in many cases. Even in these areas, therefore, political and diplomatic limits may recur, thus being able to inhibit actions of a humanitarian nature. Furthermore, the specific focus of many of these bodies on human rights, leads to a significant compression of the autonomous relevance of IHL in the evaluation of conduct relating to armed conflict, as often there are only general references to these rules or we can identify possible difficulties in coordinating these two branches. Finally, even if they also operate in relation with NIACs, these mechanisms face several limits to providing control over the unlawful conduct of NSAs.

Nevertheless, there is no doubt that these instruments provide an additional contribution towards raising awareness in respect for IHL in the international community, and have the advantage of permitting the overriding of the necessity to obtain the consent of parties to the conflict for their implementation, a typical limit for several IHL enforcement instruments. In addition, many of these mechanisms confirm some of the recent trends in the enforcement of IHL. First, these mechanisms have partly contributed to reducing gaps in the current system of IHL, particularly in relation to the area in which we can notice the most difficulties, that is, NIACs. Secondly, some of these instruments reaffirm the growing role of the individual in activating such guarantees.

Ultimately, these different mechanisms, though hardly conclusive when considered individually, can undoubtedly contribute to the enforcement of IHL and it is without doubt that in future scenarios we will observe an increasing role for instruments alien to the IHL system.

7. CONCLUSIONS: IS THERE A NEED FOR NEW MECHANISMS TO IMPLEMENT IHL?

The analysis carried out in the previous paragraphs has demonstrated both the limits of the existing implementation mechanisms of IHL and the difficulties in achieving the goal through recourse to external instruments, which, while useful, will only provide occasional interventions in relation with the numerous contemporary armed conflicts. This framework therefore implies the need to analyse, with a *de lege ferenda* approach, the possibility of developing new tools within the IHL system aiming to guarantee a better implementation of relevant provisions also taking into account such external experiences. On this point, after examining the various options that may exist, it would be necessary to make conclusive assessments of the real feasibility of developing such innovations.

Concerning the creation of new tools in the IHL system to support the implementation phase, it can be said that, currently, the most commonly discussed proposal among scholars is the creation of a permanent body devoted to this purpose, which could be an IHL Commission.[101] However, regarding the character of this body, also suggested in the past projects of the UN reform,[102] there remains deep uncertainty and divergence of views as to its nature and functions, given the possibility of suggesting very different solutions, which can have relevant effects on any subsequent capacity to act.

In essence the main purpose of this body would be to fill the gaps of current IHL guarantee mechanisms, introducing in a uniform manner within this system some of the functions carried out by monitoring bodies operating in other areas of international law, especially in the human rights field, thus also reducing the risks of fragmentation. In this way, therefore, the IHL system would adopt some of the best practices on implementation and enforcement of international rules provided by parallel experiences.

Concerning the creation of this body, several possibilities could be envisaged. On the one hand, resorting to a diplomatic conference, it could be possible to adopt a fourth additional Protocol to the Geneva Conventions or an ad hoc treaty. This solution, however, might reduce the possible concrete relevance of the IHL Commission. It is easily conceivable that only a small group of like-minded States would initially be involved in this treaty, thus making the Commission inoperative in relation to States most directly affected by armed conflicts. On the other hand, the converse solution would be to include this Commission within the UN system, as a subsidiary body of the UN General Assembly or the Human Rights Council. However, this approach, while it would facilitate the universal character of its action, would almost certainly be counterbalanced by the assignment of reduced powers and by the characterisation of this body as a diplomatic forum, thus undermining the effectiveness of its action.

As for the mandate, various hypotheses can be envisaged. First, as to applicable law, this could be identified in international treaties binding on parties to the conflict. However, a reference to customary law is also necessary, even if this inclusion might raise obvious difficulties in interpretation. In fact, this reference as to the mandate appears necessary in light of the evolution of IHL in this area, through the development of substantive rules which have a relevant impact on applicable law, mainly in relation with NIACs. Moreover, it also permits a better evaluation of activities carried out by NSAs, a fundamental aspect to be taken into account in order to render this body effective.

Concerning control functions, the best solution would obviously be to attribute a broad spectrum of activities to the IHL Commission, in order to fill existing gaps in the system. However, of course, each of these possibilities is not easy to achieve.

For example, this body could represent the forum, now absent, in which to present and discuss periodic reports on the implementation of IHL rules.[103] In this regard, therefore, a primary function would be the analysis of measures to be adopted in peacetime. However, as identified above, difficulties already experienced in other fields in carrying out the reporting duty could replicate themselves in the IHL system. It is easy to imagine that delays and shortcomings in the preparation of reports can also occur in this area, and, moreover, we should also assess the usual modest impact on subsequent state practice of concluding observations and recommendations made by monitoring bodies, given the mild nature of this mechanism of control.

Equally, taking into account the highlighted difficulties in activating the International Fact-finding Commission, the IHL Commission could develop an observation or fact-finding mechanism operating during armed conflicts or in relation to past hostilities. Even in this case, however, the feasibility of assessment, from an abstract point of view, of possible difficulties that this body could face in carrying out this mandate, especially during ongoing armed conflicts remains uncertain.

In fact, the effective functioning of this control mechanism requires the active cooperation and confidence of parties to the conflict, given the need to operate in the war theatre. On the contrary, especially in light of recent experience, the possibility that this activity could be perceived as politically-oriented, so as to induce actors involved in hostilities to deny their partnership to the Commission, is evident. However, the Commission could avoid basing this control function solely on ad hoc consent provided by parties to the conflict. This limitation would condemn this body to a forced inactivity as is the case for the current International Fact-Finding Commission. The founding instrument should therefore provide the IHL Commission with a general capacity to act in the presence of complaints of violations raised by one of the actors involved in the hostilities or, even better, by any of the parties to the treaty creating the IHL Commission or any UN Member States if it is to operate within this organisation. In these latter cases, in order to avoid possible political tensions, especially in the face of debated issues, it would be better to operate on a confidential basis, at least during the initial phases of its activities.

Finally, from an abstract point of view nothing seems to impede the extension to the IHL system of an additional function usually entrusted to human rights monitoring bodies, that is, the establishment of a complaints mechanism. Regarding this possibility, however, a set of key variables should be better defined. In particular it is necessary to identify: entities entitled to trigger the mechanism; powers pertaining to the IHL Commission in this area, with the possibility of developing judicial or quasi-judicial evaluations, for example through the adoption of binding decisions or mere recommendations; the possibility of imposing or recommending reparation measures; and the role and access of victims and parties to the conflict to such a mechanism, through, in particular, the creation of an individual right to petition.[104]

Moreover, if the final aim of the IHL Commission is to fill gaps currently existing in the IHL system, taking into account the reality of contemporary armed conflicts, it is necessary to define the role of NSAs in this regard. In the optimal scenario, NSAs should be involved in respect of all the possible tasks potentially attributable to this body.

First, this case may refer to possible war activities conducted under the command and control of an international organisation. It has been demonstrated above that the State-centric system of guarantees established by IHL does not provide specific instruments for the implementation and enforcement of these rules in respect of international organisations actively involved in hostilities. Therefore, the IHL Commission could represent an appropriate forum to intervene in respect of gaps currently existing for these peculiar NSAs, avoiding the repetition in this area of similar problems which have already occurred in other sectors of international law. In fact, in several instances, efficient control mechanisms operating against international organisations do not exist and victims of internationally wrongful acts attributable to these NSAs do not dispose of appropriate instruments in order to obtain remedies.

The nature of international organisations does not seem to preclude, *inter alia*, the establishment of control mechanisms outlined above. In fact, some of these instruments have already been operative in relation with similar contexts. For instance, with regard to the obligation of providing periodic reports on compliance measures adopted to enforce international standards, it is sufficient to make reference to reports submitted by UNMIK to human rights monitoring bodies established by conventions to which Serbia was bound.[105] Similarly, as the possible subjection of an international organisation to an individual complaints procedure, you may take into account the proposed accession of the EU to the ECHR, which presumably will lead to this possibility in front of the European Court of Human Rights (ECtHR).

However, given the present international scenario, in which it is difficult to detect an active participation of international organisations in hostilities, it is clear that the main area of interest for the proposed IHL Commission is the possible involvement in its activities of organised armed groups operating in NIACs. Taking into account an abstract and optimal model, it would be necessary, therefore, at least with regard to groups that meet certain minimal requirements, to ensure their participation in the reporting, fact-finding and complaint procedures.

At the same time, from the outset, material and political difficulties in extending control mechanisms designed with reference to States with respect to such non-state actors are obvious. The principal problems concern, for example: the intrinsic 'provisional' characters of such NSAs in the international arena; difficulties in enforcing any measures required against them; and modalities to realise their involvement and their representation in the various procedures.

Furthermore, the problem of creating incentives for the participation of these groups within these control mechanisms ought to be resolved. In fact, it is difficult to imagine that these procedures may only operate in one direction, thus only aiming to monitor possible violations attributable to organised armed groups. The failure of such an approach would be immediate. Therefore it would be necessary to ensure that non-state entities can rely on procedures exercised by the IHL Commission, in particular being able to autonomously activate fact-finding mechanisms and complaint procedures.

This body should provide legal symmetry between the parties to a conflict, thus also reflecting, at the implementation level, the situation existing in relation to the application of substantive rules. In this way, therefore, it would be possible to guarantee a basic principle of IHL, that is, the necessity to maintain equality among belligerents. In this manner, among other things, it would also be possible to realise, even at the level of guarantees, the progressive rapprochement between the systems provided in international and non-international armed conflict, which can be considered as one of the main relevant developments of recent decades.

Nevertheless, also in this case, material difficulties are immediately apparent, given, for example, the uncertainty regarding the concrete possibility of such groups to adhere and participate in these procedures and the difficulties in identifying individuals entitled to represent these non-state entities.[106] These procedural difficulties, however, do not appear insurmountable. For example, if Art. 96 I AP empowers representatives of national liberation movements engaged in an IAC to provide a unilateral declaration of acceptance of this instrument, it does not seem impossible to imagine the application of similar tools, referred to the implementation phase, for organised armed groups operating in NIACs, as structural features are not particularly divergent between these entities. Moreover, similar procedures of adhesion to international standards by organised armed groups have already been experienced for NSAs in relation to the Deed of Commitment proposed by Geneva Call.

However, apart from the IHL Commission, other options for facilitating the implementation of IHL rules could be explored. For example, especially if a less extensive mandate is attributed to such a body, excluding individual complaint procedures or avoiding a general obligation of periodic reports, thus limiting its function to an overall control on some ongoing conflicts, it is clear that this body will mostly mirror, within the IHL system, activities carried out by the HR Council. In this case, it would be more feasible to create such a Commission within the UN system, as a parallel body of the Human Rights Council or as a subsidiary organ of the latter, as is currently the case for the Advisory Committee.

In this context, this body would mainly represent a permanent forum for discussing issues pertaining to IHL, also through the appointment of working groups of independent experts, or for conducting fact-finding missions. In this case, it is conceivable, however, that limits currently faced by the Human Rights Council, such as risk of politicisation and selectivity in evaluations and in the choice of issues to analyse, could be renewed within this new body, taking into account its possible diplomatic nature. Similarly, the establishment of a subsidiary body to the Human Rights Council made up of independent experts, such as the current Advisory Committee, could have a modest impact, bearing in mind the very limited mandate and autonomy of this latter organ.

In any case, these last hypotheses, based on the attribution of modest functions of this body, imply the need to evaluate the concrete impact and innovation that this proposed organ would have in the IHL system. In fact there is the risk that such minimal proposals would not particularly improve the IHL implementation mechanism. For instance, it is clear that certain tasks attributed to this body would not introduce specific novelty with respect to existing mechanisms, except perhaps for a greater frequency in the exercise of these functions. If one of its main activities could result in the analysis and discussion of problems pertaining to the application of IHL, this duty would not be particularly different from similar activities already conducted in this area, mainly through the International Red Cross Movement, with the risk of introducing political evaluations in the assessments of current conflicts.

Similarly, one could envisage the creation of an independent expert body, such as a High Commissioner for IHL. However, this proposal is not likely to significantly modify current gaps in the implementation phase. On the one hand if that body mirrors the current model provided by the High Commissioner for HR, it would hardly improve the IHL system, as it will mainly have purely promotional functions in respect of these rights. Moreover, its activities would represent, in many respects, a substantial duplication of the mandate already given to the ICRC in this system, without even disposing of the punctual legal basis and possibilities that the ICRC can claim on the basis of the Geneva Conventions or the Statute of the International Movement.

Nonetheless, any proposals aimed at creating new IHL bodies devoted to the implementation phase have a common obvious limitation. As noted above, what clearly emerges from an analysis of current enforcement mechanisms already in force in the

IHL system is not so much the absolute deficiency of appropriate procedures to ensure this objective, but rather the absence of political will, especially by States, to activate and provide existing mechanisms with concrete substance.[107] This scenario, in our opinion, would hardly change, even if innovative mechanisms, such as the IHL Commission, were established.

Moreover, as a basic pre-condition, it is necessary to identify a specific willingness among States to create such new bodies, whether resorting to an ad hoc treaty or through the incorporation of such mechanisms within the UN system. In essence, given the current historical moment, in which it is even difficult to affirm basic substantive IHL rules, it is uncertain whether it is possible to find the appropriate political will among States to establish innovative instruments aimed at improving the control phase. Even if it were possible to identify such common consent, States could still reduce the relevance of such bodies, compressing their functions and limiting the role and involvement of victims of violations and NSAs, such as organised armed groups.

However, at the same time, it is clear that developing new mechanisms without taking into account these latter issues, thus not imputing relevance to concrete characteristics of contemporary armed conflicts and current gaps in the IHL system, would result in a vain and unproductive effort. Currently, the most pressing exigency for the implementation of IHL is the need to expand possibilities of action with regard to some peculiar actors and scenarios. First, we are referring to non-state actors, considered as comprising both individual victims of violations of IHL and active parties to conflicts. Secondly, there is an impellent necessity to improve these mechanisms in relation with NIACs, both taking into account their quantitative predominance in the international arena and a substantial lack of instruments currently available in the IHL system.

However, it is probable that States could disagree on these novelties, given the perception of such new instruments as providing potential international legitimacy for organised armed groups. In addition, States may highlight the risk that these mechanisms can be manipulated by these actors in order to attract the attention of the international community on a given conflict. Finally, States will likely emphasise the difficulties in accepting to subject the conduct of hostilities to an international scrutiny also open to non-state actors and direct victims of violations, thus abandoning the State-centred approach which characterises several IHL implementation mechanisms currently in force.

In conclusion, in order to improve the guarantees of the IHL system, the adoption of a number of coordinated actions appear desirable. On the one hand, with regard to current mechanisms, the extension to areas other than those originally envisaged or possible modifications in regard to their mechanisms of activation appear necessary to overcome the distortions already emphasised. Secondly, the establishment of innovative instruments and bodies within the IHL system would be equally useful. As noted above, these developments will require radical action as it is difficult to incorporate these developments in existing mechanisms. Thus, the most effective way would probably result in the creation of ad hoc bodies devoted to performing such additional functions, such as an IHL Commission or similar organisms. As already emphasised by the UN Secretary-General in 1970, however, 'these measures should be regarded as complementary to what already exists rather than competitive'.[108] Their main function therefore would result in filling the main gaps existing in the IHL system, rather than aiming to substitute, in a radical way, existing instruments, which, on the contrary, could play a relevant role for the implementation of IHL rules once activated.

However, the feasibility of these innovations remains deeply uncertain. For this reason we believe that in the near future, the above-mentioned control mechanisms external to the IHL system, developed as a substitute in the face of the inability of the system to self-reform and address increasingly shortcomings, will not lose their relevance. On the contrary, even if additional instruments are developed in the IHL system, other possibilities now present in the international scene are unlikely to be abandoned. These, in fact, are operating autonomously from the IHL system and provide further instruments to guarantee the enforcement of these rules, and, moreover, they shall remain available for stakeholders independently of any innovation characterising this body of law.

Consequently, any possibility to establish new mechanisms for implementing IHL rules is subject to the capacity of identifying a common political and diplomatic consent in the international community. This would primarily occur through activities conducted by a group of like-minded States, which could realise some of the above-mentioned proposals, as was the case for some recent relevant examples such as the ICC or the Ottawa Convention. On the one hand, this action would represent a first base in view of later and more numerous accessions. On the other hand, this solution would contribute to emphasising in the international agenda the need to improve the implementation phase. In this case, the most appropriate instrument could be identified in the elaboration of an international treaty.

Even this option, however, is likely to encounter difficulties. Firstly it could be possible to predict actions carried out by some States participating in the Diplomatic Conference aiming to reduce the impact of the proposed convention, even if later they would not be interested in ratifying the proposed instrument, as experienced in relation to the ICC. Secondly, the risk of elaborating an ad hoc treaty lies in the subsequent difficulty to reach a universal membership, with the self-exclusion of States most directly affected by armed conflicts. Therefore, in order to achieve the goal of a progressive development of the IHL system in this regard, it seems necessary to obtain a strong support from civil society, through lobbying activities at national and international levels.

However, before putting the final full stop to this chapter, we wish to observe that, in dealing with the subject of guarantees, every pessimistic attitude should be set aside. In IHL, a system lacking a central institution, factors granting effectiveness run at various levels and implicate the action of as many subjects of the community as possible. In this way every factor – although modest when considered singly – working together with all other factors, each at its own different level, could nevertheless produce an acceptable standard of observance of substantive rules. Moreover, it is also true that alongside violations, even though grave, everyday fulfilment of IHL also exists, a fact not constituting news.

NOTES

*   Paolo Benvenuti is Professor of International Law at the University Roma Tre (Italy). Dr Giulio Bartolini is Researcher at the Law Faculty of the University Roma Tre (Italy). Paolo Benvenuti is author of paras 1, 2, 3, 3.1, 4.1–4.5, 5.1 and 5.2. Giulio Bartolini is author of paras 3.2–3.5, 4.6, 5.3, 6 and 7.

1.   L. Condorelli and L. Boisson de Chazournes, 'Quelques remarques à propos de l'obligation des Etats de "respecter et faire respecter" le droit international humanitaire "en toutes circonstances"', in *Studies and Essays on International Humanitarian Law and Red Cross Principles in Honour of Jean Pictet*, ed. C. Swinarski (The Hague: Martinus Nijhoff, 1984), 17 ff.

2.   M. Sassòli, 'The Implementation of International Humanitarian Law: Current and Inherent Challenges', *Yearbook of International Humanitarian Law* 10 (2007): 59–60.

3.   For instance, in relation to cases of non-compliance with the obligation to destroy stockpiled anti-personnel landmines, see Second Review Conference of the States Parties to the Convention on the Prohibition of the Use, Stockpiling, Production and Transfer of Anti-Personnel Mines and on Their Destruction, 'Final Report', 17 June 2010, APLC/CONF/2009/9, 18–27.

4.   See UK Ministry of Defence, *The Manual of the Law of Armed Conflict* (Oxford: Oxford University Press, 2004), 412.

5.   For some positive assessments of technological and targeting improvements on the use of air-delivered cluster munitions by Western States during the 2003 Gulf War, see Human Rights Watch, 'Off Targets: The Conduct of the War and Civilian Casualties in Iraq' (2003), available at: http://www.hrw.org/en/node/12207/section/2 (accessed 15 November 2010).

6.   Israel Ministry of Foreign Affairs, 'Gaza Operation Investigations: Second Update, July 2010', 32–33, available at: http://www.mfa.gov.il/NR/rdonlyres/1483B296-7439-4217-933C-653CD19CE859/0/Gaza UpdateJuly2010.pdf (accessed 15 November 2010).

7.   See 'Proposals by the International Committee of the Red Cross, Special Rapporteur at the International Conference for the Protection of War Victims (Geneva, 1993)', *International Review of the Red Cross* 304 (1995): 25–27.

8.   T. Pfanner, 'Various Mechanisms and Approaches for Implementing International Humanitarian Law and Protecting and Assisting War Victims', *International Review of the Red Cross* 874 (2009): 307.

9.   Second Review Conference, 'Final Report', 11: 'Non-compliance with the obligation to destroy stockpiled anti-personnel mines is a grave concern for the States Parties.'

10.   The reference can only go, by way of example, to the activity carried out in the area of: child soldiers; anti-personnel landmines; cluster munitions and the International Criminal Court.

11.   See, for instance, Article 6, para. 11 of the Convention on cluster munitions: 'Each State Party may, with the purpose of developing a national action plan, request … non-governmental institutions to assist its authorities to determine … .' Similar provisions are included in Article 6, para. 2, 7 of the latter Convention; Article 6, paras 3, 4, 7 of the Ottawa Convention; Article 30, para. 3(b) of the 1999 Second Protocol to the 1954 Hague Convention.

12.   See, for instance, Article 11, para. 3 and Article 12, para. 3 of the Oslo Convention and Article 11, para. 4 and Article 12, para. 3 of the Ottawa Convention.

13.   See, for instance, Article 23 of the 1954 Hague Convention.

14.   'Updated European Union Guidelines on Promoting Compliance with IHL', *Official Journal of the European Union*, C 303 (15 December 2009): 12–15.

15.   This motivation seems provided by the above-mentioned Updated EU Guidelines. According to its paragraph 2, 'Whilst the same commitment extends to measures taken by the EU and its Member States to ensure compliance with IHL in their own conduct, including by their own forces, such measures are not covered by these Guidelines' and its note 2 specifies that '[a]ll EU Member States are Parties to the Geneva Conventions and their Additional Protocols and thus under the obligation to abide by their rules'.

16.   For instance, in relation to EU missions, we can record the participation of non-EU countries, such as Albania, Argentina, Morocco, Russia and Turkey.

17.   See, J.-M. Henckaerts and L. Doswald-Beck, *Customary International Humanitarian Law*, Vol. I: Rules (Cambridge: Cambridge University Press, 2005), 503; K. Dörmann, 'Dissemination and Monitoring Compliance of International Humanitarian Law', in *International Law Facing New Challenges: Symposium in Honour of Knut Ipsen*, eds W.H. von Heinegg and V. Epping (Berlin: Springer, 2007), 230; Pfanner, *supra* note 8, at 283.

18. Dörmann, *supra* note 17, at 229.
19. See Section 3 of the 1999 UN Secretary-General's Bulletin; Model Agreement between the United Nations and Member States Contributing Personnel and Equipment to United Nations Peace-keeping Operations, 23 May 23 1991, UN Doc. A/46/185, para. 28: 'The [Participating State] shall therefore ensure that the members of its national contingent serving with [the United Nations peace-keeping operation] be fully acquainted with the principles and spirit of these Conventions.'
20. S/RES/1756, 15 May 2007, para. 2.
21. See Article 19, II Additional Protocol and Rule 142 of the International Committee of the Red Cross's study on Customary IHL.
22. See, Henckaerts and Doswald-Beck, *supra* note 17, at 505; Churchill Ewumbue-Monomo, 'Respect for International Humanitarian Law by Armed Non-State Actors in Africa', *International Review of the Red Cross* 864 (2006): 918.
23. According to data provided by Blackwater, 30 per cent of its employees do not have previous military training (see, M. Schmitt, 'Humanitarian Law and Direct Participation in Hostilities by Private Contractors or Civilian Employees', *Chicago Journal of International Law* 5 (2005): 515).
24. The Montreux Document on Pertinent International Legal Obligations and Good Practices or States related to Operations of Private Military and Security Companies during Armed Conflicts (2008), 11, para. 3.
25. US DoD Directive 2311.01E, 'DoD Law of War Program', 9 May 2006, para. 5.7.4.
26. See L.A. Dickinson, 'Testimony before the United States Senate Committee on Homeland Security and Governmental Affairs', 27 February 2008, 7.8, available at: http://www.hsgac.senate.gov/ [search on Dickinson] (accessed 15 November 2010).
27. See International Stability Operations Association, Code of Conduct (Version 12), 11 February 2009, para. 6.1.1, available at: http://www.stability-operations.org/index.php (accessed 15 November 2010). In the Preamble there are references to relevant IHL instruments, such as the Geneva Conventions and Protocols, the Convention on chemical weapons and also the Montreux Document. See B. Perrin, 'Promoting Compliance of Private Security and Military Companies with International Humanitarian Law', *International Review of the Red Cross* 863 (2006): 633–635.
28. *Prosecutor v. Hadsihasanovich et al.*, ICTY, Appeals Chamber, Decision on Interlocutory Appeal Challenging Jurisdiction in relation to Command Responsibility, 16 July 2003 (Case No. IT-01-47-AR72).
29. International Committee of the Red Cross, 'Improving Compliance with International Humanitarian Law. ICRC Expert Seminars' (Geneva: International Committee of the Red Cross, October 2003), 10–12, available at: http://www.icrc.org/eng/assets/files/other/improving_compliance_with_ihl-oct_2003.pdf (accessed 15 November 2010).

    In particular, the ICRC document refers to: (1) improving knowledge of the utility of Protecting Powers; (2) establishing a list of neutral States willing and able to take on the role of Protecting Powers; (3) suggesting the appointment of a single Protecting Power common to all Parties in the armed conflict; (4) conversely, lightening the burden on one or two Protecting Powers, appointing three States with one coming from the region of the conflict; (5) entrusting to the Protecting Power the function of referral of alleged grave breaches and other serious violations of IHL to the IFFC, removing the condition of consent of/initiative by the parties to the conflict.
30. See, for instance, the case of the ICRC delegate Eugenio Vagni who was abducted in the Philippines in January 2009, and freed in June, 178 days later.
31. See Articles 52 Geneva Convention I; 53 Geneva Convention II; 132 Geneva Convention III; 149 Geneva Convention IV.
32. See, for instance, S. Sivakumaran, 'Binding Armed Opposition Groups', *International and Comparative Law Quarterly* 55 (2006): 369 ff.; L. Zegveld, *Accountability of Armed Opposition Groups in International Law* (Oxford: Oxford University Press, 2002), 9–38.
33. International Committee of the Red Cross, *Increasing Respect for International Humanitarian Law in Non-International Armed Conflicts* (Geneva: International Committee of the Red Cross, 2008), 11.
34. See, International Committee of the Red Cross, ibid., 16–21; Pfanner, *supra* note 8, at 300–303; M. Veuthy, 'Learning from History: Accession to the Conventions, Special Agreements, and Unilateral Declarations', *Collegium* 27 (2003): 139 ff.
35. Pfanner, *supra* note 8, at 301.
36. There have been many cases where, even after initial talks, the negotiations have failed. See A.-M. La Rosa and C. Wuerzner, 'Armed Groups, Sanctions and the Implementation of International Humanitarian Law', *International Review of the Red Cross* 870 (2008): 332, footnote 15.

37. For instance, we can record, general statements about the willingness of NSAs to comply with IHL; statements designed to demonstrate adherence to specific rules, such as those referring to the prohibition of anti-personnel mines; more complex instruments, with express references to the content of Additional Protocol II or to common Article 3. For some examples see, Ewumbue-Monomo, *supra* note 22, at 911–915; La Rosa and Wuerzner, *supra* note 36, at 331–332.
38. R. Geiss, 'Humanitarian Law Obligations of Organized Armed Groups', in *Non-State Actors and International Humanitarian Law*, eds M. Odello and G. Beruto (Milan: FrancoAngeli, 2010), 96–97.
39. For an overview of its activities, see http://www.genevacall.org (accessed 27 January 2012). Recently, this NGO has announced the launch of a new Deed of Commitment for the protection of children from the effects of armed conflicts.
40. See Geneva Call, 'Verification Mission Fact-Finding during Armed Conflict, Report of the 2009 Verification Mission to the Philippines to Investigate Allegations of Anti-Personnel Landmine use by the Moro Islamic Liberation Front', 2010, available at: http://www.genevacall.org/resources/other-documents-studies/f-other-documents-studies/2001-2010/2010-GC-Report-Philippines-Web.pdf (accessed 15 November 2010).
41. Pfanner, *supra* note 8, at 303; La Rosa and Wuerzner, *supra* note 36, at 332.
42. International Committee of the Red Cross, *supra* note 33, at 19–20.
43. See O. Bangerter, 'Disseminating and Implementing International Humanitarian Law within Organized Armed Groups. Measures Armed Groups Can Take to Improve Respect for International Humanitarian Law', in *Non-State Actors and International Humanitarian Law*, eds M. Odello and G. Beruto (Milan: FrancoAngeli, 2010), 195–203.
44. See J. Somer, 'Jungle Justice: Passing Sentence on the Equality of Belligerents in Non-International Armed Conflict', *International Review of the Red Cross* 867 (2007): 655 ff.
45. See, in this regard, J. de Preux, 'Article 91', in *Commentary on the Additional Protocols of 8 June 1977 to the Geneva Conventions of 12 August 1949*, eds Y. Sandoz, C. Swinarski and B. Zimmermann (Geneva: International Committee of the Red Cross, 1987), 1053–1056; R. Wolfrum, 'Enforcement of International Humanitarian Law', in *The Handbook of International Humanitarian Law*, ed. D. Fleck, 2nd edition (Oxford: Oxford University Press, 2008), 707; Henckaerts and Doswald-Beck, *supra* note 17, at 537–541.
46. See Wolfrum, *supra* note 45, at 707: 'In practice, state responsibility for breaches of international humanitarian law has widely been neglected.'
47. De Preux, *supra* note 45, at 1054–1056. See, for instance, the UN Security Council Resolution 686 (1991), para. 2, according to which the SC '[d]emands that Iraq … (b) Accept in principle its liability under international law for any loss, damage or injury arising in that regard to Kuwait and third States … as a result of the invasion and illegal occupation of Kuwait'.
48. De Preux, *supra* note 45, at 1054. See recently the UN Compensation Commission or instruments concluded by Germany to close litigations related to World War II.
49. See, for instance, Report of the International Commission of Inquiry on Darfur to the UN Secretary-General, 25 January 2005, 149–153; Report of the UN Fact-Finding Mission on the Gaza Conflict, HRC, 25 September 2009 (UN Doc. A/HRC/12/48), 399–403; Independent International Fact-Finding Mission on the Conflict in Georgia, 'Report', Vol. II, September 2009, 420, available at: http://www.ceiig.ch/Report.html (accessed 15 November 2010).
50. See Eritrea-Ethiopia Claims Commission, Eritrea's Damages Claims, Final Award, 17 August 2009; Ethiopia's Damages Claims, Final Award, 17 August 2009. See M.J. Matheson, 'The Damage Awards of the Eritrea-Ethiopia Claims Commission', *The Law and Practice of International Courts and Tribunals* 9 (2010): 1 ff.
51. International Law Association, 'Reparation for Victims of Armed Conflict. Draft Conference Report', (2010), 2, 13–21, available at: http://www.ila-hq.org/en/committees/index.cfm/cid/1018 (accessed 15 November 2010). See also UN General Assembly Resolution 60/147 (2006), Basic Principles and Guidelines on the Right to a Remedy and Reparation for Victims of Gross Violations of International Human Rights Law and Serious Violations of International Humanitarian Law.
52. 'Italian Court of Cassation, All Civil Sections, *Presidency of the Council of Ministers v. Markovic and others*, Application for preliminary order on jurisdiction, No. 8157, 5 June 2002', *Rivista di diritto internazionale* 85 (2002): 799 ff. The Court considered the bombardments against Serbia as a non-justiciable 'act of government'.

53. Dieter Fleck, 'Individual and State Responsibility for Violations of the *ius in bello*: An Imperfect Balance', in International *Humanitarian Law Facing New Challenges: Symposium in Honour of Knut Ipsen*, eds Wolff Heintschel von Heinegg, Volker Epping and Knut Ipsen (Berlin: Springer, 2007), 191–192.

54. Henckaerts and Doswald-Beck, *supra* note 17, at 545–549.

55. Henckaerts and Doswald-Beck, *supra* note 17, at 550.

56. See, for instance, Report of the International Commission of Inquiry on Darfur, para. 600; A/RES/60/147, 21 March 2006, Basic Principles, Article IX, para. 15. See also, International Law Association, 'Reparation', 12–13.

57. See, for instance, Report of the International Commission of Inquiry on Darfur, 153, para. 603.

58. See, the reparation programme provided by Colombia under Decree 1290/08, adopted on 22 April 2008, for victims of demobilized armed groups, IACommHR, Annual Report, 2009, paras 57–63.

59. You can refer, for instance, to the US practice in relation with the Alien Tort Claims Act and the Torture Victims Protection Act. For difficulties in applying such mechanisms to NSAs, see J. Kleffner, 'The Collective Accountability of Organized Armed Groups for Systems Crimes', in *System Criminality in International Law*, eds A. Nollkaemper and H. van der Wilt (Cambridge: Cambridge University Press, 2009), 255–257.

60. L. Zegveld, 'Victims' Reparations Claims and International Criminal Courts', *Journal of International Criminal Justice* 8 (2010): 79 ff.

61. Eritrea-Ethiopia Claims Commission, *Ethiopia's Damages Claims*, 18, para. 61, 64.

62. For an analysis of similar issues in relation to human rights law, see G. Bartolini, *Riparazione per violazione dei diritti umani e ordinamento internazionale* (Naples: Jovene, 2009), 596–610.

63. See, for instance, F. Kalshoven, 'Some Comments on the International Responsibility of States', in *International Law Facing New Challenges: Symposium in Honour of Knut Ipsen*, eds W.H. von Heinegg and V. Epping (Berlin: Springer, 2007), 213. In relation to his experience with cases involving 'comfort women' he assumes that: 'For the women, however, the important thing was that their voices had been heard – in terms of the ILC Draft Articles: they had been given satisfaction.'

64. See, for instance, Report of the International Commission of Inquiry on Darfur, 153, para. 603. For the necessity to involve other States and international bodies in the reparation processes, see also Human Rights Council, Report of the Commission of Inquiry on Lebanon pursuant to Human Rights Council Resolution S-2/1, 23 November 2006 (UN Doc. A/HRC/3/2), para. 349; Report of the UN Fact-Finding Mission on the Gaza Conflict, 403, para. 1873.

65. See, G. Gaja, Fifth Report on Responsibility of International Organizations, 2 May 2007 (UN Doc. A/CN.4/583); A/RES/52/247, 17 July 1998 on third-party liability resulting from UN peace-keeping operations.

66. See International Law Association, 'Reparation', 6: 'The Committee … suggests that in principle the present Declaration should also apply to peace operations of the United Nations.'

67. J.S. Lam, 'Accountability for Private Military Contractors under the Alien Tort Statute', *California Law Review* 97 (2009): 1459 ff.

68. See, Pfanner, *supra* note 8, at 290; E.-C. Gillard, 'Reparation for Violations of International Humanitarian Law', *International Review of the Red Cross* 85 (2003): 551.

69. Kalshoven, *supra* note 63, at 211–212. For a more complex analysis, see Y. Ronen, 'Avoid or Compensate? Liability for Incidental Injury to Civilians Inflicted during Armed Conflict', *Vanderbilt Journal of Transnational Law* 42 (2009): 181 ff. According to the International Law Association, 'Reparation', 9, 'It is as yet unclear whether a right to reparation is triggered in such a situation'.

70. G. Zyberi, *The Humanitarian Face of the International Court of Justice: Its Contribution to Interpreting and Developing International Human Rights and Humanitarian Law, Rules and Principles* (Antwerp: Intersentia, 2008).

71. F. Coomans and M. Kamminga, eds, *Extraterritorial Application of Human Rights Treaties* (Antwerp: Intersentia, 2004).

72. For some examples see, Concluding Observations on Burundi, Committee on the Rights of the Child, 16 October 2000 (UN Doc. CRC/C/15/Add.133), paras 71–72; Concluding Observations on Israel, Committee on the Elimination of Racial Discrimination, 14 June 2007 (UN Doc. CERD/C/ISR/CO/13), para. 13. However, a clear reference to violations of IHL rules is not present, for instance, in the Concluding Observations of the Human Rights Committee.

73. For instance, for an analysis of activities conducted by organised armed groups such as FARC and ELN in Colombia see, IACommHR, Annual Report, OEA/Ser.L/V/II. Doc. 51, Corr. 1, 30 December 2009, Chapter IV, paras 64–74, available at: http://www.cidh.oas.org/annualrep/2009eng/Chap.IV.eng.

htm#1.Colombia (accessed 15 November 2010); IACommHR, Third Report on the Situation of Human Rights in Colombia, OEA/Ser.L/V/II.102, Doc. 9, Rev. 1, 26 February 1999, Chapter IV, available at http://www.cidh.org/countryrep/colom99en/table%20of%20contents.htm (accessed 15 November 2010).

74. See, for instance, *D.R. Congo v. Burundi, Rwanda, Uganda*, AfCommHPR, Communication No. 227/1999, May 2003; *Georgia v. Russia*, ECtHR, Application No. 13255/07, Decision on Admissibility, 30 June 2009.

75. For instance, in 2009, the Commission conducted 11 fact-finding field missions and in several cases it ascertained violations of IHL rules (see Afghanistan Independent Human Rights Commission, 'Annual Report, 1 January–31 December 2009', 42–43, available at: http://www.aihrc.org.af/media/files/ Reports/Annual%20Reports/Annual2009.pdf) (accessed 15 November 2010).

76. Apart from relevant cases decided by the Israeli Supreme Court with respect to hostilities in the Occupied Territories, see for instance, Judgments related to Kosovo's air campaign: Italy, Court of Cassation, All Civil Sections, *Presidency of the Council of Ministers v. Markovic and others* (*supra* note 52); Germany, Federal High Court of Justice, 35 *Citizens of the Former Federal Republic of Yugoslavia v. Germany*, Appeal Judgment, 2 November 2006, in *Oxford Reports on International Law in Domestic Courts*, No. 887.

77. *Supra* note 52 for the solution provided by the Italian Court of Cassation in the *Markovic* case.

78. See, for instance, the position held by the Israeli Supreme Court in several cases such as *Physicians for Human Rights v. Commander of the IDF in the Gaza Strip*, 10 May 2004, Case No. 4764/04; *The Public Committee against Torture in Israel et al. v. The Government of Israel et al.*, 13 December 2006, Case No. 769/02. On this approach, see D. Kretzmer, 'The Supreme Court of Israel: Judicial Review during Armed Conflict', *German Yearbook of International Law* 47 (2004): 430–434.

79. See G. Nolte, 'The Different Functions of the Security Council with Respect to Humanitarian Law', in *The United Nations Security Council and War: The Evolution of Thought and Practice since 1945*, ed. V. Lowe (Oxford: Oxford University Press, 2008), 519 ff.; G. Schotten and A. Biehler, 'The Role of the Security Council in Implementing International Humanitarian Law and Human Rights Law', in *International Humanitarian Law and Human Rights Law: Towards a New Merger in International Law*, eds R. Arnold and N. Quénivet (Leiden: Martinus Nijhoff, 2008), 309 ff.

80. See, for instance, S/RES/1369, 14 September 2001 (generic appeal to parties to the conflict to fulfil their IHL obligations); S/RES/598, 20 July 1987 (request to release prisoners of war).

81. See the ad hoc inquiry commissions created by the SC, i.e., the Bassiouni Commission for the Former Yugoslavia (1992–1993), the inquiry Commission for Rwanda (1994) and the International Commission on Darfur (2004–2005).

82. The SC, taking note of the Report of the Commission on Darfur, decided with S/RES/1593, 31 March 2005, to refer the situation to the Prosecutor of the ICC.

83. See, for instance, S/RES/1572, 15 November 2004, para. 9, on Ivory Coast; S/RES/1591, 29 March 2005, para. 3(c), on Darfur.

84. Pfanner, *supra* note 8, at 315.

85. You can refer, for instance, to coordination of humanitarian aid, mainly through its Department of Humanitarian Affairs; reports to the SC on issues pertaining to IHL, as protection of civilians in armed conflict (see recently, UN Doc. S/2009/277, 27 May 2009); activities carried out by the Special Representative of the Secretary-General for children in armed conflict. On relevant practice, see Pfanner, *supra* note 8, at 321–323.

86. For a first example, see A/RES/2444 (XXIII) on respect for human rights in armed conflict.

87. See, for instance, Resolutions related with operation 'Cast Lead': A/RES/64/10, 1 December 2009 and A/RES/64/254, 25 March 2010.

88. See, for instance, activities carried out by Special Rapporteurs or Working Groups on extrajudicial, summary or arbitrary executions; mercenaries; terrorism; torture.

89. See, Report of the Independent Expert on the Situation of Human Rights in the Sudan, UN Doc. A/HRC/14/41, 26 May 2010, para. 52–58; Report of the Independent Expert on the Situation of Human Rights in Somalia, UN Doc. A/HRC/15/48, 16 September 2010, paras 12–18.

90. See, for instance, First Special Session (2006) devoted to Occupied Palestinian Territories; Second Special Session (2006) on Israeli campaign in Lebanon; Third Special Session (2006) on Israeli military incursions in Occupied Palestinian Territories; Fourth Special Session on Darfur (2006).

91. See, for instance, reports of commissions of inquiry created by the HRC to review Israeli campaigns in Lebanon (UN Doc. A/HRC/3/2, 23 November 2006) and Gaza (UN Doc. A/HRC/12/48, 25 September 2009).

92. See, for instance, Resolution S-8/1: *Situation of human rights in the East of the Democratic Republic of the Congo*, Human Rights Council, 1 December 2008; Resolution 4/8: *Situation of human rights in Darfur*, Human Rights Council, 30 March 2007; Resolution S-3/1: *Human rights violations emanating from Israeli military incursions in the Occupied Territories*, Human Rights Council, 15 November 2006.

93. See, Resolution 5/1: *Institution-Building of the United Nations Human Rights Council*, Human Rights Council, 18 June 2007, Annex, para. 2: 'In addition to the above and given the complementary and mutually interrelated nature of international human rights law and international humanitarian law, the review shall take into account applicable international humanitarian law.'

94. This was what happened with the Report presented to the former Human Rights Commission by the Special Rapporteur on extra-judicial, summary or arbitrary executions (UN Doc. E/CN.4/1994/7/Add.1, 11 August 1993), which gave evidence of an extremely deteriorated situation in Rwanda in 1993, a situation clearly conducive to the 1994 genocide.

95. P. Alston, J. Morgan-Foster and W. Abresch, 'The Competence of the UN Human Rights Council and its Special Procedures in Relation to Armed Conflicts: Extrajudicial Executions in the "War on Terror"', *European Journal of International Law* 19 (2008): 183 ff.

96. See, for instance, the position maintained by the United Kingdom during its periodic review: Report of the Working Group on the Universal Periodic Review. The United Kingdom of Great Britain and Northern Ireland, UN Doc. A/HRC/8/25, 23 May 2008, para. 36: 'With respect to international humanitarian law (IHL), the United Kingdom noted that in overseas military operations where IHL applies, its policy is to comply with IHL requirements, but it does not accept that IHL is a basis for the Universal Periodic Review.'

97. See, for instance, Report of the Working Group on the Universal Periodic Review, Colombia (UN Doc. A/HRC/10/82, 9 January 2009).

98. See, Council Decision 2008/901/CFSP (2 December 2008) creating an independent fact-finding mission on the conflict in Georgia competent to investigate violations of international law, humanitarian law and human rights.

99. See, Updated EU Guidelines on Promoting Compliance with IHL (15 December 2009); Update of the EU Guidelines on Children and Armed Conflict (17 June 2008).

100. In particular, the EU Council has temporarily withdrawn the special benefit granted to Sri Lanka due to shortcomings in the application of human rights standards (Implementing Regulation (EU) No. 143/2010, *Official Journal of the European Union*, L 45, 20 February 2010, 1 ff.).

101. International Committee of the Red Cross, *supra* note 29, at 17–18.

102. K. Annan, *We the Peoples: The Role of the United Nations in the 21st Century* (New York, 2000), 46: 'New approaches in this area could include establishing a mechanism to monitor compliance by all parties with existing provisions of international humanitarian law.'

103. See International Committee of the Red Cross, *supra* note 29, at 17–18.

104. J. Kleffner, 'Improving compliance with International Humanitarian Law through the Establishment of an Individual Complaints Mechanisms', *Leiden Journal of International Law* 15 (2002): 237 ff.

105. Human Rights Committee, Report Submitted by the United Nations Interim Administration Mission in Kosovo to the Human Rights Committee on the Human Rights Situation in Kosovo since June 1999, 13 March 2006 (UN Doc. CCPR/C/UNK/1).

106. For an example of these issues, see Kleffner, *supra* note 104, at 247–248.

107. See, Sassòli, *supra* note 2, at 52; International Committee of the Red Cross, *supra* note 29, at 8–9.

108. See Report of the UN Secretary-General, 'Respect for Human Rights in Armed Conflicts', 18 September 1970, UN Doc. A/8052, para. 244.

30. Reparation for individual victims of armed conflict
*Elke Schwager**

1. INTRODUCTION

The last years have seen an impressive development in the discussion about reparation for individual victims of an armed conflict.[1] Initially, the question as to whether individual victims are able to receive reparation for the violation of their rights was mainly reasoned before some courts on a case-by-case basis. Meanwhile, the topic has become institutionalised. Within the United Nations, the General Assembly adopted the *Basic Principles and Guidelines on the Right to a Remedy and Reparation for Victims of Gross Violations of International Human Rights Law and Serious Violations of International Humanitarian Law*[2] (Basic Principles and Guidelines) addressing that issue in 2005. In 2007, the *Chicago Principles on Post-Conflict Justice* were drafted by the International Human Rights Institute and other organisations.[3] The International Law Association adopted in 2010 their Principles of *Reparation for Victims of Armed Conflict* (ILA Principles of Reparation).[4]

This development is a consequence, on the one hand, of the recognition of the individual as a direct participant and holder of rights under international law. On the other hand, there is the increasing acknowledgement that persons having suffered harm in the context of an armed conflict are very often not only incidental victims of unfortunate circumstances, but victims of violations of human rights and international humanitarian law.

Additionally, there seems to be a growing awareness of the situation and the demands of persons having suffered harm in the context of an armed conflict and the need to address this issue. For the victims, the entitlement to reparation can be one way of obtaining justice. Reparation might also help to ease the consequences of the injuries. Further, it gives the possibility of holding the perpetrators accountable. In the long term, it might support compliance with the international standards applicable in armed conflicts.

As a result, a right for individuals to claim reparation under international law is increasingly recognised. However, there is no standard procedure available for the enforcement of such a right, and, based on different reasons like waiver, immunity or non-justiciability, state practice and jurisprudence have often denied an individual holder the enforcement of his or her right.

In the following, the origin of an individual right under international law will be examined. Less in the focus of international lawyers is the fact that a violation of human rights or international humanitarian law might give rise to a right to reparation under domestic law as well. Finally, the different possibilities for enforcing a right to reparation along with potential obstacles to the enforcement will be outlined.

2. REPARATION UNDER INTERNATIONAL LAW

Recent years have seen an increasing recognition of a right to reparation for victims of violations of human rights and international humanitarian law. The above mentioned institutionalised rules all deal with a right to reparation: The Basic Principles and Guidelines reiterate and confirm existing rights for victims of gross violations of international human rights and serious violations of international law.[5] The Chicago Principles on Post-Conflict Justice formulate equally carefully in its principle 3 in 2007 that 'states shall ... develop remedies and reparation' and only state in the pertinent commentary that 'victims have the right to ... effective and prompt reparations'. Only three years later, such a right for victims of armed conflict is clearly stated by art. 6 of the ILA Principles of Reparation, which were unanimously adopted in 2010.[6] There are basically two distinct possibilities to explain the origin of a right for individuals to reparation: such a right could derive from some specific rules in international law, and it could evolve from the principles of international responsibility.

Before looking at the different international rules dealing with reparation and the principles of international responsibility, it should be noted that a right under international law exists independently of the procedural capacity of the holder of the right to enforce it pursuant to international law.[7] In *LaGrand*, the International Court of Justice (ICJ) affirmed the independence of individual rights from the existence of a procedure for the individual by holding that art. 36 para. 1 of the Vienna Convention on Consular Relations 'creates individual rights, which, by virtue of Article 1 of the Optional Protocol, may be invoked in this Court by the national State of the detained person'.[8] The enforcement of rights of individuals under international law can be pursued either on the international level, by the home state representing the relevant person, or, if a procedure therefore is available at the international level, by the individual him- or herself. Alternatively, the individual can enforce his or her right on the national level before domestic courts.[9]

2.1 Human Rights

Human rights are applicable during an armed conflict.[10] Whilst states can derogate most of the rights guaranteed under human rights in times of war or emergency, no suspension is permitted from the right to life, the right to humane treatment, the freedom from slavery, the freedom from *ex post facto* laws, and of the judicial guarantees essential for the protection of such rights.[11] These non-derogable judicial guarantees include, depending on the human rights instrument, either the right or the obligation to provide for reparation.[12] Thus, individuals having their human rights violated, which are not derogative, or which are not suspended during an armed conflict, shall receive reparation. The judicial guarantees and other provisions providing for reparation are to be found in the international and regional human rights instruments of the first generation of human rights. The content of the different provisions on reparation vary.

There is, first of all, the general obligation of states to provide for, or the right of an individual to receive, an effective remedy.[13] This obligation is in most cases directed towards states, and does not, therefore, necessarily correspond to an individual right to receive reparation under international law. States are required to foresee the possibility of reparation, which can be provided for in their domestic legal order. An exception in this respect is art. 13 European Convention on Human Rights (ECHR), which not only stipulates an obligation of the state, but an individual right to an effective remedy under international law. The effective remedy rule has not just a procedural meaning. A remedy for a violation is not effective without a substantive claim, and thus it is reasonable to assume that the obligation to provide for, or the right to, an effective remedy contains also the obligation to provide for, or the right to receive, reparation.[14] In accordance with this conclusion, the Human Rights Committee found that the state should compensate the victim of a human rights violation pursuant to art. 2 para. 3 lit. a of the International Covenant on Civil and Political Rights (ICCPR).[15] The Inter-American Court on Human Rights ruled that it follows from art. 1 para. 1 American Convention on Human Rights (ACHR),[16] that states are obliged 'to provide compensation as warranted for damages resulting from the violation'.[17] As for the African Charter on Human and Peoples' Rights (ACHPR), the African Commission on Human and Peoples' Rights is inclined to deduct an obligation to compensation from art. 7 ACHPR.[18] Regarding art. 13 ECHR, the European Court of Human Rights ruled that the individual right to an effective remedy encompasses compensation, and, where appropriate, an effective investigation.[19]

Besides the general obligation to provide for reparation, there are also some provisions of international human rights treaties explicitly stating the possibility for one form of reparation, namely compensation, in case of the violation of a specific right. Most of these provisions contain an international right to compensation vis-à-vis domestic authorities,[20] and some are formulated as a state obligation to provide for compensation.[21]

As for the regional conventions on human rights, they contain provisions which give the regional courts on human rights the competence to rule on reparation for the injured party.[22] As these rules only state the competence of the courts to do so, the right to receive reparation must be stipulated elsewhere. The courts have provided different reasons in order to explain the rule their competence is based upon.[23] The European Court of Human Rights states that if it finds a violation of the ECHR, the states are obliged to follow its decision which includes, if necessary, restitution or the payment of compensation.[24] In contrast, the Inter-American Court of Human Rights relies on the principles of international responsibility, which, traditionally, were only applicable in inter-state relationships, in order to ground the entitlement of individuals to reparation.[25] This approach is meanwhile confirmed by the ICJ in its advisory opinion on the *Legal Consequences of the Construction of a Wall in the Occupied Palestinian Territory*.[26]

Thus, in case of an armed conflict, the international and regional human rights instruments provide for reparation in case of a violation of a human right they guarantee which is not derogative or which was not suspended during an armed conflict. Accordingly, the European Court of Human Rights, for example, ruled that pursuant to art. 41 ECHR, Russia had to compensate the victims of injury, torture, arbitrary killing and forced disappearance which happened during the hostilities in

Chechnya between the Russian armed forces and Chechen rebel fighters, where no state of emergency had been declared and no derogation had been made under art. 15 ECHR.[27]

2.2 Law of Armed Conflict

As for potential rights for reparation for violations of the law of armed conflict, a distinction has to be made between violations of the *ius ad/contra bellum*[28] and the *ius in bello*.

2.2.1 Reparation for violations of the *ius ad/contra bellum*

The principles of international responsibility are applicable to a violation of the *ius ad/contra bellum*.[29] Accordingly, the perpetrator of such a violation is obliged to make reparation to the injured state for the loss and damage caused by the prohibited use of force.[30] Nevertheless, in the past, reparations for an unlawful use of force were only imposed on the loser of an armed conflict.[31] As the *ius ad/contra bellum* contains rules protecting the territorial integrity of states, the equality of states and their peaceful relations,[32] the right to claim reparation is held by the state suffering from an unlawful use of force directed against it. Even though an indirect effect of the prohibition of the use of force is also the protection of individuals from violence, their welfare is not its main concern. Individuals are thus not vested with individual rights under the rules of the *ius ad/contra bellum* and are usually not the direct beneficiary of reparation paid for an infringement of these rules.[33] However, for practical reasons, it may be useful to accord rights within a specific reparation regime to individuals in order to facilitate the evaluation of damages incurred, and the distribution of means granted by way of reparation. Therefore, in some instances, peace treaties or resolutions contain an individual right to reparation resulting from a violation of the *ius ad/contra bellum*. Two of the few examples where individuals were directly entitled to compensation under international law as a result of a violation of the *ius ad/contra bellum* are illustrated as follows:

(1) The Treaty of Versailles, which ordered Germany and its allies to render reparation to the Allied and Associated Governments for their aggression and was thus a violation of the *ius ad bellum* in the First World War,[34] attributed some rights to individuals.[35] According to art. 297 lit e) of the Treaty of Versailles, for example, nationals of Allied or Associated Powers could claim compensation for damage or injury suffered as a consequence of an 'exceptional war measure or measures of transfer' concerning their property before Mixed Arbitral Tribunals.[36]

(2) In 1991, Resolutions 687 and 692 of the UN Security Council set up the system of the United Nations Compensation Commission (UNCC).[37] Resolution 687 in its para. 16 'Reaffirms that Iraq ... is liable under international law for any direct loss, damage, including environmental damage and the depletion of natural resources, or injury to foreign Governments, nationals and corporations, as a result of Iraq's unlawful invasion and occupation of Kuwait'. Furthermore, Resolution 687 determined the source from which reparation was to be paid, namely the profits from the export of petroleum and petroleum products.

As clarified by the UNCC's procedural rules and its practice,[38] the individual, suffering harm as a consequence of Iraq's unlawful use of force, was attributed a right to compensation within the system of the UNCC.[39] As the individual had no standing before the UNCC, the state acted as representative for the individual when presenting his or her claim.[40]

Relying on the wording of Resolution 687 especially, it is argued that the right for individuals to compensation within the system of the UNCC is founded on the general principles of international responsibility under international law.[41] It is more likely though that Resolution 687 relies on international law to confirm the application of the principles of state responsibility to a violation of the *ius ad/contra bellum*. There is no indication that the position accorded to individuals within the reparation regime is an expression of a change in concept of the entitlement to reparation in the case of a violation of the *ius ad/contra bellum*. As the individual is not directly protected by these rules, it seems difficult to establish that an individual should have a right to reparation in case of their violation. In accordance with the overall state practise in cases of a violation of the *ius ad/contra bellum*, where the attribution of individual rights to reparation seems to be the exception, it is thus to be assumed that the right for individuals to reparation before the UNCC is awarded to the individuals by the Resolution itself.

2.2.2   Reparation for violations of the *ius in bello*

There is still a broad spectrum of opinions when it comes to the question as to whether individuals have a right to reparation for violations of the *ius in bello*.

As for the special regime set up by the Agreement between the Government of the Federal Democratic Republic of Ethiopia and the Government of the State of Eritrea,[42] for example, it is recognised that it attributes individuals a right to reparation for violations of the *ius in bello* committed during the conflict between the countries preceding the peace agreement. It is the wording of the Agreement itself and of the Rules of Procedure[43] which shows that the state, when claiming before the Eritrea-Ethiopia Claims Commission (EECC) a loss suffered by an individual, was not invoking its own right, but acting on behalf of the individual. In its Partial Award of 17 December 2004, the EECC confirmed this classification by ruling that claims brought by Eritrea on its own behalf for non-nationals are outside the scope of the jurisdiction of the EECC. These claims should have been made on behalf of the individuals themselves, as 'the claim remains the property of the individual and that any eventual recovery of damages should accrue to that person'.[44]

Next to individual peace treaties and resolutions containing provisions for reparation for victims of an armed conflict, it is in particular art. 3 of the Convention Respecting the Laws and Customs of War on Land[45] (Hague Convention IV) and its repetition in art. 91 of the Additional Protocol to the Geneva Conventions of 12 August 1949 and Relating to the Protection of Victims of International Armed Conflicts[46] (Additional Protocol I), which gives rise to different interpretations ranging from the denial of any right for individuals to the acceptance of an individual right to reparation. Art. 3 Hague Convention IV states: 'A belligerent party which violates the provisions of the said Regulation shall, if the case demands, be liable to pay compensation. It shall be responsible for all acts committed by persons forming part of its armed forces.' Art. 91

Additional Protocol I states the same principle for 'a party to the conflict which violates the provisions of the Conventions or of this Protocol'. The rules are valid for violations of the *ius in bello* applicable in non-international armed conflict as well. It is accepted under international customary law that the scope of art. 3 Hague Convention IV extends to all violations of the *ius in bello*.[47] As for art. 91 Additional Protocol I, it refers to violations of the provisions of the Geneva Conventions, which include in their common art. 3 rules especially applicable to non-international armed conflicts.

Whilst some domestic courts have ruled that art. 3 Hague Convention IV stipulates an individual right to compensation, the majority of domestic courts still do not acknowledge such a right resulting from art. 3 Hague Convention IV and art. 91 Additional Protocol.[48] Amongst academics, the analysis seems reversed.[49] There are mainly three arguments made when denying an individual right:

(1) Some refuse to recognise that individuals have rights under international humanitarian law at all.[50] However, the terms of some of the norms of international humanitarian law already clearly suggest that they do confer rights upon individuals.[51] Furthermore, there are norms of international humanitarian law which are not only imposing obligations on states vis-à-vis foreign nationals, but also towards their own nationals, which indicates that the fulfilment of these obligations is primarily owed to the individuals and not to other state parties.[52] Indeed, in situations of international armed conflict, where the state's authority may be weak or even undergo changes, there is the need to protect an individual independently of the assistance of its state and thus to provide him or her with his or her own rights.[53] As a consequence, the argument that individuals have no rights under international humanitarian law is already strongly contested by other domestic courts.[54]

(2) In denying an individual right to compensation, the argument is also made that there is no procedure under which the individual could exercise his or her rights.[55] As already stated above, the bearing of a right has to be differentiated from the procedural capacity to enforce it.[56] The availability of a procedure at an international level is not a condition for the existence of an individual right.

(3) Finally, there is the reasoning that art. 3 Hague Convention IV and art. 91 Additional Protocol I stipulate a right to compensation for states only.[57] Even if international humanitarian law attributed rights to the individual, it would do so only with primary rules and would not give the individual the position to be able to claim secondary rights such as compensation. Besides, it is argued, there would be no sufficient state practice recognising an individual right resulting from art. 3 Hague Convention IV and art. 91 Additional Protocol I.

The wording of both articles does not specify the beneficiary of the rule. Thus, the holder of the right has to be determined by other means of interpretation. Relying on the preparatory work of the Hague Conventions, especially academics hold that art. 3 Hague Convention IV confers a right to compensation on individuals.[58] According to the explanation of the German delegate proposing the article and the statement of other delegates, the article was intended to confer a right to compensation to a neutral or enemy person.[59] As for art. 91 Additional Protocol I, the preparatory work does not serve as much of a guidance as it was intended to confirm the principle of reparation laid down in art. 3 Hague Convention IV.[60]

Pursuant to art. 32 Vienna Convention on the Law of Treaties,[61] it is possible to revert to the *travaux préparatoires* for the interpretation of a treaty.[62] Considering that at the time the Hague Conventions were adopted, it was a subjective approach investigating the intent of the lawmaker which was taken predominantly into account when interpreting a treaty, the *travaux préparatoires* are of particular relevance. However, the preparatory work of a treaty is only a supplementary means of interpretation, and according to art. 31 Vienna Convention on the Law of Treaties a rule has to be considered in good faith in the context of the treaty and in the light of its object and purpose. The object and purpose of art. 3 Hague Convention IV and art. 91 Additional Protocol I is to confirm the application of the principles of international responsibility to violations of the *ius in bello*,[63] and to extend the liability to *ultra vires* behaviour of armed forces.[64] Ultimately, by stating the liability for violations of *the ius in bellum*, the article improves the implementation of the *ius in bello* and strengthens it. However, this purpose of the article does not clarify the intended beneficiary, as it can be reached with either the state or the individual as the holder of the right. Subsequent state praxis and relevant rules of international law are relevant when determining the content of a treaty as well, see art. 31 para. 3 lit. b and c Vienna Convention on the Law of Treaties. As there is no subsequent state praxis in interpreting art. 3 Hague Convention IV, it cannot be of any guidance here.[65] There is a relevant rule of international law which has to be taken into account. At the time of the adoption of the Hague Conventions, individual rights under international law were mainly rejected,[66] and this approach might thus have resulted in the reluctance to recognise an individual right under art. 3 Hague Convention. Meanwhile, the situation has changed with the adoption of the Charter of the United Nations[67] and numerous human rights treaties. The individual is nowadays recognised as a bearer of rights under international law.[68] Further, the position of the individual is not limited to primary rules, the individual is also explicitly recognised as the holder of secondary rules deriving from the violation of primary rules.[69] Consequently, treaty provisions in international law have to be interpreted in light of the established change regarding the meanwhile established position of the individual in international law. Accordingly, the report of the International Commission of Inquiry on Darfur, for example, states that even if Art. 3 of the Hague Convention IV was initially not intended to provide for compensation for individuals, it does so now, as the emergence of human rights in international law has altered the concept of state responsibility.[70] The interpretation of art. 3 Hague Convention IV as an individual right to compensation is also confirmed by the Basic Principles and Guidelines, which name para. 1 of the Preamble art. 3 Hague Convention IV and art. 91 Additional Protocol I as provisions providing a right to a remedy for victims of violations of international humanitarian law.[71]

2.3   International Responsibility

In addition to the specific rules providing for reparation for individuals, an argument can be made that a right to reparation for victims of a violation of the law applicable in armed conflict results from the principles of international responsibility. According to these principle, a party responsible for an internationally wrongful act is under an obligation to make full reparation for the injury caused by such act.[72]

The party injured by the wrongful act is entitled to invoke international responsibility and claim reparation, which is generally the party to which the fulfilment of the obligation breach is owed or which is specially affected by its breach.[73] The question to whom a duty is owed is also determined by the kind of rule of law to which the obligation belongs. Treaties, one of the main sources of law in international law, are usually concluded between states, and thus the obligations resulting from treaties are, due to the principle of reciprocity, owed to the other state parties.[74] But when looking at treaties in the field of human rights and international humanitarian law, reciprocity is not the only reason for the existence of the treaty obligations. Pursuant to art. 2 of each of the Geneva Conventions, the validity of the Conventions is dependent on reciprocity in so far as the provisions are only applicable towards other states parties to the Conventions. But if this stipulation is met, the provisions have to be complied with independently of the adherence of the other party.[75] Furthermore, treaties in the field of human rights and international humanitarian law contain obligations and rights which states have to respect vis-à-vis their own nationals. Thus, the compliance with these rules is not dependent on any reciprocity between states,[76] but due to the specific value of the rules which is recognised by the states.[77] As a consequence, the adherence to the rules which contain a right for individuals is not only owed to other state parties, but also to the individual. And indeed, art. 2 para. 1 ICCPR and art. 1 ECHR, for example, stipulate that their rules have to be secured to individuals. The approach is confirmed by the ruling of the ICJ in *LaGrand*: 'the United States of America breached its obligation to the Federal Republic of Germany and to the LaGrand brothers under Article 36, paragraph 2, of the [Vienna] Convention [on Consular Relations of 24 April 1963]'.[78]

Apart from being laid down in international treaties, fundamental human rights like the right to life, the prohibition of torture and inhuman and degrading treatment, slavery or forced labour, are part of international customary law and are therefore valid independently of any reciprocity.[79] Violations of fundamental human rights are

> unconditionally criminal and unjustifiable, also and even specifically when they are committed by State agents, the inference is that every system of governance must by law abstain from engaging in such acts. In other words, the State – and any other addressee of commands originating from the level of international law – has a legal obligation towards every human being not to practice conduct that violates the core rights of the human person.[80]

Apart from being owed to the individual, the obligation to respect fundamental human rights is as an obligation *erga omnes* owed to the international community.[81]

As the fulfilment of obligations under human rights and international humanitarian law is owed to individuals, they themselves are entitled to invoke the principles of international responsibility in case of a violation of these rules. Indeed, traditionally, the principles of international responsibility were only applied between states. However, their application is not limited to states. International responsibility is not a consequence of the sovereignty and equality of states.[82] It is rather 'a principle of international law, and even a general conception of law, that any breach of an engagement involves an obligation to make reparation'.[83] As such, it can principally be applied to all subjects of international law including individuals.[84] In effect, international responsibility creates a new legal relationship between the perpetrator of the unlawful act and the injured party. It results in new obligations of the offender, such as the obligation to pay compensation or to make satisfaction. As the individual is a subject under international law, he or she can receive compensation or satisfaction. Additionally, the consequence of an unlawful act is the possibility for the injured or third party to engage in countermeasures vis-à-vis the party acting unlawfully.[85] The individual is able to take countermeasures like self-defence.[86] Further measures such as the use of military means are not at his or her disposal. Neither are all states in a position to employ such means, and there is a clear tendency to restrict the ability of the injured party to resort to sanctions unilaterally but rather to decide upon and apply them collectively.[87]

Recognising the individual to be the holder of the secondary rights for reparation resulting from the violation of its primary right constitutes, on the one hand, the consequent continuation of the protection of the individual by the primary rule, and, on the other hand, the stabilisation and strengthening of individual rights.[88]

In international state practice, there are more and more examples to be found where the individual is attributed a secondary right to reparation as a consequence of a violation of their primary rights under human rights and humanitarian law. Referring to the ruling of the PCIJ in the *Factory at Chorzów* Case, which deals with the general principle of international responsibility, the ICJ held in its advisory opinion on the construction of a wall in the occupied Palestinian territory that Israel had violated its obligations under human rights and international humanitarian law, and, as a consequence, 'Israel has the obligation to make reparation for the damage caused to all the natural or legal persons concerned'.[89] Likewise, the Inter-American Court of Human Rights relies on the principles of international responsibility when explaining the entitlement of individuals to reparation.[90] Domestic courts sometimes presuppose in their rulings an individual right to reparation under international law.[91] As they do not refer to a specific law in doing so, it seems conclusive to argue that they are relating to the principles of international responsibility. Whilst not dealing with the international responsibility of parties other than states, the Commentary to the Draft Articles on State Responsibility says that 'State responsibility extends, for example, to human rights violations and other breaches of international law where the primary beneficiary of the obligation breached is not a State'.[92] Whilst an earlier version of the Basic Principles and Guidelines contained a general right to reparation under international law for individuals in case of a violation of their rights,[93] the version adopted by the General Assembly makes clear that they do not 'entail new international or domestic legal obligations'.[94] Considering that so far a right for individuals to reparation resulting from the principles of international responsibility is not fully established by state practice, the Basic Principles and Guidelines cannot thus be seen as confirming the existence of such a right.[95] In contrast, according to the ILA Principles of Reparation, the obligation to make individual reparation can be traced back to the general principles of international responsibility.[96]

The Basic Principles and Guidelines limit their scope to gross violations of human rights and serious violations of international humanitarian law.[97] Equally, an earlier draft of the ILA Principles of Reparation proposed to limit the right to reparation to violations of core norms of human rights and international humanitarian law.[98] The final version no longer contains such a limitation.[99] And indeed, as apart from the problem of defining which violations exactly constitute a gross or serious violation, there is no reason or justification to limit a right to reparation to such special cases. None of the rules providing for reparation for violations of human rights and international humanitarian law restrict their application to gross or serious violations. States have the possibility of derogating all but the core rights guaranteed by the human rights instruments during an armed conflict, and thus, a right to reparation will obviously only remain for these core rights where a derogation has been declared. However, states do not always use that possibility. Russia, for example, did not suspend any rights in Chechnya and the European Court for Human Rights ruled in *Isayeva, Yusupova and Bazayeva v. Russia*[100] that the civil victims of an aerial strike are entitled to receive compensation not only for the violation of a core right such as the right to life, but also for a violation of the right to property and the failure of the authorities to carry out an adequate and effective investigation.

2.4   Forms and Standard of Reparation

According to the principles of international responsibility, reparation can take different forms such as restitution, compensation, satisfaction and assurances and guarantees of non-repetition.[101] Additionally, the Basic Principles and Guidelines mention in Principle 21 rehabilitation as a form of reparation which should include medical and psychological care as well as legal and social services. The various instruments on reparation differ when it comes to the interplay between the different forms of reparation. Whilst art. 35 Draft Articles on State Responsibility states a primacy of restitution, the ILA Principles of Reparation propose to determine the appropriate form of reparation in each case considering that restitution of property, for example, might not be in the best interests of an individual.[102] There is also the possibility of collective reparation where reparation is made vis-à-vis groups of victims or entire communities.[103]

Concerning the amount of reparation, the principles of international responsibility demand full reparation be made.[104] Whilst the text of the ILA Principles of Reparation does not appear to make any restrictions on the amount of reparation due in the wording of its relevant art. 6 and 7, it is stated in the commentary that the principles do not intend to give any clear guidance on the amount of reparation due to the conflicting interests of the individual victim to receive full reparation and the economic capacities of the responsible party. It is especially pointed out that a collective claims settlement might be the best solution in post-conflict situations.[105] And indeed, it is argued that full reparation to victims of an armed conflict is neither possible nor desirable for economic reasons, as debts which exceed the economic capacity of a state might aggravate the human rights situation in the state itself.[106] Germany especially, for obvious reasons, stated that international responsibly arising from a violation of the law of war would only trigger reparation as a claim of action but would not address the amount due as the amount would have to be negotiated between the parties.[107] Whilst in the past reparation paid as a consequence of an armed conflict has often been limited, no rule has evolved that the economic resources necessarily have to be taken into account.[108] Furthermore, such a limitation was considered usually for reparation paid as a consequence of a violation of the *ius ad/contra bellum*.[109] When contemplating reparation for violations of the *ius in bellum*, the scale of damage will generally not be as high. But independent of this consideration, the fact that mass damages have occurred cannot impact on the initial existence of the right to receive full reparation. Otherwise the grotesque situation would occur in which the one who has caused mass violations does not have to make full reparation, whereas the one who has committed a manageable amount of violation has to make full reparation.[110] Instead of limiting the amount of reparation, limited financial capacities can be taken into account, for example, in payment methods.[111] Besides, the holder of the right to reparation can waive their right to receive the full amount of reparation. An incentive to exercise such a waiver is the setting up of special reparation regimes or special claims commissions at an international or national level offering a simple and quick procedure in order to obtain a certain amount of reparation.

2.5   Non-state Actors

Reparation for violations of international law can also be claimed from non-state actors, if they have obligations under international law.[112] As for the *ius in bello*, many articles in the relevant treaties apply not only to states, but to all parties to the conflict. If a party to the conflict infringes its obligations under the *ius in bello*, it is liable to pay compensation according to the wording of art. 3 of the Hague Convention IV and art. 91 of the Additional Protocol I. Thus, not only states, but also parties to the armed conflict are liable for their violations of international humanitarian law.[113] Apart from states and other parties to the conflict, the *ius in bello* also addresses the individual, who, therefore, can also violate these norms. While the penal responsibility of individuals for an infringement of international law is meanwhile firmly established, their liability to make reparation under international law is increasingly recognised due to the obligation to provide compensation under international law laid down in art. 75 Rome Statute of the International Court of Justice (Rome Statute).[114] According to this provision, a victim can obtain reparation from the individual perpetrator through a ruling of the International Criminal Court.[115] However, a victim cannot demand reparation for every violation of the *ius in bello* as the jurisdiction of the Court is only triggered by a violation of the *ius in bello* constituting a war crime according to art. 8 Rome Statute.

Treaty-based human rights are generally only binding upon states. A direct horizontal effect between individuals (*Drittwirkung*) is traditionally not recognised.[116] Some treaties however address explicitly the individual and therefore contain individual obligations.[117] But human rights are not only valid as treaty law, as the fundamental human rights constitute customary law as well.[118] Following the conception that such rights are not granted to the individual by the states but result necessarily from the pure existence of a human being,[119] these rights are binding for all actors under international law and can thus be infringed by non-state actors as well.[120]

With non-state actors being bound to respect fundamental human rights, the question arises whether victims of their potential infringements of these rights are entitled to reparation. As the international treaties on human rights are generally not considered to contain obligations for individuals, their norms on reparation do not apply.[121] However, as the principles of international responsibility are general principles of law, they are valid for non-state actors as well.[122] The principles state that the infringement of an obligation under international law entails the responsibility of the violator. Within the scope of their obligations under international law, non-state actors can therefore be held responsible for their acts under international law.[123] Accordingly, the ILA Principles of Reparation name in its art. 5 international organisations and other non-state actors as parties responsible for a violation of rules of international law and thus liable to make reparation under its art. 6.[124]

3. REPARATION UNDER DOMESTIC LAW

Next to rights to reparation under international law, claims for reparation for violations of human rights and international humanitarian law suffered in the course of an armed conflict also exist in the framework of a domestic legal system. A violation of a human right or a right under international humanitarian law generally constitutes an unlawful behaviour under domestic law which gives rise to actions under, for example, tort law or the law of state liability.

In former times, claims against the government for unlawful acts of its organs were usually barred from jurisdiction and a claim was only possible against the individual acting for the government.[125] This situation, in which 'the King can do no wrong' has since changed.[126] Nowadays, states even have the obligation to provide for an effective remedy for individuals pursuant to international law, which means that states have to allow proceedings against the domestic government for alleged violations of human rights and international humanitarian law.[127] The domestic legal orders differ when it comes to the question as to whether the individual whose unlawful behaviour is attributable to the state is liable next to the state.[128]

Whilst domestic claims for human rights violations and especially torture are increasingly discussed and recognised before domestic courts when they are resulting from incidents which happened in times of peace,[129] domestic courts are reluctant to recognise claims under domestic law resulting from violations of human rights and international humanitarian law during an armed conflict.

3.1 Parallelism

Claims under domestic law and claims under international public law resulting from the same incident exist next to each other. This parallelism can be demonstrated by the procedure of diplomatic protection used in international public law and by the obligation of states to provide redress for individuals stipulated in international treaties.

Mirroring international customary law,[130] art. 1 of the Draft Articles on Diplomatic Protection of the International Law Commission (ILC) of 2006 defines diplomatic protection as

> the invocation by a State, through diplomatic action or other means of peaceful settlement, of the responsibility of another State for an injury caused by an internationally wrongful act of

that State to a natural or legal person that is a national of the former State with a view to the implementation of such responsibility.[131]

If the unlawful act is a violation of both international law and domestic law, the exhaustion of local remedies is the prerequisite for the exercise of diplomatic protection, as the state in which the violation occurred should have the opportunity to redress it by its own means.[132] Traditionally, the prevailing opinion was that the exhaustion of local remedies by the individual was a material condition for the existence of the state claim under international law brought forward by way of diplomatic protection.[133] By espousing the private individual claim and presenting it diplomatically to the injuring state, the private claim was considered to become international and as being merged into the international claim of the state.[134] Thus, the claim of an individual under the domestic legal order and the state claim under international public law resulting from an injury of an individual were not existing in parallel. These days, the fulfilment of the local remedies rule is no longer considered as a material condition for the existence of the state claim, but as a procedural requirement for the exercise of diplomatic protection.[135] As a consequence, a state claim can exist independently of the exhaustion of local remedies. The claim of an individual under domestic law and the claim under international public law are triggered at the same time, namely the moment the violation occurs. The claim under domestic law subsists if a state invokes a claim under international law. Both claims exist side by side.[136]

The parallelism of claims under domestic and international public law also becomes evident when looking at the international obligations of states to provide for an effective remedy and thus for a procedure to assert the violation and a right to receive reparation.[137] According to art. 2 para. 3 lit. a ICCPR, for example, the state has to provide for a possibility of redress for the individual in its domestic legal system in case of a violation of a human right guaranteed under the ICCPR. At the same time, such a violation triggers the responsibility of the injuring state under international law towards an individual and/or its home state. Thus, the violation of a human right gives rise to a claim under domestic law existing next to the international claim resulting from the principles of international responsibility.

3.2 Parallelism During an Armed Conflict

It is often stated that incidents during an armed conflict could not give rise to claims under domestic law. The three main arguments put forward are (1) that there was a rule existing under international law which demanded reparation to be made under international law and excluded claims under domestic law;[138] (2) that the domestic legal order would be suspended during an armed conflict; and (3) that the armed forces should enjoy complete legal freedom of action in the field.

(1) The theory of exclusivity of international law was brought up by *Feaux de la Croix*, the highest ranking official expert on reparation in the Federal Republic of Germany, who had a previous career during the Nazi regime where he worked at the Reich Ministry of Justice from 1934 until 1945.[139] Not surprisingly, there is no rule or principle according to which claims in the context of an international armed conflict would have to be solved under international law.[140] Indeed, in the past, states very often

waived claims of their nationals against foreign states or agreed not to pursue such claims in peace treaties.[141] But such waivers rather speak in favour of the assumption that claims of individuals are not automatically excluded under a rule of international law. If such claims did not exist initially, a waiver would not be needed. The German Federal Constitutional Court followed this assessment in a case concerning forced labour during World War II and ruled that an incident during an armed conflict may trigger claims under both a domestic legal order and under international law.[142]

(2) The German Federal Supreme Court, dealing with compensation claims of relatives of Greek civilians who were massacred in Distomo in 1944, held that the national legal order was suspended in times of war, and that therefore claims under national law did not exist – at least, according to the situation prevailing at the time of World War II. A specific international legal liability regime would overlap with an individual claim under domestic law.[143] A German Regional Higher Court applied this reasoning to a more recent incident concerning claims brought by civilian victims having suffered harm as a consequence of the destruction of a bridge in Varvarin in Serbia by NATO air raids.[144] The Court of Appeal reversed the initial ruling, holding that in the light of the German fundamental law and due to the developments in the international legal order, the individual has to have the possibility of redress, especially in times of an armed conflict where the state applies its most powerful means.[145] And indeed, there is no rule under either German[146] or international law stipulating the suspension of the national legal order during an armed conflict. In contrast, the *ius in bello*, being applicable next to the legal order during an armed conflict, requires in common art. 1 of the Geneva Conventions and art. 1 para. 1 Additional Protocol I that the parties to the instruments respect the Conventions and the Protocol under all circumstances. This obligation is not met by suspending the domestic legal order, but by ensuring that a violation of an individual right resulting from the *ius in bello* can be sanctioned, which, in turn, can be achieved by remedies before domestic courts.[147] The obligation to provide remedies is also stated, for more recent incidents, in the human rights instruments for violations of human rights adopted after World War II.[148] Equally, principle 3 lit. d of the Basic Principles formulates that the 'obligation to respect, ensure respect for and implement international human rights and humanitarian law... includes, inter alia, the duty to provide effective remedies to victims, including reparation'.

Heß points out that in the discussion about the existence of claims under domestic law very often no differentiation is made between the substantive claim and the procedural way to enforce the claim.[149] As international armed conflicts very likely result in situations of mass violations, individual domestic claims may be deferred by compensation mechanisms under international or national law including under compensation schemes in the framework of a social security system.[150] These other ways of seeking compensation for victims do not change the fact that claims under national law initially existed.

(3) Under the heading of 'combat immunity'[151] claims related to immediate operational decisions and actions in a situation of armed conflict were usually dismissed by courts in the Commonwealth. This principle was first described in 1940 by the majority of judges of the Australian High Court:

The uniform tendency of the law has been to concede to the armed forces complete legal freedom of action in the field, that is to say in the course of active operations against the enemy, so that the application of private law by the ordinary courts may end where the active use of arms begins. Consistently with this tendency the civil law of negligence cannot attach to active naval operations against the enemy.[152]

One of the judges agreed with the majority that actions of the armed forces on a battlefield are not justiciable before national courts during the armed conflict; however, he argued that if the conflict has come to an end, courts might rule upon the actions.[153] More recent decisions also excluded the application of civil liability to battlefield situations. In *Mulcahy v. Ministry of Defence*, the English Court of Appeal ruled in 1996 that a claim would be excluded as the loss was suffered in the course of an actual military action taking place during an armed conflict. It denied the claim, as 'those engaged in fighting the enemy should not have to concern themselves with the possibility of actions against them for negligence.'[154] In *Bici v. Ministry of Defence* an English Court of Appeal limited the application of the principle of combat immunity by finding that it would only apply when soldiers acted in self-defence or in a situation of necessity, as only such situations would allow the soldiers to act free from any legal fetters for negligent or intentional acts.[155] In these cases, the acts of soldiers are usually in accordance with the *ius in bello* anyway, and thus the principle of combat immunity does not seem to stipulate an exception from liability. Consequently, *Lord Bingham of Cornhill* stated in an *obiter dictum* in *Al-Skeini* regarding violations of international humanitarian law: 'An action in tort may, on appropriate facts, be brought in this country against the Secretary of State: see *Bici v Ministry of Defence* … .'[156]

Under US law, for example, actions against the US government must be authorised through an explicit waiver of the immunity by Congress. The Federal Tort Claims Act (FTCA)[157] waives the sovereign immunity of the US for claims for money damages for injury or loss of property, or personal injury or death caused by federal governmental agents. Similarly, the Administrative Procedure Act (APA)[158] makes the US liable for non-monetary suits against federal agencies under specified conditions. However, both the FTCA and the APA exclude from their review actions based on, respectively, 'combatant activities of the military or naval forces … during time of war',[159] and 'military authority exercised in the field in time of war or in occupied territory'.[160]

In Germany, the Federal Court of Justice found that armed forces were given a broad scope for judgement evaluation which escaped judicial scrutiny, and a claim under domestic state liability could only arise if the behaviour of the armed forces was evidently in violation of international law.[161]

By relying on the principle of combat immunity or excluding claims for military combat activities, statutes and courts deny claims arising out of a battlefield situation in order to protect the freedom of decision and action in military operations. However, this military freedom is already limited under the *ius in bello*, which takes military considerations and military necessity into account and ponders them in relation to humanitarian concerns. The *ius in bello*, which is especially made for the behaviour of armed forces on the battlefield, regulates military actions during an armed conflict and thus sets the standard to which military behaviour has to adhere. The freedom of military decisions and actions within these rules can be granted to the military forces without entirely denying the access to the courts and thus creating a lawless situation.

If the behaviour of military forces is in accordance with the *ius in bello*, this conformity excludes claims under the domestic law. If, in contrast, a violation of the *ius in bello* has led to harm, the violation has to be sanctioned and thus the loss can be claimed under domestic law. Accordingly, art. 13 of the ILA Principles of Reparation demands that 'States shall assure that victims have a right to reparation under national law'.

3.3 *Ius in Bello* and the Domestic Legal Order

The *ius in bello* is applicable within the domestic legal order. According to the different theories explaining the relationship between international and domestic law, the *ius in bello*, being a set of norms of international law, is either immediately incorporated into the law upon ratification of international treaties by states adhering to the monist theory, or exists within the domestic law after its transformation in domestic law in respect to states following the theory of dualism.[162] With the *ius in bello* existing in the domestic legal order, the norms of the *ius in bello* constitute binding rules. However, in a legal relationship of an individual such as a claim of the individual, a norm of international law can only be decisive if the norm is directly applicable.[163] This is the case if a norm determines legal consequences for a specific case directly without the need of any further sovereign act for its execution.[164] As for the norms of the *ius in bello*, especially those which address a party to the conflict, they contain clear and specific rules of behaviour during an armed conflict. Thus, they are directly applicable. Accordingly, the US Supreme Court, for example, held in *Hamdan v. Rumsfeld* that the Geneva Conventions can be invoked by an individual to determine his legal status, which was in this specific case to challenge the government's plan to prosecute him by a military commission established in violation of the Geneva Conventions.[165]

As the *ius in bello* is applicable in a domestic legal order and regulates behaviour during an armed conflict, it can influence claims under domestic law arising from incidents during an armed conflict. If a violation of the *ius in bello* constitutes a violation within the domestic legal order as well, there is not necessarily any influence of the *ius in bello* upon a domestic claim. The targeted killing of a civilian, for example, contradicts art. 51 para. 4 lit. a Additional Protocol I. At the same time, wrongful behaviour generally gives rise to claims for reparation under the domestic legal orders. Nevertheless, in the US, for example, the courts refer directly to the *ius in bello* when recognizing claims for reparation resulting from war crimes under the Alien Tort Claim Act of 1789.[166]

If, in contrast, the killing of a civilian during an armed conflict was in accordance with the *ius in bello*, the *ius in bello* can exclude a claim otherwise resulting from the incident under domestic law. Depending on the legal dogmatic in the domestic legal order, the compliance of a harmful act with the rules of the *ius in bello* can be invoked as justification[167] or change the standard of negligence.[168] The Court of Appeals Cologne, for example, stated in *Varvarin* that the duty of soldiers owed to the individual under the rules of state liability during an armed conflict is determined by directly applying the *ius in bello*.[169]

Allowing claims under domestic law arising from incidents during an armed conflict is, therefore, not limiting the military freedom more than it is restricted by humanitarian concerns reflected in the *ius in bello* in any event. Domestic claims only sanction a behaviour which is not in accordance with the *ius in bello* and thus strengthen the *ius in bello*. As Judge Elias puts it in *Bici v. Ministry of Defence* when considering the application of civil liability: 'Troops frequently have to carry out difficult and sensitive peace keeping functions ... whilst still being subject to common law duties of care. The difficulties of their task are reflected in the standard of the duty rather than by denying its applicability.'[170]

4. REFLECTIONS ON THE ENFORCEMENT

As the holder of a right does not necessarily need to possess the procedural capacity to enforce his or her right, the question naturally arises as to how such rights can be enforced. Individual rights under international law can be pursued at an international level by the home state or, in some instances, by the individual, and at the national level by the individual. Claims arising under domestic law can be enforced at the national level by the individual.

4.1   Enforcement at the International Level

The individual still has a rather weak position when it comes to the enforcement of his or her rights at the international level. As for human rights violations, there is, meanwhile, the European Court of Human Rights, the African Court on Human and Peoples' Rights, the Inter-American Commission on Human Rights and the Human Rights Committee of the ICCPR, all of which can be addressed directly by an individual.[171] The international human rights bodies are not competent to rule on violations of international humanitarian law as such, however, as international humanitarian law determines the scope of human rights during an armed conflict, it is directly or indirectly referred to by the international human rights bodies.[172] If the individual is the victim of a crime for which the trial is pending before the International Criminal Court, he or she can request a ruling of the Court on reparation pursuant to art. 75 Rome Statute.[173]

Apart from these procedural means, an individual is generally dependent on the assistance of its home state to enforce his or her rights at the international level. Individual rights under international law can be enforced by a state exercising its diplomatic protection, meaning the invocation by a state of the responsibility of another state for an injury caused by an internationally wrongful act.[174] For a long time, the 'Vattelian fiction' or the 'Mavrommatis principle'[175] was, to use the words of the ILC, the 'cornerstone of diplomatic protection'.[176] According to this principle, an injury to a national was considered to be an injury to the state itself. Due to the recognition of the individual as a bearer of subjective rights under international public law, this fiction can no longer be upheld.[177] To quote the ILC again: 'A State does not "in reality" – to quote *Mavrommatis* – assert its own right only. "In reality" it also asserts the right of its injured national'.[178] From the point of view of international law, a state is not obliged to exercise diplomatic protection for its national; however, such an obligation towards the individual might result from a national legal order.[179]

Within the system of the UNCC and the EECC, the individual had no standing and generally his or her home state was acting as representative for the individual.[180]

The ILA has not only adopted its Principles of Reparation, but is currently working on a Draft Model Statute of an Ad Hoc International Compensation Commission.[181] It should serve as a guideline for the actual establishment of such a commission by state agreement or resolution. The capacity of individuals to submit claims is explicitly stated in art. 4 of the current version of the Draft Model Statute, however, the claims should be forwarded by the state according to its art. 5.[182]

4.2 Enforcement at the National Level

Individuals have the capacity to participate in domestic proceedings and are thus generally able to address domestic courts without any assistance. Before domestic courts, individuals can bring actions under either international or national law. As the claims arise out of an armed conflict, they might have to overcome obstacles such as the justiciability of the claim or the immunity of a defending state or state official in another forum state during the proceedings.

4.2.1 Cause of action and proceedings

As international law is valid in the domestic legal order,[183] individuals can base their actions on rights resulting from human rights and international humanitarian law. As far as international rights to reparation for individuals are recognised by domestic courts, they can serve directly as a cause of action. Accordingly, art. 3 Hague Convention IV, for example, was invoked and recognised as an entitlement to compensation by courts in Greece and in Germany.[184] In the US, elements of international and domestic law are combined in the so-called transnational public law litigation.[185] Civil claims for compensation are filed before US courts based on a violation of international public law.

According to the domestic legal order, claims for reparation arising out of the violation of a right of an individual can be brought in administrative, civil or penal proceedings. Indeed, in jurisdictions such as Germany, Italy or the Netherlands, a victim can participate in criminal proceedings and bring a claim for compensation based on domestic law upon which the criminal court will decide.[186]

4.2.2 Obstacles

By applying the political question theory or the non-justiciability doctrine, for example, domestic courts deny jurisdiction for claims concerning highly political governmental acts as the court would not have the power to review them.[187] In the past, domestic courts have relied on these theories in order to deny the claims of individuals which have arisen during an armed conflict.[188] In *Markovic*, the Italian Supreme Court ruled that Italian courts had no jurisdiction to examine the claims against Italy for compensation for damage sustained as a result of an air strike by NATO forces.[189] *Frulli* points out that whilst the decision to participate in military operations is made by the parliament and, due to the discretion inherent to such a question, this decision might not be examinable by domestic courts, claims of individuals concerning a specific behaviour during an armed conflict are not exempted from judicial review. She states:

> It follows that judicial review should not be automatically discarded with respect to single acts of war, since such acts – in addition to the possibly breaching rules of international humanitarian law binding upon Italy – may infringe, at a national level, on fundamental human rights proclaimed in the Italian Constitution and complemented by the rights to judicial redress.[190]

Moreover, it is interesting to note that Italian courts are less hesitant to examine military acts of an armed conflict if they are attributable to a state other than Italy.[191]

As for the potential obstacle of state immunity,[192] the issue does not arise if individuals bring claims for reparation before the domestic courts of the state which is responsible for the violation triggering the reparation, as such claims are not barred by the rule of immunity under international law.[193] If, in contrast, individuals file suits for acts of a state which are considered to be *acta iure imperii* before other domestic courts, they can deny their jurisdiction because of state immunity. There are exceptions from the rule of immunity. First of all, a state can waive its immunity. Additionally, there is the tort exception found in international conventions and domestic laws according to which immunity does not apply for tortious behaviour having led to death or personal injury or damage or loss of tangible property[194] which has a certain connection to the forum state.[195] Further, there is an increasing trend to recognise an exception for violations of norms considered to *be ius cogens*.[196] *Furuya* interprets art. 41 Draft Articles on Responsibility, which stipulates that a state has a duty not to recognise as lawful a situation created by a serious breach of another state of a *jus cogens* norm, as a procedural rule demanding a forum state not to grant immunity to a behaviour constituting a violation of *ius cogens* as applying immunity in such cases would imply the recognition of the wrongful behaviour.[197]

There are domestic court decisions in which these exceptions are applied to military acts as well.[198] Others do not follow this approach, arguing that military acts 'of their very nature, may involve sensitive issues affecting diplomatic relations between States and national security'.[199] Böhmer argues that military acts have to be immune as they are not individualised violations but a mere reflex of an aggression.[200] However, military behaviour cannot be seen as being just a corollary of a violation of the *ius ad/contra bellum* on the basis that single acts might constitute violations of *ius in bello*. It should also be noted that *acta iure imperii* are always touching upon sensitive areas as they are, by nature, governmental acts. There is no reason why violations of individual rights should only be judged if they have not occurred during an armed conflict. The fact that such violations usually occur on a bigger scale during an armed conflict can be dealt with, for example, by mass claim procedures like class actions.

It seems that the rule of immunity resulting from international law is changing, and whilst there is no longer a rule demanding that immunity be granted for all *acta iure imperii*, there is equally no fully established rule yet that immunity cannot be granted for tortious behaviour or violations of *ius cogens* norms. The decisions of the Italian courts, which did not recognise Germany's immunity for its war crimes committed during World War II, have lead to a proceeding before the ICJ instituted by Germany which is pending at the date of writing this chapter.[201] The outcome will certainly influence the debate about immunity.

4.3 Competition

With parallel claims resulting from the same cause at different levels of law and potential different mechanisms to enforce the claim, the question of competition as between the different enforcement procedures naturally arises. The different claims and enforcement mechanisms should not result in a double obligation of the perpetrator.[202] Usually, this problem is solved by the local remedies rule. A state is generally only allowed to bring its or the individual claim for reparation resulting from an injury of an individual under international public law if the individual has exhausted all procedural means available under domestic law, meaning that the claims will not be enforceable by the individual under domestic law. The same solution has been chosen by most of the different mechanisms under international public law, allowing individuals to bring their claims for violations of international law. A claim before the regional court on human rights is generally only admissible if the individual has exhausted local remedies in trying to enforce his potential claims before national institutions.[203] The situation was different within the system of the UNCC and the EECC. As they were especially set up to deal with claims arising from an armed conflict, there was no need to exhaust local remedies. In order to avoid any double payment, the UNCC asked the governments to provide them with information concerning lawsuits or payments dealing with claims falling in the jurisdiction of the UNCC.[204] The EECC tried to establish its exclusive competence in art. 5 para. 8 Peace Agreement by stating that the EECC would be the sole forum where claims arising from the conflict could be heard. Nevertheless, in *Nemariam v. Federal Democratic Republic of Ethiopia*, the US Court of Appeals refused to apply the principle of *forum non convenience* in order to decline its jurisdiction, as it held that the EECC was not an adequate forum due to the possibility of the state parties to waive individual claims, and due to the fact that the decisions of the EECC were not made directly in favour of individuals.[205] Nevertheless, four years later, the case was dismissed for lack of subject matter jurisdiction as the claim was considered to be barred by immunity.[206] The competence of parallel enforcement procedures can be considered to be beneficial as it allows mutual checks. Further, if reparation has already been made, the party liable to make reparation could bring an objection that the reparation had already been made.

5. CONCLUDING REMARKS

Reparation for individual victims of violations of human rights or international humanitarian law during an armed conflict can be based on treaty norms providing for reparation under human rights and international humanitarian law. Additionally, according to the principles of international responsibility, a right to reparation for an individual emerges as a secondary right in case of a violation of rights guaranteed under human rights and international humanitarian law. A right to reparation can result from domestic law, and, especially, from tort law or the law of state liability.

Whereas it is still difficult for individuals to enforce their rights under international law at the international level without the assistance of a state, an individual has *locus standi* before domestic courts and can bring claims for reparation based on domestic and international law. However, claims arising from an incident during an armed conflict were historically seldom recognised and enforced before domestic courts. The same arguments were brought forward when examining the jurisdiction, justiciability, immunity or the question of the effectiveness of state waivers: (i) courts were not in a position to judge upon political issues such as armed conflicts; (ii) the military would need freedom of action; (iii) domestic courts would not have the capacity to deal with mass claims; and (iv) mass claims would exceed the financial resources of the debtor and could therefore not be invoked as a state should not be stripped of its financial basis. Ultimately, none of these arguments are convincing. The rules of the *ius in bello* are legal rules, compliance to which is a legal and not a political issue. Whilst the answer of a legal question can indeed have political implications, it cannot lead to the rejection of the legal examination of the situation due to a lack of standardised rules. During an armed conflict, the armed forces are not free from judicial scrutiny. The law of armed conflicts sets the pace for the radius for operation by considering military necessities. Armed forces have to respect these rules and bear the consequences in cases where they do not do so. The problem of mass claims can be solved by finding the appropriate modalities for the participation of a large number of victims,[207] as already existent in some legal orders, with the possibility, for example, of class actions. Equally, the extreme case of lack of resources of the defendant can influence the form and modalities of compensation payments. As long as there is no effective international procedure available for the reparation claims of individuals, domestic courts should take their role in ensuring respect for human rights and international humanitarian law by granting reparation in case of its violation.

NOTES

*   Elke Schwager is a judge at the District Court, Munich (Langericht München). This chapter expresses the author's personal views. It was written in 2010, and so does not take into account any later developments.

1.   For an encompassing analysis, see P. d'Argent, *Les reparations de guerre en droit international public: la responsabilité internationale des Etats à l'épreuve de la guerre* (Bruxelles: Bruylant/LGDJ, 2002); A. Gattini, *Le riparazioni di guerra nel diritto internazionale* (Padua: CEDAM, 2003); E. Schwager, *Ius bello durante et bello confecto* (Berlin: Duncker & Humblot, 2008).

2.   A/RES/60/147, 21 March 2006.

3.   Namely the Chicago Council on Global Affairs, the International Institute of Higher Studies in Criminal Sciences in Siracusa, Italy, and the Association Internationale de Droit Pénal International Human Rights Law Institute, 2007, available at: http://biblio.cdp-hrc.uottawa.ca/dbtw-wpd/docs/The%20 Chicago%20Principles%20on%20Post-Conflict%20Justice.pdf (accessed September 2010).

4.   Resolution No. 2/2010, Reparation for Victims of Armed Conflict; available at: http://www.ila-hq.org/ en/committees/index.cfm/cid/1018 (accessed September 2010).

5.   *Infra* note 94.

6.   Resolution No. 2/2010, Reparation for Victims of Armed Conflict; available at: http://www.ila-hq.org/ en/committees/index.cfm/cid/1018 (accessed September 2010).

7. H. Lauterpacht, *International Law and Human Rights* (London: Archon Books, 1950), 61. R. Provost, *International Human Rights and Humanitarian Law* (New York: Cambridge University Press, 2002), 16; E. Roucounas, 'Facteurs privé et droit international public', *RdC* 299 (2002): 48; A. Randelzhofer, 'The Legal Position of the Individual under Present International Law', in *State Responsibility and the Individual*, eds A. Randelzhofer and C. Tomuschat (The Hague: Kluwer Law International, 1999), 231, 234; for a different view, H. Kelsen, 'Unrecht und Unrechtsfolgen im Völkerrecht', *XII Zeitschrift für Öffentliches Recht* (1932): 481, 523; C. Tomuschat, 'Individual Reparation Claims in Instances of Grave Human Rights Violations: The Position under General International Law', in *State Responsibility and the Individual: Reparation in Instances of Grave Violations of Human Rights*, eds A. Randelzhofer and C. Tomuschat (The Hague: Kluwer Law International, 1999), 1, 11 *et seq.*

8. *LaGrand* (Germany v. United States), I.C.J. Reports 2001, 29, para. 77.

9. See already the Permanent Court of International Justice (PCIJ), *Jurisdiction of the Courts of Danzig*, PCIJ, Advisory Opinion, Series B, Nos 15 (1928), 17, 18: 'it cannot be disputed that the very object of an international agreement, according to the intention of the contracting parties, may be the adaptation by the parties of some definite rules creating individual rights and obligations and enforceable by national courts'. See also Roucounas, *supra* note 7, at 48–49.

10. *Legality of the Threat or Use of Nuclear Weapons*, Advisory Opinion, I.C.J. Reports 1996, 240, para. 25; *Legal Consequences of the Construction of a Wall in the Occupied Palestinian Territory*, Advisory Opinion, I.C.J. Reports 2004, 178, para. 106; *Case Concerning Armed Activities on the Territory of the Congo* (D.R. Congo v. Uganda), I.C.J. Reports 2005, 69, para. 216.

11. See Article 4, International Covenant on Civil and Political Rights (ICCPR); Article 15, European Convention on Human Rights (ECHR); Article 27, American Convention on Human Rights (ACHR).

12. General Comment 29: *States of Emergency (Article 4)*, HRC, 31 August 2001 (UN Doc. CCPR/C/21/Rev.1/Add.11), para. 14; IACtHR, Advisory Opinion, No. OC-9/87 of Judicial Guarantees in States of Emergency, Articles 27(2), 25 and 25(8), American Convention on Human Rights, 6 October 1987, Series A, No. 9, paras 22–24.

13. Article 8, Universal Declaration of Human Rights; Article 2, para. 3(a) ICCPR; Article 7 ACHPR; Article 13 ECHR.

14. E. Klein, 'Individual Reparation Claims under the International Covenant on Civil and Political Rights: The Practice of the Human Rights Committee', in *State Responsibility and the Individual: Reparation in Instances of Grave Violations of Human Rights*, eds A. Randelzhofer and C. Tomuschat (The Hague: Kluwer Law International, 1999), 27, 33; for a different view, R. Pisillo-Mazzeschi, 'International Obligations to Provide for Reparation Claims?', in ibid., 149, 164; C. Tomuschat, *Human Rights: Between Idealism and Realism* (Oxford: Oxford University Press, 2003), 298.

15. *Albert Wilson v. Philippines*, HRC, 11 November 2003 (UN Doc. CCPR/C/79/D/868/1999).

16. Article 1, para. 1, ACHR, contains the obligation to respect the rights recognised in the ACHR.

17. *Velásques Rodrígues v. Honduras*, IACtHR, Merits, Judgment of 29 July 1988, Series C, No. 7, para. 166.

18. E. Ankumah, *The African Commission on Human and Peoples' Rights* (Dordrecht: Martinus Nijhoff Publishers, 1996), 132; V. Nmehielle, *The African Human Rights System* (The Hague: Martinus Nijhoff Publishers, 2001), 103.

19. *Aksoy v. Turkey*, ECtHR, Application No. 21987/93, Judgment of 18 December 1996, para. 98.

20. Compensation is provided in case of a miscarriage of justice by, e.g., Article 10 ACHR and Article 3 of the Seventh Protocol to the ECHR; in case of spoliation according to Article 21, para. 2, ACHPR, and in case of an unlawful arrest or detention pursuant to Article 9, para. 5, ICCPR, and Article 5, para. 5, ECHR.

21. See, for instance, Article 14, para. 6, ICCPR, in case of a miscarriage of justice. The specific provisions stipulating an international right to compensation such as Article 5, para. 5, ECHR are not redundant even if the same international treaty, which foresees this specific provision, contains a general right to reparation as well, such as Article 13, ECHR. Specific provisions detail which form of reparation a state has to provide. Klein, *supra* note 14, at 27, 32; for a different view, C. Ovey and R. White, *Jacobs and White: The European Convention on Human Rights*, 4th edition (Oxford: Oxford University Press, 2006), 155.

22. Article 41, ECHR 'just satisfaction'; Article 63, para. 1, sentence 2, ACHR 'the breach of such right or freedom be remedied and fair compensation to be paid'; Article 27, Protocol to the ACHPR 'to remedy the violation, including the payment of fair compensation or reparation'.

23. The African Court on Human and Peoples' Rights has so far not pronounced an opinion in this respect.

24. *Papamichalopoulos and others v. Greece*, ECtHR, Application No. 14556/89, Judgment of 31 October 1995, Series A, No. 330-B, para. 34; *Scozzari and Giunta v. Italy*, ECtHR, Application Nos 39221/98 and 41963/98, Judgment of 13 July 2000, para. 249; *Maestri v. Italy*, ECtHR, Application No. 39748/98, Judgment of 17 February 2004, para. 47.

25. *Velásquez Rodríguez v. Honduras*, IACtHR, Reparations and Costs, Judgment of 21 July 1989, para. 25; *The Mayagna (Sumo) Awas Tingni Community v. Nicaragua*, IACtHR, Merits, Reparations and Costs, Judgment of 31 August 2001, para. 163.

26. I.C.J. Reports (2004), 136, paras. 152 *et seq.* See also *infra* section 2.3.

27. See from the long list of Decisions of the ECtHR concerning the conflict only, for example, *Isayeva v. Russia*, ECtHR, Application No. 57950/00, Decision, 24 February 2005, para. 231 *et seq.*; *Isayeva, Yusupova and Bazayeva v. Russia*, ECtHR, Application Nos 57947/00, 57948/00 and 57949/00, Decision, 24 February 2005, para. 241 *et seq.*; *Bazorkina v. Russia*, ECtHR, Application No. 69481/01, Decision, 27 July 2006, para. 181; *Chitayev and Chitayev v. Russia*, Application No. 59334/00, Decision, 18 April 2007, para. 212.

28. For the notions *ius ad bellum* and *ius contra bellum*, see *Behrami and Behrami v. France*, ECtHR, Application No. 71412/01, Decision on Admissibility, 2 May 2007, and *Saramati v. France, Germany and Norway*, ECtHR, Application No. 78166/01, Decision on Admissibility, 2 May 2007, paras 18 *et seq.*

29. Principle 1 of Resolution A/RES/2625 (XXV), 24 October 1970, Article 5, para. 2, of Resolution A/RES/3314 (XXIX), 14 December 1974, and Article 1 of Resolution A/RES/42/22, 18 November 1987.

30. German Federal Court of Justice, *Distomo*, 26 June 2003, *BGHZ*: 155, 279; F. Berber, *Lehrbuch des Völkerrechts: Kriegsrecht*, Vol. II (Munich: Beck,1962), 239, section 48; I. Brownlie, *International Law and the Use of Force by States* (Oxford: Clarendon, 1963), 147; d'Argent, *supra* note 1, at 449–461; for a different view, K.J. Partsch, 'Remnants of War', *AJIL* 78 (1984): 386, 392–393.

31. R. Wolfrum and D. Fleck, 'Enforcement of International Humanitarian Law', in *The Handbook of Humanitarian Law in Armed Conflicts*, ed. D. Fleck, 2nd edition (Oxford: Oxford University Press, 2008), 675, 707, para. 1417.3; T.V. Minh, 'Les réparations de guerre au Vietnam et le droit international', *RGDIP* 81 (1977): 1046, 1051–1054.

32. A. Randelzhofer, 'Use of Force,' in *EPIL*, ed. R. Bernhardt, *EPIL* IV(1999), 1246, 1250; d'Argent, *supra* note 1, at 476.

33. The Eritrea-Ethiopia Claims Commission (EECC) found itself competent to rule upon Eritrea's violation of the *ius ad/contra bellum*. Even though claims of individuals can be brought before the EECC by Eritrea or Ethiopia, the claims filed for a violation of the *ius ad/contra bellum* were claims of Ethiopia only. Final Award on Ethiopia's Damage Claim, 17 August 2009, available at: www.pca-cpa.org/showfile.asp?fil_id=1260

34. See Article 231 of the Treaty of Versailles, 28 June 1919, United Kingdom Treaty Series 4 (Cmd. 153). For the applicable *ius ad bellum* at that time, see Brownlie, *supra* note 30, at 135 *et seq.*

35. B. Eichhorn, *Reparation als völkerrechtliche Deliktshaftung: rechtliche und praktische Probleme unter besonderer Berücksichtigung Deutschlands (1918–1990)* (Baden Baden: Nomos, 1992), 75 *et seq.*; H.U. Granow, 'Ausländische Kriegsschäden und Reparationen', *Archiv des öffentlichen Rechts* 77 (1951–1952): 67, 68.

36. H. Jsay, *Die privaten Rechte und Interessen im Friedensvertrag* (Berlin: Vahlen, 1923), 156; d'Argent, *supra* note 1, at 47 *et seq.*

37. S/RES/687, 3 April 1991, and S/RES/692, 20 May 1991.

38. See Article 5, paras 1, 2 and 3 of the Provisional Rules for Claims Procedure, UN Doc. S/AC.26/Dec.10 (1992); V. Heiskanen, 'The United Nations Compensation Commission', *RdC* 296 (2002): 259, 328.

39. C. Alzamora, 'The UN Compensation Commission: An Overview', in *The United Nations Compensation Commission*, ed. R.B. Lillich (New York: Transnational, 1995), 3, 8–9; J.R. Crook, 'Is Iraq Entitled to Judicial Due Process?', in *The United Nations Compensation Commission*, ed. R.B. Lillich (New York: Transnational, 1995), 77, 80; N. Wühler, 'The United Nations Compensation Commission', in *State Responsibility and the Individual: Reparation in Instances of Grave Violations of Human Rights*, eds A. Randelzhofer and C. Tomuschat (The Hague: Kluwer Law International, 1999), 213, 216.

40. See Decisions Nos 1 and 18 of the Governing Council of the Commission, UN Doc. S/AC.26/Dec.1, (1991), para. 19; UN Doc. S/AC.26/Dec.18 (1994).

41. L. Lee, 'The Right of Victims of War to Compensation', in *Essays in Honor of Wang Tieya*, ed. R.S.J. Macdonald (Dordrecht: Martinus Nijhoff Publishers, 1994), 489, 493; Heiskanen, *supra* note 38, at 259, 328.

42. 12 December 2000, *ILM* 40 (2001): 260. Article 5, para. 1, sentence 2 reads: 'The mandate of the Commission is to decide through binding arbitration all claims for losses, damage or injury by one Government against the other, and by nationals (including both natural and juridical persons) of one party against the Government of the other party or entities owned or controlled by the other party that are (a) related to the conflict that was the subject of the Framework Agreement, the Modalities for its Implementation and the Cessation of Hostilities Agreement, and (b) result from violations of international humanitarian law, including the 1949 Geneva Conventions, or other violations of international law.'

43. Article 5, paras 8 and 9 of the Peace Agreement, Articles 23 and 24 (3)(b) of the Rules of Procedure of October 2001, available at: http://www.pca-cpa.org/showpage.asp?pag_id=1150 (accessed September 2010).

44. Civilians Claims, Eritrea's Claims 15, 16, 23 and 27–32, para. 19. Claims for injuries of Eritrean nationals were only brought on behalf of Eritrea and not explicitly on behalf of the individuals.

45. Convention Respecting the Laws and Customs of War on Land, 18 October 1907, in *Documents on the Law of War*, eds A. Roberts and R. Guelff, 3rd edition (Oxford: Oxford University Press, 2000), 67 *et seq.*

46. 8 June 1977, UN Treaty Series, Vol. 1125.

47. L. Oppenheim, *International Law*, Vol. II, 593 *et seq.* See also the Report of the International Commission of Inquiry on Darfur which refers to Article 3, Hague Convention IV, and thus applies it to the non-international conflict in Sudan, UN Doc. S/2005/60, 2005, para. 593 *et seq.*

48. For an overview of the different decisions, see P. Stammler, *Der Anspruch von Kriegsopfern auf Schadenersatz* (Berlin: Duncker & Humblot, 2009), 159–261; L. Zegveld, 'Remedies for victims of violations of International Humanitarian Law', *International Review of the Red Cross* 85 (2003): 497, 507 *et seq.*; S. H. Bong, 'Compensation for Victims of Wartime Atrocities', *JICJ* 3 (2005): 187.

49. R. Bank and E. Schwager, 'Is there a Substantive Right to Compensation for Individual Victims of Armed Conflict against a State under International Law?', *GYIL* 49 (2006): 367; E.-C. Gillard, 'Reparation for violations of international humanitarian law', *International Review of the Red Cross* 85 (2003): 529, 536; C. Greenwood, 'International Humanitarian Law (Law of War)', in *The Centennial of the First International Peace Conference*, ed. F. Kalshoven, (The Hague: Kluwer Law International, 2000), 161, 250; R. Hofmann, 'Victims of Violations of International Humanitarian Law: Do They Have an Individual Right to Reparation against States under International Law?', in *Common Values in International Law – Essays in Honour of Christian Tomuschat*, eds P.-M. Dupuy, B. Fassbender, M.N. Shaw and K.P. Sommermann (Kehl: Engel, 2006), 341, 357; F. Kalshoven, 'State Responsibility for Warlike Acts of the Armed Forces: From Article 3 of the Hague Convention IV of 1907 to Article 91 of Additional Protocol I and Beyond', *International and Comparative Law Quarterly* 40 (1991): 827; R. Pisillo Mazzeschi, 'Reparation Claims by Individuals for State Breaches of Humanitarian Law and Human Rights: An Overview', *JICJ* 1 (2003): 339, 342; M. Sassòli, 'State Responsibility for Violations of International Humanitarian Law', *International Review of the Red Cross* 84 (2002): 401, 419; Zegveld, *supra* note 48, at 497, 507. For a different view, see d'Argent, *supra* note 1, at 846; Tomuschat, *supra* note 14, at 294; D. Fleck, 'Individual and State Responsibility for Violations of the *Ius in Bello* – An Imperfect Balance', in *International Humanitarian Law Facing New Challenges*, eds W. Heintschel von Heinegg and V. Epping (Berlin: Springer, 2007), 190–193.

50. District Court of Tokyo, *Shimoda et al. v. The State*, 7 December 1963, *ILR* 32 (1964): 626; Tokyo High Court, *X et al. v. the State of Japan*, 7 August 1996, *Japanese AIL* 40 (1996): 117, 188; German Federal Court of Justice, *Distomo*, 26 June 2003, *Neue Juristische Wochenzeitschrift* (2003): 3488, 3491, for claims resulting from World War II; *Tel-Oren et al. v. Libyan Arab Republic*, (U.S.App.D.C. 1984), 726 F.2d 774, 810; *Goldstar (Panama) SA v. United States*, *ILM* (4th Cir. 1994): 55, 58–59; *Princz v. Federal Republic of Germany* (D.C.Cir. 1994), 26 F.3d 1166, 1175; K.J. Partsch, 'Humanitarian Law and Armed Conflict', in *EPIL*, R. Bernhard, 2nd edition (1995), 957, 959; Provost, *supra* note 7, at 27 *et seq.*, who considers the rules of international humanitarian law to be only standards of treatment or conduct and the individual merely a beneficiary of the rules rather than the holder of rights.

51. See, e.g., Article 13 of the Annex to the Hague Convention IV, Article 7 Geneva Convention III, Article 27, para. 1, Geneva Convention IV. Besides, states are not able to amend or waive, the position is granted to individuals under international humanitarian law; see, for example, Article 6, para. 1,

Geneva Convention III, Article 7, para. 1, Geneva Convention IV; and there are norms protecting individuals independently of their nationality; see, e.g., Article 6 of the Geneva Convention of 1864, Article 13 of the Geneva Convention IV of 1949 or the norms applicable during a non-international armed conflict. See J. Pictet, *Development and Principles of International Humanitarian Law* (Dordrecht: Martinus Nijhoff Publishers, 1985), 94; C. Greenwood, 'Rights at the Frontier – Protecting the Individual in Time of War,' in *Law at the Centre*, ed. B.A.K. Rider (London: Kluwer Law International, 1998), 281 *et seq.*

52. Pictet, *supra* note 51, at 94.

53. Y. Dinstein, 'Human Rights in Armed Conflict', in *Human Rights in International Law: Legal and Policy Issues*, ed. T. Meron, Vol. 2 (1984), 345, 355; T. Meron, 'The Humanization of Humanitarian Law', *AJIL* 94 (2000): 239, 253, who points out, that it was in the area of international humanitarian law, where the individual was first vested with rights and obligations under international law. Similarly, the ICJ, *Legal Consequences of the Construction of a Wall in the Occupied Palestinian Territory*, Advisory Opinion, I.C.J. Reports 2004, para. 95 in relation to the Geneva Convention IV of 1949.

54. German Federal Constitutional Court, *Italian Military Internees*, 26 April 2004, *Neue Juristische Wochenzeitschrift* (2004): 3257, 3258; German Federal Court of Justice, *Varvarin*, 2 November 2006, BGHZ 169, 348, in contrast to its earlier jurisprudence in *Distomo*, 26 June 2003, *BGHZ*: 155, 279; Gerechtshof Amsterdam, Vierde meervoudige burgerlijke kamer, *Dedovik v. Kok et al.*, 6 July 2000, para. 5.3.22, analysed by Zegveld, *supra* note 48, at 497, 504.

55. High Court Tokyo, *X et al. v. the Government of Tokyo*, 8 February 2001, *Japanese AIL* 45 (2002): 142, 143; *X et al. v. the Government of Tokyo*, High Court Tokyo, 11 October 2001, *Japanese AIL* 45 (2002): 144, 145; *Kasutani v. Iwamoto*, Japan, *YIHL* 3 (2000): 541, 544; Tomuschat, *supra* note 7, at 1, 11 *et seq.*

56. *Supra* section 2.

57. German Federal Constitutional Court, Italian Military Internees, 26 April 2004, *Neue Juristische Wochenzeitschrift* (2004): 3257, 3258; ibid., 15 February 2006, *Neue Juristische Wochenzeitschrift* (2006): 2542, 2543; High Court Tokyo, *X et al. v. the Government of Tokyo*, 8 February 2001, *Japanese AIL* 45 (2002): 143; *X et al. v. the Government of Tokyo*, 11 October 2001, *Japanese AIL* 45 (2002): 144, 145; High Court Tokyo, *So Shinto*, 30 November 2000, analysed by H. Kasutani and S. Iwamoto, Japan, *YIHL* 3 (2000): 541, 544; d'Argent, *supra* note 1, at 864; Tomuschat, *supra* note 14, at 294; B. Fassbender, 'Can Victims Sue State Officials for Torture? Reflections on *Rasul v. Myers* from the Perspective of International Law', *Journal of International Criminal Justice* 6 (2008): 357, 358.

58. Kalshoven, *supra* note 49, at 827 *et seq.*; Greenwood, *supra* note 49, at 161, 250; Zegveld, *supra* note 48, at 497, 506.

59. *Deuxième Conférence internationale de la Paix: actes et documents*, Vol. III, (1908), 144, 147, Vol. I, (1908), 103 *et seq.*

60. Official records of the Diplomatic Conference on the Reaffirmation and Development of International Humanitarian Law Applicable in Armed Conflicts, Geneva (1974–1977), Vol. III, 347, CDD/I/335 and Add. 1 and 2, IX, 355, 356: CDDH/I/SR.67.

61. Vienna Convention on the Law of Treaties, 23 May 1969, UN Treaty Series, Vol. 1155, 331.

62. Article 32, Vienna Convention on the Law of Treaties.

63. R. Bierzanek, 'The Responsibility of States in Armed Conflicts', *Polish YIL* XI (1981–1982): 93, 94.

64. *Deuxième Conférence internationale de la Paix: actes et documents*, Vol. I, (1908), 103.

65. Court rulings recognising Article 3, Hague Convention IV as an individual right: Higher Administrative Court, Münster, 9 April 1952, *ILR* (1952): 632–634; *Prefecture of Voiotia v. Federal Republic of Germany*, Court of First Instance of Leivadia, No. 137/1997, 30 October 1997, *RHDI* (1997): 595, 601, analysed by I. Bantekas, 'International Decisions, Prefecture of Voiotia v. Federal Republic of Germany', *ACIL* 92 (1998): 765. Not especially recurring on Article 3 of the Hague Convention IV, but presupposing an international right to compensation resulting from a violation of international humanitarian law: Special Supreme Court Greece, *Federal Republic of Germany v. Miltiadis Margellos*, 17 September 2002, in M. Panezi, 'Sovereign Immunity and Violation of *Ius Cogens* Norms', *RHDI* 56 (2003): 199; Corte Suprema di Cassazione, *Ferrini*, 11 March 2004, available in *Rivista di diritto internazionale* 87 (2004): 540.

66. Oppenheim, *supra* note 47, at 200.

67. 26 June 1945, *UNCIO* 15: 335.

68. Lauterpacht, *supra* note 7, at 61; Roucounas, *supra* note 7, at 24–40; R. McCorquodale, 'The Individual and the International Legal System', in *International Law*, ed. M.D. Evans, 2nd edition (Oxford: Oxford University Press, 2006), 307, 312 *et seq.*

69. See the rules providing for reparation established in the field of human rights, *supra* section 2.1.

70. Report of the International Commission of Inquiry on Darfur to the United Nations Secretary-General pursuant to Security Council Resolution 1564, 25 January 2005, para. 593 *et seq.*

71. The provision reads: 'Recalling the provisions providing a right to a remedy for victims of violations of ... international humanitarian law as found in Article 3 of the Hague Convention of 18 October 1907 concerning the Laws and Customs of War and Land (Convention No. IV, 1907), Article 91 of Additional Protocol to the Geneva Conventions of 12 August 1949 relating to the Protection of Victims of International Armed Conflicts (Protocol I).'

72. *Factory at Chorzów*, PCIJ, Judgment, Jurisdiction, Series A, No. 9 (1927), 3, 21; *Factory at Chorzów*, Judgment, Merits, PCIJ, Series A, No. 17 (1928), 29; Article 31, para. 1 of the ILC Draft Articles on State Responsibility for internationally wrongful acts (Draft Articles on State Responsibility), 9 August 2001, annexed to A/RES/56/83, 12 December 2001, and commended to states by A/RES/62/61, 8 January 2008.

73. *Factory at Chorzów*, Judgment, Merits, PCIJ, Series A, No. 17 (1928), 47; Article 42 Draft Articles on State Responsibility.

74. Provost, *supra* note 7, at 127.

75. See common Article 1 of the Geneva Conventions, J. Pictet, *Geneva Convention for the Amelioration of the Condition of the Wounded and Sick in Armed Forces in the Field: Commentary*, Vol. I (Geneva: ICRC, 1952), Article 1, 25.

76. Provost, *supra* note 7, at 128, 129.

77. When concluding the treaty, the States Parties attribute to the individual a right of their own, they conclude a Treaty containing provisions in favour of a third party; see A. Verdross and B. Simma, *Universelles Völkerrecht: Theorie und Praxis*, 3rd edition (Berlin: Duncker & Humblot, 1984), section 758, 762.

78. *LaGrand* (Germany v. United States), Judgment, I.C.J. Reports 2001, 466, 515, para. 128 (4).

79. W. Kälin and J. Künzli, *Zwischen Rigidität und Flexibilität: Der Verpflichtungsgrad internationaler Menschenrechte*, 2nd edition (Berlin: Duncker & Humblot, 2008), 78 *et seq.*; for a different view, J. Watson, *Theory and Reality in the International Protection of Human Rights* (New York: Transnational Publisher, 1999), 79.

80. Tomuschat, *supra* note 7, at 1, 12.

81. *Barcelona Traction* (Belgium v. Spain; 2nd phase), Judgment, I.C.J. Reports 1970, 3, 32; Article 33, Draft Articles on Responsibility.

82. In this sense, M. Shaw, *International Law*, 6th edition (Cambridge: Cambridge University Press, 2008), 778; C. de Visscher, *La responsabilité des Etats*, Vol. II (Leyde: Brill, 1929), 90.

83. *Factory at Chorzów*, PCIJ, Judgment, Merits, Series A, No. 17 (1928), 47.

84. See *Reparations for Injuries Suffered in the Service of the United Nations*, Advisory Opinion, I.C.J. Reports 1994, 174, 184 *et seq.*, where the International Court of Justice ruled that the United Nations are entitled to claim reparation even from states which are not members of the United Nations, and thus recurs to the general principle of international state responsibility; K. Ipsen, 'Völkerrechtliche Verantwortlichkeit und Völkerstrafrecht', in *Völkerrecht*, ed. K. Ipsen, 5th edition (Munich: Beck, 2004), section 39, footnote 4.

85. Third Report on State Responsibility, *Yearbook of the International Law Commission* II, UN Doc. A/CN.4/246/Add.1–3, 1971, 199, 208, with further references. In contrast, it was argued that the main characteristic of international responsibility would be the power of the injured party to take countermeasures; see Kelsen, *supra* note 7, at 494. This approach goes back to the classification of international law as a coercive order. However, due to the lack of comprehensive enforcement mechanisms, international law is mainly created by consensus; see H. Mosler, 'The International Society as a Legal Community', *RdC* 140 (1974): 1, 32 *et seq.*, for exceptions see, C. Tomuschat, 'Obligations Arising for States Without or Against their Will', *RdC* 241 (1993): 195, 248, 268.

86. K. Doehring, 'Handelt es sich bei einem Recht, das durch diplomatischen Schutz eingefordert wird, um ein solches, das dem die Protektion ausübenden Staat zusteht, oder geht es um die Erzwingung von Rechten des betroffenen Individuums?', in *Der diplomatische Schutz im Völker- und Europarecht aktuelle Probleme und Entwicklungstendenzen*, eds G. Ress and T. Stein (Baden-Baden: Nomos, 1996) 13, 15, 16.

87.   Third Report on State Responsibility, *Yearbook of the International Law Commission* II, UN Doc. A/CN.4/246/Add.1–3, 1971, 199, 209, 210.

88.   A. Fischer-Lescano, 'Subjektivierung völkerrechtlicher Sekundärregeln', *Archiv des Völkerrechts* 45 (2007): 299, 304.

89.   *Legal Consequences of the Construction of a Wall in the Occupied Palestinian Territory*, Advisory Opinion, I.C.J. Reports 2004, para. 152; E. Schwager, 'The Right to Compensation for Victims of an Armed Conflict', *Chinese JIL* 4 (2005): 417, 430.

90.   *Velásquez Rodríguez v. Honduras*, IACtHR, Reparations and Costs, Judgment of 21 July 1989, Series C, No. 7, para. 25; *The Mayagna (Sumo) Awas Tingni Community v. Nicaragua*, IACtHR, Merits, Reparations and Costs, Judgment of 31 August 2001, Series C, No. 79, para. 163.

91.   Corte Suprema di Cassazione, *Ferrini v. Federal Republic of Germany*, 11 March 2004, No. 5044/2004, para. 9, *ILR* (2006): 658; Special Supreme Court Greece, *Federal Republic of Germany v. Miltiadis Margellos*, 17 September 2002; in Panezi, *supra* note 65, at 199.

92.   Commentaries to the Draft Articles on Responsibility of States for internationally wrongful acts (A/56/10), Article 28, 214.

93.   Principle 6, 7 of the version of 24 May 1996, UN Doc. E/CN.4/1996/17; d'Argent, *supra* note 1, at 790.

94.   See para. 7 of the Preamble of the Basic Principles and Guidelines; General Observations in UN Doc. E/CN.4/2004/57, Appendix 2003, 5, No. 10.

95.   For a different view, R. Hofmann, 'Do Victims of Armed Conflict Have an Individual Right to Reparation?', in *Report of the Seventy-Second Conference*, ILA, 2006, 766, 767.

96.   Draft Conference Report, The Hague 2010, Article 6, Commentary (2)(b), available at: http://www.ila-hq.org/en/committees/index.cfm/cid/1018 (accessed September 2010).

97.   See para. 6 of the Preamble of the Basic Principles and Guidelines.

98.   Article 3, para. 1, 'Draft Declaration of International Law Principles on Compensation for Victims of War', in *Report of the Seventy-Third Conference*, ILA, ed., 2008, 462, 466.

99.   Draft Conference Report, The Hague 2010, Article 4, Commentary (3), available at: http://www.ila-hq.org/en/committees/index.cfm/cid/1018 (accessed in September 2010).

100. *Isayeva, Yusupova and Bazayeva v. Russia*, ECtHR, Application Nos 57947/00, 57948/00 and 57949/00, Judgment of 24 February 2005.

101. *Factory at Chorzów*, PCIJ, Judgment, Merits, Series A, No. 17 (1928), 47; Article 30, 35–38, Draft Articles on State Responsibility; Principle 15–23, Basic Principles and Guidelines; Articles 7 to 10, ILA, Principles of Reparation.

102. Draft Conference Report, The Hague, Article 7, Commentary (3), available at: http://www.ila-hq.org/en/committees/index.cfm/cid/1018 (accessed September 2010).

103. *Moiwana Community v. Suriname*, IACtHR, Preliminary Exceptions, Merits, Reparations and Costs, Judgment of 15 June 2005, para. 194; *Mayagna (Sumo) Awas Tingi Community v. Nicaragua*, IACtHR, Merits, Reparations and Costs, Judgment of 31 August 2001; Rules 97 and 98, Rules of Procedure and Evidence of the ICC; F. Rosenfeld, 'Collective Reparation for Victims of Armed Conflict', *International Review of the Red Cross* 92 (2010).

104. *Factory at Chorzów*, PCIJ, Judgment, Merits, Series A, No. 17 (1928), 47; *Case Concerning Armed Activities on the Territory of the Congo* (D.R. Congo v. Uganda), I.C.J. Reports 2005, 93, para. 259; Article 31, para. 1, Draft Articles on State Responsibility.

105. Draft Conference Report, The Hague, Article 6, Commentary (6), available at http://www.ila-hq.org/en/committees/index.cfm/cid/1018 (accessed September 2010).

106. W.M. Reisman, 'Compensation for Human Rights Violations: The Practice of the Past Decade in the Americas', in *State Responsibility and the Individual: Reparation in Instances of Grave Violations of Human Rights*, eds A. Randelzhofer and C. Tomuschat (The Hague: Kluwer Law International, 1999), 63, 67; Tomuschat, *supra* note 7, at 1, 19.

107. UN Doc. A/CN.4/488 (1998), 105; Eichhorn, *supra* note 35, at 82, 109.

108. Brownlie, *supra* note 30, at 135 *et seq.*

109. The EECC took the difficult economic conditions found in the affected areas of Ethiopia and Eritrea into account when assessing compensation for violations of the *ius in bello* as well; see Press Release of 19 August 2009. It explained in its Final Award on Eritrea's Damage Claims, 17 August 2009, para. 3: 'Moreover, as the claims addressed in this Award are almost entirely claims by the State Party for compensation for violations of law that it has suffered, rather than claims on behalf of its nationals, the Commission has been compelled to make judgements not as to appropriate compensation for individual victims, but instead as to the relative seriousness of those violations of law and

the effects they had on the Claimant State Party.' Both available at http://www.pca-cpa.org/
showpage.asp?pag_id=1151 (accessed September 2010).

110. M. Eichhorst, *Rechtsprobleme der United Nations Claims Commission* (Berlin: Duncker & Humblot, 2002), 99.

111. Report of the International Law Commission on the work of its forty-eighth session, UN Doc. A/51/10 (1996), Commentary 8(b), 153, para. 19. For the discussion, see also Bank and Schwager, *supra* note 49, at 367.

112. A. Clapham, *Human Rights Obligations of Non-State Actors* (Oxford: Oxford University Press, 2006); D. Fleck, 'Humanitarian Protection Against Non-State Actors', in *Verhandeln für den Frieden/Negotiating for Peace. Liber Amicorum Tono Eitel*, eds J. Frowein, K. Scharioth, I. Winkelmann and R. Wolfrum (Berlin: Springer, 2003), 69–94; L. Zegveld, *Accountability of Armed Opposition Groups in International Law*, (Cambridge: Cambridge University Press, 2002).

113. International Law Commission Commentaries to the Draft Articles on Responsibility of States for internationally wrongful acts (A/56/10), Article 10, para. 16.

114. Rome Statute of the International Court of Justice, 17 July 1998, UN Doc. A/CONF.183/9. Rule 106 of the Rules of Procedure and Evidence of the International Criminal Tribunal for the former Yugoslavia and the similar Rule 106 of the Rules of Procedure and Evidence of the International Criminal Tribunal for Rwanda deal with compensation for victims stating that the victim can bring a claim before the competent national authority in order to obtain compensation. According to the wording of these Rules, the claim for compensation has to be judged pursuant to domestic law. The Rules are therefore not establishing a claim under international law.

115. So far, no order was rendered under this provision. See C. Ferstman and M. Goetz, 'Reparations before the International Criminal Court: The Early Jurisprudence on Victim Participation and its Impact on Further Reparation Proceedings', in *Reparations for Victims of Genocide, War Crimes and Crimes Against Humanity*, eds C. Ferstman, M. Goetz and A. Stephens (Leiden: Martinus Nijhoff Publishers, 2009), 313.

116. See only General Comment No. 31: *Nature of the General Legal Obligation Imposed on States Parties to the Covenant*, HRC, 26 May 2004 (UN Doc. CCPR/C/21/Rev.1/Add.13), para. 8 of the Human Rights Committee of the ICCPR: 'The Article 2, Paragraph 1, obligations are binding on States [Parties] and do not, as such, have direct horizontal effect as a matter of international law.'

117. See, for example, Article VI of the Convention on the Prevention and Punishment of the Crime of Genocide, Article 1, para. 1 of the Convention Against Torture and Other Cruel, Inhuman or Degrading Treatment or Punishment.

118. *Supra* note 79.

119. C. Tomuschat, 'The Applicability of Human Rights to Insurgent Movements', in *Krisensicherung und Humanitärer Schutz*, eds H. Fischer, U. Froissart, W. H. von Heinegg and C. Raap (Berlin: Berliner Wissenschafts-Verlag , 2004), 573, 587.

120. However, an individual is not necessarily bound to respect the same content of a specific right as a state. If the potential violator of a human rights norm is an individual, its right might have to be taken into account when determining whether an infringement of the rights of another person has occurred.

121. As for Treaties containing international obligations for individuals such as the Torture Convention, the situation is different in so far as the obligation to pay compensation pursuant to Article 14 of the Convention is especially valid for the individual perpetrator. However, Article 14 of the Torture Convention does not contain an international right for the victim to obtain compensation. It only states the state obligation to provide such a right under its domestic legal order.

122. *Supra* notes 83, 84. For a different view, J. Crawford and S. Olleson, 'The Nature and Forms of International Responsibility', in *International Law*, ed. M.D. Evans (Oxford, Oxford University Press, 2006), 445, 448.

123. There are international stipulations providing for international civil responsibility for individuals. The International Convention on Civil Liability for Oil Pollution 1969, 29 November 1969, UN Treaty Series, Vol. 973, 3, and the Protocol of 1992 to amend the International Convention on Civil Liability for Oil Pollution Damage, 27 December 1992, UN Treaty Series, Vol. 1956, 255, for example, contain a provision according to which the owner of a ship is liable for any damage caused by oil as a consequence of an accident of the ship. In its commentary to Article 58, ILC Draft Articles on Responsibility, the ILC states that '[s]o far this principle [of individual responsibility] has operated in the field of criminal responsibility, but it is not excluded that developments may occur in the field of individual civil responsibility'; (A/56/10).

124. Draft Conference Report, The Hague, Article 6, Commentary (2)(b), available at: http://www.ila-hq.org/en/committees/index.cfm/cid/1018 (accessed September 2010).
125. In the tradition of common law, for example, claims against the Government and the Crown were barred by the so-called Crown Immunities, see 'English Court of Appeal, *Mulcahy v. Ministry of Defence*', *QB* (1996): 732, 740. Similarly, according to the *Kokka-Mutōseki* doctrine, the doctrine of the irresponsibility of the state, the Japanese government was not responsible to its citizens for damages caused by its acts performed in the exercise of official authority; Bong, *supra* note 48, at 187, 191.
126. The crown immunities were abolished in 1947; see the English House of Lords, *Matthews v. Ministry of Defence*, 13 February 2003, *UKHL* 4 (2003): para. 4 *et seq*. As for Japan, the State Compensation Law of 1947 provides for the responsibility of the Japanese state to pay compensation for damages caused by the illegal acts of public officials in performing their duties; Bong, *supra* note 48, at 187, 191. For an overview, see D. Shelton, *Remedies in International Human Rights Law*, 2nd edition (Oxford: Oxford University Press, 2005), 23 *et seq*.
127. *Supra* sections 2.1 and 2.2.1.
128. For an overview, see again Shelton, *supra* note 126, at 33.
129. Federal Court of Australia, *Habib v. Commonwealth of Australia*, 25 February 2010, No. NSD 956; C. Scott, ed., *Torture as Tort: Comparative Perspectives on the Development of Transnational Human Rights Litigation* (Oxford: Hart Publishing, 2001); Fassbender, *supra* note 57, at 347.
130. *Diallo* (Guinea v. D.R. Congo), Judgment, I.C.J. Reports 2007, para. 39.
131. UN Doc. A/61/10, 22, 24.
132. *Interhandel* (Switzerland v. United States), Preliminary Objections, I.C.J. Reports 1959, 6, 27; I. Brownlie, *Principles of Public International Law*, 7th edition (Oxford: Oxford University Press, 2008), 493.
133. ILC, State Responsibility, YILC 1977, Vol. II/1, Commentary to art. 22, 34 *et seq*.
134. E.M. Borchard, *The Diplomatic Protection of Citizens Abroad* (New York: The Banks Law Publishing Company, 1970), 358.
135. Brownlie, *supra* note 132, at 493.
136. Verdross and Simma, *supra* note 77, at 828 *et seq*.; German Federal Constitutional Court, 13 May 1996, BVerfGE 94, 315, 330.
137. *Supra* section 2.1.
138. E. Feaux de la Croix, 'Schadenersatzansprüche ausländischer Zwangsarbeiter', *Neue Juristische Wochenzeitschrift* (1960): 2268, 2269; Granow, *supra* note 35, at 67, 71. Gurski argued that as a war was a conflict between states, it could only provoke reparation claims between states, H. Gurski, *Außenwirtschaftsdienst des Betriebs-Beraters* (AWD) (1961), 12, 14–15.
139. He was head of the subdivision for reparation issues at the Federal Ministry of Finance from 1953 until 1959 and head of the Division of Liquidation of the War from 1959 until 1971. See the Minutes of the Cabinet of the Federal Government, Vol. 2, 2000, 669, available at: http://www.bundesarchiv.de/cocoon/barch/0000/z/z1960a/kap1_6/para2_9.html (accessed September 2010). For his role in the reparation process, see C. Goschler, *Schuld und Schulden* (Göttingen: Wallstein, 2005), 230 *et seq*.
140. M. Domke, 'Individualansprüche für Völkerrechtliche Deliktshaftung?', *Schweizerische Juristen-Zeitung* 58 (1962): 2, 4.
141. For a list of such Treaties, see ibid., 4, and German Federal Constitutional Court, 13 May 1996, BVerfGE 94, 315, 332 et seq.
142. 13 May 1996, BVerfG 94, 315, 331–332.
143. *Distomo*, 26 June 2003, *BGHZ*: 155, 279, 300.
144. Landgericht Bonn, *Neue Juristische Wochenzeitschrift* (2004): 525, 526.
145. Oberlandesgericht, 28 July 2005, *Neue Juristische Wochenzeitschrift* (2005), 2860. In the end, the court dismissed the claims as it could not find that Germany had violated its duties. After a dismissal of the case by the Federal Court of Justice, 2 November 2006, *BGHZ*: 169, 348, the case is currently pending before the German Federal Constitutional Court.
146. For an examination of the German law in this context, see Schwager, *supra* note 1, at 208 *et seq*.
147. In this sense, see German Federal Court of Justice, *Varvarin*, 2 November 2006, *BGHZ* 169, 348, para. 16, generally, for violations of international law, German Federal Constitutional Court, East German expropriation case, 26 October 2004, *BVerfG* 112: 1, para. 80: 'In the state system created by the Basic Law, irrespective of whether claims of individual persons already exist under public international law, it may be necessary to be able to assert violations of public international law as

infringements of subjective rights.' The decision is published in English under: http://www.bundesverfassungsgericht.de/entscheidungen/rs20041026_2bvr095500en.html (accessed September 2010).

148. *Supra* section 2.1.
149. B. Heß, 'Kriegsentschädigung aus kollisionsrechtlicher und rechtsvergleichender Sicht', in *Entschädigung nach bewaffneten Konflikten. Die Konstitutionalisierung der Weltordnung*, DGV, ed., 107, 116.
150. Ibid.
151. The courts refer to the principle of 'combat immunity', even though the point is not strictly one of immunity, but of the constricted scope of the duty of care. See J. Rowley, 'Combat Immunity and the Duty of Care', *Journal of Personal Injury Law* 4 (2004): 280, 281.
152. *Shaw Savill and Albion Company Ltd v. The Commonwealth*, CLR 344, 362. The owner of a ship had sued the Commonwealth of Australia in the High Court of Australia in Admiralty for damages in consequence of a collision which occurred between a military ship and a civil motor vessel.
153. Ibid., at 344, 356 *et seq.*
154. Court of Appeal, 21 February 1996, [1996] QB 732, 735. The underlying facts of the case are special in so far as the Court was not considering a claim of a civilian, but of a soldier who allegedly had suffered injury from the negligence of the gun commander during the Second Gulf War. The Court made it clear, however, that the principle would also apply to claims made by civilians: 'If during the course of hostilities no duty of care is owed by a member of the armed forces to civilians or their property, it must be even more apparent that no such duty is owed to another member of the armed forces.' Ibid., 750.
155. *Bici v. Ministry of Defence*, Queen's Bench Division [2004] EWHC 786 (QB), paras 101–102.
156. '*Al Skeinei v. The Secretary of State for Defence*, House of Lords', *UKHL* 26 (2007): para. 26.
157. 28 U.S.C. §§ 1346, 2671–2680.
158. 5 *USC* 702: 'A person suffering legal wrong because of agency action, or adversely affected or aggrieved by agency action within the meaning of a relevant statute, is entitled to judicial review thereof.'
159. *USC* 28, section 2680 (j).
160. *USC* 5, section 701 (b) (1) (g).
161. *Varvarin*, 2 November 2006, *BGHZ*: 169, 348, 360. At the time of the drafting of this chapter, the case was pending before the German Constitutional Court of Justice.
162. K.H. Partsch, 'International Law and Municipal Law', in *EPIL*, ed. R. Bernhardt, Vol. II (1995), 1183, 1190; C. Amrhein-Hofmann, *Monismus und Dualismus in den Völkerrechtslehren* (Dunker & Humblot: Berlin, 2003).
163. Verdross and Simma, *supra* note 77, at 551, section 864.
164. It is sometimes argued that international rules are only directly applicable if they confer subjective rights; see, for example, A. Bleckmann, 'Self-Executing Treaty Provisions', in *EPIL*, ed. R. Bernhardt, Vol. III (1997), 374. As the *ius in bello*, as stated above, contains individual rights, those rules conferring the rights are directly applicable according to this reasoning.
165. 29 June 2006, 126 S.Ct. 2749, Chapter VI D i. For the direct applicability of humanitarian law, see also 'German Federal Constitutional Court, *Italian Military Internees*, 26 April 2004', *Neue Juristische Wochenzeitschrift* (2004), 3257, 3258; for an overview of state practice, see E. David, *Principes de droit des conflits armés*, 3rd edition (Bruxelles: Bruylant, 2002), 226, para. 1.199.
166. *Kadic v. Karadzic* (2d Cir. 1995), 70 F.3d 232, 238. For the Alien Tort Claims Act, see *USC* 28: section 1350; and for its application, see B. Stephens, J. Chomsky et al., *International Human Rights Litigation in U.S. Courts*, 2nd edition (Koninklijke Brill NV: Leiden 2008).
167. Brownlie, *supra* note 132, at 36; German Federal Court of Justice, 12 July 1951, BGHZ 3, 94, 106. In Germany, reference is also made to the *ius in bello* in order to justify otherwise unlawful behaviour under criminal law, see German Federal Court of Justice, 30 September 1960, BGHSt 15, 214; 15 August 1969, BGHSt 23, 103, 105.
168. *Bici v. Ministry of Defence*, Queen's Bench Division, [2004] EWHC 786 (QB), para. 104.
169. Oberlandesgericht Cologne, 28 July 2005, *Neue Juristische Wochenzeitschrift* (2005), 2860, 2863. It found that at least in those cases in which a soldier had violated rules under international humanitarian law which gives individuals a subjective right, the individual would be entitled to obtain compensation according to the domestic law of state liability.
170. Ibid.

171. Article 34, ECHR; Article 3, para. 3, ACHPR; Article 44, ACHR; Article 1, Optional Protocol to the International Covenant on Civil and Political Rights, 16 December 1966.
172. Greenwood, *supra* note 49, at 61, 251. For an analysis of the jurisprudence, see Zegveld, *supra* note 48, at 497, 515.
173. *Supra* note 114.
174. Article 1 of the Draft Articles on Diplomatic Protection of the International Law Commission.
175. The notion had first been formulated by Vattel in 1758: E. de Vattel, *The Law of Nations or the Principles of Natural Law Applied to the Conduct and to the Affairs of Nations and Sovereigns*, Vol. III (1758); and has been stated in a dictum of the Permanent Court of International Justice in 1924 in the *Mavrommatis Palestine Concessions* case, PCIJ, Series A, No. 2, 1924, 12.
176. International Law Commission, Diplomatic Protection, UN Doc. A/59/0, 2004, 13, 27.
177. K.W. Geck, 'Diplomatic Protection,' in *EPIL*, ed. R. Bernhardt, Vol. I (1992), 1045, 1057; J. Dugard, First Report on Diplomatic Protection, ILC Fifty-second session, A/CN.4/506 2000, 24 para. 66.
178. ILC, UN Doc. A/61/10, 22, 25.
179. Geck, *supra* note 177, at 1045, 1051–1052; Diplomatic Protection, A/59/10, 2004, 13, 27 Art 2 Commentary 2.
180. For the UNCC, see V. Heiskanen, 'The United Nations Compensation Commission', *RdC* 296 (2002): 259; for the EECC, see W. Kidane, 'Civil Liability for Violations of International Humanitarian Law: The Jurisprudence of the Eritrea-Ethiopia Claims Commission in the Hague', *Wisconsin JIL* 25 (2007): 23.
181. 'Draft Model Statute of an Ad Hoc International Compensation Commission', in *Report of the Seventy-Third Conference*, ILA, ed., 2008, 500 *et seq.*
182. Article 4 of the Draft in its version of 1 August 2010 reads: '1. Any victim falling within the definition provided for in the previous Article, whether natural or legal person, may have the capacity to submit claims to the Commission. 2. Other persons who are in a family or civil law relationship to the victim, particularly a spouse, child or parent of the victim, may submit claims on behalf of the victim provided that there is a legal interest therein.'
    Article 5 reads: '1. Each victim shall submit his or her claim to the States of which nationality he or she has. That State shall forward whole of the claims received to the Commission after having categorized them in accordance with the criteria provide for in Article 6. 2. In spite of the previous paragraph, victims who are not in a position to have their claims forwarded by the State of their nationality may submit their claims to an appropriate person, State or international organization designated by the Commission.'
183. *Supra* section 3.3.
184. *Supra* note 65.
185. H. Koh, 'Transnational Public Law Litigation', *Yale Law Journal* 100 (1991): 2347, 2348; Stephens, Chomsky et al., *supra* note 166.
186. In *Civitella*, the Italian Supreme Court convicted the German Milde for war crimes committed during World War II and granted the victims compensation, 'Corte Suprema di Cassazione, sez. I penale, *Civitella*, 21 October 2008', *Rivista di diritto internazionale* 92 (2009): 618. In contrast, in *Van Anraat*, the Court of Appeal, The Hague rejected the claims of victims of chemical warfare as it considered them to be too complex to be decided by a criminal court, Court of Appeal, The Hague, 9 May 2007, LJN: BA4674; Dutch Supreme Court, 30 June 2009, LJN: BG4822. See A. Ciampi, 'The Italian Court of Cassation Asserts Civil Jurisdiction over Germany in a Criminal Case Relation to the Second World War', *JICJ* 7 (2009): 597; L. Zegfeld, 'Compensation for the Victims of Chemical Warfare in Iraq and Iran', in *Reparations for Victims of Genocide, War Crimes and Crimes against Humanity*, eds C. Ferstman, M. Goetz and A. Stephens (Leiden: Martinus Nijhoff Publishers, 2009), 369.
187. United States Supreme Court, *Baker v. Carr* (1962), 369 US 186, 217.
188. Israeli Supreme Court, *Ajuri v. IDF Commander,* HCJ 7015/02, IsrLR 2002, 1; *Burger-Fischer et al. V Degussa AG,* (D.N.J. 1999), 65 F.Supp. 2D 248, 282.
189. Corte di Cassatione, '*Markovic*, 8 February 2002', *Rivista di diritto internazionale* 85 (2002): 799.
190. M. Frulli, 'When are States Liable Towards Individuals for Serious Violations of Humanitarian Law? The *Markovic* Case', *JICJ* 1 (2003): 406, 412.
191. See the successful proceedings against Germany, 'Corte Suprema di Cassazione, *Ferrini*, 11 March 2004', *Rivista di diritto internazionale* 87 (2004): 54; ibid., '*Distomo*, 29 May 2008', *Rivista di diritto internazionale* 92 (2009), 594.

192. A. Gattini, 'To What Extent are State Immunity and Non-Justiciability Major Hurdles to Individuals' Claims for War Damages?', *JICL* 1 (2003): 348; P. De Sena and F. De Vittor, 'State Immunity and Human Rights: The Italian Supreme Court Decision on the Ferrini Case', *EJIL* 16 (2005): 89.

193. As for immunity resulting from domestic law for the government of the forum state, *supra* section 3.

194. Article 12, UN Convention on Jurisdictional Immunities of States and their Property, 2 December 2004; Article 11, European Convention on State Immunity; G.M. Badr, *State Immunity: An Analytical and Prognostic View* (The Hague: Martinus Nijhoff Publishers, 1984), citing section 1605(a)(5) United States Foreign Sovereign Immunities Act of 1976, Section 5(a) United Kingdom State Immunity Act of 1978; Section 7(a) Singapore State Immunity Act of 1979 and Section 6(a) South African Foreign States Immunities Act of 1981.

195. Such a link is not required by the U.S. Antiterrorism and Effective Death Penalty Act of 1996, Pub. L. 104 – 132, para. 221, codified in 28 U.S.C. §§ 1605 (a)(7) and 1610 (f) FSIA.

196. *Al-Adsani v. United Kingdom*, ECtHR, Application No. 35763/97, Joint Dissenting Opinion of Judge Rozakis and Caflisch joined by Judges Wildhaber, Costa, Cabral Barreto and Vakić, 21 November 2001, para. 3; U.S. District Court *Von Dardel v. UdSSR*, 623 F.Supp. 246 (D.D.C. 1985), 252; *Letelier v. Republic of Chile*, 488 F.Supp. 665 (D.D.C.1980); J. Bröhmer, *State Immunity and the Violation of Human Rights* (Martinus Nijhoff: The Hague, 1997), 196 *et seq.*

197. S. Furuya, 'State Immunity: An Impediment to Compensation Litigation Assessment of Current International Law', in *Report of the Seventy-Second Conference*, ILA, ed., 2006, 783, 792 *et seq.*

198. Corte Suprema di Cassazione, *Ferrini*, 11 March 2004, *Rivista di diritto internazionale* 87 (2004): 54; Greek Court of First Instance of Levadia, *Prefecture of Voiotia v. Federal Republic of Germany*, Case No. 137/1997, 30 October 1997, *RHDI* 50 (1997): 599; Hellenic Supreme Court Areios Pagos, *AJIL* 95 (2001), 200. Corte Suprema di Cassazione, sez. I penale, *Civitella*, 21 October 2008, *Rivista di diritto internazionale* 92 (2009): 618. Not accepting immunity for the execution of the Judgment of the Greek Areigos Pagos in *Distomo*: Corte di Cassazione, *Distomo*, 29 May 2008, *Rivista di diritto internazionale* 92 (2009): 594.

199. *McElhinney v. Ireland*, ECtHR, Application No. 31253/96, Judgment of 21 November 2001, para. 38. See also *Kalogeropoulou et al. v. Greece and Germany*, ECtHR, Application No. 59021/00, Judgment of 12 December 2002; Greek Supreme Special Court, *Anotato Eidiko Dikasterio*, 17 September 2002, Margellos, Panezi, *supra* note 65, at 199, 207; German Federal Court of Justice, *Distomo*, 26 June 2003, *BGHZ*: 155, 279. According to the Court of Appeal in The Hague, the United Nations enjoys immunity from legal proceedings concerning liability claims for the massacre in Srebrenica, *Mothers of Srebrenica*, 30 March 2010, LJN: BL8979.

200. Bröhmer, *supra* note 196, at 206.

201. Jursidictional Immunities of the State (*Germany v. Italy*), Application No. 2008/44.

202. *Reparations for Injuries Suffered in the Service of the United Nations*, Advisory Opinion, I.C.J. Reports 1949, 174, 185 *et seq.*

203. Article 35, para. 1, ECHR; Article 46, para. 1 (a), ACHPR; Article 56, para. 5, ACHR; see also Article 2, 5, para. 2 (b) Protocol I to the ICCPR.

204. Decision No. 13, 25 September 1992, UN Doc. S/AC.26/1992/13.

205. (D.C. Cir. 2003), 315 F.3d 390.

206. *Nemariam v. Fed. Democratic Republic of Ethiopia,* (D.C. Cir. 2007), 491 F.3d 470.

207. L. Zegfeld, 'Remedies for War Victims', in *Future Perspectives on International Criminal Justice*, eds C. Stahn and L. Van den Herik (The Hague: T.M.C. Asser Press, 2010), part VII, No. 26.

Index

9/11 World Trade Center attacks, influence on development of HRL 22

A. and Others v. UK, 2004 (UK) 127, 139
Abresch, W. 485, 498–9
access
  to court, right of 136
  to humanitarian assistance 301–2, 304
accountability
  duty to account for forcibly disappeared individuals 173–4, 182–6
  duty to account for use of force 174
  for grave violations of HRL/IHL 351–4
  and justice and peace, need for balance 351–4
accused, human rights of 577, 580–81
Additional Protocols *see under* Geneva Conventions
Afghanistan 153–4
African Charter on Democracy, Elections and Governance, 2007 (AU) 517
African Charter on Human and People's Rights, 1981 (Banjul Charter) (AU) 19, 504
  and promotion of IHL 508–9, 512–14
  Protocol Establishing Peace and Security Council 512–14
  Protocol on Rights of Women in Africa 504–5
  on rights of individual to reparation 630
African Commission on Human and People's Rights
  establishment 19
  impunity rules 511–12
  inter-states IHL cases brought by 509–12
  promotion of IHL by 508–9
African Court of Justice and Human Rights (ACtHR) 362–3, 520–22
African Union 19, 362
  African Standby Force, obligations of 515–16
  Common Position on the Illicit Proliferation, Circulation and Trafficking of Small Arms and Light Weapons (Bamako Declaration), 2000 514

Convention for the Protection and Assistance of Internally Displaced Persons in Africa, 2009 (Kampala Convention) 148, 151–2, 505–6
  Directive on the Protection of Civilians 513–14
  establishment and purpose 503
  Grand Bay Declaration and Plan of Action, 1999 506–8
  human rights agencies, powers and duties 511
  IHL, references to 503, 522–3
  condemnation of violations 518–20
  in declarations and decisions 506–8, 514–15
  by Peace and Security Council 512–15
  in regional agreements 516
  in treaties 504–6
  impunity rules 511–12, 517–18, 520–22
  judicial enforcement role under IHL 520–22
  Kigali Declaration, 2003 507–8, 514
  Non-Aggression and Common Defence Pact 517
  peacekeeping missions, protection of IHL during 512–14
  Solemn Declaration on a Common African Defence and Security Policy, 2004 514–15
Agenda for Human Rights *see* Swiss Agenda for Human Rights
Al Jedda v. UK, 2011 (ECtHR) 92–3, 103
Al-Skeini v. Secretary of State for Defence, 2007 (UK) 81, 102, 108–9, 500, 642
Albekov v. Russia, 2008 (ECtHR) 172
Aleksovski case, 2000 (ICTY) 584
Alston, P. 157–8, 167
American Convention on Human Rights, 1969 19
  applicability in wartime 56
  applicability to non-state armed groups 149
  Article 29 471–2
  extraterritorial application 400
  judicial interpretation 471–2
  and most favourable to the individual principle 254, 257–8